MANUAL OF
CULTIVATED
BROAD-LEAVED
TREES & SHRUBS

Volume III, PRU – Z

Written by GERD KRÜSSMANN
Translated by MICHAEL E. EPP
Technical Editor: GILBERT S. DANIELS

Timber Press
Portland, Oregon

Title of the German original version:
Krüssmann, Handbuch der Laubgehölze
® 1978 by Verlag Paul Parey
Berlin and Hamburg

English translation 1986 by Timber Press
Rights Reserved
Printed in Hong Kong

ISBN 0-88192-006-1

Timber Press, Portland, Oregon

Contents of Volume III

GENERAL

MAIN TEXT

APPENDIX

Acknowledgment

With the publication of this third volume, the complete set is now finished.

I must extend my thanks to my many colleagues and friends throughout the world who've readily offered assistance at my request. Unfortunately, to list all those who've assisted in this work is impossible and those which follow is only a token of my deeply felt gratitude. I'm appreciative of all the information made available to me from small insights to larger problems from those who've submitted long, detailed reports.

Above all, however, I would like to thank my dear, old friend, Mr. Harold G. Hillier, Winchester, England in whose home and arboretum I have had many pleasant discussions about dendrologic matters over the past few decades (during which we have become imperceptively older). Likewise, thanks to Mr. Roy Lancaster, Curator of the Hillier Arboretum.

Also, I would like to extend a hearty thanks to the University of Peking for illustrations from their *Iconographia Cormophytorum Sinicorum* (1972–1976). I have made much use of this work which the reader will notice as "ICS" in the credits.

Herman J. Grootendorst and Harry Van De Laar, both of Boskoop, have given me much advice of which I have made great use, and for which I thank them both. I have many other Dutch colleagues to thank, among them D. M. van Gelderen, Boskoop; F. Schneider and Dr. P. G. De Jong, both in Wageningen.

In Germany, H. Scheller of Offenbach offered insight into his work on *Fraxinus;* my dear friend Hinrich Kordes, Bilsen, repeatedly called my attention to new plants which I might otherwise have missed. The Botanic Garden and Museum of Berlin are due a hearty thanks for their literary help; as are the Kew Gardens and Dr. P. S. Green in particular.

To Monsieur R. Minier of Angers, France I offer many thanks for much information, and Dr. L. J. Metcalf in Christchurch, New Zealand. In North America, I am grateful to those at the Arnold Arboretum, Morton Arboretum and the U. S. National Arboretum for much information. Many thanks go especially to my dear friend Dr. Donald Wyman, as well as Brian O. Mulligan in Seattle, and finally Fr. Vrugtman, the Curator at the Royal Botanic Gardens in Hamilton, Ontario, Canada.

Finally, I must thank my publisher, Dr. h. c. Friedrich Giorgi for bringing my plan to reality. I sincerely hope that this new edition, even more than the first, will long be a valued source of information on the woody plants of the temperate world.

Bad Salzuflen, Spring 1978   Gerd Krüssmann

Alphabetical Reference to the Botanical Terminology

To facilitate the use of this book by readers of all language groups, the most frequently used botanical terms have been arranged in alphabetical order. The word is then followed by the scientific (generally Latin, but occasionally Greek) word and then by the equivalent terms in German, French and Dutch. Furthermore, in all cases where a plant part from the 'Guide to the Terminology' is illustrated, a reference number may be found in parentheses after the word in the English column referring to the illustration number in volume I.

English (fig. no.)	Latin	German	French	Dutch
abscising	caducus	hinfällig	caduc	afvallend
achene	achenium	Nüsschen	achaine, akène	nootje
acrodrome 23d	acrodromus	spitzläufig (Nerven)	acrodrome	acrodroom
acuminate 20i	acuminatus	lang zugespitzt	terminé en queue	lang toegespitst
acute 20a, 21g	acutus	spitz	aigu	spits
adult leaves	folia adulta	Altersblätter	feuilles adultes	ouderdomsbladeren
albumen	albumen	Eiweiss	albumen	eiwit
alternate	alternans	wechselständig	alterne	afwisselend
alternate (of leaves) 10a	alternifolius	—(von Blättern)	à feuilles alternes	afwisselend
angiosperms	angiospermae	Bedecktsamer	angiospermes	bedektzadigen
angle of nerves		Nervenwinkel	aisselle des nerves	nerfaksel
anther	anthera	Staubbeutel	anthère	helmknop
apex, top	apex	Blattspitze	pointe	top
apiculate	apiculatus	fein zugespitzt	apiculé	puntig
applanate	applanatus	abgeflacht	aplati	afgeplat
appressed	adpressus	angedrückt	appressé	aangedrukt
arrow-headed	sagittatus	pfeilförmig	sagitté	pijlvormig
ascending 6f	ascendens	aufsteigend	ascendent	opstijgend
auriculate (eared) 21e	auriculatus	geöhrt	muni d'oreillettes	geoord
awn	arista	Granne	arête	baard (van gras)
awned 19i	aristatus	grannig	aristé	met baard (van gras)
axillary	axillaris	achselständig, seitenständig	axillaire	okselstandig
bark	cortex	Rinde, Borke	écorce	bast
bearded	barbatus	Achselbart	barbé	okselbaard
berry 34	bacca	Beere	baie	bes
biennial	biennis	zweijährig	bisannuel	tweejarig
bilabiate 30i	bilambatus	zweilippig	bilabié	tweelippig
blade 9b	lamina	Blattspreite	limbe	bladschijf
blunt 20b, 21f	obtusus	stumpf	obtusé	stomp
boat-shaped	navicularis	kahnförmig	naviculaire	bootvormig
brachidodrome 23c	brachidodromus	schlingenläufig (Nerven)	brachidodrome	brachidodroom
bract	bractea	Hochblatt	bractée	schutblad
branch	ramus	Ast	branche	tak
branchlet	ramellus	Zweiglein	petite branche	twijgje
bristle	seta	Borste	soie	borstel
bristle-pointed	setosus	borstig	seteux	borstelig
bud	gemma	Knospe	bourgeon	knop
bullate	bullatus	aufgetrieben, blasig	boursoufflé, bullé	opgeblazen
calyx	calyx	Kelch	calice	kelk
campanulate (bell-shaped) 29d	campanulatus	glockig	campanulé	klokvormig
camptodrome 22c	camptodromus	bogenläufig (Nerven)	camptodrome	camptodroom
capitula (head) 32e	capitulum	Köpfchen	capitule	hoofdje
capsule 34	capsula	Kapsel	capsule	doos
carpel 25f	carpellum	Fruchtblatt	carpelle	vruchtblad
catkin 32b	amentum	Kätzchen	chaton	katje
channeled	canaliculatus	rinnenförmig	canaliculé	gootvormig
ciliate 19b	ciliatus	gewimpert	cilié	gewimperd

English (fig. no.)	Latin	German	French	Dutch
cirrhous	cirrhus	Wickelranke	vrille	rank
clavate 29f	clavatus	keulenförmig	claviforme	knodsvormig
claw	unguis	Nagel	onglet	nagel
clawed	unguiculatus	genagelt	onguicule	genageld
climbing	scandens	kletternd, klimmend	grimpant	klimmend
clustered 10f	fasciculatus	büschelig	fasciculaire	gebundeld
coarse	grossus	grob	grossier	grof
compound	compositus	zusammengesetzt	composé	samengesteld
compressed	compressus	zusammengedrängt	comprimé	samengedrukt
concave	concavus	vertieft	concave	uitgehold
conduplicate 8h	conduplicatus	zusammengefaltet	condupliqué	samengevouwen
connate 11f	connatus	verwachsen	conné	vergroeid
connective	connectivum	Mittelband	connectif	konnektief
convex	convexus	gewölbt	convexe	gewelfd
convolute 8f	convolutus	übergerollt	convoluté	opgerold
cordate 21b	cordatus, cordiformis	herzförmig	cordé, cordiforme	hartvormig
corky 5i	suberosus	korkig	subéreux, liégeux	kurkachtig
corolla	corolla	Blumenkrone	corolle	bloemkroon
corymb 32d	corymbus	Doldentraube	corymbe	schermtros
cotyledon	cotyledon	Keimblatt	cotyledon	kiemblad
craspedrome 23b	craspedromus	randläufig (Nerven)	craspedrome	craspedroom
creeping 6a	repens, reptans	kriechend	rampant	kruipend
crenate 19h	crenatus	gekerbt	crénelé	gekarteld
crescent-shaped 16h	lunatus	mondförmig	luniforme	halvemaanvormig
crispate 19k	crispus	gekraust	crispé, ondulé	gekroesd
cross-section	sectio transversa	Querschnitt	section transversale	dwarse doorsnede
cross-wise 10d	decussatus	kreuzständig	décussé	kruisgewijs
crown	corona, cacumen	Krone	couronne	kroon
cuneate (wedge-shaped) 21d	cuneatus	keilförmig	en forme de coin	wigvormig
cupulate (cup-shaped) 29b	cupulaeformis	becherförmig	cupuliforme	bekervormig
cupule	cupula	Fruchtbecher	cupule	vruchtbeker
cuspidate 20h	cuspidatus	feinspitz	cuspidé	fijn toegespitst
cyme 33b	cyma	Scheinquirl, Trugdolde	cime, cyme	bijscherm, tuil
deciduous	deciduus	abfallend	caduc	afvallend
decumbent 6e	decumbens	liegend	décombant	liggend
decurrent 11e	decurrens	herablaufend	decurrent	aflopend
decussate (deeply cut) 19e	incisus	eingeschnitten	incisé	ingesneden
deflexed	declinatus	niedergebogen	déliné	neergebogen
delicate	gracilis	zierlich	gracieux	sierlijk
dentate 19g	dentatus	gezähnt	denté	getand
digitate	digitatus	gefingert	digité	vingervormig
dioecious	dioecus, dioicus	zweihäusig	dioique	tweehuizig
distichous (2 ranked) 10e	distichus	zweizeilig	distique	tweerijig
double	bi-, plenus (of flowers)	doppelt, gefüllt	double	dubbel-, gevuld
downy	pubescens	weichhaarig	pubescent	zachtharig
drooping	cernuus	übergebogen	penché	overgebogen
drupe	drupa	Steinfrucht	drupe	steenvrucht
dull	opacus	matt	mat	mate, dof
elliptic 13	ovalis	oval	elliptique	ovaal, elliptisch
elliptical 13	ellipticus	elliptisch	elliptique	elliptisch
emarginate 20c	emarginatus	ausgerandet	émarginé	uitgerand
enclosed/covered 7e	vestitus	bedeckt	couvert	bedekt
entire 19a	integer, -rimus	ganzrandig	entier	gaafrandig
epigynous 28c	epigynus	unterständig	épigyne	onderstandig

English (fig. no.)	Latin	German	French	Dutch
equitant 8e	amplex	umfassend	amplexe	omvattend
evergreen	sempervirens	immergrun	toujours vert	groenblijvend
exserted	exsertus	vorragend	saillant	eruit stekend
falcate 16f	falcatus	sichelförmig	en forme de faux	sikkelvormig
fascicle	fasciculus	Büschel	fascicule	bundel
fastigiate	fastigiatus	fastigiat	fastigié	fastigiaat
female flower (pistillate)	flos femineus	Stempelblüte	fleur féminin	stamperbloem
filament	filamentum	Faden	filet	helmdraad
fissured	fissura	rissig	fissurer	spleet, scheur
flagellate (whip-formed)	flagellaris	peitschenartig	flagellaire	zweepvormig
flat, plain	planus	eben, flach	plat	vlak, glad, ondiep
flexuose	flexuosus	hin und hergebogen	flexueux	zigzag gebogen
floccose	floccosus	flockig-filzig	floconneux	vlokkig, viltig
follicle	folliculus	Balgfrucht	follicule	
fragrant	odoratus	duftend	odorant	geurend
fringed	fimbriatus	gefranst	fimbrié	met franjes
fruit	fructus	Frucht	fruit	vrucht
funnelform 29c	infundibuliformis	trichterförmig	infundibulé	trechtervormig
furrowed 5f	sulcatus	gefurcht	sillóné	gegroefd
gaping	ringens	rachenblütig	fleur en gueule	mondvormig
geniculate	geniculatus	geknickt	genouillé	geknikt
genus	genus	Gattung	genre	geslacht
glabrous	glaber	kahl	glabre	kaal
gland	glans	Drüse	gland	klier
glandulary-hairy 36g	glanduloso-pubescens	drüsenhaarig	glanduleux-pubescent	klierachtig behaard
glaucous	glaucus	bereift	pruineaux	berijpt
globose	globosus	kugelig	globeux	bolvormig
glossy	lucidus, nitidus	glänzend	brillant, luisant	glanzend
gymnosperms	gymnospermae	Nacktsamer	gymnospermes	naaktzadigen
habit	habitus	Habitus, Gestalt	forme	habitus
hair-covering	indumentum	Behaarung	pubescence	beharing
hairy	pilosus	behaart	pileux	behaard
hastate 21h	hastatus	spiessförmig	hasté	spiesformig
herbaceous	herbaceus	krautartig, krautig	herbacé	kruidachtig
hermaphrodite	hermaphroditus	zwittrig	hermaphrodite	hermafrodiet
hilum	hilum	Nabel	hile	navel
hirsute	hirsutus	rauhhaarig	hirsute	ruwharig
hispid	hispidus	steifhaarig	hispide	stijfharig
husk	siliqua	Schote	silique	hauw
hypanthium	hypanthium	Blütenboden	hypanthium	bloembodem
hypogynous 28a	hypogynus	oberständig	hypogyne	bovenstandig
imbricate 8a	imbricatus	dachziegelig	imbriqué	dakpansgewijze
incised	incisus	eingeschnitten	incisé	ingesneden
inflorescence	inflorescentia	Blütenstand	inflorescence	bloeiwijze
involucre	involucrum	Hüllkelch	involucre	omwindsel
involute (rolled inward) 8b	involutus	eingerollt	enroulé	ingerold
irregular	irregularis	unregelmässig	irregulier	onregelmatig
jointed	articulatus	gegliedert	articulé	geleed
juvenile leaves	folia juvenilia	Jugendblätter	feuilles juveniles	jeugdbladeren
keeled	carinatus	gekielt	caréné	gekield
kernel, stone	nucleus	Kern	noyeau	kern
kidney-shaped 16g	reniformis	nierenförmig	en forme de rein	niervormig
lanceolate 14o	lanceatus, lanceolatus	lanzenförmig, lanzettlich	lancéolé	lancetvormig
large, broad	latus	breit	large	breed
latex	latex	Milchsaft	laiteux	melksap

English (fig. no.)	Latin	German	French	Dutch
leaf 9a	folium	Blatt	feuille	blad
leaf base	basis	Blattgrund	base de feuille	bladvoet
leaf cushion	pulvinus	Blattkissen, Blattpolster	coussinet foliaire	bladkussen
leaf margin	margo	Blattrand	contour de feuille	bladrand
leaf scar	cicatricula	Blattnarbe	cicatrice foliaire	bladmerk
leaflet	foliolum	Blättchen	foliole	blaadje
leathery	coriaceus	lederartig	coriace	leerachtig
leprous 36e	lepidisotus	schülferschuppig	lepidote	schubbig
ligulate	ligula	Zungenblüte	ligule	tongetje
limb	limbus	Saum	limbe	zoom, rand
linear 12a	linearis	linealisch	linéaire	lijnvormig
lobe, loculicidal	loba	Lappen	lobe	lob
lobed 18f	lobatus	gelappt	lobé	gelobd
locule (chamber of ovary)	loculum	Fach	loge	hok
long shoot		Langtrieb	rameau longue	langlot
male flower (staminate)	flos masculus	Staubblüte	fleur mêle	meeldraadbloem
mane-like	jubatus	mähnenartig	criniforme	manenvormig
mealy	farinosus	mehlig	farineux	melig
monoecious	monoecus	einhäusig	monoique	eenhuizig
mucronate 20g	mucronatus	stachelspitz	mucroné	gepunt
mucronulate 20f	mucronulatus	stachelspitzig	mucronulé	fijn gepunt
naked 7d	nudis	nackt	nu	naakt
narrow	angustus	schmal	étroit	smal
needle-form	acerosus	nadelförmig	acéré	naaldvormig
nodding 4d	nutans	überhängend	incliné	overhangend
not shining	opacus	glanzlos	opaque	mat, dof
nut 34	nux	Nuss	noix	noot
obcordate 16c	obcordatus	obcordat, verkehrt herzförmig	obcordate	omgekeerd hartvormig
oblanceolate 15u	oblanceolatus	oblanzettlich	oblancéolé	omgekeerd lancetvormig
oblate	oblatus	oblat	oblate	oblaat
oblique 21k	obliquus	schief	oblique	scheef
oblong 12	oblongus	länglich	oblong	langwerpig
obovate 15	obovatus	obovat, verkehrt eiförmig	obovate	omgekeerd eirond, eivormig
obvolute 8d	obvolutus	halbumfassend	obvoluté	halfomvattend
opposite (of foliage) 10b	oppositus, oppositifolius	gegenständig (bei Blättern)	opposé	tegenoverstaand
orbiculate 13m	orbicularis	kreisrund	corbiculaire	cirkelrond
outspread	patulus	abstehend	étendre	afstaan
ovary	ovarium	Fruchtknoten	ovaire	vruchtbeginsel
ovate 14	ovatus, ovulum	eiförmig, eirund	ovate	eirond, eivormig
ovule	ovulum	samenanlage	ovule	eitje
palmate 17d	palmatus	handförmig, handteilig	palmé	handdelig, handvormig
panicle 32h	panicula	Rispe	panicule	pluim
papilionaceus (butterfly-like)	papilionaceus	schmetterlingsförmig	papilionacé	vlinderbloemig
papilla	papilla	warze	papille	wratachtig
pappus	pappus	Haarkelch	aigrette	zaadpluis
pectinate	pectinatus	kammförmig	pectiné	kamvormig
pedate	pedatus	fussförmig	pedatiforme	voetvormig
pedicel	pediculus	stielchen	pedicelle	steeltje
peduncle	pedunculus	Blütenstiel	pedoncule	bloemsteel
pedunculate	pedunculatus	gestielt (Blüte)	pédonculé	gesteeld
peltate 16a	peltatus	schildförmig	pelté	schildvormig

English (fig. no.)	Latin	German	French	Dutch
pendulous (weeping) 4e	pendulus	hängend	pendant	hangend
penniform 17e	pinnatiformis	fiederförmig	penniforme	veervormig
perfoliate 11d	perfoliatus	durchwachsen	perfolié	doorgroeid
perianth	perianthemum	Blütenhülle, Perigon	périanthe	bloembekleedsel
perigynous 28b	perigynus	mittelständig	périgyne	halfonderstandig
petal 25c	petalum	Blütenblatt	pétale	kroonblad
petiole	petiolus	Blattstiel	pétiole	bladsteel
petioled 11a	petiolatus	gestielt (Blatt)	petiolé	gesteeld
phylloclades	phyllocladium			
phyllode	phyllodium	Phyllodium	foliace	phyllodium
phyllotaxis	Phyllotaxis	Blattstellung	phyllotaxis	bladstand
pinnately cleft 18b	pinnatifidus	fiederspaltig	pennatifide	veerspletig
pinnately partite 18c	pinnatipartitus	fiederteilig	pennatipartite	veerdelig
pinnatisect 18d	pinnatisectus	fiederschnittig	pinnatiséqué	veervormig ingesneden
pistil	pistillum	Stempel	pistil	stamper
pistillate (see: female flower)				
pith	medulla	Mark	moelle	merg
plaited 8g	plicatus	gefaltet	plié	gevouwen
pod	legumen	Hülse	gousse	peul
poisonous	venenatus	giftig	vénéneux	vergiftig
pollen	pollen	Blütenstaub	pollen	stuifmeel
polygamous	polygamus	vielehig	polygame	polygaam
prickle 37a	acus	Stachel	aiguillon	stekel
prickly	aculeatus	stachelig	muni d'aiguillons	stekelig
procumbent	procumbens	niederliegend	tracant	neerliggend
prostrate	prostratus	niedergestreckt	couché	neerliggend
pruinose	pruinosus	bereift	pruineux	berijpt
pubescent	pubescens	feinhaarig	pubescent	fijn behaard
pulverulent	pulverulentus	bepudert, bestäubt	pulverulent	bepoederd, bestoven
punctate (dotted) 5k	punctatus	punktiert	ponctué	gestippeld
pungent	pungens	stechend	piquant	stekend
quadrangular 5e	quadrangulatus	vierkantig	à quatre angles	vierhoekig
raceme 32c	racemus	traube	grappe	tros
racemose	racemosus	traubig	en grappe	trosvormig
radiate	radiatus	strahlig	radiaire	radiaal
receptacle	receptaculum	Blütenboden	receptacle	bloembodem
reflexed	reflexus	zurückgebogen	re1flechi	teruggeslagen
regular	regularis	regelmässig	régulaire	regelmatig
resinous	resinosus	harzig	résineux	harsachtig
reticulate	reticulatus	netznervig	reticulé	netvormig
retuse 20d	retusus	eingedrückt	émoussé	ingedrukt
revolute 8c	revolutus	zurückgerollt	revoluté	teruggerold
rhizome	rhizoma	Wurzelstock	rhizome	wortelstok
rhombic	rhombicus	rautenförmig (=rhombisch)	rhombique	ruitvormig
rooting	radicans	wurzelnd	radicant	wortelend
rotate (wheel-shaped) 29a	rotatus	radförmig	rotacé	radvormig
rough	asper	rauh	rude	ruw
rounded 21a	rotundatus	abgerundet	arrondi	afgerond
roundish 13l	suborbiculatus	rundlich	arrondi	afgerond
rugose	rugosus	runzelig	rugueux	gerimpeld
runner 6b	sobol, stolon	Ausläufer, Sprössling	drageon, stolon	uitloper, wortelspruit
salver-shaped 29g	hypocraterimorphus	stieltellerförmig	hypocratériforme	schenkbladvormig
samara 35b	samara	Flügelfrucht	samare	gevleugeld nootje
scabrous	scaber	scharf	scabre	ruw

English (fig. no.)	Latin	German	French	Dutch
scaly 10g	squama	Schuppe	squameux	schub
scattered	sparsifolius	zerstreut (Blättern)	espacé	verspreid
schizocarp 35e	schizocarpium	Spaltfrucht	schizocarpe	splitvrucht
scion	vimen, virga	Rute	verger, scion	twijg, roede
seed	semen	Samen	graine, semence	zaad
semidouble	semiplenus	halbgefüllt	demi-double	half gevuld
semi-evergreen (see: wintergreen)				
semi-terete 5b	semiteres	halbrund	demi-cylindrique	halfrond
sepals 25k	sepala	Kelchblätter	sépales	kelkbladen
serrate	serratus	gesägt	serré	gezaagd
serrulate 19d	serrulatus	feingesägt	serrulé	fijn gezaagd
sessile 7a, 10b	sessilis	sitzend	sessile	zittend
shaggy	villosus	zottig behaart	poilu	donzig
shell	epicarpium	Schale	écorce	schil van vrucht opeen gehoopt
shoot	ramulus	Trieb	pousse	scheut
short branch		Kurztrieb	rameau court	kortlot
shrub	frutex	Strauch	arbuste, arbrisseau	struik, heester
silky	sericeus	seidenhaarig	soyeux	zijdeachtig
simple	simplex	einfach	simple	enkelvoudig
sinuate 18e	sinuatus	gebuchtet	sinué	bochtig
slightly drooping 4c	cernuus	nickend	penché	knikkend
smooth	laevis	glatt	lisse	glad
solitary	solitaris	einzelstehend	solitaire	alleenstaand
spathulate 16e	spathuliformis	spatelförmig	spatulé	spatelvormig
species	species (sp)	Art	espèce	soort
spike 32a	spica	Ähre	épi	aar
spindle, rachis	rhachis, rachis	Spindel	fuseau	spil
spiral	spiralis	schraubig	spiralé	spiraalvormig
spur	crus	Sporn	éperon	spoor
stamen 25a	stamen	Staubblatt	1etamine	meeldraad
staminate (see: male flower)				
standard		Hochstamm	haute-tige	hoogstam
stellate 38f	stellatus	sternhaarig	étoilé	sterharig
stem	culmus	Halm (Gramineae)	tige	halm
stem-clasping 11c	amplexicaulis	stengelumfassend	amplexicaule	stengelomvattend
sticky	glutinosus, viscosus	klebrig	poisseux, visqueux	kleverig
stigma 34	stigma	Narbe	stigmate	stempel
stipule 9b	stipula	Nebenblatt	stipule	steunblad
straggly 4f	divaricatus	sparrig	divariqué	uitgespreid
strap-form 12b	loratus	riemenförmig	loriculé	riemvormig
strap-shaped	loratus	bandformig	loriculé	bandvormig
striated	striatus	gestreift	strié	gestreept
strict 4b	strictus	straff	raide	opgaand
strigose 36	strigosus	striegelhaarig	à poils rudes	scherpharig
subspecies	subspecies (ssp)	Unterart	sous-espèce	ondersoort
subulate (awl-shaped)	subulatus	pfriemformig	subulé	priemvormig
syncarp	syncarpium	Sammelfrucht	syncarpe	vruchten
tapering	attenuatus	verschmälert	attenue	versmald
terete 5a	teres	stielrund	cylindrique	rolrond
terminal	terminalis	endständig	terminal	eindstandig
terminal bud 7g		Endknospe	bourgeon terminal	eindknop
ternate 17b	ternatus	dreizählig	terné	drietallig
tessellate 22b	tessellatus	würfelnervig	tessellé	schaakbord-vormig
thorn 37b-c	spina	Dorn	épine	doorn
thorny	spinosus	dornig	épineux	gedoornd
throat	faux	Schlund	gorge	keel

English (fig. no.)	Latin	German	French	Dutch
tomentose	tomentosus	filzig	tomenteux	viltig
tooth	dens	Zahn	dent	tand
toothed 19g	dentatus	gezähnt	denté	getand
translucent	pellucidus	durchscheinend	pellucide	doorschijnend
triangular 16b	triangularis, triangulatus	dreieckig, dreikantig	à trois angles, triangulaire	driehoekig, driekantig
trichoma	trichoma	Haare	trichome	beharing
trifoliate	trifoliatus	dreiblättrig	trifoliolé	driebladig
trioecious	trioecus	triözisch	trioïque	driehuizig
truncate 21e	truncatus	abgestutzt	tronqué	afgestompt
truncated	truncatus	gestutzt	tronqué	afgestompt
tube 29h	tubus	Röhre	tube	buis
tubercled	tuberculatus	höckerig	tuberculeux	bultig
twig (secondary branches)	ramulus	Zweig	branche	twijg
twining	volubilis	windend	volubile	windend
twisted 4i	tortus, tortuosus	gedreht	tortueux	gedraaid
two-edged 5d	anceps	zweischneidig	à deux faces	tweezijdig
umbel 32f	umbella	Dolde	ombelle	scherm
underside		Unterseite	face de dessous	onderzijde
undulate	undulatus	gewellt	ondulà	gegolfd
unisexual	unisexualis	eingeschlechtig	unisexuel	eenslachtig
upper side		Oberseite, oben	face de dessus	bovenzijde, boven
upright	erectus	aufrecht	dréssé	oprecht
urceolate	urceolatus	krugförmig	urcéiforme	kruikvormig
v-valved	valvatus, -valvis	klappig	-valve	klepvormig
variety	varietas (var.)	Varietät	variété	varieeteit
velvety	holosericeus	samthaarig	velute	fluweelhaarig
viscid	viscidus	schmierig	viscide	kleverig
warty	verrucosus	warzig	verruqueux	wrattig
whorled 10c	verticillatus	quirlig	verticillé	kransstandig
winged 5h	alatus	geflügelt	ailé	gevleugeld
wintergreen	semipersistens	wintergrün	semi-persistant	wintergroen
woolly 38	lanatus, lanuginosus	wollhaarig, wollig	laineux, lanugineux	wollig, 'zachtharig

Explanation of Symbols

To provide the reader with information relating to the use of the plants described in this work and their cultural requirements, the following symbols are used after many of the descriptions.

Light Requirements
- ○ = needs or tolerates full sun
- ◑ = needs or tolerates semishade
- ● = needs or tolerates lasting shade

Soil Requirements
- **m** = moist soil
- **w** = wet soil (most plants do not like standing water but some will tolerate it for varying lengths of time)
- **d** = dry soil
- **S** = sandy soil (light and loose)
- **H** = humus soil (loose, dark, organic loam)
- **A** = alkaline soil (even chalk soils)

Properties of the Plants
- ✧ = with ornamental flowers
- ✗ = fruit or other plant part edible or economically useful
- ∅ = especially attractive foliage or fall color
- \# = evergreen foliage
- ⚭ = ornamental fruit
- Ⓕ = cultivated for timber, countries where grown are indicated

Other Symbols or Abbreviations
N = North, S = South, E = East, W = West, M = Mid, Middle.
Dates refer to the year of introduction into cultivation.
× = hybrid, cross.
HCC (with number) = color code from the Horticultural Color Chart.
z followed by number denotes hardiness zone according to USDA Hardiness Map.

Notes on Illustrations
The abbreviation 'Fig.' always refers to illustrations within the text pages of this book. References to illustrations in other books will be found at the end of the description and are indicated by initials and numbers.

For example: DL 2: 21 = Dippel, Handbuch der Laubholzkunde, Vol. 2, Illustration #21 (or if the illustrations are not numbered, the illustration on page 21).

The list of abbreviations to the literature providing illustrations cited in this book can be found on pp. 15–17. A complete bibliography of all books used in compiling this work may be found in the last volume.
Pl. = plate (for those found in other works). Plate 31, 43 etc. refers to those found in this book.

Synonyms
Plant names in italics at the end of a description are invalid synonyms.
The cultivars are noted with single quotes '____'.

Abbreviated Temperature Conversion Chart

Fahrenheit to Celsius

°F	°C
40	4.4
35	1.7
30	− 1.1
25	− 3.9
20	− 6.7
15	− 9.4
10	−12.2
5	−15
0	−17.8
− 5	−20.6
−10	−23.2
−15	−26.1
−20	−28.9
−25	−31.7
−30	−34.4
−35	−37.2
−40	−40
−45	−42.8
−50	−45.6

Celsius to Fahrenheit

°C	°F
5	41
0	32
− 5	23
−10	14
−15	5
−20	− 4
−25	−13
−30	−22
−35	−31
−40	−40
−45	−49

Readers should note the following points relative to hardiness:

1. The majority of the plants dealt with in this book will be found in zones 4 to 8, and occasionally zone 9.
2. Areas with the same average low temperature are described by the isotherms drawn along 5°C clines.
3. Hardiness ratings of plants is given using the U.S. Dept. of Agriculture system. It is indicated in the text as "z" followed by a number indicating hardiness zone.

Winter hardiness ratings are only guidelines. It must be realized that microclimate plays an important role so a specific location within a zone may be warmer or cooler than the zone as a whole. Protected areas in woods, southern exposures or gardens within cities as well as careful cultivation may allow one to raise plants in a zone which is normally too cold.

Hardiness Zones and the British Isles

Very few of the trees, shrubs and other garden plants cultivated in Britain are native to the British Isles. Over the centuries they have been introduced from all over the world, though especially from cool and warm temperate climates. How well they thrive in the British Isles largely depends on the climate they evolved in.

Although all plants are closely adapted to the climate of the region in which they occur wild, few have rigid requirements of heat and cold. There are other factors that decide whether a plant will thrive, e.g. soil type and amount of rainfall, but these will be mentioned later; temperature is of primary importance.

The British Isles has an equable oceanic climate which is seldom very cold, hot or dry. As a result, a wide range of the world's plants can be grown outside providing they are sited intelligently. Undoubtedly, some of these plants would prefer more summer sun or a more definite cold winter rest, but their innate adaptability is catered for in the vagaries of our climate. There is, however, a point at which a plant's tolerance ceases. Low temperature is the most important of these tolerances. If a plant cannot survive an average winter outside it is said to be tender. If a plant survives average winters but not the exceptionally hard one it is said to be half-hardy. These terms are, of course, relevant only to the area in which one lives.

Large continental land masses, e.g. North America and Central Europe, have climates that get progressively colder winters as one proceeds northwards and further inland from the sea. North America provides a familiar example, the extreme south being almost tropical, the far north arctic. In the 1930s, the United States Department of Agriculture divided the USA into 7 hardiness zones based upon an average of the absolute minimum temperatures over a period of 20 years. Later, the system was revised and refined and 10 zones recognized (zone 1 is arctic, zone 10 tropical). More recently this Hardiness Zone system has been extended to Europe, including the British Isles. Gardeners in the United States and Canada soon took advantage of the hardiness zone concept and over the years, largely by trial and error, most trees and shrubs and many other plants have been assessed and given zone ratings. Nevertheless, this system, though useful, can only be considered to give approximate hardiness ratings, especially when applied to the British Isles.

Sitting as it does on the eastern edge of the North Atlantic Ocean, the British Isles occupies a unique position. Although its total length, about 650 miles (Cornwall to Orkney), lies within latitudes 50° to 60° N, it falls into zone 8! Moved into the same latitudes in North America, it would lie entirely north of the Canadian border with the tip of Cornwall level with Winnipeg (zone 2–3). Even the eastern coastal region of Canada at these latitudes is no warmer than zones 3–4. Because of the influence of the Gulf Stream the British Isles enjoys a remarkably uniform climate. Such temperature gradients as these are run east to west rather than south to north.

It is a characteristic of temperate oceanic climates to have milder winters and cooler summers than equivalent continental ones and because of their northerly position this is even more marked in the British Isles. For this reason, a number of trees and shrubs which thrive in zone 8 in USA fail to do so well in Britain e.g., *Albizia julibrissin, Lagerstroemia indica,* etc. Such plants may live but fail to bloom, or get cut back severely by the British winters. The factor is primarily lack of summer sun rather than absolute cold.

This lack of summer warmth brings us to the several important ancillary factors which affect a plant's hardiness. Apart from lack of damaging low temperatures a plant needs the right kind of soil, adequate rainfall and humidity, plus sufficient light intensity and warmth. As with low temperature most plants have fairly wide tolerances, though there are noteworthy exceptions. Most members of the *Ericaceae*, especially *Rhododendron* and allied genera, must have an acid soil or they will die however perfect the climate. For plants near the limits of their cold tolerance, shelter is essential. Protection from freezing winds is particularly important. This can be provided by planting in the lee of hedges, fences and walls or among trees with a fairly high canopy. Individual plants can also be protected by matting or plastic sheeting or the bases can be earthed up or mounded around with peat, coarse sand or weathered boiler ash. A thick layer of snow also provides insulation against wind and radiation frost! Plenty of sunshine promotes firm, ripened growth with good food reserves, notably a high sugar content in the cell sap which then takes longer to freeze. If the summer is poor a partial remedy is to apply sulphate of potash (at 10g/per square metre) in late summer. This will boost the amount of sugars and starches in the plant. Half-hardy plants will stand having their tissues moderately frozen providing the thawing-out is gradual. For this reason it is best to grow them in a sheltered site which does not get the first rays of the morning sun. This is especially relevant for species with tender young leaves or early flowers, e.g. *Cercidiphyllum, Camellia* and *Magnolia.*

Zone 9 in the USA is warm-temperate to sub-tropical with hot summers. In the British Isles it tends to have even cooler summers than zone 8, and as a result very few truly sub-tropical plants can be grown in Britain. Most of the plants in the famous so-called, sub-tropical gardens, e.g. Tresco, Logan, Inverewe, etc., are of warm-temperate origin. For the reasons set down above, in Britain, if in doubt, it is best to consider zone 8 as zone 7 and zone 9 as zone 8 for plants of unreliable hardiness.

by Kenneth Beckett

Hardiness Zones of Europe

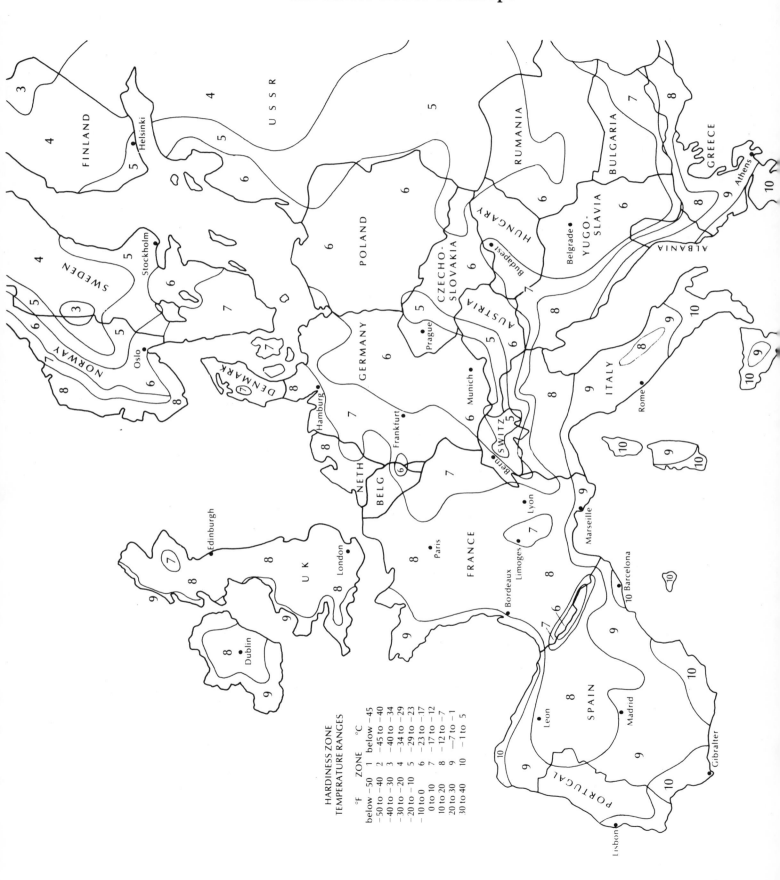

HARDINESS ZONE
TEMPERATURE RANGES

°F	ZONE	°C
below −50	1	below −45
−50 to −40	2	−45 to −40
−40 to −30	3	−40 to −34
−30 to −20	4	−34 to −29
−20 to −10	5	−29 to −23
−10 to 0	6	−23 to −17
0 to 10	7	−17 to −12
10 to 20	8	−12 to −7
20 to 30	9	−7 to −1
30 to 40	10	−1 to 5

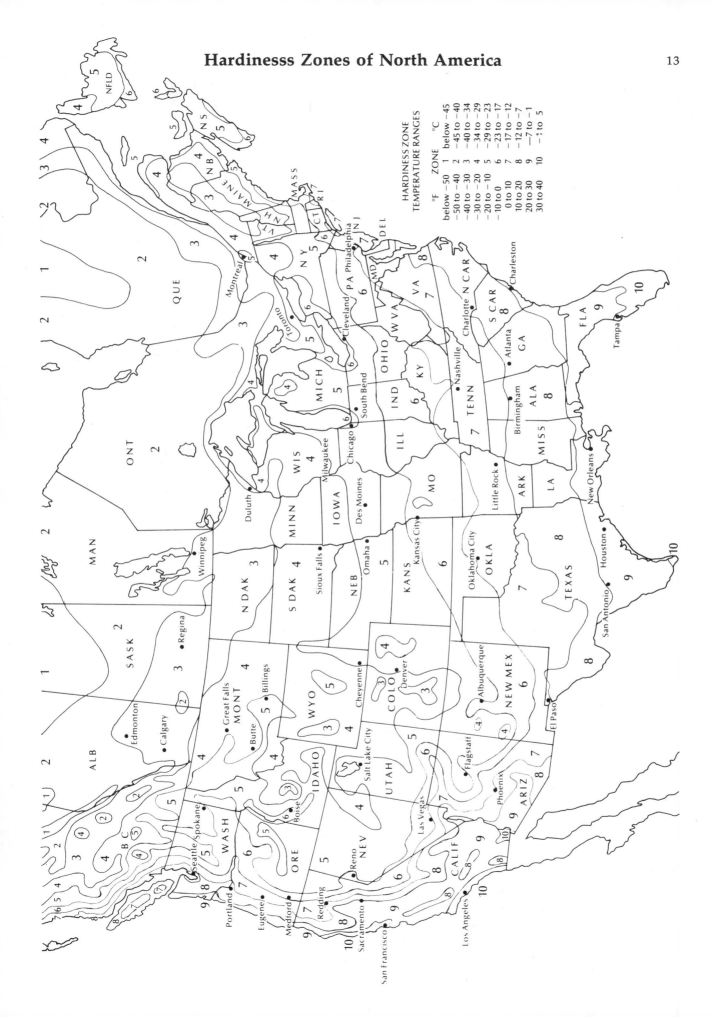

HARDINESS ZONE
TEMPERATURE RANGES

°F	ZONE	°C
below −50	1	below −45
−50 to −40	2	−45 to −40
−40 to −30	3	−40 to −34
−30 to −20	4	−34 to −29
−20 to −10	5	−29 to −23
−10 to 0	6	−23 to −17
0 to 10	7	−17 to −12
10 to 20	8	−12 to −7
20 to 30	9	−7 to −1
30 to 40	10	−1 to 5

Hardiness Zones of China

SOVIET UNION

Mongolia

Heilongjiang

Jilin

Xinjiang

Liaoning

Inner Mongolia

KOREA

Gansu

Hebei

−4° C

PEOPLE'S REPUBLIC OF CHINA

Ningxia

Shanxi

Shandong

JAPAN

Qinghai

Shaanxi

0° C

Jiangsu

Tibet

Henan

Anhui

4° C

Hubei

NEPAL

SIKKIM

Sichuan

Zhejiang

8° C

BHUTAN

Hunan

Jiangxi

INDIA

ASSAM

Guizhou

Fujian

12° C

BANGLADESH

Yunnan

Guangxi

TAIWAN

Tropic of Cancer

Guangdong

BURMA

VIETNAM

LAOS

HAINAN

PHILIPPINES

THAILAND

CAMBODIA

HARDINESS ZONE
TEMPERATURE RANGES

N. BORNEO

INDONESIA

MALAYSIA

MALAYSIA

°F	ZONE	°C
below −50	1	below −45
−50 to −40	2	−45 to −40
−40 to −30	3	−40 to −34
−30 to −20	4	−34 to −29
−20 to −10	5	−29 to −23
−10 to 0	6	−23 to −17
0 to 10	7	−17 to −12
10 to 20	8	−12 to −7
20 to 30	9	−7 to −1
30 to 40	10	−1 to 5

List of Abbreviations to Other Reference Works

The following abbreviations are found at the end of most of the plant descriptions; they refer exclusively to illustrations in the given works. Included in this list is the book's title and date of publication; more detailed bibliographical information may be found at the end of this work.

AAu	Audas: Native Trees of Australia. 1947
AB	Arnoldia; Bulletin of the Arnold Arboretum. 1911 →
ANZ	Allan, H. H.: Flora of New Zealand, Vols. 1–2. 1961–1970.
Bai	Baileya (periodical). 1953
BB	Britton & Brown: Illustrated Flora of the Northern USA and Canada, 3 Vols. 1896–1898
BC	Bailey, Standard Cyclopedia of Horticulture; 1950
BCi	Bolanos: Cistographia Hispanica. 1949
BD	Bulletins de la Société Dendrologique de France. 1906–1939
BFC	Clapham-Tutin-Warburg: Flora of the British Isles Illustrations, 4 Vols. 1957–1965
BFl	Barrett: Common Exotic Trees of South Florida. 1956
BIC	Bor & Raizada: Some beautiful Indian Climbers and Shrubs. 1954
BIT	Blatter & Millard: Some beautiful Indian Trees. 1954
BM	Curtis' Botanical Magazine, 1787–1947 ns (new series) 1948 →
BR	Botanical Register. 1815–1847
BRho	Bowers: Rhododendron and Azaleas. 1960
BS	Bean: Trees and Shrubs hardy in the British Isles, 4 Vols. 1970 →
CBa	Camus: Les Bambusées. 1913
CCh	Camus: Les Châtaigniers
CFQ	Carvalho & Franco: Carvalhos de Portugal. 1954
CFTa	Curtis: The endemic Flora of Tasmania, 5 Vols.
ChHe	Chapple: Heather Garden. 1961
CIS	Hu-Chun: Icones Plantarum Sinicarum, Vols. 1–5
CMi	Clements: Minnesota Trees and Shrubs. 1912
CQ	Camus: Monographie du genre *Quercus,* 6 Vols. 1936–1954
CS	Camus: Monographie des Saules de France. 1904–1905
CTa	Curtis: Student's Flora of Tasmania. 1956 to 1967
CWF	Clark: Wild Flowers of British Columbia. 1973
DB	Deutsche Baumschule. 1949 →
Dfl	Dendroflora (yearbook). 1964 →
DH	Dallimore: Holly, Box and Yew. 1908
DL	Dippel: Handbuch der Laubholzkunde, 3 Vols. 1889–1893
DRHS	Dictionary of Gardening, 4 Vols. 1951, Supplement 1969
EH	Elwes & Henry: Trees of Great Britain and Ireland, 7 Vols. 1906–1913
EKW	Encke: Die schönsten Kalt– und Warmhauspflanzen

ENP	Engler & Prantl: Die Natürlichen Pflanzenfamilien, 2nd Ed. 1924 →
EP	Engler: Das Pflanzenreich
EWA	Erickson: Flowers and Plants of Western Australia
FAu	Forest Trees of Australia. 1957
FIO	Fang: Icones Plantarum Omeiensium. 1942–1946
FRu	Focke: Species Ruborum 1–23, 1911 to 1914
FS	Flore des Serres et des Jardins de L'Europe, 23 Vols. 1845–1880
FSA	Coed/de Winter/Rycroft: Flora of South Africa
GC	Gardeners Chronicle. 1841 →
GF	Garden and Forest. 1888–1897
Gfl	Gartenflora. 1852–1938
GH	Gentes Herbarium. 1935 →
Gn	The Garden (periodical)
GPN	Gram-Jessen: Vilde Planter i Norden, 4 Vols.
Gs	Gartenschönheit. 1920–1942
GSP	Grimm: Shrubs of Pennsylvania. 1952
GTP	Grimm: Trees of Pennsylvania. 1950
Gw	Gartenwelt. 1897 →
HAl	Hara: Photo-Album of Plants of Eastern Himalaya. 1968
HBa	Houzeau de Lehaie: Le Bambou. 1906 to 1908
HF	Schlechtendahl-Langethal-Schenck: Flora von Deutschland, 5th Edition, Published by Hallier. 1880–1887
HH	Hough: Handbook of the Northern States and Canada. 1950
HHD	Harlow-Harrar: Textbook of Dendrology. 1941
HHS	Harrar-Harrar: Guide to the Southern Trees. 1962
HHo	Hume: Hollies. 1953
HHy	Haworth-Booth: Hydrangeas. 1951
HI	Hooker: Icones Plantarum. 1836 →
HIv	Hibbert: The Ivy. 1872
HKS	Hong Kong Shrubs. 1971
HKT	Hong Kong Trees. 1969
HL	Hendriks: Onze Loofhoutgewassen, 2nd Edition 1957
HM	Hegi: Flora von Mitteleuropa, 13 Vols. 1908–1931
HRh	Hooker: Rhododendrons of Sikkim-Himalaya. 1849–1851
HS	Hao: Synopsis of the Chinese *Salix.* 1936
HSo	Hedlund: Monographie der Gattung *Sorbus.* 1901
HTS	Harrison: Know your Trees and Shrubs. 1965
HW	Hempel & Wilhelm: Baume und Straucher des Waldes, 3 Vols. 1889–1899
IC	Ingram: Ornamental Cherries, 1948
ICS	Icones Cormophytorum Sinicorum, 4 Vols. 1972–1975
IH	L'Illustration Horticole. 1854–1896

JA	Journal of the Arnold Arboretum. 1919 →
JAm	Jones: The American species of *Amelanchier*. 1946
JMa	Johnstone: Asiatic Magnolias in Cultivation. 1955
JRHS	Journal of the Royal Horticulture Society. 1846 →
JRi	Janczewski: Monographie des Grosseilliers. 1907
JRL	Jahrbücher Rhododendron und immergrune Laubgehölz. 1937–1942; 1952 →
KD	Koehne: Deutsche Dendrologie. 1893
KEu	Kelly: Eucalypts. 1969
KF	Kirk: Forest Flora of New Zealand. 1889
KGC	Kunkel: Flora de Gran Canaria. 1974 →
KIF	Kurata: Illustrated important Forest Trees of Japan, 4 Vols. 1971–1973
KO	Kitamura & Okamoto; Coloured illustrations of Trees and Shrubs of Japan
KRA	Koidzume: Revision Aceracearum Japonicarum. 1911
KSo	Karpati: Die *Sorbus*-Arten Ungarns. 1960
KSR	Keller: Synopsis Rosarum Spontanearum Europae Mediae. 1931
KTF	Kurz & Godfrey: The Trees of Northern Florida. 1962
LAu	Lord: Shrubs and Trees for Australian Gardens. 1948
LCl	Lavallée: Les Clématites a grandes fleurs. 1884
LF	Lee: Forest Botany of China. 1935
LLC	Lloyd, C.: *Clematis*. 1965
LNH	Labillardiére: Novae Hollandiae Plantarum Specimen. 1804
LT	Liu: Illustrations of native and introduced plants of Taiwan, 2 Vols. 1960
Lu	Lustgarden (periodical). 1920 →
LWT	Li: Woody Flora of Taiwan. 1963
MB	Mitford: The Bamboo Garden. 1896
MCea	McMinn: A systematic study of the genus *Ceanothus*. 1942
MCl	Markham: *Clematis*
MD	Newsletters of the German Dendrological Society. 1892 →
MFl	Meyer: Flieder (Lilacs). 1952
MFu	Munz: A revision of the genus *Fuchsia*. 1943
MG	Moellers Deutsche Gärtner-Zeitung. 1896 to 1936
MiB	Miyoshi: Die Japanischen Bergkirschen. 1916
MJ	Makino: Illustr. Flora of Japan. 1956
MJCl	Moore & Jackman: *Clematis*
MLi	McKelvey: The Lilac. 1928
MM	McMinn & Maino: The Pacific Coast Trees. 1935
MMa	Millais: Magnolias. 1927
MNZ	Metcalf: Cultivation of New Zealand Trees and Shrubs. 1972
Mot	Mottet: Les arbres et Arbustes d'ornement. 1925
MOT	Muller: The Oaks of Texas. 1951
MPW	McCurrach: Palms of the World. 1960
MRh	Millais: Rhododendrons, 2 Vols. 1917 and 1924

MS	McMinn: Manual of the Californian Shrubs. 1951
NBB	Gleason: The New Britton & Brown, Ill. Flora
NDJ	Yearbook of the Netherlands Dendrological Society. 1925 to 1961
NF	The New Flora and Silva. 1928–1940
NH	Nat. Hort. Magazine. 1922 → (see only those after 1955), from 1960–1974 name changed to 'American Horticulture Magazine'
NK	Nakai: Flora Sylvatica Koreana. 1915
NT	Nakai: Trees and Shrubs of Japan proper. 1927
NTC	Native Trees of Canada. 7th edition 1969
OFC	Ohwi: Flowering Cherries of Japan. 1973
PB	Hesmer: Das Pappel-Buch. 1951
PBl	Pareys Blumengärtnerei, 2nd edition 1958–1960
PCa	Pertchik: Flowering Trees of the Caribbean
PDR	Poln. Dendr. Rocznik (see only after 1950)
PEu	Polunin: Flowers of Europe
PFC	Pizarro: Sinopsis de la Flora Chilena. 1959
PMe	Polunin: Flowers of the Mediterranean
PPT	Palmer, E. & N. Pitman: Trees of Southern Africa, 3 Vols. 1972
PSw	Polunin: Flowers of Southwest Europe
RBa	Rivière: Les Bambous. 1878
RH	Revue Horticole. 1829 →
Rho	Rhodora. 1899 →
RLo	Rehder: Synopsis of the genus *Lonicera*. 1903
RMi	Rosendahl: Trees and Shrubs of the Upper Midwest. 1955
RPr	Rousseau: The Proteaceae of South Africa. 1970
RWF	Rickett: Wild Flowers of the United States, 13 Vols.
RYB	Rhododendron Year Book, 1–8; from Vol. 9 Rhododendron and Camellia Year Book. To 1971
SB	Satow: The cultivation of Bamboos. 1899
SC	Sweet: Cistineae
SCa	Sealy: A revision of the genus *Camelia*. 1958
SDK	Sokoloff: Bäume und Sträucher der USSR, 7 Vols.
SEl	Servettaz: Monograph. Eleagnaceae
SFP	Salmon: New Zealand Flowers and Plants in Colour. 1967
SH	Schneider: Handbuch der Laubholzkunde, 2 Vols. 1904–1912
SL	Silva Tarouca: Unsere Freiland-Laubgehölze. 1922
SM	Sargent: Manual of the Trees of North America. 1933
SME	Schwarz: Monographie der Eichen Mitteleuropas und des Mittelmeergebietes. 1936–1939
SNp	Stainton: Forests of Nepal. 1972
SPa	Sudworth: Forest Trees of the Pacific Slope. 1908
SR	Stevenson: Species of *Rhododendron*. 1947
SS	Sargent: The Silva of North America, 14 Vols. 1891–1902
ST	Sargent: Trees and Shrubs, 2 Vols. 1905 to 1913

StP	Stern: A study of the genus *Paeonia*. 1946
THe	Tobler: Die Gattung *Hedera*. 1912
TPy	Terpo: Pyri Hungariae. 1960
TY	Trelease: The Yuccaceae. 1902
UCa	Urquhart: The *Camellia*, 2 Vols. 1956 and 1960
UJD	Uehara: Japanische Dendrologie, 4 Vols. 1959 (undated!)
UR	Urquhart: The *Rhododendron*, 2 Vols. 1958 and 1962
VG	Viciosa: Genisteas Espanoles I–II. 1953 to 1955
VQ	Vicioso: Revision del genero *Quercus* en Espana. 1950
VSa	Vicioso: Salicaceas de Espana. 1951
VT	Vines: Trees, Shrubs and Vines of the Southwest. 1960
VU	Vicioso: Ulex. 1962
WJ	Wilson: The Cherries of Japan. 1916
WR	Willmott: The genus *Rosa*, 2 Vols. 1910 to 1914
WRu	Watson: Handbook of the Rubi of Great Britain and Ireland. 1958
WT	West-Arnold: The native Trees of Florida. 1956
YTS	Yamakai Color Guide, Flowering Garden Trees and Shrubs, Vols. 1–2. 1971
YWP	Yamakai Color Guide, Flowers of Woody Plants, 1–2. 1969.

Plant Descriptions

Prunus L. — Almond, Cherry, Peach, Plum — Rosaceae

Deciduous, occasionally evergreen shrubs or trees; leaves alternate, serrate, occasionally entire, with stipules; flowers solitary or in clusters or racemes; sepals and petals 5 each, usually white, often pink to red; stamens numerous, pistil 1, with an elongated style; fruit a drupe, usually single seeded. — About 430 species, most in the temperate zones, some in the Andes of South America.

Outline of the Subgenera and Sections of the species described

★ Fruits furrowed, usually pruinose; leaves involuted.

Subgenus I. **Prunus**
(= *Prunophora* [Neck.] Focke)
Fruit furrowed, glabrous, usually pruinose, seed pit compressed, usually longer than wide, smooth or nearly so; flowers solitary or umbellate clusters, appearing before the foliage, occasionally appearing at the same time; petiole usually persisting on the fruit (except *P. simonii*).

Section 1. **Euprunus** Koehne
(= *Prunus* Benth. & Hook.). Plum
Ovaries and fruits glabrous; flowers stalked, solitary or in pairs, occasionally in 3's; seed often pitted; leaves rolled up in the bud stage:
> *P. blireana, bokhariensis, cerasifera, cocomilia, consociiflora, curdica, domestica, gigantea, gymnodonta, institia, monticola, pseudoarmeniaca, salicina, simonii, spinosa, ursina, ussuriensis*

Section 2. **Prunocerasus** Koehne
Flowers in 3's or more, occasionally solitary; seed usually smooth; leaves folded in the bud stage, occasionally rolled:
> *P. alleghaniensis, americana, angustifolia, dunbarii, gracilis, gravesii, hortulana, maritima, mexicana, munsoniana, nigra, orthosepala, reverchonii, subcordata, umbellata*

Section 3. **Armeniaca** (Mill.) K. Koch
Apricot
Ovaries and fruits pubescent (only *P. brigantina* is glabrous); flowers sessile (stalked on *P. dasycarpa*); Leaves rolled up in the bud stage:
> *P. armeniaca, brigantina, dasycarpa, mandshurica, mume, sibirica*

Subgenus II. **Amygdalus** (L.) Benth. & Hook.
Almond, Peach
Flowers sessile or short stalked, appearing before the foliage; fruit tomentose, normally dehiscent; seed pitted or smooth; leaves folded in the bud stage; buds in groups of 3, of which the laterals are flower buds; terminal bud present:
> *P. amygdalo-persica, arabica, argentea, arnoldiana, baldschuanica, bucharica, davidiana, dulcis, fasciculata, fenzliana, kansuensis, mira, mongolica, pedunculata, persica, petunnikowii, pilosa, skinneri, spinosissima, sweginzowii, tangutica, tenella, triloba, vavilovii, webbii*

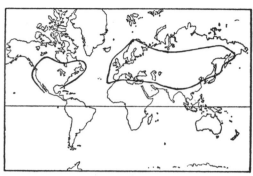

Fig. 1. Range of the genus *Prunus*

★★ Fruit not furrowed, not pruinose; seed bulging or nearly globose; leaves folded in the bud stage; terminal bud present.

Subgenus III. **Cerasus** (Adans.) Focke
Large trees or shrubs, to 18 m high or more; inflorescences never in true racemes, relatively few flowers, appearing before or with the foliage; flowers normally distinctly stalked, solitary or in clusters; calyx tube campanulate, urceolate or cupulate.

Section 4. **Eucerasus** Koehne
Large shrubs or trees, to 18 m high; leaves obtusely serrate or crenate; inflorescence usually a sessile umbel, occasionally on a short stalk (like *P. fruticosa*); involucre large, persisting while in flower; calyx cup campanulate-urceolate, glabrous; petals entire:
> *P. avium, cerasus, eminens, fontanesiana, fruticosa, gonduinii*

Section 5. **Sargentiella** Koehne
Large shrubs or trees, to 18 m high; leaves incised and usually biserrate, teeth often with an acuminate awn; inflorescence a nearly sessile umbel or corymb, appearing before or with the foliage; calyx cup tubular-campanulate, sepals narrowly triangular, erect or outspread; petals usually emarginate at the apex:
> *P. campanulata, cerasoides, concinna, hillieri, hirtipes, incisa, juddii, kurilensis, nipponica, sargentii, serrulata, speciosa, yedoensis*

Section 6. **Cyclaminium** Koehne
Trees, to 9 m high; leaves often somewhat convex, coarsely serrate; stipules usually incised (fringe-like), with stalked glands; inflorescence a loose corymb with leaflike bracts, margin with stalked glands; calyx cup broadly campanulate; sepals long, completely reflexed when in full bloom:
> *P. cyclamina, dielsiana*

Section 7. **Confusicerasus** Ingram
Trees, to 7 m high; leaves obtuse and biserrate to

finely lobed; inflorescence a corymb, these sessile on those species flowering before leafing out in spring, but distinctly stalked on those species flowering at the same time the leaves appear:

> *P. dawyckensis, pseudocerasus*

Section 8. **Microcalymma** Koehne
Trees, 9–18 m high; leaves simple or somewhat biserrate; inflorescence usually an umbel; calyx lobes distinctly bulging at the base; petals incised at the apex:

> *P. changyangensis, subhirtella*

Section 9. **Magnicupula** Ingram
Shrubs or trees, to 15 m high; leaves often coarsely serrate (but with fine, dense teeth on *P. serrula*); flowers appearing with the leaves, inflorescence a few flowered, sessile umbel (normally with only 1–2 flowers); calyx campanulate, usually relatively large compared to the corolla; calyx lobes relatively short; petals usually entire, wide; fruits usually ellipsoid:

> *P. apetala, canescens, mugus, rufa, schmittii, serrula, setulosa*

Section 10. **Phyllocerasus** (Koehne) Rehd.
Trees, to 7 m high; leaves acutely serrate; flowers in short stalked, occasionally nearly sessile umbels, with 1–4 flowers; calyx cup short campanulate; calyx lobes partly reflexed; stamens distinctly exserted and widely outspread; fruits ellipsoid, red when ripe:

> *P. litigiosa, pilosiuscula, tatsienensis*

Section 11. **Phyllomahaleb** (Koehne) Rehd.
Trees, to 10 m high; leaves with acute or acuminate teeth; flowers appearing with the foliage, grouped 4–8 in erect or nearly erect corymbs, usually (but not always) with persistent, leaflike bracts; calyx cup campanulate-cupulate:

> *P. conadenia, emarginata, maackii, macradenia, mahaleb, maximowiczii, pensylvanica, pleiocerasus*

Subgenus IV. **Padus** (Moench) Focke
Leaves deciduous; flowers grouped more than 12 in elongated racemes, these foliate at the base; bracts (subtending leaves) small; flowers appearing with the foliage; calyx cup broad cupulate:

> *P. alabamensis, buergeriana, cornuta, grayana, laucheana, padus, sericea, serotina, ssiori, vaniotii, virens, virginiana, wilsonii*

Subgenus V. **Lithocerasus** Ingram
Small shrubs, 0.3–3 m high; buds in groups of 3 together; the lateral ones are flower buds, flowers appearing with the foliage, usually more or less distinctly short stalked and grouped 1–2 or more in sessile umbels; calyx cup tubular to cupulate.

Section 12. **Microcerasus** (Spach) Schneid.
Small shrubs, about 1–3 m high, young shoots usually very thin; flowers appearing with the foliage, usually distinctly stalked; calyx cup hemispherical to cupulate; fruit always glabrous:

> *P. besseyi, cistena, glandulosa, humilis, japonica, pumila, utahensis*

Section 13. **Amygdalocerasus** Koehne

Low shrubs, usually 0.3–1 m high; flowers usually sessile or short stalked (but distinctly stalked on some species); calyx cup more or less tubular, usually somewhat bulging at the base, often also shorter and more cupulate; petals occasionally somewhat pubescent at the base on the dorsal side; fruits usually glabrous, occasionally however (particularly when young), somewhat pubescent near the apex:

> *P. bifrons, incana, jacquemontii, microcarpa, prostrata*

Section 14. **Armeniacocerasus** Ingram
Shrub, to 3 m high or more; leaves densely pubescent, particularly on the underside; flowers appearing with the foliage, usually distinctly sessile; calyx cup broadly campanulate:

> *P. tomentosa*

Subgenus VI. **Laurocerasus** (Ser.) Rehd.
Leaves evergreen, serrate, dentate or entire; flowers in elongated racemes, leafless at the base:

> *P. caroliniana, ilicifolia, laurocerasus, lusitanica, lyonii, spinulosa, wallichii, zippeliana*

Outline of the parentage of the *Prunus* cultivars

This list contains (with some exceptions) no cultivars with Latin names (i.e. 'Latifolia', 'Grandiflora', 'Alba', 'Pendula'), only those with "fancy names".

'Accolade'	→ *sargentii* × *subhirtella*
'Alberti'	→ *padus*
'Alphandii'	→ *mume*
'Amanogawa'	→ *serrulata*
'Ansu'	→ *armeniaca*
'Asagi'	→ *serrulata*
'Asano'	→ *serrulata*
'Aurora'	→ *persica*
'Autumnalis'	→ *subhirtella*
'Autumn Glory'	→ *serrulata*
'Baton Rouge'	→ *skinneri*
'Benardii'	→ *laurocerasus*
'Benden'	→ *serrulata*
"Bendona"	→ **'Benden'**
'Beni-shi-don'	→ *mume*
'Botan-sakura'	→ *serrulata*
'Bruantii'	→ *laurocerasus*
'Bunyardii'	→ *cerasus*
'Burbank'	→ *persica*
'Camelliifolia'	→ *laurocerasus*
'Cardinal'	→ *persica*
'Cartilaginea'	→ *serotina*
"Clara Meyer"	→ **'Klara Mayer'**
'Colchica'	→ *laurocerasus*
'Colorata'	→ *padus*
'Columnaris'	→ *sargentii*
'Crimson Cascade'	→ *persica*
"Dahlem"	→ *subhirtella* 'Plena'
'Daikoku'	→ *serrulata*
'Dawn'	→ *mume*
'Dawsar'	→ *dawyckensis* × *sargentii*
'Decumana'	→ *avium*
'Dropmore'	→ *padus*
'Elfenreigen'	→ *subhirtella* (× ? *concinna*)
'Erect'	→ *laurocerasus*
'February Pink'	→ *incisa*
'Festeri'	→ *cerasifera*

'Fiesseriana' → laurocerasus
'Fire Hill' → tenella
'Fudansakura' → serrulata
'Fugenzo' → serrulata
'Fukubana' → subhirtella
'Fukurokuju' → serrulata
'Gioiko' → serrulata
"Globe" → 'Schnee'
'Hally Jolivette' → subhirtella × yedoensis
'Hatasakura' → serrulata
'Helen Borchers' → persica
'Herbergii' → laurocerasus
'Hessei' → cerasifera
'Hisakura' → serrulata
"Hisakura" → 'Kanzan'
'Hollywood' → cerasifera
'Hokusai' → serrulata
'Horinji' → serrulata
'Iceberg' → persica
'Ichiyo' → serrulata
'Imose' → serrulata
'Ito-kukuri' → serrulata
'Ivensii' → yedoensis
'jamasakura' → serrulata spontanea
"James H. Veitch" → 'Fugenzo'
'Jo-nioi' → serrulata
'Kaba' → serrulata
'Kanzan' → serrulata
"Kwanzan" → 'Kanzan'
'Kiku-sakura' → serrulata
'Kiku-shidare-sakura' → serrulata
'Kirin' → serrulata
'Klara Mayer' → persica
"Kojima" → 'Shirotae'
'Kokonoye-sakura' → serrulata
'Kornicensis' → hillieri
'Kursar' → kurilensis × sargentii
'Lindsayae' → cerasifera
'Louise Asselin' → cerasifera
'Magnoliifolia' → laurocerasus
'Mandarin' → persica
"Maurice" → laurocerasus
'Mikuruma-gaeshi' → serrulata
'Mischeana' → laurocerasus
'Moerheimii' → yedoensis
"Mount Fuji" → 'Shirotae'
'Moseri' → blireana
'Muckle' → nigrella
"Naden" → 'Kanzan'
'Newport' → cerasifera
"New Red" → 'Kanzan'
'Ojochin' → serrulata
'Okame' → campanulata × incisa
'Okiku-sakura' → serrulata
'O-moi-no-wac' → mume
'Oshokun' → serrulata
'Otinii' → laurocerasus
'Otto Luyken' → laurocerasus
'Pandora' → subhirtella × yedoensis
'Peppermint Stick' → persica
'Petzoldii' → triloba
'Pink Perfection' → serrulata
'Pinto' (= 'Peen-to') → persica platycarpa
'Pissardii' → cerasifera
'Plantierensis' → domestica
'Pollardii' → amygdalo-persica
'Prince Charming' → persica
'Purpusii' → cerasifera

'Rancho' → sargentii
'Reynvaanii' → laurocerasus
'Rhexii' → cerasus
'Rosemary Clarke' → mume
'Royal Redleaf' → persica
'Ruby' → kurilensis
'Rudolf Billeter' → laurocerasus
'Ruiran' → serrulata
'Russell's Red' → persica
'Schipkaensis' → laurocerasus
'Schnee' → gondouinii
'Sekiyama' → serrulata
'Semperflorens' → cerasus
"Senriko" → 'Ojochin'
"Shidare-sakura" → 'Kiku-shidare-sakura'
'Shidare Yoshino' → yedoensis
'Shimidsu-sakura' → serrulata
'Shirofugen' → serrulata
'Shirotae' → serrulata
'Shogun' → serrulata
'Shosar' → campanulata × sargentii
'Shubert' → virginiana
'Shujaku' → serrulata
'Spaethii' → padus
'Spire' → hillieri
'Spring Joy' → kurilensis
'Sumi-zome' → serrulata
'Tai Haku' → serrulata
'Taizanfukun' → serrulata
'Takasago' → serrulata
"Taoyama-sakura" → 'Taoyame'
'Temari' → serrulata
'Thundercloud' → cerasifera
'Trailblazer' → cerasifera
'Ukon' → serrulata
'Umineko' → incisa × speciosa
'Uzu-sakura' → serrulata
'Van Nes' → laurocerasus
'Vesuvius' → cerasifera
'Wadai' → pseudocerasus × subhirtella
'Wasino-o' → serrulata
'Woodii' → cerasifera
'Yae-murasaki' → serrulata
'Yedo-sakura' → serrulata
'Yokihi' → serrulata
'Yoshino' → yedoensis
'Zabeliana' → laurocerasus

Prunus acuminata see: *P. maritima*

P. alabamensis Mohr. A tree in its habitat, to 10 m high, young shoots tomentose; leaves ovate-elliptic to more oval-oblong, 6–12 cm long, short acuminate or occasionally also obtusish, rough appressed serrate, base round or tapered, finely pubescent beneath, petiole 6–12 mm long, tomentose; flowers in pubescent, 8–15 cm long racemes, white, corolla about 8 mm wide; fruits globose, thick, eventually nearly black, with persistent calyx remnants. SM 526. Alabama. 1906 z7 Fig. 3.

P. alleghaniensis Porter. Low, irregularly growing shrub, to 5 m high trees, occasionally also smaller, slightly thorny, young shoots pubescent to glabrous, then red-brown; leaves oval-oblong to obovate, acute to acuminate, 6–9 cm long, finely and scabrous serrate, base rounded, pubescent at first, eventually totally glabrous; flowers grouped 2–4 together, 1–2 cm wide,

Fig. 2. *Prunus alleghaniensis* (from Sargent)

Fig. 3. *Prunus alabamensis* (from Sargent)

white, spent flowers pink, calyx usually pubescent (!), sepals oval-oblong, pubescent interior, petals rounded-obovate, April; fruits about 1 cm thick, globose, dark purple, pruinose, pulp pleasantly tart, seed flattened. BB 2012; GSP 241; SS 153; BC 3225. USA, Allegheny Mts. 1889. z6 Plate 6; Fig. 2, 11. ⚭ ✕

P. americana Marsh. Shrub or small tree, 3–8(11) m high, broad growing or broad crowned, stoloniferous (!), bark thick, shoots more or less thorny, young shoots pubescent, light green, later glabrous and brown; leaves ovate to obovate, 6–10 cm long, acuminate, scabrous and often biserrate, base round, dark green above, lighter beneath and somewhat pubescent, petiole without glands; flowers grouped 2–5 in umbels, appearing with the foliage, white, 2–3 cm wide, calyx glabrous on the exterior, tips acuminate, entire; fruits nearly globose, 2–3 cm thick, light violet-red, occasionally yellow, usually not pruinose, exterior tough and not glossy, seed compressed. BB 2007; KTF 109; RMi 255; VT 404; SS 150. East and central N. America. 1765. z4 Ⓕ USA, in windbreaks. Plate 6; Fig. 4. ✕ ⚭

var. *lanata* see: **P. lanata**

var. *mollis* see: **P. lanata**

var. *nigra* see: **P. nigra**

A number of cultivars are available in the USA cultivated for fruit.

P. × amygdalo-persica (West.) Rehd. (*P. dulcis × P. persica*). Tree or shrub, occasionally with somewhat thorny short shoots; leaves lanceolate, like *P. dulcis*, but more scabrous serrate; flowers 4–5 cm wide, light pink with a darker center; fruits peach-like, but dry and eventually splitting open, seed pit hard and furrowed. RH 1908: 64; Gfl 74: 477 (= *P. persico-amygdala* [Reichenb.] Schneid.). Before 1632. First discovered in Switzerland. z4 Fig. 10. ⇪ ⚭

'**Pollardii**'. The type of the cross in cultivation today. Developed before 1904 by Mr. Pollard of Ballarat, Victoria, Australia; first introduced to the trade by the R. U. Nicholls & Co. Nursery in 1904 under the name "Amygdalus communis Pollardii. ⇪

P. amygdalus see: **P. dulcis**

P. angustifolia Marsh. Chicasa Plum. Thinly branched shrub developing thickets, 2.5–4 m high, twigs bowed in

zigzag pattern, glabrous, reddish; leaves elliptic-lanceolate, acute, 2–5 cm long (!), glabrous and glossy above, lighter beneath, margins curved navicularly upward, acuminate, tapered to the base, margins serrate, petioles with or without glands; flowers grouped 2–4, white, appearing before the foliage, about 8 mm wide, stalk 5–6 mm long, calyx lobes ovate, without glands, glabrous on both sides; fruits small, cherry-like, early, red to yellow, with yellow spots, thin pruinose, pulp soft and juicy, not separating from the seed pit, pit ovate, small, rough. BB 2010; SS 152 (= *P. chicasa* Michx.). S. USA. z6 Fig. 4. ⚭

var. **watsonii** (Sarg.) Bailey. Shrub, low, usually only to 1 m high, twigs more distinctly flexuose, thornier; leaves smaller, less acute, less distinctly serrate; flowers smaller; fruits thick shelled. BB 2011; GF 7: 25; BC 3221 (= *P. watsonii* Sarg.). In dry regions from Kansas to New Mexico. 1879. z4 Fig. 11.

P. ansu see: **P. armeniaca** var. **ansu**

P. apetala (S. & Z.) France & Sav. Bushy shrub or a small tree, to 5 m high, young shoots pubescent; leaves broadly obovate, with caudate tips, 3–5 cm long, deeply and irregularly biserrate, both sides densely pubescent, petiole pubescent, 6 mm long; flowers appearing with the foliage, paired or solitary, small, 1.4 cm wide, white, stalk loosely pubescent, calyx rather large, long campanulate, 1 cm long, purple-red, pubescent, sepals rather small, petals broadly obovate, entire to slightly incised; fruits nearly globose, nearly black. MJ 1318; MD 1917: 12; KIF 3: 21; OFC 143 (= *P. ceraseidos* Maxim.; *P. crassipes* Koidz.). Japan, N. Hondo, in the mountains. 1924. Ornamental value slight. z6 Plate 7; Fig. 26.

var. **pilosa** (Koidz.) Wils. All parts less pubescent; leaves more scabrous serrate; flowers larger, calyx 2–3 times longer than the lobes, styles usually glabrous. YWP 2: 19 (= *P. matsumurana* Koehne; *P. crenata* Koehne). Japan, commonly found in the mountains of Honshu on the seaward side and there gradually blending with the type.

P. arabica (Oliv.) Meikle. Erect, broom-like shrub in appearance, 1–1.5 m high, shoots green, angular, glabrous; leaves not numerous, linear-lanceolate, 1–4 cm long, 3–5 mm wide, glabrous, margins finely crenate; flowers solitary, white to pale pink, 1.5 cm wide, petals nearly circular, April; fruits oval, somewhat compressed, to 2.5 cm long, 1.3 cm wide, the dry, leathery shell is pubescent to glabrous and eventually splitting open, seed pit acute to ovate, to 1.5 cm long. TFI 2: 29 (= *P. spartioides* [Spach] Schneid.; *Amygdalus spartioides*

Fig. 4. *Prunus americana* (left) and *P. angustifolia* (right) (from Illick, Sargent)

Spach). Orient, from Syria to Turkey and Iran, in dry regions of the mountains and steppes. 1933. z9

P. argentea (Lam.) Rehd. Divaricate, 2–2.5 m high shrub, twigs thornless, young shoots white tomentose or gray silky glossy; leaves oval-elliptic, 2.5–4 cm long, indistinctly finely serrate to nearly entire, gray-green above, white tomentose beneath, short petioled; flowers in 1's or 2's, appearing with or shortly before the leaves, nearly sessile, about 2 cm wide, light pink, ovaries pubescent, stamens about half as long as the petals; fruits ovate, 1.5 cm long, whitish tomentose (*P. orientalis* Koehne non Walp.). Asia Minor. 1756. z8–9 Fig. 10. Ø ✤

P. arkansana see: **P. mexicana**

P. armeniaca L. Apricot. Round crowned tree, 5–10 m high, or a tall shrub, bark reddish brown, glossy, glabrous; leaves broadly ovate, 5–10 cm long, abruptly short acuminate (!), glabrous; flowers usually solitary, white to pale pink, 2.5 cm wide, calyx red-brown, April; fruits yellow, most with a red cheek, quite short pubescent, flavorful, seed pit large, smooth, with a thick, furrowed margin. HM 1267 (= *Armeniaca vulgaris* Lam.). N. China and Nan Shan, Dzungaria (according to Kostina, USSR). Cultivated for centuries. z6 Plate 6; Fig. 5, 24. ⚭ ✗

var. **ansu** Maxim. Leaves broadly elliptic to broadly ovate, base truncate to broadly cuneate (!); flowers usually in pairs (!), pink; fruit nearly globose, red (!), pulp brownish, sweet, pit a freestone, finely reticulate and sharply angular. JRHS 71: 12; MJ 1300 (= *P. ansu* Komar.). Cultivated in Japan and Korea. 1880. ✤ ⚭ ✗

'**Pendula**'. Branches pendulous. Before 1884.

'**Variegata**'. Leaves white variegated. Before 1770.

P. × arnoldiana Rehd. (*P. cerasifera* × *P. triloba*). Very similar to *P. triloba*, but differing in the white flowers appearing with the foliage, flower stalks longer, sepals reflexed, pubescent interior; leaves more elliptic, not so coarsely serrate, larger, thicker, less pubescent. 1920.

P. avium L. Bird Cherry, Sweet Cherry. Tree generally no taller than 15–20 m, occasionally reaching 25(30) m, crown broadly conical, twigs thick, with many short shoots, young shoots glabrous, leaves oval-oblong, acuminate, coarse and irregularly serrate, glabrous above, only the venation more or less pubescent beneath (!), 6–15 cm long, petiole glabrous, glandular, to 3 cm long; flowers white, in sessile umbels on the previous year's wood, corolla about 2.5 cm wide, calyx glabrous, broadly urceolate, 6 mm long, sepals reflexed, inflorescences without leaflike subtending bracts, April to May; fruits black-red, sweet, somewhat bittersweet on the wild forms. HM 1252; HF 2557. Europe to Asia Minor, Caucasus and W. Siberia. Cultivated for centuries. Ⓕ W. Germany (very limited). z5 ✗ ⚭

Cultivars

'**Asplenifolia**'. Leaves narrower, sharply and deeply incised. Before 1864. Ø

'**Decumana**'. Leaves very large, 20–30 cm long, 12 to 18 cm wide, often cordate at the base, somewhat inflated-convex; flowers normal (= *Cerasus nicotianifolia* Launay; *Cerasus decumana* Launay). Discovered before 1808 in France. Plate 7, 10. Ø

'**Fastigiata**'. Habit narrowly conical (= *P. avium pyramidalis* Aschers. & Graebn.). Before 1825.

'Globe' see: **P. × gondouinii 'Schnee'**

'Multiplex' see: '**Plena**'

'**Nana**'. Dwarf form, short branched; flowers solitary. Before 1914 in England.

'**Pendula**'. Shoots bowed downward, but the branches often erect at the highest point of the arch (= *Cerasus juliana pendula* Ser.). Around 1825 in France.

'**Plena**'. Growth like the species; leaves more scabrous serrate; flowers in double rosettes, pendulous (!). HM 1253; GC 138: 162 (= *P. avium multiplex* Hort.). Known since about 1700 in England. Very beautiful cultivar, flowers abundantly, flowers appear with the light green leaves. An excellent street tree for heavy, alkaline soil. Plate 1, 7, 10. ⊕

'**Praemorsa**'. Leaves notched at the apex, deformed.

'**Rubrifolia**'. Leaves more or less purple-red. Known before 1892 in France. ∅

'**Salicifolia**'. Similar to 'Asplenifolia', leaf blade very narrow, but not so deeply incised. ∅

The fruiting types of sweet cherry are botanically distinguished as follows:

var. **duracina** (L.) K. Koch. Biggareaux. Foliage and fruits very large; fruit pulp firm (!), usually light colored, fruit black or red, occasionally yellow. ⚭ ✂

var. **juliana** (L.) K. Koch. Heart Cherries. Fruit flesh soft (!), very juicy, black or light colored. ⚭ ✂

var. *pyramidalis* see: **P. avium 'Fastigiata'**

P. baldschuanica Regel. Very closely related to *P. triloba* f. *simplex*, but a shrub, broad growing, twigs glabrous; leaves obovate to oblong-obovate, acuminate, more coarsely serrate, teeth more acute; flowers red, calyx tube campanulate, as long as wide, sepals entire, stamens 20. GF 1890: 613; Gs 5: 68. Turkestan. 1890. z5

P. besseyi Bailey. Similar to *P. pumila*, but the stem is usually prostrate, twigs ascending, scarcely over 1 m high, young shoots glabrous; leaves gray-green, more elliptic to oval-lanceolate and inclined downward (not directed upward!), 2–6 cm long, appressed and shallowly serrate, base cuneate, entire, petiole about 1 cm long; flowers white, grouped 2–4 together on the previous year's shoots, about 1.5 cm wide, calyx cupulate, sepals tiny, serrate, early May; fruits nearly globose and to 1.8 cm thick, purple-black, sweet, edible. BB 2019; RMi 255; BM 8156; BC 3231–32. USA. 1900.

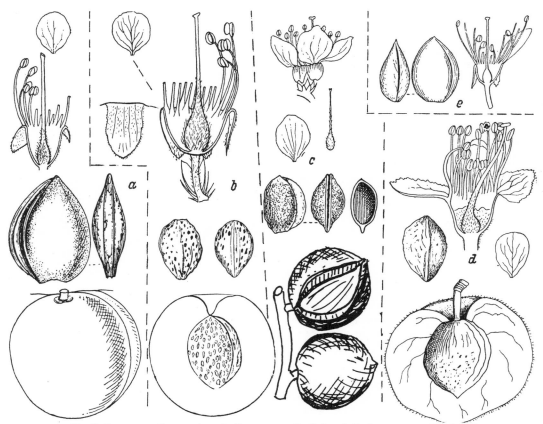

Fig. 5. **Prunus.** a. *P. armeniaca*; b. *P. mume*; c. *P. sibrica*; d. *P. dasycarpa*; e. *P. brigantina* (from Koehne, Sieb. & Zucc., Schneider)

Cultivated for fruit in the USA but seldom fruiting in Europe. z3 Plate 8. ⌀ ⅋ ✕

P. bifrons Fritsch. Very closely related to *P. jacquemontii*, but a shrub, small, only 1–1.5 m high, young shoots pubescent; leaves dimorphic, ovate to obovate on the long shoots, to 3.5 cm long and 2 cm wide, dark gray-green above, silvery tomentose beneath, about 2 cm long and 9 mm wide on the previous year's wood, finely serrate, sharply acuminate, with 6–7 distinct vein pairs; flower stalks about 3 mm long, flowers pink, appearing with the foliage, solitary or in pairs, about 2 cm wide, petals often pubescent at the base on the dorsal side, style pubescent on the basal half; fruits somewhat cordate-globose, amber-red, 8 mm thick (= *P. jacquemontii* var. *bifrons* [Fritsch] Ingram). Himalayas; SW. Afghanistan, Kashmir. 1892. z5 Fig. 14.

P. ✕ blireana André (*P. cerasifera* 'Atropurpurea' ✕ *P. mume*). A broad growing shrub, twigs somewhat nodding; leaves red-brown, oval, 3–6 cm long (reddish in back lighting), later more or less greening, petiole 1–1.5 cm long; flowers solitary, semidouble (!), pink, 3 cm wide, sepals with glands, ovaries pubescent, April. RH 1905: 392; MD 1917: 16; ChCh 77 (= *P. pissardii blireana fl. pl.* Lemoine). Developed in France around 1895; introduced into the trade in 1906 by Lemoine. z6 Plate 11. ⌖

'Moseri' (Moser). Like the above, but stronger growing; leaves somewhat lighter red; flowers smaller and lighter, sepals without glands (!). MD 1917: 16 E (= *P. pissardii moseri fl. pl.* Moser). Developed by Moser, Versailles, France around 1894. ⌖

P. bokhariensis Royle. Closely related to *P. salicina*; leaves oblong-elliptic to obovate-lanceolate, 5–8 cm long, rather tough, finely and narrowly crenate, acuminate, venation pubescent beneath, petiole 6–13 mm long, pubescent; flowers appearing with the foliage, solitary, but also clustered 5–8 (!) on short shoots, about 1.5 cm wide, white, stalks 10–13 mm long, calyx only pubescent on the interior at the base, ovaries glabrous. Kashmir? 1929.

P. borealis see: **P. nigra**

P. bornmülleri see: **P. prostrata** var. **brachypetala**

P. bracteata see: **P. maximowiczii**

P. brigantiaca see: **P. brigantina**

P. brigantina Vill. Briancon Apricot. Shrub or small tree, 3–6 m high, stem short; leaves very similar to *P. mandshurica*, ovate to elliptic, 3–7 cm long, short acuminate, base somewhat cordate, biserrate, pubescent beneath, particularly on the venation; flowers white to pale pink, 2–5 together, about 2 cm wide, May; fruit a small, pure yellow, smooth apricot (= *P. brigantiaca* Vill.). Occurs spontaneously near Briancon in SE. France. Cultivated for centuries. (Bergamot oil is obtained from the seeds; the plant is also occasionally used as an understock.) Fig. 5. ⅋ ✕

P. bucharica (Korsh.) Fedtsch. Buchara Almond. Small

shrub, scarcely over 2 m high, closely related to *P. tangutica*, but only slightly thorny; leaves oval-elliptic or more oblong, 3–4 cm long, acute, finely crenate, petiole thin, to 1.5 cm long; flowers white, sepals long haired on the margin; fruits eventually splitting open, stone ovate to oval-lanceolate, 2.5–3 cm long, smooth or nearly so. Turkestan. 1902.

P. buergeriana Miq. Tree, 9–10 m high, young shoots pubescent or glabrous; leaves elliptic to oblong-elliptic, 7–11 cm long, acuminate, appressed and finely serrate, base cuneate, light green and glabrous beneath, but with hair fascicles in the vein axils, petioles 8–12 mm long; flowers 7 mm wide, white, in slender, 6–8 cm long, finely pubescent racemes, calyx cupulate, sepals short, toothed, stamens somewhat longer than the petals, styles short (!); fruits nearly globose, black, with a persistent calyx (!). NK 5: 1; MJ 1321; KO pl. 39; KIF 2: 28. Japan, Korea. 1894. Quite hardy, but rarely cultivated. z5 Fig. 18.

P. bungei see: **P. humilis**

P. campanulata Maxim. Taiwan Cherry. A tree in its habitat, to 7 m high, or only a tall shrub, young shoots glabrous; leaves oval-oblong, sharply serrate, about 9 cm long, 4 cm wide, acuminate, base usually round, glabrous beneath; flowers grouped 2–5 in pendulous, umbellate racemes, corolla somewhat funnelform, usually a deep wine-red (!!), 1.8 cm wide, appearing before or with the foliage, sepals and the upper part of the calyx reddish, basal portion bronze-green, calyx 7 mm long, sepals partly reflexed, traingular. MCL 29; OFC 146; BM 9575 (= *P. cerasoides* var. *campanulata* Koidz.). S. Japan. 1899. The darkest red flowering *Prunus* species !! Not reliably hardy. z8 Plate 7; Fig. 6, 22. ⌖

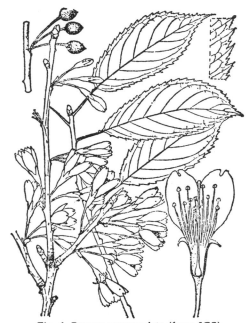

Fig. 6. *Prunus campanulata* (from ICS)

'Plena'. Flowers double, carmine-pink, small flowers.

Including 2 hybrids:

'Okamé' (*P. campanulata* × *P. incisa*). Graceful, small-leaved bush; flowers 3 in stalked clusters, appearing long before the foliage, fuchsia-pink (HCC 627/2), very densely packed on the shoot, calyx brownish red, stalk red, March. Developed before 1947 by C. Ingram, Benenden, England. z7 Plate 11. ⊕

'Shosar' (*P. campanulata* × *P. sargentii*). Medium-sized tree, broadly columnar; leaves bright green, yellow to coppery in fall; flowers large, simple, dark pink, 4 cm wide, very similar to *P. sargentii*, but flowering 3 weeks earlier, stalks and calyces dark red, late March–early April, flowering before the leaves. Developed by C. Ingram. ⊕

P. canescens Bois. Shrub, to 2 m high, twigs steeply ascending, young shoots pubescent, gray-yellow, the bark later exfoliating, exposing a glossy brown, mirror-like reflective trunk; leaves ovate, acuminate, 3–6 cm long, very coarsely serrate, pubescent above, densely gray pubescent beneath, petiole 1 cm long; flowers grouped 2–5, in dense corymbs with leaflike subtending bracts, light pink, petals not fully opening, corolla 1.2 cm wide, calyx campanulate-urceolate, reddish, usually pubescent only at the base, sepals narrowly triangular, petals oblong-obovate, style loosely pubescent on the basal half, April–May; fruit globose, 1 cm thick, light red. Mot 68. China; Hupeh, Szechwan Prov. 1898. z6 Plate 7.

P. cantabrigiensis see: **P. pseudocerasus** var. **cantabrigiensis**

P. capollin see: **P. salicifolia**

P. capuli see: **P. salicifolia**

Fig. 7. *Prunus caroliniana* (from HHS)

P. caroliniana (Mill.) Ait. Evergreen tree, 6–12 m high in its habitat; leaves oblong-lanceolate, acuminate, sparsely serrate to entire, 5–11 cm long, leathery, dark green and glossy above, margins usually somewhat involuted; flowers cream-white, in short, dense, 3–4 cm long, axillary racemes, March–April; fruits oval-rounded, black, 12 mm long, persisting for one year. SS 160; VT 387; KTF 111. S. USA. z7 Fig. 7. # ∅

P. cerasifera Ehrh. Cherry Plum. Tree-like shrub to small tree, 4–8 m high, often thorny, young shoots glabrous, bark green; leaves elliptic to ovate, 2–7 cm long, finely obtusely serrate, bright green, underside glabrous except for the venation (!); flowers solitary (!), white, interior somewhat pink, appearing before the foliage, stalks glabrous, March to early April; fruits globose, juicy, sweet, red to yellow, 2–3 cm thick, slightly pruinose. BM 5934 (= *P. domestica* var. *cerasifera* Ser.; *P. myrobalana* Loisel.). Asia Minor, Caucasus. Cultivated since about 1500. Often used as an understock for plum. Ⓕ Yugoslavia (reforestation) and USSR (windbreaks). z4 Fig. 25. ✕ ⊛

Includes many cultivars:

'Atropurpurea'. Small tree or tall shrub; leaves larger than those of the species, red-brown (!), later gradually becoming a dull purple; flowers white (!), occasionally toned light pink, appearing before the foliage, April; fruits purple-red, globose, 3 cm thick. RH 1891: 190 (= *P. pissardii* Carr.; *P. cerasifera* var. *pissardii* Bailey). Imported into France around 1880 by the Paillet Nursery from Tabris, Iran where the Shah's head gardener was M. Pissard. His name is often erroneously listed as "Pissart" as it was spelled by Carrière (see however, note 2 in Ascherson & Graebner in Synopsis 6, 2: 126). Plate 9. ∅ ⊕

var. **divaricata** (Ledeb.) Bailey. The wild form. Somewhat more slender habit, looser; leaves rounded at the base; flowers smaller, white, appearing with the foliage; fruits yellow, 2 cm thick, globose. BM 6519; HM 1269 (= *P. divaricata* Ledeb.). 1820.

f. *elegans* see: **'Louise Asselin'**

f. *feketeana* see: **'Pendula'**

'Festeri'. Leaves and flowers larger, otherwise similar to 'Atropurpurea'; flowers pink. Australian hybrid.

var. *gigantea* see: **P.** × **gigantea**

'Hessei' (Hesse). Shrub, small, slow growing; leaves narrow, irregularly incised and partly deformed, usually dark brown, teeth usually yellow or greenish, occasionally also yellow on a portion of the leaf blade. Developed around 1906 by Hesse of Weener, W. Germany.

'Hollywood'. Leaves green at first, later more brown-red, about 9 cm long; flowers light pink, appearing before the leaves; fruits rather large, red (= 'Trailblazer'). Developed around 1953 by Clarke in the USA by crossing *P. cerasifera* 'Nigra' × japanese plum 'Shiro'. ⊕ ⊛ ✕ ∅

'Lindsayae'. Graceful habit, tree-like, young shoots with a nearly black bark; leaves red-brown when first opening, later greening; flowers light pink, 2 cm wide, solitary or in pairs. Introduced from Iran before 1935 by Miss Nancy Lindsay of Manor Cottage, Sutton Courtney, Abingdon, Berkshire, England. ∅ ⊕

'Louise Asselin' (Dauthenay). Small shrub, slow growing; leaves green, white speckled (= f. *elegans* Bailey). Developed in 1899 in France.

'Newport'. Shrub to 3 m high; foliage bronze-brown, about like *P. blireana* 'Moseri'; flowers white to pale pink, rather small. Developed before 1942 at the State Fruit Breeding Farm in Zumbra Heights, Minnesota, USA. ⊕ ∅

'Nigra'. Similar to 'Woodii', but with larger leaves; foliage a deep black-red, not fading in fall; flowers pink. Developed in the USA around 1916. ∅ ⊕

'Pendula'. Branches very pendulous; leaves green (= f. *feketeana* Späth). 1901.

var. *pissardii* see: **'Atropurpurea'**

'Purpusii' (Hesse). New growth green, then becoming red-brown, later with yellow and pink zoning along the midrib. Introduced into the trade by Hesse of Weener, W. Germany in 1908.

'Rosea'. Leaves purple-bronze when young, then gradually becoming more bronze-green, totally green by late summer; flowers pure salmon-pink, fading lighter, very densely arranged on nearly thornless shoots (= *P. spinosa* 'Rosea'). Introduced by the B. Ruys Nursery of Dedemsvaart, Holland as a hybrid of *P. cerasifera* 'Nigra' × *P. spinosa*. Growth habit much more open than *P. spinosa*, twigs hardly thorned, flowers somewhat larger and more numerous in the clusters. ⊕ ∅

var. *spaethiana* see: **'Woodii'**

'Thundercloud'. Leaves red-brown, dull bronze in fall; flowers pink. Introduced in 1937 by the Housewearts Nursery, Woodbury, Oregon. Much used in the USA. ⊕ ∅

'Trailblazer' see: **'Hollywood'**

'Vesuvius'. Similar to 'Nigra', but with few flowers; leaves dark red, well colored, rather large. Hybridized by Luther Burbank in the USA. Before 1929. ⊕ ∅

'Woodii' (Späth). Shoots red in cross section; leaves small, like 'Atropurpurea', but remaining evenly black-red from spring to fall; flowers pink. Gw 17: 470 (= var. *spaethiana* Wood). Introduced into the trade by Späth in 1910. ∅ ⊕

P. cerasoides D. Don. Very closely related to *P. campanulata*, but not yet introduced into cultivation; leaves more leathery, sharply serrate, more oval-rounded. SH 1: 339a, 340f.; ICS 2345; HAL 17 and 64 (= *P. puddum* Roxb.). China, Himalayas, Lushai Mts., W. Yunnan Prov. z9 Plate 7; Fig. 22. ⊕

var. *campanulata* see: **P. campanulata**

var. **rubea** Ingram. A tree to 24 m high, shoots glabrous; leaves broadly oval-oblong to more obovate, 7 to 11 cm long, 3.5–5 cm wide, apex caudate-acuminate, finely and densely serrate, the teeth uneven and gland tipped, bright green above, lighter beneath, glabrous but for a few hairs on the venation beneath; flowers grouped 2–4 in pendulous umbels, appearing before the leaves, bud scales and bracts abscising before the flowers are fully opened, calyx tubular-campanulate, 7–9 mm long, glossy carmine on the apex, base brown, sepals ascending, ovate, obtuse, carmine, about 5 mm long, petals forming a campanulate group, pink-red, about 1.4 cm long, February–March (the species flowers in December–January); fruits ellipsoid, 1.5 cm long, red. BMns 12 (= *P. hosseusii* Diels). N. Bengal, Bhutan, Assam, Upper Burma, W. Yunnan. 1931. z9 ⊕

P. ceraseidos Maxim see: **P. apetala**

P. cerasus L. Sour Cherry. Tree, 5(8–10) m high, open crown, rounded, branches outspread, thin, often nodding, bark reddish brown, somewhat glossy, young shoots glabrous, thin, stoloniferous (!); leaves elliptic to ovate, flat, leathery, 5–8 cm long, finely serrate, glossy, only very slightly pubescent on the venation beneath; flowers appearing with the leaves, in dense clusters of 3–4, about 2 cm wide, sepals brownish, glabrous, petals nearly circular, stalks about 2.5 cm long, late April–early May; fruits black-red, globose, somewhat wider than long, sour. HM 1250; HF 2258. SE. Europe to N. India, Iran, Kurdistan. Cultivated for centuries. z3 Fig. 8. ✕

Includes the following ornamental cultivars:

'Bunyardii'. Leaves small, obtuse; flower stalks 5 cm long (!) (=

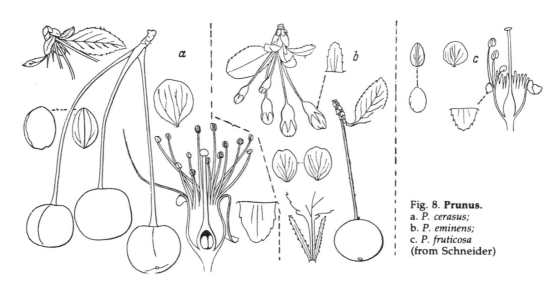

Fig. 8. **Prunus.**
a. *P. cerasus;*
b. *P. eminens;*
c. *P. fruticosa*
(from Schneider)

Fig. 9. *Prunus cerasus* 'Semperflorens' (from BC)

var. *bunyardii* Ingram). Cultivar from the hills of NW. India; grown in the Royal Botanic Garden, Edinburgh, since about 1925.

var. *caproniana ranunculiflora* see: **'Rhexii'**

'Cucullata'. Leaves convex.

f. *globosa* see: **'Umbraculifera'**

'Laciniata'. Leaves particularly deeply incised. ∅

'Persiciflora'. Flowers pale pink, double. Known in Switzerland since 1623.

'Plena'. Flowers only semidouble (!), white (= f. *semiplena* Hort.). Holland. 1851. ⊕

'Polygyna'. Branches and twigs more outspread, less pendulous; flowers often with several carpels, therefore often with several cherries on a common stalk. Switzerland (Geneva). Before 1825. ⌀

'Pulverulenta'. Leaves fine and evenly white and yellow variegated. ∅

'Rhexii'. Flowers densely double, pure white, outspread (!), not pendulous. FS 1805; GC 133: 67 (= *P. ranunculiflora* Voss; *P. cerasus caproniana ranunculiflora* Jaeg.). Known in England since 1594 and illustrated in Gerard's *Herbal*; presumably originated in England. ⊕

'Salicifolia'. Leaves only 1–3 cm wide, 8–12 cm long, coarse and doubly serrate.

'Schnee' see: **P. × gondouinii 'Schnee'**

'Semperflorens'. Densely branched shrub, with many dead short shoots; leaves elliptic, irregularly serrate; flowers usually grouped 3–4(8) in loose groups, each flower separately attached to the shoot, stalk 3–4 cm long, flowers and fruits from May to fall; fruits small, dark red and sour. RH 1871: 50; BC 3238. Origin unknown, but known in 1623. Fig. 9. ⊕ ⌀

f. *semiplena* see: **'Plena'**

'Umbraculifera'. Habit densely rounded, bushy, dwarf; narrow leaved (= f. *globosa* Späth). Introduced into the trade by Späth in 1884.

'Variegata'. Leaves white variegated, more coarsely speckled than 'Pulverulenta'. ∅

The fruit cultivars are classified as follows:

var. **austera** L. Sour Cherry, Morellos. Tree, 5–9 m high, with stout branches; flower stalks longer; fruits dark or black-red, sour to bitter, small or large, juice colored (!), stone globose. ⌀ ✗

var. **caproniana** L. Amarelles. Tree with stout branches, to 9 m high; leaves large; flower stalks shorter; fruits light red, with light, colorless (!) juice, bittersweet, stone usually globose. ⌀ ✗

var. **frutescens** Neilr. Bush Sour Cherries. Shrubby habit, to only 1 m high in dry mountainous areas, twigs thin, nodding, stoloniferous, but becoming taller in cultivation; leaves steeply ascending; fruits with light, colorless juice, always sour, stones ovate, without sharp edges. ⌀

var. **marasca** (Host) Viviani. More strongly branched, branches more or less nodding, often hanging to the ground; stipules larger; inflorescence more compact; fruits very small, black-red, bitter. The maraschino cherry is obtained from this tree. ⌀ ✗

P. changyangensis (Ingram) Ingram. Small tree, about 9–10 m high in its habitat, very similar to *P. subhirtella*, but pubescent on all parts, young shoots pubescent; stipules finely serrate, linear-lanceolate, 6 mm long, 1 mm wide, leaves ovate to oblong-obovate, usually about 5 cm long, 3 cm wide, with 10–16 vein pairs (!), densely pubescent beneath, eventually persisting only on the venation, abruptly acuminate, finely serrate; flowers appearing just before the foliage, usually in clusters of 3–5, corolla about 2.3 cm wide, whitish pink, petals distinctly incised, calyx urceolate, pubescent, base hemispherically inflated, stamens usually 18, style shaggy pubescent at the base; fruits somewhat flat-globose, 9 mm thick, purple-black. IC 18 (= *P. subhirtella* var. *changyangensis* Ingram). China, W. Hupeh Prov.; Changyang Hsien, in the mountain forests. 1907. z6 Plate 7.

P. chicasa see: **P. angustifolia**

P. × cistena (Hansen) Koehne (*P. cerasifera* 'Atropurpurea' × *P. pumila*). Slow growing shrub, scarcely over 2.5 m high and wide; leaves lanceolate-obovate, acuminate, 3–6 cm long, dark brown-red, light red on young twigs, serrate, glossy above, midrib somewhat pubescent beneath, petiole 1–1.5 cm long; flowers solitary or paired, white, calyx and stalk dark brown, May; fruits blackish purple. MD 1917: 16a. Developed by N. E. Hansen in the USA around 1910. "Cistena" is the word for baby in the Sioux Indian language. z3 Plate 2. ∅

P. cocomilia Ten. Related to *P. cerasifera*. Small tree or thorny, smooth branched shrub; leaves elliptic to obovate, 3–5 cm long, 12–15 mm wide, finely serrate, glabrous to nearly so; flowers usually paired, scarcely 12 mm wide, white, stalks about as long as the calyx tube, late April; fruits globose to ellipsoid, yellow, 3 cm long, somewhat acuminate, good flavor. SH 1: 346 m–n. Italy. 1824. z6 Fig. 25. ✗ ⌀

P. communis see: **P. dulcis**

P. conadenia Koehne. Very closely related to *P. maximowiczii*, but the glands on the leaf margin teeth and bracts much larger. A tree, to 10 m high, young shoots glabrous; leaves obovate, 4 to 9 cm long, caudate acuminate, base rounded to lightly cordate, doubly serrate, teeth with conical glands, glabrous beneath or nearly so; flowers grouped 5–8 in racemes, glabrous, flower stalks 5–15 mm long, styles pubescent; fruits red, ovate, stone pitted. W. China. 1908. z5 Plate 8.

P. concinna Koehne. Shrub or small tree, 2–4 m high, young shoots glabrous; leaves oval-oblong to obovate-oblong, long acuminate, usually about 7 cm long and 3 cm wide, base round to cuneate, fine and scabrous, simple to biserrate, dark green above with scattered pubescence, venation pubescent beneath, petioles usually reddish, somewhat pubescent, 6 mm long, with 2 glands, stipules rather small, linear; flowers usually white, occasionally soft pink, 2.5 cm wide, usually solitary or grouped 2(4) in sessile clusters, stalk 1 cm long, with leaflike subtending bracts, calyx glabrous, purple, narrowly campanulate, 7 mm long, sepals entire, narrowly triangular, petals incised, obovate, 12 mm long, flowers abundantly, appearing before the leaves; fruits ovate, purple-black. IC pl. 2. Central China. 1907. z6 ✤

P. conradinae see: **P. hirtipes**

P. consociiflora Schneid. Closely related to *P. salicina*, but with the leaves pleated (!) in the bud stage. Small tree, young shoots glabrous, brown; leaves oblanceolate to obovate, long, drawn out at the apex, base cuneate, 3–7 cm long, finely dentate, the teeth glandular, with axillary pubescence on the venation beneath; flowers grouped 2–3 together, appearing before the leaves, clustered in 2.5 cm wide fascicles on the short shoots, flowers abundantly, fragrant, calyx and flower stalks glabrous, calyx lobes narrow, ovaries glabrous. Central China. 1900. z6 ✤

P. cornuta (Royle) Steud. Tree, to 5 m high (20 m in its habitat), young twigs usually glabrous (or also pubescent), glossy brown, conspicuously thick; leaves elliptic to obovate, acute, 8–20 cm long, base nearly cordate to broadly cuneate, dark green above, bluish green beneath and rust-brown pubescent on the venation when young, petiole 1.5–3 cm long, glandular; flowers white, 6–10 mm wide, in 10–16 cm long, finely pubescent racemes, sepals glandular toothed, late May, after the leaves; fruit nearly globose, pea-sized, purple-brown. BM 9423 (= *P. pachyclada* Zab.). Himalayas, in the mountains to 4000 m. 1860. The name "cornuta" (= horned) refers to a deformity of the fruits in the plants' native habitat caused by a gall wasp making a horn-like curved fruit form. z5 Plate 5; Fig. 18. ∅

P. crassipes see: **P. apetala**

P. crenata see: **P. apetala** var. **pilosa**

P. curdica Fenzl & Fritsch. Low shrub, only about 0.5 m high, divaricately branched, not as stoutly thorned as *P. spinosa*; leaves elliptic, acute, 6–9 cm long, to 3 cm wide, both sides pubescent at first, later rather glabrous, petiole 1 cm long; flowers nearly always solitary, about 2

cm wide, flower stalk finely pubescent to glabrous, 1–6 mm long, stamens about 20, appearing with the leaves, April; fruits rounded, erect, blue-black, stone distinctly pitted. SH 1: 346 e, 347 o–q. S. Armenia. Before 1892. z6 Fig. 25.

P. cyclamina Koehne. Tree, about 5 m high (taller in its habitat), young shoots glabrous; leaves oblong-obovate or oblong, with a short tip, usually about 10 cm long and 4.5 cm wide, distinctly ribbed and somewhat rugose above, base rounded, margins often glandular serrate, petiole 1 cm long, furrowed above, with one or several glands, normally totally glabrous; flowers pink-red, 3.6 cm wide, usually 4 in stalked corymbs, with distinctly rounded bracts, calyx broadly campanulate, 4 mm long, glabrous, sepals 3 mm longer (!) than the calyx, slightly ciliate, very reflexed (!), red, petals narrowly ovate, deeply incised, April, 2 weeks earlier than the very closely related *P. dielsiana*; fruits ovate, red. BMns 338. Central China; in the mountains of Hupeh Prov. 1907. z6 Plate 7. ✤

P. damascena see: **P. domestica**

P. × dasycarpa Ehrh. Probably a hybrid between *P. armeniaca × P. cerasifera*. A tree, to 6 m high, twigs reddish, glabrous when young; leaves usually oval-elliptic, 3 to 6 cm long, acuminate, densely and finely serrate, dull green above, venation pubescent beneath, petiole 2–2.5 cm long, often with glands; flowers white, stalks 1 cm long or longer (!), pubescent, March to April; fruit globose, 3 cm thick, purple-red to black-violet (!), pruinose, finely pubescent, flesh juicy, sour, not a freestone, but fruiting only occasionally. Not observed in the wild, but often cultivated in central Asia (according to Kostina), in Afghanistan, Kashmir, Baluchistan, Transcaucasus and Iran. z5 Fig. 5. ⚭ ✕

P. davidiana (Carr.) Franch. Shrub or tree, 3–10 m high, twigs erect, rodlike; leaves lanceolate, long acuminate, 6–12 cm long, widest on the basal third, dark green and somewhat glossy above, lighter beneath, petiole 1–2 cm long, occasionally with glands (!); flowers solitary, 2.5 cm wide, light pink, darker in the center, calyx lobes totally glabrous on the exterior (!), March; fruits nearly globose, about 3 cm long, finely tomentose, yellowish, with a very thin, fleshy pericarp, stone smooth, pitted, flesh easily separated. RH 1902: 120; ICS 2337; Gfl 1412. China; Hopei, Honan, Shansi, Shensi Prov. 1865. z4 Plate 6; Fig. 10. ✤

'**Alba**'. Shoots and leaves a lighter green; flower white. Gfl 1412. First observed in France in 1872. ✤

var. **potaninii** (Batal.) Rehd. Leaves oval-lanceolate, acute to acuminate, 6–7.5 cm long, tougher, glossy above, crenate, base round; fruits ellipsoid. NW. China. 1914.

'**Rubra**'. Like the species, but flowers more intensely red. First observed in cultivation in Holland. 1887. ✤

P. dawyckensis Sealy. Tree, probably to 9 m high or more, young shoots pubescent; leaves narrowly ovate to elliptic, tapered to both ends, coarsely serrate, 9 cm long and 3 cm wide at the middle, pubescent on both sides,

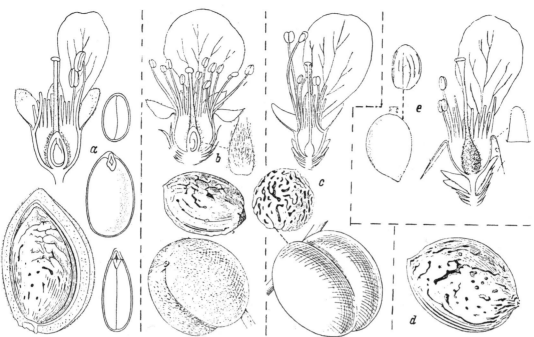

Fig. 10. **Prunus.** a. *P. dulcis;* b. *P. fenzliana;* c. *P. davidiana;* d. *P. amygdalo-persica;* e. *P. argentea* (from Focke, Fritsch, Carrière, Schneider)

venation more densely pubescent beneath, as is the petiole which is 1.5 cm long, with 1–2 red glands; flowers grouped 2–4 in short corymbs, a light mallow-pink, about 2 cm wide, calyx tube inflated, coarsely pubescent at the base, 6 mm long, sepals outspread to somewhat reflexed and pubescent, petals entire, axils pubescent, with small, serrate bracts, April; fruits ellipsoid, yellow-red, 1.5 cm long, juicy and rather sweet. BM 9519. China. 1907. Rehder's view that this plant is a natural hybrid of *P. canescens* × *P. dielsiana* is only a hypothesis and, according to Ingram, not valid. The plant described by Rehder is probably *P. pseudocerasus!* z6 Plate 7. ⊕

Includes the hybrid:

'Dawsar' (*P. dawyckensis* × *P. sargentii*). A smaller tree, upright; shoots, leaves, flower stalks, and calyx pubescent; flowers appear before the leaves, in groups of 3, 4 cm wide, opening purple-pink, later becoming lighter, calyx reddish, pubescent, calyx lobes outspread, petals deeply incised at the apex, flower stalk 2 cm long. JRHS 99: 126. Developed by C. Ingram. 1965. Differing from *P. sargentii* in the pubescence, from *P. dawyckensis* in the more attractive, larger flowers. ⊕

P. depressa see: **P. pumila** var. **depressa**

P. dielsiana Schneid. Shrub or small tree, scarely over 6 m high, young shoots finely pubescent (!); leaves obovate to oblong, 8–14 cm long, usually about 10 cm long and 4 cm wide, apex caudate-acuminate, base broadly cuneate, more finely serrate than *P. cyclamina*, glabrous above, pubescent beneath, particularly on the venation, petiole glandular, distinctly pubescent, furrowed, 1.5 cm long; flowers grouped 3–5, appearing before the leaves, in long stalked corymbs, white to

somewhat reddish, about 3.5 cm wide, axes pubescent, bracts rounded, glandular fringed, calyx broadly campanulate, about 3.5 mm long, pubescent, sepals longer than the calyx, very reflexed, petals incised, styles glabrous, April; fruit broadly ovate, 8 mm thick. IC Pl. 4; BMs 174; ICS 2347. China; W. Hupeh, E. Szechwan Prov. 1907. z6 Plate 7. ⊕

P. divaricata see: **P. cerasifera** var. **divaricata**

P. domestica L. Common Plum. Small tree, 6(10) m high, usually thornless, twigs normally only finely pubescent when young, later glabrous; leaves elliptic to obovate, 5–10 cm long, thin. finely crenate, pubescent on both sides when young, later only pubescent beneath; flowers grouped 1–3 on short shoots, greenish white, usually appearing before the leaves, sepals pubescent on the interior, April; fruits ellipsoid, occasionally nearly globose, blue-black, sweet, fruit pulp easily separating from the stone, stone nearly smooth. HM 1275 (= *P. oeconomica* Borkh.; *P. damascena* Dierb.). S. Europe, Eurasia (origin not known for sure). Cultivated for centuries and in many forms. z5 Fig. 25. ✗

Because of their large number, refer to works on fruit trees for the cultivars.

var. *cerasifera* see: **P. cerasifera**

'Plantierensis' (Simon-Louis). Flowers white, semidouble; fruit violet. Developed in France in 1884. ⊕

P. dulcis D. A. Webb. Almond Tree. Upright, broad crowned tree, to 10 m high, twigs glabrous; leaves oblong to oblong-lanceolate, widest at the middle, to 12 cm long, serrate, long acuminate, base broadly cuneate to round, light green above, glabrous on both sides petiole to 2.5 cm long; flowers solitary or paired, nearly sessile, appearing before the leaves, white to pale pink, calyx lobes oblong, margins pubescent; fruit ovate, flat, 3–6 cm long, shell velvety pubescent, dry, stone smooth, pitted. HM 1259; VT 399; SS 152 (= *P. communis* Arcang.; *P. amygdalus* Batsch; *Amygdalus communis* L.). Syria to N. Africa. Cultivated for centuries. z7 Plate 10; Fig. 10.

The fruit forms are:

var. **amara** (DC.) Focke. Bitter Almond. Basal teeth on the leaves glandular; petals longer than the calyx, style as long as the stamens; stone shell very hard, full of holes, seed bitter, rather small. ⁂ ✗

var. **fragilis** (Borkh.) Focke. Brittle Almond. Margin teeth without glands; petals as long as the calyx, whitish pink; fruit shell crusty, deeply furrowed, brittle, kernel sweet. ⁂ ✗

var. **sativa** (Ludwig) Koch. Sweet Almond. Leaf petiole glandular; petals, leaf margin teeth and fruit shell like those of var. *amara,* but the style longer than the inner stamens; kernel larger and sweet. ⁂ ✗

Ornamental forms:

'Alba Plena'. Flowers pure white, double. ✿

'Purpurea'. Leaves purple-red. ⊘

'Rosea Plena'. Flowers to 4 cm wide, very densely double, dark pink, buds the same color. RH 1875: Pl. 370. ✿

P. × dunbarii Rehd. (*P. americana* × *P. maritima*). Similar to *P. maritima,* shoots eventually glabrous; leaves larger, more scabrous serrate, more acuminate, less pubescent on the underside, flower stalk and calyx becoming glabrous; fruits larger, purple, stone more compressed. Around 1900.

P. effusa 'Schnee' see: **P. × gondouinii 'Schnee'**

P. emarginata (Hook.) Eat. Shrub or small tree, but seldom over 4 m high, young shoots partially pubescent at first, later glabrous; leaves obovate-oblong to oblanceolate, 3–6 cm long, obtuse to emarginate, finely crenate, glabrous above, slightly pubescent beneath, later usually nearly glabrous; flowers white, 1 cm wide, grouped 6–10 in corymbs, flower stalk 5–10 mm long, slightly pubescent, May, appearing after the foliage; fruits globose, red at first, then black, 12 mm wide, bitter. SPa 166; MS 220. N. America; Oregon and California to Idaho and Arizona. 1918. z5 Plate 8; Fig. 12.

var. **mollis** (Hook.) Brew. & Wats. Taller growing, often a tree, 10–12 m high, young shoots densely pubescent; leaves obovate or oblong, to 8 cm long, acute to obtuse, lightly pubescent to glabrous above, softly pubescent beneath; calyx pubescent. SS 157 (as *P. emarginata*) (= *P. prunifolia* [Greene] Shafer; *P. mollis* Walp. non Torr.). N. America; British Columbia to California.

P. × eminens Beck (*P. cerasus* × *P. fruticosa*). Upright shrub, 1–3 m high; leaves and flowers usually longer stalked and also somewhat larger than those of *P. fruticosa,* otherwise somewhat intermediate between the parents. SH 1: 341 l–n (= *P. intermedia* Host non Poir.). 1831. Fig. 8.

P. fasciculata (Torr.) Gray. Desert Almond. Divaricately branched shrub, 0.5–1.5 m high, lateral shoots short, stiff, thorned; leaves clustered on very compressed, usually only bud-sized short shoots, spathulate to linear-lanceolate, 6–12(20) mm long, usually entire or occasionally with 1–2 teeth on either side, tapered to the base, finely pubescent; flowers white, more or less dioecious, grouped 2–3 together, 6 mm wide, March–May; fruits oval-rounded, brown tomentose, about 1 cm long. MS 215. N. America; California to Arizona, on dry mountain slopes. Before 1881. z7

P. fenzliana Fritsch. A dense, stoutly thorned, densely branched, large upright shrub to small tree, 3–4 m high, twigs thin, eventually gray-green, glabrous; leaves narrowly oval-oblong, 6–8 cm long, acuminate, base usually round, bluish green on both sides (!) and glabrous, petiole 1 to 2 cm long; flowers whitish, about 3–4 cm wide, appearing in March (!); fruits with a dry pulp, like small almonds, but the stone is smaller. Caucasus. 1890. Extraordinarily tolerant of cold and dryness. z4 Plate 12; Fig. 10. ✿

P. × fontanesiana (Spach) Schneid. (*P. avium* × *P. mahaleb*). A tree, similar to *P. avium,* but with softly pubescent young shoots; leaves smaller, wider, 6–8 cm long, base often round to somewhat cordate; flowers usually distinctly corymbose, grouped 4–6–10 together, to 2 cm wide; fruits only a few, small, deep red, somewhat bitter. Gw 7: 497 (= *P. graeca* Desf.). Before 1834. z5 ⁂

P. fruticosa Pall. Steppe Cherry. Shrub, to about 1 m high (often grafted on a standard!), twigs outspread, rather divaricate, thin, short branched, glabrous; leaves small, elliptic to obovate, 3–5 cm long, crenate, glabrous, dark green, glossy, tough; flowers grouped 2–4, small, in sessile umbels, white, about 1.5 cm wide. April–May; fruits globose, 1 cm thick, dark red, sour, stone acute on both ends. HM 1249; HF 2559. Middle and E. Europe to Siberia. Before 1600. Often planted as a small crowned (when grafted on a standard) street tree. z4 Plate 6; Fig. 8. ⁂

'Pendula'. Twigs very thin, pendulous, otherwise like the species. Gw 10: 511.

'Variegata'. Twigs thin and pendulous, like 'Pendula', but the leaves yellowish speckled. ⊘

P. × gigantea (Späth) Koehne (*P. amygdalo-persica* × *P. cerasifera*). Closely related to *P. cerasifera.* Leaves elliptic-oblong to elliptic-lanceolate, 7–12 cm long, petiole usually with 2 glands; flowers nearly sessile, sterile, calyx tube hemispherical, sepals rounded, somewhat long haired or nearly glabrous, petals light pink, obovate, very convex. MD 1917: 16 B (= *P. cerasifera gigantea* Späth). 1877.

P. glandulosa Thunb. Dwarf Flowering Almond. A glabrous shrub, about 1.5 m high, occasionally with somewhat pubescent young twigs; leaves oval-oblong to oblong-lanceolate, 3–9 cm long, acute, crenate, finely serrate, base cuneate, both sides totally glabrous or somewhat pubescent on the venation beneath, petiole about 5 mm long; flowers white to light pink, solitary or paired in the leaf axils, corolla about 1.2 cm wide, simple (!), calyx like that of *P. japonica*, style glabrous or pubescent at the base, late April; fruits nearly globose, about 1 cm thick, dark purple-red, ripening in late September. MD 1909: 81; BM 8260; ICS 2348. Central and N. China; Japan. 1835. z4 Fig. 13.

'Alba'. Like the species, but with pure white flowers, single. 1894.

'Alboplena'. Flowers white, densely double, about 2.5 cm wide. 1852. Widely used cultivar. Plate 12. ⊕

'Sinensis'. Twigs and leaves darker than those of the type, leaves more lanceolate; flowers pink, densely double. NK 5: 21 (= *P. glandulosa fl. pl. roseo* Bean; *P. sinensis* Pers.). 1774. ⊕

P. × gondouinii (Poit. & Turp.) Rehd. (*P. avium × P. cerasus*). Twigs usually thin; leaves more similar to *P. avium*; fruits large, like a heart cherry, but sour (!). ⊗ ✗

The low acid, "Duke Cherries" are included here. They consist of about 65 cultivars which may be found detailed in the fruit literature.

Also included here is:

'Schnee'. Small crowned tree (when grafted on a standard) or a shrub, globose, 2–3 m wide as old plants, very densely branched, branches thin; leaves elliptic, 5–7 cm long, dark green; flowers extraordinarily numerous in clusters, single, a dazzling white, completely sterile (= *P. cerasus* 'Schnee'; *P. effusa* 'Schnee'; *P. avium* 'Globe' in the USA). Introduced in 1920 by Wilh. Pfitzer, Stuttgart. An attractive, small crowned park and street tree; cultivated far too little. ⊕

P. gracilis Engelm. & Gray. Broad growing shrubs developing thickets, similar to *P. maritima*, to 1.5 m high, but usually much lower, bark gray, young shoots red-brown and pubescent, quickly becoming glabrous; leaves ovate-elliptic, seldom oval-lanceolate, 3–5 cm long, acute at both ends, finely serrate, finely pubescent above, densely pubescent beneath with reticulate venation, petiole with 0–2 glands; flowers appear before the leaves, grouped 2–4 together, about 1 cm wide, white, stalks and calyx finely pubescent, calyx lobes acutely ovate, entire to finely serrate, without glands. pubescent on both sides; fruits nearly globose, 1.5 cm thick, usually red, somewhat pruinose, stone elliptic, obtuse at both ends, rather smooth. BB 2015; VT 397. SW. USA. 1916. z6 ⊗

P. graeca see: **P. × fontanesiana**

P. gravesii Small. Small shrub, about 1 m high, thornless, young shoots pubescent; leaves circular to oval-rounded, 2.5–4 cm long, rounded to obtuse at the apex, base obtuse to truncate, serrate, pubescent beneath, at least on the venation; flowers white, solitary or grouped 2–3 in axillary umbels, appearing with the foliage, 12 mm wide, petals circular; fruits 8 mm thick, globose, nearly black, somewhat pruinose, stone globose, acuminate at the base. BB 2014. USA; Connecticut. 1902. z5

P. grayana Maxim. Japanese Bird Cherry. Small tree, 5–7 m high in its habitat, with a slender trunk, young shoots usually pubescent or glabrous; leaves oblong-ovate, 7–14 cm long, long acuminate, base usually round, sharp awned serrate, rich green above, gray-green beneath, pubescent on the midrib, petiole about 1 cm long, without glands; flowers many in 7–9 cm long, erect, sessile racemes, foliate at the base, petals reflexed, corolla about 1 cm wide, sepals very small, styles much longer than the stamens, June; fruits globose, with a small tip, eventually black, 8 mm thick, stone smooth. MJ 1322; KO Pl. 39; YWP 2: 21, 22; KIF 1: 70 (= *P. padus* var. *japonica* Miq.). Japan. 1900. z6 Plate 8; Fig. 18.

P. gymnodonta Koehne. Closely related to *P. salicina*, young leaves however, folded in the bud stage. Shrub, much branched, thornless; leaves narrowly obovate to obovate-oblong, 5–7 cm long, short acuminate with a sharp tip, base acute to cuneate, margins serrate, teeth without glands, glabrous to somewhat pubescent beneath, stipules nearly filamentous; flowers appearing with the foliage, solitary or paired, white, about 1.5 cm wide, petals spathulate-obovate, short clawed, stalk only 1.5–3 mm long. Manchuria. Before 1910. z5

P. helenae see: **P. hirtipes**

P. × hillieri (Hillier) (*P. incisa × P. sargentii*). Small tree, densely branched; leaves a gorgeous red in fall. Flowers grouped 1–4, single, white, turning pink, flowers very abundantly, before the leaves. Plate 12.

Includes the following forms:

'Kornicensis' (Wroblewski). Tree, to 5 m, corolla ovate, shoots glabrous, red-brown; leaves elliptic, 5–12 cm long, long acuminate, base rounded, acutely biserrate, midrib pubescent beneath; flowers in clusters of 1–4, light pink, stalk and calyx pubescent; fruits dark red, larger than those of *P. incisa*. Developed in 1930 in the Kornik Arboretum, Poland. ⊕ ∅

'Spire'. Originated as a twig mutation on the species. Develops a very narrow crowned, tightly upright tree, 8 m high by 3 m wide as a 30 year old tree; fall foliage orange, yellow and red; flowers almond pink, single, early. Originated at Hillier Nursery around 1935. An excellent street tree. ⊕

P. hirtipes Hemsl. Koehne. A tree in its habitat, to 8 m, often only a tall shrub in cultivation, branching open and wide arching; leaves reddish on the new growth, broadly ovate to obovate-oblong, short acuminate, 5–10 cm long, biserrate, usually totally glabrous; flowers white, about 2 cm wide, grouped 1–4 together, in short stalked clusters, calyx campanulate-urceolate, 4 mm long, glabrous, petals narrowly ovate, deeply incised, styles glabrous in January in mild areas, otherwise in March, long before the foliage appears; fruits ovate, red. IC Pl. 3 (= *P. conradinae* Koehne; *P. helenae* Koehne). Central China. 1907. z8 Plate 7. ⊕

'Malifolia'. Flowers larger, 3–4 cm wide, appearing 2–3 weeks later (= *P. conradinae* var. *malifolia* Ingram). 1948. ⊕

'Semiplena' (Ingram). Flowers semidouble, an attractive soft pink-white, eventually almost totally white, persisting longer. BMns 551 (this reference includes a detailed explanation for the current name change from *P. conradinae*, with a thorough list of synonyms). Discovered around 1925 by Ingram. Plate 11. ⊕

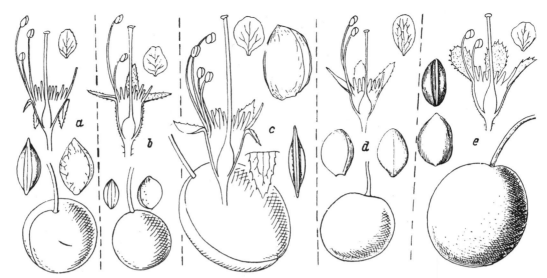

Fig. 11. **Prunus**. a. *P. hortulana*; b. *P. alleghaniensis*; c. *P. nigra*; d. *P. angustifolia* var. *watsonii*; e. *P. subcordata* (from Schneider, Sargent)

P. hortulana Bailey. Tree, growing to 10 m high, not stoloniferous, branches outspread, bark thin, deep brown, somewhat scaly, young shoots glabrous, eventually red-brown; leaves ovate-lanceolate, 7–11 cm long, long acuminate (somewhat similar to *P. persica*), glandular serrate, glossy above, midrib pubescent beneath, rather tough, petiole to 2.5 cm long, with 2 glands; flowers in umbels of 2–4, about 1.5 cm wide, white, stalk and calyx glabrous, calyx lobes glandular serrate and usually pubescent on both sides, eventually reflexed, appearing before the leaves; fruits nearly globose, 2–3 cm long, red or yellow, glabrous or pruinose, thin shelled, stone ellipsoid, bullate, reticulately grooved. BB 2009; VT 403; SS 403. Central USA; cultivated for its fruit. 1890. z6 Fig. 11. ⚭ ✻

P. hosseusii see: **P. cerasoides** var. **rubea**

P. humilis Bge. Shrub, to 1.5 m high, upright, young twigs pubescent; leaves obovate to elliptic, 3–5 cm long, acute to short acuminate, finely serrate, glabrous beneath, venation distinctly raised; flowers 1–2, whitish pink, 1.5 cm wide, style glabrous, appearing with the foliage on the previous year's wood; fruit nearly globose, bright red, about 1.5 cm thick, edible, somewhat sour. BM 7335; MD 1909: 180 (= *P. bungei* Walp.) N. China, on dry, sunny mountain slopes. z5 Fig. 13. ⚭

P. ilicifolia Walp. Evergreen shrub or small tree, *Ilex*-like, about 5(9) m high, dense crowned; leaves ovate to oval-lanceolate, obtuse to acute, 5–7 cm long, base round, margins coarse thorny toothed, blade tough and glossy, petiole 5–10 mm long; flowers white, in slender, about 4 cm long racemes, corolla 8 mm wide; fruits nearly globose, 1.5 cm thick, purple-black, stone ovate. SPa 168; GF 5: 475; SS 162. California. z9 Plate 5; Fig. 12. #∅

P. incana (Pall.) Batsch. Shrub. 1.5–2 m high, loose and upright growing, twigs thin, somewhat pubescent;

leaves ovate to obovate-lanceolate, 2.5–5 cm long, acute, fine and sharply serrate, dark green and smooth above, gray-white tomentose beneath, stipules tiny, linear; flowers 1–2, sessile, 1 cm wide, bright pink, calyx tubular-campanulate, 6 mm long, late April, appearing with the foliage; fruits pea-sized, globose, red, smooth. RH 1853: 281; BR 25: 28 (= *Amygdalus incana* Pall.). SE. Europe, Asia Minor. 1815. z6 Plate 8; Fig. 14. ⚭

P. incisa Thunb. Round crowned, small tree, hardly over 5 m high in the wild, usually only a tall shrub, young shoots glabrous; leaves reddish at first, ovate to obovate, slender acuminate, 3–6 (usually 4.5) cm long, coarsely and incised biserrate, loosely pubescent above, venation more or less pubescent beneath, petiole about 1.2 cm long, distinctly pubescent; flowers 2–3 in sessile clusters, white, corolla about 2.3 cm wide, nodding, stalks usually with oval, serrate, subtending bracts, calyx somewhat rugose, tube campanulate, reddish, as are the 5 mm long sepals, distinctly incised, late March–April; fruits oval, 6–8 mm long, purple-black. BM 8954; MJ 1320; OFC 149; KIF 3: 22. Japan, mountains on south central Hondo. Flowers abundantly and very attractively. z6 Plate 2, 6, 12; Fig. 22. ⚭

var. *moerheimii* see: **P. × yedoensis 'Moerheimii'**

Includes 2 selections:

'February Pink'. Somewhat darker pink than the following form, flowers in February or earlier (flowers susceptible to frost damage!). Selected by Hillier. ⚭

'Praecox'. Pale pink, flowers in January in mild winters or mild climates. Hillier, 1957. ⚭

Also includes the following hybrid (*P. incisa* × *P. speciosa*):

'Umineko'. Narrow crowned tree, to 8 m high and 3 m wide when full grown, wider than *P.* 'Amanogawa'; leaves orange and scarlet in fall; flower single, cupulate, pure white, 2.5 cm wide, with conspicuously golden-yellow stamen filaments, April. 1928. Very attractive. ⚭

P. insititia L. Tall shrub to small tree, 3–7 m high, sometimes thorny, twigs tomentose at first; leaves elliptic to ovate, 4–8 cm long, coarsely crenate, pubescent when young, later becoming glabrous, petiole 1–2 cm long; flowers white, paired, 2–2.5 cm wide, stalks pubescent, April; fruits, pendulous (!), globose to ovate, blue-black, flesh sweet, does not separate easily from the stone, stone smooth, somewhat compressed. HM Pl. 156. Central and Southern Europe to N. Africa. Cultivated since prehistoric times. z5 ✕ ⌀

Often used as an understock for plums.

Distinguished here are:

var. **italica** (Borkh.) L. M. Neumann. This variety comprises the fruit forms European Plum (Greengage) and Victoria Plum. ✕

var. **subsilvestris** Boutigny. The wild form with thorny twigs.

var. **syriaca** (Borkh.) Koehne. Collective name for the mirabelle plums; fruits globose, gold-yellow, sweet. ✕

P. intermedia see: **P.** ✕ **eminens**

P. involucrata see: **P. pseudocerasus**

P. iwagiensis see: **P. nipponica**

P. jacquemontii Hook. f. Shrub, 2–2.5 m high, wide spreading habit, twigs thin, reddish at first and glabrous or sparsely pubescent, later light gray; leaves dimorphic, oval-elliptic to obovate-oblong and to 6 cm long on long shoots, 3 cm wide, acute at both ends, on older wood usually oblanceolate, scarcely over 3 cm long, acuminate, scabrous and regularly but not deeply serrate, dark green above, light green beneath, finely pubescent only when young; flowers usually paired, occasionally solitary, pink, about 2 cm wide, sessile or with a 5 mm long petiole, calyx glabrous, tubular-campanulate, base slightly bulging, sepals only 2 mm long, style shorter than the stamens, appearing with the foliage; fruits nearly globose, red, about 1.5 cm long, juicy. BM 6976. NW. Himalayas, in dry areas. 1879. z7 Plate 8; Fig. 14. ⌖

var. *bifrons* see: **P. bifrons**

P. jamasakura see: **P. serrulata** var. **spontanea**

P. japonica Thunb. Japanese Almond-Cherry. Small, finely branched shrub, 1–1.5 m high, young shoots glabrous; leaves ovate to broadly ovate, long acuminate, scabrous and biserrate, 3–7 cm long, base round to cordate, glabrous on both sides or pubescent on the venation beneath, petiole 2–3 mm long; flowers

Fig. 12. **Prunus.** a. *P. ilicifolia;* b. *P. prostrata;* c. and d. *P. emarginata* (from Sudworth, Bot. Reg. and Dippel)

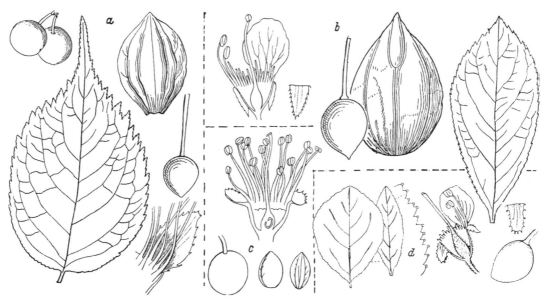

Fig. 13. **Prunus**. a. *P. japonica*; b. *P. humilis*; c. *P. pumila*; d. *P. glandulosa* (from Koehne)

grouped 2–3, whitish pink, to 2 cm wide, short stalked, calyx hemispherical, sepals rather large, serrate, petals obovate, style glabrous, appearing with the leaves, April–May; fruits nearly globose, 1 cm thick, wine-red, stone acute at both ends. MJ 1306; RH 1890; MD 18: 179; ICS 2350 (= *P. japonica* var. *eujaponica* f. *fauriei* Koehne). Central China to Korea; cultivated only in Japan. 1860. z4 Plate 8; Fig. 13. ⊕ ⚭

'Engleri'. Similar to 'Thunbergii', but with the venation on the leaf undersides short pubescent; flower stalks twice as long, about 2 cm long at fruiting, petals 8 mm long or more, pale pink, stamens 6 to 8 mm long, style glabrous or pubescent at the base; fruits 1–1.5 cm thick. Manchuria. 1903. ⚭

'Kerii'. Leaves glabrous beneath; flowers semidouble, ovaries usually 2, flower stalk 3 mm long. BM 2167; BR 27. E. China. 1808. Probably not presently in cultivation. ⊕

var. **nakai** (Lév.) Rehd. Small shrub, scarcely over 50 cm high; leaves very broadly ovate, often pubescent beneath; flowers light pink, few flowers; fruits large, plum-like. NK 5: 22 (= *P. nakai* Lév.). Manchuria. 1918. ⚭

'Thunbergii'. Leaves long acuminate, the teeth distinctly triangular, leaf apex long and narrowly acuminate, leaf base cordate; flowers light pink, petals 5 mm long, stamens shorter than the petals, flower stalk about 4 mm long, style sparsely pubescent at the base. 1910. Japanese cultivar. ⊕

P. × juddii E. Anderson (*P. sargentii* × *P. yedoensis*). Tree, similar to *P. sargentii*, but with coppery colored young leaves, carmine-red in fall; flowers larger, more intensely pink, fragrant, later April–early May, flowers very abundantly. Developed in the Arnold Arboretum in 1914. z6 ⊕

P. kansuensis Rehd. Tall shrub, closely related to *P. persica*, but flowering much earlier and with a different stone type; shoots rodlike, bark furrowed; leaves lanceolate, long acuminate, 5 to 10 cm long, finely dentate, midrib pubescent beneath, widest in the middle, petiole 3–5 mm long; flowers usually paired, clustered at the branch tips in 30–40 cm long flower shoots, white, 2 cm wide, buds pink, petals oval-rounded, stamens as long as the petals, filaments white, anthers yellow, calyx gray, exterior pubescent, often flowering as early as January–February; fruits globose, velvety pubescent, flesh white, hardly edible, a freestone, October, stone furrowed, but not pitted. JRHS 84: 165. NW. China. 1914. z4 ⊕

P. kurilensis Miyabe. Kurile Cherry. Very slow growing, small, thick stemmed, erect shrub, scarcely reaching 1 m high, young shoots pubescent, later becoming glabrous; leaves narrowly ovate, long acuminate, base cuneate, about 7 cm long, 3 cm wide, very coarsely serrate, teeth with glands at the tips, venation above somewhat indented, somewhat rough pubescent, the major veins densely pubescent beneath, petioles 9 mm long, bristly pubescent; flowers white to whitish pink, grouped 1–3 in sessile umbels, flower stalk about 1.3 cm long, pubescent, calyx tubular-campanulate, glabrous except for a few hairs, sepals entire, oval-oblong, calyx and sepals reddish, but the stalk is green (!), corolla 2.8 cm wide, petals broadly oval, white or pink toned, style glabrous, shorter than the stamens (!, longer on *P. nipponica*); fruit flat globose, 7 mm wide, purple-black. MJ 3523; OFC 142 (3 types) (= *P. nipponica* var. *kurilensis* [Miyabe] Wils.). Japan; Kurile, Sachalin, Hokkaido. 1914. z5 Plate 14. ⊕

'Ruby'. Fall foliage conspicuously carmine-red; flowers appearing slightly later, lilac-pink, fading lighter. Selected by Schiphorst in Holland, 1958.

P. kurilensis × P. sargentii. Known only in the following form:

'Kursar' (Ingram). Growth tree-like, vigorous; leaves elliptic to obovate-elliptic, long acuminate, 9–12 cm long, base round to broadly cuneate, scabrous biserrate, short pubescent on both sides, denser beneath, petiole 2–2.5 cm long, glabrous; flowers grouped 3–4, pink (HCC 527), single, early, flowers abundantly. Developed before 1952 by C. Ingram of Benenden, England. ✧

P. lanata (Sudw.) Mack. & Bush. A small tree, crown dense and round, with many root sprouts, bark red-brown, young shoots pubescent to glabrous; leaves obovate to more oblong, 6–12 cm long, acuminate, scabrous and biserrate, base usually broadly cuneate, pubescent beneath, blade rather thin, petiole without glands; flowers grouped 2–5 together, 2–3 cm wide, white, calyx pubescent on the exterior, the flower stalk similarly pubescent, calyx lobe long acuminate, entire; fruit nearly globose, 2–3 cm thick, yellow to red, edible, stone flat. SM 563 (= *P. americana* var. *mollis* Torr. & Gray p.p.; *P. americana* var. *lanata* Sudw.; *P. palmeri* Sarg.). USA, from Illinois to Texas. 1903. z5 ⊗ ✕

P. lannesiana Wils. is a name often utilized by Japanese botanists for their numerous flowering cherries, many of which are hybrids of **P. serrulata** var. **spontanea** × **P. speciosa**. In this book all these Japanese cultivars may be found listed under **P. serrulata**.

P. latidentata see: **P. mugus**

P. × laucheana Bolle (*P. padus* × ? *P. virginiana*). Tree, 8–15 m high, twigs somewhat pendulous, young shoots light brown, punctate; leaves rounded, short acuminate, base round, finely appressed-scabrous serrate, not glossy above, lighter beneath, vein axils pubescent, petiole usually glandular; flowers in short, erect racemes, longer than the leaves, petals rounded, smaller than those of *P. padus*; fruits black-red, 12 mm thick, less pitted than *P. padus* (= *P. padus* var. *rotundifolia* Hort.). Origin unknown. Around 1880. z3

P. laurocerasus L. Laurel Cherry. Evergreen shrubs, also a small tree in mild climates, 2–4(8) m high, young shoots glabrous, green; leaves oblong to obovate or elliptic, stiff and leathery, thick, 5–15(25) cm long, glossy above and dark green, pale green beneath, entire or also somewhat dentate, margins slightly involuted, glabrous on both sides, usually with 4 glands on the basal part of the blade, petiole 8–10 mm long; flowers white, about 8 mm wide, in erect, 5–12 cm long, many-flowered racemes, May, often flowering again in fall; fruits conical, 8 mm long, black-red. HM 1240 (= *Laurocerasus officinalis* Roem.). SE Europe, Asia Minor. 1576. The species is hardly ever found in cultivation, instead a large number of cultivars are used. Of these, the large-leaved forms originate from the Caucasus, the small-leaved forms from the Balkans. z7 # ∅

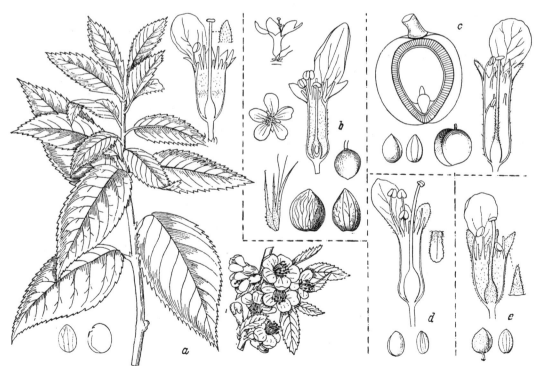

Fig. 14. **Prunus.** a. *P. jacquemontii;* b. *P. incana;* c. *P. bifrons;* d. *P. microcarpa;* e. *P. prostrata*
(from Bot. Mag., Schneider)

Key to the cultivars (from van de Laar 1970)

The key contains only the more commonly found forms; the properties described are for healthy, vigorous plants in full sun. The leaf sizes are only for the blade (without the petiole), the smaller leaves on the short lateral shoots are not considered. The appressed teeth are often very small, but usually larger on older leaves.

1. Leaves shorter than 14 cm, 5.5 cm wide at most... 2
   Leaves longer than 13 cm, often to 10 cm wide ... 12

2. Leaves 6–9 cm long, 2–3 cm wide, rough, glossy, margins distinctly dentate:
   'Rudolph Billeter'

   Leaves longer, margins less distinctly dentate 3

3. Leaves 7–11 cm long 4
   Leaves 9–14 cm long 7

4. Leaves 7–11 cm long, 2–3 cm wide, apex acutely tapered, dark green, very glossy, usually entire:
   'Otto Luyken'

   Leaves broader, less glossy...................... 5

5. Leaves 7–11 cm long, 2–3.5 cm wide, slightly glossy, margins dentate (particularly on older leaves):
   'Schipkaensis Holland'

   Leaves dark green, margins slightly dentate or entire 6

6. Leaves 7–11 cm long, 3–4.5 cm wide, flat, very deep green, slightly glossy, usually entire:
   'Van Nees'

   Leaves 7–11 cm long, 3.5–5 cm wide, more or less convex, rather dull, margins slightly dentate:
   'Schipkaensis Compacta'

7. Leaves 9–14 cm long, 2–3(3.5) cm wide, rather glossy, entire, growth more or less horizontal:
   'Zabeliana'

   Leaves broader (but only slightly so on 'Herbergii') 8

8. Leaves 9–14 cm long, 4–4.5 cm wide, dark green, glossy, margins usually undulate and very slightly dentate, growth more or less horizontal:
   'Mischeana'

   Growth upright............................... 9

9. Leaves 9–14 cm long, 4–5.5 cm wide, more or less convex, rough, apical leaves light green, rather dull, margins very slightly dentate, growth broadly erect:
   'Serbica'

   Leaves flat or channel-like plaited 10

10. Leaves 9–14 cm long, 3.5–5 cm wide, flat, slightly glossy, more or less entire, growth very broadly upright:
    'Schipkaensis'

    Growth straight upright 11

11. Leaves 9–14 cm long, 2.5–4 cm wide, apex acutely tapered, slightly glossy, flat, more or less entire:
    'Herbergii'

    Leaves 9–14 cm long, 2.5–4 cm wide, conspicuously channel-like plaited, dull, margins occasionally somewhat undulate, slightly dentate:
    'Reynvaanii'

12. Leaves 13–17 cm long 13
    Leaves 16–22(25) cm long 15

13. Leaves 13–17 cm long, 3.5–5 cm wide, more or less drooping, also more or less bullate, dark green, glossy, margins very slightly dentate, broadly upright habit:
    'Schipkaensis Macrophylla'

    Growth narrowly upright, leaves lighter.......... 14

14. Leaves 13–17 cm long, 3.5–5 cm wide, glossy, margins slightly dentate:
    'Caucasica'

    Leaves 13–17 cm long, 6–8 cm wide, rounded at the apex to more or less abruptly acuminate, light green, slightly glossy, margins distinctly dentate:
    'Rotundifolia'

15. Leaves 16–20 cm long, 5–6.5 cm wide, glossy, margins slightly dentate:
    'Bruantii'

    Leaves 18–22(25) cm long. 6–8(10) cm wide, glossy, margins slightly dentate:
    'Magnoliifolia'

'Angustifolia'. Tall growing; leaves narrowly oblong to lanceolate, 8–10(12) cm long 2–3 cm wide. RH 1863: 13 (= f. *salicifolia* Jaeg.; f. *longifolia* Jaeg.). Introduced in 1802 by A. Leroy of Angers, France. #

'Benardii'. Large-leaved form. Introduced before 1920 by G. Benard & Cie., near Orléans, France. Existence in cultivation today is questionable. #

f. *bertinii* see: **'Latifolia'**

'Bruantii'. Vigorous, growth to 3 m high or more, branches ascending, open habit, young shoots often reddish; leaves oblong-elliptic, 16–20 cm long, 5–6.5 cm wide, widest at the middle, light green, glossy, slightly dentate. Dfl 7: 60. Selected before 1913 in France. z9 #

'Camelliifolia'. Growth vigorously upright, to about 2.5 m high; leaves elliptic, narrow, curled ring-like, bullate, margins involuted and curved. 1901. Commonly cultivated in English gardens. Plate 14. #

'Caucasica'. Vigorous upright habit, to 3 m high or higher; leaves oblong to narrowly elliptic, 13–17 cm long, 3.5–5 cm wide, normally widest in the middle, usually slightly dentate at the apex and somewhat involuted, light green, glossy. GC 5: 621; Dfl 7: 46, 60. Hardiest of the large-leaved forms. #

'Colchica'. Broad habit, short branched; leaves thin (!), to 18 cm long, only 5 cm wide, dull green; flowers very abundantly. GC 6: 106 a. England. 1853. #

'Compacta' see: **'Schipkaensis Compacta'**

'Erect'. Very similar to 'Rotundifolia' and 'Reynvaanii'. Vigorous grower, to 2.5 m, twigs more outspread; leaves broadly elliptic, 9–14 cm long, 5–6.5 cm wide, slightly dentate, light green, glossy. Selected as a seedling and introduced by P. Lombarts of Zundert, Holland in 1960; not widely distributed. #

'Fiesseriana'. Tight, upright habit; leaves narrowly oblong, 11–12 cm long, 3 cm wide, margins undulate, dull green above. MG 40: 52; Gw 37: 638. Introduced in 1921 by Fiesser of Karlsruhe, W. Germany #

'**Herbergii**'. Dense pyramidal habit, to about 2 m high; leaves oblong to more narrowly elliptic, 9 to 14 cm long, 2.5–4 cm wide, acuminate, entire or with only a few teeth at the apex, margins somewhat undulate, bright green above, slightly glossy; flowers abundantly, May and September. Dfl 7: 47, 58. Brought into the trade in 1930 by Herberg of Germany as a substitute for laurel. A very hardy selection, suitable for hedging. #

'**Latifolia**'. Leaves oblong-elliptic, 20–25 cm long, dark green (= f. *bertinii* of Bertin Pere; f. *macrophylla* of Royer). Brought into the trade around 1869 in Versailles, France. z9 #

f. *laurifolia* see: '**Van Nes**'

f. *longifolia* see: '**Angustifolia**'

f. *macrophylla* see: '**Latifolia**'

"Maurice". Distributed by P. Lombarts of Zundert, Holland around 1955 by this name, but probably only a misspelling of 'Mischeana' to which it is identical. #

'**Microphylla**'. Leaves narrowly lanceolate, 3–5 cm long, 1–2 cm wide, tapered at both ends, slightly dentate (= f. *parvifolia* Hort.). France. 1873. Cultivated today? #

'**Mischeana**'. Growth flat and wide, to 1.5 m high to twice as wide and usually rather circular, new growth brownish, soon becoming dark green, glossy; leaves broadly elliptic, 9–14 cm long, 4–5.5 cm wide, margins usually undulate and slightly dentate particularly near the apex; flowers in 25 cm long, bowed racemes, August–September (and with racemes only half as long in May). Dfl 7: 49, 58 (= f. *rufescens* Hort.; 'Spaethii'). Introduced from the Balkan Mts. by Späth of Berlin and introduced into the trade in 1898. A much valued form. #

'**Otinii**'. Strong upright habit, but compact and sparsely branched; leaves more or less pendulous, 20–25 cm long, 8–10 cm wide, slightly dentate, acute at both ends, the darkest green of all the large-leaved forms, underside lighter or somewhat blue-green. Developed by Otin (or Ottin). St. Etienne, France. z9 #

'**Otto Luyken**'. Broad growing, very dense and compact, shoots erect, about 1 m high as old plants; leaves all rather vertically arranged, oblong-lanceolate, 7–11 cm long, 2–3 cm wide, acuminate, an attractive dark green, glossy, entire, occasionally with a few teeth at the apex of the older leaves; flowers very abundantly with 20 cm long racemes, May–June and August–September. Dfl. 7: 50, 58. Originated as a seedling in 1940 at the Herm. A. Hesse Nursery of Weener, W. Germany, but first introduced into the trade in 1953. Very attractive, slow growing cultivar, excellent for low hedges. #

f. *parvifolia* see: '**Microphylla**'

'**Pyramidalis**'. Habit pyramidal. Cultivated in 1920 and later in the E. Turbat & Cie. and L. Renault Nurseries, both of Orléans, France; possibly no longer in existence. #

'**Reynvaanii**'. Dense, upright habit, to about 2 m high; leaves oblong to narrowly elliptic, 9–14 cm long, 2.5–4 cm wide, widest in the middle, those at the branch tips directed upward and folded somewhat navicular, somewhat dentate, dull green, not glossy; flowers primarily on young plants, May, older plants flower only sparsely. Dfl 7: 47, 58. Developed before 1913 by A. J. Reynvaan of Velp, Holland. #

'**Rotundifolia**'. Habit broad and stoutly erect, to 3 m high; leaves broadly elliptic to obovate, 13 to 17 cm long, 6–8 cm wide, more or less rounded above and abruptly acuminate,

light green (!), not very glossy, tough, margins distinctly dentate. Dfl 7: 46, 61. Developed in 1865 by L. C. B. Billard & Barre of Fontenay-aux-Roses, France. Still widely grown. z8 #

'**Rudolf Billeter**'. Low shrub, broadly ascending habit, unattractively branched; leaves narrowly elliptic to narrow-lanceolate, 6–9 cm long, 2–3 cm wide, light green with still lighter venation, glossy, rough, margins totally coarsely dentate (!). Dfl 7: 58. Selected around 1930 in Stäfa, Switzerland; introduced into the trade in 1962 by C. Frikart. #

f. *rufescens* see: '**Mischeana**'

f. *salicifolia* see: '**Angustifolia**'

'**Schipkaensis**'. Broad growing, occasionally more vase-shaped (also hollow in the center), to 2 m high; leaves oblong to broadly elliptic, 9–14 cm long, 3.5–5 cm wide, flat, nearly entire, slightly glossy; flowers in numerous, 6–8 cm long, erect racemes, May. RH 1905: 43; HL 329; Dfl 7: 43, 53, 59. Introduced by Späth of Berlin, W. Germany from Bulgaria where the plant grows in the Schipka Pass (at 1333 m, near Kasanlik); 1889. Quite winter hardy. #

'**Schipkaensis Compacta**'. Broad habit, to 1 m high, shoots ascending; leaves convex, elliptic, 7 to 11 cm long, 3.5–5 cm wide, often somewhat twisted, slightly dentate, dark green, dull. Dfl 7: 59 (= 'Compacta' Krüssmann, not Bean). Introduced into the trade in 1914 by the W. Klenert Nursery in Graz, Austria. #

'**Schipkaensis Holland**'. This is a 'Schipkaensis' form (probably from a seedling) grown in Dutch nurseries but only named in 1970. Broad growth habit, compact; leaves lanceolate to narrowly elliptic, widest over the middle, 7–11 cm long, 2–3.5 cm wide, somewhat glossy, distinctly dentate, particularly on the basal leaves; flowers very abundantly in erect racemes, May. Dfl 7: 52, 59. Differing from the typical 'Schipkaensis' primarily in the smaller, dentate leaves. #

'**Schipkaensis Macrophylla**'. Differing from 'Schipkaensis' in the open, broadly upright habit, to 2.5 m high; leaves oblong to narrowly elliptic, 8–13(17) cm long, 3–5 cm wide, distinctly acuminate, blade somewhat convex, with indented midrib and lateral veins, more or less bowed downward and pendulous, slightly dentate on the apical half, dark green; flowers very abundantly in 20 cm long racemes, May, often flowering again sparsely in the fall, often fruits well. Dfl 7: 54, 59. Particularly winter hardy selection by G. D. Böhlje, Westerstede, W. Germany, 1930. Introduced into the trade in 1940. One of the most popular forms in cultivation today. Plate 14. #

'**Serbica**'. Broad and dense habit, twigs short and erect, somewhat rounded, low; leaves elliptic, 9–14 cm long, 4–5 cm wide, dull green above, somewhat rugose and convex, the youngest leaves light green, somewhat dentate at the apex. Dfl 7: 60 (= f. *serbica* Pancic). Geographical form from SE. Serbia (Yugoslavia); introduced into Germany in 1877 and further distributed from there. #

'Spaethii' see: '**Mischeana**'

'**Van Nes**'. According to Dutch opinion, very similar to or identical to f. *laurifolia* Schneid., a mountain form from the Caucasus Mts. Growth wide and dense, to about 1.75 m high; leaves oblong to elliptic, 7–11 cm long, 3–4.5 cm wide, very dark green (!), entire, slightly glossy; flowers in about 20 cm long, numerous racemes, August–September, contrasting well with the dark green foliage. Dfl 7: 56, 59. Cultivated by P. van Nes AZ. in Boskoop, Holland since about 1935. Particularly winter hardy and much valued. #

'Variegata'. Growth rather narrowly upright, densely branched, to 2 m high; leaves oblong-lanceolate, dense white punctate and speckled, somewhat bullate. Distributed from France in 1811, commonly grown in England today. z9 #

'Zabeliana'. Growth nearly totally horizontal, but on favorable sites reaching 1.5 m high in a few years, then to 3 m wide; leaves oblong-lanceolate, 9–14 cm long, 2–3 cm wide, light green, entire; flowers in 18 cm long, erect racemes, appearing sparsely in May, very numerous in September. Gw 5: 178; Dfl 7: 58. Introduced by L. Späth of Berlin from Bulgaria in 1898. Very winter hardy, excellent form; widely distributed. #

P. litigiosa Schneid. Small, ascending tree, to about 6 m high, but usually shrubby, to 3 m high, young shoots glabrous; leaves narrowly obovate to oval-oblong, acuminate, about 7 cm long and 3.5 cm wide, finely and scabrous serrate, both sides eventually glabrous except for a few hairs on the venation beneath; flowers usually grouped 2–3 in nearly sessile umbels, white, 2.5 cm wide, pendulous, with many, very long stamens (!), calyx broadly campanulate, sepals triangular, more or less reflexed, petals broadly oval, entire, styles long, the basal half silky pubescent; fruits ellipsoid, 1 cm long, scarlet-red, somewhat translucent. IC 21 and Pl. 6 (= *P. rehderiana* Koehne). China; Hupeh Prov. 1907. z6 Plate 8. ✧

P. lusitanica L. Portugese Laurel Cherry. Evergreen tree or shrub, to 20 m high in its habitat, twigs red, glabrous; leaves oblong-ovate, acuminate, 6–12 cm long, slightly serrate, dark green and glossy above, lighter beneath; flowers white, in 12–15 cm long racemes, corolla about 1 cm wide, June; fruits ovate, 8 mm long, dark red. HM 1240; KGC 19; MD 1914: 280. Spain, Portugal. 1648. z7 Plate 9. # ⌀

'Angustifolia'. Leaves oblong-lanceolate, 5–8 cm long. MD 1907: Pl. 1 (= f. *angustifolia* Dipp.). 1893.

ssp. **azorica** (Mouillef.). Franco. Tall shrub or also a small tree, to 4 m high, often very broad crowned; leaves large, ovate-elliptic, 8–13 cm long, 4.5–6.5 cm wide, nearly entire to finely serrate, with 3–5 pairs of lateral veins, reddish on the new growth, petiole reddish; flowers grouped 20–30 in 10–17 cm long racemes; fruits cherry-like, to 13 mm long, 11 mm thick. Azores, in the mountains. 1860. z9 Plate 15. # ⌀

'Myrtifolia'. Compact habit, conical; leaves more ovate, 3–5 cm long. 1892.

'Variegata'. Leaves small, white margined. 1865.

P. lyonii Sarg. Evergreen shrub or tree, 2.5–14 m high; similar to *P. ilicifolia*, but with much larger leaves, 5–12 cm long, ovate to oval-lanceolate, entire to sparsely and finely serrate, dark green, glabrous, leathery; flowers in 5 to 12 cm long racemes, March–May; fruits 1.2–2.5 cm thick, globose, black. MS 214. USA; California. z8 Plate 5. # ⌀

P. maackii Rupr. Manchurian Cherry, Amur Cherry. Tree, to 10 m high, crown broadly conical, bark of the older branches and trunk brownish yellow, oldest bark shaggy exfoliating (!!), young shoots pubescent; leaves oval-oblong, acute, about 7 cm long, base rounded-cuneate, finely and scabrous serrate, underside finely glandular punctate and somewhat pubescent on the

venation; flowers grouped 6–10 in irregular racemes on older wood (!), calyx campanulate-urceolate, pubescent, 3.5 mm long, sepals oblong-triangular, slightly ciliate, corolla white, 1 cm wide, style longer than the stamens, pubescent to the midpoint, April; fruits black, globose, 5 mm thick, stone rugose. NK 17: 2; SH 1: 352 h–i. Korea, Manchuria. 1910. Wonderful bark! Very winter hardy. z2 ⌀

P. macradenia Koehne. Very closely related to *P. maximowiczii*. Tree, to 10 m high, young shoots glabrous; leaves ovate to oval-elliptic, 4.5–6.5 cm long, caudate-acuminate, base cuneate to round, entire to biserrate, teeth with conical glands, pubescent beneath; flowers grouped 3–4 in pubescent racemes, calyx very densely pubescent (!!); fruits globose, dark red, stalk 6–20 mm long, stone somewhat ribbed. W. China. 1911. z5

P. mahaleb L. St. Lucie Cherry. A broad, round crowned tree, 5–7(10) m high and wide, bark longitudinally furrowed, branches divaricate, nodding, young shoots finely pubescent; leaves circular to broadly ovate, 3–6 cm long, 2–3 cm wide, obtuse to short acuminate, finely callous serrate, base slightly cordate to round, glossy green above, midrib pubescent beneath; flowers white, 1.5 cm wide, fragrant, grouped 6–10 in corymbs, bracts small, leaflike, sepals ovate, entire, May; fruit 6 mm thick, black. BB 2023; HM 1247; HW 3: 57; BS 2: 242. Europe, Asia Minor. Cultivated for centuries; used primarily as an understock for all the sour cherries. The aromatic wood was once used in the manufacture of pipe stems. Ⓕ W. Germany (on slopes), Romania, Yugoslavia (reforestation and windbreaks). z6 Plate 17; Fig. 15. ✧

'Monstrosa'. Dwarf habit, dense, compact (= f. *globosa* Dieck; var. *compacta* Späth, var. *bommii* Bean). 1864.

'Pendula'. Branches somewhat nodding, but otherwise like the species (= var. *pendula* Dipp.). 1893.

'Xanthocarpa'. Fruits yellow (= fr. *albo*; var. *chrysocarpa* Nichols.; fr. *flavo* Hort.). 1839.

P. mandshurica (Maxim.) Koehne. Manchurian Apricot. Small tree, to 6 m (by some accounts to 20 m high in its habitat with a 70 cm diameter trunk), crown divaricate and wide, twigs nodding, dark red-brown; leaves broadly elliptic to ovate, abruptly acuminate, 5–12 cm long, scabrous serrate, teeth longer than wide (!), rich green above, lighter beneath, pubescent in the vein axils; flowers solitary, pale pink, 3 cm wide, April, stalks only 2–5 mm long, ovaries pubescent (!); fruits globose, somewhat wider than long, 2.5 cm wide, yellow, somewhat sour, juicy, stone small, smooth, obtuse angled. NK 5: 25; ICS 2340. Manchuria, Korea. 1900. z6 Plate 6. ⌂ ✂

P. maritima Marsh. Beach Plum. Shrub, 1–2 m high, divaricate habit, twigs red-brown, pubescent at first; leaves elliptic, acute (!), scabrous serrate, 4–6 cm long, glossy green and glabrous above, softly pubescent beneath, petiole pubescent, often glandular (!); flowers grouped 2–3, white, stalk 5–7 mm long, calyx pubescent, April; fruits globose, purple to carmine, pruinose. BB 2013; GSP 238; BC 3226 (= *P. acuminata* Michx.; *P. pubescens* Pursh). E. USA. 1818. z3 Plate 6. ✧

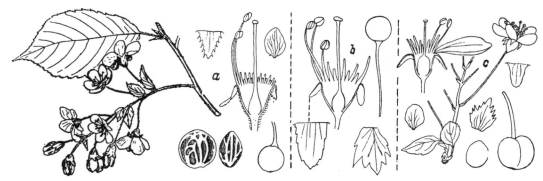

Fig. 15. **Prunus.** a. *P. maximowiczii;* b. *P. pensylvanica;* c. *P. mahaleb*
(from Sargent, Schneider)

P. matsumurana Koehne see: **P. apetala** var. **pilosa** (Koidz.) Wils.

P. maximowiczii Rupr. Small tree, about 7.5 m high, occasionally to 10 m high or more, twigs outspread, young shoots pubescent; leaves usually obovate, 4–8 cm long, abruptly acuminate, coarsely biserrate, bright green and glabrous above, lighter beneath, pubescent on the venation, fall color bright red and yellow (!!); flowers cream-white, 1.5 cm wide. grouped 5–10 in erect corymbs, axes pubescent, bracts leaflike, calyx conical-cupulate, sepals acute and serrate, style glabrous, May, appearing after the foliage; fruits globose, black, 5 mm thick. NK 5: 5; BM 8641; MJ 1310; ICS 2351; KIF 4: 12 (= *P. bracteata* Franch. & Sav.). Japan; central Hondo to Sachalin; Korea; Manchuria, Amur region. 1895. z5 Plate 8; Fig. 15. ⊘

P. mexicana S. Wats. Tree, to 12 m or only a shrub, never stoloniferous (!), young shoots pubescent to glabrous; leaves oblong-obovate, 6–12 cm long, scabrous and often biserrate, abruptly short acuminate, base round to lightly cordate, rugose above and short pubescent at least when young, with reticulate venation and pubescence beneath, somewhat leathery; flowers grouped 2–4, white, about 1.5–2 cm wide, stalk glabrous, calyx lobes usually reflexed, as long as the tube, somewhat dentate to entire at the apex, somewhat glandular, pubescent interior; fruits globose, occasionally ellipsoid, purple-red, pruinose, stone obovoid to nearly globose. ST 165; SM 519 (= *P. arkansana* Sarg.). SW. USA to Mexico. 1910. Occasionally used in the USA as a non-suckering fruit understock. z6

P. microcarpa (Boiss.) C. A. Mey. A quite variable species, closely related to *P. prostrata*, but the leaves and fruits distinctly stalked. Shrub, 2–2.5 m high, densely branched; leaves broadly ovate to elliptic, acute, base usually round, occasionally also cuneate, pubescent at first, later glabrous, 1.5–2.5 cm long, 1–1.6 cm wide, scabrous and unevenly serrate, with 5–7 vein pairs, petiole 7–12 mm long (!); flowers whitish pink, in fascicles of 2–3, about 1 to 1.5 cm wide, calyx campanulate, 4–7 mm long, base somewhat inflated, style glabrous, the 14 stamens slightly exserted, sepals triangular, pubescent interior, stalks 1–2 cm long; fruits

dark red (also occasionally yellow), 1 cm long. BM 8360; TFI 29. Transcaucasia, N. Persia; Elbrus Mts. and Astrabad Province. 1910. z5 Fig. 14. ⊕

var. **diffusa** Schneid. Divaricate habit; leaves usually glabrous, small and rather short petioled, obtuse ovate; flower stalks often shorter than the calyx tube. SW. Persia; Luristan.

var. **pubescens** (Bornm.) Meikle. Low divaricate habit; leaves often short pubescent beneath, but also occasionally glabrous, oval-oblong to obtuse elliptic, usually 1.2 cm long and 4–12 mm wide; flower stalks usually short, but occasionally to 1.5 cm long (= var. *tortuosa* [Boiss. & Hauskn.] Schneid.). Cappadocia. Kurdistan.

var. *tortuosa* see: var. **pubescens**

P. mira Koehne. Shrub or tree, 8–10m high, shoots green, thin, smooth; leaves lanceolate, 5–10 cm long, long acuminate, sparsely crenate, entire near the apex, base round, long pubescent along the midrib beneath, petiole with 2–4 glands; flowers solitary or paired, whitish pink, nearly sessile, 2–2.5 cm wide, calyx red, petals obovate-rounded, sepals ovate, margins pubescent; fruit globose, 3 cm thick, densely tomentose, fleshy, flesh white, dry, edible, but bitter, stone totally smooth (!!, the only almond with a smooth stone). BM 9548. China; W. Szechwan Prov., in the mountains to 3000 m. 1914. z5 ⊕

P. mollis see: **P. emarginata** var. **mollis**

P. mongolica Maxim. Thorny shrub, similar to *P. tangutica*, but glabrous, leaves rounded-elliptic, only about 1 cm long, margins finely crenate, with 4 vein pairs; flowers sessile; fruits smaller, about 1.5 cm long and 1 cm wide, slightly compressed, lightly tomentose, flesh adheres tightly to the stone. S. Mongolia. 1866. z5

P. monticola K. Koch. Broad growing shrub, closely related to *P. cerasifera*, 1–2 m high, but broader than high; leaves ovate to elliptic, 3–5 cm long, 2–3 cm wide, coarsely dentate, glabrous, petiole 8 mm long; flowers white, very numerous, 12 mm wide, usually in pairs on spur-like short shoots, mid April, stamens 30 or more; fruits globose, red, about 2 cm thick, flesh yellow, stone compressed, over 12 mm long. SH 1: 348 a–c, 349 k. Asia Minor. 1854. z5

P. mugus Hand.-Mazz. Low shrub, compact in its habitat and less than 90 cm high, often twice as high in cultivation, young shoots yellow-brown pubescent; leaves elliptic to obovate, dark green, acute to rounded, base broadly cuneate, appressed biserrate, with scattered bristly pubescence above, only the midrib pubescent beneath, about 4 cm long, 2.5 cm wide, petiole glabrous, 6 mm long; flowers grouped 1–2, pink, somewhat campanulate, 1.5 cm wide, few flowers, calyx tubular-campanulate, apical portion red and rugose, base swollen and rust-green, 1 cm long, sepals obtuse triangular, stalk 2 cm long, glabrous; fruits elliptic, 9 mm long, dark red. IC Pl. 5 (= *P. latidentata* var. *souliana* Cardot). SE. Tibet. 1925. z5 Plate 7.

Fig. 16. *Prunus mume* (from ICS)

P. mume S. & Z. Japanese Apricot. Round crowned tree, to 10 m high, or a tall shrub, similar to *P. armeniaca* but the bark of the twigs green (!), thin; leaves ovate to elliptic, long acuminate, 4–10 cm long, finely and scabrous serrate, base usually broadly cuneate, bright green above, lighter with persistent pubescence beneath, particularly on the venation; flowers solitary or paired, sessile, white to dark pink, to 3 cm wide, very fragrant, especially in the evening, appearing before the foliage, petals obovate, April; fruits globose, 2–3 cm thick, yellow to greenish, slightly pubescent, flesh sour to bitter, does not loosen from the stone, stone pitted. NK 5: 24; MJ 1301; GC 29: 183 (= *Armeniaca mume* Sieb.). S. Japan. 1844. z7 Plate 6; Fig. 5, 16, 23. ⚘

Includes many cultivars:

'Alba'. Strong growing form; flower single, pure white, very abundant. RH 1885: 102. ⚘

'Alboplena'. Flowers semidouble, white, appearing as early as late winter. Gn 69: 186; Gfl 1513 b. ⚘

'Alphandii'. Flowers pink, double, March (= *rosea plena*). 1885. ⚘

'Benishidori'. Flowers an intense pink, fading lighter, buds dark pink, double, very fragrant, later March–early April. JRHS 1977: 124. Introduced before 1961. Plate 1. ⚘

'Dawn'. Flowers light pink, double, late flowering. Introduced into the USA in 1925. ⚘

'O-moi-no-wac'. Flowers white, occasionally also with a few pink petals or totally pink, semidouble, cupulate, late March–early April. ⚘

'Pendula'. Small tree with pendulous branches; flowers single or semidouble, pale pink, February–March. ⚘

f. *rosea plena* see: **'Alphandii'**

'Rosemary Clarke'. Flowers semidouble, white, fragrant, calyx red. Named in 1938 by W. B. Clarke of San Jose, California, USA. ⚘

P. munsoniana Wight & Hedr. Tree, to 8 m high, young shoots glabrous, eventually dark red-brown; leaves oblong-lanceolate (!), finely glandular serrate (!), thin, 6–10 cm long, acuminate, base round, light green and glabrous above, pubescent beneath, eventually only on the venation, petiole usually with 2 glands; flowers grouped 2–4, thin stalked, about 1.5 cm wide, calyx lobes oval-oblong, glandular ciliate, exterior usually glabrous, interior pubescent at the base, petals obovate, April–May; fruit usually globose, 1.5–2.5 cm long, red or yellow, white punctate, ripening late, stone acute-elliptic, rough. SM 522; VT 402; BC 3223. Central USA. Occasionally cultivated for its fruit. z6 ⚘ ✗

P. mutabilis see: **P. serrulata** var. **pubescens** and var. **spontanea**

P. myrobalana see: **P. cerasifera**

P. nakai see: **P. japonica** var. **nakai**

P. napaulensis see: **P. sericea**

P. nigra Ait. Canadian Plum. Tree, to 9 m high, branches ascending, small crowned, bark thin; leaves ovate to oblong or obovate, long acuminate, 6–10 cm long (!), coarsely and often doubly serrate, dull dark green above, glabrous, pubescent beneath or eventually nearly so, base obtuse to somewhat cordate, petiole 1.5–2.5 cm long, with 2 red glands near the blade; flowers grouped 3–4 in umbels, appearing before the foliage, white, fading pink, 2–3 cm wide, calyx lobes glandular serrate, acute, eventually becoming red; fruits ellipsoid, to 3 cm long, orange-red, thick shelled, not pruinose, flesh clings tightly to the stone, stone large, flat, sharp angled. BB 2008; RMi 253; BM 1117 (= *P. americana* var. *nigra*

Fig. 17. *Prunus nigra* (from Sargent)

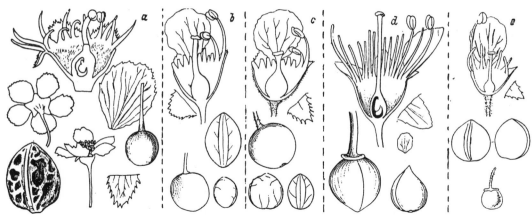

Fig. 18. **Prunus.** a. *P. padus;* b. *P. ssiori;* c. *P. cornuta;* d. *P. grayana;* e. *P. buergeriana*
(from Shirasawa, Schneider)

Wangh.; *P. borealis* Poir.). NE. America. 1773. Occasionally cultivated in Canada for its fruit. z2 Plate 6; Fig. 11, 17. ⚬✕

P. ✕ nigrella W. A. Cumming. (*P. nigra* ✕ *P. tenella*). Shrub with a globose habit, 2.5 to 3 m high; leaves oblanceolate to oblong, occasionally lanceolate, 6.5–9 cm long, 2.5–4 cm wide, acute, base cuneate, margins serrate, venation not as conspicuous as on the parents; flowers appear on 2 year old plants, purple-pink, 3.5 cm wide, of these about 10% with petals and 2 styles, sterile, May. Bai 11: 2 to 4. z3 ⚬

'**Muckle**' The type of the cross. Developed before 1949 by R. M. Muckle, Clandeboye, Manitoba, Canada. Named and introduced in 1952 by the Morden Exp. Farm, Morden, Manitoba, Canada. ⚬

P. nikkoensis see: **P. nipponica**

P. nipponica Matsum. Japanese Alpine Cherry. Tall, open shrub, about 5 m high, young shoots glabrous, twigs chestnut brown; leaves usually ovate, occasionally obovate, 4–7 cm long, to 4 cm wide, long acuminate, coarsely incised and biserrate, venation pubescent beneath when young, later totally glabrous, petiole glabrous, 8 mm long; flowers white (not pink!), grouped 2–4 in sessile clusters, stalks 2 cm long, glabrous, corolla 2.5 cm wide, petals entire to incised, calyx tube narrowly campanulate to tubular, purple, 6 mm long, sepals triangular-lanceolate, style 1 cm long, April–May; fruits globose, 8 mm thick, purple-black. MD 1917: 11; MJ 1319; OFC 150; KIF 3: 23; YWP 2: 18 (= *P. iwagiensis* Koehne; *P. nikkoensis* Koehne). Japan. 1915. z6 ⚬

var. *kurilensis* see: **P. kurilensis**

P. oeconomica see: **P. domestica**

P. orientalis see: **P. argentea**

P. ✕ orthosepala Koehne (*P. americana* ✕ *P. angustifolia* var. *watsonii*). Abundantly branched shrub, about 1–1.5 m high, twigs red-brown, broad growing; leaves oblong-lanceolate to oblanceolate (!), 4–5 cm long, acute to acuminate, base tapered, serrate, glabrous and glossy, petiole with 0–2 glands; flowers white, turning pink, 12 mm wide, calyx and lobes glabrous, margins ciliate; fruits late, globose, red, white punctate, pruinose, to 2.5 cm thick, stone elliptic, somewhat rough. BC 3224; SH 1: 344 c–d1, 3451. USA; Kansas. 1880. z5 Fig. 23. ⚬

P. pachyclada see: **P. cornuta**

P. padus L. Bird Cherry. Tree, to 15 m high, crown dense, branches somewhat nodding, young twigs finely pubescent at first, later glabrous, bark dark brown, inner bark unpleasantly scented; leaves elliptic, abruptly short acuminate, 6–12 cm long, scabrous serrate, dark green above, bluish green beneath, glabrous, leaf petiole green, normally with 2 glands; flowers white, fragrant, 1–1.5 cm wide, grouped 15–20 in loose, pendulous racemes, petals 6–8 mm long, twice as long as the stamens (!), calyx interior pubescent (!), April–May, appearing after the foliage; fruits globose, pea-sized, black, stone oval, rugose (!). HW 56; GPN 445–446 (= *P. racemosa* Lam.). Europe, N. Asia to Korea and Japan. Cultivated for centuries. Thrives in shady sites. Ⓕ Austria (screen plantings); Holland (on slopes); India (reforestation). z4 Fig. 18. ⚬

'**Alberti**' (Lemoine). Small tree, habit broadly conical, densely branched; flowers in dense (!), 15–28 cm long racemes. Most attractive cultivar. ⚬

'**Aucubifolia**'. Leaves yellow speckled. DB 5: 202. Recognized before 1845. ∅

'**Bracteosa**'. Subtending bracts of the inflorescences particularly well developed, more or less surpassing the flowers, later abscising. 1825.

'**Chlorocarpos**'. Fruits yellow green. 1818.

'**Colorata**'. Bark of the young shoots purple-brown; leaves on the new growth coppery purple, later a dull green with purple venation and a reddish underside; flower buds carmine, opening pink; fruits normally black-red (= f. *colorata* A. Nilsson). Found in 1953 in Smaland Province, Sweden. Cultivated since about 1960. Very attractive. ∅ ⚬

var. **commutata** Dipp. Vigorous habit; leaves and flowers

appearing three weeks earlier than the species, leaves coarser, more crenate, flowers in 15 cm long racemes. GC 139: 548; IC 34 (= var. *seoulensis* Nakai; *P. regeliana* Zab.). E. Asia. Around 1880.

f. *grandiflora* see: 'Watereri'

'Heterophylla'. Leaves often deeply incised. Before 1892.

var. **laxa** Rehd. Twigs more slender, nodding; leaves usually obovate, slender acuminate, lighter beneath, glabrous; flowers in loose (!) racemes, pendulous; stone small, smooth to nearly so. Korea. 1906.

'Leucocarpos'. Twigs somewhat pubescent; fruits yellowish white (= *P. salzeri* Zdarek). Discovered before 1869 in Austria.

'Nana'. Habit nearly hemispherical, only 2–3 m high, very densely branched; smaller in all respects. (St. Gallen Botanic Garden, Switzerland) Plate 15.

'Pendula' (Beauchaine). Twigs widely drooping. 1849.

'Plena'. Flowers semidouble, persisting longer than those of the species, but not as attractive. Before 1892. ⊕

var. *japonica* see: **P. grayana**

var. **pubescens** Regel & Tiling. Young shoots and leaves more or less soft pubescent, leaves more oblong and acute. NE. Asia. 1906.

var. *rotundifolia* see: **P. × laucheana**

var. *seoulensis* see: var. **commutata**

'Spaethii' (Späth). Similar to 'Watereri', flowers less abundantly, but the individual flowers are 2 cm wide, petals obovate.

'Stricta.' Flowers in erect (!) racemes.

'Watereri'. Fast growing, broad habit; leaves with distinctly pubescent vein axils beneath (!); flowers in elongated, 18–20 cm long racemes. DRHS 1699; JRHS 94: 183 (= f. *grandiflora* Hort.). 1914. Not as attractive as 'Alberti'. Plate 1. ⊕

P. palmeri see: **P. lanata**

P. paracerasus see: **P. × yedoensis**

P. pedunculata (Pall.) Maxim. Shrub, to 2 m high, twigs dark brown, finely tomentose; leaves elliptic-oblong, 2.5–4 cm long, irregularly dentate, somewhat hard, glossy, pubescent beneath at first; flowers solitary, pink, stalks as long or twice as long as the calyx, these cupulate-campanulate, late April–early May; fruits ovate, 1 cm long, pubescent, stone smooth. RH 1875: 58; SH 1: 335 a–c (= *Amygdalus boissieri* Carr.). Siberia. Before 1860. z6 Fig. 29

P. pensylvanica L. Shrub or tree, to 12 m high, round crowned, young shoots glossy red-brown, glabrous, dense yellowish punctate; leaves ovate-lanceolate, 6–11 cm long, long acuminate, finely and scabrous serrate, glossy green above, somewhat lighter beneath, glabrous on both sides, a gorgeous golden-yellow (!) in fall, occasionally also reddish; flowers grouped 3–6 in short stalked umbels, along the previous year's growth, corolla 1.5 cm wide, white, stalk glabrous, 1–1.5 cm long, May, appearing with bud break of the new leaves; fruits globose, pea-sized, red. BB 2022; BM 8486; RMi 253;

Fig. 19. *Prunus pensylvanica* (from Sargent)

GTP 243 (= *P. persicifolia* Desf.). N. America; Canada to N. Carolina and Colorado. 1773. z2 Fig. 15, 19. ∅ ⊕

var. **saximontana** Rehd. A shrubby form; leaves smaller, wider, lighter green; umbels with fewer flowers, sessile. Rocky Mts. 1882.

P. persica (L.) Batsch. Peach. Tree or a tree-like shrub, to 8 m high, twigs glabrous, red on the sunny side, opposite side often green; leaves broadly lanceolate, widest at or above the middle, glabrous on both sides, 8–15 cm long, long acuminate, petiole 1 to 1.5 cm long, with glands (!); flowers grouped 1–2, pink or red, 2–3.5 cm wide (very characteristic on the fruit cultivars!), usually appearing before the leaves, sepals pubescent on the exterior, calyx campanulate; fruits more or less globose, 5–7 cm wide, very juicy, with white or yellow flesh depending upon the variety, flesh clinging to or free from the stone, stone hard, with deep furrows and pits. HM 1263 (= *Amygdalus persica* L.; *Persica vulgaris* Mill.). China, occurring in the mountains to 2600 m. Cultivated for centuries. z5 ⚬ ✕

Includes a large number of cultivars:

'Ackerman Redleaf'. Red-leaved form, actually more often used as an understock, the basal suckers are then easily recognized. Introduced into the trade around 1950 by Ackermans Nurseries, Bridgeman, Michigan USA. Differs only slightly from 'Purpurea'. ∅

'Alba'. Wood green; leaves conspicuously light green; flowers pure white, single. BR 1586. First named in England in 1829.

'Alboplena'. Flowers pure white, densely double, otherwise like the single flowering form. FS 969. England. Around 1850. ⊕

'Alboplena Pendula'. Weeping form with double white flowers. ⊕

f. *atropurpurea* see: 'Purpurea'

'Aurea'. Bark golden-yellow to orange; flowers small, dark pink, corolla campanulate; fruits orange with red cheeks, medium-sized. RH Pl. 549 (= *Persica vulgaris ramuleis aureis* Hort.). Commonly cultivated in the vicinity of Toulouse, France around 1870. ⚬ ✕

'Aurora'. Flowers to 3 cm wide, double, deep pink, densely arranged, petal limb somewhat crispate. ⊕

'Burbank'. Leaves very acuminate; flowers very large, semidouble, light pink. ⊕

'Camelliiflora'. Flowers very large, very densely double, dark wine-red, relatively tight. FS 1299. Introduced from Japan by Siebold. Before 1854. ⊕

'Cardinal'. Flowers rosette form, semidouble, intensely pink-red. ⊕

"Clara Meyer". Incorrect spelling for 'Klara Mayer'.

'Crimson Cascade'. Weeping form with carmine-red flowers. ⊕

'Dianthifolia'. Flowers very large, semidouble, petals narrow and acuminate, dark red striped. FS 1300. Introduced from Japan by Siebold. Before 1854. ⊕

'Duplex'. Flowers small, light pink, semidouble. FS 969; RH 1852: 221. Known in France since 1636. ⊕

'Florentine'. Carmine-red, double. ⊕

'Helen Borchers' (Clarke). Strong grower; semidouble, clear pink. Clarke, San Jose, California. Before 1949. ⊕

'Iceberg' (Clarke). Strong grower; flowers pure white, semidouble, 4 cm wide. W. B. Clarke, San Jose, California. Before 1950. ⊕

'Ispahan'. Low, 3–4 m high with age, densely bushy; flowers soft pink; fruits globose with prominent tips, ripening in September. Found in cultivation in Isphahan, Iran by Brugière and Oliver around 1800 and introduced into France.

'Klara Mayer' (Späth). Shrub, of only medium vigor; flowers a good double form, bright pink-red, about 4 cm wide, flowers abundantly; fruits light green, somewhat reddish, rather large. SpB 197. Introduced around 1890 by Späth. The cultivar name is nearly always misspelled. ⊕ ✂

'Magnifica'. Flowers double, light carmine. GC 104: 331. ⊕

'Nana'. Dwarf form, only 0.6–1 m high; leaves longer than those of the species, more distinctly serrate, pendulous; flowers light pink, densely arranged; fruits like those of the species, greenish, somewhat reddish, very good eating peach. In France before 1890. Still cultivated in Orléans. ⚭ ✂

var. **nucipersica** Schneid. Nectarine. Leaves usually more serrate; fruits smaller than peaches and with a smooth skin. ⚭|✂
The commonly made assertion that nectarines are a cross between peaches and plums is totally false; it is rather, a mutation.

'Palace Peach' (Russel). Flowers double, about 2.5 cm wide, with 12–15 petals, uncommonly deep red (HCC 824/3). L. H. Russel, Windlesham, England. Before 1946. ⊕

'Pendula'. Twigs horizontally outspread, tips nodding, otherwise like the species. Imported by Siebold from Japan. Before 1845.

'Peppermint Stick'. Flowers double, white with red stripes. Introduced by W. B. Clarke, San Jose, California. ⊕

var. **platycarpa** Bailey. Flat Peach, Pinto Peach. Fruit much flattened at both ends, disk-form, as thick as the width of the stone, with a depression at the pistil end, stone small, flat, compressed, rough and irregular. RH 1870: 111; BC 2453 (= Persica platycarpa Decne.). A popular fruit type in China; also occasionally cultivated in S. Florida, USA. ⚭ ✂

'Prince Charming'. Habit tightly erect; flowers double, pink-red. ⊕

'Purpurea'. Leaves purple-red; flowers single, pink. FS 1896 (=

f. *rubrifolia* Hort.; f. *atropurpurea* Schneid.). Cultivated in Belgium since 1873. ∅

'Ramuleis aureis' see: 'Aurea'

'Royal Redleaf'. Leaves bright red on new growth, but later turning reddish green. USA. ⊕ ◌

f. *rubrifolia* see: 'Purpurea'

'Rubroplena'. Flowers dark pink, distinctly double. FS 1319. ⊕

'Russel's Red'. (Russel). A rather strong grower, densely branched; flowers double, bright red. Before 1933. Susceptible to peach leaf curl. ⊕

'Versicolor'. Slow growing shrub; leaves light green; flowers very numerous, densely double, sometimes totally white or with red or rust colored stripes. FS 1319. Before 1863 in France. ⊕

'Windle Weeping' (Clarke). Shoots spreading umbrella-form, vigorous grower; flowers cupulate, numerous, semidouble, a good pink. W. B. Clarke, San Jose, California. Before 1949. ⊕

P. persicifolia see: **P. pensylvanica**

P. persico-amygdala see: **P. × amygdala-persica**

P. petunnikowii (Litvin.) Rehd. Closely related to *P. tenella*, to 1 m high, but the twigs often thorny; leaves totally glabrous, clustered on short shoots, linear-lanceolate to narrowly oblanceolate, 1–3 cm long, acute, base long tapered, glandular serrate; fruits ellipsoid, about 2 cm long, nearly sessile, compressed, base oblique, stone somewhat rough, with a beaked point at the base. Turkestan. 1912. z6 ⊕

P. pilosa (Turcz.) Maxim. Shrub (to a small tree), to 1.5 m, very closely related to *P. pedunculata*, thornless, twigs gray pubescent; leaves obovate, 1–2 cm long, glandular serrate, gray-pubescent on both sides; flowers reddish, nearly sessile, calyx with a pubescent interior, sepals erect; fruits about 12 mm long. Mongolia. 1933. z5

P. pilosiuscula Koehne. Small, sparsely branched, rather upright tree, scarcely over 9 m high, or only a shrub, young shoots thin pubescent; leaves ovate to oblong-ovate to 4–9 (usually 6) cm long and 3.4 cm wide, acuminate, scabrous biserrate, base rounded to broadly cuneate, with scattered bristly pubescence above, usually more or less pubescent beneath or only on the venation, margin teeth medium-sized, awned acuminate; flowers grouped 2–3(5) in short stalked corymbs, white or light pink, corolla flat spreading, with about 25 long stamens, calyx broadly campanulate, 4.2 mm long, sepals triangular, somewhat reflexed, style long, pubescent on the basal half, May, appearing with the foliage; fruits elliptic, 1 cm long, red. BM 9192; NF 12: 55; ICS 2352 (= *P. polytricha* Koehne; *P. pulchella* Koehne). Central and W. China; Hupeh, Szechwan, S. Kansu Prov. 1907. z5 ⊕

var. **media** Koehne. Leaf margins more finely serrate; petals very narrowly ovate, white, partly reddish, style less pubescent.

P. pissardii see: **P. cerasifera 'Atropurpurea'**

P. pissardii blireana see: **P. × blireana**

P. pissardii moseri see: **P. × blireana 'Moseri'**

P. pleiocerasus Koehne. Small tree, 5–8 m high, open crowned, young shoots glabrous; leaves obovate-oblong to oval-oblong, 4–9 (usually about 7) cm long and 3.7 cm wide, caudate acuminate, finely and irregularly serrate, base broadly ovate, venation pubescent at first, later glabrous; flowers appear shortly before the foliage, white, hardly 2 cm wide, inconspicuous, grouped 5–7 in corymbs, bracts glandular acuminate, calyx cupulate, 4 mm long, sepals triangular, 4 mm long, petals rounded, entire or somewhat incised, style and ovaries glabrous; fruits globose, but with a small pointed tip, red to nearly black, stone furrowed. W. China; W. Hupeh to Yunnan Prov., in the mountains. 1907. z5

P. polytricha see: **P. pilosiuscula**

P. prostrata Labill. Rock Cherry. Inconsistent, divaricate, gnarled shrub, 0.5(1) m high; leaves broadly ovate, 2–3 cm long, scabrous serrate, occasionally deeply incised, dark green above, white tomentose beneath, but occasionally pubescent or (rarely) glabrous on both sides; flowers pink, solitary or paired, usually sessile, about 1.2 cm wide, calyx tubular-campanulate, somewhat inflated at the base, 7 mm long, style shorter than the stamens, long-haired at the base, May; fruits nearly globose, 1 cm thick, black-red. NF 9: 154; PSw 15. Mountains of the Mediterranean region from Spain to the Balkan Peninsula, Morocco to Tunisia and Asia Minor. 1802. z6 Plate 8; Fig. 12, 14. ⊕

var. **brachypetala** (Boiss.) Ingram. Divaricate shrub, more pubescent on all parts; leaves small, often densely tomentose, particularly on the underside (= *P. bornmülleri* [Schneid.] Hand.-Mazz.; *Cerasus brachypetala* Boiss.). SW. and W. Iran, north to Luristan and Kurdistan.

var. **concolor** Boiss. Leaves smaller, totally glabrous above, underside becoming more or less glabrous and green. N. Syria, Asia Minor, Greece.

var. **glabrifolia** J. H. Moris. Leaves nearly completely glabrous. Corsica, Sardinia, the Atlas Mts., Rif Mts. in Morocco and the Chrea Chain in Algeria.

var. **incana** Litardière & Maire. Leaves tomentose on both sides; fruits allegedly sweet, not bitter. Central Atlas Mts. ⊕

P. prunifolia see: **P. emarginata** var. **mollis**

P. pseudoarmeniaca Heldr. & Sart. Small shrub, similar to *P. cocomilia*, 1–1.5 m high, twigs thornless; leaves elliptic to obovate, 1–3 cm long, acute, quite finely obtuse crenate, base cuneate; flowers paired, white, stalks short; fruits oval-rounded, about like a cherry, 2 cm long, purple-blue, stone compressed. SH 1: 3460. Greece. 1934. z7

P. pseudocerasus Lindl. Small tree, 7–8 m high, young shoots sparsely pubescent, later becoming glabrous; leaves rather large and tough, broadly obovate to oval-oblong, 9 cm long in the center and 5 cm wide, much larger on long shoots, abruptly acuminate, uneven and rather coarsely serrate; buds pink, opening white, corolla 2 cm wide, in short-stalked clusters before the leaves or appearing with the foliage in longer stalked corymbs, petals nearly circular, calyx broadly campanulate, nearly cupulate, 4 mm long, base somewhat swollen and pubescent, stalks pubescent, March; fruits cordate-ovate, 1.5 cm long, yellow-red and somewhat sweet; tetraploid. BR 800; ICS 2353; OFC 153 (= *P. involucrata* Koehne). Cultivated as a fruit tree in China; not known in the wild. 1819. Flower and fruit inferior to that of *P. avium*! z6 Plate 7, 15; Fig. 22.

var. **cantabrigiensis** (Stapf) Ingram. Leaves more oblong-obovate, long acuminate, 5–13 cm long, 2–7 cm wide, coarsely biserrate; inflorescences usually dense, stalks and calyx less red, petals a strong pink in bud, opening a lighter pink. BM 9129; Bai 20: 15 (= *P. cantabrigiensis* Stapf). ⊕

The following hybrid is also included here:

'Wadai' (*P. pseudocerasus* × *P. subhirtella*). Multistemmed, tall shrub or small, dense crowned tree, young shoots bristly pubescent, the older branches and twigs often have many short aerial roots at the nodes (!); leaves elliptic, acuminate, 5–8 cm long; flowers small, dark pink in bud, opening light pink, fragrant, March. Developed by K. Wada in Yokohama, Japan. A beautiful flowering shrub. ⊕

P. pubescens see: **P. maritima**

P. puddum see: **P. cerasoides**

P. pulchella see: **P. pilosiuscula**

P. pumila L. Sand Cherry. Shrub, about 1 m high, twigs occasionally procumbent, young shoots thin, erect, glabrous, red-brown; leaves all directed upward, oblanceolate to narrowly obovate, 3–5 cm long, shallowly serrate on the apical half, apex acute to obtuse, base cuneate, dull green above, gray-white beneath, fall color bright red; flowers grouped 2–4, about 1.2 cm wide, on the previous year's wood, white, petals flat spreading, narrowly obovate, late April–May; fruits oval-rounded, 1 cm thick, black-purple, sour. BB 2017; VT 389; IC Pl. 7. Northeastern North America. 1765. z4 Plate 8, 16; Fig. 13, 14. ⊘ ⊕

var. *cuneata* see: var. **susquehanae**

var. **depressa** (Pursh) Bean. Shrub, prostrate; leaves thinner, more bluish white beneath, less acuminate, often obtuse spathulate; fruits rounded-ellipsoid, edible. GSP 244 (= *P. depressa* Pursh). N. America; New Brunswick to Ontario and Massachusetts. 1864. ⊘ ⊕

var. **susquehanae** (Willd.) Jäg. Erect shrub, to 1.3 m high; leaves obovate-elliptic, more scabrous serrate; fruits smaller. BB 2018; GSP 242 (= *P. susquehanae* Willd.; *P. pumila* var. *cuneata* Bailey). Northeastern N. America. 1805.

P. racemosa see: **P. padus**

P. ranunculiflora see: **P. cerasus 'Rhexii'**

P. regeliana see: **P. padus** var. **commutata**

P. rehderiana see: **P. litigiosa**

P. reverchonii Sarg. Shrub, to 2 m high, developing thickets, young shoots glabrous, red-brown; leaves lanceolate (!), acuminate, 5–7 cm long, crenate, dark green above, folded conspicuously navicular (!), light green and somewhat pubescent beneath, petiole with 2–

4 glands, pubescent above; flowers grouped 2–4, white, about 1 cm wide, glabrous, calyx lobes oblong, glandular-ciliate, pubescent on the interior, petals obovate, entire, clawed at the base, appearing with the foliage; fruits globose, 1–2 cm thick, usually yellow with carmine, occasionally totally red, ripening in August–September (!), stone elliptic, acute at both ends, somewhat reticulate. VT 400. South central USA. 1916.

P. rufa Hook. f. Small, wide tree, about 6 to 7 m high, young shoots rust-brown tomentose; leaves narrowly ovate to obovate-lanceolate, 5–10 cm long, acuminate, base usually round, finely serrate, teeth glandular, glabrous above, venation pubescent beneath, petiole 1 cm long; flowers usually solitary (or 2–3), white to pale pink, petals never fully outspread, rather funnelform, about 1.6 cm wide, calyx thick tubular-campanulate, slightly swollen at the base, apical portion rugose (!), sepals finely serrate, broadly triangular, style glabrous to pubescent, petals nearly round and entire; fruits ellipsoid, dark red. SH 1: 339 n, 340 l; SNp 44; JRHS 1977: 354. Himalayas; Assam to Nepal. 1897. z9 Plate. 7; Fig. 26. ⌀

P. rufomicans see: **P. sericea**

P. sachalinensis see: **P. sargentii**

P. salicifolia Kunth. Tree, more or less evergreen (!), 9–12 m high in its habitat, young shoots glabrous or pubescent; leaves lanceolate, gradually acuminate, about 7 to 12 cm long and 3 cm wide, base cuneate, somewhat leathery, quite finely serrate, usually glabrous on both sides or sparsely pubescent in the vein axils beneath, petiole glabrous or pubescent, 6 mm long; flowers in loose, pendulous racemes, grouped 20–30 together, white, corolla about 1 cm wide, late May; fruits nearly globose, deep purple-red, about 1.7 cm thick (!), with persistent calyx remnants. RH 1893 (= *P. serotina* var. *salicifolia* [Kunth] Koehne; *P. capuli* Cav.; *P. capollin* DC.). Mexico to Peru, in the mountains. 1820. z6 Fig. 31. # ⌀

P. salicina Lindl. Japanese Plum. Tree, 6 to 9 m high, twigs glabrous, eventually red-brown and glossy; leaves oblong to obovate, 6–10 cm long (!), obtusely biserrate, light green above, lighter beneath and glabrous except for the pubescent vein axils, petiole 1–2 cm long; flowers usually in groups of 3 (!), white, 1.5–2 cm wide, stalk 1–1.5 cm long, glabrous, calyx lobes glabrous, somewhat toothed, April; fruits oval-globose, distinctly indented at the base, yellow or red, also green, 5–7 cm wide. NK 5: 26; BC 3216; MJ 1304; ICS 2361 (= *P. triflora* Roxb.). China. Long in cultivation in Japan. z8 Fig. 24, 25. ✂ ⚭

A number of fruit cultivars are grown, but these are generally inferior to the European plums.

P. salzeri see: **P. padus 'Leucocarpos'**

P. sargentii Rehd. Tall tree, broad upright habit, 15–18 m high, all parts glabrous, bark reddish, new growth reddish; leaves broadly oblong-elliptic to obovate-oblong, 6 to 12 cm long, long acuminate, scabrous and

Fig. 20. *Prunus sargentii* (from BC)

serrate to biserrate, coarsely dentate, acuminate, eventually blue-green beneath, petiole with 2 small glands; flowers appear somewhat before the leaves, pink, nearly 4 cm wide, grouped 2–4 in sessile (!) umbels, the small basal bracts completely hidden by the involucral scales, calyx tube tubular-campanulate, about 6 mm long, stalk rather thick, 1–2 cm long, petals broadly oval-oblong to obovate, incised at the apex, April; fruits oval-oblong, 1 cm long, glossy dark red. IC Pl. 1; MiB 30–31; MJ 1314; KIF 3: 25; OFC 145; ChCh 33 (= *P. sachalinensis* Miyoshi; *P. serrulata* var. *sachalinensis* Wils.). Japan, Sachalin. Around 1870. Ⓕ England (experimental); Japan (erosion control). z5 Plate 2, 18; Fig. 20. ⌀ ⚭

'Columnaris'. Differing from the species in the broadly columnar habit. AB 21: 45. Grown in the Arnold Arboretum, Boston, USA since 1914 and distributed from there. ⚭

'Rancho'. Another columnar form, yet narrower than the previous cultivar at 7.5 m high only 1.5 m wide. Protected by US Plant Patent 2065. Discovered by J. Gerling, Rochester, N.Y., USA; introduced in 1961 by E. H. Scanlon, Olmsted Falls, Ohio. ⚭

Includes the following hybrid, of *P. sargentii* × *P. subhirtella*:

'Accolade' (Knap Hill). Open, graceful shrub; leaves elliptic to elliptic-oblong, long acuminate, 7–10 cm long, 3.5–5 cm wide, widest in the middle, base round, finely and scabrous serrate, upper surface eventually only finely scabrous, pubescent beneath, more densely so in the vein axils, midrib and petiole red; flowers in groups of 3 in pendulous clusters, about 4 cm wide, semidouble, petals 12–14, obovate, fuchsia-pink (HCC 627/1), early. JRHS 79: 97. Developed before 1952 by the Knap Hill Nursery, Woking, England. Plate 2. ⚭

P. × **schmittii** Rehd. (*P. avium* × *P. canescens*,

intermediate between the parents, but more similar to *P. canescens*). Small tree, narrow upright habit, with a glossy brown bark, but this with many wide, rough lenticel bands; leaves elliptic-oblong, 5–8 cm long, acuminate, quickly becoming glabrous above, primarily pubescent on the venation beneath, petiole 1–2.5 cm long; flower stalks 1–1.5 cm long, with large bracts at the base, petals white, 1 cm long, broadly ovate, calyx campanulate. 1923. Plate 16.

P. scoparia (Spach) Schneid. Small tree, very closely related to *P. arabica*, but to 6 m high, twigs rodlike, with only a few leaves; leaves narrowly linear, 2–4 cm long, sparsely finely dentate to nearly entire, coppery red on the new growth, later gradually becoming green; flowers pale pink, 2.5 cm wide, petals nearly circular; fruits ovate, about 2 cm long, very pubescent. SH 1: 332 e–h. Iran. 1934. z9

P. sericea (Batal.) Koehne. A tree to 20 m high in its habitat, closely related to *P. cornuta*, young shoots glabrous; leaves elliptic to obovate-oblong, 8–12 cm long, acuminate, base round to cuneate, margins finely serrate, silky pubescent beneath (!); flowers about 8 mm wide, in 10–14 cm long, pubescent racemes, calyx glabrous, stamens longer than the petals; fruits oval, black, 1.5 cm long, on thick stalks (= *P. napaulensis* var. *sericea* Batal.; *P. rufomicans* Koehne). China; Szechwan Prov. 1908. z6 ⌀

P. serotina Ehrh. Black Cherry. Tree, to 35 m high, crown narrowly oblong, branches short, horizontal, bark dark brown, inner bark aromatic, young shoots glabrous; leaves oblong, acuminate, 8–13 cm long, finely crenate, glossy dark green above, lighter beneath with rust-brown pubescence along the midrib, eventually rather tough and leathery; flowers white, in 10–14 cm long, glabrous, cylindrical racemes, late May–June, corolla 8–10 mm thick, sepals oval-oblong, often serrate, style shorter than the stamens; fruit egg-shaped, 8–10 mm thick, dark purple with remnants of the calyx at the end of the stalk, bitter tasting. BB 2026; GTP 248; VT 390; SS 159. N. America; Ontario, N. Dakota, Texas, Florida. Cultivated for centuries; an important forest tree. Ⓕ W. Germany, Romania, Yugoslavia, Holland, USA. z4 Plate 16; Fig. 21, 31. ⌀

'**Aspleniifolia**'. Leaves narrower, oblong-elliptic, deeply serrate to incised, occasionally slightly to deeply slitted. 1864.

ssp. *capuli* (Cav.) McVaugh see: **P. salicifolia**

'**Cartilaginea**'. Vigorous grower, much more densely foliate, branches more upright; leaves larger, to 15 cm long, 5–6 cm wide, brighter green and glossier, nearly laurel-like. Before 1833. Better than the species as a street tree. Plate 16. ⌀

var. *montana* (Small) Brit. Mountain form from the southern Alleghenies; leaves more elliptic, tougher, short acuminate, whitish green beneath; racemes with fewer flowers, shorter, outspread, sepals and filaments pubescent. USA; Virginia to Alabama.

'**Pendula**'. Slow growing form with pendulous branches and twigs, the latter easily broken. 1882. Plate 16.

Fig. 21. *Prunus serotina* (from Illick)

'**Pyramidalis**' (Hesse). Habit tightly conical. Before 1903.

'**Phelloides**' (Hesse). Leaves narrowly lanceolate. Selected by Hesse, Weener, W. Germany around 1900. ⌀

var. *salicifolia* (Kunth) Koehne see: **P. salicifolia**

P. serrula Franch. Tree, to 7 m or a multistemmed shrub, to 12 m high in its habitat, older branches and trunk with a mirror-smooth, glossy, mahogany-brown bark, exfoliating in narrow strips, young twigs pubescent; leaves lanceolate, 4–10 cm long, long acuminate, biserrate, dull green above, lighter beneath, midrib pubescent, with pubescent vein axils; flowers white, about 2 cm wide, grouped 1–3, nodding, style finely pubescent on the basal half, calyx campanulate, somewhat swollen at the base, 6 mm long, stamens longer than the petals, April–May, appearing with the foliage; fruits oval, about 0.6 cm long (= *P. serrula* var. *tibetica* Koehne). W. China; mountains of N. Yunnan and Szechwan Prov. 1913. z6 Plate 17.

P. serrulata Lindl. Small tree, scarcely over 3 m high, twigs stiffly outspread, sparsely branched, crown to 9 m wide (on very old plants); leaves smooth and glossy (!), short serrate (!), ovate, long acuminate, 6–12 cm long; flowers grouped 3–5 together, pure white, double (!), about 3.7 cm wide, late April to early May. China. (The plant cultivated in Japan is not the species but rather only a sport of var. *hupehensis*). z6 Fig. 22.

var. *hupehensis* Ingram. Chinese Mountain Cherry. Very similar to var. *spontanea*, but growth wider and larger, new growth not as dark red-brown; flowers appear before the foliage, usually small and white, occasionally also pink, in sessile umbels. OFC 154. China; S. Kansu, Shensi, Hupeh, Szechwan Prov., in the mountains. Around 1900. Considered by Ingram to be the prototype of the double-flowered *P. serrulata* Lindl. ⌂

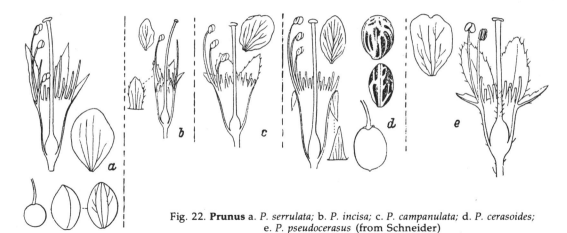

Fig. 22. **Prunus** a. *P. serrulata*; b. *P. incisa*; c. *P. campanulata*; d. *P. cerasoides*;
e. *P. pseudocerasus* (from Schneider)

var. **pubescens** Wils. Korean Mountain Cherry. Habit like that
of var. *spontanea* and var. *hupehensis*, leaf petiole and blade
underside, however, always more or less pubescent (!),
younger growth bronze-green and without reddish tones;
hardly differing in flower. MiB 33; WJ 8–9 (= *P. mutabilis*
Miyoshi p.p.). Korea to NW. Hokkaido. 1929.

var. *sachalinensis* see: **P. sargentii**

var. **spontanea** (Maxim.) Wils. Japanese Mountain Cherry (=
Jamasakura). Tree, about 12–14 m high, glabrous on all parts,
branches often outspread, bark brownish, new growth dark
coppery red, later becoming green, bluish on the underside;
leaves oblong to more obovate, with long acuminate tips, about
8 cm long and 4.2 cm wide, margins entire or nearly biserrate,
teeth medium-sized, with awn tips, petiole with 1–2 glands, to 2
cm long; flowers usually white, occasionally also pink, 3 cm
wide, grouped 2–4 (usually 3) together on about 1.4 cm long
stalks, involucre rather large, the interior reddish, stipules
linear, the fringe with glandular tips, petals incised, calyx
narrow tubular-campanulate, sepals narrow, 6 mm long,
appearing with the foliage; fruits nearly globose, 7 mm thick,
dark red. IC 18; MiB 20–26, 28, 32; MJ 1312; KO ill. Pl. 38 (= *P.
yamasakura* Sieb.; *P. mutabilis* Miyoshi). Japan; S. Hondo.
Around 1914. A very long lived tree. Ⓕ Japan (erosion
control). ✣ ∅

Key to the Japanese Flowering Cherries
(from Ingram)

● Flowers white, when fully open;
  ★ Young leaves green, golden-green or bronze-
    green;
    v Flowers single;
      x All parts glabrous (considering they are
        mature plants since young seedlings of
        most species and forms are pubescent):
        'Hatasakura', 'Jo-nioi', 'Shirotae',
        'Washi-no-o'

      xx Some parts more or less pubescent:
        var. *pubescens*
    vv Flowers semidouble or double;
      x All parts glabrous:
        'Shimidsu-sakura'
  ★★ Young leaves coppery red, reddish brown or
    reddish;
    v Flowers single;
      x All parts glabrous:

    var. *spontanea,* 'Tai Haku', Taki-
    nioi'
    xx Many parts more or less pubescent:
      'Fudansakura', var. *pubescens*

  vv Flowers semidouble to double;
    x All parts glabrous:
      'Shirofugen'
● ● Flowers reddish white or totally pale pink, when
fully open;
  ★ Young leaves greenish bronze to rust-brown-
    bronze;
    v Flowers single;
      x All parts glabrous:
        'Amanogawa'   'Botan-sakura',
        'Ojochin', 'Ruiran'

      xx Many parts more or less pubescent:
        'Shidare Yoshino', 'Yoshino'
    vv Flowers semidouble or double;
      x All parts glabrous:
        'Ichiyo', 'Ito-kukuri', 'Shujaku'
  ★★ Young leaves coppery red, reddish brown or
    reddish;
    v Flowers single;
      x All parts glabrous:
        'Benden'
    xx Many parts more or less pubescent
    (rare):
        var. *pubescens*
    vv Flowers semidouble or double:
      —

● ● ● Flowers distinctly pink to deep pink, when fully
open;
  ★ Young leaves greenish bronze or brownish
    bronze;
    v Flowers single;
      x All parts glabrous:
        'Mikuruma-gaeshi', 'Oshokun'
    vv Flowers semidouble or double;
      x All parts glabrous:
        'Asano', 'Daikoku', 'Hokusai',
        'Horinji', 'Kiku-sakura', 'Kiku-
        shidare-sakura', 'Kokonoye-sa-
        kura', 'Okiku-sakura', 'Pink Per-
        fection', 'Sumizome', 'Yedo-sa-
        kura', 'Yokihi'

★★ Young leaves coppery red, reddish brown or reddish;
    v Flowers single;
        x All parts glabrous:
            'Hisakura' (the true plant), *P. sargentii*

    vv Flowers semidouble or double;
        x All parts glabrous:
            'Fugenzo', 'Kanzan', 'Kirin', 'Taoyama', 'Yae-murasaki'

        xx Many parts more or less pubescent:
            'Taizanfukun', 'Takasago'

●●●● Flowers greenish yellow or yellowish, when fully open;
    ★ Young leaves reddish brown;
        v Flowers nearly single to semidouble:
            'Asagi', 'Gioiko', 'Kaba', 'Ukon'

'Amanogawa'. Habit, narrowly columnar, new growth yellowish brown; flower slight pink, single, occasionally slightly double, somewhat fragrant, middle-late. MiB 87; OFC 2; JRHS 1935: 107 (= *P. serrulata* f. *erecta* Miyoshi).

'Asagi'. Very similar to 'Ukon', but earliest of the "yellow" forms, single and only pale yellow (= *P. serrulata luteoides* Miyoshi).

'Asano'. Vigorous grower, narrowly upright (!), densely branched; leaves narrowly lanceolate; flowers lilac-pink, densely double, about 3.7 cm wide, with about 100 petals (= *P. serrulata* f. *geraldinae* Ingram). Found and named by Ingram in Japan, 1926. ⊕

'Benden'. Strong growing; flowers single, pale pink, early. MiB 53; OFC 12 (= *P. serrulata* f. *rubida* Miyoshi; *P.* "Bedono" Miyoshi). Somewhat like a strong growing 'Hisakura', but paler, one week earlier, and less meritorious.

'Botan-sakura'. Small tree, broad upright habit, new growth bronze; leaves awned serrate; flowers whitish pink, later becoming white, often over 5 cm wide, single to nearly so, grouped 2–4 in loose corymbs, middle early, buds pink, sepals distinctly serrate. MiB 43; BM 8012 (?); IC 39; OFC 17 (= *P. serrulata* f. *moutan* Miyoshi).

'Daikoku'. Small tree, branches rather steeply ascending, new growth yellowish green; leaves medium-sized, teeth awned; flowers double, purple-pink, with 40 or more petals, with some greener, leaflike carpels in the center, late, relatively sparse flowering, in loose, pendulous corymbs, stalk long and stiff. Introduced from Japan around 1899; named by Ingram in 1916.

'Fudansakura'. Small tree; leaves sparsely pubescent beneath, somewhat rough to the touch; flowers in sessile clusters from November to mid April (!), buds soft pink, quickly becoming white, 4 cm wide, single, calyx reddish. OFC 22 (= *P. serrulata* f. *semperflorens* Miyoshi).

'Fugenzo'. Slow growing, crown broad and flat (!), new growth coppery red; leaves awned serrate; flowers pink, semidouble, rather large, opening widely, occasionally somewhat nestled in the foliage, in long-stalked, pendulous corymbs, flowers very abundantly. MiB 78; MJ 3520; OFC 23 (= *P. serrulata* f. *classica* Miyoshi; *P. serrulata veitchiana* Bean; *P. serrulata* "James F. Veitch"). Known in Japan for more than 1000 years (easily recognized in old paintings); cultivated in England since 1878. ⊕

'Fukurokuju'. Only minutely differing from 'Hokusai'. OFC 24; MiB 8 + 63 (= *P. serrulata* f. *contorta* Miyoshi).

'Gioiko'. Flowers single, cream-white, fading to green, petal tips wine-red, about 4 cm wide, late flowering, 1 week after 'Ukon', some buds not completely developing (!). MiB 89; OFC 32 (= *P. serrulata* f. *tricolor* Miyoshi). 1914.

'Hatasakura'. Flowers single, white, petals deeply incised on the limb, rather small. MiB 39 (perhaps not quite typical?); OFC 34 (= *P. serrulata* f. *vexillipetala* Miyoshi). Worthless. Plate 19.

'Hisakura'. Rather strong growing; flowers single (!), somewhat semidouble only on older plants, pink, grouped 2–4 in loose corymbs, middle early, calyx purple-brown. MiB 74 (= *P. serrulata* f. *splendens* Miyoshi). (Not to be confused with "Hisakura" of the European nursery trade which is included under 'Kanzan'.) ⊕

'Hokusai'. About twice as wide as high, to 10 m wide by 6 m high when fully grown, new growth brownish bronze, later becoming dark green and somewhat leathery salmon-brown to orange-red in fall; flowers light pink, semidouble, 7–12 petals, about 4.7 cm wide, middle late. FS 2238 (as *P. caproniana fl. roseo pl.*); IC 28; RH 1875 Pl. (as *Cerasus julianae fl. roseo*). This was the first double pink form to come to Europe; probably introduced from Japan in 1866 by Siebold, but named by Ingram in 1925. ⊕ Ø

'Horinji'. Small tree, scarcely over 5 m high, upright, somewhat stocky; leaves long and narrow (!); flowers soft pink, semidouble, with about 14 petals in 2–3 rings, about 4.3 cm wide, middle late, densely clustered at the shoot tips. MiB 60 (= *P. serrulata* f. *decora* Miyoshi). ⊕

'Ichiyo'. Tree, medium vigor, broadly upright, to 7 m high or more, new growth bronze-green; flowers light pink, very clean, corolla rather circular, limb fringed, petals in 2 rings, middle late, grouped 3–4 together in rather long-stalked, pendulous corymbs. MiB 80; OFC 45 (= *P. serrulata* f. *unifolia* Miyoshi). 'Ichiyo' = "single-leaved" referring to the leaflike carpel in the flower, but these are also often found in pairs. ⊕

'Imosé'. Habit and crown form somewhat like 'Kanzan'; young leaves light copper-brown to nearly lobster-red, fall color deep golden-yellow just before leaf drop; flowers fully double, with 25–30 petals, soft lilac pink, 4.5 cm wide, usually grouped 3–4 in an inflorescence. OFC 46. Found by C. Ingram in Japan and introduced in 1927. ⊕

'Ito-kukuri'. Habit loose, bushy, rather erect; flowers pale pink, semidouble, only medium-sized, in loose, fascicled corymbs at the branch tips. MiB 68 (= *P. serrulata* f. *fasciculata* Miyoshi).

'Jo-nioi'. Fast growing, well branched, medium-sized and wide, new growth golden-brown, later green; flowers pure white, single, almond scented (!), grouped 3–5 in long stalked umbels, calyx green, flowering abundantly. MiB 101; OFC 54 (= *P. serrulata* f. *affinis* Miyoshi). 1900. ⊕

'Kaba'. The darkest of the yellow-green types, double, about 10 days later than 'Ukon', but less attractive in habit and flower form (= 'Kaba-sakura'). ⊕

'Kanzan'. Growth tightly upright, crown nearly obconical, fast growing, to 12 m high, new growth brown; mature leaves somewhat reddish, somewhat blue-green beneath; flowers grouped 2–5 in clusters, double, dark pink, very large, usually with 1–2 leaflike carpels, buds dark carmine. MiB 77; OFC 107 (as 'Sekiyama') (= "Hisakura" in European nurseries, 'Sekiyama, 'Kirin', 'Naden', 'New Red', 'Kwanzan' in the USA). 1913. Little known in Japan but one of the most widely used in the West. Plate 18. ⊕

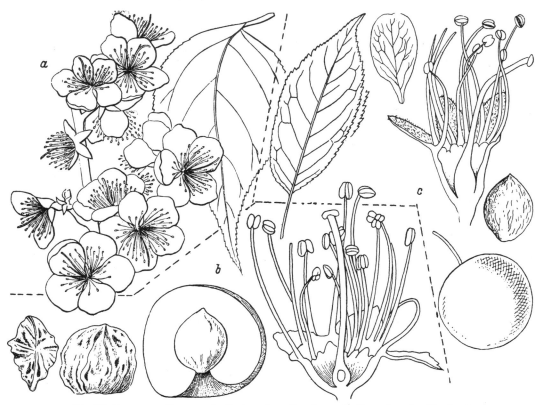

Fig. 23. **Prunus**. a. *P. mume*; b. *P. simonii*; c. *P. orthosepala* (from Lauche, Koehne)

'Kiku-sakura'. Similar to 'Asano', but larger and fuller. Shrub, slow and weak growing, erect, short branched; flowers soft pink, densely double, globose, with 200 or more petals, mid May, flowers very slow to develop, stalk short and thick. MiB 81 (= *P. serrulata* f. *chrysanthemoides* Miyoshi). ✿

'Kiku-shidare-sakura'. Shoots very pendulous; flowers double, dark pink, in dense clusters. OFC 67 (= *P. serrulata* f. *rosea* Wils.; Cheal's Weeping, Lidera Nova). According to Ingram, probably originated from China, not Japan. Plate 18. ✿

'Kirin'. Flowers large, very densely double, petals narrow, dark pink, late flowering, very attractive, buds carmine, stalks of the flowers and inflorescences rather short. OFC 70; MiB 76 (= *P. serrulata atrorubra* Miyoshi). ✿

'Kojima' see: 'Shirotae'

'Kokonoye-sakura'. Flowers semidouble, soft pink, 4.5 cm wide, very early and abundantly flowering. MiB 67 (= *P. serrulata* f. *homogena* Miyoshi).

'Mikuruma-gaeshi'. Branches long ascending, only sparsely branched, densely covered with short shoots terminating in flower clusters; flowers soft pink, single, about 5.3 cm wide, middle early, stalks rather short. MiB 61; CG 133: 85; OFC 85; ChCh 33 (= *P. serrulata* f. *densiflora* Miyoshi). Often mistakenly labeled!! ✿

'Ojochin'. Tree, to 7 m high, vigorous, stiff and coarse habit; leaves bronze-brown at first, large, broadly elliptic, rather leathery tough, some with and some without long drawn out tips; flowers normally single (rarely somewhat semidouble),

whitish pink, 4.5 cm wide. MiB 42(?); IC 36; OFC 100; JRHS 1935: 106 (= *P. serrulata senriko* Ingram). Plate 3. ✿

'Okiku-sakura'. Rather stiff upright habit, usually small; young leaves bronze-green; flowers double, pale pink, with 19 to 22 petals, about 5 cm wide, calyx rather small, sepals long, narrow, finely serrate, with a leaflike carpel, in dense, pendulous clusters.

'Oshokun'. Growth broad and flat; leaves bronze or brownish green on new growth; flowers double, buds carmine, opening soft pink-white, middle late, flowers abundantly every year and perhaps therefore a poor grower (only 2 m high in 20 years), but one of the most beautiful cultivars in flower. ✿

'Pink Perfection' (Waterer Sons & Crisp, 1935). Similar to 'Kanzan', but with somewhat lighter brown-red new growth; flowers somewhat lighter pink, 4.5 cm wide, pendulous, stalks long.

'Ruiran'. Broadly upright habit, a problem-free tree, new growth brownish green; leaves single serrate, teeth short awned, usually with only 6–7 vein pairs, glands absent or with only one, bracts and stipules rather small and incised; flowers single, plate-like, soft pink, later white, 4.7 cm wide, middle early, grouped 2–4 in umbellate panicles on long stalks, flowers less abundantly (= *P. serrulata* f. *communis* Miyoshi; 'Koshio-Yama'?).

'Senriko' see: 'Ojochin'

'Shidare Yoshino' see: **P. yedoensis**

'Shimidsu-sakura'. Broad crowned, poor grower, scarcely over 3 m high and only slightly wider, new growth bronze-green;

fall color golden-yellow; buds pink toned, opening pure white, semidouble, 5 cm wide, petals fringed on the margin, with 2 leaflike carpels, grouped 3–6 together in 15–20 cm long, pendulous corymbs, very late, often still flowering in June. JRHS 81: 46; 67: 50; ChCh 52 (= *P. serrulata longipes* Ingram; 'Oku Mikayu'). Plate 19. ⊕ ⊘

'Shirofugen'. Tree, strong growing, 7–9 m high, branches widespreading, dark brown, new growth coppery; buds pink, opening pure white, fading to purple-pink, double, in loose, pendulous corymbs, flowering very late and persisting for a long time, bracts often leaflike (!). JRHS 1935: 108; ChCh 53 + 60 (= *P. serrulata* f. *alborosea* Wils.). ⊕

'Shirotae'. Fujiyama Cherry. Small tree, branches horizontally spreading and drooping, new growth bronze-green; leaves deeply serrated (!), teeth long, curved and awn-like, fall color golden-yellow; flowers single on young plants, about 5.5 cm wide, pure white, somewhat smaller on older plants and then often semidouble, (!!), grouped 2–3 in pendulous clusters, middle late. MiB 66; OFC 113; ChCh 61; JRHS 1935: 104 (= *P. serrulata* f. *albida* Miyoshi; *P. lannesiana* f. *sirotae* Wils., 'Mount Fuji'; 'Kojima'). 1905. ⊕

'Shujaku'. Small tree, new growth yellowish bronze; leaves rather short serrate, the teeth with short awns, glands solitary or totally absent, stipules and bracts small; flowers slightly double, pink, somewhat campanulate, 4 cm wide, rather small, usually in groups of 5 together, flowering very abundantly, middle late. MiB 73 (= *P. serrulata* f. *campanuloides* Miyoshi). ⊕

'Sumizome'. New growth bronze-green; flowers soft pink, semidouble, 12–14 petals, 4.7 cm wide. OFC 120.

'Tai Haku'. Tree, strong growing, new growth attractively copper-red (!); leaves on vigorous plants to 16 cm long and 10 cm wide; flowers single, to 6 cm wide (!), snow white, sepals long and narrow, middle early; tetraploid. IC 40; JRHS 1935: 105; ChCh 69. Introduced from Japan around 1900, named by Ingram in 1927. Most beautiful of all the white flowering forms. ⊕

'Taizanfukan'. Well-branched, tightly upright shrub, bark rough on 2–3 year old shoots, new growth bronze; leaves small, leathery, dark green; flowers in dense clusters, densely double, light pink, axes pubescent (!), many flower buds developed but of these only a few actually bloom. MiB 70; OFC 122 (= *P. serrulata* f. *ambigua* Ingram).

'Takasago'. Tree, to 8 m high, slow growing, bark smooth, young shoots densely white pubescent at first, later gray and smooth, new growth yellow-brown to reddish brown; leaves densely pubescent on both sides (!), bright red-brown-orange in the fall, petiole pubescent, with 1–2 glands; flowers semidouble, light pink, 4.5 cm wide, 2–4 in short-stalked clusters, mid April, abundantly flowering. MiB 54; MJ 1316; OFC 123; RH 1866: 371 (= *P. sieboldii* Wittm.). Introduced by Siebold in 1862. ⊕ ⊘

'Taki-nioi'. Large tree, branches outspread, new growth reddish bronze, appearing with the flowers; flowers white, small, simple, loosely arranged, late. MiB 51; OFC 124 (= *P. serrulata* f. *cataracta* Miyoshi). ⊕

'Taoyame'. Strong growing, broadly upright, young shoots deep purple-red (!), new growth very dark bronze-brown; flowers semidouble, light pink, calyx and stalks wine-brown, middle late. OFC 125. ⊕

'Temari'. Flowers partly single, partly semidouble, pale pink, 4.5 cm wide, short stalked, in globose inflorescences at the shoot tips. OFC 126.

'Ukon' Strong growing, new growth red-brown; flowers semidouble, conspicuously yellowish to greenish yellow, 4.5 cm wide, older plants particularly abundant flowering. MiB 88; OFC 131; ChCh 76 (= *P. lannesiana* f. *grandiflora* Wils.; *P. serrulata* f. *luteo-virens* Miyoshi). 1905. Plate 3. ⊕

'Uzu-sakura' is only a more upright growing type of 'Hokusai'. OFC 133.

'Washi-no-o'. Vigorous growing, stout branched, new growth brownish; flowers single (5–7 petals), pure white, to 4 cm wide, slightly fragrant, short stalked. MiB 41; OFC 134 (= *P. serrulata* f. *wasinowo* Ingram). Often not true in cultivation; less valued than 'Tai Haku'.

'Yae-murasaki'. Slow grower, 20 year old plants are scarcely 3 m high, winter buds conspicuously red (!); flowers semidouble, purple-pink, 8–10 petals, flowers extraordinarily abundant and middle late. IC 37; OFC 90; ChCh 49 (= *P. serrulata* f. *purpurea* Miyoshi). ⊕

'Yedo-sakura'. Growth broadly upright, medium size, new growth golden-coppery; leaves broadly oblong to obovate (!) with a short, pronounced tip; flowers usually semidouble, with 8–10 petals, a strong pink, buds carmine, middle early. MiB 59 (= *P. serrulata* f. *nobilis* Miyoshi). 1905. ⊕

'Yokihi'. Growth medium high; flowers semidouble, 4.5 cm wide, pale pink, but the outer ring of petals somewhat darker than the inner, late April. OFC 139.

'Yoshino' see: **P. yedoensis**

P. setulosa Batal. Shrub or small tree, closely related to *P. canescens*, to 5 m high in its habitat, young shoots glabrous; stipules distinctly leaflike, with glandular acuminate teeth, leaves obovate to oval-elliptic, acuminate, about 4 cm long and 1.5 cm wide, deeply incised, the teeth biserrate with 2–4 teeth, scattered bristly pubescent above, midrib pubescent beneath, petiole glabrous and 6 mm long; flowers white, grouped 1–2 on the previous year's wood, 1.7 cm wide, calyx large, tubular-campanulate, reddish, 8 mm long, sepals partly reflexed, petals nearly round and entire, stamens longer than the style, the latter long silky pubescent at the base, appearing with the leaves; fruits ellipsoid, 1 cm long, dark red. China; Kansu Prov. 1934. z6

P. sibirica L. Small tree, erect growing, to 5 m high; leaves ovate, long acuminate, 5–8 cm long, simple and finely serrate, reddish new growth, petiole 1–3 cm long; flowers nearly sessile, solitary, soft pink or white, to 3 cm wide, stalk and calyx nearly glabrous, April; fruit nearly sessile, rather globose, 1.5–2 cm thick (!), yellow with a reddish cheek, flesh dry, hardly edible, stone smooth, winged-angular. Gs 3: 74; ICS 2342 (= *P. armeniaca* var. *sibirica* K. Koch; *Armeniaca sibirica* Pers.). E. Siberia, Manchuria, N. China. Around 1800. z5 Plate 6; Fig. 5, 24.

P. simonii Carr. Small tree, narrowly conical, twigs red-brown, glabrous; leaves oblong-lanceolate, to 10 cm long, finely crenate, dull green above, bluish green beneath, venation branched at very acute angles (!), petiole short, with 2–4 large glands; flowers grouped 1–3, white, 1–1.5 cm wide, short stalked, late April–May; fruits globose, very short stalked, 3–5 cm wide, red-brown, fragrant, flesh yellow, usually somewhat bitter

Fig. 24. **Prunus.** *P. sibirica* — *P. armeniaca* — *P. salicina* (from ICS)

with an almond flavor, stone nearly circular, rough, tightly clinging. RH 1872: 111; BC 3217. N. China, in cultivation; not observed in the wild. 1863. z6 Fig. 23. ⚥

P. sinensis see: **P. glandulosa 'Sinensis'**

P. ✕ skinneri Rehd. (*P. japonica* ✕ *P. tenella*). Low shrub, scarcely over 1 m high; similar to *P. tenella,* but with oval-oblong leaves, 3.5–5 cm long, acuminate, lightly biserrate, midrib pubescent beneath; flowers numerous, dense, short stalked, light pink, small, calyx narrowly campanulate, this and the stalk pubescent. NH 1945: 68. Around 1934. ⊕

'Baton Rouge' (Skinner). A particularly abundant flowering selection of the above, developed by F. L. Skinner in 1934, Dropmore, Manitoba, Canada.

P. speciosa (Koidz.) Ingram. Open-crowned tree, to 12 m high; leaves bronze-green on new growth, elliptic ovate to narrowly obovate, with a rather abruptly acuminate apex, about 10 cm long, 6 cm wide, glabrous, but with a sparsely pubescent midrib when young, similarly the petiole; flowers appearing with the foilage, white, in loose, more or less long-stalked corymbs, corolla about 3.2 cm wide, white, slightly fragrant, calyx narrowly tubular-campanulate, 5 mm long. MiB 46; MJ 1313; KO 38; OFC 152; YWP 2: 16 (= *P. mutabilis speciosa* Miyoshi; *P. lannesiana* f. *albida* Wils.). Japan; Hondo, Kyushu. 1882. Much used in Japan as an understock for grafting. Plate 13.

P. spinosa L. Sloe, Blackthorn. Twiggy, thorny shrub or small tree, to 4 m high, branches divaricately spreading, short shoots with thorny tips, young shoots red-brown, tomentose to finely pubescent; leaves broadly lanceolate or elliptic, 2–4 cm long, finely serrate to crenate, pubescent when young, later becoming glabrous; flowers appearing before the leaves, solitary or paired, very numerous, 1–1.5 cm wide, white, April–

May; fruits globose to nearly ovate, erect, 1 to 1.5 cm long, blue-black, pruinose, flesh very bitter, stone bulging. HF 2554; HM 1270; GPN 445–446; HW 3:89. Europe, N. Africa, Asia Minor. Cultivated since antiquity. Ⓕ W. Germany (on slopes). Plate 9; Fig. 25. ⊕

'Plena'. Flowers somewhat smaller, densely double, pure white; fruits often 2 or 3 connate. Before 1770. ⊕

'Purpurea'. Young leaves red-brown, later more green above with a reddish margin, purple and glabrous; flowers pink. Disseminated by Barbier, Orléans, France, 1903. More recently, a form was developed in Holland with much more intensely red leaves; both forms may occur in cultivation under the same name. ∅

'Rosea' see: **P. cerasifera 'Rosea'**

'Variegata'. Leaves more or less white variegated. Before 1903.

P. spartioides see: **P. arabica**

P. spinosissima (Bge.) Franch. Thorn Almond. Small thorny shrub, divaricate habit; leaves elliptic-obovate to oblanceolate, 1–2 cm long, glabrous; flowers 1.5–2 cm wide, petals oblong-obovate, whitish pink, sepals long pubescent at the apex; fruits oval-rounded, stone smooth. SH 1: 336 p–r. Turkey to Persia and the Transcaspian region. 1910. z6 Fig. 29.

P. spinulosa S. & Z. Small evergreen tree, young shoots often finely pubescent; leaves leathery tough, narrowly oblong to more obovate, 5–8 cm long, 1.5–3 cm wide, long acuminate with thorny tips, leaf margins more or less thickened and sparsely dentate or entire, teeth appressed or outspread, glossy above; flowers in 2–8 cm long, many flowered racemes, white, corolla only about 6 mm wide, petals circular, 3 mm wide, September–October; fruits broadly ovate, 8 mm long. KIF 1: 72. Japan; the warmer regions. z9 Plate 22. #

P. ssiori F. Schmidt. Tree, 10–25 m high in its habitat, broad crowned, branches broadly spreading, bark light gray-brown, fragrant, young shoots short, glabrous, brown, winter buds large, spindle-form; leaves obovate-elliptic to oblong, 7–15 cm long, long acuminate, base usually distinctly cordate, margins finely awned-serrate, dark green and glabrous above, lighter beneath with pubescent vein axils, petiole 2–3 cm long, with 2 glands; flowers white, 1 cm wide, appearing with the foliage, numerous in 10–23 cm long, narrow racemes, petals as long as the stamens; fruits flat-rounded, about 1 cm thick, eventually black, stone indistinctly rugose to smooth. MJ 1324; KIF 3: 26. Central Japan; Hokkaido. 1915. Hardy. z5 Plate 5; Fig. 18.

P. subcordata Benth. Small tree, to 8 m high, branches usually spreading horizontally, branches gray-brown, young shoots pubescent or glabrous, light red; leaves broadly ovate to nearly circular (!), 3–7 cm long, scabrous and biserrate, base usually slightly cordate (!), pubescent beneath when young, later mostly glabrous, rolled up in the bud stage (!); flowers grouped 2–4, white, turning to pink, about 1.5 cm wide, calyx tips pubescent on both sides, oblong and obtuse; fruits ellipsoid, red or yellow, pruinose, 2–3 cm long. SPa 165; MS 219; SS 154. Western N. America. 1850. z7 Fig. 11, 30.

P. subhirtella Miq. Higan Cherry. A large tree in its habitat, 15–18 m high, with a thick trunk and thin, pubescent young shoots, bark eventually gray-brown; leaves ovate, acuminate, 3–8 (5 in the middle) cm long and 2.3 cm wide, scabrous serrate, with about 10 vein pairs, bright green above, sparsely pubescent on the venation beneath; flowers grouped 2–5 together,

appearing before the leaves, in umbels, bracts small, ovate, serrate, calyx tube lightly pubescent, purple-red, distinctly bulging at the base, 6 mm long, sepals narrowly triangular, about 3 mm long, petals pale pink (white on the type!), about 2.5 cm wide, more or less distinctly incised, style longer than the stamens, April; fruits oval-rounded, 9 mm long, purple-black when ripe. MJ 1309; IC 25; MD 1917: 8; OFC 74 (= *P. miqueliana* Maxim.; *P. taiwaniana* Hayata; *Cerasus herincquiana* Lav.). Japan. Around 1894. z5–6 Plate 8, 17; Fig. 26. ✧

var. **ascendens** Wils. The erect growing, wild type. A large tree, sparsely branched; leaves elliptic-oblong, 6–10 cm long; flowers white or a washed-out pink, flowers less abundantly. MD 1917: 42 a–e; MJ 3519, 1318; OFC 144 (= *P. miqueliana* Maxim.; *P. aequinoctialis* Miyoshi). Central Japan. 1916. Of no significance in cultivation. Plate 8.

'**Autumnalis**'. Shrub or small tree, to 5 m high (allegedly only half as high in Japan!), wide branched; leaves more coarsely serrate than those of the species, frequently biserrate; flowers white, semidouble, from November to April in clear weather. NM 8733; IC 29; DB 13: 23 (= *P. microlepis* Bean). Around 1900. Known in cultivation in Japan since 1500 (!). Plate 8; Fig. 26. ✧

'**Autumnalis Rosea**'. Like the white-flowered form, but with a soft pink center in the flowers, calyx also reddish. OFC 55. 1960. ✧

var. *changyangensis* see: **P. changyangensis**

'**Elfenreigen**' (*P. subhirtella* × *P. concinna?*). Rather narrow upright habit, open branched, new growth appearing one week before *P. subhirtella*; young leaves brownish, intensely orange and red in fall; flowers white, petals very narrow, therefore appearing stellate, loosely arranged, late April. Developed by Rud. Schmidt, Rellingen, W. Germany. ✧

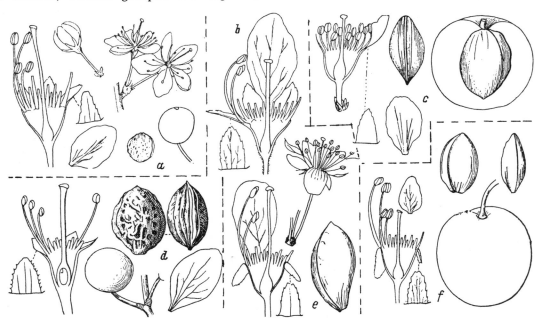

Fig. 25. **Prunus**. a. *P. spinosa*; b. *P. salicina*; c. *P. cocomilia*; d. *P. curdica*; e. *P. domestica*; f. *P. cerasifera* (from Fritsch, Schneider)

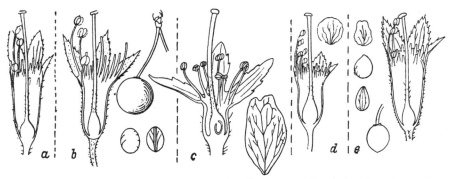

Fig. 26. **Prunus.** a.–b. *P. subhirtella;* c. *P. subhirtella* 'Autumnalis'; d. *P. rufa;* e. *P. apetala*
(from Schneider, Koehne, Lavallée)

'Fukubana'. Flowers semidouble or densely double, opening dark pink, later becoming somewhat lighter, petals 12–14, very deeply incised and then appearing somewhat crispate, flowering period a week later than the other upright forms; fertile (!), but fruiting only occasionally. 1927. The best *P. subhirtella* form. Plate 3, 17. ✣

'Grandiflora'. (Ingram). Flowers larger, to 3.7 cm wide, whitish pink, flowers less abundantly. A selection by Ingram. Before 1950. ✣

'Pendula'. Branches weeping; leaves like those of the species, but somewhat wider; flowers abundantly, but only a very faded whitish pink. BM 8034; MJ 3518; OFC 49 (= *P. pendula* Maxim.). Introduced by Siebold into Holland, 1862. Plate 8. ✣

'Pendula Plena Rosea'. Weeping form; flowers double in rosettes or semidouble, a good pink, similar to 'Fukubana', but somewhat lighter. OFC 135 (as 'Yaebeni-shidare'). 1938.

'Plena'. Flowers densely double, flat, 2.5 cm wide, a strong pink in bud, opening white (= ? "Dahlem" in Holland). 1935. Very attractive but rare form.

'Rosea'. This is the normally cultivated form of *P. subhirtella*. Upright habit. ChCh 68. ✣

'Stellata' (Clarke). Erect habit; flowers clustered 3–5 at the shoot tips, appearing like 15 cm long, dense panicles, corolla about 3.5 cm wide, petals narrowly oblong, nearly stellate in appearance. IC 26. Selection of W. B. Clarke, San Jose, California, USA. ✣

P. subhirtella × P. yedoensis. Giving rise to the following forms:

'Hally Jolivette' (Sax) ([*P. subhirtella* × *P. yedoensis*] × *P. subhirtella*). Rounded, about 3–4 m high shrub, finely and densely branched, shoots thin, red to red-brown, densely warty punctate, scattered bristly pubescent at first, later glabrous and glossy; leaves ovate, 3–4.5 cm long, 1.5–2.5 cm wide, widest at the middle, long acuminate, base round, simple to biserrate, teeth sharp, pubescent on both sides, denser beneath, particularly on the venation, midrib and the 5–8 mm long petiole red and red pubescent; flowers double, small, white, with a pink center, 3 cm wide, buds pink, flowering continuously for 2–3 weeks (!), April to May. Developed by Dr. K. Sax in the Arnold Arboretum, 1940. z5–6 Plate 13. ✣

'Pandora' (Waterer) (*P. subhirtella* 'Rosea' × *P. yedoensis*). Upright habit, tall shrub, shoots loosely arranged, slightly nodding; leaves ovate-elliptic, widest beneath the middle, 5–7 cm long, 2.5–3 cm wide, long acuminate, base rounded, rather coarse and scabrous biserrate, rugose and glabrous above, scattered pubescent beneath, denser on the venation, midrib and the 1 cm long petiole red; flowers solitary, white with a trace of pink, simple, medium size, but abundant, April. GC 1951: (I) 107. Developed before 1939 by Waterer Sons & Crisp. ✣

P. susquehanae see: **P. pumila** var. **susquehanae**

P. sweginzowii Koehne. Small, glabrous shrub, very similar to *P. tenella*, but with scabrous, biserrate leaves, stipules leaflike (!); flowers dark pink, calyx tubular, 12 mm long, sepals long and glandular fringed, petals oblong-obovate, base cuneate, about 12 mm long. MD 1910: 97. Turkestan. Before 1910. z6 Fig. 29. ✣

P. szechuanica Batal. Very closely related to *P. macradenia*, but with smaller leaves, 3–4.2 cm long, bracts only 3–8 mm long, leaf and bract glands compressed and disk form, leaf petiole usually blackish purple; stone totally smooth. China; Szechwan Prov. z6 Fig. 27.

P. tangutica (Batal.) Koehne. Dense, thorny shrub, 3–4 m high, twigs brown, very finely pubescent, later glabrous; leaves usually clustered at the buds or on short lateral shoots, oblanceolate to oblong, acute, 1–3 cm long (!), dark green above, lighter beneath, with 5–8 vein pairs, finely crenate, base cuneate; flowers solitary, sessile, 2.5 cm wide, pink-red, petals obovate, sepals elliptic, indistinctly toothed, glabrous, stamens about 30, March; fruits nearly sessile, 2 cm thick, thin fleshed, densely tomentose, eventually dehiscing, stone rounded, keeled on both sides, rough. BM 9239; DRHS 1700 (= *P. dehiscens* Koehne). W. China, Szechwan Prov. 1910. z5 ✣

P. tatsienensis Batal. Shrub, closely related to *P. litigiosa*, but glabrous; leaves caudate acuminate, the teeth with large, terminal, conical glands, bracts glandular dentate, glands rounded, disk form; fruits 1 cm thick, brown-red. W. China. z6 Fig. 27.

The wild species is not in cultivation, rather only its var. **stenadenia** Koehne. Only slightly different, primarily in the narrow oblong glands on the bracts (not disk form).

P. tenella Batsch. Dwarf Almond. Thin branched, upright shrub, to 1.5 m high, twigs glabrous; leaves narrowly elliptic to obovate or oblanceolate, 3–7 cm

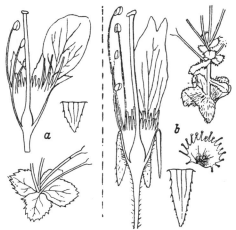

Fig. 27. **Prunus.** a. *P. tatsienensis;* b. *P. szechuanica*
(from Schneider)

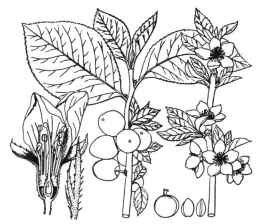

Fig. 28. *Prunus tomentosa*
(from Lauche et al)

long, scabrous serrate, acute, somewhat thick, glossy green; flowers grouped 1–3, pink-red, to 3 cm wide, very numerous, sessile, appearing with the foliage; fruits ovate, 2 cm long, gray-yellow, pubescent, stone broadly ovate, rough. HF 2551; BM 161; HM 1085 (= *P. nana* [L.] Stokes). Central Europe to E. Siberia. 1683. z2 Plate 2, 20; Fig. 29. ✤

'**Alba**' (Camuset). Leaves lighter green; flowers like the species, but pure white. Found in France around 1845. ✤

var. **campestris** (Bess.) Rehd. More vigorous growing; leaves larger, more elliptic to elliptic-oblong or elliptic-obovate; flowers red, sepals narrower, more than half the calyx length; fruits rounded (= *Amygdalus besseriana* Schott; *Amygdalus sibirica* Lodd.; *Amygdalus ledebouriana* Schlecht.). The steppes of central Russia. ✤

var. **campestris** '**Albiflora**'. Like the above, but with white flowers. ✤

'**Fire Hill**'. An English selection with intensely red, more densely arranged flowers. ✤

var. **georgica** Desf. Distinguished only by its greater height, larger, more glossy leaves, and less dentate margin (= *P. nana* var. *georgica* [Desf.] Voss). ✤

'**Speciosa**'. Shrub, only 0.5–0.8 m high; flowers larger, darker pink, particularly in bud. RH 1874: Pl. 370 (= f. *gessleriana* [Kirchn.] Rehd.; *P. nana rubra* Hort.). 1853. ✤

P. texana Dietr. Texas Almond. A low, very irregularly branched shrub, young shoots light gray, very pubescent; leaves elliptic to more oblong, 1.5–3 cm long, 6–15 mm wide on strong young shoots, obtuse, somewhat tapered toward the base, distinctly glandular serrate, green and softly pubescent above, gray tomentose beneath; flowers solitary or in pairs, most appearing with the foliage, 1 cm wide, white; fruits small, velvety pubescent, stone 1.5 cm long, 1 cm wide and 9 mm thick. HI 288 (as *Amygdalus glandulosa*) (= *P. glandulosa* [Hook.] Torr. & Gray; *P. hookeri* C. Schneid.; *Amygdalus texana* [Dietr.] W. Wight). Texas; endemic. z6

P. tomentosa Thunb. Korean Cherry. Densely growing shrub, 1–1.5 m high, twigs densely tomentose, blackish brown; leaves obovate, abruptly acuminate, 4–6 cm long, rugose and dull green above, pubescent, gray-green and tomentose beneath, margins serrate; flowers mostly solitary, appearing with the foliage, white, somewhat pink toned in the center, 1.5 cm wide, sessile, calyx tube widely campanulate, usually pubescent, inside and out, late April–May; fruits globose, scarlet-red (!), 1 cm thick, glabrous or pubescent, very ornamental. BM 8196; MJ 1307 (= *P. trichocarpa* Bge.). N. and W. China, Japan, Himalayas. 1870. z3 Plate 8, 20; Fig. 28. ✤ ♋

var. **endotricha** Koehne. Leaves elliptic; flowers white, flowering very abundantly. China; W. Hupeh Prov. 1908. ✤ ♋

'**Leucocarpa**'. Cultivar. Fruits whitish. 1930.

For other forms, see Howard & Baranov: The Chinese Bush Cherry, *Prunus tomentosa;* in Arnoldia **24**, 81–86, 1964.

P. triflora see: **P. salicina**

P. triloba Lindl. Flowering Almond. Shrub or small tree (to 5 m), often grafted on a standard, very densely branched, twigs dark brown, densely velvety pubescent; leaves broadly elliptic, often 3 lobed, biserrate, 4–8 cm long, dull green above, lighter and pubescent beneath; flowers paired or solitary, about 3.5 cm wide, dense rosette form, double, along the entire length of the previous year's growth, abundantly flowering, March–April; fruit rare, about 1 cm wide, rounded. FS 1532; BS 47. Introduced by Robert Fortune from China in 1855; not observed in the wild. In this book, as in Boom, the original name is retained for the double flowering form. z3 ✤

'**Petzoldii**'. Twigs glabrous (!); leaves elliptic to ovate, never 3 lobed (!), widest beneath the middle, eventually glabrous beneath, petiole as long as the calyx tube; flowers pink, single, 1.5–2 cm wide, with 10 (!) sepals and as many petals (= var. *petzoldii* [K. Koch] Bailey). China, known only in cultivation. 1869. ✤

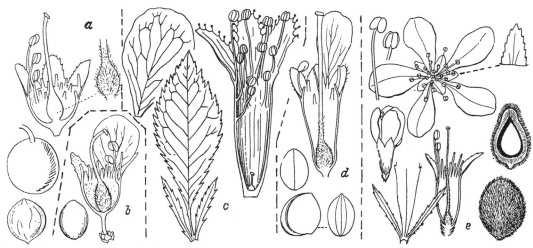

Fig. 29. **Prunus.** a. *P. triloba* f. *simplex;* b. *P. pedunculata;* c. *P. sweginzowii;* d. *P. spinosissima;* e. *P. tenella* (from André, Koehne, Schneider)

f. **simplex** (Bge.) Rehd. The wild form. Flowers single, scarcely over 2.5 cm wide, pink, less persistent; fruits nearly globose, reddish, pubescent, rather dry fleshed, stone thick, hard, rugose. BM 8061. China; on forested mountain sides in Shantung and Tsili. 1884. Rare in cultivation; less attractive than the double flowering form, flowers abscise earlier. Plate 20; Fig. 29.

P. umbellata Ell. Very densely crowned, small tree, to 6 m high, twigs very thin, often more or less thorny, somewhat pubescent only when young; leaves elliptic to lanceolate, 4 to 5 cm long, light green and thin, acute, base acute to round, finely and densely serrate, usually glabrous above, pubescent beneath, eventually persisting only on the venation, petiole without glands; flowers grouped 2–4 in umbels, appearing with or shortly before the foliage, 1 to 1.8 cm wide, calyx glabrous on the exterior (!); fruits globose, 1–2 cm thick, yellow to orange, also with a trace of red, thinly pruinose, flesh usually bitter and sour, freestone, stone oval-rounded. SS 155; DL 3: 261. E. USA. z8 Fig. 30.

P. ursina Kotschy. Shrub, to 3 m high, slightly thorny, young shoots pubescent; leaves ovate to obovate, 2–5 cm long, acute to obtuse, often short acuminate, crenate, venation yellow pubescent beneath, petiole to 12 mm long; flowers appearing before the leaves, about 1.5–2 cm wide, yellowish white, calyx and the short stalk densely pubescent; fruits nearly globose, about 2.5 cm wide, violet-red, rather smooth, stone smooth. SH 1: 346 s–t, 348 o. Syria. z7

P. ussuriensis Kov. & Kost. Ussuri Plum. Tree, 4–6(10) m high, round crowned, stout branched, shoots reddish brown, glabrous; leaves obovate to lanceolate, thin, light green; flowers grouped 2–3 together, small, white, appearing with the foliage, April; fruits globose to ellipsoid, greenish yellow to dark red, edible, juicy, pleasant tasting, August, stone not free (= *P. triflora* var. *mandshurica* Skvorc.). Manchuria and far eastern USSR. z5 ⊗ ✕

P. ✕ utahensis Koehne (= *P. angustifolia* var. *watsonii* ✕ *P. besseyi*). Very similar to *P. besseyi*, but the leaves elliptic to elliptic-oblong or oblong-obovate, 3.5–6 cm long, finely serrate, glossy above, with reticulate venation beneath; fruits dark brown-red, slightly pruinose. DL 3: 259; SH 1: 345 m–n. Originated in the USA around 1865. z4

P. vaniotii Lév. A broad crowned, 12–15 m high tree in its habitat, young shoots glabrous, surrounded at the base at first with red bud scales, these lanceolate and quickly abscising; leaves oblong to obovate, acute to gradually acuminate, about 8 cm long and 3.5 cm wide, finely serrate, base nearly cordate to cuneately rounded, new growth red-brown, later deep green above, bluish beneath, petiole about 1.3 cm long, purple-red, glandular; flowers numerous in cylindrical, loose racemes at the ends of foliate lateral shoots, corolla small, white, 8 mm wide, calyx tube broadly cupulate, yellowish brown; fruits nearly globose, orange to brown-red, 8 mm thick, stone somewhat rugose (= *P. brachypoda* var. *prattii* [Koehne] Ingram; *P. pubigera* var. *prattii* Koehne). W. China. 1908. z5 Plate 5.

var. **potaninii** (Koehne) Rehd. Tree, to 20 m; leaves oblong-obovate, 4–11 cm long, short acuminate, base cordate or nearly so, finely serrate, whitish and glabrous beneath, with reticulate venation, petiole 1–2.5 cm long, finely pubescent; flowers about 1 cm wide, in 7–14 cm long (without the stalk), glabrous, narrow racemes, calyx interior pubescent beneath the middle, stamens ⅓ shorter than the petals; fruits 8 mm thick, stone somewhat rugose (= *P. pubigera* Koehne; *P. brachypoda* var. *pubigera* Schneid.; *P. pubigera* var. *potaninii* Koehne). W. China. 1908. Plate 5.

P. vavilovii M. Pop. Shrub to small tree, 2.5–9 m high, bark dark gray to nearly black, young shoots green, pubescent; leaves oval-oblong, 4–6(8) cm long, 1.5–2(3) cm wide, finely dentate, glabrous above, lightly pubescent beneath; flowers appear before the foliage, 3.5–4 cm wide, pink, March–April; fruits almond-like, dry flesh, 2–5 cm long, to 3.5 cm wide, July–August, stone to 3 cm long and 2 cm wide (= *Amygdalus vavilovii* M. Pop.; *Amygdalus kalmykowii* O. Lincz.; *Amygdalus uzbekistanica* Sabir.) Central Asia Kopet-Dag W. Tien Shan Mts., Pamir-Alai. z4

P. virens (Woot. & Standl.) Shreve. Very similar to *P. salicifolia*, but partly evergreen, primarily differing in the smaller flowers and shorter racemes. Small tree or shrub; leaves usually elliptic, acute, occasionally acuminate, finely serrate, petiole without glands; flowers in about 10 cm long racemes; fruits purple-black, edible, bittersweet. VT 391 (= *P. serotina* var. *acutifolia* S. Wats.). USA; New Mexico to Arizona. 1916. Hardy. z6 # ⌀

P. virginiana L. Tree or shrub, stoloniferous, twigs glabrous, brownish green at first, later gray-brown; leaves broadly obovate to broadly elliptic, abruptly acuminate, 4–12 cm long, base round, margins densely serrate, bright green above, blue or gray-green beneath, glabrous on the underside except for the brownish pubescent vein axils, leaf petiole red, with 2–6 glands, often also with reddish venation; flowers white, appearing after the foliage, 8 mm wide, in 6–8 cm long, nodding racemes, calyx widely campanulate, sepals short triangular, glandular ciliate toothed, not pubescent, petals rounded, dentate, style shorter than the stamens, late May–June; fruits globose, 1 cm thick, red at first, eventually purple, bittersweet, without calyx remnants (!), stone acute, smooth. BB 2024; GTP 247; VT 392; SS 158. Western N. America. 1724. Easy to grow, but of only little ornamental value. Ⓕ USA. z2 Plate 8, 20; Fig. 31. ⌀

var. **demissa** (Torr. & Gray) Torr. Habit more shrubby, 1–3 m high, twigs and inflorescences glabrous or pubescent; leaves smaller, 5–9 cm long, ovate to obovate, shorter acuminate, base round to somewhat cordate, usually pubescent beneath, petiole with 2 glands. BB 2025; MS 221; SPa 167 (= *P. demissa* Dietr.). USA; Washington to California. 1892. Plate 8; Fig. 32.

'Duerinckii'. Leaves broadly elliptic, otherwise hardly different. Cultivated in Belgium. 1840.

'Leucocarpa'. Fruits light amber yellow. 1889.

var. **melanocarpa** (A. Nels.) Sarg. Shrub or small tree, twigs smooth; leaves smaller, thicker, glabrous on both sides, petiole without glands, the small margins teeth more appressed or inward curving; flowers white, in compact, erect to ascending racemes; fruit nearly black, bitter (= *P. melanocarpa* Rydb.). Rocky Mts.; California to British Columbia. 1879.

'Nana'. Dwarf form. Before 1903.

'Pendula'. Twigs pendulous. Before 1903.

'Shubert' (Will). Leaves green at first, soon brown, eventually deep brown colored. Will Nurseries, USA. Around 1950. ⌀

'Xanthocarpa'. Yellow fruited form of var. *melanocarpa*. 1912.

P. wallichii Steud. An evergreen species similar to *P. laurocerasus*, from E. Himalayas to W. China and Sumatra. HAl 65. Not cultivated in the West. z9 #

P. watsonii see: **P. angustifolia** var. **watsonii**

P. webbii (Spach) Vierh. Densely branched shrub or small tree, to about 6 m high, short shoots thorned, young shoots red; leaves oblong-linear, acute, 3–4.5 cm long, 6 to 9 mm wide, base cuneate, shallowly glandular crenate, glabrous on both sides, light green above, lighter beneath, petiole 5–12 mm long; flowers appear before the leaves, most solitary, occasionally grouped, about 2 cm wide, petals broadly obovate, apex usually slightly bilabiate, white, sepals short elliptic, 3 mm long, with a few hair fascicles at the apex, calyx short cylindrical, glabrous, stamens about 26, filaments eventually pink; fruits somewhat conical, nearly 2 cm long, densely velvety pubescent. BMns 118 (= *P. haussknechtii* Schneid.). Sicily to Asia Minor. Before 1930. Ⓕ Yugoslavia; reforestation in Macedonia. z6 ☾

P. wilsonii (Schneid.) Koehne. Closely related to *P. sericea*. A tree in its habitat, to 10 m; leaves obovate, 9–13 cm long, 4.5–6 cm wide, acuminate, base rounded, tough, margins finely serrate, silky pubescent beneath, petiole 7–15 mm long, with 1–4 glands; racemes pubescent, stamens about 1.5 times as long as the petals. Central China. z6 Plate 5.

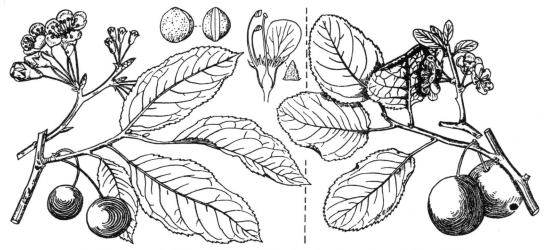

Fig. 30. **Prunus.** Left *P. umbellata*; right *P. subcordata* (from Sargent, Schneider)

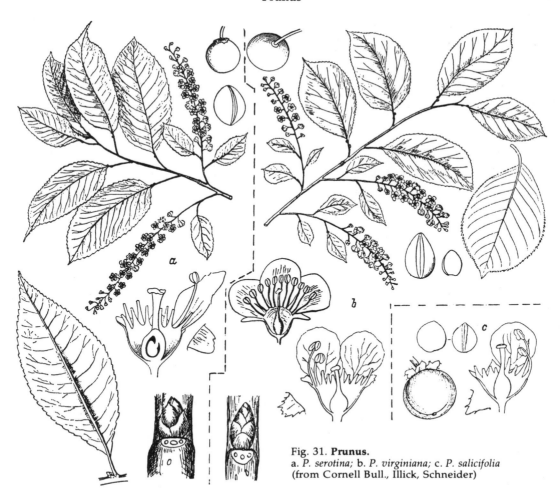

Fig. 31. **Prunus.**
a. *P. serotina*; b. *P. virginiana*; c. *P. salicifolia*
(from Cornell Bull., Illick, Schneider)

P. yamasakura see: **P. serrulata** var. **spontanea**

P. × **yedoensis** Matsum. Tokyo Cherry. Hybrids of unknown origin, not observed in the wild. Tree, broadly erect, 12–15 m high, bark smooth, young twigs lightly pubescent; leaves yellowish green on new growth, elliptic, 6–12 cm long, acuminate, biserrate, acute, bright green above, lighter beneath, pubescent on the venation, leaf petiole pubescent, fall color golden-yellow with brick-red; flowers with a touch of pink when opening, later pure white, about 3–3.5 cm wide, grouped 5–6 in short-stalked racemes, calyx, style and flower stalk pubescent, late March–April; fruits globose, pea-sized, black. BM 9062; MJ 1311; KO ill. 99; IC 38; MJ 4; OFC 117; ChCh 32 + 61 (= *P. paracerasus* Koehne; 'Yoshino'). Planted in the region around Tokyo. The famed 800 cherries planted in Potomac Park, Washington D.C. as a gift from the mayor of Tokyo are all members of this Taxon. Of relatively recent origin, totally unknown even in Japan before 1868. Very abundant bloomer and attractive tree. z6 Plate 1, 6, 21. ⊕

'Ivensii' (Hillier). Weeping form. Branches rather thin, wide, horizontally spreading at first, then nodding downward, rather long, very thin lateral shoots; flowers pink in bud, opening white. Selected by Hillier, Winchester, England. Plate 21.

'Moerheimii' (Ruys). Shrub, to 3 m high, twigs gray, pendulous; leaves on long shoots 7–10 cm long, on short shoots smaller, elliptic, somewhat acuminate, biserrate, base round to acute, with 8 to 11 vein pairs, glabrous or scattered pubescent above, densely pubescent beneath, petiole pubescent, with 2 glands; flowers usually 3 in stalked clusters, bracts deeply serrate, stalk pubescent, calyx purple, rather glabrous, sepals somewhat serrate, petals pink at first, soon becoming white, narrow, 10–14 mm long, late flowering (= *P. incisa moerheimii* Ruys). Around 1930. ⊕

var. *pendula* see: **'Shidare Yoshino**

var. *purpendens* see: **'Shidare Yoshino'**

'Shidare Yoshino'. Weeping form, grafted on a standard or trained upward and then growing sharply and vertically downward, annual growth to 1.5 m long; flowers pure white, profusely flowering only on older plants. DB 11: 12 (= *P. yedoensis purpendens* Ingram; *P. yedoensis pendula* Ingram). 1916. Plate 21. ⊕

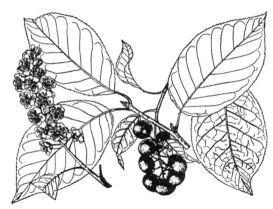

Fig. 32. *Prunus virginiana* var. *demissa*
(from Sudworth)

P. zippeliana Miq. Evergreen tree, stem with red-brown, exfoliating bark; leaves thin, leathery, narrowly oval-oblong to more elliptic, 10–20 cm long, 4–7 cm wide, gradually tapered to the apex, scabrous dentate, glabrous or finely pubescent beneath, petiole 1–1.5 cm long; flowers white, 6–7 mm wide, numerous, in short, dense, sessile racemes, petals circular, 3 mm wide, September–October. KIF 2: 30; YWP 2: 23 + 24. Japan, in the warmer regions. z9 # ⊕

The soil and site requirements of the *Prunus* species are quite variable, but general conditions can be cited for a given subgenus. Careful observance of optimal conditions is not so important with the wild types as with the fruiting types where economic concerns come into play. Apricots and their relatives require an open, sunny area in a loose, sandy, alkaline soil. Almonds and peaches (and those species belonging to this subgenus) like a warm, dry site in a light, deep and fertile soil. Plums will tolerate any soil, so long as it is not a very hard, dense clay or too hot and dry. *P. mahaleb* and *P. cerasus,* on the other hand, prefer a dry, sandy to somewhat gravelly soil; the cherries like a sandy, fertile, cool soil. The racemose cherries (bird cherries) grow particularly well on a moist, humus soil, also on a sandy humus soil, when sufficient moisture is present. Finally, the evergreen species are the only ones which dislike alkalinity and prefer a moist, humus soil in a sunny, or preferably somewhat shady site. The laurel cherries are particularly well suited as understory plants on wooded sites.

Lit. Bailey, L. H.: Native dwarf Cherries; in Cornell Univ. Agr. Exp. Sta. Hort. Div. Bull. **38**, 1892 ● Ingram, C.: Ornamental Cherries; London 1948 (259 pp., an important work!) ● Miyoshi, M.: Japanese Mountain Cherries, their wild forms and cultivars; in J. Coll. Sci. Imp. Univ. Tokyo **24**, 1–175, 1916 (with 23 plates and 89 color illustrations of cherry types) ● Wilson, E. H.; The Cherries of Japan; in Publ. Arnold Arb. **7**, 1–68, 1916; Cambridge, Mass. (Plates 1–8) ● Koehne, E.: Die Kirschenarten Japans; in Mitt. DDG 1917, 1–65 (ill.) ● Koehne, E.: Fünf Mischlinge von *Prunus cerasifera* Ehrh.; in Mitt. DDG 1917, 66–71 ● Koehne, E.: Die geographische Verbreitung der Kirschen, *Prunus* subg. *Cerasus*; in Mitt. DDG 1912, 168–183 ● Wight, F. W.: Native American species of *Prunus*; in U.S. Dept. Agr. Bull. **179**, 1915 ● Groh, H., & H. Senn: *Prunus* in eastern Canada; in Canad. J. Res. Sect. C, Bot. Sci. 1940, 318–346 (ill.) ● Russell, P.: The Oriental Cherries, USDA Agric. Circ. **313**, 1–72,

1934 ● Williams, H. A.; Edible varieties of Almonds; in J. RHS **68**, 62–65 ● Ingram, C.: Notes on Japanese Cherries (II); in J. RHS **54**, 159 ff.; (III) **70**, 10–18 (with key); The Yingtao or Chinese Fruiting Cherry; in J. RHS **68**, 307–309 (covers *P. pseudocerasus* and its forms) ● Cumming, W. A.: A new hybrid of the genus *Prunus: Prunus* × *nigrella;* Baileya **11**, 5–8, 1963 (with ills.) ● Van de Laar, H.: *Prunus laurocerasus;* in Dendroflora **7**, 42–61, 1970 ● Sano, T.: Flowering Cherries; Kyoto 1961 (101 pp., 101 plates; in Japanese and English) ● Ohwi, J., & Y. Ohta: Flowering Cherries of Japan; Tokyo 1973 (325 pp., 154 color plates; in Japanese, with Latin names, most beautiful plates of the flowering cherries) ● Chadbund, G.: Flowering Cherries; London 1972 (166 pp.) ● Zylka, D.: Die Verwendung von Wildarten der Gattung *Prunus* in der Sortenzüchtung und als Unterlage, auf Grund vorwiegend russischer Forschungsergebnisse; Wiesbaden 1970 (222 pp.) ● Löschnig-Passecker: Die Marille; Vienna 1954 (363 pp.).

PSEUDOCYDONIA Schneid. — ROSACEAE

Very closely related to *Chaenomeles* (and earlier often included in that genus), but differing in the solitary flowers, stamen filaments in a ring, and leaves with awn-like tooth apexes. — 1 species in China.

Pseudocydonia sinensis Schneid. Small tree or tall shrub, easily distinguished by the plate-like exfoliating bark, twigs without thorns; leaves elliptic-oblong, deeply serrated, 5 to 8 cm long, underside shaggy pubescent when young, very glossy above, scarlet-red and yellow in fall; flowers appear with the foliage, solitary, light pink, May; fruit woody, dark yellow, 10–15 cm long. BM 7988 (= *Cydonia sinensis* Thouin; *Chaenomeles sinensis* [Dum.-Cours.] Schneid.). China. Hardy, but rarely found in cultivation. z6 Plate 24; Fig. 228 (Vol. I). ⊕ ⚬

PSEUDOCYTISUS

Pseudocytisus spinosus see: **Vella spinosa**

PSEUDOPANAX C. Koch — ARALIACEAE

Glabrous, evergreen shrubs or small trees; leaves extraordinarily variable, simple or palmately compound; leaves on young plants often quite different from those on mature plants; leaflets leathery tough, entire or serrate or dentate; flowers dioecious, in umbels, these grouped into panicles or racemes; calyx limb entire to dentate, petals 5, valvate; stamens 5, anthers ovate to oblong; ovaries 5 chambered, style short; fruits fleshy, globose, black. — 6 species in New Zealand and S. America.

Pseudopanax arboreum see: **Neopanax Arboreum**

P. crassifolium (Soland.) C. Koch. Glabrous, evergreen, stiffly branched shrub or tree; leaves quite variable: oval-lanceolate on young seedlings, coarsely lobed, 3–5 cm long, later swordlike, only 2.5–5 cm wide and 30 to 70 cm long, margins thorny dentate (during this stage, which lasts about 20 years, the plant remains single stemmed and unbranched), leaves are 3–5 parted when the plant begins branching, becoming simple again in the final stage, oblanceolate, 7–20 cm long, 2.5–3 cm wide, then entire or sinuately toothed; flowers small, greenish, in 7–10 cm wide, terminal, compound umbels; fruits black, 5 mm thick. KF 38. New Zealand. 1846. z9 # Ø

P. discolor (Kirk) Harms. Well branched shrub, 1.5–3 m high in its habitat, twigs thin; leaves arranged along the shoots, yellow-green to bronze-brown, 3–5 parted, intermixed with simple leaves, leaflets obovate to more lanceolate or elliptic, 2.5–8 cm long, 2–4 cm wide, coarsely and scabrous serrate, terminal leaflet largest, dull above; flowers in terminal racemes. MNZ 237 (= *Panax discolor* Kirk). New Zealand. z9 # Ø

P. ferox Kirk. Small, slender, evergreen tree, 3–6 m high; leaves variable, but always simple, linear-lanceolate on seedlings, later swordlike, 30–45 cm long, 1 to 2.5 cm wide, very thick and stiff, directed downward, margins with broad, hooked, densely arranged teeth, 10–20 cm long in the final stage, entire to sparsely dentate; fruits 8 mm thick (!). New Zealand. z9 Plate 22. # Ø

P. lessonii (DC.) C. Koch. Well branched shrub or small tree, 2.5–5 m high, with thick, ascending branches; leaves clustered at the shoot tips, most 3–5 parted, larger on young plants than on mature, but otherwise similar, obovate-cuneate to oblanceolate, thick and leathery, 5–10 cm long, 2–4 cm wide, apical half sinuate or obtusely serrate, smooth and glossy above, distinctly veined on both sides, terminal leaflet largest; flowers in terminal, compound umbels (= *Panax lessonii* DC.). New Zealand. z9 Plate 22. # Ø

PSEUDOSASA Mak. — GRAMINEAE

Evergreen bamboos with creeping rootstocks, stem cylindrical, to 5 m high, with persistent stem sheaths; with a branch arising from each node; buds hardly apparent. — 3 species in E. Asia.

Pseudosasa japonica Mak. Stem 2–3(5) m high, stem sheaths bristly pubescent at first, later pale brown, persisting very long; leaves lanceolate, 10–24 cm long, 2–4 cm wide, long acuminate, base tapered, glossy dark green above, blue-green beneath except for a green marginal strip, very finely checkered venation, margins rough. NH 24: 175; NK 20: 1–2; CBa 5a (= *Arundinaria japonica* S. & Z.; *Bambusa metake* Sieb.). Japan. 1850. z7 # Ø

Very fast growing. Spreads by rhizomes. Prefers a moist, fertile soil.

PSEUDOWINTERA Dandy — WINTERACEA

Evergreen shrubs to small trees; leaves alternate, simple, aromatic, with a sharp peppery taste, translucent glandular punctate; flowers axillary, in clusters or solitary; calyx cupulate, persistent, limb entire or lobed, the petals not enclosed within the bud; petals 5–6, imbricate in the bud stage; stamens up to 15, in 3 rings; fruit berrylike, with 2–6 seeds. — 3 species in New Zealand, but only one generally cultivated.

Pseudowintera colorata (Raoul) Dandy. Peppertree, Horopito. Densely branched, small to medium-sized shrub, to 2.5 m high in its habitat, shoots yellow-brown; leaves elliptic to broadly obovate, mostly obtuse, base cuneate, 2–7 cm long, 1.5–3 cm wide, leathery tough, dull yellow-green above, red speckled and limbed, whitish or bluish beneath, petiole 3–6 mm; flowers grouped 1–6 in axils, yellow-green, with 5 to 7 petals, these about 6 mm long; fruits bright red or also black (= *Drimys colorata* Raoul; *Wintera colorata* Teigh.). New Zealand. z9 Ø

Needs a protected site and a lime free soil. The leaves have better color in full sun, occasionally nearly a metallic gold.

Lit. Vink, W.: The Winteraceae of the Old World. I. *Pseudowintera* and *Drimys*, morphology and taxonomy; Blumea 8, 225–354, 1970.

PSIDIUM L. — Guava — Myrtaceae

Evergreen shrubs or trees; leaves opposite, smooth or tomentose, pinnately veined; flowers grouped 1–3 on axillary or lateral stalks; calyx with connate sepals at first, flower tube campanulate, cylindrical or pear-shaped, petals 4–5, outspread; stamens numerous, free; ovaries usually 4–5 chambered; fruit a globose to pear-shaped berry crowned with the persistent sepals. — About 140 species in tropical America and the West Indies, many with edible fruits; some species are cultivated in tropical countries.

Psidium cattleyanum Sabine. Shrub or tree, to 8 m high, bark smooth, gray-brown, young shoots cylindrical; leaves elliptic to obovate, 5–10 cm long, leathery tough, smooth, venation hardly visible; flowers solitary, white, 2.5 cm wide, March–April; fruits oval to globose, 2.5–3.5 cm long, purple-red; flesh white, edible, tastes like strawberries. BM 2501; BR 622. Brazil. 1818. z10 # ⚬ ✕

P. guayava L. Guava, Guajava. Tall, evergreen shrub or tree, bark greenish brown, scaly, young shoots 4 sided; leaves oblong to elliptic, 7–15 cm long, venation indented above, elevated on the underside, finely soft pubescent; flowers solitary or 2–3 on a stalk, white, 2.5 cm wide, April; fruits globose to oval or pear-shaped, from 2.5–10 cm wide depending on the cultivar, shell yellow, flesh greenish yellow (becoming deep pink to salmon color when processed and canned), ripening September–November, extraordinarily rich in Vitamin C. HKT 81; ICS 3710. Tropical America. 1692. z10 # ⚬ ✕

The most important cultivars economically are **'Fan Retief'** and **'Frank Malherbe'**.

Lit. Popenoe, W.: Manual of tropical and subtropical fruits; New York 1919 (pp. 272–286) ● Mowry, H., L. R. Toy & H. S. Wolfe: Miscellaneous tropical and subtropical Florida fruits; Univ. Fla. Agr. Ext. Serv. Bull. **109**, 1941 ● Mustard, M. J.: Ascorbic acid content of some Florida-grown Guavas; Univ. Fla. Agr. Ext. Serv. Bull. **414**, 1945.

PSORALEA L. — LEGUMINOSAE

Perennials, subshrubs or shrubs; leaves mostly pinnate, with 3–5 leaflets, occasionally only 1 or more than 5; flowers in variable inflorescences, occasionally solitary; calyx lobes nearly regularly formed, standard ovate to circular, wings as long or shorter than the keel; pod ovate, single-seeded, not dehiscent. — About 130 species in the tropics and subtropics.

Psoralea pinnata L. Small shrub, 0.7–1.5 m high; leaves pinnate, leaflets 5–11, linear, about 3 cm long, slightly pubescent; flowers very numerous, blue, striped, wings white, in axillary clusters or solitary, short stalked, May–June. South Africa. 1690. z10 ⊕

PTELEA L. — "Hop tree" — RUTACEAE

Deciduous, aromatic shrubs; leaves alternate, petiolate, trifoliate, the leaflets nearly sessile, translucent punctate; flowers polygamous, greenish white, inconspicuous, in corymbs; calyx short, 4 or 5 parted, tips overlapping; petals 4 or 5, much longer than the calyx, also overlapping; fruits dry, circular, winged. — About 7–10 very closely related species in N. America and Mexico.

(There is considerable disagreement among authors as to the number of species in this genus, according to Wilson only 3, according to Greene around 60!)

Ptelea angustifolia see: **P. baldwinii**

P. aptera Parry. Shrub, to 5 m high in its habitat; leaves trifoliate, the leaflets sessile, terminal leaflets coarser than the lateral ones, about 2–2.5 cm long, the lateral leaflets about 1.5–2 cm, indistinctly crenate, finely soft pubescent; flowers in clusters of a few together; fruits broadly ovate, juicy, totally or nearly without a winged limb. GF 3: 333. USA; California. z9 Fig. 33. ⚋

P. baldwinii Torr. Shrub, to 5 m high, twigs brown, new growth silver-gray, later violet-brown; leaflets ovate-elliptic to oblong-ovate, 3–6 cm long, margins finely crenate, dark green above, lighter and pubescent beneath; flowers coarser than those of *P. trifoliata*, but in smaller corymbs at the ends of the young shoots; fruit only 1.5 cm wide (!), narrowly winged, with a small apical tip. VT 592 (= *P. angustifolia* Benth.). Texas to Mexico. 1893. z6

P. mollis see: **P. trifoliata** var. **mollis**

P. monophylla see: **Cliftonia monophylla**

P. polyadenia Greene. Differs from *P. trifoliata* in the dark brown, finely pubescent or tomentose shoots; leaflets elliptic-ovate, 3 to 6 cm long, rather leathery, very glandular punctate, obtusish to acute, margin crenate, light green above, short soft pubescent beneath. SE. USA. 1916. z6

P. trifoliata L. Shrub or tree, to 5 m high, crown round, young shoots pubescent, yellow-green or more brownish; leaflets oblong-elliptic, 6–10 cm long, entire to indistinctly crenate, eventually glabrous above, glossy, gray-green beneath, eventually usually glabrous or with pubescent venation, petiole 7–10 cm long; flowers greenish white, about 1 cm wide, in about 4–8 cm wide corymbs, June; fruits nearly circular, 2–2.5 cm wide, slightly emarginate at the apex. BB 2271; GSP 250; VT 591. Eastern N. America. Before 1886. z5 ⚋

'**Aurea**' (Behnsch). Leaves persistently bright yellow. Discovered by Behnsch before 1886. Produces rather true from seed. Plate 24. ∅

'**Fastigiata**'. Growth narrowly upright, otherwise hardly differs from the species. Before 1903.

f. *heterophylla* see: '**Pentaphylla**'

var. **mollis** Torr. & Gray. Leaflets broader than those of the species, dense and persistently pubescent on the underside (= *P. mollis* M. A. Curtis). S. USA, Texas.

'**Monophylla**'. Leaflets reduced to one. Before 1903.

'**Pentaphylla**'. Leaflets 3–5, narrower than those of the species (= f. *heterophylla* Booth). 1795.

f. **pubescens** (Pursh) Voss. Leaves dull green above (!), pubescent beneath; young shoots, petiole and inflorescences glabrous or nearly so. Occurring with the species.

Not particular as to soil type or site, thrives best, however, in a moist soil in full sun.

Lit. Greene, E. L.: The Genus *Ptelea* in western and southwestern United States and Mexico; in Contrib. U.S. Nat. Herb. **10**, 49–78, 1906.

Fig. 33. *Ptelea aptera* (from BC)

PTEROCARYA Kunth — Wingnut —
JUGLANDACEAE

Deciduous trees, twigs with chambered pith; leaves alternate, pinnate; flower monoecious, in laterally arranged, pendulous catkins; males on the previous year's shoots or at the base of the current year's growth, flowers with 1–4 sepals and 2 bracts, an elongated bract is attached; female flowers in much longer, loose catkins, ovaries unilocular, surrounded by a connate, 4 lobed hull, with 2 bracts at the base; fruits top-shaped, with 2 wings, single seeded, 4 chambered only at the base. — 10 species, from the Caucasus to Japan.

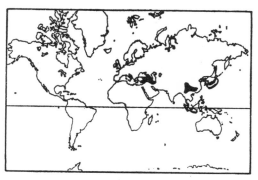

Fig. 34. Range of the genus *Pterocarya*

Outline

Section I. **Eupterocarya** Rehd. & Wils.
Winter buds naked, usually 2(3) situated one over the other; fruits with 2 distinct wings;
× Rachis winged; leaflets 11–21:
P. × rehderiana, P. stenoptera
×× Rachis cylindrical; leaflets 11–25:
P. fraxinifolia
××× Rachis cylindrical; leaflets 5–9:
P. hupehensis

Section II. **Cycloptera** Franch.
Winter buds naked, several situated over the other; fruits with an encircling wing:
P. paliurus

Section III. **Chlaenopterocarya** Rehd. & Wils.
Winter buds with 2–3 dark brown scales, abscising in winter, secondary buds absent; leaflets 11–21:
P. rhoifolia

Pterocarya caucasica see: **P. fraxinifolia**

P. fraxinifolia (Lam.) Spach. Normally a multistemmed, 15–20 m high, often picturesque tree, bark black-gray, deeply furrowed, twigs olive-brown, slightly lepidote at first, soon becoming glabrous; leaves 20–40 cm long, rachis cylindrical and glabrous (!), leaflets 11–21, oval-oblong to oblong-lanceolate, acuminate, 8–12 cm long, thin, bright green above, lighter beneath, nearly totally glabrous; fruit clusters 20–45 cm long, fruits with 2 distinct, semicircular wings, 1.5–2 cm wide. EH 121 (= *P. caucasica* C. A. Mey.; *P. sorbifolia* Dipp.; *P. spachiana* Lav.). Caucasus to N. Persia. 1782. z6 Fig. 35, 37. ∅ ⚭

'Albomaculata'. Slow growing, shrubby; leaves white speckled, especially when young.

'Dumosa'. Low growing, shrubby, densely branched, shoots yellow-brown; leaflets smaller, 5–7 cm long. Discovered in 1845 in the Segrez Arboretum, France but also found wild in the Caucasus Mts. since 1877 (van Volxem, in Gard. Chron. 1877, I: 72). Fig. 37.

P. hupehensis Skan. Tree, 4–12 m high, bark dark gray, young shoots finely lepidote; leaves 15–30 cm long, rachis cylindrical, glabrous, leaflets only 5–9 (!), oblong to oblong-lanceolate or oblong-obovate, short acuminate, 6–11 cm long, serrate to finely serrate, base round, sessile, deep green above, lighter beneath and glabrous except for the stellate pubescent vein axils; male catkins 6–10 cm long; fruit clusters 30–45 cm long,

fruits with semicircular wings, 2.5–3 cm wide. ICS 757. Central China; Hupeh, Szechwan Prov. 1903. z6 ⚭

P. japonica see: **P. stenopteka**

P. paliurus Batal. Tree, 7–12 m high, young shoots finely tomentose or lepidote (bluish green according to Lee); leaves 15–25 cm long, rachis finely tomentose, cylindrical, leaflets 7–8, oblong-ovate to oblong-lanceolate, acute, 6–15 cm long, finely serrate, tough, base very oblique, venation beneath pubescent to nearly glabrous; fruits in 15–25 cm long racemes, the individual fruits with encircling wings and forming a 3–7 cm wide disk. LF 71; ICS 756 (= *Cyclocarya paliurus* [Batal.] Iljinskaja). Central China. 1901. Fig. 36 ⚭

P. × rehderiana Schneid. (*P. fraxinifolia* × *P. stenoptera*). Intermediate between the parents, but stronger growing, stoloniferous, young shoots red-brown; leaves somewhat smaller than those of *P. fraxinifolia*, rachis more or less winged (!), at least on the strong shoots, the wings never toothed like *P. stenoptera* (!), leaflets 11–21, narrowly oblong, 6–12 cm long; fruit wings ovate to oval-oblong, longer than wide (!). JRHS 88: 35; ST 137; BC 3254. Developed in the Arnold Arboretum. 1880. z6 Plate 23. ∅

P. rhoifolia S. & Z. Tree, 20–30 m high, leaf buds (unlike all the other species) with 2–3 large hull scales (!), twigs pubescent at first; leaves 20–40 cm long, rachis cylindrical and finely pubescent at first, 20–40 cm long, leaflets 11–21, oval-oblong to more lanceolate, 6–12 cm long, finely and scabrous serrate, venation pubescent or nearly so beneath; fruit clusters 20–30 cm long, fruits 2.5 cm wide with the broadly rhombic wings. JRHS 50: 73; MJ 2004; KIF 1: 31. Japan. 1888. Ⓕ Japan. z6 Fig. 35. ⚭

P. sinensis see: **P. stenoptera**

P. sorbifolia see: **P. fraxinifolia**

P. spachiana see: **P. fraxinifolia**

P. stenoptera C. DC. Tree, 15–25 (30) m high, young shoots dense brown-yellow pubescent or nearly glabrous; leaves 20–40 cm long, rachis winged, the wing

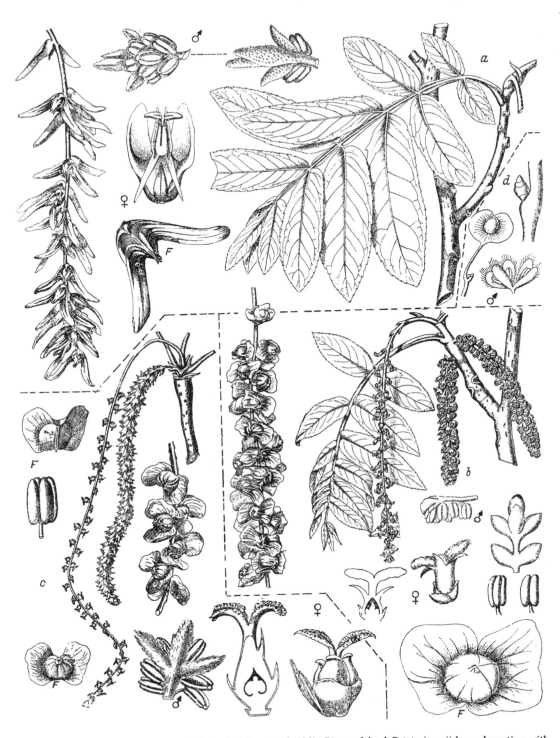

Fig. 35. **Pterocarya.** a. *P. stenoptera;* b. *P. fraxinifolia;* c. *P. rhoifolia.* **Pteroceltis.** d. *P. tatarinowii,* branch section with bud, solitary fruit, male flowers. F = fruits. (from Lavallée, Shirasawa, Maximowicz)

margins usually serrate (!), leaflets 11–21, terminal leaflets often absent, narrowly oblong, 4–10 cm long, finely serrate, venation and midrib on the underside lightly pubescent; fruit clusters 20–30 cm long, fruits with oblong, erect (!) wings, these with the nutlet 1.5–2 cm long. LF 72; RH 1920: 91; FIO 146; ICS 758 (= *P. japonica* Hort.; *P. sinensis* Hort.). China. 1860. Ⓕ E. and Central China. z7 Fig. 35, 37. ∅ ⚭

The following is a list of illustrations of some Chinese species not yet found in cultivation in the West:

P. delavayi	ICS 761
P. insignis	ICS 760
P. macroptera	ICS 759; FIO 145

All species prefer a deep, cool soil, near water; old trees are very impressive as a result of their multistemmed habit. Totally winter hardy but susceptible to damage by late frosts.

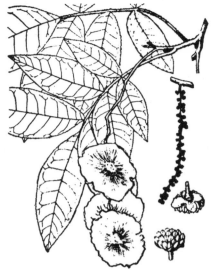

Fig. 36. *Pterocarya paliurus* (from ICS)

Fig. 37. **Pterocarya.** Left *P. fraxinifolia* 'Dumosa'; center *P. fraxinifolia;* right *P. stenoptera* (from Dippel)

PTEROCELTIS Maxim. — ULMACEAE

Monotypic genus; deciduous tree, very similar to *Celtis* in habit and foliage, but solitary fruits, like small elm fruits, arranged in the leaf axils.

Pteroceltis tatarinowii Maxim. Tree, to 15 m high, twigs quickly becoming glabrous; leaves alternate, ovate-lanceolate, acuminate, 3–8 cm long, base broadly cuneate, irregularly and scabrous serrate, base 3 veined, glabrous, petiole 1–2 cm long, thin; fruit samara, 1.5–2 cm wide, nearly circular, emarginate at the apex, stalk 1.5 to 2 cm long, solitary in the leaf axils. LF 110–111. N. China to Mongolia. 1894. Hardy. z5 Plate 24; Fig. 35. ⚭

Culture and requirements the same as *Celtis* and *Ulmus*.

PTEROSTYRAX S. & Z. — Epaulette Tree — STYRACACEAE

Deciduous trees or shrubs; leaves alternate, petiolate, dentate; flowers in large panicles on short lateral shoots, calyx 5 toothed, corolla with 5 petals, stamens 10, exserted, ovaries subinferior or nearly inferior, 3 (occasionally 4 or 5) locular, with 4 ovules in each locule; fruit an oblong, ribbed or winged drupe with 1–2 seeds. — 7 species, from Burma to Japan.

Pterostyrax corymbosa S. & Z. Shrub, 3–4 m high; leaves elliptic to ovate, 6–11 cm long, short acuminate, base cuneate, both sides somewhat stellate pubescent; flowers white, in 8 to 15 cm long, loose umbellate panicles, petals 1.5 cm long, white, stamens of unequal length, connate at the base, longer than the petals, May–June; fruits obovate, 12 mm long, 5 winged (!!), densely stellate pubescent. LF 255; EP 241: 17; KIF 3: 71; FIO 50. Japan, in mountainous regions. 1850. Hardy. Nearly always incorrectly labeled in cultivation! z6 Plate 23; Fig. 38. ⊕

P. hispida S. & Z. Tree, to 15 m high, often a tall shrub, to 5 m high or more, young shoots very pithy, finely pubescent; leaves ovate-oblong, 8–20 cm long, very thin, rich green above, light gray-green and slightly

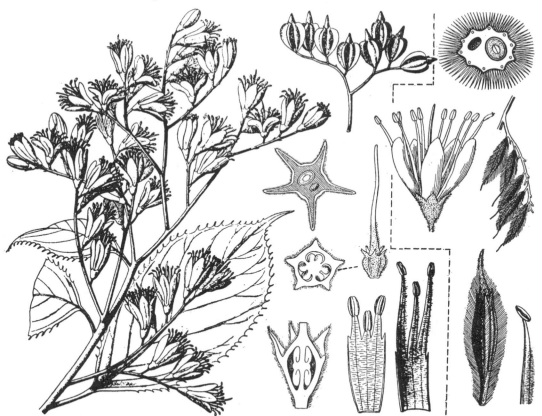

Fig. 38. **Pterostyrax.** Left *P. corymbosa,* flowering shoot, with fruiting twig, fruit cross section and flower parts; right *P. hispida,* above fruit in cross section, beneath five fruits at natural size, then a fruit enlarged, individual flower and stamen (from Perkins, Gürke)

pubescent beneath, margins finely bristly dentate (vein ends exserted past the leaf margins); flowers in axillary, pendulous, 10–20 cm long panicles, fragrant, corolla cream-white, 5 parted, lobes outspread, stamens much longer than the petals, June; fruit a rough haired, cylindrical, 10 mm long drupe with 10 fine ribs. DL 1: 202; BM 8329; EP 241; 18; KIF 3: 72; FIO 50. Japan, China; Szechwan, W. Hupeh Prov. 1875. z6 Plate 23; Fig. 38. ⊕

Fast growing shrubs for wooded sites or parks, prefer a deep humus soil and a sunny site. The long shoots of young plants should be headed back in the fall to speed hardening off and prevent frost damage.

PTILOTRICHUM C. A. Mey. — CRUCIFERAE

Stellate pubescent subshrubs or perennials, very closely related to *Alyssum* and often included in that genus, but differing in the white to pink flowers, untoothed filaments, and the presence of nectaries on the outermost stamens; fruit a stellate haired, inflated or flat pod with 2 seeds in each locule. — 15 species, from the Mediterranean region to Central Asia.

Ptilotrichum spinosum (L.) Boiss. Small, dense, thorny shrub, about 20 cm high and broad or wider, twigs rather stiff, gray-white stellate pubescent, thorns branched (modified, thorny flower axes!); leaves narrowly lanceolate, 2–4 cm long, acute, silvery; flowers many in flat corymbs, terminal and axillary, May–late June, white to soft pink, flowers very abundantly. MG 1909: 426 (= *Alyssum spinosum* L.). SW. France, Spain, Algeria. z7 Plate 24. ⊕

'Roseum'. Flowers persistently soft pink to lilac. JRHS 93:260. ⊕

For dry sunny spots in rock gardens; plant in rock crevices. Flowers very persistently and abundantly.

PUERARIA DC. — Kudzu Vine — LEGUMINOSAE

Twining perennials or shrubs, closely related to *Phaseolus*, but differing in the glabrous style (lacking tufted pubescence), knot-like swollen spots on the flower rachis at the point of attachment of the individual flowers and the monadelphous (bundled) stamens; leaves pinnate, leaflets 3, large, entire or lobed, flowers blue, purple or violet, in terminal or axillary, panicled racemes; calyx campanulate, with unequal lobes; fruit a bivalved, oblong pod. — 35 species in tropical Asia, Japan and on New Guinea.

Pueraria lobata (Willd.) Ohwi. High twining, bean-like subshrub, rootstock fleshy, twigs striped, pubescent; leaves deciduous, alternate, trifoliate, leaflets oval-rhombic, 10–18 cm long, both sides with an appressed, soft pubescence and ciliate; flowers violet-red, 1.5 cm long, in dense, to 25 cm long, erect, panicled racemes, June–August; pods linear-oblong, 4–9 cm long, pubescent. GF 6: 505; ICS 2753; LWT 128; RH 1891: Pl. 31 (= *P. hirsuta* Schneid. non Kurz; *P. thunbergiana* Benth.; *Dolichos japonicus* Hort.). China; Japan; in the mountain forests and thickets. 1885. z5 ∅ ⊕

Very fast growing in warm sites and good soil; 12–18 m in a single season when well rooted! Normally dies back to the ground in the fall.

PUNICA L. — Pomegranate — PUNICACEAE

Deciduous, very densely branched shrubs, or small trees; leaves opposite and clustered, entire, without stipules; flowers hermaphroditic, grouped 1–5 at the shoot tips, axillary and terminal; calyx campanulate to tubular, sepals 5–8, valvate, fleshy, petals 5–7, overlapping, stamens very numerous, ovaries inferior, multilocular, the locules arranged in concentric circles and layered 1–3 levels deep; ovules numerous, style single, short; fruit a globose, many seeded false berry, with a thick, leathery-woody shell. — 2 species from the Mediterranean region to the Himalayas and on the island of Suqutrā (Socotra) in the Gulf of Aden, Yemen.

Punica granatum L. Pomegranate. Very strong branched, erect shrub, to 2 m high, or a small, 3–5 m high tree, young shoots somewhat winged, occasionally thorned; leaves usually opposite, also occasionally alternate on the long shoots, clustered on short shoots, oval-lanceolate, 3–8 cm long, entire, stiff, hard, light green; flowers funnelform-rotate, sessile, coral-red, 3 cm wide, June–September; fruit globose, 2–12 cm wide, with a persistent calyx, yellow-reddish, eventually brown. HM 2170. SE. Europe to the Himalayas. 16th Century. z9 Plate 4; Fig. 39 # ⊕ ⚛

f. *alba* see: **'Albescens'**

'Albescens'. Flowers whitish, single. Andrews, Bot. Repos. Pl. 96 (= f. *alba* Voss). Before 1800. ⊕

'Flavescens'. Flowers single, yellow. Before 1830. ⊕

'Legrelliae'. Flowers densely double, petals yellow, densely red striped near the margin. FS 1385; MCL 82. Before 1858. ⊕

'Multiplex'. White, double. Before 1830. ⊕

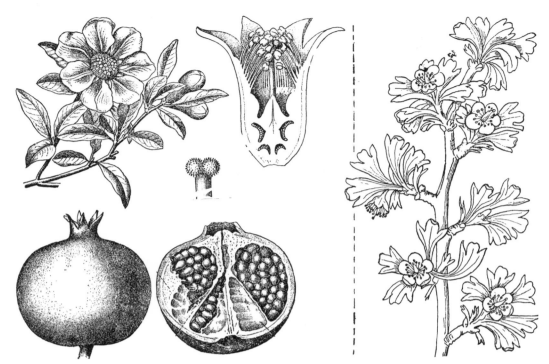

Fig. 39. Left *Punica granatum*, flowering twig, individual flower in cross section, without petals, style end beneath, fruit with a longitudinal section. Right *Purshia tridentata* (from Pursh, Berg & Schmidt)

'Nana'. Dwarf form; leaves smaller, narrower; flowers red, smaller than those of the type; fruits smaller. BM 634. Before 1806. Still widely cultivated. ⊕ ⊗

'Pleniflora'. Flowers scarlet-red, double. Hayne, Arzneyk. Gw 10: Pl. 35 (= f. *rubra fl. pl.* DC.). Before 1827. ⊕

f. *rubra* see: **'Pleniflora'**

P. protopunicea Balf. f. Leaves circular to elliptic; flowers and fruits smaller, ovaries only halfway adnate to the receptacle, developed from only 1 ring of carpels. Suqutrā, Gulf of Aden. Discovered in 1880. z8 #

Many cultivars of pomegranate are grown in the tropical regions for shipment to the cooler climates. The fruits are picked before they are fully ripe and held in cool storage for over 6 months where ripening takes place.

Pomegranates can also be cultivated in tubs, often reaching a great age in this manner.

Lit. Hegi: Fl. Mittel Europa, V, 2, 761–766 (particularly covering historical and technological aspects) ● see Bailey, Standard Cyclopedia **2**, 2751, 1950 for descriptions of 8 fruit cultivars.

PURSHIA DC. — ROSACEAE

Deciduous shrubs, closely related to *Cercocarpus;* leaves alternate, usually clustered, small, 3 toothed at the apex, base cuneate, small; flowers solitary, yellowish, calyx tubular, petals 5, spathulate, stamens numerous, styles 1 or 2; fruit a pubescent, leathery nutlet, the persistent calyx somewhat exserted. — 2 species in Western N. America.

Purshia glandulosa Curran. Erect, greenish shrub, 0.5–2.5 m high; leaves 6–9 mm long, in 3–5 linear lobed sections, occasionally dentate, lightly pubescent above when young, eventually glabrous, appressed glandular above and on the margins, margins revoluted; flowers solitary, terminal, on short lateral shoots, light yellow to white, April–June, calyx finely tomentose, without glands. MS 224. USA; desert plant from Colorado to Nevada. 1885. z6

P. tridentata (Pursh) DC. Shrub, erect, but the twigs widespreading, 0.6–2.5 m high; leaves cuneate, 6–12 mm long, to 2.5 cm long on long shoots, with 3 triangular lobes at the apex, green and finely pubescent above, white tomentose beneath, margins involuted; flowers 1.5 cm wide, light yellow, calyx with stalked glands, April–July; fruit a dry, 1 cm long nutlet. MS 224; BR 1446. USA; Oregon and California to New Mexico. 1826. In its habitat, one of the most important food sources for grazing wildlife, sheep and cattle. z6 Fig. 39.

A collector's plant for well drained soils in full sun. Ornamental value very slight.

Fig. 40. **Puya.** Left *P. chilensis;* right *P. alpestris* (from BM, Rauh)

PUYA Mol. — Puya — BROMELIACEAE

Actually herbaceous perennials, but many species develop a small, 1 m high, thick stem, on top of which is a tuft of very long, narrow, sharply acuminate leaves, smooth or scaly on the dorsal side, margins scabrous thorny dentate, base with stem-clasping sheaths; flowers on a tall (*P. gigas,* 6–9 m high!), simple or candelabrum-like branched shaft; the individual flowers attractive, all very consistent, petals distinct, somewhat tubular at the base; fruit a loculicidal, dehiscent capsule. — About 120 species in the Andes of South America.

Puya alpestris (Poepp. & Endl.) Gay. Leaves over 1 m long, 2–2.5 cm wide, in dense rosettes, margin with 5 mm long prickles, underside white scaly; shaft 60–100 cm long, inflorescence a very large, loose, compound panicle of many racemes, the bracts bright red, petals deep dark blue with a metallic green shimmer, fading to purple. BM 5732; DRHS 1718. Central Chile, on dry slopes. 1718. The hardiest species. z8 Fig. 40. ∅ ✧

P. chilensis Molina. Stem 1–1.5 m high, occasionally branched; leaves in a rosette, 50–100 cm long, only 5 mm wide, often twisted, blue-green, margins with hornlike, stout, recurved teeth; shaft 1–1.5 m high, inflorescences branched, rusty pubescent, flowers with widely exserted, yellow or yellow-green petals, 5 cm wide. BM 4715; FS 869; JRHS 87: 13 and 58; 91: 260. Chile. 1820. z9 Fig. 40. ∅ ✧

Lit. Rauh, W.: Bromelien für Zimmer und Gewächshaus, II; Stuttgart 1973.

PYRACANTHA Roem. — Firethorn — ROSACEAE

Evergreen, thorny shrubs; leaves alternate, crenate, occasionally entire, stipules tiny, abscising; flowers white, in corymbs; petals circular, outspread, stamens 20, anthers yellow, carpels 5, free on the ventral side, dorsal side adnate for half the length of the calyx tube; fruit a small, red or orange drupe with a persistent calyx; nutlets 5. — About 6 species from SE. Europe to the Himalayas and central China.

Key to the Species (from Rehder, expanded)

● Leaf undersides and calyx glabrous or leaves slightly pubescent;

  + Inflorescence axes pubescent;

    v Young shoots gray pubescent, leaves oval-elliptic, acute:
      P. coccinea

    vv Young shoots reddish, pubescent, leaves oblanceolate, obtuse:
      P. koidzumii

  ++ Inflorescence glabrous;

    v Leaves oblong to oblong-lanceolate, occasionally more obovate, 1–2 cm wide, usually with a small bristly tip:
      P. crenulata

    vv Leaves usually obovate to somewhat oblong, 1.5–2.5 cm wide, obtuse;

      x Leaves crenate, widest above the middle, obtuse, green beneath, 3–7 cm long, 1–2.5 cm wide:
        P. crenatoserrata
      1.5–3.5(–4.5) cm long, 0.5–1 cm wide:
        P. rogersiana

xx Leaves usually entire, occasionally somewhat
serrate, widest in the middle or somewhat
above, usually acute, underside blue-green:
P. atalantoides

● ● Leaf undersides and calyx fully (or nearly totally)
tomentose:

P. angustifolia

Outline of the Parentage of the Cultivars

There are between 50 to 60 cultivars, mostly from the United
States. The American cultivars are occasionally mentioned in
the European literature but are rarely found in cultivation in
Europe except for the two new fireblight resistant hybrids
'Mohave' and 'Shawnee'. The remaining American forms are
not described here, other than to show their taxonomic rela-
tionship in the following table. The European cultivars
designated as hybrids are described at the end of this section.

'Andenken an Heinrich Bruns'	→ **'Golden Charmer'** and **'Orange Charmer'**
'Bad Zwischenahn'	→ *P. coccinea*
'Buttercup'	→ hybrid
'Crimson Tide'	→ *P. koidzumii*
'Ebben'	→ *P. coccinea*
'Flava'	→ *P. rogersiana*
'Golden Charmer'	→ hybrid
'Government Red'	→ hybrid
'Graberi'	→ hybrid
'Kasan'	→ *P. coccinea*
'Lowboy'	→ *P. coccinea*
'Mohave'	→ hybrid
'Monrovia'	→ *P. coccinea*
'Moonbeam'	→ *P. crenato-serrata*
'Morettii'	→ *P. coccinea*
'Orange Charmer'	→ hybrid
'Orange Giant'	→ **'Kasan'**
'Orange Glow'	→ hybrid
'Praecox'	→ *P. coccinea*
'Rosedale'	→ *P. koidzumii*
'Runyan'	→ *P. coccinea*
'Shawnee'	→ hybrid
'Soleil d'Or'	→ hybrid
'Sungold'	→ **'Soleil d'Or'**
'Sunshine'	→ hybrid
'Taliensis'	→ hybrid
'Telstar'	→ *P. coccinea*
'Thornless'	→ *P. coccinea*
'Tiny Tim'	→ hybrid
'Variegata'	→ *P. crenato-serrata*
'Victory'	→ *P. koidzumii*
'Walderi'	→ hybrid
'Walderi Prostrata'	→ hybrid
'Watereri'	→ hybrid
'Wyatt'	→ *P. coccinea*

Pyracantha angustifolia (Franch.) Schneid. Stiff, erect
shrub, to 4 m high, occasionally also procumbent, otherwise divaricate, shoots brown-yellow tomentose; leaves
narrowly oblong to oblanceolate, 1.5–5 cm long, entire
or with a few tiny teeth on the apex, base acutely tapered
to a short petiole, glossy green above, also pubescent
above at first, later gray tomentose only on the
underside; flowers in 2–4 cm wide, dense umbellate
panicles, white, axes gray tomentose, May–June; fruits
orange-red, pea-sized, persisting until spring. BM 8345;
DRHS 1719. SW. China. 1889. z7 Plate 25, 26. # ∅ ⚭

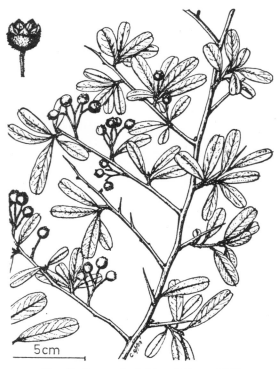

Fig. 41. *Pyracantha koidzumii* (from LWT)

P. atalantioides (Hance) Stapf. Shrub, to 5 m high; leaves
oblong-elliptic to lanceolate, 3–7 cm long (!), entire (!) or
finely serrate to crenate, bluish beneath (!), brownish
pubescent when young (!); inflorescences 3–4 cm wide;
fruits 7–8 mm wide, scarlet-red to light carmine,
persisting from October–March. BM 9099; GC 60: 309
(= *P. gibbsii* A. B. Jacks.; *P. discolor* Rehd.). SE. to W.
China. 1907. z7–8 Plate 26. # ∅ ⚭

P. coccinea Roem. Shrub, 2–3(5) m high, young shoots
gray pubescent; leaves oval-lanceolate, 2–4 cm long,
densely and finely crenate or serrate, dark green and
glossy above, glabrous, lighter beneath and somewhat
pubescent only when young; flowers 8 mm wide, many
in 3–4 cm wide umbellate panicles, axes finely
pubescent, May–June; fruit globose, 5–6 mm thick,
scarlet-red, fruits very abundantly. HM 1023; BS 2: 589
(= *Crataegus pyracantha* Borkh.). Italy to Asia Minor.
1629. z6 Plate 26. # ∅ ⚭

Includes a large number of slightly variable cultivars.

'Bad Zwischenahn'. Broadly upright habit, 2–3 m high,
branches and twigs stoutly thorned; leaves broadly elliptic to
obovate, glossy dark green above, crenate; fruits paprika-red
(redder than 'Kasan'), 8 × 9 mm thick, fruits abundantly.
Selected and introduced by Joh. Bruns, W. Germany, 1960.
Winter hardy but not totally scab resistant. # ⚭

'Ebben'. Habit rather globose to more broadly conical; leaves
broadly elliptic to obovate, rounded, margins crenate; fruits
light orange or rust-red, 7 × 8.5 mm (= 'Lalandei Major').
Discovered and introduced around 1935 by J. H. Ebben &
Zoon, Cuyk, Holland. Winter hardy but susceptible to scab.
#

'Kasan'. Broadly bushy and strong growing, young shoot tips gray pubescent, more dull green, as are the leaves, these broadly elliptic, acute, margins obtusely serrate; fruits orangered, to 9 × 11 mm, particularly abundant and regular, but very susceptible to apple scab in moist climates (= 'Orange Giant' Schiphorst 1950). Developed in the Kasan Botanic Garden, USSR. Commonly used because of its superior winter hardiness. z5–6 Plate 25. #

'Keessen' see: **'Lalandei'**

'Lalandei'. Strong growing, long shoots with short side branches (therefore, very well suited as an espalier), young shoots rather distinctly pubescent; leaves oval-oblong, 2–4 cm long, acute, dull green, margins crenate; fruits dark orange-red, 10 × 8 mm, abundant, colorful from mid September. MG 3: 7 (= *P. lalandei*; 'Keessen' from W. Keessen, Terra Nova, Aalsmeer 1891; 'Lalandei Monrovia'; 'Pirate'). Developed by Lalande in Nantes, France in 1847. Possibly a hybrid with *P. crenulata*. Susceptible to scab and less winter hardy. z6–7 #

'Lalandei Major' see: **'Ebben'**

'Lalandei Monrovia' see: **'Lalandei'**

'Orange Giant' see: **'Kasan'**

'Pauciflora'. Habit very dense and rounded; small leaved, glossy; fruits orange-red, hidden beneath the foliage and rather sparse. Very old cultivar grown in W. Germany since 1847 but much improved upon today. Still cultivated in the USA as it is very hardy. Susceptible to scab. #

'Pirate' see: **'Lalandei'**

'Telstar'. Narrowly conical habit, loosely branched (well suited as an espalier); leaves broadly elliptic, acute, deep green, margins crenate to obtusely serrate; fruits very large, 8 × 11 mm, orange, from early September. Developed by the van Klaveren Bros. in Hazerswoude, Holland, 1962. Very susceptible to scab. #

P. crenatoserrata (Hance) Rehd. Shrub, to 3 m high, young shoots rust-brown pubescent; leaves elliptic to obovate-oblong, rounded to acute at the apex, 2.5–6 cm long, margins crenate, gradually tapered and entire at the base, dark green and glossy above, light green beneath; flowers 1 cm wide, in 3–4 cm wide inflorescences, May–July; fruits globose, coral-red, 7 mm thick, fruits abundantly, October–December. RH 1913: Pl. 204; BM 9099, f. 5–10; GC 65: 132a (= *P. yunnanensis* Chitt.; *P. crenulata* var. *yunnanensis* Vilm.; *P. gibbsii* var. *yunnanensis* Vilm.; *P. gibbsii* var. *yunnanensis* Osborn; *P. fortuneana* [Maxim.] Li). Central and W. China. 1906. z7–8 # ⌀ ✧ ⚮

P. crenulata (D. Don) Roem. Shrub or small tree, young shoots and petioles rusty pubescent; leaves oblong to oblanceolate, occasionally oval-lanceolate, 2–5 cm long, acute or obtuse, with small tips, margins crenate, base cuneate, glossy green above, glabrous; flowers 8 mm wide, in loose, 2–3 cm wide inflorescences, styles spread apart from the base (!), May–June; fruits nearly globose, 6–8 mm wide, orange-red. BR 30: 52; RH 1913: Pl. 205. Himalayas. Around 1844. Serious doubt has recently arisen as to whether this species truly exists in cultivation. z7 Plate 26. # ⌀ ⚮

var. *rogersiana* see: **P. rogersiana**

var. *taliensis* see: **'Taliensis'**

var. *yunnanensis* see: **P. crenatoserrata**

P. discolor see: **P. atalantioides**

P. fortuneana see: **P. crenatoserrata**

P. gibbsii see: **P. atalantioides**

P. koidzumii (Hayata) Rehd. Shrub, 3–4 m high, loosely branched, densely foliate, young shoots reddish (!), pubescent, old shoots deep purple, glabrous, thorns 1–1.5 cm long; leaves oblanceolate, 2.5–4.5 cm long, apex rounded, entire, only exceptionally with a few small teeth on the long stout shoots, leathery tough, deep green and glossy above, lighter and pubescent to glabrous beneath; flowers abundantly along the entire branch in 3–4 cm wide clusters, axes pubescent (!); fruits flat globose, 7 mm wide, orange-scarlet, fruits abundantly. BMns 205. Taiwan. 1937. z8 Fig. 41. # ⌀ ✧ ⚮

'Rosedale'. Branches long arching with attractive foliage; fruits large, bright red. Described as the most beautiful cultivar in the USA. Particularly good to espalier. z8 # ⚮

P. lalandei see: **P. coccinea 'Lalandei'**

P. rogersiana Chitt. Dense, broadly upright shrub, branches more outspread with age, 3–4 m high, young shoots short pubescent, later glabrous and eventually dark red-brown; leaves oblanceolate to oblong-oblanceolate, rounded at the apex, 1.8–3.5 cm long, 5–10 mm wide, occasionally with some smaller leaves among them, to 4.5 cm long and 1.3 cm wide on long shoots; apical half shallowly dentate, dark green above, lighter beneath; flowering along the entire branch, usually with 4–8 small corymbs grouped to a cluster, June; fruits flat globose, 8–9 mm wide, orange-yellow, fruits abundantly. BMns 74 (= *P. crenulata* var. *rogersiana* A. B. Jacks.; *P. rogersiana* var. *aurantiaca* Bean). China; NW. Yunnan Prov. 1911. z8–9 # ⌀ ✧ ⚮

var. *aurantiaca* see: **P. rogersiana**

'Flava'. Fruits light yellow. RH 1925: Pl. 572. ✧ ⚮

P. yunnanensis see: **P. crenatoserrata**

Hybrids

'Andenken an Heinrich Bruns' (*P. coccinea* × *P. rogersiana*) Not a clone, rather an inconsistent mix of seedlings, introduced into the trade around 1950 in Westerstede, W. Germany. From this group, 2 clones have been selected ('Golden Charmer' and 'Orange Charmer', which see) and are superior cultivars. # ⚮

'Buttercup' (*P. coccinea?* × *P. rogersiana*). Shrub, broadly bushy; fruits rather small, intensely yellow. An English cultivar. #

'Golden Charmer' (*P. coccinea* × *P. rogersiana*). Shrubby habit, but slender upright, long branched, lateral shoots outspread; leaves oblong-elliptic, 2–5 cm long, acute to nearly round, finely crenate, dark green; fruits nearly globose, 9 mm thick, orange-yellow, fruits very abundantly. Selected from 'Andenken an Heinrich Bruns' by the Darthuizer Boomkwekerijen of Leersum, Holland, introduced in 1960. Winter hardy and scab resistant. # ⚮

'Knap Hill Lemon'. A very strong-growing clone, dense; fruits similar to those of 'Buttercup', but larger and lighter yellow. #

'Mohave' (*P. koidzumii* × *P. coccinea* 'Wyatt'). Strong grower, to 4 m high and 5 m wide, very densely branched; foliage deep green, tough, evergreen, resistant to *Fusicladium* and fireblight; fruits large, tight, coloring in mid August, dark red-orange at first, later more orange-red, very persistent and scarcely eaten by birds. Developed in the U.S. National Arb. in Washington D.C. in 1963 by D. E. Egolf. # ⚭

'Morettii'. Very dense habit; young leaves bronze-green; fruits bright red. Very winter hardy, but susceptible to scab. #

'Orange Charmer' (*P. coccinea* × *P. rogersiana*). Habit and foliage like 'Golden Charmer', but the fruits somewhat larger and deep orange, coloring in mid September. This clone is also selected from 'Andenken an Heinrich Bruns' and introduced into the trade by Vuyk van Nes, Boskoop, Holland, 1962. Has the same good qualities as 'Golden Charmer' and is a valuable cultivar. Plate 25. # ⚭

'Orange Glow' (presumably *P. coccinea* × *P. crenatoserrata*). Slender upright habit, loosely branched; leaves broadly elliptic to obovate, 2–4 cm long, crenate, obtuse at the apex; inflorescences not pubescent; fruits flat-globose, 9 × 7 mm, orange-red to dark orange, late September, persistent and abundant. Discovered around 1930 in the garden of Dr. Banga, Wageningen, Holland. One of the most important cultivars today. Quite resistant to scab. # ⚭

'Shawnee' (seedling of 'San Jose', a hybrid of *P. koidzumii* × *P. crenatoserrata*). Shrub, to 3.5 m high, very divaricate habit, branches strong, young shoots rust-brown pubescent at first, quickly becoming glabrous, very stoutly thorned; leaves narrowly elliptic, 1–5 cm long, finely crenate, acute or obtuse, often with a small thorny tip; fruits pure yellow to orange-yellow, flat rounded, 7 × 9 mm, fruits abundantly and persistently, ripe and colorful by August. Bai 14: 61. Developed by D. R. Egolf, U.S. National Arb., Washington D.C. Introduced in 1966. # ⚭

'Soleil d'Or' (Mutation of 'Morettii', originated on a plant in the National Arboretum Les Barres, Nogent-sur-Vernisson, France around 1970). Upright habit, medium-sized; leaves oval-lanceolate, conspicuously light green, glossy; fruits light yellow, abundant and appearing early (= 'Sungold'). Introduced into the trade by Sallé-Proust, Orléans, France. Reportedly resistant to scab. # ⚭

'Sungold' see: **'Soleil d'Or'**

'Sunshine' (*P. coccinea* × *P. rogersiana*). Open habit, twigs somewhat nodding, otherwise very similar to 'Golden Charmer', but with larger fruits, about 10 × 8 mm, dark orange-yellow. Introduced into the trade by J. Spaargaren & Zonen, Boskoop, and Sursum Corda in Schoorl, Holland. #

'Taliensis' (presumably *P. crenatoserrata* × *P. rogersiana*). Young shoots slightly pubescent; leaves totally glabrous, similar in form to those of *P. crenatoserrata*, but smaller and finely crenate nearly to the base; fruits glossy yellow, 6–7 mm thick, coloring in October, but abscising earlier than the other hybrids (= *P. crenulata taliensis* Hort.). Distributed around 1922 by L. Chenault, Orléans, France. Supposedly developed from seed from the Tali Range, Yunnan Prov., China. # ⚭

'Tiny Tim' (*P. crenatoserrata*). Dwarf from, to only 1 m high, shoots outspread, very densely foliate; leaves oblanceolate, obtuse; fruits well. Developed by F. J. Tomlinson in California, USA. Introduced in 1966 by Select Nurseries in Brea, California. #

'Watereri' (*P. atalantioides* × *P. rogersiana?*). Strong grower, to about 2.5 m high and wide, very dense, young shoots densely pubescent; leaves elliptic to more lanceolate, 2–3.5(6) cm long, 6–12(20) mm wide, acute, apical third finely crenate, venation pubescent beneath; fruits abundantly, fruits flat globose, orange. JRHS 82: 6 (= 'Waterer's Orange'). Developed before 1955 by Waterer, Son & Crisp in England. z9 #

'Waterer's Orange' see: **'Watereri'**

All species prefer a fertile, clay soil, but also thrive in a sandy humus. Very important genus as evergreen hedges and fruiting plants.

Lit. Sealy in Bot. Mag. 74 ns ● Boom, B. K.: Het huidige vuurdoorn-sortiment; in Boomkwekerij 1960, 102–103 ● De Vos, F.: Cultivated Firethorns; in Proc. Plant Prop. Soc. 8, 32–58, 1958 (48 types described!) ● Egolf, D. R., & R. F. Drechsler: Chromosome numbers of Pyracantha; Baileya 15, 82–88, 1967 (55 cultivars) ● Van de Laar, H.: Pyracantha; in Dendroflora 3, 40–46, 1966 (15 Cultivars) ● Egolf, D. R.: The USDA introduces its new Pyracantha 'Mohave'; Americ. Nurseryman 4/1/72, 7, 24–25 ● Egolf, D. R.: Pyracantha 'Shawnee' (Rosaceae); in Baileya 14, 61–63, 1966.

× PYRACOMELES Rehd. — ROSACEAE

Generic hybrids between *Osteomeles* and *Pyracantha*; differing from *Pyracantha* in the thornless shoots and pinnatisect leaves, differing from *Osteomeles* in the pinnatisect apical blade half, pinnate only at the base.

× **Pyracomeles vilmorinii** Rehd. (*Osteomeles subrotunda* × *Pyracantha crenatoserrata*). Low, semi-evergreen shrub, 1–1.5 m high, twigs thin, gray pubescent; leaves with 2.5–3.5 cm long petioles, with a total of 5–9 lobes or pinnae, rather ovate, crenate at the apex, pubescent at first, later glabrous; flowers 1 cm wide, white, many in terminal corymbs, glabrous, sepals broadly triangular, outspread, petals broadly obovate, stamens 12–15, May; fruit globose, 4 mm thick, coral-red, fruits abundantly. GC 1938, I, 49. Originated as a chance seedling in 1922 by Chenault, Orléans, France. z6 Plate 25. #

PYRETHRUM

Pyrethrum frutescens see: **Chrysanthemum frutescens**

+ PYROCYDONIA Winkl. ex Daniel — ROSACEAE

Grafted hybrid between *Pyrus* and *Cydonia*, intermediate between the parents in appearance; see the species description.

This generic hybrid was once considered the hybrid genus × *Pyronia*, but is no longer considered correct as with + *Crataegomespilus* and × *Crataemespilus*.

+ **Pyrocydonia danielii** Winkl. ex Daniel (*Cydonia oblonga* × *Pyrus communis* 'Williams Christ'). Tree-like habit, like *Cydonia*; leaves ovate, rounded at the base, 4–6 cm long, margins irregularly and bristly serrate, more or less pubescent, petiole 5–6 mm long; flowers and fruits not observed. BD 1925: 63 (= *Pyronia danielii* [Daniel] Rehd.). Developed in 1902 in the garden of St. Vincent Collège, Rennes, France as a grafted hybrid; further propagated in 1913.

'**Winkleri**' (Daniel). Shrubby habit; leaves lanceolate, 1–4.5 cm long, long acuminate, base obtuse, somewhat navicular, underside more tomentose and white dentate; flowers not observed. BD 1925: 63; RH 1914: 27 (= *Pyrocydonia winkleri* Guill.). Developed in Rennes, France in 1913, also 'Williams Christ'.

× PYRONIA Veitch — ROSACEAE

Sexual generic hybrid between *Pyrus* and *Cydonia*; for the grafted hybrid, see + *Pyrocydonia*.

× **Pyronia veitchii** (Trabut) Guill. (*Cydonia oblonga* × *Pyrus communis*). Shrub or tree, like *Cydonia* in habit, shoots brown, densely punctate; leaves elliptic, tapered at both ends, 3–8(10) cm long shoots, 2–3.5(5) cm wide, tough, entire to finely crenate, light green and glossy above, finely pubescent beneath at first, petiole 1.5–2 cm long; flowers in 3's at the shoot tips, pink-white, 5 cm wide, anthers violet, flowering continuously from May to July, sometimes flowers again in the fall; fruit ellipsoid, green, 6–8 cm long, without stone or grit cells, flesh white, sweet, edible and tasty. J. Hered. 1916: 416, Fig. 12 (= *Cydonia veitchii* 'John Seden' Trabut; *Pyrocydonia* 'John Seden' Guill.). Developed around 1895 in the Veitch nursery. z6 ✂

'John Seden' see: × **P. veitchii**

'**Luxemburgiana**' (Veitch). Strong growing tree, habit like that of *Pyrus*; leaves more ovate, acute, base rounded, 7–9 (12) cm long; flowers only 3.5 cm wide, light pink; fruits more pear-shaped, 7 × 6 cm in size, green-yellow, without stone cells, flesh white, edible. BD 1925: 68 (= var. *luxemburgiana* Guill.). Developed by Veitch before 1913. ✂

Cultivated like *Pyrus* or *Cydonia*; may be grafted to either.

PYROSTEGIA C. Presl — BIGNONIACEAE

Evergreen shrub, climbing by means of tendrils; leaves opposite, with 2 or 3 leaflets, tendrils filamentous, three parted; flowers in terminal panicles; calyx campanulate to nearly tubular, incised or dentate; corolla tubular-infundibular, bowed, stamen filaments exserted; fruit a linear, leathery capsule with elliptic, winged seeds. — 5 species in tropical South America.

Pyrostegia ignea (Vell.) Presl. Shoots somewhat angular or striped, pubescent when young; leaflets usually in 3's, elliptic to more oblong, short acuminate, oblique at the base, glabrous above, pubescent beneath, 4.5–6 cm long; flowers in dense, pendulous, short panicles, calyx campanulate, with 5 short teeth, corolla tubular-infundibular to nearly clavate, 5–7 cm long, light orange-carmine, the limb tips valvate in the bud stage (!). BM 2050; FS 743; HV 33; NF 12: 88 (= *P. venusta* Ker-Gawl; *Bignonia ignea* Vell.). Brazil. 1816. Gorgeous in bloom, but only for the warmest regions. z10 Plate 4. # ✧

P. venusta see: **P. ignea**

Cultivated like *Bignonia*.

PYRULARIA Michx. — SANTALACEAE

Deciduous shrubs, parasitic on the roots of *Kalmia*, *Calycanthus* and other woody plants; leaves alternate, entire; flowers small, in spikes or racemes, 4 or 5 parted, not conspicuous, unisexual or hermaphroditic; fruit obovoid (pear-shaped), rather large, drupe. — 3 species, one in N. America, 2 in the Himalayas.

Pyrularia pubera Michx. Loose shrub, partly procumbent, 1–3 m high; leaves obovate-oblong, acute to acuminate, 5–15 cm long, base cuneate, entire, finely pubescent when young; flowers greenish, very small, few in terminal racemes, May; fruits pear-shaped, yellowish, leathery, 2.5 cm long, with persistent calyx lobes, contains a bitter, poisonous oil (as does the entire

Fig. 42. *Pyrularia pubera*, twigs with fruits and a single fruit in cross section (from Grimm)

plant). BB 1276. USA; Pennsylvania to Georgia, in the mountains. 1800. z5 Fig. 42.

Cultivated like *Buckleya*.

PYRUS[1] L. — Pear — ROSACEAE

Deciduous trees or shrubs, twigs occasionally terminating in a thorn; leaves alternate, simple, occasionally lobed, margins usually serrate or crenate; stipules small, bristle form or awl-shaped; flowers on short lateral shoots in umbels or corymbs; calyx and corolla 5 parted, stamens usually 20, occasionally 25–30, carpels 5, sometimes only 2, partly connate, styles in equal number, distinct or constricted only at the base of the disk; flesh with stone cells, wall of the seed core cartilaginous, seeds black-brown. — About 30 species from Europe to E. Asia, and N. Africa.

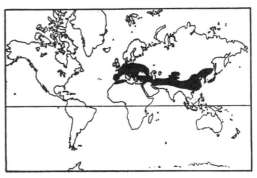

Fig. 43. Range of the genus *Pyrus*

Outline of the more important Species

● Fruits with a persistent calyx;

  x Leaves entire or crenate, simple;

    v Leaves usually oblong and obtuse, with papillae beneath, entire or slightly crenate toward the apex, becoming glabrous:
      P. amygdaliformis

    vv Leaves without papillae beneath;
      + Leaves entire, cuneate, normally pubescent beneath;
        § Leaves linear-lanceolate to lanceolate, glossy above:
          P. salicifolia

      §§ Leaves wider;
        ★ Leaves lanceolate to broadly elliptic:
          P. elaeagrifolia

    ★★ Leaves elliptic to obovate:
      P. nivalis

    ++ Leaves totally crenate, rounded ovate to oblong-ovate:
      P. communis

  xx Leaves at least somewhat pinnately partite:
    P. regelii

  xxx Leaves bristly serrate, usually ovate, glabrous:
    P. ussuriensis

● ● Fruits with a totally or partially abscising calyx; fruits brown, yellow on *P. bretschneideri*;
  x Leaves dentate or scabrous serrate;
    v Leaves scabrous serrate or finely serrate, often with appressed teeth; 6–12 cm long;
      + Fruit yellow; leaves broadly cuneate at the base, styles 5, occasionally 4:
      P. bretschneideri

---

1) The classic spelling is "Pirus"; Linnaeus, however, lapsed into the use of "y" and the often disputed name has applied ever since.

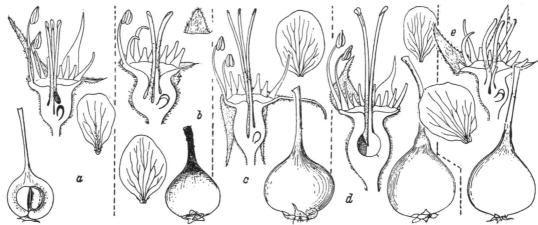

Fig. 44. **Pyrus.** Flower parts and fruit. a. *P. amygdaliformis*; b. *P. salicifolia*; c. *P. elaeagrifolia*; d. *P. nivalis*; e. *P. regelii* (from Schneider, altered)

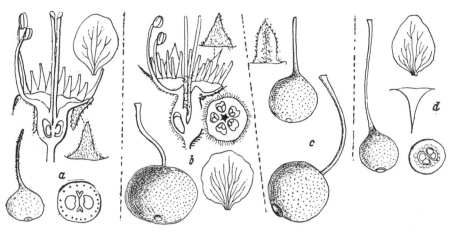

Fig. 45. **Pyrus**, flower parts and fruit. a. *P. betulifolia;* b. *P. pashia;* c. *P. pashia* var. *kumaoni;* d. *P. calleryana* (from Schneider, altered)

++ Fruits brown, leaves usually rounded to somewhat cordate at the base;
§ Styles 5; leaves bristly serrate or with appressed, acuminate teeth:
P. pyrifolia

§§ Styles 3–4; calyx occasionally partly persistent; leaves finely serrate with acute teeth:
P. serrulata

vv Leaves serrate, teeth more or less outspread, style 2–4;
+ Leaves glabrous, 6–10 cm long; styles 4–5, occasionally 2; fruits nearly globose or pear-shaped, 1.5–2 cm long:
P. phaeocarpa

++ Leaves pubescent, 4–7.5 cm long; styles 2 or 3; fruits globose, about l cm long:
P. betulifolia

xx Leaves crenate or finely crenate;
v Leaves finely crenate, oval to ovate, about 5 cm long; styles 5;
P. longipes

vv Leaves crenate;
+ Styles 3–5; stamens 25–30; leaves ovate to oblong:
P. pashia

++ Styles 2–3; leaves rounded ovate to oblong-ovate:
P. calleryana

Pyrus achras see: **P. pyraster**

P. amygdaliformis Vill. Shrub or tree, to 6 m high, divaricate, often thorny, young shoots with thin and long pubescence, later brown and glossy; leaves quite variable, ovate to obovate or oblong, acute to obtuse, 2.5 to 7 cm long, finely crenate to entire, gray tomentose when young, later glabrous above and glossy green, eventually glabrous and bluish beneath, somewhat tough, petiole thin, 1–3 cm long; flowers 8–12 in gray tomentose corymbs, corolla 2–2.5 cm wide, May; fruits

globose, 2–3 cm thick, yellow-brown, on a 2–3 cm long stalk. TPy 67; HF 2534; BS 2: 593 (= *P. parviflora* Desf.). S. Europe, Asia Minor. 1810. Slight ornamental value. z6 Plate 27; Fig. 44

var. **cuneifolia** (Guss.) Bean. Leaves smaller, narrower, tapered at the base. Gussone, Pl. Rar. Pl. 39.

var. **lobata** (Decne.) Koehne. Shrubby, twigs thin, thorny; leaves oblong, narrowly obovate to elliptic, simple or with 1–2 shallow or deep lobes, 2–3.5 cm long, 1–2 cm wide, gray-green (= *P. lobata* Decne.).

var. **oblongifolia** (Spach) Bean. Leaves elliptic to oblong, obtuse, base round, petiole 2.5–3 cm long; fruit considerably larger than the species, yellowish, reddish on the sunny side. SH 1: 361g (= *P. oblongifolia* Spach). S. France; Provence ("Gros Perrusier").

var. *persica* see: **P. persica**

P. auricularis see: **Sorbopyrus auricularis**

P. austriaca see: **P. nivalis** f. **austriaca**

P. balansae Decne. Closely related to *P. communis*, but with ovate to oblong leaves, 5–10 cm long, long acuminate, base rounded, entire to crenate (but scabrous and finely toothed on young plants!), petiole to 4 cm long; flowers white, April–May; fruits top-shaped, 2.5 cm thick, long stalked. SH 1: 361 pp. Asia Minor. 1866. z6

P. betulifolia Bge. A slender tree, 5–10 m high, fast growing, branches gracefully nodding, gray tomentose in the first year, glabrous in the second year; leaves ovate-oblong to more rhombic, acuminate, 4–7 cm long, scabrous serrate, base round or broadly cuneate, eventually glossy green above, gray-green and pubescent to nearly glabrous beneath, petiole 2–2.5 cm long; flowers white, 2 cm wide, grouped 8–10 in tomentose corymbs, styles 2–3, calyx pubescent, May; fruits nearly globose, 1–1.5 cm thick, brown with whitish spots, calyx abscising, stalk thin, 2–3 cm long. BC 3281; GF 7: 225. N. China. 1865. Long utilized as a grafting

Fig. 46. **Pyrus.** Left *P. betulifolia*; *P. calleryana* in the center; right *P. ussuriensis* (from ICS)

understock in China, more recently used in the USA and Europe. z5 Plate 27; Fig. 45, 46.

P. bourgaeana Dcne. Tree, twigs ascending on young trees, later outspread, bark finely plated, bark of young shoots brown; leaves tough, ovate-lanceolate to broadly ovate, 2 to 7 cm long, 1.5–3.5 cm wide, crenate; flowers with oblong-lanceolate sepals; fruits top-form to globose, 17–25 mm wide, dull yellow and irregularly brown speckled, with a persistent calyx, stalk thick, 2–4 cm long. W. Spain, Portugal, Morocco, on dry sites. z6–7

P. bretschneideri Rehd. Medium-sized tree, very similar to *P. ussuriensis* var. *ovoidea*, but fruits with an abscising calyz (!); twigs rather glabrous, purple-brown in the second year; leaves ovate to more elliptic, long acuminate, base broadly cuneate (!), occasionally round, 5–11 cm long, scabrous awned serrate, teeth usually appressed, floccose at first, soon becoming glabrous, petiole 2.5 to 7 cm long; flowers white, 3 cm wide, in woolly, later glabrous corymbs, April–May; fruits oval to nearly globose, yellow, 2.5–3 cm long, stalk 3–4 cm long, flesh white, juicy, eaten in China. BC 3280; MG 31: 103. N. China z5 Fig. 48. ∅ ✕

P. bucharica see: **P. koshinsky**

P. calleryana Decne. Tree with glabrous, smooth branches, but covered with short thorny shoots, winter buds finely pubescent; leaves broadly ovate, short acuminate, 4–8 cm long, totally glabrous, crenate, glossy, petiole 2–4 cm long; flowers 2–2.5 cm wide, stalk 1.5–3 cm long, axes glabrous, stamens 20, styles 2, occasionally 3; fruits globose, 1 cm thick, brown and punctate, calyx abscising, stalk thin. NK 6: 25; MG 31: 113. China. 1908. z5 Plate 27; Fig. 45, 46.∅

var. *fauriei* see: **P. fauriei**

f. **tomentella** Rehd. Young shoots densely tomentose, but glabrous in the 2nd year; leaves floccose at first, later becoming glabrous except for the midrib, leaves often finely serrate on the long shoots; axes of the inflorescences shaggy pubescent. China. 1908.

Including 2 selections:

'Bradford'. Selection lacking the thornlike short shoots, strong growing (15 m high and 9 m wide in 40 years), crown consistently oval; leaves tough, glossy green, undulate margin, fall color yellow to orange-carmine; flowers very abundant (not pollinated by *P. communis*, only by *P. calleryana*); fruits oval, only 1 cm thick, rust-brown, persisting late into the winter. Selected by the U.S. Plant Introduction Station in Glenn Dale, Maryland from seed collected in 1918 from the mountains around Ichang, China. Commonly used as a street tree in the USA. ⊕

'Chanticleer'. Another selection, distinguished by its narrow conical crown, also with yellow-carmine-red fall color. Introduced by Edward Scanlon, USA. ⊕

P. × canescens Spach (*P. nivalis* × *P. salicifolia*). Tree, similar to *P. nivalis*, but with lanceolate to narrowly elliptic leaves, finely crenate toward the apex, gray-white pubescent when young, eventually dark green above, glabrous and glossy; fruits short-stalked, light green. Before 1830. *P. canescens* in cultivation is usually nothing more than *P. salviifolia*. z6 Plate 28. ∅

P. communis L. Common Pear. Tree, to 15 m high, broadly conical habit, branches often thorny, young twigs glabrous or also thinly pubescent; leaves oval to elliptic, 2–8 cm long, acute, crenate, shaggy pubescent at first, quickly becoming totally glabrous, often brightly colored in fall, petiole thin; flowers about 3 cm wide, in shaggy pubescent or glabrous corymbs, cupula tomentose, anthers red, April–May; fruits pear-shaped to nearly globose, 2.5–5 cm long, yellow-green eventually, bitter, with a persistent calyx. HW 3: 76. Europe, Asia Minor. Cultivated for centuries. z5 Fig. 49.

var. *cordata* see: **P. cordata**

var. *pyraster* see: **P. pyraster**

var. **sativa** DC. Collective name for edible cultivars of pear. For further details, refer to the literature on fruit trees.

P. cordata Desv. Thorny shrub, 3–4 m high, branches outspread, bark thin, finely plated, young shoots purple; leaves oval, occasionally somewhat cordate at the base, 1–4 cm long, distinctly crenate, always nearly totally glabrous, petiole often longer than the blade; inflorescence seldom umbellate, usually with 1–3 cm long, distinct axes, petals obovate, 8–10 mm long; fruits globose to obovoid, 10–18 mm thick, not tapering to the stalk, glossy, red when ripe, calyx eventually abscising, stalk thin, 15–35 mm long. TPy 10 (= *P. communis* var. *cordata* [Desv.] Briggs). S. Europe; SW. England (but rare). z8

P. cossonii Rehd. Small, sparsely thorny tree, young shoots glabrous; leaves rounded-elliptic to ovate, 2.5–5 cm long, 1–3 cm wide, short acuminate to obtuse, totally finely and evenly crenate, woolly beneath at first, later glabrous on both sides and glossy green above, petiole thin, 2.5–5 cm long (!); flowers white, 3 cm wide, in 5 to 7 cm wide corymbs, April–May; fruits globose, brown, 1.5 cm thick, slightly punctate, stalk 3 cm long, thin, calyx abscising (= *P. longipes* Coss. & Dur.). Algieria. 1875. z8–9

P. depressa see: **Aronia arbutifolia**

P. elaeagrifolia Pall. Small, thorny tree, young shoots tomentose; leaves lanceolate to oblanceolate or narrowly elliptic, 4–7 cm long, obtuse to short acuminate, base cuneate, entire, gray or white tomentose on both sides, sometimes becoming glabrous above, petiole 1–4 cm long; flowers white, 3 cm wide, in tomentose pubescent corymbs, stalk 1–2 cm long, April–May; fruits globose to top-shaped, about 2 cm thick, green (= *P. elaeagrifolia* Steud.; *P. nivalis* var. *elaeagrifolia* Schneid.). Asia Minor. 1800. Similar to *P. nivalis*, but with narrower, grayer leaves. z5 Plate 27; Fig. 44 ⌀

var. **kotschyana** (Decne.) Boiss. Shrub, usually without thorns (!); leaves wider, 3–6 cm long, petiole to 3 cm long, pubescence like the species. GC 98: 405. Asia Minor. ⌀

P. fauriei Schneid. Tree, often only a large shrub, old shoots thorny, young shoots thornless, similar to *P. calleryana*, but smaller in all respects; leaves often elliptic-ovate, base broadly cuneate, 2.5–5 cm long, petiole 2–2.5 cm long, pubescent; flowers appear after the leaves (before the leaves on *P. calleryana*), in clusters of 2–8; fruits about 1.3 cm thick, without stone cells (! *P. calleryana* has stone cells). NK 6: 24 (= *P. calleryana* var. *fauriei* [Schneid.] Rehd.). Korea. 1918.

P. ferruginea see: **P. ussuriensis** var. **hondoensis**

P. firma see: **Sorbus hybrida 'Gibbsii'**

P. grandifolia see: **Aronia melanocarpa** var. **grandifolia**

P. heterophylla see: **P. regelii**

P. hondoensis see: **P. ussuriensis** var. **hondoensis**

Fig. 47. *Pyrus kawakamii* (from LWT)

P. indica see: **Docynia indica**

P. kawakamii Hayata. "Evergreen Pear". Shrub to small tree, 4–10 m high, shoots often thorny, bark dark brown; leaves grouped 3–4 together, at the tips of smaller shoots, leathery tough, evergreen, ovate to obovate, 6 to 10 cm long, finely crenate, petiole 3 cm long; flowers few in groups, calyx glabrous; fruit globose, 11 mm thick, glabrous. LWT 107. China, Taiwan. z8 Fig. 47.

P. korshinsky Litvin. Closely related to *P. communis*. Tree, young shoots tomentose; leaves oblong-lanceolate to oval-oblong, acuminate, 5–8 cm long, finely crenate, more or less glabrous, margin and leaf underside shaggy tomentose, as is the 1.5–3 cm long petiole; flowers in short, tomentose corymbs, stalk 2–3 cm long, disk pubescent, style base shaggy pubescent; fruits globose, 2 cm thick, calyx persistent, stalk thick (= *P. bucharica* Litvin). Turkestan. 1890. z6–7 Plate 27 Fig. 49.

P. kumaoni see: **P. pashia** var. **kumaoni**

P. × lecontei Rehd. (*P. communis* × *P. pyrifolia*). Medium-sized, strong, but slow growing tree, twigs stout and wavy; leaves ovate-elliptic, about 8 cm long, 3 cm wide, acuminate, finely crenate to serrate, petiole glabrous; flowers 3 cm wide, grouped 7–10 in corymbs, April; fruits ellipsoid, 6–8 cm long, 4–5 cm thick, symmetrical, yellow and punctate when ripe, flesh white, firm, granular, sour. BC 2809; Hedrick, Pears of N.Y. 180, 187 (= 'Le Conte' Pear). Developed in Philadelphia, USA before 1850 and still cultivated. Of little merit. z6 ⌀ ✕

Includes the fruit form 'Kieffer' or 'Kieffer's Seedling'. BC 2810.

P. lindleyi Rehd. Closely related to *P. ussuriensis*, but with ovate and abruptly acuminate leaves, base round, but usually cordate on the long shoots, margins finely dentate or serrate, the teeth short and appressed, not acuminate (!); fruits broadly ellipsoid, with a persistent calyx, long petiole. BR 1248; BC 3279; MG 31: 111 (= *P. sinensis* Lindle. non Poir.). China. 1820. Uncertain species, perhaps only a cultivar of another species. Known only by Lindley's description and illustrations. z6

P. lobata see: **P. amygdaliformis** var. **lobata**

P. longipes see: **P. cossonii**

P. malifolia see: **Sorbopyrus auricularis 'Bulbiformis'**

P. × michauxii Bosc (*P. amygdaliformis* × *P. nivalis*). Small, round crowned tree, twigs thornless; leaves ovate to elliptic-oblong, 3–7 cm long, obtuse or abruptly acuminate, entire, both sides white woolly when young, later becoming glabrous and glossy above, pubescent or glabrous beneath; flowers white, in very short, dense, tomentose corymbs; fruits globose to top-shaped, 3 cm long and 2 cm thick, yellow-green, sour. Orient (?). Before 1816. z6

P. nivalis Jacq. Snow Pear. Small tree, about 10 m high, occasionally taller, thornless, young shoots thickly white tomentose, outer bud scales pubescent, inner ones glabrous; leaves elliptic to obovate, acute, 5–8 cm long, base cuneate, entire or only shallowly crenate at the apex, white tomentose when young, later dark green above with scattered white hairs, light gray to white tomentose to nearly glabrous beneath, fall color dark red; flowers 2.5–3 cm wide, grouped 6–9 in white tomentose corymbs, April–May; fruits yellow-green, 3–5 cm thick, globose to top-shaped, ripening late, sour. HM 1033; TPy 45–65. SE. Europe. 1800. z6 Plate 27; Fig. 44. ✗

f. **austriaca** (Kern.) Schneid. Leaves elliptic, eventually totally glabrous. TPy 75–80 (= *P. austriaca* Kern.). Austria, Hungary.

var. *elaeagrifolia* see: **P. elaeagrifolia**

P. oblongifolia see: **P. amygdaliformis** var. **oblongifolia**

P. ovoidea see: **P. ussuriensis** var. **ovoidea**

P. parviflora see: **P. amygdaliformis**

P. pashia Hamilt. Tree, 10–12 m high, usually thorny, young shoots usually woolly at first, later glabrous, red-brown; leaves ovate to oblong, 6–12 cm long, acuminate, base usually round, crenate or obtusely serrate, but on young plants or suckers often also scabrous serrate or even trilobed (!), tomentose when young, eventually glabrous or nearly so, petiole 1.5–4 cm long; flowers 2–2.5 cm wide, white, covered with petals (!!), anthers dark red, stamens 25–30, styles 3–5, calyx lobes triangular; fruits nearly globose, 2 cm thick, brown, dense warty punctate, stalk 2–3 cm long. MG 31: 113 (= *P. variolosa* Wall.). Himalayas to W. China. 1908. z5 Plate 27; Fig. 45

var. **kumaoni** (Decne.) Stapf. Primarily differs in the glabrous shoots, glabrous inflorescences, and ovate calyx lobes, often obtuse. BM 8256; BS 2: 596 (*P. kumaoni* Decne.; *P. wilhelmi* Schneid.). Himalayas. 1825. Only this variety appears in cultivation, not the species! Fig. 45.

P. persica Pers. Small tree; leaves outspread, thick, tomentose when young, elliptic-oblong, acute, 3–6 cm long, 1.5–3 cm wide, both sides densely pubescent at first, later bluish green above and glabrous, sparsely woolly beneath, margins finely crenate; flowers 6–12 in white tomentose umbels; fruits rounded to top-shaped, about 3 cm thick, greenish, with red cheeks, stalk 2 cm. SL 321 (= *P. amygdaliformis* var. *persica* [Pers.] Bornm.; *P. sinaica* Dum.-Cours.). Asia Minor, Greek Islands (not the Sinai!). Before 1810. z7

P. phaeocarpa Rehd. Tree, young shoots tomentose, glabrous and reddish brown in the 2nd year; leaves elliptic-ovate to oval-oblong, 6–10 cm long, long

Fig. 48. **Pyrus.** Left *P. serrulata*; center *P. pyrifolia*; right *P. bretschneideri* (from ICS)

Plate 1

Prunus avium 'Plena'   *Prunus padus* 'Watereri'
both in the Dortmund Botanic Garden, W. Germany

Prunus mume 'Benishidori'
in the Hillier Arboretum, England

Prunus × *yedoensis*
in Keukenhof, Lisse, Holland

Plate 2

Prunus sargentii
Dortmund Botanic Garden, W. Germany

Prunus incisa
in the Göteborg Botanic Garden, Sweden

Prunus × cistena
in the Copenhagen Botanical Garden, Denmark

Prunus tenella
in the Dortmund Botanic Garden

Plate 3

Prunus serrulata 'Ukon'
both in the Dortmund Botanic Garden, W. Germany

Prunus subhirtella 'Fukubana'

Prunus serrulata 'Ojochin'
in the Dortmund Botanic Garden

Prunus 'Accolade'
at Keukhof, Lisse, Holland

Plate 4

Punica granatum
in its native habitat in Montenegro, Yugoslavia

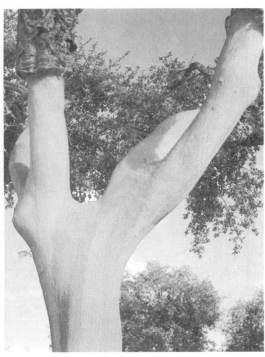

Quercus suber
debarked in Spain

Pyrostegia ignea
in a garden on the French Riviera

Quercus robur 'Atropurpurea'
in the Bad Brückenau Park, W. Germany

Plate 5

Platanus × *acerifolia* 'Tremonia'
in Dortmund, W. Germany

Populus lasiocarpa, fruits,
in Knuthenborg Park, Denmark

Prunus. a. *P. ssiori;* b. *P. wilsonii;* c. *P. vaniotti;* d. *P. cornuta;* e. *P. vaniotii* var. *potaninii;*
f. *P. lyonii;* g. *P. ilicifolia* (most collected from wild plants)

Plate 6

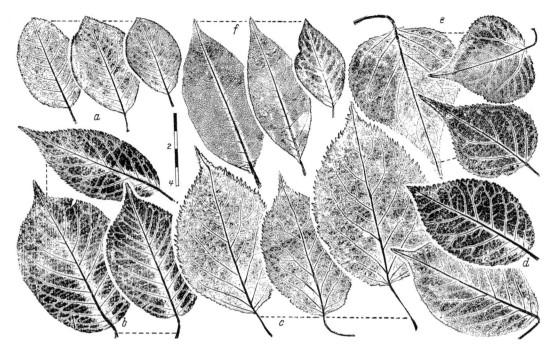

Prunus I. a. *P. maritima;* b. *P. americana;* c. *P. mandshurica;* d. *P. nigra;* e. *P. sibirica;* f. *P. alleghaniensis* (material from wild plants)

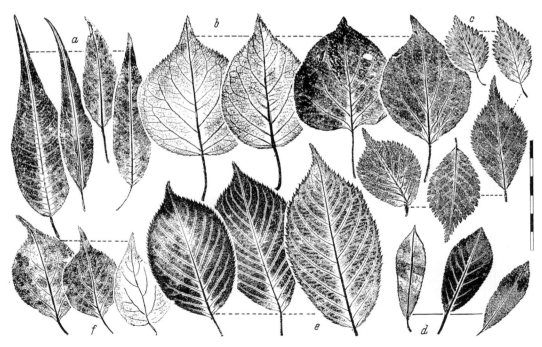

Prunus II. a. *P. davidiana;* b. *P. armeniaca* (2 leaves at left from plants in cultivation, right from wild plants); c. *P. incisa* (wild, from Japan); d. *P. fruticosa;* e. *P. yedoensis;* f. *P. mume* (from wild plants)

Plate 7

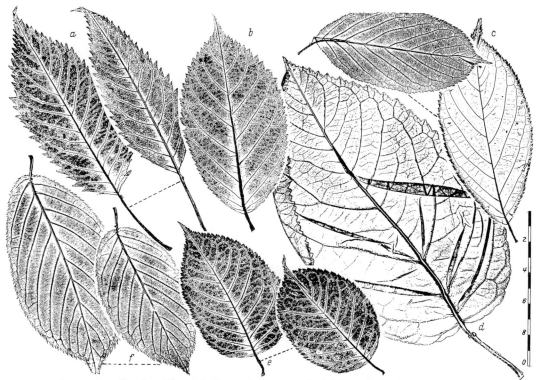

Prunus I. a. *P. avium* 'Plena'; b. *P. pseudocerasus*; c. *P. dielsiana*; d. *P. avium* 'Decumana';
e. *P. hirtipes*; f. *P. cyclamina* (from plants in cultivation)

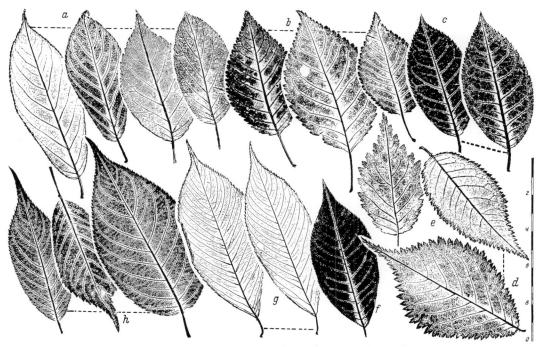

Prunus II. a. *P. campanulata* (2 leaves at left from wild plants); b. *P. dawyckensis*; c. *P. mugus*; d. *P. apetala*; e. *P. canescens* (leaf at left); f. *P. rufa*; g. *P. changyangensis*; h. *P. cerasoides* (most material from wild plants)

Plate 8

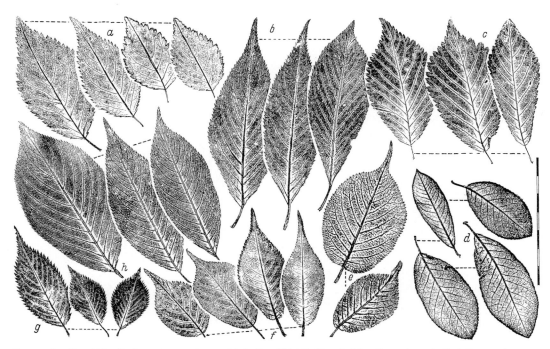

Prunus I. a. *P. subhirtella* (Japanese understock); b. *P. subhirtella* 'Pendula'; c. *P. maximowiczii;* d. *P. emarginata;* e. *P. conadenia;* f. *P. litigiosa;* g. *P. subhirtella* 'Autumnalis'; h. *P. subhirtella* var. *ascendens* (material from wild plants, except b,g,h)

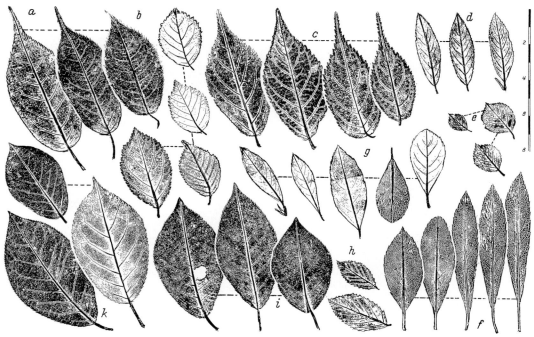

Prunus II. a. *P. campanulata* (2 leaves at left from cultivation, right from wild plants); b. *P. dawyckensis;* c. *P. mugus;* d. *P. apetala;* e. *P. canescens* (leaf at left); f. *P. rufa;* g. *P. changyangensis;* h. *P. cerasoides* (most material from wild plants)

Plate 9

Prunus lusitanica
in the Dortmund Botanic Garden, W. Germany

Prunus spinosa in fruit

Prunus cerasifera 'Atropurpurea' in the Coimbra Botanic Garden, Portugal

Plate 10

Prunus dulcis before harvest on a plantation near Barcelona, Spain

Prunus avium 'Plena'
Photo: Archivbild

Prunus avium 'Decumana'
in the Dortmund Botanic Garden, W. Germany

Plate 11

Prunus × *blireana*
Photo: Archivbild

Prunus campanulata × *incisa* 'Okamé'

Prunus hirtipes 'Semiplena'
in the Dortmund Botanic Garden, W. Germany

Plate 12

Prunus fenzliana
in the Westfalenpark, Dortmund, W. Germany

Prunus glandulosa 'Alboplena'
Photo: Archivbild

Prunus 'Hillieri'
in the Dortmund Botanic Garden, W. Germany

Prunus incisa 'Compacta'
in the Dortmund Botanic Garden, W. Germany

Plate 13

Prunus speciosa in the Dortmund Botanic Garden, W. Germany

Prunus 'Hally Jolivette'
Photo: Arnold Arboretum, USA

Plate 14

Prunus kurilensis
in the Dortmund Botanic Garden, W. Germany

Prunus laurocerasus 'Camelliifolia'
in RHS Gardens, Wisley, England

Prunus laurocerasus 'Schipkaensis Macrophylla' in the D. Hobbie Nursery, Linswege, W. Germany

Plate 15

Prunus lusitanica ssp. *azorica*
in the Hillier Arboretum, England

Prunus padus 'Nana'
in the St. Gallen Botanic Garden, Switzerland

Prunus pseudocerasus in the Dortmund Botanic Garden, W. Germany

Plate 16

Prunus pumila
in the Glasnevin Botanical Garden, Dublin, Ireland

Prunus schmittii
in the Hillier Arboretum, England

Prunus serotina (right); 'Cartilaginea' (left)
in the Dortmund Botanical Garden, W. Germany

Prunus serotina 'Pendula'
in the Wageningen Arboretum, Holland

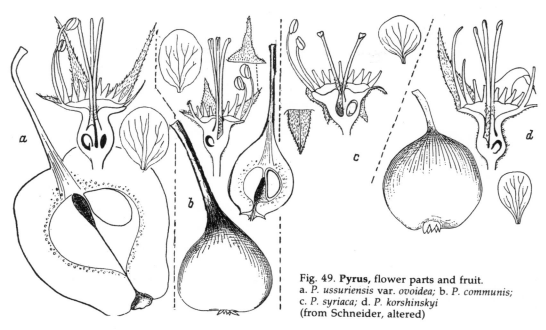

Fig. 49. **Pyrus**, flower parts and fruit.
a. *P. ussuriensis* var. *ovoidea;* b. *P. communis;*
c. *P. syriaca;* d. *P. korshinskyi*
(from Schneider, altered)

acuminate, base normally broad cuneate, dentate, the teeth outspread (!), loose and shaggy pubescent only at first, quickly becoming totally glabrous, petiole 2–6 cm long; flowers 3 cm wide, in woolly, occasionally nearly glabrous corymbs, styles 3–4, occasionally only 2; fruits pear-shaped, 2–2.5 cm long, brown with light spots, soon becoming soft. BC 3282; MG 31: 112. N. China. 1850. z5

f. **globosa** Rehd. Leaves often ovate, rounded at the base; fruits nearly globose, 1.5–2 cm thick. BC 3282. 1882.

P. pinnatifida var. *fastigiata* see: **Sorbus ✕ thuringiaca 'Fastigiata'**

P. pollveria see: **Sorbopyrus auricularis**

P. pyraster Burgsd. Small to medium-sized tree, branches and twigs usually thorny, bark thick, later breaking up into small plates, twigs ascending on younger trees, later more outspread, young shoots pubescent, eventually totally glabrous, brown, glossy; leaves rounded to ovate, thin, 3–5 cm long, with 6–8 vein pairs, somewhat pubescent at first, eventually glabrous; flowers with linear-subulate, eventually dry sepals and elliptic petals; fruits globose-top-shaped to nearly pear-shaped, 1.5–3 cm thick, dull yellow, usually brown speckled when ripe, in umbellate clusters. TPy 15 (= *P. communis* var. *pyraster* L.; *P. achras* Gaertn.). Central to SW. Europe. z6

P. pyrifolia (Burm.) Nakai. Sand Pear. Tree, 5–12 m high, young shoots glabrous or floccose at first, glabrous and reddish to dark brown in the 2nd year; leaves oval-oblong, occasionally ovate, 7–12 cm long, long acuminate, base usually round, occasionally slightly cordate, scabrous bristly serrate, teeth slightly appressed, glabrous or somewhat floccose when young,

petiole 3–4.5 cm long; flowers 6–9 in glabrous to floccose at first, corymbs, corolla 3–3.5 cm wide, stalk 3–3.5 cm long, thin, calyx lobes triangular ovate and long acuminate, twice as long as the tube, petals ovate, style 4, occasionally 5, glabrous, stamens about 20; fruits nearly globose, about 3 cm thick, brown, light punctate, calyx abscising, flesh rather hard. LF 173; BC 3276 and 2808; MG 31: 104 (= *P. serotina* Rehd.). Central and W. China. z6 Plate 26, 27; Fig. 48 ∅

var. **culta** (Mak.) Nakai. Leaves larger and wider, to 15 cm long; fruits larger, apple- or pear-shaped, brown or yellow. BC 2808. Cultivated in Japan and China. Introduced into America around 1850. ✂

Included here are the so-called "Japanese" and "Chinese" pears of pomology.

f. **stapfiana** (Rehd.) Rehd. Teeth of the leaf margin less appressed; petals tapered claw-like; fruits pear-shaped (!), to 5 cm long. BM 8226; DRHS 1722. China. 1875.

P. regelii Rehd. Shrub or small tree, 5(9) m high, twigs divaricate, often terminating in a thorn, gray tomentose when young, purple-brown in the 2nd year, glabrous, short shoots usually thorny; leaves quite variable, partly ovate-oblong and simple or with one to several shallow to deeper lobes and uneven and rather coarsely serrate, somewhat pinnately partite and with 5–7 narrow, coarse or finely serrate lobes, tomentose when young, later glabrous; flowers white, 2–2.5 cm wide, few in short corymbs; fruits pear-shaped or more globose, 2–3 cm thick. BS 2: 597 (= *P. heterophylla* Regl.& Schmalh. non Poir., non Steud.). Turkestan. 1891 z6 Plate 27; Fig. 44. ∅

P. rhamnoides see: **Sorbus rhamnoides**

P. salicifolia Pall. Tree, 5–8 m high, twigs more or less pendulous, shoots thin, short shoots often terminating in a thorn, young shoots densely gray-white tomentose, more green and glabrous in fall; leaves narrowly elliptic, tapered to both ends, 3–9 cm long, normally entire, occasionally with a few teeth, both sides silver-gray pubescent when young, later a turbid green above and more or less glabrous, persistently pubescent beneath; flowers 2 cm wide, grouped 6–8 in small, globose corymbs, calyx and flower stalk white woolly, April; fruit a 2–3 cm long, green pear with a short, thick stalk, hard, sour. SE. Europe, Asia Minor, Caucasus. 1780. z5 Plate 27, 28; Fig. 44 ⌀

'Pendula'. Hardly differs from the species.

P. × salviifolia DC. (*P. communis* × *P. nivalis*). More similar to *P. nivalis*. A tree, but with smaller leaves, twigs often very stoutly thorned; leaves elliptic to ovate, acute to acuminate, 5 cm long, base broadly cuneate to nearly round, usually finely crenate, gray pubescent when young, eventually rather glabrous, petiole long; fruits pear-shaped, long stalked, about 2.5 cm long and thick, stalk 2–3 cm long. TPy 66; BR 1482. France, W. Switzerland, Hungary. Before 1800. z6 ⌀

P. serotina see: **P. pyrifolia**

P. serrulata Rehd. Small tree, very similar to *P. pyrifolia*, but the leaves not bristly serrate (!), young shoots woolly, reddish brown in the 2nd year; leaves ovate to oval-oblong, gradually or abruptly acuminate, 5–11 cm long, base broadly cuneate to rounded, finely serrate (but the teeth are not bristly acuminate!), floccose-tomentose at first, soon glabrous, petiole 3.5–7 cm long; flowers 2.5 cm wide, in slightly woolly corymbs, styles 3–4 (!), occasionally 5, sepals acute to acuminate, as long as the tube; fruits nearly globose, 1.5 cm thick, brown with lighter spots, calyx more or less persistent. MG 31: 112. China; Kansu, Hupeh, Szechwan Prov. 1917. z6 Fig. 48

P. simonii see: **P. ussuriensis**

P. sinaica see: **P. persica**

P. sinensis see: **P. lindleyi** × **P. ussuriensis**

P. syriaca Boiss. Small, usually thorny tree, habit erect, twigs usually outspread; leaves oblong to more lanceolate, usually 2–5, rarely to 10 cm, long, glabrous or nearly so, finely crenate, petiole 2–5 cm long; flowers in tomentose corymbs, April–May; fruits pear-shaped, about 3 cm thick, stalk about 5 cm long, thick. TPy 43–44. Cypress, Asia Minor. Before 1874. z7 Plate 26; Fig. 49. ⌀

P. ussuriensis Maxim. Tree, to 15 m high, young twigs yellowish brown, glabrous; leaves rounded-ovate or ovate, acuminate, 5 to 10 cm long, base round to cordate, bristly serrate, glabrous on both sides, dark yellowish green above, lighter beneath, fall color red-brown, stalk 2–5 cm long, thin; flowers white, 3 cm wide, grouped 6–9 in dense, hemispherical, glabrous corymbs, stalk 1–2 cm long, petals obovate, gradually tapering to the base, April; fruits nearly globose, green-yellow, 3–4 cm thick,

stalk short and thick. Flesh hard, not edible. BC 3277; MJ 1412; RH 1872: 28 (= *P. simonii* Carr.; *P. sinensis* sensu Decne.). NE. Asia. 1855. z5 Plate 27; Fig. 46. ⌀

var. **hondoensis** (Kikuchi & Nakai) Rehd. Leaves rust-brown floccose-tomentose at first, as are the young shoots, ovate to oval-oblong, teeth less bristly acuminate, yet finer than the species and more appressed (= *P. ferruginea* Koidz.; *P. hondoensis* Kikuchi & Nakai). Central Japan. 1917.

var. **ovoidea** (Rehd.) Rehd. Twigs more divaricately spreading, young shoots brown; leaves ovate to oblong-ovate, narrower than the species; fruit distinctly ovate in longitudinal section, widest at the base, gradually becoming narrower toward the apex (!), flesh yellow, juicy. NK 6: 17; BC 2868; MG 31: 102 (= *P. ovoidea* Rehd.; *P. simonii* Hort. non Carr.). N. China, Korea. 1865. Plate 27; Fig. 49. ✕

P. variolosa see: **P. pashia**

P. vestita see: **Sorbus cuspidata**

P. wilhelmi see: **P. pashia** var. **kumaoni**

The *Pyrus* species prefer a sunny, warm site and a deep, fertile, not too moist soil. The gray- and white-leaved species are very tolerant of dry periods. The garden merit of many species and cultivars is only slight.

Lit. Terpo, A.: Magyar ország vadkörtéi (Pyri Hungariae); in Ann. Acad. Hort. Viticult. 6, 2, 1–258, Budapest 1960 (with summaries in German and Russian) ● Diapulis, Ch.: Beiträge zur Kenntnis der orientalischen Pomaceen (*Pyrus, Sorbus, Crataegus*); in Fedde, Rep. spec. nov. regn. veget. 34, 29–72, 1933 ● Hedrick, U.: The Pears of New York; New York 1921 ● Rehder, A.: Synopsis of the Chinese species of *Pyrus*; in Proc. Amer. Acad. 50, 225–241, 1915 ● Whitehouse, W. E., J. L. Creech & G. A. Seaton: Bradford Ornamental Pear, a promising shade tree; in American Nurseryman 4/15/1963, 7–8, 56–57 ● Anon: Growing the Bradford Ornamental Pear; Home and Garden Bull. 154, USDA 1968 ● Franco, J. do Amaral, & M. L. da Rocha Afonso: Des pereiras bravas Portuguesas; Rev. Fac. Cie. Lisbon, 2nd series, C, 13, 175–213, 1965 ● Zielinski, Q. B.: Taxonomic status of *Pyrus fauriei* Schneider (Rosacea). Baileya 13, 17–19, 1965. ● Westwood, M.N.: Comparison of *Pyrus fauriei* Schneid. with *P. calleryana* Decaisne (Rosaceae); Baileya 16, 39–41, 1968.

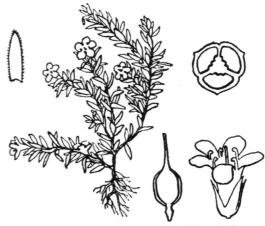

Fig. 50. *Pyxidanthera barbulata* (from BB)

PYXIDANTHERA Michx. — DIAPENSIACEAE

Evergreen, procumbent dwarf shrub; leaves very small, alternate or clustered, compacted; flowers very numerous, small, sessile, 5 parted, corolla broadly campanulate, limb lobes obovate, somewhat longer than the tube, stamens 5, with very wide, flat filaments, both pollen sacs parallel and opening by means of a cross slit (*Diapensia* has pollen sacs which are not parallel and open with longitudinal slits). — 2 species in N. America.

Pyxidanthera barbulata Michx. Moose flower. Mat-like habit, occasionally to 1 m wide, evergreen; leaves oblanceolate, 3–8 mm long, scabrous acuminate, usually pubescent toward the base; flowers usually very numerous, white to pink, 7–8 mm wide, April–May. Eastern USA; New Jersey to Virginia and North Carolina, in sandy pine forests. z6 Fig. 50.

QUERCUS L. — Oak — FAGACEAE

Deciduous or evergreen trees, occasionally shrubs; leaves alternate, short petioled, serrate or dentate or lobed, occasionally pinnatisect, occasionally entire; flowers monoecious, inconspicuous, the male flowers in pendulous catkins, female flowers solitary or in 2 to many-flowered spikes; fruit an ovate or rounded nut, more or less surrounded by a cup form, tight involucre. — Around 450 species from N. America to western tropical S. America, temperate and subtropical Eurasia and N. Africa, in the tropics only at higher altitudes.

Outline of the Genus (from Prantl)

Subgenus I. **Cyclobalanopsis** (Oerst.) Schneid.
Scales of the acorn cup in concentric circles (!); leaves leathery, evergreen, entire or slightly crenate; style short, widened at the apex; acorns ripening in the first year; aborted ovules near the apex of the fruit:
> Q. acuta, bambusifolia, gilva, glauca, lamellosa, myrsinifolia, oxyodon, stenophylla

Subgenus II. **Erythrobalanus** (Spach) Oerst.
Scales of the acorn cup not fused into concentric circles; leaves deciduous or evergreen, entire or lobed, apex and lobes bristly acuminate; style linear-elongated, capitate; acorns ripening in the 2nd year, shell often thick walled, interior tomentose; scales of the acorn cup tightly appressed; aborted ovules in the apical part of the fruit.

Section **Phellos**, Willow Oaks
Leaves usually entire, oblong-lanceolate (some hybrids also lobed or dentate), rolled up in bud, bright red or yellow in fall:
> Q. × heterophylla, imbricaria, incana, laurifolia, × leana, × ludoviciana, phellos, × rudkinii, × runcinata, × schochiana

Section **Nigrae**, Black Oaks
Leaves obovate, widest above the middle, apex 3–5 lobed or entire, folded in the bud stage:
> Q. arkansana, × bushii, marilandica, nigra

Section **Rubrae**, Scarlet Oaks
Leaves pinnately lobed, not wide at the apex; lobes usually sinuately toothed with bristly acuminate teeth, usually bright red in fall:
> Q. × benderi, × brittonii, coccinea, ellipsoidalis, falcata, georgiana, ilicifolia, kelloggii, laevis, palustris, × rehderi, × richteri, × robbinsii, rubra, shumardii, texana, velutina

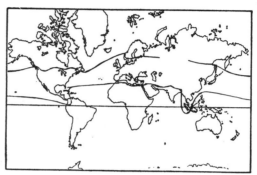

Fig. 51. Range of the genus *Quercus*

Section **Stenocarpae** Oerst.
Leaves evergreen and partly entire, partly dentate:
> Q. agrifolia, crassifolia, hypoleucoides, wislizenii

Subgenus III. **Lepidobalanus** Endl.
Scales of the acorn cup not fused into concentric circles; leaves deciduous or evergreen, lobed or dentate, with or without bristly tips; style subulate, acute; acorns ripening in the 1st or 2nd year, shell not tomentose on the interior; scales of the acorn cup outspread or appressed, shell glabrous inside (except on *Q. chrysolepis*); aborted ovules in the basal part of the fruit.

Section **Cerris**, Turkey Oaks
Leaves mucronulate to bristly serrate or dentate, or mucronulate pinnatisect; style subulate, acute, erect or reflexed; cup scales large, most outspread to recurved, at least the apical ones linear and elongated:
> Q. acutissima, aegilops, afares, baronii, castaneifolia, cerris, ehrenbergii, × kewensis, × libanerris, libani, macrolepis, pyrami, trojana, vallonea, variabilis

Section **Suber**, Cork Oaks
Style linear, rather acute, erect or reflexed; cup with reflexed or loosely appressed scales; fruits ripening in 1st or 2nd year; leaves evergreen:
> Q. alnifolia, calliprinos, coccifera, engleriana, × hispanica, leucotrichophora, semecarpifolia, suber

Section **Ilex**, Holly Oaks
Leaves evergreen, thick, leathery, entire or thorny dentate; fruits normally ripen in the 1st year; style short, rounded; cup scales appressed:

× *audleyensis, chrysolepis, gramuntia, ilex, phillyreoides, reticulata, vacciniifolia, virginiana, warburgii*

Section Gallifera, Gall Oaks
Leaves serrately lobed with usually mucronulate saw-teeth, occasionally entire; styles short, rounded; cup scales small, appressed:
Q. faginea, fruticosa, infectoria

Section Robur, English Oaks
Bark dark, deeply furrowed; leaves usually deep green above; cup scales small to relatively large, appressed or somewhat looser:
Q. canariensis, congesta, dalechampii, frainetto, haas, hartwissiana, × *hickelii, iberica, macranthera, mas, petraea, pedunculiflora, polycarpa, pontica, pubescens, pyrenaica, robur,* × *rosacea, sadleriana,* × *turneri, virgiliana*

Section Alba, White Oaks
Bark light gray, exfoliating in thick plates; leaves light green, often bluish, purple to orange or brown in the fall; cup scales small and appressed, occasionally enlarged or widely outspread:
Q. alba, aliena, austrina, × *beadlei,* × *bebbiana, bicolor, chapmanii,* × *deamii, douglasii, fabri, gambelii, garryana, glandulifera,* × *jackiana, liaotungensis, lobata, lyrata, macrocarpa, margaretta, michauxii, mongolica, muehlenbergii, prinoides, prinus,* × *sargentii,* × *saulii, stellata, undulata*

Section Dentatae, Kaiser Oaks
Leaves deciduous, very large, dentate; acorns ripening in the first year; cup scales linear, outspread, free; bark deeply furrowed:
Q. dentata

Quercus acuta Thunb. Evergreen tree, 9–12 m high in its habitat, but usually only a shrub in cultivation, young shoots and leaves brown tomentose at first, but quickly becoming totally glabrous; leaves elliptic, occasionally more ovate, long acuminate (especially on young plants), base rounded to broadly cuneate, entire, 6–13 cm long, 2–6 cm wide, limb occasionally somewhat undulate, petiole to 2.5 cm long, glossy dark green above, dull yellowish beneath, with 8–10 vein pairs; acorns clustered, cup surrounding ⅓ of the fruit, with concentric rings. KIF 1: 46; MJ 1969; CQ 22 (1 to 8); NF 9: 183 (= *Q. laevigata* Bl.). Japan. 1878. Dislikes alkaline soil. z8–9 Plate 28, 34; Fig. 52. # ⌀

Q. acutissima Carruth. Deciduous tree, usually not over 6–12 m high, young shoots softly pubescent at first, soon glabrous; leaves *Castanea*-like, quite variable, usually oblong-lanceolate, occasionally nearly ovate to obovate, 10–20 cm long, 2.5–5 cm wide, long acuminate, often asymmetrical, base round, with 14–16(20) veins on either side, these exserted past the marginal teeth as 5 mm long bristles, glossy green above, a little lighter and glabrous (!!) below, silky pubescent only when young, petiole 1.5–2.5 cm long, thin; fruit sessile, cup hemispherical, 3.5 cm wide including the outspread scales, surrounding the 2 cm long acorns by ⅔. CQ 235; FIO 124; KIF 1: 52; NK 3: 9; EH 337 (= *Q. serrata* S. & Z.). E. Asia; Japan to China, Korea. 1862. Hardy. Ⓕ China, Korea, Japan. z7 Plate 32, 44; Fig. 53. ⌀

Q. aegilops L. This is a collective name put forth by Camus to include *Q. macrolepis* Kotschy, *Q. vallonea* Kotschy, *Q. ithaburensis* Eig., *Q. brantii* Lindl., *Q. pyramii* Kotschy, *Q. look* Kotschy and others as subspecies. In this work *Q. aegilops* L. is considered to be a *nomen confusum*. The subspecies included are treated as species. *Q. aegilops* Lam. (non L.), see: **Q. macrolepis** Kotschy.

Q. afares Pomel. Very similar to *Q. castaneifolia* and often included with it, but with a more upright conical to columnar habit, bark more deeply fissured; leaves late to drop, thin, oblong-lanceolate to oval-oblong, 6–12 cm long, with 10–15 vein pairs, dark green above, gray-white tomentose beneath; fruits in clusters of 4–5 together (!), acorns 3.5–4.5 cm long, about 2 cm thick, cup surrounding about ⅓ of the acorn. CQ 58 (= *Q. castaneifolia* var. *algeriensis* Bean; *Q. castaneifolia* var. *incana* Batt. & Trabut). Algeria. 1896. z9

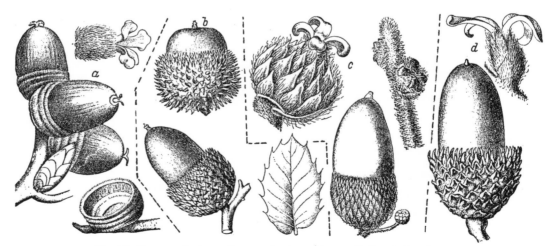

Fig. 52. **Quercus**, fruits. a. *Q. acuta*; b. *Q. coccifera*; c. *Q. ilex*; d. *Q. suber*
(from Hempel & Wilhelm, Kotschy, Shirasawa)

Fig. 53. **Quercus.** Left *Q. acutissima*; center *Q. variabilis*; right *Q. aliena* var. *acuteserrata*
(from ICS)

Q. agrifolia Née. Evergreen tree, 20–30 m high in its habitat, also often shrubby, broad crowned, young shoots softly pubescent; leaves very hard, broadly elliptic to more rounded or ovate, somewhat convex, 2.5–5 cm long, thorny dentate, dark green and smooth above, lighter beneath, glossy and glabrous except for the small pubescent tufts in the vein axils; fruits sessile, acorn tips conical, 2–3.5 cm long, cup surrounding ⅓ of the acorn (interior silky pubescent). SPa 138–140; SS 403; CQ 241 (1–21); JRHS 58: 45. USA; California. 1849. z9 Fig. 56. #

Q. aizoon see: **Q.** × **turneri 'Pseudoturneri'**

Q. alba L. White Oak. Tree, to 30 m high, broad rounded crown, bark light gray-brown, exfoliating (!), young shoots pubescent, but quickly becoming glabrous, often bluish white (!); leaves obovate-oblong, 10–20 cm long, with 3–4 entire or sparsely toothed lobes, pubescent when young, later more or less glabrous, dull green above, bluish to gray-green beneath, fall color orange to wine-red, often also violet-red; fruits short or long stalked, acorns oval-oblong, 2–2.5 cm long, about ¼ covered by a gray-white cup. GPT 181; SS 356–358; CQ 211–214; TO 172–175; MOT 4. USA. 1724. The most common species in N. America, developing forests and quite important as a timber tree. Ⓕ USA. z7 Plate 34. ∅

f. **elongata** Kipp. Leaves much narrower, 20–25 cm long, about 8 cm wide, gradually cuneate tapered toward the base, with 3–4 wide, triangular ovate lobes on either side, these often concave (!), fall color usually an intense violet or orange. ∅

f. **pinnatifida** (Michx.) Rehd. The type with deeply pinnatisect leaves, lobes narrow and often dentate; fruits slender stalked.

f. **repanda** (Michx.) Trel. Leaves with very shallow sinuses (!); fruits usually short stalked. CQ 211 (13–14) (= *Q. repanda* [Michx.] Raf.). Virginia to Illinois. Often incorrectly labeled in cultivation!

Q. aliena Bl. Deciduous tree, 20 m high or more, young shoots yellowish green, glabrous, somewhat warty; leaves obovate to oblong, acute to somewhat rounded, 10–20 cm long, base cuneate, very coarsely sinuately dentate, with 10–15 coarse, blunt teeth on either side, deep green and glabrous above, whitish beneath or bluish and finely short tomentose, petiole 12–30 mm long; fruits sessile, usually solitary or grouped 2–3, ovate, 2–2.5 cm long, ⅓ surrounded by a gray tomentose cup, scales appressed. NK 3: 14; CQ 97–99; MJ 3647; CIS 18; KIF 3: 8. Japan, Korea. 1908. z6 Plate 35, 41. ∅

var. **acuteserrata** Maxim. leaves usually somewhat smaller and narrower, the teeth more acute, somewhat inward curving and glandular tipped. CQ 98–99. Japan, central China. Fig. 53.

Q. alnifolia Poech. Golden Oak. Evergreen shrub or small tree, very slow growing, young shoots densely gray tomentose, leaves rounded to broadly obovate, 2.5–6 cm long and nearly as wide, finely dentate only at the apical end, apex round to nearly truncate, base the same, with 5–8 vein pairs, dark green and glossy above, yellow to gray-yellow tomentose beneath (!), petiole 1–1.5 cm long; acorns solitary or paired, 2.5–3 cm long, ovate, with a sharp apex, cup covering half of the acorn, with a broad ring of long, pubescent scales. CG 40. Cypress. 1885. Rare in cultivation. z8 Plate 28, 33. #

Q. ambrozyana see: **Q.** × **hispanica 'Ambrozyana'**

Q. aquatica see: **Q. nigra**

Q. arkansana Sarg. Small tree, 6–8 m high, similar to *Q. marilandica*, but the young shoots densely white pubescent at first; leaves broadly obovate, slightly trilobed at the apex, base cuneate, 5–8 cm long, broadly elliptic to ovate on sterile shoots, rounded and undulately lobed at the base, white tomentose above only when young, eventually brownish tomentose beneath, but eventually nearly glabrous, petiole 8–12 mm long; fruits grouped 1–2, broadly ovate, to 1.5 cm

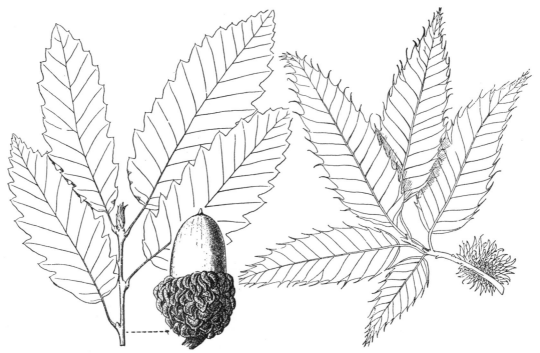

Fig. 54. **Quercus**. Left *Q. castaneifolia*; right *Q. variabilis* (from Dippel, Kotschy)

wide, acorns ⅓ covered by the cup. ST 2: 152; CQ 344 (9 to 19); KTF 14. USA; Arkansas. 1909. z6 ⌀

Q. × audleyensis Henry (*Q. ilex × Q. petraea*). Deciduous tree, shoots gray tomentose until the 2nd year, leaf drop occurs late in the fall; leaves quite variable on the same twig, some obovate-oblong, 8–9 cm long, entire and undulate or with 4–5 teeth or lobes on either side, these occasionally with 1–3 small teeth on the tip, leathery tough, eventually dark green and glossy above, lighter beneath and pubescent near the base and on the venation, petiole 1–2 cm long; sets no perfect fruit. EH 338 (59) (= *Q. koehnei* Ambrozy). First observed in Audley End, Essex, England; again in Berlin by Späth in 1912. z6 ⌀

var. *sempervirens* see: **Q. × turneri 'Pseudoturneri'**

Q. austriaca see: **Q. cerris** var. **austriaca**

Q. austrina Small. Medium-sized tree, similar to *Q. alba*, about 20 m high in its habitat, bark light gray, scaly; leaves obovate-elliptic, 7–15 cm long, 3–10 cm wide, usually with 2–3 large lobes on either side, occasionally unlobed or flatly sinuate, both apical pairs directed forward, dark green above, lighter and glabrous beneath (*Q. alba* is whitish!); acorns ripening in the 1st year, solitary, short stalked, nut 12–20 mm long, ⅓–½ enclosed by a thin, pubescent cup. KTF 39; WT 38 (= *Q. durandii* var. *austrina* [Small] Palmer). S. USA, from South Carolina to Florida and S. Texas. z7

Q. armeniaca see: **Q. hartwissiana**

Q. ballota see: **Q. ilex** var. **ballota** and **Q. i.** var. **rotundifolia**

Q. bambusifolia Hance. Tall tree, 15–18 m high in its habitat, bark gray, smooth; leaves willow-like, about 5 cm long, 1 cm wide, acute at both ends, entire, glossy dark green above, blue-green beneath, glossy on both sides, petiole 2 mm, red-brown; acorns conical, 1.5 cm long, 1 cm wide, with a small apical tip, densely silky pubescent apex, ⅓ covered by the involucral cup. LF 98; HKT 84; CQ 1: 15 (= *Q. salicina* Benth. & Bl.). China; Kwangsi, Kwangtung Prov., in the mountains. z8 # Also see: **Q. myrsinifolia**

Q. banisteri see: **Q. ilicifolia**

Q. baronii Skan. Semi-evergreen shrub or small tree, closely related to *Q. acutissima*, young shoots gray-white, thin, smooth; leaves elliptic, 4–6 cm long, 2–3 cm wide, with 5–7 pairs of small teeth with bristly tips, dark green above, bluish green beneath with finely reticulate venation, glabrous to the tomentose midrib; acorns cylindrical, 1.5 × 1 cm, half enclosed by a silky pubescent cup. W. China. 1915. z9

Q. beadlei Trel. (*Q. alba × Q. michauxii*). Occasionally encountered in the range of the parents, but seldom found in cultivation.

Q. × bebbiana Schneid. (*Q. alba × Q. macrocarpa*). Similar to *Q. alba*, leaves very large, variable, more or less lobed, pubescent beneath (!), usually with 5 lobes on either side; fruits solitary (occasionally 2–3 stunted ones together), cup deeper than that of *Q. alba*, without the fringed limb. SS 360; CQ 225 (1–18). Appears among the parents. 1880. z4 ⌀

Q. × benderi Baenitz (*Q. coccinea × Q. rubra*). A large tree, young shoots reddish, buds ovate, obtuse, somewhat pubescent at the apex; leaves obovate, acuminate, base abruptly truncated, more lobed than *Q. rubra*, with 5–7 deep lobes, the lobes with bristly teeth, eventually glabrous on both sides except for the axillary pubescence beneath, purple or yellow in fall, petiole 3–5 cm long; fruits often stunted, otherwise ovate, cup top-shaped, the fruit nearly half enclosed. CQ 343 (2–14). Discovered before 1903 in Scheiniger Park, Breslau, Silesia (now Poland), and doubtlessly in other parks as well. z5 ⌀

Q. bicolor Willd. Deciduous tree, tall, rounded, about 20 m high, bark light gray-brown, scaly, like *Platanus* (!), young shoots scaly pubescent; leaves oblong obovate, 10–16 cm long, acute to rounded, with 6–8 (10) coarse, obtuse teeth, occasionally more deeply incised, deep green above, glossy, whitish tomentose or velvety gray-green beneath, orange to red in fall, petiole 1–2 cm long; fruit 1–2 on thin, 3–8 cm long stalks, acorns oblong-ovate, 2–3 cm long, ⅓ surrounded by the gray cup. GTP 182; CQ 174 (8 to 18); TO 186 (= *Q. platanoides* Sudw.). Eastern N. America. 1800. z4 Plate 35; Fig. 75. ⌀

Q. boissieri see: **Q. infectoria** var. **boissieri**

Q. borealis see: **Q. rubra**

Q. brevifolia see: **Q. incana**

Q. × brittonii W. T. Davis (*Q. ilicifolia × Q. marilandica*). Small tree or shrub, divaricate; leaf form varying between that of the parents, leathery, 9–10 cm long, obovate to broadly obovate, widest beneath the apex, obtuse-cuneate to lyre-form tapered at the base, coarsely sinuately dentate, with 1–3 normally sinuate teeth on either side, wide, 3–4 side lobes, gray-yellow tomentose when young, later glossy deep green above with

pubescent venation, underside sparsely yellowish gray-green tomentose, venation and the vein axils denser (= *Q. ferruginea hybrida* Dipp.) W. USA, appears with the parents. 1888. z6

Q. brutia see: **Q. robur** ssp. **brutia**

Q. bungeana see: **Q. variabilis**

Q. × bushii Sarg. (*Q. marilandica × Q. velutina*). Tree, to 10 m, shoots very stout, densely tomentose, glabrous only in the fall, winter buds 1 cm long; leaves usually obovate, 10–13 cm long, most 5 lobed (3 lobed on fruiting branches, as in Plate 30), with deep, rounded sinuses, midrib distinct, base round, occasionally tapered, tough, deep green and glossy above, yellow-green beneath, glabrous, but with axillary pubescence, petiole 3 cm long; acorns ovate, half enclosed by the cup, scales large, loosely appressed. CQ 343 (20–23). USA; first found in Oklahoma among the parents. 1931. Plate 30. z6

Q. californica see: **Q. kelloggii**

Q. calliprinos Webb. Palestine Oak. Evergreen tree, very closely related to *Q. coccifera*, but often with a thick stem; leaves usually oblong, acutely serrate, occasionally thorny or entire, to 5 cm long; acorns half (or less) enclosed within the cup, scales longer than those of *Q. coccifera*. CQ 50, 51 (= *Q. fenzlii* Kotschy; *Q. palaestina* Kotschy). Asia Minor. 1855 Ⓕ Israel. z9 #

Q. canariensis Willd. Algerian Oak. Tree, 25(30) m high, young shoots glabrous and furrowed; leaves oval-oblong to obovate, 5–15(22) cm long, base slightly cordate, thick, leathery tough, with 10–12 coarse, obtuse teeth on either side, glossy dark green above, underside only floccose at first, quickly becoming glabrous, petiole 1.5–2 cm long; fruits grouped 1–3 on a short petiole, acorns about 2.5 cm long, half enclosed in a 2.5 cm long, hemispherical cup. CQ 115–118; SME 41–42; VQ 9–10 (= *Q. mirbeckii* Durieu). S. Spain, N. Africa (not endemic

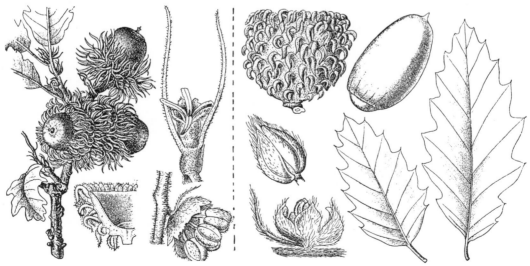

Fig. 55. **Quercus.** Left *Q. cerris;* right *Q. × hispanica* (from Kotschy, Schneider)

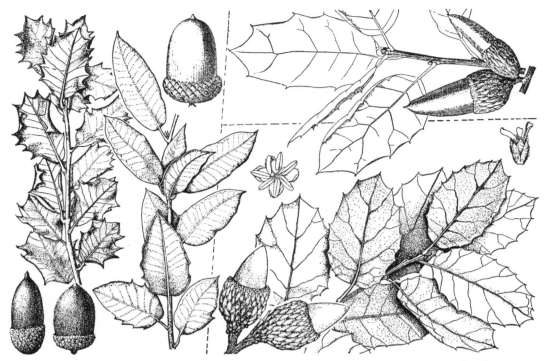

Fig. 56. **Quercus.** Left *Q. chrysolepis*; right above *Q. agrifolia*; right beneath *Q. wislizenii* (from Sudworth)

to the Canary Islands despite the name). 1844. z8 Plate 33, 45. ⊘

Q. castanea see: **Q. muehlenbergii**

Q. castaneifolia C. A. Mey. Large crowned, deciduous tree, to 25 m high, round crowned, shoots tomentose at first, later glabrous; leaves elliptic-oblong to more lanceolate, 7–16 cm long, acute, base cuneate to round, coarsely serrate, the teeth with a small mucro, the 6–14 vein pairs terminating in the teeth, glossy dark green above, finely gray tomentose beneath to nearly glabrous; acorns nearly sessile, 2–3 cm long, ovate, enclosed ½ or more by the cup, scales reflexed (!), the base ovate. CQ 59: BS 2: 466 + Pl. 57; NF 10: 45. Caucasus, Iran. 1840. Ⓕ USSR. z7 Plate 31; Fig. 54. ⊘

var. *algeriensis* see: **Q. afares**

'Green Spire'. Strong growing, broadly columnar, compact habit. Developed by Hillier of Winchester, England.

var. *incana* see: **Q. afares**

Q. catesbaei see: Q. larevis

Q. cerris L. Turkey Oak. Deciduous tree, to 35 m, broadly conical crown, bark blackish, bulging with thick checkered plates, young shoots gray tomentose, buds pubescent, surrounded by persistent, filamentous scales (!!); leaves oblong in outline, tapered to both ends, 6–12 cm long, coarsely denate to pinnately cleft, the teeth triangular and acute, dark green above and stellate pubescent when young, dull light green and pubescent

beneath, yellow-brown in fall, petiole 3–20 mm long; acorns grouped 1–4, nearly sessile, 3 cm long, about half enclosed within the cup, this with awl-shaped, reflexed lobes. CQ 63-66; EH 316–318; HF 962; HW 25 (= *Q. lanuginosa* Lam.). S. Europe, Asia Minor. 1735. z7 Fig. 55 ⊘

'Ambrozyana' see: **Q. hispanica 'Ambrozyana'**

'Argenteovariegata'. Leaves broad and irregularly cream-white margined, the border occasionally reaching to the midrib (= f. *variegata* Hort.; f. *argenteo-variegata* Ottolander). A large tree heretofore limited to Holland. Before 1864. ⊘

f. *asplenifolia* see: f. **laciniata**

'Aureovariegata'. Leaves distinctly yellow variegated (not white) (= f. *aureo-variegata* Schneid.). Before 1867. Existence in cultivation today unknown. ⊘

var. **austriaca** (Willd.) Loud. Leaves ovate, acute, tapered to both ends and evenly lobed, the lobes triangular, numerous, short, slightly leathery more pubescent beneath, petiole 10–15 mm long. CQ 65 (1–7) (= *Q. austriaca* Willd.). Tyrol to Sicily, Balkans, Asia Minor. ⊘

var. *ciliata* see: ssp. **tournefortii**

f. *dissecta* see: f. **laciniata**

var. **haliphloeos** Lam. & DC. Leaves larger than those of the species, the apical half twice as wide as the basal half, petiole 5–6 mm long. CQ 64(7–9) (= *Q. haliphoeos* Lam.). France. 1783.

f. **laciniata** (Loud.) Schneid. Leaves pinnately cleft to pinnately partite, the lobes often further pinnately cleft, usually light green beneath with scattered stellate pubescence. CQ 235 (8–

9) (= f. *dissecta*; f. *asplenifolia*; f. *laciniata* Hort.). Also many transitional forms between the species and this form. Plate 33. ∅

'Pendula'. Twigs long, pendulous or lying on the ground; leaves narrow, deeply lobed. Loudon, Arbor. et Frutic. fig. 1707. First recognized in Amsterdam, Holland.

var. **pseudocerris** Boiss. Leaves quite variable, deeply pinnatisect, the lobes linear and entire or finely lobed, somewhat pubescent above, often densely white tomentose. CQ 66 (2–10). Greece, Lebanon, Syria.

ssp. **tournefortii** (Willd.) O. Schwarz. Leaves lyre-form pinnately cleft, with a wide, open sinus in the middle of the margin, either side with 3–5, usually entire lobes, somewhat yellowish green above, yellowish white-green and short tomentose beneath. CQ 65 (11 to 17); 66 (11) (= *Q. cerris* var. *ciliata* Kotschy). Armenia, Sicily, Lebanon. ∅

f. *variegata* see: **'Argenteovariegta'**

Q. chapmanii Sarg. Semi-evergreen shrub, occasionally a small tree in its habitat, to 7 m, crown outspread, bark broken up into irregular plates, twigs stiff, olive brown to gray-brown, smooth, but with raised lenticels; leaves dropping after the new leaves appear, with a conspicuous yellow shimmer (!) at bud break, obovate to elliptic, 5–7 cm long, 2.5–3 cm wide, often indistinctly 3 lobed, the apex rounded, base cuneate, entire, margins undulate, dark green above, glossy, yellowish and pubescent beneath; acorns usually solitary, sessile, ripening in the 1st year, nut to 2.5 cm long, about half as wide, about ⅓ covered by a hemispherical cup. WT 37; KTF 41; CIS 64. USA; coastal region of South Carolina to S. Florida. z7 Fig. 66.

Q. chinensis see: **Q. variabilis**

Q. chinquapin see: **Q. prinoides**

Q. chrysolepis Liebm. Small evergreen tree, 12–18 m high in its habitat, shoots yellowish pubescent; leaves ovate to oval-oblong, 3–10 cm long, acute, base rounded to cordate, thorny dentate on young trees, usually entire on older plants, bright green above and eventually glabrous, dull and yellowish pubescent beneath, persisting for 3–4 years on the plant; fruits solitary or paired, acorn ovate, 2–2.5 cm long, ¼ surrounded by the cup. SS 398–399; SPa 132–133; CQ 237 to 238; TO 209–210. Western N. America. 1887. z8 Plate 31; Fig. 56. #

var. *vacciniifolia* see: **Q. vacciniifolia**

Q. cinerea see: **Q. incana**

Q. cleistocarpus see: **Lithocarpus cleistocarpus**

Q. coccifera L. Kermes Oak. Evergreen shrub, scarcely over 3 m high, very densely branched, young shoots stellate-lepidote; leaves elliptic to oblong or ovate, stiff and hard, 1.5–4 cm long, base round to cordate, terminating in a thorn, with 3–5 thorns on either side (nearly *Ilex*-like), dark glossy green above, lighter beneath, glabrous on both sides, petiole 3–4 mm long; acorns usually solitary, half enclosed in the cup, this with reflexed, thorny scales. CQ 48; CFQ 21; BS 2: 469. Mediterranean coast from Spain to Syria. 1683. Earlier notable as the host plant of the Kermes scale (*Chermes*

ilicis), from which a valuable dye was made in the Middle Ages. Ⓕ Israel. z9 Plate 41; Fig. 52. #

Q. coccinea Muenchh. Scarlet Oak. Tree, 20–25 m high, occasionally higher, crown round and open, young shoots somewhat pubescent at first, then glabrous and yellow-brown, buds large, oval, brownish, apex pubescent; leaves oblong-elliptic in outline, 9–15(18) cm long, sinuate pinnately lobed, most with 7(9) outspread, somewhat dentate lobes, base normally truncated, occasionally broad cuneate, bright green and glossy above, lighter and glabrous beneath except for the small pubescent tufts in the vein axils, fall color scarlet-red, petiole thin, 3–6 cm long; fruits solitary, short stalked, acorn ovate, 1.5–2 cm long, nearly half enclosed by a top-shaped cup, scales appressed. DL 2: 56; GTP 160; SS 412–413; CQ 329–331. Eastern USA, moist areas. 1691. Ⓕ W. Germany, once grown on a trial basis. z4 Plate 30. ∅

'Splendens.' Fall color particularly bright red. Introduced around 1900 by the Knapp Hill Nursery of England and propagated primarily in Holland today. ∅

Q. conferta see: **Q. frainetto**

Q. congesta Presl. Deciduous tree to tall shrub, shoots tomentose; leaves ovate to obovate-oblong, to 14 cm long, sinuately lobed to pinnatisect, with 6–8 pairs of lobes, with indented venation, underside gray-green and remaining distinctly pubescent; fruit stalks to 4 cm long, scales of the cup linear-lanceolate, erect, but not appressed. S. France, Sardinia, Sicily. z7

Q. crassifolia Humb. & Bonpl. A rather large, deciduous tree in its habitat, shoots rather thick, more or less scabby, buds glabrous, glossy, 5 mm long, 3 mm thick; leaves large, elliptic, obovate or rounded, 12–14 cm long, 6–9 cm wide (nearly twice as large on young trees!), rather truncate at the apex, base more or less cordate, more or less entire to flat sinuately dentate, with 5–7 vein pairs, stiff leathery, dark green above, densely tomentose, brown when young, petiole quite short; acorns ripening in the first year, 15–20 mm long, ⅓ enclosed in a deep cup (= *Q. spinulosa* Mart. & Gal.). Central Mexico. 1939. z9

Q. crispata see: **Q. pubescens** var. **anatolica**

Q. crispula see: **Q. mongolica** var. **grosseserrata**

Q. cuneata see: **Q. falcata**

Q. daimio see: **Q. dentata**

Q. dalechampii Ten. Small tree, young shoots glabrous; leaves oblong to obovate-lanceolate, 8–13 cm long, deeply sinuate to pinnatisect, with 5–7 ovate to oblong-lanceolate, acute lobes on either side, base truncate to nearly cordate, finely soft pubescent at first, soon more or less glabrous; fruits grouped 1–3 on 5 mm long stalks, acorns ovate, 2 cm long, cup short pubescent, scales very thick and bumpy. SME 11; CQ 139 (3–6), 127 (6–9). Italy; from Naples to Sicily. 1900. z7 Also see: **Q. virgiliana.**

Q. × deamii Trel. (*Q. macrocarpa* × *Q. muehlenbergii*). Tree, similar to *Q. muehlenbergii*, but with more deeply lobed leaves and with 7–9 (!) pairs of acute lobes, finely tomentose beneath; fruit short stalked (= *Q. fallax* Palmer). USA; Indiana. 1916.

Q. dentata Thunb. Japanese Emperor Oak. Deciduous, round crowned tree, 20–25 m high, fast growing, bark thick, deeply furrowed, twigs very thick and gray tomentose; leaves obovate with a distinctly tapered base, 15–30(50) cm long, 9–14(30) cm wide, tough, coarsely sinuately lobed, with 8–12 vein pairs, dark green above, lighter and soft pubescent beneath, both sides gray tomentose when young, acorns usually in sessile clusters, oval-rounded, 2 cm long, cup hemispherical, the acorns usually half enclosed, upper scales lanceolate, outspread. CQ 67 to 68; GF 6: 386; EH 337; KIF 1: 53 (= *Q. obovata* Bge.; *Q. daimio* Hort.). Japan, Korea, Manchuria, N. and W. China. 1830. Attractive, very large leaved species; fruits as a young plant. Ⓕ Japan, Korea; erosion control. z6 Plate 32, 42; Fig. 64. ⌀

var. **oxyloba** Franch. Leaves narrower at the base, lobes sharply acuminate, triangular. CQ 70 (106). China; Yunnan Prov.

'**Pinnatifida**'. Leaves deeply incised, incisions reaching nearly to the midrib, lobes linear, margins irregular and finely crispate. DB 1969: 228 (= *Q. pinnatifida* Franch. & Sav.). Japanese cultivar. 1880.

Q. densiflora see: **Lithocarpus densiflorus**

Q. digitata see: **Q. falcata**

Q. diversicolor see: **Q. reticulata**

Q. douglasii Hook. & Arn. Blue Oak. Usually a 10–20 m high tree in its habitat, with a thick stem and a dense, globose crown, young shoots hairy tomentose, bark cracked into light gray scales; leaves deciduous, oblong, 5–12 cm long, margins broad and flat lobed, often only undulate or rather deeply lobed, with 2–3 lobes on either side, blue-green above, lighter beneath, venation

elevated and pubescent; acorns solitary, sessile, acutely ellipsoid, 20–25 mm long, tomentose, with a flat cup of thickened scales. AI 1258. Western N. America; California. z8 #

Q. dschorochensis see: **Q. iberica**

Q. durandii see: **Q. austrina**

Q. echioides see: **Lithocarpus densiflorus** var. **montanus**

Q. edulis see: **Lithocarpus edulis**

Q. ehrenbergii Kotschy. Deciduous shrub or a small tree, twigs outspread, young twigs brown tomentose; leaves leathery tough, oval-rounded or broadly elliptic, 5–8 cm long, lobes dentate to pinnately cleft (often resembling *Crataegus orientalis*), both sides densely pubescent when young, later nearly glabrous pubescent, rounded at the apex, base lightly cordate, with 5–6 vein pairs, petiole 1–2 cm long; fruit solitary, ovate, 3–4 cm long, 2–3 cm thick, cup hemispherical, the acorns half enclosed. CQ 54 (11–20). Asia Minor, Lebanon, Syria. 1880. Often erroneously labeled in cultivation! z9 Fig. 64.

Q. ellipsoidalis E. J. Hill. A tall tree, similar to *Q. palustris*, to 25 m high, bark gray and smooth or with flat grooves, young shoots tomentose; leaves elliptic, 8–12 cm long, deeply 5–6 lobed sinuate, the lobes coarsely dentate, base truncate or broadly cuneate, soon totally glabrous except for the pubescent vein axils beneath, petiole 3–5 cm long; fruit short stalked, acorns ellipsoid to nearly globose, 1–2 cm long, often half enclosed in the cup, scales appressed, light brown, finely pubescent. CQ 32 (1 to 13); SS 721; HH 144–145. NE. USA, on light soil. 1902. z3 ⌀

Q. engleriana Seemen. Evergreen, small tree, 5–7 m high, young shoots dense gray tomentose at first; leaves leathery, narrowly ovate to oblong, 6–10 cm long, slender acuminate, base rather rounded, with 9–13 vein

Fig. 57. **Quercus.** Left *Q. engleriana*; center *Q. lamellosa*; right *Q. oxyodon* (from ICS)

pairs, terminating in small, sharp teeth, dark green and glossy above, lighter and brownish woolly beneath, petiole 6–15 mm long; acorns grouped 1–3, ovate, 12 mm long, cup only enclosing the base, scales gray pubescent. CQ 88 (13–22), 89 (1–9); FIO 122 (= *Q. obscura* Seemen; *Q. sutchuenensis* Franch.). China; Hupeh, Szechwan Prov. 1900. z9 Fig. 57. #

Q. estremadurensis see: **Q. robur** ssp. **robur**

Q. × exacta Trel. (*Q. imbricaria* × *Q. palustris*). Occasionally occurs as a natural hybrid in the range of the parents; probably not in cultivation.

Q. fallax see: **Q. × deamii**

Q. fabri Hance. Deciduous tree, to 25 m high, twigs ash-gray to brownish, angular, only yellowish pubescent when young; leaves obovate-oblong to elliptic, 6–17 cm long, with 6–10 round lobes on either side, base round to somewhat auricled, gray tomentose beneath with reticulate venation, petiole 3–5 mm long; acorns cylindrical, 2 cm long, ⅓ enclosed by the sessile, hemispherical cup. CQ 99 (6–27). Korea, China. 1908. Hardy. z5 Fig. 68.

Q. faginea Lam. Portuguese Oak. Closely related to *Q. canariensis*. A semi-evergreen tree or a shrub, to about 20 m high in its habitat, bark thick, brown to gray, checkered with rectangular plates, young shoots gray or whitish pubescent when young; leaves quite variably formed, partly oval-elliptic, partly obovate-oblong, 3–7 cm long, 1.5–4 cm wide, obtuse to rounded, margins rather regularly dentate, base cordate or rounded to truncate, upper surface loosely stellate pubescent at first, later glabrous or gray-green, densely gray tomentose beneath, eventually glabrous; acorns about 2.5 cm long, oval-oblong, about ⅓ enclosed in the cup, ripening in the 1st year, paired or solitary, stalk about 1 cm long. SME 52; VQ 12; CFQ 13–15 (= *Q. lusitanica* Webb non Lam.; *Q. lusitanica* var. *baetica* Coutinho & Webb). Spain, Portugal. 1835. z9 Plate 31; Fig. 67. #

Q. falcata Michx. Tree, 10–20 m high or more, crown broad and rounded, open, twigs outspread, rust-brown pubescent when young; leaves elliptic-oblong in outline, 8–20 cm long, deep and sinuately lobed, with 3–7 acute, often sickle-shaped lobes, entire to sparsely dentate, terminal lobes much elongated, dark green and glossy above, gray to brownish pubescent beneath, pendulous, unattractively brown in fall, petiole 3–3.5 cm long; fruits nearly globose, 1–1.5 cm high, acorns enclosed up to ⅓ by the cup, this pubescent on the interior. SS 420; GTP 420–421; DL 2: 52; CQ 311 (6–13), 312–315; MOT 94–95; KTF 2 (= *Q. digitata* Sudw.; *Q. cuneata* Dipp.; *Q. triloba* Michx.). N. America. 1763. Dry sites. z7 Plate 30. ∅

var. **pagodifolia** Ell. Tree. 30(40) m high, young shoots tomentose until the 2nd year; leaves ovate to oval-oblong, 15–20 cm long, less deeply lobed, with 5–11 broad lobes, white tomentose beneath, occasionally reddish beneath; fruits solitary, acorn half enclosed in the cup. SM 235; EH 334; SS 722; CQ 315 (5–14); KTF 43 (= *Q. padoda* Raf.; *Q. pagodifolia* Ashe). SE. USA, in swamps and along river banks. 1904. z9 ○

Q. farnetto see: **Q. frainetto**

Q. fastigiata see: **Q. robur** ssp. **robur** 'Fastigiata'

Q. fendleri see: **Q. undulata**

Q. × fernaldii Trel. (*Q. ilicifolia* × *Q. rubra*). Natural hybrid, occasionally occurring among the parents; found in 1924 in Massachusetts and Virginia, USA.

Q. ferruginea see: **Q. marilandica**

Q. ferruginea hybrida see: **Q. × brittonii**

Q. fontanesii see: **Q. × hispanica**

Q. frainetto Ten. Hungarian Oak. Tree, to 30 m high, sometimes to 40 m, crown ovate at first, later rounded, young shoots pubescent only at first, later glabrous (!); leaves obovate to oblong-obovate, 10–18 cm long, tapered at the base and auricular, usually with 7 lobes on either side, the narrow sinuses almost reaching the midrib, the apical lobe usually further trilobed, dentate, dark green and eventually glabrous above, gray-green beneath, pubescent (!), petiole short, 5–10 mm long; fruits grouped 2–5 together, sessile, acorns oval-oblong, 2–2.5 cm long, ⅓ or more enclosed within the cup, scales appressed. SME 29; EH 335; CQ 73 (= *Q. conferta* Kit.; *Q. farnetto* Ten.; *Q. hungarica* Hub.; *Q. pannonica* Booth). Balkan Peninsula, Turkey, S. Italy. 1838. Very attractive, fast growing park tree. "Frainetto" is an accepted typographical error; the author meant to use the southern Italian name "farnetto". z6 Plate 32, 36; Fig. 77. ∅

Q. fruticosa see: **Q. lusitanica**

Q. fulhamensis see: **Q. × hispanica** 'Fulhamensis'

Q. gambelii Nutt. Deciduous tree, to 6 m high, often only a shrub, stoloniferous, twigs gray-yellow pubescent at first, later olive-brown; leaves obovate to oblong, 7–12 cm long, with 3–6 oblique, uneven lobes on either side, sinuses running to the midrib, base cuneate to rounded, dull green above, light gray-green beneath, short pubescent, petiole 1–2 cm long; fruits sessile, acutely ovate, acorns 1.5–2 cm long, half enclosed by the cup. SS 366–367; CQ 209 (1–5); MOT 12. S. USA; dry mountain slopes from Colorado to New Mexico. 1894. z6 Plate 34. ∅

Q. garryana Dougl. ex Hook. Oregon Oak. Deciduous tree, about 20(30) m high, often only shrubby in its mountain habitat, young shoots tomentose or pubescent, orange, glabrous in the 2nd year; leaves obovate-oblong, 8–14 cm long, with 3–5 coarse, broadly ovate, usually obtuse, entire or dentate lobes, the incisions running nearly to the midrib, base cuneate to round, glabrous and dark green above, lighter beneath and soft pubescent or glabrous, petiole pubescent, 1.5–2.5 cm long; fruits sessile to short stalked, acorns ovate, 2.5–3 cm long, ⅓ enclosed within the cup. SPa 128; SS 364–365; CQ 209 (10–20); TO 167–168. Pacific N. America. 1873. z7 Plate 34; Fig. 58 ∅

Q. genuensis see: **Q. warburgii**

Fig. 58. *Quercus garryana* (from Sudworth)

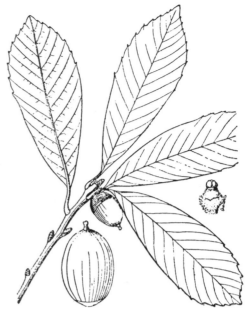

Fig. 59. *Quercus gilva* (from ICS)

Q. georgiana M. A. Curtis. Deciduous shrub, 1.5–4 m high, broad habit, twigs glabrous; leaves ovate to obovate, 6–12 cm long, acute, sinuate to pinnately cleft, lyre-form lobed, the apical lobes are largest and triangular, pubescent when young, later glabrous and bright green above, lighter beneath, slightly tomentose only in the vein axils, fall foliage orange and scarlet; fruits paired or solitary, on a very short, thick stalk, acorn oval, acute, about 1 cm long, nearly half enclosed within the hemispherical cup, this glossy on the interior. SS 425; CQ 318 (4–22). USA; Georgia, in sandy, gravelly areas. 1876. z6

Q. gilva Blume. Evergreen tree, to 30 m high in its habitat, bark dark gray, roughly furrowed, shoots dark brown, densely punctate with lenticels, current year's shoots densely rust-brown silky pubescent; leaves elliptic-oblong to oblanceolate, 8 cm long, 2 cm wide, acute, finely and simple serrate on the apical half, basal half entire, narrowly cuneate, leathery tough, light green above, brownish silky pubescent beneath, petiole 15 mm; acorns globose, 1.5 cm thick, half covered by the cup. KIF 1: 47. China; Chekiang Prov. z9 Fig. 59. #

Q. glaben see: **Lithocarpus glaben**

Q. glandulifera Bl. Deciduous tree, 7–15 m high, young shoots silky pubescent, the hairs directed forward; leaves obovate to narrowly ovate, 5–12 cm long, tapered to both ends, with 6–12 inward curving, gland-tipped teeth, 8–14 vein pairs, somewhat leathery, dark green and glossy above, bluish green and appressed silky pubescent beneath, petiole 6–12 mm long; fruits small, about 1.5 cm long, grouped 1–3 on a small stalk, acorn

half covered by a densely white pubescent cup. CQ 102–103; MJ 1974; DL 2: 37 (= *Q. serrata* Thunb. non auct.). Japan, Korea, China. 1893. z6 Plate 43. ⌀

Q. glauca Thunb. Evergreen tree, 12–15 m high, but usually only shrubby in cultivation; leaves narrowly ovate to oval-oblong, 7–13 cm long, dentate on the apical half, blue-green and appressed silky pubescent beneath, petiole 1.2–2.5 cm long; acorns ovoid, 1.5 cm long, cup flat, composed of silky, concentric rings. MJ 1966; CQ 19; FIO 126; KIF 1: 48. Japan, China, Himalayas. 1835. z8 Plate 42. # ⌀

var. *stenophylla* see: **Q. stenophylla**

Q. graeca see: **Q. macrolepis**

Q. gramuntia L. emend. Sm. Small, irregular tree; leaves evergreen, elliptic to nearly circular, 2.5–3 cm long and wide, with stout, outspread, thorny teeth, deep green above, densely woolly beneath, petiole short. CQ 87; EH 339 (= *Q. ilex* var. *gramuntia* [L.] Loud.). Discovered in the 17th century in the forest of the Gramont Estate near Montpellier in south France. Very closely related to *Q. ilex*. z8 #

Q. grisebachii see: **Q. trojana**

Q. grosseserrata see: **Q. mongolica** var. **grosseserrata**

Q. haas Kotschy. Tree, closely related to *Q. robur*, but the twigs are more slender, finely pubescent; leaves larger, 10(20) cm long, deeply lobed dull green above, yellowish tomentose beneath at first, later light gray-green and finely stellate pubescent, petiole tomentose (!), 2–6 mm long; fruits grouped 1–3 on a 4–6(10) cm long stalk, acorn elliptical, 4–5 cm long, about 2 cm thick, cup hemispherical, covering ⅓ of the acorn, the scales tomentose and tuberculate. SME 21; CQ 157. Asia Minor. 1870. As good a plant as *Q. robur*. z6 Plate 33; Fig. 71 ∅

Q. haliphoeos see: **Q. cerris** var. **haliphloeos**

Q. hartwegii see: **Q. warburgii**

Q. hartwissiana Stev. Deciduous tree, 7–9 m high, bark distinctly furrowed; leaves obovate-oblong, 7–12(15) cm long, usually obtuse to rounded at the apex, base asymmetrical, auricular or cordate, with 5–9 rather short, evenly rounded teeth on either side, dark green and glossy above, lighter beneath and sparsely pubescent on the venation, petiole yellow, 1.5–2.5 cm long; fruits grouped 2–5 on a common, 3–8 cm long stalk, acorn ovate, 2–3 cm long, cup like *Q. robur*, covering ⅓ of the acorn. SME 15; CQ 119–120 (= *Q. armeniaca* Kotschy). Bulgaria, Asia Minor to Transcaucasia. 1857. Often confused in cultivation with *Q. pubescens*! Ⓕ USSR. z6 Plate 33, 42.

Q. henryi see: **Lithocarpus henryi**

Q. × heterophylla Michx. f. (*Q. phellos* × *Q. rubra*). Tree, about 20 m high or more, young shoots glabrous, buds small, acute, glabrous; leaves quite variable on the same tree, oblong to elliptic, entire or with 3–5 teeth on either side, these often long acuminate, very unevenly outspread, eventually deep green and glossy above, occasionally brownish beneath, glabrous except for tufts in the vein axils, petiole 1.2–2.5 cm long; acorns nearly sessile, very similar to those of *Q. rubra*. CQ 338; EH 334. USA; first discovered near Philadelphia, later found in other locations. 1822. z6 Fig. 63. ∅

Q. × hickelii Camus (*Q. pontica* × *Q. robur*). Tall shrub, resembling *Q. pontica*, but taller, buds smaller; leaves usually obovate, gradually tapering to the auriculate base, to 15 cm long and 10 cm wide, partly more elliptic and with a cuneate base, with 12–16 pairs of lateral veins, margins coarsely dentate, the teeth obtuse and with a small mucro, glossy dark green above, lighter beneath, petiole very short. Developed in France, 1922. Less attractive than *Q. pontica*. z6

Q. hindsii see: **Q. lobata**

Q. × hispanica Lam. (*Q. cerris* × *Q. suber*). Semi-evergreen tree, 10–12(30) m, or only a shrub, bark thick, but only slightly corky, young shoots tomentose; leaves rather tough, oval-oblong, 4–10 cm long, acute, with 4–7 short, triangular teeth on either side, these with a small, pronounced tip, dark green and sparsely pubescent above, gray-green tomentose beneath, petiole 5–10 mm long; acorn oval-oblong, 3–4 cm long, cup covering about half of the acorn, scales long and reflexed. CQ 88; VQ 17; HW 82 (= *Q. pseudosuber* Santi; *Q. fontanesii* Guss.). S. France, Spain, Portugal, Italy, the Balkans, occurring sporadically in the range of the parents. 1830. z6 Plate 31; Fig. 55. ∅

Includes the following cultivars:

'**Ambrozyana**' (Simonkai). Semi-evergreen shrub or small tree, twigs gray tomentose, stipules abscising; leaves smaller than those of the species, obovate-oblong, 6–10 cm long, glabrous above, the lobe teeth terminating in a short, awl-like tip, glossy dark green above, gray tomentose beneath; flowers and fruits not observed. DB 10: 114–115 (= *Q. ambrozyana* Simonkai; *Q. cerris* 'Ambrozyana'). Discovered in Mlynany, Czechoslovakia in 1909. Parentage unknown, according to C. Schneider; perhaps *Q. cerris* × *Q. suber*. Plate 31, 43. ∅

'**Crispa**'. More compact habit, bark very corky; leaves nearly evergreen, only 5–8 cm long, limb densely crispate, densely white tomentose beneath. Loudon, Arboret. 3: 1715, 1717c, 1718 (= *Q. hispanica* var. *crispa* [Loud.] Rehd.). 1792. ∅

var. *crispa* see: '**Crispa**'

'**Dentata**'. Similar to 'Lucombeana' in foliage, but with a corky bark. Developed by Lucombe & Prince according to Bean, and not to be confused with 'Fulhamensis', which is occasionally mistakenly listed as 'Dentata'.

"**Dentata**" see: '**Fulhamensis**'

'**Diversifolia**'. Small tree, twigs ascending, bark very corky; leaves ovate, about 5 cm long, to 2 cm wide, usually with a broad, deep sinus in the middle of either side, with 1–4 lobes on the basal portion, apex entire to dentate, white tomentose beneath; cup hemispherical, scales partly appressed. EH 339: 71 (= *Q. hispanica* var. *diversifolia* [Henry] Rehd.).

var. *diversifolia* see: '**Diversifolia**'

'**Fulhamensis**'. Fulham Oak. Slender tree, crown rounded, branches thinner, less corky, young shoots gray tomentose; leaves only semi-evergreen, ovate, 7.5–9 cm long and 3–5 cm wide, acute, with 5–8 acute teeth on either side, white tomentose beneath, base round to somewhat auriculate; acorn not indented at the apex. CQ 78: 26; EH 335; Loudon, Arbor. 1710 (= *Q. fulhamensis* Zab.; *Q. hispanica* "Dentata"). Presumably originated as a seedling of 'Lucombeana' in the nursery of Whitley & Osborne in Fulham, England. Plate 31. ∅

'**Fulhamensis Latifolia**'. Similar to 'Fulhamensis', but with leaves larger, more elliptic, to 8 cm long and 6 cm wide, obtuse at the apex, teeth broad and shallow, gray tomentose beneath (= *Q. hispanica* var. *latifolia* [Henry] Rehd.). ∅

'**Heterophylla**'. Very closely related to *Q. cerris* var. *haliphloeos*. Leaves oblong, irregular and deeply lobed, occasionally with a deep, broad sinus in the middle of either side, reaching nearly to the midrib. Loudon, Arbor, 3: 1719 (= *Q. hispanica* var. *heterophylla* [Loud.] Rehd.).

var. *heterophylla* see: '**Heterophylla**'

var. *latifolia* see: '**Fulhamensis Latifolia**'

'**Lucombeana**'. Semi-evergreen, tall, conical tree, 25–30 m high, with bark somewhat corky; leaves semi-evergreen, more similar to *Q. cerris*, oval-oblong, 6–12 cm long, 2.5–4 cm wide, with 6–7(9) coarse triangular teeth on either side, glossy dark green and glabrous above, gray-green and tomentose beneath; acorn not indented at the apex, to 2.5 cm long, over half covered by the cup, basal scales reflexed, apical scales erect. CQ 1: fig. 35; EH 335: 23; Loudon, Arbor. 3: 1711–1714; BS 3: Pl. 56 (= *Q. hispanica* var. *lucombeana* [Sweet] Rehd.). Discovered by William Lucombe in 1765 at the nursery in St. Thomas, Exeter, England. Plate 31, 44. ∅

var. *lucombeana* see: '**Lucombeana**'

Q. humilis see: **Q. lusitanica**

Fig. 60. *Quercus hypoleucoides*

Q. hypoleuca see: **Q. hypoleucoides**

Q. hypoleucoides Camus. Silver-Leaved Oak. Semi-evergreen tree, 5–7 m high, occasionally somewhat higher in its habitat, crown obconical, young shoots rather stiff, gray tomentose in the 1st year, red-brown in the 2nd year, glabrous, glossy; old leaves dropping at bud break of the new, lanceolate to more elliptic, apex long drawn out, 5–10 cm long, 2 to 2.5 cm wide, entire or with a few undulate teeth, gray or whitish stellate pubescent above at first, later deep green and glossy, dense gray or white tomentose beneath, petiole 1 cm long; acorns solitary or paired, sessile, nut acutely ovate, 1 to 1.5 cm long, to ⅓ enclosed by the cup. SM 245; TO 226 (= *Q. hypoleuca* Engelm. non Miq.). SW. USA, in the mountains. z9 Fig. 60.

Q. iberica Bieb. Deciduous tree, closely related to *Q. petraea*, but with twigs totally glabrous; leaves obovate-lanceolate, 8–16 cm long, with 8–12 evenly sinuate lobes, base round to somewhat cordate, finely soft pubescent at first, later becoming glabrous, petiole 1.5–3 cm long; fruits grouped 1–3 together, nearly sessile or on 1.5 cm long stalks. SME 4; CQ 121 (= *Q. dschorochensis* sensu Wenz. non K. Koch). Asia Minor. 1890. z7

Q. ilex L. Holly Oak. Evergreen tree, to 20 m high, broad crowned, rounded, bark nearly totally smooth, scaly on older trunks, branches of older trees usually pendulous, young shoots gray tomentose; leaves leathery, quite variable in form, usually elliptic to narrowly ovate or oval-lanceolate, 3–7 cm long, acute, base round to broadly cuneate, either entire or more or less coarsely dentate, loosely whitish tomentose when young, but soon becoming dark green and glossy above, gray tomentose beneath, petiole 3 to 15 mm long; acorns grouped 1–3 together, 2–3 cm long, half enclosed within the cup. CQ 82 to 88; CFQ 17; BS 615. Mediterranean

region. Before 1580.⑤ Italy, Somalia, Yugoslavia, USSR, W. Pakistan. z8 Fig. 52. #

Includes a number of forms:

var. **angustifolia** DC. Leaves narrowly lanceolate, entire or nearly so. #

var. **ballota** (Desf.) A. DC. Leaves oblong, rounded at both ends, but the apex with a small mucro, 1.5–5 cm long; acorns large, edible, sweet (= *Q. ballota* Desf.; *Q. rotundifolia*). S. Spain, N. Africa. The fruits are roasted and eaten like chestnuts. Also see: var. **rotundifolia**. z10 #✂

'Crispa'. Very slow growing; leaves nearly circular, about 1.5 cm long, margins crispate dentate. In cultivation before 1838. #

var. *fastigiata* see: 'Fordii'

'Fordii'. Conical habit; leaves 2.5–5 cm long, narrowly oblong, tapered at both ends, margins undulate, entire or with a few teeth (= *Q. ilex fastigiata* Nichols.). Thought to have been developed in the Lucombe & Prince Nursery, Exeter, England. #

var. *gramuntia* (L.) Loud. see: **Q. gramuntia**

f. **microphylla** Trabut. Leaves elliptic, 2–2.7 cm long, 1.2 cm wide, acute or obtuse, thorny dentate. Algeria, in the mountains. #

var. **rotundifolia** (West.) Batt. Small tree, occasionally to 10 m high; leaves oblong, rounded at both ends, with small tips, 1.5–5 cm long, entire or sparsely dentate, dark green above, gray-white tomentose beneath; acorns cylindrical, 4–5 cm long, 1 cm thick, edible, almond flavored. CQ 87; CFQ 20 (= *Q. ilex* var. *ballota* A. DC.; *Q. ballota* Lam.). Spain, Portugal, Morocco. #✂

Q. ilicifolia Wangh. A dense, divaricate shrub or small tree, 4–6 m high, crown rounded, twigs densely light gray pubescent at first; leaves usually obovate, 5–12 cm long, usually with 2 lobes on either side, separated by a deep sinus, base broadly cuneate, entire or with some bristly teeth, dark green and glabrous above, whitish tomentose beneath, petiole 2–3.5 cm long, fall foliage yellow to red-brown; fruits oval, short stalked, acorns 1 cm long, about half enclosed in a shell-form cup. GTP 170; SM 253; SS 424; CQ 319; TO 397 (= *Q. banisteri* Michx.; *Q. nana* [Marsh.] Sarg. non Willd.). Eastern USA, on gravelly and sandy, often sterile soil, particularly in the mountains. 1800. z5 Plate 30.

Q. imbricaria Michx. Shingle Oak. Tree, to over 20 m high, conical crown when young, rounded with age, young shoots glabrous, light brown leaves elliptic to oblong, 10–18 cm long, entire (!), glossy dark green above, lighter and somewhat pubescent beneath, dark yellow to brownish yellow in fall; fruits short stalked, acorns nearly globose, 1–1.5 cm long, nearly half covered by the cup. SS 432; GTP 174; CQ 272 (6–19). Eastern N. America. 1724. z5 Plate 29; Fig. 61. ∅

Q. incana Bartr. non Roxb. Bluejack Oak. Small deciduous tree, 4–8 m high, often only a shrub, divaricate, shoots dark gray, short tomentose; leaves leathery, persisting for 2 years in its native habitat (!), oblong, 5–9 cm long, short bristly acuminate, base somewhat uneven and usually rounded, entire, eventually glabrous above or nearly glabrous or glossy,

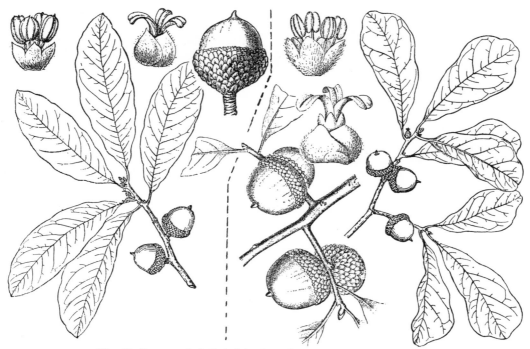

Fig. 61. **Quercus.** Left *Q. imbricaria;* right *Q. nigra* (from Sargent)

Fig. 62. *Quercus incana* (from Michaux)

white tomentose beneath, venation raised; fruits solitary, sessile, acorns ovate, about 1.5 cm long, covered nearly to the midpoint by the top-shaped cup. DL 2: 47; CQ 269 (14–16), 270; KTF 48; MOT 66–67; SNp 139 (= *Q. cinerea* Michx.; *Q. brevifolia* Sarg.). USA; Virginia to Florida. Also see: **Q. leucotrichophora** Ⓕ W. Himalaya. z8? Fig. 62. ⌀

Q. infectoria Oliv. Semi-evergreen tree, very similar to *Q. lusitanica,* but the young twigs glabrous or nearly so; leaves nearly elliptic, 4–6 cm long, rounded at the apex, base rounded to somewhat cordate, glabrous and glossy above, somewhat bluish beneath and eventually scattered pubescent, margins with 5–7 teeth on either side, petiole 8–12 mm long; fruits usually solitary, 1–1.8 cm long, cup hemispherical. CQ 108 (1 to 13); SME 49, 48. Asia Minor, Turkey, Greece. 1850. z9 Plate 31.

var. **boissieri** DC. Leaves larger, 6–9 cm long, usually with 5–7 teeth on either side, occasionally entire, 8–10 vein pairs, soft pubescent beneath, as are the young shoots and leaf petiole. CQ 110 (1–11) (= *Q. boissieri* Reuter). Syria, Asia Minor, Kurdistan, Cypress, Persia. z9

Q. × jackiana Schneid. (= *Q. alba × Q. bicolor*). Leaves similar to *Q. alba,* but softly pubescent beneath like *Q. bicolor,* the lobes acute or truncate; fruit stalk 1 cm long, acorns nearly like those of *Q. bicolor.* Occurs among the parents. 1916. ⌀

Q. kelloggii Newb. California Black Oak. Broad-crowned tree, branches thick and outspread, 15–18 m high, bark deep brown to nearly black, young shoots long pubescent at first; leaves oblong elliptic, 8–15 cm long, sinuate 7-lobed, occasionally only 5-lobed, the sinuses deep and narrow, the lobes coarsely toothed, pubescent at first, later glabrous, leathery tough, glossy above, glabrous to somewhat tomentose beneath, petiole 2–3 cm long; fruits single or paired, on about 1 cm long stalks, acorns ovate, 2.5–3 cm long, nearly half enclosed by a deep cap, scales loosely appressed, glabrous. SM 231; SS 416; SPa 145–147; CQ 333–334 (= *Q. californica* Coop.). USA; Oregon to California. 1878. z8 Plate 30. ⌀

Q. × kewensis Osborn (*Q. cerris* × *Q. wislizenii*). Evergreen tree, 10–12 m high (probably), crown ovate, twigs thin, ascending, young shoots stellate pubescent at first, light brown; leaves oval-oblong, 5–8 cm long, with 5–6 acute, coarse, triangular teeth on either side, base cordate to truncate, dull green and glabrous above, glossy green beneath (!), finely reticulate venation with scattered stellate pubescence, petiole 1.5–2 cm long; acorns to 2.5 cm long, ripening in the 2nd year. GC 90: 209; CQ 337. Originated by chance in Kew Gardens, 1914. z7 Plate 31. #

Q. koehnei see: **Q. × audleyensis**

Q. laevigata see: **Q. acuta**

Q. laevis Walt. Small tree, 6–12 m high, often only a shrub, crown irregular, young shoots glabrous; leaves obovate to triangular in outline, asymmetrical, 10–20 cm long, with 3–5 deep, irregular lobes terminating in bristly teeth, glossy green on both sides, with brownish pubescent vein axils beneath, petiole 1–2 cm long; fruits usually solitary, oval-rounded, acorns 2 cm long, about ⅓ enclosed in the stalked cup. SS 417; EH 333; CQ 30–38 (4–18), 309–311; TO 404 to 405; KTF 47 (= *Q. catesbaei* Michx.). SE. USA. 1834. z8 ⌀

Q. lamellosa Sm. Evergreen tree, huge in its habitat, to over 30 m high, young shoots tomentose; leaves variable in size and form, usually oblong to narrowly ovate, 12–25 cm long, acute, base rounded to broadly cuneate, distinctly and sharply serrate nearly to the base, glossy dark green above, blue-green beneath and pubescent at first, with 20–25 vein pairs, these indented above; acorns 1–4 in short spikes, flattened, to 2.5 cm thick, nearly totally enclosed within the cup, cup composed of 10 concentric rings. CQ 26; SNp 140; HAL 43. N. India; Nepal, Sikkim, Bhutan. 1802. Considered the most beautiful of all oaks. ℗ E. Himalayas. z9 Fig. 57. # ⌀

Q. lanuginosa see: **Q. cerris** & **Q. pubescens**

Q. laurifolia Michx. Laurel Oak. Deciduous tree, semi-evergreen in milder climates, 20(30) m high, young shoots thin, dark brown, glabrous; leaves oblong to obovate, 5–14 cm long, acute to nearly round, entire or with 1–2 small lobes or teeth on either side, base acute or nearly round, dark green and glossy above, lighter beneath and finely pubescent at first, but soon becoming glabrous, petiole yellow, 5–8 mm long; acorns solitary or paired, nearly sessile, oval-globose, 1–1.5 cm long, shell-form cup covering only the base. Rho 1031–1034; CQ 271 (1–9); MOT 61–71. S. USA. 1786. z8 Fig. 66. ⌀

Q. × leana Nutt (*Q. imbricaria* × *Q. velutina*). Large tree with an open rounded crown, fast growing, young shoots reddish, stellate pubescent; leaves oblong to obovate, 8–12(17) cm long, acute, occasionally also

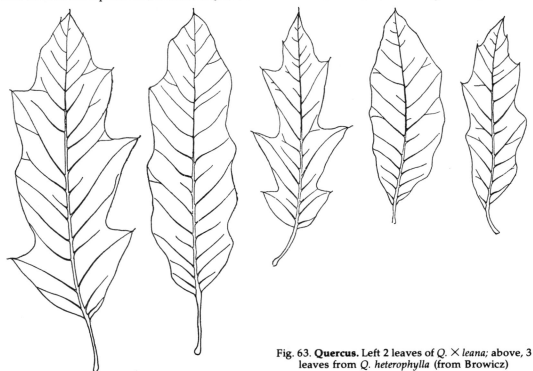

Fig. 63. **Quercus.** Left 2 leaves of *Q.* × *leana;* above, 3 leaves from *Q. heterophylla* (from Browicz)

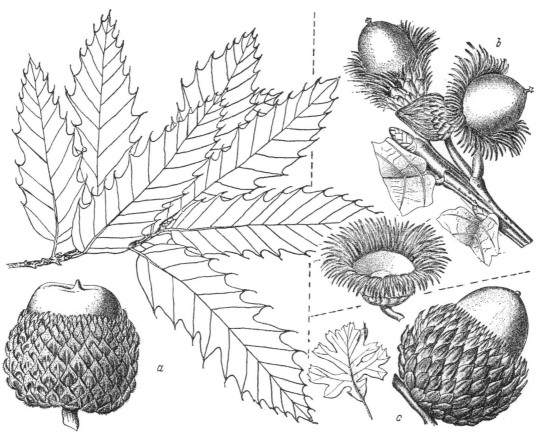

Fig. 64. **Quercus.** a. *Q. libani*; b. *Q. dentata*; c. *Q. ehrenbergii*
(from Browicz, Kotschy, Schneider, Shirasawa)

trilobed at the apex, otherwise with 1–3 shallow or deep lobes on either side, dark green and glossy above, loosely stellate pubescent beneath (!), rust-brown along the midrib, petiole 1.5–2 cm long, base round; fruits solitary or paired, acorns about 2 cm long, half covered by a deep cup. SS 434; CQ 341 (1–16); EH 334; JRHS 58: 54. Frequently occurs among the parents; USA. Before 1850. z6 Plate 29; Fig. 63. ⌀

Q. leucotrichophora A. Camus. Evergreen tree, to 25 m high in its habitat, bark exfoliating in large pieces (!), young shoots densely gray tomentose; leaves oblong-lanceolate, finely slender acuminate, base cuneate, 5 to 15 cm long, 3–5 cm wide, distinctly toothed nearly to the base, dark green above, quickly becoming glabrous, pure white tomentose beneath until leaf drop, with 8–12 vein pairs, petiole 8–15 mm long; acorns usually 1(3), ovate, 2.5 cm long, very short stalked, half covered by the cup. CQ 91 (= *Q. incana* Roxb.). Himalayas, Upper Burma, in the mountains between 1500–2500 m. Grows with *Rhododendron arboreum* in its habitat. z8 #

Q. liaotungensis Koidz. Tree, very similar to *Q. mongolica*, but the twigs are densely foliate, somewhat pubescent at first, but soon becoming glabrous; leaves obovate-oblong, 5–7(9) cm long, base tapered and round to cordate, tough, with 5–7 rounded lobes on either side, dull green above, glabrous, lighter beneath, normally glabrous, petiole 1–4 mm long; fruits ovate, 12 to 15 mm long, cup thin, scales small, smooth, somewhat concave (!). CQ 100 (= *Q. mongolica liaotungensis* Nakai). Manchuria, Mongolia, China. 1912. Hardy. z5 Fig. 68.

Q. × libanerris Boom (*Q. cerris* × *Q. libani*). Tree, similar to *Q. cerris*, but differing in the glabrous shoots, only the terminal buds with persistent linear scales (!); leaves large, with 10–16 flat lobes on either side, with rather long tips, smooth above, glabrous beneath; fruits not yet observed. z6

'Trompenburg' (van Hoey Smith). Only clone known to date. Shoots dense and finely gray pubescent at first; later nearly totally glabrous, dark gray-brown, finely punctate, buds obtuse, brown, finely pubescent to glabrous, surrounded by linear scales; leaves oblong, acute, 7–13 cm long, 2–4 cm wide, base broadly cuneate, with 10–16 oblique, forward directed lobes, these with a very short, straight or curved needlelike apex, glabrous or scattered stellate pubescent above, dull gray-green, rough to the touch, denser stellate pubescent and gray beneath, later with glabrous venation, petiole 7–12 mm. NDJ 21: 159 (4d). Discovered before 1957 by van Hoey Smith, Rotterdam, Holland. ⌀

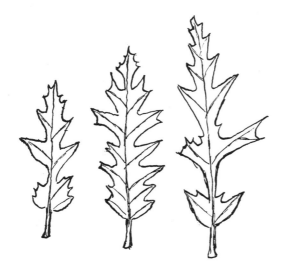

Fig. 65. *Quercus libani* var. *pinnata*

Q. libani Oliv. Lebanon Oak. Deciduous, delicately textured tree, 7–8(10) m high, finely and densely branched, the young shoots soon glabrous; leaves oblong-lanceolate, widest beneath the middle (!), 5–10 cm long, 1.5–3 cm wide, long acuminate, base round to somewhat cordate, bristly serrate, with 9–12 vein pairs, dark green and glabrous above, light green and nearly glabrous to finely short pubescent beneath; acorns solitary or paired, very large, broadly ovate, about 2.5 cm thick, ⅔ enclosed by the cup. CQ 52; SME 63; BS 2: 619. Syria, Asia Minor. 1855. Hardy and very attractive. z7 Plate 31; Fig. 64. ⌀

var. **pinnata** Hand. Mazz. Leaves much more deeply and irregularly incised. Iran; Kurdistan. Existence in cultivation uncertain.

Q. lineata var. *oxyodon* see: **Q. oxyodon**

Q. lobata Née. Deciduous tree, broad crowned, to 30 m high in its habitat, young shoots gray, short pubescent, glabrous in the 2nd year; leaves obovate, 6–8 cm long, with 4–5 deep, ovate, obtuse lobes on either side, dark green and stellate pubescent above, finely gray tomentose beneath, petiole 1 cm long, pubescent; fruits usually sessile, acorns conical and long acuminate (!), 4–5 cm long, ¼ enclosed within the cup, basal scales much thickened. SPa 123; SS 362; CQu 210 (1–21) (= *Q. hindsii* Benth.). USA; California. 1874. z9 Fig. 71, 82. ⌀

Q. × ludoviciana Sarg. (*Q. falcata* var. *pagodifolia* × *Q. phellos*). A large tree, young shoots pubescent; leaves quite variable on the same twig, some very similar to those of *Q. phellos* and then entire, 7–12 cm long, or asymmetrically lobed, then 12–15 cm long, with 1–4 pairs of long, ascending, triangular lobes, often also sickle-shaped, occasionally obovate, bright green on both sides, somewhat pubescent beneath, petiole 7–20 mm long; fruits oblong-ovate, round, 12 mm thick, ⅓ covered by the cup. CQ 339 (1–7) (= *Q. subfalcata* Trel.). S. and E. USA, but also naturalized in England. 1913. z7 Plate 29. ⌀

'**Microcarpa**'. Leaves oblong-lanceolate, 7–9 cm long, shallowly lobed. DL 2: 49 (= var. *microcarpa* [Sarg.] Rehd.). 1880.

Q. lusitanica Lam. (non sensu Webb!). Semi-evergreen dwarf shrub, scarcely over 0.30 m high in its habitat, in exceptional cases to 1.5 m, covering the ground mat-like, shoots yellowish tomentose; leaves elliptic, 2–5(9) cm

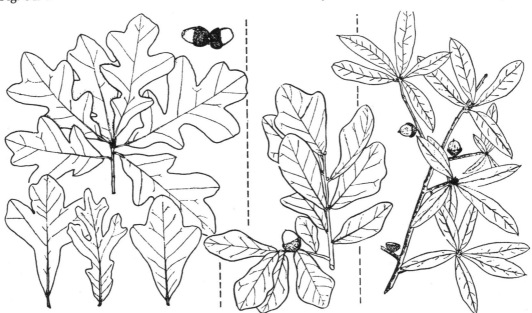

Fig. 66. **Quercus.** Left *Q. margaretta*; middle *Q. chapmanii*; right *Q. laurifolia*
(from KFT, WT and HHS)

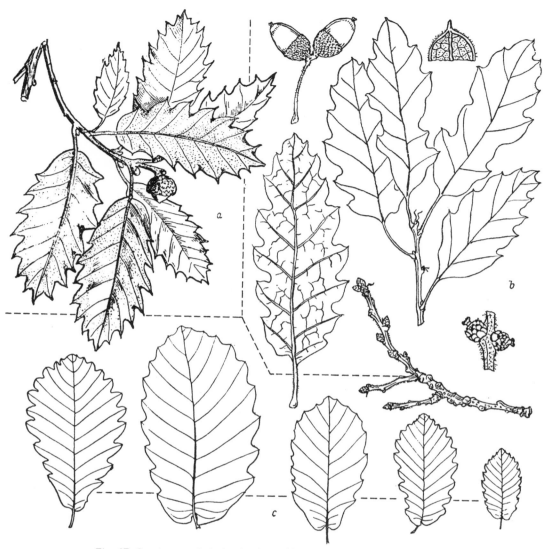

Fig. 67. **Quercus.** a. *Q. lusitanica;* b. *Q.* × *turneri;* c. *Q. faginea* var. *faginea,*
the various leaf forms (from VQ and Gard. Chron.)

long, obtuse, base round to cordate, with 4–7 thorny
teeth on either side, eventually very leathery tough, dark
green above, gray-white stellate tomentose beneath,
petiole 1–3 mm long; fruit about 1.5 cm long, stalk 12 mm
long, acorns ⅔ enclosed within a gray pubescent cup.
CQ 114; SME 47; VQ 11 (= *Q. fruticosa* Brot.; *Q. humilis*
Lam. non Walt.; *Q. lusitanica* var. *humilis* Elwes & Henry).
S. Spain, S. Portugal, Morocco. 1829. z9 Fig. 67.

var. *humilis* see: **Q. lusitanica**

Q. lusitanica sensu Webb see: **Q. faginea** Lam

Q. lyrata Walt. Round crowned tree, branches short,
twigs often pendulous, young shoots soft pubescent,
becoming glabrous in winter; leaves obovate-oblong,
14–20 cm long, lyre-shaped pinnately cleft, with 3–4
acute or obtuse lobes on either side, the 2 basal pairs

much smaller and usually triangular, the terminal lobes
usually further trilobed, dark green and eventually
glabrous above, underside white tomentose or green
and softly pubescent, base cuneate, petiole 1–2 cm long;
fruits sessile or short stalked, acorns nearly globose or
ovate, about 1.5–2.5 cm high, most fully enclosed within
the cup. HH 170–171; SS 374; CQ 218–219; TO 183.
USA, in swamps and wet spots in the central southern
states. 1786. z6 Plate 34; Fig. 82. ⌀

Q. × **'Macon'** (*Q. macranthera* × *Q. frainetto*). Foliage
more like *Q. frainetto*, but the leaf blade more obovate,
more acute and somewhat smaller; young shoots and
buds tomentose like *Q. macranthera*. JRHS 98: 113. Fig.
75. ⌀

Q. macedonica see: **Q. trojana**

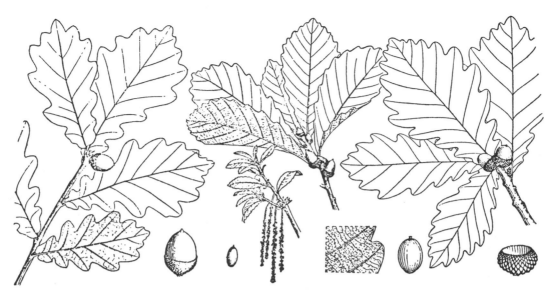

Fig. 68. **Quercus.** Left *Q. mongolica;* middle *Q. fabri;* right *Q. liaotungensis* (from ICS)

Q. macranthera Fisch. & Mey. Persian Oak. Tree, to 20 m high, young shoots thick, very distinctly gray tomentose, gradually becoming glabrous in the 2nd year, terminal buds with 2 cm long, linear, pubescent scales (!); leaves broadly obovate, tapering to the base, 6–18 cm long, rounded at the apex, with 8–10 ovate lobes on either side, the largest lobes are in the middle of the leaf blade (!), dark green and rather glabrous above, gray tomentose beneath (!!); fruits grouped 1–4, sessile, acorns about 2 cm long, half enclosed by the cup, scales lanceolate. CQ 72; SME 24. Caucasus to N. Persia. Before 1873. Ⓕ USSR. z6 Plate 32, 45. ⌀

Q. macrocarpa Michx. A broad crowned tree, 20–25(50) m high, bark deeply furrowed and scaly, young shoots stout and densely pubescent at first; leaves obovate, 15–30 cm long, irregularly lyre-shaped pinnately cleft with 5–7 lobes on either side, terminal lobes much larger than the others, dark green above, light gray-green to whitish beneath, short tomentose; acorns nearly sessile, elliptical, 3 cm long, half enclosed within the cup, cup limb with long, crispate, fringed scales (!). SS 371 to 373; GTP 177; CQ 219–233; TO 184–185. Atlantic Canada and USA, in lowlands. 1811. Highly valued in the USA as a pollution tolerant street tree. Ⓕ USA, in screen plantings. z4 Plate 34; Fig. 82. ⌀

var. **oliviformis** (Michx. f.) Gray. Leaves smaller, more deeply and irregularly lobed, the lobes narrow and often reaching nearly to the midrib; acorns elliptic-oblong, olive-shaped (!), smaller than those of the species, scarcely protruding from the cup. SS 373; CQ 224 (= *Q. olivaeformis* Michx. f.). Eastern USA, on the Hudson River. ⌀

Q. macrolepis Kotschy. Tree, 10–15 m high, bark dark brown, finely channeled, shoots rather thick and nearly smooth, yellowish or gray tomentose when young; leaves semi-evergreen, ovate to oval-lanceolate, 6–7 cm

long, 3–4 cm wide, acuminate, base lightly cordate, with 5–9 acute teeth on either side, both sides densely gray tomentose when young, later more or less glabrous above; acorns ovate, 2.5–4 cm long, 1.5–2 cm thick, somewhat indented at the apex, cup reaching slightly past the center of the acorn, 4.5–6 cm wide with the outspread scales. CQ 57 (1–19); SME 61 (= *Q. aegilops* Lam. non L.; *Q. graeca* Kotschy; *Q. aegilops* var. *macrolepis* Boiss.). Turkey, Crete, Greece to central Italy. Ⓕ Turkey, Iran, Iraq, for erosion control. z7 Plate 31. ⌗ ⌀

Q. magnifica albertii see: **Q. velutina albertsii**

Q. margaretta Ashe. Small deciduous tree, 6–8 m, or more commonly a tall shrub, usually surrounded about 3 m from the stem by a ring of 50 cm high shoots arising from underground, bark light gray, scaly, exfoliating into small, thick rectangular plates, shoots yellow-brown, glabrous (tomentose on the very similar *Q. stellata!*); leaves obovate, 5–12 cm long, 3–7 cm wide, usually with 2 rounded lobes and shallow sinuses on either side, base

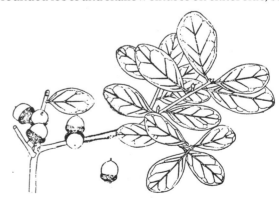

Fig. 69. *Quercus myrtifolia* (from WT)

cuneate; acorns paired or solitary, ripening in the first year, nut elliptical to ovate, 12 mm long, half enclosed within the cup. WT 51; KTF 50 (= *Q. stellata* var. *margaretta* [Ashe.] Sarg.). USA; Virginia to Texas and Florida. z6 Fig. 66.

Q. marilandica Muenchh. Blackjack Oak. A small, normally broad crowned tree, very slow growing and gnarled in appearance, 6–10 m high, with a thick, nearly black bark, shoots tomentose in the 1st year, brown in the 2nd, glabrous; leaves broadly obovate, usually truncate and bilobed at the apex, base tapered, 10–20 cm long, tough, deep green and glossy above, lighter and rusty pubescent beneath, brown or yellow in fall, petiole 1–2 cm long; fruits grouped 1–2, short stalked, long ovate, to 2 cm long, often striped, about half covered by the cup. GTP 169; SS 426–427; CQ 306–307; HH 154; TO 400–403; MOT 96–97 (= *Q. ferruginea* Michx. f.; *Q. nigra* Wangh. non L.). Eastern USA, in dry soil. 1723. z6 Plate 29. ⊘

Q. mas Thore. Deciduous tree, shoots, buds and leaf undersides silky pubescent at first, later more or less glabrous; leaves oblong-ovate, 8–18 cm long, sinuately lobed, with 8–10 pairs of rather narrow, forward directed lobes, without indented venation, petiole 15–25 mm; fruit stalks silky pubescent, scales of the fruit cup broadly ovate, obtuse, asymmetrically warty. SW. France, N. Spain. z7

Q. michauxii Nutt. Basket Oak, Swamp Chestnut Oak. Tree to 30 m high, bark light gray, scaly, young shoots pubescent at first; leaves obovate to more oblong, 10–16 cm long, acute, rather coarsely and regularly dentate, these obtuse and 10–14 on either side, bright green (!) and glossy above, gray tomentose or velvety beneath, petiole 1.5–3.5 cm long; fruits shorter stalked than the leaves (!), acorns oval-oblong, about 3 cm long, 1/3 covered by the cup, scales on the cup base much thickened, apical limb composed of stiff, fringed scales. CQ 176; SS 382–383; HH 174 (= *Q. prinus* L. p.p.). N. America, on swampy soil. 1737. Often listed as "*Q. prinus* L." after 1915. The modern nomenclature by Little, Fernald and others is followed here. z6 Fig. 71.

Q. mirbeckii see: **Q. canariensis**

Q. mongolica Fisch. ex Turcz. Tall tree, 25–30 m high, young shoots glabrous; leaves obovate to obovate-oblong, 10–20 cm long, obtuse, tapered and auriculate at the base, with 7–10 broad, usually obtuse, coarse teeth, dark green above, lighter and glabrous beneath or pubescent only on the venation, densely clustered at the shoot tips (!!), petiole 4–8 mm long; fruits ovate, 2 cm long, nearly sessile, acorns 1/3 covered by a thick cup, scales warty, the apical ones fringed-acuminate. CQ 94–96; DL 2: 82; NK 3: 11. E. Siberia, N. China, Korea, N. Japan; only occasionally found in Mongolia. 1879. Ⓕ NE. China. z4 Plate 35, 45; Fig. 68. ⊘

var. **grosseserrata** (Bl.) Rehd. & Wils. Twigs glabrous, warty; leaves somewhat smaller and more acute, 10–12 cm long, the teeth acute (!), these occasionally with a few small teeth; cup densely appressed scaly, not ciliate. CQ 101 (1–7); KIF 1: 54; MJ 1975 (= *Q. grosseserrata* Bl.; *Q. crispula* Bl.). Japan, Sachalin 1893. Plate 35–45.

var. *liaotungensis* see: **Q. liaotungensis**

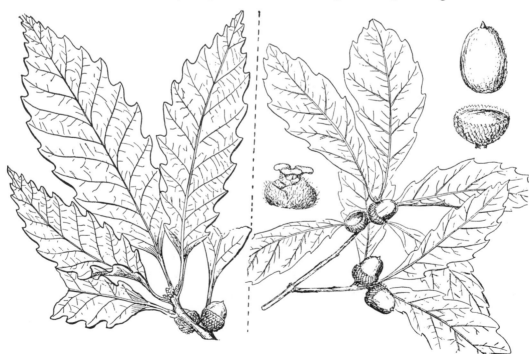

Fig. 70. **Quercus**. Left *Q. muehlenbergii;* right *Q. prinoides* (from Illick)

Q. montana see: **Q. prinus**

Q. muehlenbergii Engelm. Yellow Chestnut (Chinquapin) Oak. Deciduous tree, to 20 m high, taller in exceptional cases, young shoots reddish brown, pubescent at first, but soon becoming glabrous; leaves oblong-lanceolate to somewhat obovate-oblong, usually long acuminate, 10–16 cm long, base usually rounded, with 8–13 teeth on either side, these acute, and normally curved inward, dark green or yellow-green above, finely whitish tomentose beneath, petiole 2–4 cm long, mostly yellow; fruits usually solitary, stalk 5–6 mm long, acorns oval, 2 cm long, about ⅓ surrounded by the cup. GTP 186; SM 281; SS 377; CQ 178 (1–19); MOT 6–7 (= *Q. castanea* Willd; *Q. acutissima* [Michx.] Sarg. non Roxb.). USA. 1822. An attractive park tree. z5 Plate 35; Fig. 70. ⌀

Q. myrsinifolia Bl. Evergreen tree, 9–15 m high in its habitat, normally only shrubby in cultivation, young shoots thin, glabrous, warty in the 2nd year, new growth an attractive purple (!) or violet-brown and velvety pubescent; leaves lanceolate to oblong-lanceolate, long acuminate, base round to broadly cuneate, 5–12 cm long, serrate (often only on the apical half), glabrous on both sides, glossy green above, somewhat bluish beneath, petiole 2.5 cm long; fruits 2–4 in short spikes, acorns oval-oblong, 1.5–2 cm long, ⅓ covered by the glabrous cup. CQ 16; NK 3: 25; FIO 126; KIF 4: 2 (=*Q. bambusifolia* Fort. non Hance; *Q. vibrayeana* Franch. & Sav.). Japan; E. China. 1854. z8 Plate 29, 46. # ⌀

Q. myrtifolia Willd. Myrtle Oak. Small or shrubby evergreen tree, bark light gray, shallowly furrowed and flat checkered or transverse wrinkled; leaves elliptic to obovate or oblong, rounded, occasionally with small bristly tips, 2–5 cm long, 12–25 mm wide, base cuneate to round, entire to somewhat involuted, dark green and glossy on both sides; acorns grouped 1–2, sessile, globose, about 1 cm wide, about ¼ covered by the cup. KTF 54. USA; coastal region from S. Carolina to Florida and S. Mississippi. z7 Plate 29; Fig. 69. #

Q. nana see: **Q. ilicifolia**

Q. nigra L. Water Oak. Deciduous tree, 20 m high or more, crown rounded, symmetrical, shoots glabrous; leaves often persisting 2 years in its habitat, quite variable in form, normally obovate and slightly lobed at the apex, sometimes also ovate or oblong and entire, 3–7 cm long, tough, dull bluish green above, lighter beneath, glabrous except for the vein axils; fruits short stalked, acorns oval, 1–1.5 cm long, nearly half enclosed in the cup. SS 428; DL 2: 50; CQ 304–305; TO 308–314; MOT 77 to 79 (= *Q. aquatica* Walt.; *Q. uliginosa* Wangh.). S. USA; its habitat is in the *Taxodium* swamps, but does equally well on dry soil. 1723. Also see: **Q. marilandica** and **Q. velutina**. z6 Plate 29; Fig. 61. ⌀

Q. obovata see: **Q. dentata**

Q. obscura see: **Q. engleriana**

Q. obtusiloba see: **Q. stellata**

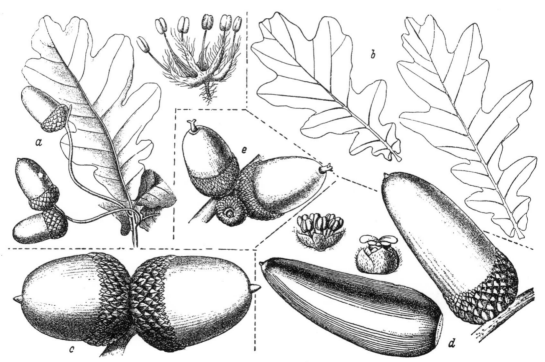

Fig. 71. **Quercus.** a. *Q. haas*; b. *Q. pedunculifolia*; c. *Q. michauxii*; d. *Q. lobata*
(from Browicz, Kotschy, Sargent, Schneider)

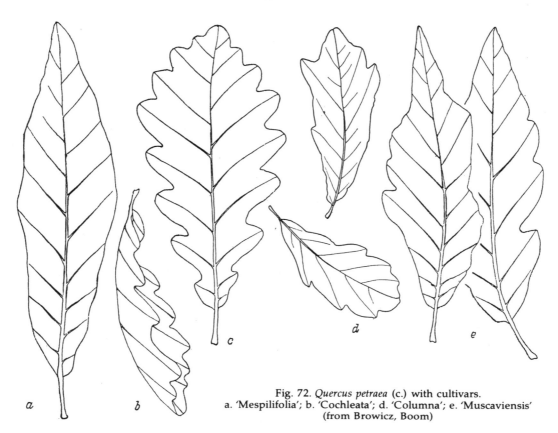

Fig. 72. *Quercus petraea* (c.) with cultivars.
a. 'Mespilifolia'; b. 'Cochleata'; d. 'Columna'; e. 'Muscaviensis'
(from Browicz, Boom)

Q. occidentalis see: **Q. suber** var. **occidentalis**

Q. olivaeformis see: **Q. macrocarpa** var. **oliviformis**

Q. oxyodon Miq. Evergreen tree, to 7 m high, twigs widely outspread, crown flat, young shoots quickly becoming glabrous; leaves narrowly oblong, long acuminate, base round, 7–20 cm long, distinctly dentate, the teeth curved inward, dark green and glossy above, blue-green and densely tomentose beneath, midrib yellowish beneath, as are the 12–20 raised vein pairs; acorns 8 mm long, cup with concentric rings, fruits sessile, several in small spikes on a 2.5–3 cm long axis. CQ 8; JRHS 58: 176; FIO 127 (= *Q. lineata* var. *oxyodon* Wenz.). China; W. Hupeh, E. Szechwan Prov. 1900. z9 Fig. 57. # ⌀

Q. pagoda see: **Q. falcata** var. **pagodifolia**

Q. pagodifolia see: **Q. falcata** var. **pagodifolia**

Q. palustris Muenchh. Pin Oak. Straight trunked (!), 20–40 m high tree, crown broadly conical, branches nearly horizontal, low ones more pendulous, covered with short stiff pin branchlets; leaves broadly oblong, wide pinnately cleft, 8–15 cm long, lobes acute, dentate, bright green on both sides, reddish in fall, petiole 2–5 cm long; fruits sessile to short stalked, acorn nearly hemisperical, 1–1.5 cm wide, ⅓ covered by a shell-form cup. SS 422–423; CQ 316–317, 318 (1 to 3). Eastern USA. Before 1770. Thrives in dry or moist soil. An excellent park tree

but should not be used in high traffic areas due to low hanging branches. Ⓕ W. Germany z5 Plate 30. ⌀

'Crownright' (Flemer). Narrowly conical habit. Patented. Introduced in 1969 (L. Beck). ⌀

'Pendula'. Branches more pendulous than those of the species.

'Reichenbachii'. New growth an attractive red (= f. *reichenbachii* Wendl.).

'Umbraculifera'. Crown globose; leaves glossy green, an attractive red in fall (= var. *umbraculifera* Chancerel). Before 1920.

Q. pannonica see: **Q. frainetto**

Q. pedunculata see: **Q. robur**
    —*bullata* see: **Q. robur** ssp. **robur** 'Cucullata'
    —*cochleata* see: **Q. robur** ssp. **robur** 'Contorta'
    —var. *heterophylla* see: **Q. robur** ssp. **robur** 'Fennessii'
    —*latimaculata* see: **Q. robur** ssp. **robur** 'Maculata'

Q. pedunculiflora K. Koch. A large tree, similar to *Q. robur*, young shoots glabrous; leaves obovate-oblong, 6–12 cm long, deeply sinuately lobed with 5–7 lobes on either side, these occasionally with 1–3 broad, obtuse teeth, base cordate, finely tomentose beneath (!), later rather glabrous, petiole 3–10 mm long; fruits grouped 1–3 on 3–6 cm long stalks; acorns 2–3 cm long, 1.5–2 cm thick, cup yellowish tomentose (!). SME 20; CQ 135 (= *Q. rhodopea* Vel.). Balkans to Asia Minor and Transcaucasia. 1870. Ⓕ Romania. z6 Fig. 71.

Fig. 73. *Quercus petraea* 'Laciniata' (from Browicz)

Q. petraea (Mattuschka) Liebl. Sessile Oak, Durmast Oak. Tree, to 45 m high, differing from most other oaks in the regular crown and central stem leading through to the tree top (percurrent); leaves obovate, 8–12 cm long, regularly short and round lobed, truncate to broadly cuneate at the base (!), petiole 1–1.6 cm long, yellow (!); fruits grouped, nearly sessile (!). SME 9; CQ 122–127; VQ 1; EH 92 (= *Q. sessilis* Ehrh.; *Q. sessiliflora* Salisb.). Europe to Asia Minor. An important forest tree in Europe and cultivated there for ages. Ⓕ W. Germany, Belgium, England, Hungary, Romania, Yugoslavia. z5 Plate 46; Fig. 72, 79.

Includes many forms:

'Albovariegata'. Leaves more or less white variegated. ∅

'Aurea'. Young shoots yellow; leaves yellow at first, later green, only the venation and the petiole remaining yellow. CQ 127 (6–9) (= var. *aurea* Schur.). Before 1857. ∅

'Aureovariegata.' Leaves more or less yellow-green.

'Cochleata'. Leaves tougher than those of the species, blade convex. First observed in Moscow, USSR. Before 1864. Fig. 72.

'Columna' (Hesse). Columnar habit; leaves narrowly oblong, flat and irregularly lobed, more gray-green. Resistant to powdery mildew! Fig. 72.

'Falkenbergensis' (Booth). Leaves 6–9 cm long, 4–6 cm wide, rounded at the apex, with 5–7 flat teeth on either side, base

emarginate to somewhat cordate (!), bright green above, whitish green beneath, venation densely pubescent.

'Giesleri' (Giesler). Leaves very long and narrow, partly entire, part slightly lobed. Boom, Ned. Dendr. 4th ed: 34m. Discovered by the head gardener (Giesler) at Glienicke near Potsdam, E. Germany. Introduced into the trade by Späth in 1885.

'Insecata'. Leaves of the primary shoots 20–25 cm long, but only 2–3 cm wide, irregularly incised and lobed, partly filamentous, dark green, occasionally whitish margined. MD 1913: 138; PDR 9: Pl. 4 (= f. *laciniata* Späth non Schwarz; f. *insecata* Rehd.). Before 1893. ∅

f. *laciniata* see: **'Insecata'** and **'Laciniata'**

'Laciniata'. Like the species, but the leaves more deeply incised, occasionally incised-lobed. SME 10 (3,4,7) (= f. *laciniata* [Lam.] Schwarz non Späth). Fig. 73. ∅

f. *louettei* see: **'Mespilifolia'**

'Mespilifolia'. Leaves of the primary shoots narrowly lanceolate, 8–18 cm long, margins undulate, without teeth, tough, deep green, petiole 3 cm long, leaves of the secondary shoots more normal. CQ 127 (12–15) (= f. *louettei* Kirchn.; f. *mespilifolia* Wallr.). Fig. 72. ∅

'Muscaviensis'. Leaves of the primary shoots often completely entire or nearly so, the secondary shoots more like the species. PDR 9: Pl. 4 (4a, b) (= f. *muscaviensis* Koehne). Fig. 72. ∅

'Pendula'. Shoots and twigs pendulous. A rare form. Before 1896.

'Pinnata'. Leaves deeply pinnatisect, somewhat analogous to *Q. robur* 'Pectinata'. SH 1: 102e (= f. *pinnata* Schneid.). ∅

'Purpurea'. Leaves brownish purple at first, later a dull dark reddish gray-green with red venation (= f. *rubicunda* Nichols.). ∅

f. *rubicunda* see: **'Purpurea'**

Q. phillyraeoides Gray. Evergreen, rounded, large shrub, also a small tree in its habitat, 5–9 m high, young shoots stellate-lepidote; leaves leathery tough, elliptic to obovate, 3–6 cm long, rounded to somewhat cordate at the base, apex obtuse acuminate to round, apical half shallow and obtuse dentate, glossy dark green and glabrous to the midrib above, lighter and similarly glossy

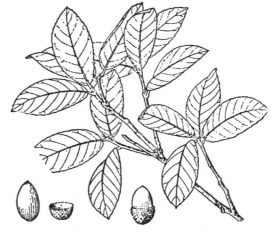

Fig. 74. *Quercus phillyreoides* (from ICS)

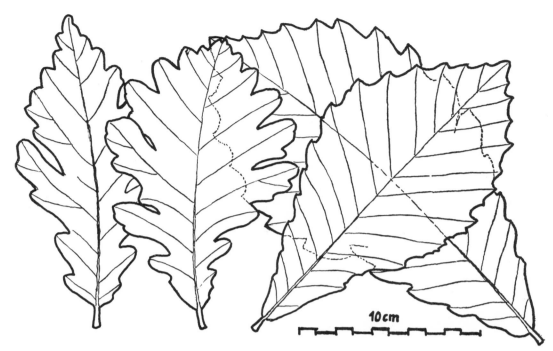

Fig. 75. **Quercus,** hybrids. Left 2, *Q.* 'Macon'; right 2, *Q.* 'Pondaim' (Original)

beneath, petiole about 6 mm long, lepidote except for part of the midrib; fruits ovate, 1.5–2 cm long. CQ 39; KIF 1: 51. China, Japan. 1862. z7 Fig. 74. #

Q. phillyreoides Gray. Evergreen, rounded tree, 20–30 m high, crown oblong-rounded, twigs red-brown, thin, glabrous; leaves linear-oblong to more lanceolate, entire (!), acute at both ends, 5–10 cm long, both sides thinly pubescent at first, later glabrous on both sides, glossy dark green above, lighter beneath, light yellow in fall; fruits solitary, short stalked, hemispherical, 1 cm long, only ⅓ covered by a flat cup. GTP 173; CQ 268; MOT 73–74. SE. USA; normally on moist to wet soil, along river banks, etc. 1723. z6 Plate 29, 41, 46. ∅

Q. pinnatifida see: **Q. dentata 'Pinnatifida'**

Q. platanoides see: **Q. bicolor**

Q. polycarpa Schur. Closely related to *Q. petraea.* Leaves obovate to oblong-lanceolate, 7 to 12 cm long, base somewhat cordate, with 5–8 shallow lobes on either side, softly pubescent beneath when young, eventually glabrous; fruits grouped 1–6 together, nearly sessile to short stalked, cup with distinctly hooked scales. SME 8; CQ 131 (7–8). SE. Europe, Asia Minor. 1900. Ⓕ Romania. z6

Q. 'Pondaim' (*Q. pontica* × *Q. dentata*). Tree-like habit (not shrubby like *Q. pontica*), buds less acute than those of *Q. pontica*; leaves broadly obovate, margins coarsely and acutely dentate, petiole very short. JRHS 98: 112. Developed around 1960 by J. R. P. van Hoey Smith, Rotterdam, Holland. Fig. 75.

Q. pontica K. Koch. Armenian Oak. Deciduous shrub or small tree, scarcely over 6 m high, twigs totally glabrous, brown-red, somewhat angular, terminal buds large, yellow-brown, angular; leaves somewhat leathery, variable in form, most broadly elliptic or obovate, 15–20 cm long, occasionally also larger, 6–10 cm wide, with 15–25 vein pairs, scabrous dentate, bright green and glossy above, light gray-green beneath, glabrous, midrib and the 1–1.5 cm long petiole yellow, glabrous, fall color dark yellow; acorns ovate, about 2 cm long, half enclosed by the cup. EH 339; CQ 71; SME 1. Caucasus, Armenia. 1885. z6 Plate 47. ∅

Q. prinoides Willd. Dwarf Chinquapin Oak. Deciduous shrub, to 2 m high (!), in its habitat occasionally a small, to 5 m high tree, shoots quickly becoming glabrous; leaves ovate-oblong, acute, 6–12 cm long, undulate toothed with 4–7 small, acute to obtuse teeth on either side, bright green above, glabrous, fine gray tomentose beneath, petiole 5–10 mm long; fruits solitary, sessile, acorns ovate, 1–1.5 cm long (!), about half covered by the cup, scales warty. GTP 189; SS 378; CQ 179 (1–18) (= *Q. chinquapin* Pursh; *Q. prinus humilis* Marsh.). Eastern USA, on dry sites. 1730. z5 Plate 35; Fig. 70.

Q. prinus L. Chestnut Oak. Tree, to 25 m high or more, bark dark and furrowed, young shoots pubescent at first or glabrous; leaves oblong, obovate to oblong-lanceolate, 12–18 cm long, acute, with 10–15 obtuse teeth, coarsely crenate toothed on either side, tapered only at the base and acute to round, glossy and yellowish green at the apex (!!), lighter beneath, finely tomentose

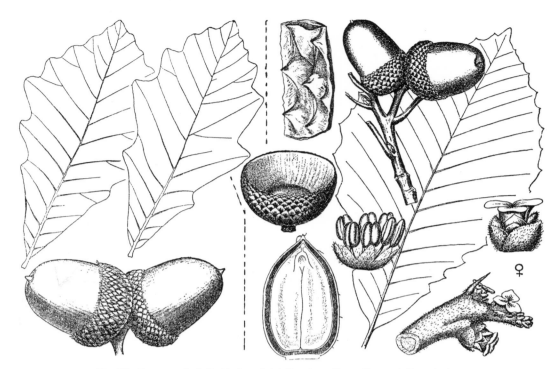

Fig. 76. **Quercus.** Left *Q. bicolor*; right *Q. prinus* (from Sargent, Browicz)

when young, later often nearly totally glabrous, orange in fall, petiole 1.5–3 cm long; fruits solitary or paired on about 2 cm long stalks (!), acorns ovate, about 3 cm long, nearly half enclosed within a tuberculate cup. SS 375, 376; HH 176, 177; GF 1: 510; CQ 177 (2–10); MOT 5 (= *Q. montana* Willd.; *Q. prinus* var. *monticola* Michx.). N. America, on dry soil (!). 1688. As with Little and Fernald, the name used here is that common in 1915 and not that cited by Willdenow, *Q. montana*, which originated in the USA before 1943. Also see: **Q. michauxii.** z6 Plate 35; Fig. 76.

var. humilis see: **Q. prinoides**

Q. pseudosuber see: **Q. × hispanica**

Q. pseudoturneri see: **Q. × turneri 'Pseudoturneri'**

Q. pubescens Willd. Downy Oak. Deciduous tree, 12–16 (20) m high, broad crowned (often wider than high), twigs soft pubescent; leaves obovate to elliptic, but quite variable in form, 5–10 cm long, round lobed, with 4–8 lobes on either side, dull dark green above and usually glabrous, light gray-green tomentose beneath, petiole 5–10 mm long; fruits grouped 1–4, sessile or on short common stalks, acorns ovate, 1.5–2 cm long, over ⅓ covered by the tomentose cup (= *Q. lanuginosa* Thuill.). S. Europe to Asia Minor. Cultivated for centuries. Ⓕ Mediterranean region. z7 Plate 33, 47; Fig. 77.

3 geographical subspecies can be distinguished:

ssp. **anatolica** O. Schwarz. Shrub or small tree, to 6 m high; leaves quite variable in outline, from nearly entire to deep pinnately cleft, 3–6 cm long, eventually glabrous; scales of the fruit cup nearly alike, acuminate. SEM 39; CQ 141 (= *Q. crispata* Stev.). Eastern part of the Balkan Peninsula and Crimea. Plate 33.

ssp. **palensis** (Palassou) O. Schwarz. Shrub or tree; leaves sinuately dentate to slightly lobed, 4–7 cm long, persistent tomentum beneath; scales of the fruit cup irregular, the basal ones short, thick and more or less connate, the apical ones longer, distinct, cuspidate. Pyrenees, N. Spain.

ssp. **pubescens.** Tree, to 25 m, or only a shrub, 3–4 m; leaves pinnately lobed, 6–12 cm long; scales of the fruit cup nearly alike, more or less obtuse. CQ 128; SEM 37–40; VQ 6. Occurs over the entire range of the species, except Spain and the Pyrenees.

'Pinnatifida'. Leaves 3–6 cm long, deeply lobed, the lobes obtuse, often coarsely dentate, tomentose beneath, venation silky pubescent. SME 37; SH 1: 122a (= var. *pinnatifida* [Gmel.] Spenner).

Q. pungens Liebm. Evergreen or semi-evergreen shrub, or also a medium-sized tree in its habitat, young shoots short tomentose to mealy pulverulent, eventually totally glabrous; leaves rather thick, very hard and stiff, elliptic to oblong, to 9 × 4 cm in size, acute or obtuse, base round to cordate, margins coarsely dentate or incised, the teeth always acute and with a mucro, margins undulate-crispate, not involuted, very glossy above and with hard stellate hairs (like sandpaper to the touch, therefore also "Sandpaper Oak"), densely rough tomentose beneath, petiole 1 cm; acorns 1 cm long. SW. USA, on dry sites in the mountains. z5 #

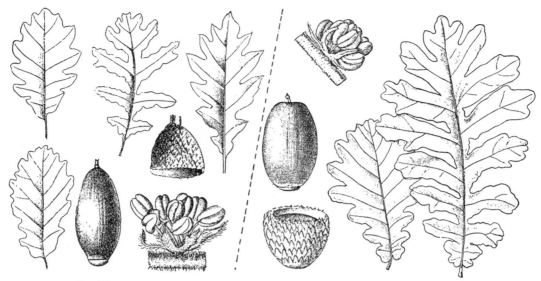

Fig. 77. **Quercus.** Left *Q. pubescens;* right *Q. frainetto* (from Hempel & Wilhelm)

Q. pyrami Kotschy. Erect, conical tree, bark deeply furrowed, young shoots ash-gray tomentose; leaves semi-evergreen, flat, somewhat dimorphic, spring foliage ovate to nearly circular, 4–7.5 cm long, with 7–8 shallow, somewhat bristly acuminate teeth on either side, fall foliage oval-oblong, acute, base round to truncate, deeply dentate or sinuately lobed, the lobes often deep and further toothed; acorn nearly elliptical, 3.5–4 cm long, 2–2.5 cm thick, cup half enclosing the acorn, hemispherical. SME 58; EH 335; CQ 56(9–15) (= *Q. aegilops* var. *pyrami* Boiss.). Asia Minor, Sicily, along the Pyramus River. z6 Ø|⚭

Q. pyrenaica Willd. Spanish Oak. Deciduous tree, stoloniferous, about 10–15 m high, often a bushy shrub, branches outspread, yellowish tomentose as are the buds; leaves obovate to more oblong, 6–15 cm long, base round to auriculate, short cuneate tapered, pinnatisect to pinnately cleft, with 5–7 teeth or sinuately open lobes on either side, pubescent above, but eventually rather glabrous and dark green or gray-green, yellowish tomentose beneath, petiole 5–10(15) mm long; fruits clustered 2–4, oval-oblong, 1.5–3 cm long, ⅓ to ½ covered by the hemispherical fruit cup, acorns floccose at the apex. SME 31–32; CQ 75 to 76; CFQ 6–7; VQ 4 (= *Q. "toza"* or *"tozza"*). Pyrenees, S. France. 1822. Ⓕ Portugal. z7 Plate 33. Ø

'Pendula'. Twigs pendulous; leaves usually with longer lobes, these usually with one or more large teeth (= *Q. toza pendula* Ottolander). Before 1879.

Q. × rehderi Trel. (*Q. ilicifolia × Q. velutina*). Shrub, occasionally a small tree, shoots very quickly becoming glabrous, with lenticels; leaves obovate, obtuse, cuneately tapered at the base, 6–11 cm long, with 2–3 flat lobes on either side, these somewhat bristly dentate (similar to *Q. ilicifolia,* but usually more markedly lobed), eventually finely tomentose to nearly glabrous beneath,

petiole 8–12 mm long. Rho 3: Pl. 29; CQ 343 (15–16). USA, occurs among the parents. Around 1905. z5

Q. repanda see: **Q. alba** f. **repanda**

Q. reticulata H. B. K. Evergreen tree or shrub, young shoots brown tomentose at first, later glabrous; leaves leathery tough, obovate to more oblong, 7–10 cm wide, obtuse to more rounded, margins undulate dentate, base round to lightly cordate, deep green and glabrous above except for the few scattered stellate hairs, yellowish stellate tomentose beneath, with about 8 vein pairs terminating in short bristles on the marginal teeth, with

Fig. 78. *Quercus reticulata*

raised reticulate venation, petiole 6 mm; acorns grouped 2–6 at the end of the 7 cm long stalk, nut about 1.5 cm long, about ¼ covered by a hemispherical, tomentose cup. MOT 40 (= *Q. diversicolor* Trel.). N. Mexico to SW. USA. 1883. z8 Plate 41; Fig. 78. # ⌀

Q. × richteri Baenitz (*Q. palustris* × *Q. rubra*). Tree, similar to *Q. palustris;* leaves deeply lobed, with 4–5 lobes on either side, base cuneate; fruit cup shell-form. Discovered in Silesia (now Czechoslovakia/Poland) before 1900. Later discovered in stands of the parents in the USA. z5

Q. rhodopea see: **Q. pedunculiflora**

Q. × robbinsii Trel. (*Q. coccinea* × *Q. ilicifolia*). Tree, to 12 m, similar to *Q. × rehderi*, but the leaves and twigs less pubescent and with a deep fruit cup, young shoots tomentose at first, like *Q. ilicifolia;* leaves similar to those of *Q. coccinea*, oblong-obovate, 10–12 cm long, sinuately lobed with 5 acute lobes, brownish tomentose beneath; acorns ovate, 1.5–2 cm long, half enclosed within the cup. Rho 24 (2). E. USA, among the parents. 1909. z5

Q. robur L. English Oak. A huge, strongly branched, irregular tree, 20–30(50) m high, stem neither (!) straight nor dominant throughout the crown, bark dark gray, deeply furrowed, young shoots glabrous; leaves obovate to oblong, 5–10(14) cm long, irregularly round lobed with 3–6 lobes on either side, base auriculate or cordate, petiole 4–8 mm long, deep green above, light blue-green beneath, glabrous; fruits usually grouped on a 5–12 cm long stalk, acorns 2–3 cm long, ⅓ covered by the cup. SME 17–19; CQ 142–152; HW 21; EH 81–91 (= *Q. pedunculata* Ehrh.). Europe, N. Africa, Asia Minor. Cultivated since antiquity and quite an important forest tree in Europe. Ⓕ W. Germany, Belgium, Romania, USSR. z5 Plate 47; Fig. 79. ⌀

This species is divided into 2 subspecies:

ssp. **brutia** (Ten.) O. Schwarz. Twigs and leaf undersides pubescent when young; leaves rather leathery, with long lobes and deep, narrow sinuses; calyx cup to 23 mm wide, thick and woody, scales wide, fused, but with distinct tips (= *Q. brutia* Ten.). S. Italy.

ssp. **robur** (including *Q. estremadurensis* O. Schwarz). Leaves thin, mostly glabrous, occasionally also somewhat pubescent when young, lobes usually broad and deep; calyx cup variable in size, usually about 12 mm wide, scales gray-green, connate except for the very small tips. Occurs over the entire range of the species.

Includes the following cultivars:
1. Habit forms
   a) ˙ Columnar and conical forms:
       'Cupressoides', 'Fastigiata', 'Fastigiata Cucullata', 'Fastigiata Purpurea', 'Granbyana'
   b) Weeping form:
       'Pendula'
   c) Globse form:
       'Umbraculifera'
   d) Twisted Dwarf forms:
       'Contorta', 'Tortuosa'

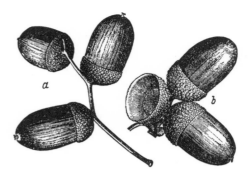

Fig. 79. Fruits of *Quercus robur* (a) and *Q. petraea* (b) (from Kerner)

2. Leaf forms
   e) Blade normal, venation red:
       var. *opaca*

   f) Margins finely incised:
       'Asplenifolia', 'Crispa', 'Cristata', 'Doumetii', 'Filicifolia', 'Pectinata', 'Strypemonde'

   g) Blade convex:
       'Cucullata', 'Cucullata Macrophylla', 'Fennessii'

   h) Leaves unlobed:
       'Salicifolia'

3. Variegated foliage forms
   i) Leaves red:
       'Atropurpurea', 'Nigra', 'Purpurascens'

   k) Leaves yellow:
       'Concordia'

   l) Leaves white to yellowish speckled:
       'Albomarmorata', 'Argenteomarginata', 'Argenteopicta', 'Argenteovariegata', 'Aureobicolor', 'Fürst Schwarzenberg', 'Maculata', 'Pulverulenta'

'Albomarmorata' (De Vos). Leaf form normal, but white marbled. NDJ 20: 5a, b, f. Probably discovered in Holland. Before 1867. Fig. 80. ⌀

'Argenteomarginata'. Leaves small, often oblique and flat lobed, rather broad at the apex, base cuneate, margin irregularly but continuously white. NDJ 20: 5g–h. First named in Holland in 1867. Fig. 80. ⌀

'Argenteopicta'. Young leaves white speckled and punctate, eventually dull dark green above and with light green spots, light gray-green beneath with distinctly white, translucent spots, 6–10 cm long, evenly sinuate, color not consistent. NDJ 20: 5d–e. Discovered before 1864 in Germany. Fig. 80. ⌀

'Argenteovariegata'. Twigs with white and reddish stripes; leaf form normally like the species, somewhat white variegated. NDJ 20; 5c (= f. *variegata* West). Cultivated in Germany since before 1810. Fig. 80. ⌀

'Asplenifolia'. Weak grower, twigs pendulous; leaves of the primary shoots irregularly linear, later leaves wider, the former irregular, the latter more regularly lobed, but the lobes always directed forward. SH 1: 126f (= f. *asplenifolia* Hartwig & Ruempl.; f. *diversifolia* Schneid.). Discovered before 1864 in Germany. ⌀

'Atropurpurea'. Slow growing, but eventually reaching 7–10 m

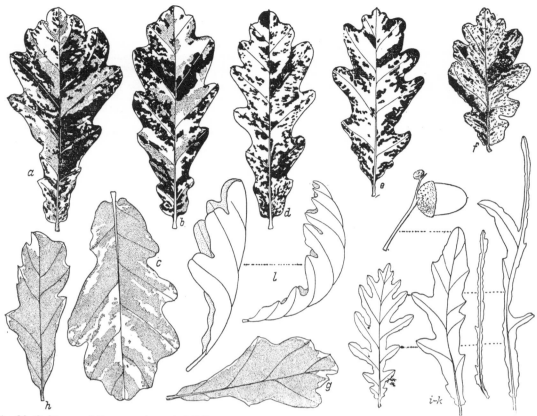

Fig. 80. Cultivars of *Quercus robur.* a,b,f. 'Albomarmorata'; c. 'Argenteovariegata'; d, e. 'Argenteopicta'; g, h. 'Argenteomarginata'; i.–k. 'Strypemonde'; l. 'Cucullata' (from Boom, altered)

high; only the young leaves deep purple, later becoming more brownish (= f. *atrosanguinea* Hort.). Before 1864. ∅

f. *atrosanguinea* see: **'Atropurpurea'**

'Aureobicolor'. Leaves of the primary shoots rather normal green with a few yellow spots, the summer shoots a beautiful yellow variegated, often turning reddish (= f. *aureo-bicolor* K. Koch; *Q. tricolor* Ottolander). Discovered in Germany before 1864. ∅

var. *comptoniaefolia* see: **'Filicifolia'**

'Concordia' (Van Geert). Shrub or small tree; leaves normally formed, golden-yellow, holds its color well throughout the summer. IH 537. Developed in Belgium by Van Geert before 1843. ∅

'Contorta' (De Vos). Weak growing; leaves convex, lobes normal, but twisted (= f. *contorta* Hort.; *Q. pedunculata cochleata* Späth). Discovered before 1874 by De Vos in Boskoop, Holland.

'Crispa'. Leaves small, margins distinctly crispate, dark green.

'Cristata'. Leaves small, densely crowded at shoot tips, plaited and twisted, asymmetrical. Discovered in 1917 in the Savernake Forest, England. ∅

'Cucullata'. Leaves rather long (!), convex, lobes less deeply incised, base cuneate. NDJ 20: 5(1); Gs 1926: 239 (= f. *cucullata*

Hartwig & Ruempl.; f. *monstrosa* Dipp.; *Q. pedunculata bullata* Hort.). Cultivated in Germany before 1864. Fig. 80.

'Cucullata Macrophylla'. Differs from 'Cucullata' in the stronger, conical habit and larger, wider, nearly "cap"-like bowed leaves, flat lobed (= f. *cucullata macrophylla* Hort.). Discovered in Germany before 1864. ∅

var. *cuneifolia* f. *laciniata* see: **'Fennessii'**

'Cupressoides'. Habit narrowly conical; leaves smaller than those of the other, much more common, conical form 'Fastigiata' (= f. *fastigiata cupressoides* Hort.). Discovered in Germany before 1867.

var. *dauvessei* see: **'Pendula'**

f. *diversifolia* see: **'Asplenifolia'**

'Doumetii'. Leaves deeply incised, nearly reaching to the midrib, the lobes twisted and undulate. RH 1894: 17. Developed in the Arboretum de Balaine, France just before 1900 and introduced by the Treyve Nursery, Moulins. Only slightly different than 'Filicifolia'.

'Fastigiata'. Pyramid Oak. Narrowly conical-upright, densely branched, all twigs erect (= *Q. fastigiata* Lam.; *Q. robur* f. *fastigiata* [Lam.] Schwarz; *Q. pyramidalis* Hort.). Very probably originated from a tree in the forest at Harreshausen (now Babenhausen), Germany, that was about 30 m high and 280 years old in 1874 (according to M. Willkomm, Forstl. Flora, p.

393, 1887). The tree was also described in 1821 by Bechstein (Forstbotanik, p. 214). In 1789 Lamarck (according to Willkomm, l.c.) reported Pyramid Oaks occurring in the western Pyrenees. This was confirmed in 1939 by A. Camus, a French oak specialist for the French portion of the western Pyrenees and parts of Spain. These oaks from the Pyrenees have more regularly lobed leaves and the undersides are more blue-green. The scales of the calyx cup are more numerous and more densely arranged. In this light, these oaks are an Atlantic race comprising most of the French plants in cultivation.

'Fastigiata Cucullata'. Columnar or conical form with erect, somewhat convex leaves (= f. *fastigiata cucullata* Hort.). Cultivated in Germany before 1864.

f. *fastigiata cupressoides* see: **'Cupressoides'**

'Fastigiata Purpurea' (Klenert). Pyramidal form, young shoots and leaves gradually greening to a very dark green. Developed by Klenert around 1895 in Graz, Austria from seed of 'Fastigiata'. ⊘

'Fennessii'. Leaf form quite variable, often convex, usually deeply incised and with rather narrow, entire lobes, not as regularly lobed as the similar 'Filicifolia'. SME 17 (8); CQ 152 (6–10); SH 1: 126a–b; PDR 9: Pl. 5 (2a–c) (= var. *cuneifolia* f. *laciniata* Schneid.; *Q. pedunculata* var. *heterophylla* Loud.). Developed and introduced around 1820 by the Fennessy & Son Nursery, Waterford, Ireland.

'Filicifolia' (Booth). Leaves deeply incised, lobes linear, curved forward with more or less crispate margins, petiole long. SME 18 (4); SH 1: 126b (= f. *filicifolia* [Topf] Schwarz; var. *comptoniaefolia* Camus). Discovered around 1850 in Germany and introduced by A. Topf in 1854.

'Fürst Schwarzenburg'. Weak growing conical form, densely foliate, spring growth a normal green, secondary growth (late July) nearly totally white at first; youngest leaves often pink, obovate, with 3–5 normally acute lobes on either side, tapered at the base, cordate auriculate, occasionally greening and then light green and rough above, more gray-green beneath, the whitish spots translucent from beneath (!), less so from above. MD 1913: 134–136. Originated as a seedling before 1884 in the Eisenberg Nursery (Czechoslovakia), introduced by Späth of Berlin, W. Germany. ⊘

'Granbyana'. Broadly conical habit. Generally cultivated only in England.

f. *holophylla* see: **'Salicifolia'**

f. *laurifolia* see: **'Salicifolia'**

'Maculata'. First growth in May a normal green, secondary growth in June a distinct yellow speckle on the leaves (= *Q. pedunculata latimaculata* Hort.). Introduced into the trade around 1867 by De Vos.

f. *monstrosa* see: **'Cucullata'**

'Nigra'. Leaves deep purple from bud break to late fall, light bluish pruinose. FS 1783–84. Cultivated in nurseries in Belgium and Germany before 1863. Plate 16. ⊘

f. **opaca** Schur. Leaves dark green, dull, petiole and venation red; fruit cup brown (= f. *rubrinervia* Hort.). Romania, Italy.

'Pectinata'. Very similar to 'Filicifolia', but the narrow, deeply incised lobes are straight, not crispate and often somewhat wider. Gs 1926: 238; SH 1: 126d; SME 18 (5) (= f. *pectinata* K. Koch). Around 1864 in Germany. Plate 47. ⊘

'Pendula'. Strong growing, annual growth up to 2 m, broad crowned, twigs distinctly pendulous; leaves falling early, not

persisting on the plant in winter (= var. *dauvessei* De Vos). First observed in England around 1788.

'Pulverulenta'. Very similar to 'Argenteopicta', but with a more vigorous, broad habit, leaves somewhat reddish on new growth, soon yellow variegated (seemingly pulverulent), later greening nearly like 'Argenteopicta'. ⊘

'Purpurascens'. Only the young leaves and shoots reddish, later nearly totally green. Described in 1808 by De Candolle from a tree found in a forest at Maule near Le Mans, France; but also observed at about the same time by Bechstein in the Lauchaer Forest, near Gotha, Thuringia (E. Germany). ⊘

f. *rubrinervia* see: f. **opaca**

'Salicifolia'. Habit broad and often picturesque, very slow growing; leaves oblong-elliptic, entire, totally without sinuses, petiole rather long; fruits long stalked. MD 1929: 107 (14); SME 18 (6) (= f. *salicifolia* K. Koch; f. *laurifolia* Hort.; f. *holophylla* Rehd.; f. *scolopendrifolia* Andrejeff). Known in Germany since 1873. ⊘

f. *scolopendrifolia* see: **'Salicifolia'**

'Strypemonde' (van Hoey Smith). Tree, slow growing, buds conspicuously thick; leaves quite variably incised, the more normal ones with small, apically oriented lobes, base auriculate, the abnormal leaves of the summer shoots are very narrow, with a few narrow lobes or totally without; fruits long stalked. NDJ 20: 5i–k. Developed in Holland around 1907 and distributed by van Hoey Smith of Rotterdam, Holland. Fig. 80. ⊘

var. *tenorei* see: **Q. virgiliana**

var. **thomasii** Wenz. Young shoots finely pubescent; leaves obovate, 10–12 cm long, 5 cm wide, long tapered at the base, with 3–5 lobes on either side, and occasionally with large, wide sinuses; fruits often solitary, stalked only 2–4 cm long, acorns 3.5–4 cm long and to 2.5 cm thick. CQ 151 (9–13); PDR 9: Pl. 5 (4) (= *Q. thomasii* Ten.). S. Italy (Calabria).

'Tortuosa'. Branches conspicuously twisted. MD 1919: Pl. 52. Discovered in Wildeshausen, near Oldenburg, W. Germany.

'Umbraculifera'. Nearly globose habit. Nederl. Fl. Pomona. Pl. 42 (3) (= var. *umbraculifera* Chancerel). Before 1879.

'Undulata'. Shrubby habit; leaves undulate-plaited, deep green. Cultivated in Moscow in 1864.

f. *variegata* see: **'Argenteovariegata'**

Q. pyramidalis see: **Q. robur** ssp. **robur 'Fastigiata'**

Q. × rosacea Bechst. (*Q. petraea × Q. robur*). Natural hybrid, intermediate between the parents. Twigs glabrous or very quickly so; leaves quite variable in form, usually obovate to nearly elliptic, base narrower than *Q. petraea*, also occasionally somewhat auriculate to cordate, petiole length intermediate between the parents; fruits on 3–5 cm long stalks, often also shorter, cup enclosing ⅓ of the acorn. CQ 159 (23–32) (= *Q. hybrida* Bechst.). Found throughout the range of the parents, but still not commonplace.

Q. rotundifolia see: **Q. ilex** var. **ballota**

Q. rubra L. Northern Red Oak. Round crowned, 20–25 m tall tree, occasionally higher, buds glabrous, to 8 mm long; leaves oblong, 12–22 cm long, with 7–11 sinuses on either side reaching to the middle of the blade, the lobes

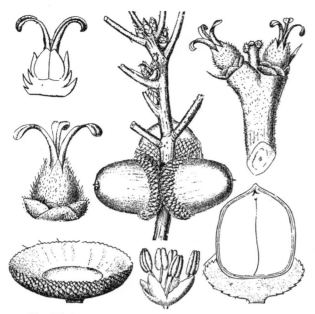

Fig. 81. *Quercus rubra*, flowers and fruit (from Sargent)

triangular to ovate, with a few irregular teeth, dull dark green above, lighter beneath, yellowish green or also gray-green, glabrous except for the brownish hair clusters in the vein axils, orange-red to scarlet or brown in fall; fruits short stalked, ovate, 2–3 cm long, only 1/3 or less covered by a flat cup. EH 314; SS 409–410; SM 241 (= *Q. borealis* Michx. f.; *Q. borealis* var. *maxima* [Marsh.] Ashe). N. America; Nova Scotia to Georgia, USA. 1724. A valuable, relatively fast growing park and forest tree. Before 1915, the name *Q. rubra* was generally accepted. Then through various interpretations, several dendrologists, principally Sudworth, preferred to use *Q. borealis* var. *maxima*. However, Fernald explained in 1947 that the old name should be given priority and that Du Roi's description of the species in 1771 typified that of Linnaeus exactly. Ⓕ Europe and USA. z5 Fig. 81. ⌀

'Aurea' (Van der Boom). Leaves golden yellow, primarily on the new growth, greening slightly toward fall. Discovered as a seedling in Oudenbosch, Holland around 1878. Comes rather true from seed. ⌀

'Heterophylla'. Leaves variable in form, oval-oblong to oblong-lanceolate or linear-lanceolate, frequently curved sickle-shaped, shallowly open dentate or with only 1–2 large teeth on either side. NDJ 21: 159 a, f, g. Discovered in Holland around 1892. ⌀

'Schrefeldii'. Leaf lobes often deeply incised and overlapping one another, incisions often very narrow, base sharply cuneate, tapered to the petiole. NDJ 21: 159k. Developed around 1890 in Muskau, E. Germany. ⌀

Q. × rudkinii Brt. (*Q. marilandica* × *Q. phellos*). Similar to *Q. phellos*, but the young shoots densely brown tomentose; leaves nearly sessile, quite variable (often even on the same shoot!), partly oblong and without dentation, apexes obtuse, base round to somewhat cordate, partly with some flat, obtuse lobes on either side, tough, pubescent when young, often rust-brown beneath. SS 437; CQ 339 (8–16). E. USA. Discovered in 1881 among the parents. A fixed hybrid (comes true from seed). z6

Q. × runcinata (A. DC.) Engelm. (*Q. imbricaria* × *Q. rubra*). Tree, young shoots pubescent at first, soon glabrous, buds ovate, 6 mm long, pubescent; leaves usually obovate-oblong, tapered to the apex, base round to truncate, 10–13(17) cm long, with 3–4 acute, often sickle-shaped lobes on either side, asymmetrical, often somewhat brownish pubescent beneath, petiole 1.5–2.5 cm long; fruits similar to *Q. rubra*. CW 342 (1–7) (= *Q. hybrida* Houba). Occurs among the parents in the USA. 1883. z5

Q. sadleriana R. Br. Low shrub, 0.5–2.5 m high, young shoots glabrous or nearly so; leaves semi-evergreen (abscising after the appearance of the new leaves in early summer), oval-oblong to broadly ovate, 5–14 cm long, obtuse, coarsely serrate, base cuneate, with raised pinnate venation, glabrous, stipules 10–15 mm long, silky; acorns solitary or several in the axils of the upper leaves, sessile, ripening the first year, cup thin, with thin, slightly warty scales, nut 15–20 mm long. TO 188; AI 1264; MS 83. Western USA; Oregon to California. z6

Q. salicina see: **Q. bambusifolia**

Q. × sargentii Rehd. (*Q. prinus* × *Q. robur*). A large tree, very similar to *Q. prinus*, but the leaves more dentate than lobed, the teeth not acuminate, base auriculate (!!); fruit cup with appressed scales. Gs 4: 26. Before 1830. z6 ⌀

Q. × saulii Schneid. (*Q. alba* × *Q. prinus*). Tree, to 15 m high, young shoots glabrous or scarcely pubescent; leaves similar to those of *Q. prinus*, but narrower at the apex, 20–24 cm long, about 10 cm wide, with 6–9 lobes on either side (!), less regular and deeper than those of *Q. prinus*, occasionally pubescent beneath; cup deeper. SS 361; CQ 226 (1–2). Occurs among the parents. 1883. z6

Q. schneckii see: **Q. shumardii** var. **schneckii**

Q. × schochiana Dieck (*Q. palustris* × *Q. phellos*). Tree; leaves oblong to more lanceolate, 6–12 cm long, entire or undulate or lobed, with small, often asymmetrical, acute lobes, glabrous above, underside without or with only small pubescent tufts in the vein axils; sterile. Discovered in 1894 in Wörlitz, Germany, but later found occurring spontaneously in E. USA. z6 Plate 29, 49. ⌀

Q. semecarpifolia Sm. Evergreen or semi-evergreen tree, to 30 m high in its habitat, young shoots soft rusty tomentose; leaves elliptic to oblong, 5–10 cm long, leathery, usually rounded at the apex, base more or less cordate, margins thorny dentate only on young plants, older plants entire, dark green above and quickly becoming glabrous except for the midrib, lighter beneath with a rust-brown tomentum, with 8–10 vein pairs, these forked before reaching the margin; acorns solitary or paired, on a short, pubescent stalk, ovate to

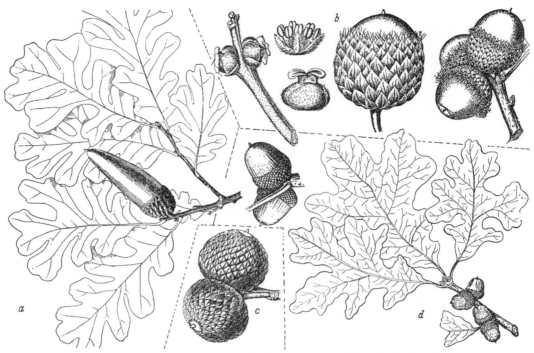

Fig. 82. **Quercus.** a. *Q. lobata*; b. *Q. macrocarpa*; c. *Q. lyrata*; d. *Q. stellata*
(from Sargent, Illick, Sudworth)

globose, 12–25 mm wide, cup flat, with erect, triangular, ciliate scales. CQ 36; SNp 142; BS 2: 914. China; Yunnan, Szechwan Prov., in the mountains at 4000 m. 1912. Ⓕ Himalayas. z8? # ⌀

Q. serrata Carruth. non Thunb. see: **Q. variabilis**

Q. serrata S. & Z. see: **Q. acutissima** Carruth.

Q. serrata Thunb. see: **Q. glandulifera** Bl.

Q. sessiliflora see: **Q. petraea**

Q. sessilis see: **Q. petraea**

Q. shumardii Buckl. Tree, similar to *Q. coccinea* and *Q. rubra*, usually not over 30 m high, bark finely scaly, buds usually glabrous and yellowish or light brown (!), shoots glabrous; leaves usually obovate to elliptic in outline, 10–15 cm long, 8–10 cm wide, usually with 7 lobes, these separated by wide sinuses reaching nearly to the midrib, the lobes often further lobed, deep green and glossy above, lighter beneath with fascicled pubescence, petiole 4–6 cm long; fruits short stalked, acorns ovate, 2–3 cm long, covered only at the base by a hemispherical to shell-like cup. CQ 327; EH 334; SS 411; KTF 59; MOT 85 to 86 (= *Q. texana* sensu Sarg. non Buckl.). Central USA. 1907. z5 Plate 30. ⌀

var. **schneckii** (Brit.) Sarg. Bark less rough, not as deeply furrowed; leaves not so variable as those of the species, less deeply lobed; fruit cup flat, hardly covering ⅓ of the acorn, with a few warty scales. CQ 327 (9–15); SM 224; BC 3310 (= *Q. schneckii* Brit.). USA; Illinois to Texas. 1897. ⌀

Q. sieboldiana see: **Lithocarpus glaber**

Q. spinulosa see: **Q. crassifolia**

Q. stellata Wangh. A dense, round-crowned tree, 10 (20) m high, bark brownish, deeply furrowed, young shoots tomentose, buds thick; leaves very tough (!), leathery thick, obovate, lyre-shaped sinuses, 10–20 cm long, base usually cuneate, occasionally rounded, with 2–3 broad, obtuse lobes on either side, the middle pair usually largest and normally with a few small lobes along the basal margin, separated from the basal lobes by a wide sinus, dark green and rough above, dull gray-green to whitish and stellate pubescent beneath, eventually becoming glabrous, petiole 1–2 cm long; fruits sessile, acorns about 2 cm long, about ⅓ to ½ enclosed by a top-shaped, tomentose cup. GTP 178; SM 269; CQ 216 (10–23), 217; TO 177–182; MOT 14–16 (= *Q. obtusiloba* Michx.). E. USA. 1819. z5 Plate 34; Fig. 82. ⌀

var. *margaretta* see: **Q. margaretta**

Q. stenophylla Mak. Evergreen tree, closely related to *Q. myrsinifolia*, but differing on the leaf underside; leaves lanceolate acuminate, serrate on the apical portion, 6–10 cm long, green above, blue-green and waxy beneath; acorns grouped 1–2 together, about 1.5 cm long, half enclosed by the cup, which is silky pubescent and with concentric rings. CQ 15 (13–20) (=*Q. glauca* var. *stenophylla* Bl.). Japan, Korea. z9 # ⌀

Q. suber L. Cork Oak. Evergreen tree, 6–10(20) m high, bark very thick, corky, young twigs yellow tomentose;

Plate 17

Prunus serrula
Photo: J. R. P. van Hoey Smith

Prunus mahaleb
in its native habitat near Sutjeska, Yugoslavia

Prunus subhirtella

Prunus subhirtella 'Fukubana'

Plate 18

Prunus serrulata 'Kanzan'

Prunus sargentii

Prunus serrulata 'Kiku-shidare-sakura'
All photos: Dortmund Botanic Garden

Plate 19

Prunus serrulata 'Shimidsu-sakura'
Both photos: Dortmund Botanic Garden

Prunus serrulata 'Hatasakura' in the Dortmund Botanic Garden, W. Germany

Plate 20

Prunus tenella
in the Dortmund Botanic Garden, W. Germany

Prunus tomentosa
in the Dortmund Botanic Garden, W. Germany

Prunus triloba 'Simplex'
in the Dortmund Botanic Garden, W. Germany

Prunus virginiana 'Aucubifolia'
in the Dortmund Botanic Garden, W. Germany

Plate 21

Prunus × *yedoensis* 'Ivensii'
in the Dortmund Botanic Garden, W. Germany

Prunus × *yedoensis* 'Shidare Yoshino'
in the Dortmund Botanic Garden, W. Germany

Prunus × *yedoensis*
Photo: Dr. Watari, Tokyo

Plate 22

Pseudopanax lessonii in Malahide Gardens, Ireland

Pseudopanax ferox in the Malahide Gardens, Ireland

Prunus spinulosa
in the Akasawa Forest Garden, Japan

Pseudopanax ferox, juvenile stage,
in the Royal Botanic Gardens, Kew, England

Plate 23

Pterostyrax corymbosa
in the Batumi Botanic Garden, USSR

Pterocarya rehderiana
in the Royal Botanic Garden, Edinburgh, Scotland

Pterostyrax hispida in the Berlin-Dahlem Botanic Garden, W. Germany
Photo: C. R. Jelitto

Plate 24

Ptelea trifoliata 'Aurea'
in the Dortmund Botanic Garden, W. Germany

Pseudocydonia sinensis in the Vilmorin Arboretum,
Verrières-les-buissons, France

Ptilotrichum spinosum
in the Royal Botanic Gardens, Kew, England

Pteroceltis tatarinovii
in the National Arboretum, Les Barres, France

Plate 25

Pyracomeles vilmorinii
in the Vilmorin Arboretum, Verrières, France

Pyracantha 'Golden Charmer'
in a Dutch nursery

Pyracantha angustifolia
in the Brissago Botanical Garden, Switzerland

Pyracantha coccinea 'Kasan'

Plate 26

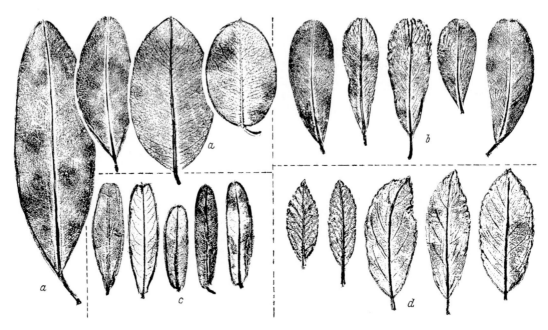

Pyracantha. a. *P. atalantoides;* b. *P. crenulata;* c. *P. angustifolia;* d. *P. coccinea*

Pyrus pyrifolia
in the Dortmund Botanic Garden, W. Germany

Pyrus syriaca in the Forestry Arboretum,
Charlottenlund, Denmark

Plate 27

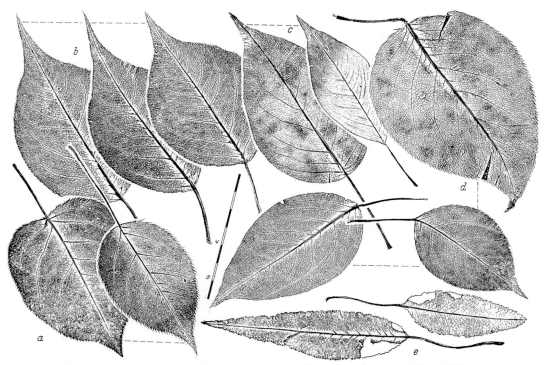

Pyrus. a. *P. ussuriensis;* b. *P. ussuriensis* var. *ovoidea;* c. *P. calleryana;* d. *P. pyrifolia;*
e. *P. korshinskyi* (most material from wild plants)

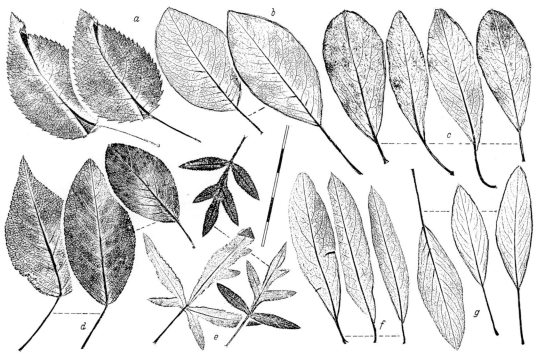

Pyrus. a. *P. betulifolia;* b. *P. nivalis;* c. *P. elaeagrifolia;* d. *P. pashia;* e. *P. regelii;*
f. *P. salicifolia;* g. *P. amygdaliformis* (most material from wild plants)

Plate 28

Pyrus × *canescens*
in the Royal Botanic Garden, Edinburgh, Scotland

Pyrus salicifolia
in the park of Birr Castle, Ireland

Quercus acuta in spring,
Jindai Botanical Garden, Tokyo

Quercus alnifolia
in Crara, Scotland

Plate 29

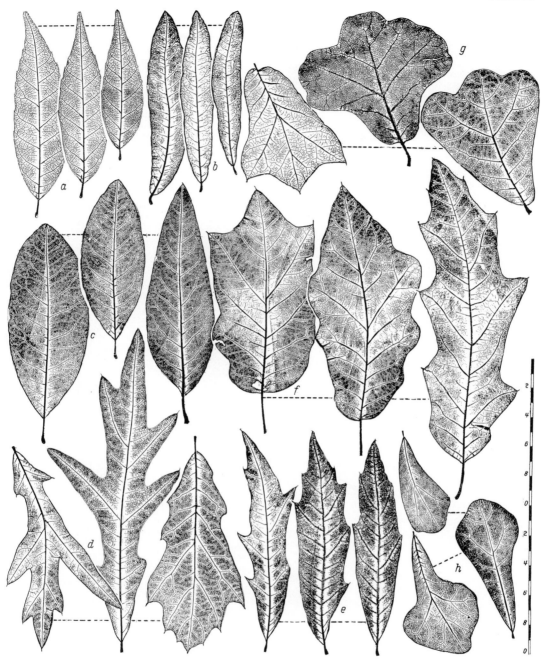

Quercus. a. *Q. myrsinifolia;* b. *Q. phellos;* c. *Q. imbricaria;* d. *Q.* ×*ludoviciana;* e. *Q.* ×*schochiana;* f. *Q.* ×*leana* (the leaf at left is from the original tree!); g. *Q. marilandica;* h. *Q. nigra* (most from plants in the wild, except d,e,f)

Plate 30

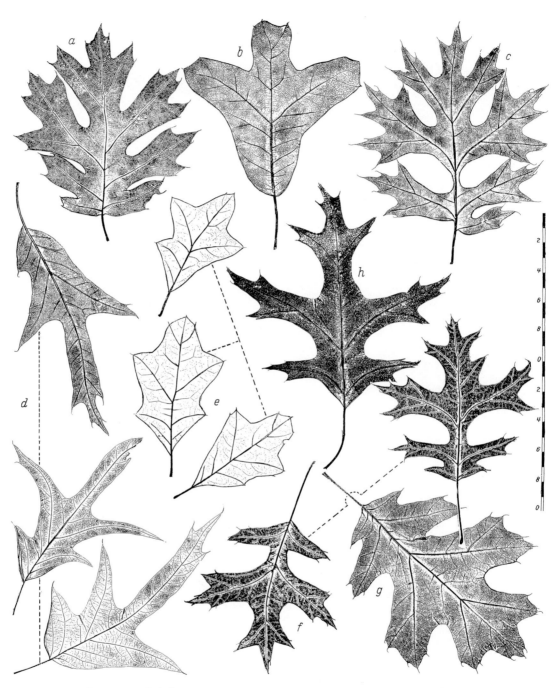

Quercus. a. *Q. kelloggii;* b. *Q. bushii;* c. *Q. shumardii;* d. *Q. falcata;* e. *Q. ilicifolia;*
f. *Q. palustris;* g. *Q. velutina;* h. *Q. coccinea* (most material from wild plants)

Plate 31

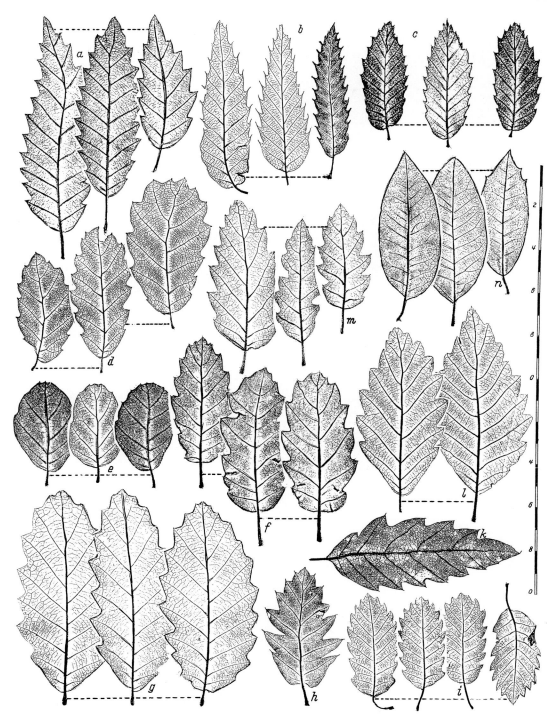

Quercus. a. *Q. castaneifolia*; b. *Q. libani*; c. *Q. trojana*; d. *Q. hispanica* 'Ambrozyana' (from original album); e. *Q. suber*; f. *Q.* × *kewensis*; g. *Q. faginea*; h. *Q. macrolepis*; i. *Q. infectoria*; k. *Q. hispanica*; l. *Q. hispanica* 'Fulhamensis'; m. *Q. hispanica* 'Lucombeana'; n. *Q. chrysolepis* (most material from wild plants)

Plate 32

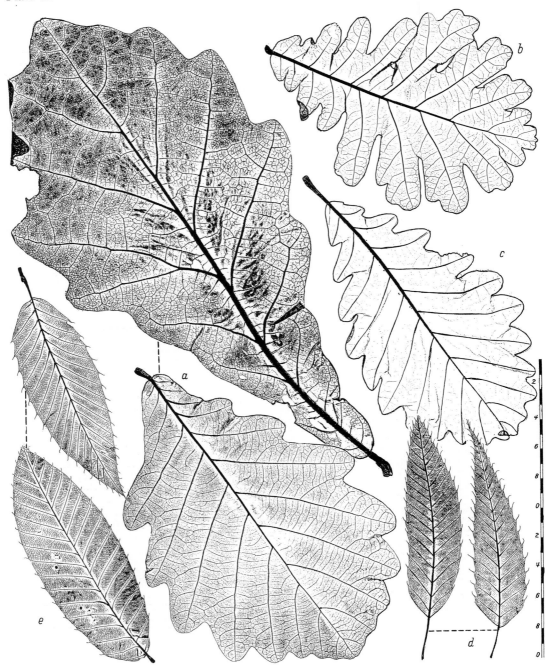

Quercus. a. *Q. dentata*, the largest leaf is from a young plant; b. *Q. frainetto*; c. *Q. macracanthera*; d. *Q. acutissima*; e. *Q. variabilis* (material from wild plants)

leaves ovate to oval-oblong, 3–7 cm long, acute, base usually rounded to lightly cordate, with 4–5 short teeth on either side, glossy dark green above, white-gray tomentose beneath, petiole 8–15 mm long; fruits oval-oblong, 1.5–3 cm long, cup distinctly cupulate, the apical scales elongated and erect or outspread. CQ 40–47; SME 55; HW 80–81; CFQ 18. S. Europe, N. Africa. Cultivated throughout history for cork. Stem nearly blood-red after the bark is removed, then becoming darker. The bark is removed every 6–7 years. Ⓕ Somalia, Portugal, France (S and SW), Ireland, USSR, USA (SW), Argentina, Brazil, Chile. z8 Plate 15, 31, 49; Fig. 52. # ∅

var. **occidentalis** (Gray) Arcang. Leaves generally evergreen, abscising in spring; fruits ripen in the 2nd year. CQ 48 (1–8) (= *Q. occidentalis* Gray). SW. Europe. 1826. As widely planted as the species. z9 # ∅

Q. subfalcata see: **Q. × ludoviciana**

Q. sutchuenensis see: **Q. engleriana**

Q. texana Buckl. Small tree, similar to *Q. shumardii*, scarcely over 10 m high, stem short, often branched to the ground, branches outspread, young shoots pubescent, as are the buds; leaves quite consistent in form (!), obovate, 6–9 cm long, usually 5 lobed, slightly pubescent on both sides, eventually glabrous and glossy above, underside more yellow-green and with hair fascicles, lobes deep, similar to those of *Q. coccinea*; fruits solitary, acorn elliptical-ovate, 1.2–1.5 cm long, cup top-form, light brown and tomentose. See also: **Q. shumardii**. SM 225; MOT 87–89; GF 7: 517; CQ 328. Texas. z8

Q. thomasii see: **Q. robur** ssp. **robur** var. **thomasii**

Q. tinctoria see: **Q. velutina**

Q. toza see: **Q. pyrenaica**

Q. tricolor see: **Q. robur** ssp. **robur** 'Aureobicolor'

Q. triloba see: **Q. falcata**

Q. trojana Webb. Small, semi-evergreen tree, 6–8 m high, often only a large, erect shrub, young shoots lepidote, gray to brown; leaves oval-oblong, leathery, 4–6(9) cm long, 1.5–2.5 cm wide, acute, rounded at the base, sinuately dentate, the 8–12 vein pairs somewhat exserted past the tooth tips, glossy dark green above, lighter beneath and short stellate pubescent or eventually totally glabrous; acorns ovate, 2.5–3.5 cm long, about 2 cm thick, over half covered by the cup, apical scales lanceolate and erect, the middle ones reflexed. CQ 57; SME 64 (= *Q. macedonica* A. DC.; *Q. grisebachii* Kotschy). Yugoslavia, Greece, Asia Minor. 1890. z8 Plate 31. ∅

Q. × turneri Willd. (*Q. ilex* × *Q. robur?*). A semi-evergreen tree to 15 m high, young shoots stellate tomentose; leaves obovate and elliptic, 6–8 cm long, acute or obtuse, sparsely sinuate dentate with 5–6 broad, obtuse but small tipped teeth, base rounded to somewhat auriculate, dark green above and eventually glabrous, eventually glabrous beneath except for the stellate pubescent venation, petiole 4–8 mm long,

pubescent; fruits grouped 3–7 on thin tomentose stalks, acorns ovate, about 2 cm long, half enclosed by the hemispherical, tomentose cup. SME 3; CQ 3; GC 133: 49. Developed around 1780 in the S. Turner Nursery in Holloway Down, Essex. z7 Plate 33; Fig. 67. ∅

'**Pseudoturneri**'. Leaves longer, narrower, 7–10 cm long, obovate-oblong, teeth usually longer and narrower, underside less pubescent, usually remaining green throughout the winter. EH 337; CQ 165 (3–9) (= *Q. pseudoturneri* Schneid.; *Q. aizoon* Koehne; *Q. austriaca sempervirens* Hort.). Presumably originated from the species in England around 1800. First propagated by Rivers in Sawbridgeworth. Plate 49. ∅

Q. uliginosa see: **Q. nigra**

Q. undulata Torr. Deciduous (also semi-evergreen in its habitat) shrub, occasionally a small tree, twigs more or less densely tomentose, rather glabrous and gray in the second year; leaves thick and leathery, elliptic to oblong, usually 4–6 cm long, 2–3 cm wide, usually acute, coarsely and irregularly dentate or lobed, with 2–4 large, triangular teeth on either side, scattered stellate pubescent and dark green above, somewhat glossy, loose or densely white stellate pubescent beneath, dull light green, petiole 5 mm; acorns solitary or paired, nearly sessile, but about 1.5 cm long, 1 cm wide, to ⅓ covered by a dense tomentose cup. MS 85 (=*Q. fendleri* Liebm.). SW. USA, in the mountains. z5

Q. vacciniifolia Kell. Broad, often also totally prostrate, evergreen shrub, twigs thin, flexible; leaves oval-oblong, 15–25 mm long, usually entire, dull glazed above, tomentose beneath; acorns ripen the second year, nut ovate, 10–15 mm long, in a flat, usually pubescent cup. AI 1268; SS 400; SPa 132 (= *Q. chrysolepis* var. *vacciniifolia* [Kell.] Engelm.). Western USA; from Oregon to California, on dry slopes in the mountains, often developing thickets. z6 #

Q. vallonea Kotschy. Large tree, 15–25 m high, in the Orient often only 5–12 m high on dry sites, bark finely scaly, young shoots yellowish or whitish tomentose until the 2nd year; leaves semi-evergreen, very tough and leathery, ovate to oval-oblong, obtuse to rounded at the apex, 5–8 cm long, base truncate, round or somewhat cordate, with 6–8 teeth on either side, both sides yellowish stellate pubescent at first, later only scattered pubescent and glossy, petiole 1–2.5 cm long; acorns globose, 2–3 cm thick, tomentose at the apex, cup enclosing ⅔ or more, with 5–6 cm wide scales. CQ 55 (1–8) (= *Q. aegilops* Boiss.; *Q. aegilops oliveriana* Tchihatchev; *Q. aegilops* ssp. *vallonea* A. Camus). Asia Minor, from the Cilician Taurus Mts. to Carmania (Iran). z9 ∅ ⚭

Q. variabilis Bl. Deciduous tree, 20–25 m high in its habitat, but usually much lower, young shoots pubescent at first, but quickly becoming glabrous; leaves abscising at bud break of the new leaves, oval-oblong or oblong-lanceolate, 8–12(20) cm long, 3–4 cm wide, acute or acuminate, base rounded to somewhat cordate, crenate, the 9–16(22) vein pairs terminating in 5 mm long bristles at the tooth tips, middle vein somewhat yellow, eventually somewhat leathery, dark green and

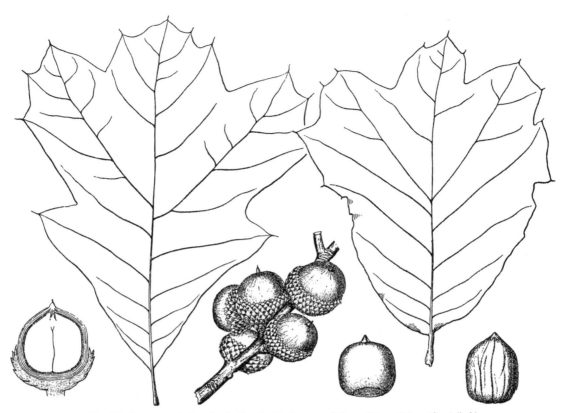

Fig. 83. *Quercus velutina* (only the fruit); leaves of the cultivar 'Magnifica' (left) and 'Nobilis' (right) (from Dippel, Sargent)

glabrous above, underside white tomentose (!!), petiole 5–25 mm long; fruits oval-globose, about 1.5–2 cm long, nearly totally surrounded by the cup, scales long and curly. CQ 61 + 225; NK 3: 10; FIO 125; CIS 19 (= *Q. chinensis* Bl.; *Q. bungeana* Forb.; *Q. serrata* Carruth. non Thunb.). N. China, Korea, Japan. 1861. Ⓕ USSR, China, Japan. z6 Plate 32; Fig. 53, 54. ⊘

Q. velutina Lam. Black Oak. Deciduous tree, 20–30 m high or occasionally taller, inner bark yellow (!), twigs tomentose in the first year, then becoming red-brown; leaves oblong-ovate to obovate, deeply and acutely lobed, 12–25 cm long, over half as wide, glossy dark green above, underside rust-brown with pubescent vein axils, tough, red-brown and orange in fall, petiole thick, 3–6 cm long; fruits short stalked, acorns ovate, 2 cm long, usually half enclosed by the cup. GTP 164; SS 414–415; CQ 320–322; MOT 99 (= *Q. tinctoria* Bartr.; *Q. nigra* DuRoi non L.). Eastern USA. Around 1800. z4 Plate 30; Fig. 83. ⊘

Variable species comprising several cultivars.

'Albertsii' (Alberts). Leaves very large, to 34 cm long and 25 cm wide, widest somewhat above the middle, incisions usually not deep (= *Q. magnifica albertii* Zab.). Discovered around 1863 by G. L. Alberts in Boskoop, Holland, introduced by De Vos. ⊘

'Macrophylla'. Violet new growth; leaves oval to broadly ovate, 16–25 cm long, 10–20 cm wide, with longer or shorter, bristly

tips, with 4 wide, triangular ovate lobes on either side, densely pubescent when young, later glabrous above, with dark red venation. DL 2: 50. Before 1892. ⊘

'Magnifica'. Leaves broadly obovate, obtuse to broad rounded at the apex, mucronate, 17–25 cm long, 12–20 cm wide at the apex, with broad, rounded sinuses, densely gray-yellow tomentose when young, later deep green above, glabrous and glossy, light yellowish green beneath with pubescent vein axils. DL 2: 58. Fig. 83. ⊘

'Nobilis'. Leaves rounded to obovate-oval, base short cuneate to rounded, to 20 cm long and 16 cm wide, with rounded terminal lobes and 2–3 short, broad rounded lobes on either side, gray tomentose when young, later deep dark green above with red-brown venation, light gray-green beneath and usually dense short tomentose. DL 2: 60. Before 1892. Fig. 83. ⊘

Q. virens see: **Q. virginiana**

Q. vibrayeana see: **Q. myrsinifolia**

Q. virgiliana Ten. Deciduous tree, very similar to *Q. pubescens*, young shoots densely gray tomentose; leaves oval-oblong, 8–16 cm long, cordate at the base, with 5–7 large lobes on either side, these 1–2.5 cm wide and commonly with 1–3 broad teeth, soft pubescent beneath at first, eventually normally blue-green and totally glabrous, petiole 5–25 mm long; fruits grouped 2–4 together on 3–8 cm long, pubescent stalks, acorns 3 cm long, cup hemispherical, fruits edible, sweet. SME 36;

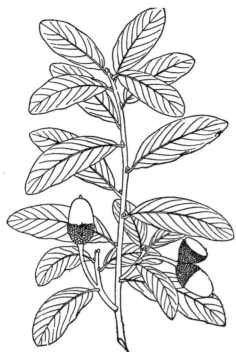

Fig. 84. *Quercus virginiana* (from Michaux)

CQ 139 (1); TO 189–190 (= *Q. robur* var. *tenorei* DC.; *Q. dalechampii* Wenz. non Ten.). SE. Europe to Italy. 1890. z7 ∅

Q. virginiana Mill. Evergreen tree, 18–20 m high in its habitat, branches often widespreading; leaves ovate to oblong, 4–7(12) cm long, entire or with a few small teeth at the apex, glabrous and glossy dark green above, gray-green and tomentose beneath, petiole 5–10 mm long, thick; fruits grouped 1–5 on a 1–8 cm long stalk, acorns ovate, about 2.5 cm long, ¼ covered by a top-shaped, tomentose cup. SS 394–395; BC 3318; GF 5: 486; DL 2: 39; CQ 167; MOT 47–49 (= *Q. virens* Ait.). S. USA. 1739. An excellent street and park tree. z8 Plate 50; Fig. 84. #

Q. warburgii Camus. Cambridge Oak. Tall semi-evergreen tree (the original tree planted around 1870 is about 18 m high), young shoots glabrous, eventually greenish brown; leaves leathery tough, persisting until bud break of the new leaves, obovate to oblanceolate, rounded, margins shallow and irregularly small lobed, basal half gradually tapered, occasionally slightly auriculate, 6–12 cm long, 3–7 cm wide, dull green and somewhat rough above, lighter green beneath, glabrous on both sides; acorns solitary or paired on rather thin stalks, nut 2.5 cm long, ovate, ⅓ enclosed in a hemispherical cup. (= *Q. genuensis* Hort.; *Q. hartwegii* var. *glabrata* Trelease). Origin unknown, but according to Bean, III, very probably distributed by the Smith Nursery, Worcester, England around 1870. Named for

the parent tree in the Botanic Garden of Cambridge University, Cambridge, England. z7

Q. wilsonii see: **Lithocarpus cleistocarpus**

Q. wislizenii A. DC. Round crowned, evergreen tree, 20–25 m high; leaves leathery tough, oblong-lanceolate to elliptic, 2.5–4 cm long, usually entire or thorny dentate on younger trees, glabrous and glossy on both sides; fruits short stalked, oblong-ovate, 2 to 3 cm long, acute, ⅔ surrounded by a top-form cup. SPa 141–142; SS 406; CQ 241 (24–42). California. 1874. z9 Fig. 56. #

Most *Quercus* species prefer a deep, fertile soil and dislike high alkalinity. However *Q. frainetto, libani, macranthera* and *canariensis* thrive on highly alkaline soils. *Q. palustris* does not require a swampy soil as the name might imply, as it grows well on dry sites. The evergreen species are generally rather susceptible to frost damage and therefore are better suited to warmer climates.

Lit. Camus, A.: Les Chénes; monographie du genre *Quercus*; Paris 1934–1949 (3 vols. text, 3 vols. of plates) ● Trelease, Wm.: The American Oaks; in Mem. Nat. Acad. Sci. **20**, 1–255, 1924 ● Andrejeff, W.: Über die homologen Reihen der Formen der Stieleiche, Traubeneiche und Flaumeiche; in Mitt. DDG 1929, 186–206 ● Kotschy, T.: Die Eichen Europas und des Orients; Vienna 1858–1862 (40 plates) ● Michaux, A.: Histoire des chênes de l'Amerique; Paris 1801 (36 plates) ● Schwarz: Monographie der Eichen Europas und des Mittelmeergebietes; Berlin 1936–1937 (text volume and 64 plates) ● Browicz, K.: The Oaks cultivated in Poland; in Rocznik Sect. Dendr. Polsk. **9**, 71–122, 1953 (in Polish with a summary in Russian) ● Houba, J.: Les Chênes de l'Amerique Septentrionale en Belgique; Hasselt 1887 (58 plates) ● Warburg, O.: Oaks in cultivation in the British Isles; Jour. RHS **58**, 176–189, 1933 ● Coker, W. W., & H. R. Totten: Trees of the southeastern States; ed. 3: *Quercus*, 110–158, 1945 ● Muller, C. H.: The oaks of Texas; in Tex. Res. Found. Contrib. **1**, 21–311, 1951 ● Palmer, E.: Hybrid Oaks of North America; in Jour. Arnold Arbor. **29**, 1–48, 1948 ● Vicioso, C.: Revision del genero *Quercus* en España; Bol. 51 Inst. Forest. Invest. Exp., 194 pp., Madrid 1950 ● Vasconcellos, J. de C. E., & J. do A. Franco: Carlvalhos de Portugal; in Ann. Inst. Sup. Agron. **21**, 1–135, Lisbon 1954 ● Schwarz, O.: *Quercus*; in Flora Europaea **1**, 61–64, 1964 ● van Hoey Smith, J. R. P.: Two promising *Quercus* hybrids in the Trompenburg Arboretum, Rotterdam; Intern. Dendrol. Soc. Year Book 1971, 97–99 ● van Hoey Smith, J. R. P.; Some new cultivars from the Arboretum Trompenburg; Jour. Roy. Hort. Soc. **98**, 205–210, 1973 ● Franco, J. do Amaral: Identification du *"Quercus lusitanica"* Lam.; Notul. Syst. Mus. Nat. Hist. Nat. Paris **15**, 212–220, 1956 ● Schwarz, O.: Über die Nomenklatur einiger europäischer Eichen; Mitt. DDG 1936, 220–225 ● Uiberlayova, E.: Die fremdländischen Eichen im Park von Pruhonice; in Wiss. Arb. Inst. Zierpflanzenbau CSSR Akad. Landw. Wiss. Pruhonice **1**, 37–81, 1961 (in Czechoslovakian with a German summary and 44 ills.)

RAPANEA Aubl. — MYRSINACEAE

Evergreen trees or shrubs; leaves alternate, simple; flowers small, polygamous or hermaphroditic, in sessile or stalked, axillary clusters; calyx small, 4–5 parted, persistent; corolla with 4–5 distinct petals; fruit a small, globose, fleshy or dry drupe. — About 200 species in the subtropics and tropics, but only the following 2 species are occasionally cultivated in milder climates.

Rapanea chathamica (F. v. Muell.) W. R. B. Oliv. Small, evergreen tree, to 5 m high, young shoots stiffly pubescent; leaves obovate, leathery tough, 2–6 cm long, 2–4 cm wide, incised at the apex, entire, pubescent on the midrib beneath and glandular punctate; flowers unisexual, tiny, petals 4, densely covered with red glands; fruits globose, 8 mm thick (= *Myrsine chathamica* F. v. Muell.; *Suttonia chathamica* [F. v. Muell.] Mez). Chatham Island. 1910. z9 #

R. nummularia (Hook. f.) W. R. B. Oliv. Dwarf evergreen shrub, procumbent, only a few centimeters high, shoots thin and wiry, lightly pubescent, red-brown; leaves densely arranged, broadly oval, 4–8 mm long, deep green, entire, occasionally incised at the apex, somewhat rugose above, underside densely translucent punctate; flowers tiny, yellowish white, solitary or in groups of three; fruits globose, blue, 5 mm thick (= *Myrsine nummularia* Hook. f.; *Suttonia nummularia* [Hook. f.] Mez). New Zealand, in the higher mountains. z9 #

Both species of easy culture in a suitable climate, but of only slight ornamental merit.

REAUMURIA L. — TAMARICACEAE

Small deciduous shrubs; leaves small, alternate, entire, more or less outspread, not scale-form; flowers solitary, terminal, corolla with ligulate tips at the base; stamens numerous; fruit a capsule with ringed pubescent seeds. — About 20 species from Asia Minor to Central Asia, most in the desert regions and the salt steppes.

Reaumuria hypericoides Willd. Shrub, erect to outspread, 20–50 cm high, shoots thin, often woody only at the base, glabrous; leaves linear to ovate or narrowly oblong, 6–20 mm long, entire, gray-green, glandular punctate; flowers purple, solitary, terminal, 2.5–3 cm wide, 5 petals, calyx deeply 5 lobed, May–August. BM 2057; BR 845; SH 2: 227. Syria, Persia, Armenia. z6 ☉

Cultural requirements unknown.

REEVESIA Lindl. — STERCULIACEAE

Evergreen shrubs or trees; leaves alternate, simple, 3 veined at the base; flowers in dense, terminal corymbs, white or pink, calyx tubular-campanulate, 4–5 toothed, petals 5, clawed, stamens attached to the style column, widely exserted past the petals; fruit a large, woody, 5 valved capsule. — 15 species, from the Himalayas to Taiwan.

Reevesia pubescens Mast. A small, evergreen tree in its habitat; leaves ovate to more oblong, 6–10 cm long, base broadly cuneate to somewhat cordate, underside brown tomentose; flowers pink, in large corymbs, style column 2.5 cm long GC 136: 104. E. Himalayas, SW. China. z9 # ☉

R. thyrsoidea Lindl. Evergreen shrub, a small tree in its habitat; leaves oval-oblong to more lanceolate, 5–12 cm long, to 5 cm wide, acute, base rounded; inflorescence 5–7 cm wide, flowers 12 mm wide, white to cream color, fragrant, style column exserted about 2 cm past the petals, July. HKT 85; BM 4199; DRHS 1748. S. China. 1826. z9 Plate 50. # ☉

Suitable only for very warm regions!

REHDERODENDRON Hu — STYRACACEAE

Deciduous trees or tall shrubs, twigs stellate pubescent; leaves simple, alternate, paper thin, finely serrate, stipules on the apical leaves; flowers in axillary, leafless panicles or racemes; calyx 5 lobed, petals 5, occasionally connate only at the base, ovaries totally inferior (!); fruit a large woody, ribbed, oblong to elliptic capsule with 1–3 seeds. — 9 species in W. China.

Fig. 85. *Rehderodendron hui*. a. flowering twig; b. fruiting twig; c. ovary, in longitudinal section and d. in cross section; e. stamens (from Hu)

Rehderodendron hui Chun. Deciduous shrub, about 2.5 m high; leaves elliptic, acute at both ends, 8–10 cm long, finely dentate, petiole 1–2 cm long; flowers in panicles of about 7, corolla about 4 cm wide, white; fruits ellipsoid to obovoid, 3 cm long, endocarp woody (!), shell smooth. NF 12: 155; CIS 246. China; NE. Kwangtung Prov. Probably not in cultivation. The most decorative species. z7 Fig. 85. ✣ ⚭

R. macrocarpum Hu. Tree, to 9 m high, young shoots glabrous, leaves elliptic to oval-oblong, 8–11 cm long, acute to acuminate, base cuneate, finely serrate, venation stellate pubescent beneath, petiole 1–1.5 cm long; flowers 6–7 in racemes, very fragrant, appearing before the leaves, corolla 2.4 cm wide, petals elliptic-oblong, 12 mm long, white, finely pubescent on both sides, April–May; fruits oblong, 6–7 cm long, glabrous, with 8–10 ribs. JRHS 63: 101; FIO 49; CIS 245. China; Szechwan Prov., Mt. Omei. This is the only species in cultivation but not as attractive as *R. hui*. z8? ✣ ⚭

Illustrations of other species:

R. kwangtungense CIS 247

R. praeteritum CIS 242

R. tsiangii CIS 243

R. yunnanense CIS 241

Little is known of the cultural requirements, but somewhat like *Styrax*. Probably also somewhat hardier than previously thought.

Lit. Hu, H. H.: *Rehderodendron*, a new genus of Styracaceae from Szechwan; in Bull. Fan Mem. Inst. Biol. **3**, 77–81, 1932 (pl. 1–2)

RESTIO L. — RESTIONACEAE

Herbaceous with a creeping rootstock; shoots cylindrical or compressed or rectangular; leaves reduced to a sheath and with awl-shaped tips, persistent; flowers very rarely hermaphroditic, styles 2–3; fruit a small capsule. — About 120 species in S. Africa, Madagascar and Australia.

Restio subverticillatus Mast. Stem about 0.7–1.2 m high, twigs whorled, sheaths about 2.5 cm long, leathery, striped above, thin, hard-shelled, outspread, the smaller sheaths leaflike. JRHS 1977: 353. S. Africa. z9 Plate 51. ∅

RETAMA see: GENISTA

R. monosperma see: **G. monosperma**

R. sphaerocarpa see: **G. sphaerocarpa**

RHAMNELLA Miq. — RHAMNACEAE

Deciduous trees or shrubs, similar to *Rhamnus*, but with persistent stipule base and a narrowly oblong fruit; leaves alternate, pinnately veined, finely serrate; stipules awl-shaped, flowers hermaphroditic, small, green, 5–15 in axillary mock umbels, 5 parted; ovaries incompletely 2 locular; style 2 lobed; fruit oblong, black, single-seeded. — 10 species in E. Asia.

Rhamnella franguloides (Maxim.) Weberb. A tree in its habitat, to 10 m; leaves oval-oblong, 5–12 cm long, long acuminate, base rounded to broadly cuneate, finely serrate, glabrous on both sides except for the pubescence beneath, petiole 3–8 mm long; flowers inconspicuous, May–June; fruits cylindrical, 8 mm long, black. NK 9: 5. Japan, Korea, E. China. 1906. Hardy. z6 Plate 54.
Cultivated like *Rhamnus*.

RHAMNUS L. — Buckthorn — RHAMNACEAE

Deciduous, occasionally evergreen trees or shrubs, twigs often thorny; leaves alternate or opposite, serrate or entire; flowers small, polygamous or dioecious, greenish or yellowish to white, usually inconspicuous, in axillary clusters or small racemes; fruit a globose drupe with 2–4 seed pits. — About 155 species, most in the northern temperate zone, a few in Brazil and S. Africa.

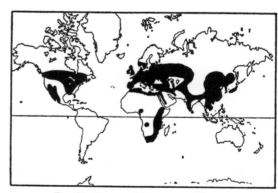

Fig. 86. Range of the genus *Rhamnus*
(from Sokolov)

Short outline of the Genus (from Dippel)

Subgenus I. **Eurhamnus** Dipp.
Thorny or thornless shrubs; winter buds distinctly scaly, without terminal buds; leaves mostly opposite; seeds with shallow or deeper channels or cracks;

Section 1. **Cervispina** Moench.
Twigs nearly opposite and terminating in a thorn; leaves more or less opposite and clustered:
R. catharticus, davuricus, erythroxylon, infectorius, japonicus, leptophyllus, lycioides, oleoides, pallasii, saxatilis, tinctorius, utilis, virgatus

Section 2. **Alaternus** DC.

Always thornless shrub, twigs alternate; leaves alternate, with 6–14 pairs of parallel lateral veins:

R. alaternus, alnifolius, alpinus, costatus, croceus, fallax, heterophyllus, hybridus, imeretinus, lanceolatus, ludovici-salvatoris, pumilus

Subgenus II. **Frangula** (Mill.) Dipp.

Thornless, upright shrubs, winter buds naked, terminal buds present; leaves always alternate; seeds without furrows or cracks:

R. californicus, carolinianus, crenatus, frangula, purshianus, rupestris

Rhamnus alaternus L. Evergreen shrub, 2–3(5) m high, young shoots finely pubescent; leaves elliptic to ovate, 2–5 cm long, acute, sparse and sharply serrate to nearly entire, dark green and glossy above, yellow-green beneath, 3–5 veins, petiole 4–6 mm long; flowers very small, yellowish green, 5 parted, in short, clustered racemes, March–April; fruits 6 mm in diameter, black. HW 3: 59; SH 2: 187 a–f, 188 g–m; PEu 71. Mediterranean region. Around 1700. z7 Fig. 87. # ⌀

'Angustifolius'. Leaves oblong-lanceolate to lanceolate, more deeply serrate (= *R. perrieri* Hort.).

'Argenteovariegatus'. Leaves narrower than those of the species, with broad white margins. Plate 52.

'Integrifolius'. Leaves usually entire, venation rather indistinct.

R. alnifolius L'Hér. Scarcely 1 m high, wide shrub, young shoots finely floccose; leaves elliptic to ovate, unevenly crenate, 4–10 cm long, acute, base usually cuneate, underside mostly light pubescent on the 6–8 vein pairs, petiole 5–12 mm long; flowers usually 2–4, without petals, 5 parted, May–June; fruits black, 6 mm thick, with 3 seeds. BB 2393; GSP 316. Western USA. 1778. Hardy. z2 Plate 53; Fig. 87.

R. alpinus L. Thornless shrub, 2–3 m high, divaricate habit, young shoots usually glabrous, eventually dull gray-brown; leaves elliptic, 5–10 cm long, round to abruptly short acuminate, base rounded to somewhat cordate, finely serrate, dark green above, underside yellow-green, glossy on both sides, with 9–12 vein pairs; flowers inconspicuous, May–June; fruits black, 5 mm in diameter. HM 1897; HF 2187. Southern European mountains, from NW. Spain to Greece. 1752. z6 Plate 53; Fig. 87. ⌀

R. billardii see: **R. × hybridus** var. 'Billardii'

R. californicus Esch. Evergreen shrub, 2.5 m high or more, shoots softly pubescent; leaves elliptic-oblong, obtuse to acute, 3–10 cm long, base round, sparsely dentate, soft pubescent on the 8–12 vein pairs beneath; flowers in short stalked, pubescent umbels; fruits flat globose, red at first, then purple-black, 8 mm in diameter. RH 1858: 198 (= *R. incanus* Carr.). USA; Oregon to California. Around 1870. z7 Plate 55. # ⌀

var. **tomentellus** Brew. & S. Wats. Twigs and leaf undersides dense yellowish or gray tomentose. SS 63 (= *R. tomentellus* Benth.). USA; California to Arizona. 1858. z9 Plate 53. # ⌀

R. carolinianus Walt. Indian Cherry. Shrub, occasionally a tree in its habitat, to 10 m high, young shoots soft pubescent; leaves elliptic to oblong-lanceolate, 5–15 cm long, indistinctly serrate to entire, acute, base round to cuneate, with 8–10 vein pairs, usually totally glabrous, golden-yellow in fall, petiole 6–15 mm long; flowers grouped 2–8 in pubescent inflorescences, May–June; fruits red at first, then black, sweet, edible, stone not furrowed. BB 2394; SS 61; KTF 148. S. USA. 1727. Hardy. z6 Plate 53. ⌀ ✂ ⚇

R. carniolicus see: **R. fallax**

R. catharticus L. Common Buckthorn. Tree-like, divaricate shrub, to 6 m high, short shoots thorned; leaves opposite, ovate-elliptic, 4–7 cm long, crenate, dull green above, light green beneath and usually glabrous, thin, with 3–5 vein pairs; flowers yellowish green, in axillary clusters of 3–5, 4 parted, May–June; berries pea-sized, black, bitter. HM 1890; GPN 567–568; BB 2392. Northern temperate zone. Cultivated throughout history; used earlier as a dye plant. Ⓕ Austria; N. Tyrol in screen plantings. z3 Fig. 87, 88.

R. chlorophorus see: **R. utilis**

R. costatus Maxim. Shrub, 3–4 m high, shoots thick and glabrous; leaves opposite (!), oval-oblong, 8–14 cm long, short acuminate, crenate, base narrowly cordate or round, rugose above, underside pubescent on the approximately 20 vein pairs, petiole 3–4 mm long; flowers greenish, May; fruits obovoid, black, 9 mm wide. MJ 1031. Japan. 1900. z6 Plate 53. ⌀ ⚇

R. crenatus S. & Z. Deciduous shrub, to 3 m high, young shoots and leaves rust-brown pubescent, soon becoming glabrous; leaves oblong-ovate to lanceolate or obovate-oblong, 5–10 cm long, acuminate, base round, finely serrate, light green above, lighter beneath and pubescent, at least on the 7–12 vein pairs, petiole 8–15 mm long; flowers in small, pubescent inflorescences, June; fruits globose, 7 mm thick, red at first, then black. NK 9: 14; MJ 1032; SH 2: 185 f–g, 186 p–q. Japan, Korea to central China. 1905. Hardy. z4 Plate 53; Fig. 87.

R. croceus Nutt. Evergreen shrub, usually not over 1 m high and wide, occasionally thorny; leaves oval-round to circular, 1.5–2.5 cm long, thorny dentate, leathery tough, dark green above, yellow-green beneath, occasionally also copper-brown; flowers 4 parted, in short fascicles; fruits obovoid, red, 8 mm long. SPa 190. California. 1848. z8 Fig. 87 #

R. davuricus Pall. Large, broad growing shrub, occasionally a small tree, to 7 m high, short shoots thick and thorned, young shoots glabrous; leaves opposite, oblong to elliptic, acuminate, base tapered, 5–10 cm long, finely crenate, glabrous, gray-green beneath, rather tough; flowers yellowish green, inconspicuous, May; fruits black, pea-sized. NK 9: 12; BC 3371; MJ 1030. Siberia to N. China. 1817. Does well on poor or eroded soil. z5 Plate 53, 54

R. erythroxylon Pall. Very thorny, divaricate shrub, 0.7–1.8 m high, young shoots finely pubescent at first; leaves

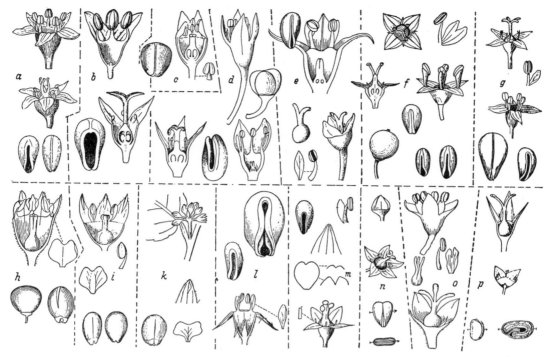

Fig. 87. **Rhamnus.** Flowers, flower parts, fruits and seeds, most enlarged. a. *R. alaternus*; b. *R. croceus*; c. *R. frangula*; d. *R. saxatilis*; e. *R. fallax*; g. *R. catharticus*; h. *R. purshianus*; i. *R. crenatus*; k. *R. rupestris*; l. *R. leptophyllus*; m. *R. alpinus*; n. *R. alnifolius*; o. *R. imeretinus*; p. *R. japonicus* (from HEMPEL & WILHELM, KOEHNE, SARGENT, SCHMIDT, SCHNEIDER)

linear-lanceolate, 3–7 cm long, finely serrate, finely pubescent when young, dark green above, lighter beneath, petiole 5–12 mm long; flowers on short lateral shoots; fruits with 3 stones, these with narrow furrows. SH 2: 193b, 194f. Siberia. 1823. z3 Plate 51; Fig. 88.

R. fallax Boiss. Upright, well branched shrub, to 3 m high, twigs glabrous, eventually red-brown; leaves oblong-elliptic, acuminate, 5–12 cm long, base round to lightly cordate, crenate, with 12–20 vein pairs, deep green above, glossy yellow-green beneath, glabrous, petiole 6–15 mm long; flowers yellow-green, in fascicles of 3–7, May–June; fruits black, 5–6 mm thick. HM 1894e; SH 2: 190 i–m, 191 b–d (= *R. carniolicus* Kern.). Carinthia, Austria, to Greece, in the mountains. 1800. z6 Plate 53; Fig. 87. ∅

R. frangula L. Alder Buckthorn. Shrub, to 2 m, occasionally a small tree, to 5 m high, twigs pubescent at first; leaves ovate-oblong, 3–7 cm long, short acuminate, entire, dull glazed and dark green above, lighter and glossy beneath, with 9–12 vein pairs; flowers small, 5 parted, hermaphroditic, 10–20 in clusters, May to June; fruits pea-sized, red at first, then black, with 2 seeds. HM 1900; HW 3: 48 (= *Frangula alnus* Mill.). Europe, Asia Minor, N. Africa. Cultivated since antiquity. Ⓕ Romania. z3 Fig. 87, 89.

'Angustifolius'. Leaves narrow-oblong to oblanceolate, 8–25 mm wide, margins uneven, often crenate.

'Asplenifolius'. Leaves linear-lanceolate, 4–6 cm long, 3–5 mm wide, margins irregularly crenate or notched and undulate. Developed before 1888 from seed in Muskau, E. Germany. Plate 52. ∅

'Columnaris' (Luedy). Columnar form, 3–4 m high, only about 80 cm wide, very dense; leaves and fruits like those of the species. Discovered in 1936 by A. E. Luedy of Bedford, Ohio (USA). Patented in 1955 under the name "Tallhedge" by the Cole Nursery Co., Painesville, Ohio. Plate 50.

'Heterophyllus'. Leaves lanceolate, margins irregular, partly undulate, often lobed.

var. **latifolius** Dipp. Leaves larger, 8–12 cm long and 5–6 cm wide; fruits larger (= *R. latifolius* Kirchn. non L'Hér.). Caucasus. 1860.

R. heterophyllus Oliv. Deciduous shrub, to 1.5 m high, twigs thin, alternate, with a dense short pubescence when young; stipules persistent and somewhat thorned, leaves ovate to rounded or oblong-lanceolate, 5–30 mm long, acute, base rounded to cuneate, sparsely and finely serrate, glabrous above, underside yellow-green and long pubescent on the 3–4 vein pairs, tough, petiole 1–2 mm long; flowers inconspicuous, paired or solitary, axillary, July; fruits globose, 5 mm thick, with 3 stones. W. China. 1910. Easily recognized by the variably formed leaves on the same twig. z6 Fig. 88.

R. × hybridus L'Hér. (*R. alaternus* × *R. alpinus*). Semi-evergreen shrub, also evergreen in mild climates, to 4 m

Fig. 88. **Rhamnus.**
Left *R. heterophyllus;*
right *R. erythroxylon*
(from ICS)

high, shoots glabrous; leaves elliptic to ovate or elliptic-oblong, 5–10 cm long, obtuse to somewhat acute, finely and shallowly serrate, with about 7 vein pairs, smooth and dark green above, yellow-green beneath, glossy on both sides, petiole 4–8 mm long. SH 2: 189 a–c. Developed before 1788. z6 Plate 55. ⊘

'Billardii'. Leaves smaller, narrower, more lanceolate, more coarsely dentate, 4–7 cm long. SH 2: 189d (= *R. billardii* Dipp.). Possibly *R. alaternus* 'Angustifolius' × *R. alpinus*? ⊘

R. imeretinus Kirchn. Shrub, to 3 m high, twigs stout, gray, slightly pubescent at first; leaves elliptic-oblong, 10–25 cm long, finely serrate, rich green and glossy above, pale green and pubescent beneath, bronze-red in fall, with 15–25 vein pairs, these indented above, petiole 1–2 cm long; flowers green, inconspicuous, in few-flowered clusters, June; fruits black, 6 mm thick. DL 2: 252 (as *R. alpina grandiflora* Dipp.); MG 1906: 405; BM 6721. Caucasus, Asia Minor. Before 1858. The most attractive species. z6 Plate 52; Fig. 87. ⊘

R. incanus see: **R. californicus**

R. infectorius L. Avignon Berry. Low, broad growing shrub, to 2 m high, divaricately branched, thorny; leaves elliptic to obovate, 1–4 cm long, dark green and usually glabrous above, somewhat pubescent beneath, petiole 4–10 mm long; flowers grouped 2–4 in clusters, calyx tube campanulate, wider than long; fruits globose to somewhat oblong, black, with 2 stones, opening by a split at one end. HF 2185; SH 2: 195a, 196 f–h. Mts. of SW. Europe. 1683. The dried fruits were at one time used to make a yellow dye and called "Graines d'Avignon". z7 Plate 51.

R. japonicus Maxim. Divaricate, 3 m high shrub, twigs yellowish brown, glossy, thorny; leaves opposite, obovate to more oblong, 5–8 cm long, short acuminate, base cuneate (!), finely serrate, bright green above, underside sparsely pubescent or glabrous, with 4–5 vein pairs, slender petioled; flowers in axillary clusters, very

numerous, brownish green, fragrant, on small, thorned shoots, May; fruits black, globose, 6 mm thick. MJ 1029. Japan. 1888. z4 Fig. 87.

R. lanceolatus Pursh. Erect, deciduous shrub, to 2 m high, young shoots pubescent, later red-brown; leaves oval-lanceolate to oblong-lanceolate, 3–8 cm long, acute (often obtuse on flowering shoots), base cuneate to rounded, finely serrate, glabrous or finely pubescent beneath, with 7–9 vein pairs, petiole 5–10 mm long; flowers hermaphroditic, on many plants short stalked and clustered with a short style, but on other plants fewer to solitary and with a longer style (!), May; fruits 6 mm wide, black, with 2 seeds. GSP 318; BB 2392. USA. 1870. z5

R. latifolius see: **R. frangula** var. **latifolius**

R. leptophyllus Schneid. Deciduous shrub, closely related to *R. japonicus*, to 2 m high; leaves obovate-elliptic, 4–7 cm long, obtusish acuminate, sparsely finely dentate, glabrous and light green beneath; flower stalks and calyx pubescent; seeds with open furrows. SH 2: 196 v–w, 198 e–h. Central to W. China. 1907. z6 Plate 51, 54; Fig. 87.

R. ludovici-salvatoris Chodat. Nearly glabrous, evergreen shrub, to 2 m high; leaves elliptic to nearly circular, stout and densely thorny dentate; inflorescences dense, flowers 5 parted, without petals, calyx lobes oval-lanceolate, yellow; fruits oval. PSw 27. Balearic Islands, SE. Spain (near Valencia). z9 #

R. lycioides L. Evergreen shrub, densely branched, glabrous or somewhat pubescent, to 1 m high; leaves evergreen or deciduous, leathery tough, 0.5–2 cm long, obovate to linear, obtuse or somewhat emarginate, entire, occasionally finely crenate; flowers in clusters, most hermaphroditic, 4 parted, petals absent or very small, calyx lobes lanceolate, acute, yellowish; fruits yellowish at first, later black. Mediterranean region to Portugal. z9 #

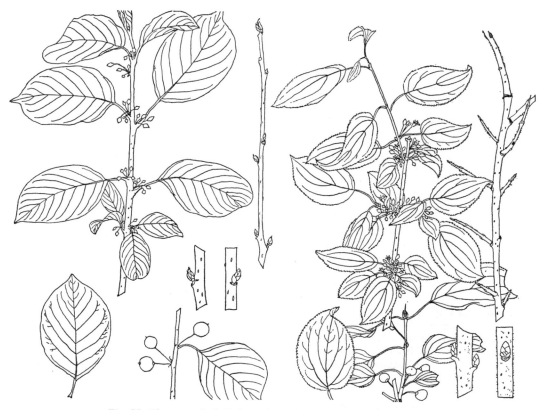

Fig. 89. **Rhamnus.** Left *R. frangula;* right *R. catharticus* (from Nose)

R. oleoides L. Evergreen shrub, 1 m high; leaves obovate, 1–2.5 cm long, obtuse, base cuneate, the 3–4 vein pairs pubescent or glabrous beneath, petiole 2–5 mm long; seeds with open furrows only at the base. SH 2: 195 c–d. Mediterranean region. 1933. z9 Plate 55. #

R. pallasii Fisch. & Mey. A broad shrub, to 2 m high, twigs thorny; leaves linear to narrow-lanceolate, 2–5 cm long, finely serrate, lightly serrate when young, lateral veins more or less distinct, petiole 5–12 mm long; flowers greenish, stalk glabrous, 3–6 mm long; fruits usually with 2 stones, these with open furrows. SH 2: 193 c–c3, 194 b–e. Asia Minor. 1890. z7 Plate 51.

R. perrieri see: **R. alaternus 'Angustifolius'**

R. pumilus L. Procumbent shrub, 10–20 cm high, very slow growing, young shoots finely pubescent; leaves rounded, elliptic, 2–5 cm long, crenate, dark green above, lighter beneath, with 5–8 vein pairs, venation pubescent beneath; flowers yellowish green, on 4–7 mm long stalks, June–July; fruits bluish black, globose. HM 1894 (= *R. pusillus* Ten.). Alps, Pyrenees, not unusual to find in rocky crags. 1752. Very attractive for the rock garden. z5 Plate 53, 51. ∅

R. purshianus DC. Loose shrub, to 3 m high (also a tree in its habitat, to 15 m high), twigs soft pubescent at first; leaves elliptic to oblong or ovate, 5–15 cm long, flat and sparsely serrate to nearly entire, base round, with 10–15 parallel vein pairs, rich green above, lighter beneath and short pubescent; flowers numerous, yellow-green, hermaphroditic, 5 parted, in stalked clusters, July; fruits obovoid, 8 mm thick, black-red. SPa 192–193; SS 62–63. N. America. 1826. The drug "Cascara Sagrada" (a mild laxative) is obtained from the bark. Ⓕ USA. z7 Plate 52, 53. Fig. 87. ∅

R. pusillus see: **R. pumilus**

R. rupestris Scop. Shrub, to 80 cm high, erect or prostrate, young shoots pubescent; leaves elliptic-oblong, often nearly circular, 2–5 cm long, finely dentate to nearly entire, dark green above, underside pubescent on the 5–8 vein pairs, base often cordate; flowers hermaphroditic, 5 parted, petals small, June–July; fruits 6 mm thick, red at first, then black. HM 1903; HF 2188; SH 2: 185e, 186 m–o (= *R. wulffenii* Spreng.). SE. Europe, Illyria (Balkan P.), Istria (Yugoslavia). 1800. z6 Fig. 87.

R. saxatilis Jacq. Low, broad shrub, 0.6–0.9 m high, finely pubescent when young, later thorny; leaves elliptic to obovate, 1–2.5 cm long, often plaited, finely serrate, glabrous, with 2–4 vein pairs, these yellowish pubescent beneath when young; flowers yellow-green, inconspicuous, April–May; fruits black, usually with 3 seeds, these with open furrows. HM 1892; HF 2186; HW 3: 57. Central and S. Europe. 1752. z6 Plate 51; Fig. 87.

R. tinctorius W. & K. Shrub, 1–1.5 m high and wide, branches partly opposite, partly alternate, young shoots soft pubescent, thorny; leaves elliptic to narrow-elliptic, 2–5 cm long, obtuse, base cuneate, finely serrate, usually with 2 vein pairs on either side, usually pubescent on both sides or also glabrous above; flowers yellow-green; fruits top-shaped, 2–4 tubercled, stone with open furrows. HF 2184. SE. Europe. 1820. z6 Plate 51.

R. tomentellus see: **R. californicus** var. **tomentellus**

R. utilis Decne. To 3 m high, deciduous, thornless shrub, twigs glabrous; leaves narrowly oblong, 6–12 cm long, finely serrate, glossy dark green above, yellowish green beneath, with 5–8 yellowish vein pairs, these yellowish pubescent beneath at first; flowers yellowish green, April–May; fruits pea-sized, black, usually with 2 seeds, these furrowed. DL 2: 250–251; SH 2: 197 t–w; MJ 3445 (= *R. chlorophorus* Dipp. non Decne.). Central and Eastern China; for dry gravelly soil, likes alkalinity. 1870.

z7 ∅ ⚭

R. virgatus Roxb. Shrub to small tree, closely related to *R. japonicus*, but the young twigs finely pubescent; leaves narrow-elliptic to lanceolate, 4–8 cm long, usually obtusely acuminate, both sides sparsely pubescent (!), finely dentate to notched, petiole 4–10 mm long; fruits blue-black, stone with open furrows. SH 2: 192 f–h. NW. Himalayas. 1919. z8

R. wulffenii see: **R. rupestris**

In general *Rhamnus* are only slightly ornamental, but they are easily cultivated. The large-leaved species, especially *R. imeretinus*, are particularly attractive. The use of *R. catharticus* must be restricted since it is an alternate host of a grain rust (*Puccinia coronata*).

Lit. Suessenguth, K.: Rhamnaceae; in Engler, Nat. Pflanzenfamilien, 2nd edition, Nr. 20d, Berlin 1953 ● Wolf, C. B.: The North American species of *Rhamnus*; in Monogr., Bot. Ser. No. 1, Rancho Santa Ana Bot. Gard. Calif., 1938.

RHAPHIOLEPIS Lindl. — ROSACEAE

Rounded, medium-sized or low evergreen shrubs; leaves leathery tough, alternate, short petioled, serrate to entire; flowers in panicles or racemes, terminal; sepals 5, oblong to obovate, stamens 15–20, styles 2–3, connate at the base, ovaries inferior; fruits globose, purple-black, without a calyx, with 1–2 large seeds. — 4 species in S. Japan and S. China.

Rhaphiolepis × delacourii André (*R. indica × R. umbellata*.) Shrub, about 2 m high, rounded, young shoots pubescent at first, quickly becoming glabrous; leaves obovate, 3–7 cm long, dentate on the apical half, base cuneate, apex obtuse to rounded, leathery thick, totally glabrous; flowers in erect, 7–10 cm long, conical panicles, pink, corolla 12–18 mm wide, stalks pubescent. BMns 362; GC 136: 225; RH 225. Developed around 1900 by Delacour in Villa Allerton, Cannes, France. z9 Plate 55. # ∅ ⊕

R. indica (L.) Lindl. Shrub, about 1 m high; leaves lanceolate, 5–7 cm long, thin (!), more sharply serrate, acute to acuminate; flowers in loose glabrous racemes with lanceolate subtending leaves (bracts), corolla 1.5 cm wide, white with a light pink center, stamens carmine-pink, February to August. RB 468; BM 1726; HKS 84 (as "*Crataegus indica*") (= *R. salicifolia* Lindl.). S. China. 1806. z9 # ∅ ⊕

Some American cultivars include:

'Springtime' (Monrovia Nursery) with brownish new growth and intensely pink flowers.

'Coates Crimson' (L. Coates) was developed by L. Coates Nurseries in San Jose, California. MCL 84; patented (1952).

R. japonica see: **R. umbellata**

R. salicifolia: see: **R. indica**

R. umbellata (Thunb.) Mak. Shrub, to 4 m high in its habitat, hardly over 1 m in cultivation, young shoots finely tomentose; leaves very thick and leathery, obovate to elliptic, nearly entire or with shallow obtuse teeth at the apex, 3–8 cm long, deep green above, underside floccose when young; flowers in erect, 5–10 cm long panicles or racemes, fragrant, corolla 1.5–2 cm wide, white, stamens carmine, May–June; fruits about 1 cm thick, blue-black. NF 1: 102; KIF 3: 29; YWP 2: 11; MJ 1395 (= *R. japonica* S. & Z.). S. Japan. 1862. z9 # ∅ ⊕

f. **ovata** (Briot) Schneid. Leaves broadly obovate, larger and wider than the species, rounded at the apex, entire or slightly dentate. BM 5510; Gw 4: 129. Japan, Korea. Before 1864. z9

Very attractive shrubs in mild climates, preferring a warm, sunny, protected site (good for the wall garden on south exposures); like a humus, acid soil, as *Rhododendron*.

RHAPHITHAMNUS Miers — VERBENACEAE

Evergreen shrubs or trees with finely pubescent twigs; leaves opposite, simple, leathery tough, nearly sessile, entire; calyx campanulate, 5 toothed; corolla tubular, with 4 or 5 uneven lobes; stamens 4; fruit a fleshy drupe. — About 10 species in Chile.

Rhaphithamnus cyanocarpus see: **R. spinosus**

R. spinosus (Juss.) Small, evergreen shrub, to 6 m high in its habitat, young shoots rough and erect pubescent, with claw-like, 1–2.5 cm long thorns, these yellowish on older twigs; leaves broadly cordate-ovate, 0.5–2 cm long, 0.4–1.2 cm wide, often in whorls of 3, glossy dark green, glabrous on both sides; flowers solitary or paired in the

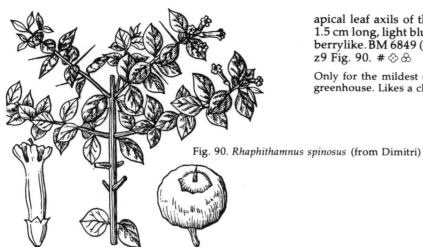

apical leaf axils of the previous year's growth, tubular, 1.5 cm long, light blue, April; fruits pea-sized, light blue, berrylike. BM 6849 (= *R. cyanocarpus* Miers). Chile. 1843. z9 Fig. 90. # ⊕ ⊗

Only for the mildest climates unless overwintered in a cool greenhouse. Likes a clay-humus soil.

Fig. 90. *Rhaphithamnus spinosus* (from Dimitri)

RHODODENDRON L. — ERICACEAE

Evergreen or deciduous shrubs, also trees in the habitat and milder regions; leaves alternate, entire, simple; flowers usually in terminal corymbs, less often axillary, occasionally solitary; corolla usually campanulate or infundibular, occasionally also tubular or cupulate to rotate, generally with a 5 lobed (also occasionally 6–10 lobed) limb; calyx normally with the same number of lobes as the corolla limb, these often much reduced; stamens 5 or 10, often twice as many as the corolla limb lobes; fruit a woody capsule, dehiscing longitudinally, seeds very small. — About 500 to 600 species (by some accounts about 900); the major region of distribution is E. Asia, from S. China to the Himalayas and Japan; a larger range but with fewer species is temperate N. America, 4 species in central and S. Europe, 5 species in the Caucasus, a few in the Arctic and finally, 250 species in Malaysia. Many species are classed as epiphytes.

Classification of the Genus Rhododendron

This book will retain the classification system used throughout the English-speaking world which divides the genus into Series and Subseries (also in Bean, 8th Edition, Vol. 3, 1976). It must be pointed out, however, that this system of classification is not completely satisfactory; botanists generally agree that the entire system must be reevaluated and many series or subseries can and must be lumped together. H. Sleumer compiled a botanical classification in 1949 which was further revised by A. Seithe/von Hoff in 1960. Those readers with an understanding of German may study the original work of these botanists (Sleumer, H.: Ein System der Gattung *Rhododendron* L.; in Bot. Jahrb. **74**, 511–553, 1949 ● Seithe, A./von Hoff: Die Haarformen der Gattung *Rhododendron* L. und die Möglichkeit ihrer taxonomischen Verwertung; in Bot. Jahrb. **79**, 297–393, 1960. For a better unnderstanding of this system, readers of English may consult Melva, N., & W. R. Philipson: The *Rhododendron* and *Camellia* Year Book **25**, 1–8, 1971. For a good review of Sleumer's system see the following chart of the characteristics of the Subgenera and Sections.

Here follows a brief outline of the more important characteristics of the Subgenera in Sleumer's system:

Subgenus	Approx. no. of species	Scales	Arrangement of flowers and foliar buds	Leaves
Hymenanthes	300	absent	Flower buds terminal (occasionally also axillary), with subtending foliar buds	evergreen
Rhododendron	495	present	as above	evergreen
Pseudazalea	13	present	as above	±evergreen
Rhodorastrum	2	present	Flower buds axillary (occasionally seemingly terminal), with subtending foliar buds	±evergreen
Pseudorhodorastrum	8	present	Flower buds axillary, foliar buds on the shoot tips	evergreen
Pentanthera	20	absent	Flower buds terminal (occasionally also axillary), with subtending foliar buds	deciduous
Tsutsutsi	54	absent	Flower buds terminal with foliar buds enclosed	evergreen and deciduous
Azaleastrum ·	25	absent	Flower buds axillary, foliar buds at the shoot tips	evergreen and deciduous

(The series *Camtschaticum* was excluded by Sleumer and included with the genus *Therorhodion* Small)

General Outline of the Series

A detailed outline of the species and a key to their identification would require a considerable amount of space. For such information, please refer to the technical literature, primarily that of Bowers, Cowan, Sleumer, Davidian, Bean, etc.

The outline that follows is designed purely from a practical point of view. A more detailed list may be found in Bowers (left column, p. 458 to 460).

A. Subgenus RHODODENDRON

Plants with scaly (lepidote) leaves

(Form and spacing of the scales should be carefully observed with a magnifying glass!)

Series Dauricum
Deciduous to evergreen shrubs; flowers solitary or paired among clustered buds at the shoot tips; flowers in late winter, pink-red:

Shrubs, often deciduous and resembling Azaleas

    R. dauricum, mucronulatum

Series Trichocladum
Deciduous to semi-evergreen shrubs; flowers grouped 2–4 together, yellow; style usually glabrous, often sharply curved; stamens 10:
    R. lepidostylum, trichocladum

Series Triflorum
Evergreen, in exceptional cases deciduous species, thin branched; flowers usually grouped 3–4 together, occasionally 6–8 in loose corymbs; calyx very small, corolla infundibular, usually speckled; style glabrous; stamens 10;

Key to the Subseries

A. Inflorescence distinctly racemose, with 5–15 flowers, rachis 8–50 mm long; calyx 5 lobed, 1–4 mm long:

Subseries Hanceanum

    R. hanceanum

A. Inflorescence short racemose or umbellate, with 3–6 (occasionally to 10) flowers; rachis 1–5 mm (occasionally to 10 mm) long; calyx more rotate or 5 lobed, often 0.1–5 mm long;

B. Flowers light or dark yellow or greenish yellow:

Subseries Triflorum
    R. ambiguum, keiskei, laticostum, lutescens, triflorum

B. Flowers white, pink, purple, lavender to strong violet:

C. Midrib pubescent on the leaf underside:

Subseries Augustinii
    R. augustinii, trichanthum

C. Midrib not pubescent on the leaf undersides:

Shrubs: often deciduous and resembling Azaleas

Subseries Yunnanense
    R. concinnum, davidsonianum, hormophorum, oreotrephes, rigidum, searsiae, yunnanense, zaleucum

— — — — — —

Series Anthopogon
Small shrubs; corolla with a slender tube and broad flared limb; calyx usually large; style very short, thick, glabrous; stamens 5–10 (including the earlier Series *Cephalanthum*):

Small alpine shrubs; corolla tubular with an outspread limb

    R. anthopogon, cephalanthum, primuliflorum, sargentianum, trichostomum

Fig. 91. **Rhododendron,** forms of the corolla. a. *R. fortunei;* b. *R. falconeri;* c. *R. smirnowii;* d. *R. barbatum;* e. *R. thomsonii;* f. *R. davidii;* g. *R. campanulatum;* h. *R. degronianum;* i. *R. griffithianum;* k. *R. arboreum* l. *R. maximum;* m. *R. fulgens* (from Hooker, B. M., Shirasawa, Franchet, Sargent; all about ½ actual size)

Series **Campylogynum**

Small shrubs, leaves small, thick; flowers usually solitary, purple, long stalked, corolla less than 2.5 cm wide; style short, thick, glabrous:
  R. campylogynum

Series **Glaucophyllum**

Usually small or low shrubs, leaves very tough, often bluish beneath; calyx large, deeply 5 lobed; style short, thick, often recurved; stamens 10; — Normally low shrubs (to 60 cm high) from high in the mountains (3300–4600m)

Key to the Subseries

A. Scales of the leaf undersides in 2 forms, the smaller light yellow, the larger brown, close or more widely spaced:

Subseries **Glaucophyllum**
R. brachyanthum, charitopes, glaucophyllum, shweliense, tsangpoense

A. Scales of the leaf underside all evenly formed and brown, spaced 0.5–10 times as far apart as their width:

Subseries **Genestierianum**
R. genestierianum

Series **Lapponicum**
Small shrubs; leaves very small, underside densely scaly; corolla broadly funnelform, calyx usually small, flower stalk very short; stamens 5 or 10; flowers purple-reddish or pink, occasionally yellow:
R.chryseum, complexum, cuneatum, edgarianum, fastigiatum, fimbriatum, flavidum, hippophaeoides, impeditum, intricatum, lapponicum, nivale, orthocladum, parvifolium, rupicola, russatum, scintillans, setosum, tapetiforme, telmateium

Series **Lepidotum**
Very similar to the Series *Lapponicum,* but the scales of the leaf underside are much denser, overlapping; corolla purple, reddish, pink or yellow; calyx well developed; style short, thick, often bowed, glabrous; stamens 8 or 10:
R. baileyi, lepidotum

Series **Uniflorum**
Low shrubs, usually not over 50 cm high; flowers solitary or paired:
R. imperator, pemakoense, pumilum

Series **Saluenense**
Low shrubs, often prostrate; leaves often ciliate; flowers grouped 1–2–3; corolla rotate-outspread, tube short; calyx large, ciliate; stamens 10:
R. calostrotum, keleticum, prostratum, radicans, saluenense

Series **Boothii**
Small shrubs, occasionally epiphytic; flowers in terminal corymbs; corolla campanulate, usually yellow; calyx large; styles short, often curved; stamens 10;

Similar to the previous group but taller; 90–120 cm high

Key to the Subseries

A. Styles short, thick, sharply curved;

B. Inflorescences 1–2 (occasionally 3) flowered; scales of the leaf undersides with a very narrow limb, nearly bullate:

Subseries **Megeratum**
R. leucaspis

B. Inflorescences 3–10 flowered; scales on the leaf undersides with a broad limb, entire:

Similar to the above group, but taller; 90–120 cm high

Subseries **Boothii**
R. boothii

A. Style long, thin, straight:

Subseries **Tephropeplum**
R. tephropeplum

— — — — — —

Series **Scabrifolium**
Thin-branched shrubs; flowers arising from axilliary buds; leaves pubescent beneath; corolla tubular, calyx well developed; stamens 10:
R. hemitrichotum, scabrifolium, spiciferum, spinuliferum

Flowers axillary, 0.5–2.5 m tall shrub

Series **Virgatum**

Similar to the above group but the leaves glabrous beneath; flowers arising from a few to many axillary buds; ovaries densely scaly; stamens 10, pubescent at the base:
R. racemosum, virgatum

Series **Heliolepsis**

Shrubs or trees; very similar to the Series *Triflorum,* but more densely scaly; flowers 3–6 together, corolla always scaly on the exterior, calyx very small, stamens 10:
R. brevistylum, desquamatum, heliolepis, rubiginosum

Flowers funnel-form, calyx very small

Series **Triflorum**

(already mentioned on p. 123)

Series **Maddenii**

Medium-sized to tall shrubs, occasionally epiphytic; flowers usually 2–6 together, corolla large to very large, usually infundibular, white, occasionally also yellow; style normally scaly; stamens 10–25;

Medium-sized to large shrubs, commonly epiphytic in the habitat

Key to the Subseries

A. Stamens 15–25; calyx usually well developed, but rarely large; ovaries with 10–12 locules; leaf petiole usually with a **V**-form furrow above:

Subseries **Maddenii**
R. crassum, maddenii

A. Stamens 10 (only occasionally to 13); calyx variably developed, from indistinct to very large; ovaries with 5–7 locules;

B. Calyx large and more or less leaflike, the lobes 8 mm long or longer; leaf petiole convex and not furrowed above (except on *R. megacalyx*):

Subseries **Megacalyx**
R. dalhousiae, lindleyi, megacalyx, nuttallii, taggianum

B. Calyx usually barely developed and often only ciliate; leaf petiole with a **V**-form furrow above:

Subseries **Ciliicalyx**
R. burmanicum, ciliatum, ciliicalyx, cubittii, johnstoneanum, parryae, valentinianum, veitchianum

Series **Moupinense**

Small shrubs, young shoots bristly; leaves leathery, ciliate; flowers grouped 1–2, corolla white or pink, exterior not scaly; stamens 10:
R. moupinense

Series **Edgeworthii**

Mostly epiphytic shrubs; leaves scaly and pubescent (!) beneath; corolla infundibular, fleshy, calyx large; style long and thick; stamens 10:
R. edgeworthii

Greenhouse plants!

— — — — — —

Series **Cinnabarinum**

Leaves more or less bluish; flowers pendulous; corolla tubular, narrowly funnelform, with erect or nearly erect limb lobes; style pubescent, stamens 10:
R. cinnabarinum, concatenans, keysii, xanthocodon

Totally different in flower form

— — — — — —

Series **Carolinianum**

Small shrubs; calyx small, ciliate; ovaries scaly, style glabrous, stamens 10, pubescent:
R. carolinianum, minus

Very hardy, 1.5–5 m tall shrubs

— — — — — —

Series **Ferrugineum**

European alpine shrubs; flowers 1.5–2 cm wide, in small corymbs; stamens 10:
R. ferrugineum, hirsutum, kotschyi

Very hardy, 0.5–1 m tall shrubs

— — — — — —

Series **Micranthum**
Small-flowered shrub, flowers resembling *Ledum* or *Spiraea*, white, many in corymbs, 8–12 mm wide, stamens 10, glabrous:
R. micranthum

Very small flowered

B. Subgenus HYMENANTHES (Bl.) K. Koch
Leaves without scales (elepidote)

Series **Albiflorum**
Deciduous shrub; flowers paired or solitary along entire shoot (totally different from other species):
R. albiflorum

Totally different in the arrangement of flowers

— — — — — —

Series **Camtschaticum**
Deciduous shrub, prostrate, 10–20 cm high; flowers on the young, current year's foliate shoots (totally different from all the other species):
R. camtschaticum

Differing in the flowers on the current year's shoots

— — — — — —

Series **Ovatum**
Thin-branched shrubs, leaves evergreen; flowers solitary from axillary buds near the shoot tips; calyx lobes large and wide; stamens 5, equal in length; ovaries bristly:
R. leptothrium, ovatum

Series **Semibarbatum**
Very similar to Series *Ovatum*, deciduous; flowers solitary, from lateral buds under the terminal foliate buds; corolla small, rotate, stamens 5, very uneven in length:
R. semibarbatum

— — — — — —

Series **Falconeri**
Large shrubs or trees, large leaved, leaves with a 2 layered indumentum; flowers grouped 20–30 in corymbs, corolla cupulate or infundibular, limb 7–10 lobed; stamens 12–18; calyx small:
R. arizelum, basilicum, coriaceum, falconeri, fictolacteum, galactinum, hodgsonii, rex

Large-leaved shrubs

Series **Grande**
Like Series *Falconeri*, but the leaves with a thicker tomentum beneath, indumentum without "cupulate" hairs; corolla limb 7–10 lobed, corolla usually widened at the base; stamens 14–20:
R. grande, macabeanum, magnificum, mollyanum, peregrinum, praestans, protistum, sinogrande, watsonii

Series **Arboreum**
Mostly very large-leaved shrubs or trees for very mild climates; leaves usually acute; flowers numerous, in dense, globose corymbs, corolla campanulate; stamens at least 10, occasionally 12–14:

Large-leaved shrubs or trees for very mild climates

Subseries **Arboreum**
R. arboreum, lanigerum, niveum

Subseries **Argyrophyllum**
R. argyrophyllum, floribundum, hunnewellianum, insigne, ririei, thayerianum

Large-leaved shrubs or trees for very mild climates

Series **Barbatum**
Tall shrubs or trees, young shoots and leaves more or less bristly or glandular pubescent; flowers deep red with distinct nectaries;

Key to the Subseries

A. Calyx large, 5–25 mm long;

    B. Leaf apex acute; indumentum absent or scattered, thick or thin, loose woolly; leaf petiole 5–10 mm; inflorescence compact; calyx 5–10 mm, more or less regular, the lobes obtuse; corolla red to carmine; range Himalayas:

Subseries **Barbatum**
R. barbatum, smithii

BB. Leaf apex acute or round; indumentum composed of coarse, scattered glandular hairs, occasionally totally glabrous or thin woolly; leaf petiole 20–30 mm, inflorescence loose; calyx 10–30 mm, more or less irregular, lobes narrow; corolla white or pink, occasionally carmine; range Yunnan Prov., Burma, SE. Tibet:

Subseries **Glischrum**
R. glischrum, habrotrichum, hirtipes, rude

BBB. Leaf apex acute; indumentum a dense, continuous tomentose layer; leaf petiole 20–30 mm; inflorescence more or less compact; calyx 10–15 mm, more or les regular, lobes narrow; corolla white to pink; range Yunnan Prov., Burma, SE. Tibet:

Subseries **Crinigerum**
R. crinigerum

AA. Calyx very small, 1–3 mm (except *R. longesquamatum.*), frequently with hairs or bristles, particularly on the midrib; inflorescence loose, few flowered; corolla white, pink or purple (red on *R. strigillosum*); range Central and E. China, Taiwan:

Subseries **Maculiferum**
R. longesquamatum, morii, pachytrichum, pseudochrysanthum, strigillosum

Series **Irroratum**
Mostly shrubs; indumentum on the leaves more or less thinning, leaves eventually usually totally glabrous, with a cuticular margin; flowers always tubular, limb 5 lobed; calyx very small to totally indistinct; stamens 10–14;

Key to the Subseries

A. Indumentum absent on mature leaves or, if present, thin and not stellate pubescent; leaves acute or abruptly long acuminate, occasionally rounded; ovaries never stellate pubescent; style glabrous or glandular, never floccose or tomentose:

Subseries **Irroratum**
R. aberconwayi, irroratum

AA. Indumentum stellate haired, always present on young leaves, later gradually shedding; leaf apexes more or less rounded; ovaries always stellate tomentose; style more or less stellate pubescent:

Subseries **Parishii**
R. elliotii, eriogynum, kyawii, venator

Series **Campanulatum**
Shrubs or small trees; leaves usually rounded at both ends, underside woolly; flowers not in elongated racemes; ovaries glabrous:
R. campanulatum, fulgens, lanatum, sheriffii, wallichii

Usually erect, medium-sized shrubs with medium-sized leaves

Series **Fortunei**
Mostly large shrubs; leaves totally glabrous or quickly becoming so; corolla large, infundibular or campanulate, limb 6–7 lobed, occasionally only 5 lobed, white to pink, never red or yellow; stamens 12–26, occasionally only 10;

Mostly erect, medium-sized shrubs with medium-sized leaves

Key to the Subseries

A. Style with glands up to the apex;

B. calyx tiny:

Subseries **Fortunei**

R. decorum, diaprepes, discolor, fortunei, hemsleyanum, houlstonii, serotinum, vernicosum

BB. Calyx large (15–20 mm):

Subseries **Griffithianum**
R. griffithianum

AA. Style glabrous or glandular only at the base;

B. Leaves circular:

Subseries **Orbiculare**
R. orbiculare

BB. Leaves much longer than wide;

C. Leaves small, 5–10 cm long, more or less evenly elliptic, rounded at both ends; floral axis usually very short; flowers 3–4 cm long:

Subseries **Oreodoxa**
R. fargesii, oreodoxa

CC. Leaves large, 10–30 cm long, more or less oblanceolate, often abruptly acuminate, base cuneate; floral axis usually elongated; flowers 4–7 cm long;

D. Corolla infundibular-campanulate; stamens 10–15; style slender, stigma capitate:

Subseries **Davidii**
R. davidii, planetum, sutchuenense

DD. Corolla campanulate, bulging at the base; stamens 15–25; style thick, stigma disk-form:

Subseries **Calophytum**
R. calophytum

Series **Fulvum**
Shrubs or trees with long, narrow leaves, widest above the middle, tomentose beneath; flowers long and thin stalked, in loose racemes; ovaries glabrous, long, narrow, later becoming a sickle-shaped capsule:
R. fulvum, uvarifolium

Series **Lacteum**
Shrubs or small trees, leaves with a thin indumentum beneath; flowers white, pink or yellow; stamens 10, pubescent at the base; ovaries tomentose:
R. beesianum, lacteum, przewalskii, traillianum, wightii

Series **Neriiflorum**
Flowers in loose inflorescences, never compact; corolla normally not speckled; ovaries usually densely pubescent, often also glandular; stamens 10–12;

Key to the Subseries

1. Leaves oblong-elliptic, indumentum absent, or narrow, acuminate and with indumentum, indumentum in this case loose and woolly, gray to dark cinnamon-brown, often later becoming glabrous; corolla very fleshy, scarlet to carmine (*R. floccigerum* occasionally also yellow); ovaries slender and gradually drawn out to the style, not truncated (!), pubescent; fruit long, curved:

Subseries **Neriiflorum**
R. floccigerum, neriiflorum, sperabile

2. Leaves oblanceolate to obovate, occasionally narrow relative to the length; indumentum absent or usually in thin layers (occasionally loose and woolly), white to light brown; corolla thin-walled on *R. citriniflorum*, the others very fleshy; ovaries short, obtuse, pubescent, occasionally densely glandular; fruits straight, short, not curved: Mostly erect, medium-sized shrubs with medium-sized leaves

Subseries **Sanguineum**
R. citriniflorum, dichroanthum, sanguineum

3. Dwarf, prostrate or creeping shrubs, leaves small, rounded or acute at the apex, indumentum absent or quickly disappearing; corolla very fleshy, scarlet to deep carmine, occasionally pink; ovaries short, obtuse, densely pubescent or glandular or both; fruit straight or lightly bowed:

Subseries **Forrestii**
R. chamaethomsonii, forrestii

> 4. Leaves broadly obovate, rounded above, indumentum woolly (not in thin layers), more or less reddish brown; corolla very fleshy, red to deep carmine, occasionally yellow or white; ovaries short, obtuse, wide relative to its length, pubescent or glandular; fruit straight, short:

Subseries **Haematodes**
R. beanianum, chaetomallum, coelicum, haematodes, pocophorum

Series **Ponticum**

Medium-sized shrubs to small trees; floral axis elongated, therefore the inflorescence often distinctly racemose; corolla deeply 5 lobed, the lobes usually as long as the tube; stamens 10 (14 on *R. degronianum* var. *heptamerum*);

Key to the Subseries

> A. Leaves glabrous when mature; flowers never yellow; range: America, Europe, Asia Minor:

Subseries **Ponticum**
R. catawbiense, macrophyllum, maximum, ponticum

> B. Leaves with a distinct indumentum (except *R. aureum* with yellow flowers and *R. fauriei* with white to yellowish flowers); range: Caucasus, N. Asia and Japan:

Subseries **Caucasicum**
R. adenopodum, aureum, brachycarpum, caucasicum, degronianum, hyperythrum, smirnowii, ungerii, yakushimanum

Series **Taliense**

Mostly shrubs, between 1–2.5 m high; leaves acute, underside nearly always thick tomentose; flowers in dense inflorescences with short axes; corolla speckled; stamens 10, pubescent at the base;

Key to the Subseries

> A. Medium-sized shrubs, neither prostrate nor dwarf; leaves broad relative to the length, occasionally narrow on SS *Adenogynum,* but this species has a distinct calyx; bud scales abscising;
>
> > B. Calyx tiny, without glands; ovaries glabrous or nearly so:

Subseries **Taliense**
R. aganniphum, clementinae purdomii, taliense

> > BB. Calyx small, not glandular; ovaries densely tomentose, without glands:

Subseries **Wasonii**
R. rufum, wasonii, wiltonii

> > BBB. Calyx usually large, ciliate with distinctly stalked glands; ovaries usually more or less glandular:

Subseries **Adenogynum**
R. adenogynum, adenophorum, balfourianum, bureavii, detonsum

> AA. Primarily dwarf species; leaves usually narrow, more or less acute, margins normally involuted, bud scales usually persistent; calyx usually small, margins not distinctly glandular ciliate; ovaries glandular or tomentose, occasionally glabrous:

Usually erect, medium-sized shrubs with medium-sized leaves

Subseries **Roxieanum**
R. roxieanum

Series **Thomsonii**

Leaves relatively wide, about equally long, usually glabrous, often bluish, base cordate; inflorescences loose, often few flowered; corolla campanulate, stamens 10; flower stalk, ovaries and styles often glandular;

Key to the Subseries

A. Style with apical glands;

B. Corolla cupulate-rotate, yellow, white or pink; calyx usually 4–12 mm long:

Subseries **Souliei**
R. litiense, puralbum, souliei, wardii

B. Corolla campanulate, light or dark pink;. calyx 1–5 mm long or only a thin marginal limb;

C. Leaves circular to ovate; low, wide shrub, shoots glandular bristled; flowers usually grouped 2–3 together:

Subseries **Williamsianum**
R. williamsianum

C. Leaves oblong to more elliptic; erect shrubs; shoots not glandular-bristly; flowers grouped 5–7 together:

Subseries **Cerasinum**
R. cerasinum

A. Styles totally without glands or glandular only at the base (occasionally ¾ glandular but never completely to the apex);

B. Corolla usually funnelform; shoots glandular-bristly or not so; fruit capsule slender, curved sickle-shaped; leaves oblong, elliptic or oblong-elliptic:

Subseries **Selense**
R. erythrocalyx, martinianum, selense

C. Ovaries not glandular:

Subseries **Thomsonii**
R. hookeri, meddianum, thomsonii

D. Leaves circular, elliptic or oblong; calyx large, 4–20 mm long; flowers carmine, pink or white (occasionally yellow); style without glands; capsule short, thick or broadly oblong, straight:

Subseries **Thomsonii**
R. cyanocarpum, eclectum, lopsangianum

D. Leaves circular to elliptic; calyx small, usually 1–3 mm long; flowers yellow, pink or white; style glandular at the base or on the basal half or not glandular; capsule slender, often bowed:

Subseries **Campylocarpum**
R. callimorphum, caloxanthum, campylocarpum, myiagrum

— — — — — —

Series **Auriculatum**
Foliar buds very long and narrow, flower buds with long, narrow scales; leaves lanceolate; shoots glandular; corolla narrowly funnelform, white, exterior pubescent; flowering in August:
R. auriculatum

Series **Griersonianum**
Foliar buds long and narrow; leaves thick woolly beneath from dendroid hairs; flowers red, exterior pubescent; shoots, petioles and calyx floccose; flowering in June:
R. griersonianum

— — — — — —

Subgenus AZALEA (L. emend. Desv.) Planch.
(=Series *Azalea*)

Primarily deciduous shrubs; flowers terminal, never axillary; leaves dimorphic on many semi-evergreen species (spring and summer leaves differing); stamens 5, but 8–10 on the semi-evergreen species; calyx usually small;

Key to the Subseries

A. Flowering and foliar shoots arising from similar terminal buds; flowers grouped 1–3, occasionally more, never yellow or with yellow patches; corolla exterior glabrous, very rarely bristly on the tube;

    B. Leaves distributed along the shoot, persistent, or abscising and then a few persisting under the terminal bud, more or less strigose; young shoots with flat, brown, appressed hairs or with soft, flat hairs:

Subseries **Obtusum**
R. indicum, kaempferi, kiusianum, macrosepalum, mucronatum, obtusum, oldhamii, pulchrum, scabrum, serpyllifolium, simsii, tosaense, tschonoskii, yedoense

    BB. Leaves usually in whorls of 2–5 at the shoot tips; also distributed along the stronger shoots;

        C. Leaves persistent, in whorls of 2–3; shoots with a few appressed, flat hairs, occasionally nearly totally glabrous; corolla campanulate; stamens 10, occasionally 12:

Subseries **Tashiroi**
R. tashiroi

        CC. Leaves abscising, in whorls of 2–5; shoots glabrous or shaggy pubescent; corolla rotate-infundibular; stamens 5–10:

Subseries **Schlippenbachii**
R. quinquefolium, reticulatum, sanctum, schlippenbachii, weyrichii

AA. Flowers from terminal buds, usually few to many, the foliate shoots arise from special buds beneath the terminal;

    B. Corolla rotate-campanulate or infundibular-campanulate, glabrous exterior, never yellow or with yellow patches;

        C. Corolla rotate-campanulate, deeply lobed, the basal lobes occasionally incised nearly to the base; stamens 10, occasionally 5–7, exserted:

Subseries **Canadense**
R. albrechtii, canadense, pentaphyllum, vaseyi

        CC. Corolla tubular-campanulate, with short, somewhat outspread lobes, white; stamens 10, enclosed:

Subseries **Nipponicum**
R. nipponicum

    BB. Corolla funnelform, exterior pubescent and frequently also glandular (*R. prunifolium* is glabrous), many species yellow, commonly with a yellow patch; stamens 5:

Subseries **Luteum**
R. alabamense, arborescens, atlanticum, austrinum, calendulaceum, canescens, flammeum, japonicum, molle, oblongifolium, occidentale, periclymenoides, prinophyllum, prunifolium, viscosum

Hardiness and Garden Merit. Many of the following species are not hardy in the colder temperate zones. For cooler and drier continental regions the microclimates should be observed at the specific planting sites for their suitability to *Rhododendron* culture. The evaluation of species in this work is based on a British system of 4 ratings for hardiness and garden merit. However, for the sake of consistency, hardiness figures will correspond with the USDA hardiness zone map.

Regarding garden merit: ★★★ excellent; ★★★ good; ★★ satisfactory; ★ slight to none.

List of the Species
(cultivars, see "Cultivar List")
(S = Series, SS = Subseries)

Rhododendron aberconwayi Cowan (S and SS Irroratum). Evergreen shrub, about 1 m high, young shoots glandular and finely pubescent; leaves oblong-elliptic, outspread, 5–8 cm long, 2–3 cm wide, acute with a small mucro; flowers grouped 6–12 in corymbs, corolla broadly campanulate to shell-form, 2.5–3 cm wide, white or white with a trace of pink and dark red spots, stamens 10, uneven, May–June. RYB 3: 17. W. China, Yunnan Prov. 1937. z7 ★★★ # ☼

R. adenogynum Diels (S Taliense, SS Adenogynum). Evergreen shrub, 1–2 m high, shoots light green; leaves obovate-oblong, 5–12 cm long, 2–4 cm wide, acuminate, base round to nearly cordate, thick yellow woolly beneath, petiole 2 cm long, without glands; flowers about 12 together, corolla funnelform to campanulate, fleshy, white to pink-lilac, with carmine patches, about 4.5 cm wide, calyx large, 1.5 cm long, light green, densely glandular as are the ovaries and style base, stamens 10, uneven, April. BM 9253; SR 633. China; NW. Yunnan Prov., east side of the Lichiang Mts., on grassy slopes at 3000–4000 m. z6 ★ Fig. 96. # ∅

R. adenophorum Balf. f. & W. W. Sm. (S Taliense, SS Adenogynum). Evergreen shrub, 1–2 m high, young shoots densely woolly and glandular; leaves lanceolate to oblanceolate, 6–10 cm long, 2–4 cm wide, acuminate, base round, eventually glabrous above, with about 14 vein pairs, rust-red to cinnamon-brown tomentose beneath, glandular beneath the tomentum; flowers about 10 together, corolla funnelform, 5 cm long, pink with a few carmine-red spots, April. Central Yunnan Prov., in gravelly meadows at 4000 m. z6 ★ # ∅

R. adonopodum Franch. (S Ponticum, SS Caucasicum). Evergreen shrub, 1–2.5 m high, young shoots thinly tomentose and glandular; leaves oblong-oblanceolate, acute, 7–15 cm long, cuneately tapered at the base, leathery, glabrous above, densely gray tomentose beneath and on the 12–25 mm long petiole; flowers in loose, terminal, clustered racemes, axis to 5 cm long, corolla broadly funnelform-campanulate, 5–7 cm wide, light pink, interior usually punctate, with 5 rounded limb lobes, ovaries densely covered with long glands, style glabrous, stamens 10, pubescent only at the base, April. China; Szechwan Prov. 1900. z6 ★★ # ☼

R. aechmophyllum see: **R. yunnanense**

R. aemulorum see: **R. mallotum**

R. aeruginosum see: **R. campanulatum** var. **aeruginosum**

R. aganniphum Balf. f. & Ward (S and SS Taliense). Evergreen shrub, 0.5–3 m high, young shoots thinly floccose at first, but very quickly becoming glabrous; leaves leathery tough, oblong-elliptic, 6–11 cm long, acute, base round to slightly cordate, with 14–16 vein pairs, underside with a dense, silver-white to light brown indumentum; flowers 15–20 in dense corymbs, corolla funnelform-campanulate, 3.5 cm long, white or with a trace of pink, and red spotted, limb with 5 emarginate lobes, stamens 10, uneven, ovaries and style glabrous, calyx composed only of an undulate limb; fruit cylindrical, distinctly curved. BMns 147 (= *R. vellereum* Tagg). SE. Tibet, Tsangpo Valley. z7 ★ Fig. 95. #

R. alabamense Rehd. (S Azalea, SS Luteum). Deciduous shrub, 1–1.5 m high, very rarely higher, habit rather globose, often stoloniferous, young shoots usually appressed rough pubescent, gray, later brown; leaves usually obovate to more elliptic, 3–6 cm long, 1–3 cm wide, acute, base cuneate, lightly pubescent above, denser beneath and light green, margins ciliate, petiole 5 mm; flowers appearing with the foliage, 5–15 in umbellate clusters, stalk glandular pubescent, calyx lobes oval, bristly, without glands, corolla funnelform and gradually widening, 1–3 cm wide, white with a large yellow patch on the upper lobes, sweet smelling, April–May. RYB 11: 3 (= *Azalea nudiflora* var. *alba* Mohr). USA; Alabama to Georgia. 1922. z7 ★★ ☼

R. albiflorum Hook. (S Albiflorum). Deciduous shrub, 1.5–1.8 m high, young shoots pubescent; leaves narrowly ovate, 2.5–6 cm long, somewhat pubescent on both sides or also glabrous; flowers solitary or paired (!) from lateral buds of the previous year's leafless shoots, corolla white, campanulate, 2 cm wide, 5 lobed, the lobes erect, stamens 10, pubescent, June–July. SR 3; BM 3670; NF 9: 128; 7: 197; RWF 254 (= *Azalea albiflora* Ktze.). N. America, Rocky Mts. Difficult to cultivate. z5 ★ Fig. 92, 114.

Fig. 92. *Rhododendron albiflorum* (from Hooker)

R. albrechtii Maxim. (S Azalea, SS Canadense). Upright, deciduous shrub, 1–3 m high, open, bushy, shoots quickly becoming glabrous, brown; leaves obovate to oblanceolate, usually 5 at the ends of short shoots, 4–15 cm long, 1.5–6 cm wide, appressed pubescent beneath, petiole short; flowers grouped 4–5, appearing before or with the foliage, corolla broadly campanulate, not parted to the base, purple-red stamens 10 (!), April to May. BM 9207; MJ 755; RYB 14: 1. N. and central Japan, in thickets and forests. z6 ★★★★ ✤

R. alpicola see: **R. nivale** ssp. **boreale**

R. ambiguum Hemsl. (S and SS Triflorum). Evergreen shrub, 1–1.5 m high, shoots thin, narrowly upright, densely glandular; leaves oblong-ovate, acuminate, 6–9 cm long, 2–4 cm wide, with variably shaped scales beneath, margin undulate; flowers 3–6, terminal, corolla infundibular, to 5 cm wide, yellow with green patches, interior somewhat pubescent, exterior slightly scaly, stamens 10, April to May. BM 8400; Gs 1926: 125. China, W. Szechwan Prov., 3500 m. 1904. Variable in form and color of the flowers. z7 ★★ Plate 57. # ✤

R. anthopogon D. Don (S Anthopogon). Small, evergreen shrub, very aromatic, compact, to 50 cm high, shoots short and branched, involucral scales of the winter buds abscising; leaves obovate-elliptic, 3–4.5 cm long, 1.5–2 cm wide, slightly scaly above, more densely so beneath, petiole 1 cm long, scaly above; flowers 4–6 in dense corymbs, corolla narrowly tubular with a broad limb, pink, stamens 6–8, calyx finely ciliate along the margin, April. BM 3947; SR 5; RYB 2: 18; SNp 110. E. Himalayas, S. Tibet, 3500–5000 m. z7 ★★ # ✤

R. apodectum see: **R. dichroanthum** ssp. **apodectum**

R. arborescens (Pursh) Torr. (S Azalea, SS Luteum). Upright, deciduous shrub, 3–4 m high, irregularly branched, young shoots glabrous, occasionally slightly pruinose; leaves thin, obovate to oblanceolate, 4–8 cm long, 1.5–3 cm wide, glossy green above, usually blue-green beneath, occasionally somewhat pubescent; flowers 3–6, appearing after the leaves, corolla infundibular, to 5 cm wide, white, pink toned, fragrant, June–July. RYB. 11: 4; HyWF 133; RWF 255 (= *Azalea arborescens* Pursh). E. USA, in the mountains. 1818. z5 ★★★ Fig. 94. ✤

R. arboreum Sm. (S and SS Arboreum). Evergreen tree, 6–12 m in its habitat; leaves tough, oblanceolate, 10–20 cm long, 3–5 cm wide, glossy green above, usually silvery beneath; flowers to 20 in dense, rounded corymbs, corolla funnelform-campanulate, 4–5 cm wide, the type deep red with black spots, but quite variable in color, stamens 10, white, glabrous, January–April. BM 3825, 4381, 5008, 5311, 7696; SR 14; HAL 161. Himalayas; Kashmir, Bhutan, Assam, Ceylon, 1500–3000 m. Only for very mild climates. z9 ★★★★ Fig. 91. # ✤ ⌀

Including 2 subspecies:

ssp. **campbelliae** (Hook. f.) Tagg. Also tree-like; leaves like the typical species in form and size, but more leathery and more brown tomentose beneath; flowers from carmine or pink to white, but occasionally with a pink limb and white center (= *R. arboreum* var. *roseum* Lindl.; *R. campbelliae* Hook. f.). Found in the range of the species in Sikkim and Nepal, but particularly at altitudes of over 2400 m. At higher altitudes the leaves become thicker with darker brown indumentum beneath. Much hardier than the typical *R. arboreum*, but flowering only on older plants and so early that the flowers are often frost damaged. # ✤

ssp. **cinnamoneum** (Wall. Cat.) Tagg. More bushy habit than both other forms; similar to ssp. *campbelliae*, but the leaf undersides cinnamon-brown or rust-brown and sometimes loosely woolly; flowers normally white, with distinct markings

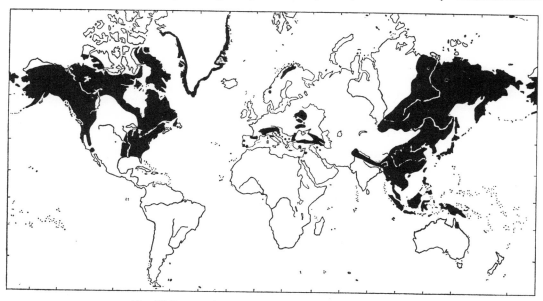

Fig. 93. Range of the genus *Rhododendron* (Original)

Fig. 94. **Rhododendron.** Left *R. arborescens;* middle *R. atlanticum;* right *R. bakeri*
(from NBB and Schneider)

or occasionally also pink or carmine. BM 3825; BR 1982 (= *R. cinnamoneum* Wall.). Higher altitudes in the range of the species. More winter hardy than ssp. *campbelliae*. Plate 62. # ☺

var. *roseum* see: ssp. **campbelliae**

R. × 'Arbutifolium' see: cultivar 'Arbutifolium'

R. argenteum see: **R. grande**

R. argyrophyllum Franch. (S Arboreum, SS Argyrophyllum). Evergreen shrub, 2–3(6) m high, young shoots thinly gray or white tomentose at first, eventually glabrous; leaves narrowly oblong, 6–13 cm long, 1.5–3 cm wide, acuminate, base round, smooth and dark green above, usually silvery beneath; flowers grouped 6–10 in loose corymbs, corolla campanulate, 3–3.5 cm wide, white, often with a pink trace or pink with darker patches, May. China; W. Szechwan Prov., 1800–2500 m. 1904. z6 ★★★ # ☺

var. **cupulare** Rehd. & Wils. Young shoots glabrous; flowers smaller, cupulate. Plate 37.

var. **nankingense** Cowan. Leaves broader and larger, silver-white beneath; flowers pink to purple-lilac, to 5 cm wide, in large inflorescences, scented like primulas. RYB 12: 15. China; Kweichow Prov. 1932. ☺

R. arizelum Balf. f. & Forrest (S Falconeri). Evergreen shrub, also a tree in its habitat, to 5 m high, young shoots and leaf undersides velvety brown; leaves obovate, 13–20 cm long, rugose above like *R. falconeri;* flowers 20

together in dense, about 15 cm wide corymbs, corolla campanulate, 4–5 cm wide, 8 lobed, white to yellowish or with a pink trace and reddish basal spot, stamens 16, ovaries densely pubescent, but not glandular (!), April. RYB 24: 36; ICS 4208. China, Burma, Tibet. 1917. z8 ★★ Fig. 95. # ⌀

R. artosquameum see: **R. oreotrephes**

R. astrocalyx see: **R. wardii**

R. atlanticum Rehd. (S Azalea, SS Luteum). Deciduous, stoloniferous shrub, about 60 cm high; leaves oval-oblong, 4–10 cm long, 2–3.5 cm wide, bristly ciliate or quite finely serrate, upper surface light or bluish green and smooth, venation somewhat pubescent beneath; flowers grouped 4–10, appearing with or shortly after the foliage, corolla tubular-funnelform, 4 cm wide, white, usually somewhat pink toned, very fragrant, when in bud has a distinct ring of long bristly glands at the apex. RYB 1: 37; LAz 27; BHR 35. E. USA, along the coast. z6. ★★★ Fig. 94. ☺

R. augustinii Hemsl. (S Triflorum, SS Augustinii). Evergreen shrub, 1.5–3 m high, young shoots soft pubescent and glandular; leaves lanceolate, sharply acuminate, 4–12 cm long, 1.5–3 cm wide, quickly becoming glabrous above, densely glandular beneath with a pubescent midrib; flowers usually in 3's, corolla broadly funnelform, deeply 5 lobed, lilac to violet-blue, exterior totally scaly, ovaries pubescent and scaly, stamens 10, very uneven, April–May. VVR 123; BM 8479; SR 764; UR 6. China; W. Hupeh, Szechwan Provs., often in open sunny, rocky sites at 3000 m. 1901. The dark violet types are (unfortunately) more tender than the lighter ones. z6 ★★★ Plate 62. # ⊕

var. **chasmanthum** (Diels) Davidian. Very similar to *R. augustinii*, but the shoots glabrous and flowering 2 weeks later. 1.5–2 m high, young shoots glabrous; leaves lanceolate, 6–10 cm long, acuminate, midrib soft pubescent beneath; flowers grouped 4–5 together, corolla deeply 5 lobed, 4–5 cm wide, lavender-blue, the apical lobes green punctate, calyx deeply 5 lobed, scaly, stamens 10, ovaries usually glabrous, May. BMns 79 (= *R. chasmanthum* Diels). China, Tibet. 1907. z7 ★★★

R. aureum Georgi (S Ponticum, SS Caucasicum). Evergreen, 15–30 cm high, procumbent habit, annual shoots very short, leaves broadly obovate, 3–6 cm long, 1–2 cm wide, margins involuted, dark green above, pale green or brownish beneath, with occasional remnants of the juvenile stage tomentum, petiole 5 cm long; flowers 3–8 together, broadly campanulate, about 3 cm long, light yellow, 10 stamen bundles, ovaries brown tomentose, style glabrous, May–June. RYB 24: 28; 25: 31 (= *R. chrysanthum* Pall.). In the Siberian-Mongolian mountains, Manchuria; Japan, Hokkaido, Honshu. Difficult to cultivate! Needs snow cover in winter, moisture (sphagnum soil) in summer; good specimens are very attractive. z2 ★ Plate 37.

R. auriculatum Hemsl. (S Auriculatum). Evergreen shrub, also a tree in its habitat, 2.5–5 m high, new growth and flowers appear in July to August (!): leaves oblong, apex rounded with a pointed tip, 15–30 cm long, with a small auricle at the base on each side, dark green above, lighter beneath and glandular pubescent; flowers grouped 7–15 together in globose corymbs, very fragrant, corolla 7 lobed, 7 cm deep and nearly as wide, white to light pink, stamens 14, glabrous, to 3 cm long, stalks 2.5–3 cm long, not glandular. BM 8786; ICS 4117. China. Flowers only on older plants. z6 ★★ # ∅

R. australe see: **R. leptothrium**

R. austrinum Rehd. (S Azalea, SS Luteum). Deciduous shrub, 1.5–2.5(4) m high, young shoots soft pubescent,

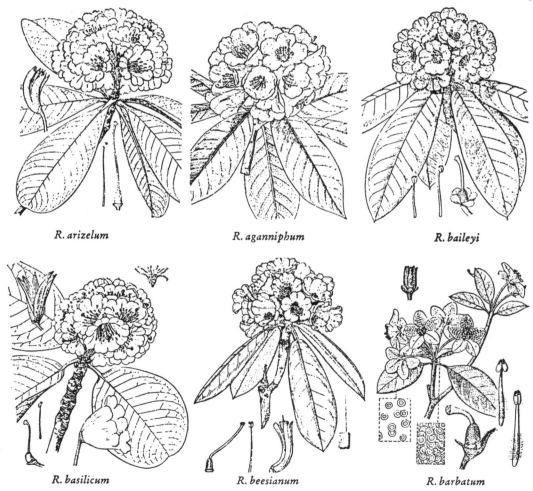

R. arizelum   *R. aganniphum*   *R. baileyi*

R. basilicum   *R. beesianum*   *R. barbatum*

Fig. 95. **Rhododendron** (from ICS)

and also with glandular bristles, bark brown, buds densely white pubescent; leaves obovate to more oblong and elliptic, 2.5–10 cm long, 1–3.5 cm wide, finely pubescent on both sides, denser beneath, margins ciliate, petiole 2–9 mm; flowers appearing with or before the foliage, 6–15 in umbellate clusters, flower stalks about 1 cm long, calyx lobes triangular-lanceolate, glandular ciliate, corolla funnelform, tube 2 cm long, abruptly flared, corolla lobes broadly ovate, to 1 cm wide, long acuminate, exterior pubescent and glandular ciliate, light yellow or dark yellow to orange, stamens 5, about 3 times as long as the tube, ovaries white strigose, more or less fragrant, March–April. (= R. nudiflorum var. luteum Curtiss ex Rehd.). USA; Florida to Mississippi. 1916. Distinguishable from R. canescens only while in flower by the flower color and presence of glands. z6 ★★ ✧

R. × 'Azaleoides' see: cultivar 'Azaleoides'

R. baileyi Balf. f. (S Lepidotum, SS Baileyi). Small, evergreen shrub, 1–1.5 m high, young shoots reddish scaly; leaves elliptic to obovate, obtuse with a distinct mucro, 2.5–6 cm long, 1–3 cm wide, base broadly cuneate, deep green and scaly above, underside bluish at first, later yellowish brown and densely covered with crenately margined scales, petiole 5–15 mm; flowers in short racemes with 8–10(12) flowers on a 2.5 cm long axis, calyx with 5 uneven, small lobes, corolla plate-like, dark purple-red, the 3 apical lobes violet speckled, 3 cm wide, exterior scaly, stamens 10, ovaries white scaly, May. BM 8942; RYB 3: 23; ICS 4011. E. Himalayas. 1913. z7–8 ★★ Fig. 95. ✧

R. bakeri Lemmon & McKay (S Azalea, SS Luteum). Deciduous shrub, 0.7–2 m high, very closely related to R. calendulaceum, but flowers 2–3 weeks later, smaller, somewhat more slender tubular-funnelform, more red or also orange, in clusters of 4–7, but often 25–30 together (!) in globose inflorescences. RYB 11: 7–8 (= R. cumberlandense Braun). N. America; Cumberland Plateau in Kentucky. 1937. z5 ★★ Fig. 92. ✧

R. balfourianum Diels (S Taliense, SS Adenogynum). Evergreen shrub, about 2 m high in its habitat, young shoots scaly at first; leaves oblong to narrowly ovate, 6–11 cm long, 2–3 cm wide, sharply acuminate, base round, dull dark green above, silver-gray scaly beneath; flowers 6–9 together, corolla campanulate, about 2.5 cm wide and deep, 5 lobed, light pink, carmine punctate, calyx with 5 deep, about 6 mm long lobes, distinctly scaly, as are the flower stalk, ovaries and style base. China; W. Yunnan Prov. 1906. z6 ★ ✧

R. barbatum Wall. (S and SS Barbatum). Evergreen shrub, a tree in its habitat, to 10 m high or more, branched from the ground up, young shoots bristly, the bristles often persisting for several years; leaves elliptic-lanceolate, 10–20 cm long, 4–7 cm wide, finely rugose and glossy above, loosely gray tomentose beneath, later glabrous and yellowish green, petiole with glandular bristles; flowers 10–15 in globose corymbs, corolla funnelform-campanulate, 3 cm wide, a bright carmine-red, base with 5 black spots, stamens 10, white, glabrous, anthers purple-black, ovaries glandular, style glabrous, April. SR 129; UR 4; FS 469. Himalayas. 1849. Much used in hybrizing. z8 ★★★ Fig. 91, 95. # ∅ ✧

R. basilicum Balf. f. & W. W. Sm. (S Falconeri). Evergreen shrub, also tree-like in its habitat, 2.5–7 m high, young shoots red-brown, tomentose; leaves elliptic to obovate, 15–30 cm long, 7–15 cm wide, red-brown tomentose beneath, petiole 3 cm long, very thick, flat above; flowers 20 or more in 12–15 cm wide corymbs, corolla broadly campanulate, 8 lobed, light yellow with a reddish trace and red basal spots, 3 cm wide, stamens 16, glabrous, ovaries densely tomentose, May. SR 239; RYB 11: 34; 12: 11; 17: 8 (= R. megaphyllum Balf. f. & Forrest; R. regale Balf. f. & Ward). China. 1913. z8 ★★★ Fig. 95. # ∅ ✧

R. beanianum Cowan (S Neriiflorum, SS Haematodes). Evergreen shrub, about 1 m high, young shoots red-brown floccose; leaves oblong to more obovate, thin leathery, 6–10 cm long, apex rounded, dark green above, glossy and finely rugose, dark red-brown woolly tomentose beneath; flowers 6–8 in terminal corymbs, calyx fleshy, cupulate, corolla funnelform-campanulate, dark blood-red, with 5 black nectary pits at the base, waxy fleshy, May. NF 10: 245; BMns 219. SE. Tibet, Upper Burma. z8 ★★★ Fig. 96. # ✧

R. beesianum Diels (S Lacteum). Evergreen shrub or tree, 3–5 m high in its habitat, shoots stiff and very thick; leaves elliptic oblanceolate, 15–30 cm long, 4–7 cm wide, dark green and smooth above, underside thinly cinnamon-brown tomentose, distinct venation, petiole 2–3 cm long; flowers 15–25 in dense corymbs, corolla broadly campanulate, to 5 cm long, white to pink with a few dark red patches, stamens 10, about 2.5 cm long, ovaries brown woolly, style smooth, exserted past the stamens, April–May. BMns 125; RYB 10: 47 (= R. collectum Balf. f. & Forrest). NW to central Yunnan Prov. 1906. z7 Fig. 95. # ∅

R. bicolor see: **R. canescens**

R. boothii Nutt. (S and SS Boothii). Evergreen shrub, 1–2 m high, open, young shoots very pubescent; leaves oval-elliptic, 7–12 cm long, 3–6 cm wide, long acuminate, deep green above, loosely pubescent and ciliate when young, eventually glabrous, scaly beneath; flowers grouped 6–10 together, corolla broadly campanulate, with 5 wide, round lobes, an intense yellow, exterior scaly, calyx deeply 5 lobed, the lobes broadly ovate, 6 mm long, ciliate, stamens 10, filaments thick, basal half very pubescent, ovaries white scaly, styles thick, bowed. BM 7149; SR 159; RYB 3: 19. Himalayas, Assam. 1849. z9 ★★ # ✧

R. brachyanthum Hutchins. (S and SS Glaucophyllum). Evergreen shrub, about 1 m high, young shoots reddish and scaly; leaves oblong to narrowly elliptic, aromatic, 3–6 cm long, a strong blue-green beneath, with light and dark scales; flowers 3–4(8) in clusters, corolla campanulate, 2–2.5 cm wide, short 5 lobed, light yellow or green toned, stamens 10, red, ovaries scaly, style

Fig. 96. **Rhododendron.** Left *R. adenogynum;* middle *R. brachyanthum* var. *hypolepidotum;* right *R. camtschaticum* (from Regel, Stevenson; middle Original)

glabrous, calyx 1 cm long, deeply 5 lobed, lobes green and outspread, exterior densely scaly, June–July. BM 8750; RYB 3: 25. China. 1906. z6 ★ #

var. **hypolepidotum** Franch. Leaves very densely scaly beneath, with very uneven, light and dark scales; flowers yellow, style very thick and straight. BM 9259 (= *R. charitostreptum* Balf. f & Ward). China, Tibet. Fig. 96. ⊕

R. brachycarpum D. Don (S Ponticum, SS Caucasicum). Evergreen shrub, 2–3 m high, shoot tips and youngest leaves white tomentose, but quickly becoming glabrous, annual shoots thick, light green; leaves oblong, 7–15 cm long, 3–7 cm wide, usually rounded at both ends, light green and smooth above, thinly brown tomentose beneath, petiole 1.5–2 cm long, eventually glabrous; flowers 10–20 in ovate racemes, corolla broadly funnelform, 2.5 cm long, cream-white with green patches or a trace of pink, style shorter than the 10 stamens, June–July. BM 7881; BHR 37 and 42 (= *R. fauriei* Franch.). S. and central Japan, in the mountains. 1861. z6 ★★ Plate 61. # ⊕

Including:

ssp. **tigerstedtii** Nitzelius. Differing in the more vigorous habit, thicker shoots, larger leaves, 15–25 cm long, 5–9 cm wide; flowers white, greenish punctate, to nearly 7.5 cm wide, calyx more fully developed, fruit stalk longer, to 5 cm long, flowers 2 weeks earlier. DB 1970: 150. Korea. Cultivated in Sweden and Finland before 1955. Very winter hardy. z4 ★★ # ∅ ⊕

R. brettii see: **R. longesquamatum**

R. brevistylum Franch. (S Heliolepis). Evergreen shrub, 1–2.5 m high, young shoots reddish, scaly; leaves elliptic-lanceolate, to 12 cm long, 2.5–3 cm wide, regularly scaly above, irregularly scaly beneath with

widely spaced scales; flowers 4–8 together, corolla broadly funnelform, 4 cm long, pink with dark red markings, exterior loosely scaly, stamens 10, very pubescent, style very short, pubescent beneath, June–July. BM 8898; RYB 2: 7. China; Yunnan Prov., Lichiang Range, 3600–3900 m, in open mountain meadows. 1906. z6 ★★ Fig. 98. # ⊕

R. bullatum see: **R. edgeworthii**

R. bureavii Franch. (S Taliense, SS Adenogynum). Evergreen shrub, to about 1.5 m high, young shoots densely tomentose; leaves leathery, elliptic to ovate, 6–11 cm long, 2.5–5 cm wide, dense red woolly beneath; flowers 10–15 together, corolla funnelform, 3 cm long, pink with carmine spots, stamens 10, base very densely pubescent, ovaries, style base, flower stalk and calyx all glandular and pubescent, April. GC 136: 101. China. 1908. z6 ★★ # ∅ ⊕

R. burmanicum Hutchins. (S Maddenii, SS Ciliicalyx). Evergreen shrub, about 1 m high or less, young shoots somewhat bristly and scaly; leaves oblanceolate to obovate, about 5–7 cm long, 3–4 cm wide, abruptly acuminate and with a mucro, base cuneate, densely scaly on both sides, scales very densely arranged and sometimes overlapping, the green leaf blade somewhat visible between the scales, petiole 1 cm, scaly and bristly; flowers 5–7 terminal, stalk 2.5 cm long, scaly, calyx tiny, with bristles, corolla narrowly funnelform-campanulate, to 5 cm long, 5 lobed, greenish yellow to yellowish white, the best form is pure yellow, very fragrant, exterior scaly, stamens 10, ovaries densely scaly, April–May. BMns 546. SW. Burma, Mt. Victoria. 1914. Abundantly flowering on young plants, but suitable only for moist, mild climates. z9 ★★★ ⊕

Fig. 97. *Rhododendron calendylaceum*
(from Watson)

R. calciphilum see: **R. calostrotum** var. **calciphilum**

R. calendulaceum Torr. (S Azalea, SS Luteum). Deciduous shrub, 1–1.5 m high, stoutly branched, young shoots pubescent; leaves wide to oblong-elliptic, 4–12 cm long, 1.5–4 cm wide, finely pubescent above, underside densely pubescent at first, particularly along the midrib, orange and carmine in fall; flowers grouped 5–7, appearing with or shortly after the leaves, infundibular, to 5 cm wide, yellow or orange to scarlet, nearly without fragrance, exterior more or less glandular, tube shorter (!) to as long as the lobes, stamens 5.3 times as long as the tube, calyx, ovaries and flower stalks glandular, June. HyWF 138; RWF 258; BM 1721, 2143, 3439. Eastern USA. Often used in hybridizing. z5 ★★★ Fig. 97. ☼

R. californicum see: **R. macrophyllum**

R. callimorphum Balf. f. & Forrest (S Thomsonii, SS Campylocarpum). Evergreen shrub, 1–2 m high, young

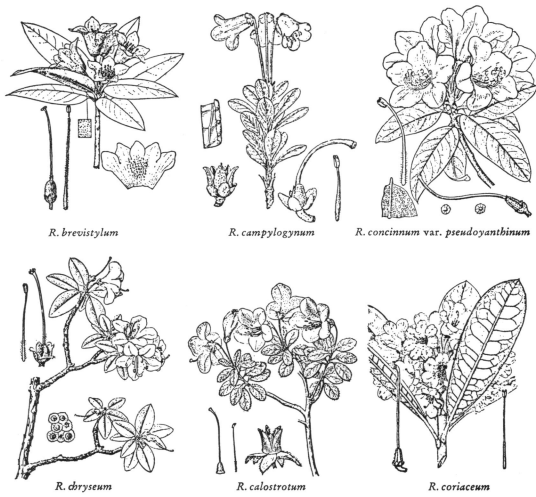

R. brevistylum   *R. campylogynum*   *R. concinnum* var. *pseudoyanthinum*

R. chryseum   *R. calostrotum*   *R. coriaceum*

Fig. 98. **Rhododendron** (from ICS)

shoots usually with stalked glands, later glabrous; leaves broadly oval-elliptic, thin leathery, 3–7 cm long, 2–4.5 cm wide, round, base lightly cordate, deep green and glossy above, blue-green beneath, glandular punctate, petiole 1.5 cm long, with stalked glands; flowers grouped 5–8, corolla broadly campanulate, 4 cm long, soft pink, buds darker, always with a carmine patch, stamens 10, uneven, glabrous, June; fruit capsule sickle-shaped, furrowed. BM 8789; RYB 8: 71 (= *R. cyclium* Balf. f. & Forrest). China; W. Yunnan Prov., 3300 m. 1912. z7 ★★★ Plate 60. # ✣

R. calophytum Franch. (S Fortunei, SS Calophytum). Evergreen shrub, 7–10 m high in its habitat, young shoots very thick, white tomentose at first, later glabrous; leaves directed downward (!), oblong-lanceolate, 20–30 cm long, 4–8 cm wide, gradually tapered to the petiole, with 20–30 vein pairs, light green above, yet lighter beneath, soon becoming glabrous, petiole 1–2 cm long; flowers to 30 in loose racemes, corolla open campanulate, base bulging, white-pink to white with a distinct carmine-red basal spot, stamens 15–20, shorter than the corolla, ovaries glabrous, styles very straight, glabrous, stigma yellow (!), capitate, March–April. BM 9173; UR 10; FIO 26; RYB 17: 6. China; W. Szechwan, forests, 2000–3000 m; Tibet. 1904. z6 ★★★★ # ⊘ ✣

R. calostrotum Balf. f. & Ward (S Saluenense). Evergreen shrub, about 30 cm high, young shoots densely scaly; leaves obovate-elliptic, to 3 cm long and 1.5 cm wide, densely greenish scaly above, densely covered with dry, reddish scales beneath; margins ciliate; flowers usually in 2's, corolla broadly funnelform, about 3 cm long, light purple-violet, exterior soft pubescent, but not scaly, calyx large, scaly and long pubescent, 8 mm long, stamens 10, stalk 2.5 cm long, late April. BM 9001; UR 9. NE. Burma. 1919. z6 ★★★★ Fig. 98. #✣

var. **calciphilum** (Hutch. & Ward) Davidian. Leaves only about 12 mm long, underside somewhat blue-green; flowers like the species, but appearing later, late May (= *R. calciphilum* Hutch. & Ward). NW. Upper Burma, occurring in limestone outcroppings. # ✣

R. caloxanthum Balf. f. & Farr. (S Thomsonii, SS Campylocarpum). Evergreen shrub, 0.7–.15 m high, young shoots glandular; leaves oval-rounded, 3–6 cm long, blue-green and glabrous beneath; flowers grouped 4–9 together, corolla campanulate, 5 lobed, 3 cm wide, sulfur yellow, but often nearly orange, orange-scarlet in bud, stamens 10, glabrous, ovaries, pistil base, calyx and stalk densely glandular, April–May. Burma. 1919. z7 ★★★# ✣

R. campanulatum D. Don (S Campanulatum). Evergreen shrub, 4–5 m tough, broadly ovate-elliptic, 7–15 cm long, 3–6 cm wide, glossy dark green above, smooth, with 14–16 vein pairs, densely rust-brown tomentose beneath, young leaves without (!) metallic gloss; flowers usually 8 in loose corymbs, corolla broadly campanulate, 4 cm long, 5 cm wide, 5 lobed, white to purple-pink, somewhat variable, apical lobes darker punctate, stamens 10, pubescent beneath, ovaries

and styles glabrous, April–May. BM 3759; UR 5. Himalayas, from Kashmir to Bhutan. 1825. Flowers poorly on young plants! The best forms (e.g. 'Knaphill') are a very attractive blue. z6 ★★★ Fig. 91. # ⊘ ✣

var. **aeruginosum** (Hook. f.) Nichols. Primarily differing when young in the conspicuously blue-green leaves with a metallic gloss, totally glabrous above; flowers grouped 10–12 together, lilac-pink to reddish purple, with darker markings. JRHS 87: 159; RYB 17: 1 (= *R. aeruginosum* Hook. f.). Himalayas, Sikkim, 4000 m. 1849. z6 ★★ #⊘✣

R. campbelliae see: **R. arboreum** ssp. **campbelliae**

R. campylocarpum Hook. f. (S Thomsonii, SS Campylocarpum). Evergreen shrub, bushy, 1–2 m high, young shoots thin, with stalked glands; leaves ovate to short elliptic, 5–8 cm long, 3–5 cm wide, rounded, dark green and glossy above, blue-green beneath with very small, scattered, brown hairs, petiole 1.5–2 cm long; flowers grouped 6–8, corolla campanulate, 4 cm long, yellow, stamens 10, anthers reddish, ovaries and calyx very glandular, April–May. SR 702. Himalayas; 3500–4500 m. 1851. Much used for hybridization in England. Progeny retain a darker yellow flower color. z7 ★★★★ Fig. 99. # ✣

var. **elatum** is the form predominantly found in English gardens. It is taller, more open, buds more orange-red, flowers sulfur-yellow, to 7 cm wide. BM 4968. Progeny usually have ivory-white or pink flowers. z7 ★★★★ ✣

Fig. 99. *Rhododendron campylocarpum*
(from Hooker)

R. campylogynum Balf. f. & Ward (S Campylogynum). Evergreen shrub, scarcely over 1 m high, dense, compact, shoots glandular; leaves obovate-lanceolate, 1–2 cm long, with a thick prickly tip, 0.8 cm wide, blue-green beneath, with scattered scales, margins somewhat curving inward; flowers 1–4 at the shoot tips, solitary on 3–5 cm long, erect stalks, corolla short campanulate, small, 1.5 cm long, limb 5 lobed, exterior violet-red, interior dark brown, exterior and calyx totally glabrous, stamens 10, pubescent at the base, May. NF 1: 164; BM 9407a; SR 183; DRHS 1768; JRHS 69: 6; VVR 78. NE. Burma, 4000–5000 m, on moist granite outcroppings. 1912. In cultivation often only cushion-form, to 15 cm high. z7 ★★ Fig. 98. # ☺

var. **myrtilloides** (Balf. f. & Ward) Davidian. Still shorter than the species, 7–10 cm high, mat-form, shoots somewhat glandular; leaves 12–18 mm long, 8 mm wide, blue-green and loosely scaly beneath; flowers solitary on 3 cm long, thin stalks, exterior plum color, interior brown. RYB 6: 66; BS 3: Pl. 70; 13: 21; NF 1: 164 (= *R. myrtilloides* Balf. f. & Ward). NE. Burma, in the higher mountains at 5000 m, needs high humidity and therefore difficult to cultivate. z6 ★★ Plate 37. # ☺

R. camtschaticum Pall. (S Camtschaticum). Procumbent, deciduous shrub, about 20–30 cm high, young shoots with long glandular hairs; leaves sessile, obovate to spathulate, 2–5 cm long, 1–2.5 cm wide, thin, ciliate, frequently with glandular hairs on the margins and the venation, light green; flowers usually solitary or paired at the shoot tips, corolla top-shaped, 2.5–3.5 cm wide, dark purple-violet with red-brown markings, exterior pubescent, stamens 10, calyx large, lobes leaflike, May. SR 189; BM 8210. Kamchatka, N. Japan, Alaska, both sides of the Bering Strait. 1799. For cool, moist gravelly slopes. z6 ★★ Fig. 96. ☺

R. canadense Torr. (S Azalea, SS Canadense). Deciduous shrub, 30–70 cm high, shoots thin, finely pubescent at first, later yellowish red, often also pruinose; leaves elliptic-oblong, 2–5 cm long, margins ciliate and involuted, dull blue-green above, thin gray tomentose beneath; flowers grouped 3–6, appearing before the foliage, corolla top-shaped, incised nearly to the base (!), lilac-purple, 3 cm wide, stamens 10, pubescent at the base, ovaries bristly pubescent. BM 474; SR 47; RFW 260. Northeastern N. America; on river banks. 1767. z3 ★ Fig. 100. ☺

R. canescens (Michx.) Sweet (S Azalea, SS Luteum). Upright deciduous shrub, about 1.5–2 m high, young shoots and buds with a soft and long gray pubescence; leaves oblong-obovate to more elliptic-oblanceolate, thickish, acute, 4–10 cm long, 1.5–3.5 cm wide, dark green above, gray tomentose beneath, particularly on the venation; flowers appearing before, with or after the foliage, grouped 5–22 together, petiole glandular and pubescent, to 1 cm long, calyx lobes very small, round, ciliate, corolla with a 2–2.5 cm long tube, exterior glandular and pubescent, limb to 4 cm wide, tube white to pink, glands green to dark red, stamens about 3 times as long as the tube, ovaries silky pubescent, April–May (= *R. bicolor* Pursh; *Azalea canescens* Michx.). Eastern USA. 1810. z7 ★ ☺

R. cantabile see: **R. russatum**

R. carolinianum Rehd. (S Carolinianum). Evergreen shrub, 1–1.5 m high, young shoots scattered glandular; leaves elliptic to obovate, 6–10 cm long, 3–4 cm wide, rounded, base broadly cuneate, glabrous above with reticulate venation, densely scaly beneath; flowers grouped 4–9 together, corolla narrowly funnelform, 3 cm long, exterior totally glabrous, pale pink, the 5 lobes longer than the tube, stamens 10, base pubescent, ovaries scaly, May–June. BR 37. Blue Ridge Mts. of eastern USA. z6 ★★ #

'**Album**'. Leaves narrower, darker, more acuminate; flowers white with yellow markings.

'**Yellow Form**'. Flowers yellow. RYB 13: 39.

R. catawbiense Michx. (S and SS Ponticum). Evergreen shrub, 2–4 m high, usually broader than high, young shoots somewhat tomentose at first, but quickly becoming glabrous; leaves oval-oblong, widest in the

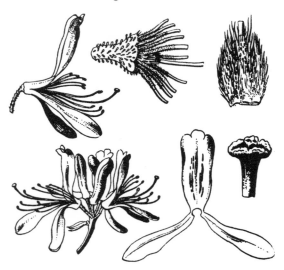

Fig. 100. *Rhododendron canadense* (from Kavka)

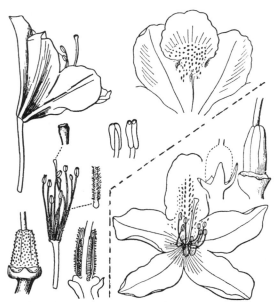

Fig. 101. **Rhododendron.** Left *R. catawbiense*; right *R. ponticum* (from Schneider)

middle, 7–15 cm long, 3–5 cm wide, deep green above, glossy, with about 16 vein pairs, glabrous beneath, minutely punctate, light green, petiole 2–3 cm long, woolly at first, later nearly glabrous; flowers grouped 15–20 together, corolla 5 cm wide at the limb, lilac-purple with greenish blotches, finely pubescent in the throat, exterior glabrous, stamens 10, base pubescent, ovaries brown tomentose (!) on the wild form, style glabrous, July. BM 1671; HyFW 139; BC 1176. N. America, developing thickets in the Allegheny Mts. Widely used for winter hardiness in hybridization (e.g. Waterer, Seidel etc.; see cultivar list). z5 ★ Fig. 101. # ⌀

R. caucasicum Pall. (S Ponticum, SS Caucasicum). Evergreen shrub, 1(2.5) m high, young shoots densely tomentose; leaves ovate to oblong, 5–10 cm long, base cuneate, dark green above, glabrous and somewhat rugose, thinly light brown tomentose beneath, petiole 1–1.5 cm long, tomentose; flowers grouped 7–10, corolla broadly campanulate, yellowish or with a pink blush and green markings, stamens 10, base pubescent, ovaries densely white tomentose, style glabrous, pink, May; fruit capsule erect. BM 1145. Caucasus. 1803. Earlier utilized in hybridizing. z7 ★ Fig. 114. # ⌀

Included here are 'Cunningham's White', 'Cunningham's Sulphur', 'Boule de Neige', 'Jacksonii' and other hybrids recognized for their early flowers and dense habit.

R. cephalanthum Franch. (S Anthopogon). Evergreen shrub, 30–50 cm high, young shoots densely thick scaly; leaves oblong-elliptic, 3 cm long, 1 cm wide, thick leathery, margins involuted, glabrous above with reticulate venation, underside densely scaly; flowers in dense, terminal capitula of about 8, corolla narrowly infundibular, 12 mm long and wide, white, limb 5 lobed, enclosing the 5 stamens, style very short, ovaries scaly, calyx scaly and ciliate, April–May. RYB 2: 19; BS 3: 361. China; Szechwan, Yunnan Provs., 1908. z7 ★★ # ☺

R. cerasinum Tagg (S Thomsonii, SS Cerasinum). Evergreen shrub, to 3 m high; leaves oblong-elliptic, 5–7 cm long, underside finely silky only when young, but very quickly becoming totally glabrous and bluish; flowers pendulous, grouped 5–6, corolla campanulate, 4–5 cm long, cream-white with a cherry-red limb, occasionally also totally scarlet-red with darker nectaries, stamens 10, glabrous, ovaries, calyx and stalk glandular (!), May. BM 9538; GC 131: 43; ICS 4179. Tibet. 1924. z7 ★★★ # ☺

R. chaetomallum Balf. f. & Forrest (S Neriiflorum, SS Haematodes). Evergreen shrub, to 2.5 m, very similar to R. haematodes, but the young shoots very bristly pubescent, not woolly, calyx much larger (to 1 cm long!); leaves densely dark brown woolly beneath; flowers grouped 4–6, corolla funnelform-campanulate, deep carmine or only dark pink, calyx similarly red, March–April. BMns 25. Tibet, China. 1917. z8 ★★★) # ☺

var. **xanthanthum** Tagg & Forrest. Shrub, only 0.5–1 m high; flowers larger than those of the species, cream-yellow with a trace of pink, calyx large and cupulate. SE Tibet, 4700 m. ☺

R. chamaecistus see: **Rhodothamnus chamaecistus**

R. chamaethomsonii (Tagg & Forrest) Cowan & Davidian (S Neriiflorum, SS Forrestii). Upright, evergreen shrub, to 0.7 m high; leaves obovate to more oblong, rounded at the apex, blue pruinose with indented venation above, glabrous beneath, 2–3 cm long; flowers grouped 4–5 together, corolla funnelform-campanulate, carmine, to 3 cm long, limb 5 lobed. UR 12: RYB 6: 58. SE. Tibet, China; Yunnan Prov. z7 ★★ # ☺

var. **chamaethauma** (Tagg) Cowan & Davidian. More upright habit, to 50 cm high or more; leaves smaller than those of the species; flowers grouped 4–5 together (= R. repens var. chamaethauma Tagg; R. repens var. chamaedoron Tagg & Forrest). SE. Tibet, Doshong La. Before 1932. Links R. chamaethomsonii with R. forrestii # ☺

R. charitopes Balf. f. & Forrest (S and SS Glaucophyllum). Evergreen shrub, to about 50 cm high, young shoots scaly; leaves obovate, 2.5–6 cm long, 8–20 mm wide, glossy green above, smooth from yellowish scales beneath; flowers usually in 3's, corolla campanulate, 5 lobed, 2.5 cm wide, pure pink, the apical lobes carmine punctate, calyx with 5 deep, about 8 mm long lobes, these scaly on the exterior, ovaries densely scaly, styles glabrous, very thick, April. BM 9358; ICS 4005. Burma. 1920. z7 ★★ # ☺

R. charitostreptum see: **R. brachyanthum** var. **hypolepidotum**

R. chartophyllum see: **R. yunnanense**

R. chasmanthum see: **R. augustinii** var. **chasmanthum**

R. chrysanthum see: **R. aureum**

R. chryseum Balf. f. & Ward (S Lapponicum). Evergreen shrub, 0.3–0.7 m high, young shoots densely scaly; leaves aromatic, ovate-elliptic, 1.5 cm long, 1 cm wide, densely scaly on both sides as is the petiole; flowers grouped 4–5; corolla top-shaped, 2–2.5 cm wide, sulfur-yellow to yellow, tube short and soft pubescent, stamens 5, widely exserted, long pubescent beneath, ovaries scaly, style glabrous, calyx with 5 oblong, ciliate and scaly lobes, April–May. BM 9246. China; Yunnan Prov., Mekong-Salween region, 4000 m. 1912. z6 ★★ Fig. 98. # ☺

R. ciliatum Hook. f. (S Maddenii, SS Ciliicalyx). Evergreen shrub, 1–2 m high, but often also procumbent, usually broader than high, young shoots bristly pubescent; leaves elliptic-lanceolate, 4–10 cm long, 2–5 cm wide, bristly pubescent above, scaly beneath, midrib bristly, petiole with long bristles; flowers 2–4 in short racemes, corolla broadly campanulate, 5 lobed, to 5 cm wide, nodding, white to light pink, calyx 8 mm long, 5 lobed, parted to the base, dense and long bristly ciliate, exterior lightly scaly, stamens 10, base pubescent, ovaries scaly, style smooth, mid April. BM 4648; SNp 102; HAL 106. Sikkim, Himalayas. 1850. Much used in hybridizing. z8 ★★★ Fig. 102. # ☺

Fig. 102. *Rhododendron ciliatum* (from Hooker)

R. ciliicalyx Franch. (S Maddenii, SS Ciliicalyx).
Evergreen shrub, to 2.5 m high; leaves narrowly elliptic,
6–11 cm long, acute, bluish and scaly beneath, petiole
bristly; flowers usually in 3's, fragrant, corolla
funnelform at the base, limb broad and 5 lobed, to 10 (!)
cm wide, pure white or with yellowish markings on both
apical lobes, stamens 10, about 5 cm long, base very
pubescent, ovaries scaly, calyx 5 lobed, the lobes 3–8 mm
long and bristly ciliate, March–May. BM 7782; ICS 4033;
DRHS 1170. China. 1892. z9 ★★★★ # ☼

R. cinnabarinum Hook. f. (S Cinnabarinum). Evergreen
shrub, upright, 1–2 m high, shoots reddish, somewhat
scaly when young; leaves obovate, to 9 cm long and 5 cm
wide, with many distinct veins above, bluish and densely
scaly beneath; flowers usually in 5's, pendulous, corolla
tubular, 5–6 cm long, apex somewhat flared and with 5
erect lobes, vermillion-red, stamens 10, May–June. ICS
4045. Sikkim, Himalayas. 1849. Very meritorious and
attractive. z8 ★★★★ # ∅ ☼

var. **aestivale** Hutch. Leaves more lanceolate; flowers like the
species, vermillion-red, limb yellowish, flowers first opening in
July (!).

var. **blandfordiiflorum** Hook. Flowers tubular, exterior red,
interior yellow to greenish. BM 4930; FS 1173. ☼

var. **pallidum** Bot. Mag. Flowers broadly funnelform-
campanulate, base narrower, limb outspread, light pink. BM
4788.

var. **purpurellum** Cowan. Tube shorter, campanulate, purple-
violet to lilac-pink.

var. **roylei** Hook. Tube more open, carmine with a trace of
violet. RYB 12: 1. ☼

R. cinnamoneum see: **R. arboreum** ssp. **cinnamoneum**

R. citriniflorum Balf. f. & Forrest (S Neriiflorum, SS
Sanguineum). Evergreen shrub, to 1 m high; leaves
obovate, 3–8 cm long, densely brownish woolly
beneath; flowers grouped 6–8, stalk bristly pubescent
and glandular, corolla campanulate, pure lemon-yellow,
without markings, 3 cm long, limb 5 lobed, stamens 10,
ovaries brownish pubescent and glandular-bristly, style
glabrous, April–May. NF 6: 8. China; Yunnan Prov.
1917. z8 ★★ # ☼

R. clementinae Forrest (S and SS Taliense). Evergreen
shrub, 1–2 m high, shoots very thick; leaves oval-oblong,
6–14 cm long, 3–7 cm wide, rounded, base nearly
cordate, dull green above, thick whitish to light brown
tomentose beneath with a glossy membranous layer at
first, petiole 2 cm long; flowers about 15 in corymbs,
corolla campanulate, cream-white with a trace of pink or
totally pink with darker markings, limb with 6–7 lobes,
stamens 12–14, calyx 1 mm long, ovaries and calyx
glabrous, May. BM 9392; ICS 4229. China; NW. Yunnan,
SW. Szechwan Provs. 1913. z6 ★ # ∅

R. coelicum Balf. f. & Forrest (S Neriiflorum, SS
Haematodes). Low evergreen shrub, about 1.5 m high in
its habitat, shoots thick, glabrous; leaves leathery,
obovate, about 7 cm long, 4 cm wide, rounded apex, base
obtuse, smooth and eventually glabrous above, thick
cinnamon-brown beneath, only the midrib visible;
flowers 12–15 in compact, globose umbels, axis very
short, tomentose, flower stalk 1 cm, densely glandular,
corolla funnelform-campanulate, fleshy, 4 cm long,
scarlet-red, 5 lobed, calyx cupulate, fleshy, 6 mm long,
with 5 irregular lobes, stamens 10, glabrous, ovaries with
red glands, April. RYB 10: 19. NE. Upper Burma. z8 ★★
☼

R. collectum see: **R. beesianum**

R. complexum Balf. f. & W. W. Sm. (S Lapponicum).
Evergreen shrub, 30–50 cm high, shoots very short, habit
often mat-like; flowers in 3's, corolla broadly
funnelform, dark purple-red, exterior densely scaly,
stamens 5, calyx glabrous on the exterior, but with a
ciliate margin, pistil much shorter than the stamens,
May. China; Yunnan Prov., 3500–4000 m, on rocky
meadows. z7 ★ #

R. concatenans Hutchins. (S Cinnabarinum). Evergreen
shrub, 1–1.5 m high, shoots red-brown, distinctly scaly;
leaves oblong-elliptic, completely glabrous above,
bluish and scaly beneath, bud scales reddish, glandular
and ciliate, quickly abscising; flowers 7–8, corolla
campanulate, to 4 cm wide, apricot colored with a
purplish blush and venation, the 5 oval lobes somewhat
outspread, April–May. UR 13; BMns 634. Sikkim,
Himalayas, SE. Tibet. 1925. z8 ★★★★ # ☼

'Copper' (Ingram). Flowers more reddish. RYB 9: 43. ☼

R. concinnum Hemsl. (S Triflorum, SS Yunnanense).
Evergreen shrub, 1–1.5 m high, shoots densely
branched, very scaly; leaves oblong-lanceolate, 4–5 cm
long, 1–2 cm wide, scaly on both sides, petiole similarly
scaly, 4 mm long; flowers in 3's, corolla funnelform, 4–5

Plate 33

Quercus. a. *Q. haas;* b. *Q.* × *turneri* (from the original tree); c. *Q. hartwissiana;* d. *Q. pyrenaica;* e. *Q. canariensis;* f. *Q. pubescens;* g. *Q. alnifolia;* h. *Q. cerris* 'Laciniata'; i. *Q. pubescens* ssp. *anatolica* (most material from wild plants)

Plate 34

Quercus. a. *Q. alba*; b. *Q. garryana*; c. *Q. stellata*; d. *Q. gambelii* e. *Q. acuta*;
f. *Q. macrocarpa*; g. *Q. lyrata* (material from wild plants)

Plate 35

Quercus. a. *Q. bicolor;* b. *Q. prinus;* c. *Q. muehlenbergii;* d. *Q. prinoides;* e. *Q. aliena;*
f. *Q. mongolica;* g. *Q. mongolica* var. *grosseserrata* (material from wild plants)

Plate 36

Quercus frainetto
in the Dortmund Botanic Garden, W. Germany

Quercus frainetto (wild!)
near Vizegrad, Yugoslavia

Forest of *Quercus frainetto* and *Q. cerris,* with *Mespilus germanica* as understory,
in the Strandsha Mts., Bulgaria
Photo: Dr. Browicz, Poznan

Plate 37

Rhododendron eximium   *Rhododendron argyrophyllum* var. *cupulare*
both in the Royal Botanic Garden, Edinburgh, Scotland

Rhododendron campylogynum var. *myrtilloides*   *Rhododendron aureum*
in the Royal Botanic Garden, Edinburgh, Scotland   in the Göteborg Botanic Garden, W. Germany

Plate 38

Rhododendron neriiflorum *Rhododendron spinuliferum*
both in the Royal Botanic Garden, Edinburgh, Scotland

Rhododendron grande with new growth;
in the Hillier Arboretum, England

Rhododendron edgeworthii
in the Royal Botanic Garden, Edinburgh, Scotland

Plate 39

Ribes fuchsioides
Photo: Dr. Schwanke

Robinia kelseyi
in the Dortmund Botanic Garden, W. Germany

Richea scoparia
in the Dublin Botanic Garden, Ireland

Rosa × harisonii
in the German National Rosarium, Dortmund

Plate 40

Rosa pomifera 'Duplex'

Rosa damascena

Rosa foetida 'Bicolor'

Rosa gallica 'Versicolor'

All photographs taken in the German National Rosarium, Dortmund

Plate 41

Quercus phellos,
Morton Arboretum 1974 (USA)

Quercus reticulata,
Pretoria Hort. Res. Station 1970 (S. Africa)

Quercus aliena,
in the Kyoto Botanic Garden, Japan

Quercus coccifera
in the Zurich Botanic Garden, Switzerland

Plate 42

Quercus dentata
in its habitat in Japan

Quercus dentata in a park near Beijing, China
Photo: F. Bencat

Quercus glauca
in the Akasawa Forest Arboretum, Japan

Quercus hartwissiana in the botanic garden
of the Copenhagen Veterinary College, Denmark

Plate 43

Quercus glandulifera in its habitat
Photo: Dr. S. Watari, Tokyo

Quercus hispanica 'Ambrozyana'
in the Hillier Arboretum, England

Quercus glandulifera in Japan
Photo: Dr. S. Watari, Tokyo

Plate 44

Quercus acutissima in flower
Photo: Dr. S. Watari, Tokyo

Quercus hispanica 'Lucombeana' in the Royal Botanic Gardens, Kew, England

Plate 45

Quercus macranthera
Photo: Archivbild

Quercus canariensis in Exbury Gardens, England

Quercus mongolica
in its native habitat in south Sakhalin

Quercus mongolica var. *grosseserrata*
in the Kyoto Botanic Garden, Japan

Plate 46

Quercus petraea, near Karlsruhe, W. Germany

Quercus phellos
Photo: Archivbild

Quercus myrsinifolia in its habitat
3 Photos: Dr. S. Watari, Tokyo

Plate 47

Quercus pontica
Photo: Archivbild

Quercus pubescens in Sutjeska, Yugoslavia (wild)

Quercus robur
Thiensen Arboretum, near Elmshorn, W. Germany

Quercus robur 'Pectinata'
in Baekkeskov Park, Denmark

Plate 48

3 clones of *Quercus robur* 'Fastigiata' from Hungary
(grown from seed of *Q. robur* 'Fastigiata'; 35 years old in this photo, 10–16 m high)
Photo: Barabits

Left:
'Hungaria'. Crown only 70 cm wide, branches and twigs nearly vertical, slightly undulate, very fast growing, new growth appears early; leaves narrowly cuneate tapering to the petiole, but cordate at the base, margins deeply round lobed and undulate; tepals of the staminate flowers nearly totally absent; acorns very long stalked.

Middle:
'Raba'. Crown about 1.5 m wide, well branched, very dense and twiggy at a 45° angle from the trunk; new growth medium early, yellow-green, leaves widest above the middle, cuneate at the base, flat lobed; tepals nearly completely absent; acorns short stalked.

Right:
'Tortuosa'. Narrow crowned, about 1.5 m wide, branches and twigs criss-crossing and twisted, young leaves light green at first, narrow, acutely lobed and slightly undulate; base cuneate, only occasionally slightly cordate; tepals of the staminate flowers slightly developed or absent; acorns medium long-stalked.

(Lit. BARABITS, E.: Neue Formen unter den ungarischen Pyramiden-Eichen; in Deutsche Baumschule 1970, 155—156.)

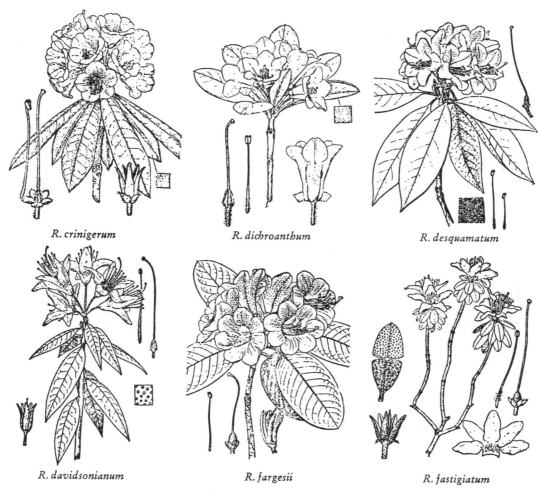

R. crinigerum   *R. dichroanthum*   *R. desquamatum*

R. davidsonianum   *R. fargesii*   *R. fastigiatum*

Fig. 103. **Rhododendron** (from ICS)

cm wide, exterior densely scaly, purple, speckled, stamens 10, densely shaggy beneath, ovaries scaly, style glabrous, calyx very small, scaly, slightly overlapped, April–May. BM 8280, 8620. China; Szechwan Prov., Mount Omei. 1904. z7 ★ Fig. 104. #

var. **pseudoyanthinum** (Balf. f.) Davidian. About 4 m high in its habitat, very similar to *R.concinnum*, but with larger flowers, these darker purple and grouped 3–5 together, corolla broadly funnelform, April–May. BM 8620 (as *R. concinnum*); RYB 6: 63. China; W. Szechwan Prov. Better than *R. concinnum*! z8 ★★★ Fig. 98. # ۞

R. coreanum see: **R. yedoense** var. **poukhanense**

R. coriaceum Franch. (S Falconeri). Thin branched (!), evergreen shrub or small tree, 2–6 m high; leaves oblanceolate, 12–25 cm long, light green and glabrous above, silvery white beneath; flowers 15–20 in loose corymbs, corolla narrowly campanulate, 3 cm long, limb 5–7 lobed, white to soft pink, with a dark red basal spot and punctate, stamens 10–14, ovaries pubescent, style glabrous, April. RYB 5: 20; 8: 25; 17: 7; GC 135: 75; BMns 462. China, Tibet. z9 ★★★ Fig. 98. # ∅ ۞

R. crassum Franch. (S and SS Maddenii). Evergreen shrub, also a small tree in its habitat, to 6 m high, young shoots thick, scaly; leaves usually at the shoot tips, elliptic to narrow obovate or oblanceolate, 7–15 cm long, 3–7cm wide, leathery tough, apex acute, base narrowed, deep green and glossy above, rugose, blue-green beneath, but densely covered with red-brown scales; flowers 3–6 in clusters, corolla white, infundibular, deeply 5 lobed, 6–8 cm long, white, often also somewhat reddish, exterior scaly, very fragrant, stamens 15–20, basal portion pubescent, ovaries scaly, also the 5–6 cm long style and the calyx with 6–12 mm long lobes, June–July; fruit capsule 2–3 cm long, very thick. BM 9673; JRHS 93: 224. China, Yunnan Prov.; Upper Burma. 1906. Only for the mildest climates! z9 ★★ # ۞

R. crinigerum Franch. (S Barbatum, SS Crinigerum). Evergreen shrub, 2–3 m high, young shoots glandular bristled and glutinous; leaves lanceolate to oblanceolate, long acuminate, 7–17 cm long, 1.5–5 cm wide, light brown tomentose beneath, midrib distinctly glandular; flowers about 12 together, corolla campanulate, 3 cm long, white to cream-yellow, limb 5 lobed, occasionally with a pink trace, a dark red basal patch and very punctate, stamens 10, ovaries glandular, calyx and flower stalk very bristly, April. BM 9464; ICS 4120. China, Tibet. 1914. z7 ★★ Fig. 103. # ∅ ✣

R. croceum see: **R. wardii**

R. cubittii Hutch. (S Maddenii, SS Ciliicalyx). Medium-sized evergreen shrub, similar to *R. veitchianum*, but the young shoots purple-brown, sparsely scaly, with scattered long bristly hairs; leaves oblong-elliptic, to 10 cm long and 3.5 cm wide, with a long mucronate apex, leathery, quickly becoming glabrous above, scaly beneath; flowers broadly funnelform, 5 lobed, interior white to soft pink, with brownish or orange-yellow markings, exterior deep pink along the ribs, upper surface scaly, limb lobes finely crispate, stamens 10, calyx thick scaled, also the ovaries. BM 9502; RYB 11: 10; JRHS 93: 227. N. Burma. z10 ★★★ # ✣

R. cumberlandense see: **R. bakeri**

R. cuneatum W. W. Sm. (S Lapponicum). Evergreen shrub, to 1 m high, young shoots very short, densely scaley; leaves elliptic, 3–5 cm long, scaly on both sides, brown beneath, the scales partly overlapping, petiole 5 mm long; flowers usually in 4's, corolla broadly funnelform, 3 cm long, pink, exterior not scaly, calyx 1 cm long, reddish, scaly and ciliate, stamens 10, pubescent beneath, style totally glabrous, April. BM 9561; NF 1: 276 (= *R. ravum* Balf. f. & W. W. Sm.; *R. cheilanthum* Balf. f. & Forrest). China; Yunnan Prov., Lichiang Range, 3500–4000 m, in limestone rock! 1906. z5 ★★ #

R. cyanocarpum (Franch.) W. W. Sm.(S and SS Thomsonii). Evergreen shrub, very closely related to *R. thomsonii*, to 5 m high, but primarily differing in the white to pink flowers, calyx large and cupulate like *R. thomsonii*; fruits plum colored, pruinose (!). BMns 155; RYB 6:70; ICS 4135. China 1906. z6 ★★ # ✣ ⚭

R. dalhousiae Hook. f. (S Maddenii, SS Megacalyx). Epiphytic, evergreen shrub, 1–2 m high, loosely branched; leaves obovate to oblanceolate, 10–15 cm long, blue-green and scaly beneath; flowers grouped 3–5, corolla funnelform, 8 cm long, very fragrant, yellowish white, later white, often with a pink blush, May–June. BM 4718; SR 492; RYB 5: 26; FS 460 to 468. Himalayas,

Fig. 104. *Rhododendron concinnum* (from B. M.)

Fig. 105. *Rhododendron dauricum* (from Dippel)

Sikkim, Bhutan. 1850. Generally only for the conservatory. z9 ★★★ # ✣

R. daphnoides see: cv. list **'Arbutifolium'**

R. dauricum L. (S Dauricum). Deciduous or somewhat semi-evergreen shrub, about 1–1.5 m high, shoots pubescent and scaly; leaves elliptic, 2–4 cm long, rounded on both ends, deep green and loosely glandular above, densely scaly beneath; flowers paired or solitary, corolla broadly open, purple-pink, to 4 cm wide, exterior soft pubescent, calyx very small, exterior densely scaly, stamens 10, pubescent beneath, style glabrous, ovaries densely scaly, February to March. BM 636; SR 226. Korea, Manchuria, N. Japan. 1780. z5 ★★ Fig. 105. ✣

var. *mucronulatum* see: **R. mucronulatum**

var. **sempervirens** Sims. Habit narrower and more tightly upright; leaves evergreen (!); flowers darker. BM 8930. # ✣

R. davidii Franch. (S Fortunei, SS Davidii). Evergreen shrub, 3–5 m high in its habitat, shoots thick; leaves leathery tough, narrowly oblong-lanceolate, 10–17 cm long, 3–4 cm wide, with 12–15 vein pairs, base cuneate, glabrous on both sides, petiole 2 cm long; flowers 8–12 in elongated racemes, corolla often campanulate, 5 cm long, lilac-pink, purple speckled on the upper margin lobes, 14–16 stamens, ovaries glandular, April–May. SR 264; FIO 28. China; W. Szechwan Prov., Mupin, 3000 m, in the forests. True existence in cultivation doubtful! z7 ★★ Fig. 91, 110. # ∅

R. davidsonianum Rehd. & Wils. (S Triflorum, SS Yunnanense). Evergreen shrub, to 2.5 m high, shoots thin; leaves oblanceolate, 3–6 cm long, dull brown and scaly beneath, blade V-shaped on the apical half (!); flowers 2–4 on the 3–4 terminal buds, corolla flat, 5 lobed, to 5 cm wide, pale pink, somewhat red punctate above, stamens 10, exserted, anthers yellow, ovaries scaly, style glabrous, flowering very abundantly, April. BM 8759 (as *R. siderophyllum*); BM 8605 (poorly chosen

Fig. 106. *Rhododendron degronianum*
var. *heptamerum* (from Siebold & Zuccarini)

example!); RYB 13: 8; Gs 1931: 85. China. 1908. z7
★ ★ ★ ★ Plate 56; Fig. 103. # ☼

R. decorum Franch. (S and SS Fortunei). Evergreen
shrub, 2–6 m high in its habitat, shoots rather thick, light
green, bluish pruinose at first, later glabrous; leaves
oblong to lanceolate, 5–15 cm long, 3–7 cm wide, apex
rounded, base cuneate, light green and waxy pruinose
above (glossy if rubbed!), blue-green beneath; flowers
8–10, corolla open funnelform-campanulate, 6–8 lobed,
whitish light pink, fragrant, stamens 12–16, densely
pubescent beneath, style quite glandular, calyx cupulate,
glandular, March–May. DRHS 177l; BM 8659; ICS 4155.
China; Yunnan, Szechwan Provs., mountain slopes and
forests, 2500 to 3000 m. 1889. z7 ★ ★ ★ # ∅ ☼

R. degronianum Carr. (S Ponticum, SS Caucasicum).
Densely foliate, evergreen shrub, 1–1.5 m high, shoots
foliate to the base, somewhat floccose; leaves oblong-
elliptic, widest at the middle, 7–15 cm long, 2–4 cm wide,
margins involuted, dark green above, glossy, glabrous,
densely reddish brown pubescent beneath, petiole 2–3
cm long, tomentose; flowers about 12 together, corolla
broadly funnelform-campanulate, 5 lobed (!), 4–5 cm
wide, soft pink or occasionally also pure white, with or
without reddish markings, stamens 10, with white
filaments and yellow anthers, ovaries densely brown
tomentose, style white, barely exserted past the stamens,
early March to mid April; fruit capsule cylindrical or
ovoid, to 2.5 cm long, deep brown, with persistent
tomentose remnants. BM 8403 (the typical 5 lobed
form); KIF 3: 61 (= *R. metternichii* f. *pentamerum* Maxim.).
Central and S. Japan, to 2000 m high in the mountains.
1894. z7 ★ ★ Plate 60; Fig. 91.

According to the most recent interpretation, the following 2
taxa, once considered separate species, must be included
here:

f. **angustifolium** (Makino) Sealy. Shrub, 1–2 m high and wide,
habit rather globose, very densely branched, young shoots
loosely white woolly tomentose at first, later brownish and
persisting so for several years; leaves narrowly lanceolate,

occasionally somewhat sickle-shaped curved, 10–17 cm long, 2
cm wide, stiff and leathery, margins involuted, dark green
above, midrib much indented, densely woolly beneath, brown,
petiole 1–1.5 cm long; flowers grouped 3–10 together, corolla
open funnelform-campanulate, 5 lobed, to 4 cm wide, soft pink,
with or without carmine patches, finely pubescent at the base,
stamens 10, ovaries brown pubescent, style glabrous, bud
scales persisting on the base, June. (= *R. makinoi* Tagg; *R.
metternichii* f. *angustifolium* Makino). Japan; Honshu, in the
mountains. # ☼

var. **heptamerum** (Maxim.) Sealy. Shrub, 1–2 m high, shoots
thinly tomentose; leaves nearly whorled, oblong, 10–15 cm
long, 1.5–3 cm wide, persisting for 4–5 years, glossy above and
slightly involuted, underside thinly light brown to reddish
tomentose; flowers grouped 10–15 together, bud scales
abscising (!), corolla somewhat unevenly campanulate, 4–5 cm
wide, limb 7 lobed(!), light pink, interior darker speckled,
stamens 14, ovaries brown tomentose, style glabrous, May–
June. MJ 749 (= *R. metternichii* S. & Z.; *R. metternichii* var.
heptamerum Maxim.). Japan; dense mountain forests on
Honshu. It remains questionable whether, as Nitzelius
explained (1961), the 7 lobed corolla justifies varietal status
since this is not the case with other *Rhododendron* spp. Plate 64;
Fig.106. # ☼

R. desquamatum Balf. f. & Forrest (S Heliolepis).
Evergreen shrub, 6 m high in its habitat, young shoots
densely scaly; leaves broadly oblong-elliptic, 6–10 cm
long, 3–5 cm wide, densely covered beneath with
irregular scales, of these the largest are dark brown,
petiole 1.5 cm long, densely scaly; flowers few in groups,
corolla broadly funnelform, lilac, speckled, stamens 10,
pubescent beneath, style glabrous, ovaries scaly, April.
ICS 4066; BM 9497. China; W. Yunnan Prov.; N. Burma.
1917. z8 ★ ★ ★ Fig. 103. # ☼

R. detonsum Balf. f. & Forrest (S Taliense, SS
Adenogynum). Evergreen shrub, 2–4 m high in its
habitat, shoots red when young, tomentose and
glandular at first, later glabrous; leaves leathery tough,
oblong, 7–12 cm long, 2–4 cm wide, smooth above and
becoming glabrous, with 14 vein pairs, thinly brown
tomentose beneath, but eventually nearly totally
glabrous, petiole 2.5 cm long; flowers about 10 together,
corolla funnelform-campanulate, 4.5 cm long, pink with
a few carmine-red speckles, 5–7 lobed limb, stamens 10–
14, except for the apical third, finely pubescent, style
glandular, except for the apical ¼, May. BM 9359. China;
Yunnan Prov., 3000 to 3500 m, on the forest's edge. z7 ★
∅

R. diaprepes Balf. f. & W. W. Sm. (S and SS Fortunei).
Very similar to *R. decorum*, but with larger leaves, to 25
cm long, flowers larger, to 12 cm wide, white to soft pink,
slightly fragrant, July. BM 9524; RYB 8: 26; ICS 4156.
China, Burma. 1913. z8 ★ ★ ★ # ∅ ☼

R. dichroanthum Diels (S Neriiflorum, SS Sanguineum). Evergreen shrub, to 1.5 m high, young shoots
white pubecsent; leaves obovate to oblanceolate, 5–10
cm long, glabrous above, white beneath; flowers
grouped 4–8, corolla tubular-campanulate, about 3 cm
long, limb 5 lobed, color quite variable, usually orange
with a pink blush, otherwise also deep orange to salmon-
pink, stamens 10, pink, ovaries densely pubescent, style

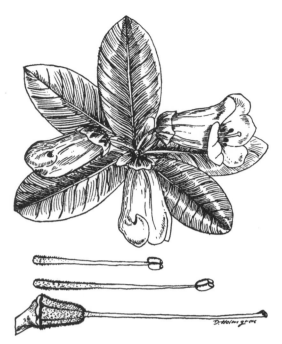

Fig. 107. *Rhododendron dichroanthum*
var. *apodectum*

glabrous, calyx colored like the corolla, large, the lobes 12–25 mm long, May. BM 8815; ICS 4146. China. 1906. z8 ★★ Fig. 103. # ☼

The following subspecies were once considered separate species:

ssp. **apodectum** (Balf. f. & W. W. Sm.) Cowan. Shrub, to about 1 m high; leaves tougher, more leathery, elliptic, 3–7 cm long, base round (!), deep green and smooth above, very densely gray pubescent beneath; flowers grouped 2–4 together, corolla tubular-campanulate, 2.5–4.5 cm long, orange to carmine and yellowish scarlet, limb 5 lobed, the lobes 8–12 mm long, erect, the same color as the corolla, calyx cupulate, stamens 10, ovaries with clustered pubescence, styles glabrous. BM 9014; ICS 4145 (= *R. apodectum* Balf. f. & W .W. Sm.; *R. jangtzowense* Balf. f. & Forrest). China; Shweli-Salween River region. (Yunnan Prov. to Burma) 1913. z8 ★★ Fig. 107. # ☼

ssp. **herpesticum** (Balf. f. & Ward) Cowan. Only about 30 cm high (!), shoots occasionally bristly pubescent; leaves oblanceolate to oblong-elliptic, to 7.5 cm long, 2–2.5 cm wide; flower stalk, calyx and ovaries glandular (!), flowers grouped 2–4 together, 3.5 cm long, dull yellow to orange-red, calyx cupulate, with rounded, 8 mm long lobes, May–June (= *R. herpesticum* Balf. f. & Ward). NE. Upper Burma, on rocky slopes in the mountains at 4000–4300 m. z8 ★ # ☼

ssp. **scyphocalyx** (Balf. f. & Forrest) Cowan. Very similar to ssp. *herpesticum*, but 1–1.5 m high (!), young shoots thinly white tomentose, not glandular; leaves obovate, 6–9 cm long, 2–4 cm wide, rounded, base slightly auriculate, dark green above and finely rugose, underside smooth with fine, white pubescence, petiole 5 mm long, without glands; flowers in 4's, corolla tubular-campanulate, orange, pink-orange, carmine with yellow or coppery, about 4 cm long, calyx cupulate, stamens 10, base pubescent, ovaries with fascicled hairs and stalked glands,

May–June (= *R. scyphocalyx* Balf. f. & Forrest). NE. Burma, China; W. Yunnan Prov., in bamboo thickets. z7 ★★ #

R. didymum see: **R. sanguineum** ssp. **didymum**

R. dilatatum see: **R. reticulatum** f. **pentandrum**

R. discolor Franch. (S and SS Fortunei). Evergreen shrub, to 6 m high in its habitat, shoots thick and glabrous, new growth appears late June to early July; leaves leathery, oblong-lanceolate, 10–20 cm long, 2–7 cm wide, base narrowly cuneate, occasionally slightly auriculate, with about 21 vein pairs, dark green above, glabrous on both sides; flowers about 10 together, corolla funnelform-campanulate, 5–8 cm long, to 10 cm wide, soft pink, later white, with 7 lobes, stamens 14–16, calyx distinctly lobed, glandular and ciliate, late June, early July (!). BM 8698; FIO 29; ICS 4161. China; Szechwan, Hupeh Provs., in forests at 1500–2000 m. Differing from *R. fortunei* in the later flowering time and taller habit. z7 ★★★★ # ∅ ☼

R. duclouxii see: **R. spinuliferum**

R. eclecteum Balf. f. & Forrest (S and SS Thomsonii). Evergreen shrub, 1–2.5 m high, young shoots thick; leaves nearly sessile (!), usually obovate to oblong, 6–12 cm long, totally glabrous except for the midrib, base somewhat cordate (!); flowers 6 or more together, corolla broadly funnelform, 3.5–5 cm long, 5 lobed, quite variable in color, white, pink, purple, occasionally yellow (the best is white with dark red sap stains), stamens 10, short, ovaries very glandular, calyx glabrous, 8 mm long, January–March (! then usually susceptible to frost damage). ICS 4136. Himalayas; Tibet, Szechwan, Yunnan Provs. z8 ★★ # ☼

R. edgarianum Rehd. & Wil. (S Lapponicum). Evergreen shrub, 0.5–0.9 m high, shoots very short, scaly; leaves broadly elliptic, about 1 cm long, both sides densely scaly, underside dark red-brown; flowers solitary, terminal, corolla open funnelform, purple-pink, exterior not scaly, stamens 10, as long as the glabrous style, anthers light brown, ovaries scaly, as is the 5 lobed, ciliate calyx, April–May. China; W. Szechwan Prov., near the Tibetan border at 4000 to 5000 m. 1908. z6 ★★ # ☼

R. edgeworthii Hook. f. (S Edgeworthii). Loose, often elliptic, shrub, to 2.5 m high, young shoots thickly brown tomentose; leaves elliptic to ovate, 5–10 cm long, rugose above, thickly brown tomentose beneath; flowers grouped 2–4 together, corolla funnelform, 8–10 cm long, white or soft pink toned, very fragrant, stamens 10, ovaries pubescent, styles woolly beneath, but not scaly, calyx deeply 5 lobed, exterior and limb not pubescent, April–May. SR 231; BM 4936; RYB 5: 29; FS 797 (= *R. bullatum* Franch.). Himalayas. 1851. In moist areas of its forest habitat this plant becomes epiphytic, otherwise normally terrestrial. z10 ★★★★ Plate 38. # ☼

R. elliottii Watt. (S Irroratum, SS Parishii). Evergreen shrub, 2–3 m high; leaves oblong-elliptic, 10–15 cm long, dull green above, lighter beneath, eventually nearly totally glabrous and glossy; flowers to about 12 together in 12 cm wide corymbs, corolla funnelform, 5 cm long, scarlet-red, interior darker speckled, limb 5 lobed, stamens 10, red, glabrous, styles and ovaries glandular, May to June. BM 9546. India. 1927. z9 ★★★★ # ☼

R. × 'Emasculum' see: cultivar **'Emasculum'**

R. eriogynum Balf. f. & W. W. Sm. (S Irroratum, SS Parishii). Tall evergreen shrub, also a small tree in its habitat; leaves oblong-elliptic, 10–20 cm long, loosely pubescent beneath at first, but later glossy green; flowers 12–15 together in 12 cm wide inflorescences, corolla campanulate, 5 cm wide, 5 lobed, bright red, with 5 dark purple-red sap stains at the base and speckled, stamens 10, pubescent at the base, ovaries and the basal style half densely pubescent, June. BM 9337; ICS 4188. China; Yunnan Prov. 1915. Very attractive species. z9 ★★★ # ☼

R. erythrocalyx Balf. f. & Forrest (S Thomsonii, SS Selense). Medium-sized evergreen shrub, densely branched, shoots thin, glandular only at first, leaves thin, ovate to more elliptic, 7–10 cm long, 3.5–5 cm wide, round with a mucro, base cordate, olive-green above, both sides with about 14 veins, thinly pubescent and somewhat glandular beneath; flowers 4–6 together, corolla funnelform-campanulate, 5 lobed, 2.5 cm wide, cream-white, with or without carmine patches and sap stains, calyx reddish, 7 mm long, fleshy and densely glandular, stamens 10, ovaries densely glandular, April–May. RYB 6: 75. China; NW. Yunnan Prov. z8 ★★ # ☼

R. euchaites see: **R. neriiflorum**

R. eximium Nutt. (S Falconeri). Very closely related to R. falconeri, very similar in total appearance, but the upper side of the developing leaves has a gorgeous orange colored pulverulence which is retained for a rather long time; leaves to 30 cm long, 7.5 cm wide; flowers asymmetrically campanulate, 4.5 cm long, limb 8–10 lobed, fleshy, lighter or darker pink, April–May. BM 7317 (= R. falconeri var. eximium [Nutt.] Hook. f.). Bhutan. In cultivation, much shorter than the yellow flowering R. falconeri. z9 ★★ Plate 37. # ∅ ☼

R. exquisitum see: **R. oreotrephes**

R. falconeri Hook. f. (S Falconeri). Evergreen tree, to 12 m high in its habitat, shoots thick, gray-brown tomentose; leaves elliptic to oblong, 15–30 cm long, 5–15 cm wide, rounded at both ends, dull dark green above and finely rugose, underside densely rust-red tomentose, petiole 4–6 cm long; flowers to 20 or more in globose corymbs, corolla unevenly campanulate, bulging on the basal half, cream-white to pale yellow and with purple basal spots, limb with 8(10) lobes, stamens 12–16, shorter than the corolla, stigma knob-like, calyx tiny, with about 8 small teeth, April–May. BM 4924; SR 244; BHR 32; FS 477 and 1166. Himalayas; Nepal to Bhutan, at 3000 m. 1850. z9 ★★★★ Plate 63; Fig. 91. # ∅ ☼

var. eximium see: **R. eximium**

R. fargesii Franch. (S Fortunei, SS Oreodoxa). Evergreen shrub, 1–5 m high, shoots glabrous, often reddish; leaves leathery, elliptic to oblong, 5–8 cm long, 3–4 cm wide, base round to lightly cordate, dark green and smooth above, blue-green beneath, petiole 1.5–2.5 cm long, often reddish; flowers 6–10 together, flowering abundantly, corolla open campanulate, 4 cm long, white to dark pink, limb with 6–7 lobes, stamens 14, glabrous, calyx and ovaries glandular, style glabrous, April. BM 8736; DRHS 1772; BHR 46. China; Szechwan, Hupeh Provs., in the forests at 2000–3000 m. 1901. Very similar to R. oreodoxa, but the leaves and ovaries differ. z8 ★★★ Fig. 103. # ☼

R. fastigiatum Franch. (S Lapponicum). Habit tightly upright or cushion-form, to about 0.9 m high, shoots scaly; leaves elliptic-oblanceolate, 1 cm long, densely scaly on both sides, but the scales of the underside only slightly touching or somewhat spaced, particularly on older leaves; flowers grouped 4–5, very short stalked, corolla broadly funnelform, purple-lilac to deeply purple-blue, 12 mm long, stamens 10, base pubescent, style glabrous, calyx with a scaly exterior and softly ciliate, April–May. ICS 4058. China; Yunnan Prov., above Ta Li. z6 ★★ Fig. 103. # ☼

R. fauriei see: **R. brachycarpum**

R. ferrugineum L. (S Ferrugineum). Alpine Rose. Evergreen shrub, to about 1 m high, often procumbent, shoots thin, densely scaly; leaves elliptic to oblong-lanceolate, 3–5 cm long, 1–1.5 cm wide, margins involuted, not ciliate, dark green above, densely red-brown scaly beneath, scales overlapping, petiole 5 mm long; flowers 6–12 in loose, terminal clusters, corolla funnelform, limb outspread, dark purple-red, 2 cm long, exterior scaly, stamens 10, ovaries densely scaly, calyx small, with rounded lobes, June to July. SR 254; HF 2029; HM 2645. Alps of Europe, also the Urgestein Mts., the Pyrenees and Apennines, scattered in the Balkans; 1500–2300 m. z5 ★ Fig. 108. # ☼

Fig. 108. *Rhododendron ferrugineum*
(from Stevenson)

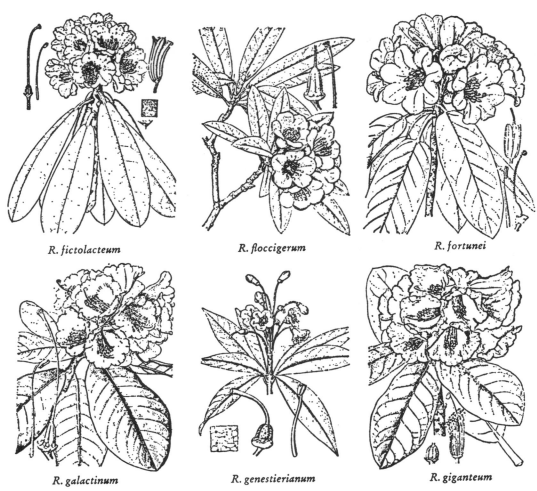

R. fictolacteum   *R. floccigerum*   *R. fortunei*

R. galactinum   *R. genestierianum*   *R. giganteum*

Fig. 109. **Rhododendron** (from ICS)

f. **album** Sweet. Flowers white. RYB 24: 20.

f. **atropurpureum** Millais. Flowers purple.

R. fictolacteum Balf. f. (S Falconeri). Evergreen shrub, a tree in its habitat, to 12 m high, young shoots cinnamon-brown tomentose; leaves elliptic to obovate, 15–30 cm long, 6–12 cm wide, variable in form, dark green above, smooth and glossy, rust-brown tomentose beneath, petiole 2.5–4 cm long; flowers 12–15 together, corolla unevenly campanulate, to 6 cm wide, limb with 7–8 lobes, white, cream-yellow or pale pink, always with a deep red basal patch, stamens 14–16, shorter than the corolla, anthers red-brown, ovaries tomentose, April–May. BM 8372 (as *R. lacteum*); RYB 4: 36; DRHS 1772. China; Yunnan Prov., 3000–4000 m in the coniferous forests. 1889. Similar to *R. rex*, but the leaves are shorter and narrower; flowers only on older plants. z8 ★★★ Plate 62; Fig. 109. # ⌀ ✧

R. fimbriatum Hutchins. (S Lapponicum). Low evergreen shrub, very similar to *R. scintillans*, but with leaves and flowers somewhat larger, the latter more purple, April–May. W. China. Not a very significant species. z6 ★ #

R. flammeum (Michx.) Sarg. (S Azalea, SS Luteum). Deciduous shrub, to 1.5 m high, young shoots finely erect pubescent and bristly; leaves obovate or elliptic to oblong, 3–6 cm long, 1.5–2.5 cm wide, somewhat bristly pubescent above, denser beneath, particularly on the long shoots; flowers appearing before or with the foliage, 6–16 in corymbs, stalk bristly, without glands, corolla funnelform, 4.5 cm long, tube narrow, exterior pubescent, 3–5 cm wide, scarlet to bright red, usually with an orange-yellow blotch on the uppermost lobes, stamens 5, basal half pubescent, ovaries bristly, but not glandular. BM 180; RYB 1: 9 (= *R. speciosum* [Willd.] Sweet non Salisb.; *Azalea nudiflora* var. *coccinea* Ait; *A. calendulacea* var. *flammea* Michx.). SE. USA; Georgia and South Carolina. 1789. Totally hardy and much used in hybridizing. z6 ★★ ✧

R. flavidum Franch. (S Lapponicum). Small evergreen shrub, 30–50 cm high, shoots densely scaly; leaves ovate to oblong, 12–25 mm long, densely scaly on both sides, more distinct beneath, base rounded; flowers grouped 3–6 together, corolla 3 cm wide, plate-like, with a quite short, pubescent tube, the limb lobes soft yellow, undulate on the margins, stamens 10, ovaries scaly, style pubescent at the base, calyx with 5 scaly lobes, about 6 mm long, April. BM 8326; ICS 4047 (= *R. primulinum* Hemsl.). China; W. Szechwan Prov. 1925. Good for the rock garden, hardy, foliage aromatic. z6 ★★ # ✣

R. flavum see: **R. luteum**

R. floccigerum Franch. (S and SS Neriiflorum). Well branched, evergreen shrub, 1–1.5 m high, current year's shoots floccose with branched hairs (!); leaves narrowly oblong to nearly lanceolate, 5–12 cm long, 1–2 cm wide, short acuminate, base cuneate, deep green above, glabrous, brown tomentose beneath at first, bluish white beneath the tomentum with a waxy papillose epidermis (!), new growth totally brown tomentose, but quickly becoming glabrous above, petiole 1 cm long; flowers 4–7, corolla tubular-campanulate, 3–5 cm long, fleshy, carmine, with 5 dark nectary pits, stamens 10, uneven, glabrous, white, anthers nearly black, calyx 1–3 mm long, with 5 undulate lobes, March–April. ICS 4140; BM 9290. China; Yunnan Prov. 1914. z8 ★★ Fig. 109. # ∅ ✣

var. **appropinquans.** Tagg & Forrest. Young shoots and leaf petiole glandular, leaf underside without tomentum. RYB 12: 33. #

R. floribundum Franch. (S Arboreum, SS Argyrophyllum). Evergreen shrub, 3–5 m high in its habitat, rather stiff, young shoots stellate tomentose; leaves leathery tough, elliptic-lanceolate, 7–15 cm long, 3–5 cm wide, base broadly cuneate, convex above and stellate pubescent at first, with 12–18 vein pairs, underside densely white tomentose with long, persistent hairs; flowers 8–12 in dense racemes, corolla broadly campanulate, 4 cm long, purple-lilac or pink, with a carmine basal patch and dots, stamens 10, ovaries bristly, calyx and flower stalk white tomentose, April. BM 9609; ICS 4240. China; W. Szechwan Prov., Mupin, forests from 1300–2500 m. 1903. z8 ★ # ∅

R. forrestii Balf. f. ex Diels (S Neriiflorum, SS Forrestii). Evergreen, creeping shrub, 10–15 cm high, developing a ground cover; leaves broadly obovate to rounded, 1.5–3 cm long, the venation distinctly indented above, total surface beneath more or less reddish (!!); flowers usually solitary (or grouped 2–3), corolla narrowly campanulate, 3 cm long and wide, limb 5 lobed, deeply incised, dark carmine, stamens 10, glabrous, style glabrous, ovaries densely glandular, calyx very small and glandular, April–May. BM 9186; UR 12; NF 1: 277; ICS 4138. NE. Yunnan Prov., SW. Tibet, moist mountain meadows and moors. 1914. A quite variable species. z8 ★★★★ # ✣

var. **repens** (Balf. f. & Forrest) Cowan & Davidian. Leaf undersides more or less blue-green (!!), not purple; flowers more scarlet-red, flower stalks and ovaries less glandular. RYB 6: 58 (= *R. repens* Balf. f. & Forrest). Tibet. # ✣

R. fortunei Lindl. (S and SS Fortunei). Broad evergreen shrub, 2(5) m high, young shoots glandular at first, later glabrous, pale green; leaves oblong, 10–20 cm long, 3–8 cm wide, both ends round or somewhat cordate at the base, dull dark green above, with 14–16 vein pairs, blue-green beneath, glabrous, petiole 2–3 cm long; flowers 6–12 in loose corymbs, fragrant, corolla funnelform-

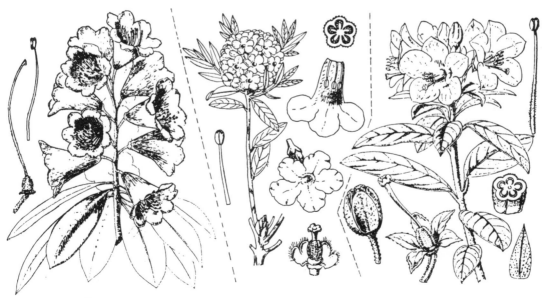

Fig. 110. **Rhododendron.** Left *R. davidii;* center *R. trichostomum* var *ledoides;* right *R. glaucophyllum* (from Bot. Mag., Plant. David.)

campanulate, 7–9 cm wide, limb 7–8 lobed, soft whitish pink, stamens 14, glabrous, ovaries and styles glandular, calyx small, with short, glandular lobes, May. BM 5596. China; Chekiang Prov., 1000 m. 1855. Much used in hybridizing for its broad habit. z7 ★★★ Fig. 91, 109. #∅⌖

R. × 'Fragans' see: cultivar **'Fragrans'**

R. × 'Fraseri' see: cultivar **'Fraseri'**

R. fulgens Hook. f. (S Campanulatum). Rounded evergreen shrub, densely branched, 1–2 m high, bark exfoliating, scales of the foliate buds carmine, young shoots green, eventually glabrous and brown; leaves elliptic, 6–11 cm long, 5–7 cm wide, rounded, base lightly cordate, dark green above, glossy, brown woolly tomentose beneath, with 12–14 vein pairs, petiole 1.5–2.5 cm; flowers 10–12 in dense, small, hemispherical corymbs, corolla campanulate, 3 cm long, 3.5 cm wide, deep blood-red with 5 black-red nectaries, otherwise without markings, stamens 10, white, glabrous, anthers brown, March–April. BM 5317; RYB 4: 50; FS 789. Sikkim, Nepal, developing thickets on mountain slopes at 3000–4000 m. 1849. z7 ★★ Fig. 91. #∅ ⌖

R. fulvum Balf. f. & W. W. Sm. (S Fulvum). Evergreen shrub, 3–6 m high in its habitat, young shoots thick, brown or gray tomentose; leaves oblong to elliptic, 10–20 cm long, glabrous above, with 13–18 vein pairs, underside light to dark cinnamon-brown, tomentose, petiole 2–2.5 cm long; flowers to 20 in corymbs, corolla campanulate, 3 cm long, white with a trace of pink or also a solid pink, with a carmine basal patch, limb 5–6 lobed, stamens 10, white to dark pink, style and ovaries glabrous, March–April. BM 9587; RYB 4: 52; DRHS 1773; ICS 4221; PBRR 60. China; W. Yunnan Prov., in thickets and the forest's edge at 2500–3500 m. 1912. z7 ★★★ #∅⌖

R. galactinum Balf. f. (S Falconeri). Evergreen shrub, to a small tree, 3–7 m high, young shoots densely brown tomentose, scales of the leaf buds obtusely rounded and fringed; leaves oval-oblong to lanceolate, 12–20 cm long, 5–8 cm wide, deep green above with a yellowish midrib, underside pale gray or light brown velvety pubescent, petiole 3.5 cm long; flowers about 15 in racemes, corolla campanulate, 3 cm long, white, exterior turning pink, interior with a carmine basal patch and punctate, limb 7 lobed, stamens 14, base usually pubescent, ovaries and styles glabrous, April–May. BMns 231; ICS 4213. China; Szechwan Prov. 1908. Quite hardy! z5 ★ Fig. 109. #∅

R. genestierianum Forrest (S Glaucophyllum, SS Genesterianum). Evergreen shrub, 1–3 m high in its habitat, young shoots bluish, glabrous; leaves lanceolate, tapering toward both ends, 5–10 cm long, 0.6–4 cm wide, thin, bright green above, distinctly bluish beneath, glabrous on both sides to slightly scaly beneath; flowers to 12 in racemes, on thin, about 2.5 cm long stalks, corolla narrowly campanulate, 12 mm long, with 5 erect lobes (!), fleshy, purple-violet, bluish pruinose, stamens 10, glabrous, ovaries scaly, style glabrous, curved, calyx very small, barely lobed, glabrous, April. ICS 4012; BM 9310;

RYB 3: 24. SE. Tibet, Upper Burma. 1919. More interesting than attractive. z9 ★ Fig. 109. #⌖

R. giganteum Tagg (S Grande). Evergreen shrub in its habitat, to 24 m, with a 60 cm thick stem, but older plants cultivated in England have only reached a few meters in height; leaves elliptic, 20–40 cm long, glabrous above, obtuse, base auriculate, densely brown woolly beneath (glabrous on young plants!), with 20–24 vein pairs, petiole thick, 2.5–5 cm long; flowers grouped 20–25 together or more in corymbs, corolla campanulate, 6.5 cm long, margin 8 lobed, dark carmine-pink, with a darker basal patch, stamens 16, glabrous as is the style, ovaries pubescent, April. BMns 253; NF 8: 269; RYB 8: 27; ICS 4215. China. 1919. The tallest growing species, but very susceptible to frost damage! z9–10 ★★★ Fig.109. #∅⌖

R. glaucophyllum Rehd. (S and SS Glaucophyllum). Evergreen, very aromatic shrub, about 1 m high, shoots densely scaly; leaves elliptic-oblong, 2.5–7 cm long, 1.5–2.5 cm wide, dull green above, blue-green beneath with small yellow and large dark brown scales, petiole 1–1.5 cm long, brown scaly; flowers grouped 5–6 together, not fragrant, corolla broadly campanulate, pink, 2.5 cm wide, the 5 rounded lobes overlapping, calyx lobes 1 cm long, long acuminate, exterior densely scaly, stamens 10, only pubescent beneath, styles thickening to the large stigma (!), May. BM 4721; SR 300; DRHS 1773; FS 672 (= *R. glaucum* Hook. f.). Himalayas. 1850. z8 ★★ Fig. 110. #∅⌖

var. **luteiflorum** Davidian. Flowers pure yellow, otherwise like the species. Upper Burma. 1953. ⌖

R. glaucum see: **R. glaucophyllum**

R. glischrum Balf. f. & W. W. Sm. (S Barbatum, SS Glischrum). Tall evergreen shrub, to 7 m high in its habitat, rather narrow upright habit, young shoots glandular-bristly, as are the leaves and petioles, calyx and ovaries; leaves narrowly oblong to lanceolate, 15–25 cm long, abruptly acuminate at the apex, base somewhat cordate, quickly becoming glabrous above, underside remaining more or less bristly pubescent; flowers to 15 or more in 12–15 cm wide corymbs, corolla campanulate, 5 cm wide, 5 lobed, distinctive in color, from lilac-pink to more purple, with a darker basal patch, stamens 10, May. BM 9035; ICS 4121; DRHS 1773. Himalayas. 1914. Garden merit varying; best suited for a moist climate. z8 ★★ Fig. 113. # ⌖

R. × 'Govenianum' see: cultivar **'Govenianum'**

R. grande Wight (S Grande). Evergreen tree, about 9 m high in its habitat; leaves oblong to oblanceolate, 15–45 cm long, 6–12 cm wide, dark green above, with 20–24 vein pairs, silver-white or light brown pubescent beneath; flowers 25–30 in broad, hemispherical corymbs, corolla campanulate, 5–7 cm long and wide, cream-white with a purple basal patch, limb 8 lobed, stamens 16, ovaries glandular and pubescent, stigma large, disk form, February–April. BM 5054, 6948; RYB 14: 11; FS 475; HAL 159; ICS 4216 (= *R. argenteum* Hook.

Fig. 111. *Rhododendron griersonianum*
(from Stevenson)

f.). Himalayas, Sikkim, Bhutan, developing entire forests at 2500-3000 m. 1849. z9 ★★★★ Plate 38. # ⌀ ☼

R. griersonianum Balf. f. & Forrest (S Griersonianum). Evergreen shrub, 1.5–3 m high, young shoots floccose, with glandular bristles, very thick, terminal buds long acuminate; leaves lanceolate, 9–20 cm long, 2–5 cm wide, dull green above, eventually glabrous, with 12–18 vein pairs, underside loose whitish to light brown woolly tomentose, petiole 2–3 cm long, often reddish, with long bristly glands; flowers 5–12 in loose corymbs, axis very densely tomentose and bristly glandular, corolla trumpet-shaped, 6 mm wide, tube very narrow and to 7 cm long, geranium-red (!), color differing from all other species, interior darker speckled, exterior densely and softly pubescent, stamens 10, bright red, ovaries and styles pubescent, May–June. BM 9195; SR 41; RYB 7: 14. China; W. Yunnan Prov., 2000–3000 m. 1917. z8 ★★★★ Fig. 111. # ⌀ ☼

R. griffithianum Wight (S Fortunei, SS Griffithianum). Evergreen shrub, 1–3 m high, young shoots light green, glabrous; leaves leathery, oblong, 10–30 cm long, 4–10 cm wide, smooth and glabrous above, with 16–24 vein pairs, underside yellow-green with a bluish cast, petiole 3–5 cm long; flowers 4–6 in loose corymbs, slightly fragrant, corolla broadly campanulate, 12–15 (!) cm wide, white with a trace of pink, limb 5 lobed, calyx 1–2 cm long, cupulate, lobed, glabrous, stamens 12–15, glabrous, style more or less glandular, curved under the large, yellow-green stigma, May. BM 5065. Himalayas, Sikkim, Bhutan. 1849. Has the largest flowers of all the Himalayan species; often used in hybridizing. z9–10 ★★★★ Fig. 91. # ⌀ ☼

R. habrotrichum Balf. f. & W. W. Sm. (S Barbatum, SS Glischrum). Evergreen shrub, to 2.5 m high, shoots densely glandular bristled; leaves ovate-oblong, short acuminate, 6–16 cm long, base round to lightly cordate, leaf margins, midrib beneath and leaf petiole bristly; flowers grouped 9–12 together, corolla campanulate, 4–5 cm wide, 5 lobed, white to light pink, with a purple basal patch, stamens 10, ovaries, calyx and flower stalk bristly, April. RYB 7: 21. China, Burma. 1912. Garden merit like that of *R. glischrum* and so similar that its inclusion in this species is sometimes considered. z8 ★★ # ☼

R. haemaleum see: **R. sanguineum** ssp. **haemaleum**

R. haematodes Franch. (S Neriiflorum, SS Haematodes). Broad evergreen shrub, usually not over 1 m high, young shoots woolly, not glandular; leaves obovate, 4–8 cm long, 2–3 cm wide, dark green above, finely rugose, underside dense red-brown woolly tomentose, petiole 1 cm long, tomentose; flowers grouped 6–8, fleshy, corolla funnelform-campanulate, 5 cm long, dark scarlet-red, limb with 5 lobes, stamens 10, glabrous, style glabrous, ovaries woolly, calyx red, 8 mm long, May. BM 9165; DRHS 1774; ICS 4141. China; Yunnan Prov., in open mountain sites and alpine meadows at 4000 m. 1911. One of the most beautiful Chinese species. z7 ★★★★ # ☼

R. × halense Gremblich (*R. ferrugineum × R. hirsutum*) (S Ferrugineum). Intermediate between the parents, but more similar to *R. ferrugineum*, occurring naturally; leaves very scaly on the underside, but less so than *R. ferrugineum*, margins slightly bristly; flowers somewhat larger than those of *R. ferrugineum*, light carmine-red, calyx lobes 1 mm long, June–July. HF 2030; HM 2652 (= *R. intermedium* Tausch). Natural hybrid, first found in 1891; occasionally found in the Alps in the range of both parents. z6 ★ #

R. hanceanum Hemsl. (S Triflorum, SS Hanceanum). Evergreen shrub, 1 m high or less, young shoots glabrous; leaves lanceolate to narrowly obovate, 2–10 cm long, tough, dark green and somewhat scaly above, lighter and more scaly beneath; flowers many in terminal clusters, corolla funnelform, 2.5 cm long, white to yellow, fragrant, basal portion pubescent, calyx 5 mm long, scaly, style glabrous, ovaries scaly, the 10 stamens pubescent at the base, exserted, April–May. FIO 34; ICS 4074. China. 1909. z8 ★★ # ☼

'Nanum'. More compact habit; flowers light yellow, more abundantly flowering. BM 8669; RYB 9: 52; 12: 35.

R. hedyosmum see: **R. trichostomum** var. **hedyosmum**

R. heliolepis Franch. (S Heliolepis). Evergreen shrub, 1–2.5 m high, shoots densely scaly; leaves oval-lanceolate, 9–12 cm long, 4–5 cm wide, densely reticulate veined above, scaly beneath, scales spaced about 1.5 times as far apart as their width, aromatic; flowers 4–5 together, corolla broadly funnelform, 3 cm long, pink to purple-pink, exterior lightly scaly, stamens 10, these pubescent on the basal portion as is the style, ovaries and stalks scaly, June. ICS 4068. China. 1912. z8 ★★ Fig.113. # ☼

Fig. 112. *Rhododendron hirsutum*
(Original, the flower parts from Schroeter)

R. hemitrichotum Balf. f. & Forrest (S Scabrifolium). Evergreen shrub, about 1 m high, shoots soft pubescent, branched; leaves lanceolate, acute, 3 cm long, 0.8 cm wide, soft pubescent above, blue-green and densely scaly beneath, spacing between the scales about equal to their width, petiole very short, soft pubescent; flowers paired or solitary, axillary, clustered at the shoot tips, buds with a brick-red apex, corolla short funnelform, 2 cm wide, 5 lobed, white-pink, margin darker, exterior densely scaly, style glabrous, April. China; SW. Szechwan Prov., Muli Mts. 1919. z8 ★★ # ☀

R. hemsleyanum Wils. (S and SS Fortunei). Tall evergreen shrub, 3–5 m high or more, young shoots thick, slightly pubescent; leaves oblong to more oval-oblong, 15–20 cm long, 6–8 cm wide, rounded, base deeply cordate or auriculate (!), leathery tough, deep green above, lighter beneath, with 13–15 vein pairs, margins occasionally also undulate; flowers 10–12 in corymbs with a thick, glandular rachis, corolla funnelform-campanulate, 5–8 cm long, 7 lobed, white, exterior glandular, interior finely pubescent at the base, stamens 10, filaments glabrous, ovaries and style densely glandular, calyx very small, only visible as a marginate limb, densely covered with long stalked glands, May. FIO 36; RYB 2: 29; ICS 4160. China; Szechwan Prov., Mt. Omei. z8 ★★ Fig. 113. # ☀

R. herpesticum see: **R. dichroanthum** ssp. **herpesticum**

R. hippophaeoides Balf. f. & W. W. Sm. (S Lapponicum). Upright, evergreen shrub, about 1 m high, branches thin, scaly, aromatic; leaves distributed along the entire shoot, erect, narrowly lanceolate, 3–4 cm long, scaly on both sides, particularly dense beneath, scales light gray,

evenly formed, overlapping; flowers 6–8 in clusters, corolla short funnelform, 2.5 cm wide, lilac-pink, not speckled, tube short and pubescent, stamens 10, alternately longer and shorter, ovaries scaly, style red, April. BM 9156; NF 1: 261; ICS 4057. China; Yunnan Prov., Lichiang Mts. 1913. Easily cultivated, likes moist sites. z5 ★★★ Fig. 113. # ☀

R. hirsutum L. (S Ferrugineum). Semi-evergreen shrub, to 1 m high, densely foliate, branches short, well branched; leaves leathery tough, elliptic, bright green, 3 cm long, margins finely crenate, bristly, ciliate, scattered scaly beneath; flowers 3–10 in corymbs, corolla funnelform-campanulate, bright red, interior pubescent, stamens 10, base pubescent as is the style, June. BM 1853; HF 2031; HM 2652. Alps, Tatra Mts. (Czechoslovakia), on dry gravelly slopes and on calcareous soils (!). z5 ★ Fig. 112. ☀

f. **albiflorum** Goiran. Leaves lighter green; flowers white. RYB 17: 27.

'**Laciniatum**'. Margins more or less deeply incised-dentate. HM 2652. Before 1903.

R. hirtipes Tagg (S Barbatum, SS Glischrum). Evergreen shrub, in its habitat a small gnarled tree, young shoots glandular bristled; leaves oblong-elliptic to broadly elliptic, 6–12 cm long, 4–7 cm wide, leathery thin, apex rounded (!), base round to somewhat cordate, apex and margins bristly at first, later becoming glabrous, underside eventually brown punctate, petiole glandular pubescent, 1–2 cm; flowers 3–5 in loose corymbs, corolla broadly funnelform-campanulate, 5 lobed, red in bud, opening pink to nearly white, interior carmine speckled, exterior brightly carmine striped, stamens 10, ovaries glandular, April. SE. Tibet. z6–7 ★★ # ☀

R. hodgsonii Hook. f. (S Falconeri). Tall evergreen shrub, to 6 m high, bark exfoliating (!); leaves elliptic to obovate, to 30 cm long, 13 cm wide, very tough and leathery, new growth with a thin white indumentum, deep green above, underside gray or brown woolly, petiole very thick, cylindrical; flowers 15–20 in globose, about 15 cm wide corymbs, corolla campanulate, 3.5–5 cm wide, 6–10 lobed, lilac-pink, never speckled (!!), stamens usually 16, rather short, ovaries pubescent as is the flower stalk, calyx very small, fleshy, with 7 short teeth, April. BM 5552; SNp 108; RYB 9: 52; ICS 4210. Himalayas, Nepal to Bhutan, in mountain forests at 3000–4000 m. 1849. z9 ★★ Fig. 113. # ⌀ ☀

R. hookeri Nutt. (S and SS Thomsonii). Evergreen shrub, totally glabrous except for the tiny, but prominent black hair clusters on the venation of the leaf underside, 3–4 m high; leaves elliptic-oblong, 9–15 cm long, rounded at both ends, bluish beneath; flowers 12–15 together, corolla campanulate, 5 lobed, blood-red, 4–5 cm wide, lobes incised in the center, stamens 10, calyx 6 mm long, March–April. BM 4926; ICS 4133. Bhutan. 1852. Very easily recognized by the black "spots" on the leaf underside. z8–9 ★★ # ⌀ ☀

R. hormophorum Balf. f. & Forrest (S Triflorum, SS Yunnanense). Shrub, deciduous, to 2.5 m high, young shoots scaly; leaves lanceolate, acute at both ends, 4–6 cm long, soft ciliate, scaly on both sides, the scales light, widely spaced, underside yellow between the scales; flowers 3–5, 3 cm long, pink with brown speckles, limb 5 lobed, calyx only a narrow limb, stamens 10, pubescent at the base, style glabrous, May. China; SW. Szechwan Prov., Muli Mts. at 3500–4000 m on dry, gravelly meadows. z8 ★★ # ✛

R. houlstonii Hemsl. & Wils. (S and SS Fortunei). Evergreen shrub, to 5 m high in its habitat, new growth a beautiful red (!); leaves obovate-lanceolate, 7–15 cm long, 2–5 cm wide, dark green above, with about 17 vein pairs, lighter beneath, glabrous on both sides, base round to cuneate, petiole 1.5–2.5 cm long, reddish; flowers 6–10 in corymbs, axes glabrous, corolla funnelform-campanulate, 4–6 cm long, white to light pink, exterior green and blood-red striped, stamens 14, glabrous, sepals small, somewhat glandular, but not ciliate, May. BHR 47. China; Hupeh, E. Szechwan Provs. z8 ★★★ # ✛ ∅

R. hunnewellianum Rehd. & Wils. (S Arboreum, SS Argyrophyllum). Evergreen shrub, slow growing, somewhat stiff, compact, to about 5 m high in its habitat, young shoots gray tomentose; leaves oblanceolate, 5–11 cm long, 6–25 mm wide, gradually acuminate at both ends, deep green above with indented venation, loose gray-white tomentose beneath, petiole about 1 cm; flowers grouped 5–8 together, corolla campanulate, 5 lobed, 5 cm wide, pink to lilac-pink, brown punctate, stamens 10, anthers deep brown, ovaries and style base white pubescent, March–April. (= *R. leucoclasium* Diels). China; W. Szechwan Prov. 1908. z9 ★★ # ✛

R. hyperythrum Hayata (S Ponticum, SS Caucasicum). Evergreen shrub, broad and dense habit, about 1 m high, 2 m wide, young shoots thick, glabrous; leaves oblong-elliptic or more lanceolate, acute, 8–15 cm long, 2.5–4 cm wide, margins distinctly involuted, deep green above, glabrous, finely punctate beneath, petiole to 2.5 cm long, pubescent at first, as is the midrib; flowers about 10 in

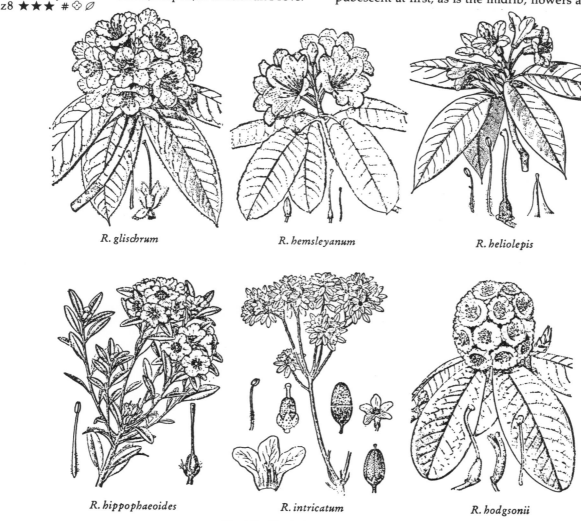

R. glischrum   R. hemsleyanum   R. heliolepis

R. hippophaeoides   R. intricatum   R. hodgsonii

Fig. 113. **Rhododendron** (from ICS)

racemes (appearing on young plants), corolla funnelform-campanulate, about 4.5 cm long and wide, 5 lobed, pink to white and more or less punctate (on plants in the wild; plants cultivated in England are pure white and nearly without punctation!), ovaries appressed pubescent, April–May. BMns 109; ICS 4153; RYB 3: 4 (= *R. rubropunctatum* Hayata non Lévl. & Van.). Taiwan. After 1930. Very attractive for the small garden. z8 ★★-★★★ # ☉

R. imbricatum see: **R. ponticum 'Imbricatum'**

R. impeditum Balf. f. & W. W. Sm. (S Lapponicum). Evergreen shrub, very densely branched, wide, about 15–40 cm high, shoots very short, with small, black scales; leaves elliptic-ovate, to 1.5 cm long, 0.8 cm wide, both sides densely scaly, petiole 2 mm long, scaly and somewhat pubescent; flowers grouped 2–3 together, somewhat fragrant, stalk very short, corolla open funnelform, about 2.5 cm wide, deeply lobed, purple-violet to lilac, the lobes outspread, stamens 10, shaggy at the base, style glabrous, calyx with 5 small lobes, late April. NH 39: 60; Gs 1930: 90; BMns 489; VVR 92. China; Yunnan Prov., Lichiang Mts. in moist, open areas at 5000 m. 1911. z5 ★★★★ # ☉

R. imperator Hutchins. & Ward (S Uniflorum). Evergreen, mat-like shrub, about 10 cm high, young shoots sparsely scaly; leaves aromatic, oblanceolate to narrowly elliptic, 2.5–3 cm long, blue-green and very thin scaled beneath; flowers paired or solitary, corolla funnelform, 2.5–3 cm wide, purple-pink, not speckled, limb 5 lobed, the lobes reflexed, total exterior soft pubescent, stamens 10, pubescent, style glabrous, carmine, ovary scaly, May. NH 39: 69; RYB 3: 27; 6: 65. Burma. 1926. z6 ★★★★ # ☉

R. indicum Sweet (S Azalea, SS Obtusum). Not to be confused with the *"Azalea indica"* of garden origin (!!). Evergreen shrub, broad growing, 0.7–1.8 m tall, shoots bristly pubescent; leaves lanceolate to oblanceolate, 2.5–3 cm long, bristly on both sides; flowers solitary or paired, corolla broadly funnelform, 3 cm long, bright red or scarlet or pink, stamens 5, style glabrous, ovaries bristly, June. BR 1700 (= *Azalea indica* L. non Sims). S. Japan. 1883. See also: *R. simsii.* z7 ★★ Fig. 114. #

Including the following forms:

'Balsaminiflorum'. Only about 10 cm high; leaves 1.5–2.5 cm long, 3–4 mm wide, glossy green above, more gray beneath, both sides bristly; flowers densely double, salmon-red (= *Azalea rosaeflora* R. Dean). Imported from Japan around 1877. z8 ★★★ # ☉

'Crispiflorum'. Leaves tougher than the species; flowers a strong pink, corolla limb undulate. BM 4726 (= *Azalea crispiflora* Hook.). Imported from Japan around 1850 by Fortune. #

R. indicum smithii see: **R. pulchrum**

R. insigne Hemsl. & Wils. (S Arboreum, SS Argyrophyllum). Evergreen shrub, 1–4 m high, young shoots thick and straight, ash-gray and thinly tomentose, 2–3 year shoots glabrous and green, all parts without glands; leaves leathery, oblong-lanceolate, 7–13 cm

long, 2–4 cm wide, margins lightly involuted, dark green above, with 14–16 vein pairs, underside with a silvery, occasionally coppery membranous layer; flowers 8 or more in broad corymbs, corolla broadly campanulate, 4 cm long, soft pink-white, darker toned and carmine speckled on the interior, limb 5 lobed, stamens 10–14, densely pubescent, style glabrous, May–June. BM 8885; RYB 24: Pl. 13; NF 7: 49; UR 14. China; Szechwan Prov., forests at 2500-3500 m. 1908. z6 ★★★ Plate 63. # ⊘ ☉

R. intermedium see: **R × halense**

R. intricatum Franch. (S Lapponicum). Evergreen shrub, 0.3(0.9) m high, shoots reddish scaled; leaves rounded-elliptic, 6–12 mm long, scaly on both sides, underside with overlapping, gray-green scales, petiole densely scaly; flowers 4–6 in nearly capitate inflorescences, corolla 1.5 cm wide, the 5 rounded limb lobes outspread, violet-purple in bud, later becoming lilac colored, the short tube softly pubescent, stamens 10, enclosed within the tube, style glabrous, very short, ovaries scaly, the 5 calyx lobes short triangular, April. BM 8163; DRHS 1775; ICS 4054. China; W. Szechwan Prov., in meadows and moors at 4000–5000 m. 1904. z5 ★★★ Fig. 113. # ☉

R. irroratum Franch. (S and SS Irroratum). Evergreen shrub, a tree in its habitat, 3–7.5 m high; leaves narrowly elliptic, 5–12 cm long, tough, eventually glabrous above, lighter beneath, glabrous, with 12–16 vein pairs; flowers in loose corymbs, rachis brown glandular, corolla narrowly campanulate with 5 rounded, incised lobes, 4–5 cm wide, pure white to yellowish, always densely carmine punctate, stamens 10, white or yellow, style, ovaries and flower stalk glandular, March–April. BM 7361; SR 346; RYB 12: 33; ICS 4182. China. 1904. z7 ★★★ # ☉

R. jangtzowense see: **R. dichroanthum** ssp. **apodectum**

R. japonicum (Gray) Suring. (S Azalea, SS Luteum). Well branched deciduous shrub, 1–2 m high, shoots somewhat bristly or glabrous, scales of the winter buds finely ciliate; leaves narrowly oblanceolate, 8–10 cm long, 2–4 cm wide, obtuse, base cuneate, ciliate, dull green above with scattered pubescence, bluish beneath, glabrous; flowers 6–10 in clusters, appearing before the leaves, not fragrant, corolla broadly funnelform, 6–8 cm wide, salmon-pink to orange with a large orange patch, exterior finely pubescent, as are the small calyx and ovaries, style glabrous, stamens 5, anthers dark brown. BM 5905; LAz 31; FS 2032–36 (= *Azalea japonica* Gray; *A. mollis* [S. & Z.] André). N. and central Japan. 1861. Excellent plant much used in hybridizing. z6 ★★★★ Fig. 114. ☉

R. johnstoneanum Watt ex Hutch. (S Maddenii, SS Ciliicalyx). Attractive, open growing, evergreen shrub, to 1.5 m high; leaves elliptic, 5–10 cm long, to 4 cm wide; flowers in 4's, corolla 5–6.5 cm long, infundibular, 5 lobed, white to slightly yellowish, interior red punctate, exterior reddish on the midline of the limb lobes, very fragrant, stamens 10, pubescent on the basal half, ovaries

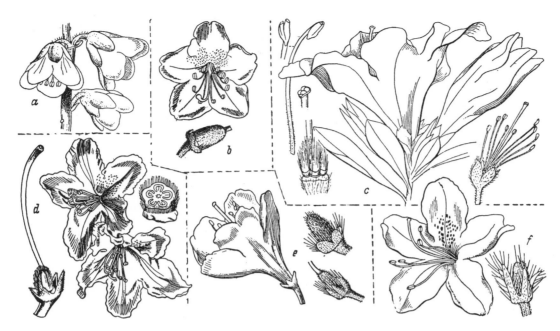

Fig. 114. **Rhododendron**, flowers and flower parts. a. *R. albiflorum;* b. *R. caucasicum;* c. *R. indicum;* d. *R. macrophyllum;* e. *R. molle;* f. *R. japonicum* (from B. M., Schneider, Shirasawa, Suringar)

and styles scaly, May. RYB 8: 30. India; Assam and Manipur. 1927. Suited only to the mildest climates. z7–8 ★★★ Fig. 130. # ✥

A double flowering form also exists in English gardens by the name **'Double Form'**.

R. kaempferi Planch. (S Azalea, SS Obtusum). Semi-evergreen or (in cooler climates) nearly deciduous shrub, to 2 m high and wide, young shoots appressed pubescent, bristles directed forward; leaves elliptic to somewhat rhombic, 2.5–6 cm long, 1.5–2.5 cm wide, glossy green above, lighter beneath, both sides somewhat bristly pubescent; flowers 2–4 in terminal clusters, pink, purple-pink to scarlet-red, corolla 5 cm wide, broadly campanulate, with 5 rounded lobes, calyx with 5 narrowly ovate to obovate lobes, these pubescent on the margin and exterior, flower stalk silky pubescent, 6 mm long, stamens 5, mid May. BM 2667; KIF 3: 63 (= *R. obtusum* var. *kaempferi* Wils.; *Azalea indica* var. *kaempferi* Rehd.). Japan. 1892. z5 ★★★ Fig. 124. ✥

R. keiskei Miq. (S and SS Triflorum). Compact, evergreen shrub, to 2.5 m high, shoots somewhat scaly only when young; leaves lanceolate, base rounded, 4–9 cm long, 1–2 cm wide, distinctly veined above, midrib somewhat pubescent, scaly beneath, spacing of the scales about the same as their diameter, petioles of younger leaves with white bristly hairs (!!); flowers 3–5 together, corolla broadly campanulate, 4 cm wide, light yellow, exterior scaly, stamens 10, somewhat pubescent, styles glabrous, calyx hardly noticeable, exterior scaly and ciliate, April–May. MJ 752; KIF 4: 35; VVR 75. Japan, central Honshu. 1908. Flower color not always pure yellow. z6 ★★★ # ✥

R. keleticum Balf. f. & Forrest (S Saluenense). Evergreen, ground cover shrub, to 15 cm high, shoots procumbent; leaves obovate to elliptic, 1.5 cm long, 1 cm wide, with a small mucro, glabrous and ciliate above, underside densely scaly, petiole scaly; flowers 1–3, terminally arranged, corolla rotate or broadly funnelform, purple-red with carmine markings, about 2.5 cm wide, stamens 10, base woolly, ovaries scaly, style glabrous, calyx 5 mm long, with 5 ovate, somewhat scaly lobes, June. SE. Tibet. 1919. z6 ★★ Fig. 115. # ✥

R. keysii Nutt. (S Cinnabarinum). Evergreen shrub, 1.5–3 m high, shoots and petioles densely scaly; leaves oblong-lanceolate, 5–10 cm long, scaly beneath; flowers about 6 together, in terminal and axillary clusters, corolla tubular (!), 2 cm long, with 5 short, erect lobes, scarlet-red, lobes yellow or orange with dark red apexes, May–June. BM 4875; SR 223; GC 128: 78; FS 1110; HAL 168. Bhutan. 1851. z7 ★★ Fig. 126. # ✥

R. kiusianum Mak. (S Azalea, SS Obtusum). Densely branched, evergreen shrub, broad growing, about 0.7 m high; leaves dimorphic, spring leaves oval-elliptic, 1–2 cm long, bright green, summer foliage more oblanceolate and adpressed pubescent on both sides; flowers 2–5, corolla funnelform, salmon-red or pink to carmine, stamens 5, anthers light brown (yellow on *R. obtusum*!), May–June. MJ 766 (= *R. obtusum* var. *japonicum* Wils.). S. and central Japan, primarily on Mt. Kiushima, an active volcano. This is the origin of the "Kurume" Azaleas, named for the town Kurume on Kiushiu island. z6 # ✥

R. kotschyi Simonk. (S Ferrugineum). Densely branched, evergreen shrub, 0.5–1 m high; leaves oblanceolate, apex rounded with a small mucro, 1.5 cm long, 0.7 cm wide, finely crenate, glabrous above, densely scaly beneath, scale spacing as wide as their diameter; flowers 2–4, pink, funnelform, finely and short pubescent on both sides, stamens 10, not exserted, styles shorter than the densely scaly ovaries, mid May. BM 9132. Higher mountains of the Balkans; also on calcareous soils. Rarely found in cultivation. z6 ★ ★ #

R. kyawii Lace & W. W. Sm. (S Irroratum, SS Parishii). Evergreen shrub, to 6 m high in its habitat, young shoots stellate pubescent at first, later glabrous; leaves oblong-elliptic, 15–30 cm long, 7–10 cm wide, loosely tomentose above at first, soon becoming glabrous, stellate tomentose beneath, later largely glabrous and glossy green, petiole to 6 cm long; flowers 12–16 in 15–18 cm wide corymbs, corolla funnelform, 5–7 cm wide, 5 lobed, carmine, with black basal spots, exterior finely pubescent, as are the flower stalk and ovaries, stamens 10, calyx glandular, July–August. BM 9271; SR 367. Upper Burma. 1919. z9 ★ ★ ★ # ☼

R. lacteum Franch. (S Lacteum). Evergreen shrub or tree, 5–9 m high; leaves leathery tough, oblong-elliptic, widest just above the center, 10–17 cm long, 6–8 cm wide, with 16–18 vein pairs, base cordate; flowers 20–30 in 15–20 cm wide corymbs, corolla broadly campanulate, cream-white to light yellow, 4–5 cm wide, limb 5 lobed, without markings, stamens 10, base pubescent, style glabrous, April–May. BM 8988; NF 5: 276; SR 381; RYB 10: 42. China; Yunnan Prov., forests at 3500 m. 1910. One of the best yellow-flowering species. z7 ★ ★ ★ ★ Fig. 116. # ∅ ☼

R. × 'laetevirens' see: cultivar **'Laetevirens'**

R. lanatum Hook. f. (S Campanulatum). Evergreen shrub, 1–2 m high, young shoots densely white to brown tomentose, entire plant without glandular scales; leaves crowded at the shoot tips, obovate to narrowly elliptic, 6–12 cm long, obtuse, base acute to nearly obtuse (not cordate), light yellow-green and glabrous above except for the woolly midrib, underside densely yellow-brown to white woolly, with 8–10 vein pairs, petiole 1.5 cm long, woolly; flowers 6–10, corolla broadly campanulate, 4.5 cm long, sulfur yellow, interior red punctate, limb 5 lobed, stamens 10, pubescent at the base, style glabrous, ovaries densely tomentose, April. FS 684; RYB 4: 51. Himalayas, Sikkim. 1849. The indumentum is utilized in Tibet in wicks for oil lamps. z7 ★ Fig. 126. # ∅

R. lancifolium see: **R. ponticum 'Lancifolium'**

R. lanigerum Tagg (S and SS Arboreum). Tall, evergreen shrub, a tree in its habitat, to 12 m, young shoots white to gray woolly; leaves oblong to lanceolate or oblanceolate, 15–25 cm long, 4–7 cm wide, obtuse to rounded at the apex, base cuneate to round, eventually glabrous above, underside persistently densely white to gray tomentose, petiole 2 cm long, woolly; flowers 40 (!) together in dense corymbs, corolla campanulate or somewhat more tubular, 5 lobed, 5 cm wide, carmine or purple-pink, stamens 10, ovaries white woolly, February–April (!). RYB 13: 29 (= *R. silvaticum* Cowan). Assam, SE. Tibet. z7 ★ ★ ★ # ☼

R. lapponicum Wahlb. (S Lapponicum). Dwarf evergreen shrub, 15–25 cm high, shoots thin, only

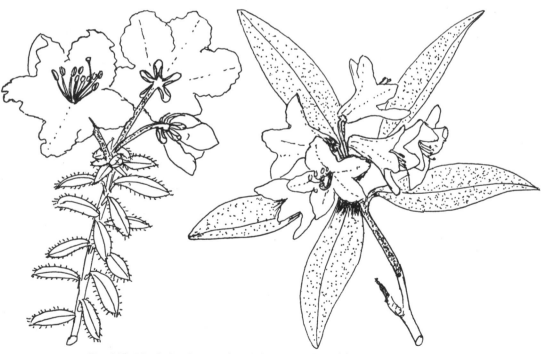

Fig. 115. **Rhododendron.** Left *R. keleticum;* right *R. × laetevirens.* (Original)

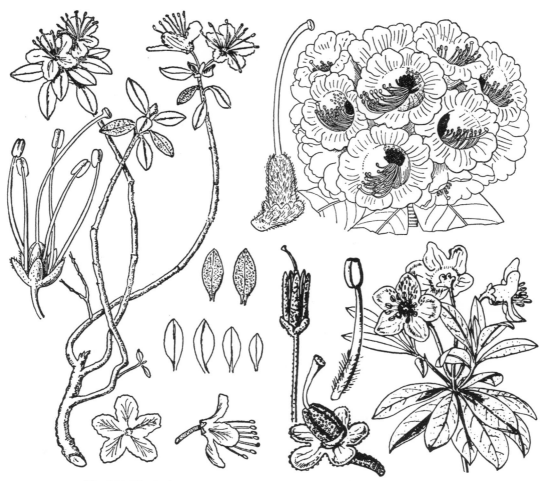

Fig. 116. **Rhododendron.** Left *R. lapponicum* (Original); right above *R. lacteum*;
right below *R. lepidotum* (from Stevenson, B. M.)

sparsely foliate, densely scaly; leaves at the shoot tips, oblanceolate, 0.8–1.2 cm long, with indented scales above, underside very densely and finely scaly, scales overlapping; flowers usually in 3's, corolla funnelform, purple-violet, stamens 5–10, style glabrous, calyx small, lobed, exterior scaly, June–July. BM 3106; GPN 650; JRHS 1934: 227. Lapland, in open spots in the mountains. Seldom found in cultivation; difficult to cultivate. z2 ★ Fig. 116. #

R. laticostum Ingram (S and SS Triflorum). Evergreen shrub, very closely related to *R. keiskei* (and often found under this name in cultivation), but differing in the 50–60 cm ultimate height; leaves broadly oblong to ovate, 3–4.7 cm long, 1.7–2 cm wide, midrib much thickened at the base, always totally glabrous; flowers pure light yellow, without markings, grouped 3–4 together. RYB 25: 22–24. Japan. z6 ★ # ✧

R. ledoides see: **R. trichostomum** var. **ledoides**

R. lepidostylum Balf. f. & Forrest (S Trichocladum). Compact evergreen shrub, about 50 cm high, often

lower, young shoots densely bristly and scaly; leaves bluish (!), often only semi-evergreen, ovate to obovate, 3 cm long, bristly ciliate, bluish and densely scaly beneath; flowers in 2's, broadly funnelform, 2.5 cm wide, light yellow, corolla short pubescent and scaly on the exterior, stamens 10, exserted, base shaggy, ovaries densely scaly and bristly (!), as is the flower stalk, May–June. RYB 6: 55; 24: 23. China; W. Yunnan Prov. z6 ★ Plate 56. #

R. lepidotum Wall. (S Lepidotum). Evergreen shrub, 0.5–1 m high, young shoots finely warty, thin, aromatic, later glabrous and smooth; leaves narrowly obovate to elliptic, 3–5 cm long, underside densely covered with more or less fleshy glands; flowers grouped 3–4 together, flower stalk 2.5 cm long, corolla short and broadly tubular, 3 cm wide, light yellow, pink or purple, exterior densely scaly, stamen filaments 8, base pubescent, styles thick and short, glabrous, calyx deeply lobed, June. BM 4657; SR 442; RYB 3: 28; SR 439. NW. Himalayas, Nepal to Szechwan and Yunnan Provs., 2600–5300 m. 1850. Hardiness quite variable, depending upon the area of its origin. z6–9 ★ Fig. 116. ∅ ✧

R. leptothrium Balf. f. & Forrest (S Ovatum). Open branched, evergreen shrub, to 6 m high, shoots very thin, quite finely pubescent, eventually gray; leaves oval-lanceolate, 4–7 cm long, acuminate, new growth reddish, later glossy green, glabrous to the midrib on both sides; flowers solitary (!) in the uppermost leaf axils, 3 cm wide, 5 lobed, deep lilac-pink, stamens 5, ovaries glandular and glutinous (!), calyx with 5 oblong, nearly 1 cm long, ciliate lobes, April–May. BMns 502; ICS 4265 (= *R. australe* Balf. f. & Forrest). China; W. Yunnan Prov. 1914. Garden merit slight, but of botanical interest. z7–8 ★ # ☼

R. leucaspis Tagg (S Boothii, SS Megeratum). Small evergreen shrub, 30–60 cm high, young shoots and petioles pubescent; leaves elliptic to obovate, rounded at the apex, 3–6 cm long, base cuneate, dark green above, blue-green and scaly beneath; flowers solitary or 2–3, corolla rotate with a short tube, 5 cm wide, pure white, the 5 limb tips overlapping, stamens 10, short, pubescent, anthers brown, styles short, thick, curved, calyx deeply 5 lobed, February–April. NF 7: 92; BM 9665; UR 11; NH 39: 65; RYB 3: 20. Tibet. 1925. Flowering on 3 year old seedlings! z8 ★★★★ # ☼

R. leucoclasium see: **R. hunnewellianum**

R. lindleyi Moore (S Maddenii, SS Megacalyx). Evergreen shrub, often epiphytic, to 3 m high, very open habit; leaves elliptic, 6–15 cm long, bluish and scaly beneath; flowers 4–6 in clusters, fragrant, corolla funnelform, about 7 cm long and wide, milk-white, occasionally with an orange or yellowish patch, April. UR 8; RYB 7: 24; 11: 31; BMns 363; HAL 163. Himalayas. 1849. z9–10 ★★★★ # ∅ ☼

R. linearifolium see: **R. macrosepalum 'Linearifolium'**

R. linearifolium var. *macrosepalum* see: **R. macrosepalum**

R. litiense Balf. f. & Forrest (S Thomsonii, SS Souliei). Evergreen shrub, to 3 m high; leaves oblong, 5–8 cm long, 2–3 cm wide, blue-green beneath; flowers grouped 6–8, corolla broadly funnelform, about 5 cm wide, light yellow, without markings, calyx about 2 cm wide, with 5 ovate to oblong, yellowish lobes, limb very densely glandular, as is the flower stalk, May. DRHS 1776; RYB 6: 73; 8: 5. China; Yunnan Prov. 1913. z7 ★★★ # ☼

R. × 'Loderi' see: cultivar **'Loderi'**

R. longesquamatum Schneid. (S Barbatum, SS Maculiferum). Evergreen shrub, to 3 m high, young shoots densely covered with long brown hairs, bud scales persisting at least 2 years; leaves oblong to obovate, acute, 7–12 cm long, 2.5–4.5 cm wide, dark green and glabrous, glandular punctate beneath; flowers 10 or more on about 2.5 cm long stalks, corolla campanulate, 5 lobed, 5 cm wide, white to pink with a dark red patch, stamens 10, ovaries and style base densely glandular, May. BM 9430; RYB 24: 29; ICS 4126 (= *R. brettii* Hemsl. & Wils.). China; Szechwan Prov. 1904. Quite winter hardy. z5 ★★ # ☼

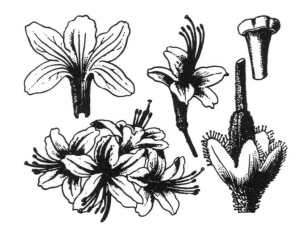

Fig. 117. *Rhododendron luteum* (from Kavka)

R. lopsangianum Cowan (S and SS Thomsonii). Closely related to *R. thomsonii*, but shorter, leaves smaller, only 3–6 cm long, more blue-green beneath; flowers smaller, narrowly campanulate, fleshy, dark carmine, calyx not distinctly cupulate, April. SE. Tibet. z7 ★ # ☼

R. lowndesii Davidian (S and SS Lepidotum). Deciduous, dwarf shrub, 15 cm high, leaves obovate to oblanceolate, apex rounded with a mucro, 2 cm long, 1 cm wide, margins and stalk bristly, underside sparsely pubescent or glabrous; flowers paired or solitary, scaly, stalks thin, pubescent, corolla campanulate, 5 lobed, 15 mm long, light yellow, with darker or carmine markings, exterior scaly, calyx and corolla reddish on the exterior. Nepal. 1950. Difficult to cultivate. z6 ★★ # ☼

R. ludlowii Cowan (S Uniflorum). Dwarf evergreen shrub, hardly over 30 cm high, young shoots glandular; leaves nearly sessile, petiole only 1 mm long, obovate to more elliptic, 9–17 mm long, 5–10 mm wide, rounded, base cuneate, margins finely crenate (!), deep green above, lighter and more loosely scaly beneath; flowers paired or solitary, stalk 18–25 mm long, thick, reddish, corolla cupulate, 2.5–3 cm long, to 4 cm wide, the 5 lobes outspread and undulate, yellow, exterior turning reddish, silky pubescent and scaly at the base, interior at the corolla apex with dark red markings, calyx 5–7 mm long (!), May. BMns 412; JRHS 92: 35; ICS 4013. SE. Tibet. By far the best of the yellow dwarf types. z6–7 ★★★★ Fig. 120. # ☼

R. lutescens Franch. (S and SS Triflorum). Evergreen shrub, 1–2 (4.5) m high, branches long and slender, sparsely glandular; leaves bronze-red on new growth, lanceolate, long acuminate, 4–5 cm long, 1–2 cm wide, less numerous and more loosely arranged, base rounded, dull green above with a few scattered scales, light green with somewhat indented sessile scales above; flowers 3–6, occasionally solitary, corolla broadly funnelform, 4–5 cm wide, light primrose-yellow with 5 distinct green spots on the exterior at the base, tube exterior somewhat pubescent at the apex, stamens 10, pubescent on the basal third, March–April. BM 8851; SR

Fig. 118. *Rhododendron macrosepalum* 'Linearifolium' (from Hooker)

789; FIO 35; ICS 4073; VVR 28. China; W. Szechwan, Yunnan Provs. 1904. z7 ★★★★ # ⊕

R. luteum Sweet (S Azalea, SS Luteum). Deciduous shrub, 1–4 m high and wide, densely branched, young shoots glandular shaggy at first, glutinous; leaves oblong-lanceolate, 6–12 cm long, 2–4 cm wide, base cuneate, with scattered, appressed glandular bristles on both sides and ciliate, gray pubescent when young; flowers grouped 7–12, appearing before the foliage, corolla funnelform, to 5 cm wide, golden-yellow, very fragrant, exterior glandular-glutinous, stamens 5, pubescent at the base, as is the style, ovaries glandular, calyx 3 mm long, glandular like the stalk, May. BM 433; SR 63 (= *R. flavum* [Hoffm.] G. Don; *Azalea pontica* L.). E. Europe to the Caucasus and Black Sea region. 1793. Very popular in Europe, quite hardy and meritorious; much used in hyridizing. z5 ★★★ Fig. 117. ⊕ ⊘

R. macabeanum Watt. (S Grande). Large evergreen shrub or tree, to 14 m high in its habitat, young shoots densely chestnut-brown tomentose; leaves leathery tough, oblong-elliptic, to 30 cm long, 20 cm wide, smooth and dark green above, densely gray-white woolly beneath; flowers many in compact corymbs, corolla campanulate-bulging, 5–6 cm long, yellow or pale yellow, with large reddish patches at the much inflated base, limb with 8 lobes, April–May. BMns 187; JRHS 84: 67; RYB 5: 45; 9: 25. India; Manipur, Assam. 1928. z8 ★★★★ # ⊘ ⊕

R. macrophyllum D. Don (S and SS Ponticum). Evergreen shrub, 1–1.5 m high, young shoots green; leaves ovate to oblong, 7–15 cm long, 3–6 cm wide, base cuneate, glabrous on both sides, with about 14 vein pairs, dark green above, lighter beneath; flowers about 20 in racemes, corolla broadly campanulate, 3–4 cm long, purple-pink with yellow markings, interior becoming lighter, margin undulate, stamens 10, calyx 1 mm long, ovaries densely white pubescent (brown pubescent on the similar *R. catawbiense*), May–June. BM 4863 (= *R. californicum* Hook. f.). N. America, Pacific Coast. 1849. z7 ★★ Fig. 114, 119. # ⊘

R. macrosepalum Maxim. (S Azalea, SS Obtusum). Semi-evergreen shrub, to 1 m high, young shoots with short, straight hairs, these usually gland tipped; spring foliage narrow-oblong to ovate, 4–7 cm long, 1–3 cm wide, acute at both ends, both sides and the 3–7 mm long petiole erect pubescent, summer foliage often persisting over winter until spring, smaller, oblanceolate; flowers grouped 1–5, corolla broadly funnelform, to 5 cm wide, pale purple-pink, 5 lobed, the apical lobes purple speckled, stamens usually 5, ovaries with a white, appressed pubescence, glandular, calyx with 2–3 cm long, linear-lanceolate lobes (!), April–May. (= *R. linearifolium* var. *macrosepalum* [Maxim.] Makino; *Azalea macrosepala* [Maxim.] K. Koch). Japan; Honshu and Shukoku. 1914. Rather rare in cultivation. z6–7 ★ ⊕

'**Linearifolium**'. Branches, leaves and flower stalks very distinctly pubescent; leaves linear to linear-lanceolate, 5–9 cm long, only 3–8 mm wide; flowers in terminal clusters of about 3, corolla divided into narrow, linear-lanceolate lobes (!), these about 3 cm long, 5 mm wide, pink, fragrant, pubescent at the base, stamens 5. BM 5769; MJ 770 (= *R. linearifolium* S. & Z.; *Azalea linearifolia* [S. & Z.] Hook.). Unique, very attractive mutation, cultivated in Europe since 1867. z6–7 ★ Fig. 118. ⊕

R. maddenii Hook. f. (S and SS Maddenii). Evergreen shrub, about 2 m high, bark papery, otherwise rather scaly; leaves lanceolate to oblong-lanceolate, 7–15 cm long, blue-green beneath; flowers 2–4, corolla funnelform, to 10 cm long and wide, white, often with a trace of soft pink, very fragrant, stamens 20, glabrous, calyx lobes 4 mm long, June–August. SR 488; BM 4805; FS 912. Himalayas. 1849. z9–10 ★★★ Fig. 121. # ⊘ ⊕

Fig. 119. *Rhododendron macrophyllum* (from Hooker)

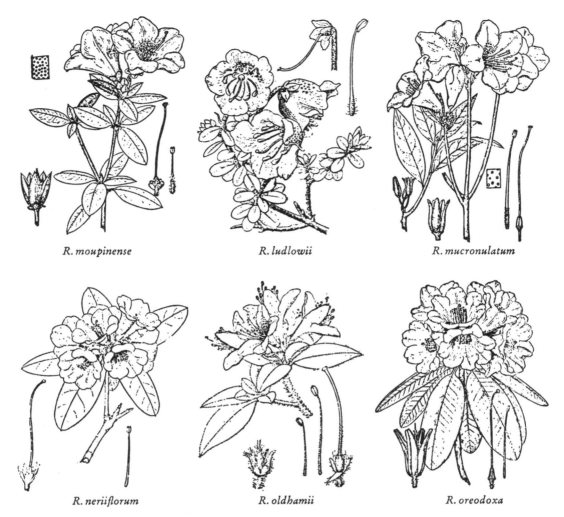

R. moupinense   *R. ludlowii*   *R. mucronulatum*

R. neriiflorum   *R. oldhamii*   *R. oreodoxa*

Fig. 120. **Rhododendron** (from ICS)

R. magnificum Ward. Tall, evergreen shrub, a tree in its habitat, to 18 m; leaves oblong to obovate, 25–35 cm long, 10–15 cm wide, broadly rounded at the apex, dull green and finely rugose, underside with a white "spider web-like" indumentum, later glabrous; flowers 20–30 together in large, hemispherical umbels, corolla campanulate or tubular, to 6 cm long, 8 lobed, lighter or darker pink, interior with 8 purple sap stains at the base, February–March. RYB 5: 37, 38; GC 127: 60. Himalayas; Burma, Tibet. 1931. z9 ★★★ #.∅ ✧

R. makinoi see: **R. degronianum** f. **angustifolium**

R. mallotum Balf. f. & Ward (S Neriiforum, SS Haematodes). Evergreen shrub, 1–3 (5) m high, young shoots densely tomentose; leaves obovate to elliptic, 7–15 cm long, dull green and rugose above, underside densely and soft red-brown tomentose; flowers broadly funnelform, 12–18 in dense, about 11 cm wide corymbs, dark scarlet-red, with 5 black bulges at the base, stamens 10, glabrous, ovaries woolly, March–April. BM 9419;

ICS 4112 (= *R. aemulorum* Balf. f.) China; W. Yunnan Prov. 1914. z7 ★★★★ #.∅ ✧

R. martinianum Balf. f. & Forrest (S Thomsonii, SS Selense). Evergreen shrub, 0.7–1.5 m high, shoots glandular; leaves arranged at the shoot tips, elliptic, 2.5–5 cm long, abruptly tapered at both ends, with a conspicuous mucro at the apex, more or less glandular when young, bluish beneath, petiole 6 mm long; flowers 3–6 in loose clusters, corolla broadly funnelform, 5 lobed, 2.5 cm long, 5 cm wide, light pink, base deep red, often also carmine speckled, stamens 10, pubescent at the base, ovaries and style base glandular, stalk 3 cm, glandular, April. China, SE. Tibet, Upper Burma. 1914. z7 ★★-★★★ # ✧

R. maximum L. (S and SS Ponticum). Evergreen shrub, 1–4 (7–10 in the wild) m high, open habit, young shoots pink glandular at first, later glabrous; leaves leathery, oval-lanceolate to oblanceolate, 10–30 cm long, 4–7 cm wide, acute, base round, eventually dark green and

Fig. 121. *Rhododendron maddenii* (from Hooker)

2.5 cm (!) long, lobes broadly ovate, not ciliate, stamens 10, short, April–May. BM 9326; RYB 2: 5; ICS 4022. NE. Upper Burma. 1914. Beautiful but very tender; grown only in the milder climates. z9 ★★★★ # ⌀ ⊕

R. megaphyllum see: **R. basilicum**

R. metternichii see: **R. degronianum** var. **heptamerum**
—f. *angustifolium* see: **R. degronianum** f. **angustifolium**
—var. *heptamerum* see: **R. degronianum** var. **heptamerum**
—f. *pentamerum* see: **R. degronianum**

R. micranthum Turcz. (S Micranthum). Small, evergreen shrub, 1–1.5 m high, shoots thin, well branched, loosely scaly; leaves oblanceolate, gradually tapered to the base, 2–5 cm long, 1–1.5 cm wide, loose scaled above, light brown and scaly beneath, partly overlapping; flowers densely clustered in terminal racemes, corolla broadly campanulate, 8–12 mm wide, white, stamens 10, May–June. BM 8198; SR 500. N. and W. China. 1901. This species is easily grown from seed and in some respects more similar to a *Spiraea* than *Rhododendron*. z6 ★ Fig. 122. #

R. minus Michx. (S Carolinianum). Evergreen shrub, 1–3 m high, densely foliate, shoots loosely scaly; leaves elliptic, triangular acuminate at both ends, 3–7 cm long, 2–4 cm wide, lightly scaly above, more densely so beneath, scale spacing about half the scale width; flowers many in racemes, corolla narrowly funnelform, purple-pink, exterior densely scaly, 2.5 cm wide, stamens 10, densely pubescent at the base, ovaries scaly, calyx 3 mm long, ciliate, May–June (!). BM 2285; SR 196. SE. USA. 1786. Resembling *R. carolinianum*, but taller and flowering later. z6 ★★ Fig. 123. # ⌀ ⊕

glabrous above, with 12–14 vein pairs, underside with a thin, more or less temporary pubescent layer, petiole 2–4 cm long; flowers 16–24 in corymbs, corolla campanulate, 3 cm long, light pink, lilac or white, yellow-green speckled on the apical lobes, finely pubescent on the throat, base glandular on the exterior, June–July. BM 951; HyFW 135; HM 2649. N. America. 1736. Of little garden merit, somewhat poor bloomer; flowers usually covered by the new foliage. z6 Plate 59; Fig. 91. # ⌀

R. maxwellii see: **R. pulchrum 'Maxwellii'**

R. meddianum Forrest (S and SS Thomsonii). Stiff, thick branched evergreen shrub, to 1.5 m high, totally glabrous; leaves elliptic to more obovate, 7–12 cm long, 5–7 cm wide, rounded at the apex with a small mucro, narrower and rounded at the base, dull green above, lighter beneath, petiole thick, 15–30 mm long; flowers grouped 5–10 together, corolla 5 lobed, campanulate, 6 cm long and wide, dark carmine, limb lobes round and incised, stamens 10, filaments white, ovaries and flower stalk glabrous and without glands, calyx cupulate, 1 cm long, fleshy, glabrous, March–April. RYB 9: 50; BM 9636; ICS 4134. China; W. Yunnan Prov., and NE. Upper Burma. 1914. z7 ★★ # ⌀ ⊕

R. megacalyx Balf. f. & Ward (S Maddenii, SS Megacalyx). Tall evergreen shrub, open habit, young shoots loose scaly; leaves elliptic to more obovate, 10–15 cm long, 3–7 cm wide, glabrous above, bluish beneath and densely scaly, the scales small and indented, spaced about the same distance apart as their width, with about 15 vein pairs, distinctly elevated beneath; flowers 5 together, stalk and calyx not scaly, corolla broadly funnelform, with 5 erect lobes, 7–10 cm wide, white, base yellow, often also turning reddish, fragrant, calyx to

Fig. 122. *Rhododendron micranthum*
(from Bot. Mag.)

Fig. 123. *Rhododendron minus* (from Bot. Mag.)

R. molle (Bl.) G. Don (S Azalea, SS Luteum). Deciduous shrub, 1–3 m high, branches rather erect, shaggy and often bristly pubescent when young; leaves oblanceolate, 5–15 cm long, pubescent above (at least when young), underside dense velvety gray-white pubescent (!!), petiole 0.5 cm long; flowers not fragrant, abundant, appearing before the leaves, corolla broadly funnelform, 5–6 cm wide, golden-yellow with a large, greenish patch, this actually composed of many smaller spots together, limb lobes ovate, longer than the tube, style glabrous, ovaries pubescent, stamens 5, pubescent on the basal half, calyx small, pubescent and ciliate, May. BR 1253 (= *R. sinense* Sweet; *Azalea sinensis* Lodd.; *A. pontica* var. *sinensis* Lindl.). E. to central China, particularly in the mountains. 1824. Not to be confused with "*Azalea mollis*"; for this see **R. japonicum**! Earlier used for hybridizing but the true species is rarely found in cultivation today and is not very winter hardy. z7 ★★★★ Fig. 114. ☼

R. mollyanum Cowan & Davidian (S Grande). Tall evergreen shrub or a small tree, to 5 m (in cultivation), young shoots thick, thin gray woolly; leaves oblong to oblanceolate, to 30 cm long, 8 cm wide, leathery tough, somewhat rugose above, silver-white woolly and glossy beneath, apex rounded, tapered to the base; flowers to 20 together, corolla campanulate and bulging, pink with a carmine basal patch, 8 lobed, to 5 cm long, stamens 15–16, ovaries pubescent, styles glabrous, calyx very small, April–May. RYB 12: 1. SE. Tibet. 1924. z7 ★★★ # ∅ ☼

R. morii Hayata (S Barbatum, SS Maculiflorum). Evergreen shrub, a tree in its habitat, branches eventually green and glabrous, with remnants of floccose hairs and glands; leaves oblong-oblanceolate,

6–13 cm long, 2–3 cm wide, abruptly short acuminate, dark green above, glabrous and glossy, lighter and somewhat glossy beneath, otherwise glabrous to the pubescent and glandular midrib, 14–16 vein pairs; flowers 12–15 in loose corymbs, corolla broadly campanulate, 3–4.5 cm long, pure white or with a trace of pink, carmine speckled, stamens 10–14, pubescent at the base, style white, glandular, April–May. RYB 11: 33; BMns 517. Taiwan, forests at 2000–3000 m. z7 ★★ #

R. moupinense Franch. (S Moupinense). Evergreen shrub, 0.5–1 m high, broad growing, branches pubescent at first; leaves obovate-elliptic, rounded at both ends, 2–3 cm long, half as wide, thin scaled beneath, glossy above; flowers 1–3 together, fragrant, corolla funnelform, 5–6 cm wide, 5 lobed, white or light to dark pink, purple speckled apex, stamens 10, ovaries scaly, style glabrous, calyx 4 mm long, glandular and lightly ciliate, February–March. SR 509; BM 8598; NH 39: 68; DRHS 1778; JRHS 96: 200. China. 1909. Quite meritorious. z7 ★★★★ Fig. 120, 126. # ☼

R. mucronatum G. Don (S Azalea, SS Obtusum). Evergreen or semi-evergreen shrub, abundantly branched, rather hemispherical, broader than high, to 1.5 m high, young shoots dense gray or brownish pubescent; leaves dimorphic: spring foliage elliptic, acute at both ends, 4–9 cm long, these leaves deciduous (!), summer leaves lanceolate, 1–4 cm long, lanceolate, dark green and persisting over winter, both forms pubescent, often also glandular; flowers 1–3, corolla broadly funnelform, to 6 cm wide, pure white, fragrant, occasionally also with a trace of pink, calyx green, lobes glandular pubescent, about 12 mm long, stamens 10 or only 8, glabrous, ovaries bristly, style glabrous, May. BM 2901; DRHS 1778 (= *Azalea ledifolia* Hook.). From Japan and China, but known only in cultivation and never found in the wild. 1819. z6 ★★★★ Fig. 125 # (#) ☼

'Narcissiflorum'. Flowers pure white, double (= 'Shiro-manyo-tsutsuji'). Introduced by Fortune from Japan, 1855. ☼

Fig. 124. *Rhododendron kaempferi* (from Stevenson)

Fig. 125. *Rhododendron mucronatum* (from Kavka)

var. **ripense** Wils. The wild type, differing in the pale lilac flowers (= *R. ripense* Mak.). Japan, along river banks in the southern part of the country.

R. mucronulatum Turcz. (S Dauricum). Deciduous shrub, densely branched with short shoots, branches thin, somewhat scaly; leaves elliptic-lanceolate, 4–10 cm long, 1–4 cm wide, very thin, with distinct tips, scattered scaly; flowers solitary from each of the terminally clustered buds, appearing before the foliage, corolla broadly funnelform, purple-pink, 3 cm wide, limb 5 lobed, stamens 10, base pubescent, anthers deep purple, ovaries scaly, style glabrous, January–March. BM 8304; RYB 12: 34 (= *R. dauricum* var. *mucronulatum* Sims). NE. Asia, Japan. 1907. Very attractive winter and spring flowering plant. z5 ★★★ Fig. 120. ⊕

'**Cornell Pink**' (Skinner). Sport with pink-red flowers. Found in the USA. ⊕

R. myiagrum Balf. f. & Forrest (S Thomsonii, SS Campylocarpum). Evergreen shrub, about 1 m high, shoots thin, very glandular at first, later glabrous and then more gray-white; leaves rather circular, 2–6 cm long and wide, base lightly cordate, dark green above, bluish beneath, with fine papillae, glandular toward the base, as is the 1–5 cm long, glandular petiole; flowers 4–5, corolla campanulate, to 2.5 cm long, white, with or without a red basal patch, with or without spots, stamens 10, glabrous, style glabrous, somewhat glandular at the base, flower stalk very glutinous-glandular ("flypaper"), May. RYB 6: 78. China; W. Yunnan Prov., in bamboo thickets at 3000 m. 1919. z7 ★★ # ⊕

R. myrtilloides see: **R. campylogynum** var. **myrtilloides**

R. neriiflorum Franch. (S and SS Neriiflorum). Evergreen shrub, 1–2.5 m high in its habitat, young shoots white tomentose at first, later glabrous and often reddish, without glands; leaves oblong to narrowly obovate, rounded at both ends, 5–10 cm long, 2–3.5 cm wide, dark green above, smooth, white to bluish white beneath, petiole 1.5 cm long, eventually glabrous and reddish; flowers grouped 5–12 together, fleshy, quite variable in size, corolla funnelform-campanulate, 3–4 cm long and nearly as wide, limb with 5 lobes, bright carmine-red, stamens 10, white, anthers deep brown, ovaries tomentose, styles slightly longer than the stamens, April–May. BM 8727; ICS 4139 (= *R. euchaites* Balf. f. & Forrest). China; Yunnan Prov., shady valleys, gravelly sites at 3000–4000 m. 1906. The species name *neriiflorum* is a long retained typographical error; the original author had written "*neriifolium*" (see Gard. Chron. 1936: 77). z7 ★★★★ Plate 38; Fig. 120. # ∅ ⊕

R. nigropunctatum see: **R. nivale** ssp. **boreale**

R. niphargum see: **R. uvarifolium**

R. nipponicum Matsum. (S Azalea, SS Nipponicum). Deciduous shrub, 1–1.5 m high, shoots glandular

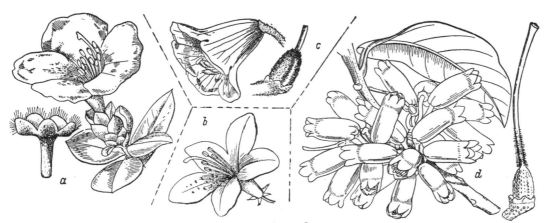

Fig. 126. **Rhododendron.** a. *R. moupinense*; b. *R. obtusum*; c. *R. lanatum*; d. *R. keysii* (from B. M., B. R., Hooker, Franchet)

bristled; leaves obovate, 5–15 cm long, 3–7 cm wide, ciliate and somewhat bristly pubescent on both sides, fall color orange and carmine; flowers 6–15 together, inconspicuous and hidden in the foliage, corolla campanulate to more tubular, white, about 2.5 cm long, with 5 nearly straight, 8 mm long limb lobes, stamens 10, calyx, flower stalk and leaf petiole glandular pubescent, May–June. SR 73; BMns 491. Japan. 1914. z7 ★

R. nivale Hook. f. (S Lapponicum). Compact evergreen shrub, 50–75 cm high or procumbent; leaves elliptic to rounded, 1 cm long, rounded above, scaly on both sides, scales denser beneath, mostly light brown mixed with a few dark brown scales; corolla broadly funnelform, 2 cm wide, purple to pink, stamens 10, basal half pubescent, style usually glabrous and longer than the stamens, calyx scaly, as large as the ovary. ICS 4063 (= *R. paludosum* Hutch. & Ward). Himalayas, in the higher mountains. z5 ★ # ☺

ssp. **boreale** Philipson & Philipson. Differing from the species in the flat cupulate calyx, style usually shorter than the stamens, color of the scales on the leaf underside often more uniform than that of *R. nivale*, flowers violet-purple. BM 8529; ICS 4062 (= *R. nigropunctatum* Franch.; *R. alpicola* Rehd. & Wils.; *R. violaceum* Rehd. & Wils.; *R. stictophyllum* Balf. f.). China; W. Szechwan Prov. to Tibet and NW. Yunnan Prov., in swampy areas at 4000–5000 m. Hardy. z5 ★ # ☺

R. niveum Hook. f. (S and SS Arboreum). Somewhat stiff, evergreen shrub, to 4 m high, young shoots white tomentose; leaves narrowly oblong, 7–15 cm long, 2.5–6 cm wide, apex rounded, tapered to the base, new growth snow-white tomentose (!), eventually deep green and glabrous above, underside remaining white, eventually light brown tomentose; flowers to 20 or more together in dense, globose corymbs, corolla funnelform-campanulate, 5 lobed, 4–5 cm long, purple to violet-lilac, with dark sap stains at the base, stamens 10, shorter than the corolla, style glabrous, ovaries tomentose, April–May. BM 4730. Himalayas, Sikkim. 1848. z7 ★★★ # ☺

R. nudiflorum see: **R. periclymenoides**

R. nudiflorum var. *luteum* see: **R. austrinum**

R. nuttallii Booth. (S Maddenii, SS Megacalyx). Evergreen shrub or tree, to 9 m high, occasionally also epiphytic in its habitat, young shoots very thick and stiff, scaly; leaves stiff and leathery, elliptic, 12–30 cm long, 6–11 cm wide, somewhat inflated at the apex, new growth reddish, later very rugose, gray beneath, then distinctly reddish reticulate veined and very scaly; flowers nearly lily-form in appearance, horizontally outspread at first, 3–6 together, very fragrant, corolla funnelform, 10–12 cm long and wide, very fleshy, ivory-white with a yellow tube and red lobes or totally pure yellow, stamens 10, 6 cm long, ovaries scaly, 7 cm long, base scaly, calyx with 2.5 cm long and 1.2 cm wide deeply incised lobes, April–May. BM 5146; MRh 218; RYB 11: 13; FS 1326; JRHS 88: 37; ICS 4025 and 4028 (= *R. sinonuttallii* Balf. f. & Forrest). Himalayas, Bhutan. 1852. Has the largest flowers of the entire genus. z10 ★★★★ # ☺ ∅

R. oblongifolium (Small) Millais (S Azalea, SS Luteum). Texas Azalea. Dense, deciduous shrub, 1–2 m high, branches finely shaggy pubescent or sparsely strigose to nearly glabrous, buds gray pubescent; leaves obovate to more oblong-lanceolate, 4–10 cm long, acute, pubescent beneath to nearly glabrous and occasionally bluish; flowers appearing with or after the leaves, 5–12 together, pure white, tube very narrow, to 3 cm long, then abruptly widening, the 5 lobes lanceolate, exterior shaggy pubescent and often also loosely glandular, sepals oval-oblong, 1–2 mm long, stamens 5, about 5 cm long, basal half pubescent, as is the ovary, July (= *Azalea oblongifolia* Small). USA; Arkansas to Texas, in moist woodlands or along streams. 1917. Closely related to *R. viscosum*, but less attractive and more tender. z8 ★ ☺

R. obtusum Planch. (S Azalea, SS Obtusum). Evergreen or semi-evergreen shrub, about 0.7 m high, occasionally taller, habit very dense and broad, occasionally procumbent, shoots densely covered with brown, appressed hairs; leaves dimorphic; spring foliage elliptic to ovate, 1.5–4 cm long, bright green above, lighter beneath, both sides with an appressed, brown, bristly pubescence, summer foliage smaller, narrower and tougher, these persisting through the winter, deep green above, petiole appressed pubescent; flowers in clusters of 1–3, corolla funnelform, about 1 cm wide, quite variable in color and somewhat variable in form, usually bright red, scarlet to carmine, stamens 5, glabrous, styles glabrous, ovaries densely bristly pubescent, calyx ciliate, May. BR 32; SR 95. N. to S. Japan. 1844. The typical species is rarely found in cultivation, but hundreds of cultivars exist. Wilson introduced many of these around 1919, about 50 of which comprise the "Kurume" Azaleas. See also: Cultivar List. z6 ★★★ Fig. 126, 127. # ☺

var. *japonicum* see: **R. kiusianum**

var. *kaempferi* see: **R. kaempferi**

Fig. 127. *Rhododendron obtusum* (from Lindley)

Fig. 128. *Rhododendron occidentale*
(from Bot. Mag.)

R. occidentale Gray (S Azalea, SS Luteum) Deciduous shrub, 1–2 m high, shoots erect, usually soft pubescent at first, later glabrous and brown, winter buds long acuminate; leaves elliptic to oblong-lanceolate, 4–10 cm long, 2–4 cm wide, ciliate, sparsely pubescent on both sides, sometimes only on the venation beneath, fall color yellow to carmine; flowers grouped 6–12 together, appearing with the first leaves, fragrant, corolla funnelform, to 6 cm wide, white to light pink, with a yellow patch, exterior glandular pubescent, stamens 5, style 5 cm long, base pubescent, as are the stamens, ovaries glandular, calyx ciliate, May–June. BM 5005; FS 1432. W. USA. 1851. Often used in hybridizing. z6 ★★★ Fig. 128. ✣

R. oldhamii Maxim. (S Azalea, SS Obtusum). Evergreen shrub, 1–2.5 m high, young shoots and leaf petiole very pubescent (!!); leaves oblong-lanceolate, tapered to both ends, 3–8 cm long, dull green to yellowish green; flowers 2–4 in loose clusters, corolla funnelform, 5 cm wide, 5 lobed, orange-red (!) with a purple-red patch, stamens 10, red, anthers purple, ovaries bristly, calyx and flower stalk glandular pubescent, May. BM 9059; ICS 4261. Taiwan. 1878. z9 ★★★ Fig. 120. # ✣

R. oleifolium see: cultivar **'Laetvirens'**

R. orbiculare DC. (S Fortunei, SS Orbiculare). Evergreen shrub, compact, scarcely over 1 m high in cul-

ture, allegedly over 3 m high in its habitat, shoots light green in the first year, bluish pruinose, light brown and somewhat glossy in the 2nd year; leaves broadly oval, 4–10 cm long and nearly as wide, deeply incised at the base, dull light green above, bluish beneath; flowers 7–10 in loose corymbs, corolla very regularly campanulate, limb 7 lobed, carmine pink, often with a bluish shimmer, interior somewhat lighter, 5–6 cm wide, stamens 14, white, glabrous, styles glabrous, ovaries glandular, April. BM 8775; BHR 41; SR 280; UR 17. China; W. Szechwan Prov. 1904. Much valued for its hardiness. z6 ★★★★ Fig. 129. # ∅ ✣

R. oreodoxa Franch. (S Fortunei, SS Oreodoxa). Evergreen shrub, 2–3 m high in cultivation, a small tree in its habitat, narrowly upright, branches somewhat foliate only at the tips, otherwise leafless, gray-white tomentose on the new growth, soon becoming totally glabrous; leaves thin and leathery, rolled up in frosty weather (!), narrowly elliptic, 5–10 cm long, 2–3.5 cm wide, rather rounded at both ends, dark green above, with 13–15 vein pairs, bluish beneath and finely warty; flowers 10–12 in corymbs, corolla broadly campanulate, limb 7 lobed, 5 cm wide, light pink, occasionally also purple speckled, stamens 14, white, ovaries and style glabrous, March (!). ICS 4165. W. to NW. China. 1904. Needs a protected site for the very early flowers, but the buds are quite hardy. z6 ★★★ Fig. 120. # ✣

R. oreotrephes W. W. Sm. (S Triflorum, SS Yunnanense). Evergreen shrub, 1–2.5 m high, young shoots reddish, somewhat scaly, leaves oblong-elliptic, rounded on both ends, 4–7 cm long, 2–3 cm wide, loosely scaly above, denser and bluish beneath; flowers 5–10 in loose corymbs, flowering very abundantly, corolla funnelform, 5–6 cm wide, lilac with darker patches, limb 5 lobed, undulate, exterior not scaly,

Fig. 129. *Rhododendron orbiculare* (from B. M.)

Fig. 130. *Rhododendron ovatum* (from Bot. Mag.)

stamens 10, white, ovaries scaly, May. BM 8784; SR 778; NF 5: 8; SR 774; BM 9597 (= *R. artosquameum* Balf. f. & Forrest; *R. exquisitum* Hutchins; *R. timeteum* Balf. f. & Forrest). China; Yunnan Prov., and SE. Tibet. 1906. Flower buds easily frost damaged, therefore needs a protected site! z6 ★★★★ Fig. 132. # ⊕

R. orthocladum Balf. f. & Forrest (S Lapponicum). Evergreen shrub, about 1 m high, usually lower, densely branched, shoots thin, scaly; leaves narrowly oblong to lanceolate, 1.5 cm long, densely scaly on both sides, scales of the underside overlapping, petiole scaly; flowers grouped 1–3, corolla broadly funnelform, 2 cm wide, soft lilac to lavender-blue, limb 5 lobed, tube short and pubescent, stamens 10, purple, anthers red, style short, reddish, ovaries scaly, late April. China; N. Yunnan Prov., on chalk at 3000–4000 m. z6 ★ #

R. ovatum Maxim. (S Ovatum). Evergreen shrub, 1–3 m high, young shoots softly pubescent and with scattered petiole glands; leaves broadly ovate, acuminate, 2.5–5 cm long, base rounded, glabrous on both sides, without glands; flowers solitary, axillary from buds clustered at the shoot tips, corolla rotate, 2.5 cm wide, with 5 outspread lobes, white pubescent, glabrous exterior, stamens 5, style glabrous, ovaries bristly, calyx lobes 5 mm long, ovate, May. BM 5064; NF 111: 177; SR 565; RYB 4; 56. E. China; Chekiang Prov. 1814. z7 ★ Fig. 130. #

R. pachytrichum Franch. (S Barbatum, SS Maculiferum). Evergreen shrub, 2.5–4.5 m high, young shoots, flowers and leaf petiole densely covered with moss-like branched hairs; leaves narrowly oblong to obovate, 7–15 cm long, ciliate, midrib pubescent beneath; flowers 7–10 together, corolla 5 lobed, campanulate, 3 cm wide, white to light pink with a purple basal patch, stamens 10, shorter than the corolla, pubescent ovaries bristly, style

glabrous, calyx tiny, usually glabrous, April. ICS 4128. China; W. Szechwan Prov. 1903. Quite hardy. z6 ★-★★ # ⊕

R. paludosum see: **R. nivale**

R. parryae Hutch. (S Maddenii, SS Ciliicalyx). Evergreen shrub, occasionally epiphytic in its habitat, or also a small tree, bark pink, exfoliating; leaves narrowly oblong-elliptic, acute to round with a mucro, 6–9 cm long, 3–4 cm wide, scaly on both sides, denser and blue-green beneath, petiole 12 mm, scaly; flowers 3–5, terminal, on a 2.5 cm long stalk, very fragrant, corolla broadly funnelform, to 11 cm wide, pure white, with an orange-yellow patch, the 5 lobes undulate and somewhat scaly near the middle, the tube pubescent on the exterior and near the base, stamens 10, base pubescent, ovaries densely scaly, calyx very small, scaly and ciliate margined. RYB 12: 31; RJB 1973: 4. Himalayas, SE. Assam. 1927. z10 ★★★★ # ⊕

R. parviflorum Adams. (S Lapponicum). Evergreen shrub, 30 cm high, shoots densely scaly; leaves oblong-lanceolate, acutish, 2 cm long, 7 mm wide, evenly densely scaly on both sides, the green leaf blade more or less visible between the scales; flowers usually 5 in umbels, corolla broadly funnelform, 2.5 cm wide, pink, interior and exterior totally glabrous, stamens 10, early April. BM 9229; GC 128: 31; ICS 4056. NE. Asia, Altai Mts. to Kamchatka and Sachalin Island. z3 ★ #

R. patulum Ward. Creeping dwarf shrub, very similar to *R. imperator* from which it is practically indistinguishable, except for the more densely arranged scales on the leaf undersides, spaced about half the scale diameter apart (spacing on *R. imperator* about 2–6 times the scale diameter); flowering abundantly, purple, but also pink and speckled. JRHS 1977: 19. Upper Burma, Mishni Hills, 4000 m. z8

R. pemakoense Ward (S Uniflorum). Evergreen shrub, about 30 cm high, erect, habit rather dense and globose, usually twice as wide as high; leaves obovate, rounded at the apex, 1–2 cm long, somewhat bluish and scaly beneath; flowers solitary or paired, broadly funnelform, about 3 cm long and wide, lilac-pink to purple, corolla totally fine pubescent, March–April. NF 11: 300; RYB 3: 29; ICS 4016. Tibet. 1930. z5 ★★★★ Fig. 132. # ⊕

R. pentaphyllum Maxim. (S Azalea, SS Canadense). Deciduous shrub, to 2.5 m high, branched, shoots quickly becoming glabrous, somewhat angular at first, but later cylindrical, winter buds with about 15 glossy, red-brown, ciliate scales; leaves 5 together at the shoot tips, elliptic to lanceolate, 4–7 cm long, 2–4 cm wide, ciliate and finely serrate, dark green above, midrib distinctly pubescent on both sides, fall color orange to carmine, petiole about 5–10 mm long, glandular bristled; flowers solitary or paired, appearing before the leaves, corolla rotate-campanulate, to 6 cm wide, purple-pink, stamens 10, ovaries glabrous, April–May. MJ 756. Central and S. Japan. z7 ★★★★ ∅ ⊕

R. peregrinum Tagg (S Grande). Tall, evergreen shrub, a small tree in its habitat, 4–5 m high, shoots very thick, gray tomentose at first; leaves elliptic-oblong, 10–18 cm long, 5–8 cm wide, short acuminate, base cordate to rounded, dull light green above, underside gray to yellowish pubescent, with 17–20 vein pairs, petiole l.5–2.5 cm long, gray-tomentose; flowers 15–20 together, corolla campanulate, to 4.5 cm long, white, exterior soft reddish, interior with a bright red basal patch, limb 6–7 lobed, stamens 14, March–May. China; SE. Szechwan Prov. Attractive, but very slow growing. z7 ★★ # ∅ ⊕

R. periclymenoides (Michx.) Shinners (S Azalea, SS Luteum). Deciduous shrub, 0.9–1.5 (3) m high, shoots bristly pubescent, winter buds glabrous or nearly so, scales abruptly acuminate (!); leaves elliptic to obovate, 3–10 cm long, limb and midrib often bristly, bright green above (!), petiole without stalked glands (!); flowers 6–12 together, only slightly fragrant (!!), corolla tubular-funnelform, the limb lobes longer (!) than the tube, light pink or more whitish pink, with or without a yellow patch, filaments 3 times longer than the tube (!!), May; fruit capsule bristly, but without glands. HyWF 130; RWF 256; BR 120 (= *R. nudiflorum* [L.] Torr.). N. America. 1734. Much used in hybridizing. Often confused with *R. prinophyllum*. z3 ★ Fig. 131. ⊕

R. phoeniceum see: **R. pulchrum**

R. planetum Balf. f. (S Fortunei, SS Davidii). Evergreen shrub, 1–3 m high, rather thick branched, with white, later exfoliating indumentum; leaves oblong, 10–20 cm long, obtuse, base cuneate, bright green above, underside somewhat loosely floccose, both sides with about 20 vein pairs; flowers about 10 together, rachis thick, somewhat tomentose, corolla funnelform-campanulate, 4–5 cm long, with 6–7 lobes, fleshy, soft pink, without patches (!!), stamens 12–14, uneven, style shorter than the corolla, ovaries glabrous, calyx only 1 mm long, glabrous. BM 8953; ICS 4171. China; Szechwan Prov. Very similar to *R. sutchuenenses* and *R.*

Fig. 131. *Rhododendron periclymenoides*
(from Guimpel)

calophytum, but the corolla differently formed and without blotches! z7 ★★ # ∅ ⊕

R. pocophorum Balf. f. ex Tagg (S Neriiflorum, SS Haematodes). Evergreen shrub, to 2 m high, very closely related to *R. haematodes*, but differs in the glandular young shoots, calyx, ovary, flower and petiole; leaf underside dense brownish woolly indumentum; flowers deep carmine or scarlet-red, 6–15 together, March–April. Tibet. 1922. z7 ★★ Plate 58. # ⊕

R. ponticum L. (S and SS Ponticum). Evergreen shrub, also occasionally a small tree, 3–5 m high, usually branched from the base up, young shoots glabrous; leaves oblong-lanceolate, 10–15 cm long, dark green above, lighter beneath, both sides totally glabrous, with 12–16 vein pairs; flowers 10–15 in corymbs, corolla broadly funnelform, 4–5 cm wide, light purple-violet with yellow-green blotches, stamens 10, base pubescent, style and ovaries glabrous, June. BM 650. From Spain and Portugal to Asia Minor. 1753. Also used as a grafting understock. z6 ★-★★ Fig. 101. # ∅ ⊕

ssp. **baeticum** (Boiss. & Reuter) Hand.-Mazz. This is the typical plant occurring in the wild in S. Portugal and S. Spain (S. Andalusia) as opposed to the species which occurs in the Caucasus and Turkey. The distinguishing characteristics are very slight, particularly the tomentose flower rachis, this glabrous on the species. #

'Album'. Flowers white. Relatively rare.

'Cheiranthifolium'. Habit denser, more compact; leaves smaller, 5–7 cm long, only 8–12 mm wide; flowers light purple, limb undulate.

'Imbricatum'. Dwarf form, short branched; leaves nearly rosette-like at the shoot tips, elliptic, usually rounded at both ends, 3–6 cm long, 1.5–3 cm wide, somewhat convex; flowers small, violet, May–June (= *R. imbricatum* Hort.). ∅

'Lancifolium'. Habit shorter than that of the type, 1.5–2 m high; leaves 5–10 cm long, 12–20 mm wide, margins always even (!!); flowers in small corymbs, center nearly white, turning more purple toward the margin (= *R. lancifolium* Moench). ∅

'Roseum'. Very strong grower, young shoots red; leaves somewhat smaller and narrower than those of the species; flowers in large corymbs, lilac-pink, lighter in the center, very late (!), mid June. ⊕

'Variegatum'. Leaves more slender and smaller than those of the species, often somewhat deformed, limb yellowish white. Poor bloomer. ∅

R. poukhanense see: **R. yedoense** var. **poukhanense**

R. × 'praecox' see: cultivar **'Praecox'**

R. praestans Balf. f. & W. W. Sm. (S Grande). Tall, evergreen shrub, a tree in its habitat, to 9 m; leaves oblong to lanceolate, 25–35 cm long, 12 cm wide, glossy dark green above, scabby beneath with a thin, glossy, light gray or light brown indumentum, rounded above, tapered to the base and becoming winged along the flat petiole, both sides with 13–16 vein pairs; flowers 15–20 together, corolla 8 lobed, obliquely campanulate, 3.5–4.5 cm long, lilac-pink, with a carmine basal spot, stamens 16, style glabrous, ovaries pubescent, calyx tiny, with 8

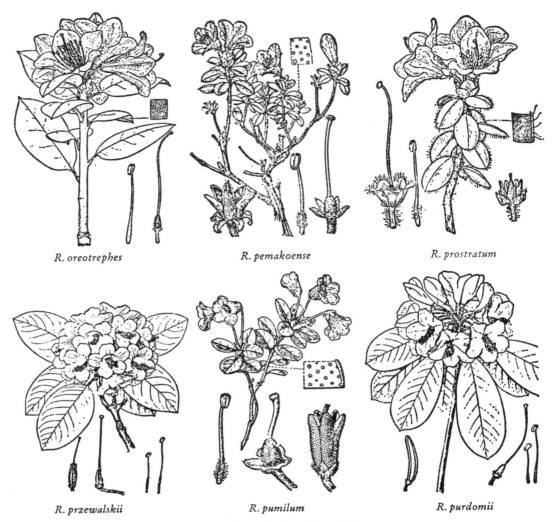

R. oreotrephes   *R. pemakoense*   *R. prostratum*

R. przewalskii   *R. pumilum*   *R. purdomii*

Fig. 132. **Rhododendron** (from ICS)

short teeth, tomentose. ICS 4218; RYB 24: 1 ('Sunte Rock'). China; Yunnan Prov., in open coniferous forests at 4000 m high. 1914. z7 ★★ # ∅ ☼

R. primuliflorum Bur. & Franch. (S Anthopogon). Evergreen shrub about 1 m high, very aromatic; leaves elliptic-oblong, 1.5–2.5 cm long, acute, base rounded, densely reddish scaly beneath; flowers 6–15 in dense corymbs; corolla narrowly tubular, 2 cm long, yellow, the 5 rounded limb lobes white (occasionally also light pink), stamens 5, enclosed, pubescent beneath, style very short and thick, stigma wide, flat, calyx 6 mm long, ciliate, April–May. ICS 4107 (= *R. tsarongense* Balf. f. & Forrest). SE. Tibet. 1917. z6 ★★ # ∅

R. primulinum see: **R. flavidum**

R. prinophyllum (Small) Millais (S Azalea, SS Luteum). Deciduous shrub, 1–3 m high, young shoots finely pubescent, winter buds gray pubescent, bud scales

obtuse or with a mucro; leaves elliptic to obovate-oblong, 3–7 cm long, acute, dull blue-green above (!) and somewhat pubescent, gray pubescent beneath; flowers very fragrant, 5–9 together, appearing with the foliage, flower pedicel with stalked glands, corolla broadly tubular, 4 cm wide, pink, tube as long or shorter than the limb lobes, filaments bristly glandular, calyx pubescent on the exterior and glandular ciliate. RYB 10: 21; RWF 257 (= *R. roseum* [Loisel.] Rehd.). N. America. z3 ★★★ ☼

R. prostratum W. W. Sm. (S Saluenense). Evergreen, procumbent shrub, only 10 cm high, in cultivation to 30 cm high, young shoots and the leaf petiole bristly; leaves oblong-elliptic, 12–20 mm long, smooth above, scaly beneath; flowers grouped 1–2–3, corolla rotate to broadly funnelform, 2.5–3 cm wide, with 5 rounded lobes, purple pink to carmine with darker patches, stamens 10, purple, base pubescent, style glabrous, ovaries scaly, calyx deeply lobed and ciliate, April–May. BM 8747; RYB 8: 21; 9: 51; NF 1: 164; JRHS 86: 82; ICS 4042. China; Yunnan Prov. 1910. z6 ★ Fig. 132. #

R. protistum Balf. f. & Forrest (S Grande). Evergreen tree, 7–12 m high in its habitat; leaves oblanceolate to obovate, 20–45 cm long, 10–18 cm wide, glabrous on young plants; flowers 20–30 together, corolla campanulate, 5 cm long, 8 lobed, cream-white, with a trace of pink, stamens 16, style glabrous, ovaries pink pubescent, May. China. 1919. This species is very similar to *R. giganteum* and *R. magnificum*, with only slight botanical differences. They were all once considered a single species (lit. Bean III: 748); *R. protistum*, being the first named species, was the name given for all three. z9 ★★★ # ∅ ✧

R. pruniflorum see: **R. tsangpoense** var. **pruniflorum**

R. prunifolium (Small) Millais (S Azalea, SS Luteum). Deciduous shrub, to 2 m high, young shoots glabrous, purple-red; leaves oblong-elliptic to obovate, 3–12 cm long, usually totally glabrous, midrib pubescent; flowers 4–5 together, corolla tubular-funnelform, orange to carmine, to 5 cm wide, tube about 2.5 cm long, stamens 5–6 cm long, overies pubescent, appearing in July–August (!!). RYB 11: 9; 13: 38; 5: 58. N. America. 1918. z6 ★★★ ✧

R. przewalskii Maxim. (S Lacteum). Very dense, evergreen shrub, scarcely over 1 m high in cultivation, to 2 m in its habitat; leaves leathery, oval-elliptic, 5–10 cm long, 2–4 cm wide, obtuse with a small tip, base round, finely rugose above, light or dark brown tomentose beneath, indumentum eventually more or less sloughing off, petiole 1–2 cm long, yellowish, glabrous; flowers grouped 12–15, corolla campanulate, white to pink, 3–4 cm wide, limb 5 lobed, stamens 10, April–May. RYB 10: 48; ICS 4206. NW. China; Yunnan, Szechwan Provs. A poor bloomer. z6 ★ Fig. 132. #

R. pseudochrysanthum Hayata (S Barbatum, SS Maculiferum). Evergreen shrub, habit quite variable, to 3 m high, young shoots rather thick, gray, floccose and with stalked glands; leaves clustered at the shoot tips, lanceolate to oblong-elliptic or also oblanceolate, thick and stiff, 3–7 cm long, 2–4 cm wide, apex round and abruptly terminating in a short, stiff point, base rounded, deep green above, lighter beneath, both sides floccose, later gradually becoming glabrous, petiole 12 mm; flowers grouped 10–20 in rather dense corymbs, corolla campanulate, 5 lobed, pale pink to white, 3–4 cm long and wide, interior speckled, exterior darker striped, stamens 10, ovaries glandular pubescent, April. BMns 284; RYB 11: 23. Taiwan. 1918. z8 ★★★ # ✧

R. pubescens see: **R. spiciferum**

R. pulchrum Sweet (S Azalea, SS Obtusum). Presumably *R. mucronulatum* × *R. scabrum*; not observed in the wild. Evergreen shrub, about 1–1.5 m high, young shoots with appressed, forward-directed bristly hairs; leaves obovate to oval-lanceolate, 2.5–7.5 cm long, appressed pubescence on both sides; flowers grouped 2–4 together, corolla funnelform, 5 lobed, 5 cm wide, purple, stamens 10, base pubescent, style glabrous, ovaries with erect bristly hairs, calyx lobes awl-shaped, 8–12 mm (!) long, exterior pubescent along the margin, as is the 12 mm long flower stalk, May. BM 2667; ICS 4259; MJ 769 (= *R. indicum smithii* Wils.; *R. phoeniceum* G. Don). Introduced from China. z7 ★★ # ✧

'Calycinum'. More vigorous growing; flowers larger, purple-pink with carmine patches, abundantly blooming (= 'Omurasaki'). Better than the species. Much cultivated in Japan.

'Maxwellii'. About 50 cm high; flowers larger, carmine-red, late May (= *R. maxwellii* Millais). Japan. Very meritorious form. ✧

R. pumilum Hook. f. (S Uniflorum). Dwarf evergreen shrub, shoots scaly and finely pubescent; leaves elliptic to more obovate, 12–18 mm long, half as wide, rounded above, bright green, scaly and blue-green beneath, petiole very short; flowers solitary or 2–3 at the shoot tips, corolla campanulate, 5 lobed, 12–18 mm long, pink, exterior pubescent and somewhat scaly, calyx scaly, 3 mm long, stamens 10, ovaries densely scaly. BS 3: Pl. 87; ICS 4014; FS 667. Sikkim, Himalayas, E. Nepal. 1924. Hardy, attractive but rare. z6 ★ Fig. 132. # ✧

R. punctatum see: cultivar **'Puncta'**

R. puralbum Balf. f. & W. W. Sm. (S Thomsonii, SS Souliei). Evergreen shrub, to 4.5 m high in its habitat; leaves oblong, 5–12 cm long, 3–5 cm wide, obtuse, base round, dark green and glabrous above, with 9–12 vein pairs, bluish green beneath, eventually glabrous, petiole glabrous except for a few glands; flowers in loose clusters of about 8, corolla broadly shell-form, pure white (!!), 4 cm long, limb with 5 rounded, emarginate lobes, calyx 7–10 mm long, with 5 uneven, rounded to oblong lobes with green glands, stamens 10–12, uneven, 1–2 cm long, style 3 cm long, ovaries glandular, May. RYB 7: 4. China; Yunnan Prov. 1913. Occasionally erroneously labeled in cultivation. z8 ★★★ # ✧

R. purdomii Rehd. & Wils. (S and SS Taliense). Vigorous, thick branched, evergreen shrub, young shoots finely pubescent; leaves oblong-lanceolate to more elliptic, 6–8 cm long, 2.5–3.5 cm wide, margins involuted, glossy light green above and somewhat rugose, lighter beneath, glabrous, distinctly reticulate veined between the 10–12 vein pairs on either side; flowers in corymbs of about 10, corolla campanulate, 2.5–3 cm long, 5 lobed, white to pink, stamens 10, ovaries whitish pubescent, calyx small, cupulate. ICS 4227. Central China; Shensi Prov. 1914. z6 ★★ Fig. 132. # ✧

R. quinquefolium Biss. & Moore (S Azalea, SS Schlippenbachii). Deciduous shrub, 1 (3) m high, shoots thin, glabrous, partly spiraled, partly whorled in arrangement, glossy brown, stem gray-brown, somewhat corky; leaves 4–5 at the ends of short shoots, obovate to rhombic, 4–6 cm long, 2–4 cm wide, ciliate, often narrowly red margined, glabrous except for the midrib and petiole; flowers solitary or paired, appearing just before or with the foliage, pendulous (!), broadly funnelform, 4 cm wide, white with greenish patches, stamens 10, greenish, ovaries and styles glabrous, April–May. MJ 760; KIF 3: 65. Central Japan. 1896. z8 ★★★ # ◐ ✿

R. racemosum Franch. (S Virgatum). Evergreen shrub, to 1 m high, erect, but also sometimes procumbent, red, finely pruinose; leaves oblong elliptic, 2–6 cm long, with a small apical tip, 1–3 cm wide, blue-green and densely scaly beneath; flowers axillary (!!), in groups of a few together, along the entire shoot and developing a form of raceme, corolla funnelform, limb 5 lobed, 2.5 cm wide, pink to whitish, exterior scaly, but not pubescent, stamens 10, calyx and flower stalk very scaly, March–April. BM 7301; UR 2; NF 6: 171. China; Yunnan Prov., 2500–3000 m. 1889. z6 ★★★★ # ✿

R. radicans Balf. f. & Forrest (S Saluenense). Evergreen, carpet-like shrub, 5–10 cm high, shoots nearly glabrous, bud scales persistent; leaves narrowly oblanceolate, 1.5 cm long, very acute, soft ciliate, loosely scaly above, much denser beneath; flowers solitary, terminal, on 1.5 cm long stalks, corolla rotate, 2 cm long, deeply 5 lobed, purple, exterior pubescent and scaly, stamens 10, base pubescent, style glabrous, ovaries scaly, calyx 5 mm long, lobes ciliate and scaly, May. RYB 8: 22; 13: 22. SE. Tibet, Tsarong. 1921. z6 ★★★ # ✿

R. radinum see: **R. trichostomum** var. **radinum**

R. ravum see: **R. cuneatum**

R. regale see: **R. basilicum**

R. repens see: **R. forrestii** var. **repens**
— var. *chamaedoron* see: **R. chamaethomsonii** var. **chamaethauma**
— var. *chamaethauma* see: **R. chamaethomsonii** var. **chamaethauma**

R. reticulatum D. Don (S Azalea, SS Schlippenbachii). Deciduous shrub, 1–5 m high, young shoots light brown, quickly becoming glabrous; leaves usually 2–3 at the ends of the short shoots, broadly ovate to rhombic, 3–7 cm long, 2–5 cm wide, pubescent above when young, eventually glabrous, reticulately veined beneath with pubescent venation, petiole 5 mm long, pubescent, purple in fall; flowers 1–2 (4) together, appearing before the leaves, corolla rotate to funnelform, purple to purple-pink, normally without markings, stamens 10, glabrous, 5 of these quite short, curved upward, ovaries and style pubescent, April–May. BM 6972; SR 116; NF 1: 21; MJ 758 (= *R. rhombicum* Miq.; *R. wadanum* Mak.). Japan; widely distributed on volcanic ash soils. z6 ★★★ Fig. 133. ○ ⌀ ✿

f. **pentandrum** Wils. Leaves bright red in fall; flowers with only 5 stamens, ovaries glandular (not pubescent!), style glabrous. BM 7681 (= *R. dilatatum* Maxim.).

R. rex Lév. (S Falconeri). Evergreen shrub or small tree, 4–5 m high, shoots very thick (flower stalk to 1.5 cm thick!), young shoots gray-white tomentose; leaves oblanceolate, about 25 cm long, 8 cm wide, broadly

Fig. 133. *Rhododendron reticulatum* (from Regel)

obtuse, narrower at the base, deep green and somewhat rugose above, gray to light brown beneath, with a more or less persistent indumentum, petiole 4–4.5 cm long, cylindrical, not furrowed above; flowers 20–30 in corymbs, rachis tomentose, corolla tubular campanulate, 5 cm long, pink, basal patch red, also punctate, stamens 16, uneven, base pubescent, style glabrous, ovaries gray pubescent, calyx small, with 8 broadly triangular, tomentose teeth, April–May. ICS 4211; RYB 10: 25. China; NE. Yunnan, SW. Szechwan Provs. Very similar to *R. fictolacteum*. z7 ★★★★ Fig. 140. # ⌀ ✿

R. rhabdotum Balf. f. & Cooper (S Maddenii, SS Megacalyx). Evergreen shrub, to 3 m high in its habitat, young shoots densely scaly and bristly pubescent; leaves obovate-oblong-elliptic, obtuse to rounded, 8–15 cm long, 3–5 cm wide, scaly beneath; few flowered, corolla funnelform, without scales, 7.5 cm long, 5 lobed, cream-white, with red lines on the underside, very similar to *R. dalhousiae*, stamens 10, with large anthers, filaments woolly pubescent beneath, ovaries densely scaly, style loosely scaly on the basal half. BS 3: Pl. 88; RYB 6: 3; JRHS 93: 218; 100: 50. Himalayas, Bhutan, Assam. 1925. z9 ★★★ # ✿

R. rhombicum see: **R. reticulatum**

R. rigidum Franch. (S Triflorum, SS Yunnanense). Evergreen shrub, 1–2 m high, shoots slightly scaly, somewhat stiff; leaves oblanceolate, tapered toward the base, 4–6 cm long, 1–2 cm wide, glandular scaly on both sides, leaf base and petiole with a few bristles; flowers usually 4 together, small, corolla funnelform, 5 lobed, pale pink with carmine markings, exterior not scaly, stamens 10, base pubescent, May. ICS 4087. China; Yunnan Prov., on cliffs at 2500–3000 m. A good bloomer. z7 ★★ Fig. 140. #

R. ripense see: **R. mucronatum var. ripense**

R. ririei Hemsl. & Wils. (S Arboreum, SS Argyrophyllum). Evergreen shrub, 3–4 m high, shoots long, rigid, greenish with white tomentum; leaves arranged in horizontal whorls under the inflorescences, narrowly ovate to oblanceolate, 7–15 cm long, 3–5 cm wide, base cuneate, bright green above, dull, glabrous, silver-white to gray-green and tomentose beneath, as is the 1–2 cm long petiole; flowers 8–10 in loose corymbs, corolla campanulate, 4–5 cm long, purple-red, base blackish speckled, limb 5–7 lobed, stamens 10, glabrous, ovaries gray-tomentose, February–March. FIO 21; ICS 4192. China; Szechwan Prov. 1904. z7 ★★★ # ✧

R. roseum see: **R. prinophyllum**

R. roxieanum Forrest (S Taliense, SS Roxieanum). Slow growing, evergreen shrub, hardly 1 m high, shoots thick woolly pubescent, bud scales persisting for several years; leaves narrowly lanceolate, 5–10 cm long, 0.8–2 cm wide, margin involuted, glossy and finely rugose above, thick rust brown woolly tomentose beneath, petiole the same, 1 cm long; flowers 10–15 in corymbs, corolla campanulate, white to cream-white or with a trace of pink, limb 5 lobed, carmine speckled above, stamens 10, basal half densely pubescent, calyx very small, April–May. BM 9383; ICS 4240. China; Yunnan Prov., in open, moist mountain meadows at 4000 m. 1913. z7 ★★ # ✧

R. rubiginosum Franch. (S Heliolepis). Evergreen shrub, to 7 m high in its habitat, young shoots reddish, scaly; leaves elliptic-lanceolate, sharply acuminate, 3–7 cm long, 2–3 cm wide, smooth and glabrous above, densely rust-brown scaly beneath, the scales partly overlapping, petiole 1.5 cm long, scaly; flowers 4–8 together, terminal, corolla funnelform, about 4 cm long, lilac-pink, exterior scaly, particularly the lobes, stamens 10, basal half pubescent, ovaries densely scaly, style glabrous, calyx undulately lobed, April–May. BM 7621; SR 330. China; Yunnan Prov., at 2000–3000 m in open forest. 1889. Very attractive, abundantly flowering, hardy. z6 ★★★ Fig. 134. # ✧

R. rubropunctatum see: **R. hyperythrum**

R. rude Tagg & Forrest (S Barbatum, SS Glischrum). Evergreen shrub, very similar to *R. glischrum*, but the leaves to 19 cm long and 7.5 cm wide, covered with glandular hairs on both sides; flowers smaller, exterior often red striped, otherwise carmine-purple, stamens 10, style and ovaries with stalked glands, calyx cupulate, fleshy, with bristly glands, the 5 lobes about 13 mm long, bristly and ciliate. China; NW. Yunnan Prov. z7 ★★ # ✧

R. rufum Batal. (S Taliense, SS Watsonii). Evergreen shrub to a small tree, young shoots rather thick, floccose

Fig. 134. *Rhododendron rubiginosum* (from Bot. Mag.)

only when quite young; leaves elliptic to oblong or obovate, 7–11 cm long, 3–4.5 cm wide, obtuse, eventually glabrous and finely rugose above, midrib indented, light brown or rust-brown tomentose, also the 2 cm long, thick, petiole; flowers 6–10 in corymbs, corolla funnelform-campanulate, to 3 cm long, white to pink-purple, interior carmine speckled, 5 lobed, stamens 10, style densely rust-red pubescent, calyx 1 mm long. ICS 4233. China; Szechwan, Kansu Provs., in the forests. z5 ★ #

R. rupicola W. W. Sm. (S Lapponicum). Evergreen shrub, 30–50 cm high, densely branched, shoots densely scaly; leaves broadly elliptic, 12 mm long, 8 mm wide, densely scaly on both sides; flowers 3–5 together, terminal, petiole very short, corolla broadly funnelform, 12 mm long, 2 cm wide, purple-violet, the short tube pubescent, the 5 lobes rounded, stamens usually 10 (occasionally only 7), purple, white pubescent at the base, calyx 4 mm long, with 5 ciliate purple lobes, April–May. China; Yunnan Prov., on chalk! 1910. z6 ★★ # ✧

R. russatum Balf. f. & Forrest (S Lapponicum). Upright, evergreen shrub, 50–80 cm high, shoots densely scaly; leaves oblong-lanceolate, 3 cm long, 1 cm wide, densely scaly on both sides, the rust-brown scales on the underside partly touching, partly overlapping, petiole 8 mm long; flowers grouped 4–5, terminal, good bloomer, corolla open funnelform, dark violet with a white throat, about 2.5 cm wide, interior lightly pubescent, exterior not scaly, stamens 10, base long pubescent, style red, calyx deeply 5 lobed, lobes 4 mm long, ciliate, April–May. BM 8963; ICS 4050; BHR 49 (= *R. cantabile* Balf. f.).

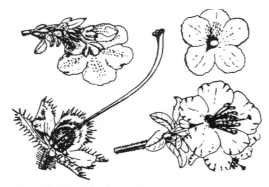

Fig. 135. *Rhododendron saluenense* (from Bot. Mag.)

China; NW. Yunnan Prov. One of the most attractive species of the series and indispensable for the rock garden. z6 ★★★★ Fig. 140. # ☉

R. saluenense Franch. (S Saluenense). Evergreen shrub, 40–50 cm high, shoots densely scaly and bristly; leaves oblong-elliptic, 3 cm long, 1 cm wide, loosely scaly and glossy above, underside with small, densely overlapping scales, petiole bristly pubescent; flowers grouped 2–3, terminal, corolla broadly campanulate, 3 cm long, 4 cm wide, purple-red with darker markings, exterior densely scaly and softly pubescent, stamens 10, base long pubescent, style glabrous, calyx and ovaries scaly, April–May. BM 9095; SR 599; DRHS 1782. China; NW. Yunnan Prov., 4000–4300 m on stone and gravel. 1914. Much valued for its large flowers, quite hardy. z6 ★★★ Fig. 135. # ☉

R. sanctum Nakai (S Azalea, SS Obtusum). Deciduous shrub, rust-brown pubescent, to 5 m high in its habitat; leaves usually 3 at the shoot tips, broadly rhombic to oval-rhombic, 4–8 cm long, 3–6 cm wide, somewhat glossy above with long brown hairs, underside lighter with a pubescent midrib; flowers grouped 3–4, dark pink, petiole 5–8 mm, calyx teeth small, corolla glabrous, stamens 10, style glabrous, May–June. Japan; Honshu, in the mountains. z7 ★★ ☉

R. sanguineum Franch. (S Neriiflorum, SS Sanguineum). Evergreen shrub, about 0.7 m high, branches short and thin, without glands, loose white tomentose; leaves leathery, ovate to narrowly oblong, 4–6 cm long, 2–2.5 cm wide, rounded, base obtuse, deep green and glabrous above, underside thinly gray-white tomentose with raised venation, petiole 1 cm long; flowers 3–4(6), corolla tubular-campanulate, fleshy, bright carmine-red, limb 5 lobed, stamens 10, white, glabrous, style glabrous, ovaries densely stellate tomentose, May. ICS 4149. China; W. Yunnan Prov., SE. Tibet. z8 ★★★ # ☉

Including, according to Cowan (see also Bean III: 761–762) 10 subspecies. Most once considered separate species. Of these, the most important are:

ssp. **didymum** (Balf. f. & Forrest) Cowan. 20–50 cm high, shoots bristly pubescent, scales of the leaf buds persistent (!); leaves somewhat whorled, leathery tough, obovate, 2–5 cm long, 1–1.8 cm wide, obtuse, base cuneate, dark green above, thinly gray tomentose beneath; flowers usually in 4's, corolla tubular-campanulate, 2.5 cm long, black-red (!), fleshy, stamens 10, filaments red, glabrous, ovaries very densely glandular, but not pubescent, styles red, glabrous, calyx glandular-bristly on the exterior, June–July. BM 9217; ICS 4148 (= *R. didymum* Balf. f. & Forrest). SE. Tibet, on limestone outcroppings and moist alpine meadows. 1917. z8 ★ Fig. 136. ☉

ssp. **haemaleum** (Balf. f. & Forrest) Cowan. To 1 m high, young shoots gray pubescent, scales of the foliar buds abscising (!), otherwise like the typical *R. sanguineum* in all respects, but the flowers are blackish carmine. BM 9283 (as *R. sanguineum*); ICS 4150 (= *R. haemaleum* Balf. f. & Forrest). SE. Tibet, Mekong and Salween River region, 4000 m. 1904. z8 ★★ # ☉

R. sargentianum Rehd. & Wils. (S Anthopogon). Aromatic, evergreen shrub, 30–50 cm high, shoots short and very well branched; fine bristly pubescent and scaly in the 1st year; leaves broadly ovate, with a small mucro, 1.5 cm long, 0.8 cm wide, apex soon glabrous and reticulately veined, glossy, loosely scaly beneath, petiole 5 mm long, scaly; flowers a few in loose umbels, stalk 1 cm long, corolla tubular, limb 12 mm wide, lemon-yellow, exterior densely scaly, interior shaggy pubescent, stamens 5, enclosed within the tube, style very short and thick, ovaries scaly, calyx with 5 erect, ovate, scaly and ciliate lobes, May. BM 8871; NF 4: 27; RYB 2: 21; 13: 19; JRHS 87: 167; ICS 4105. China; W. Szechwan Prov., at 3000 m. 1903. z8 ★★★ # ☉

R. scabrifolium Franch. (S Scabrifolium) Evergreen shrub, thin, stiffly erect, 1–2 m, shoots thin, long pubescent and woolly; leaves arranged along the branch, narrowly ovate to oblong-lanceolate, acute, tapered to the base, 3–8 cm long, 2–2.5 cm wide, dark green above with short, stiff hairs, underside pubescent only on the major veins; flowers 2–4 in the axils of the uppermost leaves, developing a 7–10 cm wide inflorescence, corolla broadly funnelform, 3 cm wide, with a short tube, with 5 deep lobes, white to light pink, stamens 10, ovaries scaly and short pubescent, calyx acute, March–April. BM 7159; ICS 4276; SR 604. China; Yunnan Prov. 1885. z8 ★★ Fig. 137. # ☉

Fig. 136. *Rhododendron sanguineum* spp. *didymum* (Original)

Fig. 137. *Rhododendron scabrifolium*

Fig. 138. *Rhododendron schlippenbachii*
(from Kavka)

R. scabrum G. Don (S Azalea, SS Obtusum). Evergreen shrub, 0.7–1.5 m high, branches covered with flattened hairs; leaves elliptic-lanceolate to oblanceolate, 4–9 cm long; flowers in clusters of 3–4, corolla broadly funnelform, 6–8 cm wide, pink-red to blood-red, stamens 10, ovaries glandular bristly, calyx lobes usually rounded, ciliate, 6 mm long, May. Bm 8478 (as *R. sublanceolatum*). Japan; Liukiu Island. 1909. Very attractive and large flowered, but quite tender. z9 ★★★ # ⊕

R. schlippenbachii Maxim. (S Azalea, SS Schlippenbachii). Deciduous shrub, to 4 m high in its habitat, branches irregular and divaricately spreading, glandular pubescent when young, light brown, later glabrous; leaves in 5's, whorled, at the ends of the shorter shoots, obovate, 6–10 cm long, 4–7 cm wide, limb somewhat undulated, cuneate at the base, bright green above, lighter beneath, scattered pubescent to glabrous on both sides, yellow to carmine in fall; flowers 3–6, appearing with or immediately before the foliage, corolla broadly funnelform, lighter to darker pink, 7–8 cm wide, red-brown punctate, stamens 10, pubescent on the basal half, style glandular bristled, April–May. BM 7373; SR 119. Korea, NE. Manchuria, central Japan, in open forests. 1893. One of the most attractive Azaleas; quite hardy. z5 ★★★★ Fig. 138. ∅ ⊕

R. scintillans Balf. f. & W. W. Sm. (S Lapponicum). Evergreen shrub, 0.5–0.7 m high, young shoots erect, thin, branches densely scaly; leaves oblong-lanceolate, 6–20 mm long, to 5 mm wide, densely scaly on both sides, scales on the underside just touching or overlapping; flowers 3–6 together, involucral scales abscising after flowering, corolla open funnelform, to 2.5 cm wide, lilac to rather blue, exterior glabrous, stamens 10, style glabrous, ovaries scaly, calyx lobe fringed, April–May. UR 16. China; Yunnan Prov., Lichiang, in open grassy areas at 4000–4500 m. 1913. z6 ★★★★ # ⊕

R. scyphocalyx see: **R. dichroanthum** ssp. **scyphocalyx**

R. searsiae Rehd. & Wils. (S Triflorum, SS Yunnanense). Evergreen shrub, 1–3 m high, young shoots scaly; leaves lanceolate, short and sharply acuminate, 6–9 cm long, 1–2 cm wide, bluish beneath, rather dense and very irregularly scaly, spacing of the scales about as wide as their radius; flowers 3–4(8) in loose clusters, corolla broadly funnelform, 3–4 cm wide, soft lilac to nearly white, exterior not scaly, limb 5 lobed, calyx with uneven-sized, long ciliate lobes, stamens 10, base pubescent, ovaries densely scaly, April–May. ICS 4089; BM 8993; SR 808. China; W. Szechwan Prov., 2500–3000 m. Quite variable species, not as attractive as *R. triflorum*. z6 ★ Fig. 140. #

R. selense Franch. (S Thomsonii, SS Selense). Upright, evergreen shrub, 1–2 m high, young shoots with tufted pubescence and stalked glands, later glabrous; leaves thin and leathery, oblong to obovate, 3–5 cm long, 1.5–3 cm wide, rounded, base rounded, never cordate, deep green above, lighter beneath with remnants of glands and hairs; flowers 4–5(8), corolla funnelform-campanulate, about 3 cm long and wide, 5 lobed, white or pale pink to pure pink, with or without a carmine basal patch, otherwise usually without markings, calyx 3 mm long, densely glandular, stamens 10, pubescent at the base, April–May. ICS 4175. China; W. Yunnan Prov., Siela region. 1917. Garden merit normally only slight, except for the selections. z8 ★★ #

R. semibarbatum Maxim. (S Semibarbatum). Irregularly branched, deciduous shrub, 1–2.5 m high, young shoots glandular pubescent, glabrous in the 2nd year, gray-yellow to dark brown; leaves elliptic-oblong, 2–6 cm long, 1–3 cm wide, rather acute at both ends, very finely bristly serrate, dark or light green above, glabrous on

Fig. 139. *Rhododendron semibarbatum*
(from Regel)

both sides except for the pubescent midrib, yellow to carmine in fall; flowers small, solitary, but clustered at the ends of the previous year's shoots, nearly hidden by the young new growth, corolla nearly plate-like, 2 cm wide, deeply 5 lobed, yellowish white, also pink toned, red punctate, stamens 5, of these 3 are long and only slightly pubescent, the other 2 shorter and densely shaggy pubescent, June. BM 9147; SR 609. Mountains of central and southern Japan. Garden merit slight, but with attractive fall foliage. z6 ★ Fig. 139. ∅

R. serotinum Hutchins. (S Fortunei, SS Fortunei). Evergreen shrub, very similar to *R. fortunei*, but with a very open, divaricate habit; flowers white, with red patches and red punctate, flowering in September (!). ICS 4157: BM 8841. China. 1889. z8 ★★ Fig. 140. # ☼

R. serpyllifolium Miq. (S Azalea, SS Obtusum). Broad, evergreen shrub, 0.5–1 m high, the thin shoots densely covered with flat hairs; leaves only 6–18 mm long, narrowly elliptic to obovate, half as wide, lightly pubescent; flowers usually solitary, corolla about 2 cm wide, light pink to nearly white, 5 lobed, stamens 5, calyx and ovaries bristly, May. BM 7503. Japan. Easily distinguised by its very small leaves and thin shoots. z6 ★ # ☼

R. setosum D. Don (S Lapponicum). Low evergreen shrub, 0.3–0.5 m high, shoots densely bristly (!)

pubescent; leaves oblong-elliptic, 1–2 cm long, 0.8 cm wide, glandular scaly above, also beneath and densely bristly ciliate, bristles however quickly abscising, spacing of the scales equal to their diameter; flowers usually terminal in 3's, occasionally to 8, corolla broadly funnelform, limb deeply lobed, about 2.5 cm long and wide, purple-pink, exterior not scaly, calyx conspicuously red, exterior and limb glandular, stamens 10, pubescent at the base, ovaries scaly, May. BM 8523; SR 428; SNp 105. S. Tibet, Sikkim, Himalayas, 3500–5000 m. 1850. z6 ★ Fig. 142. #

R. sherriffii Cowan (S Campanulatum). Evergreen shrub, to 3 m high, young shoots pubescent; leaves elliptic to obovate, 5–6.5 cm long, 3–4 cm wide, eventually totally glabrous above, underside covered with a thick brown indumentum; flowers 4–6 together in short racemes, corolla funnelform-campanulate, 4 cm long, fleshy, intensely dark carmine, with darker markings at the base of the lobes, pruinose, March–April. BMns 337; ICS 4225. S. Tibet. 1936. z8 ★★ Fig. 140. # ☼

R. shikokianum see: **R. weyrichii**

R. shweliense Balf. f. & Forrest (S Glaucophyllum). Low, evergreen, aromatic shrub, branches and leaves densely scaly, as is the corolla exterior; leaves oblong to obovate, 2.5–5 cm long; flowers campanulate, pink with a trace of yellow and purple markings, May. China; Yunnan Prov. 1924. Very similar to *R. brachyanthum* var. *hypolepodotum*, but with different colored flowers. z6 ★ # ☼

R. silvaticum see: **R. lanigerum**

R. simsii Planch. (S Azalea, SS Obtusum). Broad growing, evergreen shrub, branches densely pubescent; leaves lanceolate to narrowly oblanceolate, 3–7 cm long, bristly pubescent; flowers 2–5 together, corolla funnelform, 5–7 cm wide, pink-red to dark red on the type, stamens 10, occasionally only 8, sepals 2–6 mm long, bristly ciliate, May. FS 13; BM 1480; FIO 17; ICS 4247 (= *Azalea indica* Ait. pp.; *R. indicum* Hemsl. pp.). E. China, Taiwan. 1808. Primarily found in E. China's Yangtse Valley; one of the parent forms of the "Indica" or "Indian" azaleas. z9–10 ★★★

For detailed descriptions of the many cultivars, refer to Scheerlinck.

R. sinense see: **R. molle**

R. sinogrande Balf. f. & W. W. Sm. (S Grande). Evergreen shrub, a tree in its habitat, 6–10 m high, flower shoots very thick, gray-tomentose; leaves elliptic to oblong or obovate, 30–60 cm long (occasionally longer in cultivation!), 8–30 cm wide, widest just above the middle, glabrous above, with about 17 vein pairs, silver-gray beneath, seemingly covered with a membranous layer, petiole 2–5 cm long; flowers about 20 in racemes, corolla campanulate, bulging, 5–6 cm long, limb with 8–10 lobes, yellowish white with a carmine basal patch, stamens 18–20, irregularly long, half as long as the style, ovaries without glands, April. BM 8973; NF 3: 155; SR 318; RYB 4: 40; 9: 25. China, Burma, Tibet, at altitudes

Plate 49

Quercus schochiana
in the Dortmund Botanic Garden, W. Germany

Quercus suber
in Killerton Park, England

Quercus turneri 'Pseudoturneri'
Thiensen Arboretum, near Elmshorn, W. Germany

Quercus alnifolia
in Crarae Park, Scotland

Plate 50

Quercus virginiana, 130 years old,
in Pisa Botanic Garden, Italy

Reveesia thyrsoidea
in the Sotchi Dendrarium, USSR

Rhamnus frangula 'Tallhedge' as a hedge in Whitnall Park, Chicago, Illinois, USA

Plate 51

Restio subverticillatus in Bell Park, Fota Island, Co. Cork, Ireland

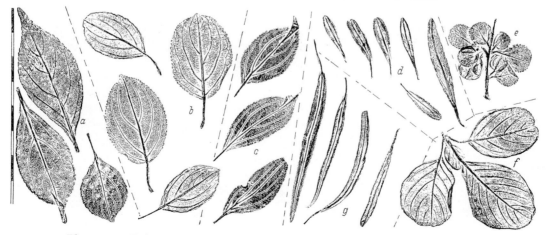

Rhamnus. a. *R. leptophyllus;* b. *R. saxatilis;* c. *R. tinctorius;* d. *R. pallasii;* e. *R. infectorius;*
f. *R. pumilus;* g. *R. erythroxylon* (material from wild plants)

Plate 52

Rhamnus alaternus 'Variegatus'
in Malahide Gardens, Ireland

Rhamnus frangula 'Aspleniifolia'
in the Morton Arboretum, Lisle, Illinois, USA

Rhamnus imeretinus
in the Bern Botanic Garden, Switzerland

Rhamnus purshianus in the Forestry
Botanic Garden, Charlottenlund, Denmark

Plate 53

Rhamnus. a. *R. purshianus*; b. *R. crenatus*; c. *R. alnifolius*; d. *R. alpinus*; e. *R. davuricus*; f. *R. californicus* var. *tomentellus*; g. *R. carolinianus*; h. *R. fallax*; i. *R. costatus* (material from wild plants)

Rhamnus pumilus in the Lyon Botanic Garden, France

Plate 54

Rhamnella franguloides in its habitat
Photo: Dr. S. Watari, Tokyo

Rhamnus davuricus in its habitat
Photo: Dr. S. Watari, Tokyo

Rhamnus leptophyllus
in the Bergianska Arboretum, Stockholm, Sweden

Plate 55

Rhamnus californicus
in the Dublin Botanic Garden, Ireland

Rhamnus oleoides
in the Dublin Botanic Garden, Ireland

Rhamnus hybridus
in the Dublin Botanic Garden, Ireland

Rhaphiolepis delacourii
in Claremont Park, Cape Town, S. Africa

Plate 56

Rhododendron vaseyi in the Arnold Arboretum, USA
Photo: Arnold Arboretum

Rhododendron davidsonianum
in Lochinch, Scotland

Rhododendron lepidostylum with bluish leaves in the Royal Botanic Garden, Edinburgh, Scotland

Plate 57

Rhododendron taggianum
in Logan, Scotland

Rhododendron ambiguum
in the Royal Botanic Garden, Edinburgh, Scotland

Rhododendron sinogrande on Garnish Island, Ireland

Plate 58

Rhododendron pocophorum with new growth,
Benmore, Scotland

Rhododendron angustinii
in the Royal Botanic Garden, Edinburgh, Scotland

Rhododendron uvariifolium in the Royal Botanic Garden, Edinburgh, Scotland

Plate 59

Rhododendron maximum in its native habitat in the Great Smoky Mts. National Park,
North Carolina, USA
Photo: National Park Service

Rhododendron strigillosum with new growth, RHS Gardens, Wisley, England

Plate 60

Rhododendron degronianum in Japan
Photo: Dr. S. Watari, Tokyo

Rhododendron callimorphum in the Royal Botanic Garden, Edinburgh, Scotland

Plate 61

Rhododendron brachycarpum in Japan
Photo: Dr. S. Watari, Tokyo

Rhododendron wardii in the Royal Botanic Garden, Edinburgh, Scotland

Plate 62

Rhododendron arboreum ssp. *cinnamoneum*
in Lochinch, Scotland

Rhododendron angustinii
in the Royal Botanic Garden, Edinburgh, Scotland

Rhododendron fictolacteum in Crarae, Scotland

Plate 63

Rhododendron 'Louis Pasteur'
in the Boskoop Experiment Station, Holland

Rhododendron insigne
in the Royal Botanic Garden, Edinburgh, Scotland

Rhododendron falconeri in Crarae, Scotland

Plate 64

Rhododendron 'Jacksonii', one of the earliest flowering cultivars

Rhododendron degronianum var. *heptamerum*
Both photos: Dortmund Botanic Garden, W. Germany

between 3000 and 4500 m, a part of the *Rhododendron* forests. 1913. The most beautiful foliage of the entire genus. z8 ★★★★ Plate 57. # ∅ ⊕

R. sinonuttallii see: **R. nuttallii**

R. smirnowii Trautv. (S Ponticum, SS Caucasicum). Evergreen shrub, 1–2 m high and wide, young shoots densely white tomentose, but glabrous in the 2nd year; leaves leathery tough, oblong-lanceolate, 6–15 cm long, 2–3 cm wide, apex usually rounded, new growth densely white woolly tomentose, quickly becoming glabrous above, with about 10 vein pairs, underside densely light brown tomentose, petiole 1–1.5 cm long; flowers 10–12 together in loose corymbs, corolla about 5 cm wide, funnelform-campanulate, the 5 lobes undulate, purple-pink to lilac, interior finely pubescent, exterior glabrous, stamens 10, base pubescent, ovaries white tomentose, May–June. BM 7495; VVR 110. Caucasus at 1500–2500 m. 1886. Very hardy species but garden merit only slight; used by Seidel for hybridizing before 1900. z5 ★ Fig. 91. # ∅

R. smithii Nutt. (S and SS Barbatum). Evergreen shrub, 3–4.5 m high, very closely related to *R. barbatum* and actually only differing in the more bristly young shoots and leaf petioles, margins otherwise smooth and plum colored pruinose; flowers 10–16 together, corolla tubular-campanulate, scarlet-carmine, March–April. BM 5120. Bhutan. 1852. z8 ★★★ # ∅ ⊕

R. smithii aureum see: cultivar **'Norbitonense Aureum'**

R. sordidum see: **R. tsangpoense** var. **pruniflorum**

R. souliei Franch. (S Thomsonii, SS Souliei). Evergreen shrub, 1–2.5 m high, young shoots reddish or bluish, more or less glandular, older shoots red-brown, glossy; leaves leathery, broadly ovate to nearly circular, 3–7 cm long, 2–5 cm wide, cordate to round at the base, dark green above, underside light blue-green, glabrous on both sides, with 8–12 vein pairs, young leaves glandular at the base, petiole 1.5–2.5 cm long, with stalked glands; flowers 5–8 in loose racemes, corolla broadly cupulate, about 5 cm wide, limb 5–6 lobed, white to soft pink,

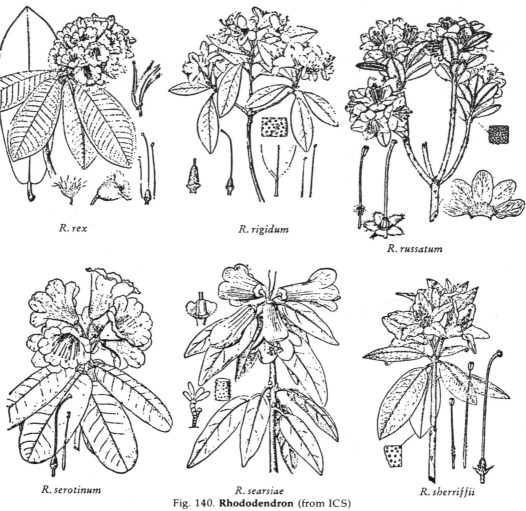

R. rex   *R. rigidum*

R. russatum

R. serotinum   *R. searsiae*   *R. sherriffii*

Fig. 140. **Rhododendron** (from ICS)

stamens 10, calyx with 5 oblong, rounded lobes, glandular, as are the flower stalk, ovaries and style, glands red, May. BM 8622; UR 5; SR 732; RYB 6: 35; GC 129: 102. China; W. Szechwan Prov., in the forests and thickets. 1905. Very attractive species. z8 ★★★★ Fig. 142. # ⌀ ✿

R. speciosum see: **R. flammeum**

R. sperabile Balf. f. & Farr. (S and SS Neriiflorum). Evergreen shrub, 0.5–1.5 m high, shoots woolly and glandular at first; leaves oblong-lanceolate, somewhat bullate with an involuted limb, 5–10 cm long, 1–3 cm wide, white pubescent and bristly glandular above at first, eventually glabrous and with gland remnants, underside thick woolly tomentose, white at first, later cinnamon-brown, petiole 5–10 mm long; flowers 4–6 in loose corymbs, corolla fleshy, tubular campanulate, about 3.5 cm long, pure scarlet-red with 5 black-red basal blotches, stamens 10, glabrous, ovaries and the basal half of the style densely glandular and pubescent, as is the small calyx, April–May. NF 3: 104; BM 9301. NE. Upper Burma. 1919. z8 ★★ # ⌀ ✿

R. sphaeranthum see: **R. trichostomum**

R. spiciferum Franch. (S Scabrifolium). Evergreen shrub, about 1 m high, shoots soft pubescent, with scattered, long hairs; leaves distributed along the entire shoot length, narrowly lanceolate, 1.5–2 cm long, shaggy pubescent on both sides, underside also scaly; flowers 2–3 from the clustered buds at the shoot tips, corolla funnelform, 1.5–2 cm wide, pink to whitish-pink, the 5 lobes erect, exterior somewhat scaly, stamens 8–10, exserted, style glabrous, ovaries distinctly pubescent, April–May. BM 9319; RYB 10: 20; ICS 4278 (= *R. pubescens* Balf. f. & Forrest). China; SW. Yunnan Prov., in the Muli Mts. at 3000 m. 1919. z8 ★★★ # ✿

R. spinuliferum Franch. (S Scabrifolium). Upright, evergreen shrub, young shoots bristly and pubescent; leaves lanceolate to more oblanceolate, 5–7.5 cm long, somewhat bullate, soft pubescent and scaly; flowers 3–5 together in erect clusters, corolla tubular (!!), 2.5 cm long, the 5 lobes straight and inward curving at the apex (!), brick-red, stamens 10, exserted, glabrous, shorter than the style, ovaries densely pubescent, calyx and flower stalk densely pubescent, April. BM 8408; DRHS 1783; ICS 4279 (= *R. duclouxii* Lévl.). China; Yunnan Prov. 1910. Easily recognized by the totally unique flower form. z8 ★★ Plate 38. # ✿

R. strictophyllum see: **R. nivale** ssp. **boreale**

R. strigillosum Franch. (S Barbatum, SS Maculiferum). Evergreen shrub, 1–2(5) m high, young shoots and leaf petiole densely bristly pubescent and with stalked glands; leaves narrowly oblong-lanceolate, 7–15 cm long, underside pubescent, particularly on the midrib; flowers grouped 8–12 in 10–12 cm wide corymbs, corolla campanulate, 5 cm wide, with 5 rounded lobes, bright scarlet-carmine, with 5 small, black-red blotches at the base, stamens 10, March–April. BM 8864; FIO 23; JRHS 87: 157. China. 1904. Resembling *R. barbatum*, but

Fig. 141. *Rhododendron sutchuenense* (from B. M.)

with larger flowers. z8 ★★★★ Plate 53; Fig. 143. # ⌀ ✿

R. sutchuenense Franch. (S Fortunei, SS Davidii). Evergreen shrub or small tree, 2–3(5) m high, young shoots thick, gray-white tomentose at first, later glabrous; leaves oblong-elliptic, 15–25 cm long, 3–7 cm wide, gradually tapered from the widest part to the cuneate or rounded base, eventually dark green above, dull, glabrous, with 17–22 vein pairs, underside glabrous except for the woolly midrib; flowers 8–10 in nearly 20 cm wide corymbs, corolla broadly campanulate, 5–7 cm long, an attractive pink, without a basal blotch (!), but purple punctate, interior dense and finely pubescent, stamens 12–15, white, base pubescent, anthers nearly black, ovaries and styles glabrous, stigma large, reddish, February–March (!). BM 8362; UR 15. China; Szechwan, Hupeh Provs. 1901. One of the most attractive species from China. z6 ★★★ Fig. 141. # ⌀ ✿

var. **geraldii** Hutchins. Flowers intensely pink-red, with a distinct chocolate-brown basal blotch (!). BHR 58.

R. taggianum Hutchins. (S Maddenii, SS Megacalyx). Open evergreen shrub, 1–2 m high, young shoots scaly; leaves oblong-elliptic, 7–15 cm long, 2.5–5 cm wide, underside bluish and scaly; flowers usually 3–4 together, erect, very pleasantly fragrant, corolla tubular-funnelform, 7–10 cm long and wide, pure white with a yellow spot at the base, limb 5 lobed, stamens 10, pubescent at the base, ovaries and style scaly, April–May; fruit capsule 5 cm (!) long. NF 6: 16; BM 9612; RYB 11: 32; 15: 14. Burma. 1925. z10 ★★ Plate 57. # ⌀ ✿

R. taliense Franch. (S and SS Taliense). Evergreen shrub, 1–3 m high, compact habit, branches thick, woolly tomentose when young, later glabrous; leaves broadly oval-lanceolate, 4–10 cm long, 2–3 cm wide, margins somewhat involuted, dark green and finely rugose above, nearly glabrous, underside brownish and

Fig. 142. **Rhododendron.** Left *R. trichocladum;* middle *R. setosum;* right *R. souliei*
(from Hooker and Bot. Mag.)

densely tomentose, petiole 1–1.5 cm; flowers 10–15 in dense, compact corymbs, corolla funnelform-campanulate, 3.5 cm long, cream-white, sometimes pink toned, limb 5 lobed, stamens 10, pubescent at the base, flower stalk densely pubescent, May. ICS 4226. China; W. Yunnan Prov., Tali Mts., in open areas at 3500–4000 m. z6 ★ Fig. 143. # ⌀

R. tapetiforme Balf. f. & Ward (S Lapponicum). Evergreen, mat-like shrub, 10–50 cm high, young shoots scaly; leaves broadly elliptic, 1.5 cm long, densely scaly on both sides, scales red-brown, overlapped on the underside, petiole scaly; flowers 2–4, open funnelform, about 1.5 cm long, lilac-pink to deeply purple-blue, exterior not scaly, stamens 10, base shaggy pubescent, flower stalk softly pubescent and scaly, April–May. China; Yunnan Prov., Tibet, in the higher mountains at 5000 m. z5 ★ #

R. tashiroi Maxim. (S Azalea, SS Tashiroi). Medium-sized, evergreen or semi-evergreen shrub, 1–4 m high, well branched, branches with scattered brown, appressed hairs; leaves leathery, 2–3 at the shoot tips, elliptic-obovate or rhombic to oblong-elliptic, 3–6 cm long, 1–3 cm wide, acuminate, base cuneate, finely crenate, both sides appressed brown haired at first, later glabrous and glossy above, underside eventually glabrous except for the midrib; flowers 2–3, corolla campanulate-funnelform, 3 cm long and wide, 5 lobed, pale pink, with purple-brown markings, stamens 10, calyx tiny, brown pubescent, April–May. SR 123. Japan; Liukiu Island; Taiwan. z7 ★★ # ☺

R. telmateium Balf. f. & W. W. Sm. (S Lapponicum). Low shrub, 30–70 cm high, strictly upright, branches densely scaly; leaves elliptic-lanceolate, about 1 cm long, 5 mm wide, densely scaly on both sides, scales overlapping on the underside, light brown, some darker, petiole scaly; flowers 1–2, corolla open funnelform, 1.5 cm long and wide, dark purple-pink with a white throat (!), limb exterior scaly, stamens 10, ovaries scaly and ciliate, April–May. NF 1: 269. China; 3500–4000 m. 1914. Resembles *R. impeditum*. z6 ★ #

R. tephropeplum Balf. f. & Farr. (S Boothii, SS Tephropeplum). Stiffly erect, evergreen shrub, 0.5–1 m high, branches scaly; leaves oblong-obovate, with a small mucro, tapered to the base, 3–6 cm long, 1.3 cm wide, both sides with small black scales, more open above, denser beneath; flowers 3–5 together, corolla broadly funnelform, 4 cm long, limb 5 lobed, bright carmine-purple to magenta-red, tube darker, exterior not scaly, flowering very abundantly, stamens 10, ovaries and basal half of the style scaly, style thin, erect (!), stigma large, carmine, calyx deeply 5 lobed, April–May. NF 9: 58; 3: 188; NH 39: 64; BM 9343; ICS 4019. SE. Tibet, Tsarong, Upper Burma, 4500 m on limestone cliffs. 1921. z8 ★★★ Fig. 143. # ☺

R. thayerianum Rehd. & Wils. (S Arboreum, SS Argyrophyllum). Evergreen shrub, to 3 m high, young shoots glutinous; leaves in whorls at the shoot tips and persisting for 4–5 years, oblanceolate, 5–20 cm long, acuminate, underside very densely covered with a yellowish brown indumentum; flowers 10–16 together in loose, erect, delicate, 10–12 cm wide inflorescences, corolla broadly funnelform, 5 lobed, 3 cm long, white, exterior with a reddish trace, interior punctate, stamens 10, calyx, ovaries and flower stalk glandular, June–July. BM 8983; ICS 4194. China. 1910. z7 ★★ # ☺

R. thomsonii Hook. f. (S and SS Thomsonii). Broad evergreen shrub or a small tree, 2–5 m high, young shoots with a temporary wax layer, bark exfoliating on older plants; leaves oval-rounded, 5–10 cm long, with a small mucro, rounded at the base to lightly cordate, deep green above, with about 9 vein pairs, underside bluish to whitish; flowers 5–8 in loose corymbs, but appearing only on older plants (!), corolla broadly campanulate, blood-red, fleshy and waxy, stamens 10, white, glabrous, ovaries and style glabrous, calyx cupulate, with 5 uneven lobes, April. BM 4997; SR 745; UR 1; RYB 6: 69; FS 688. Sikkim, Nepal, 3500–4500 m. 1849. Much used in hybridizing. z8 ★★★★ Fig. 91. #∅ ✛

var. **candelabrum** (Hook.f.) Clarke. Flowers lighter, calyx smaller, ovaries glandular.

R. timeteum see: **R. oreotrephes**

R. tosaense Makino (S Azalea, SS Obtusum). Densely branched, evergreen shrub, to 2 m high, young shoots very thin, pubescent; leaves lanceolate to oblanceolate, 1–3 cm long, appressed pubescent on both sides, "summer foliage" (at the tips of the young shoots) smaller than the "spring foliage" (at the base of the shoot, these turning carmine, abscising in the fall), petiole very short; flowers 2–6, short stalked, corolla funnelform, 5 lobed, 3 cm wide, purple-lilac, calyx white pubescent, stamens 5–10, ovaries bristly, style glabrous, April–May. BMns 52. Japan. 1914. z7 ★ ✛

R. traillianum Forrest & W. W. Sm. (S Lacteum). Evergreen shrub, with an aromatic resin scent, a tree in its habitat, to 9 m, shoots gray to light brown tomentose, older wood glabrous; leaves elliptic to lanceolate, 6–11 cm long, 2–4 cm wide (never as wide as *R. lacteum*), eventually glabrous above and finely rugose, with 14 vein pairs, underside greenish gray or dull brownish and tomentose, petiole 1.5–2.5 cm long; flowers 10–15 in corymbs, corolla funnelform-campanulate, 3.5 cm long, white to pink, with or without carmine-red spots, stamens 10, pubescent at the base, ovaries glabrous or with scattered hairs, style glabrous, calyx very small,

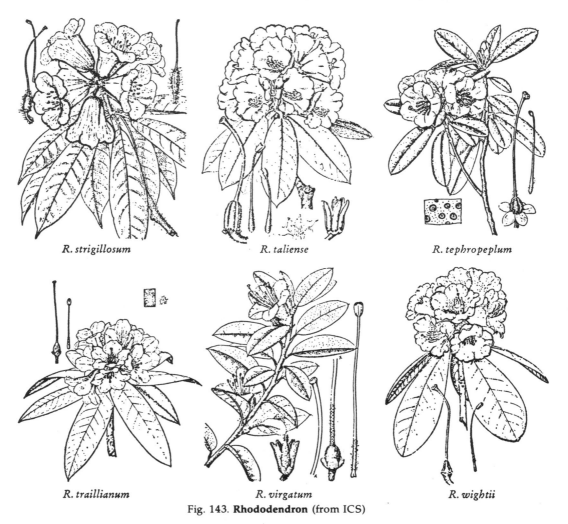

R. strigillosum   R. taliense   R. tephropeplum

R. traillianum   R. virgatum   R. wightii

Fig. 143. **Rhododendron** (from ICS)

ciliate, April–May. BM 8900; ICS 4204; BHR 59. China; NE. Yunnan Prov., a part of *Rhododendron* forests. z7 ★ Fig. 143. # ∅

R. trichanthum Rehd. (S Triflorum, SS Augustinii). Evergreen shrub, to 5 m, branches very thin, scaly and pubescent; leaves scattered along the long shoots and somewhat clustered at the apexes of the short shoots, ovate to oblong, acute, 5–8 cm long, 2–3 cm wide, rounded at the base or tapered to the petiole, sparsely scaly above with scattered bristles, underside more scaly, but less pubescent; flowers 3–5, corolla funnelform, 4.5 cm wide, lighter or darker purple, stamens 10, May–June. BM 8880. China; Szechwan Prov. 1904. z7 ★★ # ⊕

R. trichocladum Franch. (S Trichocladum). Deciduous shrub, about 1 m high, rather stiffly erect, young shoots with long and soft pubescence; leaves oblong to obovate, acute to rounded at both ends, 2.5–3 cm long, dull green and pubescent above, underside finely scaly, margins bristly ciliate; flowers 3–5 together, corolla broadly funnelform, flat, 3 cm wide, greenish yellow with green spots, tube interior woolly, stamens 10, ovaries scaly, styles bent at a right angle (!), calyx lobes lanceolate, April–May. BM 9073; SR 757. China; W. Yunnan Prov., NE. Burma. 1910. z6 ★ Fig. 142.

R. trichostomum Franch. (S Anthopogon). Evergreen shrub, to 1.2 m high, current year's shoots often short and branched, densely scaly and short bristled; leaves linear-lanceolate or narrowly oblanceolate, acute or obtuse, 8–32 mm long, 4–8 mm wide, with or without scales above, underside densely scaly, similarly the 2–4 mm long petiole; flowers several in heads, flower stalk 1–5 mm long, scaly, corolla narrowly tubular, 8–20 mm long, white to pink, exterior more or less scaly, interior long pubescent, calyx very small, 1–2 mm long, with or without scales and ciliate hairs, stamens 5, enclosed, base pubescent or glabrous, ovaries scaly, styles very short, glabrous, May–June. GC 81: 447 (= *R. sphaeranthum* Balf. f. & W. W. Sm.). China; Yunnan, Szechwan Provs. z7 ★★ #

var. **hedyosmum** (Balf. f.) Cowan & Davidian. Leaves oblong, not linear or linear-lanceolate; flowers much larger and with a longer tube. BM 9202 (= *R. hedyosmum* Balf. f.). Szechwan Prov.

var. **ledoides** (Balf. f. & W. W. Sm.) Cowan & Davidian. Leaves linear-lanceolate, dull green above, yellowish and densely scaly beneath; flowers 12–20 in dense, globose heads, pale pink, corolla 1 cm long, exterior scaly. BM 8831; NF 1: 161; 7: 115; SR 211; RYB 2: 20; ICS 4104 (= *R. ledoides* Balf. f. & W. W. Sm.). Yunnan, Szechwan Provs. 1914. z6 ★★★ Fig. 110. ⊕

var. **radinum** (Balf. f. & W. W. Sm.) Cowan & Davidian. Scales of the foliar buds persistent, abscising very late on plants in culture (subpersistent); flower stalk 1–2 mm long, flowers 8–10 together, corolla white, turning pink, exterior normally densely scaly (!). RYB 15: 26 (= *R. radinum* Balf. f. & W. W. Sm.). Yunnan, Szechwan Provs. 1917. z6 ★★★ ⊕

R. triflorum Hook. f. (S and SS Triflorum). Evergreen shrub, to 3 m high, branches thin, with small, black glands, bark of older shoots red-brown and exfoliating

(!); leaves oblong-lanceolate, 3–7 cm long, glabrous above, underside densely glandular and scaly; flowers in 3's, opening after development of the young shoots, fragrant, corolla broadly funnelform, 4–5 cm wide, pale yellow with green spots, stamens 10, ovaries very scaly, style glabrous, May–June. SR 791; FS 673; SNp 101; HAL 162. Himalaya, Sikkim, Bhutan. 1850. (z9; but hardier forms with blue-green foliage are also known.) z7 ★ Fig. 145.

R. tsangpoense Ward (S and SS Glaucophyllum). Evergreen shrub, 0.3–0.6 m high, current year's shoots thin scaled; leaves obovate, 2–4 cm long, apex rounded, narrowed at the base, glabrous above, underside bluish and thin scaly; flowers 3–5 together, flower stalk thin, 2.5 cm long, corolla open campanulate, 2.5 cm long, 5 lobed, cherry-red to violet, calyx lobes 6 mm long, stamens 10, pubescent, style slightly bent downward, May–June. RYB 3: 26. Tibet, Tsangpo River. 1924. z7 ★★ # ⊕

var. **pruniflorum** (Hutchins.) Cowan & Davidian. 30–50 cm high; leaves 2.5–5.5 cm long, underside more gray and very densely scaly (!!), scales just touching each other, with another layer of smaller, browner quickly abscising scales, crushed leaves have an unpleasant scent; flowers like the species (= *R. pruniflorum* Hutchins.; *R. sordidum* Hutchins.). Burma, Tibet, Assam. 1926.

R. tsarongense see: **R. primuliflorum**

R. tschonoskii Maxim. (S Azalea, SS Obtusum). Deciduous shrub, densely branched, 1–2 m high, branches densely appressed brown pubescent, winter buds broadly ovate, red-brown pubescent; leaves clustered at the shoot tips, narrowly lanceolate to broadly oblanceolate, 0.6–2.5 cm long, 0.5–1 cm wide, both sides with an appressed, red-brown pubescence, fall color a wonderful orange-red; flowers 3–6, small and inconspicuous, corolla tubular, white, limb outspread, 4 (!) or 5 lobed, only 8 mm wide, stamens 4–5, exserted, basal half short pubescent, May. NK 8: Pl. 17. Japan, S. Korea. z6 ★ ∅

R. ungernii Trautv. (S Ponticum, SS Caucasicum). Evergreen shrub, to 6 m high in its habitat, scarcely over 2 m high in cultivation, slow growing, young shoots white tomentose at first, later glabrous; leaves leathery thick, oblong-lanceolate, 10–19 cm long, 4–7 cm wide, deep green above and eventually glabrous, with 12–14 indented vein pairs and a distinct, sharp mucro (!), underside densely gray to light brown tomentose-woolly, with scattered stalked glands; flowers 20–30 in loose corymbs, often hidden beneath the foliage, corolla funnelform with 5 outspread lobes, 3.5 cm long, to 5 cm wide, pale pink, exterior glabrous, interior pubescent, stamens 10, base pubescent, ovaries glandular, style glabrous, calyx margin glandular pubescent, July. BM 8332; RJB 1974: 20–21. Caucasus. 1866. Very hardy, but not very attractive. z6 ★ # ∅

R. uvarifolium Diels (S Fulvum). Evergreen shrub or tree, 4–6 m high, young shoots thin white or gray tomentose at first, later glabrous, young new growth an attractive silver-gray (!); leaves leathery, oblanceolate,

10–20 cm long, 4–6 cm wide, deep green and finely rugose above, glabrous, with 15 vein pairs, thinly gray tomentose beneath, becoming glabrous on the venation, petiole 1–2 cm long, tomentose, later glabrous; flowers 15–20 together in about 15 cm wide, globose corymbs, corolla campanulate, 3–5 cm long, white with a pink blush and carmine patches, stamens 10, finely pubescent at the base, anthers deep brown, ovaries finely pubescent, style glabrous, March–April. BM 9480; RYB 4: 54 (= *R. niphargum* Balf. f. & Ward). China; Yunnan Prov.; Lichiang Mts. z7 ★★ Plate 58. # ⌀

R. valentinianum Forrest (S Maddenii, SS Ciliicalyx). Evergreen shrub, 0.5–1 m high, young shoots very bristly; leaves elliptic, 2.5–5 cm long, half as wide, bristly and ciliate above, underside very scaly; flowers 2–6 together, corolla broadly funnelform, 3 cm long, pure yellow (!), stamens 10, anthers pink, ovaries very scaly, calyx 8 mm long, the 5 lobes scaly and ciliate, April. UR 7; BMns 623. China. 1917. z9 ★★★ # ⌖

R. vaseyi Gray (S Azalea, SS Canadense). Deciduous shrub, to 2 m high, irregularly branched, young shoots finely pubescent at first, light brown, later glabrous and gray brown; leaves elliptic-oblong, 5–10 cm long, margins somewhat undulate, dark green above, lighter beneath, glabrous on both sides or somewhat pubescent only on the midrib; flowers 5–8, appearing before the leaves, corolla deeply 5 lobed, 3 cm wide, pale pink, red speckled, stamens usually 7, occasionally 5–6, ovaries glandular pubescent, as are the calyx and flower stalk, April–May. BM 8081; SR 50; RWF 259. N. America, Blue Ridge Mts. 1878. One of the best wild species. z5 ★★★ Plate 56; Fig. 144. ⌖

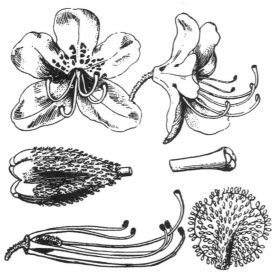

Fig. 144. *Rhododendron vaseyi* (form Kavka)

R. veitchianum Hook. (S Maddenii, SS Ciliicalyx). Evergreen, in its habitat frequently an epiphytic shrub, 1(3) m high, young shoots scaly, without bristles; leaves obovate, 5–10 cm long, obtuse to acuminate, scaly on both sides, but only scaly above on young plants, bluish beneath, spacing of the scales about as wide as their diameter; flowers 3–5 terminal, corolla 5 lobed, broadly funnelform, 6–7 cm long, 10 cm wide, white, exterior turning greenish, limb of the lobes crispate, exterior soft pubescent, stamens 10, pubescent, ovaries very scaly, calyx very short, limb often somewhat pubescent, April–May. FS 1416, 1519; BM 4992. Burma, Thailand, Laos. 1857. z9 ★★★★ # ⌖

R. vellereum see: **R. aganniphum**

R. venator Tagg (S Irroratum, SS Parishii). Evergreen shrub, young shoots with white hairs and stalked glands; leaves oblong-lanceolate, 6–12 cm long, sharply acuminate, base round to slightly cordate, quickly becoming glabrous on both sides except for some scattered stellate hairs on the venation beneath, petiole thick, 12–15 mm long; flowers 5–10 in dense, terminal corymbs, corolla 5 lobed, funnelform, scarlet-red, with 5 black-red nectar spots at the base, about 3 cm long, fleshy, stamens 10, anthers purple-black, styles glabrous, ovaries pubescent, May–June. SE. Tibet. 1924. z8 ★★ # ⌖

R. vernicosum Franch. (S and SS Fortunei). Evergreen shrub or small tree, 1.5–5 m high, resembling *R. decorum*, but the flower stalk and calyx have stalked glands (!); leaves elliptic, 6–12 cm long, glabrous, bluish beneath; flowers about 10 together, corolla funnelform-campanulate, white to pink or lilac, with or without carmine patches, limb 7 lobed, stamens 14, glabrous, ovaries very glandular, style with red stalked glands along its entire length (!!), April–May. BM 8834; 8904 and 8905; ICS 4162 (= *R. adoxum* Balf. f. & Forrest). Tibet. 1924. The upper leaf surface becomes "lacquered" (glossy) in warm weather, hence the name, "vernicosum" = varnished. z7 ★★★ # ⌖

R. violaceum see: **R. nivale** ssp. **boreale**

R. virgatum Hook. f. (S Virgatum). Evergreen shrub, to about 1 m high in cultivation, branches thinly and brown scaly when young; leaves narrowly elliptic to oblong-lanceolate, 3–7 cm long, 1–2.5 cm wide, tapered to both ends, underside with scattered brown scales; flowers 1–2 in the leaf axils at the shoot tips, bud scales persisting while in flower, corolla funnelform, 2–3.5 cm long, the 5 lobes outspread, pale purple-pink (but also other tones between white and purple), exterior more or less scaly and pubescent, stamens 10–12, ovaries very scaly, as is the style, April. BM 5060; 8802; HAL 167; FS 1408. Himalayas; from E. Nepal and Sikkim to Yunnan Prov., China. 1841. z7 ★★ Fig. 143. # ⌖

R. × viscosepalum Rehd. (*R. molle* × *R. viscosum*). The clones 'Daviesii' and 'Altaclarensis' are included here. See: Cultivar List.

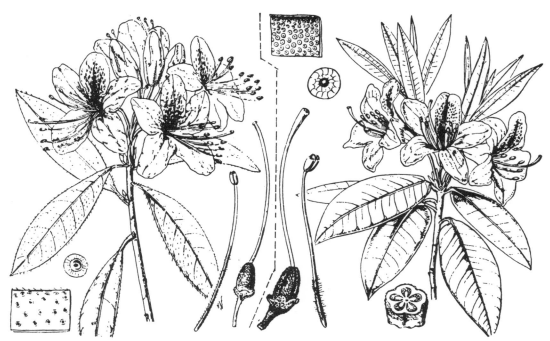

Fig. 145. **Rhododendron.** Left *R. yunnanense*; right *R. triflorum* (from Stevenson)

R. viscosum Torr. (S Azalea, SS Luteum). Deciduous shrub, 1.5–2 m high, branches irregularly whorled, young shoots with a densely appressed rough pubescence, winter buds ovate, brown, with 8–12 ovate, ciliate scales; leaves obovate, 3–5 cm long, glabrous above, underside pubescent, petiole rough pubescent; flowers 5–10 together, very pleasantly fragrant, corolla narrowly tubular with funnelform spreading lobes, 3 cm wide, white, occasionally pink, exterior finely glutinous-glandular pubescent, interior finely pubescent, calyx very small, glandular ciliate, stamens 5, base pubescent, ovaries bristly, July (!!). NF 1: 20; Hy WF 130. Eastern N. America, in coastal marsh areas. 1734. Much used in hybridizing. z3 ★★ Fig. 146.

R. wadanum see: **R. reticulatum**

R. wallichii Hook. f. (S Campanulatum). Evergreen shrub or small tree, 2–4 m high, very closely related to *R. campanulatum*, branches somewhat twisted, with a thicker, brown bark, young shoots glabrous; leaves leathery elliptic, 7–10 cm long, 2–5 cm wide, base somewhat cordate, margins involuted, dark green and smooth above, light green with scattered rust-brown hair fascicles beneath, these however, not forming a total cover (!), 10–12 vein pairs; flowers 6–10 in corymbs, corolla broadly campanulate, 4–5 cm long, lilac to lilac-pink and more or less red punctate or also pure white, stamens 10, underside pubescent, ovaries and style glabrous, April. Bm 4928; SR 853; RYB 4: 53; ICS 4223. Himalayas, Sikkim. 1849. z7 ★ #

R. wardii W. W. Sm. (S Thomsonii, SS Souliei). Evergreen shrub, broad growing, 1–3(5) m high, young shoots glandular at first, later glabrous; leaves leathery, elliptic to broadly elliptic, 5–10 cm long, rounded at both ends, dark green and eventually glabrous above, with 10–15 distinct vein pairs, underside blue-green; flowers

Fig. 146. *Rhododendron viscosum* (from Guimpel)

7–14 together, corolla somewhat fleshy, cupulate, 3–4 cm long, yellow, stamens 10, glabrous, ovaries and the entire style glandular (!), calyx distinctly 5 lobed and glandular, like the style, May. NF 6: 7; JRHS 84: 60; ICS 4176 (= *R. croceum* Balf. f. & W. W. Sm.; *R. astrocalyx* Balf. f. & Forrest). China; W. Yunnan Prov., Mekong and Salween River Region. 1913. z7 ★★★ Plate 61. # ☼

R. wasonii Hemsl. & Wils. (S Taliense, SS Wasonii). Evergreen shrub, young shoots stiff, thick, gray-white pubescent at first; leaves elliptic to narrowly ovate, 5–7.5 cm, very leathery tough, eventually deep green above, underside deep brown tomentose, particularly dark tomentum on the 2nd year shoots; flowers 6–9 at the shoot tips, corolla campanulate, 4–5 cm wide, 5 lobed, the lobes erect, cream-white to lemon-yellow, occasionally with a somewhat pink blush, always carmine speckled, stamens 10, anthers deep brown, style glabrous, light yellow, ovaries white pubescent, calyx very small and pubescent, March–April. BM 9190; ICS 4232. China; Szechwan Prov. 1904. z7 ★★ # ☼

R. watsonii Hemsl. & Wils. (S Grande). Evergreen shrub, a tree in its habitat, to 9 m, young shoots to 15 mm thick, scaly at first, later yellowish; leaves oblanceolate to obovate, apex abruptly tapered to a short point, underside drawn out to a winged base, 15–25 cm long, 5–10 cm wide, dark green above, dull, with a broad yellow midrib, underside dense and light lepidote, petiole only 2.5 cm long (!!), 12 mm wide; flowers 12–18 in 15 cm wide corymbs, corolla campanulate, 5 cm wide and long, 7 lobed, white, with a small purple blotch at the base, stamens 14, ovaries and style totally glabrous (!!), February–April. ICS 4220. China; Szechwan Prov. 1904. z9 ★ # ☼ ∅

R. websterianum Rehd. & Wils. (S Lapponicum). Evergreen shrub, about 50 cm high, young shoots densely gray-yellow and glossy scaled; leaves oval-elliptic, 6–18 mm long, obtuse at both ends, deep green and scaly above; underside densely gray-yellow scaly; flowers usually solitary (or grouped 2–3), broadly funnelform, deeply 5 lobed, 2.5 cm wide, purple-pink, the short tube pubescent on the interior, calyx deeply 5 lobed, the lobes 3 mm long, scaly and ciliate, stamens 10, ovaries scaly. ICS 4052. China. 1908. Hardy. z4 ★ # ☼

R. weyrichii Maxim. (S Azalea, SS Schlippenbachii). Deciduous shrub, 1–2 m high (taller in its habitat), young shoots with forward directed hairs, eventually glabrous; leaves usually in 3's at the shoot tips, obovate to rhombic, 3–8 cm long, 2.5–5 cm wide; flowers 2–4 at the shoot tips, corolla broadly funnelform, the 5 lobes outspread, brick-red (!!), the upper lobes punctate, stamens 6–10, usually glabrous, ovaries dense and reddish pubescent, May. BM 9475 (= *R. shikokianum* Makino). Japan, Korea. 1914. Quite hardy; similar to *R. reticulatum,* but the flower color is different. z5 ★★ ☼

R. wightii Hook. f. (S Lacteum). Evergreen shrub, 2.5–3.5 m high, open, divaricate habit, young shoots gray-white floccose, thick, later glabrous; leaves leathery,

Fig. 147. *Rhododendron williamsianum* (Original)

elliptic to obovate, 12–18 cm long, 5–7 cm wide, bright green and finely rugose above, with 12–14 vein pairs, underside of the young leaves white tomentose, later brown to orange-red, finally glabrous, petiole gray tomentose; flowers 12–20 in broad corymbs with very glutinous scales, corolla campanulate, 4 cm long, light yellow or lemon-yellow (occasionally white with a pink blush), interior with a dark red basal patch and spots, stamens 10, pubescent at the base, short, ovaries densely woolly, style very long, glabrous, April–May. BM 8492; DRHS 1786; FS 792. E. Himalayas, Sikkim, Nepal, Burma at 3500–4000 m. 1851. z7 ★ Fig. 143. # ∅

R. williamsianum Rehd. & Wils. (S Thomsonii, SS Williamsianum). Very dense evergreen shrub, broad globose habit, 0.5–1 m high, divaricately branched, thin, loosely covered with stalked glands when young, later glabrous, new growth an attractive bronze-brown (!); leaves broadly oval, cordate at the base, 2–4 cm long, 1.5–3 cm wide, bright green and glabrous above, underside blue-green and finely warty, with small glands and hairs, petiole glandular; flowers 2–3, pendulous, corolla campanulate, 3–4 cm long, pure pink, stamens 10, glabrous, ovaries green, glandular, as is the entire style, the small calyx and the flower stalk, April. BM 8935; FIO 32; ICS 4178. China; Szechwan Prov., 2500–3000 m. 1908. One of the most attractive species, but often flowering only sparsely. Nonetheless, much used recently in hybridization. z6 ★★★ Fig. 147. # ∅ ☼

R. wilsonii see: cultivar **'Laetvirens'**

R. wiltonii Hemsl. & Wils. (S Taliense, SS Wasonii). Evergreen shrub, 1–2 m high, young shoots with thick, brown wool; leaves obovate, 5–10 cm long, abruptly tapered at the apex, glossy green and deeply rugose above, underside thick brown woolly, petiole 12 mm; flowers 10 in clusters, corolla campanulate, white to pink, interior carmine speckled or punctate, the 5 lobes erect, stamens 10, ovaries brown woolly. BM 9388; FIO 25; RYB 14: 9; ICS 4230. China; Szechwan Prov. 1904. Beautiful foliage. z6 ★★ # ☼

Fig. 148. *Rhododendron yedoense* var. *poukhanense*
(from Kavka)

R. xanthocodon Hutchins. (S Cinnabarinum). Narrowly erect, evergreen shrub, a small tree in its habitat, 3.5–6 m high; leaves elliptic, 3–7 cm long, scaly, underside bluish green; flowers about 5 together, corolla campanulate, 2.5 cm long, cream-yellow and without speckles (!), limb 5 lobed, stamens 10, yellowish, anthers light brown, ovaries densely scaly, as is the small calyx, May. Tibet. 1924. z7 ★ ★ ★ # ✿

R. yakusimanum Nakai (S Ponticum, SS Caucasicum). Dense, evergreen shrub, 0.5–1 m high and wide or wider, young new growth silvery tomentose, later glabrous; leaves oblong to obovate and spathulate convex, limb much involuted, 5–10 cm long, 2.5–3 cm wide, stiff and leathery tough, dark green and glossy above, underside thick light brown tomentose; flowers about 12 in flat, loose corymbs, buds carmine-pink, corolla broadly campanulate, 3 cm long, 5–6 cm wide, soft pink at first, later pure white (!), stamens 10, anthers light brown, style longer, ovaries tomentose, flowering very abundantly, May. UR 18; RYB 5: 34; VVR 80; PBRR 61; JRHS 72: 154. Japan, Yaku-shima Island, in the mountains. 1937. Very attractive and hardy species closely related to *R. degronianum* and sometimes included as such. z5 ★ ★ ★ ★ # ∅ ✿

Including the clone **'Koichiro Wada'**, a particularly beautiful plant from RHS Gardens, Wisley, England; received the First Class Certificate (F.C.C.) in 1947 from the Royal Horticulture Society.

R. yedoense Rehd. (S Azalea, SS Obtusum). Deciduous shrub, about 1 m high, densely branched, branches very thin, young shoots roughly pubescent, glabrous in the 2nd year; leaves narrowly elliptic to lanceolate, 3–7 cm long, acute at both ends, often finely crenate, dark green above, lighter beneath, rough haired on both sides, but somewhat more so beneath; flowers 1–3, appearing before the leaves, double (!), 4 cm wide, lilac-purple, interior darker speckled, without stamens (!), calyx with

1.5 cm long, ovate lobes, April (= *Azalea yodogawa* Grig.). Japanese cultivar. 1884. Not observed in the wild. z5 ★ ★ ✿

var. **poukhanense** Nakai. Shrub, 1–1.5 m high; leaves elliptic to oval-lanceolate, 3–8 cm long; flowers 2–4 together, not double (!), fragrant, corolla funnelform, about 5 cm wide, lilac-pink, darker punctate, the 5 lobes nearly circular and undulate, stamens 10, anthers purple, ovaries bristly, April. BMns 455 (= *R. coreanum* Rehd.; *R. poukhanense* Lév.). Korea. 1913. This is the wild form of *R. yedoense*, first discovered many years after the species and therefore only given varietal rank. Fig. 148.

R. yunnanense Franch. (S Triflorum, SS Yunnanense). Evergreen, occasionally only a semi-evergreen, rounded shrub, 2–3 m high and wide, young shoots blackish glandular; leaves elliptic-lanceolate to oblanceolate, 5–7 cm long, 2–3 cm wide, somewhat bristly above and on the margins, particularly when young, both sides loosely scaly, petiole 1 cm long; flowers 3–5, terminal and axillary at the shoot tips, corolla broadly funnelform, to 5 cm wide, pale pink to white, red punctate, stamens 10, pubescent at the base, style glabrous, ovaries densely scaly, as is the calyx and flower stalk, abundantly flowering, May. BM 7614; SR 815; RYB 7: 25 (= *R. aechmophyllum* Balf. f. & Forrest; *R. chartophyllum* Franch.). China; Yunnan Prov., 3000 m. 1889. z7 ★ ★ ★ ★ Fig. 145, 149. # ✿

Fig. 149. *Rhododendron yunnanense*

R. zaleucum Balf. f. & W. W. Sm. (S Triflorum, SS Yunnanense). Evergreen shrub, to 5 m high, a tree in its habitat; leaves lanceolate, 3–7 cm long, dark green above, milk-white beneath (!, particularly with age), scaly; flowers 3–6, lightly fragrant, corolla funnelform, white to pale pink, to 4 cm long, exterior loosely scaly over the entire surface, 2.5–3 cm wide, the 5 limb lobes outspread, calyx small, lobed, exterior densely scaly, limb somewhat ciliate, April. BM 8878; SR 816; ICS 4079. China; W. Yunnan Prov., E. Upper Burma, 3000–3500 m as a tree in the rain forest. 1912. z9 ★ ★ ★ # ∅ ⊕

Cultivar List
(Alphabetical listing of the most important cultivars)

The cultivar list contains the most prominent cultivated varieties from Belgium, Germany, England, Holland and America. Where possible, the name of the hybridizer and the year of introduction into the trade are given, after the cultivar name, as well as the parents of each cultivar; and in most cases also the cultivar group as follows:

A. Deciduous Azaleas

EXBURY Azaleas. Hybrids of the 'Knap Hill' azaleas with other, unnamed, orange colored azaleas; introduced by L. Rothschild in Exbury, England and practically included in the 'Knap Hill' class. In the "International *Rhododendron* Register" the 'Exbury' types are not considered a totally separate group.

GANDAVENSE types, also called "Ghent Hybrids". Originated in Holland and Belgium, mainly between 1830 and 1840 as crosses between American wild species (*R. calendulaceum, roseum, viscosum* and others) and *R. luteum*. Flowers have longer tubes (!), some are double.

KNAP HILL types. English hybrids, whose origin is not known for certain (apparently *R. gandavense* × *R. molle, R. calendulaceum* × *R. molle* and others); named for the Knap Hill Nursery (Anthony Waterer) in Woking, England, where they were developed. The large flowers open widely in many flowered inflorescences, some types are double.

MOLLIS types. This title from the "*Rhododendron* Register" will be retained here since it is generally accepted in horticultural circles; this group contains selections of *R. japonicum, R. kosterianum* (= "Mollis" × "Sinensis") and their hybrids.

OCCIDENTALE types. Originated in England (around 1864) and Holland (1901 and later) from *R. molle* × *R. occidentale*. Corolla wide open, white to light pink, fragrant.

RUSTICA types (= *R. mixtum*, see under this name in the list). Originated as a hybrid of the double *gandavense* types and *R. japonicum*.

B. Evergreen Azaleas

AMOENA types. Descendants of *R. obtusum* 'Amoenum'. Small flowered.

ARENDSII types. German hybrids of G. Arends from Wuppertal-Ronsdorf; mostly *R. mucronatum* crossed with other Japanese types.

DIAMOND Azaleas. Hybrids of *R.* 'Multiflorum' (Arends) with *R. kiusianum* descendants; very flat, compact habit, very abundantly flowering, small flowered, flower color pink, red to violet. Hybridizer C. Fleischmann of Wiesmoor, W. Germany (1969). The cultivars are named by color: 'Rosa' (Pink), 'Rot' (Red), 'Lachs' (Salmon), 'Purpur' (Purple), 'Violett', (Violet), etc.

FRISIA Azaleas. Hybrids of "Indica" azaleas with Japanese azalea hybrids (the latter is the pollinator). Breeder C. Fleischmann, of Wiesmoor, W. Germany (1970). All cultivars are primarily cultivated as pot plants. Including: 'Jan Hinrichs', 'Hans Bickel', 'Erwin Bauer', 'Gregor Mendel', etc.

GLENN DALE types. American hybrids developed in 1935 from species of the Subseries Obtusum, mostly crosses of *R. kaempferi* hybrids with *R. mucronatum, indicum, simsii*, etc. Large flowered.

INDICA azaleas, see *R. simsii*. Not covered for its lack of hardiness.

KAEMPFERI types. Developed in Holland in 1920 as a cross between *R. kaempferi* and 'Malvatica'. Large flowered.

KURUME types. Hybrids between *R. kiusianum, kaempferi* and perhaps also *R. obtusum*, which were crossed and selected originally in Japan and later the USA and Holland. E. H. Wilson in 1917 introduced a collection of the best types into the USA. All cultivars small flowered, most not over 2.5 cm wide.

VUYKIANA types. Dutch and (later) also Belgian hybrids of 'J. C. van Tol' crossed with *R. kaempferi* types and others. Flowers very large.

C. Azaleodendron

Hybrids between deciduous azaleas and evergreen species appearing somewhat intermediate between the parents; the leaves therefore usually only semi-evergreen, abscising in spring. Some of the cultivars include 'Galloper Light', 'Glory of Littleworth', 'Govenianum'.

D. Evergreen Rhododendrons

All these cultivars are considered evergreen although, as with the wild species, the leaves will drop after 2–3 years and are constantly being replaced. A number of groups could be included here, but because of the many various combinations this would only lead to confusion. Some of the more significant groups are the 'Catawbiense', 'Williamsianum' and 'Repens' hybrids.

The CATAWBIENSE hybrids have been developed for more than 100 years in England, later in Germany and Holland and are exceptionally hardy. The flowers, however, are only small to medium in size and surpassed by more recent hybrids.

The REPENS hybrids are crosses of *R. forrestii* var. *repens* with (usually) garden hybrids to develop low to medium-sized, early and abundantly flowering forms with bright colors. The hybridizing was begun by Lord Aberconway in Wales around 1935; soon thereafter this work was taken up by D. Hobbie of Oldenberg, W. Germany whose hybrids may be found throughout the world (e.g., 'Elisabeth Hobbie', 'Scarlet Wonder', 'Salute', 'Baden-Baden', etc.)

Registration of New Hybrids. The Royal Horticultural Society, London, England is the official registrar of new introductions into the international register.

'A. Bedford' ('Arthur Bedford') (Lowinsky, before 1936) [*R. ponticum* × hybrids]. Lavender-lilac with large, deep red, nearly black markings, 8 cm wide, late May; vigorous grower. Gw 1974: 447; VVR 2. # ︶

'Abendglut' (Hobbie) ['Elisabeth Hobbie' grex]. Deep red, darkest of the entire group, early; more vigorous than most of the other types. # ⊕

'Addy Wery' (den Ouden 1940) [Kur.; 'Flame' × 'Malvatica']. Blood-red with an orange blush, flowers funnelform, 1–2 together; compact habit. # ⊕

'**Adonis**' (Felix & Dijkhuis 1952) [Kur.; 'Truus' × 'Azuma-kagami']. White, hose-in-hose*, limb fimbriate; broad habit. ⊕#

'**Adriaan Koster**' (Koster & Sons 1920) [R. campylocarpum hybrids × 'Mrs. Lindsay Smith']. Cream-white, throat red punctate. Plate 65. # ⊕

'**Agger**' (Arends 1951) [Arendsii]. Soft lilac, middle early; compact habit.

'**Aida**' (Vuylsteke 1888) [Rust.]. White with a lilac blush, double, middle early.

'**Aksel Olsen**' (D. Hobbie 1965) ['Essex Scarlet' × R. forrestii repens]. Deep red, 3–5 together, first half of May; flat growth habit; small leaved. # ⊕

'**Aladdin**' (Hage 1943) [Kur.]. Geranium-red, early; upright habit. # ⊕

'**Albatross**' (Rothschild 1930) [R. discolor × 'Loderi']. Dark pink buds, opening white, dorsal side soft pink, fragrant. PBRR 58. #

'**Albert Schweitzer**' (Ad. van Nes 1960). Light pink, reddish markings, large, globose corymbs. Dfl 6: 58. # ⊕

'**Album Elegans**' (H. Waterer, Knap Hill 1847) [R. catawbiense hybrid]. Pale lilac, becoming white, 5 cm wide, late. VVR 14. Exceedingly winter hardy. #

'**Album Novum**' (van Houtte) [R. catawbiense hybrid]. White with a lilac-pink blush, green-yellow punctate, middle early. BHR 76. #

'**Alfred**' (Seidel 1899) ['Everestianum' × 'Everestianum']. Lilac, middle early. #

'**Alice**' (J. Waterer 1910) [R. griffithianum hybrids]. Dark pink, opening lighter, without spots, calyx with 12 mm long lobes (!), early. VVR 36. #

'**Alice**' (C. B. van Nes 1922) R. kaempferi × 'Malvativa']. Salmon-pink with darker markings; upright habit.

'**Alice de Stuers**' (Koster & Sons, before 1939) [Moll.; R. kosterianum clone]. Yellow with salmon-pink and an orange patch (= 'Lady Alice de Stuers'). ⊕

'**Allah**' (Seidel 1926) [R. catawbiense hybrids]. Pale lilac-pink, late. #

'**Alphonse Lavallée**' (L. van Houtte 1863) [Moll.; R. japonicum clone]. Orange with a pink trace and a bright orange spot.

'**Altaclarensis**' [Origin unknown; ? R. luteum × R. molle]. Orange-yellow, in large inflorescences (= 'Aurea Grandiflora').

'**America**' (Koster & Sons 1920) ['Parsons Grandiflorum' × dark red hybrid]. Dark red, middle early. DBl 59. Very winter hardy. # ⊕

'**Ammerlandense**' (Hobbie 1946) ['Britannia' × R. williamsianum]. Clear, light pink, 6–7 cm wide, later April to early May; compact globose habit. Gw 1973: 9. Good winter hardiness. #

---

* "hose-in-hose": a generally accepted term for flowers whose sepals are connate in a tube form and the same color and form as the corolla; hence appearing like 2 corollas fitted one inside the other.

'**Amoena**' [Kur.] Japanese cultivar of R. obtusum, small flowered, hose-in hose, purple-red. FA 885; BM 4728. Imported from Japan in 1950 by Fortune. # ⊕

'**Annabella**' (Rothschild 1947) [Knap Hill]. Orange and yellow in bud, opening golden yellow with an orange-pink blush. ⊕

'Anna Louise' see: '**Dr. Charles Baumann**'

'**Anna Rose Whitney**' (Whitney 1954) ['Countess of Derby' × R. griersonianum]. Pink-red, to 11 cm wide, with 18–20 flowers together. VVR 60. Somewhat frost sensitive. # ⊕

'**Anny**' (C. B. van Nes 1922) [R. kaempferi × 'Malvatica']. Orange-red; upright habit. ⊕

'**Anthony Koster**' (Koster & Sons 1892) [Moll.; R. kosterianum clone]. Yellow, bronze toned in bud, middle late. GC 1893: 76.

'**Antilope**' (Felix & Dijkhuis) [R. viscosum]. Pink with a trace of salmon, a darker mid stripe, a yellow patch, fragrant.

'**Antje**' (Hobbie) ['Essex Scarlet' × R. forrestii repens]. Blood-red, very free flowering, early; habit erect-rounded. #

'**Antoon van Welie**' (Endtz) ['Pink Pearl' descendant]. Clear, dark pink, late; habit unattractively wide. VVR X. Surpassed by 'Bel Air'. #

'**Apple Blossom**' (Wezelenburg & Son) [Moll.] Soft pink. ⊕

'**Apricot**' (Gable 1933) [? R. poukanense × 'Hexe']. Apricot-pink, later becoming lighter. Very winter hardy. #

'**April Glow**' (A. C. van Wilgen) ['Wilgen's Ruby' × R. williamsianum]. Carmine-pink, limb interior somewhat lighter, campanulate, 6–7 cm wide, 7–10 together, new growth bronze; habit broad and flat (= 'April Shower'). #

'April Shower' see: '**April Glow**'

'**Arbutifolium**' [R. ferrugineum × R. minus]. Shrub, to 1 m high and somewhat broader; leaves elliptic to narrowly elliptic, 3–6 cm long, acute at both ends, dull and dark green above, with scattered, glossy, light scales beneath, these intermixed with a few larger, darker scales; flowers pink, small, calyx tiny (= R. daphnoides Hort.; R. arbutifolium Rehd.). Origin unknown, presumably France. Around 1877. #

'**Ardy**' (Boskoop Experiment Station) ['Britannia' × R. williamsianum]. Pink, campanulate, large, 7–8 together, late April, abundantly flowering; habit flat-globose, 60 cm; leaves cordate-elliptic. Dfl 3: 53. # ⊕

'**Armistice Day**' (C. B. van Nes 1930) [R. griffithianum hybrid × 'Maxwell T. Master']. Scarlet-red. #

ARONENSIS Azaleas (G. Arends). Hybrids of 'Multiflora' with 'Arendsii' types and the hardiest "Indica" azaleas. Low growing; leaves deep green, usually red-brown in fall; flowers small, in all shades between pink, lilac, purple to red, some hose-in-hose. #

'**Arpège**' (Boskoop Experiment Station, before 1965) [R. viscosum × R. japonicum]. Dark yellow with salmon-pink, 4–4.5 cm wide, about 10 together, late May, very fragrant; strong growing, upright. Dfl 3: 72. ⊕

'**Ascot Brilliant**' (Standish 1861) [R. thomsonii hybrid]. Dark carmine-red, short trumpet form. #

'**Atalanta**' (C. B. van Nes) [R. kaempferi × 'Malvatica']. Soft lilac, early; upright habit.

'**Attraction**' (Koster and Sons) [R. ponticum hybrid]. Lilac, late; broad habit. Surpassed today. Extremely rare in cultivation. z8

Plate 65. Fig. 150. #

'**August Lamken**' (Hobbie 1971) ['Dr. V. H. Rutgers' × *R. williamsianum*]. Dark pink, 6–7.5 cm wide, mid May. Gw 1973: 9. Good winter hardiness. #

'Aurea Grandiflora' see: '**Altaclarensis**'

'**Azaleoides**' [*Azaleodendron; R. ponticum* × ? *R. periclymenoides*]. Semi-evergreen, upright shrub, young shoots glandular; leaves oblong-elliptic, 8–10 cm long, dark green above, somewhat bluish beneath, glabrous; flowers 10–20 together, corolla broadly campanulate, monochromatic, light pink, without markings, limb undulate, fragrant, June–July. Bot. Repository Pl. 379; 1804 (= *R. azaleoides* Dum.-Cours.). Developed around 1800 in the Thomson Nursery, Mile End, near London, England; existence yet today uncertain; if so, extremely rare. z8 #

'**Azuma-kagami**' [Kur.]. Pink with lighter tones, medium greenish. Imported from Japan by E. H. Wilson as his "Nr. 16". #

'**Babeuff**' (Kersbergen 1918) [Moll.]. Salmon-red with a trace of orange. ☽

'**Baccarat**' (A. van Nes). Deep red with a large, black patch, inflorescence globose. Particularly good for forcing. # ☽

'**Bad Eilsen**' (Hobbie) ['Essex Scarlet' × *R. forrestii repens*]. Deep red, early May, buds reddish. Very similar to, but not surpassed by 'Scarlet Wonder'. # ☽

'**Baden-Baden**' (Hobbie) ['Essex Scarlet' × *R. forrestii repens*]. Dark scarlet-red, mid April; habit flat, to 60 cm high; foliage somewhat twisted. Flowers well, not sensitive to sunlight. # ☽

'**Ballerina**' (Rothschild) [Knap Hill]. White. ☽

'**Bagshot Ruby**' (J. Waterer 1900). [*R. thomsonii* hybrid]. Blood-red. Foliage unattractive. #

'**Balzac**' (Rothschild, before 1934) [Knap Hill]. Bright red, with darker markings, fragrant. PBRR 43. ☽

'**Barclayi**' (Barclay Fox) ['Glory of Penjerrick' × *R. thomsonii*]. Dark carmine-scarlet. JRHS 73: 83. Including 2 further clones, 'Robert Fox' and 'Helen Fox', both carmine-scarlet. #

'**Bartholo Lazzari**' (Rinz, before 1869) [Ghent hybrid]. Orange-yellow with a reddish trace, double, limb flat spreading, to 5 cm wide.

'Bas de Bruin' see: '**B. de Bruin**'

'**Basilisk**' (Rothschild, before 1934) [Knap Hill]. Buds cream-yellow, opening dark cream-yellow with golden-yellow markings. ☽

'**B. de Bruin**' (A. Waterer) [*R. catawbiense* descendant]. Scarlet-red, limb fringed (= 'Bas de Bruin'). #

'**Beauté Celeste**' (before 1822) [Ghent hybrid]. Pink with a trace of orange, small flowered, only 2.5 cm wide, fragrant (= 'Cardinal').

'**Beauty of Littleworth**' (Mangles, around 1900). [*R. griffithianum* hybrid]. Pure white, upper limb lobes and throat with pomegranate-red punctate spots, buds lilac-pink. VVR 131. #

'**Beethoven**' (Vuyk van Nes) ['J. C. van Tol' × 'Maxwellii']. Lilac with darker spots and an undulate limb. ☽

'**Bel Air**' (P. van Nes). Dark carmine-pink in large corymbs. Dfl 6: 60. A very good cultivar.

Fig. 150. *Rhododendron* 'Azaleoides' (from Guimpel)

'**Belle Heller**' (Shammarello) [*R. catawbiense* 'Album' × white *R. catawbiense* seedlings]. White with a large, yellow patch, late May. VVR 111. Good foliage. # ☽

'**Bengal**' (Hobbie 1960) ['Essex Scarlet' × *R. forrestii repens*]. Dark red, 4–5 together, later April; habit broad and low; leaves 5–7 cm long, flat. Gw 1966: 230. #

'**Bengal Fire**' (Rothschild 1934) [*R. kaempferi* × 'Oldhamii']. Brick-red, 5–6 cm wide. #

'**Berlin**' (Hobbie/J. Bruns 1964) [*R. williamsianum*]. Pink, campanulate, somewhat pendulous; habit flat-globose, to 1.5 m high. z8 # ☽

'**Berryrose**' (Rothschild) [Knap Hill]. Orange-red, yellow patch, midseason to late. ☽

'**Betty**' (C. B. van Nes) [*R. kaempferi* × 'Malvatica']. Pink, with a darker center, early; upright habit. ☽

'**Betty Wormald**' (Koster & Sons, before 1922) ['Georgy Hardy' × red hybrids]. Pink, with a lighter center and soft purple patch. BRho 79; VVA 58. Surpassed by 'Marinus Koster'. #

'**Bever**' (Arends 1951) [Arendsii]. Lilac, middle early.

'**Bibber**' (Seidel 1900) [*R. catawbiense* × 'Mrs. Milner']. Carmine-red. JRL 1937: 15. #

'**Bismarck**' (Seidel 1900) [*R. catawbiense* × 'Viola']. White with red stripes. #

'**Blaauw's Pink**' (Blaauw 1953) [Kur.]. Salmon-pink, turning darker, hose-in-hose, very early. # ☽

'**Bluebird**' (Aberconway 1930) [*R. augustinii* × *R. intricatum*]. Violet-lilac, 8–10 together, without markings, 4 cm wide, late April. JRHS 71: 67. # ☽

'**Blue Diamond**' (Crosfield) [*R. angustinii* × 'Intrifast']. Violet-blue, low. VVR 17; JRHS 71: 68. Good hardiness and attractive. # ☽

'**Blue Ensign**' (W. C. Slocock 1934). Pale lavender-blue with large, black patches. Dfl 6: 60; VVR 126. # ☽

'**Blue Peter**' (Waterer Sons & Crisp, before 1933). Soft lilac with a purple patch, limb finely undulate. VVR 17 and 68. # ☽

'**Blue Tit**' (J. C. Williams 1913) [*R. augustinii* × *R. impeditum*]. Very attractive blue, small flowered, low, hardy. VVR 30. # ☽

'Bonito' (Rothschild 1934) [*R. discolor* × 'Luscombei']. White with a chocolate-brown blotch. #

'Boskoop' (A. van Nes). Deep pink with a dark brown patch, early; foliage yellowish. # ☺

'Boule de Neige' (Odieu, around 1878) [*R. caucasicum* × *R. catawbiense* hybrid]. White, buds light pink, very early; habit very dense. Brho 142; VVR 31. #

'Bouquet de Flore' (Introduced before 1869) [Ghent hybrid]. Salmon-pink with a lighter midline, orange spot, becoming darker toward the base. ☺

'Bow Bells' (Rothschild 1934) ['Corona' × *R. williamsianum*]. Buds dark cherry-red, opening light coral-pink, 5–6 together; new growth bronze; about 1 m high in 10 years. VVR 10; PBRR 24. # ☺

'Brazil' (Rothschild 1934) [Knap Hill]. Orange-red, later somewhat darker, rather small flowered, limb slightly crispate. ☺

'Bremen' (Joh. Bruns) [*R. williamsianum* × ?]. Brilliant, bright red, May; 80 cm high. Good for forcing. z7 # ☺

'Bric-à-brac' (Rothschild 1934) [*R. leucaspis* × *R. moupinense*]. Pure white, with light markings on the upper portion of the corolla, anthers deep brown. JRHS 70: 46. #

'Bright Forecast' (Rothschild) [Knap Hill]. Salmon-pink, deep orange blotched, fragrant.

'Britannia' (C. B. van Nes 1921) ['Queen Wilhelmina' × 'Stanley Davies']. Scarlet-red, limb undulate; leaves yellow-green. BRho 79. # ☺

'Broughtonii Aureum' (before 1935) [*Azaleodendron (R. maximum* × *R. luteum)* × *R. japonicum*]. Soft yellow with orange spots on the back side. VVR 129; BS 2: 345; MRh 148 (= 'Norbitonense Broughtonianum'). z9 Plate 65. #

'Buccaneer' (U.P.P.I. 1941) [Glenn; 'Hinodegiri' × 'Late Salmon']. Bright orange-red, upper middle of the corolla darker.

'Burgemeester Aarts' (Koster & Sons) ['L. L. Liebig' × *R. maximum*]. Dark red; tall growing. #

'Butterfly' (Slocock) [*R. campylocarpum* × 'Mrs. Milner']. Totally light yellow, light red punctate. VVR 50. #

'Bycendron' (Ant. van Eeckeren, before 1966) [Kaempf.]. Salmon-pink, rather large flowered, early. Surpassed by 'Fedora'. #

'Bryon' (Vuylsteke 1888) [Rust.]. White, outer limb lobes somewhat reddish, hose-in-hose, buds cream-yellow and carmine.

'Campfire' (Gable 1942) [Kur.]. Deep red, hose-in-hose, flowers abundantly, appearing before the leaves; habit broad and open upright. Dfl 6: 40 (= 'Hino-scarlet'). First class plant, also good for forcing. ☺

'Canary' (Koster & Sons 1920) [*R. campylocarpum* × *R. caucasicum* 'Luteum']. Lemon-yellow; leaves yellow-green in a sunny position. #

'Caractacus' (A. Waterer, before 1865) [*R. catawbiense* clone]. Purple-red with a lighter center. Very winter hardy. # ☺

'Cardinal' see: 'Beauté Celeste'

'Carita' (Rothschild 1935) [*R. campylocarpum* × 'Naomi']. Totally soft lemon-yellow. VVR 79; PBRR 6 and 7. #

'Carmen' (Rothschild 1935) [*R. didymum* × *R. forrestii repens*]. Deep red; very slow growing and quite low. VVR 41; JRHS 86: 92. #

'Caroline Spencer' (Hobbie 1955) [*R. fortunei* × *R. williamsianum*]. Light pink, deeply funnelform, 5–7 lobed, 3–6 together, early May, long stalked, somewhat pendulous; medium height. Dfl 3: 50. # ☺

'Catalgla' (Gable) [Selection from *R. catawbiense* 'Album']. White, blooms well, but the foliage is sometimes not good. #

catawbiense 'Album' (A. Waterer) [Selection]. White, buds soft lilac. BRho 78; VVR 55; Dfl 6: 48. # ☺

catawbiense 'Boursault' (Boursault) [Selection]. Lilac with a reddish blush. DBl 55. #

catawbiense 'Grandiflorum' (A. Waterer) [Selection]. Lilac. VVR 4. Very winter hardy. # ☺

'Catharina Rinke' (M. Koster & Sons) ['Florodora' × seedling; Moll.]. Orange with a salmon blush, brown-red markings, 9–10 cm wide, 9–10 flowers together. ☺

'Catharine van Tol' (J. C. van Tol) [*R. catawbiense* descendant]. Red. JRL 1959: 49. Surpassed by 'Homer'. #

'Cavalier' (R. Henny) ['Pygmalion' × 'Tally Ho']. Scarlet-red; broad, flat habit. z8–9 #

'C. B. van Nes' (C. B. van Nes) ['Queen Wilhelmina' × 'Stanley Davies']. Scarlet-red, very early. Surpassed by 'Unknown Warrior'. #

'Cecile' (Rothschild 1947) [Knap Hill]. Buds deep pink, opening salmon-red with a trace of yellow, very large flowered. Dfl 6: 41. #

'Cheer' (Shammarello 1955) ['Cunningham's White' × a red *R. catawbiense* seedling]. Light pink, very early. VVR 4. #

'Chevalier de Réali' (L. van Houtte 1875) [*R. japonicum* clone]. Maize-yellow, fading quickly, 3 cm wide. ☺

'Chevalier Felix de Sauvage' (Sauvage, around 1870) [*R. caucasicum* × hardy hybrids]. Light red with darker speckles, very early, limb undulate. GC 1940: 345; VVR 19. Surpassed by 'Boskoop'. #

'China' (Slocock 1936) [*R. fortunei* × *R. weightii*]. Cream-white, yellow throat. GC 137: 52. Surpassed by 'Goldfort'. # ☺

'Chopin' (Vuyk van Nes 1945) ['Schubert' × seedling]. Deep pink with a darker blotch, 6 cm wide.

'Christiane' (Joh. Bruns 1979) ['Goldsworth Orange' × 'Prof. F. Bettex']. Pale rose, fading to cream-white when full.

'Christina' (Vuyk van Nes, before 1965) ['Florida' × 'Louise Gable']. Carmine, double, very large flowered; semi-evergreen, foliage light-green. #

'Christmas Cheer' [Kur.]. Opal-pink, single, the sepals partly petaloid. VVR 81 (= 'Ima-shojo').

'Christopher Wren' (L. J. Endtz & Co.). Orange-yellow, with a red blush, markings darker orange-brown. DBL 63 (= 'Goldball'). ☺

'Clementine Lemaire' (Moser). Dark pink, with an attractive light brown blotch. #

'Coccinea Speciosa' (Sénéclause, before 1846) [Ghent hybrid]. Bright orange-red; branches of older plants horizontal. BRho 142; SAz 1; Dfl 4: 16. One of the best cultivars. ☺

'**Comte de Gomer**' (L. van Houtte 1872) [Moll.]. Red-orange with a lighter spot, 6 cm wide (= 'Consul Cérésole').

'**Comte de Quincey**' (L. van Houtte 1873) [*R. japonicum* clone]. Light yellow, throat darker. SAz 5.

'Consul Cérésole' see: '**Comte de Gomer**'

'Corall Bells' see: '**Kirin**'

'**Corneille**' (Vuylsteke) [Ghent hybrid]. Pink, double. BHR 94. ⊕

'**Coronation Day**' (Crossfield 1937) ['Loderi' × 'Pink Shell']. Pink with a dark red spot, very large flowered. RYB 4: 23. #

'**Coronation Lady**' (Waterer Sons & Crisp) [Knap Hill]. Salmon-pink with an orange-yellow spot. ⊕

'**Corry Koster**' (Koster & Sons 1909.) [*R. griffithianum* × ?]. Light red, darker blotched, margin crispate. #

'**Cosmopolitan**' (Hagen) ['Cunningham's White' × 'Vesuvius']. Pink, with large red-brown markings, early May. Dfl 6: 48. z8 #

'**Countess of Athlone**' (C. B. van Nes 1923) [*R. catawbiense* 'Grandiflorum' × 'Geoffrey Millais']. Lilac, large inflorescences. #

'**Countess of Derby**' (Sunningdale 1913) ['Cynthia' × 'Pink Pearl']. Light carmine-pink, fully open blooms yet lighter, interior carmine punctate. VVR 30. Surpassed by 'Marinus Koster'. #

'**County of York**' (Gable, before 1936) [*R. catawbiense* 'Album' × 'Loderi King George']. Buds greenish white, opening white with olive-green markings, May; tall growing, quite winter hardy. VVR 76. #

'**Cowslip**' (Aberconway 1930) [*R. williamsianum* × *R. wardii*]. Light primrose-yellow with a trace of soft pink. z8 #

'**Creeping Jenny**' (Aberconway) [*R. griersonianum* × *R. forrestii repens*]. Scarlet, large flowered; totally flat habit. #

'**Crest**' (Rothschild, before 1953) [*R. wardii* × 'Lady Bessborough']. Primrose-yellow, darker yellow in the throat. PBRR 23. #

'**Cunningham's Sulphur**' (Cunningham). Presumably only a yellow *R. caucasicum* variety. #

'**Cunningham's White**' (Cunningham 1850) [*R. caucasicum* × *R. ponticum* 'Album']. White with greenish yellow markings, very early. BM 3811; JRL 1953: 34; VVR 22. # ⊕

'**Cynthia**' (Standish & Noble, before 1870) [*R. catawbiense* × *R. griffithianum*]. Carmine-pink, early. VVR 71 (= 'Lord Palmerston'). Very hardy. # ⊕

'**Dairy Maid**' (Slocock 1930) [*R. campylocarpum* hybrid]. Lemon-yellow with a trace of pink and a pink blotch. # ⊕

'**David**' (Swaythling, before 1939) ['Hugh Koster' × *R. neriiflorum*]. Deep red, interior somewhat punctate above, surpassed by 'J. H. Montague'. #

'**Daviesii**' (I. Davies, around 1840) [*R. japonicum* × *R. viscosum* (= *R. viscosepalum*)]. Cream-yellow to white, with a yellow patch, 6 cm wide; leaves blue-green. JRL 1960: 67; BRho 142.

'**Daybreak**' (Waterer Sons & Crisp) [Knap Hill]. Orange with a pink tone, large flowered. See also: '**Kirin**'.

'**Day Dream**' (Rothschild, before 1940) ['Lady Bessborough' × *R. griersonianum*]. Dark carmine, exterior scarlet shaded, very bright in bud, eventually more pale. PBRR 65. #

'**Debutante**' (Rothschild 1948) [Knap Hill]. Carmine-pink with an orange spot, large flowered, late. Surpassed by 'Cecile'.

'**Delicatissima**' (Koster & Sons 1895) [*R. occidentale* clone]. Cream-white, turning pink, with a yellow blotch.

'**Delta**' (Boot & Co., before 1964). Violet-pink, with pale brown-green markings, 6.5 cm wide, about 15 flowers together. #

'**Devon**' (Slocock, before 1952) [Knap Hill]. Pink-red, dull, an unattractive color.

'**Diamant**'. A crossing of *R.* 'Multiflorum' with *R. kiusianum* by C. Fleischmann. Flat growing, low, to about 50 cm wide in 5 years; leaves semi-evergreen; flowers only 2–3 cm wide, but very numerous. All types with only colored markings; 7 tones selected to date ('Salmon', 'Pink', 'Purple', 'Red', etc.) All quite hardy. #

'**Diana**' (Joh. Bruns 1979) ['Goldsworth Orange' × 'Gotthard Zaayer']. Salmon-pink.

'**Diane**' (Koster & Sons 1920) [*R. campylocarpum* hybrid × 'Mrs. Lindsay Smith']. Cream-white with primrose-yellow, compact inflorescence. #

'**Dietrich**' (Seidel, before 1902) ['Mrs Milner' × *R. smirnowii*]. Carmine-pink. JRL 1939: 13. #

'**Directeur Moerlands**' (Binken) [*R. kosterianum* clone]. Golden-yellow, interior darker, olive-brown markings (= 'Golden Sunlight'). ⊕

'**Direktör E. Hjelm**' (D. A. Koster) [*R. fortunei* hybrids]. Dark carmine-pink, with a brown blotch. JRL 1953: 41. # ⊕

'**Doncaster**' (A. Waterer) [*R. arboreum* hybrid]. Bright scarlet-red; rather slow growing. PBRR 76. # ⊕

'**Dr. A. Blok**' (L. Endtz & Co., before 1937) ['Pink Pearl' × *R. catawbiense* hybrid]. Light pink, center lighter yet. VVR 32. #

'**Dr. Arnold W. Endtz**' (Endtz) [*R. catawbiense* hybrid × 'Pink Pearl']. Carmine-pink, limb crispate. DBl 52; Dfl 6: 49. # ⊕

'**Dr. Charles Baumann**' (before 1822) [Ghent hybrid]. Carmine-pink, with a yellow blotch, limb fimbriate, late (= 'Anna Louise', 'Julda Schipp').

'**Dr. Ernst Schäle**' (Hobbie 1946) ['Prometheus' × *R. forrestii repens*]. Light scarlet-red, large flowered, flowering abundantly, very early; habit hemispherical. #

'**Dr. H. C. Dresselhuys**' (den Ouden 1920) ['Atrosanguineum' × 'Doncaster']. Aniline-red; very winter hardy. # ⊕

'**Dr. Jacobi**' (W. Hardijzer & Co. 1944) [Moll.]. Signal-red.

'**Dr. M. Oosthoek**' (Oosthoek 1920) [Moll.; *R. kosterianum* clone]. Dark orange-red. ⊕

'Dr. Nolans' see: '**Koningin Emma**'

'**Dr. Reichenbach**' (M. Koster & Sons 1892) [*R. kosterianum* clone]. Light salmon-orange, interior turning yellow, with a yellow blotch.

'**Dr. Stocker**' (North) [*R. caucasicum* × *R. griffithianum*]. Ivory-white, brown speckled. #

'**Dr. Tjebbes**' (C. A. van den Akker, before 1966) [Parentage unknown]. Carmine-red, fading somewhat lighter, with very large, dark brown markings, 9 cm wide, 14–16 flowers together, late May; habit broadly upright. # ⊕

'**Dr. V. H. Rutgers**' (den Ouden 1925) ['Charles Dickens' × 'Lord Roberts']. Aniline-red, limb undulate. VVR 66. # ⊕

'Duchess of Teck' (Waterer Sons & Crisp, 1892.) White, lilac limbed, brown patch. #

'Duchess of York' (Paul) [*R. fortunei* × 'Scapio']. Carmine-pink, cream-yellow patch, young shoots appearing while still in flower, therefore surpassed by the very similar 'Direktör E. Hjelm'. #

'Earl of Athlone' (C. B. van Nes, before 1933) ['Queen Wilhelmina' × 'Stanley Davies']. Blood-red. DBl 51. Surpassed by 'Jean Marie Montague'. #

'Earl of Donoughmore' (M. Koster & Sons 1953). Bright red and orange.

'Edmund de Rothschild' (E. de Rothschild) ['Fusilier' × 'Kilimanjaro']. Deep red. PBRR 21. #

'Edward S. Rand' (A. Waterer 1870) [*R. catawbiense* hybrid]. Carmine with a yellow center. # ✧

'El Alamein' (Kluis 1946) [*R. griffithianum* hybrid]. Cardinal-red with a distinct, brown blotch. Surpassed by 'Britannia'. # ✧

'Elisabeth Hobbie' (grex, Hobbie 1945) ['Essex Scarlet' × *R. forrestii repens*]. Translucent scarlet-red. JRL 1961: 49; VVR 136; BRH 127. # ✧

'Elizabeth' (Aberconway 1933) [*R. forrestii repens* × *R. griersonianum*]. Scarlet-red, large flowered, 4–6 together, 7 cm long, late April; leaves dull green, somewhat brownish in winter. RYB 4: 1; VVR 72. z8–9 # ✧

'Elsie Frye' [*R. ciliicalyx* hybrid]. White with a soft pink blush, throat yellow, 3–6 flowers together, 10 cm wide, fragrant. VVR 78. z9 #

'Elsie Straver' (Straver) [*R. campylocarpum* hybrid]. Cream-yellow, campanulate, in compact corymbs; foliage attractive. #

'Elspeth' (Slocock, before 1937) [*R. campylocarpum* × hardy hybrid]. Carmine-pink and apricot-yellow, darker in bud. #

'Emasculum' (*R. ciliatum* × *R. dauricum*). Semi-evergreen to evergreen shrub, to 1.5 m high, bushy, young shoots and leaves scaly; leaves elliptic, acute at both ends, 3–5 cm long, dark green and glossy above, brown scaly beneath; flowers solitary or paired, at the shoot tips, corolla 4–5 cm wide, broadly funnelform, pale lilac-purple, not speckled, limb 5 lobed, lobes undulate, stamens absent or stunted (!), March–April, after *R. praecox* (= *R. emasculum* W. Wats.). Developed by Waterer.

'English Roseum' (A. Waterer). *R. catawbiense* hybrid or a sport of 'Roseum Elegans'. Dfl 6: 48. #

'Ennepe' (Arends) [Arendsii]. Pink, medium-sized, middle early; upright habit.

'Esmeralda' (Koppeschaar) [Kur.]. Pink; broad and low habit. #

'Essex Scarlet' (G. Paul 1899). Deep carmine-scarlet with a black blotch. Surpassed by 'Baccarat'. #

'Evening Glow' (M. Koster & Sons 1920) [Moll.]. Bright dark red. VVR 19.

'Everestianum' (A. Waterer, before 1850) [*R. catawbiense* hybrid]. Lilac-pink, limb crispate, interior punctate. BRho 79. # ✧

'Exbury' azaleas see p. 182.

'Fabia' (Aberconway 1934) [*dichroanthum* × *griersonianum*]. Scarlet to salmon-orange, campanulate. VVR 72. #

'Faggeter's Favourite' (Slocock) [chance seedling of *R. fortunei*]. Cream-white with a trace of pink, interior brown punctate, fragrant. VVR 7. #

'Fanny' [Ghent hybrid]. Dark purple-pink with a bronze patch. JRL 1953: 84; BRho 142 (= 'Pucella').

'Farrall Yellow' (Haworth-Booth, before 1957 [Knap Hill; 'Marion Merryman' × 'Marmelade']. Bright yellow with a somewhat darker spot.

'Fastuosum Plenum' (Francoisi, before 1846) [*R. catawbiense* × *R. ponticum*]. Lilac, double. FS 134; Gs 1924: 104; VVR 28. #

'Favorite' (C. B. van Nes 1920) ['Hinodegiri' × *R. kaempferi*]. Dark pink with an undulate limb. Dfl 6: 40.

'Fedora' (C. B. van Nes 1922) [*R. kaempferi* × 'Malvatica']. Dark pink, large flowered, early to middle-late; upright habit.

'Fireball' (Rothschild 1951) [Knap Hill]. Dark red. ✧

'Firecracker' (Waterer Sons & Crisp) [Knap Hill]. Currant-red; grows stiffly erect; young leaves bronze. ✧

'Firefly' (Rothschild 1947) [Knap Hill]. Dark pink with a light orange blush, very large flowered. Difficult to cultivate. ✧

'Fireglow' (Knap Hill 1926) [Knap Hill]. Orange-vermilion.

'Flamingo' (Knap Hill) [Knap Hill]. Carmine-pink with a yellow-orange blotch, exterior darker, margin crispate.

'Floriade' (Adr. van Nes, before 1960). Flowers red, with a dark brown blotch, 16–20 in globose corymbs; foliage yellow-green. Poor flower bud set.

'Florida' (Vuyk van Nes, before 1958.) [Seedling × 'Vuyks Scarlet'; Vuyk.]. Dark red, hose-in-hose; semi-evergreen. ✧

'Florodora' (M. Koster & Sons 1910) [Moll.]. Light orange with a red spot.

'Fragrans' (Paxton) [Azaleodendron; catawbiense × viscosum]. Small, evergreen shrub, very similar to *R. azaleoides*, but the leaves shorter and wider; flowers in numerous corymbs, pale lilac-pink, center lighter to whitish, fragrant. Paxt. Bot. Mag. 107, Pl. 147 (= *R. fragrans* Paxt.). Originated in England around 1820. z9 #

'Fragrantissimum' (before 1868) [*R. edgeworthii* × *R. formosum*]. White with a pink blush, very fragrant. RYB 4: 28; GC 126, 35; JRHS 75: 67. z9 #

'Frans van der Bom' (Koster & Sons 1892) [*R. kosterianum* clone]. Light salmon-orange. Dfl 4: 56. ✧

'Fraseri' [*R. canadense* × *R. japonicum*]. Deciduous shrub, young shoots and winter buds finely pubescent; leaves elliptic to oblong, 4–6 cm long, acute at both ends, pubescent on both sides; flowers 8–15 together, corolla bilabiate, lilac-pink, speckled, with a very short tube, lower lip deeply incised, not fragrant, April (= *R. fraseri* W. Wats.). Developed in 1912 by G. Fraser in Ucluelet, B.C., Canada.

'Freya' (Vuylsteke 1888) [Rust.]. Double, salmon colored with a yellowish blush. BHR 95. ✧

FRISIA Azaleas. Hybrids between *R. simsii* and the Japanese azaleas, by C. Fleischmann of Wiesmoor, W. Germany around 1960–1970. All cultivars only suited to pot culture. #

'Frühlingszauber' (Hobbie/Bruns 1962) ['Essex Scarlet' × *R. forrestii repens*]. Deep red, similar to 'Scarlet Wonder'; winter hardy, also tolerant of full sun. # ✧

'Furnivall's Daughter' (Knap Hill, before 1957). Fuchsia-pink, intensely strawberry-red speckled above, about 15 flowers together; winter hardy. Dfl 6: 58; Gw 1947: 447. # ☼

'Gallipoli' (Rothschild 1947) [Knap Hill]. Orange-pink, very large flowered, buds carmine striped. ☼

'Galloper Light' [*Azaleodendron* clone]. Soft salmon-pink with a dark yellow eye. Plate 67. # ☼

'Gartendirektor Glocker' (Hobbie 1966) ['Doncaster' × *R. williamsianum*]. Pink-red at first, then pink, May; new growth bronze; habit rather globose; leaves oval-elliptic; quite winter hardy. # ☼

'Gartendirektor Rieger' (Hobbie) ['Adriaan Koster' × *R. williamsianum*]. Light yellow, large flowered, wide open; medium height. RJB 1973: 85. #

'General Eisenhower' (Kluis 1946) [*R. griffithianum* hybrid]. Dark carmine, large flowered. VVR 122; Dfl 6: 49. # ☼

'Genoveva' (Seidel) [*R. catawbiense* hybrid]. Soft lilac-white with a yellowish green blotch. JRHS 1937: 9. #

'George Cunningham' (Cunningham, before 1875) [*R. arboreum* × *R. campanulatum*]. White, interior and the entire limb black punctate. #

'George Reynolds' (Rothschild) [Knap Hill]. Dark butter-yellow with a greenish center, deeply yellow spot, very large flowered; slow growing. PBRR 47. ☼

'Gertrud Schäle' (Hobbie 1951) [*R. forrestii repens* × 'Prometheus']. Scarlet-red, large flowered. # ☼

'Gibraltar' (Rothschild 1947) [Knap Hill]. An intense orange with a red blush, margin crispate, large flowered. Dfl 6: 41. ☼

'Giganteum' (H. Waterer, before 1851) [*R. catawbiense* descendant]. Light carmine. VVR 99. Not a good color! #

'Ginger' (Rothschild 1947) [Knap Hill]. Bright orange with a trace of pink and a darker middle band on each lobe, also a deep orange-yellow blotch. PBRR 46.

'Gloria Mundi' (Sénéclause 1846) [Ghent hybrid]. Orange, 6 cm wide, limb crispate.

'Glory of Littleworth' (Mangels, before 1911) [*Azaleodendron* clone]. Lemon-yellow with a deep orange spot. #

'Glowing Embers' (Rothschild) [Knap Hill]. Orange-red with an orange blotch.

'Görlitz' (V. v. Martin/J. Bruns 1946) ['Rinaldo' × *R. williamsianum*]. Similar to 'Gartendirektor Glocker', but a brighter pink, 5.5–7.5 cm wide, May; globose habit, to 1.5 m high, quite winter hardy. Gw 1973: 9. # ☼

'Gog' (Knap Hill 1926) [Knap Hill]. Brownish orange, inflorescences rather loose.

'Goldball' see: **'Christopher Wren'**

'Gold Dust' (Rothschild 1951) [Knap Hill]. Deep yellow. ☼

'Golden Eagle' (Knap Hill 1949) [*R. calendulaceum* clone]. Orange with red. ☼

'Golden Flare' (Metselaar, before 1965) [Seedling of 'Aurea Grandiflora']. Golden-yellow with an orange-red blotch, in very large corymbs. ☼

'Golden Horn' (Rothschild 1947) [*R. dichroanthum* × *R. elliottii*]. Deep golden-yellow at first, later lighter with a pink blush and pinkish apex, large flowered. z9 # ☼

'Golden Sunlight' see: **'Directeur Moerlands'**

'Golden Sunset' (Rothschild, before 1948) [Knap Hill]. Deep yellow with an orange blotch. Dfl 6: 41. ☼

'Goldfort' (W. C. Slocock 1937) ['Goldsworth Yellow' × *R. fortunei*]. Pure yellow, with a green center, limb pink, later cream-yellow with a trace of pink. # ☼

'Goldlack' (H. A. Hesse 1900) [Ghent hybrid]. Golden-yellow. BHR 90.

'Goldsworth Crimson' (W. C. Slocock 1926) [*R. griffithianum* × hardy hybrid]. Carmine; strong growing. VVR 24. #

'Goldsworth Orange' (W. C. Slocock 1938) [*R. dichroanthum* × *R. discolor*]. Light orange with a trace of pink; low growing. #

'Goldsworth Yellow' (Slocock 1925) [*R. campylocarpum* × *R. caucasicum*]. Buds apricot colored, opening yellow, with green-brown markings. VVR 38 and 125. Surpassed by 'Dairy Maid'. # ☼

'Gomer Waterer' (J. Waterer, before 1900) [*R. catawbiense* hybrid]. Buds lilac-pink, opening white with a soft lilac blush, large flowered, late. VVR 20; Dfl 6: 48. # ☼

'Govenianum' (Goven, Highclere, before 1825) [*R. viscosum* or *R. periclymenoides* × (*R. ponticum* × *R. catawbiense*)]. Semi-evergreen shrub, similar to *R. azaleoides*; leaves oblanceolate, 5–10 cm long, bluish beneath; flowers small, darker lilac, corolla longer and narrower, calyx lobes narrower. Sweet, Brit. Flow. Gard. III: Pl. 263. z8 #

'Graciosa' (Koster & Sons 1901) [*R. occidentale* clone]. Soft pink, orange blotch, exterior red striped. ☼

'Gräfin Kirchbach' (J. Bruns) ['Scharnhorst' × *R. forrestii repens*]. Deep red, buds red; flat habit, to 80 cm high and 1 m wide; small leaved. # ☼

'Graf Zeppelin' (C. B. van Nes) ['Mrs. C. S. Sargent' × 'Pink Pearl']. A strong pink. VVR 87. #

'Grandeur Triomphante' (L. van Houtte, before 1872) [Ghent hybrid]. Dark violet-pink. JRL 1960:56.

'Gretchen' (C. B. van Nes 1922) [Kaempf.]. Dark lilac with a violet patch, 5 cm wide.

'Gristede' (Joh. Bruns) [*R. impeditum* seedling]. Violet-blue, May; to only 50 cm high, 60 cm wide. #

'G. Stresemann' see: **'Hollandia'**

'Gudrun' (T. J. R. Seidel 1905) ['Eggebrechtii' × 'Mme Linden']. White, with large red-brown markings, mid to late May, buds red-brown. Very winter hardy.

'Gustav Lüttge' (Hobbie) ['Mrs. Lindsay Smith' × *R. williamsianum*]. Soft pink-white, large flowered; habit broadly globose. #

'Halopaenum' see: **'White Pearl'**

'Hamlet' (M. Koster & Sons) [Moll.]. Deep salmon-orange with a dark red spot.

'Hardijzer Beauty' (W. H. Hardijzer, before 1958) [*R. racemosum* × Kur.; *Azaleodendron*]. Light pink, 3 cm wide, 2–4 together, with 5–6 stamens. #

'Harvest Moon' (Knap Hill 1938) [Knap Hill]. Amber-yellow with a lighter spot, slightly fragrant. SAz 8. ☼

'Harvest Moon' (M. Koster & Sons, before 1948) ['Mrs. Lindsay Smith' × *R. campylocarpum* hybrid]. Lemon-yellow, with red-brown markings, later cream-white with a carmine patch. VVR 102. Surpassed by 'Adriaan Koster'. # ☼

'Hassan' (Seidel) [*R. catawbiense* hybrid]. Carmine. JRL 1942: 2. #

'Hatsugiri' [Kur.]. Carmine-pink. ☼

'Helena' (Felix & Dijkhuis 1952) [Kur.]. Pure pink, hose-in-hose.

'Helena Vuyk' see: **'P. W. Hardijzer'**

'Helene Schiffner' (Seidel, before 1893). Pure white. VVR 83. #

'Henriette Sargent' (A. Waterer 1891) [*R. catawbiense* hybrid]. Deep pink, very similar to 'Mrs. Charles Sargent', but lower in habit. VVR 108. #

'Herbert' (Gabele 1931) ['Hexe' × *R. yedoense poukhanense*]. Reddish violet with a darker blotch, 4.5 cm wide, limb crispate, hose-in-hose.

'Hino-crimson' (J. Vermeulen, N.Y.) [Kur.; 'Amoenum' × 'Hinodegiri']. Red. ☼

'Hinodegiri' [Kur.] Carmine-red, small flowered. BRho 302 (= 'Red Hussar'). Imported from Japan by E. H. Wilson as No. 42. # ☼

'Hinomayo' [*R. obtusum* cultivar]. Soft pink, interior somewhat punctate. SAz 15. Imported from the Imperial Garden, Tokyo, Japan around 1910 by C. B. van Nes. # ☼

'Hino-scarlet' see: **'Campfire'**

'Holbein' (Seidel 1906) ['Alexander Adie' × 'Carl Mette']. Lilac-pink. #

'Hollandia' (Endtz) ['Charles Dickens' × 'Pink Pearl']. Carmine. Dfl 6: 49 (= 'G. Stresemann'). # ☼

'Homebush' (Knap Hill, before 1925) [Knap Hill]. Pink, semidouble, in dense corymbs. ☼

'Homer' (Seidel 1906) ['Agnes' × 'Kaiser Wilhelm']. Cool pink. Gs 1924: 108. # ☼

'Hortulanus H. Witte' (Koster & Sons 1892) [Moll.; *R. kosterianum* clone]. Light orange-yellow with a yellow patch. Dfl 4: 9. ☼

'Hotspur' [Knap Hill]. Deep orange, large flowered, margin somewhat crispate. PBRR 48. ☼

'Hotspur Red' [Knap Hill]. Vermilion-red, late. Older plants are nearly horizontally branched (!).

'Hugh Koster' (Koster & Sons 1915) ['Doncaster' hybrid × 'George Hardy']. Light carmine. # ☼

'Hugh Wormald' (Rothschild) [Knap Hill]. Deep golden-yellow with a darker blotch. ☼

'Hugo Hardijzer' (Hardijzer) [Moll.]. Light red. ☼

'Hugo Koster' (Koster & Sons 1892) [Moll.; *R. kosterianum* clone]. Salmon-orange with a red gloss. ☼

'Humboldt' (Seidel 1926) [*R. catawbiense* hybrid]. Pink with darker markings. RL 1959: 69; BHR 121. #

'Humming Bird' (J. C. Williams 1933) [*R. haematodes* × *R. williamsianum*]. Deep pink, campanulate, 2–3 together, late April. Flowering sparsely on young plants. # ☼

'Hyperion' (Aberconway 1931) ['Cardinal' × *R. forrestii repens*]. Blood-red. ☼

'Idealist' (Rothschild, before 1945) ['Naomi' × *R. wardii*]. Pale greenish yellow, very large flowered, grouped 10–12 together. VVR 97; PBRR 4 and 5. # ☼

'Ignatus Sargent' (A. Waterer) [*R. catawbiense* hybrid]. Light carmine-pink. VVA 99. #

'Ignea Nova' (before 1876) [Ghent hybrid]. Carmine-red, yellow patch. # ☼

'Il Tasso' (Vuylsteke 1892) [Rust.]. Pink-red with salmon, double. ☼

'Ima-shojo' see: **'Christmas Cheer'**

'Inamorata' (Rothschild, before 1950) [*R. discolor* × *R. wardii*]. Sulfur-yellow with small, carmine-red punctate markings, wide open. RJB 1970: 68; BHR 70. An attractive, vigorous form. # ☼

'Irene Koster' (Koster) [*R. occidentale* hybrid]. Light pink, with a small yellow blotch, fragrant. ☼

'Jacksonii' (Herbert 1835) [*R. caucasicum* × 'Nobleanum']. Soft pink, exterior with a darker midline, very early. Plate 64. # ☼

'Jackwill' (Hobbie 1967) ['Jacksonii' × *R. williamsianum*]. Soft pink at first, later pink-white; habit very dense and wide. Gw 1973: 9. #

'James Gable' (Gable 1942) ['Caroline Gable' × 'Purple Splendour']. Red with a darker patch, hose-in-hose.

'James Marshall Brooks' (A. Waterer, before 1870). Scarlet-red with a brown patch. JRL 1939: 14. #

'Jan Dekens' (Blaauw 1940). A strong pink, with a fimbriate limb. VVR 41. # ☼

'Jan Steen' (Rothschild, before 1950) ['Fabia' × 'Lady Bessborough']. Cream-white, pink and orange, with red-brown markings. PBRR 8. #

'Jan Wellen' (Boskoop Experiment Station) [('Aladdin' × 'Amoena') × 'Vuyk's Scarlet']. Pink with a dark red blotch, 5–6 cm wide, 2–3 flowers together, late April; broad growing. # ☼

'J. C. van Tol' (van Tol) [Mill.]. Red, nearly 7 cm wide. ☼

'Jean Marie de Montague' (C. B. van Nes). Bright scarlet-red, a beautiful color. VVR 21 (= 'The Honorable Jean Marie de Montague'). # ☼

'J. H. van Nes' (J. B. van Nes) [*R. griffithianum* hybrid × 'Monsieur Thier']. Soft pink. VVR 82. #

'Jingle Bells' ['Lem's Goal' × 'Fabia']. Yellow with pink and orange, funnelform, early May; half size. VVR 132. # ☼

'J. Jennings' [Knap Hill]. Deep red; fast growing. Surpassed by 'Satan'.

'Johanna' (Vuyk van Nes) ['Florida' × seedling]. Deep red, simple; foliage brownish, semi-evergreen. #

'John Cairns' (Endtz) [*R. kaempferi* clone]. Dark red. # ☼

'John P. Albert' (J. A. Boer 1970) [*R. japonicum*]. Carmine-pink. Quite winter hardy. #

'John Walter' (J. Waterer, before 1860) [*R. arboreum* × *R. catawbiense*]. Carmine, small flowered. Surpassed by 'Wilgen's Ruby'. VVR 63. #

'Joseph Baumann' (before 1875) [Ghent hybrid]. Blood-red.

'Joseph Haydn' (Vuyk van Nes) ['J. C. van Tol' × *R. mucronatum*]. Soft lilac with a brown blotch, 6.5 cm wide. #

'Joseph Whitworth' (J. Waterer, before 1867. [*R. ponticum* hybrid]. Deep purple with darker markings. #

'Julda Schipp' see: 'Dr. Charles Baumann'

'Juwel' (Hobbie 1960) ['Essex Scarlet' × *R. forrestii repens*]. Deep red, 3–5 together, mid May; broad habit; leaves deep green, 4–7 cm long, somewhat twisted. # ☺

'Karin' (Boskoop Experiment Station, before 1966) ['Britannia' × *R. williamsianum*]. Pink, large, shell form, limb crispate, 8–10 together, early May; flat globose habit; leaves cordate-ovate, 5–8 cm long. Dfl 3: 53. # ☺

'Kate Waterer' (J.Waterer, before 1890). Pink, yellow center, late. VVR 103. Surpassed by 'Clementine Lemaire'. # ☺

'Kathleen' (C. B. van Nes 1922) [*R. kaempferi* clone]. Pink-red. Dfl 6: 40. # ☺

'Kermesina' [Kur.] Carmine, very small flowered, mid to late season; habit low and wide. Very hardy, a good semi-evergreen. # ☺

'Kestrel' [Knap Hill]. Orange, small flowered, middle-late; strong growing.

'Kiev' (Rothschild) [*R. elliottii* × 'Barclay']. Deep blood-red with darker sap stains at the base, about 8 flowers together. # ☺

'Kilauea' [Knap Hill]. Orange-red, orange above, limb undulate, new growth deep brown, late; strong growing. ☺

'King Tut' (Shammarello 1962) [*R. catawbiense* hybrid]. Light red with a large white center. VVR XII. Very hardy. #

'Kirin' [Kur.]. Coral-pink, hose-in-hose, 2.5 cm wide (= 'Daybreak', 'Corall Bells'). Imported from Japan by E. H. Wilson as No. 22. #

'Klondyke' [Knap Hill]. Deep golden-yellow, large flowered, new growth dark brown, middle late; habit broadly upright. Dfl 6: 41. ☺

'Kluis Sensation' (Kluis 1946) ['Britannia' descendant]. Light scarlet-red, slightly punctate. VVR 60. # ☺

'Kluis Triumph' (Kluis). Deep red, late. Slightly scorched in sunny sites. #

'Knap Hill Yellow' [Knap Hill]. Dark canary-yellow, somewhat pink margined; slow growing.

'Konningin Emma' (Wezelenburg) [Moll.; *R. kosterianum* clone]. Dark orange with salmon. DBl 64 (= 'Dr. Nolans', 'Queen Emma'. ☺

'Koningin Wilhelmina' (Ottolander 1896) [Moll.; *R. kosterianum* clone]. Light orange (= 'Queen Wilhelmina').

kosterianum Schneid. [*R. japonicum* × *R. molle*]. Intermediate between the parents. Leaves only slightly pubescent beneath; flowers white to yellow and orange as well as salmon, pink to red.
  Included here are a large number of cultivars primarily developed in Holland and Belgium between 1860 and 1900.

'Koster's Brilliant Red' (Koster & Sons 1918) [Moll.; *R. kosterianum* seedling (!)]. Orange-red. SAz 3. ☺

'Lady Alice de Stuers' see: 'Alice de Stuers'

'Lady Alice Fitzwilliam' Pure white, strongly fragrant. z9 #

'Lady Annette de Trafford' (A. Waterer 1874) [*R. maximum* hybrid]. Soft pink, deep brown blotch, late. GC 135: 82; BHR 71. #

'Lady Chamberlain' (Rothschild 1930) [*R. cinnabarinum* var. *roylei* × 'Royal Flush', orange form]. Like *R. cinnabarinum*, but the flowers twice as large, orange with red and pink, somewhat pendulous. GC 133: 169; PBRR 36. #

'Lady Clementine Mitford'. Soft pink. Poor flower bud set. VVR 53. #

'Lady Eleanor Cathcart' (J. Waterer, before 1850) [*R. arboreum* × *R. maximum*]. Pure pale pink with a purple-red blotch. JRL 1959: 36. #

'Lady Grey Egerton' (J. Waterer, before 1888) [*R. catawbiense* hybrid]. Light lilac-pink. #

'Lady Roseberry' [Knap Hill]. Light carmine-red, orange patch, quickly fading, new shoots elongating while in flower.

'Laetvirens' [*R. carolinianum* × *R. ferrugineum*]. Broad, dense, evergreen shrub, about 1 m high, similar to *R. arbutifolium*; leaves narrowly lanceolate-elliptic, 3–7 cm long, 1–2 cm wide, somewhat acuminate, bright green, densely scaly beneath; flowers in loose, small corymbs, corolla narrowly tubular, pink, limb 3 cm wide, May–June (= *R. laetevirens* Rehd.; *R. wilsonii* Hort. non Nutt.; *R. oleifolium* Hort.). 1903. Fig. 115. #

'Lamplighter' (Koster & Sons 1955) ['Britannia' × 'Mme. Fr. J. Chauvin'] A glowing bright red with a salmon blush. VVR 128. # ☺

'Lapwing' (Knap Hill 1935) [Knap Hill]. Straw-yellow with pink tips and a dark yellow blotch.

'Lavender Girl' (Slocock 1950) [*R. fortunei* × 'Lady Grey Egerton']. Soft lilac, limb pink, center more white. VVR II. #

'Lavender Queen' [Kur.]. Lavender-lilac, small flowered, early. #

'Lavendula'. Lavender-lilac, May, flowers abundantly; to 60 cm high; small leaved. # ☺

'Lee's Dark Purple' (Lee, before 1851) [*R. catawbiense* hybrid]. Deep violet-purple. # ☺

'Lemonora' (Wezelenburg) [Moll.]. Apricot-yellow, exterior with a pink tinge. ☺

'Leo' (Rothschild, around 1949) ['Britannia' × *R. elliottii*]. Carmine-scarlet, 21–25 together. # ☺

'Leopardi' (cultivated before 1868 in Scotland) [*R. arboreum* hybrid]. White with a reddish blush and large, red-brown spots. JRL 1953: 63. #

'Le Progrès' see: 'Progrès'

'Letty Edwards' (Clarke, before 1946) [*R. campylocarpum* × *R. fortunei*] Light sulfur-yellow, shaded darker. #

'Lilac Time' (Endtz) [*R. kaempferi* clone]. Soft lilac, large flowered; broad habit. Dfl 6: 40. #

'Lilian Harvey' (W. H. Hardijzer) [*Azaleodendron*]. White with a trace of pink, 2 cm wide, 3–4 together, in many clusters along the branch. #

'Lily Marleen' (Vuyk van Nes, before 1965) ['Little Ruby' × 'Dr. W. F. Wery']. Deep pink, hose-in-hose, double, 4 cm wide, very abundantly flowering, mid May; broad, low habit; semi-evergreen. Dfl 4: 62 (= 'Marlene Vuyk'). # ☺

'Linda' (Boskoop Experimental Station) ['Britannia' × *R. williamsianum*]. Pink-red, broadly campanulate, 7–8 together, flowering abundantly, mid May, buds red; leaves elliptic-cordate, dull green, new growth bronze. Dfl 3: 53. # ✣

'Linswege' (Selected in Boskoop from 'Linswegeanum' ['Britannia' × *R. forrestii repens*; Hobbie] in 1974). Deep red, distinctly campanulate, 3–7 together, late April; compact habit; leaves flat, smooth. #

'Lissabon' (V. von Martin/J. Bruns 1964) ['Nova Zembla' × *R. williamsianum*]. Carmine-red, 5–7 cm wide, early May; to 1.5 m high; new growth red-brown. # ✣

'Little Gem' ['Carmen' × *R. elliottii*]. Deep blood-red, funnelform, calyx red, cupulate, early May; habit broad and flat. VVR 84. # ✣

'Loderi' (Loder 1901) [*R. fortunei* × *R. griffithianum*]. White to soft pink, very large flowered, very fragrant. JRL 1959: 12. # ✣
From this often repeated cross by Loder, a large number of clones have been selected; the more prominent ones are listed here.

'Loderi King George' (Loder). Pink, then gradually becoming pure white. RYB 5: 15; VVR 26 and 118. # ✣

'Loderi Venus' (Loder). Soft pink, fragrant. # ✣

'Lord Beaconsfield' see: **'Viscount Powerscourt'**

'Lord Palmerston' see: **'Cynthia'**

'Lord Roberts' (B. Mason). Deep red, with a black blotch, late May, but sparsely flowering; vigorous growing and leggy. #

'Louis Pasteur' (Endtz) ['Mrs. Tritton' × 'Viscount Powerscourt']. Bright red, interior pink. DBl 5. # ✣

'Lucky Hit' (van Gelderen & de Wilde) [from *R. davidsonianum*]. Pure lilac-pink with a darker spot, 3–4 cm wide, 7–9 together; habit broadly upright. #

'Luscombei' (Luscombe 1880) [*R. fortunei* × *R. thomsonii*]. Pink. #

'Magnifica' (Koster & Sons 1901) [*R. occidentale* hybrid]. Cream-yellow, later pale pink, orange spot. SAz 5. ✣

'Mahler' (Vuyk van Nes, before 1965) [Japanese Azalea × 'Vuyks Rosyred']. Lilac, with darker markings, 7 cm wide, late May, 2–3 flowers together; habit broad and low. Semi-evergreen and hardy. # ✣

'Malvatica' (Koster, around 1910) [presumably 'Hinodegiri' × *R. mucronatum*]. Lilac. Surpassed by 'Beethoven'. #

'Marchioness of Lansdowne' (A. Waterer, before 1915) [*R. maximum* hybrid]. Lilac with a large, black patch. VVR 107. Plate 66. # ✣

'Marcia' (Swaythling) [*R. campylocarpum* × 'Gladys']. Primrose-yellow, to 10 flowers together. #

'Marconi' (M. Koster & Sons, before 1924) [Moll.]. Dark red, with an orange spot.

'Marinus Koster' (Koster & Sons, 1937) [*R. griffithianum* hybrid]. Dark pink, lighter shaded. # ✣

'Marion' (Felix & Dijkhuis) [*R. catawbiense* 'Grandiflorum' × 'Pink Pearl']. Pink, large flowered. DBl 54. Surpassed by 'Queen Mary'. ✣

'Marion Merriman' (Knap Hill, before 1925). Yellow with an orange spot, flat, 18–30 flowers together.

'Marlene Vuyk' see: **'Lily Marleen'**

'Mars' (Waterer Sons & Crisp, before 1875) [*R. griffithianum* hybrid]. Deep red. DBl 61; VVR 76. Difficult to cultivate. # ✣

'Martine' (W. H. Hardijzer) [*R. racemosum* × Kur. clone]. Pink, 3 cm wide, 2–4 together, in densely arranged clusters, stamens 5–6. # ✣

'Matador' (Aberconway 1931) [*R. griersonianum* × *R. strigillosum*]. Dark orange-red, 7–8 together. PBRR 65. # ✣

'Max Sye' (Frets, around 1935) ['Chevalier Felix de Sauvage' × ?]. Deep red, with a black patch, early. Surpassed by 'Baccarat'. # ✣

'Maxwellii' [*R. pulchrum* clone]. Carmine with a darker blotch, large flowered, mid-late. #

'May Day' (A. M. Williams 1932) [*R. griersonianum* × *R. haematodes*]. Cherry-red. JRL 1959: 42; PBRR 53. #

'Medusa' (Aberconway 1928) [*R. scyphocalyx* × *R. griersonianum*]. Vermilion red. VVR 111. #

'Metternianum' (Selected from *R. metternichii* by Wada). Pink, with a better habit and hardier. Used for hybridizing by Hobbie. #

'Michael Waterer' (J. Waterer, before 1894) [*R. ponticum* hybrid]. Dark red, speckled. VVA 23. # ✣

'Midwinter' see: **'Wintertime'**

'Mimi' (B. Bunschoten, before 1958). [*R. kaempferi*]. Soft pink, with dark red markings, large flowered, semi-evergreen. # ✣

mixtum Wils. [Ghent hybrid × *molle*]. Flowers double, most in light colors, from white to soft pink and salmon-pink to salmon-red and yellow. Often found in the trade as *"Azalea rustica"*. Brought into the trade in 1888 by Ch. Vuylsteke, who obtained the cross from Louis de Smet (according to Grootendorst, l. c. 130).

'Mme Carvalho' (J. Waterer 1866) [*R. catawbiense* hybrid]. White with yellow-green speckles. VVR 101. Surpassed by 'Belle Heller'. # ✣

'Mme de Bruin' (Koster & Sons) ['Doncaster' × 'Prometheus']. Light red. DBl 53; VVR 39. Foliage unattractive. # ✣

'Mme Fr. J. Chauvin'. Pink with a red blotch. VVR 33. Surpassed by 'Direktör E. Hjelm'. #

'Mme Ida Rubinstein' (Moser) Light pink. # ✣

'Mme Masson' (Bertin 1849) [*R. catawbiense* × *R. ponticum*]. White with a yellow blotch. VVR 33. Surpassed by 'Belle Heller'. # ✣

'Moederkensdag' see: **'Muttertag'**

'Moerheim's Pink' (Hobbie) [*R. williamsianum* × 'Genoveva']. Pink. #

'Monica' (Hobbie/W. de Jong & Sons 1973) [*R. forrestii repens* seedling]. Flowers deep red, larger than those of 'Scarlet Wonder', 4–7 together, late April; habit vigorous; leaves dull green, flat. #

'Moonstone' (C. V. C. Williams 1933) [*R. campylocarpum* × *R. williamsianum*]. Light yellow, good bloomer, late April. Dfl 3: 51; VVR 85; Gw 1973: 9. z8–9 # ✣

'Moser's Maroon' (Moser, before 1932). Red brown, interior darker speckled, young growth red-brown, late. # ✣

'Mother of Pearl'. Totally soft pink to nearly white, middle late. VVR 104. Surpassed by 'Virgo'. # ✣

'Mother's Day' see: **'Muttertag'**

'Mrs. A. T. de la Mare' (C. B. van Nes) ['White Pearl' × 'Sir Charles Butler']. White with a green patch, fragrant. VVR 66. # ☼

'Mrs. Betty Robertson' (M. Koster & Sons 1920) ['Mrs. Lindsay Smith' × *R. campylocarpum* hybrid]. Light yellow with a pink tinge, later cream-yellow. # ☼

'Mrs. Charles E. Pearson' (Koster & Sons 1909) [*R. catawbiense* 'Grandiflorum' × 'Coombe Royal']. Soft lilac with brown spots. VVR 30. # ☼

'Mrs. Charles S. Sargent'. Dark carmine-pink. VVR 88. Difficult to cultivate. #

'Mrs E. C. Stirling' (J. Waterer, before 1906) [*R. griffithianum* hybrid]. Soft lilac-pink. VVR 11. Plate 66. # ☼

'Mrs. Furnivall' (A. Waterer 1920) [*R. griffithianum* hybrid × *R. caucasicum* hybrid]. Pink with a large, carmine-red blotch, funnelform. VVR 8. Surpassed by 'Albert Schweitzer'. # ☼

'Mrs. G. W. Leak' (Koster & Sons 1934 ['Chevalier Felix de Sauvage' × 'Coombe Royal']. Light pink with a large, purple-brown blotch. VVR 49. Surpassed by 'Furnivall's Daughter'. z8–9 # ☼

'Mrs. J. C. Williams' (A. Waterer). White or soft reddish, red speckled. #

'Mrs. J. G. Millais' (A. Waterer). White with a large yellow spot, large flowered, late May; vigorous. Gw 1924: 20 and 477. #

'Mrs. John Clutton' (A. Waterer, before 1865) [*R. maximum* hybrid]. White with a small yellow-green blotch. #

'Mrs. John Russell' (M. Koster & Sons, before 1939) [Moll.; *R. kosterianum* clone]. Pink with a yellow spot.

'Mrs. Lindsay Smith' (Koster & Sons 1910) ['Duchess of Edinburgh' × 'George Hardy']. White, somewhat red punctate, fragrant, very large flowered; shoots long, flexuose. Gs 1927: 114; DBl 62. # ☼

'Mrs. Norman Luff' (M. Koster & Sons, before 1939) [Moll.]. Orange with a large yellow blotch.

'Mrs. P. den Ouden' (den Ouden 1912) ['Atrosanguineum' × 'Doncaster']. Lilac-red. Surpassed by 'Dr. V. H. Rutgers'. # ☼

'Mrs. Peter Koster' (Koster & Sons). Interior totally soft pink, exterior darker pink. # ☼

'Mrs. R. S. Holford' (A. Waterer 1866). Salmon-pink. #

'Mrs. Tom H. Lowinsky' (A. Waterer-Lowinsky) [*R. griffithianum* × 'White Pearl']. Pale pink to white, with a red-brown blotch. GC 135: 83; VVR 81. #

'Mrs. W. C. Slocock' (Slocock 1929) [*R. campylocarpum* hybrid]. Apricot-pink and yellow. #

'Multiflorum' (Arends) [*R. kiusianum*]. Soft lilac, very small flowered; semi-evergreen. Hardy. # ☼

'Muttertag' (van Hecke, Belgium). Deep carmine, double, medium-sized; habit broad; semi-evergreen (= 'Mother's Day, 'Moederkensdag'). # ☼

'Myrtifolium' [*R. minus* × *R. hirsutum*]. Similar to 'Arbutifolium', low, compact growth habit; leaves 2.5–6 cm long, but lighter green, somewhat glossy, more acuminate, margins lightly ciliate, at least when young, underside densely brown scaly; flowers pink, in small racemes, June. #

'Nancy Waterer' (A. Waterer, before 1876) [Ghent hybrid]. Golden-yellow, large flowered. BHR 91. # ☼

'Naomi' (Rothschild 1926) ['Aurora' × *R. fortunei*]. Soft pink with a distinct yellow tinge, very fragrant. # ☼

'Naomi Glow'. Intensely pink. VVR 63. # — **'Naomi Nautilus'**. Pink with a trace of light orange-yellow, base greenish. # — **'Naomi Pink Beauty'**. Dark pink. PBRR 64. #

'Narcissiflora' (Louis van Houtte, before 1871) [Ghent hybrid]. Light yellow, double, fragrant. BRho 366. ☼

'Neptun' (Joh. Bruns 1975). Pink at first, when fully open more cream color with a pink blush and brown markings.

'Nicolaas Beets' (Koster & Sons 1892) [*R. kosterianum* clone]. Apricot-yellow to corn-yellow. ☼

'N. N. Sherwood' (Sibray). Pink, yellow center, flowers abundantly. # ☼

'Nobleanum' (A. Waterer, before 1835) [*R. arboreum* × *R. caucasicum*]. A strong pink, flowers very abundantly and early. #

'Noordtiana' (P. van Noordt & Sons 1900) [*R. mucronatum* clone]. White, large flowered, middle-late (occasionally with lilac and pink sports on the same shoot); upright habit. # ☼

× norbitonense W. Sm. (Subg. *Azaleodendron*) [*R. molle* × (*R. maximum* × *R. ponticum*)]. Developed around 1830 by William Smith in Norbiton, near Kingston, England and known by two names:

   'Aureum'. Semi-evergreen shrub, about 1 m high, young shoots pubescent; leaves oblong, 5–12 cm long, blue-green beneath, finely pubescent on both sides; flowers 8–16 in dense, rounded corymbs, corolla broadly funnelform, limb deeply 5 lobed, light yellow. FS 8 (= *R. smithii aureum* Paxt.). z7 ★★ # ☼

'Broughtonianum' see: **'Broughtonii Aureum'**

'Norma' (Vuylsteke 1888) [Rust.]. Pink with a salmon gloss, double, 3 cm wide. SAz 2. ☼

'Nova Zembla' (Koster & Sons 1902) [red hardy hybrid × 'Parsons Grandiflorum']. Dark red. Dfl 3: 48; VVR 3. # ☼

'Oberbürgermeister Janssen' (Joh. Bruns 1975). Fiery red. #

'Oldenburg' (Hobbie 1953) [*R. discolor* × *R. williamsianum*]. Light pink, long stalked, early May; new growth appears very early, bronze-brown. # ☼

'Old Port' (A. Waterer 1865) [*R. catawbiense* hybrid]. Dark plum colored. # ☼

'Orange Beauty' (C. B. van Nes 1920) [*R. kaempferi* hybrid]. Light orange; broad habit. SAz 16. Needs a shady site. ☼

'Orange Giant' (Vuyk van Nes 1970) [*R. yedoense poukhanense* × 'Louise Gable']. Deep orange, very large flowered, 10 cm wide; semi-evergreen. # ☼

'Ostfriesland' ['Mme de Bruin' × *R. forrestii repens*]. Scarlet-red; tall growing. #

'Oudijk's Favorite' (Le Feber 1958). Origin unknown, presumably a seedling of 'Blue Diamond' or 'Blue Tit', but with a less vigorous habit; young leaves reddish, later deep green, 3 cm long; flowers violet-blue, 4.5 cm wide, early May. # ☼

'Oudijk's Sensation' (Hobbie/Le Feber 1961) ['Essex Scarlet' × *R. williamsianum*]. Dark pink (similar to 'Lissabon', but lighter), to 7.5 cm wide, early May; slow growing; new growth bronze. Gw 1973: 9. # ☼

'Oxydol' [Knap Hill]. White, margin somewhat undulate. PBRR 42. Surpassed by 'Ballerina' and 'Persil'.

'Palestrina' (Vuyk van Nes 1944) ['C. J. van Tol' × R. kaempferi hybrid]. Ivory-white, narrowly upright. SAz 14; RJB 1970: 4 (= 'Wilhelmine Vuyk'). ⊕

'Pallas' (before 1875) [Ghent hybrid]. Orange-red with an orange-yellow blotch, 6 cm wide. ⊕

'Parsons Gloriosum' (A. Waterer, around 1860) [R. catawbiense hybrid]. Soft lilac-pink. VVR 74. # ⊕

'Pelopidas' (J. Waterer) [R. catawbiense hybrid]. Light carmine. # ⊕

'Persil' (Knap Hill) [Knap Hill]. White, with a yellow blotch. Dfl 6: 41. ⊕

'Peter Koster' (M. Koster & Sons 1909) ['Doncaster' × 'George Hardy']. Magenta-red with a lighter limb. DBl 50. #

'Phebe' (Vuylsteke 1888) [Rust.]. Sulfur-yellow, double. Dfl 4: 16 (= 'Phoebe'). ⊕

'Phidias' (Vuyksteke 1888) [Rust.]. Light orange-yellow, buds reddish, double, 3 cm wide. ⊕

'Phoebe' see: 'Phebe'

'Picotee' (A. Waterer). White, limb punctate. #

'Pink Cameo' (Shammarello) ['Boule de Neige' × red R. catawbiense seedling]. Light pink, middle early. #

'Pink Delight' (Rothschild 1951) [Knap Hill]. Dark pink with a yellow blotch. ⊕

'Pink Drift' (Sunningdale, before 1955) [R. calostrotum × R. scintillans]. Lilac-pink, very low and dense. DB 1961: 120. # ⊕

'Pink Goliath' (P. van Nes). Pink, very large flowered, middle late. A first class cultivar. #

'Pink Pearl' (J. Waterer, before 1897) ['Broughtonii' × 'George Hardy']. Soft pink, buds darker, large flowered. JRL 1958: 49; 1960: 4; VVR 80; Dfl 6: 49. # ⊕

'Pinnacle' (Shammarello) [R. catawbiense descendant]. Deep pink, very early, in tight corymbs; compact habit. VVR 85. #

'Polar Bear' (Pryor, USA). White, hose-in-hose, medium-sized, early; compact and upright habit. # ⊕

'Polly Claessens' (M. Koster & Sons) [Moll.; R. kosterianum clone]. Pure orange.

'Praecox' [R. ciliatum × R. dauricum]. Semi-evergreen, very open, upright shrub, 1–1.5 m high; leaves elliptic, 5–7 cm long, dark green, very glossy, somewhat bristly and ciliate above, underside loosely scaly, mostly abscising in fall; flowers to about 3 together at the shoot tips, corolla broadly funnelform, about 4 cm wide, lilac-pink, flowers very abundantly, February–April (= R. praecox Carr.). Developed around 1855 by I. Davies of Brook Lane Nursery, Ormskirk, England. A gorgeous hybrid, but the flowers are occasionally frost damaged. z6 ★★★★ # ⊕

'Primeur' (Vuyk van Nes 1975) ['Rijneveld' × 'Scarlet Surprise']. Pure light pink, with a purple-red blotch from small spots, 7 cm wide, 13–20 flowers together, late April; low growing; leaves long and very narrow. Dfl 11: 54. # ⊕

'Prince Camille de Rohan' (1865) [R. caucasicum hybrid]. Light pink, dark brown blotch, limb fringed. FS 1073. Surpassed by 'Cosmopolitan'. # ⊕

'Prins Bernhard' (Vuyk). Vermilion-red, large flowered, middle-late; habit broad and low. Very attractive, but hardy only in z8–9. # ⊕

'Prinses Irene' (Vuyk van Nes 1941). Light geranium-red. ⊕

'Prinses Juliana' (Vuyk van Nes, before 1941). Pure orange. Surpassed by 'Orange Beauty'. ⊕

'Prinses Marijke' (Felix & Dijkhuis 1948). Dark pink, lighter interior. DBl 58. # ⊕

'Professor F. Bettex' (den Ouden 1912) ['Atrosanguineum' × 'Doncaster']. Red, surpassed by 'Nova Zembla'. # ⊕

'Professor Hugo de Vries' (Endtz, before 1940) ['Doncaster' × 'Pink Pearl']. Pink, darker than 'Pink Pearl'. Gs 1940: 83. # ⊕

'Professor J. H. Zaayer' (Endtz) ['Pink Pearl' × red R. catawbiense hybrid]. Red; with an unattractive, navicular leaf form. #

'Progrès' [R. caucasicum hybrid]. Lilac-pink, with a purple spot, somewhat darker than 'Camille de Rohan'. BHR 79. #

'Prominent' (Boskoop Exp. Station before 1961) ['Alphonse Lavallée × 'Anthony Koster']. Orange-red, 8 cm wide, 7–8 together. ⊕

'Psyche' (Hobbie) ['Sir Charles Butler' × R. williamsianum]. Pink, campanulate, in large corymbs. # ⊕

'Pucella' see: 'Fanny'

'Puncta'. Very similar to R. minus and presumably R. ferrugineum × R. minus, but the leaves 3.5–4(5) cm long, 1.5–2 cm wide, underside green, somewhat brownish green from the lighter and darker scales, spacing of the scales at least as much as their diameter; flowers light pink, 2–2.5 cm long, exterior lightly scaly (R. minus more scaly and flowers to 3 cm long) (= R. punctatum Hort. Holl. non Andrews). #

'Purple Pillow' (J. Streng jr. 1964) [R. russatum hybrid?) Dark violet, 3 cm wide, to 4–5 together, early to late May; habit dwarf, flat globose; leaves 2 cm long, deep green. #

'Purple Splendour' (A. Waterer, before 1900) [R. ponticum hybrid]. Deep purple, violet at the base. BRho 79; VVR 40; Dfl 6: 49. # ⊕

'Purple Triumph' (Vuyk van Nes 1951) ['Beethoven' × unknown seedling]. Deep purple. ⊕

'Purpureum Elegans' (H. Waterer, before 1850). Deep purple. VVR 6. #

'P. W. Hardijzer' (Vuyk de Nes). Dark carmine-pink (= 'Helena Vuyk').

'Queen Emma' see: 'Koningin Emma'

'Queen Mary' (Felix & Dijkhuis 1950) ['Marion' × 'Mrs. C. S. Sargent']. Pink. DBl 56; VVR 38. # ⊕

'Queen of Hearts' (Rothschild 1949) [R. meddianum × 'Moser's Maroon']. Carmine, black speckled above, to 16 flowers together. PBRR 34. # ⊕

'Queen Wilhelmina' see: 'Koningin Wilhelmina'

'Raphael de Smet' (before 1889) [Ghent hybrid]. Light pink, double. SAz 2; JRL 1959: 3.

'Red Carpet' (Hobbie) ['America' × R. forrestii repens]. Bright red, late April; grows very flat, eventually only about 30 cm high. # ⊕

'Red Hussar' see: 'Hinodegiri'

'Remo' (Stevenson 1943) [R. valentinianum × R. lutescens]. Deep yellow. # ⊕

'Rêve Rose' (Lester E. Brandt 1956) ['Bow Bells' × R. forrestii repens (pink form)]. Salmon-pink with a somewhat pink blotch, 4 cm wide, 3–5 together, late April; habit dwarf and creeping; small leaved. # ⊕

'Ria Hardijzer' (W. H. Hardijzer, before 1958) [R. racemosum × 'Hinodegiri']. Light pink, 2 cm wide, densely arranged in clusters of 3–4 flowers. # ⊕

'Rijneveld' (Hobbie/Vujk van Nes ['Metternianum' × hybrid]. Coral-pink, early May, flowering well on young plants; habit very compact. Quite winter hardy. # ⊕

'Rödhätte' (Hobbie) [R. didymym × R. williamsianum]. Blood-red, broadly funnelform, in loose umbels, late May; broad habit. #

'Romany Chal' (Rothschild 1932) ['Moser's Maroon' × R. eriogynum]. Brownish scarlet-red with darker markings. VVR 58. # ⊕

'Rombergpark' (Arends/Böhlje 1968) [Selection of 'Ronsdorfer Frühblühenden']. White, exterior with a soft pink blush, limb 6 lobed, latter half of March; habit very bushy; densely foliate. # ⊕

'Ronsdorfer Frühblühenden' (Arends) [R. oreodoxa × red hybrid]. Red to pink toned flowers. #

'Rosamundii' (Standish & Noble) [R. caucasicum hybrid]. Light pink. VVR 130. #

'Rosa Perle' (Joh. Bruns) [R. degronianum × 'Kluis Triumph']. Deep pink. #

'Rosata' (Boskoop Experiment Station, before 1965) [R. viscosum × R. mollis]. Carmine-pink with darker mid-stripes, 4.5 cm wide, late May, very fragrant; habit broadly upright. ⊕

'Rosebud' (Chisholm 1930) [Kur.]. Silvery pink, double, small flowered. #

'Roseum Elegans' (A. Waterer, before 1851) [R. catawbiense hybrid]. Lilac-pink. JRL 1960: 49; VVR 105. # ⊕

'Rothenburg' (V. von Martin/J. Bruns 1968) ['Diane' × R. williamsianum]. Lemon-yellow at first, later cream-yellow, very large flowered, 8–10 cm wide, late April; to 2.5 m high; leaves glossy green. BHR 79. z8–9 # ⊕

'Royal Command' (Rothschild) [Knap Hill]. Vermilion-red. ⊕

'Rubescens'. Dark red, very early; slow growing.

'Sabine' (Joh. Bruns) ['Goldsworth Orange' × 'May Day']. Purple-red with darker markings. #

'Salute' (Hobbie 1964) ['Essex Scarlet' × R. forrestii repens]. Deep red, 5–8 together, early May; grows somewhat taller than most of the other repens hybrids; leaves 4–8 cm long, undulate. # ⊕

'Sandpiper'. Light yellow, flushed with red, yellow blotch, small flowered.

'Sang de Gentbrugge' (L. van Houtte 1873) [Ghent hybrid]. Signal-red. ⊕

'Sapphire' (Knap Hill Nursery) ['Blue Tit' × R. impeditum]. Lavender-blue. VVR 70. # ⊕

'Sappho' (A. Waterer, before 1876). White with a large, nearly black blotch. BRho 79; VVR 25 and 106. # ⊕

'Satan' (Knap Hill, before 1926) [Knap Hill]. Dark geranium-red. Dfl 6: 41. ⊕

'Saturnus' (Boskoop Exp. Station) [Moll.]. Dark orange-red with a reddish blush. Dfl 4: 57.

'Scandinavia' (Koster & Sons) ['Betty Wormald' × 'Hugh Koster']. Cardinal-red, base pink, with a blackish spot. # ⊕

'Scarlet Surprise'. Like 'Scarlet Wonder', but taller and more open growing. #

'Scarlet Wonder' (Hobbie/Le Feber 1960) ['Essex Scarlet' × R. forrestii repens]. Deep red, to 6 cm long and wide, opening wide, 4–6 together, early May, buds red-brown; leaves distinctly twisted and veined. VVR 50. # ⊕

'Schubert' (Vuyk van Nes 1931) ['J. C. van Tol' × R. kaempferi hybrid]. Light pink. ⊕

'Scintillation' (West Rose Nurseries) [Dexter hybrid]. Pure light pink, in large, tight corymbs. Dfl 6: 48; VVR 32. Winter hardy. # ⊕

'Seville' (Knap Hill, before 1926) [Knap Hill]. Orange. ⊕

SHAMMARELLO Hybrids. Crosses between 'Boule de Neige' and 'Cunningham's White' with old, red flowering Waterer types; producing very early, pink and red toned flowers (see 'Cheer', 'Tony', 'Prince Cameo', 'Pinnacle', 'King Tut' and others). Hybridized by A. M. Shammarello, South Euclid, Ohio, USA. #

'Sham's Ruby' (Shammarello). Dark red. Not any better than 'Nova Zembla'. #

'Silver Slipper' (Waterer). Cream-white, somewhat lilac-pink toned, with a yellow blotch, very large flowering, middle-late. PBRR 45.

'Silvester' (Boskoop Experiment Station 1963) ['Aladdin' × 'Amoena'; Kur.]. Pink, with a darker center, 3 cm wide, very early; broad habit. An excellent cultivar; good for forcing. # ⊕

'Sir Charles Butler' (Paul) [presumably only a seedling of R. fortunei]. Soft lilac-pink, fragrant. BRho 335. #

'Sir John Ramsden' (Waterer Sons & Crisp 1926) ['Corona' × R. thomsonii]. Exterior carmine with a pink limb, enterior light pink, limb undulate. DB 8: 308. #

'Snow' [Azalea]. White, double, small flowered. Surpassed by 'Adonis'. #

'Snow Queen' (Loder 1926) ['White Pearl' × 'Loderi'[. Pure white when fully open with a slightly reddish basal patch, pink in bud. #

'Soir de Paris' (Felix & Dijkhuis) [R. viscosum hybrid]. Dark salmon-pink, with a light orange blotch, darker mid-stripes, fragrant; very vigorous.

'Souvenir de D. A. Koster' (D. A. Koster, before 1922) ['Charlie Waterer' × 'Doncaster']. Dark scarlet, darker speckled, flowering abundantly. DBl 60. # ⊕

'Souvenir de Dr. S. Endtz' (Endtz 1927) ['John Walter' × 'Pink Pearl']. Light pink, but darker than 'Pink Pearl', carmine punctate. # ⊕

'Souvenir of Anthony Waterer' (A. Waterer). Darker salmon-pink, with a yellow blotch. # ⊕

'Souvenir of W. C. Slocock' (Slocock, before 1935) [R.

campylocarpum hybrid]. Apricot-yellow at first, later somewhat lighter. VVR 14. # ☼

'Spek's Brilliant' (Spek) [Moll.; *R. kosterianum* clone]. Orange-red with yellow anthers. ☼

'Spitfire' (Kluis 1946) [*R. griffithianum* hybrid]. Carmine, with a deep blue blotch. #

'Spring Beauty' (den Ouden). Pink with a trace of vermilion, medium-sized, middle-late; habit broad; semi-evergreen. Good for forcing. # ☼

'Stanley Davies' (Davies 1890). Dark red. Surpassed by 'Britannia'. #

'Stewartsonian' (Gable, USA). Dark orange-red, small flowered, very early; broad, vigorous habit. Dfl 6: 40. Needs a shady site. # ☼

'Stockholm' (Joh. Bruns 1972) ['Catagla' × *R. decorum*]. White, with distinct yellow-green markings; 1.5 m high. #

'Strategist' (J. Waterer) [*R. griffithianum* hybrid]. Light red. #

'Strawberry Ice' (Rothschild) [Exb.]. Light pink, with an orange blotch, limb crispate, large flowered.

'Sunbeam' (Koster & Sons 1895) [Moll.; 'Altaclarense' hybrid]. Orange-yellow.

'Sun Chariot' [Waterer Sons & Crisp] [Knap Hill]. Golden-yellow, to 10 cm wide, limb crispate.

'Superba' (Koster & Sons 1901) [Ghent hybrid]. Soft pink with an orange blotch, fringed.

'Super Star' (Joh. Bruns) [*R. yakushimanum* × 'Doncaster']. Pink. #

'Susan' (C. J. Williams, before 1930) [*R. campylocarpum* × *R. fortunei*]. Amethyst-violet, dark purple punctate above. BHR 78. # ☼

'Sylphides' (Knap Hill). Monochromatic, pure light pink, large flowered, inflorescences loose. ☼

'Temple Belle' (Kew Gardens 1916) [*R. orbiculare* × *R. williamsianum*]. Soft pink; low growing. RYB 7: 36. # ☼

'The Bride' (Standish & Noble 1850) [*R. caucasicum album* descendant]. White, green punctate. #

'The Honorable Jean Marie de Montague' see: **'Jean Marie de Montague'**

'Thomwilliams' (Magor 1915) [*R. thomsonii* × *R. williamsianum*]. Light to dark pink, campanulate, not abundantly flowering, late April; dwarf (half normal height); leaves elliptic-cordate, 4–7 cm long, dull green. #

'Tibet' (Gebr. Boer) ['Bismarck' × *R. williamsianum*]. Buds pink, opening white; dwarf, dense; leaves elliptic-rounded, 4–8 cm long. #

'T. J. Seidel' (Koster & Sons 1892) [Moll.; *R. kosterianum* clone]. Salmon-orange with a darker blotch. ☼

'Toucan' [Knap Hill]. Cream-yellow, with a large, golden-yellow blotch, large flowered, very early.

'Trilby'. Dark red. VVR 103. #

'Tunis' (Knap Hill, before 1926) [Knap Hill]. Orange-red to brick-red. Surpassed by 'Fireball'. ☼

'Ulrike' (Joh. Bruns) ['Goldsworth Orange' × 'May Day']. Red with a darker margin. #

'Unique' (Slocock, before 1934) [*R. campylocarpum* hybrid]. Yellow with a salmon blush. VVR 61; BHR 92. #

'Unique' (before 1875) [Ghent hybrid]. Yellowish orange, long auriculate, inflorescences globose. SAz 1. ☼

'Unknown Warrior' (C. B. van Nes & Sons, before 1922) ['Queen Wilhelmina' × 'Stanley Davies']. Light red, early. VVR 53. # ☼

'Van der Hoop' (den Ouden 1912) ['Atrosanguineum' × 'Doncaster']. Dark carmine-pink. # ☼

'Van Weerden Poelman' (den Ouden 1912) ['Charles Dickens' × 'Lord Roberts']. Carmine. # ☼

'Vater Böhlje' (Hobbie 1970) [*R. catawbiense* 'Compactum' × *R. williamsianum*]. #

'Velasquez' (Vuylsteke 1888) [Rust.]. Cream-white, lightly pink toned, later totally white, double. ☼

'Victorine Hefting' (Adr. van Nes) [Seedling of 'Hinomayo'; Kur.]. Deep pink, 2.5–3 cm wide, flowers very abundantly, early; broad growing. Excellent for forcing. #

'Virgo' (van Nes). White with a pink trace, and a small dark red blotch, large flowered, margin undulate, middle-late. #

'Viscount Powerscourt' (Waterer, Bagshot, before 1888). Carmine-pink, to 7 cm wide, with a large, nearly black spot, early June. Gw 1974: 20 and 447 (= 'Lord Beaconsfield'). Very attractive. #

'Von Gneist' (van Noordt) [Moll.; *R. kosterianum* clone]. Orange-red with a salmon tone. ☼

'Vulcan' (Waterer Sons & Crisp, before 1937) [*R. griersonianum* × 'Mars']. Bright red. VVR 12. #

'Vuyk's Rosyred' (Vuyk van Nes 1954). Pink-red. ☼

'Vuyk's Scarlet' (Vuyk van Nes 1954). Dark red to carmine-red. Dfl 6: 40. ☼

'W. E. Gumbleton' (L. van Houtte 1872) [Moll.; *R. japonicum* clone]. Yellow with a slight greenish patch. ☼

'Westfalenpark' (Arends/Böhlje 1968) [Selection from 'Rohnsdorfer Frühblühende']. Dark pink, funnelform, 4 cm long, limb 5–7 lobed, early April; habit broad and open. DB 1968: 92. # ☼

'White Pearl' (Halope, Belgium, 1896) [*R. griffithianum* × *R. maximum*]. Opening soft pink, soon becoming pure white. VVR 45 (= 'Halopeanum'). Plate 67. #

'Whitethroat' [Knap Hill]. Pure white, double, small flowered, middle late.

'Wilgen's Ruby' (van Wilgen 1951). Interior pink-red with a darker patch, exterior deep red. VVR 45; Dfl 6: 49. # ☼

'Wilhelm Schacht' (D. Hobbie 1973) [*R. discolor* × 'Prof. Hugo de Vries']. Soft pink, large flowered; growth, very vigorous. Very attractive. # ☼

'Wilhelmine Vuyk' see: **'Palestrina'**

'Willbrit' (Le Feber 1964) ['Britannia' × *R. williamsianum*]. Dark pink with darker markings, 7.5 cm wide, 5–8 flowers together, mid May; dwarf, flat-rounded. Similar to 'Oudijk's Sensation', but less winter hardy. #

'Willem III' [Ghent hybrid]. Orange-yellow, with an orange-red blotch. ☼

'William Austin' (J. Waterer, before 1915) [*R. catawbiense* hybrid]. Dark carmine-purple, speckled. #

'Willy' (C. B. van Nes [*R. kaempferi*]. Light pink. Surpassed by 'Betty'. # ☼

'Winston Churchill' (Felix & Dijkhuis 1949) [*R. kosterianum* clone; 'Koster's Brilliant Red' × an unknown seedling]. Dark orange-red. ☼

'Wintertime' (Boskoop Exp. Station, before 1963) ['Aladdin' × 'Amoena'; Kur.]. Geranium-red, 4 cm wide (= 'Midwinter'). # ☼

'Wyrneck' [Knap Hill]. Sulfur-yellow with a pink limb, late.

'Yodogawa' see: **R. yedoense**

'Zuidersee' (Koster & Sons 1936) [*R. campylocarpum* hybrid × 'Mrs. Lindsay Smith']. Cream-yellow, throat finely red punctate. Surpassed by 'Adriaan Koster'.

CARE. Within the scope of this book, the care of each individual species and cultivar cannot be covered. Generally speaking, however, it can be said that the susceptibility to frost damage increases with leaf size. The large leaved, evergreen types prefer a protected, woodland site in an acid, humus soil, or also in alkaline soils well prepared with organic material. The small leaved types usually grow in the mountains in full sun on open slopes; therefore preferring an open site in the garden. Many will also succeed in an alkaline soil.

Lit. The literature on *Rhododendron* is quite extensive; a good recent bibliography is contained in Bean, Trees and Shrubs, 8th Edition, Vol. 3 (1976), which lists 108 titles; also Schwartz, D.: *Rhododendron*, a selected, annotated Bibliography; New York Botanic Garden, 1975 (a valuable list of works in the English language).

General and Culture
Berg, J., & L. Heft: *Rhododendron* und immergrüne Laubgehölze; Stuttgart 1969 ● Berg, J., & G. Krüssmann: Freiland-*Rhododendron*; Stuttgart 1951 ● Clarke, J.: Rhododendrons; Portland, Oregon, 1956 ● Cox, E. H. M. & P. A.: Modern Rhododendrons; London 1956 ● Cox, P. A.: Dwarf Rhododendrons; London 1973 ● Hume, H. H.: Azaleas, kinds and culture; New York 1949 ● Krüssmann, G.: Rhododendron, andere immergrüne Laubgehölze und Koniferen; Hamburg 1968.

Botanical and Taxonomic
Batta, J.: *Rhododendron*-Nomenklatur und -Taxonomie; in Jahrb. Dtsch. Rhod. Ges. 1972, 60–88 ● Bowers, C. G.: Rhododendrons and Azaleas, 2nd ed.; New York 1960 ● Cowan, J. M.: The *Rhododendron* Leaf; Edinburgh 1950 ● Hedegaard, J.: Beiträge zur Kenntnis der Morphologie von *Rhododendron*-Samen; in Jahrb. 1968 der Dtsch. Rhod. Ges. ● Hooker, J. D.: Rhododendrons of the Sikkim Himalaya; 1849–1851 ● Hutchinson, J.: Evolution and Classification of Rhododendrons; RYB 1946, 42–47 ● Leach, D.: Rhododendrons of the World; London 1962 ● Nitzelius, T. G.: Notes on some Japanese species of the genus *Rhododendron*; in Acta Hort. Gotob. 24, 135–173, 1962 ● Nitzelius, T. G.:

Mitteilungen über einige japanische *Rhododendron*; in Jahrb. Dtsch. Rhod. Ges. 1963, 41–73 ● Philipson, M. N. & W. R.: The Classification of *Rhododendron*; RYB 1971, 1–8 ● Philipson, M. N. & W. R.: The History of *Rhododendron* Classification; Not. Roy. Bot. Gard. Edinb. **32**, 223–238, 1973 ● Rehder, A., & E. H. Wilson: A monograph of Azaleas; Cambridge, Mass., USA, 1921 ● Royal Horticulture Society: The *Rhododendron* Handbook, Part I, *Rhododendron* Species (1967); Part II, *Rhododendron* Hybrids (1969) ● Schwartz, D.: *Rhododendron*; a selected annotated Bibliography; New York Bot. Garden 1975 ● Seithe, A.: Die Haarformen der Gattung *Rhododendron* L.; in Bot. Jahrb. 79, 1960 ● Sleumer, H.: Ein System der Gattung *Rhododendron* L.; in Bot. Jahrb. 74, 511–553, 1949 ● Sleumer, H.: Ericaceae-*Rhododendron*; in Flora Malesiana I, **64**, 474–668, 1966 ● Stevenson, J. B. (publisher): The Species of *Rhododendron*, ed. 2; London 1947 ● Urquhart, B. L.: The *Rhododendron*, vol. I (1958), vol. II (1962); Sharpthorne, England ● von Hoff, A.: Bestimmungsschlüssel für die gärtnerisch wichtigen *Rhododendron*-Arten; in Jahrb. Dtsch. Rhod. Ges. 1956, 57–92 ● Wright, D.: The grouping of Rhododendrons; in RYB 1964, 47–62; 1965, 105–118; 1971, 73–77.

Hybrids
Fleischmann, C.: Ein Beitrag zur Herkunft der japanischen Azaleen; in Dtsch. Baumschule Nr. 5 and 6, 1966 ● Fleischmann, C.: Die 'Diamant'-Azaleen, eine neue Rasse; Erwerbsgärtner 1971, 174 ● Fleischmann, C.: Die 'Frisia'-Azaleen; Erwerbsgärtner 1971, 782–784 ● Fleischmann, C.: Die 'Wiesmoor-Imperial'-Azaleen; Erwerbsgärtner 1971, 964–965 ● Fleischmann, C.: Sommerblühende 'Juwel'-Azaleen; Erwerbsgärtner 1972, 321 ● Fletcher, R. H.: The International *Rhododendron* Register; R.H.S., London 1958/ including annual supplements to the *Rhododendron* Year Books, later also *Rhododendron* and *Camellia* Year Books and after 1972, "Rhododendrons"/ also F. Schneider (Wageningen, Holland): Additions to the International *Rhododendron* Register 1959–1971 (59 pp.) ● Grootendorst, H. J.: Rhododendrons en Azaleas; Boskoop 1954 ● Lee, F. P.: The *Azalea* Book; Princeton 1958 ● Lucas Phillips, C. E., & P. N. Barber: The Rothschild Rhododendrons; London 1967 ● Millais, J. G.: Rhododendrons and the various hybrids, vol. II; London 1917 and 1924 ● Scheerlinck, H.: De *Azalea indica* L.; Antwerpen 1938 (as vol. I of the Tuinbouw Encycl.; contains also portraits of nearly all the Belgian hybridizers) ● Schmalscheidt, W.: Die Gruppe der *Rhododendron caucasicum*-hybriden; in Jahrb. Dtsch. Rhod. Ges. 1970, 48–67 ● Schmalscheidt, W.: Knap Hill-Azaleen in Aurich, erste Erfahrungen und Beurteilung; in Jahrb. Dtsch. Rhod. Ges. 1971, 37–57 ● Street, F.: Hardy Rhododendrons; London 1954 ● Van Veen, T.: Rhododendrons in America, a picture book; Portland, Oregon, 1969.

Periodicals
The *Rhododendron* (later "and *Camellia*") Year Book of the Roy. Hort. Soc. London, Vol. 1–25, 1956–1971 and its supplement "Rhododendrons" from 1972→ ● *Rhododendron* und immergrüne Laubgehölze; Jahrbücher der Deutschen Rhodendron Gesellschaft, 1937–1942; from 1952.→

RHODOLEIA Champ. ex Hook.—
RHODOLEIACEAE

Small, evergreen trees; leaves clustered at the branch tips, alternate, erect, oblong, entire, leathery tough, bluish beneath, long petioled; flowers in axillary, nodding, stalked heads, to 5 together, surrounded by a reddish calyx (somewhat resembling *Parrotia*); petals 2 or 4, pink, very irregular, clawed; stamens 7–10; flowers hermaphroditic.— 7 species from S. China to Java.

Rhodoleia championii Hook. Small, evergreen tree, about 10 m high; leaves elliptic-oblong, obtuse, light green and glossy, to 9 cm long and 4 cm wide, blue-green beneath, glabrous (!), tough, petiole 2–3 cm long; flowers dark pink, in about 3 cm wide capitula, outermost involucral leaves thin and scaly, brown silky pubescent, interior thick tomentose, February; fruits composed of about 5 hazelnut-size capsules. LF 152; BM 4509; HKT 86; FS 561. E. Tibet, China; Yunnan Prov. 1852. z9

R. forrestii Chun ex Exell. About 7 m high, but a large tree in its habitat; leaves elliptic-ovate, acuminate, 8–14 cm long, deep green above, venation on both sides yellowish, bluish beneath, with tiny golden-yellow stellate hairs (!! visible when magnified); flower heads solitary, about 2 to a branch, petals narrowly spathulate, carmine, calyx brownish and pink, February–March. BMns 27. NE. Upper Burma, China; NW. Yunnan Prov. 1920. z9

Prefers a woodland, humus soil, otherwise treated somewhat like *Rhododendron*.

RHODOTHAMNUS Riechenb.—ERICACEAE

Monotypic genus. Small evergreen shrub, very similar to *Rhododendron*, but the flowers 1–2(3) at the tips of the previous year's growth; calyx with 5 deep incisions, large, persistent; corolla rotate, with 5 large, outspread lobes; stamens 10, the corolla somewhat exserted; ovaries 5 locular, with many ovules; fruit a globose, 5 locular capsule.— E. Alps to Karawanken (Yugoslavian-Austrian border).

Rhodothamnus chamaecistus (L.) Reichenb. Evergreen shrub, with a bushy, tangled branching habit, 20–30 cm high, twigs glandular pubescent; leaves alternate, narrowly elliptic, 8–15 mm long, ciliate margined, leathery thick, dark green and glossy above, lighter beneath and somewhat pubescent; flowers 1–3, terminal, corolla flat-rotate, 2–2.5 cm wide, light purple, calyx lobes acute-lanceolate, stalk glandular pubescent, May–June. FS 1962; HF 2032; FFA 25 (= *Rhododendron chamaecistus* L.). Alps, on limestone; E. Siberia. 1786. z6 Fig. 151.

Difficult to cultivate; prefers a semishaded rock garden site, soil must be cool and top dressed with limestone chips; very slow growing.

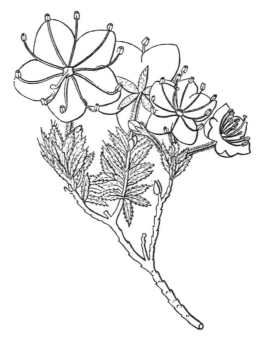

Fig. 151. *Rhodothamnus chamaecistus*

RHODOTYPOS Sieb. & Zucc.—Jetbead—
ROSACEAE

Monotypic genus. Deciduous shrub, branches opposite, brown, scaly at the base; leaves decussate, petioled, oval, acuminate, coarsely serrate; flowers solitary at the shoot tips, 4 parted, sepals small, lanceolate; stamens very numerous, carpels 2–6, distinct, style filamentous; fruitlets 1–6, but usually 4, nut-like, with a glossy black, brittle shell.

Rhodotypos kerrioides see: **R. scandens**

R. scandens (Thunb.) Mak. Often 1–2 m high in cultivation, to 5 m high shrub in Japan, twigs greenish brown, buds greenish with brown tips; leaves ovate, acute, 4–8 cm long, biserrate, rather glabrous; flowers solitary, white, 4–5 cm wide, May–June; fruits pea-sized, black, glossy, long persistent. BM 5805; Gfl 505; HM 1000 (= *R. kerrioides* S. & Z.). Japan, central China. 1866. z5

Easily cultivated in any good soil, prefers a lightly shaded site.

RHUS L. — Sumac — ANACARDIACEAE

Deciduous or evergreen trees or shrubs, sometimes climbing, usually more or less poisonous; leaves alternate, simple or 3 parted or odd pinnate, the leaflets entire or serrate; flowers usually inconspicuous, dioecious or polygamous, in axillary or terminal panicles; calyx deeply 5 parted, persistent, the 5 petals small, stamens 5, attached to the disk; ovaries unilocular; fruit a small, dry drupe. — About 250 species in the tropics and subtropics; many species have some varnish content.

Outline of the genus and the species covered in this work

Section 1. Sumac DC.
Leaves pinnate; flowers in terminal panicles; fruits red, pubescent:
R. chinensis, copallina, coriaria, glabra, michauxii, potaninii, pulvinata, punjabensis, typhina

Section 2. Toxicodendron Gray
Leaves pinnate or trifoliate; flowers in axillary panicles; fruits whitish to brownish, glabrous or bristly:
R. diversiloba, orientalis, radicans, silvestris, succedanea, toxicodendron, trichocarpa, verniciflua, vernix

Section 3. Lobadium DC.
Leaves trifoliate; flowers in short, catkin-like spikes, appearing before the leaves; fruits red, pubescent:
R. aromatica, trilobata

Rhus aromatica Ait. Deciduous shrub, prostrate, about 1 m high, shoots soft pubescent, entire plant pleasantly scented; leaves trifoliate, leaflets 3–7 cm long, the lateral ones ovate, sessile, the terminal leaflet ovate to obovate, to 7 cm long, base cuneate, coarsely crenate, fall foliage orange to red; flowers yellowish, in about 2 cm long spikes at the shoot tips, April; fruits globose, 6 mm thick, red, finely pubescent, dry. BB 2350; GSP 262 (= *R. canadensis* Marsh.). Eastern USA. 1759. Grows on dry, gravelly, stream banks in full sun in its habitat. z3 Fig. 154.

R. canadensis see: **R. aromatica**

R. chinensis Mill. Rounded, deciduous shrub or small tree, to 8 m high, twigs yellowish, pubescent at first, later glabrous; leaves pinnate, leaflets 7–13, ovate-oblong, 6–12 cm long, coarsely crenate, dark green above, brownish pubescent beneath, bright red in fall, rachis and leaf petiole distinctly winged (!!); inflorescences cream-white, in about 30 cm long and wide, terminal panicles (!), August–September; fruits rounded, flat orange-red, pubescent. MJ 1114; Gw 1: 99; SDK 4: 38; BC 3397 (= *R. javanica* Thunb. non L.; *R. osbeckii* Decne.; *R. semialata* Murr.). China, Japan. 1784. Prefers dry to moist soil. z8 Plate 68.

R. copallina L. Shining Sumac. Deciduous shrub, occasionally a small tree in its habitat, to 7 m high, twigs reddish and finely pubescent; leaves pinnate, 15–30 cm long, leaflets 9–21, oval-oblong to oval-lanceolate, 4–10 cm long, entire or with a few small teeth at the apex, glabrous and glossy above, pubescent beneath, purple-red in fall, rachis narrowly winged between the pinnae

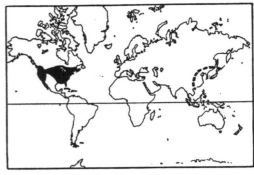

Fig. 152. Range of the genus *Rhus*

(!); flowers dioecious, in dense, axillary and terminal panicles, greenish, July; fruits carmine, pubescent, compressed. SS 104; SDK 4: 37; BB 2347; GTP 264. N. America. 1688. Very attractive fall color. z5 Plate 68.

R. coriaria L. Deciduous shrub, 1–3 m high, twigs finely and densely pubescent; leaves pinnate, to 18 cm long, with 9–15 leaflets, these ovate to elliptic, 3–5(7) cm long, coarse and obtusely serrate, gray-green, pubescent on both sides, but more densely so beneath, rachis somewhat winged between the apical leaflet pairs; flowers hermaphroditic, yellow-green, in densely pubescent, 10–25 cm long terminal panicles, June–July; fruits purple-brown, rough haired. HW 3: 33. S. Europe, Mediterranean region. 1629. The young shoots and leaves can be used in tanning leather. Ⓕ Italy, Sicily and S. Italy for tanning. z9! Fig. 153.

R. coriarioides see: **R. punjabensis**

R. diversiloba Torr. & Gray. Poison Oak. Erect shrub or also climbing by aerial roots, similar to *R. toxicodendron*, but the leaflets are obtuse (not acute !!), margins crenate (not serrate !); young shoots soft pubescent; leaves trifoliate, leaflets ovate to elliptic or obovate, 3–7 cm long, coarsely crenate or lobed, somewhat pubescent when young; flowers yellowish green, in stalked, small, 5–7 cm long, axillary panicles; fruits whitish, glabrous, abscising soon after ripe. MS 303; BR 31: 38. W. coast of N. America. 1845. Poisonous! Hardy! z6 Fig. 153.

R. glabra L. Smooth Sumac. Deciduous shrub, rarely over 3 m high, branches totally glabrous (!!), violet and pruinose; leaves pinnate, 20–30 cm long, leaflets 11–31, oblong-lanceolate, narrow and scabrous serrate, totally glabrous, underside usually blue-green, 5–12 cm long, fall color a beautiful red, rachis red; flowers greenish, in dense, erect, finely pubescent, 10–25 cm long panicles, July–August; fruits scarlet-red, finely glandular pubescent. BB 2349; GSP 258. N. America. 1620. The typical plant is almost always glabrous with pruinose shoots, distinguishing it from *R.* × *pulvinata* with which it is often confused in cultivation. Ⓕ USA, in windbreaks and for erosion control. z2

'Laciniata'. Leaflets deeply pinnatisect, otherwise like the species. RH 1863: 1. 1863.

R. henry see: **R. potaninii**

R. hirta see: **R. typhina**

R. hybrida see: **R. × pulvinata**

R. javanica see: **R. chinensis**

R. michauxii Sarg. Deciduous, stoloniferous shrub, 1 m high, branches densely pubescent; leaves pinnate, leaflets 9–15, oval-oblong, 5–10 cm long, coarsely serrate, densely brownish pubescent beneath (!), rachis winged under the terminal leaflet; flowers in 10–20 cm long panicles, green-yellow, June–July; fruits red, densely pubescent, compressed. GF 8: 405. SE. USA. 1806. Poisonous! z6

R. orientalis (Greene) Schneid. Deciduous, climbing shrub, very similar to *R. radicans*, but easily distinguished by the bristly fruits and the geographical range of the plant; young shoots soft pubescent; leaves trifoliate, entire, dull green above, pubescent only in the vein axils beneath. MJ 1113. Japan, China. 1865. z6

R. osbeckii see: **R. chinensis**

R. potaninii Maxim. Round crowned, deciduous tree, 5–8 m high, branches glabrous or finely pubescent; leaves pinnate, 20–35 cm long, leaflets 7–11, short, but distinctly stalked (!), oval-oblong to more lanceolate, 6–12 cm long, acuminate, entire, but often coarsely serrate on young plants, base oblique rounded, occasionally somewhat cordate, venation beneath lightly pubescent, rachis occasionally somewhat winged between the apical leaflets; flowers in 10–20 cm long, pendulous panicles, whitish, anthers yellow, May–June; fruits dark red, densely pubescent, pendulous. MD 1910: 103 (= *R. sinica* sensu Koehne non Diels; *R. henryi* Diels). Central and W. China. 1902. z5

R. × pulvinata Greene (*R. glabra* × *R. typhina*). Intermediate between the parents, branches totally finely and short pubescent, as is the inflorescence; fruit clusters bristly (= *R. hybrida* Rehd.). 1923. Occasionally occurring among the parents in the wild. Often erroneously labeled "*R. glabra*" in cultivation. z3

R. punjabensis Stewart var. **sinica** (Diels) Rehd. & Wils. Deciduous tree, 10–12 m high, branches short pubescent; leaves pinnate, leaflets 7–11, sessile, oval-oblong, 8–12 cm long, entire, base round to somewhat cordate, venation pubescent beneath, rachis narrowly winged on the apical portion, also totally winged on younger plants, then also with 11–17 leaflets; flowers whitish, in pendulous, pubescent, 12–20 cm long panicles, June–August; fruits red, 4 mm thick, in pubescent, pendulous panicles (= *R. sinica* Diels; *R. coriarioides* Dipp.). Central and W. China. 1890. Similar to *R. potaninii*, but pubescent. The species is not found in cultivation. z6

R. quercifolia see: **R. toxicodendron**

R. radicans L. Poison Ivy. Deciduous shrub, climbing by means of aerial roots (!), branches somewhat pubescent, leaflets 3, ovate-rhombic, 3–12 cm long, sparsely coarsely dentate or also entire, dark green and glabrous above, lighter and pubescent beneath, bright red to orange in fall; flowers greenish white, in small panicles,

Fig. 153. **Rhus.** Left, *R. diversiloba*; right *R. coriaria* (from Hooker, Hempel, & Wilhelm)

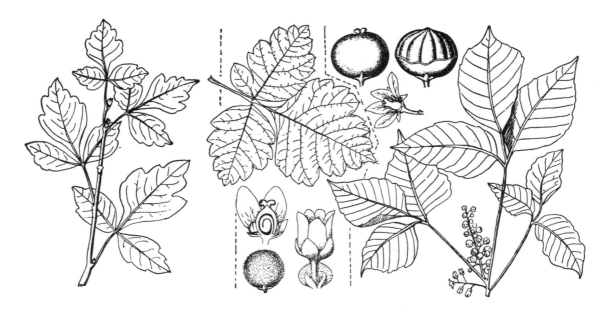

Fig. 154. **Rhus.** Left *R. trilobata;* center *R. aromatica;* right *R. radicans*

June–July; fruits globose, 5–6 mm thick, whitish to yellowish, glabrous or short pubescent. BB 2353; GSP 266; Rho 683 (1) (= *Toxicodendron radicans* Ktze.). Eastern USA. 1640. Inflammatory to the skin upon contact, handle only with gloves! z4 Fig. 154.

var. **rydbergii** (Small) Rehd. Shrubby habit (!), less than 1 m high; leaflets thickish, sinuately dentate, underside glabrous or pubescent only on the venation. Rho 43: 594 (2) (= *R. rydbergii* Small). Texas to Montana. 1918.

R. rydbergii see: **R. radicans** var. **rydbergii**

R. semialata see: **R. chinensis**

R. silvestris S. & Z. Small tree, to 10 m high, much shorter in cultivation, young shoots short pubescent, later rather glabrous, red-gray (!); leaves thin, to 40 cm long, leaflets 7–13, short stalked, oval-oblong, 4–10 cm long, with 15–28 distinct vein pairs (spaced at less than 5 mm apart!), slightly pubescent above, more densely so beneath, fall foliage an attractive scarlet-red; inflorescences about 15 cm long, pubescent, with outspread branches, June; fruits very oblique, nearly 1 cm wide, wider than high, yellow-brown. MJ 1110; SDK 4: 38. China, Korea, Japan. 1881. z8 Plate 68, 69.

R. sinica see: **R. potaninii** and **R. punjabensis**

R. succedanea L. Deciduous shrub or small tree, to about 9 m high; leaves pinnate, leaflets 9–11(15), elliptic-oblong to lanceolate, 6–12 cm long, glossy green above, with 12–15 vein pairs, gray or bluish beneath, glabrous, each blade half uneven in width; flowers very small, yellowish, in 9–12 cm long, axillary panicles; fruits kidney-shaped, 7–9 mm wide, yellow-brown, in pendulous panicles. MJ 1109; SDK 4: 39; LWT 174. China, Japan, Himalayas. 1863. In earlier times, the fruits of this plant provided the basis for candle wax in Japan and China. z5 Plate 68.

R. toxicodendron L. Poison Ivy, Poison Oak. Deciduous, not climbing (!) shrub, without aerial roots, only about 50 cm high, stoloniferous, shoots erect; leaflets 3, ovate-rhombic, rather tough, with 3–7 lobes, occasionally entire, pubescent beneath, fall color an attractive scarlet-red to orange; flowers greenish white, in loose, axillary, 3–7 cm long panicles; fruits greenish white, usually pubescent, globose, 5 mm thick. BB 2783; Rho 685 (1–2) (= *R. quercifolia* Steud.). 1937. N. America. Very poisonous! z4 Plate 68.

R. trichocarpa Miq. Small, deciduous, flat crowned tree, 4–8 m high, young shoots soft pubescent; leaves pinnate, leaflets 13–17, short stalked, broadly ovate, entire, 4–10 cm long, acuminate, base round, usually pubescent on both sides, with 10–16 vein pairs, fall color orange-red, rachis cylindrical, pubescent; flowers not very conspicuous, in pubescent panicles on 6–15 cm long stalks, June; fruits yellowish, bristly, 6 mm thick, the pubescent outer shell quickly abscising. MJ 1112; GF 10: 384. Japan, China. z8

R. trilobata Nutt. Deciduous shrub, usually rather erect, 1(2) m high, similar *R. aromatica,* but unpleasant smelling and with smaller leaves, less pubescent; young shoots pubescent but quickly becoming glabrous; leaves trifoliate, leaflets sessile or nearly so, elliptic to obovate, 2–3 cm long, with a few rounded teeth, cuneate at the base, terminal leaflet usually 3 lobed, somewhat pubescent only when young; flowers greenish (!), inconspicuous, March–April; fruits globose, red, pubescent, 6 mm thick. BB 2351; MS 304; SDK 4: 39. SW. USA. 1877. ⓕ USA, in windbreaks and screen plantings. z5 Fig. 154.

R. typhina L. Staghorn Sumac. Small, usually multistemmed, deciduous tree, seldom over 5 m high, or only a shrub, twigs with a dense velvety pubescence;

leaves pinnate, leaflets 11–31, oblong-lanceolate, deep green, acuminate, serrate, blue-green beneath, pubescent when young, fall color scarlet-red and orange; flowers greenish, in dense, very pubescent, 15–20 cm long, terminal panicles, June–July; fruits red, densely pubescent, in pyramidal clusters. BB 2348; GSP 263 (= *R. hirta* Sudw.). Eastern N. America. 1629. Ⓕ USA, erosion control. Likes a well drained to dry, but fertile soil; short lived. Bark rich in tannin content, particularly the root epidermis. z3 Plate 69.

'Dissecta'. Leaflets pinnatisect, nearly fern-like; inflorescence normal, like the species. MG 15: 211; RH 1907: 10; SL 353 (= var. *filicina* Spreng.). 1898. Plate 70.

'Laciniata'. Leaflets as finely incised as 'Dissecta', but the inflorescence contains many deeply incised bracts.

R. venenata see: **R. vernix**

R. vernicifera see: **R. verniciflua**

R. verniciflua Stokes. Varnish Tree. Deciduous tree, 15–20 m high, narrowly upright when young (!), young shoots pubescent, later glabrous and gray-yellow, with lenticels; leaves pinnate, 25–50 cm long, with 7–13 leaflets, these ovate-oblong, 7–15 cm long, 3–6 cm wide, with 8–16 vein pairs (spaced more than 5 mm apart [!], see *R. silvestris*), acuminate, entire, pubescent beneath when young, eventually only pubescent on the midrib, rachis cylindrical; flowers yellowish white, in loose, pendulous, 15–20 cm long panicles, June; fruits straw-yellow, nearly pea-sized. LF 206; MJ 1111; MD 21: Pl. 12; SL 307 (= *R. vernicifera* DC.). Japan, middle and W. China, Himalayas. 1874. This is the source of lacquer in Japan and China. Poisonous! z9 Plate 68.

R. vernix L. Poison Sumac. Generally only shrubby, 2–3 m high, occasionally a small tree, crown usually broad and round, stiffly branched, orange, later light gray; leaves pinnate, with 7–13 leaflets, these short stalked, elliptic to more oblong, 4–10 cm long, acuminate, entire, base cuneate, slightly pubescent when young, later totally glabrous, with 8–12 vein pairs, underside usually bluish (!), fall color orange-red; flowers greenish yellow, in 10–20 cm long, narrow, pendulous panicles, June–July; fruits globose, about 5 mm thick, yellowish white, pendulous and long persistent. SS 107–108; BB 2353; GTP 267; SDJ 4: 38; KTF 126 (= *R. venenata* DC.). Eastern N. America, particularly in swampy sites. 1713. Poisonous! z3 Plate 68.

The above mentioned species are fast growing, hardy, usually with very attractive fall foliage color, but are often very poisonous. The poisonous species should be avoided. All like a good, fertile soil in a sunny site.

Lit. Graebner, L.: Die in Deutschland winterharten *Rhus*; in Mitt. DDG 1906, 100–107 ● Barkley, F. A.: A monographic study of *Rhus* and its immediate allies in North and Central America, including the West Indies; in Mo. Bot. Gard. Ann. **24**, 265–498, 1937 (ill.). ● Barkley, F. A.: *Schmaltzia*; in Amer. Midl. Nat. **24**, 647–665, 1940 (ill.).

RIBES L. — Currant, Gooseberry — SAXIFRAGACEAE

Deciduous, occasionally evergreen, low to medium-sized, prickly or thornless shrubs; leaves alternate, simple, petiolate, folded in the bud stage, occasionally involuted, frequently lobed, crenate or incised; flowers hermaphroditic, sometimes unisexual, usually 5, occasionally 4 parted, in few or many flowered racemes; petals 4–5, inserted in the calyx throat, often only small and scale-like, usually shorter than the calyx; stamens 4 or 5; ovaries inferior, unilocular, styles 2, distinct or connate; fruit a juicy, few or many-seeded berry, crowned by the calyx limb. — About 150 species in the northern cool and temperate zones, also in S. America from the Andes to Patagonia.

Outline of the species and hybrids mentioned in this book

Subgenus I: Berisia (Spach) Jancz.
Shrubs, thornless, occasionally with small prickles at the leaf nodes; flowers dioecious, usually in racemes.

Section 1: Euberisia Jancz.
Flowers in erect racemes; male flowers without ovaries, anthers on the female flowers without pollen, petals tiny; stamens much shorter than the sepals; leaf buds with dry scales; branches always thornless:
R. alpinum, distans, glaciale, luridum, maximowiczii, orientale, vilmorinii

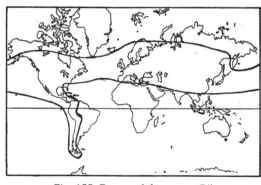

Fig. 155. Range of the genus *Ribes*

Section 2: Diacantha Jancz.
Flowers and buds like that of Section 1; young twigs with paired, small prickles at the nodes, often with small, scattered bristles:
R. diacanthum, giraldii, pulchellum

Section 3: Davidia Jancz.
Flowers like those of Section 1, but with evergreen leaves:
R. henryi, laurifolium

Section 4: **Hemibotrya** Jancz.
Flowers grouped 2–9 in clusters; male flowers with sterile ovules in the ovaries, female flowers with sterile pollen; leaf buds with leafy scales; branches always thornless:
R. fasciculatum

Section 5: **Parilla** Jancz.
Flowers in racemes, otherwise like Section 4; leaves often evergreen:
R. gayanum

Subgenus II: **Ribesia** Berl.
Flowers hermaphroditic, usually in racemes; thornless shrubs; bud scales leafy (but membranous in Section 12).

Section 6: **Microsperma** Jancz.
Flowers 1–2, greenish; calyx cupulate; flower stalk with 2 bracts; ovaries glandular bristled; style not divided; seeds tiny, more than 50 in a fruit:
R. ambiguum

Section 7: **Symphocalyx** Berl.
Flowers in racemes, yellow, calyx tubular, ovaries glabrous; fruits smooth, black or yellow; leaves rolled up in the bud stage (!):
R. aureum, odoratum

Section 8: **Calobotrya** Spach
Flowers in racemes, red, white or yellow, protogynous, calyx cupulate to tubular; plants glandular-glutinous; fruits often glandular, usually black and pruinose:
R. bethmontii, fontenayense, glutinosum, gordonianum, malvaceum, nevadense, sanguineum, viscosissimum, wolfii

Section 9: **Cerophyllum** (Spach) Jancz.
Flowers small, white or pink, protogynous, 2–7 in racemes; calyx cylindrical, angular (!); ovaries glandular or smooth; phyllotaxy 3/8 (all other sections 2/5!):
R. cereum, inebrians

Section 10: **Botrycarpum** A. Rich.
Floral racemes erect or pendulous, greenish or brown, red or white, bracts usually linear; calyx tubular to campanulate; ovaries usually glandular; fruits black or brown; plants with resin glands:
R. americanum, bracteosum, culverwellii, fragrans, fuscescens, hudsonianum, nigrum, petiolare, procumbens, ussuriense, viburnifolium

Section 11: **Heritiera** Jancz.
Flower racemes erect, stalks usually thin, flowers whitish to reddish, rotate to cupulate, protandrous; anthers reflexed after flowering; ovaries glandular-bristled; fruits black or red; low or procumbent shrubs:
R. coloradense, glandulosum, laxiflorum

Section 12: **Ribesia** Berl.
Flower racemes pendulous or outspread, usually many flowered; flowers rotate to top-shaped, occasionally campanulate, green reddish or purple; fruits red or purple, occasionally black; buds with dry membranous scales; erect, occasionally procumbent shrubs:
R. emodense, gondouinii, holosericum, houghtonianum, koehneanum, mandshuricum, meyeri, moupinense, multiflorum, petraeum, silvestre, spicatum, triste, urceolatum, warszewiczii

Subgenus III: **Grossularioides** Jancz.
Shrubs, prickly and stiff bristled; flowers cupulate, hermaphroditic, 6–20 in pendulous racemes; bracts tiny; fruits black or red, glandular bristly, separated from the stalk; buds with dry membranous scales.

Fig. 156. **Ribes.** Flowers and their parts. a. R. distans; b. R. vilmorinii; c. R. orientale; d. R. glaciale; e. R. luridum; f. R. maximowiczii; g. R. giraldii; h. R. gayanum; i. R. ambiguum; k. R. wolfii; l. R. aureum (most from Janczewski)

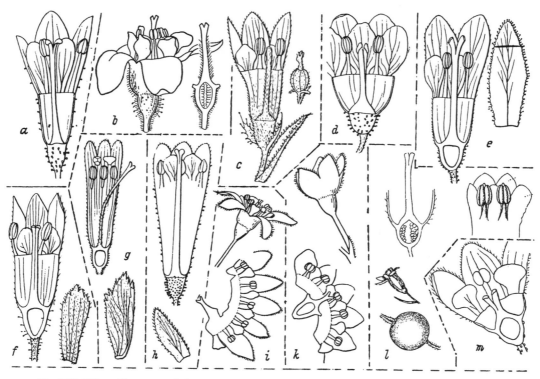

Fig. 157. **Ribes.** Flowers and their parts. a. *R. sanguineum*; b. *R.* × *fontenayense*; c. *R. malvaceum*; d. *R. nevadense*; e. *R. glutinosum*; f. *R. viscosissimum*; g. *R. cereum*; h. *R. inebrians*; i. *R. hudsonianum*; k. *R. petiolare*; l. *R. americanum*; m. *R. fragrans* (most from Janczewski)

Section 13: Grossularioides (Jancz.) Rehd.
    With the characteristics of the Subgenus:
        R. lacustre, montigenum

Subgenus IV: Grossularia (Mill.) A. Rich.
    Flowers hermaphroditic, 1–4 in small racemes; calyx top-shaped to tubular, never rotate; fruits not separated from the stalk; buds with dry membranous scales; twigs with paired prickles at the nodes, occasionally nearly absent, often also bristly.

Section 14: Eugrossularia Engl.
    Petals flat or somewhat concave; anthers obtuse, never glandular; styles pubescent or glabrous; flowers greenish, whitish or purple, occasionally red:
        R. aciculare, alpestre, burejense, cynosbati, darwinii, divaricatum, grossularioides, hirtellum, inerme, irriguum, leptanthum, lydiae, magdalene, missouriense, niveum, oxyacanthoides, pinetorum, quercetorum, rotundifolium, setosum, succirubrum, uva-crispa

Section 15: Robsonia Bert.
    Petals convolute, involute or convex; anthers sagittate or obtuse and glandular, occasionally without glands; style always glabrous; flowers usually red to scarlet, 5 or only 4 parted; fruits bristly or glandular, never smooth:
        R. californicum, kochii, lobbii, menziesii, roezlii, speciosum

Ribes aciculare Sm. Very similar to *R. burejense*. Shrub, to 1 m or more in height, branches short prickled and bristly, occasionally with 5–7 (!) prickles at a node;

leaves rounded, 3 cm wide, 3–5 lobed, glossy above, occasionally glandular pubescent; flowers pink or light green, ovaries usually glabrous, occasionally somewhat glandular bristled, style split to the middle; fruits globose, red, green or yellow. JRi 100. Siberia. 1903. z3 Fig. 160.

R. affine see: **R. laxiflorum**

R. albidum see: **R. glutinosum 'Albidum'**

R. albinervium see: **R. triste**

R. alpestre Wall. Strong growing, erect shrub, to 3 m high, very prickly or bristly, young shoots reddish, prickles usually 3 parted, to 2 cm long; leaves rounded, 2–5 cm wide, 3–5 lobed, incised dentate, slightly pubescent to nearly glabrous, cordate at the base; flowers inconspicuous, greenish red and white, grouped 1–2 on short stalks, ovaries glandular bristled, April–May; fruits globose to ellipsoid, 1.5 cm long, purple-red, glandular bristled, sour. JRi 102. Himalayas, W. China. z6 Plate 77; Fig. 160

var. **giganteum** Jancz. To 5 m high, with up to 3 cm long, stiff thorns; flowers glabrous; fruits green, smooth. W. China. 1908. Much used in China for very dense, tall, impenetrable hedges.

R. alpinum L. Alpine Currant. Deciduous shrub, 1–2 m high, densely bushy and well branched, branches glabrous, thornless, light gray, later somewhat exfoliating; leaves 3–5 lobed, rounded, breaking from bud very early, to 5 cm long, usually smaller, somewhat pubescent above, underside glossy, yellow or whitish yellow in fall; flowers dioecious, inconspicuous, in erect racemes, yellowish green, male racemes medium long, with many flowers, female racemes few-flowered, April–May; fruits dark red, mealy and dull tasting, long persistent. GPN 437–438; HM Pl. 144. Mountain forests in Europe and Siberia. 1588. z2 ∅ ⚭

'Aureum'. Slow growing; leaves yellow at first, later only yellow-green. Found in Belgium around 1878.

'Compactum' (Berndt). Particularly dense growth, a low selection. Berndt, Zirlau, Germany. ∅

'Laciniatum'. Leaves deeply lobed and incised dentate. Before 1864.

var. *mandshuricum* see: **R. distans**

'Pumilum'. Only about 1 m high, very densely branched, branches thin; leaves smaller than those of the species. Found around 1828 in England and widely planted today. ∅

'Verno-aureum'. Leaves golden-yellow on new growth, later normal green. Developed in 1927 by Wroblewski, Kornik, Poland.

A number of cultivars exist today such as, **'Weber'**, **'Schmidt'**, **'Green Mound'** and others which have better growth habits and foliage than the species.

R. ambiguum Maxim. Small shrub, scarcely 60 cm high, occasionally epiphytic (!); leaves small, rounded kidney-shaped, 2–5 cm wide, 3–5 lobed, lobes short, obtuse, usually glabrous above, glandular-glutinous beneath; flowers grouped 1–2 (!), greenish, 12 mm wide, stalks 1 cm long, sepals elliptic; fruits nearly globose, green (!), glandular pubescent, translucent. JRi 41–42. Japan, China; Szechwan Prov., commonly found on older trees. 1915. Interesting and hardy, but seldom found in cultivation. z6 Fig. 156.

R. americanum Mill. Deciduous shrub, 1–1.5 m high, branches thin, nodding, yellow glandular; leaves with yellow gland spots on both sides (!), 3 lobed, the lobes acute, serrate, 5–8 cm long and wide, fall color scarlet to red-brown; flowers numerous in about 10 cm long racemes, pendulous, tube greenish yellow, April–May; fruits about 6 mm long, black, pulp greenish, July. BB 1874; GSP 160; RMi 149; JRi 81–82 (= *R. floridum* Mill.). Northern N. America, woodlands. 1727. z2 Plate 72; Fig. 157. ∅ ⊕

R. amictum see: **R. roezlii**

R. appendiculatum see: **R. petiolare**

R. aureum Pursh. Golden Currant. Upright, deciduous shrub, to 2 m high, bark brown, young twigs glabrous or finely pubescent; leaves rounded, usually 3 lobed, 3–5 cm wide, coarsely dentate, the lobes widespread, most only ciliate on the margins, otherwise glabrous, fall color red, petiole ciliate at the base; flowers yellow, fragrant, petals often becoming reddish, sepals outspread, inclined together after flowering (!), racemes

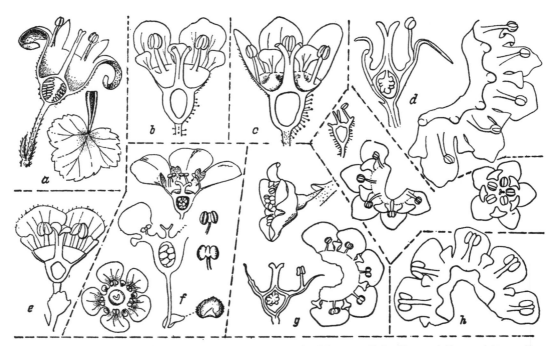

Fig. 158. **Ribes.** Flowers and their parts. a. *R. nigrum*; b. *R. glandulosum*; c. *R. laxiflorum*; d. *R. urceolatum*; e. *R. spicatum*; f. *R. silvestre*; g. *R. warszewiczii*; h. *R. koehneanum*; i. (shown above h) *R. coloradense* (from Janczewski, Schmidt, Baillon)

Plate 65

Rhododendron 'Attraction'
in the Boskoop Experiment Station, Holland

Rhododendron 'Adriaan Koster'
in RHS Gardens, Wisley, England

Rhododendron 'Broughtonii Aureum' in the Royal Botanic Gardens, Kew, England

Plate 66

Rhododendron 'Marchioness of Lansdowne'
in the Boskoop Experiment Station, Holland

Rhododendron 'Mrs. Helen Koster'
in the Boskoop Experiment Station, Holland

Rhododendron 'Mrs. E. C. Stirling' at the entrance to the Royal Botanic Gardens, Kew, England

Plate 67

Rhododendron (Azaleodendron) 'Galloper Light' in the Boskoop Experiment Station, Holland

Rhododendron 'White Pearl' (= 'Halopeanum') in the Royal Botanic Garden, Edinburgh, Scotland

Plate 68

Rhus. a. *R. vernix;* b. *R. copallina;* c. *R. silvestris;* d. *R. succedanea;* e. *R. verniciflua;*
f. *R. chinensis;* g. *R. toxicodendron*
(material from wild plants)

Plate 69

Rhus typhina, after leaf drop in the Dortmund Botanic Garden, W. Germany

Rhus silvestris in its native habitat in Japan
Photo: Dr. S. Watari, Tokyo

Plate 70

Rhus typhina 'Dissecta'
in the Dortmund Botanic Garden, W. Germany

Ribes speciosum in the Park of Lord Bruntisfield,
near Kenmare, Ireland

Ribes × *magdalenae*, enlarged

Ribes × *darwinii*

Both photos: Friedrich Koch

Plate 71

Ribes. a. *R. orientale;* b. *R. glaciale;* c. *R. luridum;* d. *R. longeracemosum;* e. *R. giraldii;* f. *R. pulchellum;* g. *R. moupinense;* h. *R. inebrians;* i. *R. nevadense;* k. *R. petraeum;* l. *R. bracteosum;* m. *R. meyeri*
(material from wild plants)

Plate 72

Ribes. a. *R. glutinosum;* b. *R. sanguineum;* c. *R. americanum;* d. *R. malvaceum;* e. *R. ussuriense;*
f. *R. viscosissimum;* g. *R. viburnifolium;* h. *R. lacustre* (material from wild plants)

Plate 73

Salix lanata
in the Copenhagen Botanic Garden, Denmark

Rosa richardii
in the National Rosarium, Dortmund, W. Germany

Salix × *boydii*
both in the Dortmund Botanic Garden, W. Germany

Rubus cockburnianus

Plate 74

Salix alba 'Tristis'
both in a park in Bade

Salix × *sepulcralis*
ienna, Austria

Sambucus nigra 'Purpurea'
in the Hillier Arboretum

Salix helvetica
in the Zurich Botanic Garden, Switzerland

Plate 75

Sarmienta repens
in the Royal Botanic Garden, Edinburgh, Scotland

Schisandra rubriflora
in the Royal Botanic Gardens, Kew, England

Sassafras albidum var. *molle*
in its habitat in Oregon, USA

Solandra grandiflora
in a garden in Spain

Plate 76

Solanum aviculare
in the Dublin Botanical Garden, Ireland

Sparmannia africana 'Plena'
in a garden in Spain

Stachyurus praecox 'Gracilis'
in the Royal Botanic Gardens, Kew, England

Staphylea holosericea 'Rosea'
in RHS Gardens, Wisley, England

Plate 77

Robinia pseudoacacia 'Microphylla'
in the Gisselfeld Park, Denmark

Robinia pseudoacacia 'Tortuosa'
in the Royal Botanic Gardens, Kew, England

Ribes. a. *R. setosum;* b. *R. alpestre;* c. *R. divaricatum;* d. *R. menziesii;* e. *R. hirtellum;*
f. *R. burejense;* g. *R. cynosbati;* h. *R. leptanthum* (material from wild plants)

Plate 78

Rosa wichuraiana in its native habitat in Japan

Rosa laevigata in its native habitat in Japan
Both photos: Dr. Watari, Tokyo

Plate 79

Rosa willmottiae
Photo: Archivbild

Rosa foetida in its native habitat in Asia Minor
Photo: Wilh. Schacht, Munich

Plate 80

Rosa hugonis
Photo: Archivbild

Rosa sericea f. *pteracantha*
in Dortmund, W. Germany

Rosa roxburghii in Pruhonice Park,
near Uhrineves, Czechoslovakia
Photo: Dr. A. Pilat, Prague

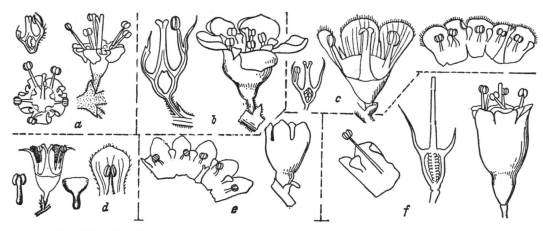

Fig. 159. **Ribes.** Flowers and their parts. a. *R. mandshuricum;* b. *R. emodense;* c. *R. meyeri;*
d. *R. petraeum;* e. *R. moupinense;* f. *R. longeracemosum* (most from Janczewski)

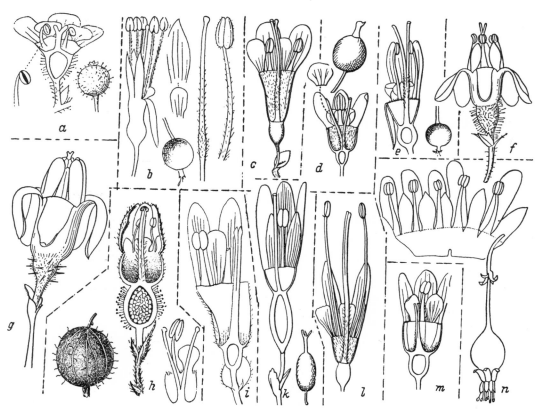

Fig. 160. **Ribes.** Flowers and their parts. a. *R. lacustre;* b. *R. neveum;* c. *R. setosum;* d. *R. oxycanthoides;* e. *R. divaricatum;* f. *R. alpestre;* g. *R. pinetorum;* h. *R. uva-crispa* var. *reclinatum;* i. *R. leptanthum;* k. *R. stenocarpum;* l. *R. rotundifolium;* m. *R. aciculare;* n. *R. grossularioides* (most from Janczewski)

Fig. 161. **Ribes.** Left *R. aureum;* middle *R. bracteosum;* right *R. triste* (from Abrams)

pendulous, 5–6 cm long, with 5–15 flowers, April–May; fruits pea-sized, purple-brown to black, sour. JRi 66; BB 1877; HM 980 (= *R. tenuiflorum* Lindl.). Western N. America to Mexico. 1812. Used as an understock for currants and gooseberries, but not as frequently as *R. odoratum* (with which it is often confused!). Ⓕ USA, in windbreaks. See also: **R. odoratum.** z2 Fig. 156, 161.

'Chrysococcum'. Fruits yellow. 1895. ♂♀

R. × bethmontii Jancz. (= *R. malvaceum* × *R. sanguineum*). Habit like that of *R. sanguineum;* leaves more rugose, like those of *R. malvaceum,* abscising early, both sides short glandular, pubescent beneath; flowers 10–20 in drooping racemes, carmine-pink, exterior pubescent, tube nearly urceolate, stamens shorter than the petals, pollen sterile (!), style nearly twice as long as the tube (!), conical at the base; fruits black, sets fruit only by cross pollination with another species. JRi 192. Discovered around 1904 by Daniel Bethmont, Chateau Ruffec, France. z6 ✛

R. biebersteinii see: **R. petraeum** var. **beibersteinii**

R. billardii see: **R. fasciculatum** var. **chinense**

R. bracteosum Dougl. Upright, deciduous shrub, 1.5–2 (3) m high, young shoots scattered pubescent and glandular; leaves thin, circular, 5–7 lobed (!), 5–20 cm (!) wide, lobes deep, ovate to lanceolate, scabrous biserrate, resin glands beneath; flowers greenish or reddish, in long, to 20 cm (!), erect racemes, fruits globose, pea-sized, black, white pruinose, with yellow gland spots, edible. JRi 69–70; MS 140; BM 7419. Alaska to N. California. 1895. z7 Plate 71; Fig. 161. ∅|♂♀|✗

R. burejense F. Schmidt. Thorny shrub, similar to *R. cynosbati,* to about 1 m high, branches usually very bristly, with thorns at the nodes; leaves rounded, 2–6 cm wide, deeply 3–5 lobed, with obtuse, dentate lobes, base cordate, soft pubescent and glandular; flowers grouped 1–2, brownish, stalks 3–6 mm long, calyx broadly

campanulate, stamens longer than the petals, style glabrous (!); fruits 1 cm thick, green, very bristly (!), edible. NK 15: 9; JRi 99. NE. Asia. 1903. z5 Plate 77. ♂♀✗

R. californicum Hook. & Arn. Deciduous shrub, closely related to *R. menziesii,* but branches without bristles (!); leaves totally or nearly glabrous; flowers green or reddish, ovaries bristly, but only the shorter bristles occasionally glandular, petals obovate, about half as long as the filaments; fruits globose, densely bristled. JRi 95–96; MS 167. California. z7 Fig. 166.

R. caucasicum see: **R. petraeum** var. **biebersteinii**

R. cereum Dougl. Deciduous shrub, much branched, to 1 m high, young shoots finely glandular pubescent; leaves rounded kidney-shaped, 1–4 cm wide, 3–5 lobed, the lobes round, crenate, rather glabrous above, underside glandular pubescent and gray-green; flowers white, greenish to yellowish, tubular, 6–8 mm long, few in short, pendulous racemes, sepals 2 mm long, petals tiny, circular, styles long pubescent (!!), April–May; fruits bright red, pea-sized, globose, smooth and glossy. BB 1876; MS 142; JRi 68; BM 3008. Western N. America, dry hills. z5 Fig. 157, 165. ✛ ♂♀

var. **farinosum** Jancz. Habit somewhat weeping, young shoots violet; leaves gray-white glandular-resinous; flowers white or pink. N. America, mountains along the Columbia River. ✛

R. coloradense Cov. Procumbent shrub, to about 50 cm high, young shoots pubescent, similar to *R. glandulosum;* leaves thin, wider than long, rounded, 5–8 cm wide, most 5 lobed, base deeply cordate, glabrous above, venation somewhat pubescent beneath, with tiny glands, lobes triangular, irregularly crenate; flowers 6–12 in erect, glandular, pubescent, 2–5 cm long racemes, greenish to reddish, sepals outspread, petals purple, fan-shaped, June–July; fruits black, 1 cm thick, not pruinose, sparsely glandular. JRi 48. SW. USA. 1905. z6 Fig. 158.

R. cruentum see: **R. roezlii** var. **cruentum**

R. × **culverwellii** MacFarlane (*R. nigrum* × *R. uva-crispa*). Habit like that of *R. nigrum*, vigorous, densely branched, branches totally thornless; leaves like *R. uva-crispa*, nearly totally without resin glands (!); calyx cup glabrous inside, style somewhat pubescent; fruits 2–4 together, black-red, sour, seedless, finely pubescent, usually not developing fully. GC 12: 271; 44: 120; JRHS 28: 169 (= *R. schneideri* Maurer). Around 1880. Looks almost like a gooseberry without the bristles. z6 ⚭

R. cynosbati L. Deciduous shrub, thorny, 1 (1.5) m high, branches thin, pendulous, with simple to 3-part thorns, occasionally also thornless, prickles about 1 cm long, thin; leaves rounded, 3–5 cm wide, 3–5 lobed, incised serrate, more or less soft haired; flowers in racemes of 2–3, cupule campanulate, sepals brownish green, stamens slightly longer than the petals, ovaries bristly; fruits globose to ellipsoid, 1 cm thick, wine-red, bristly, edible. JRi 108; BC 3406; BB 1865; RMi 152. Eastern USA. 1759. z2 Plate 77; Fig. 162. ⚭✖

R. × **darwinii** F. Koch (*R. menziesii* × *R. niveum*). Intermediate between the parents, strong upright habit, young twigs light brown, prickles simple or 3-part compound; leaves similar to those of *R. niveum*, variable in size, 5 lobed, crenate, brown speckled in spring, finely pubescent; flowers grouped 1–4 in pendulous racemes, sepals red, whitish at the apex, reflexed, petals white, style to 15 mm long, reddish; fruits globose, black, sourish, glabrous. DB 9: 27. Originated in 1952. z6 Plate 70. ⊕

R. davianum see: **R. glutinosum** 'Albidum'

Fig. 162. *Ribes cynosbati* (from Schmidt, Guimpel)

R. diacanthum Pall. Upright, deciduous shrub, to 2 m high, branches glabrous, with small paired prickles under the nodes, next to these, other smaller, scattered prickles, new growth appears early; leaves rounded, ovate to obovate, 2.5–3.5 cm long, slightly 3 lobed, the lobes obtuse, sparsely dentate, glossy above; flowers in

Fig. 163. **Ribes.** Left *R. diacanthum,* middle *R. niveum;* right *R. menziesii* (from Bot. Reg., Schmidt)

small, erect racemes, greenish yellow, April–May; fruits globose, small, scarlet-red, sourish, glabrous. JRi 161; NK 15: 2 (= *R. saxatile* Pall.). N. Asia; Tianshan to N. Korea and Turkestan. 1781. z2 Fig. 163. ✛

R. dikuscha see: **R. petiolare**

R. distans Jancz. Deciduous shrub, very similar to *R. alpinum*, 60–70 cm high; leaves rounded, to 5 cm long and 6 cm wide, 3–5 lobed, the lobes acute (!), base cordate (!); flowers dioecious, male racemes with 8–12 flowers, erect, 1–2 cm long, calyx top-shaped, greenish, pistillate flowers grouped 2–6; fruits globose, scarlet-red, nearly sessile, mid August. JRi 166 (= *R. alpinum* var. *mandshuricum* Maxim.; *R. maximowiczianum* Komar.). Manchuria. 1915. z5 Fig. 156.

R. divaricatum Dougl. Shrub to 3 m high, branches gray to brown, occasionally bristly, thorns 1–2 cm long, stiff, stout, hooked (!); leaves rounded-cordate, 2–6 cm wide, mostly 5 lobed, venation beneath usually pubescent; flowers greenish purple, grouped 2–4, on thin stalks, calyx campanulate, sepals oblong, April–May; fruits globose, 1 cm thick, dark red to black, distinctly pruinose. MS 154; JRi 112 b-c; BR 1359. Western N. America, in the mountains. 1826. Used in hybridizing mildew-resistant gooseberries ('Robustenta', 'Resistenta', etc.). z4 Plate 77; Fig. 160, 167. ⚮

R. echinatum see: **R. lacustre**

R. emodense Rehd. Closely related to *R. petraeum*, young shoots glabrous and red; leaves 3–5 lobed, to 12 cm wide, base cordate, the lobes acute and glandular, pubescent beneath; flowers greenish with a trace of red, in 10–12 cm long racemes, calyx nearly campanulate, pubescent or nearly glabrous, sepals broadly obovate, mostly outspread, petals cuneate, erect, style as long as the stamens; fruits large, red to black, seeds large. JRi 32–33 (= *R. himalayense* Decne. non Royle; *R. meyeri* sensu Schneid. non Maxim.). Himalayas, China; Yunnan Prov., in the mountains. 1908. z6 Fig. 159.

R. fasciculatum S. & Z. Deciduous shrub, 1–1.5 m high, branches stiff, thick, brownish, grooved, usually totally glabrous when young; leaves appearing very early, but persisting for a long time, rounded, 4–7 cm wide, usually wider than long, 3–5 lobed, glabrous or somewhat pubescent; flowers 2–9 in clustered racemes, yellow, fragrant, cupulate, April–May; fruits globose, scarlet-red, pulp yellowish, dry-mealy, ripening in October. JRi 116; ST 38. Japan, Korea. 1884. z5 Fig. 165.

var. **chinense** Maxim. More vigorous habit, taller; leaves to 10 cm long, rather semi-evergreen. NK 15: 1; MG 14: 571 (= *R. billardii* Carr.). N. China, Korea, Japan. 1867. z9

R. floridum see: **R. americanum**

R. × fontenayense Jancz. (*R. sanguineum* × *R. uva-crispa*). Intermediate between the parents, but thornless, about 1 m high; leaves tough, rounded, 3–5 lobed, about 6–8 cm long and wide, truncate at the base, somewhat cordate, pubescent beneath; flowers wine-red, grouped 3–6 in small, horizontally spreading to somewhat pendulous racemes, tube cupulate, broader than long, ovaries glandular pubescent, style pubescent, flowering rather abundantly; fruits seldom develop, purple-black, pruinose and glandular. JRi 193 to 194. Probably originated before 1906 by Billard in Fontenay-aux-Roses, France. z5 Fig. 157. ✛

R. fragrans Pall. (non Lodd.!). Deciduous shrub, similar to *R. hudsonianum*, 30–70 cm high; leaves rounded kidney-shaped, tough, 5–6 cm wide, 3 lobed, the lobes only slightly developed, sparsely pubescent beneath, but very glandular, entire plant aromatic (scented like balm!); flowers white, 1 cm wide, about 15 in loose, erect, to 7 cm long racemes, sepals oblong; fruits brownish, juicy, 8 mm thick. JRi 74. Manchuria, E. Siberia, on gravelly slopes. 1917. See also: **R. odoratum**. z3 Fig. 157. ✛

R. × fuscescens (Jancz.) (*R. bracteosum* × *R. nigrum*). Very similar to *R. bracteosum*, but with reddish brown flowers (!), bracts smaller and linear (spathulate on *R. bracteosum*), flower racemes shorter, erect to nodding, fruits larger. Before 1905.

R. gayanum (Spach) Steud. Evergreen shrub, to 1.5 m high, young shoots glandular or soft pubescent; leaves tough, rounded, 3–6 cm long, 3–5 lobed, lobes obtuse, pubescent on both sides; flowers campanulate, yellow, fragrant, pubescent, in 3–6 cm long, erect racemes, May; fruits globose, black, good tasting, pubescent, late July. JRi 141–142; BM 7611 (as *R. villosum*) (= *R. villosum* C. Gay non Nutt.). Chile, in the mountains. 1858. Hardiest of the evergreen species from S. America. z8 Fig. 156. # ✛

R. giraldii Jancz. Divaricate shrub, less than 1 m high, branches outspread, bristly and prickly, also finely pubescent when young, prickles stout at the nodes; leaves small, rounded to kidney-shaped, about 3.5 cm long and wide, 3–5 lobed, glandular pubescent, persisting long into the fall; flowers greenish brown, in erect to nodding, 3–7 cm long, dry (!) racemes, May; fruits globose, red, glandular pubescent. JRi 163. N. China; Shensi Prov. 1905. Closely related to *R. pulchellum*, but pubescent. z6 Plate 71; Fig. 156.

R. glaciale Wall. Upright, deciduous shrub, 2(4) m high, similar to *R. alpinum*, young shoots reddish, glabrous; leaves rounded-ovate, 3–5 lobed, the lobes acute, middle lobe usually much longer, loosely glandular bristled; flowers appearing soon after the new leaves, purple-brown (!), small, grouped 3–20 in 2–5 cm long racemes, calyx usually very finely pubescent, April–May, fruits globose, scarlet-red, glabrous, fleshy, sourish. JRi 173; SNp 61. China; Yunnan, Hupeh Provs., Tibet, in the higher mountains. 1823. z5 Plate 71; Fig. 156.

R. glandulosum Grauer ex G. H. Weber. Deciduous shrub, procumbent, fast growing, broad habit, scarcely 40 cm high, branches to 1 m long, new growth appears very early, young shoots sparsely pubescent, glandular; leaves thin, rounded, 3–8 cm wide, 5–7 lobed, very unpleasantly scented (!), glabrous above, venation beneath pubescent; flowers 8–12 in ascending racemes,

Fig. 164. *Ribes glandulosum* (from Schmidt)

these finely pubescent, shorter than the leaves, reddish white, April; fruits red, glandular bristly, 8 mm thick. BB 1872; GSP 162; RMi 147; JRi 46–47 (= *R. prostratum* L'Hér.). N. America, in the mountains; moist sites. 1641. z2 Fig. 158, 164.

R. glutinosum Benth. Deciduous shrub, 3–4 m high, young shoots, leaf petiole and floral racemes glandular-glutinous and soft pubescent; leaves rounded, 3–5 lobed, 4–8 cm long and wide, eventually glabrous above, underside green and slightly pubescent; flowers pink, to 30 in 4–8(11) cm long, pendulous racemes, sepals somewhat longer than the cylindrical tube, styles glabrous, ovaries glandular bristly, otherwise glabrous, April–May; fruits black, pruinose, scattered pubescent, oblong. MS 148; JRi 55–56 (= *R. santae-luciae* Jancz.). California, in the coastal mountains. 1832. z6 Plate 72; Fig. 157, 169. ✧

'Albidum'. Flowers white, soft pink toned. FS (1): 17 (= *R. albidum* Paxt.; *R. davianum* Hort.). Developed around 1840. Often confused in cultivation with *R. sanguineum* 'Albescens', which has gray tomentose leaf undersides. ✧

R. × gondouinii Jancz. (*R. petraeum* × *R. silvestre*). Shrub, vigorous, upright, intermediate between the parents, young shoots red, glabrous, appearing early; leaves to 10 cm wide, 3–5 lobed, truncate at the base, somewhat cordate, underside lightly pubescent; flowers in 5 cm long, nearly horizontal racemes, calyx short, bell-shaped; fruit red, medium size. JRi 186–187 (= 'Frühe Hochrote'; 'Gondouin'). Around 1907 by Gondouin, St. Cloud. ⚥

R. × gordonianum Beaton (*R. odoratum* × *R. sanguineum*). Shrub, 1.5–2.5 m high, branches brown, stiffly erect, glabrous; leaves 3–5 lobed, incised dentate, glossy, finely glandular pubescent on both sides; flowers more erect than those of the parents, reddish yellow (!) or with a red and yellow tube, calyx lobes red on the exterior, interior yellow, racemes to 7 cm long, April–May. FS 165. Discovered by Beaton in Shrubland Park, Ipswich, England around 1837. z6 ✧ ✗

Fig. 165. **Ribes.** Left *R. cereum;* middle *R. inebrians;* right *R. fasciculatum* (from B. M., Dippel)

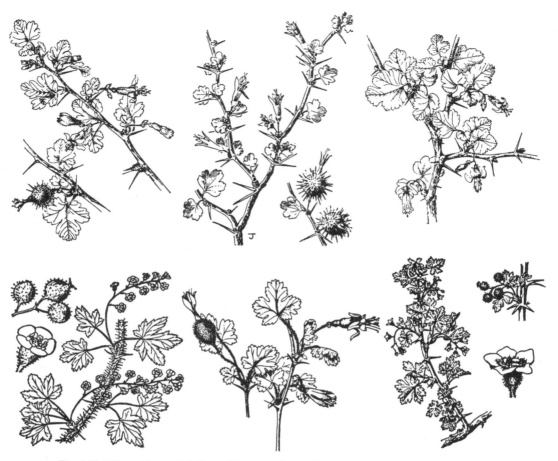

Fig. 166. **Ribes.** Above: left *R. roezlii;* center *R. roezlii* var. *cruentum;* right *R. californicum;*
Below: left *R. lacustre;* center *R. lobbii;* right *R. montigenum* (from Abrams)

R. gracile see: **R. hirtellum, R. missouriense,** and **R. rotundifolium**

R. grossularia see: **R. uva-crispa**

R. grossularioides Maxim. Closely related to *R. alpestre.* Shrub, to 2 m high, branches bristly or glandular bristled or smooth; leaves rounded, to 4 cm wide, 3–5 lobed, somewhat cordate, glabrous or somewhat silky pubescent; flowers 1–2 in elongated racemes, stalk about 1.5 cm long, calyx cup rather campanulate, greenish and reddish, style as long as the stamens, anthers without glands at the tip (!). JRi 183. Japan in the mountains. 1881. Rarely found in cultivation, often erroneously labeled! See also: **R. lacustre.** z6 Fig. 160.

R. henryi Franch. Evergreen shrub, to 1.2 m high, branches thornless, twigs glandular bristly; leaves obovate to more rhombic, 5–10 cm long, tapered to both ends, 3–5 cm wide, glandular dentate, underside glandular and bristly; flowers greenish yellow, 8 mm wide, in 3–5 cm long racemes, stalk glandular pubescent February to March; fruit ellipsoid, 12 mm long, glandular bristled. Central China. 1908. Similar to *R.*

laurifolium, but shorter, shoots pubescent, leaves larger and thinner. z8 #

R. himalayense see: **R. emodense**

R. hirtellum Michx. Shrub, to 1 m high, branches thin, occasionally bristly, gray when young, later dark brown, thornless or with only small prickles (!); leaves oval-rounded, 3–5 lobed, base broadly cuneate, petiole thin, often long pubescent; flowers in 2's (1–3), in very short racemes, late, cupule greenish, narrowly campanulate, as long as the greenish or reddish, erect or outspread sepals; fruits purple to black, 8–10 mm thick, mostly glabrous. GSP 157; JRi 111; BC 3405; BM 6892 (as *R. oxyacanthoides*) (= *R. oxyacanthoides* sensu Hook. f. non L.; *R. gracile* sensu Jancz.). Northern N. America. 1847. The older American, disease-resistant gooseberries were developed by crossing this species with the European cultivars. z4 Plate 77. ⚥ ✂

R. × holosericeum Otto & Dietr. (*R. petraeum* var. *caucasicum* × *R. spicatum*). Upright shrub, 1–1.5 m high, young shoots reddish; leaves rounded, 3 lobed, medium-sized, 6–7 cm wide, glabrous above, very pubescent beneath (!), petiole tomentose; racemes 3–7 cm long, with 10–25 red-brown flowers, calyx distinctly campanulate (!); fruits small, blackish red, compressed, sour. JRi 185. Before 1842. z4 ⚥ ✂

'Pallidum' (*R. petraeum* 'Bullatum' × *R. spicatum*). Leaves larger, to 8 cm wide, 3–5 lobed, less pubescent beneath; racemes to 8 cm long, with brownish flowers; fruits large, bright red, sour. JRi 183; Sorge, Beerenobst, Pl. 74 (= 'Rote Holländische'; called 'Prince Albert' in Holland). Cultivated since about 1665. ⚥ ✂

'Prince Albert' see: **'Pallidum'**

'Rote Holländische' see: **'Pallidum'**

R. 'Houghton Castle' see: **R. × houghtonianum**

R. × houghtonianum Jancz. (*R. silvestre* × *R. spicatum*). Intermediate between the parents, vigorous habit, new growth appears late, branches somewhat pubescent and glandular; leaves pubescent, 6 cm wide, 3–5 lobed, base somewhat cordate; racemes 3–5 cm long, with 8–18 flowers, these larger than those of *R. spicatum*, green with some brown; fruits globose, pure red, good tasting. JRi 181; Sorge, Beerenobst, Pl. 72 (= 'Houghton Castle'). Developed in England. Before 1901. z5 ⚥ ✂

R. hudsonianum Richards. Upright, deciduous shrub, 1–1.5 m high; leaves kidney-shaped, wider than long, 3–10 cm wide, more or less pubescent with resin glands, lobes ovate, obtuse or more acute, coarsely dentate; flowers white, in 3–6 cm long racemes, these erect, loose, bracts bristly, sepals ovate, outspread, longer than the cupulate tube, ovaries with resin glands, May–June; fruits globose, 5–10 mm thick, black. BB 1873; RMi 147; JRi 76. Hudson Bay to Alaska; in woodlands. 1899. z2 Fig. 157.

R. inebrians Lindl. Very similar to *R. cereum*, hardly differing in habit and foliage characteristics; leaves 1–3 cm wide; flowers normally pink, few in pendulous racemes, ovaries mostly glabrous (!), May–July; fruits pea-sized, light red, usually glandular. BR 1471; BC 3403 (= *R. pumilum* Nutt.; *R. spaethianum* f. *majus* Koehne). Western N. America, in the mountains. 1827. z6 Plate 71; Fig. 157, 165. ✣

var. **spaethianum** (Koehne) Jancz. More delicate than the species in all respects, scarcely over 50 cm high, glabrous, branches very thin; leaves glossy; flowers pink, very abundant; fruits dark red. JRi 67 (= *R. spaethianum* Koehne). USA; Colorado, Utah, Montana. ✣

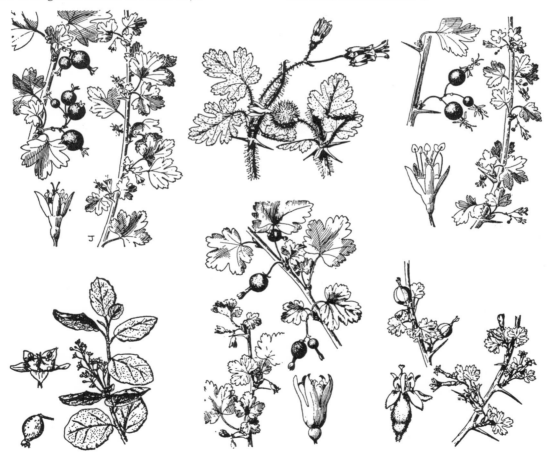

Fig. 167. **Ribes.** Above: left *R. inerme;* center *R. sericeum;* right *R. divaricatum;*
Below: left *R. viburnifolium;* center *R. irriguum;* right *R. quercetorum* (from Abrams)

R. inerme Rydb. Glabrous shrub, 1–2 m high, prickles not numerous, to 1 cm long or totally absent; leaves cordate or truncate, 1–6 cm wide, 3–5 lobed, lobes obtuse and crenate, glabrous to somewhat glandular pubescent beneath; flowers grouped 1–4, reddish or greenish, cupule glabrous, tube somewhat longer than the glabrous sepals, petals pink to white, May–July; fruits purple-red, glabrous, 8 mm thick, edible. JRi 110 a-b, d-e (= *R. oxyacanthoides* L. sensu Jancz. p. p.). N. America. z6 Fig. 167.

Mention should be made here of **R. purpusii** Koehne from Colorado, which differs from the above species only in the glandular pubescent flower stalk and bracts.

R. irriguum Dougl. Thorny, upright shrub, 1–3 m high, young shoots usually soft pubescent, gray, often also totally without bristles; leaves 3–7 cm wide, glabrous or nearly so, 3–5 lobed, pubescent and finely glandular beneath; flowers greenish white, grouped 1–3, nodding, stalks shorter than the leaves, petals obovate, half as long as the sepals, May–June; fruits globose, 7–13 mm thick, smooth, black. JRi 110c. Western N. America, in the mountains. 1920. z4 Fig. 167.

R. jessoniae see: **R. maximowiczii** var. **floribundum**

R. × kochii Krüssm. (*R. niveum* × *R. speciosum*). Deciduous shrub, about 1 m high, slow growing, thorns very similar to those of *R. speciosum*, but somewhat darker, glossy; flowers mostly in 3's and 2's, 4–5 parted (!), sepals narrowly ligulate, red, reflexed, petals white to reddish, stamens twice as long as the sepals, anthers brown, ovaries very small, glabrous or slightly bristly glandular, April; fruits brownish, bristly pubescent, occurs only rarely. Switzerland. Beitr. Dendr. 2: 74. Developed 1941. Much hardier than *R. speciosum*. z7 ✧

R. × koehneanum Jancz. (*R. multiflorum* × *R. silvestre*). Garden Currant. Rounded shrub; leaves medium-sized, 3–5 lobed, to 6.5 cm wide; racemes to 10 cm long, with up to 35 small, shell-form, brownish flowers, stamens pink, style and stamens equally long; fruits numerous, medium-sized, red, ripening in late July. JRi 188. Around 1904. z6 Fig. 158. ⚭ ✂

R. lacustre (Pers.) Pour. Swamp Gooseberry. Shrub, about 1 m high, branches thin, slightly pendulous, densely covered with fine, bristly, erect prickles, prickles and bristles 2–4 mm long; leaves nearly circular, 3–6 cm wide, 5 lobed, deeply incised, glabrous or somewhat glandular pubescent; flowers 4–10, greenish red, in loose, pendulous racemes to 9 cm long, May; fruits small, black, densely glandular bristled. JRi 83–84; BM 6492; RMi 145; BB 1871 (= *R. grossularioides* Michx.; *R. echinatum* Lindl.). Northern N. America, in swamps and moist sites. 1812. z4 Plate 72; Fig. 160, 166.

var. *molle* see: **R. montigenum**

R. laurifolium Jancz. Evergreen shrub, to 1.5 m high, branches glandular at first, later glabrous; leaves oval-oblong, 5–10 cm long, acute, crenate, base round, leathery tough, petiole bristly; flowers greenish yellow, grouped 6–12, in 3–6 cm long, nodding racemes, May; fruits ellipsoid, pubescent, black-red, in long pendulous racemes. BM 8543; NF 5: 201; GC 129: 4; JRHS 99: 252. W. China. 1908. z9 # ✧

R. laxiflorum Pursh. Procumbent (!) shrub, with soft pubescent young shoots; leaves circular, base cordate (!), 6–8 cm wide, deeply 5 lobed, glabrous above, somewhat pubescent beneath, the lobes ovate, serrate; flowers 6–12 in 4–8 cm long, erect, very loose (!) racemes, pubescent, glandular, reddish to red, petals fan-shaped, flower stalk much longer than the bracts, May–July. JRi 45 (= *R. affine* Dougl.). Alaska to N. California; in woodlands. 1818. z5 Fig. 158, 169.

R. leiobotrys see: **R. odoratum 'Leiobotrys'**

R. leptanthum Gray. Deciduous shrub, divaricate, very dense, stoutly thorned, upright, 1(2) m high, prickles 1 cm long; leaves rounded, 2 cm wide, 3–5 lobed, bud break very early, glabrous or pubescent and somewhat glandular; flowers grouped 1–2, white, very numerous, stalk very short, cupule greenish, sepals greenish white, pubescent, petals spathulate, white or softly reddish, April–May; fruits 6–8 mm thick, black, very numerous. JRi 105; Gfl 53: 409. SW. USA, in the mountains. 1893. z6 Plate 77; Fig. 160. ✧

R. lobbii Gray. Stoutly thorned shrub, to 2 m high, young shoots pubescent, prickles in 3's, about 1–2 cm long; leaves rounded-cordate, 2–3.5 cm wide, 3–5 lobed, obtuse, usually thinly pubescent above; flowers grouped 1–2, very large, sepals dark purple, petals pink, often only 4 (!), anthers black, filaments pink, pistil green, April–May; fruits ellipsoid, purple, densely covered with stalked glands. MS 162; JRi 89; BM 4931 (as *R. subvestitum*); BC 3407. British Columbia to California. 1852. One of the most attractive species. z7(–8) Fig. 166, 170. ✧

R. longeracemosum Franch. Deciduous shrub, to 3 m high, thornless, shoots glabrous; leaves 3–5 lobed, to 14 cm long and wide, the lobes acute, glabrous, petiole to 12 cm long, base cordate; racemes pendulous, to 30 cm (!) long, but very loose, with 15 flowers at most, these reddish-greenish, tubular-campanulate, sepals and petals erect, stamens and style exserted; fruits black, glossy. JRi 38. Tibet, W. China; Szechwan, Hupeh Provs., in the higher mountains. 1908. z6 Plate 71; Fig. 159. ✧

R. luridum Hook. f. & Thoms. Similar to *R. glaciale*, but with larger leaves, new growth appears later, fruits black. Deciduous shrub, about 1 m high, young shoots glabrous, carmine-red; leaves broadly ovate, 3–5 lobed, about 5–6 cm long and wide, the lobes short and obtuse, base usually cordate, underside with scattered silky glandular hairs; flowers top-shaped, dark purple, 10–25 together in 3–5 cm long, erect racemes, May; fruits black, flesh purple, sour, ripening late. JRi 174. Himalayas; Tibet, Sikkim, Nepal, in the higher mountains. Around 1900. z5 Plate 71; Fig. 156.

R. × lydiae F. Koch (*R. leptanthum × R. quercetorum*). Growth strong, upright, like the parents, branches gray, new growth appears very early, prickles 1–3; leaves small, bright green, like *R. leptanthum;* flowers usually in 2's, light yellow (!); fruits small, globose, black. Developed in cultivation, 1944. ⊕

R. × magdalenae F. Koch (*R. leptanthum × R. uva-crispa*). Intermediate, but more similar to *R. leptanthum,* to 1.5 m high; flowers pink and white; fruits black, ellipsoid, with only a few viable seeds. Developed spontaneously in 1929. Plate 70.

R. malvaceum Sm. Upright, deciduous shrub, very similar to *R. sanguineum,* 2 m high, branches red-brown, finely light gray shaggy and glandular; leaves 3 lobed, 2–5 cm long and wide, dull dark green and rough pubescent above (!), underside gray tomentose and glandular; flowers 15–25 in horizontal racemes to 7 cm long, pink, cupule tubular, exterior and interior pubescent, ovaries white pubescent (!), eventually pruinose. MS 150; JRi 59. California. 1832. z7 Plate 72; Fig. 157, 169. ⊕

R. mandshuricum (Maxim.) Komar. Shrub, to 2 m high, bark nearly black; leaves rather large, usually 3 lobed, to 11 cm wide and 9 cm long, lobes usually acute; flowers to 50 in 12–16(20) cm long, pendulous racemes, calyx shell-form, sepals reflexed, interior with 5 distinct "warts", these not interconnected by an elevated ring; young fruits blue-green, later red, about 1 cm thick. NK 15: 8; JRi 17. NE. Asia. 1906. z6 Fig. 159. ⊕

R. maximowiczianum see: **R. distans**

R. maximowiczii Batal. Deciduous shrub, closely related to *R. luridum,* but with glandular bristly young shoots; leaves ovate, medium-sized, 4–6 cm long, nearly undivided or shallowly 3–5 lobed, coarsely serrate, pubescent on both sides, denser beneath; flowers 10–20 in erect, 3–5 cm long racemes, red, May; fruits globose, to 1 cm thick, red, yellow or greenish, glandular pubescent. JRi 178. Central China; Kansu Prov., along river banks. z6 Fig. 156.

var. **floribundum** Jesson. Flower racemes 10–15 cm long; fruits not as bristly, bristles thinner. BM 8840 (= *R. jessoniae* Stapf). W. China. 1903. ⊕

R. menziesii Pursh. Deciduous shrub, to 2 m high, young shoots soft haired, densely bristly, prickles 1–2 cm long; leaves tough, rounded, 2–4 cm wide, 3–5 lobed, usually glabrous above or slightly glandular, underside velvety pubescent and glandular (!); flowers 1–2, purple, calyx tubular-campanulate, sepals 3 times as long as the calyx, petals whitish, shorter than the filaments, anthers sagittate; fruits globose, bristly, black. MS 172; JRi 91–92; GC 45; 242 (= *R. subvestitum* Hook. & Arn.). USA; Oregon to California. 1830. z7 Plate 77; Fig. 163. ⊕

R. meyeri Maxim. Closely resembling *R. petraeum.* Shrub, about 1 m high or more, young shoots glabrous, reddish, buds small; leaves usually 5 lobed, to 9 cm wide, the lobes acute or obtuse, base cordate, glabrous; flowers small, tubular-campanulate, nearly sessile, reddish, sepals and petals erect, style somewhat longer than the stamens, racemes 3–5 cm long, horizontally spreading, loose; fruits black, glossy. JRi 34–35. Central Asia, from the Pamir Mts. to Dzungaria. 1882. Plate 71; Fig. 159.

var. **turkestanicum** Jancz. Leaves more or less obtuse (!), glabrous beneath. Turkestan, Dzungaria.

R. meyeri see: **R. emodense**

R. missouriense Nutt. Thorny shrub, 1–2 m high, branches gray or whitish and bristly, glabrous, prickles red-brown, 1–2 cm long, straight; leaves rounded, 2–6 cm wide, thin, slightly pubescent above, more densely pubescent beneath, 3–5 lobed, coarsely and obtusely dentate; flowers 2–3, greenish white, thin stalked, sepals linear, 2–3 times longer than the tubular calyx, petals much shorter, April–June; fruits purple to brownish, 1 cm thick, glabrous. JRi 113; BB 1867; RMi 152 (= *R. gracile* sensu Brit. & Brown). N. America. 1907. z5

R. mogollonicum see: **R. wolfii**

R. montigenum McClatchie. Small, open shrub, 0.5–1 m high, branches only slightly thorned, with short, thick prickles at the nodes, otherwise more or less bristly; leaves kidney-shaped, 1–4 cm wide, 5 lobed, the lobes acute, pubescent; flowers few in short, nodding racemes, brownish green, tube glandular bristly, May; fruits pea-sized, dark red, densely glandular bristled. JRi 85–86; MS 153 (= *R. lacustre* var. *molle* A. Gray). Western N. America, in the higher mountains. 1905. z6 Fig. 166.

R. moupinense Franch. Thornless shrub, 1–2(5) m high, branches sometimes twisted, glabrous; leaves quite variable, usually large, to 16 cm wide, usually 3(5) lobed, the lobes acuminate, with scattered stalked glands on either side, otherwise glabrous; racemes 4(12) cm long, with 5–7(25) flowers, these sessile top-form campanulate, red or green-red, sepals and petals erect, glabrous, stamens half as long as the sepals, style shorter than the stamens; fruits black, glossy. JRi 36. Tibet, Moupi region, in the higher mountains; also in Yunnan, Hupeh and Kansu Provs., China. 1908. z5 Plate 71; Fig. 159.

R. multiflorum Kit. Upright, thornless shrub, 1.6–2 m high, branches ash-gray, pubescent when young, buds large (!); leaves nearly cordate, to 10 cm long and wide, obtuse 3–5 lobed, dentate, gray-white beneath, densely pubescent; flowers to 50 (!) together in elongated racemes, these outspread or eventually pendulous, to 12 cm long, calyx yellow-green, glabrous, campanulate, sepals reflexed, stamens widely exserted (!!), April–May; fruits dark red. BM 2368; JRi 15–16. SE. Europe, Balkan Peninsula in the mountains. z6 Fig. 168. ⊕ ⊛ ✂

R. nevadense Kellogg. Upright, deciduous shrub, 1–1.5 m high, shoots glabrous or somewhat pubescent when young; leaves rounded, 3–6 cm wide, the 3(5) lobes obtuse, crenate, thin, scattered pubescent, light green beneath; flowers in pendulous racemes, smaller than *R. sanguineum*, sepals pink, petals white, the latter rounded-oblong (!), June–July; fruits blue, 8 mm thick, glandular. MS 146; JRi 53. USA; California, Sierra Nevada. 1907. z7 Plate 71; Fig. 157, 169.

R. nigrum L. Black Currant. Deciduous shrub, to 2 m high and wide, branches strong, with yellow glands, pubescent to glabrous when young, yellowish, entire plant aromatic; leaves rounded, 5–10 cm wide, 3–5 lobed, underside pubescent and glandular punctate; flowers 4–10 together, in soft pubescent, pendulous racemes, tube campanulate, exterior greenish, interior reddish white, May; fruits globose, about 1 cm thick, black, edible, with a strong scent. JRi 77–78. Europe to central Asia and Himalayas. 1588. Ⓕ USSR, in W. Kasachstan in screen plantings. z5 Fig. 158. ⚭ ✂

f. *aconitifolium* see: 'Heterophyllum'

f. *albidum* see: 'Xanthocarpum'

f. *dissectum* see: 'Apiifolium'

f. *fructu luteo* see: 'Xanthocarpum'

f. *laciniatum* see: 'Heterophyllum'

var. *reticulatum* see: 'Marmoratum'

Including many cultivars (see the fruit literature):
Differing in leaf form:
'Apiifolium', 'Heterophyllum'
Differing in leaf color:
'Coloratum', 'Marmoratum'
Fruits a different color:
'Chlorocarpum', 'Xanthocarpum'

'Apiifolium'. Leaves 3 lobed, usually incised to the base, the lobes pinnatisect with narrow sections (= f. *dissectum* Nichols.). 1864.

'Chlorocarpum' (Späth). Fruits green. Gfl 562. Before 1838. ⚭

'Coloratum'. Leaves white variegated.

'Heterophyllum'. Leaves deeply incised, except at the base, the lobes irregular (!) and deeply incised (= f. *laciniatum* Ktze.; f. *aconitifolium* Kirchn.). ∅

'Marmoratum'. Leaves densely yellow-white marbled (= var. *reticulatum* Bean). ∅

'Xanthocarpum'. Fruits yellowish to whitish (= f. *albidum* Hort.; f. *fructu luteo* Hort.). Before 1827. ⚭

R. niveum Lindl. Deciduous shrub, thorned, 1–3 m high, branches reddish to brown, very stoutly thorned, otherwise glabrous, prickles 1–3, thick, brown; leaves rounded, lobed, to 3 cm wide, dark green, appearing early, occasionally somewhat pubescent; flowers 1–4, nodding, pendulous on thin stalks, white, cupule campanulate, white, 2 mm long, sepals and petals white, April–May; fruits blue-black, glabrous, 8 mm thick. BR 1692; JRi 114; DL 3: 156. Northwest N. America. 1826. z6 Fig. 160, 163.

R. odoratum Wendl. Clove Currant. Very similar to *R. aureum* (and very often grown under this name in cultivation!), but easily distinguished by the always pubescent young shoots; leaves oval-rounded, 3–8 cm wide, 3–5 lobed, the lobes coarsely dentate; flowers 5–10 in nodding racemes, fragrant, cupule 12–15 mm long and 2.5 mm wide, sepals scarcely half as long as the tube, reflexed and rolled, not straightening and inclining together on spent flowers (on *R. aureum*: cupule 6–10 mm long, 1.5 mm wide, sepals outspread, longer than half of the tube length, on spent flowers erect and inclined together), April–May; fruits globose, about 1 cm thick, black. BC 3402; HyWF 75; RMi 145 (= *R. aureum* Hort; *R. fragrans* Lodd.). Central N. America. 1812. Ⓕ USA, in screen plantings. z5

'Crandall'. Fruits to 15 mm thick. Planted as a fruit form in the USA. 1888. (Others in cultivation include 'Jelly', 'Utah', 'Golden') ⚭ ✂

'Leiobotrys'. Young shoots and flowers not pubescent, but with a few glands, calyx lobes reflexed, but not involuted; fruits black (= *R. leiobotrys* Koehne).

'Xanthocarpum'. Fruits orange-yellow. ⚭

R. orientale Desf. Deciduous shrub, 1–2 m high, young shoots red-brown, glandular glutinous (!), thornless; leaves usually 3 lobed, about 4.5 cm long and 5.5 cm wide, bright green above, soft pubescent beneath, new growth appears very early, crushed leaves very fragrant; flowers green, turning reddish, 5–20 in 1–5 cm long, erect racemes, rachis pubescent and glandular, April–May; fruits scarlet-red, glandular pubescent. BM 1583; JRi 164; Br 1278 (= *R. villosum* Wall.; *R. resinosum* Pursh; *R. punctatum* Lindl.). Greece to Himalayas and Siberia; always in the mountains. 1805. z6 Plate 71; Fig. 156.

var. *heterotrichum* (C. A. Mey.) Jancz. Young branches reddish; leaves glossy; flowers reddish; fruits not glandular. Siberia. 1907.

R. oxyacanthoides L. "American Mountain Gooseberry". Shrub, about 1 m high, branches prickly bristled and with 1–3 thorns at the nodes, these 1 cm long, stiff, brown; leaves cordate, 2–4 cm long, somewhat rugose, glabrous, glossy green; flowers greenish white, usually 1–2 on short stalks, cupule broadly tubular, sepals somewhat longer than the tube, April–May; berries globose, 1 cm thick, purple-red, smooth. BMi 154; BB 1868. N. America, in moist thickets and along river banks. 1705. See also **R. hirtellum** and **R. inerme**. z2 Fig. 160.

R. petiolare Fisch. Upright, deciduous shrub, to 1.5 m high, young shoots glabrous; leaves rounded, 10–15 cm wide, 3–5 lobed, base cordate, lobes ovate, acute, scabrous serrate, thin, glabrous or slightly pubescent at first, with resin glands beneath; flowers white, pubescent, shell-form, in erect, 5–12 cm long racemes, sepals ovate, obtuse, 7 mm long, April–May; fruits nearly globose, 1 cm thick, blue-black, not pruinose. MS 141; JRi 75 (= *R. dikuscha* Fisch.; *R. appendiculatum* Krylof). E. Siberia, Manchuria, western N. America. 1827. z5 Fig. 157, 169. ⟳

Fig. 168. **Ribes.**
Left *R. procumbens;*
right *R. multiflorum*
(from B. M., Pallas)

R. petraeum Wulf. Upright shrub, 1.5 m high or more, branches thick, gray-brown, glabrous; leaves rounded, 7–10 cm wide, cordate to truncate at the base, usually 3 lobed, the lobes acute, dentate, soft pubescent beneath, eventually pubescent at least on the venation; flowers small, distinctly campanulate, greenish to reddish, in dense, many flowered racemes, sepals short, round, ciliate (!), petals only half as long, style conical (!), April–June; fruits red to black-red, sour. HM 987; JRi 29 (= *R. petraeum* var. *bullatum* [Otto & Dietr.] Schneid.). W. and central Europe, in the mountains, particularly on moist slopes. Also utilized in the development of the garden currant. z6 Plate 71; Fig. 159. ⚙✂

var. **altissimum** (Turcz.) Jancz. Shrub, to 3 m high; leaves 3–5 lobed, occasionally very large, to 15 cm wide; floral racemes 5–7 cm long, with about 20 small, light red flowers; fruits black-red. Siberia. 1910.

var. **atropurpureum** (C. A. Mey.) Schneid. Leaves 3 lobed, smooth and flat, to 15 cm wide, without bristles; flowers about 15 together in 2–4 cm (!) long racemes, exterior purple, interior lighter, disk without callus; fruits black-red. Siberia. 1878.

var. **biebersteinii** (Berl.) Schneid. Leaves normally 5 lobed (!), rounded, about 12 cm long and wide, lobes obtuse and short, underside richly pubescent (!); racemes to 10 cm long, flowers reddish; fruits blackish (= *R. caucasicum* Bieb.; *R. biebersteinii* Berl.). Caucasus.

var. *bullatum* see: **R. petraeum**

var. **carpathicum** (Schulte) Schneid. Leaves flat and smooth, 3 lobed, to 9 cm wide; racemes short (!), loose, flowers flesh pink. Tatra and Carpathian Mts. 1838.

R. pinetorum Greene. Shrub, thorned, to 2 m high, branches drooping, without bristles, prickles grouped 1–3, about 1 cm long; leaves thin, cordate, 2–3 cm long, deeply 3–5 lobed, dull green and glabrous, underside somewhat pubescent; flowers usually solitary, occasionally paired, orange-red, rather large, stalk finely pubescent, sepals twice as long as the campanulate, pubescent calyx cupule, style glabrous, April–May; fruits purple, 1–1.5 cm long, densely prickly bristled. JRi

98. USA; Arizona to New Mexico. 1898. Hardy. z6 Fig. 160. ⚘

R. procumbens Pall. Procumbent shrub, similar to *R. fragrans,* but with tougher leaves, these kidney-shaped, to 8 cm wide, 3–5 lobed; racemes erect, 1–4 cm long, flowers glabrous, glandular, reddish, bracts absent; fruits brownish, smooth. JRi 342; NK 15: Pl. 7. E. Siberia. 1907. z3 Fig. 168.

R. prostratum see: **R. glandulosum**

R. pulchellum Turcz. Shrub, 1–2 m high, closely related to *R. diacanthum,* but with larger leaves, to 5 cm long, more deeply trilobed, base cuneate to slightly cordate. Shrub, 1–2 m high, nodes with small, stout, paired prickles, these red when young; flowers about 12–20 together in 2.5–6 cm long, erect racemes, reddish, rachis red glandular; fruits ellipsoid, glabrous, red. JRi 162. N. China. 1905. Often confused in cultivation with *R. orientale* var. *heterotrichum.* z5 Plate 71.

R. pumilum see: **R. inebrians**

R. punctatum see: **R. orientale**

R. purpusii see: **R. inerme**

R. quercetorum Greene. Upright, thorny shrub, 1–1.5 m high, branches gracefully nodding, new growth breaks bud quickly, even in winter after leaf drop (!); leaves thin, rounded, 1–2 cm wide, bright green, deeply 3–5 lobed, lobes dentate, finely pubescent on both sides; flowers yellowish or whitish, with a slight honey scent, calyx short tubular, lobes yellow, outspread, petals shorter than the sepals, ovaries smooth, style glabrous, not split, May–June; fruits globose, 6 mm thick, black, smooth. USA; California, in the mountains. 1914. z8 ⚘

R. resinosum see: **R. orientale**

R. roezlii Regel. Thorny, deciduous shrub, to 1.5 m high, branches pubescent at first, but not bristly (!!), prickles thin, to 1.5 cm long; leaves rounded, thin, truncate to

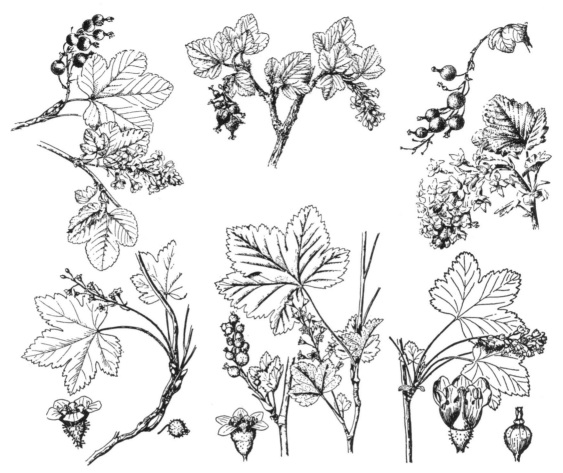

Fig. 169. **Ribes.** Above: left *R. sanguineum;* middle *R. malvaceum;* right *R. glutinosum;* Below: left *R. laxiflorum;* middle *R. petiolare;* right *R. nevadense* (from Abrams)

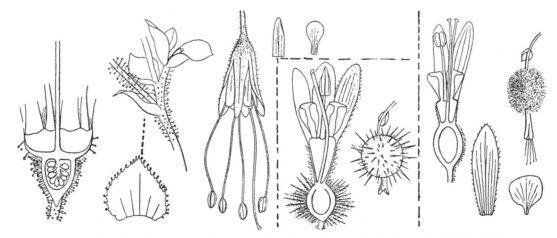

Fig. 170. **Ribes.** Flowers and their parts. Left *R. speciosum;* middle *R. roezlii;* right *R. lobbii* (from Janczewski)

nearly cordate, 1.5–2.5 cm wide, 3–5 lobed, incised crenate, usually finely pubescent on both sides; flowers grouped 1–3, purple, petals white, half as long as the sepals, equally long as the filaments, calyx cup campanulate, finely pubescent, ovaries bristly and white haired, anthers sagittate, May; fruits purple, 1–1.5 cm thick, bristly. MS 164; Gfl 982 (1–3); DRHS 1795 (= *R. amictum* Greene). USA; California. 1899. Hardy. z7 Fig. 170. ⊕

var. **cruentum** (Greene) Rehd. Plant nearly totally glabrous; leaves somewhat leathery; bracts more or less abscising; ovaries and fruit not pubescent, fruits globose, very bristly-prickled. JRi 93–94; MS 165; BS 3: 169; BM 8105 (= *R. cruentum* Greene). Northwestern North America, coastal regions. ⊕

R. rotundifolium Michx. Thorny shrub, about 1 m high or shorter, branches thin, brown, prickles only few and small; leaves broadly cuneate to nearly cordate, 2–5 cm wide, usually 3 lobed with obtuse lobes, finely pubescent; flowers grouped 1–3, greenish red, sepals twice as long as the campanulate calyx, stamens nearly twice as long (!) as the sepals, equally long as the pubescent based style, April–May; fruit purple, 6–8 mm thick, smooth. JRi 113; BB 1869; GSP 154 (= *R. triflorum* Willd.; *R. gracile* sensu Pursh non Michx.). Eastern and central USA. 1809. Often confused with *R. divaricatum*!! z6 Plate 72; Fig. 169.

R. rubrum L. Red Currant. Collective name. See: **R. spicatum** Robson and **R. silvestre** (Lam.) Mertens & Koch.

R. sanguineum Pursh. Winter Currant. Deciduous shrub, 2(4) m high, branches aromatic, red-brown, soft pubescent and somewhat glandular; leaves rounded, 3–5 lobed, 5–10 cm wide, base cordate, dark green pubescent above, whitish tomentose beneath (!), petiole glandular pubescent; flowers in ascending to pendulous, many flowered, glandular pubescent, 8 cm long racemes, calyx tubular, red or reddish, sepals somewhat longer than the tube, petals white to reddish, half as long as the sepals, spathulate, April–May; fruits black, densely blue-white pruinose, to 1 cm thick, somewhat glandular bristled. MS 147; JRi 57; BM 3335. Western N. America to California. 1826. z6 Plate 72; Fig. 169.

Including many cultivars:

Flowers dark red:
'Atrorubens', 'Atrorubens Select', 'Grandiflorum', 'King Edward VII', 'Koja', 'Lombartsii', 'Pulborough Scarlet', 'Splendens'

Flowers whitish to pink:
'Albescens', 'Carneum'

Flowers double:
'Plenum'

Leaves yellow:
'Brocklebankii'

'Albescens'. Flowers whitish. Gn 58: 208. Before 1894. Often confused in cultivation with the similar *R. glutinosum* 'Albidum', the undersides rather glabrous and more deeply scabrous serrate lobed.

'Atrorubens'. Compact habit; flowers deep red, small, in short, dense racemes (= 'Atrosanguineum'). Selected in England around 1838. ⊕

'Atrorubens Select' (Hort. Boskoop). Like 'Atrorubens', but taller growing, flowers larger, racemes wider. ⊕

'Atrosanguineum' see: **'Atrorubens'**

'Brocklebankii'. Rather slow growing; leaves yellow (!). Gn 78: 311. England. Best planted in the shade to avoid sunscald to the foliage. ∅

'Carneum'. Flowers pale pink, in broad racemes. Found in Germany around 1870.

Grandiflorum' (Hesse). Flowers pure red in large racemes.

'King Edward VII' (Cannell & Sons). Rather low and compact habit, less than 2 m; flowers larger than those of the species, pure red, in large racemes. ⊕

'Koja'. Flowers dark red, in vertically pendulous, short racemes. Selected in the Hornum Experiment Station, Denmark. 1975. Considered meritorious.

'Lombartsii' (Lombarts). Vigorous growth; flowers rather large, red in bud, later becoming much lighter, racemes small. Selected around 1945 by P. Lombarts of Zundert, Holland.

'Plenum' (Dick). Rather slow growing; flowers double, red, late, FS (I): 247. Found by David Dick, gardener of the Earl of Selkirk in St. Mary Isle, Scotland in 1839.

'Pulborough Scarlet' (N. J. Prockter). Flowers deep red with a white center, racemes particularly large, flowering very abundantly. Discovered in 1933 in Sussex, England. One of the best cultivars today. ⊕

'Splendens'. Dark red. RH 1913: 428. It is uncertain whether this plant, distributed by Smith, Newry in England around 1900, is even in existence today. In 1913, Barbier of Orléans, France described a French hybrid by this name from the Tourrès Nursery of Macheteaux-les-Tonneins (Lot-et-Garonne).

R. santae-luciae see: **R. glutinosum**

R. sativum see: **R. silvestre**

R. saxatile see: **R. diacanthum**

R. saximontanum see: **R. setosum**

R. schlechtendahlii see: **R. spicatum**

R. schneideri see: **R. × culverwellii**

R. setosum Lindl. Bristly branched shrub, usually less than 1 m high, prickles awl-shaped, usually less than 1 cm long; leaves thin, rounded, 1–4 cm wide, 3–5 lobed, base cordate to truncate, finely pubescent, petiole shorter than the blade; flowers 1–3 together, sepals white, calyx tubular-campanulate, twice as long as the recurved sepals, April–June; fruits red to black, about 1 cm thick, somewhat bristly to smooth. JRi 107; BB 1866 (= *R. saximontanum* E. Nels.). NW. USA. 1810. z2 Plate 72.

R. silvestre (Lam.) Mertens & Koch. Red Currant. Shrub, upright, broad, young shoots usually slightly pubescent and with glands; leaves rounded, to 6 cm wide, base deeply cordate with a narrow sinus (!), lobes acute, eventually glabrous or slightly pubescent beneath;

racemes pendulous or outspread and curved downward, rachis and stalk glabrous or slightly pubescent, calyx cup plate-like, style base surrounded by a pentagonal ring (!!), flowers greenish to reddish, anther halves outspread, separated by a broad middle band; fruits red, translucent. JRi 18–21; RMi 148; GPN fig. 435 (I) (= *R. sativum* [Reichenb.] Syme; *R. vulgare* Lam.; *R. rubrum* L. p.p. sensu Jancz.). W. Europe; Upper Rhine, France, Belgium, England. Cultivated since about 1600. Ⓕ Romania, in windbreaks. z6 Fig. 158. ⚥ ✗

Included here are most of the red and white fruited garden currants.

'Macrocarpum'. Garden Currant. Racemes very long, pendulous, flowers larger, flat-cupulate, very early. JRi 22–23. ⚥ ✗

'Variegatum'. Leaves irregularly white marbled and bordered. Before 1770.

R. spaethianum see: **R. inebrians**

R. speciosum Pursh. Evergreen, shrub to 4 m high in its habitat, branches and twigs light gray-brown at first, the prickles usually 2–3 at a node, 1–2 cm long, the numerous bristles 2–3 mm long; leaves rounded, glabrous, 3–5 lobed, margins crenate, 1–4 cm long, cuneate; flowers usually in 3's, 4 parted (!!), resembling a fuchsia with the purple-red, very narrow sepals and the twice as long stamens, calyx broadly campanulate, red, glandular bristly, anthers ovate, April–May; fruits densely glandular-bristled, red. MS 176; JRi 87; BC 3408; BM 3530. California. 1828. The most attractive species of the entire genus. z7 Plate 70; Fig. 170. # ☉

R. spicatum Robson. Nordic Currant. Upright shrub, to 2 m high, branches usually glabrous; leaves rounded, to 10 cm wide, 3–5 lobed, glabrous, base truncate to shallowly cordate with a wide sinus (!!), underside usually pubescent or also nearly glabrous; flower racemes erect at first, later more outspread or somewhat nodding, but not pendulous, except at fruiting, rachis and flower stalk more or less pubescent and finely glandular, flowers 7 mm wide, light green, usually brown-red toned, calyx cupulate, interior distinctly circular, without the bulging ring around the style base (!), anther halves tightly adjacent, April–May; fruits red, translucent. BB 1875; JRi 27; GPN fig. 435; Pl. 436 (= *R. rubrum* L. p.p.; *R. schlechtendahlii* Lange). N. Europe and N. Asia, from Scandinavia to Manchuria, in the south from N. Germany to Poland. Cultivated since antiquity, but always rare, usually only in botanic gardens. z3 Fig. 158. ☉ ✗

R. stenocarpum Maxim. To 2 m high, thorny shrub, branches light brown, wavy, very prickly and bristly; leaves rounded, about 3 cm wide, deeply 3–5 lobed; flowers grouped 1–3 together, reddish, calyx campanulate, petals white, 3/5 as large as the sepals (!); fruits cylindrical, to 2.5 cm long, greenish, reddish, somewhat translucent. JRi 101. NW. China. 1903. z6 Fig. 160.

R. subvestitum see: **R. menziesii**

R. × succirubrum Zab. (*R. divaricatum* × *R. niveum*). Very vigorous growing shrub, erect, glabrous, prickles at the nodes to 2 cm long, leaves rounded, 3–5 cm wide, 3–5 lobed, the lobes obtuse, small, nearly glabrous; flowers 2–4 in small, pendulous racemes, carmine-pink, stamens widely exserted, half again as long as the sepals; fruits somewhat pruinose, otherwise black, the juice is a strong dye. JRi 201 to 202. 1888.

R. tenuiflorum see: **R. aureum**

R. triflorum see: **R. rotundifolium**

R. triste Pall. Deciduous shrub, thornless, usually procumbent or creeping, about 0.5 m high; leaves thin, kidney-shaped rounded, 6–10 cm wide, mostly 3 lobed, deep green and glabrous above, lighter and pubescent beneath, distinctly veined, lobes coarsely serrate, base usually cordate; racemes somewhat glandular, most shorter than the leaves, flowers reddish, calyx broadly campanulate, sepals obtuse, outspread, May–June; fruits smooth, red, 6 mm thick. RMi 148; JRi 24; GSP 157 (= *R. albinervium* Michx.). Northern N. America, in woodlands. 1820. z2

R. × urceolatum Tausch (*R. multiflorum* × *R. petraeum*). Shrub, similar to *R. multiflorum*, very thickly branched, robust, new growth and flowers appear late; leaves rounded, 3–5 lobed, to 8 cm wide; flowers about 25 in loose (!), 7–12 cm long racemes, calyx broadly campanulate, brownish, stamens somewhat shorter than the sepals; fruits globose to somewhat pear-shaped, deep red, like a large currant. JRi 189. Origin unknown. 1838. z6 Fig. 158.

R. ussuriense Jancz. Deciduous, stoloniferous shrub, to 1 m high, young shoots somewhat pubescent, covered with yellow resin glands, scented like camphor (!); leaves large, 3–5 lobed, 5–8 cm wide, middle lobe largest, petiole rather glabrous; flowers 5–9 in racemes, yellowish green, campanulate, sepals ligulate, petals sagittate, style short, not exserted past the stamens; fruits bluish black, 8 mm thick, flesh green, not aromatic, abscising when ripe. JRi 79–80; NK 15: 6. Manchuria to Korea. 1904. z5 Plate 72.

R. uva-crispa L. Gooseberry. Low, broad growing shrub, to 1 m high, shoots and leaves pubescent, prickles 1–3, gray with yellow-brown tips, stout; leaves rounded, 3–5 lobed, incised crenate, 2–6 cm wide, base cordate, soft pubescent beneath; flowers 1–3 in racemes, greenish, cupule hemispherical, sepals as long as the cup, stamens about half as long as the sepals, these becoming erect after flowering, ovaries tomentose, with or without a few glands, April–May; fruits yellowish or green, not pruinose, small, pubescent. JRi 110a; BB 1870 (= *R. grossularia* var. *uva-crispa* Sm.; *R. grossularia* var. *pubescens* Koch). NE. and central Europe. Cultivated for centuries. Most of the modern European gooseberry cultivars stem from this species and the following form. Ⓕ Romania, in windbreaks. z5 ⚥ ✗

var. **reclinatum** (L.) Berl. Differing in the soft pubescent ovaries, often also glandular; fruits globose to ellipsoid, red or yellow,

Fig. 171. *Ribes viscosissimum* (from Hooker)

smooth or pubescent or glandular bristled. JRi 109, 109b (= *R. grossularia* L.). Europe, N. Africa, Caucasus. Fig. 160. ⊗ ✕

R. viburnifolium A. Gray. Evergreen, thornless shrub, 1.5 m high; leaves broadly ovate to elliptic, 2–4 cm long, obtuse, base round, nearly entire or with a few small teeth, densely glandular punctate, pleasantly scented when crushed; flowers pink, in erect, 2.5 cm long racemes, April; fruits ellipsoid, red, 8 mm long. BM 8094. USA; California. z9 Plate 72. # ⌀ ⊕

R. villosum see: **R. gayanum** and **R. orientale**

R. vilmorinii Jancz. Deciduous, upright shrub, similar to *R. alpinum*, to 2 m high, finely branched, young shoots red (!), new growth appears very late (!); leaves about 2–3 cm long and wide, 3–5 lobed, base cordate to truncate; male flowers in 5–20 mm long racemes, greenish brown, very small, May; fruits globose, black, glabrous or glandular, August. JRi 167 to 168. W. China; Yunnan Prov. 1902. z6 Fig. 156.

R. viscosissimum Pursh. Deciduous shrub, to 1 m high or less, young shoots and inflorescences glandular pubescent; leaves rounded kidney-shaped, 5–8 cm wide, the lobes round, short and wide, pubescent and glandular on both sides; flowers few in erect or ascending, 10 cm long racemes, tubular-campanulate, 6–7 cm long, light green or reddish, sepals oblong, obtuse, as long as the calyx, ovaries glandular, May–July; fruits

black, 1 cm thick, glandular bristled, not pruinose. MS 144; JRi 62. West coast of N. America, in the mountains. 1827. z7 Plate 72; Fig. 171. ⊕

R. vulgare see: **R. silvestre**

R. warszewiczii Jancz. Similar to *R. spicatum*. Upright shrub, to 1.5 m high; leaves rounded, to 9 cm wide, 3–5 lobed, base cordate, slightly pubescent beneath, particularly on the venation; flowers light reddish, in 5–7 cm long, nodding racemes, calyx cup interior with a slightly recognizable ring (!) around the style base, April–May; fruits globose, about 1 cm thick, black-red, sour. JRi 25–26. E. Siberia. 1860. z4 Fig. 158.

R. wolfii Rothr. Upright, deciduous shrub, 2(3) m high, young shoots finely pubescent or glabrous; leaves rounded, 4–9 cm wide, 3–5 lobed, base cordate, the lobes acutely serrate, venation pubescent beneath and glandular; flowers greenish white (!), in dense, erect, 2–4 cm long, glandular pubescent racemes, ovaries glandular-bristly, calyx cupulate (!), soft pubescent, sepals 3–4 times longer than the cup, petals much shorter, white, April–May; fruits globose, black, pruinose, glandular bristly. JRi 52; BM 8121 (= *R. mogollonicum* Greene). SW. USA, in the mountains. 1900. z6 Fig. 156.

Most species easily cultivated in any normal garden soil; many species exceptionally winter hardy. The thornless types are generally more ornamental. The evergreen species should only be considered for the mildest climates. Many species leaf out soon after leaf drop in the fall, as early as December and, weather permitting, are in full foliage by January.

Lit. Berger, A.: A taxonomic review of currants and gooseberries; in Techn. Bull. N.Y. State Agr. Exp. Sta. 109, 1–118, 1924 ● Hylander, N.: Nomenklatorische und systematische Studien über nordische Gefässpflanzen; Uppsala 1945 (194–196) ● Janczewski, E.: Monographie des Grosseilliers, *Ribes* L.; in Mém. Soc. Phys. Hist. Nat., Genève 1907, 199–517 (the most important work yet today!) ● Thory, C.-A.: Monographie du genre Grosseillier; Paris 1829 (12 pp., 23 plates).

Fruit literature

Maurer, L.: Stachelbeerbuch; Stuttgart 1913 (1 to 346; 14 color and 136 other plates) ● Oldham, C. H.: The cultivation of berried fruits in Great Britain; London 1946 (1–374, ill.; very thorough work with many literature references) ● Sorge, P.: Beerenobst; Arten- und Sortenkunde; Arbeiten des Sortenamtes für Nutzpflanzen Nossen 4, 1–152, 1953.

RICHEA R. Br. — EPACRIDACEAE

Evergreen shrubs and trees; leaves alternate, narrow, with a sheath-like base encircling the stem; flowers in single, terminal heads or compound spikes; corolla "barrel"-shaped, fully closed (!), opening after the abscission of the stamens and pistils. — About 10 species, most in Tasmania, one in Australia, some in Madagascar.

Richea scoparia Hook. f. Evergreen, multi-stemmed

shrub, about 1 m high or more in cultivation, densely foliate, the branches resembling many *Dracaena* species; leaves linear-lanceolate, 2–3.5(7) cm long, drawn out from the sheath-like base to a narrow apex, light green, somewhat curved, glabrous; flowers densely clustered in stiffly erect, terminal, spike-form racemes, 5–20 cm long, corolla obovate or ovate, 6–8 mm long, mostly white, but also pink or orange (as a specimen in the Dublin Botanic Garden, Ireland), filaments short, May.

NF 12: 218; BM 9632; LAu 231; CFTa 111. Tasmania. 1930. Overwintered in conservatories in cooler climates. z9 # ⊕

Illustrations of further species
| R. acerosa | CFTa 28 |
| R. gunnii | CFTa 27 |

R. procera	CFTa 29
R. dracophylla	CFTa 25; BMns 468
R. sprengelioides	CFTa 26

Cultivated like *Epacris*, full sun; superb in flower. Growing among *Eucalyptus* in its mountain habitat.

RICINUS L. — Castor Oil Plant — EUPHORBIACEAE

Monotypic genus with properties as described below.

Ricinus communis L. Castor Bean, Castor Oil, "Palma Christi". Grows 10–12 m high in its habitat, cultivated as an annual in cooler climates, then 1.5–2.5 m, becomes woody in warmer regions, total plant glabrous, occasionally somewhat prickly; leaves alternate, very long petioled, shield-like (peltate), palmately lobed, with 5–12 lobes, margins serrate or dentate; flowers monoecious, in nearly paniculate inflorescences at the branch tips, the uppermost (staminate) green and clustered, the lower ones (pistillate) short stalked, July; fruit a smooth or prickly capsule with 3 large, marbled, very poisonous seeds. BM 2209; PBl 1: 922. Tropical Africa, but distributed throughout the world in cultivation. z9

Many cultivars are available in cultivation, varying in size and color of their leaves and seeds. Particularly well known is 'Zanzibariensis', with green, 50 cm wide leaves, white venation and very large seeds. Plate 90.

Easily propagated as an annual from seed.

ROBINIA L. — Locust — LEGUMINOSAE

Deciduous trees or shrubs, branches often somewhat angular, smooth, bristly or glutinous; leaves alternate, odd pinnate, leaflets opposite, short petioled, entire; stipules often in the form of stout thorns; flowers white to lilac or purple-pink, in dense, pendulous racemes, usually fragrant, calyx with 5 lobes, both apical ones nearly connate, standard broad, style inward curving, rough haired or bristled at the apex; pod linear, flat, bivalved dehiscent. — About 20 species in N. America and Mexico.

Robinia × ambigua Poir (*R. pseudoacacia* × *R. viscosa*). Intermediate between the parents but more similar to *R. pseudoacacia*, differing in the somewhat glutinous branches with small thorns; leaflets 15–21; flowers light pink. Add. 19: 624 (= *R. dubia* Foucault; *R. intermedia* Soul.-Bod.). Known since 1812. z3

'Bella-rosea'. Branches more glutinous, thorns stouter; flowers larger and somewhat darker, calyx less pubescent (= *R. bella-rosea* Nichols.; *R. viscosa* var. *bella-rosea* [Nichols.] Voss). Developed around 1860 in Leiden, Holland.

'Decaisneana'. Branches slightly glutinous, thorns small or totally absent; calyx rather strongly pubescent, flowers light pink. FS 2027; RH 1873: 151 (= *R. pseudoacacia* var. *decaisneana* Carr.). Developed around 1860 by Villevieille in Manosque, France. ⊕

R. bella-rosea see: **Robinia × ambigua 'Bella-rosea'**

R. boyntonii Ashe. Shrub, to 3 m high, branches thornless, smooth or finely pubescent; leaflets 7–13 together, elliptic-oblong, 1.5–2.5 cm long, rachis finely pubescent; flowers purple-pink with white, 8–10 in loose racemes, calyx lobes ovate, pod glandular bristled, May–June (= *R. hispida rosea* Pursh). Southeastern USA. 1914. z5

R. coloradensis see: **R. × holdtii**

R. dubia see: **Robinia × ambigua**

R. elliottii (Chapm.) Ashe. Shrub, only 1 m high, branches rodlike with short thorns, small lateral twigs at the shoot tips, densely gray tomentose at first; leaflets 11–15, elliptic, 1.5–2.5 cm long, densely gray pubescent beneath (!!); flowers purple-pink, occasionally with some white, about 2 cm long, 5–10 in racemes, stalk and calyx gray pubescent, lobes shorter than the tube; fruits bristly (= *R. rosea* Ell.). Southeastern USA. 1901. Lowest growing species. z5

R. fertilis Ashe. Stoloniferous, 2 m high shrub, branches and petioles bristly; leaflets 9–12, elliptic to oblong (!!), 2–5 cm long, mostly acute, pubescent beneath when young; flowers pink, about 2.5 cm long, calyx densely bristled, lobes lanceolate, half as long as the tube, June; fruits abundantly developed (!!), 5–7 cm long, densely bristly. USA. 1900. z5

'Monument' (Wayside Gardens). Narrow conical habit, 3–4 m high, sparsely bristled; flowers larger, soft lilac-pink, racemes to 10 cm long. Brought into the trade in 1948 by Wayside Gardens of Mentor, Ohio, USA. ⊕

R. glutinosa see: **R. viscosa**

R. hartwigii (Koehne). Small tree, 8–10 m high (usually found listed as a "4 m high shrub"), young branches, leaves, and petioles densely soft pubescent with stalked glands (!!), as are the calyx and fruit pods; leaflets elliptic-lanceolate, 3–4 cm long, loosely pubescent above, underside silky gray haired; flowers purple-pink to whitish, in 8 cm long racemes, rachis with stalked glands, June–fall; pods 5–9 cm long, glandular bristly (= *R. viscosa* var. *hartwigii* [Koehne] Ashe). USA; N. Carolina to Alabama. 1904. z6

R. hillieri see: **R. × slavinii 'Hillieri'**

R. hispida L. Shrub, 1(1.5) m high, sparsely branched, stoloniferous, branches densely covered with long, red bristles; leaflets 7–13, nearly circular to broad elliptic, 3–5 cm long, obtuse, dark green above, gray beneath, glabrous; flowers purple or pink, about 2.5 cm long, 3–6 in bristly pubescent racemes, not fragrant, June and September; pods 5–8 cm long, bristly. BM 311; BB 2123; RMi 264. Southeastern USA. 1758. Very attractive, but easily broken by wind, particularly those grafted on standards; does particularly well on sandy, sterile soil where it spreads rapidly by stolons. z5 ⊕

'Macrophylla'. Total plant somewhat more vigorous, not so brittle, branches only soft pubescent (!) or totally free of bristles, similarly the leaf petiole; leaflets and flowers somewhat larger (= *R. macrophylla* Schrad.). Developed in France in 1825. ⊕

R. hispida f. *nana* see: **R. nana**

R. hispida rosea see: **R. boyntonii**

R. × holdtii Beissn. (*R. neomexicana* × *R. pseudoacacia*). Tree, only medium-sized, crown rounded, branches thorny; leaflets 3–5 cm long, dark green, tough (!); racemes looser and longer than those of *R. neomexicana*, keel and wings nearly white, standard pink, pod with scattered glands (= *R. coloradensis* Dode). Developed in Alcott, Colorado by F. von Holdt around 1890; first brought into the trade in 1902. z4

'Britzensis' (Späth). Differing in the lighter, whitish flowers, June and August–September; leaves 3–5 cm long, light green at first, later more gray-green; pods 6 cm long, glandular. Developed around 1900 by Späth in Berlin, W. Germany.

R. intermedia see: **Robinia × ambigua**

R. kelseyi Hutchins. Open, glabrous shrub, 2–3 m high, branches covered with many thin bristles; leaflets 9–11, oblong, 2–3.5 cm long, acute, glabrous, darker above, gray-green beneath; flowers appearing with the foliage (!!), pink-lilac, 2 cm long, 5–8 in extraordinarily dense, 5–6 cm long racemes along the entire previous year's shoots, calyx densely glandular pubescent, turning purple, lobes triangular, acute, May; pods 3–5 cm long, densely covered with red glandular bristles. MD 1910: 102; BM 8213; BS 3: 183. Southeastern USA. 1901. z5 ⊕

R. leucantha Rehd. Stoloniferous shrub, low; flowers white, in 7 cm long racemes. Discovered in 1926 in Georgia, USA and first named in 1945. Cultivated by Kelsey Highland Nurseries in East Boxford, Mass. and considered an excellent ornamental shrub. z5

R. luxurians (Dieck.) Schneid. Shrub or tree, to 10 m high, branches thorny, glandular pubescent at first; leaflets 15–21, elliptic-oblong, 2–3.5 cm long, rounded, underside silky pubescent at least when young, petiole shaggy pubescent; flowers pale pink to nearly white, in dense, many flowered racemes, stalks glandular, calyx lobes triangular, June–August; pods 6–10 cm long, glandular bristly. BM 7726 (as *R. neomexicana*); SDK 4: 18; SS 114 (= *R. neomexicana* Auct. non A. Gray).

Southeast USA. 1881. z5.

R. macrophylla see: **R. hispida 'Macrophylla'**

R. × margaretta Ashe (*R. hispida* × *R. pseudoacacia*). Shrub, 3–4 m high, closely related to *R. pseudoacacia*, but pubescent on the leaflet undersides; flowers pale pink, about 2 cm long, in soft pubescent, 15 cm long racemes, calyx pubescent and somewhat glandular. USA: North Carolina. 1920. z5

'Idaho'. Tree-like habit, broad, open crown; flowers dark reddish purple, the darkest of the genus. Am. Nurseryman, 9/1/1962.

'Pink Cascade' (Flemer). Vigorously stoloniferous; very abundantly flowering, pink, large flowered (= 'Purple Crown' in USA). Developed in the USA around 1934.

'Purple Crown' see: **'Pink Cascade'**

R. nana Elliott. Shrub, to 1 m high, occasionally higher, branches bristly pubescent, shoots, leaves and flower stalks only soft pubescent or also more or less bristly; leaflets 9–15, elliptic to ovate, acute, base tapered or rounded, underside appressed pubescent at least when young, 12–25 mm long, May–June; pods oblong, bristly (= *R. hispida* f. *nana* Torr. & Gray). USA; North and South Carolina. z5

R. neomexicana A. Gray. Shrub, to 2 m high (!), branches thorny, similar to *R. holdtii*, young shoots and leaf axes finely gray pubescent; leaflets 9–15, elliptic to more lanceolate, 1–4 cm long, obtuse to acute, finely appressed pubescent and rough on both sides; floral racemes soft pubescent and glandular bristled, flowers pink, June and August–September; pods sparsely pubescent, not glandular, reticulately veined. VT 567. New Mexico. 1921. Often confused with var. *luxurians*! See also: **R. luxurians**. z5

R. pseudoacacia L.*. Black Locust, False Acacia. Tree, to 25 m high, crown open, bark deeply furrowed, young branches and twigs very thorny, olive-green to dark red-brown; leaflets 9–19, elliptic, 3–4 cm long, rich green above, gray-green beneath, yellow in fall; flowers white, 2 cm long, in dense, 10–20 cm long racemes, fragrant, June; pods to 10 cm long, smooth. SS 112–113. Eastern and central USA, much naturalized in Europe. Around 1635. A valuable park and utility tree with very durable wood. The bark and young branches are poisonous, particularly to horses! Ⓕ W. Germany, Austria, Hungary, Yugoslavia, Romania, Bulgaria, USSR, Greece, Ireland, Holland, France, Japan, China, USA, Argentina, Uruguay, Chile, and New Zealand. z3 ⊕

Including a large number of cultivars:

Outline of the cultivars

A. Number of leaflets about normal;

    l. Like the species, but without thorns:
       'Inermis'

*Linnaeus wrote *Pseudo-acacia* in 1753 and *Pseudacacia* in 1763.

2. Like the species, but flowering from June to fall:
   'Semperflorens'

3. Color of the leaves variable:
   'Aurea' (yellow-green)
   'Frisia' (golden-yellow)
   'Glaucescens' (gray-green)
   'Purpurea' (new growth reddish)

4. Differing in habit, number of leaflets normal;
   Globose forms:
   'Bessoniana', 'Rehderi', 'Umbraculifera'

   Weeping forms:
   'Pendula', 'Ulriciana'

   Narrow forms:
   'Appalachia', 'Pyramidalis', 'Rectissima', 'Stricta'

   Branches twisted:
   'Tortuosa' (tree-like)
   'Volubilis' (shrubby)

   Compact, dwarf form:
   'Nigra Nana'

   Branches thick:
   'Cylindrica'

5. Differing in the form of the leaflets;
   Leaflets smaller or narrower:
   'Amorphifolia',   'Coluteoides',   'Linearis',
   'Microphylla', 'Myrtifolia'

   Leaflets with a variable blade:
   'Bullata' (convex)
   'Crispa' (crispate)
   'Dissecta' (incised)

   Leaves pendulous:
   'Pendulifolia', 'Pendulifolia Purpurea', 'Rozyn-skiana'

B. Number of leaflets fewer (1–3–5–7);

6. Leaflets 1(3):
   'Unifoliola' (habit normal)
   'Monophylla Fastigiata' (habit very narrow)
   'Monophylla Pendula' (weeping habit)

7. Leaflets usually 3–7; shoots very thorny:
   'Sandraudiga'

'Amorphifolia'. Thornless, slower growing than the species; leaves smaller, similar to 'Coluteoides', but oblong, to 2 cm long. SH 2: 51c. Discovered in England around 1798.

f. *angustifolia* see: **'Microphylla'**

'Appalachia' (Hopp). Narrowly upright habit, very vigorous growing when young, with only small thorns on the current year's growth. For a detailed description see Bk 1954: 76–77 (= "Clone Nr. 4138"). Valued for forestry use; best propagated by root cuttings.

'Aurea'. Leaves yellow, later more or less green-yellow. Discovered in Germany in 1859. Not particularly attractive.

'Bessoniana'. Vigorous growing, open crowned, rounded-ovate, somewhat divaricate with age and then easily wind damaged, branches usually totally thornless; leaves normal, flowers very rarely. SL 375. Origin debatable; either in the Laurentius Nursery in Leipzig, E. Germany around 1860 or from Besson in Marseille, France.
Including a Dutch clone called 'Rotterdam' with a straight stem and more conical crown.

'Bullata'. Slow growing shrub, branches very thin; leaflets bullate.

'Coluteoides'. Smaller tree or shrub; leaflets bright green, elliptic, to 15 mm long; flowering very abundantly. HL 228, 230 (= f. *sophorifolia* Link). Discovered in England around 1765.

'Crispa'. Vigorous grower; leaflets smaller and narrower than those of the species, margins very crispate, particularly on the summer shoots. SH 2: 51a. Found in France before 1825. ⊘

'Cylindrica'. Slow growing form with compressed, stiff, short, thick, nearly cylindrical shoots; leaflets larger than those of the species, oblong, blue-green (= f. *monstruosa* Hort. ?). Before 1900 in France.

'Decaisneana' see: **R. ambigua**

f. *dependens* see: **'Monophylla Pendula'**

'Dissecta'. Low growing, compact, branches short; leaflets linear to oblong, blade often reduced to only a midrib. RH 1875: 62. In France before 1865. ⊘

f. *elegantissima* see: **'Microphylla'**

f. *erecta* see: **'Monophylla Fastigiata'**

var. *fastigiata* see: **'Pyramidalis'**

'Frisia' (W. Jansen). Young shoots with wine-red prickles; leaves an attractive golden-yellow, retaining this color to leaf drop. Found in Willem Jansen Nursery in Zwollerkerspel, Holland in 1935. Much better than 'Aurea' and particularly strong growing as a young tree. ⊘

'Glaucescens'. Branches very thin, short prickled; leaflets densely arranged, most folded upward, gray-green.

f. *heterophylla* see: **'Unifoliola'**

'Inermis'. Growth like the normal species, but the branches with or without stunted prickles; leaflets somewhat larger (= R. *spectabilis* Dum.-Cours.; f. *inermis* Mirbel). Around 1800 in France. This form is almost always confused with 'Umbraculifera', the so-called "Globe Acacia".

'Linearis'. Habit broad and open; leaflets linear. Before 1864 in Muskau, E. Germany.

'Microphylla' (Loddiges). Very graceful form with small, very narrow, to 15 mm long leaflets, occasionally also branches with wider leaves are found. SH 2: 51d (= f. *angustifolia* Koehne; f. *elegantissima* Hort.; var. *tragacantha* Kirchn.). In England before 1813. Plate 77.

f. *monophylla* see: **'Unifoliola'**

'Monophylla Fastigiata' (Dieck). Habit very narrow and columnar upright; leaflets 1–7, terminal leaflet enlarged (= f. *erecta* Rehd.). Developed around 1880 by Dr. Dieck in Zöschen, E. Germany.

'Monophylla Pendula' (Dieck). Branches widely drooping; leaflets 1–7, terminal leaflets much enlarged (= f. *dependens* Rehd.; f. *pendula monophylla* Zab.). Discovered before 1883 by Dr. Dieck in Zöschen, E. Germany.

f. *monstruosa* see: **'Cylindrica'**

'Myrtifolia'. Leaflets 11–19, broadly ovate, 10–15 mm long, apex round to emarginate. SH 2: 51f. Before 1850.

'Nigra Nana'. Dwarf form, branches clustered almost like witches'-brooms; leaflets very fine, often filamentous.

'Pendula'. Branches nodding, otherwise normal. Germany, around 1822.

f. *pendula monophylla* see: **'Monophylla Pendula'**

'Pendulifolia'. Leaves pendulous and more or less bullate. Originated from seed of 'Tortuosa' before 1864.

'Pendulifolia Purpurea'. Leaves pendulous, new growth purple. Brought from Belgium by Späth before 1840, and then introduced to the trade by him.

'Purpurea'. Branches very thorny; leaves on new growth reddish, but inconsistent. Originated in Muskau, E. Germany before 1893.

'Pyramidalis'. Columnar habit, like the "Lombardy Poplar", branches all upright, thornless or nearly so. IH 6: 20 (= var. *fastigiata* Lem. non Neumann). France. Around 1839.

'Rectissima'. The so-called "Ship's Mast Acacia". Habit straight and upright, not flowering. Originally found in large stands on Long Island, New York, but later disseminated as a forest tree.

'Rehderi'. Ovate-rounded dwarf form, stoloniferous, branches erect (!). Gw 2: 217. Developed from seed in Muskau, E. Germany around 1842.

'Rozynskiana' (Zamoyski). To 20 m high, branches horizontally spreading or nodding; leaves vertically weeping, to 40 cm long, leaflets narrow, limb undulate; flowers large, abundant. Gs 7: 153. Developed in the nursery of Count Zamoyski in Podzamcze, in central Poland around 1900. Introduced by Späth in 1903. Not identical to 'Ulriciana' as is often cited. ∅ ✧

'Sandraudiga' (Lombarts). Very vigorous growing, conical, branches very thorny; leaves 3–7 parted, leaflets elliptic, rounded or somewhat emarginate, very large, pure gray-green; flowers like those of the type or somewhat smaller. Discovered by P. Lombarts of Zundert, Holland around 1937.

'Semperflorens'. Strong growing tree, branches less thorny; flowering twice, first in June, then August–September. RH 1875: 191. Discovered by Durousset around 1870 in Genouilly (Sâone-et-Loire), France. Excellent park tree. ✧

f. *sophorifolia* see: **'Coluteoides'**

'Stricta'. Habit broadly conical and narrowly upright (not so narrow as 'Pyramidalis'), branches directed upward. Discovered in Germany before 1822.

'Tortuosa'. Large tree, limbs and twigs wavy, young shoots twisted corkscrew-like; leaves often pendulous; only occasionally flowering. Gw 2: 218. Found in France around 1813. Plate 77.

f. *tortuosa nana* see: **'Volubilis'**

var. *tragacantha* see: **'Microphylla'**

'Ulriciana' (Reuter). Branches thin and long, weeping; leaves normal, like the species. Found on Pfauen Island near Potsdam, E. Germany before 1892.

'Umbraculifera'. "Globe Acacia". Shrubby, 3–4 m high, very slow growing, with very many thin, nearly witches'-broom-like, totally thornless shoots; leaves smaller, light green; flowers never observed. MG 18: 630; HL 229 (= f. *inermis*. Kirchn. non Mirbel). Found in Austria in 1813.

'Unifoliola'. Thornless; leaves mostly simple (composed of only 1, 15 cm long leaflet), often, however, with 2 or 4 small additional leaflets. RH 1860: 121 (= f. *monophylla* Carr.; f. *heterophylla* Zab.). Developed around 1858 in the Deniaux Nursery, Bezirk Maine-et-Loire, France.

'Volubilis'. Like 'Tortuosa', only shrubby, branches more twisted; leaves limp, drooping, often also twisted (= f. *tortuosa nana* Hort.).

R. rosea see: **R. elliottii**

R. × slavinii Rehd. (*R. kelseyi* × *R. pseudoacacia*). Similar to *R. kelseyi*, but with wider leaflets, acute to obtuse; flowers light pink, much more abundantly flowering than the parents, rachis of the inflorescence somewhat shaggy pubescent, not glandular, pod rough with tiny warts. Developed in 1915.

'Hillieri'. Small, elegant tree, with a round crown; flowers lilac-pink, slightly fragrant, June (= *R. hillieri* hort. Hillier). Developed by Hillier in 1962.

R. spectabilis see: **R. pseudoacacia 'Inermis'**

R. viscosa Vent. Tree, to 12 m, crown broad and rounded, annual shoots black-brown, glandular pubescent and glutinous, with small thorns; leaflets 13–21, ovate, dark green above, loosely gray pubescent beneath; flowers light pink, standard with a yellow (!) blotch, racemes to 8 cm long, dense pendulous, June and August; pods to 8 cm long, glandular bristled and glutinous. SS 115; BB 2122; DB 5: 41 (= *R. glutinosa* Sims). Southeastern N. America. 1791.

var. *bella-rosea* see: **R. × ambigua 'Bella-rosea'**

var. *hartwigii* see: **R. hartwiggii**

All species require full sun; thriving on a light soil, unfortunately easily damaged by wind. *R. psuedoacacia*, however, is a significantly important forest tree.

Lit. Rydberg, P. A.: *Robinia*; in North American Flora **24**, 221–228, 1924 ● Wyman, D.: Locust popular for flowers in arid areas but beset by borers; in American Nurseryman, Sept. 1, 1962, **15**, 44–46.

ROSA L. — Rose — ROSACEAE

Deciduous, occasionally evergreen, upright or climbing shrubs, shoots usually more or less prickly and bristled; leaves alternate, odd pinnate, occasionally simple, with stipules; flowers solitary or in umbellate panicles at the ends of short lateral shoots; sepals and petals 5, occasionally 4; stamens numerous, pistils numerous, the latter enclosed in a normally urceolate receptacle, this becoming fleshy and berrylike (hip) when ripe and sometimes containing a few to many, single seeded, hard shelled fruits; chromosome number x = 7. — Over 100 species (according to many authors to 200!) in the temperate and subtropical regions of the Northern Hemisphere; in Europe, N. America to N. Mexico, Africa to Ethiopia, in Asia to the Himalayas and the Phillipines.

The species of this genus are quite variable and easily hybridized, making species classification very difficult and causing many divergent opinions among botanists.

Of the so-called "garden roses" there are probably around 12,000 with hundreds added each year. There are very many good books on garden roses as well as catalogues of the larger rose growers which the reader may consult for further details.

Regarding the genus outline, a detailed key to the entire genus would require a disproportionately large amount of space for the purpose of this book. Rather, a taxonomic outline of the genus is used here, including the species and hybrids mentioned.

Outline of the Genus

Subgenus I. **Hulthemia** (Dumort.) Focke*
Leaves simple, without stipules; flowers solitary, yellow; fruits prickly-bristled (smooth on *R. kopetdaghensis*):
R. hardii, kopetdaghensis, persica

Subgenus II. **Eurosa** Focke
Leaves pinnate, with stipules; flowers mostly in corymbs, occasionally solitary; fruits fleshy; calyx cup narrowed at the mouth to a disk; fruitlets borne on basal or parietal placentation;

Series 1. **Pimpinellifolia** (Ser.) Rehd.
Mostly low shrubs, stems usually with straight prickles and bristles; leaflets 7–9, stipules narrow, with abruptly widening, distinctly outspread auricles; sepals entire, erect and persistent; distributed in Europe and Asia:
R. ecae, foetida, harisonii, hemisphaerica, hibernica, hugonis, involuta, koreana, penzanceana, pimpinellifolia, primula, pteragonis, reversa, sericea, xanthina

Series 2. **Gallicanae** (Ser.) Rehd.
Mostly erect, low shrubs, stems usually with hooked prickles intermixed with bristles; stipules narrow, adnate to the petiole, leaflets 3–5, mostly tough; flowers few, often with narrow bracteoles or solitary and then without bracteoles; sepals often pinnatisect, reflexed after flowering, abscising; styles not exserted; in Europe and Asia Minor:
R. alba, centifolia, collina, damascena, gallica, macrantha, richardii, waitziana

Key to the most important species of this Series

+ Prickles very irregular; leaves usually doubly glandular serrate;
x Leaves tough, leathery; flower stalks erect, very finely pubescent:
R. gallica

xx Leaves thin, often only single serrate; flower stalks nodding, glutinous-glandular, somewhat fragrant:
R. centifolia

++ Prickles all regularly formed; leaves simple, not serrate, not glandular;

x Calyx cup glandular-bristled; leaflets oval-oblong, often pubescent beneath:
R. damascena
xx Calyx cup usually smooth; leaflets broadly elliptic, undersides pubescent:
R. alba

Series 3. **Caninae** (Ser.) Rehd.
Stems erect or bowed, usually with regularly formed, straight, bowed or hook-like prickles; middle leaves on the flowering shoots mostly 7 parted; bracteoles present, more or less widened, as are the stipules; inflorescences usually many flowered; outer sepals pinnatisect, reflexed after flowering, either abscising or remaining erect:
R. agrestis, andersonii, britzensis, canina, coriifolia, corymbifera, dumalis, glauca, glutinosa, horrida, inodora, macrantha, marginata, mollis, obtusifolia, orientalis, pokornyana, rubiginosa, serafinii, sherardii, sicula, stylosa, tomentosa, tuschetica, villosa

Series 4. **Carolinae** (Crép.) Rehd.
Mostly erect, low shrubs, stems thin, with normally straight, paired prickles, often also bristly; apical stipules usually narrow; inflorescences usually few flowered; sepals outspread after flowering, quickly abscising, the outermost entire or with only a few erect lobes; flower stalk and calyx cup glandular-bristly, occasionally smooth; ovules only basal in the flat globose calyx cup:
R. carolina, foliolosa, mariae-graebnerae, nitida, palustris, rugotida, scharnkeana, virginiana

Series 5. **Cinnamomeae** (Ser.) Rehd.
Erect shrub; stems usually with straight prickles, often paired under the leaves, stems often also bristly, flower stalks often thornless or glandular bristled; leaflets 5–11, stipules more or less widened, gradually blending into the broadly outstretched auricles; inflorescences usually many flowered; sepals usually entire, erect and persistent after flowering, occasionally abscising; calyx cup usually smooth:
R. acicularis, amblyotis, arkansana, aschersoniana, banksiopsis, beggeriana, bella, blanda, bruantii, californica, calocarpa, caudata, coryana, corymbulosa, davidii, davurica, elegantula, engelmannii, fedtschenkoana, forrestiana, giraldii, gymnocarpa, hemsleyana, highdownensis, holodonta, kamtchatica, kochneana, laxa, lheritiereana, macounii, macrophylla, marriettii, majalis, micrugosa, moyessii, multibracteata, murielae, nutkana, oxyodon, paulii, persetosa, pendulina, pisocarpa, prattigosa, prattii, pricei, proteiformis, pruhoniciana, pyrifera, rubrosa, rugosa, sertata, setipoda, spaethiana, spinulifolia, suffulta, sweginzowii, wardii, warleyensis, webbiana, willmottiae, wintoniensis, woodsii

Series 6. **Synstylae** (DC.) Rehd.
Stems climbing or creeping, occasionally erect, prickles hook-like, stipules mostly adnate to the petiole, occasionally filamentous, free and abscising; flowers in umbellate panicles; sepals reflexed after flowering, outer sepals pinnatisect or all undivided, abscising; styles nearly always connate in a slender column and exserted past the flat or slightly conical disk:
R. anemoniflora, arvensis, brunonii, cerasocarpa, dupontii, filipes, helenae, iwara, jacksonii, kordesii, longicuspis, luciae, maximowicziana, moschata, mulliganii, multiflora, phoenicia, polliniana, rehderiana, rubus, ruga, sempervirens, setigera, sinowilsonii, soulieana, wichuraiana

---

* Hulthemia and Hulthemosa. *Rosa persica* Mich. (1789) was singled out in 1824 by Dumortier and given its own genus name, *Hulthemia*. Some modern authors (i.e. Hurst, Boulenger and Rowley) have resurrected this generic name, while others retain the old name *Rosa persica*. — With the use of *Hulthemia* one would have to refer to the 2 known hybrids of *Rosa persica* with the genus name × *Hulthemosa* (established in 1941 by Juzepchuk in Komarov, Flora of the USSR 10: 507.)

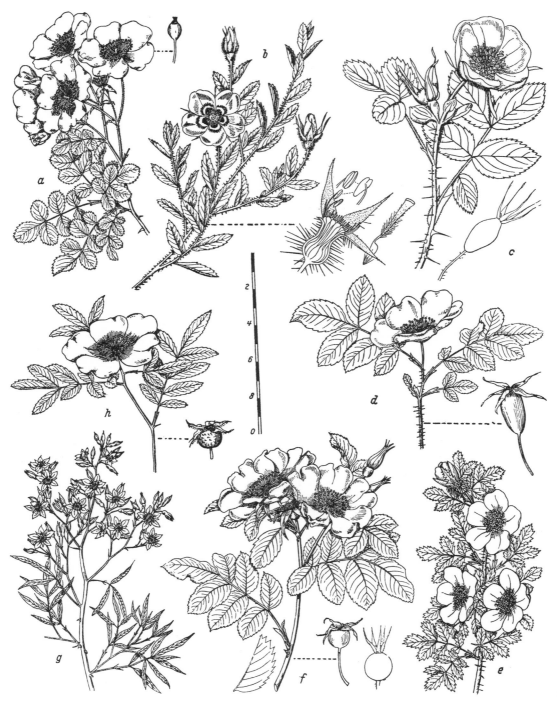

Fig. 172. **Rose.** a. *R. wichuraiana*; b. *R. persica*; c. *R. acicularis*; d. *R. acicularis* var. *bourgeauiana*; e. *R. minutifolia*; f. *R. nutkana*; g. *R. multiflora* 'Watsoniana'; h. *R. foliolosa* (from Gard. & For., Lindley, Redouté)

Series 7. **Chinenses** (Ser.) Rehd.
Stems climbing or creeping, with scattered, hook-like prickles; leaflets 3–5, occasionally 7; stipules and bracteoles narrow; inflorescences 1 to many flowered; sepals entire or sparsely pinnatisect, reflexed after flowering; styles distinct, only about half as long as the inner stamens:
R. *borboniana, chinensis, dilecta, gigantea, noisettiana, odorata*

Series 8. **Banksianae** (Lindl.) Rehd.
Evergreen climbing shrubs, branches thin and glabrous, with hook-like prickles or thornless; leaflets 3–7, stipules free, awl-shaped, abscising; flowers in umbellate panicles, white or yellow; sepals entire, reflexed after flowering, abscising:
R. *banksiae, cymosa, fortuniana*

Series 9. **Laevigatae** (Thory) Rehd.
Evergreen shrubs, stems with scattered, hook-like prickles; leaflets usually 3; stipules free or only attached at the base, abscising; flower solitary, large, without bracts; sepals erect, entire, persistent; flower stalk and calyx cup densely bristly:
R. *anemonoides, laevigata*

Series 10. **Bracteatae** (Thory) Rehd.
Evergreen shrubs, stems erect or creeping, tomentose or pubescent, prickles paired; stipules somewhat adnate and comb-like incised (pectinate); inflorescence surrounded by large bracts; sepals entire, reflexed after flowering; calyx cup tomentose:
R. *bracteata, clinophylla*

Subgenus III. **Platyrhodon** (Hurst) Rehd.
Leaves pinnate; stipules adnate, very narrow, with awl-shaped, outspread auricles; flowers 1–2, with small, abscising bracts; calyx cup prickly, fruitlets on a somewhat raised hump on the receptacle;
R. *roxburghii*

Subgenus IV. **Hesporhodos** Cockerell
Leaves pinnate; stipules adnate, with spreading auricles; flowers solitary, without bracts; calyx cup prickly, cupulate, without a disk; fruitlets on an elongated, conical hump in the receptacle; sepals pinnatisect, erect, persistent; fruit not fleshy:
R. *minutifolia, stellata*

Rosa acicularis Lindl. Shrub, to 1 m high, stem densely soft bristled, twigs occasionally also thornless, prickles straight, thin; leaflets 3–7, elliptic to oblong, 2–5 cm long, single serrate, dull green above, glabrous, soft pubescent beneath, petiole glabrous to pubescent, stipules broad; flowers solitary, dark pink, fragrant, 4–5 cm wide, petals obovate, incised, May–June; fruits pear-shaped, rounded, glabrous, about 1.5 cm long. WR 46; YWP 2: 29 (= R. *carelica* Fries; R. *sayi* Schwein.). N. America, N. Europe, NE. Asia. 1805. The only circumpolar species occurring above the Arctic Circle. Not often used in hybridizing since it is difficult to cross and usually produces sterile progeny. z2 Fig. 172.
The most significant hybrids are 'Pikes Peak' and 'Dornröschen'.

var. **bourgeauiana** (Crép.) Crép. Flowers larger, to 5 cm across; fruits more globose and with a very short throat. BC 3453 (= R. *bourgeauiana* Crép.). N. America. Before 1875. Fig. 172.

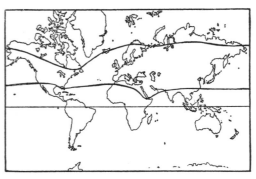

Fig. 173. Range of the genus *Rosa*.

var. *engelmannii* see: **R. engelmannii**

var. **fennica** Lallemant. Tetraploid form (= R. *acicularis* var. *gmelinii* Bge.; R. *gmelinii* Bge.). Finland to Siberia.

var. *gmelinii* see: var. **fennica**

var. **nipponensis** (Crép.) Koehne. Leaflets 7–9, 1–3 cm long, single serrate, glabrous, petiole bristly; flower stalk glandular bristled (= R. *nipponensis* Crép.). Japan; Fujiyama. 1894.

R. agrestis Savi. Shrub, 1–2(3) m high, shoots thin, prickles stout, wide, hooked; leaflets 5–7, oblong-elliptic, 1.5–5 cm long, base usually cuneate, pubescent to nearly glabrous; flowers 1–3, pale pink or whitish, sepals narrow, quickly abscising, style somewhat exserted, stalk without glands; fruits oblong-ovate, orange-red. WR 147; HM 1225; KHL 2: Pl. 158; KSR 21; KRR 156 (= R. *sepium* Thuill.). All of Europe but rare in the north and east; N. Africa. 1878. z6 Fig. 179.

R. × alba L. (presumably R. *canina*. [female] × R. *damascena*). White Rose; White Rose of York. To 2 m high, erect, stems with irregular, hook-like prickles, often also with bristles; leaflets 5–7, broadly elliptic, pubescent beneath; flowers white to soft pink, double, occasionally single, 6–8 cm wide, fragrant, stalk glandular-bristly, June; fruit oblong-rounded, red, 2.5 cm long, smooth. WR 139. Commonly cultivated since the Greek and Roman times. G. S. Thomas suggested that this rose is possibly a natural hybrid originating in the Crimea with R. *canina* var. *froebelii* Christ (white flowers, few prickles) as the mother plant, since the plant occurs in the wild in Kurdistan and also reaches the Crimea and the Caucasus. z5

Of the forms included here, the following are the most prominent:

'Great Double White' see: '**Maxima**'

'**Maxima**'. Jacobite Rose. Vigorous growth, 2 m high or more; leaves gray-green, usually situated only at the shoot tips, rather "leggy"; flowers irregularly, open double, rather large, opening cream-white with a trace of soft pink, but quickly becoming pure cream-white. GSR 62 (= 'Great Double White').

'Nivea' see: '**Semiplena**'

'**Semiplena**'. The type of this rose. Shrub, to 2 m or more, multistemmed, densely foliate; flowers only slightly double, milk-white, finely fragrant, flowering only once, anthers numerous, golden-yellow, flowers abundantly, June; with many red fruits in the fall. WR 136 (= *R. alba* 'Suaveolens', *R. alba* 'Nivea'). This rose is widely cultivated in Kazanluk, Bulgaria for its oil content.

'Suaveolens' see: **'Semiplena'**

Included with *R. alba* are about 20 cultivars:
'Blush Hip', 'Céleste', 'Chloris', 'Félicité Parmentier', 'Königin von Dänemark', 'Mme Legras de St. Germain', 'Maiden's Blush', 'Pompon Blanc Parfait'.

R. alpina see: **R. pendulina**

R. amblyotis C. A. Mey. Similar to *R. majalis,* but the branches with slender, straight, upward-directed prickles; leaflets 7, occasionally 9, elliptic-oblong to more oval-oblong, 3–5 cm long, acute, scabrous serrate, underside soft pubescent at least on the midrib; flowers red, 5 cm wide, sepals drawn out caudate-like, flower stalks thin, 2 cm long, glabrous; fruit flat-globose to more pear-shaped, 12 mm thick. Kamchatka. 1917. z5

R. × 'Andersonii' (Hillier & Sons 1912) (*R. canina* × ? *R. gallica*). Shrub of medium vigor, 2 m high, branches drooping, very thorny; leaflets 5, long acuminate, underside soft pubescent; flowers pure pink, single, 5–7.5 cm wide, shell form, flowers abundantly and over a long period; fruit very similar to *R. canina,* scarlet-red. WR 380. 1912. Sometimes cultivated under the name *R. collina* 'Andersonii'. z5

R. anemoniflora Fort. Climbing rose, branches with a few, small, hook-like prickles; leaflets usually 3 (!), oval-lanceolate, acuminate, serrate, glabrous; flowers white, 2.5–3 cm wide, in small panicles, single on the wild type, semidouble on the cultivars, sepals acuminate, usually somewhat pinnate, styles grouped into a column, on the double flowering forms, the inner petals are narrow and totally different from the outer ones (!), stalk usually somewhat glandular, June–July. WR 21 (= *R. triphylla* Roxb.; *R. sempervirens anemoniflora* Regel.). Discovered in 1844 by Robert Fortune in a garden in Shanghai and later in other parts of E. China. Shepherd and G. S. Thomas pointed out that this is probably a natural hybrid between *R. banksiae* and *R. moschata,* however as yet only observed in cultivation. z7

R. × anemonoides Rehd. (*R. laevigata* × *R. odorata*). Vigorous climbing rose; leaflets 3(5), glabrous, glossy, stipules half free; flowers solitary, single, 7 cm wide, pink, stalks bristly like the calyx. WR 41; MG 11: 345; RH 1901: Pl. 542. Developed in 1895 by J. C. Schmidt in Erfurt, E. Germany and first disseminated under the name "Anemone Rose". z8

Including a dark pink sport: **'Ramona'**.

R. apennina see: **R. serafinii**

R. arkansana Porter. Often a low subshrub in its habitat, similar to *R. acicularis,* but smaller, only about 50 cm high, flowering period longer, shoots prickly and bristly; leaflets 9–11, elliptic, 2.5–5 cm long, scabrous serrate, glossy above, glabrous on both sides or the venation pubescent beneath, stipules glandular dentate; flowers light red, 3 cm wide, in umbellate panicles, sepals reflexed, glabrous or glandular beneath, outermost sepals often pinnate, stalk glabrous, June–July; fruits globose, 1.5 cm thick, red. BB 1968 (= *R. rydbergii* Greene). Central and W. USA. 1917. When hybridized, can produce "herbaceous" roses; i.e. ones that can be cut back to the ground each year and resprout from the base. z5

R. arkansana suffulta see: **R. suffulta**

R. arkansanoides see: **R. suffulta**

R. arvensis Huds. Climbing rose, 1–2 m high, but branches thin and often much longer, creeping or developing thickets, with many, small, hook-like prickles; leaflets usually 7, ovate, 1–4 cm long, coarsely serrate, dull green above, underside soft pubescent; flowers solitary or in few-flowered umbellate panicles, white, 2.5–3 cm wide, not fragrant, sepals acutely ovate, much shorter than the petals, glabrous, abscising, June–July; fruits ovate, nearly 2 cm long, bright red. BM 2054; HM Pl. 154; WR 3; KSR 7 (= *R. repens* Scop.). S. Germany, S. Europe, Turkey. 1750. z6

The so-called "Ayrshire" roses were produced in the first half of the 19th century by crossing this species with other garden roses. This resulted in very winter hardy plants with vigorous habits, single or double, white to pink flowers (see Shepherd, 19–23, l. c.).

'Splendens'. Vigorous habit; leaves remaining green long into fall; flowers small, loosely double, soft pink-white, fragrant. Known in England as the "Myrrh-scented rose".

R. arvina see: **R. × polliniana**

R. × aschersoniana Graebn. (*R. blanda* × *R. chinensis*). Shrub, 1.5 m high, stoutly erect, stems with hook-like prickles; leaves light green; flowers small, but very numerous, light purple, sepals erect after flowering or reflexed, styles distinct, very irregular, late May to late June; sterile. Gfl 1504. Developed around 1880 by Zabel in Hannover-Münden, W. Germany. z5

R. austriaca pygmaea see: **R. gallica 'Pumila'**

R. balearica see: **R. sempervirens**

R. banksiae Ait. Evergreen shrub, to 3 m high, but often also to 5 m, drooping branches thornless, glabrous, bark green; leaflets 3–5, acutely lanceolate, 3–6 cm long, finely serrate, margins often undulate, glossy above, stipules bristle-form, abscising (!!); flowers rather small, delicate, white or yellow, single or double, very numerous, very pleasantly scented, sepals not pinnate, May–June; fruits globose, pea-sized, red. WR 35 (= *R. banksiana* Abel). Central and W. China. 1796. Winter hardy in only the mildest climates. z7

'Alba Plena' see: var. **banksiae**

var. **banksiae**. The type of the species. Flowers double, pure white, very fragrant. GSR 1; BM 1954; BR 397 (= *R. banksiae* 'Alba Plena'). Discovered by William Kerr in a garden in Canton, China in 1907. Widely cultivated in Japan and China but not found in the wild. The plant found under this name in Western culture is often *R. fortuniana* with larger flowers and better winter hardiness. z8 Plate 82; Fig. 178

'**Lutea**'. Flowers double, yellow, fragrance somewhat less than that of the other forms. GSR 2; BR 1105; WR 34. Cultivated since 1824. z9

f. **lutescens** Voss. Flowers single, sulfur-yellow, fragrant. GSR 3; BM 7171. W. China. One specimen found by E. H. Wilson on a grave and never in the wild. Introduced into England by Hanbury, La Mortola (Italy). z9

var. **normalis** Regel. The wild form, 6 m high, to 15 m high in its habitat, branches thornless; flowers small, white, single, fragrant. China; Hupeh and Szechwan Provs. Cultivated in Scotland since 1796, but first flowered in 1909 in Nice, Italy. (see Thomas, Climb. Roses, 146). z9

R. banksiana see: **R. banksiae**

R. banksiopsis Baker. Resembling *R. caudata*, but less prickly, stems often thornless on the apical half; leaflets 7–9, oblong, usually pubescent beneath, single serrate; flowers pink, 2.5 cm wide, in umbellate panicles, sepals longer than the petals, leaflike at the apex, glabrous beneath, persistent, stalk smooth, June–July; fruits red, bottle-shaped. WR 505. W. China. 1907. Differs only slightly from *R. caudata*. z6

R. beggeriana Schrenk. Well branched, multistemmed, 2.5 m high shrub, stems with paired, scattered and hook-like prickles; leaflets 5–9, oval-elliptic to obovate, 8–25 mm long, serrate, usually pubescent and blue-green to gray-green beneath; flowers several to many in umbellate panicles, white, 2–3 cm wide, stalks glandular to smooth, sepals abscising, June: fruits nearly globose, red, later becoming deep purple, 6–8 mm thick. WR 54; KHL 2: Pl. 159 (= *R. regelii* Reuter; *R. silverhjelmii* Schrenk.). N. Persia to Altai and Dzungaria. 1868. Not good for hybridizing. z4 Fig. 178.

The best cultivar:

'**Polstjärnan**' (Wasastjärna 1932). Very vigorous, to 5 m high; flowers very small, white, flowering abundantly in clusters for one period. Exceptionally frost hardy.

R. belgica see: **R. × damascena**

R. bella Rehd. & Wils. Very similar to *R. moyesii*, but with bristly stems, leaflets smaller, flowers pink. Shrub, to 2.5 m high, prickles less numerous, straight; leaflets 7–9, elliptic, bluish, glabrous, midrib glandular beneath, serrate; flowers 1–3, pink, fragrant, 4–5 cm wide, petals obcordate, stalks and fruits glandular, June; fruits ellipsoid to ovate, as long as the stalk, orange-scarlet, gradually narrowing to the apex. CIS Pl. 79. N. China. 1910. z6

R. bengalensis see: **R. chinensis** var. **semperflorens**

R. berberifolia see: **R. persica**

R. bifera see: **R. × damascena**

R. blanda Ait. Meadow Rose. Closely related to *R. pendulina*. A shrub, to 2 m high, branches slender, brown, nearly thornless, with scattered, straight prickles when young, later abscising; leaflets 5–7, elliptic to obovate-oblong, dull gray-green, underside lighter and finely pubescent, coarsely single serrate; flowers 1–3, pink, 5–6 cm wide, stalk and floral axis glabrous, as is the calyx,

May–June; fruits globose, 1 cm thick, red, occasionally ellipsoid. WR 104; BB 1966; GSP 234 (= *R. fraxinifolia* Lindl.; *R. solandri* Tratt.). Eastern N. America; on moist and gravelly sites. 1773. Variable. z2

R. bodinieri see: **R. cymosa**

R. × borboniana Desp. (*R. chinensis* × *R. damascena*). Vigorous habit; leaves large; original plant had dark pink, medium-sized flowers, with about 20 petals, flowering continuously, but less floriferous in fall than in early summer. WR 114. Developed on the Isle Bourbon (now Réunion), in the W. Indian Ocean. Sent to France in 1817 where it was named. Somewhat tender in winter. The opinion of some authors that the Bourbon Rose is a hybrid of *R. chinensis* × *R. gallica*, is probably not correct. Since the repeat flowering character of *R. chinensis* is recessive, a hybrid between this and the once flowering *R. gallica* will most probably be once flowering (according to Shepherd). z6

Including a number of descendants with the following characteristics: height 1–1.5 m, erect, branches prickly, often glandular bristled; flowers solitary or a few together, usually densely double, attractively formed, particularly the fall flowers (the summer flowers are not as attractive).
Including 'Boule de Neige' (Lacharme 1867), 'Souvenir de la Malmaison' (Beluze 1843), 'Variegata di Bologna' (Lodi 1909), 'Zéphirine Drouhin' (Bizot 1868), etc.
The Bourbon hybrids were later crossed with *R. odorata*, the Tea Rose, producing the REMONTANT Roses, which have larger, more abundant flowers than the Bourbon Roses. They are also hardier and flower over a longer period and have therefore virtually replaced the Bourbon Roses.

R. bourgeauiana see: **R. acicularis** var. **bourgeauiana**

R. boursaultiana see: **R. × lheritieranea**

R. bracteata Wendl. Macartney Rose. Upright, to 3 m high, bushy evergreen shrub, stems pubescent and with stout, hook-like, often paired prickles; leaflets 5–9, oblong-obovate, apex rounded, very shallowly dentate, dark green and glossy above, underside tomentose, stipules finely pinnate; flowers large, solitary, terminal, milk-white, fragrant, stalks and sepals densely pubescent, calyx surrounded by large bracts (!), stamens very numerous, about 300–400, July–August; fruits globose, orange, 3 cm thick. WR 42; BM 1377; LWT 109; CIS 78 (= *R. macartnea* Dum. Cours.). Named for Lord Macartney, who brought this S. Chinese and Taiwan native to England in 1793. z7

Including: '**Mermaid**' (Wm. Paul 1918), with very large, light yellow flowers, climbing (to the rooftops in southern England.)

R. britzensis Koehne. Shrub, vigorously upright, 2–3 m high, branches glabrous, prickles slender, small, 6–8 mm long, only scattered on the flowering shoots; leaves 12–14 cm long, leaflets usually 11 (occasionally 7–9), elliptic, gray-green, 2.5–3.5 cm long, serrate; flowers nearly always solitary, soft pink, finally white, 7–8(10) cm wide, petals emarginate, calyx and stalk bristly, as are the petals, mid May to late June; fruits ovate, dark red, about 3 cm long, somewhat glandular bristled. MD 1910: 94. Kurdistan. 1901. z6

R. × bruantii Rehd. 1922. Considered today a superfluous name for the hybrids of *R. rugosa × R. odorata* (= *rugosa* hybrids × tea roses and tea hybrids). Rehder included here the cultivars of Bruant ('Mme Georges Bruant') and Cochet ('Blanche Double de Coubert') among others.

R. brunonii Lindl. Himalayan Musk Rose. Strong growing climber, branches to 5 m high or more, usually pubescent and glandular when young, prickles stout, hook-like; leaflets 5–7, elliptic-lanceolate, 3–5 cm long, acuminate, soft pubescent, finely serrate; flowers white, 2.5–5 cm wide, many in umbellate panicles, fragrant, sepals narrowly lanceolate, somewhat glandular and pubescent, later reflexed, then abscising, stalk somewhat pubescent and glandular, June–July; fruits ovate, 8 mm thick, brown. SNp 56; BR 829; WR 11; RA 1930: 214 (= *R. moschata* var. *nepalensis* Lindl.). Himalayas. Very similar to *R. moschata*, but differing in the narrower leaflets, somewhat smaller flowers, but these in larger panicles, pubescent shoots, less winter hardy. Usually confused with *R. moschata* and much more frequently cultivated in the warmer climates. z7

'La Mortola'. A still more vigorous form.

R. burgundensis see: **R. centifolia 'Parvifolia'**

R. calendarum see: **R. × damascena**

R. californica Cham. & Schlechtd. Shrub, to 3 m high, stems with flat, curved prickles, young shoots occasionally bristly, flowering shoots usually prickly; leaflets 5–7, broadly elliptic, 1–3 cm long, serrate (not glandular), dull green and appressed pubescent above, shaggy beneath; flowers in corymbs with bracts, dark pink, 4 cm wide, sepals with shaggy exteriors, stalks shaggy or glabrous, June–August; fruits small, globose, with a distinct neck, 1–1.5 cm thick. MS 196; KHL 2: Pl. 157. California. 1571. z6 Fig. 184.

'Ardens' (Späth). Flowers intensely carmine-red, 6–7 cm wide, anthers golden-yellow, June. Originated from seed by Späth of Berlin before 1930.

'Nana'. Dwarf habit; flowers pink, single. 1914.

'Plena'. Very delicate habit, to 2 m high, branches drooping; flowers loosely double, a warm pink to light carmine, fragrant, June–July. GSR 4(= 'Theano' Geschwind 1894).

'Theano' see: 'Plena'

R. × calocarpa (André) Willm. (*R. chinensis × R. rugosa*). A vigorous, upright shrub, 2–2.5 m high, branches densely prickly, prickles straight, intermixed with bristles; flowers pink-red, single, 7–8 cm wide, smaller than *R. rugosa*, but in umbellate panicles, sepals glandular-bristly, finally abscising, stalks bristly, June–July; fruits globose, light red, many together, persistent. WR 60; RH 1891: 35; RZ 1907: 32 (= *R. rugosa calocarpa* André). Developed in Poitiers, France by Bruant, named in 1891 by Edouard André, introduced by Bruant in 1895 but soon disappeared from cultivation. z5

R. campanulata see: **R. × 'Francofurtana'**

Fig. 174. *Rosa canina* (from Lauche)

R. canina L. Dog Rose. Shrub, to 3 m high, branches bowed downward, prickles stout, hook-like; leaflets 5–7, ovate-elliptic, 2–4 cm long, double or only serrate, glabrous or lightly pubescent on either side; flowers 1–3, pink to white, 4–5 cm wide, sepals later reflexed and finally totally abscising, becoming reddish before fruiting (!), style glabrous or pubescent, the stigmas usually developing a small, conical head, June; fruits ellipsoid, scarlet-red, 2–3 cm long. WR 379 to 380; GPN 473; KSR 27–28. All of Europe to the 62nd parallel in Scandinavia. Quite variable; Wolley-Dod differentiated no less than 60 varieties and forms. 1737. Ⓕ Austria, Romania; in windbreaks and green screens. z3 Fig. 174.

var. *tomentella* see: **R. obtusifolia**

Since the wild forms are of no horticultural significance they will not be mentioned here.

The following wild species also belong to the Canina Group and can be studied in further detail in the *"Rosa"* section of Flora Europaea 2: 25–32, 1968: *R. abietina* Gren. ex Christ., Alps; KSR 26 ● *R. andegavensis* Bast., W. to S. and central Europe ● *R. deseglisei* Boreau, central Europe ● *R. nitidula* Bess., Great Britain and N. Portugal, eastward to S. Sweden, the Carpathians and Greece ● *R. pouzinii* Tratt., Mediterranean region ● *R. rhaetica* Gremli, Alps; KSR 29 ● *R. squarossa* (Rau) Boreua, central Europe ● *R. subcanina* (Christ) Dalla Torre & Sarnth., Europe ● *R. subcollina* (Christ) Dalla Torre & Sarnth., Europe and far to the North.

R. cantabrigiensis see: **R. × pteragonis** f. **cantabrigiensis**

R. carelica see: **R. acicularis**

R. carolina L. Carolina Rose. Shrub, 1–1.5 m high, slender branched, with many stolons (!), stems bristly at first, branches often thornless; leaflets 5, elliptic to lanceolate, 1–3 cm long, scabrous serrate, dull green above, glabrous, slightly glossy, gray-green beneath, usually glabrous; flowers usually solitary, pink, 5 cm wide, sepals lanceolate, acuminate or widened, abscising, glandular-pubescent, stalk glandular bristled, July–August; fruit flat globose, 8 mm thick, rather bristly. WR 64; BB 1971; GSP 231; KHL 2: 157 (= *R. humilis* Marsh; *R. virginiana* var. *humilis* Schneid.). Eastern N. America. 1826. z5 Fig. 184.

var. **grandiflora** (Baker) Rehd. Leaflets usually 7, elliptic to obovate; flowers 5–6 cm wide. WR 207 (as *R. humilis grandiflora*) (= *R. lindleyi* Spreng.). NE. USA. Before 1870.

'**Plena**'. Dwarf shrub, scarcely over 50 cm high, densely bushy, thinly branched, with stolons, prickles paired under each leaf axil; leaflets small, narrow, acute, serrate; flowers pure salmon-pink, somewhat darker in the center, densely double, later nearly white, sepals very long and narrow, finely glandular pubescent, as are the calyx and stalk. TRT 32 (= *R. pennsylvanica* Marsh.).

R. carolinensis see: **R. virginiana**

R. carteri see: **R. multiflora 'Nana'**

R. caryophyllacea see: **R. inodora**

R. caudata Baker. Shrub to 4 m high, stems with scattered, thick, straight, 8 mm long prickles, much widened at the base; leaflets 7–9, oval-elliptic, 2.5–5 cm long, serrate, glabrous and bluish beneath, stipules wide, glandular ciliate; flowers few in umbellate panicles, 3.5–5 cm wide, red, stalk and calyx glandular bristled, occasionally nearly smooth, sepals erect, entire, long caudate (!), apex leaflike, June; fruits oblong-ovate, 2.5 cm long, with a long throat, orange-red. WR 163. W. China. Around 1896. z6

R. centifolia L. Cabbage Rose, Provence Rose. Similar to *R. gallica*, but taller, to about 2 m high, slightly stoloniferous, prickles rather uneven, partly bristle form and glandular, the stouter ones very compressed, nearly straight and only slightly widened at the base; leaflets usually 5, often pubescent on both sides or only beneath, large, somewhat limp, ovate-rounded, rachis without prickles; flower buds short, sepals always outspread, never reflexed, pinnatisect, fruit cup ovate, stiffly glandular bristled like the flower stalk, flowers densely double, to several together, on long stalks, white to dark red (never yellow!), very fragrant, stalk under the flower glandular-glutinous and fragrant, particularly so on the "Moss Roses", June–August. WR 115; HM Pl. 154; KHL 2: Pl. 156, 162. The once steadfast opinion that this rose came from the east Caucasus and was known to the ancient Greeks and Romans is no longer valid, according to studies first done by E. Bunyard, and especially by C. C. Hurst. This rose is a complex hybrid developed gradually from the late 16th to the early 18th centuries. Included in the parentage are *R. gallica, moschata, canina* and *damascena*. The whole process from the first steps around 1710 to its completion around 1850 took place in Holland. The plant is recorded in many paintings by the Dutch masters. Fig. 175, 177.

Of the cultivars in existence today, the more prominent ones are:

'**Bullata**'. Very broad habit; leaflets very large, limply drooping,

Fig. 175. *Rosa centifolia*

blistery bullate, very reddish when young, soft; flowers pink, densely double, pendulous, calyx and stalk slightly glandular. WR 123; RJb 33: 48 (= Rose à feuilles de Laitue, Salad-Rose). Around 1801.

"Centifolia Alba" = '**Mme Hardy**'

'**Cristata**'. Very broad growing; flowers an attractive pink, but only the margins of the sepals "mossy" (glandular), not the calyx cup. WR 118; BM 3475; GSR 92; PWR 178; 180 (= 'Chapeau de Napoléon'). Found in 1820 on a fortress embankment in Fribourg, Switzerland.

'**De Meaux**'. Rarely over 1 m high, foliage more finely textured than that of *R. centifolia*, flowers deep pink, early summer, 2.5 cm wide, scented. Origin unknown.

"Major" see: **R. centifolia**

'**Minima**'. Flowers double, only 15 mm wide or less, light pink with a dark pink center. Very attractive form.

'Minor' = '**Petite de Holland**'

'**Mme Hardy**'. Medium-sized plant, to 1.8 m high, with good green foliage, flowers in creamy white clusters in midsummer, double, becoming pure white with a green eye in the center, scented, one of the finest white roses. Developed by M. Hardy in France in 1832.

'**Parvifolia**'. Burgundy Rose. To only 50 cm high, branches nearly thornless; leaflets oval, very small, dark green, underside and the stalks somewhat floccose; flowers small, many together, flat double, purple-red with a violet trace or dark pink, calyx nearly glabrous. WR 120 (= *R. burgundensis* West; *R. ehrhardtiana* Tratt.). Known since before 1664.

'**Petite de Holland**'. Shrub to 1.2 m high, flowers double, pale pink with deep pink centers, 6.4 cm across, appearing in midsummer, scented. Origin unknown.

'Pomponia' = 'De Meaux', Dijon Rose

var. *sancta* see: **R. × richardii**

'Simplex'. Like the species, but with single flowers, dark pink (= 'Ciudad de Oviedo'). Spain.

'Variegata'. Vigorous habit, very thorny; leaves deep green, coarsely serrate; flowers solitary or several, densely globose double, soft cream-white with pink stripes, abundant. WR 122 (as *R. provincialis variegata*). Around 1845 in Angers, France. Under several names in cultivation; e.g., 'Belle des Jardins', 'Village Maid', etc.

Other *centifolia* types: 'Duc de Fitzjames', 'Fatin-Latour', 'Juno', 'Paul Ricault', 'Robert le Diable', 'Spong', 'The Bishop', 'Tour de Malakoff', 'Unique Blanche'.

Moss Roses

'Andrewsii'. Single flowered Moss Rose. Flowers dark pink (= *R. muscosa simplex* Andr.). Discovered by Shailer in Little Chelsea, England in 1807 as a mutation on the Moss Rose, later also found in France.

'Muscosa' (sport of *R. centifolia*). Moss Rose. Usually not over 1 m high; flowers attractive, dense and tightly double, pink, several together, flower stalk and calyx densely "mossy" (glandular). BM 69; WR 116. Cultivated in England since 1724, but even earlier on the continent.

'Muscosa Alba' (mutation on the normal Moss Rose with pure white, double flowers). Habit more open; leaves soft green, elliptic, buds and petioles densely and long "mossy" (glandular); flowers white, center nearly soft pink tinged, but later also pure white, very fragrant, occasionally also with some pink colored petals. Mutation observed in 1954 by G. S. Thomas.

Further Moss Rose forms: 'Baron de Wassenaer', 'Black Boy', 'Blanche Moreau', 'Blue Boy', Capitaine John Ingram', 'Comtesse de Murinais', 'Gloire des Mousseux', 'Golden Moss', 'Henri Martin', 'Jeanne de Montfort', 'Marie de Blois', Mme Louis Levêque', 'Mousseline', 'Nuits d' Young', 'Parkjuwel', 'Reine Blanche', 'Salet', 'Striped Moss', 'William Lobb' and others.

R. cerasocarpa Rolfe. Climbing rose, to 3 m high, branches with only a few, stout, hook-like prickles; leaflets 5, leathery tough, oval-elliptic-acuminate, to 7 cm long, glabrous, serrate, petiole glabrous, stipules narrow, entire; flowers white, 2.5–3 cm wide, in panicles, sepals entire or pinnate, 6 mm long, glandular and pubescent, abscising, stalks and calyx densely glandular, buds abruptly acuminate, June; fruit globose, 1 cm thick, red. BM 8688. W. China. 1914. z5

R. cherokeensis see: **R. laevigata**

R. chinensis Jacq. China Rose. Low, erect shrub, stems with or nearly without prickles; leaflets 3–5, broadly ovate to oblong, acuminate, 3–6 cm long, glossy and deep green above, underside lighter and glabrous stipules very narrow; flowers usually several, occasionally solitary, on long stalks, pink on the originally introduced plant, 5 cm wide, but also dark red to nearly white, sepals simple, acuminate, smooth, reflexed after flowering, later abscising, June to fall; fruits ovate to pear-shaped, 1.5–2 cm long, remaining green long into

Fig. 176. *Rosa chinensis* 'Viridiflora' (from Gartenflora)

fall, eventually brown-green. WR 26 (as *R. indica*); YTS 1: 14 (= *R. sinica* L.; *R. indica* sensu Lour. non L.; *R. indica* var. *bengalensis* [Pers.] K. Koch; *R. nankinensis* Lour.). China. The year of introduction into European gardens is not known for sure. The opinions of the authors is varied (McFarland 1759; Rehder, Thomas 1768; Jaeger, Bean 1789; Glasau 1792; Ascherson, Park "end of the 18th century"). In any case, the single flowering wild form was found in 1885; it was classified as f. *spontanea* by Rehd. & Wils. z6 Fig. 178.

'Longifolia'. To 60 cm high, branches nearly thornless; leaflets 3–5, linear-lanceolate, to 5 cm long, serrate to entire; flowers usually single, dark pink-red (= *R. longifolia* Willd.; *R. indica longifolia* Lindl.; *R. chinensis* var. *longifolia* [Willd.] Rehd.). 1820. Presumably rarely cultivated today.

'Minima'. Miniature Rose, Fairy Rose. Delicate shrubs, about 20–50 cm high, multistemmed, very thinly branched; flowers on the oldest form single to slightly double, pale pink, about 3 cm wide, persistently flowering. BM 1762; PWR 161 (= *R. indica pumila* Thory; *R. lawranceana* Sweet; *R. indica minima* Bean; *R. indica humilis* Ser.). The origin is not known for certain; however it is believed (G. S. Thomas), that it was developed in England in 1805 from *R. chinensis* × *R. gigantea*. The version of the English botanist Sweet, citing the origin as the island Mauritius in 1810, is no longer valid since Sweet himself had never verified this claim.

Included here are very many cultivars, most from Ralph S. Moore, USA; P. Dot in Spain; Jan de Vink, Holland; the oldest form is 'Pompon de Paris' which is today considered identical to 'Rouletii'.

'Mutabilis'. A slender, open, upright shrub, about 1 m high, also to 2 m in particularly favorable conditions, young shoots purple-red, prickles red, young leaves coppery; flowers single, shell form, about 5 cm wide, opening with a soft leather-yellow interior, exterior orange, on the 2nd day the interior becomes coppery salmon, gradually becoming dark carmine-red and then abscising, flowering repeatedly. RH 1934: 60; TRT 124 (= *R. mutabilis* Corr.; *R. chinensis* f. *mutabilis* [Corr.] Rehd.). First cultivated in 1932, but possibly identical with 'Tipo Ideale' as described by Redoute.

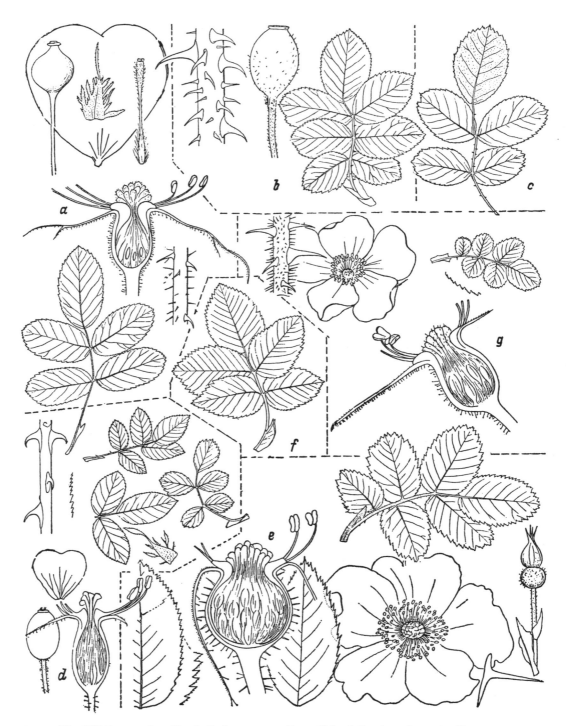

Fig. 177. **Rosa.** a. *R. gallica*; b. *R. damascena*; c. *R. centifolia*; d. *R. micrantha*; e. *R. villosa*;
f. *R.* 'Francofurtana'; g. *R. glutinosa* (most from Schneider, altered)

var. **semperflorens** (Curtis) Koehne. Monthly Rose, Bengal Rose. Delicate, thinly branched shrub, 1–1.5 m high, prickles evenly formed, small, few in number, red; leaflets 3–5, small, ovate, serrate, usually turning a good red, glabrous; flowers dark red, medium-sized, loosely semidouble, fragrant, with a very long flowering period, often solitary or grouped 2–3 together, long stalked, stalks thin and glabrous, ovaries glabrous, oblong, sepals lanceolate, long acuminate, entire, 15 mm long, erect, abscising; fruits light red. WR 89; BM 284 (= *R. semperflorens* Curtis; *R. bengalensis* Pers.; *R. diversifolia* Vent.; 'Slater's Crimson China', 'Crimson China', 'Old Crimson China'). Discovered in a garden in Calcutta, India in 1789 by a captain in the English East India Company and given to Gilbert Slater of Knots Green, England (a director of the same company) who propagated and distributed the plant. Before the introduction of this rose there were no forms with such deep red flowers; all dark red roses are somehow descended from this one. Slater classified the plant as the "Bengal Rose". After this period the plant was forgotten in Europe and thought to have died out, but was later found in England and Bermuda.

f. **spontanea** Rehd. & Wils. The wild form. A 1–2 m high shrub, flowers dark red or pink, single, usually solitary. GC 1902: 170 (= *R. indica* Hemsl. 1887 non L. nec Lour.). China; N. to central Szechwan Prov., in thickets and along river banks in Shih-ch'uan Hsien, but not common. First found in 1885 by A. Henry in Ichang, later also in other parts of China and (naturalized) in India. Presumably not yet in cultivation.

'Viridiflora'. "Green Rose". Small shrub; flowers medium-sized, double, green, about 5 cm wide, petals green (leaflike), margins serrate, occasionally somewhat bronze toned, usually in clusters, occasionally solitary, very long and persistent flowering. GSR 127; FS 1136; RŽ 1909: 41 (= *R. chinensis* var. *viridiflora* Dipp.; *R. indica* var. *monstrosa* Bean; *R. monstrosa* Breiter). Presumably cultivated since 1743 (but not verified!); perhaps more correct is the opinion of G. S. Thomas, that this rose originated around 1833 in Charleston, South Carolina, USA as a mutation on *R. chinensis*. From there in 1837 it came to Thomas Rivers in England and finally in 1856 was further disseminated by the English nursery of Bembridge & Harrison. Fig. 176.

R. cinnamomea see: **R. majalis**

R. clinophylla Thory. Similar to *R. bracteata*, but somewhat less vigorously climbing, branches becoming glabrous, pubescence shaggier, prickles straight; leaflets oblong-elliptic, usually somewhat larger toward the leaf apex, underside more or less pubescent, acuminate (!), rachis shaggy pubescent; flowers white; fruits large, often containing up to 150 seeds. BR 739; SH 1: 331; RŽ 1888: 72 (= *R. involucrata* Roxb.; *R. lyellii* Lindl.; *R. lindleyana* Tratt.). India; from Kumaon to Burma, in moist lowlands. Introduced to the West before 1817. Often used in religious ceremonies in India. z10

R. × collina Jacq. (? *R. corymbifera* × *R. gallica*). Shrub, about 1.5 m high, branches smooth, prickles stout, hooked, red when young, later gray; leaflets 5(7), finely serrate, glabrous above, lighter beneath with pubescent venation, petiole pubescent, occasionally somewhat glandular, stipules acute; flowers pink, fragrant, grouped 1–3 on short shoots, sepals persistent, leaflike at the apex, glandular on the dorsal side like the stalk, June–July; fruit occasionally also glandular, ovate, glossy, orange-red like *R. canina*. Central Europe. 1778. z6

'Andersonii'. Leaflets only slightly pubescent above; flowers to 7.5 cm wide, pink-red, later somewhat fading.

R. "cooperi" Hort. ('Cooper's Burmese Rose' by G. S. Thomas; presumably a natural hybrid of *R. gigantea* × *R. laevigata*). Vigorous growth, to 6 m high, branches purple-brown, rather stiff; leaves evergreen, to 18 cm long, leaflets 7, lanceolate, long acuminate, very glossy, finely serrate; flowers white, single, 10 cm across, old flowers turning pink with red spots. GSR 5. Raised from seed collected in the wild in Burma in 1931 by Cooper, Curator (1934–1950) of the Royal Botanic Garden, Edinburgh, Scotland. z6

R. coriifolia Fries. Closely related to *R. corymbifera*, but lower, to 1.5 m high, densely branched, branches and twigs often bluish pruinose, prickles curved, evenly formed; leaflets 5–7, medium-sized or small, rather stiff, oblong to broadly oval, base cuneate, usually glandular serrate, underside soft tomentose and gray-green, usually glabrous above; flowers a good pink, styles in woolly heads, stalk very short, with a large bract, sepals gray, pubescent, persisting until the fruits ripen and usually erect; fruits globose to ovate, to 2.5 cm long. WR 391; GPN 474–475 (= *R. frutetorum* Bess.). Europe; Asia Minor. 1878. z5

var. **froebelii** (Lambert) Rehd. Smaller shrub, compact, older stems tough, with many thin branches; leaves long petioled, leaflets large, gray-green on both sides, pubescent, stipules long and narrow; flowers grouped 1–3 together, white; fruits long, ellipsoid to oval-oblong, red, ripening early (= *R. laxa* Hort. non Retz.; *R. froebelii* Christ; *R. dumetorum* 'Laxa'). Brought into the trade around 1890 by O. Froebel of Zurich, Switzerland and still an important graft understock today.

R. coryana Hurst (*R. macrophylla* × *R. roxburghii*). Shrub, to 2.5 m high, strong growing, densely bushy, branches only slightly prickly, resembling that of *R. macrophylla*; leaves very similar to *R. roxburghii*; flowers dark pink, single, 6–7 cm wide, June; fruits not observed to date. GSR 154 (= *R. macrophylla* 'Coryana'). Originated in the Cambridge Botanic Garden, England in 1926. Recently used in hybridizing by S. McGredy but usually erroneously listed in catalogues as "*R. koreana*"! z6

R. corymbifera Borkh. Closely related to *R. canina*, primarily differing in the pubescent leaflets. Shrub, 1.5–2.5 m high, broad growing, prickles stout, hooked; leaflets 5–9, elliptic, to 5 cm long, densely arranged, serrate, usually pubescent on both sides (!); flowers usually in umbellate panicles, white to soft pink, 4–5 cm wide, sepals usually glabrous, occasionally somewhat glandular beneath, abscising, stalks usually glabrous, June; fruits ovate, orange-red, 12–18 mm long. WR 130; KHL 2: Pl. 158 (as *R. dumetorum*) (= *R. dumetorum* Thuill.). N. Africa, Asia Minor; throughout Europe, not as common in the N. and NW, mainly in the plains. 1838. z6 Fig. 179.

R. corymbulosa Rolfe. Shrub, to 2 m, stems erect or also procumbent, with only a few, thin, straight prickles or thornless; leaflets 3–5, oval-oblong, 2–4 cm long, acute, finely biserrate, dull green and somewhat pubescent above at first, underside bluish and pubescent, stipules glandular ciliate, fall foliage purple; flowers an attractive red with a white "eye", 20–25 mm wide, many in umbellate inflorescences, stalks and calyx cup glandular bristled, June–July; fruits scarlet-red, oval, 1–1.3 cm long. BM 8566. W. China. 1908. Very attractive, small flowered, but abundantly flowering species. z6

R. cymosa Tratt. Evergreen shrub, climbing to 4.5 m high, stems thin, with a few, hook-like prickles; leaflets 3–5, widely spaced, elliptic, oval-lanceolate, dark green and glossy above, lighter beneath, glabrous, serrate, stipules filamentous, free, occasionally absent (!!); flowers very numerous, in large, compound umbellate panicles, white, small flowered, sepals pinnate, style woolly, June; fruit scarlet-red, globose, small. WR 156, 157 (= *R. microcarpa* Lindl.; *R. bodinieri* Lév. & Van.; *R. esquirolii* Lév. & Van.; *R. indica* L. p. p.; *R. sorbiflora* Focke). China. 1904. The most common rose species in the warmer parts of China, particularly in Ichang; extraordinarily variable in the size of the leaves and inflorescences as well as the degree of pubescence. z9

R. dalmatica see: **R. glutinosa** var. **dalmatica**

R. × damascena Mill. (*R. gallica* × *R. phoenicia*; *R. gallica* × *R. moschata*). Shrub, to 2 m high, branches very stoutly thorned, with many hook-like, regular thorns, these laterally compressed at the base; leaflets 5–7, ovate, serrate, glabrous and more gray-green above, underside softly pubescent; flowers usually many in groups, pink to red, occasionally white and red striped, double, usually fragrant, flower stalks often limp, calyx cup tapered at the apex, never globose (like *R. gallica*), sepals reflexed at flowering time, glandular bristled on the dorsal side, abscising, June–July; fruits more or less top-shaped, to 2.5 cm long, bristly. BTR 2; KHL 2: Pl. 156b; WR 124 (not good!) (= *R. gallica* var. *damascena* Voss; *R. belgica* Mill.; *R. calendarum* Borkh.; *R. polyanthos* Roessig). While the origin of this rose has never been completely clear, it is generally thought that the "Summer Damascenes" were brought with the Crusaders returning from Asia Minor to Europe around 1520–1570. However, the last large Crusade ended 300 years earlier! On the "Fall Damascenes" the authors are in total agreement that these roses were not only cultivated in ancient Rome, but were on Samos Island (Greece) around 1000 B.C. The plant was used by the Aphrodite Cult and thus eventually reached Athens and Rome.

Often confused with *R. gallica* and *R. centifolia*, but easily distinguished by the more vigorous habit, the long, usually bowed stems with stout hooked prickles, lighter and softer leaves with normally 5–7 leaflets, only semidouble, very fragrant flowers in only pink tones, with a conspicuous transparency to the petals; fruits very bristly. z5 Fig. 177.

var. *bifera* see: paragraph following "2."

C. C. Hurst (1941) divided the Damascene Roses into 2 "natural and distinct" groups:
1. *R. × damascena* (= *gallica* × *phoenicia*), Summer Damascene Rose;
2. *R. × bifera* Pers. (= *gallica* × *moschata*), Fall Damascene Rose.

While the name for the Summer Damascene Roses has not changed, G. D. Rowley suggested for the Fall Damascenes, the combination *R. damascena* var. *semperflorens* (Loisel. & Michel) Rowley 1959 (= *R. semperflorens* Loisel. & Michel 1819; *R. bifera* var. *semperflorens* Loisel. & Michel 1819; *R. damascena* var. *bifera* hort non. Regel 1877).

The most important types of the Damascene Rose:

'Perpetual White Moss' see: var. **semperflorens**

var. **semperflorens** (Loisel. & Michel) Rowley (better known as 'Quatre Saisons' or 'Rose des Quatre Saisons' in France, as 'Monthly Rose' in England). A fall flowering Damascene Rose. Shrub, just over 1 m high; leaves partly yellow-green; flowers pure pink, densely double, often also quadrupled and with an "eye", June–July, then sparsely flowering until fall (this somewhat uncertain and dependent upon growing conditions). Twice in recent times (Thomas 1950) this form has been observed as a mutation on 'Quatre Saisons Blanc Mousseux' (= 'Perpetual White Moss'). This form is a forerunner of the Bourbon and Remontant Roses; it is probably the same rose grown in Roman times in Paestum near Pompeii and elsewhere in large numbers. It has been identified in old murals.

'Trigintipetala'. Shrub, about 1.5 m high, flowers pink (somewhat like 'Ballerina' in color), semidouble, about 30 petals, 8 cm wide, very fragrant, June–July. Disseminated since about 1889 by Dr. Dieck in Germany. This is the "Rose of Kazanluk", the most important type for the production of rose oil (attar) brought from Turkey to Bulgaria more than 300 years ago. The center of "Rose oil" culture is in southern Bulgaria.

There are several selections of this form propagated vegetatively, but of little horticultural significance outside of Bulgaria.

'Versicolor'. "York and Lancaster Rose". Shrub, about 1 m high, branches green; leaves light gray-green, soft pubescent; flowers medium-sized, loosely double, some half white, half pink or only white or pink, but never red or striped (sports with pure pink flowers occasionally appear and have been cultivated under the name 'Professeur Emile Perrot'). Named "York and Lancaster" in 1551 by a Spanish doctor Monardes in remembrance of the English "War of the Roses" (1455–1485) between the houses of York and Lancaster, whose symbols were a white and red rose respectively. This rose (only introduced into English gardens in the early 17th century) had nothing to do with the war, but is still planted in England as a traditional commemoration. A careful pruning is required of this form to remove mutations with solid colored flowers.

Other Damascene types cultivated today include: 'Blush Damask', 'Celsiana', 'Coralie', 'Gloire de Guilan', 'Hebe's Lip', 'Ispahan', 'La Ville de Bruxelles', 'Leda', 'Mme Hardy', 'Marie Louise', 'Oeillet Parfait' and 'Omar Khayyam'.

R. davidii Crép. Shrub, to 3 m high, stems with thick, straight, 4–6 mm long, scattered prickles, base much widened; leaflets 7–9(11), elliptic-oblong, 2–4 cm long, serrate, glabrous above, bluish and pubescent beneath; flowers in umbellate panicles, pink, 4–5 cm wide, stalk and calyx glandular bristled, style exserted 3 mm, June–July; fruits ovoid, to 2 cm long, scarlet-red, with a long throat. NF 6: 130; BM 8679. W. China. 1908. z6

var. **elongata** Rehd. & Wils. Leaflets 5–7 cm long; flowers less numerous; fruits to 2.5 cm long. Gs 16: 1 (= *R. macrophylla* var. *robusta* Focke). 1908.

R. davurica Pall. Shrub, closely related to *R. majalis*, about 1 m high, branches nearly smooth, prickles large, paired under the leaf base, somewhat hooked, but otherwise straight and slender; leaflets 7, oblong-lanceolate, 3 cm long, acute, glandular and pubescent beneath, biserrate, petiole pubescent, stipules narrow; flowers pink, grouped 1–3, sepals longer than the petals (!), leaflike at the apex, persistent, limb pubescent, June–July; fruits ovate, 12 mm long, smooth. NK 7:9; KHL 2: Pl. 157 (= *R. willdenowii* Spreng.). N. China, NE. Asia. 1910. z5 Fig. 184.

R. deserta see: **R. woodsii**

R. × **dilecta** Rehd. This is the botanical name of the modern Hybrid Tea Roses. Rehder coined this term in 1922 for the hybrids between *R. borbonia* × *R. odorata* (Bourbon Roses × Tea Roses) This name has proven somewhat erroneous in practice since many modern cultivars have neither of the above species in their parentage. It would, however, make little sense to assign a scientific name to the so-called "Tea Hybrids" since they are so diverse. Therefore in many Rose works the term is omitted altogether.

R. diversifolia see: **R. chinensis** var. **semperflorens**

R. dumalis Bechst. Shrub, to 2 m high, branches often bluish pruinose, prickles hooked with a wide base; leaflets 5–7, nearly touching, medium-sized, broadly ovate to more rounded, glabrous on both sides and usually bluish pruinose, stipules usually conspicuously wide; flowers solitary or several, rather large, pink-red, sepals with lanceolate-linear appendages, margin softly pubescent, calyx globose, pruinose, June to July; fruits globose to ovate, very large (= *R. glauca* Vill. non Pourr.; *R. reuteri* [Godet] Reuter). Europe, Asia Minor; in the mountains. z5

R. dumetorum see: **R. corymbifera**

R. dumetorum 'Laxa' see: **R. coriifolia** var. **froebelii**

R. × **dupontii** Déségl. Shrub, 2–2.5 m high, stems erect at first, later more outspread, with only a few, weak prickles; leaflets usually 5, oval-elliptic, to 5 cm long, biserrate, gray-green beneath with pubescent venation, petiole glandular; flowers usually 4–7 in umbellate panicles, buds pink, opening white, fading to a pink trace, 6–7 cm wide, fragrant, single, sepals glandular, abscising, anthers occasionally petaloid (!), style distinct, silky pubescent, stalk glandular, June; fruit ellipsoid, 12 mm long, red, ripening very late, October–January. WR 13; Gfl 57: 60; GC 127: 75; GSR 6 (= *R. freundiana* Graebn.; *R. moschata nivea* Lindl.). The earlier opinion of this plant's origin (a hybrid of *R. gallica* × *R. moschata* found in southern France in 1817) has been recently thrown into doubt as a result of chromosome research. z6

R. earldomensis see: **R.** × **pteragonis** 'Earldomensis'

R. ecae Aitchis. Shrub, not over 1 m high, densely branched, branches very prickly; leaflets 5–9, mostly obovate, only 4–8 mm long, serrate, glandular beneath; flowers solitary, 2 cm wide, a good golden-yellow, short stalked, stalks brown, sepals reflexed, persistent, May–June; fruit globose, pea-sized, red, glossy. WR 277 (as *R. xanthina*); BM 7666; GSR 7. Afghanistan, Turkestan. 1880. Found and introduced by Dr. Aitchison who derived the name "ecae" from the initials of his wife "E. C. A.". z7

Only one hybrid known to date; 'Golden Chersonese'.

R. eglanteria see: **R. rubiginosa**

R. ehrhardtiana see: **R. centifolia** 'Parvifolia'

R. elegantula Rolfe. A delicate shrub, 1–1.5 m high, but to 2 m wide, open, stoloniferous, young shoots densely red bristled, but only slightly prickly; leaflets 7–9, oval-elliptic, 1.2–1.8 cm long, bluish on both sides, purple to carmine in fall, serrate, rachis somewhat glandular, stipules narrow, glandular margined; flowers pink, 2.5 cm wide, solitary or several, but flowering abundantly, sepals finely pubescent, persistent, June; fruits ovate, coral-red, abundantly fruiting. BM 8877; GC 94: 112 to 113; 81: 70. W. China. 1900. Rehder and Shepherd cite *R. farreri* Stapf as a synonym to this plant, while Modern Roses (7), Bean and Mulligan (in Dict. of Gardening 4; 1951) consider it a separate species. This author would tend to agree with Rehder since the distinguishing characteristics are so slight that to name a separate species would be superfluous. z6

On the other hand, the following forms should be retained:

f. persetosa Stapf. Growth rate generally somewhat slow, stems more bristly to the shoot tips, prickles somewhat reddish; leaves somewhat smaller; flowers somewhat smaller, salmon-pink to whitish. GSR 14 (= "Three-penny-bit-Rose"). Developed by Mr. Bowles from seed collected by R. Farrer in the fall of 1915 in S. Kansu Prov., China.

R. elliptica see: **R. inodora**

R. × **engelmannii** S. Wats. (natural hybrid of *R. acicularis* × *R. nutkana*; proven artificially by Erlanson; fertile.). Similar to *R. acicularis* var. *bourgeauiana*, but with oblong fruits, to 2.5 cm long, shoots more bristly, leaves glabrous beneath (= *R. acicularis* var. *engelmanii* [S. Wats.] Crép.). N. America. 1891. z3

R. ernestii see: **R. rubus**

R. esquirolii see: **R. cymosa**

R. fargesii Boul. Similar to *R. moschata*. Not in cultivation! Cultivated plants with this name are *R. moyesii*.

R. farreri see: **R. elegantula**

R. fedtschenkoana Regel. Shrub, 1–1.5 m high, branches erect, bristly, prickles paired and mostly straight; leaflets 5–7, elliptic, 2.5 cm long, acute, finely serrate, bluish on both sides (!), petiole somewhat bristly; flowers mostly white, 1–4 at the shoot tips, 5 cm wide, unpleasantly scented, sepals glandular beneath, persistent, apexes filamentous (!), calyx and stalk glandular, June–July; fruits pear-shaped, red, 1.5 cm long. BM 7770; WR 49; GSR 15; TRT 37. Turkestan, central Asia. Found in 1875 by Olga Fedtschenko and subsequently released by the Leningrad Botanic Garden, USSR. z4

Fig. 178. **Rosa.** a. *R. laxa;* b. *R. webbiana;* c. *R. beggeriana;* d. *R. gymnocarpa;* e. *R. soulieana;*
f. *R. chinensis;* g. *R. phoenicea;* h. *R. banksiae;* i. *R. laevigata* (most from Schneider and Willmott)

Plate 81

Rosa oxyodon f. *haematodes*
Photo: Archivbild

Rosa gallica in its habitat in Bialowodska, near Roznow, Poland
Photo: Dr. Browicz, Poznań

Plate 82

Rosa banksiae in a park in Lugano, S. Switzerland

Rosa paulii in the Dortmund Botanic Garden, W. Germany

Plate 83

Rosa xanthina f. *spontanea* in the Royal Botanic Garden, Edinburgh, Scotland

Rosmarinus lavandulaceus
in Jardin Pinya de Rosa, Santa Cristina, Spain

Rosmarinus officinalis
in Nikita Botanic Garden, Jalta, USSR

Plate 84

Rubus phoenicolasius in its native habitat in Japan

Rubus rosifolius in Japan
Both photos: Dr. Watari, Tokyo

Plate 85

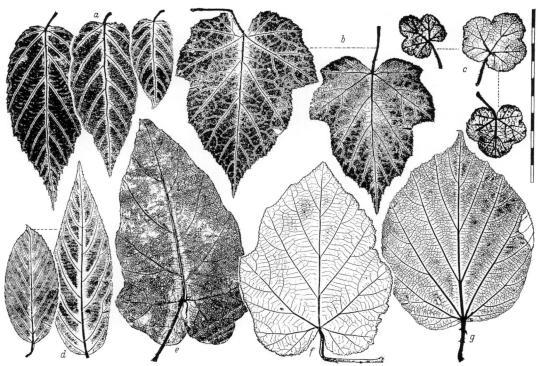

Rubus. a. *R. hupehensis;* b. *R. lambertianus;* c. *R. calycinoides;* d. *R. malifolius;* e. *R. ichangensis;*
f. *R. flagelliflorus;* g. *R. chroosepalus* (most material from wild plants)

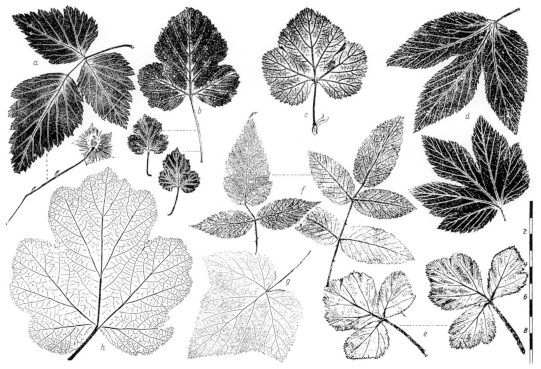

Rubus. a. *R. spectabilis;* b. *R. microphyllus;* c. *R. deliciosus;* d. *R. trifidus* (2); e. *R. parvifolius;*
f. *R. rosifolius;* g. *R. trilobus;* h. *R. setchuenensis* (most material from wild plants)

Plate 86

Rubus buergeri in its habitat in Japan
Photo: Dr. Watari, Tokyo

Rubus parvus in the Royal Botanic Garden, Edinburgh, Scotland

Plate 87

Rubus mesogaeus
in the Royal Botanic Gardens, Kew, England

Rubus calycinoides
in the Dortmund Botanic Garden, W. Germany

Rubus idaeus 'Phyllanthus'
in the Dortmund Botanic Garden, W. Germany

Rubus eustephanus var. *coronarius*
Photo: Dr. Watari, Tokyo

Plate 88

Rubus corchorifolius
in the Kyoto Botanic Garden, Japan

Rubus henryi
Photo: Archivbild

Rubus ellipticus
in the Sochi Botanic Garden, USSR

Rubus platyphyllus
in the Frohnleiten Alpine Garden, Steiermark, Austria

Plate 89

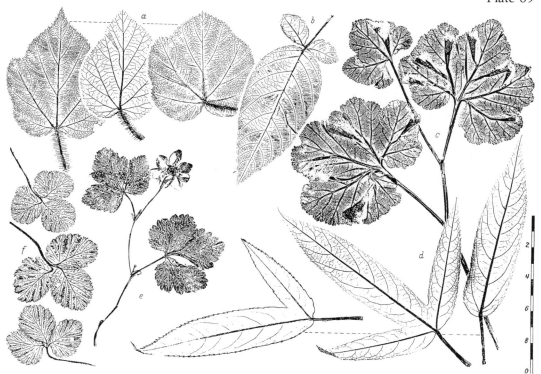

Rubus. a. *R. tricolor;* b. *R. playfairianus;* c. *R. chamaemorus;* d. *R. henryi;* e. *R. arcticus;* f. *R. fockeanus* (material from wild plants)

Rubus parvifolius in Japan

Plate 90

Rubus trilobus
in Malahide Gardens, Ireland

Ricinus communis 'Zanzibariensis'
in San Antonio, on Ibiza, Balearic Islands

Russelia equisetiformis in the Coimbra Botanic Garden, Portugal

Plate 91

Sabal palmetto
in the Suchumi Botanic Garden, USSR

Sabal blackburniana
in Marimurtra Garden, Blanes, Spain

Salix sachalinensis in its native habitat in Japan
Photo: Dr. Watari, Tokyo

Plate 92

Salix babylonica 'Crispa'
in the Dortmund Botanic Garden, W. Germany

Rumex lunaria
in the Lisbon Botanic Garden, Portugal

Salix babylonica along the Rio Tajo, Aranjuez, Spain

Plate 93

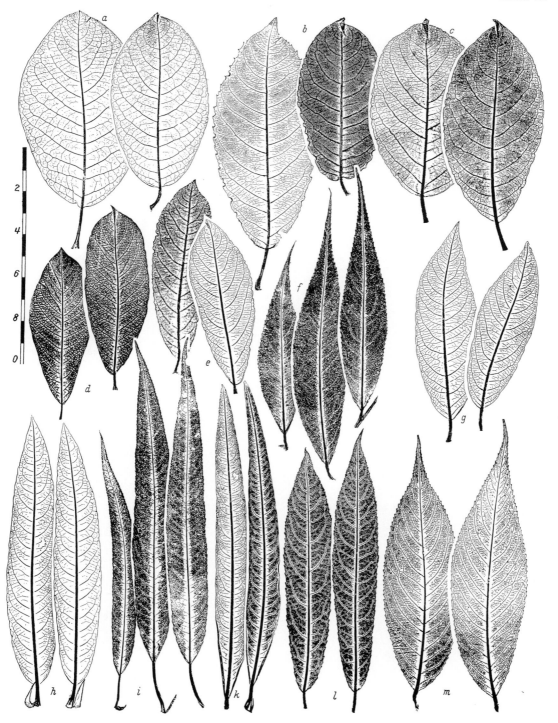

Salix. a. *S. hookeriana;* b. *S. aegyptiaca;* c. *S. caprea;* d. *S. sitchensis;* e. *S. cinerea;* f. *S.* × *blanda;* g. *S.* × *smithiana;* h. *S.* × *stipularis;* i. *S. acutifolia* 'Pendulifolia'; k. *S. viminalis;* l. *S. nigra;* m. *S. fragilis* (most material from wild plants)

Plate 94

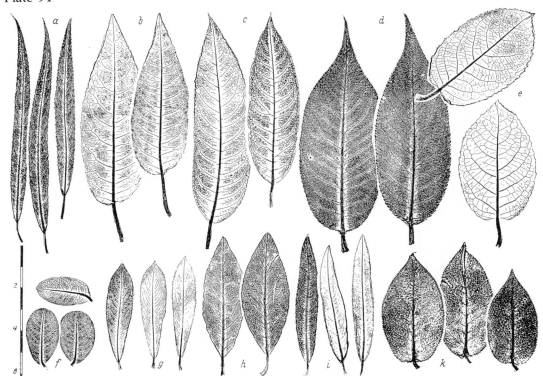

Salix. a. *S. medwedewii*; b. *S. pyrifolia*; c. *S. triandra*; d. *S. pentandra*; e. *S. myrsinifolia*; f. *S. caesia*; g. *S. purpurea*;
h. *S. phylicifolia*; i. *S. irrorata*; k. *S. syrticola*
(most material from wild plants)

Salix daphnoides
in the Dortmund Botanic Garden, W. Germany

Salix elaeagnos
in the Aarhus Botanic Garden, Denmark

Plate 95

Salix apoda
in the Dortmund Botanic Garden, W. Germany

Salix × boydii
in the Royal Botanic Garden, Edinburgh, Scotland

Salix lanata 'Stuartii' in the Royal Botanic Garden, Edinburgh, Scotland

Plate 96

Salix × *blanda* in the Botanic Garden of the
Royal Veterinary College, Copenhagen, Denmark

Salix alba 'Tristis'
in Heltorf Park near Düsseldorf, W. Germany

Salix acutifolia 'Pendulifolia' in the Dortmund Botanic Garden, W. Germany

R. fendleri see: **R. woodsii** var. **fendleri**

R. fenestrata see: **R. setigera**

R. ferox see: **R. horrida**

R. ferruginea see: **R. glauca**

R. filipes Rehd. & Wils. Climbing rose, 2.5–5 m high, branches with a few hook-like prickles; leaflets 5–7, oval-lanceolate, 5–7 cm long, glabrous, glandular beneath, serrate; flowers white, 2–2.5 cm wide, in many-flowered panicles, sepals narrow, widened at the apex, as long as the narrow petals, abscising, stalk very thin (!), smooth or glandular, style pubescent, fused into a column, June–July; fruit oval, red, 1 cm long. BM 8894; DRHS 1814. W. China. 1908. z5

Including:

'Kiftsgate'. White, flowering very abundantly. JRHS 86: 127.

R. florida see: **R. multiflora 'Carnea'**

R. foecundissima see: **R. majalis 'Foecundissima'**

R. foetida Herrm. Fox Rose. Shrub, to 3 m high in its habitat, scarcely over 1.5 m in cultivation, stems slender, brown, with a few, straight, unevenly large prickles; leaflets 5–9, elliptic, 2–4 cm long, doubly glandular serrate, bright green above, glandular and pubescent beneath; flowers usually solitary or in pairs, deep yellow, about 5 cm wide, strong, unpleasantly scented, stalks and calyx smooth, sepals lanceolate, leaflike, June; fruits globose, brick-red, occasionally also somewhat bristly. WR 90; BM 363; HF 2622; KHL 2: Pl. 151; 133 (= *R. lutea* Mill.). Asia Minor, Iran to Afghanistan and NW. Himalayas; occasionally found naturalized in Austria. Taken from there to Holland and England around 1593 by Clusius and therefore given the name 'Austrian Briar'. Supposedly taken by the Moors into Spain in the 13th century. Grown in the garden of Gerard in England in 1596 but also possibly cultivated there before that time. First hybridized by Pernet-Ducher around 1883–1888 with poor results at first; but later giving rise to the "Pernetiana Roses" (= Lutea Hybrids). These hybrids and *R. foetida* are however, very susceptible to black spot (*Diplocarpon rosae*) for which reason they are seldom cultivated. *R. foetida* and all its forms should also not be pruned for this reason! Plate 79; Fig. 182

'Bicolor'. 'Austrian Copper'. To 2 m high; flowers single, interior bright orange-scarlet, exterior yellow. GSR 16 (= *R. punicea* Mill.; *R. lutea bicolor* Sims). Originated as a bud mutation before 1590 and often reverting back to the yellow form, then called 'Austrian Yellow'. All modern orange and yellow colored roses are descendants of this plant, these originally called "Pernetiana" roses.

'Persian Yellow'. Flowers golden-yellow, small, densely double, globose. FS 374 (= *R. lutea persiana* Lemaire). Introduced from Iran in 1837. ⊕

R. foliolosa Nutt. Shrub, 0.3–0.7 m high, branches reddish, with short, straight or somewhat curved prickles or nearly thornless, occasionally bristly; leaflets 7–9, narrowly oblong, 12–25 mm long, glabrous and glossy above, occasionally with pubescent venation beneath; flowers light red, solitary or few, 3 cm wide, sepals lanceolate, long acuminate, to 2.5 cm long, glandular bristled, as are the calyx and short stalk, July–August (!); fruits rather globose, 8 mm thick, red. WR 70; BM 8513; BC 3445; KHL 2: 154. SE. USA. 1880. Very attractive foliage, quite winter hardy, also very tolerant of dryness. z6 Fig. 172.

R. forrestiana Bouleng. Shrub, to 1 m high, stems stiffly erect, prickles paired, straight or bowed upward, brown; leaflets 5–7, ovate to obovate, 1–2 cm long, apex rounded, glabrous beneath or with a pubescent midrib, serrate; flowers solitary or several, pink, 2–3 cm wide, sepals small, filamentous, persistent, bracts large (!), oval, glandular bristly, June–July. Bull. BG Brux. 14: 126; GRS 17. W. China. 1922. Similar to *R. multibracteata*, but shorter and flowering less abundantly. z8

R. forrestii see: **R. roxburghii** f. **normalis**

R. × fortuniana Lindl. (*R. banksiae* × *R. laevigata*). Evergreen climber, 7–10 m high, branches thin, prickles scattered, sickle-form curved, small; leaflets 3–5, oval-lanceolate, finely serrate, thin, light green, glossy, stipules small, awl-shaped, abscising; flowers solitary (!!), or short, bristly stalks, cream-white, double, 7 cm wide, petals more loosely and irregularly arranged, June. WR 36; FS 7: 256. China, known only in cultivation. Brought to England around 1845 by R. Fortune. Very similar to *R. banksiae*, but larger in all respects. Often cultivated under this name, but easily distinguished by the glandular flower stalks. z9

R. franchetii see: **R. luciae**

R. × 'Francofurtana' (*R. gallica* × *R. majalis*). Shrub, to 2 m high, stems with partly straight, partly bowed prickles, flowering shoots nearly thornless; leaflets 5–7, occasionally 3, oval-rounded, serrate, densely ash-gray floccose beneath, stipules on the flowering shoots larger and wider than those of the other shoots; flowers solitary, terminal, 5–7 cm wide, single to semidouble, purple, lightly fragrant, receptacle top-shaped, glandular bristled at the base, as is the stalk, sepals erect after flowering, rather entire, June. HF 2628 (= *R. turbinata* Ait.; *R. campanulata* Ehrh.). Known before 1770. z6 Fig. 177. ⊕

R. fraxinifolia see: **R. blanda**

R. freundiana see: **R. × dupontii**

R. froebelii see: **R. coriifolia** var. **froebelii**

R. frutetorum see: **R. coriifolia**

R. fujisanensis see: **R. luciae** var. **fujisanensis**

R. gallica L. (1759). French Rose. Shrub, 40–80(150) cm high, with underground, densely prickly and bristly stoloniferous suckers, young branches green to dull red, prickles compact and uneven, intermixed with prickly bristles; leaflets tough, 3–5, broadly elliptic, 2–5 cm long, serrate or biserrate, dark green and rough above, lighter and pubescent beneath, petiolules and rachis bristly glandular; flowers solitary, pink to red, 5–6 cm wide, mostly single, fragrant, sepals with numerous lanceolate-linear pinnae, abscising before the fruits ripen, June; fruits top-shaped, brick-red, glandular bristled, but the bristles dropping from the ripe fruits. WR 325; BM 1377; HM Pl. 155; KHL 2: Pl. 153 and 156; KSR 5–6 (= R. rubra Blackw.). S. and central Europe, to Belgium and central France and in Asia Minor. Very winter hardy. Cultivated since antiquity and a forebear of our modern garden roses. Much planted in the 18th century in Provins, France (a small village about 50 km southeast of Paris) giving rise to the name "Provins Rose". This name was, however, later to cause considerable confusion for the similarity to the name "Provence Rose" for Rosa centifolia. z6 Plate 81; Fig. 177.

During the first half of the 19th century, more than 1000 R. gallica forms were cultivated. Empress Joséphine of France had no less than 167 R. gallica cultivars in her rose garden at Malmaison in 1811. Aside from collectors' gardens, only a few gallica cultivars are grown today. Among those are:

'Conditorum'. The "Hungarian Rose". Shrub, about 1 m high; flowers magenta-pink, semidouble, purple veined, very fragrant. Probably a very old cultivar, but first introduced and named by Dieck in 1889. Used in Hungary in the preparation of rose water and pastries.

var. damascena see: R. × damascena

'Officinalis'. Apothecary Rose; "Red Rose of Lancaster". Scarcely higher than 70 cm, branches with small, sparse, uneven, straight prickles; leaflets 5, ovate, glabrous above, pubescent beneath; flowers carmine-red, semidouble, yellow anthers, very fragrant, mid-late; fruits large, nearly globose, dark red. WR 121 (as R. provincialis); GSR 86; SOR 1 (= R. provincialis Mill.). Probably the best known R. gallica cultivar, grown as early as 1310 in France where apothecaries used the dry, crushed petals in the production of a scented powder.

'Pumila'. Only 20–30 cm high, creeping; leaflets oval-rounded; flowers single, red, flower stalks and calyx sparsely glandular. WR 109 (= R. pumila Jacq.; R. austriaca pygmaea Wallr.). Known before 1789; occasionally occurring naturally in Spain and Italy.

variegata see: 'Versicolor'

'Versicolor'. Sport of 'Officinalis' and the same in habit, thorns and foliage; flowers white-red-pink, striped and dappled, with many yellow anthers in the center, 7–8 cm across, summer flowering, fragrant. WR 110; GSR 92 (= R. rosamundi West; R. gallica variegata Andr.). First introduced in 1583 by Clusius, but surely much older.
    Some additional R. gallica forms are: 'Belle des Jardins', 'Camaieux', 'Cardinal de Richelieu', 'Charles de Mills', 'Georges Vibert', 'Sissinghurst Castle', 'Tuscany' and 'Violacea'; the newest cultivar is 'Scharlachglut'.

R. gebleriana see: R. laxa

R. gentiliana see: R. multiflora f. cathayensis

R. germanica see: R. × polliniana

R. gigantea Coll. ex Crép. Climbing rose, to 10 m high (15 m in its habitat), prickles stout, hook-like, but scattered and often totally absent; leaflets 5–7, lanceolate, about 7 cm long, glabrous and glossy, deeply and often glandular serrate, stipules long and narrow, with linear tips; flowers usually solitary, white to yellowish, 10–12 cm wide, fragrant, sepals 3 cm long, occasionally widened at the apex, reflexed, glabrous, eventually abscising, May–June; fruits globose to pear-shaped, 2–3 cm long, thick walled, yellow to orange. WR 34; BM 7972; NF 1: 260 (= R. odorata var. gigantea [Crép.] Rehd. & Wils.; R. xanthocarpa Watt ex Willm.). Upper Burma, SW. China. 1889. z9

f. erubescens Focke. Flowers single, light to dark pink, smaller (= R. odorata f. erubescens [Focke] Rehd. & Wils.). Presumably the type of this species. z9

R. giraldii Crép. Closely related to R. sertata, 1–2 m high, branches with thin, straight, often paired prickles, occasionally also thornless; leaflets 7(9), rounded to ovate, 1.5–2.5 cm long, pubescent on both sides, also often glandular beneath, serrate; flowers pink, solitary or 3–5, 2.5 cm wide, stalk short, glandular bristled like the calyx, sepals persistently glandular, stalk very short, glandular pubescent, June–July; fruits ovate, 1 cm long, scarlet. Central and N. China. 1897. z5

R. glabrata see: R. × spinulifolia

R. glauca Pourr. Red Leaf Rose. Shrub, to 3 m high, erect habit, slender branched, shoots brown-red, pruinose, sparsely prickly, prickles straight or hooked; leaves brownish purple and bluish pruinose (!), leaflets 5–7, elliptic, glabrous, scabrous serrate; flowers numerous, carmine pink, 3–4 cm wide, calyx erect at fruiting time, later abscising, June; fruits globose, 1.5 cm thick, red. WR 133; BR 430; KHL 2: Pl. 158; KSR 11 (= R. rubrifolia Vill.; R. ferruginea Déségl.). Pyrenees to Yugoslavia, in the mountains. 1814. Susceptible to rust! See also: R. dumalis. z2–7 Fig. 179.

R. glaucophylla see: R. hemisphaerica

R. glutinosa Sibth. & Sm. Southern Wine Rose. Shrub, 30–70 cm high, growth dense, very prickly, prickles sometimes thick and rather straight, sometimes bristly glandular; leaves 3–7 parted, rounded, elliptic, small, biserrate, glandular on both sides, also glandular on the margins, petiole and stipules; flowers light pink, solitary on short stalks, small, sepals pinnate, calyx and stalk glandular bristled, style pubescent, June; fruit scarlet-red, glossy, bristly, 1.5 cm thick. WR 150; KHL 2: Pl. 156; KSR 18 (= R. pulverulenta Bieb.). Eastern and central Mediterranean region, Balkan Peninsula, Asia Minor. 1821. Similar to R. sicula, but having the prickles densely intermixed with stalked glands. Fig. 177.

var. dalmatica (Kern.) Schneid. Less pubescent, prickles straight; leaflets larger, to 2.5 cm long; fruits larger, ovate, to 2.5 cm long. BM 8826 (= R. dalmatica Kern.). Dalmatia. 1882.

R. gmelinii see: R. acicularis var. fennica

R. graveolens see: R. inodora

R. grosseserrata see: R. macounii

R. guilelmi-waldemarii see: R. webbiana

R. gymnocarpa Nutt. Shrub, 0.5–1.5 m high, stems glabrous, with thin, paired prickles and bristly; leaflets 5–9, glabrous, rather widely spaced (!!), oval-elliptic to round, sharply biserrate and glandular; flowers pink, solitary or paired, to 3 cm wide, sepals ovate, acuminate, abscising, stalk glabrous to glandular bristled, June–July; fruit globose, 6–8 mm thick, with many small seeds. MS 195; WR 71; KHL 2: Pl. 159. Western N. America. 1893. One of the few shade tolerant wild roses. z6 Fig. 178.

R. hakonensis see: **R. luciae** var. **hakonensis**

R. × **hardii** Cels. (*R. clinophylla* × *R. persica*). Resembling *R. persica*, but much taller, to 2 m; leaves sometimes simple, sometimes 7-part pinnate, dark green, oval-oblong, deeply incised, glabrous, with stipules; flowers light yellow, with a red basal spot on each petal, to 5 cm wide; fruits obtusely ovate, somewhat prickly bristled, yellow and orange when ripe, 3 cm long, infertile. WR 2; BM 195; JRHS 91: 163 (= *Hulthemosa hardii* [Cels.] Rowley). Developed before 1836 in the Jardin de Luxembourg, Paris, France. z8

R. × **harisonii** Rivers (? 'Persian Yellow' × *R. pimpinellifolia*). Shrub, about 50–100 cm high, branches short; leaflets 5–9, elliptic, biserrate, glandular beneath, as is the thinly pubescent petiole; flowers solitary, semidouble, light yellow, 5–6 cm wide, sepals lobed at the apex, calyx and stalk bristly, May; fruit nearly black. GSR 20; RJb 35: 48. 1830. This is the well-known "Yellow Rose of Texas". z6

'Vorbergii'. Flowers cream-white, single, to 5 cm wide, calyx and stalk smooth, mid May, flowering very abundantly; fruit globose, about 15 mm thick, black. GS 1923: 102 (= *R. vorbergii* Graebn.). Originated before 1902 in the Forest Botanic Garden at Hannover-Münden, W. Germany.

R. helenae Rehd. & Wils. Strong growing climber, to 5 m high, branches stoutly thorned, thorns hook-like, young shoots reddish; leaflets usually 7–9, oval-lanceolate, 2.5–5 cm long, glabrous, gray-green and pubescent beneath, mostly scabrous and single serrate; flowers white, 2–3 cm wide, several in flat umbellate panicles, fragrant, sepals lanceolate, finely acuminate, shorter than the reflexed petals and abscising, calyx glabrous, stalk glandular, June–July; fruit ovate, red, to 12 mm long. NF 12: 120; GSR 21; CIS 77. Central China. 1907. Found by E. H. Wilson and named for his wife. z6

R. hemisphaerica Herrm. "Sulfur Rose". Shrub, 1–2 m high, branches somewhat stiffly erect, with hook-like prickles, these compressed at the base; leaves dark gray or blue-green above, leaflets 5–9, obovate, coarsely serrate, 3–4 cm long, underside usually lighter and finely pubescent; flower buds green-yellow, flowers sulfur-yellow, to 5 cm wide, very densely double, globose, mostly solitary, nodding, without fragrance, sepals erect, persistent, June–July, not flowering in wet soils; fruit globose, dark red. WR 93; BR 46 (= *R. glaucophylla* Ehrh.; *R. sulphurea* Ait.). Introduced from Turkey around 1600 by Clusius; not observed in the wild. Thrives best in a dry, warm climate. z6 Fig. 182.

var. **rapinii** (Boiss. & Bal.) Rowley. This is the single flowering wild form of *R. hemisphaerica!* Shrub, only about 1 m high, branches with prickles, often also with bristles intermixed; leaflets usually 7, velvety pubescent on the venation beneath;

flower single, light yellow, solitary or 2–3 together, calyx hemispherical; fruit globose, smooth, yellow to red, about 1.5 cm long (= *R. rapinii* Boiss. & Bal.). Asiatic Turkey to NW. Iran. First introduced in 1933. Very rare in cultivation and difficult to grow.

R. hemsleyana Täckholm. Shrub, to 2 m high, stems only slightly prickly, prickles short, straight, with a broad base; leaflets 7–9, elliptic, 2–5 cm long, double glandular serrate, underside glabrous or pubescent on the venation, stipules broad, glandular ciliate, rachis glandular; flowers 3–11, pink, 3–5 cm wide, stalk 1–3 cm long, densely glandular bristled, sepals caudate, with a wide, serrate apex, June; fruit oval-oblong, with a long neck, 2.5 cm long. BM 8569 (as *R. setipoda!*). Central China. 1904. z6

R. heterophylla see: **R.** × **proteiformis**

R. × **hibernica** Templeton (*R. canina* × *R. pimpinellifolia*). Shrub, 1–2 m high, stems dark red, erect or bowed, prickles scattered, hook-like, with a few bristles intermixed; leaflets 7–8, ovate, about 18 mm long, scabrous serrate, mostly glabrous; flowers pink, 1–2–3 together, 3–5 cm wide, slightly fragrant, sepals persistent, glabrous, calyx and flower stalks glabrous; fruit globose to ovate, 12 mm thick, dull red. WR 289; GSR 22. N. Ireland, N. England, Scotland. 1802. z4

R. × **highdownensis** Hillier (*R. moyesii* × ?). Tall growing shrub, similar to *R. moyesii*, but flowers carmine-red with a white center, on nodding branches; fruit large, bottle-shaped. GSR 23, 24. Developed in 1925 by Sir Fred Stern, Highdown, England.

R. hillieri see: **R.** × **pruhoniciana**

R. hirtula see: **R. roxburghii** var. **hirtula**

R. holodonta Stapf. Very similar to *R. moyesii*, but the leaflets to 5 cm long, 2.5 cm wide, loosely pubescent beneath, particularly on the venation; flowers pink (!), 5 cm wide, solitary or in umbellate panicles of 2–6; fruit bottle-shaped, bristly or smooth, red to scarlet, to 6 cm long. BM 9248; GSR 25 (= *R. moyesii* f. *rosea* Rehd. & Wils.). W. China. 1908. z5

R. horrida Fisch. Closely related to *R. micrantha*. Lower shrub, branches rather stiff, spreading, prickles short and irregular, very much hooked, widened at the base; leaflets 5–7, oval-elliptic, 10–15 mm long, glandular beneath, occasionally also above, biserrate, stalk and stipules also glandular; flowers solitary, white, 3 cm wide, short stalked, sepals pinnate, often leaflike at the apex, as long as the petals, glandular beneath, abscising, calyx long, glandular-bristly, as is the stalk, June; fruit oval-rounded, smooth or bristly, blood-red. WR 154 (as *R. ferox*); KHR 2: Pl. 158; KSR 35 (= *R. turcica* Rouy; *R. ferox* Bieb. non Lawr.; *R. horridula* Fisch. non Spreng.). SE. Europe, Turkey, Caucasus. 1796. Similar to *R. sicula*, but with stiff, thick, crooked prickles, intermixed with bristles and stalked glands, sepals reflexed and abscising. z6 Fig. 179.

R. horridula see: **R. horrida**

R. hudsoniana see: **R. palustris**

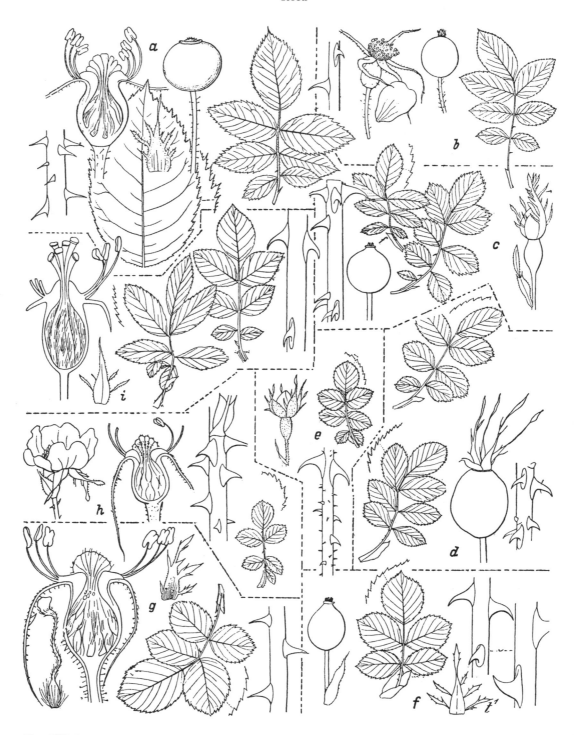

Fig. 179. **Rosa.** a. *R. marginata*; b. *R. glauca*; c. *R. agrestis*; d. *R. inodora*; e. *R. horrida*; f. *R. obtusifolia*; g. *R. corymbifera*; h. *R. sicula*; i. *R. stylosa* (most from Schneider, altered)

R. hugonis Hemsl. Shrub, 2–2.5 m high, branches deep brown, straight or bowed, prickles flat, straight, also with intermixed bristles on long shoots (!), this at least at the base of the shoot; leaflets 7–13, obovate to elliptic, 8–20 mm long, glabrous above, serrate, underside pubescent at least when young (!); flowers solitary on short lateral shoots, light yellow, 5 cm wide, stalk and calyx glabrous, May to June; fruit broadly globose, to 1.5 cm wide, deep red to blackish red. KHL 2: Pl. 152; 155f.; WR 95; BM 8004; GSR 26. Central China; on gravelly, semi-arid soil in its habitat. 1899. Named for "Father Hugo" (Rev. Hugh Scallon). z6 Plate 80; Fig. 182.

'Canary Bird' = *R. hugonis* × *R. xanthina*

R. hugonis × *R. sericea* f. *pteracantha* see: **R.** × **pteragonis** f. **pteragonis**

R. humilis see: **R. carolina**

R. hystrix see: **R. laevigata**

R. indica see: **R. chinensis** and **R. cymosa**
—*noisettiana* see: **R. noisettiana**
—*odorata* see: **R. odorata**

R. inodora Fries. Closely related to *R. rubiginosa*, to 2 m high, but leaflets elliptic to obovate-oblong, 1.5–3 cm long, not glandular, pubescent beneath; flowers pink to white, flower stalk short, normally glandular, fragrance stronger but less pleasant than that of *R. rubiginosa*; fruit ovate, bright red. WR 496; KHL 2: Pl. 158; KSR 23 (= *R. elliptica* Tausch; *R. caryophyllacea* Bess.; *R. graveolens* Gren. & Godr.). W. and Central Europe in the mountains, southeast to Albania and W. Ukraine, particularly on calcareous soils. 1875. z5 Fig. 179.

R. involucrata see: **R. clinophylla**

R. × **involuta** Sm. (*R. pimpinellifolia* × *R. villosa* or *R. tomentosa*). Shrub, 0.5–1 m high, profusely stoloniferous, the older stems chocolate-brown, bristly and prickly; leaflets 7–9, ovate, 1 cm long, overlapping, dull gray-green, venation green pubescent beneath, coarse and usually serrate, flowers solitary, white, red striped in bud, 5 cm wide, on short lateral shoots, sepals, stalk and calyx smooth, fruit globose to top-shaped, deep brown, 12 mm thick. WR 96. N. Scotland, Hebrides, but also similar hybrids observed in W. Ireland and SE. France. z6

R. × **iwara** Sieb. (*R. multiflora* × *R. rugosa*). Intermediate between the parents. Broad growing, stems gray tomentose, with wide, bowed prickles; leaflets 5–7, elliptic, gray tomentose beneath, stipules with long, bristle-formed teeth; flowers small, white, many in umbellate panicles. WR 61 (= *R. yesoensis* [Franch. & Sav.] Makino). Originated spontaneously in Japan. Brought to Europe in 1832 by Siebold; not particularly ornamental ("iwara" is Japanese for "rose thorn"). z5

R. jackii see: **R. maximowicziana** var. **jackii**

R. × **jacksonii** Willm. (*R. rugosa* × *R. wichuraiana*). Low shrub, with bowed branches, prickles very irregular, loosely arranged, straight, slender; leaflets 7–9, oblong, obtuse, tough, serrate, glossy above, stipules connate, with ovate, distinct apexes; flowers carmine, several together, flowering abundantly, calyx globose, sepals oval-lanceolate, somewhat glandular beneath, petals large, style distinct; fruit light red, urceolate to globose or bottle-shaped, but much smaller than that of *R. rugosa*. WR 20. Developed in the Arnold Arboretum by Jackson Dawson before 1897 and first given to the trade as 'Lady Duncan' but reclassified as the type of the cross in 1910 by E. Willmott. Sterile. z5

'Max Graf' is included here.

R. jasminoides see: **R. luciae** var. **hakonensis**

R. jundzillii see: **R. marginata**

R. × **kamtchatica** Vent. (*R. davurica* × *R. rugosa*). Differing from *R. rugosa* in the thinner, less prickly branches, but equally gray tomentose and short bristly; leaflets oblong, dull, less rugose above, underside usually gray-green and less pubescent; flowers 3–5 on smooth, short stalks, smaller, sepals long, inclined together; fruit smaller, globose, smooth. BR 419; BM 3149 (= *R. rugosa* var. *kamtchatica* [Vent.] Regel). E. Siberia, Kamchatka. 1770. z4

R. kelleri see: **R. maximowicziana** var. **jackii**

R. klukii see: **R. obtusifolia**

R. × **kopetdaghensis** Meff. (*R. hemisphaerica* var. *rapinii* × *R. persica*). Habit like that of *R. persica*, to 50 cm, shoots wiry, stiff, to 5 mm thick, moderately prickled, more or less finely pubescent; leaves pinnate, leaflets 3–7, elliptic, gray-green, short tomentose on both sides, with stipules; flowers like *R. hardii*, but without a basal blotch, 4 cm wide, sepals simple, densely tomentose; fruits globose, 1 cm thick, thornless. KRR 121 (= *Hulthemosa kopetdaghensis* [Meff.] Juz.). Turkmenia (USSR); Kopet-Dagh. Not completely familiar to Western botanists. z5

R. kordesii Wulff (*R.* × *jacksonii* 'Max Graf', self-hybrid). Shrubby habit, branches drooping, leaves and prickles like those of *R. wichuraiana*; leaflets usually 7, occasionally 5, light green and glossy, not rugose; flowers light red to red, single to double, 7–8 cm wide, long flowering, not fragrant; fruit ovate to ellipsoid. This plant, originated as a spontaneous chromosome doubling of 'Max Graf' by W. Kordes in 1940, is not in general cultivation, but occasionally found in botanic gardens. Kordes worked further with this plant to develop a number of 'Kordes Roses', some of the best of the modern climbing roses, notable for their vigorous habit, good health, glossy foliage and abundant, persistent flowers. z5

The more prominent cultivars: 'Hamburger Phoenix' (1954), 'Leverkusen' (1954), 'Dortmund' (1955), 'Wilhelm Hansmann (1955), 'Parkdirektor Riggers' (1957), 'Gruss an Heidelberg' (1959), 'Raymond Chenault' (1960), 'Morgengruss' (1962), 'Ilse Krohn Superior' (1964), 'Sympathie' (1964) and others.

R. koreana Komar. Shrub, to 1 m high, very dense, branches dark red, densely bristly; leaflets 7–11, elliptic,

1–2 cm long, underside glabrous to somewhat pubescent, scabrous glandular serrate; flowers white with a trace of pink, about 3 cm wide, stalks glandular; fruit ovate, orange-red, about 1.5 cm long. Korea. 1917. Alleged hybrids of this wild species by S. McGredy are not correct! See: *R.* × *coryana* Hurst (= *R. macrophylla* × *R. roxburghii*). z6

R. laevigata Michx. Cherokee Rose. Strong growing, evergreen climber, to 5 m high, stems usually glabrous, with thick, hook-like prickles; leaflets usually 3, ovate to lanceolate, glossy, smooth, midrib and petiole occasionally somewhat prickly, stipules distinct or abscising; flowers white, solitary, 7 cm wide, fragrant, sepals very bristly, entire, persistent, erect, May to June; fruit orange, pear-shaped. BM 2847; WR 40; MJ 1332; KHL 2: Pl. 150; 159 (= *R. cherokeensis* Donn; *R. triphylla* Roxb.; *R. ternata* Poir.; *R. hystrix* Lindl.). Taiwan, China; W. Hupeh, Fukien Provs., particularly common in W. Hupeh in gravelly sites. Only known in cultivation in Japan. z7 Plate 78; Fig. 178.

R. lawranceana see: **R. chinensis 'Minima'**

R. laxa Retz. Closely related to *R. majalis*. Usually somewhat lower in habit, stems with a green bark, often also somewhat reddish, prickles hook-like or also straight, widened at the base; leaflets 5–9, glabrous, or pubescent beneath, to 4 cm long; flowers white, single, solitary or several together, sepals entire, persistent, stalk glandular, July; fruit ovate, red, 1.5 cm long, sepals erect. WR 53; KHL 2: Pl. 159 (= *R. soongarica* Bge.; *R. gebleriana* Schrenk). Turkestan. 1800. Not to be confused with the understock rose "Rosa laxa" (see *R. coriifolia* var. *froebelii*). z6 Fig. 178.

R. × **lheritieranea** Thory (*R. chinensis* × ?). Climbing to 4 m high, stem only slightly prickly or totally thornless, reddish on the sunny side, otherwise green, prickles light, soft; leaflets 3–7, oval-oblong, serrate, glabrous; flowers more or less double, flat shell-form, bright red with a white center, several in umbellate panicles along the branches, not fragrant, buds recurved before blooming, June; fruit globose, smooth. WR 301 (= *R. reclinata* Thory; *R. boursaultiana* Desp.). Originated before 1820. As stated by G. S. Thomas, the general assumption that the Boursault Roses stem from a cross between *R. chinensis* × *R. pendulina* is improbable due to the results of recent chromosome counts. z6

> From the few cultivars included here, the following should be noted: 'Amadis', 'Morletii', 'Mme Sancy de Parabère'.

R. lindleyana see: **R. clinophylla**

R. lindleyi see: **R. carolina** var. **grandiflora**

R. longicuspis Bertol. Semi-evergreen, strong growing, climber or prostrate shrub, branches red-brown; leaves very large, 12–28 cm long, leaflets oval-elliptic to oval-oblong, 5–10 cm long, leathery tough, dark green, very glossy, long acuminate, base round, glabrous, reticulately veined beneath, stipules finely dentate; flowers white, 5 cm wide, exterior silky pubescent, in large, umbellate panicles, strongly scented (like bananas), stalk pubescent; fruit ovate, scarlet-red to orange. GSR 27 (= *R. lucens* Rolfe). W. China; Himalayas. 1915. z9

R. longifolia see: **R. chinensis 'Longifolia'**

R. lucens see: **R. longicuspis**

R. luciae Franch. & Rochebr. Shrub, procumbent or climbing to 3 m high, very similar to *R. wichuraiana*, all parts glabrous or nearly so, branches very long, prickles rather flat; stipules membranous, entire, margins somewhat glandular, the free portion short and filamentous, leaflets 5(7), rather thin, somewhat glossy above, lighter beneath, terminal leaflet ovate or narrowly ovate, 2–4 cm long, 1–2 cm wide, acuminate to long acuminate, the basal pair often smaller; flowers in umbellate panicles, white, 2–3 cm wide, fragrant, stalk 6–10 mm long, May–June (= *R. luciae* var. *oligantha* Franch. & Sav.; *R. franchetii* Koidz.). E. China, Japan, Korea; in the lower mountains, in thickets. z7

var. **fujisanensis** Makino. Leaflets 5(7), lighter beneath, glabrous to nearly so, lateral leaflets somewhat smaller, terminal leaflets rather leathery, ovate to oval elliptic, 15–25 mm long, 10–15 mm wide, acute; flowers only a few, June–July (= *R. fujisanensis* [Makino] Makino). Japan; Honshu, Shikoku. z7

var. **hakonensis** Franch & Sav. Leaflets thin, glabrous, whitish beneath, terminal leaflets ovate to broadly ovate, acute to abruptly long acuminate; flowers grouped 1–2 together, May–June (= *R. hakonensis* Koidz.; *R. jasminoides* Koidz.). Japan. z7

var. *wichuraiana* see: **R. wichuraiana**

> Including the cultivars: 'Albéric Barbier', 'Albertine', Fräulein Oktavia Hesse', 'Gerbe Rose', and others.

R. lucida see: **R. virginiana**

R. lutea see: **R. foetida**

R. lyellii see: **R. clinophylla**

R. macartnea see: **R. bracteata**

R. macounii Greene. Closely related to *R. woodsii*, but stems with straight prickles, also bristly when young; leaflets obovate, bluish and finely pubescent beneath; flowers small, light pink; fruit flat globose. RMi 204; BR 976 (as *R. woodsii*) (= *R. grosseserrata* E. Nelson; *R. subnuda* Lunell). Western N. America. Before 1826. z4

R. × **macrantha** Desp. (*R. gallica* × ?; in any case, not crossed with *R. canina*). Shrub, 1–1.5 m high, stems green, bowed, prickles scattered, bowed, also with a few bristles intermixed; leaflets 5–7, ovate, 3 cm long, serrate to biserrate, pubescent at least on the underside, petiole glandular pubescent; flowers usually several together, soft pink at first, later nearly totally white, 7 cm wide, very fragrant, single to semidouble, calyx, sepals and stalk glandular, sepals abscising, June; fruits globose, dull red, to 1.5 cm thick. NF 12: 120; WR 134; RA 1930: 260 (= *R. waitziana* var. *macrantha* [Desp.] Rehd.). Originated in France in the 18th century.

R. macrophylla Lindl. Shrub, 3–4 m high, branches dark red, with only a few, light brown, stout, straight prickles;

leaves to 20 cm long, leaflets 9–11, ovate-elliptic, to 4 cm long, acute, pubescent beneath; flowers grouped 1–3, light red, to 5 cm wide, stalk and calyx glandular bristled or smooth, sepals nearly as long as the petals, usually glandular bristly, persistent; fruit bottle-shaped, bright red, to 3 cm long, bristly. JRHS 94: 93; SNp 49; WR 50; KHL 2: Pl. 157. Himalayas. 1818. z7 Fig. 184.

var. *acicularis* see: **R. persetosa**

'Coryana' see: **R. coryana**

var. *crasseaculeata* see: **R. setipoda**

'Glaucescens' (Forrest Nr. 14985). Shoots bluish pruinose; leaves blue-green on both sides, narrower than those of 'Rubricaulis'; flowers purple-pink. Disseminated by Hillier.

f. *gracilis* see: **R. sertata**

var. *robusta* see: **R. davidii** var. **elongata**

'Rubicaulis' (Forrest Nr. 15309). Stems distinctly red, bluish white pruinose; petiole, flower stalk, bracts and major veins distinctly red. Disseminated by Hillier. Not as winter hardy as the species!

R. majalis Herrm. May Rose, Cinnamon Rose. Stoloniferous shrub, erect, to 1.5 m high, branches thin, brown-red, often thornless, prickles short and hooked, with 2 stout thorns at each leaf petiole base; leaflets 5–7, elliptic-oblong, dull green and pubescent above, more densely gray pubescent beneath, serrate; flowers grouped 1–3, often solitary, to 5 cm wide, carmine-red, petals somewhat emarginate, sepals entire, narrow, eventually erect and closing upon each other, May–June; fruit flat-globose, 1 cm thick, dark red, glabrous and smooth. WR 45; HM Pl. 155; 1233; KHL 2: Pl. 157; KSR 1 (= *R. cinnamomea* sensu L. [1759] non L. [1753], nom. ambig.). N. and central Europe to the USSR, except the southwestern part. Cultivated before 1600. The old name *R. cinnamomea* should no longer be used since it was originally a synonym for *R. pendulina* and according to nomenclatural rules must be thrown out. z6 Fig. 184.

'Foecundissima'. Flowers pink, double. WR 45; BC 3456 (= *R. cinnamomea* f. *plena* West.; *R. foecundissima* Muenchh.). 1596.

R. majalis × *R. gallica* see: **R. × 'Francofurtana'**

R. manettii see: **R. noisettiana 'Manettii'**

R. marginata Wallr. Upright shrub, 2–2.5 m high, closely related to *R. canina*, but differing in the straight or nearly straight prickles; leaves double glandular serrate, underside also usually glandular; flowers solitary or grouped, pink, later white, to 7 cm wide, sepals pinnate, dorsal side glandular, shorter than the petals, sepals abscising, June; fruit ovate, dark red, smooth. WR 149; KHL 2: Pl. 158; KSR 9–10 (= *R. jundzillii* Bess.). Central and E. Europe, west Asia. 1870. z5 Fig. 184.

R. × mariae-graebnerae Aschers & Graebn. (*R. palustris* × *R. virginiana*). Shrub with a rather globose habit, to 1.5 m high, resembling *R. palustris*, prickles slightly bowed, scattered bristly or totally lacking bristles on the long shoots; leaflets more glossy and more coarsely dentate, fall color of the leaves a conspicuous red and yellow; flowers bright pink, lasting the entire summer, also

flowering with the fruit; fruit red. Developed around 1900 by H. Zabel in the Botanic Garden of Hannover-Münden, W. Germany, but occasionally found naturally in the habitat of the parents. z5

R. marrettii Lév. Upright shrub, 1.5–2 m high, branches reddish, with a few, slender, upward curving prickles, mostly paired; leaflets 7–9, oblong, 2–3 cm long, rather glabrous, serrate; flowers few together, pink, 4–5 cm wide, sepals wider at the apex, pubescent beneath, longer than the petals, persistent, stalk glabrous, June; fruit rather globose, 12 mm thick, red. WR 162; MJ 3526 (= *R. rubro-stipulata* Nakai). Sachalin Island. 1908. z2

R. maximiliani see: **R. woodsii**

R. maximowicziana Regel. Climbing rose, densely branched, stems with only a few small, hooked prickles, also bristly on young shoots; leaflets 7–9, oval-elliptic, 2.5–5 cm long, smooth, glossy, single serrate, petiole pubescent, loosely glandular and prickly, stipules very narrow, glandular ciliate; flowers white, in small umbellate panicles, 2.5–3 cm wide, sepals long, narrow, pinnate, eventually abscising, styles fused into a glabrous column; bracts persistent, June–July; fruit ovate, 12 mm thick, red, smooth. NK 7: 1. Manchuria, Korea. Before 1880. z6

var. **jackii** (Rehd.) Rehd. Branches purple, with scattered, hook-like prickles, without bristles; leaflets to 6 cm long, stipules entire; panicles with about 20 flowers, petals obovate; fruits pear-shaped, 5–7 mm thick, red. NK 7: 3 (= *R. jackii* Rehd.; *R. kelleri* Baker). Korea. 1905.

var. **pilosa** (Nakai) Nakai. Primarily differing in the pubescent petioles and flower stalks (= *R. jackii* var. *pilosa* Nakai). Korea. 1916. This form was crossed with some hybrid teas at the Iowa State College, USA. The best were named and introduced in 1953.

R. micrantha Sm. Similar to *R. rubiginosa*. Shrub, upright, to about 1.5 m high, densely branched, stems bowed, all prickles alike, curved; leaflets 5–7, broadly ovate, 2–3 cm long, glabrous or pubescent above, underside densely glandular and pubescent; flowers 1–4, pink to white, 3 cm wide, sepals pinnate, abscising early, enlarged at the apex, glandular, styles glabrous, June; fruit ovate, 12–18 mm long. WR 148; HM 1224; KHL 2: Pl. 156; KSR 19–20. W. central and south Europe to N. Ukraine. Before 1800. z6 Fig. 177.

R. microcarpa see: **R. cymosa**

R. microphylla see: **R. roxburghii**

R. × micrugosa Henkel (*R. roxburghii* × *R. rugosa*). Large shrub, narrowly upright, to 2 m high, branches very prickly and straight; leaves very densely arranged; flowers solitary, 7–10 cm wide, clear pink; fruit orange, very prickly, like *R. roxburghii*. Gfl Pl. 1581; RH 1905: Pl. 144; GSR 28 (= *R. vilmorinii* Bean). Developed before 1905 by Henri de Vilmorin. Seedlings are sometimes attractive plants with fragrant, white flowers. z5

R. minutifolia Engelm. Shrub, about 1 m high, young stems soft pubescent, densely covered with slender, brown prickles; leaves only 2–4 cm long, leaflets 3–5, occasionally to 7, elliptic to obovate, 3–8 mm long, deeply incised, underside soft pubescent; flowers solitary or grouped, pink to nearly white, 2.5 cm wide; fruit globose, very prickly, red, 8 mm thick. BC 3457; DL 3: 247; KHL 2: 154. USA; California. 1888. Needs a dry, hot climate; not very winter hardy. z9 Fig. 172.

R. mirifica see: **R. stellata** var. **mirifica**

R. mitissima see: **R. pimpinellifolia** var. **inermis**

R. mokanensis see: **R. wichuraiana**

R. mollis Sm. Small shrub, upright, about 1 m high, branches reddish, pruinose, with evenly formed, thin, rather straight prickles; leaflets 5–7, smaller than those of the similar *R. villosa* and more rounded, silky pubescent beneath, less glandular, biserrate; flowers 1–4 together, pink, 4–5 cm wide sepals somewhat pinnate, glandular bristly, persistent, June–July; fruit globose, scarlet-red, somewhat bristly or totally smooth, ripening early. WR 138; KSR 14 (= *R. mollissima* Fries; *R. villosa* var. *mollissima* Rau). Mainly in N. and W. Europe, eastward to south central Russia. 1818. Distinguished from the similar *R. villosa* by the pruinose young shoots and the smaller leaflets (12–35 × 8–18 mm). z6

R. mollissima see: **R. mollis**

R. monstrosa see: **R. chinensis** 'Viridiflora'

R. moschata Herrm. Musk Rose. Open growing shrub with 3–4 m high, glabrous, reddish, sparsely thorned shoots; leaflets 5–7, ovate, acute, deep green and glabrous above with a reddish trace at the leaf apex, underside more gray, glabrous, serrate, petiole glandular bristled, stipules small, linear, ciliate; flowers white, 5 cm wide, petals soon becoming reflexed, with a strong musk scent, in 3's, in large terminal clusters from August to frost, sepals sub-pinnate, stalk tomentose. GSR 200; SOR 32. Habitat unknown, perhaps Asia Minor. 1651. Originally described with semidouble flowers but single flowers also occur on the same plant. Very rare and only relatively recently rediscovered! The commonly cultivated *"Rosa moschata"* is a vigorous, summer blooming climber, and probably identical to *R. brunonii* (!!). *R. moschata* was much used in hybridizing and when crossed with *R. multiflora* produced the long flowering shrub roses once called "Lambertiana Roses". z7

var. *autumnalis* see: **R. noisettiana**

var. **nastarana** Christ. Leaflets smaller, denser and scabrous dentate, blue-green, glabrous, petioles glandular; flowers whie with a trace of pink, in clusters (= *R. pissardii* Carr.). Iran. 1879.

var. *nepalensis* see: **R. brunonii**

var. *nivea* see: **R. × dupontii**

'Plena'. Prickles less numerous and weaker; leaflets pubescent beneath; flowers semidouble. Cultivated since before 1629.

R. moyesii Hemsl. & Wils. Shrub, to 3 m high, stems brown-red, prickles yellowish, paired, straight; leaflets 7–13, ovate-elliptic, 1–4 cm long, finely serrate, totally glabrous except for the pubescent midrib; flowers grouped, 5–6 cm wide, dark wine-red, petals obcordate, stamens golden-yellow, stalk glandular bristly, calyx often the same or smooth, sepals ovate, long caudate, erect, June; fruit bottle-shaped, 5–6 cm long, with a distinct neck, dark orange-red. WR 74; BM 8338; GSR 30. W. China; Szechwan Prov. Found in 1890, introduced in 1894 and 1903. z6

Including the form:

'Fargesii'. A tetraploid form with shorter, more obtuse leaflets; most *moyesii* hybrids have this form as a parent! Not to be confused with *R. fargesii* (not generally cultivated) which is similar to *R. moschata*.

f. *rosea* see: **R. holodonta**

> Hybrids of *R. moyesii*: 'Eddie's Crimson', 'Eddie's Jewel', 'Eos', 'Fred Streeter', 'Geranium', 'Heart of Gold', 'Langley Gem', 'Nevada', 'Sealing Wax', 'Superba'.

R. mulliganii Bouleng. Growth habit like that of *R. rubus*, vigorous, prickles with a broad base; leaflets 5–7, elliptic, acute to acuminate, to 6 cm long, serrate, underside pubescent; flowers white, about 5 cm wide, fragrant, stalks somewhat pubescent, 2.5–3.5 cm long, sepals pinnate, 12–15 mm long; fruit orange-red, smooth or somewhat glandular, to 12 mm long. W. China. 1917–1919. Distinguished from *R. rubus* in the larger flowers on longer stalks and pinnate sepals. z5

R. multibracteata Hemsl. & Wils. Shrub, 2.5(4) m high, branches thin, bowed, prickles paired, straight, slender; leaflets 7–9, broadly ovate, 5–15 mm long, biserrate, dull green above, gray-green beneath, usually glabrous; flowers light pink, 3 cm wide, solitary or grouped in narrow, terminal, 30 cm long, nodding panicles, with clustered bracts (!!), July; fruit ovate, about 1.5 cm long, glandular bristly like the stalk, orange-red, ripening late. WR 158 (as *R. reducta*); TRT 20 (= *R. reducta* Baker). W. China; Szechwan Prov. 1910. z7

R. multiflora Thunb. Shrub, to 3 m high and wide, very vigorous, densely branched, climbing, stems moderately prickly, sometimes nearly thornless; leaflets usually 9, obovate to oblong, 2–3 cm long, persisting into winter; flowers white, 2 cm wide, many in large, conical umbellate panicles, sepals ovate, abruptly acuminate, style glabrous, June–July; fruit pea-sized, red (= *R. polyantha* S. & Z.). Japan, Korea. 1862. Much valued for dense hedges, but primarily as grafting understock for the almost totally thornless form "Thornless Multiflora". *R. multiflora* is much used in hybridizing; the descendants of which normally flower once a year (June–July) and are ascending in habit, while the *wichuraiana* types are drooping to procumbent. z5 Fig. 180.

'Carnea'. Descended from f. *cathayensis*, but with double flowers, pink. BR 425; BM 1059 (= *R. florida* Pour.). 1804.

f. **cathayensis** Rehd. & Wils. Flowers light pink, 2–4 cm wide, single, in rather flat umbellate panicles, stalks glabrous or somewhat glandular. CIS 76; WR 171; NF 8: 244; GSR 18 (= *R. gentiliana* Lév. & Van.). China. 1907.

Fig. 180. *Rosa multiflora*

'Nana' (Lille 1891). Shrub, 60–80 cm high, not climbing; flowers 2.5–4 cm wide, white to light pink, semidouble, occasionally with a few double flowers, flowering the entire summer; fruit pea-sized, red, like the species (= *R. polyantha nana* Hotr.; *R. carteri* Hort.). First developed from seed in 1891 by Léonard Lille in Lyon-Villeurbanne, France, and brought into the trade as "Rose multiflore naine remontante". Young seedlings flower after reaching 15–20 cm in height.

'Platyphylla'. Very strong growing hybrid with small, partly pink, partly carmine-red, double flowers in flat umbellate panicles, the individual flowers much larger than those of *R. multiflora*. BR 1372; MJ 1335; SOR 37 (= *R. thoryi* Tratt.; *R. platyphylla* [Thory] Takasima non Rau). Introduced from China around 1817. Also known in England as the "Seven Sisters Rose" for the 7 (although usually many more) flowers of the panicle in 7 different colors from carmine to pink.

f. watsoniana (Crép.) Matsum. Shrub, scarcely 1 m high; leaflets only 3–5 (!), very long and narrow, limb undulate, nearly bamboo-like in appearance; flowers white or pale pink, small, but in large umbellate panicles, only few flowered, June; fruit pea-sized, red. WR 16; KHL 2: Pl. 154 (= *R. watsoniana* Crép.). Japan; known only in cultivation. 1870. Fig. 172.

> Particularly prominent *multiflora* descendants: 'Aglaia', 'Crimson Rambler', 'Paul's Scarlet Climber', 'Tausend-schön', 'Veilchenblau', etc.

R. murielae Rehd. & Wils. Shrub, erect or broad growing, 1.5–3 m high, stems slender, reddish with a few thin, straight prickles or thornless; leaflets 9–15, elliptic-oblong, 2 cm long, glandular dentate, midrib pubescent beneath, petiole woolly and bristly, stipules glabrous; flowers in small umbellate panicles, 2–2.5 cm wide, white, sepals 15 mm long, long acuminate, leaflike at the apex, persistent, densely pubescent or glabrous on the dorsal side, petals circular, flower stalk very slender, 2.5 cm long, often glandular, June–July; fruits bottle-shaped, 15 mm long, orange-red. W. China. 1904. Rarely seen in gardens. z6

R. muscosa simplex see: **R. centifolia 'Andrewsii'**

R. mutabilis see: **R. chinensis 'Mutabilis'**

R. nankinensis see: **R. chinensis**

R. nipponensis see: **R. acicularis** var. **nipponensis**

R. nitida Willd. Shrub, erect, 50–70 cm high, stems densely short bristled, prickles slender, 3–5 mm long; leaflets 7–9, elliptic-oblong, 1–3 cm long, very glossy above, dark green, deep brown-red in fall; flowers solitary or groups of few, pink, 4–5 cm wide, sepals erect, narrow, entire, glandular bristly, as is the stalk, June–July; fruit globose, 1 cm thick, scarlet-red, somewhat bristly. WR 69; BB 1972; KHL 2: 157. Eastern N. America. 1807. z4 Fig. 184.

'Superba' see: **R. × rugotida 'Dart's Defender'**

> Including some cultivars (presumably hybrids with *R. rugosa*) from A. A. Nijveldt, Boskoop, Holland: 'Dutch Hedge', 'English Hedge', 'Pink Hedge' and 'Red Hedge'.

R. noisettiana Thory (*R. chinensis* × *R. moschata*). A climbing rose, stems erect, limp, prickles red, hooked; leaflets 5–7, oblong-lanceolate, single serrate, light green beneath, petiole usually pubescent and with fine prickles; flowers yellow, white or pink, no red tones, occasionally to 100 flowers in an inflorescence, but only medium-sized, fragrant. WR 32; BS 3: 216 (= *R. indica noisettiana* Ser.; *R. moschata autumnalis* Hort.). All forms very sensitive to frost and seldom found in cultivation. Original cross made in 1810 by John Champney in Charleston, South Carolina, USA and named 'Champney's Pink Cluster'. z7

Included here is the once well-known form **'Maréchal Niel'** (Pradel 1864), flower sulfur-yellow, very fragrant.

'Manettii' (Crivelli). Shrub, to over 2 m high, branches and twigs with white longitudinal stripes, young shoots reddish, prickles numerous, nearly black; leaflets 7–9, broadly elliptic; flowers semidouble, pink (= *R. manettii* Crivelli). Originated around 1837 in the Milan Botanic Garden, Italy. Valued as an understock since it roots easily from cuttings.

R. nutkana Pall. Shrub, to 1.5 m high, erect, branches thin, dark brown, narrowly upright, prickles broad and straight, young shoots usually bristly; leaflets 5–9, broadly oval-elliptic, 2–5 cm long, dark green and glabrous above, underside somewhat glandular pubescent, doubly glandular serrate; flowers usually solitary, lilac-pink, 5–6 cm wide, stalk usually somewhat glandular-bristly, calyx smooth, June–July; fruit globose, smooth, red, to 2 cm thick. WR 75; MS 190; KHL 2: Pl. 154. Western N. America, along the coast of Alaska to N. California. *R. nutkana* has been occasionally used in hybridizing. z6 Fig. 172.

'Cantab' (Hurst 1927) (*R. nutkana* × 'Red-Letter Day'). Shrub, 1.5–2 m high, foliage deep green; flowers single, to 8 cm wide, shell form, deep pink with a white center, stamens yellow, flowering once.

var. **hispida** Fern. Leaves coarsely serrate; fruit glandular bristly (= *R. macdougalii* Holzinger). British Columbia to Utah.

R. obtusifolia Desv. Similar to *R. canina*, about 1.5 m high, prickles usually very hooked; leaflets 5–7, deep green and often glossy above, more or less pubescent, underside the same; flowers small, white to pale reddish, style short-haired, sepals eventually abscising; fruit scarlet to orange, globose, smooth. KHL 2: 158 (as *R. tomentella*); KSR 25 (= *R. tomentella* Léman; *R. canina* var. *tomentella* [Lém.] Baker; *R. klukii* Bess.). Central, south and NW. Europe, primarily in the mountains. 1905. z6 Fig. 179.

R. ochroleuca see: **R. pimpinellifolia** f. **luteola**

R. odorata (Andr.) Sweet (*R. chinensis* × *R. gigantea*). Tea Rose. Evergreen or semi-evergreen climber with long, often procumbent shoots, climbing to 10 m high under ideal conditions, prickles scattered, hook-like; leaflets 5–7, elliptic-oblong, 2–7 cm long, scabrous serrate, glossy above; flowers white, light pink or yellowish, single or double, 5–7 cm wide, solitary or several together, fragrant, stalk short, occasionally glandular, sepals entire or lightly pinnate, style distinct, exserted, June–September. WR 179–180; PWR 193 (= *R. indica odorata* Andr.; *R. thea* Savi). Origin unknown; found in cultivation in China, 1810. The hybridizing of Tea Roses occurred shortly thereafter in France since the plants would not set fruit in the open in England and cultivation under glass was not yet common. See also: **R. gigantea**. z7

Here follows the most prominent forms of the species cultivated in China since time immemorial, in order of their introduction:

'Hume's Blush Tea-scented China'. Presumably a natural hybrid of *R. chinensis* × *R. gigantea*. Branches very long, prickles scattered, hooked; leaflets 5–7; flowers semidouble, pink, persistently flowering, fragrant (= *R. indica odorata* Andrews, Roses Pl. 77; *R. indica fragrans* Thory in Redouté, Roses 1: Pl. 19; *R. indica odoratissima* Lindl. in BR 804). Discovered in 1809 by an officer of the English East India Company in the Fan Tee Nursery near Canton, China. Introduced into England and named by Sir Abraham Hume. Only known through illustrations today. The fragrance of this rose (opinions differ as to whether it is the flowers or the crushed leaves) resembles that of crushed tea leaves. Later, as new forms were introduced the typical fragrance was lost and the name "Tea Rose" was adopted.

'Parks' Yellow Tea-scented China'. Presumably also a natural hybrid of *R. chinensis* × *R. gigantea*. Flowers light yellow, double (= *R. odorata ochroleuca* Lindl.). Discovered in 1824 by John Damper Parks in the same nursery as the previous cultivar. Later much hybridized; while a good seed producer, no lasting pure yellow flowers were obtainable and the plant was eventually lost in cultivation.

'Fortune's Double Yellow'. Strong growing, to 3 m high; flowers 4–8 together, loosely double, salmon-yellow, exterior reddish, very fragrant, 7–10 cm wide. FS 769; BM 4679; WR 28 (= *R. odorata* var. *pseudindica* [Lindl.] Rehd.; 'Gold of Ophir'; 'Beauty of Glazenwood'). Discovered by Robert Fortune in 1845 in the garden of a mandarin in Ningpo, China.

R. omeiensis see: **R. sericea**

R. omissa see: **R. sherardii**

R. orientalis Dupont ex Ser. Dwarf habit, young shoots densely pubescent, prickles extraordinarily sparse, slightly bowed to straight, needlelike with a broad base; leaflets 5, elliptic, usually about 15 mm long, light green above, gray beneath, pubescent on both sides, teeth broad and directed forward; flowers solitary, pink, short stalked, pedicel and calyx with long stalked glands and bristles, sepals erect; fruits ellipsoid, 1 cm long. KSR 36. S. Yugoslavia, N. Albania, Greece, Asia Minor. 1905. z7

R. oxyodon Boiss. Very similar to *R. pendulina*, but to about 2 m high or more, branches reddish, sparsely prickly; leaflets normally 9, elliptic, 2.5–5 cm long, venation pubescent beneath, doubly serrate and often glandular, stipules large, midrib reddish, limb red glandular; flowers 3–7 in umbellate panicles, dark pink, 5–6 cm wide, slightly fragrant, stalk glandular bristly (!); fruits ovate to bottle-shaped, red, smooth, nodding (not pendulous) (= *R. pendulina* var. *oxyodon* [Boiss.] Rehd.). E. Caucasus. 1904. z6

f. **haematodes** (Crép.) Krüssm. To 3 m high; leaves more blue-green, petiole bright red; flowers similar to those of the species, but in smaller umbellate panicles; fruits larger, bottle-shaped, pendulous, scarlet-red. KHL 2: 153 (= *R. pendulina* f. *haematodes* [Crép.] Krüssm.). Caucasus. 1863. Plate 81.

R. palustris Marsh. Swamp Rose. Erect, very broad shrub, 1–1.8 m high, branches reddish, prickles somewhat hooked with a broad base; leaflets usually 7, broadly elliptic, acute at both ends, 2–5 cm long, finely and scabrous serrate, tough, dark green and glabrous above, underside lighter and pubescent; flowers pink, 5 cm wide, in umbellate panicles, June to late July; fruits globose, red, glabrous, pea-sized, glossy, stalk glandular. GSP 232; BB 2: 1970; WR 68 (as *R. carolina*!) (= *R. hudsoniana* Thory; *R. pensylvanica* Michx.). Eastern N. America. Always in swamps in its habitat. 1726. Relatively little cultivated and quite variable; often confused with the glossy green (!) leaved *R. virginiana* Mill. or the stoloniferous *R. carolina* L. Not well suited for the small garden! z5

R. × paulii Rehd. (*R. arvensis* × *R. rugosa*). Intermediate between the parents. Branches to 4 m long, vigorous, prostrate, very prickly; flowers white, single, to 6 cm wide, in clusters. KHL 2: Pl. 160; GSR 34 (= *R. rugosa repens alba* Paul). Before 1903. Plate 82.

'Rosea'. Like the species, but having pure pink flowers with a somewhat lighter center. GSR 35 (= *R. rugosa repens rosea* Hort.). Before 1903.

R. pendulina L. Alpine Rose. Shrub, 1–1.5 m high, branches usually reddish or also green, often totally thornless (!); leaflets 7–9, oval-oblong, 2–6 cm long, doubly glandular serrate, pubescent or also glabrous on both sides; flowers 1–5, but usually solitary, pink to purple, to 4 cm wide, sepals persistent, erect; fruit pendulous, ovate to bottle-shaped, light red, May–June. KHL 162; WR 99; HM 1233; HF 2625; KSR 2–3 (= *R.*

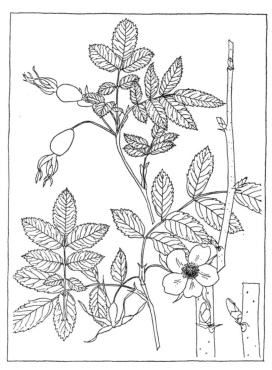

Fig. 181. *Rosa pendulina*

alpina L.). Mountains of S. and central Europe. 1789. z6 Fig. 181.

f. *haematodes* see: **R. oxyodon** f. **haematodes**

var. *oxyodon* see: **R. oxyodon**

f. **pyrenaica** (Gouan) Keller. Lower habit, branches bluish green, only slightly reddish; leaflets usually ovate, venation glandular beneath, as are the biserrate margins; petiole and flower rachis always glandular bristly. BM 6724 (as *R. alpina*). Pyrenees. 1815.

R. pennsylvanica see: **R. carolina 'Plena'**

R. pensylvanica see: **R. palustris**

R. × penzanceana Rehd. (*R. rubiginosa* × *R. foetida* 'Bicolor'). This is the correct botanical name for the hybrid 'Lady Penzance' (Lord Penzance 1894). The other so-called "rubiginosa hybrids" are not of this cross; e.g. 'Lord Penzance' is of *R. harisonii* × *rubiginosa*. The others are of Remontant types × *R. rubiginosa*.

R. persetosa Rolfe. Similar to *R. setipoda*, but stems densely bristly, also the flower stalks, 1.5 m high; leaflets 5–9, about 2–5 cm long, serrate, underside soft pubescent, as is the rachis; flowers 2–3 cm wide, deep pink, grouped in large panicles, flower stalk and calyx cup glabrous, sepals entire, June. JRHS 27: 487 (= *R. macrophylla* var. *acicularis* Vilm.). W. China. 1895. Not to be confused with *R. elegantula* var. *persetosa*! z6

R. persica Michx. Small shrub, 20–50 cm high, very stoloniferous, branches yellow-brown, finely prickly; leaves simple (not pinnate!), sessile, elliptic-oblong, 2–3 cm long, blue-green, finely pubescent, serrate; flowers solitary, 5 cm wide, yellow with a deep red "eye", sepals lanceolate, persistent, simple, May–August; fruits globose, densely bristly, green. JRHS 88: 63; WR 1; BM 7096; KHL 2: Pl. 154 (= *R. berberifolia* Pall.; *R. simplicifolia* Salisb.). Afghanistan to Dsungaria, on salt-laden soil near the Caspian and Aral Seas. 1790. Easily propagated from seed but difficult to cultivate. z5 Fig. 172.

R. phoenicia Boiss. Somewhat similar to *R. moschata*. Vigorous habit, branches thin, whip-like, several meters long, glabrous, green, with a few, small, hook-like prickles; leaflets 5–7, usually ovate-elliptic, obtuse, scabrous and serrate, somewhat pubescent, particularly on the underside, petiole pubescent and prickly; flowers in many-flowered umbellate panicles, white, 4–5 cm wide, buds oval, sepals shorter than the petals, pinnate, tapered at the apex, abscising, calyx and the much elongated style column glabrous, June; fruit ovate, red, 12 mm long, October. KHL 2: Pl. 159. Turkey, Syria, Lebanon. Around 1885. Very difficult to transplant because of its deep rooting habit; thrives on hot, dry soil and flowers abundantly. z9 Fig. 178.

R. pimpinellifolia L. Scotch Rose. Vigorously stoloniferous shrub, about 1 m high, branches thin, divaricate or bowed or also more upright, very densely prickly and bristly, particularly at the branch base; leaflets 5–11, but normally 7–9, nearly circular, 1–2 cm long, glandular biserrate, glabrous; flowers to 5 cm wide, mostly white, occasionally also more or less yellow or pink, numerous, but solitary and arranged on short lateral shoots, sepals entire, persistent, much shorter than the petals, May–June; fruits flat globose, brown-black, smooth, stalk thick and fleshy. WR 82; HM 1233; KHL 2: Pl. 155; KSR 4 (= *R. spinosissima* L.). Europe to Asia. Cultivated for centuries. Quite variable! z5 Fig. 182.

var. **altaica** (Willd.) Thory. Habit more upright, to 1.8 m, branches less prickly; leaflets usually 9, stipules narrow, margins glandular; flowers about 7 cm wide, white, opening light yellow, petiole and calyx smooth; fruits larger, brown-red. GSR 52; PWR 186 (= var. *grandiflora* Ledeb.). Siberia, Dsungaria, Altai Mts. 1818.

'Andrewsii'. Low; flowers light red, semidouble, floriferous; fruit smooth. WR 89. Origin unknown, but growing in French gardens before 1806.

'Flava'. Whitish yellow.

var. *grandiflora* see: var. **altaica**

var. **hispida** (Sims) Boom. Shrub, to 2 m high, branches densely covered with thin prickles and bristles; leaflets 7–9, 2–3 cm long, serrate; flowers pale yellow, 5–6 cm wide, sepals entire, calyx glabrous; fruits flat globose, black. JRHS 83: 132; WR 87; BM 1570; GSR 53. Siberia. Before 1781.

var. **inermis** DC. Shrub, medium height, branches nearly thornless; flowers light pink, abundant (= *R. mitissima* Gmel.).

'Lutea' (Bean). About 90 cm high; leaflets broadly ovate, to 2.5 cm long, soft pubescent beneath; flowers light yellow. Origin unknown, perhaps a hybrid.

f. **luteola** (Andr.) Krüssm. 1–2 m high, very stoloniferous, branches densely bristly and prickly; leaflets 7, elliptic, nearly 2 cm long, coarsely dentate; flowers pale yellow, to 5 cm wide; fruit globose, dark purple, fleshy. WR 85 (= *R. ochroleuca* Sw.). Russia. Before 1802.

var. **myriacantha** (Lam. & DC.) Sér. Only 50–70 cm high, very densely prickly, prickles very slender, very numerous, the basal ones often recurved; leaflets very small, densely glandular; flowers small, white with a pink trace, stalk and calyx stiffly bristly. WR 88. Spain and S. France to Armenia. Before 1820.

'Nana'. Dwarf form; flowers rather large, white, semidouble. Andrews, Roses: 122. Before 1806.

'Plena'. Flowers white, double. 1819 in France.

'Rubra'. Flowers pink-red. Around 1770 in England.

var. *tuschetica* see: **R. tuschetica**

R. pisocarpa A. Gray. Shrub, to 2 m high, branches thin, gracefully nodding, sparsely prickly, very bristly at the base, prickles very small; leaflets 5–7, elliptic-oblong, 1–4 cm long, coarsely serrate, finely pubescent beneath; flowers to 3 cm wide, lilac-pink, in umbellate panicles with leaflike bracts, sepals bristly glandular beneath, June–August; fruit globose, orange, 8 mm thick, occasionally also with a short neck. WR 73; MS 197; KHL 2: Pl. 157; GRS 36. Western N. America. 1882. z6 Fig. 184.

R. pissardii see: **R. moschata** var. **nastarana**

R. platyphylla see: **R. multiflora 'Platyphylla'**

R. poetica see: **R. woodsii** var. **fendleri**

R. × pokornyana Borb. (*R. canina* × *R. glauca*). Intermediate between the parents, 1.5–2 m high, branches and twigs very pruinose, light blue, prickles scattered, straight to slightly bowed; leaflets 5–7, medium-sized to small, serrate, glabrous on both sides, pruinose, underside often violet-red; flowers grouped 1–3 together, dark red, 3.5–4 cm wide, sepals slender, with a few narrow pinnae, calyx globose to oblong; fruits small, globose (= *R. scopulosa* Briqu.). Hungary. 1916. z3

R. × polliniana Spreng. (*R. arvensis* × *R. gallica*). Growth habit like that of *R. arvensis*, stems blue-green, prickles small, scattered, hook-like; leaflets 5–7, small, rather tough and leathery, bluish green above, underside somewhat pubescent; flowers solitary or paired on long, segmented, glandular bristly stalks, about 6 cm wide, white with a trace of pink, single, fragrant; fruits only rarely developed, WR 333; KSR 37 (= *R. germanica* Märklin; *R. arvina* Schwenkf.). First observed in N. Italy, but cultivated since about 1800. z7

R. polyantha see: **R. multiflora** and **R. × rehderiana**

R. polyanthos see: **R. × damascena**

R. pomifera see: **R. villosa**

R. pratincola see: **R. suffulta**

R. × 'Prattigosa' (Kordes 1953) (*R. prattii* × *R. rugosa*).

Shrub, to 4 m high and 5 m wide, bushy; leaves light green, leathery; flowers very large, single, pink, somewhat fragrant, abundant, buds red, long acuminate; fruit flat globose, similar to *R. rugosa*, but smaller and very numerous.

R. prattii Hemsl. Resembling *R. davidii* but with smaller inflorescences. Shrub, 1–2 m high, stems reddish, glabrous, thornless or with a few straight, thin, light yellow prickles; leaves 5–7 cm long, with 11–15, ovate-lanceolate, about 2 cm long leaflets, often only half as long, obtuse serrate, venation pubescent; flowers 3–7 in umbellate panicles, pink, 2.5 cm wide, sepals abruptly acuminate, pubescent on both sides, eventually abscising, June–July; fruit ovate, scarlet-red, glandular. W. China. 1908. z6

R. pricei Hayata. Upright shrub, branches loosely prickly, nearly glabrous to somewhat bristly; leaflets usually 7, thin-leathery, oval-oblong, 1–2 cm long, 6–8 mm wide, terminal leaflet largest, acute at both ends, finely serrate, particularly toward the apex, stipules linear, connate, densely shaggy pubescent; sepals reflexed, lanceolate, finely bristly on both sides; fruit globose. Taiwan; in the mountains at 1500–2000 m.

R. primula Bouleng. Upright shrub, to about 2 m high, stems slender, red-brown at first, prickles stiff, wide, with a flat base, paired at the nodes; leaves small, 3–8 cm long, underside glandular at the margins and myrtle (*Myrtus*)-scented (!), leaflets 7–13, elliptic, 8–12 mm long, double serrate, stipules narrow, glandular, apexes filamentous; flowers solitary, flat light yellow, 3 cm wide, fragrant, petals obcordate with a flat incision, stalk short and glabrous, May; fruits globose to top-shaped, brown-red as is the stalk (!), 12–15 mm thick. NF 8: 83; 2: 193; GSR 39; PWR 184. Turkestan to N. China. 1910. Often confused with *R. ecae*, but easily distinguished by the taller habit, lighter flowers and red-brown fruits. Hybrids with this species as yet not observed. z7–8

R. × proteiformis Rowley (*R. rugosa* 'Alba' × unknown diploid). Shrub, about 1.2 m high; leaves normal at first, then gradually becoming narrower, paler and more crispate, nearly fern-like (similar to *R. multiflora* f. *watsoniana*), perhaps a virus condition; flowers white, 3 cm wide, semidouble, 5–10 together, occasionally with a second flowering period (= *R. heterophylla* Cochet-Cochet 1897, non Woods 1818). Erroneously listed by Cochet as *R. rugosa* × *R. foetida*! *R. foetida* is a tetraploid. Perhaps identical to 'Adiantifolia'.

R. provincialis see: **R. gallica 'Officinalis'**

R. × pruhoniciana Kriechbaum (*R. moyesii* × *R. willmottiae*). Shrub, strong growing, densely branched, very similar to *R. willmottiae*, but with deep red-brown flowers (!); fruits persisting long after leaf drop. GSR 40 (= *R. hillieri* Hillier). Developed by F. Zeman in 1924 in Pruhonice (near Uhrineves), Czechoslovakia. z6

R. × pteragonis Krause (*R. hugonis* × *R. sericea*). Intermediate between the parents, but the flowers with 5 petals, larger, yellow; branches with more or less broad, stout, wing-like prickles. z6

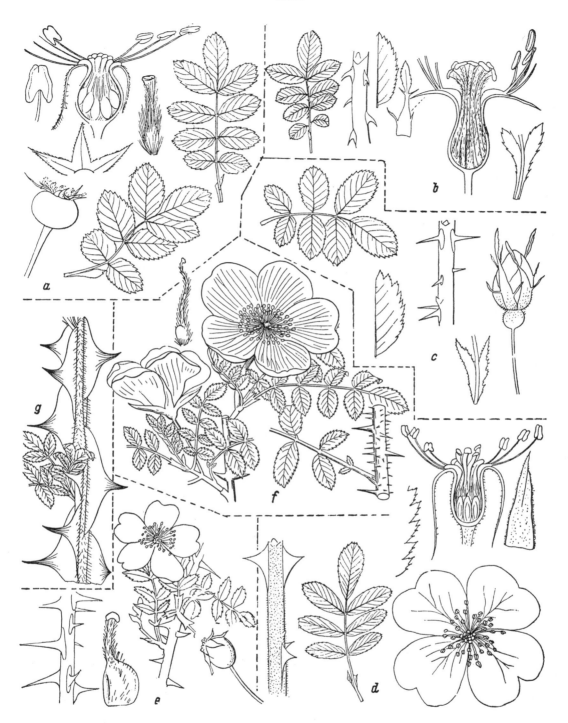

Fig. 182. **Rosa.** a. *R. pimpinellifolia;* b. *R. hemisphaerica;* c. *R. foetida;* d. *R. sericea;* e. *R. xanthina;*
f. *R. hugonis;* g. *R. sericea* var. *pteracantha* (from B. M. and Schneider, altered)

f. **pteragonis** (*R. hugonis* × *R. sericea* f. *pteracantha*). Bushy habit, to 2 m high, prickles very wide, dark red; flowers with 5 petals, light yellow, large, very numerous along the branch. Developed in 1938 by Max Krause in Holstein, W. Germany.

Including also:

f. **cantabrigiensis** (Weaver) Rowley (*R. hugonis* × *R. sericea* var. *hookeri*). Shrub, about 2 m high, branches very bristly, stiff, erect; leaflets 7–11, venation pubescent and densely glandular beneath, as are the teeth; flowers solitary, light yellow 5 cm wide, stalks 2 cm long, glandular, sepals glandular on the exterior, June. GSR 41 (= *R. cantabrigiensis* Weaver). Developed in the Cambridge Botanic Garden, England before 1931.

'Earldomensis' (*R. hugonis* × *R. sericea* var. *omeiensis*). Shrub, about 1.5 m high, outspread habit, branches nearly fern-like, fine; flowers canary-yellow. GSR 42 (= *R. earldomensis* Page 1934).

Also: 'Red Wing'.

R. pulverulenta see: **R. glutinosa**

R. pumila see: **R. gallica 'Pumila'**

R. punicea see: **R. foetida 'Bicolor'**

R. pyrifera Rydb. Very similar to and lumped together with *R. woodsii* by many authors; differing in the pear-shaped fruit. Shrub, about 1 m high or more, prickles straight, slender, 4–8 mm long; leaflets usually 7, elliptic, 2–4 cm long, coarsely serrate, deep green, glabrous above, underside finely pubescent and glandular, like the stipules, petiole and rachis finely pubescent, often also glandular; flowers white, 4–5 cm wide, in umbellate panicles, petals obcordate, sepals glandular, June–July; fruits ellipsoid to pear-shaped, 1 cm thick and 2 cm long, with a distinct neck at the apex. USA; Rocky Mts. Before 1937. z4

R. rapa see: **R. virginiana 'Plena'**

R. rapinii see: **R. hemisphaerica var. rapinii**

R. reclinata see: **R. × lheritieranea**

R. reducta see: **R. multibracteata**

R. regeliana see: **R. rugosa**

R. regelii see: **R. beggeriana**

R. × rehderiana Blackburn. The botanical name for the so-called "Polyantha Roses"; *R. chinensis* × *R. multiflora* (= *R. polyantha* Carr.). The name is, however, not very functional since the modern Polyantha Roses have not only the above parentage but many others as well. z6

The following list of Polyantha cultivars are matched with their parents by easily recognizable common characteristics:
    'Eblouissant' from *R. chinensis*
    'Minima', 'Masquerade', 'Tip-Top' from *R. foetida* Bicolor'
    'Florence Mary Morse' from *R. rubiginosa*
    'Rosenmärchen' from *R. moschata*
    'Langley Gem' from *R. moyesii*
    'Floradora' from *R. multibracteata*
    'Orange Triumph' from *R. wichuraiana*
    'Tantus Triumph' from *R. roxburghii*
    'Erna Grootendorst' from *R. rugosa*

In the process of hybridizing the many Polyantha Roses, several classes or groups were originated and were classified as follows:

POLYANTHA Roses (actually the "true" Polyantha Roses). Flowers relatively small, but very numerous and in large umbellate panicles.
    e.g.: 'Ruby', 'Paul Crampel', 'Dick Koster', 'Orléans Rose', Orange Triumph', etc.

FLORIBUNDA Roses. Flowers large, well formed, in large or small clusters.
    e.g.: 'Kordes Sondermeldung', 'Schweizer Gruss', 'Rosenelfe', 'Gruss an Aachen', etc.

FLORIBUNDA GRANDIFLORA. Flowers very large, long stalked, only a few in umbellate panicles; plants very vigorous; leaves deep green, very healthy.
    Including: 'Queen Elizabeth.'

The name "Polyantha Hybrid" for the older Floribunda types is not often used in England and America today. The term most often used, "Floribunda Tea Hybrid" is not very accurate and should probably be reduced to simply, "Floribunda".

R. repens see: **R. arvensis**

R. reuteri see: **R. dumalis**

R. × reversa Waldst. & Kit. (*R. pendulina* × *R. pimpinellifolia*). Shrub, 1–2 m high, branches usually purple, very unevenly prickled, often densely bristly on the flowering shoots; leaflets 7–11, densely glandular, 1–3 cm long, dentate; flowers solitary, reddish to milk-white, sepals simple, linear, erect on the fruits; fruit globose-ovate, 2 cm long, pendulous, dark red (= *R. rubella* Sm.). S. France, Switzerland, SE. Europe. 1820. z6

R. × richardii Rehd. (presumably *R. gallica* × *R. phoenicia*). Low shrublet, 50–70 cm high, branches green, glabrous, very prickly, prickles very uneven, small, hooked; leaflets 3–5, elliptic-oblong, obtuse, margins glandular, rugose above, somewhat pubescent beneath; flowers in small umbellate panicles, light pink, 5–7 cm wide, sepals large, pinnate, margin and dorsal side glandular, style soft pubescent, stalk glandular bristly, to 3 cm long, calyx smooth, June. WR 113 (= *R. sancta* Rich. non Andr.; *R. centifolia* var. *sancta* Zab.). Ethiopia; supposedly also growing in the wild in the E. Caucasus. 1902. The name "sancta" stems from the use of this plant near churches and graves in Ethiopia; this is also the rose (according to Crépin) that adorned tombs in Egypt from 500–200 B.C. The true parentage of this rose is still not completely clear. z7 Plate 73.

R. rosamundi see: **R. gallica 'Versicolor'**

R. roxburghii Tratt. Divaricate habit, to 2.5 m high, bark of older shoots exfoliating annually, gray, prickles paired at the leaf petiole base; leaflets elliptic-oblong, 7–15, somewhat pubescent, about 1.5–2.5 cm long, finely serrate; flowers double (!), light pink, 5–6 cm wide, June; fruit flat globose, green, quite prickly, like a small chestnut, prickles longitudinally furrowed. BM 3490; WR 135; MJ 1331; BR 919; SOR 42 (= *R. microphylla* Roxb. ex Lindl.). China. Introduced into Western cultivation in 1824 from the Calcutta Botanic Garden (India) which had obtained it from Canton, China. Little used in hybridizing. z6 Plate 80.

var. **hirtula** (Regel) Rehd. & Wils. Differing from f. *normalis* only in the leaflets, 15–25 mm long and pubescent beneath; flowers single, pale pink. KIF 4: 11; BM 6548 (= *R. hirtula* Nakai). Japan. Found along the coast of the Hakone Sea in central Japan by Maximowicz in 1862.

f. **normalis** Rehd. & Wils. Habit much more vigorous, 3–4 m high and wide, stems stout; leaflets obovate to elliptic, rounded or acute, glabrous (!); flowers white to pale pink, solitary or grouped. MJ 1330; KHL 2: 152; GSR 45, 46 (= *R. forrestii* Focke). China; Szechwan Prov. Wild form found in 1908.

R. rubella see: **R. × reversa**

R. rubiginosa L. Sweet Briar. Vigorous growing shrub, 2–3 m high, branches very prickly, prickles hooked, stout, often with bristles intermixed; leaflets 5–7, oval-rounded, dark green, glandular, scented much like apples (!); flowers 1–3, light pink, 3 cm wide, flower stalk short, glandular bristly, as is the calyx, sepals more or less outspread, late absciscing, June; fruit scarlet-red, ovate, to 1–2 cm long, smooth or somewhat glandular bristled at the base, occasionally totally bristly. WR 145; HF 2630; KHL 2: Pl. 163; KSR 22–23 (= *R. eglanteria* L.; nom. ambig.); (Hylander urgently recommended the elimination of the then valid name *R. eglanteria* since this was later used by Linnaeus also for *R. foetida* which would have resulted in a lasting confusion.). All of Europe to 61° N latitude. Caucasus, Asia Minor, naturalized in N. America. Cultivated before 1594. Much used in hybridizing but most of the so-called "Rubiginosa hybrids" of commerce belong to *R. × penzanceana*. Ⓕ N. Tyrolea. z6 Fig. 183.

'Duplex'. Flowers semidouble, 10 petals, pink, more fragrant than the species, but the leaves less fragrant. WR 449 (as 'Jannet's Pride'). Known since 1629 but possibly no longer cultivated. (According to Modern Roses VII, this is identical to the 'Lucy Ashton' seedling 'Magnifica'.)

Other hybrids with 'Magnifica' by Kordes: 'Fritz Nobis', 'Rosenwunder'.

R. rubra see: **R. gallica**

R. rubrifolia see: **R. glauca**

R. × rubrosa Preston (*R. glauca × R. rugosa*). More vigorous than *R. glauca*, flowers larger, but the leaves not so attractively blue, rachis glabrous, shoots less prickly; fruitless. GC 1926: 150. Brought into the trade as 'Carmenetta'. 1923. z3

R. rubro-stipulata see: **R. marrettii**

R. rubus Lév. & Van. Long-branched climbing rose, stems to 6 m long in its habitat and mild climates, prickly, reddish, glabrous or pubescent, prickles hook-like; leaflets usually 5, oval-elliptic, 3–6 cm long, scabrous and coarsely serrate, glossy green above, underside pubescent and reddish when young; flowers in dense umbellate panicles, white, fragrant, 3 cm wide, styles fused into a pubescent column, sepals glandular pubescent, as is the stalk, June–July; fruit globose, pea-sized, red. WR 168; BM 8894; JRHS 65: 102 (= *R. ernestii*

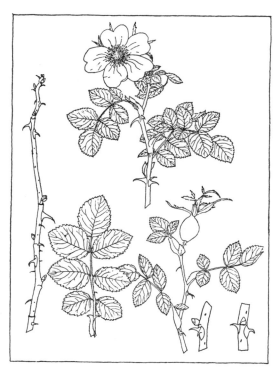

Fig. 183. *Rosa rubiginosa*

Stapf.). Central and W. China, 1907. Distinguished from *R. helenae* in the 5 larger, pubescent leaflets with reddish undersides when young. z8–9

R. × ruga Lindl. (*R. arvensis × R. chinensis*; Shepherd thought that *R. odorata* and not *R. chinensis* was the second parent because of the very strong, typical fragrance). Climbing shrub, branches 2.5–3 m long, prickles scattered, hooked; leaflets 5–7, serrate, 4–5 cm long, glabrous on both sides; flowers several in large, terminal, loose umbellate panicles, individual flowers ball-form, loose, double, 4–6 cm wide, light pink, fragrant, sepals absciscing, stalks long, smooth, June–July; fruits globose, red, smooth, but only rarely developed. WR 17; Br 1389. Originated in Italy before 1830. z7

R. rugosa Thunb. Rugosa Rose. Shrub, 1–2 m high, stems thick, tomentose, very prickly and bristly; leaflets 5–9, elliptic, 3–5 cm long, glossy dark green and rugose above, tough, thick, golden-yellow in fall, bluish beneath, reticulately veined, pubescent; flowers solitary or few together, pink-red, 6–8 cm wide, stalk short and bristly, June to fall; fruits flat globose, smooth, to 2.5 cm wide, of considerable economic use. WR 58; BR 420 (= *R. regeliana* Linden & André). N. China, Korea, Japan; naturalized in N., W., and central Europe. The hardiest of all roses. 1854. Ⓕ Denmark (windbreaks); Holland (dune stabilizing). z2

Including the following forms:

'**Adiantifolia**' Cochet 1907. Similar to 'Crispata' but normally only 7 (not 9) leaflets, these larger and longer, stipules very broad and long, fimbriately incised along the margins ('Crispata' only finely dentate).

'**Alba**' (Ware). Flowers white. Gn 1876: 452; GSR 129; RZ 1907: 32.

'**Albo-plena**'. Flowers white, double. Presumably a mutation of 'Alba'. Before 1902.

'Atropurpurea' see: '**Rubra**'

var. chamissoniana C. A. Mey. Branches nearly thornless; leaflets narrower, smaller, less rugose.

'**Hollandica**' (J. Spek, Boskoop, around 1888) (*R. rugosa* × *R. majalis*). Also known as "Boskooper Rugosa", known in Holland now as "Scherpe Boskoop" and much used as an understock. Shrub, rather tall, well branched, stems bristly, prickles and bristles very numerous, light, variable in size; leaflets large, light green; flowers 5–10, single, dark red; fruits pendulous, globose, dark red, glandular. Used for understock on standards for humus soil, but suckers easily.

'**Nitens**'. Like the species, but the leaves glossy green and glabrous on both sides.

'**Plena**'. Purple-red, double, very winter hardy. 1879. Earlier disseminated as 'Kaiserin des Nordens' or 'Empress of the North'.

var. *repens alba* see: **R.** × **paulii**

var. *repens rosea* see: **R.** × **paulii** '**Rosea**'

'**Rosea**'. (*R. rugosa* × *R. rugosa* 'Alba'). Flowers pink, single.

'**Rubra**'. Vigorous; flowers carmine purple; fruit bright red. GSR 136 (= 'Atropurpurea'). Red flowering wild form, usually listed as a cultivar.

'**Tenuifolia**'. Branches with the typical prickliness of *R. rugosa*; leaves somewhat more widely spaced, leaflets (5)7(9), very long and narrow, irregularly undulate, stipules much widened.

> Perhaps more important than the little-known forms are the cultivars: 'Carmen', 'Conrad Ferdinand Meyer', 'Dr. Eckener', 'F. J. Grootendorst', 'Hansa', 'Nova Zembla', 'Pink Grootendorst', 'Ruskin', 'Scabrosa', 'Schneezwerg' and others.

R. × **rugotida** Darthuis Nursery 1950 (*R. nitida* × *R. rugosa*). Strong growing, to 1 m, with stolons; leaves very similar to *R. rugosa*, but smaller; flowers pink, like *R. nitida*; fruitless. z2

Including:

'**Dart's Defender**' Darthuis Nursery 1971 (*R. nitida* × *R. rugosa* 'Hansa'). More vigorous the *R. nitida*; flowers violet-pink (= *R. nitida* 'Superba' Darth. Nursery.).

R. rydbergii see: **R. arkansana**

R. sancta see: **R.** × **richardii**

R. sandbergii see: **R. woodsii**

R. sayi see: **R. acicularis**

R. × **scharnkeana** Graebn. (*R. californica* × *R. nitida*). Low shrub, branches with thin prickles, mostly bristly, leaflets 7–9, oblong, base cuneate; flowers purple-pink, 1–5 together. Gfl 1902: 1501. Cultivated before 1900. z5

R. scopulosa see: **R.** × **pokornyana**

R. semperflorens see: **R. chinensis** var. **semperflorens** and **R. damascena**

R. sempervirens L. Climbing rose, to 5 m high, branches green, thin, flexible, with thin, red prickles; leaflets 5–7, oval-lanceolate, short acuminate, 2.5–6 cm long, glossy on both sides, serrate, stipule margins glandular; flowers rather large, 2.5–5 cm wide, white, fragrant, few in umbellate panicles, sepals ovate, glandular beneath, abscising, style pubescent, calyx globose, glandular, June–July; fruit oval-rounded, 12 mm long, orange-red. WR 5; BR 465; KSR 7 and 34 (= *R. balearica* Pers.). Mediterranean region, SW. Europe, N. Africa. 1629. Once used for hybridizing. z7

> Originating from this species are 'Félicité et Perpétué', 'Spectabilis' and 'Adelaide d'Orléans' as well as the 'Ayrshire Roses'.

var. *anemoniflora* see: **R. anemoniflora**

R. sepium see: **R. agrestis**

R. serafinii Viv. Similar to *R. sicula*, but with curved or falcate prickles, occasionally with bristles intermixed. Low shrub, 30–80 cm high, never stoloniferous (see *R. sicula*), branches short and bowed, very densely covered with short, thick, hooked, irregular prickles; leaflets 7–11, oval-rounded, 8–12 × 6–10 mm large, very glossy, scabrous serrate, glandular beneath, otherwise glabrous; flowers solitary (or 2–3), whitish pink, 3 cm wide, stalk very short and without glands, sepals lobed, reflexed after flowering, quickly abscising, style glabrous, May; fruit oval, 8–12 mm thick, light red. WR 153 (= *R. appenninia* Woods). Mediterranean Islands, Bulgaria, S. Yugoslavia. 1914. z7

R. sericea Lindl. Tightly upright shrub, 2–2.5 m high, branches gray or brown, with large, wide, often flat, straight or curved prickles, these paired under the leaves; leaves compact, 3–7 cm long, with 7–11 small, rounded-elliptic leaflets, scabrous serrate toward the apex, silky pubescent beneath, primarily on the venation; flowers solitary, white, 2.5–5 cm wide, normally with 4, occasionally with 5 petals, May; fruits top-shaped, red to orange-yellow, without (!) a fleshy, thick stalk, seeds only at the base of the fruit. SNp 53; WR 52; BM 5200; KHL 2: Pl. 155d (= *R. tetrapetala* Royle). Himalayas. 1822. z7

Key to the Varieties (from Rowley)

Fruits red;
    Plant thornless:
            var. *denudata*

    Plant with prickles and bristles;
        Leaflets numerous, to 17:
            var. *polyphylla*

        Leaflets seldom more than 11;
            Fruit stalk thin, green:
                var. *sericea*

            Fruit stalk fleshy, red:
                var. *omeiensis*

    Plant densely covered with prickles, bristles and thick glands: var. *hookeri*

Plant with long decurrent, wing-like prickles:
var. *pteracantha*

Fruits yellow:
var. *chrysocarpa*

f. **chrysocarpa** (Rehd.) Rowley. Fruits yellow, otherwise like the species (= *R. omeiense* f. *chrysocarpa* Rehd.).

var. **denudata** (Franch.) Rowley. Branches practically thornless; fruits red (= *R. sericea* f. *denudata* Franch.). 1890.

'Hicote Gold' (Hilling 1948). Flowers canary-yellow, several together. Exact origin unknown.

var. **hookeri** Regel. Like var. *sericea*, but mostly glandular. China; Kumaon.

f. *inermis eglandulosa* see: var. **polyphylla**

var. **omeiensis** (Rolfe) Rowley. Omei Rose. Grows taller, 3–4 m high, strictly upright, stems gray-brown, prickles hard, flat, much wider at the base, with many bristles among them, young shoots often only bristly; leaflets 9–11(17), oblong, 1–3 cm long, glabrous beneath or finely pubescent on the midrib; flowers white, to 3 cm wide, petals 4, exceptionally 5, stalk and calyx glabrous, May–June; fruits pear-shaped, 1–1.5 cm long, bright red, with an equally long, fleshy thick (!!), red to yellow stalk. BM 8471 (= *R. omeiensis* Rolfe). Central China. 1901. z5

var. **polyphylla** Geier. Stems and twigs only slightly thorny; leaflets to 17, otherwise like the species (= *R. sericea* f. *inermis eglandulosa* Focke).

var. **pteracantha** Bean. Prickles much larger, wing-like decurrent, bright red and translucent when young; leaflets usually distinctly veined; fruit stalk usually shorter than that of the species. BM 8218; GSR 50; KHL 2: Pl. 152, 155 (= *R. omeiensis* f. *pteracantha* Rehd. & Wils.). China; W. Szechwan Prov., in the mountains at 3000–3600 m. 1890. Plate 80; Fig. 182.

var. **sericea**. The type of this species (see species' description), with a characteristic thin, green, persistent fruit stalk; fruit dropping early. WR 52. W. Himalayas; not found to date in China. 1822. Fig. 182.

R. sertata Rolfe. Similar to *R. webbiana*, but with larger flowers, more intensely colored, habit taller and more open, leaflets more serrate. Shrub, 0.7–2 m high, stems red-brown, bluish pruinose, bowed, with only a few, straight, mostly paired prickles; leaves 6–10 cm long, leaflets 7–11, elliptic, 1.5–2 cm long, scabrous serrate, bluish beneath, glabrous; flowers in 4's on short shoots, 3–5 cm wide, pink, sepals acuminate, entire, persistent (!), calyx smooth or bristly, June; fruits ovate, 2 cm long, dark red. BM 8473; DRHS 1820 (= *R. macrophylla* f. *gracilis* Focke). W. China; Kansu, Yunnan Provs. 1904. z6

R. setigera Michx. Prairie Rose. Shrub, climbing 1–2 m high, stems glabrous, with stout, slightly curved prickles; leaflets usually only 3(5), oval-oblong, 3–9 cm long, serrate, light green above, underside gray-green with pubescent venation, petiole glandular; flowers dark pink, 5–6 cm wide, in loose umbellate panicles, few flowered, stalk usually glabrous; June–August; fruit small, globose, glandular bristly, brown-green. WR 23; BC 3438; BB 1965 (= *R. trifoliata* Raf.; *R. fenestrata* Donn). N. America, from the Atlantic to the Rocky Mts. 1810. This species was much used in the mid 19th century for hybridizing winter-hardy climbing roses. Shepherd noted that this species is "functionally dioecious", that is, the fruit bearing plants often have sterile pollen while the pollen of fruitless plants is exceptionally fertile. In its native habitat, it is common to see large shrubs full of fruit next to fruitless ones. z5

The old hybrids, developed between 1840 and 1850 are scarcely seen today. Of the modern hybrids, those worth noting include: 'Doubloons' and 'Long John Silver'.

R. setipoda Hemsl. & Wils. Dense, stemmy, upright shrub, 3 m (to 5 m in cultivation) high, prickles few, straight, large, broad based, to 8 mm long; leaflets 7–9, elliptic, underside glabrous or glandular pubescent, margins usually deeply serrate, stipules large, densely glandular ciliate, rachis glandular and somewhat prickly; flowers pink, to 5 cm wide, 12 or more in panicles, sepals long caudate with a leaflike, serrate apex, petals somewhat pubescent on the exterior, caylx glandular-bristled, June; fruit bottle-shaped, red, 2.5 cm long, 6–7 cm long in cultivation (!) (possibly somewhat interbred with *R. moyesii*.). WR 55; GSR 51 (= *R. macrophylla* var. *crasseaculeata* Vilm.). Central China. 1895. z6

var. *inermis* see: **R. wardii**

R. sherardii Davies. Dense shrub, to 2 m high, branches often somewhat crooked, prickles often very hooked; leaflets broadly ovate to elliptic, pubescent above, underside blue-green and tomentose; flowers usually grouped, dark pink, nearly hidden by foliage around the base; fruit top-shaped, 1.2–2 cm thick, with very long, persistent sepals, these separating very late. HM 1223; KSR 15 (= *R. omissa* Déségl.). N., W. and central Europe, to SW. Finland, and southward to Bulgaria. 1933. z5

R. sicula Tratt. Low shrub, 20–80 cm high, similar to *R. serafinii*, but with stolons, prickles straight or somewhat curved, slender, of nearly equal length, young shoots red; leaflets 5–9, rounded, 6–12 mm long, glabrous, but glandular beneath, somewhat fragrant; flowers solitary, pink, 2.5–3 cm wide, sepals persistent (eventually abscising on *R. serafinii*); fruit oval-rounded, 1.3 cm long, red. BM 7761; KHL 2: Pl. 158; KSR 18. S. Europe, N. Africa. Before 1894. z8 Fig. 179.

R. silverhjelmii see: **R. beggeriana**

R. simplicifolia see: **R. persica**

R. sinica see: **R. chinensis**

R. sinowilsonii Hemsl. Climbing rose, to 5 m high, young shoots reddish, prickles few, short, hooked; leaves semi-evergreen or evergreen (!), leaflets 5–7, oblong-elliptic, 7 cm long or longer, scabrous serrate, somewhat pubescent beneath, petiole glabrous, prickly, flowers 3–5 cm wide, white, in loose umbellate panicles, petals entire, pubescent on the exterior, sepals ovate, caudate, to 2.5 cm long, abscising, stalk thick, reddish, somewhat glandular, June to July; fruits ellipsoid, red, 12 mm long. WR 73; PWR 233. SW. China. 1904. z9

R. solandri see: **R. blanda**

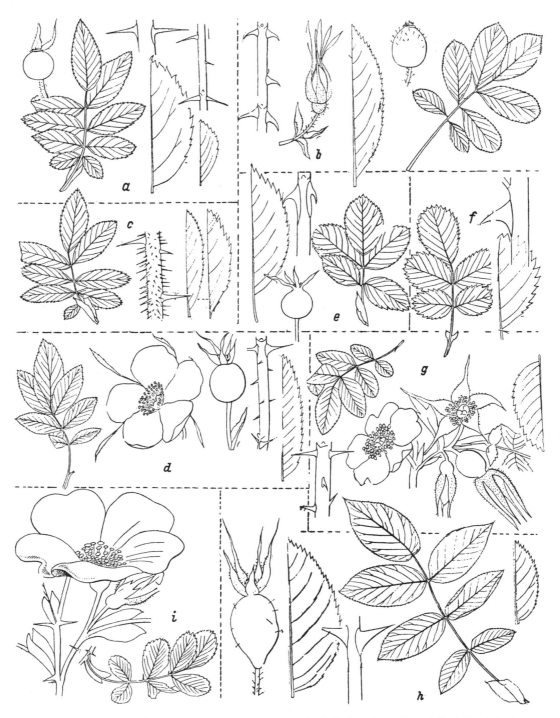

Fig. 184. **Rosa.** a. *R. virginiana;* b. *R. carolina;* c. *R. nitida;* d. *R. davurica;* e. *R. majalis;* f. *R. californica;* g. *R. pisocarpa;* h. *R. macrophylla;* i. *R. woodsii* (most from Schneider, altered)

R. soongarica see: **R. laxa**

R. sorbiflora see: **R. cymosa**

R. soulieana Crép. Shrub, to 4 m high, branches widely outspread, young shoots green, later more blue-green, very prickly, prickles reddish, straight, widened at the base; leaves gray-green, leaflets 5–9, oblong-elliptic glabrous, stipules narrow, margins glandular; flowers many in 10–15 cm wide corymbs along the entire branch, cream-yellow at first, later pure white, 3 cm wide, fragrant, sepals ovate, short acuminate, reflexed, usually glabrous and entire or somewhat pinnate, calyx glandular, June–July; fruit oval, 1 cm long, orange-yellow. WR 18; BM 8158; KHL 2: Pl. 159. W. China. 1896. Of significant ornamental merit but primarily for mild climates. Actually not a climbing rose but just a strong growing shrub rose. z7–8 Fig. 178.

Including the hybrids: 'Chevy Chase', 'Navigator'.

R. × spaethiana Graebn. (*R. palustris* × *R. rugosa*). Strong growth habit, upright; leaflets narrow, light green; flowers carmine-pink, 7–8 cm wide, several together; fruits abundantly developed, scarlet-red. Gfl 1902: Pl. 1504 (as *"carolina × rugosa"*.) z4

R. spinosissima L. As suggested by Hylander, this name should no longer be used and considered *nomen ambiguum*. See: **R. pimpinellifolia**.

The numerous cultivars of this plant (called Burnet Roses in England and numbering 70 according to Paul!) have been nearly totally lost in cultivation. Most originated in Scotland and numbered over 100 cultivars around 1822.

R. × spinulifolia Dematra (*R. pendulina* × *R. tomentosa*). Shrub, 1–3 m high, stems stout, well branched, prickles irregular, partly needlelike, primarily on the basal part of the shoot, flowering shoots often thornless; leaflets 5–7, medium-sized, glabrous above, underside pubescent; flowers pink-red, large; fruits bottle-shaped, large, soft prickly, with only 1–2 nutlets. KSR 38 (= *R. glabrata* Déségl.). Switzerland, Alsace, Hungary. z6

R. stellata Woot. Shrub, upright, 30–50 cm high, young shoots soft pubescent, densely branched, prickles slender, straight, often paired, with bristles intermixed; leaflets 3(5), about 12 mm long, obovate to cuneate, deeply toothed at the apex, glabrous or lightly stellate pubescent, stipule margins glandular; flowers solitary, bright pink, 4–6 cm wide, style woolly, stamens very numerous, about 160 or more, sepals pinnate, bristly on the dorsal side, June–August; fruits top-shaped, brown-red, bristly, to 2 cm thick, usually infertile. WR 103 (= *R. vernonii* Greene). USA; New Mexico, Organ Mts. Found in 1897; introduced in 1902. Winer hardy, but a dry, sunny site is suggested. z6

var. **mirifica** (Greene) Cockerell. Vigorous habit, to about 1 m high, branches glabrous and glandular, but not stellate pubescent; leaflets usually in 5's, deeply dentate, usually glabrous or nearly so; flower dark pink, 3.5–6 cm wide; fruits globose, bristly, dull red, 1.5–2 cm thick. BM 9070; ARA 1932; TRT 64 (= *R. mirifica* Greene). Mountains in northern New Mexico; Sacramento Mts., hence the common name "Sacramento Rose". 1910.

R. stylosa Desv. Shrub, to 3 m high, stems bowed, prickles stout, hooked, wider at the base; leaflets 5–7, mostly narrow-ovate to lanceolate, 1.5–5 cm long, acuminate, serrate, underside usually soft pubescent, occasionally also above, or also with both sides glabrous, without glands, stipules and bracts rather narrow; flowers 1–8 or more, white to light pink, 3–5 cm wide, long stalked, usually glandular bristly, style column glabrous, shorter than the stamens, stigmas in an ovate ball, disk conical, sepals reflexed after flowering, abscising before the fruits ripen, June; fruits ovate, red, smooth, 1–1.5 cm thick. WR 14; HM 1226; KHL 2: Pl. 158; KSR 8 (= *R. systyla* Bast.). W. Europe; Ireland to W. Germany (Rhine region), Switzerland, S. France, NW. Spain; Bulgaria. 1838. z6 Fig. 179.

R. subnuda see: **R. macounii**

R. suffulta Greene. Only about 50 cm high, often a subshrub, branches green, densely fine prickled and bristly, dying back to the ground after flowering (!!), simultaneously new shoots develop for the next year; leaflets 7–11, broadly elliptic to oval-oblong, 2–4 cm long, serrate, bright green, pubescent on both sides, normally becoming glabrous above, petiole and rachis finely pubescent; flowers in umbellate panicles, pink, 3 cm wide, stalk and calyx glabrous, sepals occasionally lobed, June; fruit globose, 1 cm thick, red, with erect sepals. WR 105 (= *R. pratincola* Greene; *R. arkansana suffulta* Cockerell; *R. arkansanoides* Schneid.). Eastern and central USA. 1880. z5

R. sulphurea see: **R. hemisphaerica**

R. sweginzowii Koehne. Shrub, to 5 m high, stems densely covered with large, flat, triangular prickles, prickles varying in size; leaflets 7–11, elliptic to oval-oblong, 2–5 cm long, biserrate, bright green and glabrous above, underside pubescent, more densely so on the venation; flowers light pink, 4 cm wide, grouped 1–3 together, rachis prickly, stalk and calyx glandular bristled, sepals only slightly lobed and serrate, June; fruits bottle-shaped, light red to bright red. CIS 80; MD 1910: 96; GSR 58, 59. NW. China. 1909. z6

'Macrocarpa' (Vogel, Sangerhausen). Selection with larger, to 5 cm long and 2 cm thick fruits. Otherwise like the species.

R. systyla see: **R. stylosa**

R. taquetii see: **R. wichuraiana**

R. ternata see: **R. laevigata**

R. tetrapetala see: **R. sericea**

R. thea see: **R. odorata**

R. thoryi see: **R. multiflora 'Platyphylla'**

R. tomentella see: **R. obtusifolia**

R. tomentosa Sm. Shrub, 2 m high, branches crooked, young shoots often pruinose, prickles thick, straight or bowed; leaflets 5–7, elliptic to ovate, 2–4 cm long, finely pubescent above, tomentose and glandular beneath; biserrate, stipules with short, triangular, erect auricles;

flowers light pink to nearly white, 4 cm wide, stalk often glandular bristly, sepals lobed, abscising before the fruits ripen; fruits nearly globose, 1–2 cm thick, with stalked glands. WR 139; HM Pl. 154; GN 77: 511; RZ 1919: 51; KSR 16–17. Over all of Europe except the far north; Caucasus and Asia Minor. 1820. z6

R. trifoliata see: **R. setigera**

R. triphylla see: **R. anemoniflora** and **R. laevigata**

R. turbinata see: **R. × 'Francofurtana'**

R. turcica see: **R. horrida**

R. tuschetica Boiss. Very closely related to *R. glutinosa*, but leaflets ovate (not obovate or elliptic), sepals long and caudate, erect on the fruits, not outspread (= *R. pimpinellifolia* var. *tuschetica* Christ.). Dagestan Mts., USSR. 1945.

R. unguicularis see: **R. webbiana**

R. vernonii see: **R. stellata**

R. villosa L. Apple Rose. Densely branched, short stemmed shrub, 1.5–2 m high, often stoloniferous, shoots reddish and somewhat pruinose at first, prickles thin, straight, scattered; leaflets 5–7(9), elliptic-oblong, 3–5 cm long, gray-green and pubescent above, underside tomentose and glandular, glandular biserrate, somewhat resin scented; flowers grouped 1–3 together, pink, to 5 cm wide, stalk glandular bristly, as is the calyx, sepals pinnate, upward directed, June–July; fruits globose-oblong, to 2.5 cm thick, dark red, bristly, of some commercial use. WR 141; BM 7241; HF 2632; KHL 2: Pl. 156; KSR 12–13; GSR 37 (= *R. pomifera* Herrm.). Europe, primarily in the mountains; Orient. 1771. z6 Fig. 177.
'Duplex'. "Wolley-Dod's Rose". Leaves gray-green; flowers large, semidouble, pure pink, more floriferous than the species. GSR 38 (as *R. villosa duplex* West). Known in England before 1770, but disseminated much later by Rev. Wolley-Dod in Edge Hall, Chechester.

var. *mollissima* see: **R. mollis**

R. vilmorinii see: **R. × micrugosa**

R. virginiana Mill. Virginia Rose. Shrub, about 1.5 m high, shoots erect, red-brown, only slightly or not stoloniferous, prickles hooked, but frequently bristle-form on the young shoots; leaves glossy green, leaflets 7–9, elliptic to obovate, 2–6 cm long, scabrous serrate, venation pubescent beneath; flowers light pink, few or solitary, flowering abundantly, June–July; fruits flat-globose, 1.5 cm wide, smooth, red, stalk glandular-bristly. WR 197; BB 2: 285; KHL 2: 157 (= *R. lucida* Ehrh.; *R. carolinensis* Marsh.). Eastern N. America. Before 1807. z4 Fig. 184.

var. *humilis* see: **R. carolina**

'Plena' More compact growth habit but habit and foliage otherwise similar to the species; buds well developed, flowers with broad, circular outer petals, pure pink, inner ones smaller, acute, somewhat darker pink, slightly fragrant, July–August (= *R. rapa* Bosc; *R. lucida* var. *plena* hort. ex Rehd.). 1768.

R. vorbergii see: **R. × harisonii 'Vorbergii'**

R. × waitziana Tratt. (*R. canina* × *R. gallica*). Shrub, about 2 m high, prickles scattered, irregularly formed and usually slighly curved; leaves rather tough, usually serrate, glabrous or with the midrib pubescent beneath; flowers usually solitary, 6–8 cm wide, usually dark pink, sepals glandular on the dorsal side, style short haired, somewhat elongated; fruit usually abscising before ripe. Central Europe; on the forest's edge. 1874. z5

var. *macrantha* see: **R. × macrantha**

R. wardii Mulligan ("White Moyesii"). Shrub, growth upright, about 1.5 m high or more, branch tips nodding, young stems with a bluish green covering; leaves light green, leaflets 7–11, ovate-elliptic; flowers shell-form, grouped 1–3 together, white, with a dark brown center, like *R. moyesii* in form; fruit small, not numerous. GC 131: 36 (= *R. setipoda* var. *inermis* Marquand & Shaw). SE. Tibet. 1924. This plant is very similar to *R. sweginzowii*, but has white flowers and is nearly thornless. z7

The species is not cultivated, rather only a form called **"culta"** (Mulligan) with smaller flowers, about 3–3.5 cm wide, flower stalk often glandular. Grown from seed collected by Kingdon Ward (K. W. 6101).

R. × warleyensis Willm. (*R. blanda* × *R. rugosa*). Shrub with very thorny shoots, prickles straight, slender; leaflets 5–7, oblong, medium-sized, 25–35 mm long, not as rugose as *R. rugosa*, glabrous above, thinly pubescent beneath; flowers solitary, pink-red, 6 cm wide, ovaries glabrous, sepals long drawn out. WR 185. Before 1911. z2

R. watsoniana see: **R. multiflora f. watsoniana**

R. webbiana Royle. Shrub, 1.5–2 m high, branches thin, with a few, straight prickles, these light, paired; leaflets 5–9, rounded to broadly elliptic, 1.5–2 cm long, glabrous or somewhat pubescent beneath; serrate, entire at the base, obtuse, petiole often prickly glandular pubescent, stipules glandular ciliate; flowers grouped 1–3, light pink, 4–5 cm wide, sepals glandular, often pubescent at the base, apex usually widened, shorter than the petals, persistent, June; fruits oblong-bottle-shaped, to 2.5 cm long, bright red. WR 76; KHL 2: Pl. 159 (= *R. unguicularis* Bertol.; *R. guilelmi-waldemarii* Klotzsch). W. Himalayas; Afghanistan, Turkestan. 1879. z6 Fig. 178.

R. wichuraiana Crép. Semi-evergreen climber, stems 2.5–5 m long, often procumbent, green, branches with thick, hooked prickles; leaflets 7–9, broadly ovate, dark green above, lighter beneath, very glossy on both sides (!); flowers in small, conical umbellate panicles, white, 4–5 cm wide, fragrant, sepals much shorter than the petals, glabrous or lightly glandular, as is the stalk, July–August; fruits ovate, 15 mm long, deep red. BM 7321; WR 19; 169 (as *R. taquetii*); 170 (as *R. mokanensis*); MJ 1336 (= *R. luciae* var. *wichuraiana* Koidz.; *R. taquetii* Lév.; *R. mokanensis* Lév.). Japan, Korea, E. China. 1891. With a procumbent habit in its native habitat, branches easily rooting along their length, therefore a good plant for future hybridizing for ground cover roses. Used in hybridizing for climbing roses since 1893. Its descendants usually have small, glossy, dark green leaflets, with slender branches which must sometimes be tied up. Called the "Memorial Rose" in N. America for its use at grave sites. z6 Plate 78; Fig. 172.

The more prominent cultivars are: 'American Pillar' (1902), 'Hiawatha' (1904), 'Minnehaha' (1905), 'Dr. W. van Fleet' (1910), 'New Dawn' (1930), 'Blaze' (1932), 'Direktor Benschop' (1945).

R. willldenowii see: **R. davurica**

R. willmottiae Hemsl. Shrub, to 3 m high, stems long, drooping, well branched, current year's growth brown-red, very pruinose, with straight, paired prickles; leaflets 7–9, elliptic to circular, 6–15 mm long, densely and usually biserrate, glabrous; flowers usually solitary, carmine-pink, intensely colored in bud, 3 cm wide, somewhat fragrant, flowering along the entire shoot, sepals abscising (!), June; fruits ovate, 1.8 cm long, orange-red. WR 177; BM 8186; KHL 2: Pl. 151; GSR 60. W. China. 1904. z6 Plate 79.

R. × wintoniensis Hillier (*R. moyesii × R. setipoda*). Very similar in appearance to *R. holodonta*, about 2 m high, branches nodding; leaves with the scent of *R. rubiginosa*; flowers carmine-red with a white center, velvety, grouped 7–10 in umbellate panicles, June; fruit large, bottle-shaped. Developed in 1928 by Hillier, Winchester, England. z6

R. woodsii Lindl. Shrub, upright, 1.5–2 m high, stems reddish, later gray, prickles numerous, thin, straight or somewhat bowed, only a few on flowering shoots; leaflets 5–7, obovate to more oblong, 1–3 cm long, scabrous and serrate, finely pubescent and bluish beneath, stipules narrow, entire to slightly serrate and without glands; flowers pink, grouped 1–3, 3.5–4 cm wide, stalk and calyx smooth, June–July; fruits globose, about 1 cm thick, most with a distinct neck. WR 77; KHL 2: Pl. 157 (= *R. deserta* Lunell; *R. sandbergii* Greene; *R. maximiliani* Nees). Central and western N. America. 1880. Quite variable species and therefore, once much subdivided by many botanists. z4 Fig. 184.

var. **fendleri** (Crép.) Rehd. Shrub, low, prickles slender, straight; stipules and petiole glandular, leaflets usually biserrate; flowers and fruit somewhat smaller. BB 1969; GSR 61 (= *R. fendleri* Crép.; *R. poetica* Lunell). Western N. America. 1888.

R. xanthina Lindl. Upright shrub, 1.5–3 m high, stems brown, with thick, straight prickles, long shoots totally thornless (!!); leaflets 7–13, 1–2 cm long, obtusely serrate, glabrous above, somewhat pubescent beneath, stipules narrow and glandular; flowers 4–5 cm wide, golden-yellow, solitary or paired, double or semidouble (!), style stunted, May to June; fruit not yet observed. NK 7: 6 (= *R. xanthina allardii* Hort.; *R. xanthina plena* Hort.). N. China, Korea, found in cultivation. 1906. First known only through Chinese paintings, then the double form was found in the garden of a Chinese mandarin, later the single flowering species was found in the wild. z6 Fig. 182.

f. *normalis* see: f. **spontanea**

f. **spontanea** Rehd. The wild form. Somewhat taller; leaves often somewhat pubescent on the midrib; flowers single, larger, 5–6 cm wide, sepals erect, persistent; fruit rather globose, 12–15 mm wide, light red. GC 127: 112; KHL 2: Pl. 155, 161 (= f. *normalis* Rehd. & Wils.). N. China, Mongolia, Turkestan. 1906. Often confused with 'Canary Bird' (possibly *R. hugonis × R. xanthina*), which has lighter flowers and blackish red fruits. Plate 83.

R. xanthocarpa see: **R. gigantea**

R. yesoensis see: **R. × iwara**

NEW ROSES. The International Rose Register is kept by the American Rose Society, International Registration Authority for Roses, P.O. Box 30000, Shreveport, Louisiana 71130, USA. All new cultivars should be cleared with this authority before their introduction.

LITERATURE

Taxonomic

Almquist, S.; Studier öfver Bergianska Trädgardens spontana *Rosa*-Former; in Act. Hort. Bergian. **4**, 1–88, Stockholm 1907 (1 Plate) ● Boulenger, G. A.: Les Roses d'Europe de l'herbier Crépin; Bull. Jard. Bot. Bruxelles **10**, 1–417, 1924–1925; loc. cit. **12**, 1–192, 1931 ● Boulenger, G. A.: Revision des Roses d'Asie; Bull. Jard. Bot. Bruxelles **9**, 203–348; **12**, 165–276; **14**, 115–121; **14**, 274–278, 1933 to 1936 ● Boulenger, G. A.: Introduction à l'étude du genre *Rosa*; Bull. Jard. Bot. Bruxelles **14**, 242–278, 1937 ● Christ, H.: Die Rosen der Schweiz, mit Berücksichtigung der umliegenden Gebiete Mittel- und Süd-Europas; Basel 1873 ● Crépin, F.: Note sur les Roses à fleurs jaunes; Flore des Serres **23**, 104–105 ● Crépin, F.: Primitiae Monographiae Rosarum; Bull. Soc. Bot. Belg. **8**, 226–349, 1869; loc. cit. **11**, 15–130, 1872; loc. cit. **13**, 242–290, 1874; loc. cit. **14**, 3–46, 137–168, 1874; loc. cit. **15**, 12–100, 1876; loc. cit. **18**, 221–416, 1879; loc. cit. **21**, 7 to 196, 1882 (reprint Lehre W. Germ. and London 1972) ● Crépin, F.: Tableau analytique des Roses européennes; Bull. Soc. Bot. Belg. **31**, 66–92, 1892 ● Keller, R.; *Rosa*; in P. Ascherson and P. Graebner, Syn. Mittel-Eur. Fl. **6** (1), 32–384, 1900–1905 ● Keller, R.: Synopsis Rosarum Spontanearum Europae Mediae; Denkschr. Schweiz. Naturf. Ges. **65**, 1931 (pp. x + 796 + 40 plates) ● Klastersky, I.: *Rosa*; in Tutin et al., Flora Europaea, II, 25–32, London 1968 ● Rehder, A.: *Rosa*; in Rehder & Wilson, Plantae Wilsonianae, vol. **2**, 304–345, Cambridge, Mass. 1915 ● Saakov, S. G.: Wild- und Gartenrosen; E. Berlin 1976 (432 pp., also contains the wild roses of the Soviet Union) ● Schwertschlager, J.: Die Rosen des südlichen und mittleren Frankenjura; Munich 1910 ● Thory, C. A.: Prodrome de la monographie des espèces et variétés connues du genre rosier; Paris 1820 (190 pp., 2 plates) ● Vicioso, C.: Estudios sobre el genero "*Rosa*" en España; Madrid 1964 (2nd edition, 134 pp. with plates) ● Wolley-Dod, A. H.: A revision of the British Roses; Suppl. J. Bot. **68** and **69**, 1930–1931 (111 pp.) ● Woods, J.: A synopsis of the British species of *Rosa*; Trans. Linn. Soc. **12**, 159–234, 1818 ● Willmott, E.: The genus *Rosa*; London 1910–1914 (2 vols.).

Cytology and Hybridizing

v. Rathleff, H.: Die Rose als Objekt der Züchtung; Jena 1937 (82 pp.) ● Täckholm, G.: Zytologische Studien über die Gattung *Rosa*; in Act. Hort. Bergian. **7**, 97–281, 1922.

Cultivar descriptions

Gault, S. Millar & Patrick M. Synge: Dictionary of Roses in Color. New York, 1971 ● Gravereaux, J.: Les Roses cultivées à l'Hay en 1902; Paris 1902 (232 pp.) ● Jäger, A.: Das Rosenlexikon. General catalogue of all known cultivars and wild roses up to 1936; Uftrungen, Harz, 1936 (768 pp., private printing) ● Mansfield, T. C.: Roses in Colour and Cultivation; London 1947 (261 pp., 80 color plates) ● McFarland, J. H.: Modern Roses VIII; Shreveport, La., USA, 1978 (contains nearly all the rose hybrids) ● Park, B.: Collins Guide to Roses; London 1956 (288 pp., 130 ills.) ● Simon, L., & P. Cochet: Nomenclature de tous les noms de Rose; Paris 1906 (2nd edition contains 10,953 names!) ● Suzuki, S.: Roses of the World; Tokyo 1956 (420 pp., 200 color plates; in Japanese, names in Latin).

Judging Methods

Lewis, C. H.: The Judging of Roses; official Judges Manual; American Rose Society, Columbus, Ohio, USA, 1960 (89 pp.).

Historical Works

Döring, W. L.: Die Königin der Blumen oder die höhere Bedeutung der Rose usw.; Crefeld 1835 (743 pp.) ● Joret, C.: La rose dans l'antiquité et au moyen age; Paris 1892 (480 pp.) ● Hurst, C. C.: Notes on the origin and evolution of our garden Roses; in Jour. Roy. Hort. Soc. **66,** 73–82; 242–250; 282 to 289, 1941 ● Johnson, A. T.: Notes on the Burnet Roses; in Jour. Roy. Hort. Soc. **68,** 30–33, 1943 ● Krüssmann, G.: Rosen — Rosen — Rosen; Berlin 1974 (The Complete Book of Roses, Timber Press, Portland, OR, USA) ● Leroy, A.; L'Histoire des Roses; Paris 1954 (66 pp., 16 plates) ● Shepherd, R. E.: History of the Rose; New York 1954 (264 pp., 28 ills., 8 pp. of bibliography) ● Thomas, G. S.: The old Shrub Roses; London 1961 (2nd ed., 232 pp., 39 plates) ● Redouté, P. J.: Les Roses; Paris 1835 (3rd. ed., 3 vols., 183 plates; not seen personally. Only 2 facsimile volumes at the Ariel Publishing Co., London, each with 16 pp. of text and 24 plates, 1954 and 1956; wonderful plates!) ● Schleiden, M. J.: Die Rose; Symbolik und Geschichte; 1873.

Popular Rose Books

Glasau, F.: Rosen im Garten; Hamburg 1961 (217 pp., 140 ills.) ● Harvey, N. P.: The Rose in Britain; London (4th ed., 212 pp., 22 plates) ● Kordes, W.: Das Rosenbuch; Hannover 1960 (8th ed., 284 pp., 137 ills.).

Also the yearbooks of the various Rose Societies.

ROSMARINUS L. — LABIATAE

Low, aromatic, evergreen shrubs; leaves opposite, narrow, entire, margins involuted; flowers in short, axillary racemes, few flowered, densely arranged, nearly sessile, bluish to white; calyx ovate-campanulate, short bilabiate; tube exserted, limb bilabiate, upper lip erect, emarginate, lower lip 3 parted, middle lobes largest; stamens 2; fruits composed of 4 ovate nutlets. — 4 species in the Mediterranean region (monotypic according to some botanists).

Rosmarinus lavandulaceus de Noe ex Balansa. Evergreen, mat-form procumbent shrub or (in cultivation) trailing over slopes; leaves light green, only about 1–1.5 cm long; flowers light blue, in 3 cm long, dense racemes, May, but with scattered flowers appearing the whole season long, calyx more pubescent than that of *R. officinalis,* not glandular (!). GC 1951: 94 (= *R. officinalis* f. *prostratus* Hort.). Capri; commonly found in gardens around the Mediterranean. z9 Plate 83. # ☉

R. officinalis L. Rosemary. Evergreen, more or less woody shrub, 0.5–1 (2) m high, older branches with scaly bark, shoots densely foliate, gray tomentose; leaves linear-oblong, 3–5 cm long, sessile, glossy green above, underside gray tomentose; flowers in short, axillary racemes on the previous year's wood, corolla pale blue to whitish, calyx bluish red, ovate-campanulate, glandular, May. BS 3: 230; HM 3360. S. Europe, Asia Minor. Cultivated since antiquity. z7–8 Plate 83. # ☉

'Albiflorus'. Flowers white.

'Angustifolius'. Habit broadly upright, bushy; leaves only about 1.5 mm wide.
> Including the selection **'Benenden',** brought by Collingwood Ingram from Corsica to England, particularly floriferous, sky-blue. ☉

'Erectus'. Tightly upright habit, dense and compact. (= f. *fastigiata* Hort.; f. *pyramidalis* Hort.). For a sunny, calcareous soil in a warm site; otherwise easily cultivated.

f. *fastigiata* see: **'Erectus'**

f. *prostratus* see: **R. lavandulaceus**

f. *pyramidalis* see: **'Erectus'**

Lit. Turrill: The Genus *Rosmarinus;* in Kew Bulletin 1920, 105–108.

ROTTLERA

Rottlera japonica see: **Mallotus japonicus**

ROYSTONEA O. F. Cook — PALMAE

Thornless palms with slender stems, crown a crest of large pinnate leaves with long sheathes, these clasping the stem tube-like; leaves regularly pinnate, the pinnae narrow, linear-lanceolate, tapered at the apex and unevenly twice incised; flowers monoecious, small, white. — About 6 or 7 species in tropical America, but commonly cultivated in all frost free parts of the world; very ornamental.

Roystonea oleracea (Jacq.) O. F. Cook. Stem 30–40 m high in its habitat, swollen at the base; leaves 3–4 m long, gracefully drooping, pinnae linear-lanceolate, 30–90 cm long, dark green, the middle leaflets to 5 cm wide, the basal ones much narrower; fruits 2 cm long (= *Oreodoxa oleracea* Mart.). West Indies. 1844. # ∅

R. regia O. F. Cook. Royal Palm. Stem 9–13 m high, normally thickened in the middle; leaves 2.5–3 m long, the pinnae to 70 cm long and 2.5 cm wide, bright green, the leaves somewhat nodding only at the apex, otherwise more horizontal; fruit ovate, 12 mm long (= *Oreodoxa regia* H. B. K.). Cuba. 1836. z10 # ∅

RUBUS L. — Raspberry, Blackberry, Dewberry — ROSACEAE

Deciduous or evergreen shrubs, erect, climbing or prostrate, occasionally herbaceous, thorned or thornless; leaves alternate, simple, lobed or palmate or pinnately compound, stipules fused; flowers mostly in terminal or axillary umbellate racemes or panicles, white or pink; calyx and corolla 5 parted; calyx 5 lobed, persistent; stamens numerous, disk ring form; ovaries numerous, situated on a convex or obtusely conical receptacle; drupaceous fruit single seeded, usually grouped into an aggregate fruit form, separating as a unit from the receptacle or persistent. — About 400 species, primarily in the Northern Hemisphere, but also in Africa, Australia, New Zealand and on the Pacific Isles.

Only a relatively small number of species are ornamental and more or less winter hardy.

Outline of the Species Covered in this Work

● Shoots herbaceous; rootstock creeping and stoloniferous; stipules wide, free and situated on the stem;

Subgenus **Chamaemorus** (Hill) Focke
Stems thornless, herbaceous; leaves simple, lobed; flowers dioecious, solitary, terminal, white; fruit large, orange-yellow:
R. chamaemorus

Subgenus **Cyclactis** (Raf.) Focke
Stems more or less prickly, herbaceous; leaves palmately lobed or pinnate; flowers hermaphroditic; fruit red to deep purple or yellow:
R. arcticus, saxatilis, xanthocarpus

●● Shoots woody, usually biennial (except *R. fockeanus*), usually sterile in the first year, flowering and fruiting in the 2nd year; stipules more or less adnate to the leaf petiole;

Subgenus **Dalibarda** Focke
Shoots appressed to the ground, only slightly woody, thornless; leaves nearly strawberry-like in appearance, trifoliate; fruitlets to 20 together:
R. fockeanus

Subgenus **Dalibardastrum** Focke
Shrubs or subshrubs; shoots thornless, procumbent, covered with flexible bristles; leaves simple to trifoliate; stipules wide, free; calyx bristly:
R. barbatus, tricolor

Subgenus **Malachobatus** Focke
Evergreen or deciduous, creeping or climbing plants, usually prickly; leaves usually simple, often lobed or palmate; stipules free, wide, usually split into several narrow lobes; flowers small, in racemes or panicles, occasionally only few flowered; sepals uneven, erect after flowering; fruit abscising from the receptacle:
R. buergeri, calycinoides, chroosepalus, flagelliflorus, henryi, hupehensis, ichangensis, irenaeus, lambertianus, lineatus, malifolius, parkeri, playfairianus, setchuenensis

Subgenus **Anoplobatus** Focke
Stems erect, occasionally procumbent, thornless, bark exfoliating; stipules lanceolate, lightly fused to the leaf petiole; leaves simple, palmately lobed; flowers large, with erect petals, style clavate form, receptacle flat:
R. deliciosus, fraseri, odoratus, parviflorus, trifidus, trilobus

Subgenus **Idaeobatus** (Focke) Focke. Raspberries.
Shrubs with deciduous, erect or climbing or procumbent shoots, these usually prickly, bristly, glandular, normally biennial; leaves usually trifoliate or pinnate, occasionally palmately compound, occasionally also simple; stipules linear, adnate; fruit composed of many fruitlets, loosening from the receptacle when ripe:
R. adenophorus, amabilis, biflorus, cockburnianus, corchorifolius, coreanus, crataegifolius, ellipticus, flosculosus, idaeus, illecebrosus, incisus, innominatus, inopertus, lasiostylus, leucodermis, mesogaeus, microphyllus, niveus, nobilis, occidentalis, parvifolius, pedunculosus, peltatus, phoenicolasius, rosifolius, spectabilis, thibetanus

Subgenus **Lampobatus** Focke
Evergreen, usually very high climbing, prickly shrubs; inflorescences situated on many rodlike shoots; tropical shrubs:
R. australis, barkeri, parvus, squarrosus

Subgenus **Eubatus** Focke. Blackberries.
Stems usually angular, occasionally cylindrical, prickly, usually biennial; leaves trifoliate or 5 part palmate, occasionally 7 parted (*R. ursinus*, but this pinnate!), stipules adnate to the leaf petiole; petals always present; fruits abscising with the receptacle, usually black or dark purple:
R. caesius, canadensis, candicans, flagellaris, fruticosus, hispidus, laciniatus, linkianus, platyphyllos, setosus, ulmifolius, ursinus

Rubus adenophorus Rolfe. Deciduous shrub, about 2 m high or more, stems erect, drooping at the tips, prickly, densely covered with long-stalked glands and these with conspicuous, black heads (!!), particularly numerous on the flowering stalks and sepals; leaves pinnate, leaflets usually in 3's, also to 5 on long shoots, acutely ovate, 5–12 cm long, dull green and soft pubescent above, underside denser and gray-green, base of the terminal

Fig. 185. **Rubus.** Left *R. adenophorus;* center *R. amabilis;* right *R. rosifolius* (from ICS)

leaflet somewhat cordate, biserrate; flowers light pink, small, in 10–12 cm long, densely glandular panicles, July; fruits about 1 cm thick, black, edible. FRu 80 (= *R. sagatus* Focke). China; W. Hupeh Prov. 1907. z6 Fig. 185 ∅ ⚭

R. amabilis Focke. Deciduous shrub, upright, delicate textured, to 2 m high, young shoots somewhat pubescent and with small prickles, branch tips thornless; leaves pinnate, 10–20 cm long, with 7–11 leaflets, these ovate, 2–5 cm long, terminal leaflets somewhat larger, scabrous and incised biserrate, venation usually pubescent on the underside and with small prickles, similarly the rachis and flower stalk; flowers solitary, white, 4–5 cm wide, nodding, petals overlapping, June–July; fruits conical, red, 1.5 cm long, edible. FRu 70. China; W. Szechwan Prov. 1908. z6 Fig. 185. ∅ ⊕ ⚭ ✗

R. arcticus L. Herbaceous perennial, 10–20 cm high, with a creeping rootstock, stems wiry thin; leaves trifoliate, leaflets ovate to obovate, obtusely serrate, 2–3 cm long, glabrous or nearly so; flowers usually solitary and terminal, 2 cm wide, with 5–7 petals, pink-red, rounded, incised, June; fruit yellow-brown, sweet, edible, with only a few fruitlets. PAr 281; PEu 43; GKN 453; HM 1077. Northern Hemisphere, circumpolar. Good rock garden plant, not difficult to cultivate. z1 Plate 89; Fig. 187. ⊕

R. australis Forst. Evergreen climber (!), stems thin, zig-zagging, glabrous, with small, hooked prickles; leaves 3(5) parted, leathery tough, leaflets quite variable in form and size, either ovate with a cordate base or linear, 5–12 cm long, petiole, rachis and midrib prickly; flowers dioecious, white, reddish or yellowish, fragrant, in panicles; fruit 6 mm thick, orange. FRu 86 and 87. New Zealand; climbing to the tops of tall trees in its habitat. z9 Fig. 186 #

R. bambusarum see: **R. henryi** var. **bambusarum**

R. barbatus Edgew. Evergreen shrub, procumbent (!), stems rooting, densely covered with purple bristles, not prickly; leaves trifoliate, leaflets obovate to rhombic, obtusish, scabrous serrate and somewhat lobed, terminal leaflets 3–6 cm long, lateral leaflets somewhat smaller, deep green and glossy above, venation bristly beneath, petiole 3–5 cm long, bristly; flowers grouped 1–3, white, 3 cm wide, on thin, bristly stalks; fruits globose, edible, dark red. BM 5023 (= *R. nutans* Wall. non Vest). Himalayas. 1860 z9 # ⚭ ✗

R. × barkeri Cock. (? *R. parvus* × *R. australis*). Evergreen shrub, twiggy, thinly branched, spreading, usually procumbent, never climbing, shoots soft pubescent and thornless; leaves usually trifoliate, occasionally with only 1 or 2 leaflets, these lanceolate to more oblong, 6–11 cm long, 2–3 cm wide, acute, scabrous serrate, smooth and glossy above, brick-red new growth, later bronze-green or also glossy dark green, petiole, petiolules and midrib beneath with hooked prickles; scarcely ever flowering. GC 128: 10; MNZ 70. Found in the wild in New Zealand in 1898. z9 Fig. 186. #

R. bellidiflorus see: **R. ulmifolius 'Bellidiflorus'**

R. biflorus Buch.-Ham. Upright, deciduous shrub, to 3 m high, branches upright or somewhat climbing, very blue-white pruinose, prickles scattered, rather stout and curved; leaves 10–20 cm long, pinnate, with 3–5 leaflets, these ovate to elliptic, acute, 4–10 cm long, terminal leaflets often 3 lobed, the lateral ones narrower, dark green above, white tomentose beneath, irregularly and incised serrate, petiole prickly; flowers grouped 1–3, white, fragrant, May to June; fruit yellow, globose, 2 cm thick, edible. BM 4678. Himalayas. 1818. z9 Fig. 189 ⚭ ✗

var. **quinqueflorus** Focke. Strong growing, taller than the species; flowers grouped 5–8 at the shoot tips. GC 66: 212; 73: 32. W. China. 1908.

R. buergeri Miq. Sterile shoots procumbent, flowering shoots erect, softly tomentose and with small prickles; leaves broadly cordate, similar to those of *R. irenaeus*, but slightly open sinuate (!), about 8 cm long and wide, unevenly scabrous serrate, eventually smooth above, underside reticulately veined and gray pubescent, stipules pinnatisect, petiole 3–8 cm long; flowers 1 cm wide, inconspicuous, in small, axillary clusters, September; fruit hemispherical, black. FRu 53; MJ 1383. Japan, China; Hupeh Prov. z6 Plate 86. ⊘

R. caesius L. "Dewberry". Procumbent shrub, stems erect at first, occasionally somewhat climbing, but usually finally procumbent, thin, cylindrical, bluish pruinose, smooth or somewhat pubescent, with scattered, weak, nearly straight prickles; leaves trifoliate, occasionally 5 parted, oval-rhombic, 3–7 cm long, occasionally with a 3-lobed terminal leaflet, unevenly and incised serrate, plaited above and rugose, glabrous, green, soft pubescent beneath and gray, lateral leaflets smaller, oblique; flowers white, 3 cm wide, in few flowered, glandular pubescent prickly corymbs, May–October; fruits black, blue pruinose, sour, composed of only a few fruitlets. HM 1104; Pl. 148; HF 2576; PEu 133. Europe, N. Asia to the Altai Region (USSR) on the forest's edge and in open fields. Hardly cultivated! z5 Fig. 187.

R. calycinoides Hayata. Evergreen shrub, creeping or rooting along the stems, 5–10 cm high, very densely foliate, shoots shaggy pubescent, with solitary, small prickles; leaves broadly oval-rounded, 3 lobed, base deeply cordate, 2–4 cm long and wide, margins undulate, irregularly crenate, glabrous above, deep green, somewhat bullate, densely white to brownish tomentose beneath, petiole 6–12 mm long, to 3.5 cm long on sterile shoots; flowers paired or solitary on bowed, ascending, to 10 cm long shoots, about 1.5 cm wide, white, not very conspicuous, May–June; fruit bright red, 1.5 cm long, receptacle orange, fleshy. BM 9644; DB 13: 139. Taiwan. z8–9 Plate 85, 87. # ⊘

R. canadensis L. Shrub, to 2 m high, stem to 4 m long, curving in a large arch, finely pubescent, reddish, with a few weak prickles or nearly totally thornless, furrowed and rounded-angular; leaves usually 5 parted on the long shoots, thin, ovate to obovate, long acuminate, terminal leaflets 7–15 cm long, the lateral ones shorter, usually with pubescent venation beneath, but without prickles, leaves on the lateral shoots trifoliate, acute; flowers white, in foliate, pubescent, 8–15 cm long racemes, petals obovate, 1–1.5 cm long, June; fruits black, globose, sour. BM 8264; BB 1906; FRu 121. N. America. z3 1727.

R. candicans Wiehe. Shrub, 2–3 m high, stems nearly upright, bowed in fall, cylindrical to obtuse-angular and more or less deeply furrowed, sparsely pubescent, with long, straight or curved prickles; leaves 5 parted, 3 parted on flowering shoots, 5–10 cm long, oval-oblong to obovate, base round to somewhat cordate, deep and unevenly serrate, dull dark green above and somewhat pubescent at first, white tomentose beneath, flowers white to pale pink, about 2.5 cm wide, in long, narrow,

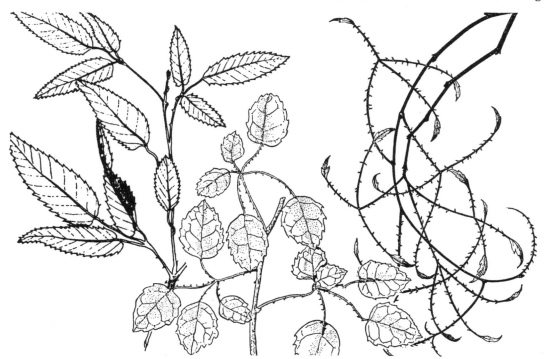

Fig. 186. **Rubus.** Left *R. barkeri;* center *R. australis;* right *R. squarrosus* (from Metcalf; Kerner)

Fig. 187. **Rubus.** Left *R. arcticus;* center *R. crataegifolius;* right *R. caesius*

simple or compound racemes, petals oblong, sepals acutely ovate, June–July; fruits globose, glossy, black. HM 1092 (= *R. thyrsoideus* Wimm.; *R. thyrsanthus* Focke; *R. coarctatus* P. J. Muell.). Central Europe. z6

'Linkianus' see: **R. linkianus**

R. carolinianus see: **R. idaeus** var. **canadensis**

R. chamaemorus L. Herbaceous perennial, 10–20 cm high, shoots thin, thornless, with 3–4 simple, rounded, lobed leaves, arising from the rootstock, base cordate, 3–8 cm wide, serrate; flowers solitary, about 3 cm wide, dioecious, June; fruit light orange-yellow, very good tasting, with large seeds. HF 2573; GPN 455–456; HM 1080; PAr 279; PEu 44. N. Europe, in peat bogs. 1789. Difficult to cultivate. z2 Plate 89. ✣ ⚬ ✕

R. chroosepalus Focke. Semi-evergreen shrub, luxuriant, with prickles and glabrous shoots, prickles short, bowed; leaves broadly ovate, abruptly short acuminate, 7–12 cm long, scabrous and unevenly serrate, occasionally shallowly lobed, dark green above, silvery tomentose beneath (nearly like the leaves of *Tilia tomentosa!*), tough, petiole 3–6 cm long, prickly; flowers in large, terminal, 12–20 cm long panicles, without petals (!), but the calyx interior is red, August; fruit small, black. FRu 15. China; Hupeh Prov., in the mountains. 1900. z6 Plate 85; Fig. 191. # ∅ ✣

R. cissoides var. *pauperatus* see: **R. squarrosus**

R. clemens see: **R. setchuenensis**

R. coarctatus see: **R. candicans**

R. cockburnianus Hemsl. Deciduous shrub, stems erect at first, to 3 m high, apical half usually horizontally spreading and branched, bluish white pruinose,

sparsely prickly; leaves pinnate, leaflets 7–9, oblong-lanceolate, 3–6 cm long, terminal leaflets larger and more rhombic, unevenly and coarsely serrate, glabrous above, underside white tomentose, stalk and rachis somewhat prickly; flowers purple-pink, small, in terminal, 10–12 cm long panicles, June; fruits black. FRu 78; GC 65: 248 (= *R. giraldianus* Focke). China; Shensi, Szechwan Provs. 1907. z6 Plate 73. ∅

R. commersonii see: **R. rosifolius 'Coronarius'**

R. corchorifolius L. f. Deciduous shrub, very stoloniferous, 1.5–2 m high, shoots prickly, tomentose when young, branched at the tips; leaves oval-lanceolate, 8–16 cm long, 6–10 cm wide, base cordate, very deeply 3 lobed on sterile shoots, irregularly serrate, venation pubescent above, underside gray tomentose, stalk 1–2 cm long, prickly; flowers white, solitary or several on short lateral shoots, 3 cm wide, April; fruits large, light red, edible. NK 7: 20a; MJ 3543; GC 51: 149 (= *R. kerriifolius* Lév. & Van.). Japan, China. 1907. z6 Plate 88. ∅ ⚬ ✕

var. **oliveri** (Miq.) Focke. Shoots smooth; leaves pubescent only on the venation beneath, otherwise glabrous (= *R. oliveri* Miq.). China, Japan. 1907.

R. coreanus Miq. Deciduous shrub, vigorous, to 3 m high, shoots branched and nodding at the apex, angular, brown, white pruinose, very prickly, prickles to 1.5 cm long; leaves pinnate, to 25 cm long, usually with 7 leaflets, these ovate-elliptic, acute, base broadly ovate to round, unevenly and scabrous serrate, terminal leaflets obovate, all parallel veined, bright green and glossy above, underside white tomentose or with pubescent venation; flowers pink, small, in 3–7 cm wide umbellate panicles, May–June; fruits small, globose, red at first, then black, edible, but stale tasting. NK 7: 29; GC 51: 149; MJ 3544. Korea, Japan, China. 1906. z6 Fig. 193. ∅

R. crataegifolius Bge. Deciduous, stoloniferous shrub, to 3 m high, shoots furrowed, red-brown, pubescent when young, with scattered prickles; leaves palmate, 3–5 lobed, 5–12 cm long, base cordate, smaller on flowering shoots and only 3 lobed, otherwise the lobes oval-lanceolate, unevenly coarsely serrate, venation beneath soft pubescent, fall color an attractive red and yellow; flowers white, 2 cm wide, several in clusters, petals narrow, sepals lanceolate, very recurved, June; fruits small, red. NK 7: 21; BC 3490. Japan, Korea, N. China. 1875. z5 Fig. 187.

R. deliciosus Torr. Deciduous shrub, 1–3 m high, not stoloniferous, shoots drooping, soft pubescent when young, totally thornless, bark exfoliating; leaves kidney-shaped to ovate, 3–7 cm long, 3–5 lobed, irregularly serrate, base cordate to truncate, lobes obtuse, glandular with somewhat pubescent venation beneath; flowers mostly solitary, to 5 cm wide, pure white, appearing on the previous year's shoots in May, sepals pubescent, ovate; fruits hemispherical, 1.5 cm wide, dark purple, dry, tasteless. BS 3: 239; GH 5: 425; FRu 54; FS 2404. USA; Rocky Mts. 1870. One of the best species of all. z6 Plate 85; Fig. 188. ⊕

R. ellipticus Smith. Strong growing shrub, 1.8–3 m high, habit narrowly upright, shoots stiff, densely covered with straight, brown or red bristly hairs with some thick, short, straight prickles intermixed; leaflets 3, terminal leaflet much larger than the others, ovate, not lobed, regularly finely biserrate, underside soft pubescent with raised venation, midrib prickly; flowers small, white, in few-flowered clusters; fruits yellow, good tasting (= R. flavus Hamilt.). Himalayas. Known in California as "Golden Evergreen Raspberry". z8 Plate 88.

R. euleucus see: **R. pedunculosus**

R. eustephanos see: **R. rosifolius 'Coronarius'**

R. flagellaris Willd. Procumbent shrub, shoots to 2 m long, with scattered, weak prickles; leaves on long shoots 3–5 parted, terminal leaflets oval-rhombic, 3–10 cm long, acute to obtuse, scabrous and irregularly serrate, thin, rather glabrous above, sparsely pubescent beneath, lateral leaflets smaller, short petioled; flowers white, 2.5 cm wide, mostly 2–4 together, May–June; fruits hemispherical, black, glabrous; sweet, 1.5 cm thick. RMi 174; GSP 214 (= R. procumbens Muhl.). Eastern N. America. 1809. z4 ⚮✗

R. flagelliflorus Focke. Evergreen climber or procumbent shrub, to 3 m high, current year's growth to 1.5 m long, finely whitish tomentose when young, with small, very thin, curved prickles; leaves ovate to oval-lanceolate, 8–16 cm long, crenate toothed and shallowly lobed, appressed pubescent and deep green above, underside dense brown tomentose (!); flowers white, very quickly abscising, sepals with purple interior (!), in short, axillary clusters, June; fruits black, edible. FRu 51. Central and W. China. 1901. Very attractive; leaves often finely green marbled in the shade. z7 Plate 85. # ∅ ⊕

R. flavus see: **R. ellipticus**

R. flosculosus Focke. Upright, deciduous shrub, shoots to 3 m long, branched at the tips, finely pubescent or totally glabrous, usually purple-brown, often also pruinose, with only a few prickles; leaves pinnate, with 5–7 leaflets, these ovate, 3–5 cm long, to 7 cm long on long shoots and somewhat rhombic, unevenly serrate, glabrous, above, underside white tomentose; flowers small, only 6–8 mm wide, pink, in narrow, 5–10 cm long, terminal and axillary racemes, June; fruit small, deep red to black. FRu 77. Central China; Hupeh, Szechwan Provs. 1907. z6

R. fockeanus Kurz. Herbaceous perennial, strawberry-like, lying on the ground, shoots rooting at the nodes; leaves trifoliate, leaflets rounded, the lateral ones obliquely obovate, 2–3 cm long; flowers solitary, white;

Fig. 188. *Rubus deliciosus* (from BM)   Fig. 189. *Rubus biflorus* (from Bot. Reg.)

fruits composed of about 20 fruitlets, bright red. Central China, E. Himalayas, in mountain forests at 3000–4000 m. Existence in cultivation unknown. (The plant cultivated in England under this name is normally *R. calycinoides!*) z5 Plate 89.

R. × fraseri Rehd. (*R. odoratus × R. parviflorus*). Very similar to *R. odoratus*, but the shoots and leaf petioles less glandular pubescent; leaves with more acuminate lobes; flowers pink, quickly fading. GC 73: 24 (= *R. robustus* G. Fraser non Presl). 1918.

R. fruticosus L. Common European Blackberry. Shrub, to 2 m high, open bushy, shoots later drooping, obtuse angular, sharp angular above, glabrous, reddish on the sunny side, densely covered with stout, usually somewhat bowed prickles; leaves 5 parted, leaflets plaited, coarse and scabrous biserrate, somewhat glossy above and dark green, lighter or gray-green beneath, more or less densely soft pubescent, terminal leaflets broadly ovate, 7–10 cm long, base cordate, lateral leaflets narrower; flowers white to pink, 2 cm wide, in many-flowered corymbs, stamens somewhat shorter than the style, June–July; fruit black, glossy, edible. HM 1089; HF 2580 (= *R. plicatus* Weihe & Nees). Europe. Linnaeus considered nearly all the European blackberries to be *R. fruticosus* with *R. plicatus* being the type of the species. ℗ W. Germany on slopes. z6 ⚥ ✗

laciniatus see: **R. laciniatus**

'Plenus' see: **R. linkianus**

R. giraldianus see: **R. cockburnianus**

R. gracilis see: **R. niveus** and **R. pedunculosus**

R. hokonensis see: **R. lambertianus** var. **hakonensis**

R. henryi Hemsl. & Ktze. Evergreen climber, to 6 m high in its habitat, shoots thin white floccose-tomentose when young, with a few, hooked prickles; leaves deeply 3–5 lobed, occasionally simple or with 1 lobe, 10–15 cm long, the lobes lanceolate, long acuminate, sparsely finely serrate, deep green above, white tomentose beneath; flowers light red, nearly 2 cm wide, in axillary and terminal, glandular racemes, June; fruit black, glossy, 1–1.5 cm wide. FRu 12; MG 30: 7. Central China. 1900. z7 Plate 88, 89; Fig. 193. # ⌀

var. **bambusarum** (Hemsl.) Rehd. Shoots more thorny with small hooked prickles; leaves distinctly trifoliate (!), leaflets narrowly lanceolate, 7–12 cm long. BMns 33 (= *R. bambusarum* Hemsl.). China; Hupeh Prov., primarily in bamboo forests. 1900. # ⌀

R. hispidus L. Procumbent, semi-evergreen shrub, shoots to 1.5 m long, densely covered with downward directed bristles; leaves 3(5) parted, tough, leaflets oval-rhombic, the lateral ones oblique, acute, coarsely biserrate, 3–6 cm long, more or less glabrous on both sides; flowers white, 2 cm wide, in few-flowered corymbs, on 15–25 cm long erect stalks from the leaf axils; fruit purple, eventually black, small, sour. BC 3505; BB 1902; HyWF 82 (= *R. sempervirens* Bigel.). Eastern N. America. 1768. z4 Fig. 190.

R. hupehensis Oliv. Deciduous to semi-evergreen climbing shrub, shoots dark, lightly floccose when young, tomentose, slightly prickly; leaves simple, oblong-lanceolate, base round, 7–11 cm long, finely and irregularly serrate, gray tomentose beneath, petiole 1 cm long; flowers 3–7 in small, very glandular (!) racemes, white, calyx gray tomentose, July–August; fruits purple-black, bitter. SH 2: 591 e–f; GC 61: 166 (= *R. swinhoei* Bean non Hance). China; Hupeh Prov. 1907. z6 Plate 85; Fig. 191. ⌀

R. ichangensis Hemsl. & Ktze. Deciduous shrub, to 2 m high, climbing or procumbent, shoots thin, with stalked glands and scattered, hook-form prickles; leaves simple, oval-lanceolate, 8–15 cm long, base deeply cordate, sparsely mucronulate-serrate, somewhat lobed at the base, glabrous above, midrib prickly beneath, as is the 2–3 cm long stalk; flowers tiny, white, 6–8 mm wide, in slender, 15–25 cm long panicles, July; fruits small, red, good tasting. FRu 18; GC 48: 275. W. and central China. 1900. z6 Plate 85; Fig. 191.

R. idaeus L. Raspberry. Deciduous shrub, upright, to 2 m high, stems tomentose at first, basal portion occasionally somewhat prickly, otherwise stiff bristly, often also pruinose; leaves pinnate, leaflets 3–5, broadly ovate, 5–10 cm long, coarsely biserrate, finely pubescent above, underside more or less white tomentose; flowers small, white, in short, axillary and terminal, somewhat prickly racemes, petals shorter than the sepals, May–July; fruit hemispherical to more conical, purple-red, finely pubescent, sweet. HM 148; 1082; HF 2573; GSP 211. Europe, N. America, Siberia; circumpolar. Cultivated for ages and available in many cultivars. z4 ⚥ ✗

Special Lit. for the fruit varieties: Leemans, J. A., & E. T. Nannenga: A morphological classification of Raspberry Varieties; Wageningen, Holland 1957 (140 pp., 139 ills., bibliography with 100 works).

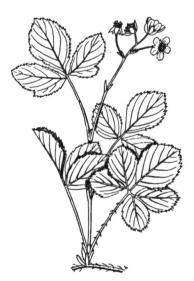

Fig. 190. *Rubus hispidus* (from Hooker)

Fig. 191. **Rubus.** Above: left *R. irenaeus*, center *R. ichangensis*, right *R. malifolius.*
Below: left *R. hupehensis*, center *R. setchuenensis*, right *R. chroosepalus* (from ICS)

var. **aculeatissimus** Rgl. & Tiling. Young shoots glabrous, often pruinose, bristly, usually with stout prickles, widened at the base (= *R. melanolasius* Focke). N. America, E. Asia. Before 1894.

'**Albus**'. Form of var. *strigosus* with amber-yellow fruits. ⚭ ✂

var. **canadensis** Richardson. Young shoots ash-gray tomentose, with bristle-like fine prickles (= *R. subarcticus* Rydb.; *R. carolinianus* Rydb.). N. America; Labrador and Alaska, southward to Colorado; also in Eastern Asia.

'**Phyllanthus**'. Inflorescences branched, but instead of flowers, with tassel-like, green, compact shoots. PBl 1: 813. First observed in Denmark. 1888. Plate 87. ✜

var. **strigosus** (Michx.) Maxim. Young shoots smooth, often bluish pruinose, densely bristly and often also glandular, with or without bristle-like prickles; inflorescence glandular and prickly; fruit hemispherical. BB 1894; GH 5: 403 (= *R. strigosus* Michx.). N. America. With many cultivars. ⚭ ✂

R. illecebrosus Focke. Strawberry-Raspberry. Only slightly woody, mostly herbaceous plant, shoots 0.5–1 m high, angular, prickly, erect; leaves 15–20 cm long, pinnate, leaflets 5–7, on short shoots only 3, oblong-lanceolate, acuminate, 4–8 cm long, biserrate, glabrous; flowers white, solitary, to 4 cm wide, July to September; fruits scarlet-red, large, sweet-stale, 3 cm long. FRu 64; BM 8704; MJ 1382. Japan. 1895. Grows well in the shade of tall trees. z6 ⚭

R. incisus Thunb. Deciduous shrub, low, leaves quite variable, shoots thin, erect to ascending, white pruinose, with medium-sized, straight or bowed prickles; leaves ovate in outline, with a broad, cordate base, 3–5 cm wide, deeply 3 lobed on long shoots, more ovate on flowering shoots, indistinctly lobed, unevenly serrate, stalk 4 cm long, thin, prickly; flowers mostly solitary, 1 cm wide, white, petals erect at first. FRu 58. Japan. z6

var. **subcrataegifolius** (Lév. & Van.). Shrub, to 1 m high, erect, with stolons, shoots somewhat striped, purple pruinose, smooth or somewhat prickly; leaves always 3–5 lobed or in some cases unlobed, 3–12 cm long, base deeply cordate, crenate toothed, green above, white pubescent beneath; flowers white, few in loose, terminal corymbs, anthers purple, calyx pubescent on the interior, late May; fruits orange, with only a few fruitlets. FRu 60; Gfl 53: 78; BM 8246 (= *R. incisus* sensu Späth non Thunb.; *R. koehneanus* Focke). Japan. 1890.

R. inermis see: **R. ulmifolius 'Inermis'**

R. innominatus S. Moore. Deciduous shrub, upright, to 2 m high, shoots densely glandular (!!), shaggy and prickly; leaves pinnate, leaflets 3–5, the lateral ones obliquely oval-oblong, 5–10 cm long, base rounded, terminal leaflets larger, ovate, long acuminate, nearly cordate at the base, irregular and coarsely serrate, green and lightly pubescent above, gray-white tomentose beneath; flowers small, about 1 cm wide, pink, in terminal, 25–40 cm long panicles, petals quickly abscising, rachis (like the shoots) tomentose and prickly, axes glandular pubescent, July–August; fruits globose, orange, 1.4 cm thick, edible. GC 38; 290. Central and S. China; Szechwan, Yunnan Provs. 1901. Nearly always labeled erroneously in cultivation! z6 ⊕ ⚭ ✕

var. **kuntzeanus** (Focke) Bailey. Shoots, stalks and inflorescences without glands; fruit red, edible (= *R. kuntzeanus* Hemsl.). Central China. 1887. ⚭ ✕

R. inopertus Focke. Deciduous climbing shrub, similar to *R. niveus* (but differing in the 7–9 leaflets and the short-stalked flowers), stems stout, rather cylindrical; leaves pinnate, with 7–9 leaflets, these ovate or oval-lanceolate, usually long acuminate, 5–7 cm long, totally glabrous or only slightly pubescent; flowers in short-stalked, axillary clusters at the shoot tips. China; Szechwan, Yunnan, Hupeh Provs., in the mountains. z6

R. irenaeus Focke. Evergreen shrub, procumbent, shoots to 2 m long, thornless or with small prickles; leaves nearly circular, somewhat acuminate, occasionally rounded at the apex, base broadly cordate, 10–15 cm wide, dark green and somewhat metallic above, underside whitish or brownish tomentose, petiole 4–8 cm long, stipules large, incised; flowers about 2 cm wide, white, in the leaf axils and in terminal clusters, calyx tomentose, July; fruits red, large. FRu 52. China; Hupeh Prov., Nan Shan. 1900. z9 Fig. 191. # ⊘ ⚭

R. kinashii see: **R. mesogaeus**

R. koehneanus see: **R. incisus** var. **subcrataegifolius**

R. kuntzeanus see: **R. innominatus** var. **kuntzeanus**

R. laciniatus (West.) Willd. Deciduous shrub with climbing or procumbent stems, these usually pubescent, but quickly becoming glabrous, angular with curved prickles; leaves always 5 parted, leaflets deeply pinnatisect, the lobes incised, dark green above, underside soft pubescent; flowers pink-white, 2 cm wide, in large, pubescent, prickly panicles, June to July; fruits black, rounded, to 1.5 cm long, good tasting. HM 1086; BC 3499 (= *R. fruticosus laciniatus* West.). Origin unknown, but cultivated since 1770; widely naturalized today. z5 ⊘ ⚭ ✕

R. lambertianus Ser. Semi-evergreen, luxuriant shrub, climbing or procumbent, densely foliate, stems thin, 4 sided, glutinous and usually finely tomentose when young, with a few, hooked prickles; leaves ovate to more oblong, base cordate, 7–12 cm long, long acuminate, crenate toothed and shallowly lobed, occasionally also distinctly 3 lobed, pubescent on both sides, petioles 2–4 cm long; flowers white, 8 mm wide, in 8–14 cm long panicles, August to September; fruits small, red, October. MJ 3553; GC 48: 270. Central China. 1907. Hardy. z6 Plate 85. # ⊘

var. **hakonensis** (Franch. & Sav.) Focke. Very similar to the species, but the stems not angular and glabrous; leaves glabrous. KO ill. 217; MJ 1384 (= *R. hakonensis* Franch. & Sav.). Japan, Central China. 1907. # ⊘

R. lasiocarpus see: **R. niveus**

R. lasiostylus Focke. Upright, deciduous shrub, stems to 2 m high, prickles bristle form, bark bluish white; leaves pinnate, leaflets 3–5, terminal leaflets to 15 cm long, broadly cordate-ovate, uneven and biserrate, somewhat lobed, acuminate, lateral leaflets ovate, nearly sessile, 5–10 cm long, light green and scattered pubescent above, underside white tomentose; flowers 1–5 together, small, nodding, reddish, petals smaller than the sepals, quickly abscising, June; fruits globose, 2.5 cm wide, red, white woolly. FRu 71; BM 7426. Central China; Hupeh Prov. z7 ⊘ ⚭

R. leucodermis Dougl. Upright deciduous shrub, to 2 m high, shoots upright, very bluish white pruinose, covered with flat, curved prickles; leaves pinnate, leaflets 3, often 5 on long shoots, broadly ovate, acute, 6–10 cm long, base round to nearly cordate, coarsely biserrate, gray tomentose beneath, petiole and midrib prickly; flowers white, few in terminal clusters, petals shorter than the sepals, May–June; fruits purple-black, globose, pruinose, edible. MG 16: 429; MS 187; GH 5: 411. Western N. America. 1829. With some fruit cultivars grown in the USA. z5 ⊘ ⚭ ✕

R. lineatus Reinwardt. Semi-evergreen or deciduous shrub, shoots to 3 m long, somewhat climbing, thin, finely pubescent and nearly thornless; leaves palmately pinnate, 5 parted, leaflets oblong-lanceolate to oblong, middle leaflets 10–15 cm long, the others shorter, each with 30–50 parallel vein pairs, regularly dentate, deep green above, glossy silvery silky beneath; flowers in short, axillary clusters, small, white. FRu 14. Himalayas, China. 1905. One of the most beautiful plants of the entire genus. z9 Fig. 192. ⊘

R. linkianus Ser. Vigorous growing, deciduous shrub, shoots finely pubescent and with many stout, sharp hooked prickles, the petiole and leaf midrib also prickled; leaves 3–5 parted, leaflets ovate to elliptic, acute, terminal leaflets 7–10 cm long and long stalked, the others smaller, coarsely and usually doubly dentate, dark green and usually glabrous above, white tomentose beneath; flowers in short, usually foliate, pubescent or tomentose, prickled panicles, white to soft pink, flowers large and double. Gw 17: 553 (= *R. thyrsoideus* 'Plenus';

R. fruticosus 'Plenus'; *R. candicans* 'Linkianus'). Garden origin; exact location unknown but existing before 1770. Very attractive and abundantly flowering, also in semishade. z6 ⊕|⌀

R. loganobaccus see: **R. ursinus** 'Loganberry'

R. malifolius Focke. Deciduous climber or procumbent shrub, to 2.5 m high, shoots with short, hooked prickles; leaves simple, elliptic to more oblong, long acuminate, base rounded, 5–12 cm long, glabrous above, underside pubescent on the 7–10 vein pairs, sparsely crenate, petiole about 1 cm long; flowers white, 2.5 cm wide, in terminal racemes, these glabrous and to 12 cm (!) long, calyx tomentose, petals circular, June; fruits black, not edible. China; Szechwan Prov. 1904. z6 Plate 85; Fig. 191. ⌀

R. melanolasius see: **R. idaeus** var. **aculeatissimus**

R. mesogaeus Focke. Strong growing deciduous shrub, to about 2.5 m high, stems slender, cylindrical, densely tomentose, with small, bowed prickles, shoots unbranched in the 1st year, curving at the tips; leaves trifoliate, leaflets elliptic to broadly ovate, quite variable in size, terminal leaflets much larger, 5–8(16) cm long, unevenly coarsely serrate and lobed, pubescent above only when young, underside gray-white tomentose, terminal leaflets with a round or slightly cordate base, lateral leaflets with a more oblique base; flowers white to pale pink, small, in small, axillary clusters, petals 6–8 mm long, May to June; fruits globose, small, black. FRu 76, 82; MJ 1380 (= *R. kinashii* Lév. & Van.). Central China. 1907. z6 Plate 87. ⌀

R. microphyllus L. f. Deciduous shrub, 1–1.5 m high, shoots glabrous, prickly; leaves palmately 3–5 lobed, 5 veined at the base, 3–8 cm long, cordate-ovate in outline, the lobes unevenly and coarsely dentate, finely lobed,

Fig. 192. *Rubus lineatus* (Original)

venation soft pubescent beneath, midrib prickly; flowers white, solitary in the apical leaf axils, petals narrowly ovate, May–June; fruit globose, yellow, juicy, nearly 2 cm thick. FRu 56; MJ 1375; BM 7801 (= *R. palmatus* Thunb.). Japan, China. 1899. z9 Plate 85.

'Variegatus'. Leaves 3 lobed, 4–7.5 cm long, cream-white and pink marbled. Pretty. ⌀

R. niveus Thunb. Very vigorous, deciduous shrub, stout stemmed, to 4 m high, apexes gracefully nodding, finely tomentose at first, later glabrous and pruinose, with hooked prickles; leaves pinnate, leaflets usually 5–7, elliptic to more ovate, 3–6 cm long, acute, simple and coarsely serrate, base round, dark green above, underside white tomentose; flowers purple-pink, in many-flowered, terminal panicles, stalk and calyx white tomentose; fruit dark red, eventually black, globose, sourish, edible (= *R. lasiocarpus* Sm.; *R. gracilis* Roxb.). Himalayas to S. India and Ceylon, in the mountains. 1934. See also: *R. pedunculosus*. z9 Fig. 193. ⌀ ⊗|✕

R. × nobilis Regel (= *R. idaeus* × *R. odoratus*). Habit and stems like those of *R. odoratus*, also with exfoliating bark, but lower and not so glandular-glutinous; but the leaves trifoliate, large, pubescent on both sides; flowers purple-red, in terminal corymbs, June–July. Originated in 1855 by C. de Vos in Hazerswoude, near Boskoop, Holland. ⊕

R. nutans see: **R. barbatus**

R. nutkanus see: **R. parviflorus**

R. occidentalis L. Deciduous shrub, 2–3 m high, shoots drooping, with small prickles, very pruinose and often purple; leaves pinnate, trifoliate, 5 parted on long shoots, leaflets ovate, abruptly short acuminate, 5–8 cm long, base round to cordate, biserrate, underside white tomentose, petiole somewhat prickly; flowers 1–1.5 cm wide, white, few in tomentose-prickly corymbs, petals elliptic, shorter than the sepals, May–June; fruits black-red, pruinose, hemispherical, edible. BB 1896; GSP 211; GH 5: 409–410. N. America. 1696. Frequently used in hybridizing fruit cultivars. z4 ⊗|✕

R. odoratus L. Deciduous shrub, stoloniferous, 1–2 m high, shoots erect, woody, sparsely branched, shaggy glandular when young; leaves large, palmately 3–5 lobed, base cordate, 10–25 cm wide, the lobes broadly triangular, middle lobes longer than the others, all acute, usually abruptly acuminate, soft tipped to finely serrate, pubescent on both sides, stipules nearly free, abscising; flowers 3–5 cm wide, purple, fragrant, in short, many-flowered panicles, sepals broadly ovate, abruptly caudate, exterior glandular, June–August; fruit red, broadly hemispherical. BB 1890; GSP 208; HM 1079; BM 323. N. America. 1770. For a moist, humus soil; excellent understory plant. z4 Fig. 194. ⌀ ⊕

'Albus'. Bark lighter, leaves lighter, flowers whitish.

R. oliveri see: **R. corchorifolius** var. **oliveri**

R. omeiensis see: **R. setchuenensis**

R. pacatus see: **R. setchuenensis**

Fig. 193. **Rubus.** Left *R. coreanus;* center *R. henryi;* right *R. niveus* (from ICS)

R. palmatus see: **R. microphyllus**

R. parkeri Hance. Deciduous shrub, climbing, stems biennial, slender, round, gray tomentose, with scattered, hooked prickles, these occasionally glandular at the apex; leaves simple, acutely oval-oblong, 10–16 cm long, base cordate, crenate and sinuately lobed, pubescent above, dark green, underside gray or brownish tomentose, petiole 5–20 mm long, pubescent and prickly; flowers white, 8 mm wide, in loose, large, glandular pubescent panicles, calyx reddish glandular haired, June; fruits black, with only a few fruitlets. FRu 24; GC 51: 166. Central China, Szechwan Prov. 1907. z6

R. parviflorus Nutt. Deciduous shrub, 1.5(2) m high, stems flexuose, thornless, bark exfoliating; young shoots soft pubescent on both sides, stipules somewhat adnate to the petiole; flowers white (!), 3–6 cm wide, only 4–8 (!) in short, dense corymbs, sepals ·glandular, but not stiff haired, petals broadly ovate, May–July; fruit hemispherical, to 2 cm wide, red, inedible. BB 1891; MS 184; GH 5: 424; BM 3453 (= *R. nutkanus* Mocino). Western N. America. 1827. z5 Fig. 194. ∅

R. parvifolius L. Low shrub, shoots rather short, about 50–70 cm long, nodding, short shaggy pubescent, prickly; leaves trifoliate, occasionally 5 parted or only 3 lobed, leaflets rounded to broadly obovate, the lateral ones more elliptic, 2–5 cm long, unevenly dentate, terminal leaflets often lobed, appressed pubescent above, underside white tomentose; flowers small, few, axillary at the shoot tips, purple-pink, petals erect, calyx with a green exterior, sepals outspread, later reflexed, June; fruits red, globose, edible. NK 7: 31; MJ 1379; YWP 2: 26 (= *R. triphyllus* Thunb.). China, Japan. 1818. z6 Plate 85, 89. ⚭✂

R. parvus Buchan. Evergreen, procumbent shrub, shoots thin, often rooting at the nodes, prickles small, not numerous; leaves simple, linear, 3–10 cm long, to 1 cm wide, long acuminate, densely and regularly thorny toothed, base cordate, midrib prickly beneath; flowers 1–3 axillary, white, about 2.5 cm wide, petals ovate, outspread, dioecious, May–June; fruits to 2.5 cm long, juicy. MNZ 71. New Zealand; South Island. z9 Plate 86. #

R. pedunculosus D. Don. Very strong growing, 5 m high shrub, stems 2.5–3 cm thick, densely velvety pubescent and covered with small prickles when young; leaves 15–30 cm long, pinnate, with 3–5 leaflets, terminal leaflet ovate, acuminate, cordate at the base, 8–12 cm long, biserrate, strigose pubescent above, underside white tomentose, lateral leaflets only half as large, base oblique, sessile; flowers white to pale pink, in few-flowered corymbs, petals obovate, shorter than the lanceolate sepals, June–July; fruit small, blue-black (= *R. gracilis* Roxb.; *R. niveus* Wall. non Thunb.; *R. euleucus* Focke). Himalayas, China. 1901. z9

R. peltatus Maxim. Evergreen shrub, to 1 m high, erect, shoots thin, round, glabrous; leaves nearly circular in outline, flat 3–5 lobed, the lobes with small, abruptly tapered tips, petiole attached shield-like (peltate) (totally different from the other species!!); flowers large, terminal, white, petals circular; fruits elongated, very large, edible. MJ 3548. Japan, mountain forests; China, Hupeh Prov. z7 ∅ ✣ ⚭✂

R. phoenicolasius Maxim. Deciduous shrub, upright-drooping, to 3 m high, shoots densely pubescent, with red stalked glands and bristles, with a few, thin prickles; leaves pinnate, usually 3, occasionally 5 parted, broadly ovate, 4–10 cm long, acuminate, coarse and irregularly acute serrate, somewhat pubescent and dark green above, underside white tomentose, 4–10 cm long, lateral

Plate 97

Salix fargesii
in Crarae, Scotland

Salix magnifica
in Birr Castle Park, Ireland

Salix moupinensis in a garden in Kolding, Denmark

Plate 98

Salix lapponum
in the Royal Botanic Garden, Edinburgh, Scotland

Salix pentandra
in the Arnold Arboretum, USA

Salix reticulata in the Royal Botanic Garden, Edinburgh, Scotland

Plate 99

Sambucus nigra 'Linearis' in the Dortmund Botanic Garden, W. Germany

Salix matsudana 'Tortuosa'
in the Dortmund Botanic Garden, W. Germany

Sambucus nigra 'Laciniata'
in the Dortmund Botanic Garden, W. Germany

Plate 100

Sambucus sieboldiana in Japan
Photo: Dr. S. Watari, Tokyo

Sambucus nigra 'Pyramidalis'
in the Dortmund Botanic Garden, W. Germany

Sambucus racemosa 'Plumosa Aurea'
in the Dortmund Botanic Garden, W. Germany

Sarcococca saligna
in Caerhays Castle garden, SW. England

Plate 101

Sarcococca confusa
in Knighthayes Court, England

Sarcococca hookeriana var. *digyna*
in Knighthayes Court, England

Sarcococca humilis in the Dortmund Botanic Garden, W. Germany

Plate 102

Sasa palmata in the Royal Botanic Gardens, Kew, England

Sasa veitchii in its habitat
Photo: Dr. Watari, Tokyo

Plate 103

Sasa variegata in the Lyon Botanic Garden, France

Sinowilsonia henryi in the Royal Botanic Garden, Edinburgh, Scotland

Plate 104

Schefflera venulosa
in S'Avall Garden, Majorca, Spain

Schefflera impressa
in the Hillier Arboretum, England

Schinus molle
in Jardin Marimurtra, Blanes, Spain

Sassafras albidum var. *molle*
in the Dortmund Botanic Garden, W. Germany

Plate 105

Schisandra rubriflora
in the Lismore Castle garden, Ireland

Securinega fruticosa
in the Dortmund Botanic Garden, W. Germany

Schisandra sphenanthera in the Royal Botanic Gardens, Kew, England

Plate 106

Sedum populifolium
in Whitnall Park, Chicago, USA

Schizophragma hydrangeoides
in the Dortmund Botanic Garden, W. Germany

Schizophragma integrifolium in Bagatelle Park, Paris, France

Plate 107

Semiarundinaria fastuosa in its habitat
Photo: Dr. Watari, Tokyo

Senecio rotundifolius
in Malahide Gardens, Ireland

Senecio reinoldii
in the Hillier Arboretum, England

Shepherdia argentea
in the Dortmund Botanic Garden, W. Germany

Plate 108

Senecio monroi
in the Royal Botanic Gardens, Kew, England

Senecio 'Sunshine'
in the Royal Botanic Gardens, Kew, England

Senecio elaeagnifolius
in the Dublin Botanic Garden, Ireland

Senecio platanifolius,
Son El Salt, Majorca, Spain

Plate 109

Sinarundinaria nitida
in Pitt White, England

Shibataea kumasaca in its habitat
Photo: Dr. Watari, Tokyo

Sinarundinaria nitida in the Göteborg Botanic Garden, Sweden

Plate 110

Sinojackia rehderiana
in the Royal Botanic Gardens, Kew, England

Sibiraea laevigata
in the Oslo Botanic Garden, Norway

Smilax megalantha in Dublin, Ireland

Sinomenium acutum
in the Essen Botanic Garden, W. Germany

Plate 111

Smilax herbacea in Malahide Gardens, Ireland

Sophora japonica 'Pendula', flowering type,
Son Julia on Majorca, Spain

Skimmia japonica in Bell Park, Fota Island, Ireland

Plate 112

Sophora tetraptera in the Royal Botanic Gardens, Kew, England

Sophora japonica 'Dot' in Jardin Pinya de Rosa, Santa Cristina, Spain

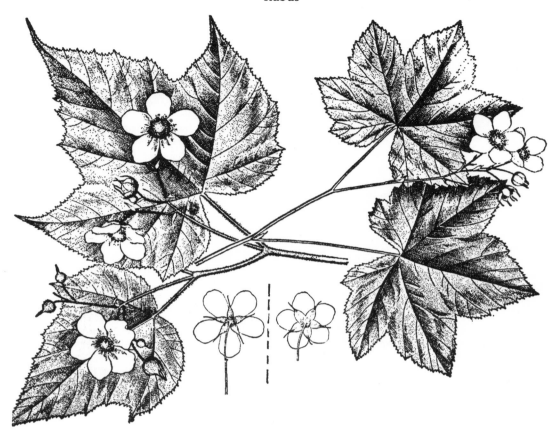

Fig. 194. **Rubus.** Left *R. odoratus;* right *R. parviflorus* (from New Britton & Brown)

leaflets smaller; flowers light pink, in dense, axillary, glandular pubescent, short racemes, petals shorter than the sepals, June–July; fruits hemispherical, orange-red, sourish-sweet, edible ("Japanese Wineberry"!). NK 7: 28; BC 3492; BM 6479. Korea, Japan. 1876. z6 Plate 84. ∅ ✛ ⚬ ✕

R. platyphyllos K. Koch. Luxuriant, procumbent, semi-evergreen shrub, shoots thick, very prickly and glandular bristly; leaves normally trifoliate, leaflets broadly ovate, 12–14 cm long, unevenly serrate, base cordate, green pubescent on both sides, underside gray-green; flowers white, in loose, glandular bristly panicles, these foliate at the base; fruits purple-violet, to 3 cm long, edible, but developing fully only in mild climates. RH 1906: 570; DB 1962. Caucasus. 1904. z6 Plate 88. # ∅

R. playfairianus Focke. Evergreen or semi-evergreen shrub, shoots climbing or procumbent, very dark, thin, with small, hooked prickles, floccose-tomentose; leaves 3(5) parted, leaflets stalked, oblong-lanceolate, terminal leaflets much larger, 6–14 cm long, scabrous serrate, lateral leaflets 3–7 cm long, dark green above, gray tomentose beneath; flowers in small, axillary and terminal racemes, 1–1.5 cm wide, not very conspicuous, calyx densely shaggy, but not glandular, May–June; fruit black. GC 51: 166. China; Hupeh Prov. 1907. z7 Plate 89. # ∅

R. plicatus see: **R. fruticosus**

R. polytrichus see: **R. tricolor**

R. procumbens see: **R. flagellaris**

R. robustus see: **R. ✕ fraseri**

R. rosifolius Sm. Evergreen shrub, upright, to 2 m high or more in the tropics, bushy, shoots somewhat angular, loosely pubescent, with scattered prickles; leaves pinnate, 5–7 parted on long shoots, otherwise usually 5 or 3 parted, occasionally also simple, leaflets thin, ovate to oblong-lanceolate, 5–7 cm long, with 8–10 vein pairs, coarsely biserrate, pubescent and nearly equally colored on both sides; flowers solitary or 2–3 together, terminal, 2.5–3 cm wide, white, August; fruits 2 cm long, fruitlets very small, red, stale tasting. FRu 65; BM 6970. Mountain forests from the Himalayas to China and Japan. 1816. Conservatory plant! z9 Plate 84, 85; Fig. 185. # ✛

'Coronarius'. Flowers to 5 cm wide, densely double, white, like small roses. FS 1714; BM 1783 (= *R. commersonii* Poir; *R. eustephanos* Focke var. *coronarius* Koidz.). Originally from China, but cultivated longer in Japan. 1827. z9 Plate 87. # ✛

R. sagatus see: **R. adenophorus**

R. saxatilis L. "Stoneberry". Perennial, developing 0.7–1.5 m long, procumbent shoots from a creeping, woody rootstock, fertile shoots erect, 30 cm high, these pubescent and with fine straight prickles; leaves trifoliate, leaflets ovate to rhombic, about 3 cm long, coarse and scabrous serrate, rather glabrous, petiole 5–6 cm long; flowers few in the apical leaf axils, small, white to greenish, petals 8 mm long, 3 mm wide, June–July; fruits red, with 3–4 fruitlets, each somewhat pea-sized, edible. PAr 281; HF 2574; GPN 451. Europe, in deciduous forests, on calcareous soil. z4

R. sempervirens see: **R. hispidus**

R. setchuenensis Bur. & Franch. Deciduous shrub, luxuriant, to 2.5 m high, shoots cylindrical, velvety pubescent, totally thornless, stellate pubescent; leaves nearly circular in outline, indistinctly 5–7 lobed, 10–16 cm wide, cordate, the lobes broad and obtuse, irregularly crenate, rugose above, gray tomentose beneath with reticulate venation, petiole 5–7 cm long; flowers purple, 1–1.5 cm wide, in axillary clusters or also in many-flowered panicles, July to August; fruits black, ripening late, good tasting. FRu 46 (= *R. clemens* Focke; *R. omeiensis* Rolfe; *R. pacatus* Focke). W. China, Mt. Omei. 1908. Hardy. z5 Plate 85; Fig. 191. ⌀ ✧

R. setosus Bigel. Procumbent shrub, similar to *R. hispidus*, but with stronger shoots, occasionally also ascending, older shoots densely covered with stiff, downward directed bristles; leaflets on long shoots usually 5, normally 3 on flowering shoots, obovate, usually acute to short acuminate, 5–10 cm long, short petioled to sessile, deciduous; flowers white, small, in elongated, glandular bristly racemes, July–August; fruits small, red, sour. Eastern N. America, on dry and moist soils. z6

R. spectabilis Pursh. Upright, deciduous shrub, 1–2 m high, shoots somewhat prickly only on the basal portion, otherwise thornless and glabrous; leaves nearly glabrous, trifoliate, leaflets ovate, long acuminate, membranous, somewhat pinnatisect to incised serrate, terminal leaflet stalked, whole leaf 10–15 cm long, stipules bristle form; flowers solitary, purple-red, 2.5 cm wide, fragrant, nodding, on short lateral shoots, calyx pubescent, May; fruit yellow or orange, large, edible, translucent. MS 185; GH 5: 419; FS 2260; BC 3491. Western N. America. 1827. z5 Plate 85. ✧ ✿ ✂

R. squarrosus Fritsch. Evergreen shrub, habit climbing or spreading mat-like, shoots thin, covered with many small, yellow prickles as are the leaf petiole and midrib; leaves usually completely lacking from young plants, occasionally present on older plants, oval-lanceolate, to 5 cm long, scabrous, irregularly serrate and lobed; flowers dioecious, in panicles, yellowish white, 8 mm wide, calyx tomentose; fruit orange-red (= *R. cissoides* var. *pauperatus* Kirk). New Zealand, throughout the country in forests and thickets, on the plains and in the hills. z9 Fig. 186. #

R. strigosus see: **R. idaeus** var. **strigosus**

R. subarcticus see: **R. idaeus** var. **canadensis**

R. swinhoei see: **R. hupehensis**

R. thibetanus Franch. Deciduous shrub, upright, to 1.8 m high or more, stems biennial, glabrous, round, bluish red pruinose, irregularly covered with thin, straight prickles; leaves pinnate, 10–20 cm long, with 7–13 leaflets, rachis prickly, leaflets ovate, base oblique, 2.5–5 cm long, the basal pairs largest, then becoming smaller toward the leaf apex, terminal leaflet long, deeply incised, otherwise all leaflets incised serrate, silky pubescent above, gray tomentose beneath, flowers 3–8, purple, 1.5 cm wide, in the leaf axils, June; fruits globose, black, pruinose, 1.5 cm thick. FRu 74; GC 51: 149 (= *R. veitchii* Rolfe). W. China. One of the prettiest species. z6 ⌀

R. thyrsanthus see: **R. candicans**

R. thyrsoideus see: **R. candicans**

R. thyrsoideus 'Plenus' see: **R. linkianus**

R. tricolor Focke. Procumbent shrub, deciduous, shoots finely gray tomentose and very densely covered with 3–4 mm long, erect, thin bristles; leaves oval-rounded, 6–10 cm long, short acuminate, scabrous and irregularly serrate, occasionally slightly lobed, base cordate, dark green above, white tomentose and bristly on the venation beneath, stipules persistent, incised at the apex; flowers 3–4 in short, terminal, bristly racemes, white, 2–2.5 cm wide, July–August; fruits about 1.5 cm thick, light red, bristly, edible. BM 9534 (= *R. polytrichus* Franch. non Progel). China; Yunnan, Szechwan Provs. 1908. z7–8 Plate 89. ⌀ ✿

R. × **'Tridel'** (Ingram) (*R. deliciosus* × *R. trilobus*). Deciduous shrub, similar to *R. deliciosus*, but the flowers somewhat larger, more regular, pure white, looking like rose flowers from a distance. Developed by Collingwood Ingram of Benenden, Cranbrook, England, 1950. Protected by plant patent in the USA. z6? ✧

'Benenden'. The type of this cross. Description as above. JRHS 89: 12. 1950. ✧

R. trifidus Thunb. Evergreen to semi-evergreen shrub, upright, to 2 m high, shoots glandular pubescent at first, quickly becoming glabrous, zig-zagged at the apex, unbranched in the first year; leaves nearly circular in outline, deeply 5–7 lobed (occasionally only 3 lobed), 10–20 cm wide, the lobes oblong-lanceolate, coarsely biserrate, venation slightly pubescent on both sides, petiole 3–6 cm long; flowers pink-white, 2.5–3 cm wide, solitary in the leaf axils or a few in terminal corymbs, calyx tomentose, April to May; fruits red, edible. MJ 1372. Japan. 1888. z6 Plate 85. # ⌀ ✿ ✂

R. trilobus Moc. & Sesse. Deciduous shrub, upright, 1–1.5 m high, similar to *R. deliciosus*, but leaves always 3 lobed, the lobes acute, occasionally indistinctly 5 lobed; leaves 6–8 cm long and wide, base cordate, irregularly serrate, underside densely and soft pubescent; flowering shoots short, usually single flowered, flowers white, 5–8 cm wide, sepals oval-lanceolate, exterior gray haired, interior carmine-red; fruits like those of *R. deliciosus*. FRu 55; BMns 452. S. Mexico, in the higher mountains. z6 Plate 85, 90. ✧

R. triphyllus see: **R. parvifolius**

R. ulmifolius Schott. Shrub, semi-evergreen, 3–4 m high, stems ascending, usually pubescent, angular and furrowed, pruinose (!), stellate pubescent at the shoot tips, prickles with a broad base, straight on the stems, on the lateral shoots curved (!); leaves 3 and 5 parted, leaflets broadly ovate to obovate, coarsely biserrate toward the apex, deep green and somewhat pubescent or glabrous above, white tomentose beneath; flowers pink, in long, tomentose prickly panicles, petals obovate to nearly circular, June–July; fruits ovate, small, rather dry. HM 1094. Europe. z7

'Bellidiflorus'. Shrub, 2–3 m high; flowers densely double, like *Bellis* flowers, petals very narrow, pink-red, July–August, in long, slender panicles (= *R. bellidiflorus* Kirchn.). Cultivated before 1864. z7 # ✣

'Inermis'. Plants totally thornless; leaflets normally 3; flowers single (= *R. inermis* Willd.). Before 1770.

'Variegatus'. Blade green, venation yellow. Old cultivar of unknown origin. For sunny sites. ∅

R. ursinus Cham. & Schlechtd. Evergreen shrub, procumbent or also erect, shoots pubescent when young, prickles straight; leaves 3–5 parted, the apical leaves also simple; leaflets broadly ovate, 3–6 cm long, acute, coarsely biserrate, base rounded, pubescent above, white tomentose or shaggy pubescent beneath; flowers dioecious, white, in prickly corymbs, petals about 1 cm long, sepals caudate; fruit black, pubescent, oblong. California. 1910. z7 #

'Loganberry' (Logan). Shoots to 4 m long, not stoloniferous; leaves on long shoots usually 5-part pinnate, underside densely pubescent; fruit black, oval-conical, 3–4 cm long, born abundantly, somewhat sourish. GH 5: 19–20 (= *R. loganobaccus* Bailey). Developed by J. H. Logan in Santa Cruz, California, 1880. # ⚥ ✗

Special Literature: Logan, M. E.: The Loganberry; Oakland, California. 1955 (20 pp., 3 ills.)

R. veitchii see: **R. thibetanus**

R. xanthocarpus Bur. & Franch. Subshrub, with a woody rootstock, annual growth 20–50 cm high, erect, angular, prickly; leaves pinnate, with 3–5 leaflets, these ovate to lanceolate, terminal leaflets to 7 cm long, lateral leaflets only 3 cm long, petiole and midrib very prickly; flowers small, white, grouped 1–3 terminal, June; fruits golden-yellow, glossy, about 1.5 cm long, with a raspberry taste. Gfl 41: 25. China; Szechwan, Yunnan Provs. 1885. Hardy. z6 ⚥ ✗

The species mentioned are mostly very decorative, either for their attractive bark, or for their foliage or flowers; the fruit of most species is good tasting. Most species flower on the shoot tips of the previous year's wood. Therefore the current year's shoots should not be cut back. Soil preference is a fertile, clay-sand. Tolerates semishade; many species require a mild climate.

Lit. The literature on *Rubus* is voluminous: a recent bibliography may be found in Watson (l.c., 265 to 266). For the ornamental Asiatic species, see Focke, W. O.: Species Rubrorum; in Bibl. Bot. 72 and 83, 1910–1914 ● For the American species see Bailey, L. H.: *Rubus* in North America; Gentes Herbarium, **V**, 1–932, 1941–1945 (426 ills.).

RUMEX L. — POLYGONACEAE

Perennials, only a few subshrubs or shrubs; leaves basal or alternate; petals and sepals (tepals) 6 in total, occasionally 4, sometimes equal in size when in full bloom, the outermost tepals unchanging, the innermost greatly enlarged around the fruit, ovaries triangular; fruit a triangular, non-winged (at fruiting) nutlet (*Polygonum* fruits are winged).— 200 species in the temperate Northern Hemisphere, with the following species occasionally found in culture.

Rumex lunaria L. Evergreen shrub, to about 1.5 m high, erect; leaves ovate, truncate to slightly cordate at the base, 5–7 cm long and nearly as wide, rounded at the apex, thickish, bright green and dull glazed, petiole 4–5 cm long; flowers reddish, small, in loose, terminal, about 15 cm long panicles, January–March. Canary Islands. z10 Plate 92. #

RUSCUS L. — RUSCACEAE

Low evergreen shrubs with green stems and small scaly leaves, in the leaf axils are large, glossy green, prickly or soft modified stems (phylloclades); in the middle of the phylloclades are small, monoecious, inconspicuous, white flowers, paired or solitary in the axil of a bract; perianth with 6 petals, the innermost smaller, stamens 3, connate, ovaries surrounded by the stamen tube; fruit usually single seeded. — 6 species in the Mediterranean region.

Ruscus aculeatus L. Butcher's Broom. Shrub, 30–60(80) cm high, divaricate and well branched, shoots round; phylloclades prickly, sessile, ovate, 2–3 cm long, with a very small linear-lanceolate leaf at the base; flowers usually paired, on the underside, very short stalked, stamen tube purple, April; fruits red, broadly globose, 1

cm thick. HM Pl. 64. S. Europe, S. France, Orient to Iran. z7 Fig. 196.

var. **angustifolius** Boiss. Phylloclades particularly narrow. Fig. 196.

var. **barrelieri** Goir. Stronger and stiffer than the species in all respects; phylloclades less numerous, 2–3 times longer than wide. Tyrol.

var. **burgitensis** Briq. Low, often less than 20 cm high; phylloclades 1–1.5 cm long, 0.5–0.8 cm wide, very stiff; fruits much smaller. French Jura Mts.

var. **platyphyllus** Rouy. Phylloclades to 5 cm long and 2 cm wide.

R. hypoglossum L. Subshrubby, 20–40 cm high, shoots unbranched, angular; phylloclades narrowly lanceolate,

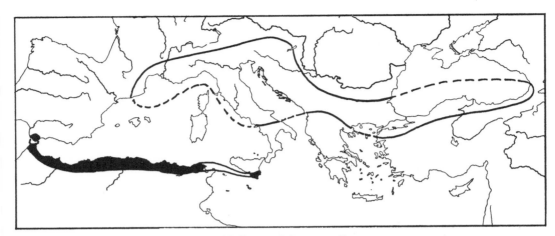

Fig. 195. Range of the genus *Ruscus*

glossy, 7–11 cm long, 3–4 cm wide, not prickly, with a small, oblong leaf on the twisted base; flowers situated on the upper side (!), yellowish, grouped 3–5, in the axil of a leaflike bract, tube violet, March–April; fruit globose, 1 cm thick, red. HM 378. S. Europe. Good for shady sites, even among tree roots! z8 Fig. 196.

R. hypophyllum L. Similar to *R. hypoglossum,* but only 20–30 cm high, shoots angular; phylloclades elliptic, long acuminate, 3.5–7 cm long, 2–3 cm wide, not prickly, in the axil of a small, linear leaf; flowers grouped 5–6,

thin stalked (!), situated on the underside, in the axil of a small bract, May–June; fruit nearly 2 cm thick, red. BM 2049. Canary Islands to the Caucasus. 1625. z9

Easily cultivated plants for dry sites, under strees, prefer shade but *R. aculeatus* also thrives in full sun. Propagated by division.

Lit. Yeo, P. F.: *Ruscus;* in (Synge, P. M.) Dictionary of Gardening, 2nd edition; Roy. Hort. Soc., Suppl., 494–495, 1969 ● Yeo, P. F.: A contribution to the taxonomy of the genus *Ruscus;* in Not. Bot. Gard. Edinb. **28,** 237–264, 1968.

Fig. 196. **Ruscus.** a. *R. aculeatus;* b. *R. aculeatus* f. *angustifolius;* c. *R. hypoglossum* (from Kerner and Original)

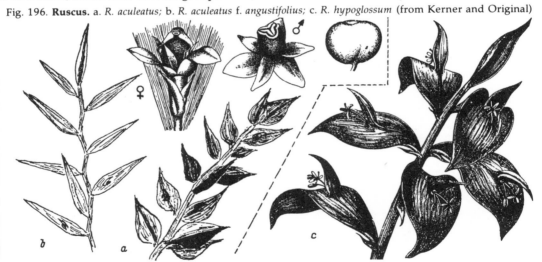

RUSSELIA Jacq. — SCROPHULARIACEAE

Evergreen shrubs with long, rodlike, green nodding shoots; leaves opposite or whorled, often scaly; flowers bright red; calyx deeply incised; corolla tubular, limb bilabiate, these further 5 lobed, lobes rounded, stamens 4, not exserted, style filamentous with a small stigma. — About 40 species in Central America and Mexico.

Russelia equisetiformis Schlechtd. & Cham. Shrub, 0.7–1 m high, broom-like in appearance (like *Cytisus scoparius*), but with outspread and nodding twigs; leaves

linear to ovate, usually reduced to a small scale; flowers scarlet-red, 2.5 cm long, in loose racemes, June–September. BR 1773; Gfl 1: 5 (= *R. juncea* Zucc.). Mexico. 1833. z9 Plate 90.

R. juncea see: **R. equisetiformis**

Very attractive shrub, suitable for the open landscape only in frost free climates! Best overwintered in a cool greenhouse. Very attractive in flower.

RUTA L. — Rue — RUTACEAE

Perennials or subshrubs with strongly scented oil glands; leaves alternate, simple unlobed to multipinnatisect; flowers in terminal cymes, the individual flowers 4 or 5 parted, yellow, stamens 8–10; carpels 4 or 5; fruit a capsule. — About 60 species in the Northern Hemisphere, most from the Mediterranean to central Asia.

Ruta graveolens L. Rue. Subshrubby, rootstock woody, shoots rather stiff, sparsely branched, very aromatic; leaves odd pinnate, the pinna with 1–3 incisions, lobes spathulate to lanceolate, blue-green; flowers in cymes, terminal flowers 5 parted, lateral flowers 4 parted, greenish yellow, the petals concave, June–August. Mediterranean region, on dry, warm slopes. z5 Fig. 197.

var. **vulgaris** Willk. Garden Rue. Usually about 50 cm high; leave more blue-green, more aromatic; petals longer clawed, fruit capsule more deeply incised, with larger, indented glands, flowers later than the wild form (= *R. hortensis* Mill.). 1562.

R. hortensis see: **R. graveolens** var. **vulgaris**

R. patavina L. Subshrub, 15–30 cm high, shoots soft pubescent, erect; leaves linear-oblong, 3–4 cm long, obtuse, base cuneate, the apical leaves 3 cleft; flowers in tight, terminal, 3–6 cm wide corymbs, yellow, June–July. Orient. z6 ⊕

Culture simple; requires a sunny location in average garden soil.

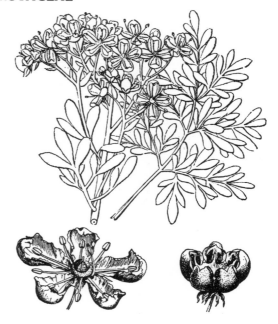

Fig. 197. *Ruta graveolens*
(from Lauche and Baillon)

SABAL Adans. — Sabal Palm — PALMAE

Bushy palm or tree, stem obliquely ascending at the base, stout or thin, ringed or smooth, upper portion covered with the persistent leaf sheaths; leaves circular or cuneate at the base, deeply fan-like incised, the segments linear, 2 cleft, limb fringed, leaf petiole channeled above, with a sharp, smooth margin, leaf sheaths large; flower and fruit clusters usually as long as the leaves, erect, much branched, flowers white or green; fruits small, globose, black. — About 25 species in the warmer Americas, from the southern USA to Venezuela and the Lesser Antilles. The following species are more commonly found in cultivation.

Sabal blackburniana Glazebr. Fan Palm. A 9–12 m high tree in its habitat, stem thickened in the middle; crest with about 20–30 large leaves, these circular, to 2 m long and wide, blue-green, rather stiff, with about 40 segments, stalk to 2 m long; inflorescence about 1 m long, abundantly branched; fruit reverse pear-shaped, about 3 cm long. West Indies. 1826. z10 Plate 91. # ⊘

S. palmetto (Walt.) Lodd. Palmetto Palm. 6–18 m high or more, stem erect, with a characteristic pattern (inverted Y) from leaf scars; leaves 1.5–2.5 m long, cordate, drooping for their entire length, shorter than the petiole, with 30–40 deeply incised segments on either side, each with a few long filaments, petiole smooth; inflorescence shorter than the leaves, ascending, horizontal or weeping; fruit black. Southern USA. 1825. z10 Plate 91. # ⊘

Cultivated only in frost free regions, otherwise overwintered in a palm house.

SALIX L. — Willow — SALICACEAE

Deciduous or (rarely) semi-evergreen trees or shrubs, occasionally a small, creeping dwarf shrub; winter buds with only 1 mitre-shaped scale; shoots usually cylindrical; leaves alternate, by exception nearly opposite, stalked or sessile, variable in form, but usually lanceolate, stipules present; flowers usually appearing before, but also with or after the leaves, usually in lateral, sessile or stalked, dioecious catkins, these often foliate and erect, the individual flowers situated in the axil of a normally entire bract and with 1–2 nectaries or a small, lobed disk; staminate flowers with 2–12 stamens, filaments thin, distinct or connate, exserted past the bracts; pistillate flowers with sessile or stalked, unilocular ovaries and with sessile or stalked, usually divided stigma; ovules usually several; fruit a bivalvate capsule; seeds with a pubescent tuft. — About 500 species in the cool or temperate northern zones, some also in South America, but not in Australia.

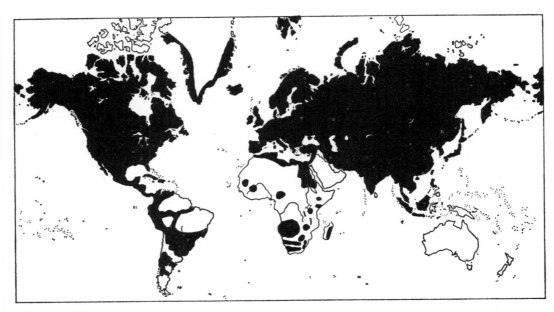

Fig. 198. Range of the genus *Salix*

Key to the Series (excluding hybrids)

● Stamens 3–9; ovaries glabrous; scales yellowish, glabrous, flowers with 2 nectaries;

    Ser. **Nigrae** (Loud.) Rehd.
        Leaves green on both sides, linear:
            S. nigra

    Ser. **Pentandrae** (Hook.) Moss.
        Leaves elliptic to lanceolate:
            S. ehrhartiana, lasiandra, lucida, meyeriana, pentandra

    Ser. **Amygdalinae** (Koch) Rehd.
        Leaves lanceolate; pistillate with 1 nectary:
            S. amygdaloides, medwedewii, triandra

●● Stamens 2, occasionally 1;
  + Pistillate flowers with 2 nectaries, scales yellowish or reddish, darker at the apex; catkins on foliate shoots, appearing with or after the leaves;

    × Upright trees or shrubs;

      ★ Filaments long pubescent at the base;

    Ser. **Fragiles** (Koch) Moss.
        Leaves lanceolate to elliptic, glabrous or soon glabrous; pistillate flowers with 2 nectaries:
            S. fragilis, matsudana

    Ser. **Albae** (Hook.) Rehd.
        Leaves lanceolate to elliptic, more or less silky pubescent; pistillate flowers with 1 nectary:
            S. alba, babylonica, jessoensis, oxica

    Ser. **Longifoliae** (Anders.) Rehd.
        Leaves linear:
            S. interior

    ★★ Filaments glabrous, scales persistent;

Ser. **Eriostachyae** (Schneid.) Rehd.
  Leaves finely serrate, venation pubescent beneath; catkins 5–13 cm long:
    S. fargesii, moupinensis

Ser. **Magnificae** (Schneid.) Rehd.
  Leaves entire, glabrous beneath; catkins 10–30 cm long:
    S. magnifica

✕✕ Low or prostrate shrub, not over 1 m high; leaves never linear, not over 8 cm long; catkins on foliate shoots; scales persistent;

  ★ Ovaries glabrous, pistillate flowers with 1, occasionally 2 nectaries;

    Ser. **Herbaceae** (Hook.) Moss.
      Creeping shrubs, leaves glabrous:
        S. herbacea, polaris, retusa, rotundifolia, serpyllifolia, uva-ursi

  ★★ Ovaries pubescent, pistillate flowers with 2 nectaries;

    Ser. **Reticulatae** (Fries) Moss.
      Style absent; leaves reticulately veined:
        S. nivalis, reticulata, saximontana, vestita, yezoalpina

    Ser. **Ovalifoliae** Rydb.
      Style present, filaments glabrous, leaves eventually glabrous:
        S. arctica, petrophila

    Ser. **Glauca** (Fries) Moss.
      Style present, filaments pubescent, leaves pubescent at least beneath:
        S. glauca, glaucosericea, pyrenaica, reptans

++ Pistillate flowers with only 1 nectary; scales usually darker at the apex, persistent; catkins usually sessile or nearly so, appearing before or with the leaves;

  ✕ Stamens 2, always totally distinct;

    ★ Style absent or very short, shorter or as long as the stigmas;

      Ser. **Capreae** (Bluff & Fingerh.) Moss.
        Ovaries pubescent; large shrubs or small trees; leaves usually large and wide:
          S. aegyptiaca, ambigua, appendiculata, aurita, atrocinerea, balfourii, caprea, cinerea, discolor, pedicellata, salviifolia, silesiaca, starkeana, xerophila

      Ser. **Incubaceae** (Fries) Rehd.
        Ovaries pubescent; low shrubs, occasionally 3–4 m high; leaves usually small:
          S. arenaria, gracilis, humilis, repens, rosmarinifolia, sericea, subopposita

      Ser. **Myrtilloides** (Loud.) Rehd.
        Ovaries glabrous, stalked; shrub, to 1 m high:
          S. myrtilloides

      Ser. **Balsamiferae** (Schneid.) Rehd.
        Ovaries glabrous, stalked; leaf base rounded to cordate; large shrub:
          S. pyrifolia

    ★★ Style present, longer than the stigmas;

      Ser. **Candidae** (Schneid.) Rehd.
        Ovaries stalked, pubescent, style shorter than half the ovary; leaves lanceolate, white pubescent beneath:
          S. candida

      Ser. **Phylicifoliae** (Fries) Moss.
        Ovaries stalked, pubescent, style shorter than half the ovary, leaves green beneath, glabrous or pubescent:
          S. apoda, arbuscula, bicolor, foetida, hegetschweileri, hibernica, laggeri, mielichhoferi, nigricans, petiolaris, phylicifolia, pulchra, waldsteiniana

      Ser. **Hastatae** (Hook.) Rehd.
        Ovaries stalked, glabrous, style shorter than half the ovary, leaves silky pubescent or blue-green beneath:
          S. cordata, eriocephala, hastata, irrorata, japonica, pyrolifolia, syrticola

      Ser. **Myrsinites** (Hook.) Moss.
        Ovaries sessile, pubescent; style half as long as the ovary; leaves elliptic to lanceolate, 1–5 cm long:
          S. myrsinites

      Ser. **Chrysantheae** (Koch) Rehd.
        Ovaries nearly sessile, glabrous, style half as long as the ovary; leaves broad, pubescent to tomentose, 3–7 cm long:
          S. hookeriana, lanata

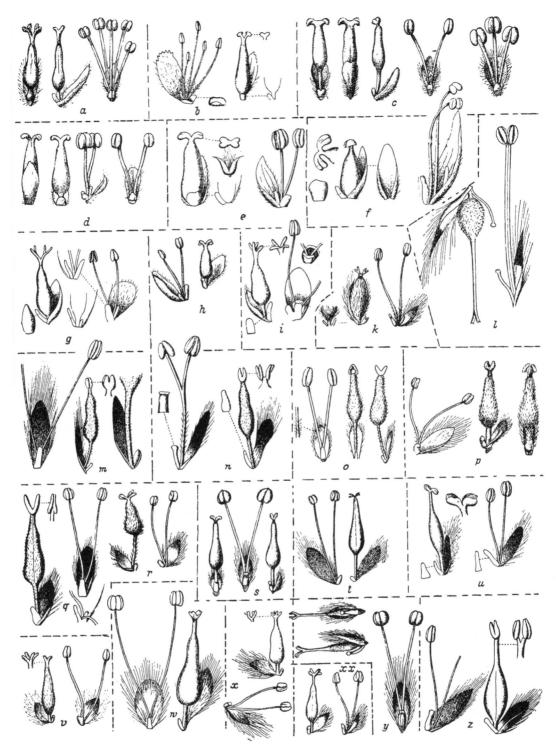

Fig. 199. **Salix**. Flowers, enlarged. a. *S. pentandra;* b. *S. lasiandra;* c. *S. triandra;* d. *S. fragilis;* e. *S. alba;* f. *S. babylonica;* g. *S. herbacea;* h. *S. retusa;* i. *S. serpyllifolia;* k. *S. glauca;* l. *S. gracilistyla;* m. *S. caprea;* n. *S. aegyptiaca;* o. *S. cinerea;* p. *S. aurita;* q. *S. repens;* r. *S. sericea;* s. *S. myrtilloides;* t. *S. pyrifolia;* u. *S. cordata;* v. *S. phylicifolia;* w. *S. hookeriana;* x. *S. hastata;* xx. *S. nigricans;* y. *S. myrsinites;* z. *S. daphnoides* (most from Schneider, Koehne)

Ser. **Pruinosae** (Koch) Rehd.
Ovaries sessile, glabrous, style half as long as the ovary; leaves lanceolate, glabrous; shoots usually pruinose:
S. acutifolia, daphnioides

Ser. **Viminales** (Bluff & Fingerh.) Moss.
Ovaries sessile, pubescent (glabrous on *S. rehderiana!*), style half as long as the ovary; leaves usually tomentose beneath, narrow:
S. dasyclada, friesiana, helvetica, kinuyanagi, lapponicum, rehderiana, sachalinensis

✕✕ Stamens 2, but more or less connate, or only 1;

★ Stamens 2, connate;

Ser. **Canae** (Kern.) Rehd.
Style absent or very short, up to half as long as the ovary; ovary glabrous; filaments half connate or less; catkins stalked; leaves white tomentose beneath:
S. elaeagnos

Ser. **Purpureae** (Fries) Moss.
Style absent or short, to half as long as the ovary; ovary pubescent; filaments totally connate; leaves glabrous or silky pubescent beneath;
S. bockii, caesia, integra, koriyanagi, microstachya, miyabeana, purpurea, wilhelmsiana

Ser. **Gracilistylae** (Schneid.) Rehd.
Style longer than the pubescent ovary; leaves elliptic to oblong:
S. gracilistyla, melanostachys

★★ Stamens 1 or 2 in the same catkin;

Ser. **Sitchenses** (Bebb) Rehd.
Style distinctly conspicuous, ovary stalked, pubescent; leaves oblong-obovate to oblanceolate, 5–12 cm long:
S. sitchensis

Note on identification. Keys for the *Salix* species are difficult to make since there is considerable cross pollination in nature which results in many forms and transition forms. Chmelar lumped closely related species as "relatives"; Rechinger (in Flora Europaea) called them "groups". In this work, the Series or Sections by Rehder (bibliography) are retained. Since only a small part of the 500 described *Salix* species will be covered here, the above short taxonomic outline to the mentioned species and hybrids should be sufficient. In reference to Rechinger (in Flora Europaea I), the following hints on identification should also be noted:

1. Procumbent plants, shoots appressed to the ground:
   S. apoda, arctica, myrsinites Group, *pyrenaica, reptans, reticulata, rotundifolia*

2. Partly rhizomatous
   a) Alpine and arctic species:
      S. herbacea, polaris
   b) Grows in swamps or sand:
      S. myrtilloides, repens Group

3. Shoots bluish pruinose:
   S. acutifolia, daphnoides

4. Debarked shoots with elevated ridges:
   S. aegyptiaca, appendiculata, atrocinerea, aurita, bicolor, cinerea

5. Leaves narrowly linear and more or less entire:
   S. caspica, elaeagnos, rosmarinifolia, viminalis Group, *wilhelmsiana*

6. Leaves very glossy above:
   S. glabra, lucida, pentandra

7. Leaves becoming black when dry:
   S. glabra, nigricans, purpurea

8. Leaves always totally glabrous:
   S. caesia, fragilis, glabra, pentandra, purpurea, triandra

9. Leaves appressed silky pubescent:
   S. alba, glauca Group, *repens* Group, *viminalis* Group with its hybrids

10. Leaves rust colored pubescent beneath:
    S. atrocinerea and hybrids

11. Stamens distinct:
    most species except those in Nr. 12

12. Stamens connate:
    S. amplexicaulis, caesia, purpurea

13. Stamens always 2:
    most species, except *S. pentandra* (usually 5) and *S. triandra* (3)

14. Ovaries glabrous or pubescent, stalked or sessile (must be observed with a hand lens).

Salix acutifolia Willd. Shrub, to 4 m high, branches slender, dark red-brown and very bluish pruinose, particularly the older shoots, glabrous, inner bark yellow; leaves lanceolate, 6–12 cm long, long acuminate, finely serrate, glabrous on both sides, dark green and glossy above, more bluish beneath, base cuneate, stipules lanceolate; catkins appearing before the leaves, usually widely spaced, thick, scales acutely ovate, long pubescent, stamens 2, filaments occasionally partly connate, ovary nearly sessile. HW 2: 29 (= *S. pruinosa* Bess.; *S. violacea*, Andr.; *S. daphnoides* var. *acutifolia* Döll). Russia to E. Asia. 1809. z4

'Pendulifolia' (Späth). To 6 m high and wide, branches very slender, weeping in a large arch; leaves nearly always vertically pendulous (!), 10–16 cm long, long acuminate, base cuneate, bright green above, bluish beneath at first, midrib yellow, petiole 1–3 cm long, stipules small; only staminate catkins observed, very early, slender, 4–6 cm long. DB 9: 8 (= *S. pendulifolia* Späth). First sent by Schneider to Späth around 1916, but introduced in 1939. Widely cultivated today. Plate 93. Ø ✛

S. adenophylla Hook. see: **S. cordata**

S. aegyptiaca L. Shrub, to 4 m high, or a small tree, thick branched, current year's shoots tomentose; leaves oblong, occasionally obovate, 6–15 cm long, acute, irregularly crenate or rather coarsely dentate, base round, pubescent on both sides at first, later glabrous above, somewhat pubescent and blue-green beneath, petiole 2 cm long, stipules subcordate; catkins thick, sessile, very early, February–March, staminate catkins to 3.5 cm long, filaments distinct, base pubescent, pistillate catkins to 9 cm long in fruit. GC 77: 129; BMns 91; DB 10: 81 (= *S. medemii* Boiss.). Armenia, Iran. 1874. Very meritorious, early species. z6 Plate 93; Fig. 199. ✛

S. aemulans see: **S. saximontana**

S. alba L. White Willow. Tree, 6–25 m high, fast growing, crown abundantly branched, younger shoots nodding at the tips, olive-brown, silky pubescent when young, bark longitudinally furrowed; leaves lanceolate, 6–10 cm long, widest in the middle, finely serrate, acuminate at both ends, appressed silky pubescent on both sides at first, later dull green above and rather glabrous, bluish and silky beneath, stipules lanceolate; flowers 4–6 cm long, on foliate stalks, stamens 2, ovaries sessile, conical, glabrous, style short. HW 100; HM Pl. 79; CS 2; BB 1178. Europe, W. and N. Asia, open forests and moist lowlands. Cultivated through the ages. z2 Fig. 199, 201.

f. *argentea* see: **'Sericea'**

'Aurea'. Growth habit less vigorous, shoots yellowish green; leaves yellowish.

var. *britzensis* see: **'Chermesina'**

'Calva'. Larger, broadly conical tree, branches more erect, without a single, central stem, branches arise at about 60° from the stem, shoots red-brown on the sunny side at the apex; leaves lanceolate, about 9.5 cm long, 1.5 cm wide, glossy green above, underside somewhat gray, silky pubescent at first, eventually totally glabrous or nearly so on the underside, often with a brown margin, petiole 7 mm long, red; ovary somewhat stalked. EH 381 (= var. *coerulea* [Sm.] Koch; *S. coerulea* Sm.; *S.* 'Coerulea'; *S. alba* ssp. *coerulea* [Sm.] Rech. f.). The original tree was allegedly found around 1700 in Norfolk, England. In England, cricket bats were once made from the wood of this tree, hence the colloquial name "Cricket-bat Willow".

'Chermesina'. Conical habit when young, branches bright red or orange, particularly in winter. (= *S. alba britzensis* Späth). Found in Germany around 1840.

ssp. *coerulea* or var. *coerulea* see: **'Calva'**

f. *regalis* see: **'Sericea'**

'Sericea'. Silver Willow. Habit somewhat slower growing and more graceful than the species; leaves more or less densely silver-gray pubescent on both sides, glossy (= f. *splendens* Anderss.; f. *regalis* Hort.; f. *argentea* Wimm.). In Germany around 1840. Ø

f. *splendens* see: **'Sericea'**

'Tristis'. Yellow Weeping Willow. Tree, to 20 m high, stem thick, often unsound, branches usually somewhat outspread, with thin, distinctly yellow, pendulous shoots; leaves not remaining green until frost (see *S. sepulcralis*), turning yellow rather early, then gray and falling (!!); flowers pistillate. MG 13: 88 (= *S. alba tristis* Baumann 1815; *S. alba* var. *vitellina pendula* Rehd. 1896). Found in France around 1815. Tree often suffers, unfortunately, from insect and disease problems. Plate 74, 76.

A clone was selected in Holstein (W. Germany) which is somewhat stronger growing and more resistant to the typical problems; known in the trade as **'Tristis Resistenta'**.

'Vitellina'. Normally upright willow with (especially in winter) yellow current year's shoots. HF 918. In Switzerland around 1671.

var. *vitellina pendula* see: **'Tristis'**

A number of clones have been selected and are widely grown in Holland for rapid growing street trees. They are briefly described as follows:

'Barlo' (Geessink 1968) Female tree with a very narrow crown and many short, steeply ascending shoots, these rather light brown-green, densely foliate, with wide crotch angles; leaves only 7–9 cm long, 1.5 cm wide, light green above, gray-blue beneath, petiole 6–8 mm long, brown-green, leaves dropping late. Dfl 6: 71.

'Belders' (Ned. Alg. Keuringsdienst) Male tree, narrow crowned, stem often somewhat wavy, young shoots green at the apex, crotch angle about 60°; leaves to 11.5 cm long, 1.5 cm wide, petioles about 10 mm long, partly red, foliar buds in the summer with a distinct green spot at the base. 1967.

'Bredevoort' (Geessink 1968) Female tree with a narrow, conical crown and rather short, steeply ascending branches, stem rather straight, shoots dark green in the middle; leaves 11–13 cm long, 2.5 cm wide, green above, gray-blue beneath, petiole 1 cm, red-brown, with about 4 mm long stalked glands.

'Drakenburg' (Staatsbosbeheer) Female tree with a rather wide, conical crown, stem straight, crotch angles about 70–80°, young shoots green and somewhat brown at the apex; buds red-brown; leaves to 12 cm long and 1.5 cm wide, petiole 7 mm long, stipules to 9 mm long and 1 mm wide. Cultivated since 1955.

'Het Goor' (Geessink 1968) Male tree with a straight stem, broadly ovate crown, branches rather widely outspread with wide crotch angles, shoots olive-green to brown; leaves 7.5–9 cm long, 1.5 cm wide, light green above, blue-green beneath, petiole 7–8 mm long, light green and somewhat red, leaf drop late. Dfl 6: 72.

'Lichtenvoorde' (Geessink 1968) Male tree, stem straight, crown very narrowly cylindrical, branches rather short, ascending, somewhat pendulous at the tips, shoots glossy green in the middle; leaves 8–10 cm long, 1.5 cm wide, green above, blue-green beneath, petiole 11 mm, light green, leaf drop late.

'Liempde' (H. C. van Vleuten) Male tree, crown rather narrowly conical with a straight, dominant leader (percurrent trunk), crotch angles about 50°, young shoots red at the tips; leaves 9–11 mm long, red, stipules 3–5 mm long. Dfl 6: 70. 1949. The most commonly planted willow tree in Holland.

'Lievelde' (Geessink 1968) Male tree, conical habit, branches ascending, the basal ones conspicuously long, crotch angles about 45°, shoots usually gray-brown, with large buds; leaves about 6–7 times longer than wide, leaf drop late.

'Rockanje' (Sipkes 1950) Female tree, with 60° crotch angles, young shoots brown-green to red at the apex; leaves 9–10.5 cm long, 1.5 cm wide, green above, gray-green beneath, petiole 9 mm long, light green and somewhat red, stipules 4 mm long. 1955. This clone is particularly tolerant of strong winds.

S. albicans see: **S. laggeri**

S. × alopecuroides Tausch. (*S. fragilis × S. triandra*). Large shrub or tree, branches brittle, shoots brown to yellowish, glossy; leaves oblong-lanceolate, 4–12 cm long, unevenly serrate, dark green above, lighter to bluish green beneath, stipules rather large, obliquely semicircular, acute, serrate; catkins on foliate lateral shoots, slender cylindrical, 6–8 cm long, open flowered, bracts light yellow, pubescent, ovary stalked. DL 2: 110; CS 23 (= *S. speciosa* Host). Austria, Romania. 2 male clones in cultivation. z5

S. alpina Scop. (*myrsinites* Group). Low shrub, branches more or less appressed to the ground, branch tips ascending (decumbent); leaves small, elliptic, 1–2 cm long, obtuse at the apex, base cuneate, nearly entire and ciliate, otherwise glabrous on both sides, green, persisting for some time after coloring in the fall; flowers appearing with the leaves, catkins slender, stalked, anthers violet before the flowers fully open, stamens 2. CSI 63; CWE 3. E. Alps, Carpathian Mts. z5

S. 'Americana'. A commonly used name in forestry and willow culture for a hybrid of (?) *S. cordata × S. gracilis*, developed in the USA. Shrub, low growing with long shoots, annual growth green to red; leaves lanceolate, branch tips light red and pendulous in summer, stipules large, kidney-shaped; stamen filaments half connate. Commonly grown by basket makers. Only the male plant is known.

S. americana pendula see: **S. purpurea 'Pendula'**

S. amygdalina L. see: **S. triandra**

S. amygdaloides Anderss. Tall shrub or small tree, 10(20) m high in its habitat, branches ascending, young shoots glabrous, glossy, red-brown to orange; leaves oval-lanceolate, 8–12 cm long, acuminate, finely and scabrous serrate, base round to broadly cuneate, lighter or bluish beneath, somewhat pubescent only when young; staminate catkins 3–5 cm long, pistillate 4–10 cm, on foliate shoots, stamens 5–9, somewhat pubescent at the base, fruit stalk as long as the capsule. BB 1175; SPa 87; SS 467. Western N. America. 1895. z5 Fig. 200.

S. andersoniana see: **S. nigricans**

S. angustifolia see: **S. wilhelmsiana**

S. angustifolia f. *microstachya* see: **S. microstachya**

S. apoda Trautv. Dwarf shrub, similar to *S. hastata*, 10–30 cm high, shoots partly underground, glabrous; leaves elliptic, to 4 cm long in cultivation, obtuse, base broadly cuneate, finely crenate, bright green above, somewhat blue-green beneath; catkins appearing with the leaves (before the leaves in cultivation!), foliate at the base, male catkins to 4 cm long and nearly 2 cm thick, gray woolly, scales blackened, anthers orange, turning red, April, female catkins much smaller, gray-green, capsule sessile, narrowly conical, glabrous. Caucasus; Elbrus Mts. 1935. Male plants very attractive; female much more vigorous and of only slight garden merit. Often confused with *S. retusa* or *S. simulatrix* in cultivation. z6 Plate 95.

Fig. 200. **Salix.** Left *S. amygdaloides;* right *S. humilis* (from NBB)

S. appendiculata Vill. Tall shrub to small tree, branches short and outspread, debarked branches with a few, occasionally indistinct raised ridges, shoots short pubescent, later more or less glabrous; leaves rather variable in form and size, obovate to oblanceolate, usually widest at the middle, becoming more or less glabrous above, pubescence persistent beneath with very dense, raised reticulate venation, rugose above from the indented venation, coarsely dentate to entire, petiole 10 mm; catkins 3 × 1 cm, filaments with a few long hairs at the base. CSI 37 (*S. grandifolia* Ser.). Central Europe, Apennine Mts., NW. Balkans. Easily and often crossed with *S. caprea*. z6

S. arbuscula L. Small, upright shrub, 30–50 cm high, also prostrate at the higher elevations, very bushy and densely foliate, twigs and leaves somewhat pubescent only at first, soon totally glabrous; leaves lanceolate-elliptic, 5–20(40) mm long, glandular serrate, with 7–12 vein pairs, glossy green above, blue-green beneath, stipule occasionally present and very small; catkins appearing with the leaves in May, 1–3 cm long, stamens 2, distinct, anthers red or reddish, scales obovate, yellow-brown, pubescent, ovaries oval-conical, pubescent, very short stalked (!). HM Pl. 83; HW 118; CS 9; VSa 18; CSI 50 (= *S. formosa* Willd.; *S. prunifolia* Sm.). Scandinavia, Scotland, N. Russia; in the mountains. z3 Fig. 206.

S. arctica Pall. Arctic Willow. Creeping, thick branched shrub, branches cylindrical; leaves thick and leathery, obovate to elliptic, 2.5–5 cm long, obtuse to round, entire, base broadly cuneate, petiole thin, 1–3 cm long, dull green above, bluish beneath; catkins 2–4 cm long, scales obovate, dark purple, shallowly soft pubescent, persistent, stamens 2, filaments glabrous, style filamentous, longer than the stigma, capsule conical, pubescent, nearly sessile. BB 1197; PAr 137; ASA 12; CSI 56. Arctic Europe, America and Asia. z1 Fig. 214.

S. arenaria L. Creeping habit, stems ascending, previous year's shoots thick, pubescent, dark; leaves obovate, more or less outspread, short, firm, with widely spaced, sharp, glandular teeth, both sides dense and long silky pubescent, eventually dull gray-green above and with hook-form hairs, margin revoluted, 5–8 vein pairs, stipules frequently present; catkins ovate, as are the bracts, filaments and capsule, stigma short, globose (= *S. repens* var. *nitida* [Ser.] Wender; *S. repens* var. *argentea* [Sm.] Wimm. & Grab.). Atlantic Coast of Europe, but also to Poland, primarily in the dunes. z6 Fig. 207.

S. atrocinerea Brot. Tall shrub or small tree, to 10 m, young shoots somewhat pubescent, later glabrous, glossy in the 2nd year, debarked wood with ridges; leaves obovate or oblong-lanceolate, finely dentate to nearly entire, quickly becoming nearly glabrous and somewhat glossy above, underside blue-green and with quite short, brown, curved hairs, 2–5 cm long, cylindrical, dense, sessile, rachis gray pubescent. VSa 24; CSI 33 (= *S. oleifolia* Sm.). W. Europe, from England to Portugal. Easily hybridized with *S. aurita* and *S. caprea*. z7

S. aurita L. Eared Willow. Shrub, 2–3 m high, branches usually short, outspread, young shoots soft pubescent at first, later glabrous, somewhat glossy, red-brown to black-brown; leaves obovate to oblanceolate, 2.5–5 cm long, abruptly acuminate, saw-toothed, dull green above and very rugose, gray-green to gray beneath, densely pubescent on both sides at first, later only pubescent or tomentose, stipules large, kidney-shaped, dentate; catkins sessile to very short stalked, 1–2 cm long, male more ovate, erect, with 2 pubescent stamens at the base, female to 3 cm long, ovary white tomentose, stigma sessile, April. CS 16; HM Pl. 81; HM 116; HF 928; CSI 31. Europe to the Arctic Ocean, Asia to Altai; usually on moist sites. z5 Fig. 199, 207.

S. babylonica L. Babylon Weeping Willow. Tree, smaller than the other "weeping willows", 10–12 m, crown form quite variable in its habitat (according to Wilson, in Rehder & Wilson, Pl. Wils. III: 42–43), branches arching outward, annual growth very long and nearly string-like pendulous, bark greenish, but always somewhat reddish on the sunny side (!!), never yellow, somewhat pubescent when young; leaves lanceolate to linear lanceolate, 8–16 cm long, long acuminate, finely serrate, deep green above, gray-green with distinctly reticulate venation beneath, not pubescent (!!), petiole 3–5 mm long, stipules half lanceolate, somewhat revoluted; catkins usually pistillate, short stalked, to 2 cm long, curved, stamens 2, ovaries sessile, glabrous, stigmas distinctly bilabiate, bracts oblong, acute. LWTP 96; CS 1; LF 64–65; BB 1179 (= *S. heteromera* Hand.-Mazz.). E. Asia, common on the bank of the Yangtse River and elsewhere; Manchuria, Turkestan. Brought into Europe around 1730. A popular tree in the warmer parts of China and from there reaching Japan where it is also widely planted. See also: **S. matsudana**. z5 Plate 92; Fig. 199, 201.

f. *annularis* see: '**Crispa**'

'**Crispa**'. Much slower growing; leaves rolled into ringlets, very unique (= f. *annularis* Aschers.; *S. napoleonis* F. Schultz). Exact origin unknown; Belgium. 1827. Plate 92. ∅

var. *dolorosa* see: **S.** × **blanda**

'**Sacramento**'. As yet a relatively little known clone with a less conspicuous weeping habit, crown open, large leaved.

var. *salamonii* see: **S.** × **salamonii**

S. × **balfourii** Linton. (*S. caprea* × *S. lanata*). Resembles *S. caprea*, but lower, usually 1–1.5 m high; leaves elliptic, ovate, 4–6 cm long, short and usually obliquely acuminate, shallowly serrate to entire; catkins usually very attractive, golden-yellow while in flower. HS 74. Discovered in England around 1890.

S. balsamifera see: **S. pyrifolia**

S. × '**Basfordiana**'. Descendant of *S.* × *rubens*. Medium-sized to tall tree, young shoots particularly attractive orange-red in winter; leaves lanceolate, 10–15 cm long, 1.5–2 cm wide, long acuminate, finely and scabrous serrate; catkins appearing with the leaves, 5–10 cm long, slender, pendulous, ovaries 2 mm long, short stalked (=

Fig. 201. **Salix.** Left *S. babylonica;* center *S. fragilis;* right *S. alba* (from NBB)

S. fragilis var. *basfordiana* Bean; *S. basfordiana* Salter; *S. sanguinea* Scaling). Discovered in the Arden district of England around 1863 by Scaling, a gardener in Basford, Nottinghamshire and widely grown in England today.

S. bebbiana Sarg. Few-stemmed shrub, 2–5 m high, branches short, divaricate, brown, pubescent to glabrous; leaves narrowly elliptic, 2–5 cm long, 1.5–2.5 cm wide, acute at both ends, entire or nearly so, dull green above, bluish and with raised reticulate venation beneath, more or less pubescent on both sides, eventually becoming glabrous, petiole 1–2 cm; pistillate catkins 4–6 cm long, 1–2 cm wide, very open in fruit, bracts on the male and female catkins lanceolate, 1–2 mm long, yellowish, fruit on a 2–5 mm long stalk, stigma nearly sessile, deeply parted. AFP 131 (= *S. rostrata* Richardson). Northern N. America, from Alaska to California. Fig. 203.

S. bicolor Willd. Medium-sized shrub, similar to *S. phylicifolia,* shoots thick, with short, but distinct ridges on the debarked wood, buds short, yellowish to orange in winter, bud scales persisting after the buds open; leaves obtuse obovate-oblanceolate, silky pubescent on both sides when young, later dark green above and with a dull glaze, blue-green beneath; catkins appearing with the leaves, anthers red at first, later yellow. HM 462 (= *S. schraderiana* Willd.). Mountains of Europe, from central Germany to N. Spain and Bulgaria, but not in the Alps.

S. ✕ blanda Anderss. (*S. babylonica* ✕ *S. fragilis*). Weeping willow with a broad crown and short, pendulous branches, these dull green or brown, easily

broken at the base (!), much shorter than those of *S. alba* 'Tristis' (!), buds very dark from the drying scales; leaves lanceolate, 8–15 cm long, long acuminate, finely serrate, base cuneate, dark green and glossy above (!), blue-green beneath, glabrous, becoming yellow in fall and quickly dropping, petiole 5–12 mm long, stipules ovate; catkins slender, 2–3 cm long, stamens 2, pubescent at the base, ovaries short stalked, style short, stigma emarginate. CS 22; MG 13: 89 (= *S. babylonica* var. *dolorosa* Rowlee; *S. pendulina* Wender.). Presumably originated in Germany before 1831. Much less common in cultivation than the other weeping willows; female. z4 Plate 93, 96.

S. bockii Seem. Shrub, 1–3 m high, growth open and wide, shoots densely gray-tomentose; leaves myrtle-like, fine, oblong to obovate, 6–15 mm long, dark green above, silvery beneath, entire to finely dentate, margins involuted; catkins appearing first in the fall in the leaf axils, small, filaments usually totally connate, ovaries sessile, pubescent. BM 9079. W. China. 1908. Only the female in cultivation. z6 ∅

S. ✕ boydii Linton. (*S. lanata* ✕ *S. reticulata*). Small, narrowly upright shrub, 0.5–0.7 m high, branches short and outspread, thinly pubescent when young; leaves nearly circular or broadly obovate, 1–1.25 cm long, round to slightly emarginate, base usually slightly cordate, entire, both sides white pubescent at first, later dark green above, rugose and rather glabrous, short white woolly beneath; catkins ovate, 1.5–2 cm long, scales obovate, silky pubescent, anthers golden-yellow,

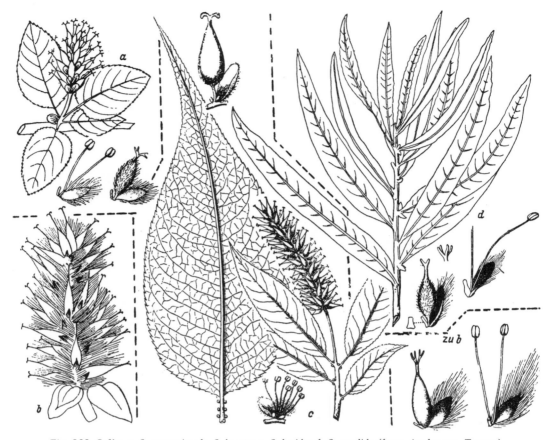

Fig. 202. **Salix**. a. *S. pyrenaica*; b. *S. lanata*; c. *S. lucida*; d. *S. candida* (from Anderson, Torrey)

May. Found around 1900 by W. Boyd in Scotland in the mountains. z6 Plate 73, 95. ∅

S. bracteosa see: **Chosenia bracteosa**

S. breviserrata B. Flod. (*myrsinites* Group). Low shrub, branches appressed to the ground, branch tips ascending (decumbent), older branches with exfoliating bark (!); leaves small, ovate, margins glandular serrate, appressed coarsely pubescent, green on both sides, somewhat translucent in fall and persisting on the branch after coloring; flowers appear before the leaves, catkins oblong, stalked, thick, with 2 stamens, anthers violet at first, ovary more or less stalked, style distinct, stigma violet, bracts pink. CSI 62; CWE 11. Alps, Pyrenees, Abruzzi (Italy); on various soils but not alkaline soil. z6

S. caesia Vill. Small, erect, short branched shrub, scarcely 1 m high, branches glossy brown, smooth; leaves elliptic, tapered or obovate at both ends, 2–3 cm long, gray-green above, whitish beneath, glabrous, petiole 2–3 mm long; catkins only 1 cm long, on short, foliate stalks, appearing with the leaves, filaments connate at the base, anthers violet, ovaries sessile, stigma nearly sessile, red. CSI 15; CS 10; HM 465; HF 939. Alps and S. Ural Mts. 1871. Female clone in cultivation. z6 Plate 94.

S. × calliantha Kern. (*S. daphnoides* × *S. purpurea*). Upright, 3 m high shrub, branches glabrous, not pruinose (!), yellow-green to brown-yellow, buds large, yellow; leaves oblanceolate or lanceolate, acute, 6–10(12) cm long, cuneate at the base, crenate, silky pubescent when young (!), later totally glabrous, dark green and glossy above, bluish green beneath, stipules absent or small, petiole about 1 cm long; catkins appearing before the leaves, 2–3.5 cm long, scales obovate, blackish at the apex, pubescent, stamens 2, filaments connate at the base (!), somewhat pubescent, ovary nearly sessile, anthers yellow at first, later reddish. HW 29. Found in the wild in the vicinity of Vienna, Austria around 1865. z7 ⊕

S. calodendron Wimm. (if considered a hybrid, then probably *S. atrocinerea* × *S. caprea* × *S. viminalis*) (*viminalis* Group). Shrub to small tree, 3–6 m high, branches more or less erect, densely velvety tomentose, the tomentum persistent and black in winter, debarked stems with stripes; leaves oblong-lanceolate to obovate-lanceolate, 7–18 cm long, 2.5–4 cm wide, acute, crenate, dull green above and somewhat pubescent, stipules large, lanceolate, petiole 1–1.5 cm; catkins appearing with the leaves, nearly sessile, apparently only the female is known, 3–7.5 cm long, bracts silky pubescent, style long, stigma thick, shorter than the style. Europe; Germany, Denmark, Sweden, England; in cultivation and often naturalized. z6

S. candida Fluegge. Shrub, 1–2 m high, erect, new shoots white woolly at first, later glabrous and glossy red-brown; leaves narrow-lanceolate, 4–10 cm long, gradually tapering to the tip, base cuneate, entire or finely dentate, margins somewhat involute, finely rugose above, both sides pubescent at first, later glabrous and dull green above, with a persistent white tomentum beneath, lanceolate; catkins usually sessile, 2–3 cm long, stamens 2, filaments glabrous, anthers red, ovaries white pubescent, with a long style, April. BB 1193; GSP 86; HM Pl. 80 (= *S. incana* Michx. non Schrank). N. America, moist sites. 1811. z5 Fig. 202. ∅

S. caprea L. Goat Willow. Tall shrub or small tree, twigs gray pubescent at first, later glabrous and glossy red-brown, usually totally green on female plants, with very thick catkin buds; leaves broadly elliptic, to 10 cm long, rugose above, dull green, gray-green beneath, more or less densely pubescent; catkins nearly or totally sessile, appearing before the leaves, staminate catkins to 4.5 cm long, with 2 stamens, anthers golden-yellow, pistillate catkins eventually to 7 cm long, ovary tomentose, bottle-shaped, stalked, stigma sessile. CS 7; HM Pl. 80; HW 32; HF 927. Europe (except farthest north and south) to NE. Asia. Cultivated through the ages. The male plants were once cultivated as *"Salix caprea mas"* and propagated by grafting. See also: **S. cinerea 'Tricolor.'** z5 Plate 93; Fig. 199. ✣

'Pendula'. Less vigorous, branches rather stiff, weeping in a short arch, densely branched. Only the male plants are cultivated in continental Europe; the English 'Kilmarnock Willow' is, however, a female. Cultivated since before 1835 but not particularly attractive.

S. caspica Pall. Large shrub or small tree, shoots long and thin, brown when young, later yellowish white, glossy and glabrous, inner bark yellow; leaves narrowly linear-lanceolate, very acute, 5–8 cm long, 4–10 mm wide, quite straight, serrate, occasionally nearly entire, eventually glabrous, venation raised beneath, stipules absent; catkins 2.5 cm long; ovaries white silky, but eventually more glabrous, nearly sessile. CSI 16. SE. Russia, W. and central Asia. Rather rare in cultivation. z6

S. chrysocoma Dode see: **S. sepulcralis**

S. cinerea L. Gray Willow. Upright shrub, to 5 m high, occasionally also a small tree, 1st and 2nd year shoots and winter buds gray tomentose; leaves elliptic to oblanceolate, 5–9 cm long, acute, crenate or sparsely serrate, base cuneate to round, both sides pubescent at first, later rather glabrous and dull green above, underside gray-green or blue-green, densely tomentose, petiole 1 cm long; catkins nearly sessile, with 4–7 leaves at the base, male catkins to 5 cm long, with 2 stamens, these long pubescent at the base, female catkins to 8 cm long in fruit, ovary usually tomentose. CS 16; HM Pl. 80; HW 116. Europe to W. Asia; in moist areas. z2 Plate 93; Fig. 199.

'Tricolor'. Slow growing; leaves smaller, white with green or white-red-green speckled and marbled (= *S. caprea tricolor* Hort.; *S. caprea variegata* Hort.). Originated in Germany around 1772. Female. ∅

S. coerulea or *S.* 'Coerulea' see: **S. alba 'Calva'**

S. cordata Michx. Very similar to *S. syrticola*, also the twigs and leaves white pubescent, but with larger leaves, 6–12 cm long, finely serrate, but coarser than those of *S. syrticola*, teeth about 2 mm apart (only 1 mm on *S. syrticola!*), eventually without glands, acuminate on the basal half, petiole 13 mm long; male catkins always with

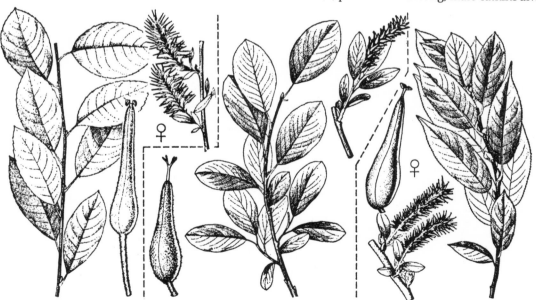

Fig. 203. **Salix.** Left *S. bebbiana;* center *S. cordifolia;* right *S. eriocephala* (from NBB)

fully (!) developed leaves at the base, female catkins 3–6 cm long. Rho 997–1000; BB 1203; NBB 13; ASA 22 (= *S. adenophylla* Hook.). Northeastern N. America. 1900. Much more rare in cultivation and often confused with *S. syrticola*. Only the female is cultivated. See also: **S. eriocephala.** z2 Fig. 199, 203.

S. × cottetii Kern. (*S. myrsinifolia × S. retusa*). Small shrub, procumbent or with the shoots somewhat ascending, young shoots white pubescent, later yellow-brown, glabrous, winter buds obtusish, pubescent; leaves elliptic-oblong, 2–4 cm long, obtuse or acute, finely serrate, both sides soft pubescent when young, later glabrous above, venation pubescent beneath, reticulately veined; catkins cylindrical, short, on white pubescent stalks, scales darker and pubescent at the apex, ovary ovate, usually glabrous, style long. CS 2: 12; Gw 9: 542. Alps, 1905. Only the male in cultivation. z6

S. cremensis see: **S. × erdingeri**

S. cuspidata see: **S. × meyeriana**

S. cutleri see: **S. uva-ursi**

S. daphnoides Vill. Violet Willow. Tall, usually broad crowned tree, 10(20) m high, twigs erect to outspread, somewhat pubescent when young, later glabrous, red, blue pruinose (!), inner bark yellow; leaves oblong to more lanceolate, 5–10 cm long, acute, large, adnate to the leaf petiole; catkins erect, about 3 cm long, densely silky pubescent, scales obovate-oblong, dark brown, stamens 2, filaments glabrous, ovary conical-ovate, glabrous, stalked, flowering very early. HM Pl. 79; HW 110; VSa 15; HF 920; CS 21; CSI 17 (= *S. pulchra* Wimm.; *S. praecox* Hoppe). Europe to Central Asia and Himalayas. 1829. Catkins effectively ornamental. z5 Plate 94; Fig. 199. ⊕

var. *acutifolia* see: **S. acutifolia**

var. *aglaia* see: '**Latifolia**'

'**Latifolia**'. Vigorous, branches normally not or only slightly pruinose; leaves larger, wider, pubescent at first (= *S. daphnoides aglaia* Schneid.). 1864.

var. *pomeranica* (Willd.) Koch. Usually shrubby; leaves much narrower, lanceolate, to 12 cm long; catkins more slender, to 8 cm long, often as early as March (= *S. pomeranica* Willd.) Europe (not only in Pomerania!). 1813. Highly valued. ⊕

'**Ruberrima**' to 8 m high, shoots very long, glossy red; catkins reddish (= *S. pulchra* '**Ruberrima**').

S. dasyclados Wimm. Large shrub, 3–6 m high, shoots thick, with a thick, velvety tomentum, 2nd year shoots still tomentose, striped beneath the bark, winter buds pubescent; leaves lanceolate, 8–20 cm long, widest in the middle, acute, crenate, dull green and somewhat pubescent above, underside dense gray woolly pubescent, petiole 1–2 cm long, stipules large, lanceolate; catkins appear before the leaves, 3–6 cm long, glands long and narrow, ovary to 6 mm long, conical, tomentose, style long, stigma thick, March–April. CSI 10. Central and E. Europe. 1829. z7

S. discolor Muhlenb. Pussy Willow. Shrub or small tree,

5–7 m high, young shoots pubescent at first, quickly becoming glabrous, purple-brown; leaves elliptic-oblong to more obovate, 4–10 cm long, acute at both ends, irregularly crenate to nearly entire, both sides pubescent at first, later glabrous, bluish beneath, thin, petiole 8–25 mm long; catkins appear in March–April, before the leaves, sessile, male catkins dense, to 3.5 cm long, with 2 glabrous stamens, female catkins 7 cm long in fruit, ovary short-haired, stalked, style very short, stigma arms split. BB 1187; HH 92; SS 478; GTP 112. N. America. 1811. z2 Fig. 208.

S. × doniana Sm. (*S. purpurea × S. repens*). Small to medium-sized shrub, young shoots thinly pubescent at first, but soon glabrous; leaves oblong-lanceolate, finely serrate toward the apex, finely silky pubescent when young, later glabrous on both sides and blue-green beneath; catkins appear before the leaves in spring, oblong, anthers red at first, later yellow, filaments more or less connate. CS 27 (= *S. parviflora* Host.). Europe, among the parents. 1829. z6

S. × ehrhartiana Sm. (*S. alba × S. pentandra*). Tree, similar to *S. pentandra*, but the young shoots less easily broken; young leaves with a distinct balsam scent (!), oblong, slender petioled, usually silky pubescent when young, green beneath; stamens usually 4 (= *S. hexandra* auth. non Ehrh.). Europe. 1894. z6

S. elaeagnos Scop. Hoary Willow. Tall shrub or small tree, occasionally 10–15 m high, shoots erect to outspread, slender, gray pubescent at first, later glabrous and brownish; leaves linear to narrowly lanceolate, 6–15 cm long, acute at both ends, margins involuted, finely serrate toward the apex, both sides gray pubescent at first, later dark green and glabrous above, white tomentose beneath, fall color golden-yellow, stipules usually absent, petioles 4–8 mm long; catkins bowed outward, small, to 3 cm long, slender, on short, foliate stalks, scales ovate, somewhat emarginate, stamens 2, filaments connate at the base or half their length, ovary glabrous, stalked, style long. CS 21; Gs 4: 48; CSI 17 and 18; HW 109; VSa 12 (= *S. incana* Schrank. non Michx.). Mountains of central and southern Europe, Asia Minor. z4 Plate 94. ∅

'**Angustifolia**'. Shrub, to 3 m high, shoots tightly upright; leaves to 10 cm long, only 3–5 mm wide, involuted (= f. *lavandulifolia* K. Koch; var. *rosmarinifolia* Hort.). France. 1806. ∅

f. *lavandulifolia* see: '**Angustifolia**'

var. *rosmarinifolia* see: '**Angustifolia**'

S. elegantissima K. Koch. Weeping willow with long branches, nodding in a wide arch, twigs pendulous, brown, smooth, glossy, youngest shoots green (!); leaves lanceolate, 8–15 cm long, 1–2 cm wide, long acuminate, scabrous serrate, not glossy above (!), blue-green beneath, petiole 1–1.5 cm long, stipules semicordate; catkins to 5 cm long, with a few entire leaves at the base, ovary short stalked, pubescent at the base, style short, stigma parted, outspread; only the female known. MG 13: 88. Origin unknown, perhaps *S. babylonica × S. fragilis*. z5

Fig. 204. **Salix**. Left *S. fargesii;* center *S. gracilistyla;* right *S. xerophila* (from ICS)

S. × erdingeri Kern. (*S. caprea × S. daphnoides*). Tall shrub, shoots erect to outspread, pubescent at first, later glabrous, yellow- to red-brown; leaves elliptic to oblanceolate, 4–8 cm long, acute at both ends, crenate to nearly entire or also undulate, silky tomentose at first, later glabrous above, smooth, glossy dark green, gray-green and reticulately veined beneath, venation pubescent; only the female catkins observed, slender, eventually to 8 cm long, scales ovate, long pubescent, ovary stalked, oval-conical, silky, style elongated. CS 46 (= *S. cremensis* Kern.). Discovered in Vienna, Austria before 1861. z6 ⊕

S. eriocephala Michx. Shrub, to 4 m high, young shoots finely pubescent or glabrous; leaves oblong-lanceolate, 5–14 cm long, acuminate, scabrous serrate, base rounded to somewhat cordate, dull green above, lighter beneath and glabrous or slightly pubescent, petiole 0.5–1.5 cm long, stipules usually large oval to kidney-shaped; catkins appear shortly before the leaves, foliate at the base, slender, male catkins 2–5 cm long, female 2.5–6 cm long. BB 1198; GSP 77 (= *S. cordata* Muhlenb. non Michx.; *S. rigida* Muhlenb.). N. America. 1812. z6 Fig. 203, 212.

S. × erythroflexuo̊sa Rag. (*S. alba* 'Tristis' × *S. matsudana* 'Tortuosa'). Small tree, similar to *S. matsudana* 'Tortuosa' in appearance, but with branches and twigs widely arching or outspread, wavy and twisted like a corkscrew, bark golden-yellow to orange; leaves oblong-lanceolate, similarly crispate and twisted (= *S. matsudana* 'Tortuosa Aurea Pendula'). Discovered in 1971 in Argentina and brought into the trade by the Beardslee Nursery, Perry, Ohio, USA in 1972. Unique, ornamental tree. z6 ∅

S. fargesii Burkh. Shrub, to 3 m high, shoots purple, glabrous, thicker than on the similar *S. moupinensis,* winter buds also larger, red; leaves narrowly ovate to elliptic, acuminate, 7–15 cm long, 4–6 cm wide, tapered at the base, finely serrate, glabrous above, deep green and glossy, with 15–25 indented vein pairs, lighter green and silky pubescent (!) beneath, small leaves occasionally nearly circular and densely pubescent beneath, petiole 5–18 mm long; male catkins 4–6 cm long, female 7–10 cm, to 20 cm in fruit, erect, 6 mm wide, ovary ovate, short stalked, glabrous, bracts pubescent and silky ciliate on the margins (!!). ICS 723. China; W. Hupeh, E. Szechwan Provs. 1911. More meritorious than *S. moupinensis.* z6 Plate 97; Fig. 204. ∅

S. × finnmarchica Willd. (*S. myrtilloides × S. repens*). Shrub, only 30(50) cm high, shoots procumbent-ascending, thin, glabrous; leaves broadly elliptic to obovate, about 2.5 cm long, finely dentate, underside pubescent when young, later glabrous and light blue-green; catkins appear shortly before or with the leaves, densely clustered, bracts yellow-green. Sweden, northern Norway. Cultivated in Berlin in 1800. Good species for the rock garden. z4 Fig. 210.

S. foetida Schleicher. Dwarf shrub with procumbent shoots; leaves elliptic-lanceolate, small, to 3 cm long, dense and scabrous serrate, with large, white glands, deep green above, with 5–10 vein pairs, unpleasantly scented when crushed (!); catkins 2–3 times longer than wide, short stalked. CSI 51. W. and central Alps, Pyrenees. z6

S. formosa see: **S. arbuscula**

S. fragilis L. Crack Willow. Tall shrub or tree, to 15 m high, crown rather globose, branches outspread (often at nearly right angles (!), yellowish to brownish, smooth, glossy, easily broken off (!); leaves oblong-lanceolate to narrowly lanceolate, 5–15 cm long, long acuminate, glandular serrate, cuneate at the base, glossy dark green above, light green or somewhat bluish beneath, silky pubescent at first, quickly becoming totally glabrous, stipules subcordate, serrate, quickly abscising; catkins on foliate, short lateral branches, rachis pubescent, male 3–4 cm long, female 3–6 cm long, stamens usually 2, basal half of the filaments pubescent, ovary conical, stalked. BB 1177; GTP 113; CS 3; CSI 2; HW 2: 28. Europe, Orient. Cultivated since antiquity. z5 Plate 93; Fig. 199, 201.

var. *basfordiana* see: S. × 'Basfordiana'

'Bullata' (Späth). Compact habit, globose, bushy, to 6 m high and 9 m wide as very old plants. MD 1935: 20 (= f. *sphaerica* Hryniewecki & Kobendza). Originated in Sweden around 1785.

f. *sphaerica* see: 'Bullata'

S. friesiana see: **S. rosmarinifolia**

S. fruticulosa see: **S. hylematica**

S. × gillotii A. & E. G. Camus (*S. lapponicum × phylicifolia*). Small, very strong branched shrub, shoots brown and glossy, warty from the leaf scars, finely pubescent at first, then glabrous; leaves oblong-lanceolate, about 7 cm long and 3 cm wide, sharply acuminate, entire to finely crenate, base usually round to cuneate, pubescent on both sides, white tomentose beneath at first, later more or less glabrous, stipules very

small, ovate, abscising. CS 33. France. z7

S. glabra Scop. Medium-sized shrub, to 1.5 m high, branches thick, strong, red-brown, somewhat glossy; leaves elliptic, flat toothed, 4–6 cm long, 1.5–2.5 cm wide, obtuse to acuminate, base cuneate to somewhat round, dark green and glossy above, light gray-green beneath, glabrous; catkins appear before the leaves, large, ellipsoid, sessile, to 7 cm long, with a few quickly abscising small leaves at the base, male flowers with 2 stamens, pubescent at the base, ovary stalked, glabrous, style distinct, stigma short stalked, bracts light brown, long pubescent. CSI 11; CWE 22. E. Alps, in the higher mountains. z6

S. glauca L. Arctic Gray Willow. Shrub, erect, 30–100 cm high, divaricately branched, twigs brown, white tomentose or silky at first when young, later yellow-brown, glossy; leaves obovate-lanceolate, 3–8 cm long, acute at both ends, entire, silky above at first, eventually glossy dark green, silky or white tomentose beneath at first, later gray-green or bluish, petiole to 1.5 cm long; catkins appearing with the leaves in June–July, to 4.5 cm long, scales long pubescent, stamens 2, pubescent at the base, anthers yellow, eventually brown, ovaries silky tomentose, short stalked. CS 11; HM Pl. 83; GPN 221; PAr 142; CSI 52; HW 122. Alps, N. Asia, on gravelly slopes along mountain streams. 1813. z3 Fig. 199k.

var. *acutifolia* (Hook.) Schneid. Stipules normally well developed, stalked longer than the glands, filaments becoming glabrous. BB 1192 (= *S. seemannii* Rydb.; *S. stipulifera* Flod.). Arctic N. America.

S. glaucosericea B. Flod. Alpine Gray Willow. Small shrub, scarcely 1 m high, with short, thick, gray

Fig. 205. **Salix.** Left *S. hookeriana;* center *S. lasiandra;* right *S. lasiolepis* (from Sudworth)

Fig. 206. **Salix**. Left *S. arbuscula;* center above *S. myrsinites;* center beneath *S. uva-ursi;* right *S. herbacea* (from Lid)

pubescent shoots; leaves oblanceolate, 5.5–7.5 cm long, 1.5–2 cm wide, pale green and somewhat glossy above, blue-green beneath, gray silky pubescent on both sides, with 7–9 vein pairs, stipules usually absent. CSI 53. Alps (Austria, Switzerland, Italy, France). z6

S. gracilis Anderss. Low shrub, current year's shoots thin and soon glabrous, purple; leaves lanceolate to narrowly lanceolate, 4–8 cm long, acuminate, finely serrate, cuneate at the base, silky pubescent beneath when young, soon becoming glabrous, petiole 4–10 mm long; catkins appearing with the leaves, with bracts at the base, male 1–2 cm, female 4 cm long in fruit, scales yellow-brown, stamens 2, ovary ovate, drawn out in a long tip, pubescent, stigma sessile. GSP 70; BB 1189 (= *S. petiolaris* sensu Pursh). N. America. 1802. Used in basket making. z5

S. gracilistyla Miq. Shrub, erect, 1–3 m high, shoots gray tomentose in the first year, glabrous in the 2nd year; leaves elliptic-oblong to more obovate, 5–10 cm long, acute at both ends, finely serrate, both sides silky pubescent at first, later glabrous above, pubescent and bluish gray beneath, petiole 4–8 mm long; catkins appearing before the leaves, sessile, densely silky, about 3.5 cm long, the female catkins to 8 cm long in fruit, scales lanceolate, filaments connate, glabrous, anthers yellow, ovary nearly sessile, style slender, longer than the ovary (!). BM 9122; NK 18: 17; YWP 2: 97; MJ 2012 (= *S. thunbergiana* Bl.). Korea, Japan, 1900. Very attractive, early species with large catkins. z6 Fig. 199, 204. ✣

var. *melanostachys* see: **S. melanostachys**

S. × grahamii Borrer. (*S. herbacea × S. phylicifolia*). Prostrate shrub, to 30 cm high, developing a large, flat nest-form; leaves elliptic to obovate, 2.5–4 cm long, acuminate or rounded above, base tapered, bright green, glossy; catkins erect, appearing with or without the leaves. Found among the parents in Scotland around 1865. z4

S. grisea see: **S. sericea**

S. hastata L. Upright shrub, to 1 m high, densely branched and densely foliate, young shoots pubescent, quickly becoming glabrous and red-brown; leaves quite variable, elliptic to obovate, 2–8 cm long, acute, sparsely appressed serrate, base cordate, dark green above, lighter to blue-green beneath with reticulate venation, midrib yellowish, usually somewhat pubescent when young, stipules usually large, subcordate, petiole 3–8 mm long; catkins appear with the leaves, on foliate shoots, 3–5 cm long, scales long pubescent, stamens 2, distinct, glabrous, anthers golden-yellow, later brown, ovaries oval-conical, glabrous, style about as long as the stigma. CS 13; HM 464; GPN 227; PAr 144; ASA 21; CSI 40 to 42. Mountains of Europe to NE. Asia and Kashmir. 1780. z6 Fig. 199.

'Wehrhahnii' (Bonstedt). To 1.5 m high, branches thick; leaves 3–6 cm long, oval-rounded, short acuminate, both sides densely pubescent at first, later glabrous and green beneath, reticulately veined; catkins very densely arranged, light yellow,

Fig. 207. **Salix.** From left: *S. aurita; S. starkeana; S. lapponum; S. myrtilloides* (below); *S. arenaria* (from Lid)

only the male observed (= *S. wehrhahnii* Bonstedt). Originally thought to be found in Engadin, Switzerland in 1930 but this is doubted today; presumably from Scandinavia. ∅ ⊕

S. hegetschweileri Heer. Medium-sized , upright shrub, strongly branched, glabrous; leaves elliptic to obovate, widest past the middle, dark green above, lighter beneath, margins with very indistinct, scattered glandular teeth, totally glabrous, petiole 3–6 mm long; catkins appearing before the leaves, elliptic, sessile, 3–4 cm long, filaments with crispate hairs on the basal half. CSI 48 (= *S. rhaetica* Kern.). Alps, Switzerland. z6 Fig. 210.

S. helvetica Vill. Swiss Willow. Small shrub, branches thick, curved, shoots pubescent at first and densely white tomentose, later glabrous and somewhat glossy; leaves obovate to more lanceolate, 4 cm long, 2 cm wide, usually widest past the middle, short acuminate to rounded apex, dark gray-green and eventually somewhat glossy above, white tomentose beneath; catkins appearing shortly before the leaves, rather large and thick, 3–5 cm long, densely pubescent, sessile, ovary with a very long style, stigma parted, forked, 2 filaments, glabrous. CS 12; CSI 43; HM Pl. 83 (= *S. nivea* Ser.). Alps; Switzerland; Tyrol, Tatra Mts. 1872. z6 Plate 74.

S. herbacea L. Dwarf Willow. Procumbent shrub, branches filamentous, cylindrical, to 15 cm long, also rhizomatous, to 5 cm high, slightly pubescent at first, quickly becoming glabrous; leaves nearly circular, 8–20 mm wide, emarginate at the apex, crenate, glossy and bright green on both sides; flowers on 2-leaved, small shoots, stamens 2, anthers yellow, ovary ovate, glabrous, very short stalked; style very short. BB 1206; HM 83; PAr

132; CSI 67; CS 8. Higher mountains of Europe and N. Asia, arctic N. America. 1789. Very adaptable to dry or moist sites. z2 Fig. 199, 206.

S. heteromera see: **S. babylonica**

S. hexandra see: **S. × ehrhartiana**

S. hibernica Rech. f. Medium-sized shrub, similar to *S. hegetshweileri*, but the leaves broadly lanceolate to nearly elliptic, nearly entire, widest at or below the middle, base broadly cuneate, short acuminate at the apex, with 9–12 vein pairs, petiole 2–3 mm thick; catkins 3 cm long, dense. NW. Ireland. z7

S. hippophaifolia see: **S. mollissima**

S. hookeriana Barratt. Normally only a small shrub, to 1 m high, occasionally also prostrate branched, but observed to be tree-like in its habitat, young shoots densely tomentose; leaves oblong to more obovate, 5–15 cm long, acute, entire to finely crenate, both sides tomentose at first, thickish, later rather glabrous above, blue-green and tomentose beneath, petiole 5–15 mm long; catkins nearly sessile, somewhat foliate at the base, male catkins 3–5 cm long, female 8–12 cm in fruit, dense, thick, ovary glabrous, conical, style long. SPa 98; SS 485; ASA 25. Western N. America. 1891. z6 Plate 93; Fig. 199, 205. ∅ ⊕

S. humilis Marsh. Prairie Willow. Shrub, to 2.5 m high, branches pubescent to tomentose; leaves oblong-lanceolate to oblanceolate, 5–10 cm long, acute at both ends, margins finely dentate and somewhat involuted, dull deep green and usually glabrous above, blue-green and tomentose beneath; catkins appear before the leaves, sessile, brick-red. BB 1: 600. NE. N. America. 1876. z4 Fig. 200.

S. hylematica Schneid. Dwarf shrub, shoots short, rather thick, red-brown, shaggy pubescent when young; leaves lanceolate to oblanceolate, about 10 mm long, 4 mm wide, finely dentate, occasionally entire, short petioled; male catkins 1–1.5 cm long, 9 mm wide, female catkins 1 cm long, fruit capsule sessile, glabrous (= *S. fruticulosa* Anderss. non de Lacroix). W. Himalayas, Kumaun Mts. 4000 m. z4

S. incana see: **S. candida**

S. integra Thunb. Tall shrub to small tree, shoots glabrous, glossy; leaves nearly sessile and usually opposite, narrowly oblong, 3–6 cm long, 7–20 mm wide, rather thin, glabrous, indistinctly serrate to entire, rounded to slightly cordate at the base, underside whitish; flowers appear before the leaves, slender, dense, style short, stigma very short, forked, April (= *S. purpurea* auct. jap. non L.; *S. savatieri* Camus; *S. multinervis* Fr. & Sav.). Japan, Korea. z6

S. interior (Rowlee) Muhlenb. Very stoloniferous shrub, 1–2 m high, also a small, slender tree in its habitat, to 8 m high, bark rather smooth, new growth orange or reddish, smooth; leaves linear-lanceolate, 6–12 cm long, sparsely dentate, acuminate, base cuneate, light green and distinctly veined above, underside silky when young, later glabrous, stipules very small or totally absent; catkins on rather long, foliate shoots, male catkins 2–4 cm long, stamens 2, pubescent at the base, female catkins to 5 cm long, rather loose when in fruit, ovary glabrous, short stalked, stigma nearly sessile. GF 8: 463; BB 1181; HH 84; ASA 3 (= *S. longifolia* Muhlenb.). N. America. 1873. z2 Fig. 208.

S. irrorata Anders. Shrub, to 3 m high, but also to 5 m wide, current year's shoots purple, very pruinose; leaves oblong to linear-lanceolate, 6–10 cm long, acuminate, sparsely serrate to nearly entire, base cuneate, glossy green above, blue-green beneath, petiole 3–10 mm long, yellow; catkins nearly sessile, usually leafless at the base, short and thick, 1–2 cm long, scales nearly black, densely white haired, style very short, stigma short and thick. SW. USA. 1898. Only the male in cultivation. The pruinose shoots attractive in winter. z5 Plate 94.

S. japonica Thunb. Tall shrub, shoots slender, brown; leaves elliptic-oblong, 5–12 cm, long acuminate, base cuneate, scabrous glandular serrate, silky pubescent when young, but soon glabrous, bright green above, blue-green beneath; catkins appearing with the leaves, slender, 8–10 cm long, filaments long pubescent at the base. MJ 2021; SH 1: 20 and 23. Japan. 1874. z6

S. jessoensis Seemen. Tall tree, branches spreading, bark light gray-brown, somewhat scaly, current year's shoots light brown, somewhat pubescent when young; leaves lanceolate, 5–9 cm long, acuminate, finely and acutely serrate, both sides silky pubescent when young, later less so above, underside always densely silky and bluish, petiole 2–5 mm long, stipules ovate-lanceolate, small,

silky; catkins only 2–3 cm long, on short, foliate stalks, stamens 2, scales broadly ovate, ovaries pubescent, stigmas oblong, undivided. HS 41. Japan. 1897. z6

S. kinuyanagi Kimura. Strong growing, upright shrub or small tree, shoots rather thick, long, gray-tomentose; leaves narrowly lanceolate, 10–20 cm long, long acuminate, base acute, margins indistinctly undulate and somewhat reflexed, pubescent above when young, densely appressed beneath, silvery silky pubescent; flowers 2.5–3.5 cm long, catkins dense, sessile, filaments distinct, glabrous, anthers yellow, only the male observed (= *S. viminalis* auct. japon. non L.). Japan. Widely cultivated there for basket making and wicker work. z6

S. kitaibeliana Willd. (*retusa* Group). Dwarf shrub, branches and shoots more or less ascending, shoots long, glabrous, green; leaves obovate, 2–3.5 cm long, 7–11 mm wide, obtusish, nearly entire, glabrous, yellow in fall, stipules absent; flowers appearing with the leaves, catkins oblong-ellipsoid, stalked, male with 2 stamens, glabrous, female catkins with a stalked, glabrous ovary. CSI 65. Carpathian Mts. z6

S. koriyanagi Kimura. Large, upright shrub or small tree, shoots brown to yellow-brown, thin and rodlike; leaves alternate to partly opposite, linear-lanceolate, 6–8 cm long, 5–10 mm wide, gradually acuminate above, base rounded, sparsely serrate, thin leathery, deep green above, blue-green beneath, glabrous, lateral veins numerous; catkins slender, 2–3 cm long, many flowered, anthers deep purple, ovary sessile, white shaggy, stigma very short (= *S. purpurea* var. *japonica* Nakai). Korea; widely cultivated in Japan for weaving. z6

S. 'Kurome' see: **S. melanostachys**

S. 'Kuroyanagi' see: **S. melanostachys**

S. laggeri Wimm. Shrub, 2–3 m high, branches spreading, thick knotty, dark brown to blackish, shoots pubescent, buds pubescent, flat; leaves narrowly elliptic to lanceolate, large, serrate, becoming glabrous above, scattered pubescent beneath; flowers appearing shortly before the leaves, catkins large, to 4 cm long, 1.7 cm wide, filaments long pubescent on the basal half, ovary stalked, styles distinct, stigma oblong, parted. CSI 24 (= *S. albicans* Bonj.; *S. pubescent* Schl.). Central Alps, on the edge of the forest, particularly on silica soils. z6

S. lanata L. Woolly Willow. Low, divaricate shrub, branches thick, gnarled (less conspicuously so in cultivation), densely white woolly pubescent, as are the winter buds; leaves elliptic-rounded to more ovate-obovate, 3–7 cm long, acute, entire to somewhat cordate, tough, both sides densely white silky-long haired when young, later becoming glabrous and then dull green above, underside more bluish and reticulately veined, petiole 5–15 mm long, stipules often large, entire; catkins appearing with the leaves, densely yellowish silky pubescent (*S. brachypoda* is the only other species in the whole genus with this characteristic), male catkins to 5 cm long, female to 8 cm in fruit, stamens glabrous, anthers golden-yellow, ovaries glabrous, style long. GPN 228; CS 36; CSI 58; PAr 139. N. Europe, N. Asia. 1789. One of the most attractive willows! z1 Plate 73; Fig. 202. ∅ ⊕

'Stuartii' (*S. lanata* × *S. lapponum?*). More procumbent habit; leaves more oblong, densely white woolly; catkins particularly dark yellow. Found in the mountains of Scotland before 1912 by Charles Stuart. Plate 95. ∅ ⊕

S. × lanceolata Sm. (*S. alba* × *S. triandra*). Large shrub, bark exfoliating, shoots olive-green, eventually glabrous, pubescent only when very young; leaves broadly lanceolate, gradually tapering to the apex, 7–12 cm long, 1.2–1.5 cm wide, finely serrate, silky pubescent at first, quickly becoming glabrous, dull green above, lighter beneath; catkins appearing with the leaves, to 8 cm long, dense, scales evenly colored, pubescent, capsule glabrous, style short, stigma bilabiate, stalk scarcely longer than the nectaries, only the female is known (= *S. undulata* Ehrh.?). Europe; particularly in S. England. Widely used in basket weaving. z4

S. lancifolia see: **S. lasiandra**

S. lapponum L. Lapland Willow. Shrub, upright, densely branched, 0.5–1.5 m high, shoots silky pubescent at first, later glabrous and red-brown, thin; leaves broadly ovate to lanceolate or elliptic, acute, 2.5–6 cm long, entire, soft pubescent and dull green above, underside gray to white tomentose, petiole 1 cm long; catkins conspicuously silvery silky, nearly sessile, with a few small bracts, scales long pubescent, filaments glabrous, anthers yellow or reddish, ovaries nearly sessile, densely silky pubescent, style thin, April. CS 12, 33; HW 12; HF 937. The higher mountains of Europe and Scandinavia, to Altai. 1789. z3 Plate 98; Fig. 207. ∅

Including:

var. **daphneola** Tausch. Glabrous in all respects. Only occurring in the highest mountains.

S. lasiandra Benth. Shrub or tree, to 15 m, very similar to *S. pentandra*, but the young shoots pubescent or tomentose at first; leaves lanceolate or narrowly oval-lanceolate, 7–12 cm long, long acuminate, totally finely glandular dentate, dark green and glossy above, midrib often distinctly yellow, underside bluish and pubescent at first, petiole with a few wart-like glands, male catkins 2.5–3 cm long, stamens 3–8, but usually 5, anthers pubescent. SPa 8; SS 469 to 470; ASA 1 (= *S. lyallii* Heller; *S. lancifolia* Anderss.). Western N. America. 1883. z5 Fig. 199, 205.

S. lasiolepis Benth. Tall shrub or small tree, 2–12 m high, multistemmed, shoots brown-black, occasionally yellowish, usually pubescent; leaves narrow or broad oblanceolate, 6–10 cm long, 1–2 cm wide, glabrous to pubescent beneath and blue-green, entire and somewhat involuted; flowers appear before the leaves, 3–7 cm long, nearly sessile, bracts obovate, dark brown, densely tomentose, capsule 5 mm long, glabrous, style 0.5 mm long, stamens 2, connate at the base. AI 1208. W. USA. z6 Fig. 205.

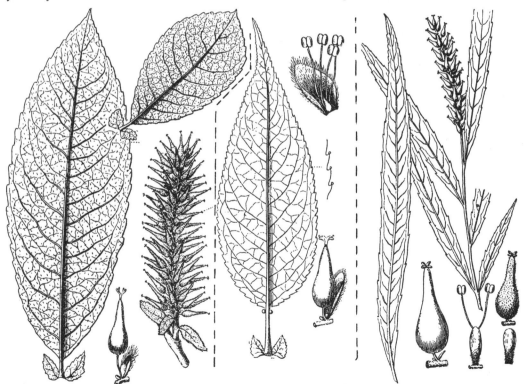

Fig. 208. **Salix.** Left *S. discolor*; middle *S. × meyeriana*; right *S. interior* (from Anderson)

S. laurifolia see: **S. pentandra**

S. × laurina Sm. (*S. caprea* × *S. phylicifolia*). Large shrub or small broad crowned tree, crown rounded, branches red-brown, very glossy; leaves obovate to more oblong, 4–8 cm long, short acuminate, glossy above, blue-green beneath, finely pubescent at first, eventually glabrous; catkins appearing before the leaves, stigma thick, usually not parted, about as long as the style. 1809. Only found in cultivation. z6

S. lindleyana Wall. apud Anderss. Procumbent dwarf shrub, to 30 cm high, totally glabrous; leaves spathulate, 5–12 mm long, to 4 mm wide, glossy and leathery above, underside light green and glabrous, ovate at the apex, tapered to the base, petiole yellow-brown and glossy like the young wood; male catkins very small, terminally arranged, 10 mm long, stamens 2, base lightly pubescent, female catkins nearly capitate, very small, ovaries short stalked, glabrous, capsule 3.5 mm long, glabrous. China; Yunnan Prov., 4200 m; Nepal. z6

S. longifolia see: **S. interior**

S. lucida Muehlb. Shining Willow. Shrub or small tree, 3–5 m high, branches yellow-brown, glossy, glabrous; leaves ovate-lanceolate, 7–12 cm, conspicuously long acuminate (!), glandular serrate, base round, glabrous and glossy on both sides, petiole 6–12 mm long, stipules subcordate, very glandular; catkins 3–6 cm long, stamens usually 3, long pubescent to the middle, stigma nearly sessile. BB 1176; GTP 109; SS 453. Eastern N. America; wet sites. 1830. Attractive species with golden-yellow catkins. z2 Fig. 202. ✿

S. lyallii see: **S. lasiandra**

S. magnifica Hemsl. Shrub to 2 m high, also to 6 m high in its habitat, glabrous in all respects, branches thick, purple at first; leaves elliptic, *Magnolia*-like, tough, to 20 cm long and 10 cm wide, bluish green above, gray-green beneath, also often somewhat reddish, petiole and venation red; flowers in erect, slender catkins in May, after the leaves, male to 15 cm long, female to 20 cm long in fruit. HS 23; Gfl 75: 29. China; Szechwan Prov. 1903. z7 Plate 97. ∅

S. matsudana Koidz. Small tree, 4–13 m high, branches upright to outspread, twigs erect to pendulous, brittle, finely pubescent at first, quickly becoming glabrous, olive-green to yellowish, older shoots eventually gray to brown; leaves narrow lanceolate, 5–10 cm long, 10–15 mm wide, distinctly scabrous glandular serrate, long acuminate, base obtuse to rounded, bright green above, underside bluish to whitish and loosely silky pubescent at first, quickly becoming glabrous, petiole 2–8 mm long, stipules lanceolate, short, glandular serrate, often absent; catkins 1–2.5 cm long, stamens 2, filaments pubescent on the base, bracts ovate, obtuse, yellow-green, ovaries sessile, glabrous, stigma sessile, glands 2 (!!). LF 66; BS 3: 20; BD 1923: 14 (*S. babylonica* Franch. non L.; *S. babylonica* var. *pekinensis* Henry). N. China, Chile, NE. Asia, Transbaikal region, Ussuri, Amur, Korea. 1905. Also thrives on dry soil. z5

'**Pendula**'. Branches pendulous, otherwise like the species; with 4–5 small, entire leaves at the base of the catkins. 1908.

'**Tortuosa**'. Branches twisted, corkscrew-like, also the leaves. 1924. Best kept as a large shrub which requires a seasonal hard pruning. ("Lung Chao Liu" in China). Plate 99. ∅

'Tortuosa Aurea Pendula' see: **S. × erythroflexuosa**

'**Umbraculifera**'. Crown flat globose to umbrella form. BD 1923: 15. Often cultivated in the vicinity of Beijing, China. (= "Man T'Ow Liu" in China). 1906.

S. medemii see: **S. aegyptiaca**

S. medwedewii Dode. Small shrub, glabrous in all respects; leaves linear-lanceolate, 6–10 cm long, only 5–6 mm wide, sparsely glandular serrate, underside bluish white; female catkins dense. Asia Minor. 1910. z7 Plate 94.

S. melanostachys Mak. Glabrous shrub, leaves oblong-lanceolate, 8–10 cm long, light green on both sides, finely glandular dentate, glabrous; catkins sessile, naked, 1–2 cm long, black (!), appearing nearly like small *Alnus* cones, scales rather dry, totally glabrous, oval-oblong, stamens 1, only the male known (= *S. gracilistyla* var. *melanostachys* [Mak.] Schneid.; *S.* 'Kurome' Hort.; *S.* 'Kuroyanagi' Hort.). Japan. Disseminated since about 1950 by J. Spek, Boskoop, Holland. Very easy to recognize by the black catkins. z5

S. × meyeriana Rostk. (*S. fragilis* × *S. pentandra*). Divaricate tree, shoots brownish green, glabrous, brittle; leaves oblong-elliptic, acuminate, finely glandular dentate, 3–12 cm long, broadly cuneate at the base, dark green and glossy above, underside blue-green; male catkins 3–5 cm long, usually with 4 stamens. CS 23; HF 916 (= *S. cuspidata* Schultz). Europe. 1829. z6 Fig. 208.

S. microstachya Turcz. Shrub, see also *S. wilhelmsiana* which is similar, but the shoots pubescent, leaves silky pubescent at first, ovaries glabrous (= *S. angustifolia* f. *microstachya* [Turcz.] Anderss.; *S. spaethii* Koopm.). W. Siberia to Mongolia. z4

S. mielichhoferi Saut. Medium-sized, upright shrub, similar to *S. nigricans*, but the branches thicker and more gnarled, shoots glabrous; leaves lanceolate to obovate, usually entire, scabrous serrate, with thick, raised venation, stipules well developed; flowers appearing shortly before the leaves, catkins elliptic, sessile, stamens 2, filaments pubescent, ovaries stalked, style long, stigma erect, short parted, bracts dark brown, sparsely pubescent. CSI 25. Alps, south central region on the forest's edge. z6

S. miyabeana Seemen. Shrub or small tree, to 5 m high, young shoots glabrous, light brown; leaves lanceolate to narrowly lanceolate, 5–15 cm long, acute at both ends, crenate, underside glabrous and bluish, petiole 3–10 mm long, stipules lanceolate, leaflike; catkins appearing before the leaves, 3–5 cm long, sessile, scales ovate, dark brown, pubescent, filaments totally connate (!), anthers yellow, ovary sessile, tomentose, stigma short, undivided, sessile. HS 86. Japan. 1897. z6

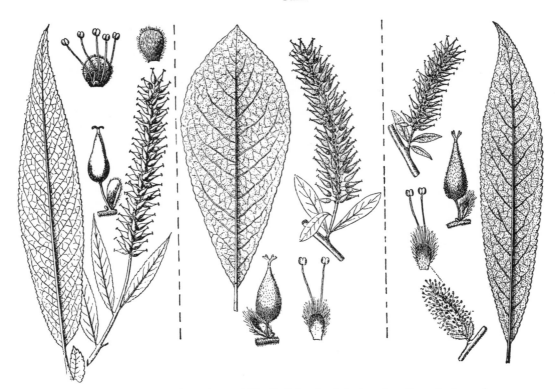

Fig. 209. **Salix.** Left *S. nigra;* middle *S. sitchensis;* right *S. sericea* (from Anderson)

S. mollissima Ehrh. (*S. triandra* × *S. viminalis*). Large, bushy shrub, branches spreading to erect, shoots more or less soft pubescent when young, later glabrous and reddish green; leaves narrow lanceolate, 8–12 cm long, glandular serrate, margins undulate, later usually flat, dull dark green above, underside thin gray tomentose and silky glossy, stipules semi-ovate; catkins cylindrical, 3–4 cm long, on slightly foliate, pubescent stalks, male catkins with 2–3 stamens, female flowers with pubescent ovaries, distinct style and outspread, 2 parted stigma. CS 24 (= *S. undulata* Ehrh.; *S. hippophaifolia* Thuill.; *S. treviranii* Spreng.). Central Europe. 1809. z6

S. × moorei F. B. White (*S. herbacea* × *S. phylicifolia*). Habit broadly procumbent, nest form, with many, spreading, thin shoots; leaves small, glossy green; catkins appear before the leaves, female. Found in the wild in Scotland. Excellent ground cover. z5

S. myrsinifolia see: **S. nigricans**

S. moupinensis Franch. Shrub, to 6 m high, shoots orange to red-brown, smooth; leaves narrowly elliptic-oblong, 6–10 cm long, short acuminate, broadly cuneate at the base, yellowish green and glabrous above, petiole 10–15 mm long; flowers whorled in the catkins (like *S. magnifica*), male catkins 6–9 cm long, female to 14 cm, ovary totally glabrous, 4–5 mm long, stalk 1–2 mm, bracts totally glabrous (!!), only the female in cultivation. China; W. Szechwan Prov. 1911. Often confused with *S. fargesii*, which has larger leaves and thicker shoots. z6 Plate 97. ⌀

S. multinervis see: **S. integra**

S. myrsinifolia see: **S. nigricans**

S. myrsinites L. Myrtle Willow. Low, erect, often gnarled shrub, scarcely over 0.4 m high, seasonal growth very short, red-brown, glossy, pubescent at first, very densely foliate; leaves tough, elliptic-obovate to lanceolate, 1–5 cm long, usually acute at both ends, usually glandular serrate, pubescent at first, later green and glossy on both sides, stipules slightly developed, very short petioled; catkins clustered at the shoot tips, on foliate stalks, 4–5 cm long, scales reddish, blackish on the apical limb, pubescent, stamens 2, filaments reddish, anthers purple, ovary short stalked, pubescent at first. CS 9; HM 466; GPN 220; PAr 144; VSa 19; CSI 61 (= *S. myrsinites* var. *serrata* Neilr.). Higher mountains in N. Europe. 1789. z5 Fig. 199, 206.

S. myrtilloides L. Swamp Willow. Upright shrub, stem procumbent, seasonal growth 20–50 cm long, slender, somewhat pubescent at first, later yellow-brown, glabrous; leaves ovate to narrowly oblong, 1.5–2(3.5) cm long, acute, usually entire, occasionally sparsely dentate, eventually dark green and somewhat glossy above, underside lighter to blue-green, reticulately veined; catkins foliate stalked, 1–1.5 cm long, scales somewhat reddish at the apex, stamens with long filaments, anthers yellow to reddish, later violet-red, ovaries glabrous. HM Pl. 81; HF 934; CSI 21; BB 1204. N. Europe, N. Asia, NW. America. 1772. Difficult to cultivate. z2 Fig. 199, 207.

S. napoleonis see: **S. babylonica 'Crispa'**

S. nigra Marsh. Black Willow. Tree, to 30 m high, bark rough, dark brown, branches slender and outspread, young shoots yellowish, somewhat pubescent when young; leaves linear-lanceolate, 6–12 cm long, acuminate, finely serrate (!), base cuneate, light green beneath, venation occasionally somewhat pubescent, petiole 3–6 mm long, stipules subcordate, persistent; catkins on foliate shoots, male 3–5 cm long, female 4–8 cm long, stamens 3–7, ovary glabrous, stigma nearly sessile. BB 1173; GTP 106; SPa 85; SS 462. N. America. 1809. z4 Plate 93; Fig. 209.

var. **falcata** (Pursh) Rehd. Leaves falcate, narrower, only 4–6 mm wide, green on both sides. SS 463. Eastern N. America.

S. nigricans Sm. Shrub, to 4 m high, quite variable, habit usually broad, young shoots densely tomentose, later becoming glabrous; leaves rounded or elliptic to oblong-lanceolate, 2–10 cm long, acute to rounded, irregularly undulate serrate, base round to nearly cordate, dark green and rather glabrous above, underside gray or blue-green, pubescent, occasionally tomentose; catkins appearing before or with the foliage, male to 3 cm long, female to 6 cm long in fruit, stamens 2, filaments pubescent, anthers golden-yellow, later blackish, ovary narrowly conical. CS 18; HM Pl. 81; HF 931 (= *S. myrsinifolia* Salisb.; *S. andersoniana* Sm.). Europe, Asia Minor, W. Siberia; moist, swampy sites. Of no particular garden significance. z5 Plate 94.

S. nivalis Hook. Snow Willow. Creeping dwarf shrub, only 1.5 cm high; leaves elliptic to circular, 1 cm long or smaller, glabrous, deep green above, blue-green beneath; catkins at the tips of foliate shoots, July to August, 1 cm long, few flowered; fruit capsule gray, 3 mm, sessile, short pubescent. N. America, Rocky Mts. z4

S. nivea see: **S. helvetica**

S. nummularia see: **S. rotundifolia**

S. oleifolia see: **S. atrocinerea**

S. opaca see: **S. sachalinensis**

S. oxica Dode. Vigorous, broad upright tree, branches deep red-brown, glabrous, silky pubescent when young; leaves lanceolate, 10–15 cm long, coarsely serrate, base cuneate, light green above, blue-gray and appressed silky pubescent beneath; ovaries glabrous, short stalked, scales lanceolate. Turkestan, Bukhara (USSR) 1910. z6

S. parviflora see: **S. × doniana**

S. pedicellata Desf. Tall shrub or tree, to 10 m, debarked shoots with well developed stripes, young shoots gray tomentose, older shoots gradually becoming glabrous; leaves oblong to obovate-lanceolate, 6–8 cm long, 3.4 cm wide, slightly dentate, crenate or nearly entire, becoming glabrous above, underside thinly pubescent, with at least 10–12 pairs of lateral veins, indented above, elevated beneath; flowers appear shortly before the

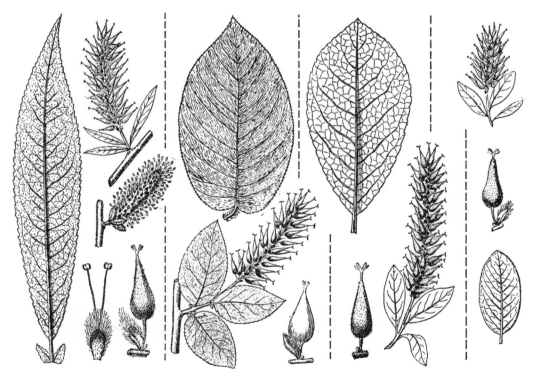

Fig. 210. **Salix.** From left: *S. petiolaris; S. syrticola; S. hegetschweileri; S. finnmarchica* (from Anderson)

leaves, catkins elliptic, 3–6 cm long, 1–1.5 cm wide, ovary long stalked, short pubescent, style distinct, stigma short, bracts small, slightly pubescent. VSa 21; CS 20. Mediterranean region, from S. Spain to Asia Minor. z7

S. pendulifolia see: **S. acutifolia 'Pendulifolia'**

S. pendulina see: **S. × blanda**

S. pentandra L. Bay Willow. Shrub or tree, to 10 m or more, bark gray, furrowed, young shoots brownish green glossy, easily broken at the point of attachment, new growth somewhat glutinous; leaves elliptic-ovate, 5–12 cm long, short acuminate, base round to slightly cordate, finely glandular dentate, deep green and glossy above, underside lighter, midrib yellow, glabrous, petiole 6–10 mm long; male catkins golden-yellow, 3–5 cm long, stamens 5–12, long pubescent to the middle, female catkins 3–6 cm long, ovary glabrous, flowers first appearing in May–June, after the leaves (!); the seeds persist over winter in the capsule. CS 4; HM 453; HF 916; CSI 4; GPN 229 (= *S. laurifolia* Wesm.). Europe to Caucasus. Cultivated for ages. z5 Plate 94, 98; Fig. 199.

S. petiolaris Sm. Low shrub, shoots thin, quickly becoming glabrous, purple; leaves lanceolate, 4–8 cm long, long acuminate, finely serrate, base cuneate, silky pubescent when young, but quickly becoming glabrous, petiole 4–10 mm long; flowers appearing with the leaves, on short, foliate shoots, male catkins 1–2 cm long, female to 4 cm in fruit, capsule ovate, narrowing to the apex, pubescent, stigma nearly sessile. BB 599. Eastern N. America. See also: **S. gracilis**. z2 Fig. 210.

S. petrophila Rydb. Dwarf shrub, creeping to 10 cm high; leaves obovate to elliptic or oblanceolate, 1–3 cm long, obtusish, entire, base cuneate, bright green above, underside somewhat lighter and with distinctly reticulate venation, totally glabrous or also somewhat silky when young, petiole 3–6 mm long; catkins on foliate shoots, 2–3 cm long, scales obovate, blackish, somewhat silky pubescent, style distinct, 0.5 mm long, stigma elongated, capsule sessile, white pubescent. Mountains of western N. America. 1922. z4

S. phylicifolia L. Bushy, upright shrub, usually not over 1–2 m high, seasonal growth short, pubescent only when young, later yellow-brown and glossy; leaves tough, elliptic-obovate to lanceolate, 3–5(8) cm long, acute, entire to crenate, base cuneate to round, bright green above, glossy, blue-green to gray-green beneath, glabrous, petiole about 1 cm long, stipules subcordate; catkins appearing before or with the leaves, male to 2.5 cm long, female to 6 cm long in fruit, stamens 2, filaments glabrous, anthers yellow, later reddish, ovaries oval-conical, pubescent. GPN 225; CS 19; CSI 45; HM 462 (= *S. weigeliana* Willd.). Europe to NE. Asia. 1809. Moist sites in the mountains and on the plains. z4 Plate 94; Fig. 199.

S. polaris Wahlenb. Polar Willow. Creeping, dwarf shrub, 3–5 cm high; leaves rounded-elliptic, 7–10 mm long, somewhat emarginate, otherwise usually entire, bright green above, lighter beneath and reticulately veined; catkins small, ovate, terminal on small lateral shoots, male catkins with 2 stamens, female with pubescent ovaries. PAr 131; MG 25: 141; ASA 5; CSI 69. Arctic Europe and Asia. 1910. Difficult to cultivate. z1 Fig. 211.

S. pomeranica see: **S. daphnoides** var. **pomeranica**

S. × pontederana Schleich. (*S. cinerea* × *S. purpurea*). Medium-sized to tall shrub, shoots velvety pubescent when young, later glabrous; leaves obovate-lanceolate, 4–8(10) cm long, to 3 cm wide, serrate toward the apex, both sides appressed pubescent when young, later glabrous and somewhat glossy above, deep green, blue-green and more or less silky pubescent beneath; flowers appearing before the leaves, March; catkins always foliate at the base, bracts lanceolate, stamen filaments connate to the middle, anthers reddish at first, later yellow, ovaries stalked, silky tomentose, style very short or sessile. CS 26 (= *S. sordida* Kern.). Europe; cultivated since 1820. z5

S. praecox see: **S. daphnoides**

S. pruinosa see: **S. acutifolia**

S. prunifolia see: **S. arbuscula**

S. pubescens see: **S. laggeri**

S. pulchra Cham. (non Wimm. !!). Low shrub, branches procumbent or more or less ascending, dark purple-brown, glossy, leaves narrow lanceolate, 4–6 cm long, 1 cm wide, glandular serrate, glabrous on both sides, finely reticulate venation, petiole short, stipules narrow, acute, glandular serrate, much shorter than the leaf petiole; catkins 4–5 cm long, 1.5 cm wide, stalk not foliate, bracts dark, acute, ovaries silky pubescent, style long, stigma narrow, long. PAr 143; ASA 33. Arctic Asia and N. America. See also: **S. daphnoides**. z1

'Ruberrima' see: **S. daphnoides 'Ruberrima'**

S. purpurea L. Purple Willow. Medium-sized shrub, but generally not over 3 m high, shoots slender, gray, glabrous, glossy; leaves on the apical part of the shoot appearing opposite (!!), oblanceolate, 5–10 cm long, acute, base cuneate, serrate toward the apex, dull green above, lighter or bluish beneath, glabrous, without stipules; catkins sessile, slender, 1.5–3 cm long, usually

Fig. 211. *Salix polaris* (from Kerner)

Fig. 212. **Salix.** Left *S. pyrifolia;* middle *S. purpurea;* right *S. eriocephala* (from NBB)

somewhat curved, stamens 2, but the filaments totally connate (!), anthers reddish at first, later black, ovaries ovate, tomentose. BB 1180; CS 7; CSI 13; HM Pl. 79; HW 30. Europe to N. Africa. Cultivated for ages and a very useful willow. See also: **S. integra.** z5 Plate 94; Fig. 212.

ssp. **amplexicaulis** (Bory & Chaub.) Schneid. Very similar to ssp. *lambertiana,* but the leaves mostly or totally opposite, often also somewhat smaller, sessile to nearly so, base truncate to cordate, or half stem-clasping (!). CSI 37. Balkans, Asia Minor. 1904.

'**Gracilis**'. Dwarf form, finely branched and narrow leaved; female (= var. *nana* Dieck; var. *uralensis* Späth). Around 1900. Particularly useful for weaving, also for small hedges.

var. *japonica* see: **S. koriyanagi**

ssp. **lambertiana** (Sm.) A. Neumann ex Rech. f. Branches thicker; leaves only partly opposite, obovate to oblong, 4–8 times longer than wide on the long shoots, margins nearly totally serrate. CS 7 (= var. *latifolia* Kern.). Widely distributed over the range of the species, particularly in the plains.

var. *latifolia* see: ssp. **lambertiana**

var. *nana* see: '**Gracilis**'

'**Pendula**'. Branches very thin, pendulous; female (= *S. purpurea scharfenbergensis* Bolle; *S. americana pendula* De Vos). Around 1830. Switzerland.

var. *scharfenbergensis* see: '**Pendula**'

var. **sericea** (Ser.). K. Koch. Young shoots and leaf undersides silky pubescent, later glabrous.

var. *uralensis* see: '**Gracilis**'

S. pyrenaica Gouan. Dwarf shrub, 20–50 cm high, branches erect, ascending or also creeping, shoots densely foliate, pubescent in all respects when young; leaves oval-oblong, to 3 cm long, obtuse or acute, entire, both sides floccose when young, later glabrous and green on both sides, with raised reticulate venation beneath; catkins ovate, 1–1.5 cm long, June–August, scales obovate, rust-brown, white woolly, filaments glabrous, anthers yellow, style long, each arm of the branched stigma further parted, dry fruit catkins persisting over winter; only the female is found in cultivation. CS 10; Gs 5: 90; VSa 9. Pyrenees, N. slopes of the alpine regions. 1875. z6 Fig. 202.

S. pyrifolia Anderss. Tall, strong branched shrub, occasionally also a small tree, to 7 m high, annual shoots glabrous, glossy, red-brown; leaves oval-elliptic to oval-lanceolate, 4–9 cm long, acute, slightly crenate, base round to somewhat cordate, deep green above, blue-green and reticulately veined beneath, petiole 6–15 mm long; catkins appearing with the leaves, male catkins about 2 cm long, female to 7 cm long at fruiting time and rather loose, ovaries glabrous, beaked, style of medium length, stigma short and thick. BB 1201; ASA 29; SS 728 (= *S. balsamifera* Barratt). Eastern N. America. 1880. The only species with a strong balsam scent. z6 Plate 94; Fig. 199, 212.

S. pyrolifolia Ledeb. Tall shrub or tree, branches rather thick, reddish brown, smooth, glossy or with scattered

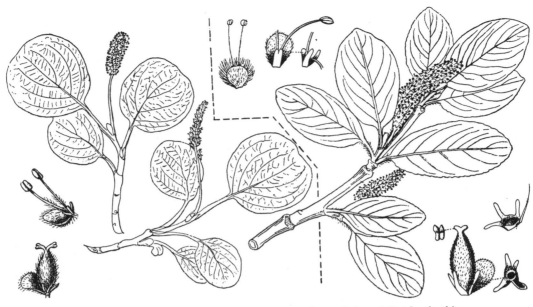

Fig. 213. **Salix.** Left *S. reticulata;* right *S. vestita* (from Guimpel, Reichenbach)

hairs; leaves to 5 cm long and 4 cm wide, ovate to more elliptic, whitish with raised venation beneath, petiole to 3 cm long, often brown or pink, as is the midrib, stipules round kidney-shaped, 1–1.5 cm wide; catkins small, with about 100 flowers, stalk very short, often nearly leafless, capsules 3–4 mm, yellow-brown, glabrous, style 1 mm, stigma short. CSI 39. N. Finland, N. Russia, Urals. z3

S. rehderiana Schneid. Shrub or small tree, to 7 m high, young shoots somewhat pubescent or glabrous, then red-brown; leaves lanceolate, 5–12 cm long, short acuminate, irregularly glandular serrate, base round to broadly cuneate, gray-white and silky beneath, or later bluish and glabrous; catkins sessile, with 2–3 leaves at the base, 2–3 cm long, scales oblong, somewhat silky, stamens 2, filaments glabrous or pubescent at the base, anthers red at first, ovaries usually glabrous, nearly sessile, April. HS 58. W. China. 1908. z6 ✧

S. repens L. Creeping Willow. Shrub, to 1 m high, branches procumbent-ascending, thin, young shoots soft pubescent at first, later brown, glabrous; leaves elliptic-lanceolate, 1.5–4(5) cm long, acute, usually recurved at the apex, entire with involuted margins, both sides silky pubescent at first, later usually totally glabrous above, with 6–8 vein pairs, petiole 2–3 mm long; catkins appearing with or shortly before the leaves, the male catkins 1–1.5 cm long, female to 5 cm long at fruiting, stamens 2, an attractive yellow, ovaries oblong-conical, pubescent. CS 14; CSI 19; HM Pl. 81; HW 123; GPN 222. Europe, Asia Minor, Siberia. Cultivated since antiquity and quite variable. z5 Fig. 199.

var. *angustifolia* see: **S. rosmarinifolia**

var. *argentea* see: **S. arenaria**

'Golden Dwarf'. Shoots ascending, an attractive red-brown; leaves a good yellow. Seedling found in France; brought into the trade by J. Legendre of Wachapreague, VA., USA. ⌀

var. *nitida* see: **S. arenaria**

var. *rosmarinifolia* see: **S. rosmarinifolia**

var. *subopposita* see: **S. subopposita**

S. reptans Rupr. Arctic Creeping Willow. Dwarf shrub, branches procumbent, eventually glabrous, green with a trace of red; leaves ovate to lanceolate, entire, 15–30 mm long, rounded to acute at the apex, cuneate at the base, both sides with persistent, long dense hair, dull green and often somewhat rugose above, gray-green with indistinctly reticulate venation beneath; catkins ovate to cylindrical, 20–45 mm long, capsule oval-conical, sessile, pubescent, style very short, stigma brown, often with long, narrow lobes. PAr 132. Arctic Asia. z1 Fig. 214.

S. reticulata L. Dwarf shrub, creeping mat-like along the ground, shoots glabrous, cylindrical, brown, winter buds large; leaves broad elliptic to broad obovate, 2–5 cm long, obtuse to emarginate, tough, entire, deep green and rugose above, gray silvery with distinctly reticulate venation beneath, petiole long, red; catkins terminal, long stalked, 2–3 cm long, cylindrical, May. CS 9; BB 1182; HM Pl. 83; GPN 218; CSI 60. Alps, N. Asia, arctic N. America. 1789. For cool sites and north exposures in the rock garden. z1 Plate 98; Fig. 213. ⌀

S. retusa L. Creeping, strong branched, ground cover willow, current year's shoots brown or more green, glabrous, finely pubescent when young; leaves clustered at the shoot tips, obovate to spathulate, 8–35 mm long, obtuse, occasionally emarginate or with a few small teeth, green on both sides, underside somewhat pubescent on the venation only when young, petiole 2–5 mm long; catkins 2 cm long, May–June, terminally arranged on foliate stalks, these on lateral shoots, scales yellowish and usually glabrous, male catkins with 2 stamens, glabrous, female with glabrous, short stalked ovaries, style short and thick. CS 8; HM 83; VSa 6; HF 948; PEu 3; CSI 64. High European mountains on chalk and rock outcrops. 1763. Easily cultivated. z1 Fig. 199.

var. *serpyllifolia* see: **S. serpyllifolia**

S. rhaetica see: **S. hegetschweileri**

S. rigida see: **S. eriocephala**

S. rosmarinifolia L. Small shrub, usually prostrate, spring growth erect, thin, often with many short shoots at the base, with scattered short hairs; leaves more or less directed upward, thin, linear-lanceolate, tapered to both ends, 2–5 cm long, 2–8 mm wide, later dark green above, persistently gray silky beneath, with 10–12 vein pairs, entire or slightly sinuate, finely glandular, leaf apex not recurved, stipules absent; catkins globose, bracts pubescent, filaments glabrous, capsule pubescent. HF 935; CSI 20 (= *S. repens* var. *rosmarinifolia* [L.] Wimm. & Grab.; *S. repens* var. *angustifolia* Neilr.; *S. friesiana* Anderss.). Central and E. Europe, westward to N. Italy, Belgium, and north to Sweden. z5 ∅

S. rostrata see: **S. bebbiana**

S. rotundifolia Trautv. Round-leaved Willow. Low shrub, spreading habit, branches and shoots lying on the ground, often very long, but not rooting, the small branchlets usually with only 4 leaves, glabrous, buds small, glabrous; leaves circular to elliptic, 5–15 mm long, base somewhat cordate, emarginate on the apex, entire or finely serrate on the basal half, glabrous, without stipules, light green with distinct reticulate venation above, 4–5 vein pairs, petiole 2–3 mm; catkins appearing with the leaves, small, usually with only 3 flowers, filaments glabrous, ovaries short stalked, style distinct, stigma thick, reddish, bract wide, yellow-green. PAr 136; ASA 6 and 7 (= *S. nummularia* Anderss.). Arctic Russia. z2 Fig. 214.

S. × rubens Schrank (*S. alba* × *S. fragilis*). Quite variable in similarity to one or the other parent, usually a medium-sized tree, 10 m high or more, branches and twigs more pendulous, young shoots not easily broken at the base; leaves lanceolate, somewhat stiff, 8–15 cm long, long and often somewhat obliquely acuminate, finely glandular serrate, bright green, bluish green beneath and silky pubescent at first, but quickly becoming glabrous; male flowers usually with 2 stamens, female flowers with short stalked, conical, glabrous ovaries (= *S. russeliana* Willd. non Sm.). Central Europe. z6

S. × rubra Huds. (*S. purpurea* × *S. viminalis*). Shrub, 1–3 m, shoots long, pubescent at first, later glabrous and yellowish; leaves lanceolate to oblanceolate, 7–15 cm long, long acuminate, eventually dull green above, underside bluish green and quickly becoming glabrous or occasionally pubescent, petiole 5–10 mm long, stipules small and quickly abscising; catkins 2–3 cm,

filaments more or less connate, anthers reddish at first, style distinct. CS 25. Europe. Important willow for basket weaving. z5

S. russeliana see: **S. × rubens**

S. sachalinensis F. Schmidt. Large shrub to small tree, young shoots thinly pubescent, later becoming glabrous; leaves lanceolate, to 14 cm long and 2.2 cm wide, dark green above, more blue-green and slightly pubescent beneath, later becoming glabrous, stipules cordate, serrate; stalk of the ovary as long as the bulb or somewhat shorter. TM 22; MJ 2019; KIF 1: 27; YWP 2: 98 (= *S. opaca* Seemen). Sachalin, Japan. 1905. z5 Plate 91.

f. *ligulata* see: **'Sekka'**

'Sekka'. Habit less vigorous, shrubby, branch tips usually fasciated, occasionally to 5 cm wide, densely covered with catkins; leaves 5–10 cm long, 1–2 cm wide, glossy green above, silvery beneath; catkins appear before the leaves, to 5 cm long, silvery, only the male known (= *S.* 'Setsuka' Hort.; *S. sachalinensis* f. *ligulata* Kimura). Frequently cultivated in Japan, also often found in the wild ("Dzyariu-yanagi" = Dragon willow). First introduced into Western cultivation by Jan Spek, Boskoop, Holland in 1950.

S. safsaf Forsk. Tall tree; leaves lanceolate, 5–10 cm long, 1–1.5 cm wide, long acuminate, base cuneate, margins finely dentate, petiole 10–15 mm long; stamens 5, pubescent on the basal half, ovaries oval-conical, glabrous, stalked, stigma nearly sessile, thick, split. TFA 28. NE. and tropical Africa. Not winter hardy! z10

S. × salamonii Carr. (*S. alba* × *S. babylonica*). Tall tree with a straight stem, branches ascending and developing a conical crown when young, twigs pendulous, but not as much or as long as *S. babylonica*, greenish; leaves similar in form, size and color to those of *S. babylonica*, but with scattered long hairs on both sides; rachis of the catkins more pubescent, bract long ciliate, only the female is known (= *S. babylonica salamonii* Carr.). Found around 1860 on the estate of the Baron de Salamon, near Manosque, Basses Alpes, France; given to the trade in 1896 by Simon-Louis, Metz, France. z5

S. salviifolia Brot. Salvia-leaved Willow. Medium-sized shrub, occasionally a tree, to 6 m high, young shoots gray tomentose and remaining so, debarked shoots with raised stripes, buds pubescent; leaves linear-lanceolate to obovate, slightly serrate, 3–5 times longer than wide, scattered pubescent above, underside densely pubescent or white tomentose; flowers appearing before the leaves, catkins elliptic, stamens 2, pubescent beneath, catkins 3–4 × 1 cm in size, capsule tomentose, style very short, stalk short. VSa 20; CSI 34. Spain, Portugal, along water courses. z7

S. sanguinea see: **S. × 'Basfordiana'**

S. savatieri see: **S. integra**

S. saximontana Rydb. Dwarf shrub, dense, carpet-form, creeping, scarcely over 5 cm high; leaves oblong or elliptic, 1.2 cm long, acute at both ends, light green above, blue-green beneath, glabrous, reticulately

Fig. 214. **Salix.** Left *S. arctica;* center *S. rotundifolia;* right *S. reptans* (from Polunin)

veined; catkins loose, fruit capsule ovate, densely gray pubescent, sessile, 3 mm long, style indistinct (= *S. aemulans* Seem.). N. America, Rocky Mts. z4

S. schraderiana see: **S. bicolor**

S. seemannii see: **S. glauca** var. **acutifolia**

S. × sepulcralis Simonk. (*S. alba* 'Tristis' × *S. babylonica*). Strong growing tree, to 20 m high, stem to 1 m thick, straight and usually very sound, branches very thin, long, pendulous, yellowish (!); leaves linear-lanceolate, glossy green above, blue-green beneath at first, remaining green until frost in the fall (!!), then gradually abscising; flowers usually male, but also abnormal catkins are often found with female and hermaphroditic flowers, these then drying brown and forming shaggy catkins which are very ornamental particularly in winter. CWE 83 (= *S. chrysocoma* Dode). Recognized by Dode as a hybrid in 1910. The variably sexed catkins were first established in 1899 by Camus. z5 Plate 74.

S. sericea Marsh. Shrub, upright, to 4 m high, annual shoots thin, reddish, soft pubescent when young; leaves lanceolate, 4–10 cm long, finely serrate, acuminate, base cuneate, both sides silky at first, later persisting only beneath, petiole 4–14 mm long, stipules narrow and abscising; catkins appear before the leaves, sessile, male about 2 cm long, stamens 2, ovaries silver-gray pubescent, stalked, stigma short, sessile. BB 1188; GSP 73 (= *S. grisea* Willd.). Eastern N. America. 1809. z4 Fig. 199, 209.

S. serpyllifolia Scop. Thyme-leaved Willow. Closely related to *S. retusa,* but yet lower and finer, stem well branched, developing a dense ground cover; leaves spathulate, 6–10 mm long, clustered nearly rosette-form at the shoot tips, 10–12 mm long in cultivation; catkins few flowered, 6–12 mm long, stalk shorter than the ventral gland. HM Pl. 82; CSI 66 (= *S. retusa* var. *serpyllifolia* [Scop.] Ser.). Alps and the mountains of SE. Europe. 1898. z6 Fig. 199.

S. 'Setsuka' see: **S. sachalinensis 'Sekka'**

S. silesiaca Willd. Silesian Willow. Shrub, to 3 m high, young shoots gray, smooth, wood without stripes; leaves oblanceolate, more or less broadly cuneate at the base, coarsely and often wavy serrate, becoming glabrous above, underside scattered pubescent, somewhat rugose, new growth blood-red (!), stipules well developed; flowers appear shortly before the leaves, stamens 2, nearly glabrous, anthers red at first, ovaries long stalked, glabrous, style distinct, stigma short, nearly undivided. CSI 38. Sudetic, Carpathian and Balkan Mts., along water courses and pools. z5

S. × simulatrix F. B. White (*S. arbuscula* × *S. herbacea*). Creeping, rather thick branched shrub, annual shoots brown, with large winter buds, somewhat pubescent only when young, then glabrous; leaves nearly circular or more ovate, 1.5–2.5 cm long, slightly crenate to nearly entire, both sides glossy dark green; catkins numerous, on foliate shoots, erect, ovaries pubescent, only the male is found in cultivation. Fs 5: 91. Switzerland, but rare. 1922. z3

S. sitchensis Bong. Tall shrub or also a small tree, to 10 m high, branches tomentose at first, becoming glabrous in the second year and then brown to orange, occasionally pruinose; leaves obovate-oblong, 5–12 cm long, acute to obtuse, entire to glandular dentate, pubescent above at first, later glabrous and glossy green, underside glossy silky tomentose, petiole to 1 cm long; catkins appear before the leaves, on short, foliate stalks, 3–5 cm long, with 1–2 stamens, filaments more or less connate, ovaries short stalked, pubescent, style short. SS 486; ASA 40; SPa 99–100. Western N. America to Alaska. 1918. z4 Plate 93; Fig. 209.

S. × smithiana Willd. (*S. caprea* × *S. viminalis*). Strong growing shrub, 4–6 m high, annual shoots rather thick and stiff, long, usually narrowly upright, very tomentose at first, later more or less glabrous, not striped under the bark; leaves oval-lanceolate, 6–12 cm long, acute, limb flat, usually rather entire, eventually glabrous and green above, underside gray, soft pubescent, reticulately veined; catkins appear before the leaves, nearly sessile, large, ovate, 3–4 cm long, scales blackish at the apex, obovate, silky, ovary tomentose, large, style as long as the stigma. CS 29; HF 927. Europe. 1829 or earlier. A good catkin effect. z5 Plate 93. ⊕

S. sordida see: **S. × pontederana**

S. spaethii see: **S. microstachya**

S. speciosa see: **S. × alopecuroides**

S. starkeana Willd. Low shrub, rarely over 1 m high, branches ascending, thin, glabrous in the first year, buds appressed, greenish orange, flat on the apex; leaves broad lanceolate to ovate, obovate, reddish and slightly pubescent when young, later glabrous, bright green and glossy above, underside gray-green with raised venation, margins glandular serrate, with 5–7 vein pairs, stipules developed, half-kidney-shaped, petiole to 5 mm long; flowers appear before the leaves, stamens 2, filaments glabrous, ovaries long stalked, pubescent, style distinct, stigma parted. CSI 30. N. and central Europe, to N. Ukraine and central Russia. z5 Fig. 207.

S. × stipularis Sm. (*S. atrocinerea* × *S. viminalis* ?). Large, upright shrub, 3–5 m high, shoots with a persistent tomentum (!), brown in winter, striped under the bark; leaves lanceolate, 8–18 cm long, tapered to the apex, margins somewhat undulate and entire to indistinctly crenate, eventually glabrous above, underside more or less silvery silky, stipules large, to 2.5 cm long (!), at least on the long shoots; catkins appearing before the leaves, nearly sessile, thick, to 4 cm long, densely silky, ovaries tomentose, style long, stigma linear, undivided, only the female is known. CS 29. Europe. 1829. z6 Plate 93.

S. stipulifera see: **S. glauca** var. **acutifolia**

S. subopposita Miq. Small, low growing shrub, to 30 cm high, nest form, with many thin, erect shoots, these densely gray pubescent when young; leaves broad lanceolate to narrow oblong, 2.5–4 cm long, 5–12 mm wide, acute, entire, glabrous and blue-green above, underside with a loose gray-yellow appressed pubescence, denser when young, petiole 1–5 mm long; male catkins to 2.7 cm long, 7 mm wide, very densely arranged, female 1–2 cm long, 8–10 mm wide in fruit (= *S. repens* var. *subopposita* [Miq.] Seem.). Japan, Korea. z5 ⊕

S. syrticola Fern. To 2 m high, loose shrub, shoots silky pubescent; leaves ovate-oblong, 4–9 cm long, finely glandular serrate, rather abruptly acuminate on the apical half (!), both sides densely silky long haired, whitish, petiole about 6 mm long, stipules large; catkins appearing with the leaves, distinctly stalked and with small leaves at the base (!), female catkins 6–8 cm long. Rho 1001–1002 (= *S. adenophylla* Hort. non Hook.). Northeastern N. America. 1913. z5 Plate 94; Fig. 210.

S. tenuifolia see: **S. × tetrapla**

S. × tetrapla J. Walker (*S. myrsinifolia* × *S. phylicifolia*). Tall shrub, occurring with the parents and quite variable; leaves more or less pubescent when young, leaf form intermediate between the parents, dry leaves becoming black, leaflike stipules usually present; filaments shaggy pubescent at the base, ovaries often only partly pubescent (= *S. tenuifolia* Sm.). Europe. 1829. z5

S. thunbergiana see: **S. gracilistyla**

S. treviranii see: **S. mollissima**

S. triandra L. Almond-leaved Willow. Shrub or tree, 1–4(10) m high, bark exfoliating in thin plates (nearly like *Platanus*), young shoots somewhat pubescent at first, then glabrous and red-brown; leaves lanceolate, 5–10 cm long, acuminate, finely serrate, base cuneate to round, dark green and glossy above, bluish or green beneath, glabrous, stipules subcordate; catkins on foliate twigs, late, April–May, 3–7 cm long, male catkins with 3 stamens, anthers golden-yellow, filaments pubescent on the base, ovaries distinctly stalked, glabrous, style very short. CS 5–6; HW 2: 29; HF 919; CSI 5 and 6 (= *S. amygdalina* L.). Distributed nearly from Europe to Japan. One of the more important willows, cultivated for ages for basket weaving. z5 Plate 94; Fig. 199.

Many races and forms of this species are known.

S. × tsugaluensis Koidz. (*S. integra* × *S. vulpina*). Shrub, branches yellow-green; leaves lanceolate, 7.5–10 cm long, to 3.5 cm wide, green above, silvery beneath; catkins appear before the leaves, silvery, scales brown. Japan. z6

'Ginme'. New growth reddish; catkins an attractive silvery, only the female is known. Japanese cultivar. Distributed by Jan Spek of Boskoop, Holland around 1950 as *S*. 'Ginme'.

S. undulata see: **S. × lanceolata** and **S. mollissima**

S. uva-ursi Pursh. Bearberry Willow. Procumbent, mat form shrub, shoots usually short and brown, glabrous; leaves elliptic-obovate, 5–25 mm long, obtuse to acute, entire or somewhat dentate, glossy above, underside usually glabrous, bluish, tough, distinct reticulate venation, petiole 2–4 mm long; catkins about 1 cm long, the female 1–4 cm long at fruiting, scales obovate, pink at the apex, silky pubescent, stamens only 1(2), style short. PAr 139; BB 1205 (= *S. cutleri* Tuckerm.). Arctic Canada, W. Greenland. 1880. z1 Fig. 206.

S. vestita Pursh. Dwarf shrub, similar to *S. reticulata*, but erect, 0.5–1 m, young shoots soft pubescent; leaves entire, long petioled, obovate to elliptic, 2–5 cm long, obtuse to emarginate, pubescent beneath, base broadly cuneate, finely crenate, both sides silky pubescent at first, later dark green and rugose above, underside silvery silky tomentose; catkins on foliate shoots, 3–4 cm long. BB 1185; PAr 134. Eastern N. America, also in the Rocky Mts., Altai and Baikal Mts. z4 Fig. 213.

S. viminalis L. Hemp Willow. Usually long branched, tall shrubs, 3–4 m high, young shoots densely pubescent, as are the buds; leaves linear-lanceolate, 10–25 cm long, widest below the middle, then gradually acuminate, entire, margins somewhat involuted, dark green above, underside silky silver-gray, petiole 4–12 mm long; catkins nearly sessile, scales obovate, black-brown, pubescent, stamens 2, distinct, anthers golden-yellow, later brown, ovary conical, pubescent, short stalked, style long. BB 1194; CSI 9; CS 21; HM Pl. 80; HW 112. Europe to NE. Asia and Himalayas. Cultivated since antiquity for basket making and comprising many races. See also: **S. kinuyanagi.** z4 Plate 93.

'Cinnamomea'. Brown Hemp Willow. Branches very long and red-brown. Old cultivar.

'Gigantea' (Harms). Giant Hemp Willow. Branches to 4 m long.

'Regalis'. Yellow Hemp Willow. Annual growth to 3 m long. Already widely cultivated before 1887.

S. violacea see: **S. acutifolia**

S. waldsteiniana Willd. Low, well branched shrub, bark gray, shoots glabrous, yellow-green, buds small; leaves elliptic, 3–5 cm long, nearly entire to crenate serrate, with many lateral veins; flowers appearing with the leaves, stamens 2, glabrous, catkins short stalked and with a few leaves, ovaries short stalked, pubescent, style long, stigma short, parted. CSI 49. E. Alps, NW. Balkans. z5 ✤

S. wehrhahnii see: **S. hastata 'Wehrhahnii'**

S. weigeliana see: **S. phylicifolia**

S. wilhelmsiana Bieb. Large, but graceful shrub, young shoots very thin and flexible, often nearly spreading at right angles, more or less silky pubescent, occasionally nearly glabrous; leaves linear, 2–6 cm long, 5–10 mm wide, entire to finely glandular serrate, both sides densely silky pubescent, later becoming more or less glabrous, petiole very short, stipules usually absent; catkins on foliate stalks, 2–3 cm, slender, anthers yellow, ovaries densely silky pubescent, stigma sessile (= *S. angustifolia* Willd. non Wulf.). Caucasus to E. Asia. 1887. z5

S. × wimmeriana Gren. & Godr. (*S. purpurea* × *S. caprea*). Tall shrub, young shoots thin, gray pubescent, later glabrous and glossy; leaves oblong to lanceolate, finely and irregularly serrate, silky pubescent at first, then glabrous, deep green above, underside more gray to blue-green; catkins nearly sessile, filaments connate at the base and somewhat long haired, stigma oblong, nearly sessile. CS 26 (= *S. daphnoides* × *S. elaeagnos*). Europe. 1872. Not to be confused with *S.* × *wimmeri* Kern. z4

S. xerophila Flod. Medium tall, bushy shrub, abundantly branched, bark gray, shoots finely pubescent; leaves oblong-obovate, dentate, finely scattered pubescent, stipules well developed; flowers appear shortly before

the leaves, elliptic, sessile, stamens 2, pubescent at the base, ovary stalked, pubescent, style distinct, stigma parted and deeply incised. CSI 29. Lapland to Ural Mts., on rather dry sites. z3 Fig. 204.

S. yezoalpina Koidz. Low shrub, branches lying on the ground and rooting, somewhat pubescent when young, later purple-brown; leaves elliptic to circular, 2–4.5 cm long, 1–3.5 cm wide, usually entire, silky pubescent when young, base broadly cuneate to nearly cordate, blue-green beneath with reticulate venation; male catkins 1.5–3 cm long, densely flowered, female catkins becoming 5 cm long after flowering, fruit capsule nearly sessile, glabrous, style slender, as is the stigma, stigma parted, filaments glabrous, July. Japan; Hokkaido, in the higher mountains. z5

By far most willows prefer or at least tolerate moist soils; they will also thrive, however, in any good garden soil with sufficient moisture. The species with gray to white tomentum on both sides of the leaves prefer dry sites. The dwarf alpine willows are best suited for rock garden culture which most simulates their mountain habitat.

Lit. Anderson, J. N.: Salices boreali-americanae; a Synopsis of North American willows; Cambridge 1858 (32 pp.) ● Ball, C. R.: New or little known west America Willows; Univ. Calif. Publ. Bot. **17**, 399–434, 1934 ● Camus, A., & E.-G. Camus: Classification des Saules d'Europe et monographie des Saules de France; Paris 1904 (386 pp.; including an atlas with 40 plates) ● Forbes: Salicetum Woburnense; London 1829 (294 pp., 140 plates) ● Hao, K.-Sh.: Synopsis of Chinese *Salix*; Berlin 1936 (123 pp., 44 plates) ● Hoffmann, G. F.: Historia Salicum iconibus illustrata; Leipzig 1785–1791 (2 vols., 80 pp., 109 plates) ● Schneider, C.: Notes on American Willows; in Bot. Gaz. **66**, 117–142, 318–353, 1918; **67**, 27–64, 309–396, 1919; continued in Journ. Arnold Arb. **1**, 1–32, 67–97, 147–171, 211–232, 1919; **2**, 1 to 25, 65–90, 185–204, 1920; **3**, 61–125, 1921 ● Seemen, O. v.: *Salix*; in Ascherson & Graebner, Synopsis Mitteleur. Fl. **4**, 54–350, 1908 ● Vicioso, C.: Salicaceas de España; Madrid 1951 (131 pp., 28 plates) ● Wimmer, F.: Salices Europaeae; Bratislava 1866 (288 pp., text in Latin; with a complete list of the older *Salix* literature) ● Kimura, A.: Symbolae Iteologicae; in Sci. Rep. Tôhoku Univ., 4th series, to 1961 published in 18 parts (only a few parts seen by the author) ● Meyer, F. G.: Identification of some willow (*Salix*) cultivars from Japan; Baileya **10**, 19 to 20, 1962 ● Rechinger, K. H.: *Salix*; in Flora Europaea I, 43–54, 1964 ● Mang, F.: Zur Kenntnis der gegenwärtigen Vertreter der *Salix*-Section *Incubaceae* Dumortier und ihrer häufigsten Bastarde in Schleswig-Holstein, Hamburg and the adjacent districts; Kiel 1962 ● Argus, G. W.: The genus *Salix* in Alaska and Yukon; Nat. Sci. Publ. Bot. **2**, 1–279; Ottawa 1973 ● Raup, H. M.: The willows of the boreal Western America; in Contr. Gray Herb. **185**, 1–95, 1959 ● Chmelar, J.: Iconographia Salicis generis, I; Brno 1975 ● Chmelar, J., & W. Meusel: Die Weiden Europas; Wittenberg 1976 (143 pp.).

Plate 113

Sorbaronia fallax
in the Wageningen Arboretum, Holland

Sorbaria arborea
in the Göteborg Botanic Garden, Sweden

Sorbaria sorbifolia in the Dortmund Botanic Garden, W. Germany

Plate 114

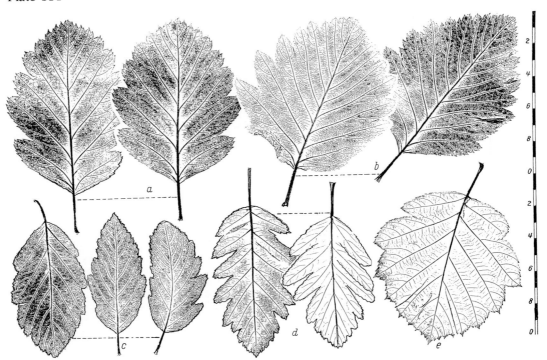

Sorbus (I). a. *S. intermedia*; b. *S. austriaca*; c. *S. minima*; d. *S. arranensis*; e. *S. latifolia*

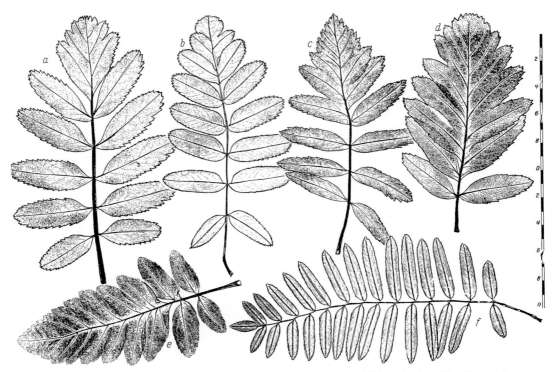

Sorbus (II). a. *S.* × *meinichii*; b. *S.* × *thuringiaca* 'Decurrens'; c. *S.* × *thuringiaca* 'Neuillyensis';
d. *S. hybrida*; e. *S.* × *thuringiaca* 'Fastigiata'; f. *S. scalaris*

Plate 115

Sorbus. a. *S. esserteauiana* 'Flava'; b. *S. sargentiana*; c. *S. occidentalis*; d. *S. insignis*; e. *S. tianshanica*

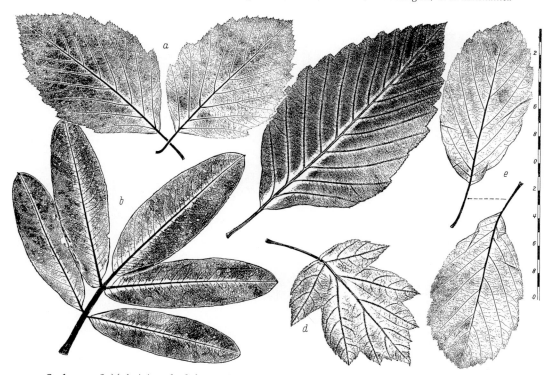

Sorbus. a. *S.* × *decipiens*; b. *S. harrowiana*; c. *S. cuspidata*; d. *S. torminalis*; e. *S.* × *paucicrenata*

Plate 116

Sorbus americana
in the Uppsala Botanic Garden, Sweden

Sorbus aria 'Majestica'
in the Uppsala Botanic Garden, Sweden

Sorbus alnifolia in the Charlottenlund Arboretum, Denmark

Plate 117

Sorbus aucuparia 'Fastigiata'
in the Dortmund Botanic Garden, W. Germany

Sorbus commixta
in the Dortmund Botanic Garden, W. Germany

Sorbus esserteauiana 'Flava'
in the Dortmund Botanic Garden, W. Germany

Sorbus gracilis (grafted on a standard)
in the Dortmund Botanic Garden, W. Germany

Plate 118

Sorbus koehneana
in the Dortmund Botanic Garden, W. Germany

Sorbus megalocarpa
in the Rowallane Park, N. Ireland

Sorbus 'Mitchellii'
in RHS Gardens, Wisley, England

Sorbus reducta
in the Dortmund Botanic Garden, W. Germany

Plate 119

Sorbus thomsonii
in RHS Gardens, Wisley, England

Sorbus vestita
in RHS Gardens, Wisley, England

Sorbus rufo-ferruginea in Japan
Photo: Dr. Watari, Tokyo

Plate 120

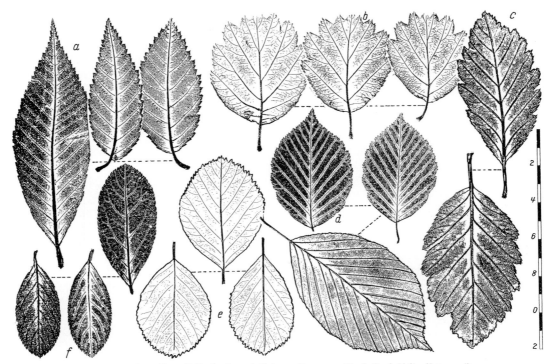

Sorbus. a. *S. meliosmifolia;* b. *S. umbellata;* c. *S. mougeotii;* d. *S. alnifolia* (2 types!);
e. *S. umbellata* var. *cretica;* f. *S. chamaemespilus*

Sorbopyrus auricularis
in Geisenheim Arboretum, W. Germany

Spiraea cana
in the Munich Botanic Garden, W. Germany

Plate 121

Spiraea bullata
in the Dortmund Botanic Garden, W. Germany

Spiraea bumalda 'Coccinea'

Spiraea × *vanhouttei*

Plate 122

Spiraea cantoniensis
in Taranto Gardens, Pallanza, Italy

Spiraea × arguta
Photo: Archivbild

Spiraea japonica 'Macrophylla'
in the Dortmund Botanic Garden, W. Germany

Spiraea nipponica
in the Dortmund Botanic Garden, W. Germany

Plate 123

Spiraea japonica in its habitat
Photo: Dr. S. Watari, Tokyo

Spiraea × *sanssouciana* (BM 5169)   *Spiraea douglasii* (BM 5151)

Plate 124

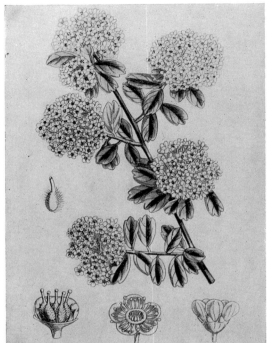

Spiraea wilsonii (BM 8399)

Spiraea nipponica var. *rotundifolia* (BM 7429)

Spiraea veitchii (BM 8383)

Spiraea henryi (BM 8270)

Plate 125

Syringa 'Monique Lemoine'
in the Lilac Park, Aalsmeer, Holland

Syringa 'Primrose'

Streptosolen jamesonii
in a park in Spain

Sutherlandia frutescens in the
Harrismith Botanic Garden, S. Africa

Plate 126

Telopea speciosissima
in the Royal Botanic Gardens, Kew, England

Ulmus elegantissima 'Jacqueline Hillier'
in the Hillier Arboretum, England

Tibouchina urvilleana
in the Dortmund Botanic Garden, W. Germany

Vaccinium vitis-idaea 'Koralle'
at J. D. zu Jeddeloh Nursery, W. Germany

Plate 127

Vitis vinifera 'Purpurea'
in the Mount Usher Park, Ireland

Vestia lycioides
in the Herbert Park, Llanover, Wales

Vella pseudocytisus in its native habitat
in the Sierra Nevada, Spain

Vaccinium nummularia
in the Royal Botanic Garden, Edinburgh, Scotland

Plate 128

Weigela maximowiczii
in the Dortmund Botanic Garden, W. Germany

Wisteria venusta
in a garden in southern England

Wisteria floribunda 'Macrobotrys'
in the Herbert Garden in Llanover, Wales

Zauschneria californica
in the Dortmund Botanic Garden, W. Germany

SAMBUCUS L. — Elderberry — CAPRIFOLIACEAE

Deciduous shrubs or small trees, occasionally perennials, branches thick, with a solid pith; leaves opposite, odd pinnate, pinnae equal, serrate; flowers in broad corymbs or panicles, corolla rotate, on the mentioned species all evenly 5 parted; stamens 5, style 3 parted; fruit a berrylike drupe with 3–5 nutlets. — About 40 species in the temperate and subtropical zones of both hemispheres.

Outline of the Most Important Species

Section **Ebulus** Spach
  Plants only herbaceous; inflorescence umbrella form:
        S. ebulus L. (not covered in this work)

Section **Eusambucus** Spach
  Inflorescence umbrella form, flat; pith of the twigs white; fruit black or deep purple, occasionally whitish or greenish;

  ★ Fruits not blue pruinose;

    x Leaflets usually 5; fruits black; branches distinctly covered with lenticels:
        S. nigra

    xx Leaflets usually 7; fruits dark purple; branches only slightly covered with lenticels:
        S. canadensis

  ★★ Fruits blue pruinose:
        S. glauca

Section **Botryosambucus** Spach
  Inflorescence panicle-like, branches opposite or alternate; pith of the twigs usually brown;

  ★ Fruit black, occasionally reddish brown; inflorescences corymbose, about as wide as high:
        S. melanocarpa

  ★★ Fruit scarlet or red, occasionally yellow:
    x Inflorescence corymbose, about as wide as high, the branches ascending; pith white or pale brown at first:

        S. microbotrys

    xx Inflorescences few-flowered, ovate, the branches ascending or recurved; pith brown;

      + Inflorescences compact, the basal arms usually recurved, only about 5 mm long; plants glabrous:
        S. racemosa

      ++ Inflorescence rather loose, the basal arms outspread, 5–15 mm long;

        * Plants more or less soft pubescent, leaflets rather coarsely serrate; fruits 4–5 mm thick:
        S. pubens

        ** Plants glabrous; leaflets densely and finely serrate, long acuminate; fruits about 3 mm thick:
        S. sieboldiana

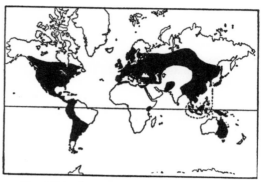

Fig. 215. Range map of the genus *Sambucus*

Sambucus californica see: **S. glauca** var. **velutina**

S. callicarpa Greene. Closely related to *S. microbotrys*, but to 3 m high, pith of the current year's shoots yellowish, yellow-brown in the second year, new growth appears in late March; leaflets 5–7, narrow, oblong-lanceolate, to 10 cm long, 2 cm wide, nearly sessile, scabrous serrate; slightly pubescent beneath when young; inflorescences somewhat larger, in flattened-cupulate panicles, yellowish white, April; fruits scarlet-red, 5 mm thick. MD 1909: Pl. (8). Western USA. 1900. Often incorrectly labeled in cultivation. z6 Fig. 216. ⚭

S. canadensis L. Shrub, 3–4 m high, stoloniferous (!), branches with only a few lenticels; leaflets usually 7, ovate, short stalked, elliptic to lanceolate, 5–15 cm long, scabrous serrate, light green above, slightly soft pubescent beneath, basal leaflets occasionally somewhat lobed; inflorescences 20–25 cm wide, somewhat vaulted (!), yellowish white, June–July; fruit purple-black, 4–5 mm thick. BB 3432; NBB 3: 296; GSP 465; MD 1909: 36a. N. America. 1761. z4 Fig. 216, 217. ⊕

'Aurea'. Shoots light green; leaves golden-yellow; fruits light red, good tasting (= f. *delicatissima* Scherw.). 1902. ⊘

'Acutiloba' (Ellw. & Barry). Thin branched; leaflets finely divided, symmetrical, very dark green. 1902. ⊘

'Chlorocarpa'. Leaves light yellowish green; fruits pale green when ripe (= 'Speer's Elderberry'). Disseminated around 1911 from the Agr. Exp. Station, Brooking, South Dakota, USA.

f. *delicatissima* see: **'Aurea'**

'Maxima' (Hesse). Very strong growing; inflorescences 30–40 cm wide (= *S. pubens* var. *maxima* Hesse). 1898. ⊘ ⊕⚭

'Rubra'. Fruits light red. 1932. ⚭

'Speer's Elderberry' see: **'Chlorocarpa'**

var. **submollis** Rehd. Leaflets with a persistent soft pubescence beneath, above only along the midrib. USA; Illinois to Texas. 1911.

S. coerulea see: **S. glauca**

S. ebulus L. Dwarf Elder. Perennial! HM Pl. 250; PEu 133. Europe, N. Africa, Asia Minor to Iran. Not covered here.

S. × fontenaysii Carr. (*S. glauca × S. nigra*). Intermediate between the parents, strong growing, pith of the young shoots white; leaves bluish green, widely and only slightly serrate, petiole with flat arching protuberances (!); inflorescences large, buds reddish, May, but often flowering again in summer; fruit black, dense blue pruinose. Originated around 1865 by Billard in Fontenay-aux-Roses, near Paris. z6 ⚭

S. glauca Nutt. Tree-like in its habitat, only 2–3 m high in cultivation, branches rather thin, somewhat bluish pruinose at first; leaflets usually 5–7, glabrous, oblong to more lanceolate, 6–16 cm long, bright bluish green, coarsely serrate; flowers yellowish white, in somewhat vaulted, 10–15 cm wide inflorescences, June–July; fruit blue-black, very pruinose, 4 mm thick. SPa 207; NF 5: 21; SS 222; Fs 5: 181 (= *S. coerulea* Raf.). Western N. America. 1850. z6 Fig. 218. ⚭

var. **neomexicana** A. Nelson. Leaflets only 3–5, narrow lanceolate, more gray-green, underside and petiole sparsely pubescent, eventually nearly glabrous; fruits very pruinose; SH 2: 635 (= *S. intermedia* Carr.). Arizona to New Mexico. 1875. Fig. 216. ⚭

var. **velutina** Johnst. Young shoots and young leaves densely and short whitish pubescent, otherwise like the species (= *S. velutina* Durand; *S. californica* K. Koch). California. Around 1870. z9 ⚭

S. intermedia see: **S. glauca** var. **neomexicana**

S. kamtschatica E. Wolf. Closely related to *S. racemosa*, but shorter; leaflets elliptic, rounded at the apex with a small protruding tip, finely serrate; inflorescence pubescent, usually wider than high, petals much longer than the tube, conspicuously toothed (!), pistil long; berries red, small. MD 1923; 32–33. Kamchatka; Transbaikal. 1923. z4 Fig. 216. ⚭

S. melanocarpa Gray. Shrub, to 4 m high, branches red-brown, pith white to pale brown in the first year, darker in the 2nd year; leaflets 5–7, long stalked, oblong-lanceolate, 8–15 cm long, coarsely serrate, dark green, pubescent beneath at first, later glabrous; flowers yellowish white, in 5–7 cm wide, hemispherical inflorescences, July to August; fruits black (!), 6 mm thick, in ovate (!) fruit clusters. MD 1909; 45 (= *S. racemosa* var. *melanocarpa* McMinn). Western N. America. 1894. z6 Fig. 216. ⚭

'Fuerstenbergii' (Schwer.). Fruits red-brown, otherwise like the species. Found in British Columbia. 1903.

S. microbotrys Rydb. Low shrub, scarcely 2 m high, bark light brown, pith white at first; leaflets 5–7, nearly sessile, oval-lanceolate, 5–10 cm long, scabrous serrate, long acuminate, light green, glabrous; flowers whitish, in nearly hemispherical, about 5 cm wide umbellate panicles, June–July; fruits scarlet to orange-red, 4 mm thick. MD 1909: 44. SW. USA. 1900. z6 Fig. 216. ⚭

S. nigra L. Black Elder. Shrub or small tree, to 6 m high, bark deeply furrowed, corky, branches gray, densely covered with large lenticels, pith white; leaflets usually 5, acute to elliptic, 10–15 cm long, dark green above,

Fig. 216. **Sambucus**, fruit clusters. a. *S. canadensis*; b. *S. glauca* var. *neomexicana*; c. *S. melanocarpa*; d. *S. callicarpa*; e. *S. racemosa*; f. *S. pubens*; g. *S. microbotrys*; h. flowers of *S. kamtschatica* (from Schwerin, Wolf)

Fig. 217. *Sambucus canadensis* (from Bailey)

Fig. 218. *Sambucus glauca* (from Sudworth)

lighter and somewhat pubescent beneath, crushed leaves unpleasant smelling; flowers yellowish white, in 10–20 cm wide, flat inflorescences, fragrant, June–July, fruits red at first, then black, glossy, 6–8 mm thick. HM Pl. 250; HF 1908. Europe, Caucasus, Asia Minor, Armenia, W. Siberia. Cultivated since antiquity. Ⓕ Germany, Austria, Holland, France. z6 Fig. 219. ⊕ ⅋ ✄

Outline of the Cultivars

1. Deviant habit

    Habit dense and low:
    'Nana', 'Dwarf Form'

    Weeping habit:
    'Pendula'

    Narrowly columnar habit:
    'Pyramidalis'

2. Differing in leaf color

    Leaves totally yellow:
    'Aurea'

    Leaves yellow speckled:
    'Luteovariegata'

    Leaves with yellow margins:
    'Aureomarginata'

    Leaves totally fine, white pulverulent:
    'Albopunctata'

    Leaves totally purple-brown:
    'Purpurea'

3. Differing in leaf form

    Leaflets with 3–4 crenate indentations on either side:
    'Latisecta'

    Leaflets regularly and deeply incised:
    'Laciniata'

    Leaflets irregularly incised, also partly filamentous:
    'Linearis'

    Leaflets linear, without incisions:
    'Hessei'

    Leaflets nearly circular, usually 3:
    'Rotundifolia'

4. Flowers differing

    Flowers turning pink:
    'Roseiflora'

    Flowers double:
    'Plena'

5. Differing in fruit color

    Berries green:
    'Viridis'

    Berries white:
    'Alba'

'Alba' Fruits dull white, somewhat translucent (= f. *leucocarpa* Hayne; f. *albo-pellucida* van Houtte). Around 1650. ⅋

f. *albo-pellucida* see: **'Alba'**

'Albopunctata'. Somewhat less vigorous than the species; leaves pure white pulverulent, marbled and finely striped, consistent, new growth often soft pink (= f. *tricolor* Zab.; f. *pulverulenta* Sweet; f. *nana bicolor* Hesse). England. Around 1740. ∅

'Albovariegata'. Leaves coarsely white speckled. England. 1770.

f. *argenteomarginata* see: **'Marginata'**

'Aurea'. Leaves golden-yellow, petiole more or less red. Gw 2: 565. England. 1826. ∅

'Aureomarginata'. Leaflets yellow margined.

f. *aureovariegata* see: **'Luteovariegata'**

f. *cannabinifolia* see: **'Laciniata'**

f. *chlorocarpa* see: **'Viridis'**

f. *dissecta* see: **'Linearis'**

'Dwarf Form'. Only about 30 cm high, shoots short and dense; leaves small, trifoliate, leaflets round.

f. *fastigiata* see: **'Pyramidalis'**

f. *filicifolia* see: **'Linearis'**

'Hessei'. Habit somewhat nodding; leaflets nearly sessile, to 12 cm long and 5 mm wide, linear, without lobes and teeth, margins slightly undulate, dark green and very glossy above. Originated by Herm. A. Hesse, Weener, W. Germany. ∅

f. *heterophylla* see: **'Linearis'**

'Laciniata'. Leaflets regularly (!) and deeply incised, without filamentous leaflets. SH 2: 408a (= f. *cannabinifolia* Kirchn.). Germany. 1650. Plate 99. ∅

'Latisecta' (Hesse). Leaflets 4–5 crenate on either side, similar to oak leaves, dark green. Developed before 1909 by Hesse, Weener, W. Germany. ∅

f. *leucocarpa* see: **'Alba'**

Fig. 219. *Sambucus nigra*. Inflorescence, individual flowers and fruits (from Berg & Schmidt)

'Linearis'. Leaflets unequal (!) and incised nearly to the midrib, many leaflets reduced nearly to a filamentous remnant. Gs 238: 7 (= f. *dissecta* K. Koch; f. *filicifolia* Kache; f. *heterophylla* Schwer.). Germany. 1853. Plate 99. ∅

'Luteovariegata'. Leaves dark golden-yellow at first, later light yellow speckled and striped (= f. *aureovariegata* Dipp.). France 1770.

'Marginata'. Leaflets with broad golden-yellow margins at first, but later paling to white-yellow (= f. *argenteomarginata* Kirchn.). England. 1846. Very common form.

'Nana' (Schwer.). Very slow growing, globose, open branched, about 1 m high (= f. *pumila* Barbier). Germany. 1907.

f. *nana bicolor* see: **'Albopunctata'**

'Pendula'. Branches lying flat on the ground, but vigorous, a weeping form normally grafted on a high standard. France in 1884.

'Plena'. Flowers semidouble, otherwise like the species. Germany. 1847. ⊕

f. *pulverulenta* see: **'Albopunctata'**

f. *pumila* see: **'Nana'**

'Purpurea'. Foliage metallic purple-bronze, with scattered green specks; flowers with a pink trace particularly in bud, anthers pink. Found in Yorkshire, England in 1954 but the actual place of origin is unknown. Plate 74. ∅

'Pyramidalis'. Columnar upright habit, slow growing, very thickly branched, bark very furrowed; leaves much smaller, crispate (= f. *pyramidata* Lav.; f. *fastigiata* Beckett; f. *stricta* Lav.). Germany. 1865. Plate 99.

f. *pyramidata* see: **'Pyramidalis'**

'Roseiflora'. Flowers single, turning a light pink. France. 1877.

'Rotundifolia'. Rather slow growing; leaflets usually trifoliate, short and wide, ovate to round, pure green; inflorescences less abundantly flowered. HM 6: 1; 130; SH 2: 408b (= f. *trifoliata* Dipp.; *S. rotundifolia* Lodd.). England. 1830.

f. *stricta* see: **'Pyramidalis'**

f. *tricolor* see: **'Albopunctata'**

f. *trifoliata* see: **'Rotundifolia'**

'Viridis'. Habit normal; leaves and the whole inflorescence light green; fruits light green, whitish striped, eventually translucent. HM Pl. 250; MD 1909: 8 (Pl.) (= f. *chlorocarpa* Hayne). Switzerland. Known since 1650. ⊗

S. pubens Michx. Shrub, to 4 m high, also a small tree in its habitat, young shoots yellowish brown, finely pubescent when young, as are the young leaves; leaflets 5–7, long-ovate to oblong-lanceolate, 5–10 cm long, serrate, soft pubescent beneath, occasionally also eventually nearly glabrous; inflorescences taller than wide, major rays straight (not curved like the very similar *S. racemosa*), flowers loosely arranged, yellowish white, spent flowers becoming brown, June–July; fruits a good scarlet-red, 5 mm thick. MD 1909: 44; BB 3433; GSP 467. N. America, in moist forests. 1812. Fig. 216. ⊗

'Dissecta'. Leaflets deeply and regularly incised. 1815.

'Leucocarpa'. Fruits white. 1841. ⊗

var. *maxima* see: **S. canadensis 'Maxima'**

'Xanthocarpa'. Fruits amber-yellow. 1891. ⚭

S. racemosa L. European Red Elder. Upright shrub, 2–3 m high, occasionally higher, branches thin, smooth, pith light brown (!), new growth appears very early; leaflets 5, ovate, nearly sessile, 4–8 cm long, scabrous and coarsely serrate; flowers yellow-green, in dense, ovate, 4–6 cm long panicles, rays bowed (see *S. pubens*), April–May; fruits 5 mm thick, scarlet-red. HM Pl. 250; PEu 134. Europe, Asia Minor to N. China; shady forests and forest perimeters. Cultivated through the ages. Ⓕ Tyrol. Fig. 216, 220.

'Goldenlocks'. Seedling of 'Plumosa Aurea', but only about 75 cm high; leaves yellow, deeply incised, retains color well in full sun. Introduced in 1971 by W. L. Kerr, Sutherland, Saskatoon, Saskatchewan, Canada. ∅

'Laciniata'. New growth green; leaves symmetrical, leaflets deeply incised into ribbonlike segments (= f. *serratifolia* Behnsch). Before 1815.

var. *melanocarpa* see: **S. melanocarpa**

'Moreheimii' (Ruys). Very similar to 'Plumosa', but more delicate; flowers white (!); fruits red. Holland, around 1935. ⚭

'Ornata'. New growth violet; leaves variably formed, the first 8–10 are like 'Plumosa', those that follow are more finely incised like 'Laciniata' (= f. *plumosa pteridifolia* Carr.). 1891.

'Plumosa' (Späth). New growth violet; leaflets incised to about the middle of the blade, teeth long and narrow. 1886. ∅

'Plumosa Aurea' (Wezelenburg). Slow growing; leaf form like that of 'Plumosa', but a gorgeous golden-yellow, best in full sun. JRHS 89: 133. Around 1894 in Holland. Plate 100. ∅

f. *plumosa pteridifolia* see: **'Ornata'**

f. *serratifolia* see: **'Laciniata'**

f. **simplicifolia** Hylander. Leaves simple on sterile shoots, more or less ovate, acute, some simple on flowering shoots, some trifoliate. Lustgarden 1950–51: 107. Discovered in 1943 in Sweden. ∅

'Sutherland Golden'. Seedling of 'Plumosa Aurea', with a similar foliage, yellow, yet better sun tolerance. Introduced in 1971 by W. L. Kerr. ∅

'Tenuifolia'. Slow growing, new growth violet; leaflets

Fig. 220. *Sambucus racemosa,* flowers (from Guimpel)

threadlike incised, nearly creating a smoke-like effect. France in 1893. ∅

S. rotundifolia see: **S. nigra 'Rotundifolia'**

S. sieboldiana (Miq.) Graebn. Shrub or small tree, to 6 m high, young shoots brownish and totally glabrous, pith light brown, with 2 blue rings at the nodes (!); leaflets usually 7, to 11 on long shoots, oblong to more lanceolate, 6–20 cm long, long acuminate to caudate, scabrous and densely serrate, light green, glabrous; flowers small, yellowish white, in about 7 cm long and 5 cm thick, ovate panicles, April to May; fruits scarlet-red, 3–4 mm thick. MD 1920: 226; KIF 4: 45. Japan, China. 1907. z6 Plate 100.

S. velutina see: **S. glauca var. velutina**

All species prefer a moist, fertile, humus soil; the variegated foliage types, particularly the yellow ones, occasionally freeze back. Older shrubs are difficult to transplant, therefore they are best planted where they will ultimately remain.

Lit. Schwerin, F.: Monographie der Gattung *Sambucus;* in Mitt. DDG 1909, 1–56. ● Revisio generis Sambucis; in Mitt. DDG 1920, 194–231 (with maps).

SANTOLINA L. — Lavender Cotton —COMPOSITAE

Aromatic shrubs or subshrubs; leaves evergreen, alternate, pinnatisect or comb-like incised (pectinate); flowers in long stalked capitula; individual florets tubular, no ray florets, hermaphroditic, receptacle somewhat bulging, involucre imbricate; corolla yellow, tubular-campanulate, with a somewhat outspread, 5 parted limb; achenes usually 3–4 sided, without a pubescent crest. →10 species in the Mediterranean region.

Key to the Species

Mature leaves green;

  Flowers yellow:
    S. virens

  Flowers white:
    S. pinnata

Mature leaves gray, flowers light yellow;

Leaf lobes narrow:
  S. neapolitana

Leaf lobes short, thick:
  S. chamaecyparissus

Santolina chamaecyparissus L. Subshrub, 30–50 cm high, very densely branched, shoots procumbent-ascending, shoots and leaves soft tomentose; leaves densely crowded, 2–4 cm long, finely pinnatisect, the segments short and thick, not over 2 mm long (!), arranged in 2 or 4 rows; flower heads deep yellow, on terminal stalks about 15 cm long, held up over the plant, involucre usually tomentose, July–August. BS 3: 285; HM 6, 2: 381. S. Europe. 1539. z7 # ⌀

var. **corsica** Fiori. Lower growing, denser, only about 30–40 cm high (= 'Nana'). Corsica, Sardinia. #

ssp. **insularis** (Genn. ex Fiori) Yeo. Usually tall growing; leaves gray tomentose, segments longer than 2.5 mm; involucre usually tomentose, flowers yellow. Central Mediterranean region. #

'Nana' see: var. **corsica**

ssp. **tomentosa** (Pers.) Arcang. Usually tall growing, gray-white; some or all the leaves usually glabrous or eventually becoming so, segments 2.5–7 mm long, involucre usually glabrous, flowers usually whitish to pale yellow (= *S. incana* Lam.; *S. tomentosa* Pers.). Pyrenees to central Italy. # ⌀

S. incana see: **S. chamaecyparissus** ssp. **tomentosa**

S. neapolitana Jord. Very similar to *S. chamaecyparissus*, but with a more open habit; leaves with longer segments, thus with a more "feathery" effect, gray; flowers lemon-yellow. NW to central Italy. z6

Including 2 clones in English gardens:

'**Edward Bowles**'. Leaves more gray-green; flower heads cream-yellow. # ⌀

'**Sulphurea**'. Similar to the above, but the leaves more gray; flowers light primrose-yellow. # ⌀

Another cultivar which presumably belongs here is **S. 'Lindavica'**, developed by F. Sündermann in Lindau, W. Germany; also with gray, distinctly pendulous, feathery leaves with narrow segments. # ⌀

S. pinnata Viv. Evergreen shrub, 40–70 cm high, very densely foliate, glabrous; leaves green (!), 2.5–3 cm long, segments 4–5 mm long, in 2 or 4 rows; flower heads hemispherical, dull white, solitary on 15 cm long stalks, July. Italy. 1791. z6 #

S. tomentosa see: **S. chamaecyparissus** ssp. **tomentosa**

S. virens Mill. Evergreen shrub, about 50 cm high, dark green and glabrous, segments in 2 rows, awl-shaped; flower heads small, light yellow, solitary on thin, 15–25 cm long stalks, July (= *S. viridis* Willd.). S. Europe. 1727. z7 #

S. viridis see: **S. virens**

Easily cultivated subshrub for very sunny, dry sites; otherwise with no particular cultural requirements.

Lit. Lancaster, R.: Santolinas; in Gard. Chron. of May 7, 1971.

SAPINDUS L. — Soapberry — SAPINDACEAE

Deciduous or evergreen trees or shrubs; leaves alternate, pinnate (one species simple), leaflets entire, occasionally serrate; flowers small, regular, polygamous-dioecious, in large, terminal or axillary panicles; sepals and petals 4–5 each, the latter with 1–2 scales over the claw, disk ring-form, stamens 8–10; ovaries unilocular, later forming a drupe. — About 13 species, mostly in the tropics, some also in temperate zones.

Sapindus drummondii Hook. & Arn. Deciduous tree, to 15 m high, bark scaly, red-brown, young shoots soft pubescent; leaflets 8–18, short stalked, obliquely lanceolate, 4–7 cm long, pubescent beneath; flowers yellowish white, 5 mm wide, in 15–25 cm long, pubescent panicles, May–June; fruits about 1–1.5 cm thick, yellow, eventually black. SS 76–77. SW. USA. 1900. Hardiest species. z6 Fig. 221. ✧ ⊛

S. mukorossi Gaertn. Evergreen tree; leaflets 8–13, oval-oblong to oblong-lanceolate, 8–15 cm long, glabrous beneath with reticulate venation, rachis with a narrow

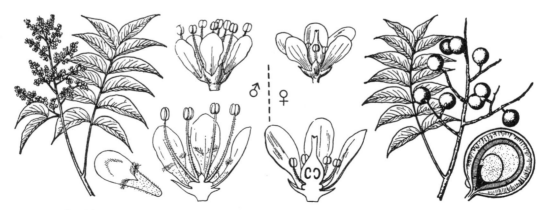

Fig. 221. *Sapindus drummondii*. Left staminate, right pistillate plant parts (from Sargent)

margin; flowers white, in large, terminal panicles; fruit a fleshy, 2 cm thick drupe, grouped 1–2 together, keeled on one side of the base, yellow-brown, seeds black, hardy. LF 219; SDK 4: 74; LWT 193; KIF 1: 86. E. Asia, Himalayas. 1877. z9 # ⊕ ⚭

Illustrations of further species:

S. *marginatus* KFT 147 ● S. *saponaria* SDK 4: 74

While varying reports are given as to its hardiness, the adaptability of the plant in temperate climates is somewhat difficult. Only of botanical interest.

SAPIUM P. Br. — Tallowtree — EUPHORBIACEAE

Evergreen trees with a poisonous, milky sap; leaves alternate, simple, usually entire with 2 distinct glands at the tip of the petiole, stipules small; flowers in terminal spikes, male flowers 3 at the base, female solitary at the apex, all without petals, stamens 2 or 3, free; fruit a capsule; seeds globose. — 120 species in the tropics and subtropics, only a few in cultivation.

Sapium japonicum (S. & Z.) Pax & Hoffm. Glabrous tree, branches gray; leaves broad ovate, 7–12 cm long, 5–10 cm wide, abruptly acuminate, deep green above, blue-green beneath, fall color carmine, petiole 2–3 cm long; inflorescence 5–10 cm long, catkin-like, inconspicuous, greenish yellow, June–July; fruit capsules flat globose, 8 mm wide, yellow with brown spots, pendulous. KIF 2: 36. China, Korea, Japan. z9 # ⊘ ⚭

S. sebiferum (L.) Roxb. Chinese Tallowtree. Tree, to 12 m high, poplar-like in appearance; leaves ovate-rhombic, to 7 cm long, 3–7 cm wide, abruptly acuminate, attractively yellow and red in fall; flowers yellowish green, in terminal panicles; fruit capsules about 12 mm thick, the 3 seeds covered with a white waxy layer. HKT 91. China, but also cultivated in other tropical countries for the useful waxy substance on the seeds. 1850. Cultivated in many botanic gardens. Ⓕ China. z9 # ⊘ ⚭

Illustrations of further species:

S. *discolor* HKT 90

SARCOCOCCA Lindl. — BUXACEAE

Evergreen, often low, glabrous shrubs; leaves alternate, petiolate, leathery; flowers very small, whitish, axillary, monoecious; petals absent, sepals and stamen filaments 4–6, styles 2–3; fruit a fleshy, ovate to globose berry. — 16–20 species in India, China and Malaysia.

Key to the Species and Varieties
(from Sealy)

1. Young shoots, leaf petioles and midrib dull reddish; stigmas 2:

   S. *hookeriana* var. *digyna* (form)

2. All vegetative plant parts green;

+ Shoots glabrous; plants with rhizomes; stigmas 3:
   S. *saligna*

++ Shoots pubescent;

* Plants with rhizomes; stigmas 2 (occasionally some flowers with 3 stigmas); fruit reddish black to black;

   x Leaves narrowly elliptic to narrowly oblong-elliptic, acute or acuminate at the apex, also at the base, usually 4–8 cm long, 0.8–1.5 cm wide, to 11.5 cm long and to 2.4 cm wide on strong shoots; anthers cream-yellow:
   S. *hookeriana* var. *digyna*

   xx Leaves elliptic, apex acute to long acuminate, not so distinctly tapered at the base, usually 3.5–7 cm long, 1–2 cm wide, to 8.8 cm long and 2.4 cm wide on strong shoots; anthers pink-red:
   S. *humilis*

** Plants densely bushy, with a few main shoots and a distinctly fibrous root system;

   v Stigmas 2–3 in each flower; fruits black and glossy:
   S. *confusa*

   vv Stigmas 3 (very rarely a few flowers with only 2 stigmas); fruit red;

      § Leaves elliptic-lanceolate or lanceolate to oval-elliptic or ovate, 2.5–5.5 cm long and 1–1.8 cm wide:
      S. *ruscifolia* var. *chinensis*

      §§ Leaves broadly ovate to ovate, 3–5.5 cm long, 1.5–3.5 cm wide:
      S. *ruscifolia*

Sarcococca confusa Sealy. Evergreen shrub, upright and densely branched, to 2 m high and wide, not stoloniferous, shoots green, soft pubescent; leaves elliptic to oval-elliptic, 2.5–5.5 cm long and 1–1.8 cm wide, glabrous, dark green above, lighter beneath; flowers like those of S. *humilis*, but the anthers yellowish, female flowers with 2 or 3 styles, very fragrant, winter bloomer; fruit black, glossy. BM 9449 (as S. *humilis*). Known only in cultivation. Around 1916 or earlier. z6 Plate 101. # ⊘ ⚭

S. hookeriana Baill. Evergreen shrub, to 1.8 m high, shoots totally fine pubescent; leaves narrowly lanceolate to oblong-lanceolate, acuminate, base cuneate, 5–8 cm long, 1.2–1.8 cm wide, petiole about 6 mm long; flowers fragrant, white, in axillary clusters, styles 3, September–November; fruit nearly globose, 6 mm thick, black (= S. *pruniformis* var. *hookeriana* Hook.). E. Himalayas, Sikkim, Bhutan, N. Assam, SE. Tibet. z6 # ⊘

var. **digyna** Franch. Stoloniferous, shoots green (reddish on the other forms, as is the leaf petiole and midribs!); leaves narrowly elliptic to oblong-lanceolate, usually 4–8(11.5) cm long, 0.8–1.5(2.4 cm) wide; anthers cream-white; fruits reddish black. DRHS 1870. China; Szechwan, NW. Yunnan Provs. 1908. Good hardiness. Plate 101. # ⊘ ⚭

var. *humilis* see: **S. humilis**

S. humilis Stapf. Evergreen shrub, very stoloniferous, not over 50 cm high; leaves acutely elliptic, usually 3.5–

7(8.8) cm long clusters, white, very fragrant, stamens widened petal-like, female flowers with 2 styles, anthers pink-red. January to March; fruit globose, 6 mm thick, black. NF 9: 271 (= *S. hookeriana* var. *humilis* Rehd. & Wils.). China; Hupeh, Szechwan Provs. 1907. z6 Plate 101. # ∅ ⚭

S. pruniformis see: **S. hookeriana** and **S. saligna**

S. ruscifolia Stapf. Evergreen shrub, 0.6–0.9 m high, shoots soft pubescent at first; leaves ovate, long acuminate, 2.5–6 cm long, half as wide, glossy green, petiole 3–4 mm long; flowers milky white, fragrant, in few flowered, axillary clusters, styles 3, stamens 6 mm long, December–March; fruits globose, 6 mm thick, scarlet to carmine. BM 9045. W. China; NW. Yunnam Prov., Tibet. 1901. z9 # ∅ ⚭

S. saligna (D. Don) Muell. Arg. Glabrous, evergreen shrub, 0.6–1.2 m high; leaves narrowly lanceolate, tapered toward both ends, 7.5–12.5 cm long, 1.3–3 cm wide, glabrous; flowers unscented, greenish, in short, axillary clusters, anthers yellow, styles 2, December to March; fruits ovate, purple, 8 mm long. BR 1012 (= *S. pruniformis* Lindl.). W. Himalayas; Afghanistan to Kumaon. Before 1908. z9 Plate 100. # ∅ ⚭

Very useful as a shade tolerant plant; for fertile, humus garden soil; should be covered in winters without snow cover. The tender species only for quite mild areas.

Lit. Sealy, J. R.: Species of *Sarcococca* in cultivation; in Jour. Royal Hort. Soc. 73, 301–306, 1949.

SARCOPOTERIUM

Sarcopoterium spinosum see: **Poterium spinosum**

SARGENTODOXA Rehd. & Wils. — SARGENTODOXACEAE

Monotypic genus. Deciduous, twining shrub; leaves alternate, long petioled, trifoliate, flowers dioecious, campanulate, in pendulous racemes, thin stalked, sepals 6, petaloid, nectaries 6, tiny, nearly circular; male flowers with 6 stamens, ovules stunted, filaments short, anthers oblong; female flowers with numerous, spirally arranged ovules; fruits berrylike. — China.

Sargentodoxa cuneata (Oliv.) Rehd. & Wils. Twining to 7 m high or more; leaflets 3, uneven, middle leaflets rhombic-ovate, 7–12 cm long, petiole 5–10 mm long, lateral leaflets nearly sessile, somewhat larger, half ovate, base very oblique; male flowers about 1 cm long, greenish yellow, fragrant, in pendulous, 10–15 cm long racemes, attractive, May; fruits in clusters of globose, dark blue, pruinose berries, about 8 mm thick and grouped 10–20 together in a short, fleshy cone, September–October. HI 1817; BM 9111–9112; and DRHS 1871 (= *Holboellia cuneata* Oliv.). E. and central China. 1907. z9 ⊕|⚭

Only for the mildest regions; must have a protected site; otherwise about like *Lardizabala*, etc.

SARMIENTA Ruiz & Pavon — GESNERIACEAE

Monotypic genus with the characteristics of the following species:

Sarmienta repens Ruiz & Pavon. Creeping, evergreen shrub, shoots light brown, glabrous; leaves opposite, rounded elliptic, 1–2 cm long, entire or with a few obtuse teeth at the apex, convex and rather fleshy, dark green above, glabrous; flowers stalked, solitary in the leaf axils, calyx distinct, with 5 sepals, corolla tubular, bulging, with a somewhat oblique limb and 5 outspread limb lobes, carmine, stamens 2, June–August. FS 1646; BM 6720. Chile. 1862. z9 Plate 75. # ⊕

Found in its habitat on moist, mossy sites, creeping and thereby climbing on rocks and tree trunks; not easily cultivated, best for a moist, temperate greenhouse.

SAROTHAMNUS See: CYTISUS

SASA Mak. & Shibata — GRAMINEAE

Low to medium-sized bamboos with stolons; stalks not always vertical, cylindrical (those of *Phyllostachys* always more or less flattened on one side of the node), nodes always with 1, occasionally 2 lateral shoots (always more on *Arundinaria*); nodes more or less thickened; leaf sheaths with rough, erect bristles; flowers with 6 stamens, style either short and with 3 stigmas or 2 styles. — About 200 species in E. Asia, however, only a few are found in cultivation.

Sasa auricoma see: **Arundinaria viridi-striata**

S. disticha (Mitford) E. G. Camus. Stem slender, 25–75 cm high, wavy, green, hollow, internodes 3–8 cm long, stem sheaths softly pubescent when young, ciliate; leaves distichous, 2–6 cm long, 5–8 mm wide, narrowly acuminate, base tapered to a small petiole, fine bristly serrate, dark green on both sides (!), with 2–3 vein pairs. NH 24: 183; SB 15 (= *Arundinaria disticha* [Mitford] Pfitzer; *Bambusa disticha* Mitford). Japan. 1870. Hardy! z6 #

S. humilis see: **Arundinaria humilis**

S. palmata (Burbridge) A. Camus. Stems to 2 m high, stoloniferous, waxy pruinose, particularly under the nodes, hollow, internodes 12–15 cm long, stem sheaths with an abscising, checkered, lanceolate ligule at the top, margins ciliate; leaves 12–32 cm long, 7–8 cm wide, long acuminate, drawn together at the base, finely serrate, light green and glossy above, bluish green and finely pubescent beneath, finely checkered, with 7–13 vein pairs. BS 1: Pl. 4; NH 24: 186; CBa Pl. 2cD (= *S. senanensis* sensu Rehd. p.p.; *Bambusa palmata* Marliac). Japan. 1913. Hardy. z7 Plate 102. # ∅

S. pumila (Mitford) E. G. Camus. Stems slender, 30–60 cm long, hollow, stem sheaths checkered, the apical ones turning purple; leaves 7–15 cm long, 0.8–2 cm wide, most abruptly long acuminate, finely serrate, base rounded, light green and somewhat pubescent on both sides, with 4–5 vein pairs. NH 24: 175; CBa Pl. 7f.a. (= *Arundinaria pumila* Mitford). Japan. 1806. Hardy. z6 #

S. pygmaea (Miq.) E. G. Camus. Stems densely clustered, thin, to 50 cm high, hollow, well branched, the branches 3 mm thick; leaves distichous, closely spaced, lanceolate, acuminate, 5–12 cm long, base round and very short petioled, 2.5–13 mm wide, margins rough and occasionally finely ciliate, green above, usually lighter beneath, with 2–4 vein pairs, ligule short truncated, finely striped, ciliate. CBa 5B; NH 24: 183 (= *Arundinaria pygmaea* Kurz). Japan. z7 #

S. sensanensis see: **S. palmata**

S. tessellata (Munro) Mak. & Shibata. Stems to 1.5 m high, somewhat hollow, soon nodding, internodes 3–8 cm long, stem sheaths persistent, each sheath enclosing the next 2 or 3 above it and tightly appressed; leaves long acuminate, to 60 cm long and 10 cm wide, scabrous serrate, abruptly narrowed together at the base, light green above, blue-green beneath and finely pubescent, pubescent at the base on one side of the yellow midrib, with 15–18 vein pairs, with a checkered vein pattern (tessellated). BS 1: Pl. 5; CBa 3B; 7B (= *Arundinaria tessellata* Bean; *Arundinaria ragamowskii* Pfitzer). Japan; strong growing, developing dense thickets. 1845. z8 # ⌀

S. variegata (Miq.) E. G. Camus. Stems 0.3–0.8 m high, very thin, scarcely over 3 mm thick, narrow tubular, slightly wavy, internodes 3–18 cm long, stem sheaths persistent, pubescent at the base; leaves 8–15 cm long, 1–2 cm wide, long acuminate, base rounded, finely serrate, dark green with white longitudinal stripes, soft pubescent on both sides, with 3–5 vein pairs. NH 24: 181 (= *Arundinaria fortunei* var. *variegata* Bean; *Arundinaria fortunei* Mitford). Japan. 1863. z7 Plate 102. # ⌀

S. veitchii (Carr.) Rehd. Strong grower, stems usually 0.3–0.5 m high, but occasionally also to about 1 m, narrow caned, internodes 8–12 cm long, stem sheaths persistent, very pubescent at first, with a cluster of bristles at the apex; leaves 10–20 cm long, 3–6 cm wide, rather abruptly acuminate, base drawn out to a point, dark green above, bluish and finely pubescent beneath, with a broad, dry yellowish marginal band in the fall and winter (!!), midrib yellow beneath, with 6–9 vein pairs. NH 24: 184 (= *Arundinaria albomarginata* Mak.; *A. veitchii* N. E. Br.). Japan. 1880. Of little ornamental value because of the unattractive dry leaf margins. z8 Plate 103. #

Like all the other Bamboo types, *Sasa* species prefer a fertile soil, best in a clay sand, sufficient moisture and a protected site. The latter is particularly important in winter; planting somewhat as understory is best.

Lit. See Bambusaceae (Vol. I p. 188).

SASSAFRAS Nees & Eberm. — LAURACEAE

Deciduous, aromatic trees; leaves alternate, entire or with 1–3 lobes at the apex, base three veined; flowers dioecious, unisexual or nearly hermaphroditic, several in small racemes before the leaves; calyx 6 parted, male with 9 stamens; female with ovate ovaries, thin style and 6 atrophic stamens; fruit an ovate drupe on a thick, fleshy stalk. — One species each in N. America, China and Taiwan.

Sassafras albidum (Nutt.) Nees. Tree, 12–15(20) m high, also higher in its habitat, occasionally shrubby, somewhat stoloniferous, bark furrowed, branches smooth, glossy green; leaves elliptic, but quite variable in form, usually 3 lobed, base cuneate, light green on both sides, glabrous, orange and scarlet in fall; flowers greenish yellow, April–May; fruits oblong, nearly pea-sized, black and pruinose when ripe, petiole fleshy, red; male trees occasionally produce female flowers and fruit. GTP 214; BS 2: 22 (= *S. officinale* var. *albidum* Blake; *S. variifolium* var. *albidum* [Nutt.] Fern.). Eastern N. America, to Texas. 1630. z5 ⌀ ⚭

var. **molle** (Raf.) Fern. Buds and young shoots pubescent; leaves more bluish and pubescent beneath at first. BB 1654; SS 304 (= *S. officinale* Nees & Eberm.; *S. variifolium* [Salisb.] Ktz.). 1903. N. America. Plate 75, 104; Fig. 222.

S. officinale see: **S. albidum**

S. tzumu (Hemsl.) Hemsl. Tree, young shoots and leaves usually soft pubescent; leaves to 20 cm long, acute, petiole to 6 cm long; flower racemes with a 4–8 cm long stalk, appearing hermaphroditic, with 9 fertile stamens and 3 staminodes. LF 144. Central China. 1900. z9 ⌀

S. variifolium see: **S. albidum**

For open sites in a deep, fertile soil; particularly impressive is an older specimen of *S. albidum*.

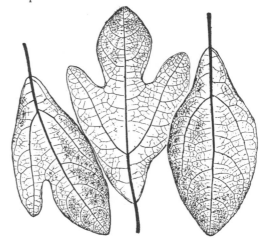

Fig. 222. *Sassafras albidum* var. *molle* (Original)

SCHEFFLERA J. R. & G. Forst. — ARALIACEAE

Evergreen trees or shrubs; leaves alternate, palmately compound; flowers in large panicles, racemes or umbels; the individual flowers are 5 or 6 parted, not very conspicuous. — About 200 species widely distributed in the tropics and subtropics.

Schefflera impressa (C. B. Clarke) Harms. Evergreen, tree-like in its habitat; leaves usually 7 parted, petiole 15–50 cm long, leaflets lanceolate to oblanceolate, leathery, 12–20 cm long, 3–5 cm wide, entire, occasionally sparsely serrate on young plants. China; Yunnan Prov. Rare in cultivation. z9 Plate 104.

S. venulosa (Wight & Arn.) Harms. Evergreen shrub; leaves 5(7) part palmate, petiole 10–12 cm long, leaflets elliptic, 7–15 cm long, 3–10 cm wide, acute to acuminate, base round, entire; flowers only about 1 cm wide, not very conspicuous, in loose, terminal, somewhat tomentose (but quickly becoming glabrous), 10–20 cm long panicles, summer; fruit ovate, distinctly 5 sided. China; Yunnan Prov. z10 Plate 104.

Both species hardy in the landscape only in the mildest climates.

SCHIMA Reinw. ex Bl. — THEACEAE

Evergreen trees or shrubs; leaves alternate; flowers attractive, sepals 5, usually evenly formed, petals 5, much larger than the sepals, connate at the base and much overlapped, stamens numerous; flowers solitary, erect, in the axils of the apical leaves and grouped into a short, clustered raceme. — 15 species in the tropics of E. Asia and E. India.

Schima arborea see: **S. wallichii**

S. argentea Pritzel. Evergreen shrub, 1–1.5 m high, but much wider, young shoots silky pubescent, light brown, later reddish, always with distinct lenticels; leaves narrowly elliptic-oblong to oblanceolate, 7–15 cm long, 3–4 cm wide, entire, glossy green above, blue-green and short pubescent beneath, with 10–12 vein pairs; flowers cream-white, shell form, to 6 cm wide, exterior silky pubescent, similar to those of *Gordonia*. NF 8: 206; BM 9558; GC 138: 181. China; Yunnan, Szechwan Provs. 1928. z9 Fig. 223. # ⌀│⊕

S. khasiana Dyer. Evergreen shrub to medium-sized tree; leaves ovate-elliptic, 12–15 cm long, 5–8 cm wide, distinctly serrate, acute, glabrous; flowers 5 cm wide, white, anthers golden-yellow, very numerous, exterior silky pubescent, stalks thick, 2 cm long, finely warty, September–October on young wood. BMns 143. Assam, Burma, China. z9 # ⊕

S. noronhae see: **S. wallichii**

S. oblata see: **S. wallichii**

S. superba see: **S. wallichii**

S. wallichii (D.C.) Korth. A tree in its habitat to 40 m high, but much shorter in cultivation, quite variable; leaves usually elliptic, occasionally wider, to 18 cm long (to 25 cm on suckers), 4–5 cm wide, acuminate, entire to serrate, glossy, reddish when young; flowers scarlet-red in bud, opening a soft reddish cream color to white, 6 cm wide, fragrant, exterior not pubescent, anthers golden-yellow, flower stalk to 5 cm long, tiny warty, appearing in late summer on young wood; fruits 2.5 cm thick, whitish at first, then red to violet, eventually black and dry. HAl 12; SNp 20; HKT 93 (as *S. superba*) (= *S. arborea* Hort.; *S. noronhae* Reinw. ex Bl.; *S. oblata* [Roxb.] Kurz; *S. superba* C. Gardn. & Champ.). India, eastward to Indonesia and Taiwan. z9 Fig. 223. # ⊕

Illustrations of other species:
   S. bambusifolia CIS 172 ● *S. confertiflora* CIS 92

Cultivated somewhat like *Gordonia*, but only for the warmest climates.

Fig. 223. **Schima.** Left *S. argentea;* center *S. wallichii;* right *S. noronhae* (from ICS)

SCHINUS L. — Peppertree — ANACARDIACEAE

Evergreen trees or shrubs, branch tips often thorny; leaves alternate, odd pinnate or simple, dentate or entire, leathery; flowers small, white or yellow, in axillary or terminal panicles; calyx 5 parted, petals 5, stamens 10; fruit a pea-sized drupe, somewhat fleshy, with a leathery rugose kernel. — About 30 species from Mexico to Argentina.

Schinus dependens see: **S. polygamus**

S. molle L. Round crowned, evergreen tree, branches gracefully nodding; leaves pinnate, 12–20 cm long, with a peppery scent, leaflets about 21–41, linear-lanceolate, 3–5 cm long, acute, dentate, glabrous: flowers yellowish white, in 2.5–5 cm long panicles, April; fruits pea-sized, carmine-pink. HM 1815; BM 3339. Central and S. America. Ⓕ Israel, Argentina, Chile, Peru; in windbreaks. z9 Plate 104. # ∅ ⚭

S. polygamus (Cav.) Cabr. Evergreen shrub, to 4 m high, or also a small tree, shoots stiff, often thorny tipped; leaves simple, obovate, 1.5–2.5 cm long, rounded at the apex, entire, tapered to the base, very short petioled; flowers very small, yellowish, very numerous in axillary, short racemes, May; fruits peppercorn-sized, red. SDK 4: 36 (*S. dependens* Ort.). Chile. z9 # ∅ ⚭

S. terebinthifolius Raddi. Brazilian Peppertree. Shrub or small tree, to 5 m high, habit not as delicate as *S. molle*, shoots not pendulous; leaves pinnate, 10–17 cm long, rachis winged, with 5–13 leaflets, variable in form, oval-lanceolate to obovate, acute or rounded, 3–6 cm long, pubescent when young, like the shoots, deep green above, lighter beneath; flowers small, white, in 5–15 cm long axillary and terminal panicles; fruits red, peppercorn-sized. LWTP 440. Chile. Of great ornamental value. z9 # ∅ ⚭

Lit. Barkley, F. A.: *Schinus* L.; in Brittonia 5, 160–198, 1944 ● Barkley, F. A.: A study of *Schinus* L.; in Lilloa 28, 5–110, 1957.

SCHISANDRA Michx. — SCHISANDRACEAE

Evergreen or deciduous, twining shrubs, more or less aromatic; leaves alternate, usually cuneate, slender petioled; flowers dioecious, solitary or few in axillary clusters, at the base of the young shoots, red, yellowish or white; sepals and petals regularly formed, 7–12, stamens 5–15, ovaries numerous, in capitate clusters, developing a spike-form elongated false fruit after flowering. — 25 species in E. and SE. Asia, 1 in N. America.

Schisandra chinensis (Turcz.) Baill. Deciduous shrub, twining 5–7 m high, totally glabrous, branches somewhat angular; leaves very thin, obovate to elliptic, short acuminate, sparsely dentate, 5–10 cm long, glossy green above, occasionally more bluish beneath, venation usually slightly pubescent when young; flowers white to pale pink, to 1.5 cm wide, stamens 5 (!!), fragrant, May–June; female plants with attractive scarlet-red fruit spikes in fall, these 10 cm long and pendulous. FS 1594; Gfl 382 (2–3); NK 20: 20; ICS 1600. Japan, Korea. 1860. z6 Fig. 224. ⊕ ⚭

var. *rubriflora* see: **S. rubriflora**

S. coccinea Michx. f. Wild Sarsaparilla. High climbing shrub; leaves ovate to elliptic, fleshy, to 12 cm long, entire to sparsely undulate dentate, petiole thin, to 5 cm long; corolla lobes 9–12, carmine, about 1 cm long, stamens 5, grouped into a 3 mm wide disk, style 12–30, June; berries grouped 7–12 together, red. BM 1413; Hortus Third 1017 (= *S. glabra* [Brickell] Rehd.). SE. USA. z7 ⊕ ⚭

S. glabra see: **S. coccinea**

S. grandiflora (Wall.) Hook. f. & Thoms. Glabrous twining shrub, shoots nearly cylindrical, brown; leaves obovate to elliptic-oblong, 6–10 cm long, acuminate, leathery tough (!), always light green beneath; flowers white to waxy white or pale pink, 2.5–3 cm wide, petals nearly circular, stalks 2–3 cm long, May–June; fruit scarlet-red, 12–20 cm (!) long, edible, July–October. Himalayas. z9 ⊕ ⚭

S. henryi Clarke. Glabrous shrub, shoots triangular and winged (!); leaves broad elliptic to ovate, 6–10 cm long, short acuminate, sparsely finely dentate, base round to broadly cuneate, blue-green beneath, leathery tough; flowers white, 1.5 cm wide, stalk thin, 4–7 cm long, April–May; fruits red, 5–7 cm long. FIO 70; ICS 1604; GC 38: 35 (= *S. hypoglauca* Lév.). Central and S. China. 1900. z9 Fig. 224. ⚭

S. hypoglauca see: **S. henryi**

S. nigra see: **S. repanda**

S. propinqua (Wall.) Baill. Shrub, deciduous, twining to 7 m high, shoots angular; leaves narrowly ovate to oblong-lanceolate, 7–12 cm long, short acuminate, sparsely dentate, base round or broadly cuneate, leathery, bluish or pale green beneath, petiole 1–1.5 cm long; flowers orange, about 1.5 cm wide, petals oblong, stalk 5–10 mm long, with small bracts, June; fruit spikes to 15 cm long, red. BM 4614; BR 201. Himalayas to Malaya. 1812. z8 ⊕ ⚭

S. repanda (S. & Z.) C. A. Smith. Strong growing glabrous shrub, shoots brown to gray-brown, cylindrical; leaves broadly ovate to elliptic-obovate, 5–7 cm long, short acuminate, base cuneate to round, very thin (!), petiole 2–4 cm long; flowers white, 1.5 cm wide, stalk 2–3 cm long, May to June; fruits black, blue pruinose, 2–5 cm long, seeds warty. NK 20: 19 (= *S. nigra*

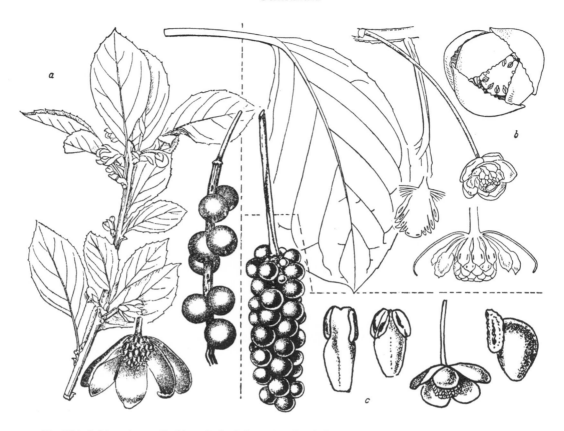

Fig. 224. **Schisandra.** a. *S. chinensis;* b. *S. henryi;* c. *S. rubiflora;* twig, individual flower, above right as seen from below, flower parts, fruit clusters (from Gfl., Gard. Chron., Bot. Mag., Lavallée)

Maxim.). Japan, Quelpaert, S. Korea, in thickets. 1892. Hardy. z6 ⊕

S. rubriflora (Franch.) Rehd. & Wils. Shrub, 4–5 m high, twining, shoots thin, reddish, glabrous; leaves obovate to oblanceolate, 6–12 cm long, dentate, acuminate, base cuneate, glabrous; flowers solitary, axillary, 2.5 cm wide, pendulous on red stalks, sepals and petals totaling 7, dark carmine, April–May; fruits in densely clustered, 5–6 cm long spikes, berries globose, red, pea-sized, stalk 5–12 cm long. BM 9146 (= *S. chinensis* var. *rubriflora* Franch.). China; W. Szechwan Prov. and Sikang to E. Assam. 1908. The most attractive species of the entire genus. z9 Plate 75, 105; Fig. 224. ⊕ ⚭

S. sphaerandra Stapf. Shrub, 2–6 m high, twining; leaves densely clustered on short shoots, lanceolate to narrowly lanceolate-elliptic, 4–11 cm long, 1.5–4 cm wide, acute, finely glandular dentate; flowers dark crimson-red, stalks about 1.5 cm long, stamens 20–50, nearly sessile; fruits to 5 cm long, berries red, 1.5 cm thick. China; Szechwan, Yunnan Provs. ⊕ ⚭

S. sphenanthera Rehd. & Wils. Shrub, to 4 m high, twining, glabrous, shoots reddish brown, cylindrical; leaves obovate to elliptic or rounded, acuminate, 5–11 cm long, base cuneate, sparsely dentate, light green beneath, petiole thin, 2–3 cm long; flowers dioecious, solitary, orange, axillary, stamens numerous, April–May; fruits in 5–7 cm long spikes, berries red, globose, 6 mm thick, stalk 10–20 cm long. BM 8921; FIO 71; ICS 1603. Central and W. China. 1907. z7 Plate 105. ⊕ ⚭

All species prefer a fertile soil in simishade and somewhat protected, particularly wooded sites.

Lit. Smith, A. C.: The Families Illiciaceae and Sandraceae; in Sargentia 7, 86–156, 1947.

SCHIZOPHRAGMA S. & Z. — HYDRANGEACEAE

Deciduous climber, covering structures by means of aerial roots, bark still tight on the 2nd year shoots, splitting open on the older shoots; leaves opposite, long petioled, dentate, or entire; flowers small, white, in flat corymbs, similar to those of *Hydrangea*, but the ray florets with only one petal (enlarged sepal), white, 3–7 cm long; fertile flowers with 4–5 sepals and petals, one style with a 4–5 parted stigma; fruit a 10 ribbed, top form capsule. — 8 species in Asia.

Schizophragma hydrangeoides S. & Z. Shrub, climbing to 10 m high, young shoots yellow-brown, somewhat long pubescent, later dark gray; leaves rather long petioled, 7–12 cm long, rounded-ovate, abruptly acuminate, base broadly rounded to somewhat cordate, stiffly pubescent when young, light green above, whitish green beneath; inflorescences 15–20 cm wide, the sterile ray florets sometimes with an ovate, about 3 cm long sepal, July. BM 8520; DL 3: 176. Mountain forests of Japan and Korea. 1880. Hardy. z5 Plate 106. ⊕

S. integrifolium Oliv. Climber, reaching 4 m high or more; leaves ovate, 10–15 cm long, thickish, entire to sparsely dentate, base cordate, venation pubescent beneath; inflorescences to 25 cm wide, sepals of the ray florets oval-oblong, to 7 cm long and 3 cm wide (!), July. GC 134: 19; BM 8991; CIS 30. Central and W. China. z7 Plate 106. ∅ ⊕

S. viburnoides see: **Pileostegia viburnoides**

Illustrations of other species:

S. macrosepalum CIS 163 ● *S. obtusifolium* CIS 164

Cultural requirements like those of *Hydrangea*.

SECURINEGA Comm. ex Juss. — EUPHORBIACEAE

Deciduous shrubs; leaves alternate, short petioled, entire, flowers dioecious or monoecious, small, greenish, without petals, male flowers clustered in the leaf axils, with 5 stamens and 5 alternating disk glands; female flowers 1–8 in axillary clusters; fruit a dehiscent capsule with 3–6 seeds. — About 25 species in the temperate and subtropical zones of central and S. America, Asia, S. Europe and Africa.

Securinega flueggeoides see: **S. suffruticosa**

S. ramiflora see: **S. suffruticosa**

S. suffruticosa (Pall.) Rehd. Divaricate shrub, to 2 m high, branches thin, brown or yellowish green; leaves elliptic, to 6 cm long, slightly bluish green beneath; flowers small, greenish, male in small clusters, female flowers solitary, July–August; fruits globose, 5 mm thick, greenish or brownish. SDK 4: 31 (= *S. ramiflora* Muell. Arg.; *S. flueggeoides* Muell. Arg.). Mongolia to N. China. 1783. z5 Plate 105.

Without particular requirements; likes full sun. The young shoots usually freeze back to the ground in winter.

SEDUM L. — Stonecrop — CRASSULACEAE

Perennials, occasionally subshrubs; leaves usually alternate, fleshy; flowers usually hermaphroditic and 5 parted, white or yellow, occasionally pink to red; stamens twice as many as sepals, the latter often fleshy and leaflike; petals free or slightly connate at the base; fruit a follicle dehiscing along the ventral seam. — About 600 species, most in the temperate or cool zones of the Northern Hemisphere.

Sedum populifolium Pall. Upright, 30 cm high subshrub, shoots usually reddish, thin, glabrous, branched; leaves ovate, to 4 cm long, thickish, irregularly and coarsely obtuse dentate, long petioled; flowers in terminal, branched corymbs, whitish or more pink, anthers red, fragrance like that of *Crataegus*, July–August. BM 211. Siberia. 1780. Hardy. z3 Plate 106. ⊕

For the rock garden or border planting, needs a dry and very sunny site; otherwise not particular.

SEMIARUNDINARIA Mak. — GRAMINEAE

Bamboo with short rhizomes; internodes of the rhizomes, stem and lateral shoots cylindrical; stem sheaths abscising soon, but not completely, persisting for a short time after becoming dry and loose; auricles and bristles absent from the stem sheaths; leaf sheaths with erect, rough bristles. — 20 species in Japan and E. Asia.

Semiarundinaria fastuosa (Mitford) Mak. Stems upright, 2–3 m high, but to 15 m high in its habitat and very imposing, stems very thin walled, 3.5–8 cm thick, cylindrical, but the uppermost internodes flattened, dark green with reddish markings, lateral shoots 1–3 in the apical nodes, erect, stem sheaths to 22 cm long, green at first, then purple, tough, smooth, interior glossy, many of these remaining attached by a short middle segment of the base for a time after drying; leaves 5–9 on the lateral shoots, long acuminate, 10–18 cm long, 1.5–2.5 cm wide, gradually tapering to the petiole, dark green above, bluish on one side beneath, soft pubescent, with 5–6 vein pairs. CBa 7(c) and 13(A) (= *Phyllostachys fastuosa* E. G. Camus; *Arundinaria narihira* Mak.). Japan. 1892. z7–8 Plate 107. # ∅

Cultivated like *Phyllostachys*.

SENECIO L. — Groundsel, Cineraria — COMPOSITAE

Perennials, deciduous or evergreen shrubs or trees; leaves alternate, entire, serrate or pinnate; flower heads in axillary or terminal corymbs or panicles; capitula either with female ray florets and hermaphroditic disk florets, or all flowers tubular and hermaphroditic; involucre cylindrical to hemispherical, bracts usually in a single row; receptacle flat or vaulted; disk florets yellow, ray florets yellow or whitish, occasionally in other colors; anthers with appendages on the base; achenes nearly round or somewhat compressed, with 5–10 stripes, with a pappus. — About 2000–3000 species throughout the world.

Key to the Species Mentioned in this Work

+ Capitula with ray florets;
    X Ray florets white; leaves pinnate at the base:
        S. hectori

  XX Ray florets yellow;
    ★ Leaves entire;
     § Leaves acute:
        S. laxifolius

      §§ Leaves obtuse;
       4–9 cm long:
        S. greyi

       to 4 cm long:
        S. compactus

    ★★ Leaves crenate;
     § Leaf margins distinctly crenate:
        S. monroi

      §§ Leaf margins indistinctly crenate:
        S. compactus

++ Capitula disk form;
    Leaves nearly as long as wide:
        S. reinoldii

    Petioles not over 7 cm long, very thick and leathery:
        S. bidwillii

    Leaves very stiff, underside densely tomentose:
        S. elaeagnifolius

    Leaves circular, thin, coarsely dentate:
        S. platanifolius

Senecio bidwillii Hook. f. Compact, evergreen shrub, thickly branched, to 1 m high, shoots, petiole and flower rachis densely white to brownish tomentose; leaves elliptic to obovate-oblong, very tough and leathery, 2–2.5 cm long, 1–1.5 cm wide, petiole thick, glabrous and glossy above, thickly tomentose beneath, without a distinctly recognizable midrib; flowers in up to 5 cm wide corymbs, capitula disk form, to 1.5 cm wide, not particularly ornamental. PRP 101. New Zealand. z9 Fig. 225. # Ø

S. compactus Kirk. Compact, evergreen shrub, well branched, to 1 m high, thickly branched, shoots and petioles with a thick, soft white tomentum; leaves sometimes rather loose, sometimes more densely arranged, obovate to oblong, obtuse 2–4 cm long, 1–2 cm

wide, margins distinct or indistinctly crenate and undulate, tapering to the petiole, white tomentose above only at first, later glabrous, white tomentose beneath with a distinctly recognizable midrib, petiole 1–2 cm long; capitula 3 cm wide, solitary or in few-flowered racemes, with 10 or more yellow ray florets. New Zealand. z9 #

S. elaeagnifolius Hook. f. Evergreen shrub, about 1 m high in its habitat, young shoots somewhat furrowed, brownish white tomentose, as is the leaf underside, petiole and inflorescences; leaves leathery, elliptic to obovate, obtuse, 5–12 cm long, glabrous and glossy above; flowers in terminal, conical, 7–12 cm long panicles, without ray florets, in summer, capitula 8–12 mm wide. DL 1: 196; MNZ 72. New Zealand. z9 Plate 108; Fig. 225. # Ø

S. greyi Hook. f. Evergreen shrub, upright at first, becoming broad and bushy with age, to about 2 m high in the wild, young shoots thick, densely covered with a dense, soft, white or somewhat brownish tomentum, as are the leaf undersides and petioles; leaves oblong to somewhat elliptic, 3–9 cm long, obtuse, entire, base usually round, deep green and glabrous above, somewhat tomentose on the margins; flowers in 10–15 cm long and nearly as wide panicles in summer, captitula about 2.5 cm wide, with 12–15 golden yellow ray florets, stalk glandular pubescent. MNZ 44. New Zealand, N. Island. That cultivated under this name is almost without exception the hybrid **S. 'Sunshine'**, see below. z9 Fig. 225. # Ø ⊕

S. hectori Buchan. Evergreen shrub, to 4 m high in its habitat, branches thick, outspread, tomentose; leaves densely clustered at the branch tips, 10–25 cm long, 4–12 cm wide, broadly oblanceolate, coarsely crenate, pinnatisect toward the base, white tomentose beneath when young; flowers in large, terminal corymbs, capitula to 5 cm wide, with white ray florets. New Zealand. 1910. Needs a well protected area, particularly out of the wind. z9 #

S. laxifolius Buchan. Bushy evergreen shrub, 0.5–1 m high, young shoots gray tomentose, as are the leaf undersides; leaves ovate to lanceolate or oval-elliptic, obtuse, entire, tapered toward the base, covered with a "spider web"-like white indumentum above at first, but later glabrous, leathery, petiole to 2.5 cm long; flower heads about 2.5 cm wide, with 12–15 golden-yellow ray florets, grouped into loose (!), terminal, broadly conical, 15–20 cm long and 12 cm wide panicles, July. BM 7378; GC 139: 739. New Zealand. Often confused with *S. greyi*, but much more rare in cultivation. z9 Fig. 225. # Ø ⊕

S. monroi Hook. f. Broad, evergreen shrub, 0.5–1.5 m high and wide, shoots, leaf undersides, petioles and flower stalks white tomentose; leaves leathery, ovate, oblong to obovate, 1.5–3 cm long, rounded, base tapered, margins distinctly undulate (!), finely rugose above, dull green and glabrous; disk florets 12–18 mm

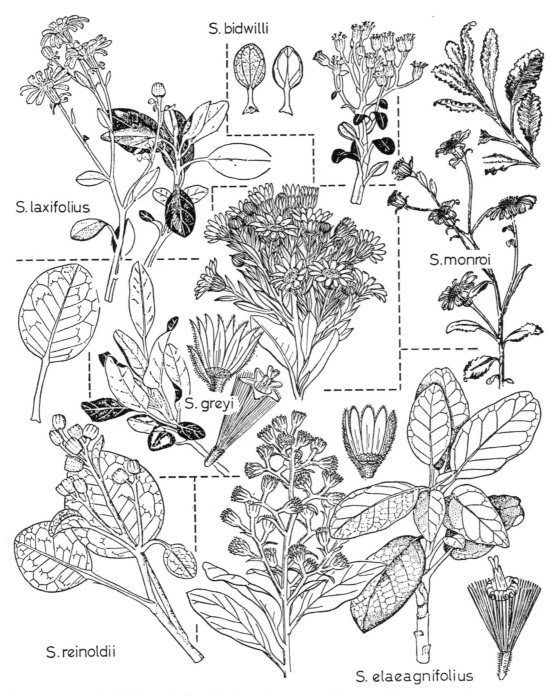

S. bidwilli

S. laxifolius

S. monroi

S. greyi

S. reinoldii

S. elaeagnifolius

Fig. 225. **Senecio** (from Poole & Adams, Gard. Chron. and Hooker, altered)

wide, with 10–15 light yellow ray florets, grouped into 10–15 cm wide, terminal corymbs, flower stalks thin, somewhat glandular, July. BM 8698; MNZ 45; PRP 99. New Zealand. Very attractive. z9 Plate 108; Fig. 225. # ∅ ⊕

S. platanifolius Benth. Upright shrub, shoots to 1 m long, becoming woody only at the base, upper parts herbaceous, soft pubescent; leaves rather circular, 5–12 cm wide, 5–9 lobed, dentate, base cordate, crispate pubescent above, underside with long, soft hairs on the venation, petiole 3–15 cm long; capitula usually few, but rather large, with 12 ray florets, yellow. S. Mexico. z10 Plate 108. #

S. reinoldii Endl. Evergreen shrub or tree, 1.5 m high (or to 15 m in its habitat), shoots, leaf undersides and petioles densely white tomentose; leaves very stiff and leathery tough, circular to ovate, 5–12 cm long and wide, entire, base cordate, deep green above, glossy glabrous, petiole 2.5–8 cm long; capitula without ray florets, yellowish, in terminal, 12–15 cm wide corymbs, June–July. KF 116; CIS 114 (= *S. rotundifolius* Hook. f.). New Zealand. Flowers without ornamental value, but a meritorious shrub, tolerates sea winds in mild climates. z9 Plate 107; Fig. 225. # ∅

SERISSA Commers ex Juss. — RUBIACEAE

Monotypic genus with the following characteristics of the species; presumably 3 species according to many modern botanists.

Serissa foetida (L. f.) Lam. Densely branched, evergreen shrub, upright, scarcely over 60 cm high, shoots glabrous or pubescent, bark unpleasantly scented when crushed; leaves opposite, with persistent stipules, nearly sessile, ovate to elliptic, 1–2 cm long, 5–8 mm wide, acute, entire, deep green above, lighter beneath, often with clusters of smaller leaves in the normal leaf axils; flowers solitary or few, axillary and terminal, corolla salver shaped, limb 4–6 lobed, the lobes often further indistinctly 3 lobed, white, May; fruit a small berry with 2 stony seeds. HKS 92; BM 361 (as *Lycium japonicum*) (*S. japonica* Thunb.). SE. Asia. 1878. Often used as a hedging shrub in Japan. z9 Fig. 226. #

S. japonica see: **S. foetida**

SESBANIA Scop. — LEGUMINOSAE

Perennials or shrubs, somewhat resembling *Colutea;* leaves even pinnate, leaflets entire, stipules subulate, very quickly abscising; flowers red or yellow, in axillary racemes, standard recurved, wings falcate oblong, keel inward curving; fruits linear, 4 sided or 4 winged. — About 50 species in the tropics and subtropics; very easily cultivated in a suitable climate.

Sesbania punicea (Cav.) Benth. Deciduous shrub,

S. rotundifolius see: **S. reinoldii**

S. 'Sunshine' (Dunedin Hybrid). Evergreen, broad growing shrub, to 1 m high and 2 m wide; leaves petiolate, ovate to elliptic or broadly elliptic, entire and flat or slightly undulate, rounded at the apex, base broadly cuneate, 3–6 cm long, 1.5–3 cm wide, thinly tomentose above, green, eventually glabrous, densely white tomentose beneath, petiole 1–2.5 cm; flower heads an attractive yellow, 2–3 cm wide, many together in large, loose corymbs, the lowest bracts of the involucre leaflike. This plant has been cultivated in England and W. Europe since about 1910 as *S. greyi* Hort. and *S. laxifolius* Hort. It is actually a clone from a hybrid complex of *S. greyi* Hook. f., *S. laxifolius* Buchanan and *S. compactus* Kirk, which are today considered collectively the 'Dunedin Hybrids' for the Dunedin Botanic Gardens, Otaga, New Zealand (see C. Jeffrey, in The Garden, 102: 161–163; 1977, with color illustrations). z8–9 Plate 108. # ∅ ⊕

Very easily cultivated given a sufficiently mild climate; well proven along the Atlantic coast of western Europe where it tolerates strong sea winds without leaf damage.

Lit. Cheeseman, T. F.: Manual of the New Zealand Flora; Wellington 1906 (368–384)

Fig. 226. *Serissa foetida* (from BM)

similar to *Colutea* in appearance, about 1.5 m high; leaves in 6–20 pairs, leaflets 2–2.5 cm long; flowers in about 10 cm long racemes, the individual flowers vermilion-red, 2 cm long, standard wide, nearly circular, calyx truncate, calyx teeth small, July; pods leathery, 5–10 cm long, 4 sided with leathery wings. DRHS 1945; BM 7353. Brazil. 1820. z10 ⊕ ⚭

SHEPHERDIA Nutt. — Buffalo Berry — ELAEAGNACEAE

Deciduous or evergreen shrubs (the only evergreen species, *S. rotundifolia* Parry, from Utah is not yet generally cultivated), branches and leaves lepidote, branch tips often thorned; leaves opposite, petiolate, oblong-ovate, entire; flowers dioecious, very small, in short spikes or racemes, appearing before the leaves; male flowers deeply 4 parted, stamens 8; female flowers tubular, ovaries enclosed, style elongated; fruits berrylike. — 3 species in N. America.

Shepherdia argentea (Pursh) Nutt. Tree-like shrub, 4–6 m high, branch tips often thorny, silvery lepidote, otherwise gray-brown; leaves narrowly oblong, 4–6 cm long, rounded, base narrowing, silvery on both sides; flowers inconspicuous, yellowish, stamens pubescent (!), March–April; fruits oval-rounded, pea-sized, red, sourish-sweet. DL 3: 116; Gfl 625; NBB 2: 573. N. America. 1818. Along rivers. Fruits can be made into a jelly. Ⓕ USA, Canada, in windbreaks. z2 Plate 107; Fig. 227. ⚭✗

S. canadensis (L.) Nutt. Divaricate shrub, to 2.5 m high, not thorny, branches glossy red-brown, lepidote; leaves ovate (!), to 6 cm long, dull green above, stellate pubescent at first, silvery beneath and often with brown scales; flowers yellowish, 4 mm wide, stamens glabrous (!), March–April; fruits yellowish red, 4–6 mm long, tasteless. NBB 2: 573. N. America, Canada; on dry, sandy-gravelly, calcareous soil. 1759. z2 Fig. 227.

S. × gottingensis (Rehd.) Rehd. (*S. argentea × S. canadensis*). Intermediate between the parents and only positively identified with a hand lens; scales split to the base (on *S. canadensis* only toothed on the margin, on *S. argentea* only split to half the radius). Discovered around 1892 in the Göttingen Botanic Garden, W. Germany.

Cultivated like *Hippophae*; if planted for fruit, both sexes must be used. Difficult to transplant as older specimens.

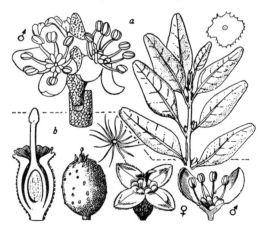

Fig. 227. **Shepherdia**. a. *S. argentea*, branch, flowers, scale; b. *S. canadensis*, flowers, ovary, fruit, stellate hair (from De Wild., Gilg, Original)

SHIBATAEA Mak. — GRAMINEAE

Closely related to *Phyllostachys*, but differing in the sometimes 3–5 shoots at the nodes in the middle of the cane, these shoots thin, very short and of nearly equal length. Low shrubs, stems flexuose, slightly hollow, distinctly flattened; leaves terminal on short shoots, short petioled. — 6 species in E. Asia.

Shibataea kumasaca (Zoll.) Nakai. Bushy, low bamboo, usually not over 1 m high, stems erect, zig-zagging, very flat, usually green, internodes 3–8 cm long, with 2–5 shoots at each node; leaves oval-oblong, 6–12 cm long, 2–2.5 cm wide, long acuminate, glossy green above, somewhat bluish beneath and floccose at first, with 6–7 vein pairs. CBa 31 (= *S. kumasasa* [Steud.] Mak.; *Phyllostachys ruscifolia* Nichols.). Japan. 1870. ("kumasaca" is pronounced like "kumasasa".) z8 Plate 109. # ⊘

S. kumasasa see: **S. kumasaca**

See *Phyllostachys* for cultivation.

SIBIRAEA Maxim. — ROSACEAE

Low, deciduous shrubs; leaves alternate, entire, without stipules; flowers unisexual or polygamous, white, in umbellate-racemose, terminal panicles, these foliate at the base and composed of simple racemes; sepals 5, erect, broadly triangular, petals 5, those of the male flowers twice as long as those of the female flowers; carpels connate at the base; fruit an oblong follicle. — 5 species in Siberia, W. China, SE. Europe.

Sibiraea altaiensis see: **S. laevigata**

S. laevigata (L.) Maxim. Somewhat stiff, to 1 m high; bushy shrub, bark somewhat tough, furrowed, branches glabrous; leaves clustered on the short shoots, narrowly obovate to oblong, 4–10 cm long, round, base cuneate, blue-green on both sides, glabrous; flowers white, in glabrous, 8–12 cm long, basally foliate panicles, May; follicles parallel, 4 mm long. BS 3: 355 (= *S. altaiensis* Schneid.). Siberia. 1774. z3 Plate 110. ⊘

var. **angustata** Rehd. Leaves narrowly lanceolate to oblanceolate, occasionally oblong, acute; inflorescences finely pubescent. W. China. 1908.

var. **croatica** (Degen) Schneid. Leaves sessile to nearly so, obtuse; sepals acute, triangular. SE. Europe; Velebit (mountains along the Croatian coast). 1905.

S. tomentosa Diels. Shrub, 40–60 cm high; leaves oblong-lanceolate to oblanceolate, acute, with a small mucro, densely silky pubescent beneath, glabrous above; flowers yellowish green, in 5 cm long, dense panicles. SW. China. 1915. z6

Cultivated and used like *Spiraea*.

SIDA

Sida pulchella see: **Plagianthus pulchellus**

SINARUNDINARIA Nakai — GRAMINEAE

Tall bamboo, rootstock creeping, forming dense thickets; stem sheaths with appendages, these weak and unsubstantial; with several lateral shoots at every node; leaves glabrous, 0.6–1.5 cm wide, with 2–4 vein pairs; leaf sheaths with flexible, smooth bristles; inflorescences panicled on foliate shoots; stamens 3; style short, with 3 stigmas. — 23 species in China and the Himalayas.

Sinarundinaria murielae (Gamble) Nakai. Very similar to the following species, but the stems yellow (!), pruinose when young, stem sheaths glabrous and ciliate; leaves 7–12 cm long, 1–1.5 cm wide, petiolate, long acuminate at the apex and drawn out to a bristly point (= *Arundinaria murielae* Gamble). Central China. 1907. z7 # ∅ ◗

S. nitida (Mitford) Nakai. Stems about 2.5–3 m high, to 6 m in its habitat, thin, erect, blackish brown (!!), erect in the 4th year and leafless, in the 2nd year branching and nodding, stem sheaths reddish, finely pubescent; leaves 5–8 cm long, 0.6–1.2 cm wide, bright green above, blue-green beneath, curling up in a frost, also abscising for the most part in fall. CBa 9 + 12 (= *Arundinaria nitida* Mitford). Central and W. China. 1889. Requires a semi-shaded location and sufficient moisture; will not tolerate full sun and dry soil! z7 Plate 109. # ○ ◗

Cultivated like *Bambusaceae*.

SINOFRANCHETIA Hemsl. — LARDIZABALACEAE

Monotypic genus. Twining shrub, similar to *Holboellia* and *Akebia*; leaves long petioled, trifoliate; leaflets with a distinct midrib and pinnate venation; flowers inconspicuous, unisexual, sepals and petals 6, carpels 3, fruit a many-seeded berry.

Sinofranchetia chinensis (Franch.) Hemsl. Deciduous, twining shrub, 5–10 m high, young shoots and leaf petioles reddish pruinose; leaflets 6–10 cm long, middle leaflets obovate to nearly circular, larger than the lateral ones and twice as long stalked, the lateral leaflets obliquely ovate to obovate, entire, with a short apex, deep green above, bluish beneath, petiole 5–10 cm long; flowers small, white, in about 10 cm long, pendulous racemes, May; fruits globose, lilac, 1.5 cm long, in 3's. BM 8720. Central and W. China. 1908. Hardy. z6 Fig. 228. ⚭

Cultivated like *Akebia*.

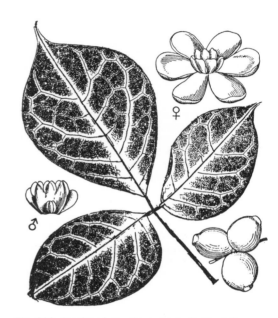

Fig. 228. *Sinofranchetia chinensis.* Individual flowers, enlarged; fruit (from Hemsley; leaf Original)

SINOJACKIA Hu — STYRACACEAE

Deciduous tree, closely related to *Pterostyrax*, but the leaves long stalked and 3–5 in racemes; fruits not ribbed; leaves deciduous, alternate, short petioled; flowers axillary, in foliate, loose racemes; calyx with 5–7 short teeth, petals 5–7, stamens 10–14, flower stalks very thin; fruit a single seeded, woody capsule. — 3 species in China.

Sinojackia rehderiana Hu. Shrub or tree, to 6 m high; leaves obovate, 2–9 cm long, acuminate, base cuneate to slightly cordate, very finely serrate, finely pubescent beneath on the venation; flowers 5–6 in loose, foliate racemes, white, petals usually 6–7, oblong, stalks to 2.5 cm long, June; fruit to 2.5 cm long, cylindrical, beaked. BMns 466; CIS 199; JRHS 1938: 99. E. China. 1930. z8 Plate 110. ✥

S. xylocarpa Hu. Tree, 5–6 m high, shoots, petioles, flower stalks and calyx stellate pubescent; leaves elliptic to nearly obovate, 3–7 cm long, short acuminate, base round, smaller on flowering shoots and with a cordate base, finely dentate, glabrous, midrib beneath stellate pubescent only at first, petiole 3–5 mm long; flowers to 2.5 cm wide, white, to 3–5 in foliate racemes, petals usually 6–7, elliptic-oblong, May; fruits ovate, with a broadly conical apex, to 2 cm long and 1 cm thick. NF 12: 153; CIS 98. E. China. 1934. z9 Fig. 229. ✥

For a deep, loose, humus soil with sufficient moisture and a mild climate; otherwise handled like *Styrax*.

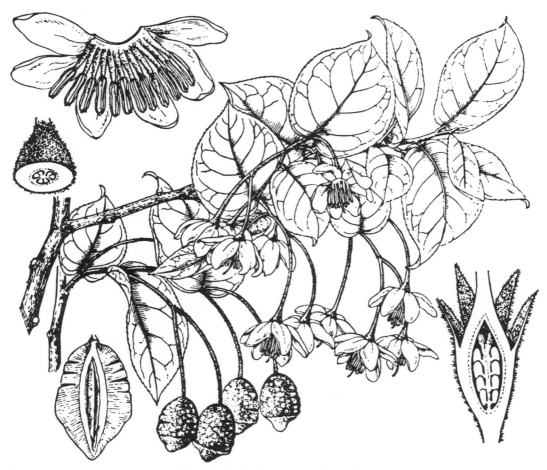

Fig. 229. *Sinojackia xylocarpa* (from Hu)

SINOMENIUM Diels — MENISPERMACEAE

Monotypic genus, very closely relatd to *Cocculus,* but the inflorescences in long, pendulous panicles (not in clusters or spikes!) and with 9–12 (not 6–9) stamens; fruit a drupe.

Sinomenium acutum (Thunb.) Rehd. & Wils. Deciduous, glabrous, shrub, twining to 5 m high, shoots glabrous, striped; leaves quite variable, partly cordate-ovate and entire, partly 3–7 lobed, the lobes long and acute, base 3–5 veined, deep green above, bluish beneath and somewhat pubescent at first; flowers unisexual, small, yellow, in conical, 8–15 cm long, pendulous panicles, June; fruit globose, 6 mm thick, black-blue. GC 52: 411; MJ 1629 (= *Cocculus heterophyllus* Hemsl. & Wils.). Central and W. China, Japan. 1901. z7 to 8 Plate 110; Fig. 230. ∅

No particular requirements; cultivated like *Menispermum.*

SINOWILSONIA Hemsl. — HAMAMELIDACEAE

Monotypic genus. Deciduous tree, branches and leaves stellate pubescent; leaves large, thin, membranous, short petioled, stipules linear, abscising; flowers inconspicuous, monoecious, without petals, in terminal spikes or racemes, male flowers appear before the leaves, sepals 5, stamens 5, ovaries absent; female flowers in short, pendulous spikes, to 15 cm long as fruit clusters, sepals spathulate, staminodes 5, ovaries nearly distinct, 2 locular; fruit a woody capsule, with 2 valves; seeds black.

Sinowilsonia henryi Hemsl. Small tree, about 6 m high

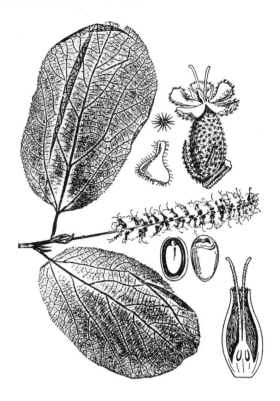

Fig. 230. *Sinomenium acutum* (Original)

Fig. 230a. *Sinowilsonia henryi*. Branch with female flowers; female flower enlarged and in longitudinal section, seeds, stellate hairs (from Hemsley; branch Original)

or more, linden-like in appearance; leaves obovate to oblong or nearly circular, acuminate, finely dentate, base nearly cordate, 10–18 cm long, 6–11 cm wide, stellate pubescent, teeth with bristly tips; flowers green, inconspicuous, male inflorescences 3–5 cm long, female to 2–3 cm long at first, but to 15 cm long in fruit, May. MD 1932: 6. Central China; Hupeh Prov. 1908. Hardy. z6 Plate 103; Fig. 230. ∅

Cultivated like *Hamamelis*; only of botanical interest, otherwise giving the general impression of a linden and not particularly meritorious.

SIPHONOSMANTHUS

Siphonosmanthus delavayi see: **Osmanthus delavayi**

S. suavis see: **Osmanthus suavis**

SKIMMIA Thunb. — Skimmia — RUTACEAE

Glabrous, evergreen shrubs, laurel-like in appearance, leaves alternate, leathery, thick, translucent punctate, short petioled, smooth, entire; flowers small, white, 4 or 5 parted, in attractive, terminal panicles, hermaphroditic or polygamous, the staminate flowers in large, fragrant inflorescences, ovaries of the female flowers 2–5 locular; fruit pea-sized, fleshy, red, with 2–4 single seeded stones. — About 7–8 species in E. Asia and the Himalayas.

While the species occurring in the W. Himalayas, E. China and Japan all have red fruits, the species in the E. Himalayas and W. China (*S. arborescens* T. Anders. and *S. melanocarpa* Rehd. & Wils.) are black fruited.

Skimmia × foremanii Knight (*S. japonica × S. reevesiana*). Intermediate between the parents, about 50 cm high;

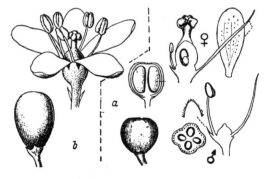

Fig. 231. **Skimmia.** a. *S. japonica*, flowers in longitudinal section, fruit; b. *S. × foremanii*, flowers and fruits (from Gard. Chron., Schneider)

leaves more lanceolate to oblanceolate, yellow-green (!), petiole reddish (!); flowers hermaphroditic, but usually staminate; fruits quite variable in form within the same fruit cluster, some nearly globose, some pear-shaped (!), scarlet-red, persistent. GC 5: 553 (*S. intermedia* sensu Rehd. non Carr.) Developed before 1881 by Foreman, Eskbank Nurseries, Dalkeith, Midlothian, Scotland. z7 Fig. 231. # ∅ ⚭

Including both the following forms:

'Rogersii'. Differing in the deep green leaves (!), green petioles (!); flowers also hermaphroditic; fruits carmine-red, flattened at the apex and more globose-angular (= *S. rogersii* Mast.; *S. foremanii* var. *rogersii* [Mast.] Rehd.). Originated before 1878 by W. H. Rogers in Southampton, England. # ⚭

'Rogersii Nana'. Like 'Rogersii', but lower growing, leaves smaller, flowers staminate. # ⚭

S. fortunei see: **S. reevesiana**

S. japonica Thunb. Evergreen, dioecious shrub, to 1.5 m high, glabrous except for the flower rachis, shoots gray, ascending; leaves often appearing whorled, narrowly oblong to narrowly obovate, 6–12 cm long including the short petiole, 2.5–3.5 cm wide, abruptly acuminate and terminating in a short tip, gradually tapering to the base, entire, glossy green above, yellowish green beneath; cymes 4–8 cm wide, flowers 4 parted, small, 5–6 mm wide, stalk soft pubescent, sepals and bracts tiny, broadly triangular, totally finely ciliate, petals narrowly oblong, 4–5 mm long, with translucent glands, stamens as long as the petals, April; fruits globose to somewhat flattened (!), about 8 mm thick, red, style abscising, 8 mm long, with a somewhat capitate, 4 parted stigma. BM 8038; Gw 5; 261; MJ 388. Japan. 1838. In many gardens the female plants are often labeled *S. oblata* Moore, the male as *S. fragrans* Carr. or *S. fragrantissima* T. Moore, the latter because of the normally fragrant flowers. z8 Plate 111; Fig. 231. # ∅ ⊕ ⚭

'Macrophylla'. Leaves and inflorescences larger. Selection from Foreman. Before 1889. # ∅

var. *variegata* see: **S. reevesiana 'Variegata'**

var. **veitchii** Rehd. Leaves obovate; flowers often hermaphroditic. RHL 1880: 57. Japan. # ⚭

S. laureola S. & Z. Evergreen, totally glabrous shrub, 0.9–2.5 m high in its habitat; leaves glandular punctate, oblong-lanceolate, 7–15 cm long, clustered at the shoot tips, crushed leaves with a strong orange scent; flowers in erect, terminal, 4–5 cm long, compact panicles, unisexual or hermaphroditic, 5 parted, white or yellow, petals oblong, much longer than the calyx, stamens 5 (absent in female flowers), filaments as long as the petals, April–May; fruits ovoid, red, 8–12 mm long. SNp 24. Himalayas. 1850. z9 # ⚭

S. melanocarpa Rehd. & Wils. Small shrub (but also a tree in Yunnan Prov., to 5 m high); leaves oblong-lanceolate, 3–8 cm long, 2–3 cm wide, deep green and glossy above; flowers hermaphroditic, in about 3 cm long, finely pubescent panicles; fruits purple-black (!), globose, about 1 cm thick. Himalayas; W. China. z9 # ⚭

S. reevesiana Fort. Low shrub, occasionally taller than 0.5(1) m, glabrous; leaves lanceolate to oblong-lanceolate, 5–10 cm long, 2–3 cm wide, long acuminate, deep green above, light green beneath; flowers hermaphroditic, 5 parted (!), in 5–8 cm long panicles, April–May; fruits dull red, obovoid, 8 mm long. BM 4719; LWT 138 (as *S. japonica*) (= *S. fortunei* Mast.). China, Taiwan. 1849. z9 # ⊕ ⚭

Including 2 forms:

'Rubella'. Petiole, flower stalks and buds very reddish, particularly in winter; flowers in large panicles, March, male. RH 1874: 311; 1885; 189 (= *S. rubella* Carr. 1874; *S. fortunei* var. *rubella* Rehd). # ⊕

'Variegata'. Leaves white margined (= *S. fortunei* var. *argentea* Mast. 1889; *S. japonica variegata* Hort. 1887). # ⊕ ⚭

S. repens Nakai. About 30 cm high, shoots creeping and rooting, well branched; leaves biennial, nearly whorled, oblanceolate to oblong, 2–8 cm long, tapered to both ends, 8–35 mm wide, very dark green (!); flowers white, female panicles 2 cm long, stamens absent, male panicles 3 cm long, ovate, calyx lobes, triangular, green, May–June; fruits globose, red, 8–9 mm thick, with white stigmas. Japan, 1927. z8 # ⊕ ⚭

S. rogersii see: **S. × foremanii 'Rogersii'**

S. rubella see: **S. reevesiana 'Rubella'**

For protected areas and mild climates; the bright red fruits are very ornamental and persist all winter. Likes a mild humus soil and sufficient moisture.

Lit. Masters, M. T.: Skimmias; in Gard. Chron. 1889, 519–521 and 552–553 (with ills. 89–91 and 94).

SLOANEA L. — ELAEOCARPACEAE

Evergreen or deciduous tropical trees; leaves alternate, occasionally also nearly opposite, entire or dentate, pinnately veined; flowers in axillary or terminal racemes, panicles or clusters, occasionally solitary, with 4 or 5 valve-like, occasionally connate sepals; petals usually absent, or if present, then 1–4, calyx leaflike; stamens numerous; fruit a prickly, dehiscent capsule with 4 or 5 valves. — About 120 species in tropical Asia and America.

Sloanea hemsleyana (Ito) Rehd. & Wils. A tall tree in its habitat, branches outspread, thick, foliage very dense; leaves deciduous, thin, oblong-lanceolate, 12–25 cm long, 5–6 cm wide, long acuminate, base broadly cuneate to rounded, petiole 3–4 cm; flowers numerous in corymbs, terminal, pure white, fragrant; fruits globose, prickly, yellowish at first, brown-purple when ripe, seeds black, glossy, with a large, orange-red aril, then very attractive. ICS 3304; HI (as *S. hanceana*) (= *Echinocarpus sinensis* Hemsl.; *Echinocarpus hemsleyanus* Ito). China; W. Hupeh Prov. z10 ⊕ ⚭

S. sterculiacea (Benth.) Rehd. & Wils. Tall tree, young shoots pubescent; leaves 20–25 cm long, totally finely serrate, glabrous above, finely soft tomentose beneath, venation raised, petiole 5 cm long; flowers white; fruit capsules pendulous, red, 5 cm thick, with 5 or 6 locules, densely covered with subulate, straight, sharp, 12–18 mm long prickles. HA1 33 (= *Echinocarpus sterculiaceus* Benth.) Sikkim, Bhutan, 900–1500 m; Yunnan Prov., 2000 m. z10 ⊙ ⚬

Illustrations of other species:

   S. sinensis ICS 3303 ● *S. tsinyunensis* ICS 3305

SMILAX L. — Greenbriar, Catbriar — LILIACEAE

Deciduous or evergreen shrubs with a creeping rootstock and upright or twining and climbing shoots; leaves alternate, variably formed, rounded, elliptic to cordate, stipules modified into tendrils; flowers dioecious, in axillary umbels or grouped into terminal racemes; perianth 6 parted, greenish, yellowish or whitish, stamens 6; pistils usually 3, style short, with 3 stigmas; fruit a globose, 1 or 3 locular, black, blue-black or red berry. — About 350 species in the tropical and temperate zones of both hemispheres, but only a few in cultivation.

Smilax aspera L. Evergreen climbing shrub, about 60 cm high, shoots somewhat curving back and forth, angular, with prickles; leaves usually narrowly oval-lanceolate, 3–10 cm long, abruptly tapered, base cordate, margins thorny, with 5–9 veins, occasionally white speckled above (!); flowers yellowish green, in clusters of 5–7 together, these grouped into 3–10 cm long, axillary and terminal racemes, fragrant, August–September; berries globose, dark red to black, usually 3 seeded. S. Europe to India. 1650. z9 # ⊘

var. **mauritanica** (Desf.) Gren. & Godr. Vigorous habit, plants less thorny; leaves larger. FS 1049 (= *S. mauritanica* Desf.). Mediterranean region. z9

S. bona-nox L. Deciduous or semi-evergreen climber, underground shoots thorny, shoots green, 4 sided, very prickly on the basal portion and with stiff stellate hairs; leaves quite variable, rounded cordate to triangular-ovate or lanceolate, 4–12 cm long, margins and midrib thorny at the base, green and glossy on both sides; flowers greenish white, umbels 1.5–3 cm long stalked (!), June; fruits black, bluish pruinose, 6–12 together, 6 mm thick, single seeded. BB 1057. N. America. 1739. z8 ⊘

S. china L. Deciduous climber, to 5 m high, shoots more or less angular, thornless or somewhat prickly; leaves usually broadly elliptic to ovate, occasionally wider than long, abruptly acuminate, 5–7 cm long, 5 veined, base somewhat cordate, green beneath; flowers yellow-green, umbels with 2.5 cm long stalks, May; fruit red, nearly 1 cm thick, many seeded. JM 2173. China, Japan, Korea. 1759. z8 ⊘

S. discotis Warb. Deciduous climber, 4–5 m high, shoots angular, with hooked, 4 mm long thorns; leaves ovate to narrowly elliptic, acute, 4–9 cm long, 2–4 cm wide, base usually cordate, bluish beneath, with 3–5 veins, petiole 2–4 mm long; flowers in June; fruits black-blue. China. 1908. z9 ⚬

S. hispida Muhlenb. Deciduous climber, reaching to 10 m high or more in trees, rootstock woody, not stoloniferous, shoots cylindrical, basal part densely covered with straight, thin, blackish bristles and prickles; leaves ovate to broadly ovate, 6–12 cm long, the larger ones cordate at the base, margins somewhat rough, venation 5–9, green beneath; flowers greenish yellow, numbering 25 in umbels, stalk 2–5 cm long, June; fruit black, 8 mm thick, many together. BB 1055; GF 5: 53. Eastern N. America. 1688. Hardy. z6 Fig. 232. ⊘

S. lanceolata L. Florida Greenbrier. Evergreen climber, to 8 m high, rhizome thick, short, tuberous, in clusters (like potatoes), shoots thick, often to 2 cm thick,

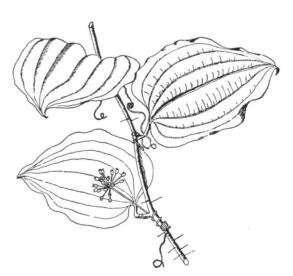

Fig. 232. **Smilax.** Left. *S. rotundifolia*; right *S. hispida* (from Watson and Original)

somewhat rough, bluish when young, with hook form prickles on the basal portion, apical parts thornless; leaves ovate to lanceolate, 5–10 cm long, slender acuminate, thin, glossy above, bluish beneath, with 5–7 veins; flowers numerous, in short stalked, axillary umbels, June; fruits globose, ripening in the following year, 6–7 mm thick. SE. USA. 1785. The best of the American species. z9 # ⚬|∅

S. laurifolia L. Tall, evergreen climbing shrub, rootstock tuberous, branches cylindrical, prickly, young shoots angular and mostly thornless; leaves leathery, narrowly oblong to more lanceolate, 5–10 cm long, 2–5 cm wide, green on both sides, fading to dark brown; flowers greenish, July–August; fruits 6 mm thick, black, ripening in the 2nd year. BB 1: 530. USA; always near water. 1739. z10 # ⚬ ∅

S. mauritanica see: **S. aspera** var. **mauritanica**

S. megalantha C. H. Wright. Evergreen climber, to 5 m high, shoots angular, gray, with thick, to 12 mm long thorns; leaves broadly ovate, the largest to 20 cm long and 15 cm wide, the smallest more lanceolate, base rounded, leathery tough, 3 veined, dark green and glossy above, bluish beneath, petiole 1.5–2.5 cm; flowers greenish, in cymes; fruit coral-red, 12 mm thick. HI 3130. China. 1907. Of great garden merit. z7 Plate 110. # ∅⚬

S. rotundifolia L. Deciduous or semi-evergreen climber, 7–10 m high, usually multistemmed, shoots usually cylindrical, with a few, thick prickles (but never at the nodes!), new growth 4 sided; leaves ovate to nearly circular, acute, 4 sided; leaves ovate to nearly circular, acute, 3–15 cm long, base rounded to cordate, entire or with rough margins, glossy green on both sides; flowers greenish yellow, in umbels, June; fruits black, usually bluish pruinose, globose, 6 mm thick, 3–6 in umbels, stalk 6–12 mm long, with 1–3 seeds. BB 1054; GSP 56. N. America. 1760. Quite winter hardy. Very strong growing. z5 Fig. 232. ∅

Despite the large number of species, only rarely found in cultivation, no particular soil preference; a warm, protected site is suggested whenever hardiness is in question. The strong growing species (*S. hispida, rotundifolia*) climb into the crowns of small trees.

SOLANDRA Sw. — Chalice Vine — SOLANACEAE

Shrubs or woody climbers; leaves alternate, simple, entire, usually leathery tough, glossy; flowers solitary, axillary, on thick, short stalks, calyx long tubular, 2–5 incised at the apex, corolla white to yellow, often also with purple markings, infundibular with a cylindrical tube and a campanulate mouth, limb 5 lobed, overlapping in the bud stage, reflexed when open; stamens 5, adnate to the corolla; fruit a fleshy, globose, 2 locular berry, more or less surrounded by the calyx. — 10 species from Mexico to tropical S. America.

Solandra grandiflora Swartz. Evergreen shrub, climbing to 5 m high or more, glabrous; leaves elliptic to obovate, to 17 cm long, acute, petiole shorter than 2.5 cm; calyx tubular, to 7 cm long, bilabiate, as long as the narrow part of the corolla tube, corolla white, becoming yellow to brownish yellow on the 2nd day, 10–15 cm long, slightly narrowed in the throat and outspread past the calyx. BIT 28; BM 1874. Jamaica, Puerto Rico, Lesser Antilles. 1781. z10 Plate 75.

S. guttata D. Don ex Lindl. Cup of Gold. Evergreen climber, to 2.5 m high, pubescent; leaves elliptic-oblong, 7–15 cm long, acute, soft pubescent on the underside, petiole to 5 cm long; flowers erect, terminal, yellow, purple speckled or striped in the throat, to 20 cm long, cup-shaped, limb outspread, crispate, calyx to 7.5 cm long, 3 lobed at the apex. DRHS 1975; BR 1551. Mexico. 1830. Often confused with *S. maxima*. z10

S. hartwegii see: **S. maxima**

S. maxima (Sessé & Moc.) P. S. Green. Climbing shrub, similar to *S. guttata*, to 4 m high, totally glabrous (!); leaves elliptic, to 15 cm long, obtuse to short acuminate, petiole to 7 cm long; calyx to 7 cm long, unevenly 3–4 lobed, tube 5 ribbed, the ribs with a green exterior, corolla glabrous, yellow, interior with 5 purple ridges, cup form, about 20 cm long, the 5 limb lobes crispate and more or less reflexed. BMns 506; MCL 95; BC 3627 (= *S. hartwegii* N.E. Br.; *S. nitida* Zuccagni). Mexico. z10

S. nitida see: **S. maxima**

Widely planted in frost free climates for the large, very fragrant (especially at night) flowers; needs to remain dry in summer until the leaves fade or abscise, then it should be watered well. Won't flower if the summer dry period is not observed.

SOLANUM L. — Nightshade — SOLANACEAE

Herbaceous plants or shrubs, also evergreen and tree-like in the tropics, branches occasionally thorny; leaves alternate, simple or compound; flowers solitary (rarely) or in umbellate panicles, often opposite the leaves; calyx 5–10 parted or dentate, persistent, corolla rotate to flat campanulate, the tips folded in the bud stage; stamens 5, inclined together, dehiscing at the apex, ovaries usually 2 locular; fruit a many seeded berry. — Over 1700 species, most in the tropics and subtropics of both hemispheres.

Solanum aviculare G. Forst. Kangaroo Apple. Deciduous, upright, thornless, glabrous shrub, to 2.5 m high; leaves lanceolate to ovate, to 25 cm long, simple to pinnatisect on young plants or irregularly lobed; flowers many in axillary cymes, corolla violet blue, 2.5–3 cm wide, calyx lobes short, corolla tip short and wide; fruit an ovate, 2–2.5 cm long, yellowish, edible berry. BM 9154 (= *S. laciniatum* Ait.). New Zealand, Australia. The name *S. laciniatum* refers to a tetraploid form with larger flowers and an increased number of grit cells in the fruits. z9 Plate 76. ∅ ✤

Fig. 233. *Solanum dulcamara* (from Lauche)

Fig. 234. *Solanum wendlandii* (from Gard. Chron.)

S. crispum Ruiz & Pav. Climbing shrub, 3–4 m high, older shoots woody, young shoots often only herbaceous, finely pubescent; leaves evergreen in mild climates, otherwise abscising, ovate to lanceolate, 7–12 cm long, base round to cordate, acute, limb often undulate-crispate (!), finely pubescent on both sides; flowers lilac-blue, at first in 7–10 cm wide, terminal corymbs, fragrant, corolla 5 lobed, to 3 cm wide, anthers yellow, calyx 5 toothed, June–September; fruits yellowish white, pea-sized. JRHS 84: 44; BM 3795. Chile. 1824. z9 ⊕

S. dulcamara L. Climbing subshrub, to 2.5 m high, shoots angular, usually glabrous, gray-yellow; leaves oblong-ovate, usually with 1–3 basal lobe pairs, 4–10 cm long, often also undivided, dark green above, lighter beneath, usually glabrous or totally finely pubescent on both sides; flowers light violet, in cymes, petals oblong-lanceolate, reflexed, sometimes with 2 green basal spots, July–August; fruits ovate, bright red, 1 cm long, poisonous. HF 252. Europe, Asia, N. Africa. 1561. z6 Fig. 233.

S. jasminoides Paxt. Deciduous climber, abundantly branched, shoots 1 m long or more; leaves usually small at the shoot tips, oval-lanceolate and entire, the basal leaves normally 3–5 parted, leaflets then ovate, 4–6 cm long, entire; flowers in short racemes, grouped into 5–7

cm wide clusters, corolla 2–2.5 cm wide, stellate form, white with a trace of blue, calyx short 5 toothed, stamens lemon-yellow, July to August. DRHS 1977; BR 33: 33; BMns 568. S. America, Brazil. 1838. Very attractive, but only for mild climates. z9 ⊕

S. laciniatum see: **S. aviculare**

S. rantonnetii Carr. "Blue Potato Shrub". Shrub or subshrub, 1–1.5 m high, thornless, nearly totally glabrous; leaves ovate, 10 cm long, usually long acuminate and undulate; flowers 2–5 in the leaf axils, 2.5 cm wide, corolla violet with a light yellow center; fruits red, about 2.5 cm thick, cordate, pendulous, very ornamental. RH 1859: 135. Argentina to Paraguay, on the forest's edge. 1870. z10

Including:

'Grandiflorum', with larger flowers. Mostly in cultivation. ⊕

S. valdiviense Dun. Deciduous shrub, to 3 m high, open, branches drooping, shoots distinctly angular, finely pubescent on the edges; leaves oval-lanceolate, simple, acute, tapered toward the base or occasionally rounded, quite variable in size, 2–4 cm long, with scattered, stiff hairs on either side; flowers lilac to white, 8–10 in cymes, fragrant, corolla about 12 mm wide, anthers yellow, summer; fruit pea-sized, olive-green, somewhat translucent. BM 9552. Chile; Valdivia. 1927. z9 ⊕

S. wendlandii Hook. f. Climber, to 5 m high or more, branches and shoots glabrous, with a few scattered, short, hook form prickles; leaves quite variable, usually pinnate, 10–25 cm long, with a large terminal leaflet, the apical leaves simple, oblong or 3 lobed, cordate, often also with the lateral leaflets lobed or otherwise incised, bright green, pinnate leaves with 9–13 leaflets, lobed leaves with ovate or oblong, entire lobes; flowers in pendulous, branched, terminal cymes, 15 cm wide or wider, corolla lilac-blue, 5 cm wide, August; fruits globose to ovate, 7–10 cm thick. BM 6914; BC 3633; MCL 124. Costa Rica. 1882. The most attractive species of the genus. z10 Fig. 234. ✥

All species need a protected area, if not a frost free climate. Require a loose, humus soil and sufficient moisture; may be overwintered in a temperate greenhouse. Only *S. dulcamara* is generally winter hardy.

Lit. Lawrence, G. H. .M.: The cultivated Species of *Solanum;* in Baileya 1960, 21–35 (with ills.)

SOLLYA Lindl. — PITTOSPORACEAE

Graceful evergreen climbers; leaves small, narrow, entire or somewhat undulate margined; flowers in few-flowered cymes, occasionally solitary at the shoot tips, nodding, blue; sepals small, distinct, petals spreading wider from the base, obovate, anthers in a conical arrangement around the ovary, fruit an indehiscent berry. — 2 species in W. Australia.

Sollya drummondii see: **S. parviflora**

S. fusiformis see: **S. heterophylla**

S. heterophylla Lindl. Small shrub, twining 0.5–1.5 m high, shoots thin; leaves variable in form, from lanceolate or linear-oblong to more ovate, obtuse to acuminate, 2.5–5 cm long, entire, usually tapering to the short petiole; flowers usually 4–8(12) in terminal (or with 1 opposite leaf) cymes, petals 8 mm long, blue, July. BM 3523; BC 3641 (= *S. fusiformis* Payer). Australia. 1830. z9 # ✥

S. parviflora Turcz. Graceful, slender and more twining than the previous species and usually with a loose, soft pubescence; leaves lanceolate to oblong-linear, the larger ones to about 2.5 cm long, very short petioled with a thin blade; flowers solitary or grouped 2–3 together, petals 6 mm long, blue, July, stalks very thin; fruits 12–18 mm long, acuminate at both ends (= *S. drummondii* Morr.). W. Australia. 1838. z9 # ✥

Very attractive, twining shrubs, easily cultivated in the proper climate; prefer a moist, peaty, but well drained soil.

SOPHORA L. — Pagoda Tree — LEGUMINOSAE

Deciduous or evergreen trees or shrubs; occasionally subshrubs; leaves alternate, odd pinnate, stipules small; flowers in racemes or panicles, calyx with 5 short teeth; stamens 10, distinct or short connate at the base; fruit a fleshy, cylindrical, segmented pod. — About 50 species in N. Asia, New Zealand and Chile.

Sophora affinis Torr. & Gray. Small, round crowned tree, to 6 m high; leaves 10–20 cm long, with 13–19 elliptic leaflets, these 2–4 cm long, obtuse to emarginate, base broadly cuneate, glabrous or scattered pubescent beneath, distinctly veined (!); flowers white, turning pink, in 5–15 cm long, pubescent panicles, June; pods 3–8 cm long, pubescent, black, long persistent on the plant. SS 122; SDK 4: 10. USA; Texas to Arkansas, on limestone. 1890. z8 Fig. 236. ✥

S. davidii (Franch.) Skeels. Deciduous shrub, to 2.5 m high, branches outspread and thorny, young shoots pubescent; leaves 2–6 cm long, leaflets 13–19, elliptic-oblong, 6–10 mm long, silky pubescent beneath; flowers bluish violet to whitish, 6–12 together in terminal racemes on short side shoots, flowering abundantly, calyx violet, short 5 toothed, June; pods 5–6 cm long, 1–4 seeded, long beaked, nearly glabrous. DM 7883; BS 3: 320 (= *S. viciifolia* Hance; *S. moorcroftiana* var. *davidii* Franch.). W. China. 1897. Hardy. For a dry, sandy soil. z5 ✥

S. flavescens Ait. Subshrub, annual shoots erect, about 90 cm long (shrubby in mild climates, to 1.5 m high); leaves 15–22 cm long, with 15–19 leaflets, these narrowly ovate, 3–5.5 cm long; flowers yellowish white, 12 mm long, in cylindrical panicles or racemes, to 30 cm long, terminal on the current year's wood, July–August. China. z6 ✥

S. japonica L. Tree, to 25 m high, crown broad and rounded, young shoots dark green, glabrous; leaves to 25 cm long, leaflets 7–17, stalked, elliptic to ovate, 3–5 cm long, glossy green above, gray-green pubescent beneath; flowers yellowish white, in loose, terminal, 25 cm long panicles, August; pods to 8 cm long, cylindrical, seeds black. BM 8764; SDK 4: 10. China, Korea (not Japan, as may be inferred by the name!). 1747. Valuable street tree. Ⓕ Yugoslavia, China. z5 ✥

'Columnaris'. Columnar habit. Distributed from French nurseries before 1907.

'Dot' (Dot). Small tree, branches partly weeping, twisted; leaves crispate. Originated around 1920 by Simon Dot, of San Feliu de Llobregat near Barcelona, Spain. (or = 'Crispa'?) Plate 112.

'Pendula'. Very slow growing, developing a picturesque tree, branches very pendulous, very stiff. Cultivated before 1927 in England. Should be grafted on a standard. The most generally cultivated form never flowers (Fig. 235); but there is also a loosely branched, abundantly flowering, weeping form, as depicted in Plate 111.

var. **pubescens** (Tausch) Bosse. Tree, young shoots finely soft pubescent (!); leaflets larger, oval-oblong to oval-lanceolate, to 8 cm long, with a navicular curve, underside dense and finely pubescent; flowers greenish white, keel and wings often turning reddish. MD 1922: 20 (= *S. korolkowii* Hort.; *S. tomentosa* Hort.; *S. sinensis* Hort.). 1830. ✥

'Regent' (Plant Patent 2338). Growth twice as strong as the species; leaves larger, darker green, distributed along the entire shoot; flowering earlier. Introduced by Princeton Nurseries, USA. Very tolerant of summer heat.

var. *rubella* see: **'Violacea'**

Fig. 235. *Sophora japonica* 'Pendula' (from Decaisne)

'**Variegata**'. Leaves cream-white margined. ⌀

'**Violacea**'. Leaves light green, leaflets long, narrow, somewhat undulate; flowers with a white standard, wings and keel purple-red, first flowering in September (= *S. violacea* Hort.; *S. japonica violacea* Carr.; *S. japonica rubella* Sprenger). Introduced from China in 1858. ✣

S. korolkowii see: **S. japonica** var. **pubescens**

S. macrocarpa Sm. Evergreen tree, 10–20 m, or only a shrub, young shoots densely tomentose; leaflets in 10–20 pairs, elliptic to obovate, obtuse, 2–2.5 cm long, silky pubescent beneath; flowers 12 together in short, axillary racemes, 2.5–3 cm long, yellow, banner as long as the wing, all petals directed forward, calyx campanulate, dentate, finely pubescent, May; pods cylindrical (!), with 1–4 seeds. DRHS 1984; BM 8647 (= *Edwardsia chilensis* Miers). Chile. 1822. z9 # ✣

S. microphylla Ait. Large shrub or small tree, very similar to *S. tetraptera*, but with rounded-obovate to broadly oblong leaflets, usually emarginate, usually glabrous above or nearly so, sparsely pubescent beneath, often only on the midrib, 6–12 mm long, flowers about 3 cm long, standard about as long as the wing. MNZ 47; KF 51; BM 1442, 3735; PFC 154 (= *S. tetraptera* var. *microphylla* [Ait.] Hook. f.; *Edwardsia macnabiana* Curt.). New Zealand. z9 Fig. 236. # ✣

S. moorcroftiana var. *davidii* see: **S. davidii**

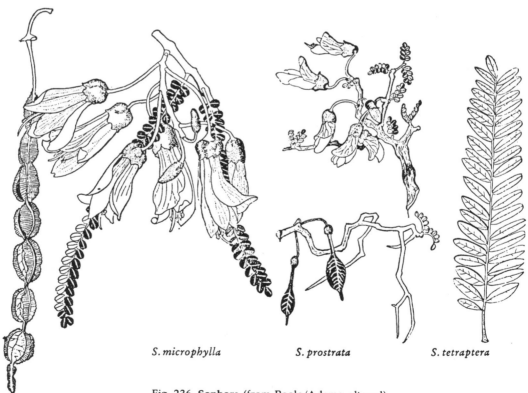

S. microphylla   S. prostrata   S. tetraptera

Fig. 236. **Sophora** (from Poole/Adams, altered)

S. prostrata Buchan. Evergreen shrub, procumbent or ascending, usually composed of a mass of chaotically branched, wiry shoots; leaves with 6–8 pairs of leaflets, these oblong, only 5–6 mm long; flowers 1–3 together, 2 cm long, brownish yellow to orange, May, on thin, silky pubescent stalks; pods 2.5–5 cm long, very narrow winged. MNZ 48. New Zealand. z8 Fig. 236. # ✣

S. sinensis see: **S. japonica** var. **pubescens**

S. tetraptera Ait. Evergreen or semi-evergreen, small tree or shrub, 3–10 m high in its habitat, shoots, stalks and calyx with a short brownish tomentum, young shoots flexuose, thin; leaves 3–11 cm long, with 7–9 leaflets on young plants, conspicuously more leaflets on older plants (31–41 and more), these linear-oblong, silky pubescent; flowers 3–5 cm long, golden-yellow, somewhat tubular, grouped 2–8 in short, pendulous racemes, calyx obliquely campanulate, May; pod 5–20 cm long, 4 winged, constricted between the individual seeds. SDK 4: 10 (= *Edwardsia tetraptera* Pour.). New Zealand, Chile. 1722. z9 Plate 112; Fig. 236. # ✣

'Grandiflora'. Leaflets linear-oblong, obtuse, both sides with a silky, appressed pubescence, about 25 mm long, 10–25 pairs; flowers to 4 cm long, banner shorter than the wings. BM 167; KF 50 (= *Edwardsia grandiflora* Salisb.). # ✣

var. microphylla see: **S. microphylla**

S. tomentosa L. "Silver Bush". Shrub, to 3 m high, totally white tomentose, but later becoming glabrous, shoots numerous, steeply ascending; leaves to about 20 cm long, with 13–21 leaflets, these elliptic to oblanceolate, 2.5–5 cm long, obtuse or emarginate; flowers about 2 cm long, in 10–20 cm long racemes, yellow, banner 2 cm wide, reflexed; fruits 6–15 cm long, with 4–9 yellow seeds. LWT 129; BIC 48. The tropics of the old world originally, but cultivated throughout the tropics today. See also: **S. japonica** var. **pubescens**. z10 # ∅ ✣

S. viciifolia see: **S. davidii**

S. violacea see: **S. japonica** 'Violacea'

SORBARIA (Ser.) A. Br. — False Spirea — ROSACEAE

Deciduous, mostly large shrubs, annual shoots cylindrical; leaves alternate, pinnate, leaflets serrate, with stipules; flower small, white, but grouped into large, terminal panicles; calyx cupulate, sepals 5, petals 5, imbricate in bud, stamens 20–50, as long or longer than the petals, carpels 5, opposite the sepals, connate at the base; follicles dehiscing along the ventral seam, with several locules. — 10 species in E. Asia.

Sorbaria aitchisonii Hemsl. Shrub, to 3 m high, shoots glabrous, usually red when young; leaflets 15–21, lanceolate, less than 15 mm wide, long acuminate, simple or nearly simple serrate (!), reddish glabrous on new growth; flowers 1 cm wide, in erect, 20–25 cm long, glabrous panicles, panicle branches erect (!), stamens longer than the petals, July–August; follicles with a recurved stalk. BS 3: 343; GC 28: 75 (= *S. angustifolia*

Zab.). W. China, Kashmir, Afghanistan. 1815. z6 Fig. 237, 238. ✣

S. alpina see: **S. grandiflora**

S. angustifolia see: **S. aitchisonii**

S. arborea Schneid. Shrub, broad growing, to 6 m high, young shoots and leaf petioles usually somewhat stellate pubescent; leaflets 13–17, oval-oblong to lanceolate, long acuminate, 4–10 cm long, scabrous and biserrate, stellate pubescent to glabrous beneath (!); flowers 6 mm wide, panicles widespreading to nodding, to 40 cm long, stamens much longer than the petals, July–August; fruits on recurved stalks. Central and western China. 1908. z6 Plate 113. ✣

var. **glabrata** Rehd. Young shoots and leaf petioles glabrous, often reddish; leaflets lanceolate to narrow lanceolate, glabrous; stamens 2–3 times longer than the petals. ✣

var. **subtomentosa** Rehd. Young shoots and leaf petioles pubescent; leaflets elliptic-oblong to oblong-lanceolate, densely stellate pubescent beneath, lateral veins very densely arranged. W. China. ✣

S. assurgens Vilm. & Bois. Shrub, to 3 m high, upright; leaves often over 30 cm long, leaflets 13–17, oblong-lanceolate, often falcate (!), long acuminate, 5–8 cm long, scabrous and biserrate, densely and regularly veined, with about 25 (!) vein pairs; panicles erect, 10–16 cm long, loose, calyx glabrous, stamens about 20 (!), shorter than the petals, July; fruits with a somewhat curved or outspread style. MG 32: 169. Central China. 1896. z7 ✣

S. grandiflora (Sweet) Maxim. Scarcely over 50 cm high, shoots pubescent, red-gray, bark later exfoliating; leaves 8–18 cm long, rachis reddish, usually pubescent, leaflets 9–13, sessile, oblong-acute, scabrous biserrate, 2.5–5 cm long, glabrous; flowers 1–1.5 cm wide (!), in few-flowered corymbs, white, stamens as long as the petals, July; follicle pubescent, with recurved styles. DL 3: 227 (= *S. alpina* Dipp.; *Spiraea pallasii* G. Don). E. Siberia. 1852. Hardy. z4 ✣

S. kirilowii Maxim. Shrub, similar to *S. sorbifolia*, 1.5–3 m high; leaflets 13–19, glabrous; flower panicles broadly conical, stamen filaments as long as the corolla, style at fruiting situated far beneath the fruit apex. N. China. z5 Fig. 237.

S. lindleyana see: **S. tomentosa**

S. sorbifolia (L.) A. Br. Shrub, to 2 m high, stems erect, rather stiff, brown, very pithy, glabrous or finely pubescent; leaves to 25 cm long, leaflets 13–23, usually 17, nearly sessile, lanceolate or oblong, acuminate, usually with 20 vein pairs, scabrous and biserrate, light green; panicles erect, 10–25 cm long, flowers about 8 mm wide, white stamens 40–50 (!!), twice as long as the petals, calyx and fruits glabrous, June–July. Gn 23; 248 (= *Spiraea sorbifolia* L.; *Spiraea tobolskiana* Hort.). Ural Mts. to Kamchatka, Sachalin, Japan. 1759. z2 Plate 113; Fig. 237. ✣

var. **stellipila** Maxim. Leaves more or less stellate pubescent beneath (!), petiole and calyx soft pubescent; fruits pubescent.

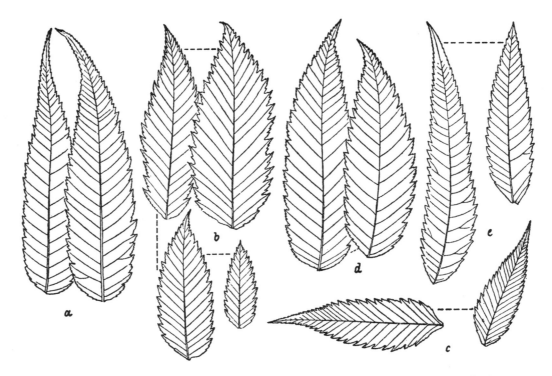

Fig. 237. **Sorbaria.** a. *S. tomentosa;* b. *S. sorbifolia;* c. *S. kirilowii;* d. *S. sorbifolia* var. *stellipila;*
e. *S. aitchisonii* (from Schneider, altered)

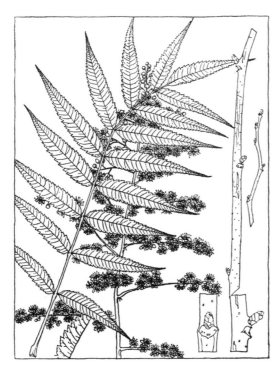

Fig. 238. *Sorbaria aitchisonii* (drawn by Nose)

Gw 15: 651; MJ 1413; Gs 1921: 156 (= *S. stellipila* Schneid). E.
Asia. 1900. Fig. 237. ⊕

S. stellipila see: **S. sorbifolia** var. **stellipila**

S. tomentosa (Lindl.) Rehd. Shrub, 2–4 (6) m high,
branches widespreading, totally glabrous, as are the
young shoots; leaflets 15–21, lanceolate to narrowly
lanceolate, 5–10 cm long, narrowly acuminate, biserrate,
venation usually with simple (!) hairs beneath; panicles
25–30 cm long, outspread, loose, branches limp, soft
pubescent, flowers yellowish white, 6 mm wide, stamens
as long as the petals, July to August; fruits glabrous. FS
108; BR 31: 33 (= *S. lindleyana* Maxim.). Himalayas. 1840.
z8–9 Fig. 237. ⊕

Prefer full sun, but protect from wind and damage from an
early frost; soil preference, deep, fertile and moist; very good
specimen plants.

× **SORBARONIA** (*Aronia* × *Sorbus*) Schneid. — ROSACEAE

Hybrids between *Aronia* and *Sorbus*, intermediate in appearance. Deciduous shrubs or small trees; leaves partly pinnate or simple, finely serrate; flowers white, in small, dense corymbs; styles 3–4; fruits red to nearly black.

1. Leaves partly pinnate or lobed;

    + Underside pubescent; fruits deep purple:
        S. hybrida

   ++ Underside nearly glabrous; fruits blackish:
        S. fallax

2. Leaves simple; margins finely serrate;

    + Fruits red to brown-red:
        S. alpina

   ++ Fruits blackish red:
        S. dippelii

× **Sorbaronia alpina** (Willd.) Schneid. (*Aronia arbutifolia* × *Sorbus aria*). Deciduous shrub, 1–3 m high, resembling *Sorbus aria*, young shoots and buds gray tomentose; leaves oblong-elliptic, acuminate, 5–7 cm long, glandular serrate, scattered pubescent above at first, later glabrous, underside densely gray tomentose; inflorescences small, gray tomentose, petals circular, white, styles 3–4, May; fruits ovate, red to brown, 8 mm thick; SH 1: 384 f–h (= *Sorbus alpina* Heynh.). Originated in cultivation around 1800, presumably in France. z5

S. dippelii (Zab.) Schneid. (*Aronia melanocarpa* × *Sorbus aria*). Bushy, deciduous shrub, occasionally a small tree (if grafted on a standard), young shoots thickly gray tomentose; leaves narrowly elliptic to oblanceolate, 3–8 cm long, shallowly glandular serrate, bright green and glabrous above, underside gray tomentose, eventually rather glabrous; flowers 8 mm wide, white, anthers pink, in small, pubescent, but eventually glabrous inflorescences; fruits to 8 mm thick, globose to pear-shaped, blackish (!). SG 1: 384i (= *Sorbus dippelii* Zab.). Originated in cultivation around 1870. z5

S. fallax (Schneid.) Schneid. (*Aronia melanocarpa* × *Sorbus aucuparia*). Tree-like shrub, branches outspread to nodding, appressed pubescent at first; leaves partly ovate to oval-oblong and simple, partly pinnately lobed at the base on one side or both or with 1–2 paired pinna, 3–8 cm long, rounded (!) at the apex, crenate, eventually dark green and somewhat glossy above, underside tomentose, eventually nearly glabrous (!), gray-green; flowers in small corymbs, petals rounded, white, slightly pink in bud, style (3–4) to 5, inflorescences eventually rather glabrous, May–June; fruits blackish red, ovate (= *Sorbus heterophylla* sensu Dipp.; *Aronia heterophylla* Zab.). Developed in cultivation around 1878 near Kassel, W. Germany. z5 Plate 113. ⚥

S. hybrida (Moench) Schneid. (*Aronia arbutifolia* × *Sorbus aucuparia*). Shrub to small tree, branches thin, often pendulous, tomentose when young; leaves oval-oblong, 3–8 cm long, with 2–3 pairs of lobes or leaflets, crenate toward the apex, pubescent beneath; inflorescences about 3 cm wide, many flowered, flowers white or reddish, styles 5; fruits globose to ovate, 8–10 mm long, deep purple. BR 1196; SH 1: 384 k–n (= *Sorbus heterophylla* Reichenb.; *Sorbus spuria* Pers.). Originated before 1785. z5 ⚥

S. sorbifolia (Poir.) Schneid. (*Aronia melanocarpa* × *Sorbus americana*). Very similar to *S. fallax*, but the leaves light green beneath (!) and totally glabrous or nearly so, leaf segments more acuminate and ovate (= *Sorbus sargentii* Dipp.; *Sorbus sorbifolia* Hedl.). Developed in 1893 in the Darmstadt Botanic Garden, W. Germany. z5

Cultivated like *Sorbus*.

Fig. 239. × *Sorbocotoneaster pozdnjakovii.* Branch of a *Sorbus*-similar plant (Original)

× **SORBOCOTONEASTER** (*Cotoneaster* × *Sorbus*) Pojark. — ROSACEAE

Hybrids between *Cotoneaster* and *Sorbus*, intermediate. Leaves either totally pinnate or only partly so and lobed or simple; flowers white, in corymbs; fruits red or black.

× **Sorbocotoneaster pozdnjakovii** Pojark. (*Cotoneaster niger* × *Sorbus sibirica*). Shrub, shoots thin, red-brown, sparsely pubescent at first, later glabrous and glossy; leaves pinnate, bright green, somewhat glossy above, underside light green, both sides with scattered, long, appressed hairs at first, petiole about 1–2 cm long, leaflets usually 5, sessile, obtuse ovate, usually somewhat navicular convex, 2–3 cm long, base oblique, often somewhat decurrent on the petiole, occasionally with a small, about 5–8 mm long leaflet situated on the rachis between the leaflet pairs; inflorescences numerous; fruits red. Found as a natural hybrid in Siberia. Around 1950. z3 Fig. 239. ∅ ⚥

There also exists another, more *Cotoneaster*-like form with partly simple leaves and black fruits which has not been observed by the author.

Lit. Pojarkowa, A. P.: *Sorbocotoneaster* Pojark.; in Bot. Material. **15**, 92–108 (Moscow 1953).

× SORBOPYRUS (*Pyrus* × *Sorbus*) Schneid. — ROSACEAE

Hybrids between *Pyrus* and *Sorbus*. To date only known in the following combination.

× **Sorbopyrus auricularis** (Knoop) Schneid. (*Pyrus communis* × *Sorbus aria*). Deciduous tree to 15 m high, branches thornless, young shoots gray tomentose at the apex; leaves elliptic-oblong, short acuminate, 6–10 cm long, irregularly serrate, dark green and glossy above, both sides gray tomentose at first, eventually persisting only beneath and on the 3–5 cm long petiole, teeth acute, without glands; flowers white, 2 cm wide, in white tomentose corymbs, May; fruits pear-shaped, 2.5 cm thick, yellow with a red cheek, sweet, but not juicy, edible, mealy. HF 2533; BS 3: 322; BR 1437 (= *Pyrus pollveria* L.; *P. auricularis* Knoop). Originated before 1690 in Bollweiler, Alsace, N. E. France. z5 Plate 120; Fig. 240.

'**Bulbiformis**'. Resembling the species, but more similar to *Pyrus*; leaves shorter, wider, often elliptic-rounded, less

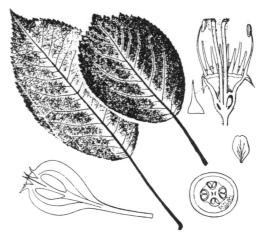

Fig. 240. × *Sorbopyrus auricularis*. Leaves (Original), flowers and fruits in cross section (from Schneider)

coarsely serrate, nearly always cordate at the base, underside less tomentose; flowers larger, to nearly 3 cm wide, less numerous in corymbs, May; fruits larger, to 5 cm long, pear-shaped, dark yellow (= *Pyrus malifolia* Spach). ⊕

Origin unknown, but present in 1834 in Paris (Ménagerie du Jardin du Roi) as a 10 m tall tree. ⊕

Cultivated like *Pyrus*. Relatively rare in cultivation.

SORBUS L. — Mountain Ash — ROSACEAE

Deciduous trees or shrubs; buds usually very large, scales imbricate; leaves alternate, with stipules, either simple and serrate or odd pinnate, usually folded in the bud stage; flowers usually white, in exceptional cases pink, in compound, terminal corymbs; sepals and petals 5, stamens 15–20, carpels 2–5, ovaries either partly free and subinferior or fully connate and inferior; styles free or connate at the base; fruits apple-like, small, core with cartilaginous walls, each locule with 1–2 seeds. — About 100 species in the Northern Hemisphere; many apomictic.

Outline of the Species Contained in this Work

Section 1. **Sorbus** (L.) Pers. "Mountain Ash"
Leaves always pinnate; carpels 2–4, occasionally 5, apex more or less free, ovary partly superior; fruits red, yellow or white, 5–15 mm thick:
> *S. americana, arnoldiana, aucuparia, commixta, decora, discolor, esserteauiana, filipes, gracilis, harrowiana, hupehensis, insignis, koehneana, matsumurana, occidentalis, pluripinnata, pohuashanensis, poteriifolia, prattii, pygmaea, randaiensis, reducta, rehderiana, rufoferruginea, sambucifolia, sargentiana, scalaris, scopulina, serotina, sitchensis, splendida, tianshanica, vilmorinii, wilsoniana*

Section 2. **Cormus** (Spach) Schneid.
Leaves pinnate, carpels 5, fully connate, ovary inferior;

fruits green to brown, 15–30 mm long:
> *S. domestica*

Section 3. **Sect. Sorbus × Sect. Aria**
Characteristics intermediate:
> *S. hybrida, thuringiaca*

Section 4. **Aria** Pers. "Whitebeam"
Leaves simple, lobed or also only serrate; calyx lobes persistent:
> *S. anglica, aria, arranensis, bristoliensis, chamaemespilus, cuspidata, decipiens, devoniensis, intermedia, lanata, latifolia, megalocarpa, minima, mougeotii, pallescens, torminalis, umbellata*

Section 5. **Micromeles** (Decne.) Rehd.
Leaves simple; fruits small, calyx lobes abscising:
> *S. alnifolia, caloneura, folgneri, japonica, keissleri, meliosmifolia, rhamnoides*

Parentage of some Cultivars

Cultivars with Latin names such as 'Nana', 'Fastigiata', 'Pendula' etc., are excluded since these names apply to many species. Many of these are further described (as noted) in the "Cultivar and Garden Hybrids" list at the end of this section.

'Apricot Lady'	→ Cultivar List
'Atrovirens'	→ *S. latifolia*
'Beissneri'	→ *S. aucuparia*
'Brouwers'	→ *S. intermedia*

'Belmonte'   → *S. americana*
'Chamois Glow'   → Cultivar List
"Cheerwater Seedling"   → 'Sheerwater Seedling'
'Decurrens'   → *S. thuringiaca*
'Dirkenii'   → *S. aucuparia*
'Dulcis'   → *S. aucuparia* 'Edulis'
'Edwin Hillier'   → Cultivar List
'Edulis'   → *S. aucuparia*
'Embley'   → Cultivar List
'Ethel's Gold'   → Cultivar List
fifeana   → *S. aucuparia*
                               'Xanthocarpa'
'Ghose'   → Cultivar List
'Gibbsii'   → *S. hybrida*
'Golden Wonder'   → Cultivar List
'Jermyns'   → Cultivar List
'Joseph Rock'   → Cultivar List
'Kewensis'   → Cultivar List
'Kirsten Pink'   → Cultivar List
'Konzentra'   → *S. aucuparia* 'Edulis'
'Lemon Drop'   → *S. folgneri*
'Leonard Springer'   → *S. thuringiaca*
'Lombarts Hybrids'   → *S. arnoldiana*
'Lowndes'   → Cultivar List
'Lutescens'   → *S. aria*
'Magnifica'   → *S. aria*
'Majestica'   → *S. aria*
'Mitchellii'   → Cultivar List
moravica   → *S. aucuparia* 'Edulis'
'Neuillyensis'   → *S. thuringiaca*
'November Pink'   → *S. hupehensis*
'Pearly King'   → Cultivar List
'Quercoides'   → *S. thuringiaca*
'Red Marbles'   → Cultivar List
'Red Tip'   → Cultivar List
'Rose Queen'   → Cultivar List
'Rosina'   → *S. aucuparia* 'Edulis'
'Rossica'   → *S. aucuparia*
'Rossica Major'   → *S. aucuparia*
'Rufus'   → *S. hupehensis*
'Schouten'   → Cultivar List
'Sheerwater Seedling'   → Cultivar List
'Signalman'   → Cultivar List
'Theophrasta'   → *S. devoniensis*
'Warleyensis'   → *S. sargentiana*
'White Wax'   → Cultivar List
'Wilfrid Fox'   → Cultivar List
'Winter Cheer'   → Cultivar List

Sorbus alnifolia (S. & Z.) K. Koch. Upright tree, to 20 m high in its habitat, crown dense and rounded, young shoots glossy, red-brown, occasionally somewhat pubescent only at first; leaves ovate, to more elliptic, short acuminate, 5–10 cm long, irregularly serrate, base round, with 6–10 vein pairs, also usually totally glabrous beneath or slightly pubescent on the long shoots, orange to scarlet in fall; flowers 1 cm wide, usually grouped 6–10 together, nearly glabrous (!), styles usually 2 (!), May; fruits pea-sized, red and yellow. LF 168; Bm 7773; KIF 1: 73; YWP 2: 3–4. Central China to Korea and Japan. 1892. z6 Plate 116, 120.

var. **submollis** Rehd. Leaves ovate, 4–6 cm long, underside loosely pubescent at first, later persisting only on the venation; inflorescences pubescent (= *S. zahlbruckneri* Hort. non Schneid.). Around 1900.

S. alpina see: **Sorbaronia alpina**

S. americana Marsh. Tree, to about 9 m high, or also a shrub, branches red-brown, winter buds large, brown, glabrous (!), glossy and glutinous; leaves to 25 cm long, leaflets 11–17, these oblong-lanceolate, 4–10 cm long, acuminate, scabrous serrate, the teeth acuminate, bright green, light gray-green beneath and somewhat pubescent when young, golden-yellow in fall; flowers 5–6 mm wide, in dense, 14 cm wide corymbs, rachis glabrous, calyx lobes very small, inclined together, May–June; fruits peppercorn-sized, scarlet-red. BB 1975; SM 347; SS 171–172; GTP 229. Central and eastern N. America; on the edge of open water holes and swamps; rather slow growing and short lived. 1811. z2 Plate 116. ⚭

'Belmonte'. Selection with a particularly attractive, dense, ovate crown; leaflets in the fall with the margin curved at the apex; fruits flat globose, to 8 mm wide and 7 mm high. Dfl 2: 4. Selected in 1964 in the Belmonte Arboretum in Wageningen, Holland. Very rapid growing; cultivated in the nursery without staking. ⚭
var. *nana* see: **S. scopulina**

S. anglica Hedl. Shrub, 1–2 m high, shoots rather thick; leaves obovate to rhombic-obovate, 7–11 cm long, 5–6 cm wide, obtuse to acute, base cuneate, margins with forward directed lobes, incisions 5–7 mm deep, otherwise serrate, deep green and glabrous above, underside more or less irregularly whitish gray tomentose, 8–10 vein pairs, petiole 12–20 mm, fall foliage a good golden-brown; inflorescences small to rather large, petals 6 mm long, anthers pink or reddish, May; fruits nearly globose, 7–12 mm, carmine to scarlet, with a few to many lenticels, particularly at the base. England, Ireland, nearly always on calcareous soil. z7 ∅ ⚭

S. arbutifolia see: **Aronia arbutifolia**

S. aria (L.) Crantz. Whitebeam. Tree or tree-like shrub, often multistemmed, 6–12 m high, crown broadly conical, branches gray tomentose at first, as are the winter buds, later olive-brown; leaves elliptic-ovate, 8–12 cm long, tough, dull green above, densely white tomentose beneath (!), with 10–14 vein pairs; flowers about 1.5 cm wide, white, in up to 5 cm wide, branched corymbs, sepals lanceolate, styles 2, May; fruits oval-rounded, orange to red, mealy, 10–12 mm thick. HM Pl. 174; CF 2: 636; HF 2539. Europe; in the mountains, nearly exclusively on chalk. Cultivated for ages. Ⓕ Tyrol. z6

var. *angustifolia* see: f. **longifolia**

'Aurea' (Hesse). Strong growing, new growth snow-white; leaves golden-yellow later and persisting so until fall (= f. *chrysophylla* Zab.). 1893. ∅

f. *chrysophylla* see: **'Aurea'**

var. *decaisneana* see: **'Majestica'**

var. *edulis* see: f. **longifolia**

var. *flabellifolia* see: **S. umbellata**

'Gigantea' (*aria* × *aria* 'Majestica'?). Similar to 'Majestica', but much faster growing, crown broadly conical; leaves very large, to 17 cm long and 10 cm wide; fruits to 17 × 14 mm in size. Selected around 1953 by P. Lombarts of Zundert, Holland. ∅ ⚭

f. **longifolia** (Pers.) Rehd. Leaves elliptic to oblong, 7–14 cm long; calyx lobes short triangular; fruits larger, more ovate, orange, good tasting. SH 1: 377 h–i (= var. *edulis* Wenz.; var. *angustifolia* Dipp.; *S. edulis* [Willd.] K. Koch).

'Lutescens'. Crown conical at first and dense, later wider; leaves silvery white on both sides on the new growth, slightly yellowish above, later silvery green above, underside remaining white, abscising early in warm summers; fruits an attractive orange-red. 1892. ∅ ⚭

'Magnifica'. Crown narrowly conical, later wider; leaves large, glossy dark green above, snow-white tomentose beneath, thick, stiff and leathery, persisting long into fall; fruits not very conspicuous. Developed by Herm. A. Hesse of Weener, W. Germany from seed in 1917. ∅

'Majestica'. Crown broader than that of 'Magnifica'; leaves large, dull green above, underside white, later greenish tomentose; fruits dark orange-red, not very conspicuous (= *S. aria* var. *decaisneana* [Lavall.] Rehd.). Cultivated in France before 1858. Plate 116. ∅

'Quercoides'. Smaller, denser, compact shrub, very slow growing; leaves oblong, scabrous and regularly lobed, margins curved upward. ∅

var. *salicifolia* see: **S. rupicola**

var. *theophrasta* see: **S. devoniensis**

S. × arnoldiana Rehd. (*S. aucuparia × S. discolor*) More similar to *S. aucuparia*, but differing in the often more or less glabrous winter buds; smaller leaflets, pubescent only when young, dark green above, gray-green beneath, stipules more or less persistent; fruits pink, but also whitish pink. 1907.

Included here are the so-called 'Lombarts Hybrids', a number of seedling forms developed around 1950 by J. Lombarts of Zundert, Holland between *S. prattii, discolor* and *aucuparia* (refer to Fontane, Een nieuwe *Sorbus*-collectie; in Boomkwekerij 13: 26 to 27, 1958; there are no less than 20 [!] forms described). ⚭

S. arranensis Hedl. Medium-sized tree; leaves more or less deeply lobed, with 8 vein pairs, 8–12 cm long, tapered toward the apex, base cuneate, thinly white tomentose beneath; fruit red, globose, 10 mm long (= *S. subarranensis* Hyl.). HSo 12, 13. West coast of Scotland; Arran Island; Norway. z6 Plate 114; Fig. 242.

S. aucuparia L. Common Mt. Ash. Tree, 5–15 m high, occasionally multistemmed, young shoots soft pubescent, later smooth and gray-brown, winter buds tomentose (!), not glutinous; leaves to 20 cm long, leaflets 9–15, oblong-lanceolate, to 6 cm long, acute, scabrous serrate, dull green and glabrous above, gray-green and pubescent (at least when young) beneath, base always distinctly asymmetrical (see *S. domestica*); flowers about 1 cm wide, stamens about as long as the petals, inflorescences to 15 cm wide, May; fruits pea-sized, bright red, in color from August to September. HM 147; HF 2538; GPN 494–495. Europe to Asia Minor and Siberia. Cultivated through the ages. Ⓕ W. Germany, Austria. z2 ∅ ✧ ⚭

Including many cultivars.

Outline of the Cultivars

Differing in habit

Columnar:	'Fastigiata'
Weeping:	'Pendula'
	'Pendula Variegata'
Dwarf form:	'Nana'

Leaves green, differing in form

Leaflets coarsely incised:	'Asplenifolia'
Some leaflets pinnate:	'Beissneri'
Leaflets nearly entire:	'Integerrima'

Leaves differing in color

Yellow, later turning green:	'Dirkenii'
Yellow variegated:	'Variegata'

Fruits differing

Normal size, yellow-orange:	'Xanthocarpa'
To 10 mm in diameter, not bitter:	'Edulis'
To 15 mm in diameter, sour:	'Rossica'
Over 15 mm in diameter, sour:	'Rossica Major'

'Asplenifolia'. Leaflets deeply serrate, occasionally also with 1–2 small lobes, underside densely pubescent; fruits bitter (= f. *laciniata* Hartm.).

'Beissneri'. Like 'Edulis', but the bark of the young shoots an attractive coral-red, also often the leaf petiole, bark of the branches and stem a warm coppery red, often with a silvery shimmer (!); leaves more or less deeply incised (like 'Asplenifolia'); fruit not bitter (= var. *dulcis laciniata* Beissn.). Found by Ordnung in the Bohemian Erz Mts. (E. Germany) in 1899.

'Dirkenii' (Dirken). Leaves bright golden-yellow at first, later greenish. Found in 1880 in the Dirken Nursery in Oudenbosch, Holland. ∅

var. *dulcis* see: **'Edulis'**

var. *dulcis laciniata* see: **'Beissneri'**

'Edulis'. Leaves nearly glabrous, petiole reddish, leaflets 4–7 cm long, only serrate in the center; flower rachis only slightly pubescent; fruits about 1 cm in diameter, sourish (not bitter!), of economic value for its fruits. (= var. *dulcis* Kraetzl; var. *moravica* Zengerl.). First discovered around 1810 near Spornhau, Germany (800 m). ⚭ ✂

'Fastigiata'. Narrowly conical, shoots stiff and thick; fruits larger than those of the species (= f. *pyramidalis* Hort.). Found in 1838 in Dunganstown, Co. Down, N. Ireland. Plate 117.

'Integerrima'. Growth tightly upright; leaflets nearly entire. Found on Bornholm Island (Denmark). 1832.

f. *laciniata* see: **'Asplenifolia'**

var. *moravica* see: **'Edulis'**

'Nana'. Shrubby; fruits larger than those of the species.

'Pendula'. Branches irregularly wavy, pendulous if grafted on a standard. MD 1911: 247.

'Pendula Variegata'. Weeping form with yellow variegated leaves. Before 1887.

f. *pyramidalis* see: **'Fastigiata'**

'Rossica' (Späth). Habit like the species, also alike in the leaf size and fruits; leaflets however, more obtuse and somewhat bullate between the lateral veins, somewhat wider than the

Plate 129

Stachyurus praecox
in the Dortmund Botanic Garden, W. Germany

Staphylea colchica 'Pyramidalis'
in the Munich Botanic Garden, W. Germany

Spiraea gieseleriana
in the Munich Botanic Garden, W. Germany

Stauntonia hexaphylla
on Madre Island, Italy

Plate 130

Stranvaesia davidiana (in hoarfrost)
Photo: Archivbild

Stewartia sinensis
in Wakehurst Place, England

Strelitzia nicolai
in a park in Malaga, Spain

Strelitzia alba
in Ultramar Garden, Lisbon, Portugal

Plate 131

Symplocos paniculata, fruiting
in the Dortmund Botanic Garden, W. Germany

Symphoricarpos chenaultii 'Hancock'
in the Dortmund Botanic Garden, W. Germany

Symphoricarpos albus 'Turesson'
Photo: Archiv

Symphoricarpos 'White Hedge'
Photo: Archiv

Plate 132

Syringa sweginzowii

Syringa × *nanceiana* 'Floréal'

Syringa reflexa

Syringa × *swegiflexa*
All photos: Fr. Meyer

Plate 133

Syringa ✕ *persica*

Syringa laciniata
Both photos: F. Meyer, Hamburg

Plate 134

Syringa vulgaris 'Mme Antoine Buchner'
in the Dortmund Botanic Garden, W. Germany

Syringa vulgaris 'Catinat'
in the Dortmund Botanic Garden, W. Germany

Syringa vulgaris 'Mirabeau'
Photo: Fr. Meyer

Syringa vulgaris 'Sensation'
Photo: Fr. Meyer

Plate 135

Syringa vulgaris 'Léon Gambetta'

Syringa vulgaris 'Edith Cavell'

Syringa vulgaris 'Mont Blanc'

Syringa vulgaris 'Jan van Tol'
All photos: Fr. Meyer

Plate 136

Syringa pinnatifolia
Photo: Fr. Meyer

Syringa patula
in the Dortmund Botanic Garden, W. Germany

Tamarix juniperina
in Fey Garden, Meckenheim, W. Germany

Tamarix tetranda
in the Berlin Botanic Garden, W. Germany
Photo: Archivbild

Plate 137

Tamarix parviflora
in a park in Locarno, Italy

Tamarix gallica
in Locarno, Italy

Tamarix ramosissima

Tecoma stans, fruit clusters,
in the Lisbon Botanic Garden, Portugal

Plate 138

Tilia cordata 'Rancho' in the USA
Photo: Scanlon

Tilia flaccida
in the Leningrad Botanic Garden, USSR

Camellia sinensis var. assamica
in the Brissago Botanic Garden, Switzerland

Tetrapanax papyrifer
in the Hamburg Botanic Garden, W. Germany

Plate 139

Tilia. a. *T. tomentosa;* b. *T.* × *flaccida* 'Diversifolia'; c. *T. petiolaris;* d. *T. henryana;* e. *T. americana* 'Dentata'; f. *T.* × *euchlora;* g. *T. heterophylla*

Plate 140

Tilia. a. *T. tuan;* b. *T. oliveri;* c. *T.* × *orbicularis;* d. *T. platyphylla* 'Laciniata'; e. *T. miqueliana;*
f. *T. japonica;* g. *T. mongolica*

Plate 141

Tripterygium regelii
in the Wageningen Arboretum, Holland

Tilia maximowicziana
in the Villa Taranto Gardens, Italy

Tilia petiolaris, young tree
in the Dortmund Botanic Garden, W. Germany

Tilia japonica
in the Tokyo Botanic Garden, Japan

Plate 142

Trachycarpus fortunei, flowering,
on Madre Island, N. Italy

Trachycarpus fortunei in fruit,
in Sotchi Dendrarium, USSR

Ulex gallii in the Royal Botanic Garden, Edinburgh, Scotland

Plate 143

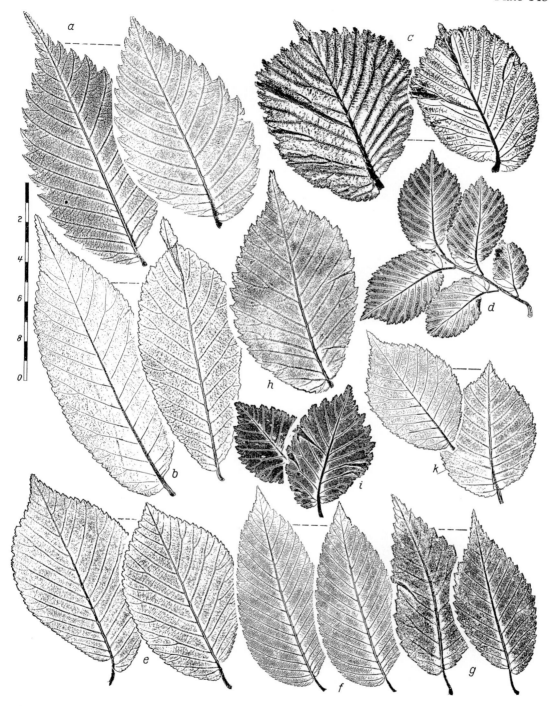

Ulmus. a. *U. americana*; b. *U. rubra*; c. *U. glabra* 'Exoniensis'; d. *U. carpinifolia* 'Sarniensis'; e. *U.* × *hollandica* 'Superba'; f. *U. wilsoniana*; g. *U. pumila* var. *arborea*; h. *U. procera*; i. *U. hollandica* 'Wredei'; k. *U. procera* 'Louis van Houtte'

Plate 144

Ulmus carpinifolia 'Umbraculifera'
in Aliszer Nawoi, Tashkent, USSR
Photo: Browicz, Warsaw

Ulmus carpinifolia var. *italica*
in Gisselfeld Park, Denmark

Ulmus hollandica 'Wredei'
in Gisselfeld Park, Denmark

Ulmus carpinifolia 'Hoersholm'
on a street in Hoersholm, Denmark
Photo: J. Oestergaard

species and entire on the basal third; fruits 12–15 mm in diameter. Introduced by Späth from Russia, brought into the trade in 1898. ⚭ ✗

'Rossica Major' (Späth). Strong growing, narrowly upright; leaflets to 8 cm long and 2.7 cm wide, petiole and rachis always red (!), always more or less woolly tomentose, margins of the leaflets at the apical half of the leaf serrate to the base, the basal leaflets always entire on the basal third of the margins, apex obtuse, somewhat tomentose beneath, somewhat bullate between the lateral veins; fruits often over 15 mm in diameter, sour. Introduced by Späth from Russia and brought into the trade in 1903. A good street tree. ⚭ ✗

'Variegata'. Leaves yellow variegated. Known since before 1821.

'Xanthocarpa'. Fruits orange-yellow, usually not taken by the birds (= f. *fifeana* Hort.). Origin unknown. Named by Lord Fife before 1893. ⚭

S. austrica Hedl. Small tree, similar to *S. intermedia*, but with a more pyramidal habit, leaves also more serrate; leaves broadly elliptic, about 1.3 times as long as wide, usually 7 cm wide, the larger incisions to about a third of the leaf blade half, the lobes often somewhat overlapping, underside pure gray-white tomentose (!); fruits rather globose, 13 mm long, red, densely punctate. HSo 16. Switzerland to Austria, Hungary, Siebengebirge. z6 Plate 114.

S. bristoliensis Wilmott. Small tree, crown compact, rather globose; leaves obovate or more oblong to rhombic, 7–9 cm long, 5–5.5 cm wide, short and broadly triangular lobed primarily past the middle, otherwise finely serrate, eventually bright green and somewhat glossy above, underside dense and evenly gray tomentose (not white!), inflorescences rather small, anthers pink; fruits light orange, longer than wide, sometimes 9–11 mm long, sometimes much smaller, with many small lenticels. England; only in the Avon Gorge, near Bristol. z7 ⚭

S. caloneura (Stapf) Rehd. Shrub or small tree, 4–5 m high, branches black-brown, glabrous, like the winter buds; leaves elliptic-oblong, 5–9 cm long, acute, doubly crenate, quickly becoming glabrous or nearly so, with 10–12 vein pairs, petiole 1 cm long (!); flowers 6–7 mm wide, white, many in dense, about 7 cm wide, flat inflorescences, anthers violet-purple, May; fruits pear-shaped, 1 cm long, brown, punctate. BM 8335. Central China. Hardy. z6 Fig. 241.

S. cashmiriana Hedl. Tree, to 10 m (?), young shoots glabrous, reddish; leaflets 15–19, oval-elliptic to oblong, 2–3 cm long, short acuminate, scabrous and appressed serrate, entire at the base, dull dark green above, glabrous, underside light green, midrib and rachis brownish pubescent only when young, rachis later more or less reddish; flowers about 1.5 cm wide, in loose, 7–12 cm wide, glabrous inflorescences, petals pink-white, buds dark pink, styles 5, anthers white, May; fruits to 18 mm in diameter, white. SH 1: 375m; GC 132: 82. Himalayas, Kashmir. Hardy. z5 ✧ ⚭

S. chamaemespilus (L.) Crantz. Dwarf Whitebeam. Shrub, 1–2 m high, branches loosely pubescent at first, later red-brown and glabrous; leaves elliptic, 3–7 cm long, acute to obtuse, finely serrate, somewhat leathery, dark green above, yellowish green beneath, glabrous to somewhat tomentose, with 6–9 vein pairs; flowers light pink-red, in dense, to 3 cm wide corymbs, styles 2, shaggy at the base, petals erect (!), May–June; fruits ovate, red. HM 1048; HF 2541. Central Europe, in the mountains. 1683. z6 Plate 120. ✧

var. **sudetica** (Tausch) Wenz. Leaves larger, oval-oblong to ovate biserrate, with 7–10 vein pairs, underside white tomentose at first, later thinly tomentose; flowers larger, calyx cup tomentose; fruits to 1 cm thick. Sudeten Mts. (N. Czechoslovakia), Black Forest (W. Germany), Vosges. 1908. z6 ✧

S. commixta Hedl. Tree, to 7 m high or more, somewhat columnar when young, winter buds glabrous, glutinous, young shoots red-brown; leaflets 11–15, elliptic-lanceolate, long acuminate, scabrous serrate, 4–8 cm long, new growth brownish and appearing early, later light green, bluish beneath, fall color yellow-red; inflorescences loose, 8–12 cm wide, glabrous, flowers 8

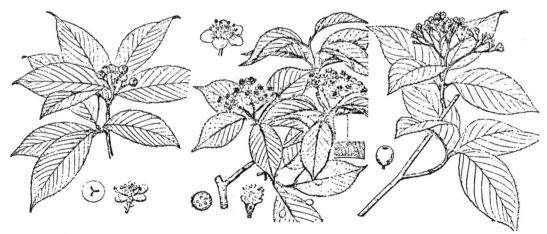

Fig. 241. **Sorbus.** Left *S. xanthoneura;* middle *S. caloneura;* right *S. folgneri* (from ICS)

mm wide, white, styles usually 3, June; fruits globose, pea-sized, scarlet-red. NK 6: 3; MJ 1399; KIF 1: 74 (= *S. japonica* Koehne non Sieb.). Korea, Sachalin, Japan. 1906. z6 Plate 117.

var. *rufo-ferruginea* see: **S. rufo-ferruginea**

S. conradinae see: **S. esserteauiana** and **S. pohuashanensis**

S. cretica see: **S. umbellata** var. **cretica**

S. cuspidata (Spach) Hedl. Tree, branches purple-brown; leaves large (!), to 22 × 16 cm, elliptic to more oblong, biserrate, densely tomentose beneath, tough; flowers many in 10 cm wide, white tomentose inflorescences, sepals lanceolate, styles 5, distinct, May; fruits nearly globose, 2 cm thick, orange-red, very quickly becoming stone hard (!!). BM 8259; SNp 46 (= *S. nepalensis* Hort.; *Pyrus vestita* Wall.). Himalayas. 1820. z7 Plate 115. ∅ ⊕

S. × decipiens (Bechst.) Hedl. (*S. aria* × *S. torminalis*?). Closely related to *S. latifolia*, but the leaves thinner, not as leathery, about 1.5 times longer than wide, to 12 cm long, base cuneate to rounded (cordate on *S. latifolia*), with 9–12 pairs of lateral veins (9–10 pairs on *S. latifolia*), underside only thinly tomentose and the venation visible (thickly tomentose on *S. latifolia*, venation not discernible); styles to ¾ connate; fruits more oval, brown-yellow, without fertile seeds. HSo 30. Thuringia (E. Germany), Switzerland, NE. France, occurring among the parents. z6 Plate 115.

S. decora (Sarg.) Schneid. Shrub or tree, to 10 m high; leaflets 11–17, but usually 15, elliptic to oval-lanceolate, to 7 cm long, obtuse to short acuminate, dark blue-green and glabrous, lighter beneath and pubescent when young, petiole and midrib usually red; inflorescences rather loose, somewhat pubescent, 5–10 cm wide, flowers nearly 1 cm wide, May; fruits oval-rounded at first, calyx lobes erect, 7–10 mm thick, bright red. BB 2319; DL 3: 191; SS 173–174; RMi 217 (= *S. sambucifolia* sensu Dipp.; *S. scopulina* sensu Hough). Northeastern N. America. 1636. Valued for its attractive fruits. z2 ∅ ⚭

var. *nana* see: **S. scopulina**

S. decurrens see: **S. × thuringiaca 'Decurrens'**

S. devoniensis Warb. **'Theophrasta'**. Tree with a dense, globose crown, somewhat resembling *S. latifolia*, winter buds conical, to 10 mm long, green to brown, the scales only pubescent on the margins; leaves elliptic-ovate, 9–12 cm long, 5–8 cm wide, acute, base broadly cuneate to round, nearly entire on the basal ⅓, otherwise coarsely biserrate, with 8–10 vein pairs, dark green above, glabrous and glossy, gray-green tomentose beneath; inflorescences to 10 cm wide; fruits globose, to 15 mm wide and high, orange, brown before dropping, with many, large, light lenticels, particularly at the base. Dfl 1966: 61 (= *S. theophrasta* Lombarts 1947; *S. aria* var. *theophrasta* Bean). The species occurs in the wild in Devon and Cornwall (England); the cultivar originated in the Royal Botanic Gardens, Kew, England. z7 ⚭

S. dippelii see: **Sorbaronia dippelii**

S. discolor (Maxim.) Maxim. Small tree, 7–10 m high, winter buds glabrous or somewhat pubescent, as are the young shoots, reddish; stipules leaflike, palmately toothed, persistent, leaflets 11–15, oblong-lanceolate, acute to acuminate, scabrous serrate nearly to the base, 3–8 cm long, dark green above, blue-green beneath (!), glabrous, finely veined; inflorescences 10–14 cm wide, loose, practically glabrous, flowers 1 cm wide, white, styles usually 3, May; fruits oval-globose, white to somewhat yellowish, occasionally turning pink, 6–7 mm thick. SH 1: 366 l–m, 367g (= *S. pekinensis* Koehne). N. China. 1883. Fall foliage red, effective with the white fruits. See also: cv. list **'Embley'**. z6 Fig. 244. ⚭

S. domestica L. Tree, to 20 m high, bark rough (like a pear tree), branches quickly becoming glabrous, winter buds glutinous, glossy; leaflets 11–21, narrowly oblong, 3–8 cm long, scabrous serrate, glabrous above, underside floccose, base always symmetrical (!), flowers 1.5 cm wide, in about 6–10 cm wide, conical corymbs, styles usually 5, shaggy pubescent at the base, May–June; fruits apple- or pear-shaped, to 3 cm long, yellow-green to brownish, reddish on the sunny side, bitter. HF 2537; HM 1047. Central and S. Europe, N. Africa, Asia Minor. Cultivated for ages for its fruits, which are pressed for juice. Ⓕ W. Germany. z6 ⚭ ✕

f. **pomifera** (Hayne) Rehd. Fruits apple-shaped, 2–3 cm long.

f. **pyriformis** (Hayne) Rehd. Fruits pear-shaped, about 3–4 cm long.

S. edulis see: **S. aria** f. **longifolia**

S. epidendron Hand.-Mazz. Shrub or also a tree, closely related to *S. folgneri*, but the shoots, leaf petioles and undersides densely rust-brown tomentose (!); leaves obovate to narrowly elliptic, 8–15 cm long, long acuminate, base cuneate, finely serrate, with 10–12 vein pairs; flowers cream-white, many in 10 cm wide, dense inflorescences, also brown tomentose; fruits 8 mm thick, globose. W. China. 1925. Very conspicuous for the brown pubescence. z6 ∅

S. esserteauiana Koehne. Tree, 8–15 m high, new shoots 5–7 mm thick, winter buds reddish, white pubescent; stipules persistent, coarsely dentate, 1–2 cm wide, leaves 18–29 cm long, leaflets 11–13, lanceolate to broadly oblong, 6–10 cm long, acute to acuminate, leathery tough, bright green and glabrous, underside with a persistent thick white tomentum (!!) or gray white tomentose, margins coarsely and often biserrate (!), fall color red; inflorescences 9–15 cm wide, rachis densely gray-white tomentose, flowers 8 mm wide, petals nearly circular; fruits globose, scarlet-red, 7–8 mm thick. BM 9403; GC 138: 262 (= *S. conradinae* Koehne). W. China. 1907. Highly valued, good hardiness. z6 ∅ ⚭

According to some authors, *S. conradinae* is a separate species with the following distinguishing characteristics (according to Fox):

S. conradinae: Better growth habit, winter buds pubescent and brown; leaves thinner, underside not as white, young leaves green, appearing late; fruits light red, ripening in August.

S. esserteauiana: Stocky growth habit, winter buds pubescent and red; leaves tough, underside lighter, young leaves brown; fruits still green in August and half the size of those on *S. conradinae.*

'Flava'. Fruits orange-yellow. JRHS 90: 243. Plate 115, 117.

S. fennica see: **S. hybrida**

S. filipes Hand.-Mazz. Shrub, to 4 m high, closely related to *S. vilmorinii*, but the shoots glabrous or nearly so; leaflets 19–27, elliptic, only 8–14 mm long, with 3–4 teeth on either side; inflorescences with 3–12 flowers, these red (!); fruits red, 7 mm thick (= *S. poteriifolia* Hand.-Mazz.). W. China. 1932. Very promising, but too little known. z6 ⊕

S. flabellifolia see: **S. umbellata**

S. folgneri (Schneid.) Rehd. Small tree or a tall graceful shrub, shoots long, thin, widely arching, white tomentose at first; leaves lanceolate to narrowly ovate, 5–10 cm long, finely acuminate, serrate, dark green above, underside snow-white tomentose (!), with 8–9 parallel vein pairs; flowers about 1 cm wide, white, many in about 10 cm wide inflorescences, May; fruits 12 mm long, red. JRHS 40: 216. China. 1901. Hardy. z6 Fig. 241. ∅ ⊛

'Lemon Drop'. Like the species, but the fruits glossy yellow. Developed by Hillier, Winchester, England. ⊛

S. foliolosa see: **S. vilmorinii**

S. gracilis (S. & Z.) K. Koch. Shrub, to 2 m high, shoots thin, new growth and young leaves bronze-red; leaflets 7–9, the apical ones larger, the basal leaflets only 1–2 cm long, elliptic-oblong, 2–6 cm long, obtuse, serrate on the apical half; inflorescences only 2–4 cm wide, with large bracts, styles 2, May; fruits pear-shaped, 1 cm long, red. MJ 1402; DB 10: 186. Japan. 1934. z6 Plate 117. ∅

S. graeca see: **S. umbellata** var. **cretica**

S. "Grondesia" see: **S. hybrida**

S. harrowiana (Balf. f. & W. W. Sm.) Rehd. Tree, 7–10 m high, often only a shrub in cultivation, shoots rather thick and stiff, totally glabrous as is the entire plant; leaflets only 5–9 (!!), narrowly oblong, 6–20 cm long (!!), finely serrate, base oblique, blue-green beneath, margins somewhat involuted; flowers in about 10–15 cm wide, loose inflorescences, stalk somewhat pubescent, May; fruits pear-shaped, 8 mm long, pink. DB 1960: 212. W. China. 1912. Very attractive and totally different species. z9 Plate 115. ∅ ⊛

S. heterophylla see: **Sorbaronia fallax** and **Sorbaronia hybrida**

S. × hostii (Jacq. f.) K. Koch (*S. chamaemespilus* × *S. mougeotii*). Shrub, scarcely over 3–4 m, divaricate, more similar to *S. hostii* in leaf and habit, but the leaves narrower, oblong, acute, to 10 cm long, scabrous biserrate and shallowly lobed, underside gray woolly pubescent, with 8–12 pairs of lateral veins, base cuneate; flowers light pink (!), in 6–8 cm wide inflorescences,

May; fruits about 1 cm thick, ovate, red. HM 1050; SH 1: 381 a–b; HSo 34. Alps, Jura Mts.; occurring among the parents. 1826. z6 ⊕ ⊛

S. hupehensis Schneid. Tree, to 10 m high, winter buds glabrous (!!), not glutinous, young shoots scattered pubescent at first; leaflets 13–17, elliptic-oblong, 2–3–5 (in cultivation also 5–6!) cm long, obtuse and with a small tip, entire, finely serrate only at the apex, gray-green beneath, glabrous or with a pubescent midrib, rediculately veined; inflorescences to 12 cm wide, glabrous or pubescent, long stalked, loose, flowers yellowish white, petals only 3 mm long, stamens 2–3 times longer than the petals, styles 4–5; fruits white, turning pink, globose, 6–8 mm thick, BMns 96; GC 138: 262 (= *S. oligodonta* [Card.] Hand.-Mazz.). Central and W. China. 1910. z6 Fig. 244. ⊛

var. **aperta** Schneid. Only 9–11 leaflets, these larger, acute (!), 3–6 cm long (as opposed to 2–4 cm on the type). W. China; Hupeh Prov. 1910.

var. **obtusa** Schneid. Leaflets 9–11, obtuse (!), 3–5 cm long, only serrate at the apex. GC 125: 32. Hupeh Prov. 1912. Not unusual in cultivation, but normally under the name "S. wilsoniana".

'Rufus'. Fruits deep pink-red, very prolific. JRHS 93: 44. Selected before 1968 in Windsor Great Park, England. ⊛

'November Pink'. Very vigorous, smaller, round crowned tree, young shoots red-brown, glabrous, glossy; leaves with 11–13 leaflets, these on flowering shoots to 4.5 cm long, oblong, serrate only on the apical ⅓, dull dark green above, blue-green beneath; anthers pink; fruits flat globose, to 9 mm wide, whitish to pale pink at first, later purple-red, persisting to late in the winter. Clone of *S. hupehensis* var. *obtusa*; brought into the trade in 1963 by F. J. Grootendorst, Boskoop, Holland. ⊛

S. hybrida (L.) L. Tree, 10–12 m high, older branches horizontally spreading (!!), often nodding at the tips, young shoots and leaf petioles floccose; leaves ovate to oval-oblong, with 8–10 vein pairs, apex usually broadly rounded, obtuse (!), usually with 1–2 pairs of leaflets at the base, coarsely serrate, all teeth acuminate, dark green above, underside gray tomentose, eventually leathery tough; inflorescences 6–10 cm wide, tomentose, flowers about 1.5 cm wide, May; fruits globose, red, sparsely punctate, 10–12 mm thick. NDJ 20: 132; 21: 192; HSo 9 (as *S. fennica*); GPN 493 (= *S. fennica* Fries.; *S.* "Grondesia" Hort.). NW. Europe, from SW. Finland to central and south Norway. This plant, although intermediate between *S. aria* and *S. aucuparia*, is not a hybrid, rather a tetraploid apomict; 2n = 68; comes true from seed. Plants often cultivated in nurseries by this name are actually *S. thuringiaca* or one of its forms. z5 Plate 114. ⊛

'Gibbsii'. Smaller, 7 m high tree, crown broad, but tight, branches ascending; leaves 10–15 cm long, 5–8 cm wide, with about 8 distinct lobes on either side and 1–2 free leaflets at the base, petiole 2–3 cm; fruits to 15 mm long, deep red, August–October. GC 77: 243 (= *S. pinnatifida* 'Gibbsii' Hort.; *Pyrus firma* Hort.). England before 1924. Presumably selected as a clone of *S. hybrida*.

var. *meinichii* see: **S. × meinichii**

S. insignis (Hook. f.) Hedl. Small tree; leaves to 30 cm

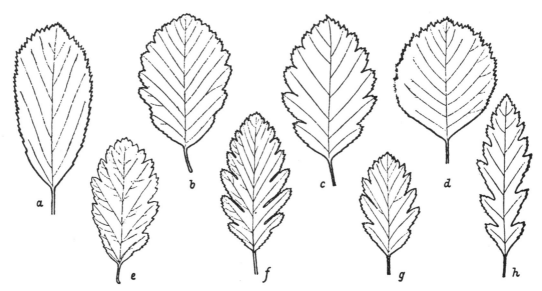

Fig. 242. Northern **Sorbus** species. a. *S. rupicola;* b. *S. subsimilis;* c. *S. intermedia;*
d. *S. obtusifolia;* e. *S. neglecta;* f. *S. subpinnata;* g. *S. arranensis;* h. *S. lancifolia* (from Lid)

long, leaflets 9–13, the middle ones largest, elliptic-
oblong, 5–10 cm long, obtuse, base oblique, shallowly
toothed only at the apex (!), apical leaflets sessile, basal
ones distinctly stalked (to 1 cm long); inflorescences
dense rust-brown silky pubescent, as are the foliate buds
at bud break, flowers with 3 styles; fruits pink.
Himalayas, Sikkim. z9? Plate 115. ⚲ ∅

S. intermedia (Ehrh.) Pers. Swedish Whitebeam. Tree,
10–12 m high, occasionally only a shrub, young shoots
very woolly, glabrous by fall; leaves broadly ovate, 6–10
cm long, thin, obtuse (!), base broadly cuneate to round
(!), lobed, occasionally pinnatisect on the basal half, with
7–9 pairs of lateral veins, irregularly serrate, glossy
above, gray tomentose beneath (not white!); inflorescences 8–10 cm wide, many branched, petals oblong to
lanceolate, styles 2, May; fruits ellipsoid, to 13 mm thick,
somewhat longer than wide, orange-red, with an erect
calyx (!). HM 1045; GPN 492 (= *S. scandica* Fries; *Aria
suecica* Koehne). Scandinavia; occasionally in Scotland
and N. Germany. Cultivated through the ages. Tetraploid apomict. Ⓕ Denmark, Great Britain. z6 Plate 114;
Fig. 242. ∅

'Brouwers'. Habit tightly upright, with a percurrent central
leader. Selected in 1956 by Brouwers of Groenekan, Holland. A
good street tree.

var. *minima* see: **S. minima**

S. japonica (Decne.) Hedl. Tree, to 20 m high, young
shoots tomentose; leaves ovate to oval-oblong, 7–10 cm
long, short acuminate, base cuneate, biserrate and small
lobed, with 10–12 vein pairs, dark green above, gray-
white tomentose beneath, petiole 1–2 cm long; flowers
in dense, tomentose inflorescences, stalk white
tomentose, May; fruits ellipsoid, scarlet-red, 1.2 cm long,
finely punctate. MJ 1398 (= *S. koehnei* Zab.). Japan,
Korea. 1915. See also: **S. commixta.** z6

var. **calocarpa** Rehd. Leaf undersides snow-white tomentose,
fall color bright yellow; fruits larger, orange. SH 1: 386 g–h, 387
m (= *Micromeles japonica* Koehne). Central Japan.

S. kamunensis see: **S. lanata**

S. keissleri Rehd. Large shrub or small tree, to 12 m,
branches stiffly erect; leaves leathery, obovate, 5–8 cm
long, crenate, with 8–10 vein pairs, glossy green; flowers
in dense, tomentose, terminal cymes, greenish white,
sweet smelling, styles usually 3, connate on the basal
portion; fruits apple-like, green, red on the sunny side
and pruinose, calyx abscising. SH 1: 389 (= *Micromeles
keissleri* Schneid.). China; Hupeh, Szechwan Provs.
1907. z6 ⚲

S. koehneana Schneid. Upright shrub, 2–3 m high,
young shoots glabrous, red-brown, winter buds light
red-brown pubescent; leaflets 17–25, oblong, 2–3 cm
long, scabrous serrate from the base up (!), bright green
above, gray-green beneath, somewhat pubescent only
when young, without papillae (!), rachis lightly winged;
inflorescences glabrous (!), 4–8 cm wide, flowers 1 cm
wide, anthers brown, May–June; fruits globose, white, 7
mm thick, on red stalks. SH 1: 3740. Central China. 1907.
z6 Plate 118. ⚲

S. koehnei see: **S. japonica**

S. lanata (D. Don) Schau. Tree, closely related to *S. aria,*
but very sensitive to frost (!), leaves much larger (!),
branches furrowed; leaves elliptic, 10–16 cm long,
scabrous and densely serrate, slightly lobed, both sides
densely white tomentose when young, later gray shaggy
tomentose beneath and occasionally becoming totally
glabrous; styles 2–3, woolly, sepals glabrous on the
exterior, petals tapered to a claw; fruits flat globose, 1.5–
3 (!) cm thick. MD 1935; 145 (4–5), SH 1: 38 a–b, 380 o–p
(= *S. kamunensis* Schau.). Himalayas. 1870. z9 ∅

S. lancifolia Hedl. Shrub, to 4 m; leaves narrowly oblong, 8–10 cm long, with about 6 pairs of large, triangular, acute lobes, incised halfway to the midrib; flowers 15 mm wide, June; fruit 8–9 mm long. N. Norway. z5 Fig. 242.

S. latifolia (Lam.) Pers. Not a hybrid between *S. aria* × *S. torminalis,* as often cited. Fast growing tree, 15 m high or more, crown broadly conical, branches glossy olive-brown; leaves ovate, 7–10 cm long, penniform lobed and scabrous serrate, dark green and dull glazed above, gray-yellow tomentose beneath (!); flowers 1.5 cm wide, cream-white, in about 10 cm wide umbellate panicles, rachis tomentose, styles usually 2, May; fruits brown, punctate, ellipsoid, about 1.5 cm long. HW 3: 85; HM 1050; DB 4: 33. Central Europe, occasionally occurring together with *S. aria* and *S. torminalis*. First discovered before 1750 in the forest at Fontainebleau, France. An attractive park tree. z5 Plate 114. ∅ ⚬

'Atrovirens' from Herm. A. Hesse is, upon examination (Dendroflora 5: 35, 1968) no different from the species.

S. matsumurana (Mak.) Koehne. Small tree, shoots reddish, winter buds glabrous; leaflets 9–13, oblong, 3–6 cm long, serrate only on the apical half, usually rounded at the apex, occasionally acute, dark green above, lighter beneath, pubescent only at the base, fall color orange; flowers 1 cm wide, white, in 5–7 cm wide clusters, styles 5, May–June; fruits ovate, about 12 mm long, orange-red. MJ 1400; SH 1: 366 e–f, 367c; JHRS 84: 27; YWP 2: 1–2. Japan. 1912. True existence in cultivation as yet uncertain; often confused with *S. serotina* or *S. americana*. z6 ∅

S. megalocarpa Rehd. Small tree, 5–6 m high, or only a large shrub, shoots thick and stiff, reddish, winter buds 1.5 cm long; leaves ovate or obovate to elliptic, 12–25 cm long, bronze-brown on new growth, crenate, glabrous, fall color red; flowers dull white, in 10–12 cm wide inflorescences, styles 3–4, connate, glabrous, May; fruits ovate, rust-brown, 1.5–3.5 cm long, to 2 cm thick. BMns 259; JRHS 86: 47. W. China. 1908. Hardy. z6 Plate 118. ∅ ⚬

S. × meinichii (Lindeb.) Hedl. Transition form between *S. aria* and *S. aucuparia,* but more similar to the latter, crown wider; leaves tougher and darker green, larger, with 4–6 pairs of leaflets, terminal leaflets rhombic, obtuse, often 3 lobed; fruits red. HSo 8 (= *S. hybrida* var. *meinichii* [Lindeb.] Rehd.). S. Norway; Oslofjord, Hordaland. Cultivated since 1904. Comes true from seed (tetraploid apomict; $2n = 68$). z5 Plate 114.

S. melanocarpa see: **Aronia melanocarpa**

S. meliosmifolia Rehd. Small tree, 5–10 m high, shoots glabrous, red-brown; leaves ovate-elliptic, long acuminate, 10–18 cm long, half as wide, with 18–24 vein pairs (!), petiole about 1 cm long; inflorescences 5–10 cm wide, white, April; fruits nearly globose, red-brown, 12 mm long, calyx abscising. W. China. 1910. Hardy. z6 Plate 120. ∅

S. minima (Ley) Hedl. Shrub, to about 3 m high, many branches, shoots thin; leaves elliptic to oblong-elliptic, 4–8 cm long, acute, cuneate to somewhat rounded at the base, shallowly lobed with obtuse to acute lobes, teeth of the outer margin forward curving, eventually dull green above, underside thin gray tomentose (not white or yellowish), usually with 7–9 vein pairs; inflorescences small, narrow, globose-convex, finely tomentose, petals 4 mm long, anthers yellowish, May–June; fruits small, nearly globose, scarlet, 6–8 mm, with small spots. CFl 2: 636 (= *S. intermedia* var. *minima* [Ley] Bean). England; Wales. Triploid. z6 Plate 114.

S. mougeotii Soy.-Willem. & Godr. Shrub to small tree, very closely related to *S. latifolia* and *S. intermedia,* but with 9–12 vein pairs, these running out to the sinuses

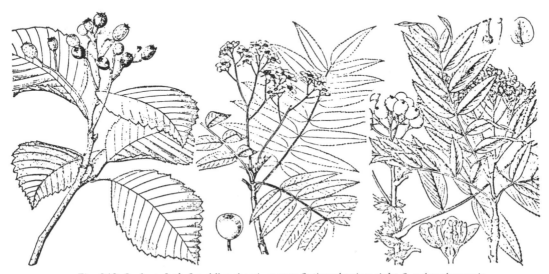

Fig. 243. **Sorbus.** Left *S. zahlbruckneri;* center *S. tianschanica;* right *S. pohuashanensis* (from ICS)

between the lobes (not in the middle of the lobes like the other 2 species); leaves oblong-elliptic, to 10 cm long, dark green above, light gray beneath, deepest lobes only incised ¼ into the blade half, lobes never overlapping, teeth sharply acuminate; fruits ellipsoid, 8 mm long, red. HM 1046; HSo 15. Alps and Jura Mts., from France to Austria. Tetraploid apomict. z6 Plate 120.

S. munda see: **S. pratti**

S. neglecta Hedl. Shrub, to 3 m; leaves elliptic, about 7 cm long, 3–4 cm wide, both sides with 5–6 toothed lobes, incised about ⅓ into the blade half; fruits 9–10 mm long. Norway. z5 Fig. 242.

S. nepalensis see: **S. cuspidata**

S. neuillyensis see: **S. × thuringiaca 'Neuillyensis'**

S. norvegica see: **S. obtusifolia**

S. obtusifolia (DC.) Hedl. Shrub, to 4 m high; leaves ovate, obtuse on the apex, base broadly cuneate, margins finely and scabrous serrate, not lobed, with 7–9 vein pairs, gray tomentose beneath; fruit 10 mm long (= *S. norvegica* Hedl.). S. Norway, S. Sweden. z6 Fig. 242.

S. occidentalis (S. Wats.) Greene. Shrub, 1–3 m high; leaflets 7–11, elliptic to oblong, rounded at the apex with a few teeth, otherwise entire (!), 2–4 (6) cm long, dull blue-green above; inflorescences 3–6 cm wide, compact, reddish pubescent to glabrous; fruits purple-red, 6–8 mm thick, pruinose. HSo 39: 3 (= *S. pumila* Raf.). British Columbia to Oregon, in the mountains. 1913. z6 Plate 115.

S. ochrocarpa see: **S. pallescens**

S. oligodonta see: **S. hupehensis**

S. pallescens Rehd. Small, erect tree, bark of older stems exfoliating; leaves narrowly elliptic to more lanceolate, long acuminate, scabrous and biserrate, 4–10 cm long, 2–5 cm wide, green above, gray-white tomentose beneath, distinctly veined; inflorescences small, sessile; fruits ovate to globose, 6 mm thick, green with a red cheek, in loose clusters (= *S. ochrocarpa* Rehd.). China; W. Szechwan Prov., 3000 m. 1908. z5 ♠ ∅

S. × paucicrenata (Ilse) Hedl. (*S. aria × S. decipiens* [!]). Resembles *S. latifolia*, but differing in the elliptic leaves, these shallowly lobed only on the apical half, thin, light green (!), base cuneate; ripe fruit seldom develops. HSo 29. Alps, Thuringia (E. Germany). Rare. z6 Plate 115.

S. pekinensis see: **S. discolor**

S. pinnatifida see: **S. × thuringiaca**

S. pinnatifida 'Gibbsii' see: **S. hybrida 'Gibbsii'**

S. pluripinnata (Schneid.) Koehne. Closely related to *S. scalaris*, but the leaflets are smaller, more densely arranged, inflorescences smaller. Shrub or small tree, young shoots, leaves and flower stalks dense gray tomentose; leaves 8–12 cm long, leaflets 21–25, linear-lanceolate, round with a small apex, base oblique, 1.5–3 cm long, with a few teeth at the apex, dark green and

smooth above, underside blue-gray woolly; inflorescences 5–8 cm wide, on short lateral shoots, flowers only small, petals 3 mm long, calyx glabrous, May; fruits bright red, ovate, 5 mm thick. SH 1: 374e. China; Szechwan Prov. Introduced around 1910. z6

S. pohuashanensis (Hance) Hedl. Small tree, young shoots pubescent, winter buds white woolly; leaflets 11–13, elliptic to oblong-lanceolate, acute, 3–6 cm long, usually scabrous serrate to just beneath the middle of the blade, underside gray-green and soft pubescent, stipules very large, half-ovate, persistent (!) or at least persisting on the leaves beneath the inflorescences; flowers about 1 cm wide, grouped in about 10 cm wide inflorescences, rachis floccose, May; fruits nearly globose, 6–8 mm thick, orange-red. BMns 133; JRHS 66: 119–120 (= *S. conradinae* Hort.). N. China. 1883. Named for Po-Hua'Shan = "Mountain of the flowers" (in N. China). Of great garden merit with a good growth habit and very winter hardy; perhaps the best Chinese Mountain Ash. z5–6 Fig. 243. ♠

S. poteriifolia Hand.-Mazz. Very slow growing shrub, 10 cm–2.5 m, shoots erect, purple-brown; leaves pinnate, 5–10 cm long, with 9–19 leaflets, elliptic, 1–2 cm long, scabrous serrate, deep green above, lighter and pubescent beneath; fruits globose, a good dark pink, in large, loose clusters. China; NW. Yunnan Prov.; upper Burma. Similar to *S. reducta*. ∅ ♠

See also: **S. filipes.** z7

S. pratti Koehne. Very similar to *S. koehneana*, but becoming taller, 5–7 m or more; leaflets 21–27, entire on the basal third (or half), underside blue-green and with papillae, usually pubescent, at least on the midrib; inflorescences 5–7 cm wide, glabrous or pubescent, petals 5 mm long; fruits white, 6–8 mm thick (= *S. munda* Koehne). W. China. 1910. z6 ♠

var. subarachnoidea (Koehne) Rehd. Differing in the rather dense, red-brown, spider web-like pubescence beneath. BM 9460 (as *S. prattii*); BS 3: Pl. 28 (= *S. munda* var. *subarachnoidea* Koehne). China; W. Szechwan Prov. 1910. ♠

var. tatsiensis (Koehne) Schneid. Leaflets smaller, only 1–2 cm long, frequently entire at the base, glabrous beneath or only pubescent on the midrib. GC 68: 153; 72: 226. W. China. 1904.

S. pumila see: **S. occidentalis**

S. pygmaea (Hort.?). Dwarf shrub, 7–25 cm high, very graceful and thin branched, shoots thinly pubescent; leaves pinnate, to 7 cm long, with 9–15 leaflets, these oval, acute, 12 mm long, 6 mm wide, scabrous serrate; flowers 2–3 in terminal clusters, light pink to carmine-red, July; fruits globose, pearl-white, 8 mm thick, in small, pendulous clusters along the shoot. Burma, Tibet, Yunnan Prov. Totally differing from *S. reducta* in the color of the flowers and fruits. z5 ✛ ♠

S. randaiensis (Hayata) Koidz. Small tree, 3–8 m high, branches ascending, shoots bowed outward, buds light chestnut-brown, glabrous, somewhat glutinous; leaves pinnate, glabrous, to 17 cm long, with 15–19 leaflets, these oblong-lanceolate, the middle ones largest, 2.5–4 cm long, 8–12 mm wide, long acuminate, scabrous serrate, deep green above, gray beneath, petiole to 3.5 cm; flowers in 8 cm wide, terminal corymbs, glabrous; fruits globose, 6–7 mm thick, 2–5 locular, reddish, in erect clusters. LWT 111 (= *S. rufo-ferruginea* var. *trilocularis* Koidz.). Taiwan, forests of the high mountains. z7

S. reducta Diels. Dwarf shrub, only 15–40 cm high, developing thickets in its habitat, young shoots sparsely bristly, very thin, winter buds glabrous; leaves 7–10 cm long, leaflets 9–15, ovate to elliptic, coarsely serrate, 1.5–2.5 cm long, acute, somewhat pubescent above, glabrous beneath, fall foliage carmine; flowers few in terminal clusters, white, 1.2 cm wide, calyx glabrous on the exterior, interior pubescent; fruits globose, carmine, 6 mm thick. Burma, W. China. 1943. Very attractive for the rock garden. z6 Plate 118. ⌀ ⚭

S. rehderiana Koehne. Shrub or small tree, closely related to *S. hupehensis*, but the shoots 5–8 mm thick; leaflets 15–19, oblong-lanceolate, 2.5–5 cm long, finely serrate, glabrous; inflorescences 3–7 cm wide, loose red-brown pubescent, styles 5; fruits whitish to reddish, 6–7 mm thick. W. China. Existence in cultivation still unknown. z6 ⊕

S. rhamnoides (Decne.) Rehd. Shrub to small tree, corolla loose, shoots only pubescent when young; leaves elliptic, 13–15 cm long, serrate, with 10–14 vein pairs, green above, underside gray pubescent at first, petiole thin; fruits green, calyx abscising. SH 1: 386b (= *Micromeles rhamnoides* Dcne.; *Pyrus rhamnoides* Hook.). Sikkim, in the mountains at 3000 m. z6 ⌀

S. rufo-ferruginea (Schneid.) Schneid. Small tree, very similar to *S. commixta*, but the winter buds brown shaggy, as are the flower stalks and the midrib on the leaf underside; styles usually 5. MJ 3557 (= *S. commixta* var. *rufo-ferruginea* Schneid.). Japan. 1915. z6 Plate 119.

var. *trilocularis* see: **S. randaiensis**

S. rupicola (Syme) Hedl. Shrub, to 2 m high, occasionally a small tree, rather stiff; very similar to *S. aria*, but the leaves widest above the middle, with 8–10 vein pairs, basal third or quarter entire, obtuse at the apex, deep green above, tough, white tomentose beneath, petiole usually somewhat reddish; inflorescences woolly, petals 7 mm long, May–June; fruits wider than long, carmine, 12–15 mm thick, often green on one side, very punctate. CFl 646; GPN 490 (= *S. salicifolia* [Myrin] Hedl.; *S. aria* var. *salicifolia* Myrin). British Isles; S. Scandinavia. z7 Fig. 242.

S. salicifolia see: **S. rupicola**

S. sambucifolia (Cham. & Schlechtd.) Roem. Shrub (!), 1–2.5 m high, winter buds nearly black, glutinous, young shoots somewhat pubescent; leaflets 9–11, ovate-lanceolate, acuminate, 3–7 cm long, very uneven at the base, dark green and glossy above (!), lighter beneath and quickly becoming totally glabrous; inflorescences only 4–5 cm wide, flowers to 1.5 cm wide (!), calyx glabrous, lobes ciliate, June; fruits nearly globose, to 12 mm thick, with large, erect (!) sepals, somewhat

pruinose. SH 1: 366a, 367 a–b; MJ 1401. NE. Asia, Ussuri region to Kamchatka; Japan; in moist, mossy coniferous forests. 1906. Very rare in cultivation, short lived; usually confused with *S. decora, S. matsumurana, S. scopulina* and *S. sitchensis.*

S. sargentiana Koehne. Tree, 7–10 m high, winter buds glutinous and somewhat pubescent, shoots thick; leaves very large, leaflets 7–11, oblong-lanceolate, 8–13 cm (!) long, 2.5–3 cm wide, finely serrate, underside densely greenish tomentose, fall color orange-brown; inflorescences about 15 cm wide, densely shaggy pubescent, May; fruits only 6 mm thick, scarlet, very numerous. GC 140: 431. W. China. 1908. Plate 115. ⚭

'Warleyensis'. Leaflets smaller, rachis dark red; inflorescences larger, looser; fruits smaller. GC 94: 177. 1931. ⊕

S. sargentii see: **Sorbaronia sorbifolia**

S. scalaris Koehne. Tall shrub, or small tree, to 6 m high, shoots soft pubescent; leaves 10–20 cm long, with 21–37 leaflets, these narrowly oblong, shallowly dentate only on the apical third or the apex, 2–3 cm long (usually twice as large on young plants!), deep green above, underside densely gray (spider web-like) tomentose, carmine-red in fall, rachis reddish, pubescent, furrowed above; inflorescences 12–14 cm wide, very dense, long pubescent, convex or flat, very well branched, flowers dull white, 6 mm wide, styles 3–4, May to June; fruits bright red, 5–6 mm thick. BMns 69; JRHS 89: 2. W. China. 1904. Plate 114. ⌀ ⚭

S. scandica see: **S. intermedia**

S. scopulina Greene. Shrub, to 4 m high, stiff branched, winter buds black pubescent; leaflets 11–15, oblong-lanceolate, acute or short acuminate, 3–6 cm long, dark green and glossy above, glabrous and blue-green beneath; inflorescences large, sparsely pubescent; fruits very numerous, pea-sized, bright red, glossy. RWF 189 (= *S. sitchensis* Piper p. p.; *S. americana nana* Hort.; *S. decora nana* Hort.). Western N. America. 1917.

S. semipinnata see: **S. × thuringiaca**

S. serotina Koehne. Tall tree, similar to *S. americana*; leaflets usually 13, oblong-lanceolate, to 5 cm long, scabrous serrate, dark green above, light gray-green beneath, bright brown-red and persisting long into fall; flower stalks shaggy pubescent, petals reflexed; fruits globose, scarcely pea-sized, red. Gs 1: 183; BMns 166. Japan? 1900. Highly valued for its beautiful fall color. z6 ⌀

S. sitchensis Roem. Shrub, to 1.8 m high, also tree-like in Alaska; leaves very large, leaflets 7–11, ovate to oblong, tough, 6–8 cm long, 2–3 cm wide, obtuse to acute, coarsely serrate at the base or to the middle, dull green above (!), underside glabrous; young inflorescences globose at first, later flatter, 5–10 cm wide, red-brown pubescent to nearly glabrous, flowers 8 mm thick, coral-red, pruinose. MS 200. Northwest N. America. 1918. Very often confused with other species. See also: **S. scopulina.** z5 ⌀

S. sorbifolia see: **Sorbaronia sorbifolia**

S. × splendida Hedl. (*S. americana × S. aucuparia*). Very similar to *S. americana*, but with wider leaflets, about 2.5–3 times longer than wide (those of *S. americana* about 3.5–5 times longer than wide); fruits larger; winter buds more pubescent and glutinous. HSo 6; Gs 5: 181. Originated in cultivation around 1850. z2 ⚥

S. spuria see: **Sorbaronia hybrida**

S. subarranensis see: **S. arranensis**

S. subpinnata Hedl. Small tree, to 5 m high; similar to *S. intermedia*, but the leaves narrower, at least the basal 3–4 lobe pairs very deeply incised (⅓ of the blade), the incisions very narrow; flowers often with 3 styles; fruits 10 mm long. Norway. z6 Fig. 242.

S. subsimilis Hedl. Tree, to 6 m high; leaves tough, with 8–9 pairs of lateral veins, similar to *S. intermedia*, but the lobes much less deeply incised; flowers 15 mm wide; fruits 10–12 mm long. Norway, on dry sites in the mountains. z5 Fig. 242.

S. theophrasta see: **S. devoniensis**

S. thomsonii (King) Rehd. Large tree, totally glabrous in all respects; leaves undivided, elliptic-lanceolate or oblanceolate, 5–8 cm long, serrate on the apical half, petiole 6–8 mm long, glabrous; inflorescences glabrous, flowers 8 mm wide; fruits 1.8 cm wide, red with white spots. India. z7 Plate 119.

S. × thuringiaca (Ilse) Fritsch. (*S. aria × S. aucuparia*). Resembles *S. hybrida*, but the leaves on the fertile short shoots becoming narrower toward the apex, with 10–14 pairs of lateral veins, more finely serrate, teeth shorter and acute, but not acuminate, leaves occasionally with 1–4 pinnae at the base, decreasingly lobed toward the apex, finally only dentate; flowers only 12 mm wide; fruit smaller, red. KSo 24 (1) (= *S. pinnatifida* [Ehrh.] Bean; *S. semipinnata* [Roth] Hedl.; *S. hybrida* Hort. non L.). First found in 1773 near Eisenach in Thuringia (E. Germany), later also found in the Carpathian Mts. z6

Including the following hybrid forms:

'Decurrens' Transition form between *S. thuringiaca* and *S. aucuparia*. Leaves pinnate nearly to the apex, leaflets in 5–7 pairs, terminal leaflet deeply incised at the base, apical leaflets with a broad, decurrent base (!), all leaflets finely serrate, stipules small and narrow. NDJ 21: 197 (= *S. decurrens* [Koehne] Hedl.). Presumably originated in cultivation as a seedling of *S. thuringiaca*. 1834. Plate 114.

'Fastigiata' (*S. aria var. longifolia × S. aucuparia*). Tree with a narrower, more conical crown, branches ascending, later more spreading and then with a wider crown; leaves oval-oblong, obtuse acuminate, with 1–4 leaflets at the base, these with a free or somewhat decurrent base, tough, dark green; fruits very numerous, dark red. NDJ 21: 192; 20: 132 (as *S. thuringiaca*) (= *S. hybrida* f. *fastigiata* Rehd.; *Pyrus pinnatifida* var. *fastigiata* Bean; *S. thuringiaca* 'Quercifolia'). Brought into the trade before 1907 by Backhouse of York, England. The best form of the group. Widely used in Europe today as a street tree but usually mistakenly labeled "*S. hybrida*". Plate 114. ∅ ⚥

'Leonard Springer' (Lombarts). Transition form; leaves only with 4–5 pairs of leaflets, these coarsely serrate, apical leaflets with the base scarcely decurrent on the rachis, terminal leaflet 6–7 cm long, rhombic, tapered toward the apex, deeply incised at the base, less deep in the middle, only biserrate at the apex, leaf petiole red (!); fruits large, to 12 mm thick, persistent. NDJ 21: 198. Developed in cultivation by J. Lombarts of Zundert, Holland and introduced to the trade in 1938. ⚥

'Neuillyensis'. Leaves resembling those of 'Leonard Springer', but the stipules larger (to 2 × 1 cm), leaf petiole green; leaflets usually in 4–5 pairs, oblong, 3–5 cm long, the apical leaflets somewhat decurrent on the rachis, terminal leaflet triangular-ovate, 6–9 cm long, base broadly cuneate, pinnately lobed and incised biserrate. NDJ 21; 198 (= *S. neuillyensis* Dipp.). First discovered in a garden in Neuilly, Lorraine before 1893. Plate 114.

'Quercifolia' see: 'Fastigiata'

S. tianshanica Rupr. Shrub or small tree, to 5 m high, branches usually totally glabrous, eventually glossy and red-brown, winter buds densely white pubescent; leaflets 9–15, lanceolate (!), acuminate, 3–5 cm long, finely serrate, entire toward the base, dark green and glossy above (!), underside lighter and glabrous, rather tough; inflorescences axillary, grouped into a terminal, 8–12 cm wide corymb, flowers nearly 2 cm wide, glabrous, stamens half as long as the petals, June; fruits globose, bright red, 8 mm thick. BM 7755. Turkestan, Tian Shan Mts., to Kansu Prov. 1895. z6 Plate 115; Fig. 243. ∅ ⚘ ⚥

S. torminalis (L.) Crantz. Round crowned tree, 10–15 m high or more, branches loosely tomentose at first, later glabrous and olive-brown; leaves broadly ovate, deeply acutely lobed, to 10 cm long, base truncate to cuneate, lobes acute, scabrous serrate, bright green and somewhat glossy above, underside light green, red in fall, petiole 2–5 cm long; flowers white, 12 mm wide, in loose, tomentose, to 12 cm wide corymbs, styles usually 2, May–June; fruits ellipsoid, brown, lighter punctate, to 1.5 cm long. HM 1047; HF 2540. Europe, Asia Minor, N. Africa. Cultivated since antiquity; popular park tree. Likes calcareous soils. Ⓕ W. Germany, USSR; in screen plantings. z6 Plate 115. ⚥

S. umbellata (Desf.) Fritsch. Shrub or small tree, 5–7 m high, very similar to *S. aria*; leaves nearly circular to broadly elliptic, obtuse, 3.5–6 cm long, incised lobed on the apical blade half, base cuneate, the lobes short, coarsely serrate, with 5–6 (!) vein pairs, dark green above, white tomentose beneath, leathery tough, petiole to 1 cm long at most; flowers in May; fruits flat-globose, orange-red, ripening in October. SH 1: 378, 379; KSo 13 (= *S. flabellifolia* Schau.; *S. aria* var. *flabellifolia* Wenz.). SE. Europe, Asia Minor. z6 Plate 120.

var. **cretica** (Lindl.) Schneid. Shrub, occasionally a tree, branches more outspread; leaves elliptic-obovate, 5–9 cm long, rounded to the apex, but not lobed (!), with 6–11 vein pairs, simple to biserrate, glossy dark green above, silver-white and thickly tomentose beneath, tough; fruits nearly globose, brown-green at first, later brown-red, nearly without lenticels. KSo 10–11 (= *S. cretica* [Lindl.] Fritsch; *S. graeca* Lodd.). Greece, Syria, Asia Minor; more recently also found in central Europe. 1830. Plate 120.

Fig. 244. **Sorbus.** Left *S. wilsoniana;* center *S. hupehensis;* right *S. discolor* (from ICS)

S. vilmorinii Schneid. Shrub or small tree, 3–6 m high (often grafted on a standard in cultivation), branches spreading, glabrous or somewhat red-brown pubescent, as are the winter buds; leaflets 19–25, elliptic to oblong-elliptic, apical half scabrous serrate, occasionally only so at the apex, 1.5–2.5 cm long, gray-green beneath, rachis usually slightly winged (!); inflorescences loose, to 10 cm wide, flowers small, 6 mm wide, styles 5, June; fruits globose, 8 mm thick, red at first, then light pink. BM 8241 (= *S. foliolosa* Hort.). China; Szechwan, Yunnan Provs. 1889. z6 ♂♀

S. wilsoniana Schneid. Closely related to *S. pohuashanensis.* Tree, 7–10 m high, shoots 5–7 mm thick, winter buds silvery pubescent at the apex; leaves to 25 cm long, leaflets 11–15, oblong-lanceolate, 6–8 cm long, acute to acuminate, gray-green beneath, pubescent on the midrib; flowers small, white, with 3–4 styles, inflorescences 10–15 cm wide; fruits carmine. SH 1: 367k, 368 p–q. Central China. Existence in cultivation unknown. Always confused with *S. hupehensis* var. *obtusa* Schneid. z6 Fig. 244.

S. xanthoneura Rehd. Tree, very similar to *S. pallescens,* but easily distinguished by the larger fruits with many lenticels, petiole and venation on the underside totally glabrous and yellowish; leaves oblong to more obovate, long acuminate, 8–13 cm long, 3.5–5.5 cm wide, margins biserrate, densely white tomentose beneath, except for the glabrous venation; fruits grouped 1–3 together, nearly globose, 8 mm wide, red. China; Hupeh Prov. z7 Fig. 241.

S. zahlbruckneri Schneid. (non Hort.!). Tree, branches nearly glabrous, purple; leaves simple, elliptic to more ovate, acute, 6–10 cm long, 3.5–5 cm wide, with 10–15 vein pairs, margins with short and acute serrate lobes, glossy green above, whitish gray-green beneath. China; Szechwan Prov. Presumably not true in cultivation and not to be confused with *S. zahlbruckneri* Hort.; see: **S. alnifolia** var. **submollis.** z6 Fig. 244.

Cultivars and Garden Hybrids

'Apricot Lady' Seedling of *S. aucuparia.* Foliage bright green, good fall color; fruits apricot-yellow. Developed by Hillier, Winchester, England. ♂♀

'Chamaois Glow'. From *S.* × *arnoldiana;* Lombarts Hybrid. Strong growing, winter buds lilac, white pubescent; foliage very large; fruits buff colored. Around 1950. ♂♀

'Cheerwater Seedling' see: **'Sheerwater Seedling'**

'Edwin Hillier'. Originated from seed of *S. poteriifolia,* but possibly fertilized by a species from the *Aria* section. Slow growing shrub or small tree, winter buds globose, rust-brown; leaves ovate to elliptic or lanceolate, the basal half with 1–3 pairs of serrate pinnae or lobes, apical half distinctly lobed and serrate, deep green above, underside densely gray to brownish gray tomentose; flowers in terminal cymes; fruits oval, pink. ♂♀

'Embley'. *Aucuparia* Section. Small to medium-sized, upright tree, apparently closely related to *S. commixta,* winter buds similarly acute, glutinous; leaves also with 11–15 sharply acuminate leaflets, fall color a glowing red and persistent; fruits in large clusters, glossy orange-red (= *S. discolor* Hort.). Developed from seed sent by E. H. Wilson or G. Forrest from China. Around 1908. Original plant is in Embley Park, Hampshire, England. Widely planted in England. ♂♀

'Ethel's Gold'. *Aucuparia* Section. Small tree; leaves pinnate, bright green, scabrous serrate; fruits amber-yellow, persisting until deep in the winter. Presumably a seedling of *S. commixta;* found by Hillier. ♂♀

'Ghose'. *Aucuparia* Section. Small tree, upright habit, somewhat resembling *S. insignis,* but more winter hardy; leaves large, pinnate, with 11–19 leaflets, these oblong-lanceolate, scabrous serrate, dull green above, bluish beneath, brownish pubescent at least along the midrib; fruits pink-red, in dense, heavy cymes, persistent. Introduced by Hillier from the Himalayas. ♂♀

'Golden Wonder'. From *S.* × *arnoldiana;* Lombarts Hybrid. Small tree, 5–7 m high; leaves deep green, yellow to orange in fall; fruits golden-yellow. ♂♀

'Jermyns'. *Aucuparia* Section; *S. aucuparia* × *S. sargentii.* Small tree, shoots erect, buds red, glabrous, glutinous; leaves intermediate in form and size, but without the conspicuous stipules of *S. sargentiana*, good fall foliage; fruits in large clusters, dark amber-yellow, later orange-red. Developed by Hillier from seed of *S. sargentiana*. ⊘ ♿

'Joseph Rock'. *Aucuparia* Section; botanical parentage as yet unclear, partly considered a separate species, otherwise also a possible hybrid with *S. serotina*. Small, narrowly upright tree, to 9 m; leaves pinnate, about 6 × 15 cm long, leaflets 15–19, narrowly oblong, scabrous serrate, red or orange to purple in fall; fruits cream-yellow at first, later amber-yellow, persisting until leaf drop. BMns 554; JRHS 89: 1 (= *S.* Rock No. 23657). Cultivated since before 1950. ⊘ ♿

'Kewensis'. *Aucuparia* Section; *S. pohuashanensis* × *S. esserteauiana*. Small tree; leaves pinnate, leaflets 19–23, narrow and long, rather regular and deeply serrate to nearly pinnatisect, deep green above, gray pubescent beneath, coloring an intense purple in fall; fruits small, oval, vermilion-red, ripening late. Originated before 1947 in the Royal Botanic Gardens, Kew, England. ⊘ ♿

'Kirsten Pink'. *Aucuparia* Section; Lombarts Hybrid. Shrubby habit, medium vigor; leaf petiole red; fruit pink. Around 1950. ♿

'Lowndes'. *Aucuparia* Section; related to *S. poteriifolia*. Small upright tree, shoots ascending, thick, gray, buds red, rust-brown pubescent at the apex; leaves pinnate, with 15–21 leaflets, these elliptic-lanceolate, scabrous serrate, distinct reticulate venation; fruits white or with a trace of pink, in dense clusters. Brought from the Himalayas by Col. D. Lowndes. ♿

'Mitchellii'. *Aria* Section; ? *S. aria* × *S. cuspidata*. An attractive, medium-sized to tall tree, original tree is 19 m high, broad crowned; leaves rounded, to 20 cm long and 15–18 cm wide, obtuse at the apex, underside white tomentose, base nearly entire, apical half finely obtuse and irregularly serrate, with 9–10 vein pairs, petiole 1.5 cm long. Developed by the Westonbirt Arboretum, England from seed collected in the Himalayas. Plate 118. ⊘ ♿

'Pearly King'. *Aucuparia* Section; *S. vilmorinii* × ?. Small, thinly branched tree; leaves finely and delicately pinnate, with 13–17 narrow, scabrous serrate leaflets; fruits globose, to 15 mm thick, pink at first, later white with a trace of pink, in large, loose, pendulous clusters. Developed by Hillier. ♿

'Red Marbles'. *Aucuparia* Section; ? *S. aucuparia* 'Edulis' × *S. pohuashanensis*. Small, thickly branched tree; leaves pinnate, with 13–15 wide, serrate leaflets, petiole purple; fruits 12–17 mm thick, red, with light lenticels, in loose, heavy clusters. Developed in 1961 by Hillier. Very attractively fruiting tree. ♿

'Red Tip' *Aucuparia* Section. Small tree with a conical crown; leaves small, light green; fruits white with red spots. Developed by Lombarts of Zundert, Holland around 1950. ♿

'Rose Queen'. *Aucuparia* Section; 'Embley' × *S. poteriifolia*. Small tree; leaves with 13–17 scabrous serrate leaflets; fruits bright pink-red, in large, loose clusters. Developed by Hillier in 1963. ♿

'Schouten'. From *S. arnoldiana*. Narrowly ovate crown, dense; fruits orange-yellow, 8–10 mm thick, but only sparsely fruiting. Selected around 1950 by Brouwers of Groenekan, Holland, from seedlings of *S. discolor* and first disseminated as *S. pekinensis*. A popular street tree in Holland. ♿

'Sheerwater Seedling'. *Aucuparia* clone. Small tree, with an ovate crown, shoots ascending, vigorous habit; fruits orange-red, in particularly large clusters, but dropping early (= "Cheerwater Seedling"). Introduced by Jackman, Woking, Surrey, England. ♿

'Signalman'. *Aucuparia* Section; *S. domestica* × *S. scopulorum*. Small tree, crown rather narrowly conical; leaves similar to those of *S. domestica*, but somewhat smaller and more densely arranged; fruits large, light orange, in dense clusters. Developed by Hillier in 1968. ♿

'White Wax'. Lombarts Hybrid. Shrubby habit; fruits white, appearing early. ♿

'Wilfrid Fox'. *Aria* Section; *S. aria* × *S. cuspidata*. Medium-sized tree, to 12 m, broad crowned, but broad columnar when young, densely branched, branches and twigs ascending; leaves elliptic, 15–20 cm long, flat and biserrate, deep green and glossy above, petiole 2.5–5 cm long; fruits globose, about 2 × 2 cm in size, green at first, then amber-yellow with gray spots. Developed by Hillier before 1920. ⊘ ♿

'Winter Cheer'. *Aucuparia* Section; *S. esserteauiana* 'Flava' × *S. pohuashanensis*. Small to medium-sized, open crowned tree; fruits bright yellow, ripening orange-red, showing color in September, persisting into winter. Developed by Hillier in 1959. ♿

All species prefer a sunny, open site and a deep, fertile soil. Unless cited otherwise, all species are quite hardy and do not require winter protection. Besides the abundant fruit display, many species also have a beautiful fall color.

Lit. Hedlund, T.: Monographie der Gattung *Sorbus*; in Kgl. Svensk Vetensk.-Akad. Handl. **35**, 1 to 147, 1901 ● Hensen, K. J. W.: De *Sorbus*-collectie in de Botanise Tuinen en het Belmonte-Arboretum van de Landbouwhogeschool te Wageningen (I); in Jaarb. Ned. Dendr. Ver. **20**, 121–139, 1957; (II) **21**, 180–187, 1959; (III) seen in manuscript, 1962 ● Hensen, K. J. W.: In Nederland gekweekte Overgangsvormen tussen *Sorbus aria* (L.) Crantz en *Sorbus aucuparia* L.; in Jaarb. Ned. Dendr. Ver. **21**, 189–204, 1959 ● Hensen, K. J. W.: In Nederland gekweekte Tussenvormen tussen *Sorbus aria* en *S. torminalis*; Dendroflora 1967, 51–60 ● Hensen, K. J. W.: Het *Sorbus latifolia*-Complex; in Misc. Papers **6**, Landb. Hoogeschool Wageningen 1970, 181–194 ● Karpati, Z.: Die *Sorbus*-Arten Ungarns und der angrenzenden Gebiete; in Feddes Repert. **62**, 71–334, 1960 (with 13 pp. of bibliography) ● Düll, R.: Unsere Ebereschen und ihre Bastarde; in Brehm-Bücherei **226**, 1–122, 1959 ● Jones, G. N.: A Synopsis of the North American Species of *Sorbus*; in Jour. Arnold Arb. **20**, 1–43, 1939 ● Koernicke, M.: Zur Kenntnis der mährischen "süssen" Ebereshe; in Die deutsche Heilpflanze **9**, 1943 (20 pp.) ● Liljefors, A.: Studies on Propagation, Embryology and Pollination in *Sorbus*; in Act. Hort. Berg. **16**, 227–329, 1953 ● Liljefors, A.: Cytological Studies in *Sorbus*; in Act. Hort. Berg. **17**, 47–113, 1955.

SPARMANNIA L. f. — TILIACEAE

Tall deciduous shrubs; leaves alternate, simple, unlobed or with 3–7 lobes, dentate; flowers in long-stalked, axillary or nearly terminal umbels; sepals 4, abscising, petals 4, oblanceolate, stamens numerous, the outermost occasionally sterile; fruit a prickly capsule, with 4–5 locules, many seeded. — 7 species in the tropics and S. Africa.

Sparmannia africana L. f. Usually multistemmed shrub, 3–6 m high in frost free climates, wood soft, shoots soft pubescent; leaves cordate-ovate, acuminate, about 15 cm long, 10 cm wide, also larger on strong shoots, 7–9 veined, very irregularly dentate, covered with long, soft hairs on both sides, petiole 10–15 cm long; flowers many in long-stalked umbels, white, attractive, stamens yellow, very numerous, May. BM 516; PBl 2: 30. S. Africa. 1790. z10 ⌀ ✢

'Plena'. Like the type, but with double flowers. Plate 76.

Very fast growing, but unconditionally requiring a frost free climate; otherwise overwintering under glass or as a tub plant.

SPARTIUM L. — Spanish or Weaver's Broom — LEGUMINOSAE

Monotypic genus. Very closely related to *Cytisus* and *Genista,* but differing in the single lipped, later 5 part calyx; flowers in loose racemes, standard large, reflexed, wings shorter than the inward curving keel, claw of the wing and the keel adnate to the stamen filament tube; fruit a linear, many-seeded pod.

Spartium biflorum see: **Cytisus fontanesii**

S. grandiflorum see: **Cytisus grandiflorum**

S. junceum L. Deciduous, 2–3 m high shrub, young shoots green, with fine, whitish stripes; usually leafless or with scattered, lanceolate, only about 1 cm long leaves; flowers golden-yellow, large, broom-like, to 2.5 cm wide, in terminal, loose racemes, fragrant, May–September; fruits 5–10 cm long. BM 85; HF 2293. Mediterranean region. 1584. z8–9

'Ochroleucum'. Flowers light yellow to nearly white.

'Plenum'. Flowers double, but not exceedingly attractive.

S. scoparius see: **Cytisus scoparius**

S. supranubius see: **Cytisus supranubius**

Cultivated like *Cytisus,* but more tender.

Lit. Sprenger, C.: Der spanische Ginster; in Mitt. DDG 1913, 212–218.

SPARTOCYTISUS

Spartocytisus filipes see: **Cytisus filipes**

S. supranubius see: **Cytisus supranubius**

SPATHODEA Beauvois — BIGNONIACEAE

Evergreen trees; leaves opposite or in whorls of 3, odd pinnate; leaflets entire; flowers large, in terminal panicles or racemes, very attractive; calyx sheath-like, opening on one side and reflexed, corolla large, campanulate, tube bulging on one side, slightly bilabiate, stamens 4; fruit an oblong-lanceolate, capsule, acuminate at both ends. — 2–3 species in tropical Africa, but otherwise widely distributed in the tropics.

Spathodea campanulata Beauvois. African Tuliptree. A tree to 15 m high or higher; leaves to 35 cm long, with 9–19 leaflets, these ovate-oblong, to 4 cm long, entire, rather glabrous, petiolate; flowers in short, somewhat branched racemes, calyx about 6 cm long, leathery tough, densely pubescent, corolla broadly campanulate, about 70 cm long, 6 cm wide, scarlet-red, slightly bilabiate, June. BM 509; FS 830. Tropical Africa. 1858. Ⓕ Philippines. z10 Fig. 245. # ✢

Only planted in totally frost free climates. Very attractive flowering tree.

Fig. 245. *Spathodea campanulata*

SPHACELE Benth. — LABIATAE

Sage-like shrubs and subshrubs; leaves opposite, often blistery-rugose bullate, smaller at the shoot apex; flowers red, violet, blue or white; calyx 5 toothed; corolla large, with a broad tube and a short, slightly bilabiate limb, 4 lobed with wide, more or less erect lobes; stamens 4; with 2–6 flowers in loose racemes or spikes or 6 to many in dense whorls. — 25 species in Mexico, Venezuela, the Andes and SE. Brazil.

Sphacele chamaedryoides Briquet. Small shrub, 50–70 cm high; leaves oblong-lanceolate, 1.5–2.5 cm long, tapered to a short petiole, the apical leaves very rugose-bullate; flowers tubular, light blue, 15 mm long, limb lobes broadly crenate, calyx 8 mm long, paired in loose racemes, July–August. BR 1382. Chile. 1875. z9 ✧

Only for particularly mild climates, but otherwise easy to cultivate.

SPHAERALCEA St. Hil. — MALVACEAE

Perennials, subshrubs or shrubs; leaves alternate, simple, triangular or lobed; flowers solitary or in clusters, axillary or in axillary, spike-like racemes, usually only short stalked; calyx 5 incised with a 3 or 2 parted involucre, corolla cupulate, yellowish, orange, lilac or whitish; fruit a densely pubescent, globose schizocarp. — 60 species in the warmer parts of America and S. Africa.

Sphaeralcea fendleri A. Gray. Subshrub, to 60 cm high, shoots erect or outspread; leaves ovate, flat or deeply 3 lobed, finely stellate pubescent on both sides; flowers mallow-like, usually in pairs and developing segmented inflorescences, corolla 2.5 cm wide, light reddish orange, July–September. BMns 140. S. USA, N. Mexico. z9 ✧

Needs a sunny, dry site and winter protection.

SPIRAEA L. — Spirea — ROSACEAE

Deciduous shrubs; leaves alternate, usually petiolate, simple, serrate, dentate or lobed, without stipules; flowers nearly always hermaphroditic, in racemes, panicles or corymbs, petals 4–5; stamens usually numerous, carpels 5, occasionally only 1–4, inserted into the calyx base, distinct or slightly connate at the base, alternating with the sepals, not opposite the sepals; fruit a follicle, dehiscing along the ventral suture, later also splitting along the dorsal suture, with 2–10 oblong seeds. — About 100 species, mostly in temperate Asia, in Europe, N. America and Mexico.

Outline of the Species Covered in this Work

+ Inflorescences compound; flowers white or pink;
  × flowers in panicles;
  Section 1. **Spiraea**

  ×× Flowers in corymbs:
  Section 2. **Calospira** K. Koch

++ Inflorescences a simple umbel or an umbellate raceme; flowers white:
  Section 3. **Chamaedryon** Ser.

Key to the Species and Hybrids
(from Rehder)
Section SPIRAEA

A. Inflorescence a broad panicle, about as wide as high (including hybrids from this section and *Calospira*);

  B. Panicles rather small, on lateral branches at the tip of the previous year's wood;
    S. fontenaysii

  BB. Panicles large, terminal, on long, erect shoots;

    C. Leaves glabrous or nearly so;

      D. Leaf blade acute:
        S. conspicua

      DD. Leaf blade obtuse or somewhat acute;

        E. Blade broad ovate to obovate:
          S. notha

        EE. Blade oblong to oval-oblong:
          S. pyramidata

    CC. Leaves pubescent or tomentose on the underside;

      D. Leaf base acute:
        S. sanssouciana

      DD. Leaf base rounded:
        S. watsoniana

AA. Inflorescence an elongated panicle, longer than wide (only Section *Spiraea*);

  B. Leaves glabrous or nearly so;

    C. Leaves scabrous serrate, except at the base;

      D. Panicles finely tomentose;

        E. Flowers light pink:
          S. salicifolia

        EE. Flowers white:
          S. alba

      DD. Panicles totally glabrous:
        S. latifolia

    CC. Leaves coarsely serrate beyond the middle, flowers pink:
      S. menziesii

  BB. Leaves pubescent or tomentose on both sides;

    C. Follicle glabrous; leaves gray or whitish tomentose beneath;

      D. Leaves acute at both ends:
        S. billardi

      DD. Leaves rounded at both ends:
        S. douglasii

    CC. Follicle pubescent; leaves usually brownish pubescent beneath:
      S. tomentosa

Section CALOSPIRA

A. Corymbs usually on short lateral shoots along the generally bowed previous year's wood:

  B. Leaves 12–25 mm long, crenate-serrate or serrate only at the apex; corymbs on very short shoots;

    C. Shoots angular; leaves usually elliptic, obtuse; winter buds with 2 outer scales:
      S. canescens

    CC. Shoots cylindrical; leaves usually oblong; winter buds with several scales:
      S. sargentiana

  BB. Leaves 2–7.5 cm long;

    C. Flowers hermaphroditic, white;

      D. Winter buds short, ovate, with several outer scales; leaves entire or only serrate on the apical half;

        E. Blade glabrous above, entire; flowering shoots 5–7.5 cm long:
          S. veitchii

        EE. Blade more or less pubescent above, margins usually dentate toward the apex;

          F. Inflorescences glabrous:
            S. wilsonii

          FF. Inflorescences pubescent:
            S. henryi

      D. Winter buds elongated, acute, with 2 outer scales; leaves biserrate or incised serrate;

        E. Leaves pubescent only on the venation beneath, incised serrate:
          S. rosthornii

        EE. Leaves totally glabrous, deeply serrate:
          S. longigemmis

    CC. Flowers dioecious, pink or white; leaves scabrous serrate; winter buds ovate, with several scales;

      D. Shoots angular; leaves usually oval-oblong; flowers pink:
        S. bella

      DD. Shoots cylindrical, leaves usually ovate to elliptic; flowers white:
        S. fastigiata

AA. Corymbs erect at the apex, on the current year's shoots;

  B. Inflorescences pubescent, occasionally glabrous, very densely compound, with lateral corymbs appearing beneath the terminal ones, only the weaker shoots with a solitary corymb;

    C. Shrub, 30 cm high or less, leaves bullate, shorter than 2.5 cm:
      S. bullata

    CC. Shrub, 0.3–1.5 m high, leaves larger;

      D. Shoots cylindrical;

        E. Ripe follicles spreading:
          S. japonica

        EE. Ripe follicles straight erect;

          F. Flowers pink:
            S. margaritae

          FF. Flowers white or with a trace of pink:
            S. foxii

      DD. Shoots more or less angular, rather stiff, nearly glabrous;

        E. Flowers pink, occasionally whitish:
           S. bumalda

         EE. Flowers white:
           S. albiflora

  BB. Inflorescences composed of only one solitary, terminal corymb, usually glabrous; follicle not spreading;

    C. Corymbs usually pubescent;

      D. Sepals in fruit reflexed; leaves usually oblong, acute or long acuminate; flowers pink or whitish:
        S. superba

      DD. Sepals erect in fruit; leaves usually ovate or elliptic; flowers white:
        S. corymbosa

    CC. Corymbs glabrous (frequently pubescent on *S. betulifolia*);

      D. Stamens longer than the petals;

        E. Flowers pink, gland ring absent:
           S. densiflora

        EE. Flowers white, gland ring present;

          F. Leaves oblong, entire or with a few teeth on the apical half, acute:
            S. virginiana

          FF. Leaves elliptic, dentate;

           G. Margins scabrous, often biserrate, acute:
             S. lucida

           GG. Margins crenate, rounded at the apex:
             S. betulifolia

      DD. Stamens as long as the petals; procumbent shrub; leaves 12–25 mm long, scabrous serrate:
        S. decumbens

Section CHAMAEDRYON

A. Flowers in sessile umbels with or without a few leaves at the base or only the lowest umbels on foliate shoots;

  B. Leaves entire or crenate only at the apex, often 3 veined, gray-green:
    S. hypericifolia

  BB. Leaves dentate or serrate, usually pinnately veined, light green;

    C. Blade linear-lanceolate, glabrous:
      S. thunbergii

    CC. Blade ovate to oblong-lanceolate, finely pubescent when young;

D. Umbels stalked on the basal portion of the shoots;

    E. Leaves oblong:
        S. arguta

    EE. Leaves obovate:
        S. multiflora

DD. Umbels all sessile, with 3–6 flowers:
    S. prunifolia

AA. Flowers in umbellate racemes on foliate stalks;

B. Blade entire or only crenate or dentate near the apex;

    C. Leaves gray pubescent on both sides:
        S. cana

    CC. Leaves nearly glabrous;

        D. Blade elliptic to oblong-lanceolate;

            E. Leaves pinnately veined; shoots angular:
                S. alpina

            EE. Leaves all or partly 3 veined;

                F. Shoots striated; leaves all 3 veined:
                    S. crenata

                FF. Shoots cylindrical; leaves partly pinnately veined, partly 3 veined:
                    S. pikoviensis

        DD. Leaves nearly circular, 12–25 mm wide:
            S. nipponica

BB. Leaf margins incised serrate and often slightly lobed (occasionally entire on *S. media*);

    C. Stamens shorter or as long as the petals; sepals erect or outspread on the fruits;

        D. Leaves glabrous;

            E. Leaves circular to ovate;

                F. Leaf apex obtuse;

                    G. Leaves pinnately veined, elliptic:
                        S. blumei

                    GG. Leaves palmately veined, 3–5 veined, circular:
                        S. trilobata

                FF. Leaf apex acute:
                  S. vanhouttei

            EE. Blade rhombic-lanceolate:
                S. cantoniensis

        DD. Leaves pubescent, at least beneath;

            E. Umbels and follicles pubescent;

                F. Pubescence gray:
                  S. blanda

                FF. Pubescence yellowish:
                  S. chinensis

            EE. Umbels and follicles glabrous:
                S. pubescens

    CC. Stamens longer than the petals; sepals reflexed;

        D. Shoots cylindrical, frequently pubescent:
            S. media

DD. Shoots angular, glabrous;

    E. Leaves doubly and irregularly serrate on the basal half:
        S. chamaedryfolia

    EE. Leaves serrate, usually only on the apical half:
        S. flexuosa

Parentage of the more Prominent Spiraea Cultivars

'Anthony Waterer'	→ *S. bumalda*
'Coccinea'	→ *S. bumalda*
'Crispa'	→ *S. bumalda*
'Dart's Red'	→ *S. bumalda*
'Froebelii'	→ *S. bumalda*
'Goldflame'	→ *S. bumalda*
"Graciosa"	→ 'Grefsheim'
'Grefsheim'	→ *S. cinerea*
'Halward's Silver'	→ *S. nipponica*
'Lenneana'	→ *S. billardii*
'Little Princess'	→ *S. japonica*
'Macrothyrsa'	→ *S. billardii*
'Pruhoniciana'	→ *S. bumalda*
'Rosabella'	→ *S. betulifolia*
'Ruberrima'	→ *S. japonica*
'Snowmound'	→ *S. nipponica*
'Snow White'	→ *S. trichocarpa*
'Summer Snow'	→ *S. betulifolia*
'Triumphans'	→ *S. billardii*
'Walluf'	→ *S. bumalda*

Spiraea alba Duroi. Shrub, to 1.5 m high, erect, similar to *S. salicifolia*, but with white flowers, panicles wider at the base, branches more outspread and finely tomentose; leaves oblong-oblanceolate, 3–6 cm long, scabrous serrate, venation pubescent beneath or totally glabrous; sepals erect, June–August; fruits glabrous. GSP 170 (= *S. lanceolata* Borkh.) Eastern USA. 1759. z5

S. albiflora (Miq.) Zab. Shrub, 30–60 cm high, shoots stiffly erect, brown, very angular, striated, finely pubescent; leaves lanceolate, long acuminate, 6–7 cm long, 1–2 cm wide, serrate or biserrate, light green; flowers white, rather small, in terminal (one larger and surrounded by many smaller) corymbs, July–August; petals somewhat shorter than the stamens, styles bowed outward; fruits glabrous. DL 3: 223; BC 3667 (= *S. callosa* var. *albiflora* Miq.). Japanese cultivar, not known in the wild. Before 1876. z5 Fig. 247. ⊕

S. alpina Pall. Shrub, 1–1.5 m high, very densely branched, branches erect to spreading, red-brown angular, pubescent at first; leaves partly clustered, short petioled, oblanceolate to narrowly oblong, 1–2.5 cm long, entire, glabrous; flowers yellowish white, 5 mm wide, in small, terminal umbels on short shoots, petals nearly circular, somewhat shorter than the stamens, May–June; fruit glossy red-brown, diverging outward, style remnants bowed erect. SH 1: 289i, 290e; PAr 282. NE. Asia to W. China. 1886. Attractive for its delicate foliage. z4

S. amurensis see: **Physocarpus amurensis**

S. aquilegiifolia see: **S. trilobata**

S. arbuscula see: **S. densiflora** ssp. **splendens**

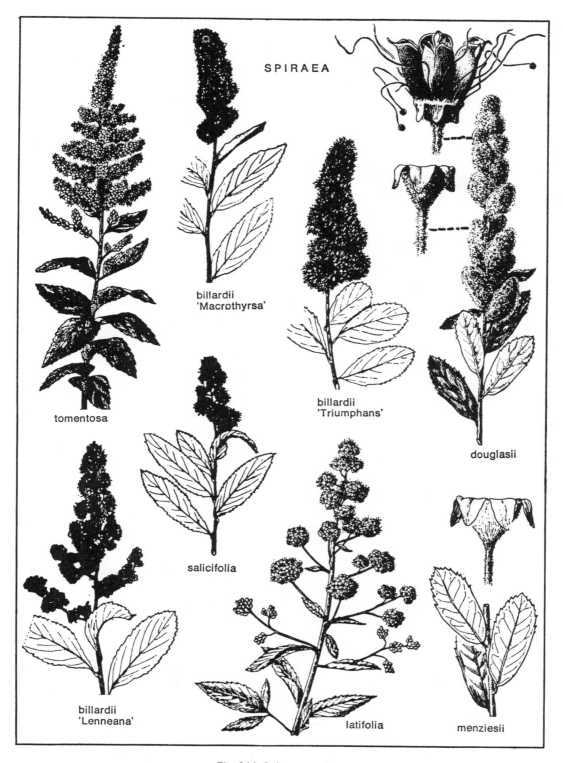

Fig. 246. **Spiraea** species

Fig. 247. *Spiraea albiflora* (from Dippel)

S. arcuata Hook. f. Similar to *S. gemmata*. Small, short and strong branched shrub, branches purple, slightly pubescent, striated; leaves oblong-elliptic, 8–15 mm long (!), entire or occasionally with a few small teeth; flowers about 6 mm wide, 10–15 in 2 cm wide umbels, on small, foliate short shoots; fruits glabrous. SH 1: 291i; SNp 47. Himalayas; Sikkim. 1908. True existence in cultivation as yet unknown. z9 Fig. 251.

S. × arguta Zab. (*S. multiflora × S. thunbergii*). Shrub, 1–2 m high, erect, branches very thin, gracefully nodding, more vigorous than *S. thunbergii*; leaves oblong-obovate or more lanceolate, to 4 cm long, bright green, scabrous and often biserrate, eventually glabrous; flowers pure white, 8 cm wide, in many-flowered corymbs along the entire branch, late April to May. Gs 1921: 81; Gw 1926: 129. Developed by Zabel before 1893. One of the prettiest early flowering spireas; good for forcing and remarkably tolerant of dryness. z5 Plate 122. ⊕

"Compacta" and *"Nana"* see: **S. cinerea**

'Grefsheim' see: **S. cinerea 'Grefsheim'**

S. baldschuanica B. Fedtschenko. Very low shrub, habit compact globose, densely branched, shoots thin, glabrous; leaves small, obovate, only serrate at the apex, bluish green; flowers in small, terminal corymbs, June to July. SE. Russia. z6

S. beauverdiana see: **S. betulifolia var. aemiliana**

S. bella Sims. Shrub, to 1 m high, branches thin, outspread, angular, somewhat pubescent; leaves elliptic to ovate, 2.5–5 cm long, biserrate to beneath the middle, venation pubescent beneath or glabrous, gray-green; flowers dioecious, pink to white, 5 mm wide, in pubescent, terminal, 2–4 cm wide corymbs, stamens longer in the male flowers, short in the female flowers, May to July; fruits pubescent, style remnants outspread.

BM 2426; SNp 48 (= *S. expansa* Wall.). Himalayas. 1823. z7 Fig. 248.

S. bethlehemensis see: **S. latifolia**

S. betulifolia Pall. Shrub, densely bushy, 0.5 (1) m high, shoots red-brown, glabrous, striated; leaves broadly ovate to elliptic, usually rounded at the apex, base usually broadly cuneate, 2–4 cm long, doubly or only simple crenate, dark green above, gray-green and reticulately veined beneath, usually glabrous; flowers white, in dense, 3–6 cm wide corymbs, petals half as long as the stamens, sepals at fruiting very reflexed (!), June; fruits glabrous, parallel, style remnants erect. MJ 1417; SH 1: 194n, 195s; Bai 20: 25–27; YWP 2: 32. NE. Asia to central Japan. 1892. z5 Fig. 252.

var. **aemiliana** (Schneid.) Koidz. Dwarf habit, 20–30 cm high; leaves broadly rounded, regularly crenate, 1.7–2.7 cm long, tough, distinct reticulate venation; flowers 4–5 mm wide, inflorescences 2–2.5 cm wide. PAr 282 (= *S. beauverdiana* Schneid.). Japan; on the volcano Mori; Kurile Islands; Kamchatka.

'Rosabella'. *Betulifolia* Hybrid. 3–4 m high; flat cymes in summer, pink. Hybridizer F. L. Skinner, Dropmore, Manitoba, Canada. ⊕

'Summer Snow' (*S. betulifolia × S. media*). Only 60 cm high; flowers in flat cymes, white, late June to late August. Hybridized by F. L. Skinner, Canada. ⊕

S. × billardii Herinq (*S. douglasii × S. salicifolia*). Shrub, to 2 m high, resembling *S. douglasii* (but the leaves acute at both ends, gray-green tomentose beneath), shoots finely pubescent, brown; leaves oblong-lanceolate, 5–8 cm long, scabrous and coarsely serrate, except for the basal third; flowers pink, in narrow, 10–20 cm long, dense panicles, stamens twice as long as the petals, June–August; fruits glabrous, parallel, style remnants

Fig. 248. *Spiraea bella* (from B. M.)

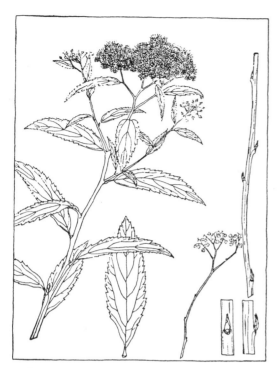

Fig. 249. *Spiraea* × *bumalda* 'Anthony Waterer'
(from Nose)

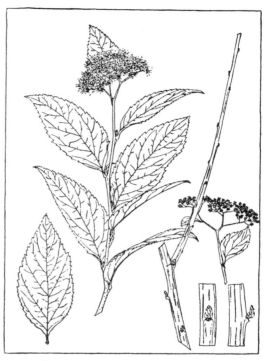

Fig. 250. *Spiraea* × *bumalda* 'Froebelii'
(from Nose)

outspread. Developed by Billard of Fontenay-aux-Roses before 1854. Easily naturalized. z5 ⊕

'Lenneana'. Shoots glabrous; leaves oblong-elliptic to obovate, 6–8 cm long, 10–18 mm wide, serrate to biserrate, base broadly cuneate and entire, light gray-green and thinly tomentose beneath; flowers to 7 mm wide, pink, in narrow panicles, broadly conical at the base, apex more cylindrical. Introduced from Leningrad before 1893. Fig. 246.

'Macrothyrsa'. Leaves broad-obovate, about 5 cm long, often more than half as wide, tomentose and light green beneath; flowers bright pink, in dense, 15–20 cm long panicles with horizontal branches (= *S. menziesii* var. *macrothyrsa* Zab.). 1870. Fig. 246.

'Triumphans'. Leaves elliptic-lanceolate, 3–6 cm long, 12–15 mm wide, serrate nearly to the base, green and somewhat pubescent beneath; panicles broadly conical, branched at the base, to 20 cm long and 10 cm wide, bright purple-pink, July–September. BS 3: 358. Before 1893. The best form of the group. Fig. 246. ⊕

S. × blanda Zab. (*S. cantoniensis* × *S. chinensis*). Shrub, 1.5–2 m high, branches nearly straight, angular striated, finely pubescent, brown; leaves ovate-oblong, 2.5–6 cm long, acute, scabrous to incised serrate, glabrous above, underside gray tomentose; flowers pure white, in pubescent corymbs, petals circular, longer than the stamens, May–June; fruits parallel, styles directed backward. SH 1: 293 d–e. Originated before 1876, presumably in France. z6

S. blumei G. Don. Medium-sized shrub, to 1.5 m high,

very similar to *S. trilobata*, but the leaves more rhombic and pinnately veined, branches outspread-nodding, cylindrical, glabrous; leaves ovate-rhombic, obtuse, 2–4 cm long, incised crenate-serrate, blue-green and distinctly veined beneath; flowers white, polygamous, many in small corymbs, petals rounded-obovate, about as long as the stamens, June; style remnants outspread. MJ 3563; NK 4: 11 (as *S. trilobata*) (= *S. obtusa* Nakai). Japan, Korea. 1858. Often confused with *S. trilobata* in cultivation. Quite variable. z6 Fig. 246.

S. bodinieri see: **S. japonica** var. **acuminata**

S. × brachybotrys Lange (*S. canescens* × *S. douglasii*). Most similar to *S. fontenaysii*, but the leaves densely gray tomentose beneath with reflexed sepals. To 2 m high, shoots brown, angular striated, finely pubescent; leaves narrowly elliptic-oblong, 3–4 cm long, serrate on the apical half with only a few teeth at the apex; flowers light pink, in dense, 3–10 cm long, somewhat tomentose panicles, with short lateral axes (= *S. pruinosa* Zab.). Originated in the Moscow Arboretum before 1867. z5 ⊕

S. bracteata see: **S. nipponica**

S. bullata Maxim. Dwarf shrub, habit dense and compact, 35–40 cm high, shoots rust-brown pubescent (!); leaves oval rounded, somewhat leathery, 1.5–3 cm long, to 2 cm wide, very rugose (!), coarsely serrate, somewhat bullate, dark green above, light green beneath; flowers dark pink at first, in small, 4–9 cm wide, compound corymbs, faded flowers a dirty light red, stamens reddish, somewhat longer than the petals, July; fruits and style remnants stunted. Gfl 1216 (= *S. crispifolia* Hort.; *S. japonica* var. *bullata* [Maxim.] Mak.). Japan, known only in cultivation. 1879. z6 Plate 121; Fig. 246. ⊕

S. × bumalda Burvénich (*S. albiflora* × *S. japonica*). Low shrub, very similar to *S. japonica* and not easily distinguishable, but lower, shoots distinctly striated; flowers white to dark pink, disk rather conspicuous, lobed; fruit style remnants terminal (= *S. pumila* Zab.). Before 1890. z3

Including the following forms:

var. *alpina* see: **S. japonica 'Little Princess'**

'Anthony Waterer' (Waterer 1875). Shrub, to 80 cm high, branches angular striated, pubescent, new growth red, occasionally with white variegated leaves intermixed (!!), but these not consistent; leaves oblong-lanceolate, to 7 cm long, scabrous and biserrate, dark green; flowers bright carmine, in flat corymbs, July–September. GC 14: 57; DB 10: 141. Fig. 249. ⊕

'Atrorosea'. To 80 cm high, nearly glabrous, habit dense and globose; leaves oblong-lanceolate, to 7 cm long and 2.5 cm wide, long and scabrous acuminate; flowers 7–8 mm wide, dark pink, sepals red-brown on the interior, horizontally arranged at fruiting. Before 1893.

'Coccinea'. Mutation of 'Anthony Waterer'. Flowers only slightly darker, otherwise hardly differing. Disseminated from Holland around 1950. Plate 121.

'Crispa' (Hesse 1923). Slow growing; leaves red at first, 5–10 cm long, margins undulate and very deeply incised serrate (!); flowers red. ⊕

'Dart's Red'. Mutation of 'Anthony Waterer', but flowers deep carmine, spent flowers lighter. Originated in England, first called 'Dart's Improved' in Holland. 1972. ⊕

'Elegans' (Lemoine). Similar to 'Anthony Waterer', but somewhat taller, densely branched, more globose; flowers light pink.

'Froebelii' (Froebel 1892). Taller growing, about 1 m high, dense and broad, new growth brown-red, never with white variegated leaves; flowers dark purple-red, in large, branched corymbs. DB 10: 135. Widely distributed and highly valued. Fig. 250. ⊕

'Goldflame'. Foliage golden-yellow in spring, greener in summer, coppery orange in fall; flowers carmine-pink, small. Introduced in 1972 by F. J. Grootendorst, Boskoop, Holland. ∅ ⊕

'Pruhoniciana' (Zeman, before 1925). Similar to 'Anthony Waterer', but only to 50 cm high; flowers pink. Developed in Pruhonice, Czechoslovakia.

'Walluf' (Goos & Koenemann, before 1930). Compact growth habit; young leaves red, not white variegated; flowers bright pink-red, but somewhat lighter than those of 'Anthony Waterer'.

S. caespitosa see: **Petrophytum caespitosum**

S. caespitosa elatior see: **Petrophytum elatius**

S. calcicola W. W. Sm. Closely related to *S. hypericifolia*,

0.7–1.5 m high, shoots long, thin, drooping, reddish, glabrous; leaves obovate to elliptic, obtuse, entire, only 4–7 mm long, glabrous; flowers white, exterior somewhat reddish, 6–8 in umbels, these grouped into 10–12 cm long inflorescences, June. China; Yunnan Prov. 1910. Occurring on limestone. Very delicate, unique species.

S. callosa see: **S. japonica**
  —*albiflora* see: **S. albiflora**
  —*superba* see: **S. × superba**

S. cana Waldst. & Kit. Dense shrub, scarcely over 1 m high, branches thin, soft pubescent, cylindrical, winter buds small; leaves elliptic-oblong, 1–2.5 cm long, entire or occasionally with a few small teeth at the apex, gray pubescent on both sides, denser beneath; flowers white, 6 mm wide, in dense, pubescent umbels on foliate stalks, petals circular, as long as the stamens, May; fruits pubescent, style remnants outspread. SE. Europe to Italy. 1825. Plate 120.

S. canescens D. Don. To 2 m high shrub, densely branched, habit nearly hemispherical, branches angular, soft pubescent; leaves elliptic to obovate, dentate at the apex, 1–2 cm long, pubescent on the margins above, gray-green beneath, pubescent; flowers white, very numerous, in hemispherical, 3–5 cm wide, delicate corymbs situated on the upper side of the drooping shoots, petals somewhat shorter than the stamens, July; fruits long pubescent, style remnants ascending. GC 43: 90; Gn 62: 410; FS 712; SNp 51 (= *S. vaccinifolia* Hort. non D. Don; *S. flagelliformis* Hort.; *S. laxiflora* Lindl.). Himalayas. 1843. Fig. 252. ⊕

'Myrtifolia' Leaves narrowly oblong, occasionally cuneate, toothed at the apex to nearly entire, bluish beneath, 12–15 mm long, 5–6 mm wide; flowers somewhat smaller, petals as long as the stamens. MG 21: 385. Before 1893. Very attractive!

S. cantoniensis Lour. Shrub, to 1.5 m high, totally glabrous, shoots cylindrical, slender; leaves rhombic-lanceolate, 2.5–5.5 cm long, coarsely serrate or trilobed, dark green above, blue-green beneath, with distinct reticulate venation; flowers many in numerous, hemispherical, 5 cm wide corymbs, pure white, at the tips of young shoots, stalk foliate, petals rounded to elliptic, longer than the stamens, May–June; fruits parallel, style remnants outspread. MJ 1421; BR 30: 10 (= *S. reevesiana* Lindl.). China, Japan. 1824. A beautiful species. z7 Plate 122. ⊕

'Lanceata'. Leaves more lanceolate, to 5.5 cm long, but only 1.2–1.5 cm wide; flowers pure white, attractively double, May. FS 1097. Cultivar from China and Japan. 1855. z8–9

S. capitata see: **Physocarpus capitatus**

S. carpinifolia see: **S. latifolia**

S. chamaedryfolia L. Upright, stoloniferous shrub, to 1.5 m high, branches usually bowed outward, glabrous, angular, flexuose; leaves ovate-elliptic to oblong-lanceolate, acute, 4–6 cm long, incised serrate, bright green, usually totally glabrous on both sides, petiole 5–10 mm long; flowers white, many in somewhat convex corymbs at the ends of short shoots, petals circular, shorter than the stamens, May–June; fruits outspread, exterior tubercled, style remnants terminal, somewhat outspread. SH 1: 290 k–o, 291 a–c (= *S. flexuosa* Fisch.). NE. Asia. 1789. z5 Fig. 251, 257.

var. **ulmifolia** (Scop.) Maxim. Taller growing, shoots stiffer, less spreading; leaves ovate at the base, biserrate; inflorescences nearly twice as large, hemispherical, on longer stalks; fruits with erect style remnants. HM 1010 (= *S. ulmifolia* Scop.). SE. Europe to NE. Asia and Japan. 1790.

S. chinensis Maxim. Shrub, to 1.5 m high, shoots nodding, yellowish tomentose when young (!!); leaves oval-rhombic to obovate, 3–5 cm long, incised serrate, occasionally somewhat 3 lobed, deep green above and totally finely pubescent, yellowish tomentose beneath; flowers pure white, 1 cm wide, many in densely pubescent corymbs, May; style remnants outspread. BR 33: 38. E. China. 1843. z7

S. cinerascens see: **Petrophytum cinerascens**

S. × cinerea Zab. (*S. cana* × *S. hypericifolia*). Shrub, 1.5 m high or more, tomentose, branches angular striated, brown; leaves oblong, acuminate, 2.5–3.5 cm long, entire or with 1–2 teeth at the apex, with short recurved leathery tip, gray-green above, lighter beneath; flowers pure white, in small, sessile umbels at the shoot tips and in 2 cm long stalked umbels toward the branch base, petals oblong-rounded, longer than the stamens, styles usually obliquely erect, usually abscising before the fruits ripen, May. Origin unknown. Around 1880. z5

'Grefsheim'. To 1.5 m high, branches gracefully nodding, finely pubescent, older branches glabrous; leaves lanceolate, acute at both ends, entire or with a few teeth at the apex, to 25 mm long and 7 mm wide, dull green and nearly glabrous above, persistently pubescent beneath; flowers 2–6 together, very short stalked, white, flowering very abundantly, 10 days earlier than *S. arguta* (= *S. arguta* 'Grefsheim'; *S.* 'Graciosa'). Found in 1949 in the Grefsheim Nursery in Nes, Norway. ✧

S. confusa see: **S. media**

S. × conspicua Zabel (*S. albiflora* × *S. alba*). Upright, about 1 m high shrub, young shoots dark brown, pubescent; leaves elliptic-oblong, acute at both ends, 3–6 cm long, serrate or biserrate, nearly glabrous; flowers light pink-white, in wide, finely pubescent panicles, petals shorter than the stamens, July–September. z6

S. corymbosa Raf. Shrub, 0.3–0.9 m high, sparsely branched, young shoots glabrous or somewhat pubescent, brown-red, cylindrical; leaves rounded-elliptic, 3–8 cm long and nearly as wide, coarsely and often biserrate on the apical half, underside bluish and glabrous, petiole 3–8 mm long; flowers white, in dense,

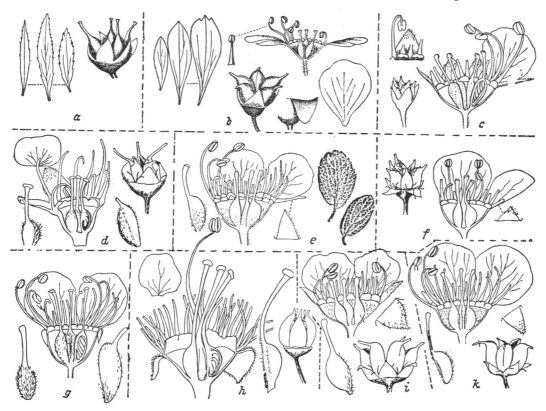

Fig. 251. **Spiraea.** a. *S. thunbergii*; b. *S. hypericifolia*; c. *S. crenata*; d. *S. nipponica*; e. *S. arcuata*; f. *S. gemmata*; g. *S. media*; h. *S. chamaedryfolia*; i. *S. trilobata*; k. *S. blumei* (from Siebold & Zuccarini, Schneider and Original)

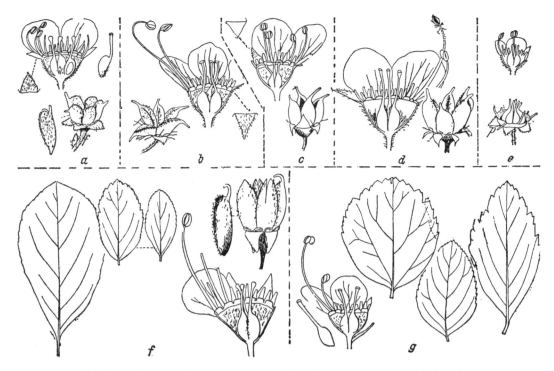

Fig. 252. **Spiraea**. a. *S. canescens;* b. *S. longigemmis;* c. *S. decumbens;* d. *S. japonica;*
e. *S. bullata;* f. *S. betulifolia;* g. *S. corymbosa* (most from Schneider)

somewhat convex, 5–10 cm wide corymbs, rachis
pubescent, sepals erect at fruiting (!!), June–July; fruits
erect, glabrous, glossy. BB 1884; GSP 174 (= *S.
crataegifolia* Link). Eastern USA. 1819. Very closely
related to *S. betulifolia.* z6 Fig. 252.

S. crataegifolia see: **S. corymbosa**

S. crenata L. Densely bushy shrub, about 1 m high,
shoots cylindrical, thin, finely pubescent at first, red-
brown; leaves obovate-oblong, 3 veined, 2–3.5 cm long,
usually with a few crenate teeth at the apex or entire,
gray-green, soft pubescent at first; flowers white, 5 mm
wide, in densely foliate umbels on small, foliate stalks,
inflorescences hemispherical; petals rounded obovate,
usually shorter than the stamens, May; fruits finely
pubescent, with erect style remnants enclosed by the
eventually inward closing sepals. HM 1900 (= *S.
crenifolia* C. A. Mey.; *S. vaccinifolia* Hort.). SE. Europe to
the Caucasus and Altai Mts. 1800. z6 Fig. 251.

S. crenifolia see: **S. crenata**

S. crispifolia see: **S. bullata**

S. decumbens W. Koch. Dwarf shrub, only 25 cm high,
shoots wiry thin, ascending, glabrous; leaves elliptic-
oblong, acute at both ends, 1–3 cm long, serrate or
biserrate; flowers white, in small, 3–5 cm wide corymbs
at the ends of foliate shoots, petals as long as the stamens,
June; fruits glabrous and parallel, with terminal, erect
style remnants. MG 27: 186. Southern Germany to S.
Tyrol. 1830. A good rock garden plant. z6 Fig. 252. ⊕

var. tomentosa see: **S. lancifolia**

S. densiflora Nutt. ex Rydb. Shrub, to 60 cm high, shoots
cylindrical, dark red-brown, glabrous; leaves elliptic,
2.5–4 cm long, rounded at both ends, apical margin
crenate or serrate, lighter green beneath; flowers in
glabrous, rather dense, 2–4 cm wide corymbs, pink,
sepals obtuse, ovate, erect, June; follicles parallel,
glabrous. NW. USA. z6

Including:

ssp. **splendens** (E. Baumann ex K. Koch) Abrams. Shrub, to 1.2
m high, young shoots finely pubescent; leaves ovate to elliptic-
lanceolate, sometimes acute, serrate or biserrate, teeth long
acuminate, base entire; corymbs finely pubescent, also the
acute, triangular sepals, flowers pink (= *S. splendens* E.
Baumann ex K. Koch; *S. arbuscula* Greene). USA; Oregon to
California. ⊕

S. discolor see: **Holodiscus discolor**

S. douglasii Hook. Upright shrub, to 2 m high, very
stoloniferous, shoots slender, brown, pubescent when
young, later glabrous; leaves oblong, rounded at both
ends, 4–9 cm long, serrate on the apical half, often also
entire on leaves beneath the inflorescences, white
tomentose beneath (!), flower rachis also white
tomentose; flowers purple-pink, in narrowly conical,
dense, 20 cm long panicles, July–August. BC 3669; FS
65; BM 5151; DB 10: 105. Western N. America. 1827. z5
Plate 123; Fig. 246.

S. esquirolii see: **S. japonica** var. **acuminata**

S. expansa see: **S. bella** and **S. fastigiata**

S. fastigiata Wall. Closely related to *S. bella*, but more vigorous, to 1.8 m high, shoots cylindrical, tomentose when young; leaves ovate to more oblong, acute at both ends, scabrous serrate on the apical half, 3–7.5 cm long, venation usually pubescent beneath; flowers in 3–12 cm wide corymbs, often terminally arranged on very long shoots, white, July; follicle pubescent, not wide-spreading (= *S. expansa* Koch). Himalayas. z6

S. flagelliformis see: **S. canescens**

S. flexuosa Fisch. Very similar to *S. chamaedryfolia*, but lower and broader growing, shoots thin, very angular and distinctly flexuose; leaves oval-oblong to more lanceolate, usually serrate above the middle, 2.5–5 cm long; flowers white, few in short-stalked umbels, May–June (*S. chamaedryfolia* var. *flexuosa* Maxim.). NE. Asia. z5 ✧

S. fontenaysiensis see: **S. × fontenaysii**

S. × fontenaysii Lebas. (*S. canescens* × *S. salicifolia*). Upright, thin branched shrub, to 2 m high, shoots angular, pubescent when young; leaves short petioled, elliptic-oblong, 2–5 cm long, crenate on the apical half, obtuse at both ends, blue-green and nearly glabrous beneath; flowers white, in pubescent, 3–8 cm long and equally wide, conical panicles, on short, lateral shoots at the tips of the previous year's wood, petals as long as the stamens, June–July; fruits nearly glabrous, widely outspread (= *S. fontenaysii* f. *alba* Zab.; *S. fontenaysiensis* Dipp.). Developed before 1866 by Billard in Fontenay-aux-Roses, near Paris. z6

'Rosea'. Flowers light pink, otherwise like the white-flowered species.

S. fortunei see: **S. japonica** var. **fortunei**

S. × foxii (Vos) Zab. (*S. corymbosa* × *S. japonica*). Similar to *S. margaritae*, but less attractive, shoots flexuose, nearly glabrous and brown; leaves elliptic, 5–8 cm long, biserrate, entire on the basal third, glabrous on both sides, dull green above, often with brown patches (!), light green beneath; flowers 6 mm wide, whitish or with a trace of pink, in wide, branched, finely pubescent corymbs, June–July; fruits obtuse at the apex, style remnants outspread. Before 1870. z5

S. fritschiana Schneid. Low shrub, similar to *S. japonica*, but the young shoots nearly glabrous, sharp angular, purple-brown, glossy; leaves obovate to oval-elliptic, 3–8 cm long, 1.5–3.5 cm wide, simple and coarsely dentate, usually pubescent on the venation, petiole 5–10 mm long; flowers light pink, in dense, 6–7 cm wide umbellate panicles. China. z6 Fig. 257.

S. gemmata Zab. Shrub, 2–3 m high, nearly totally glabrous, shoots slender, brown-red, angular striated, nodding, winter buds to 5 mm long, twice as long as the leaf petiole (!); leaves short stalked, narrowly elliptic to oblong, 1–2.5 cm long, entire, occasionally with a few teeth at the apex, bright green above, gray-green beneath; flowers white, 6–8 mm wide, grouped 2–6 in

sessile corymbs, petals nearly circular, somewhat longer than the stamen filaments; fruit apexes divergent, usually pubescent on the ventral side, usually acuminately tapered to the terminal style remnants. SH 1: 290 f–g (= *S. mongolica* Koehne non Maxim.). NW. China. 1886. z5 Fig. 251.

S. × gieseleriana Zabel (*S. cana* × *S. hypericifolia*). Medium-sized, gray pubescent shrub, shoots obtuse angular, somewhat flexuose; leaves ovate, acute, 3–4 cm long, 1–2 cm wide, scabrous serrate or occasionally also entire (basal third always entire), pubescent; flowers large, white, in very foliate corymbs, on 3–6 cm long stalks, calyx lobes totally reflexed at flowering (!!), petals as long or somewhat shorter than the stamens, late May; follicle pubescent on the interior. Developed by Zabel before 1884. z6 Plate 129. ✧

S. glabrata see: **S. japonica** var. **glabra**

S. 'Graciosa' see: **S. × cinerea 'Grefsheim'**

S. grossulariifolia vera see: **S. trilobata**

S. hacquetii see: **S. lancifolia**

S. hendersonii see: **Petrophytum hendersonii**

S. henryi Hemsl. Shrub, 2–2.5 m high, habit broad and open, shoots somewhat pubescent only when young, cylindrical; leaves oblanceolate, acute or rounded, 2–7 cm long, coarsely serrate on the apex, also entire on smaller leaves, glabrous or somewhat pubescent above, tomentose beneath; flowers white, 6 mm wide, in 5 cm wide, compound corymbs, petals circular, longer than the stamens, June; fruits pubescent, somewhat outspread. BM 8270; BC 3665. Central and W. China. 1900. z6 Plate 124. ✧

S. hypericifolia L. Shrub, to 1 m high, finely pubescent, shoots brownish, erect-nodding, nearly cylindrical; leaves nearly sessile, obtuse obovate to more lanceolate, to 3.5 cm long, entire or finely crenate at the apex, gray-green above, lighter to bluish beneath, 3 veined at the base, soft pubescent to nearly glabrous, new growth appears very early; flowers small, white, usually 5 in nearly sessile umbels, petals nearly circular, somewhat longer than the stamens, late April–May; fruit style remnants erect-recurved. HM 1008; SH 1: 2881. SE. Europe to Siberia and central Asia. 1640. z5 Fig. 251.

ssp. hypericifolia. Leaves narrowly elliptic, acute, entire; sepals shorter than the calyx cup, petals ovate, somewhat longer than the stamens. Ukraine to S. Russia.

ssp. obovata (Waldst. & Kit.) Dostal. Leaves narrowly obovate, entire or with 3–5 crenate teeth on the apex; sepals as long as the calyx cup, petals about 3 mm long, obovate, as long as the stamens (= *S. obovata* Waldst. & Kit.). SW. Europe.

S. japonica L. f. Shrub, to 1.5 m high, shoots stiffly erect, usually only slightly branched, glabrous or only pubescent when young, striated or nearly cylindrical; leaves oval-oblong, acute, 2–8 cm long, doubly incised serrate, underside gray-green and pubescent only on the venation; flowers lighter or darker pink-red, 6 mm wide, in 15–20 cm wide, flat, terminal corymbs, foliate at the base, stamens much longer than the petals, June–July; fruits rather glabrous, apexes outspread, style remnants terminal. MJ 1415 (= *S. callosa* Thunb.). Japan. 1870. z3–8 Plate 123; Fig. 252. ⊕

var. **acuminata** Franch. Leaves oval-oblong to lanceolate, green and pubescent beneath, at least on the venation; flowers pink, in 10–14 cm wide corymbs (= *S. bodinieri* Lév.; *S. esquirolii* Lév.). Central and W. China. 1908.

var. *alpina* see: '**Little Princess**'

'**Atrosanguinea**'. Shoots with a persistent thin pubescence, new growth reddish; flowers dark pink, inflorescences very tomentose pubescent. Before 1893. ⊕

var. *bullata* see: **S. bullata**

var. **fortunei** (Planch.) Rehd. Taller than the species, shoots totally cylindrical, pubescent when young; leaves oblong-lanceolate, acuminate, 5–10 cm long, scabrous and biserrate, teeth inward curving and calloused at the tips, rugose above, bluish and glabrous beneath; inflorescences well branched, soft pubescent, flowers pink, disk usually only slightly developed or absent. BM 5164; FS 871 (= *S. fortunei* Planch.; *S. callosa* Lindl. non Thunb.). E. and central China. 1850.

var. **glabra** (Regel) Koidz. Leaves ovate, glabrous; inflorescences glabrous, flowers pink (= *S. glabrata* Lge.). Before 1870.

'**Little Princess**'. Low, erect, well branched shrub, to 50 cm high, becoming wider than tall; leaves ovate, about 25 mm long, 12 mm wide, dull green above, often somewhat rugose, underside usually totally glabrous; flowers in short stalked, short pubescent, about 4 cm wide cymes, flowering very abundantly, pale lilac-pink (= *S. japonica alpina* Hort. non Maxim.; *S. bumalda alpina* Grootendorst Catalog 1953). Allegedly hybridized by L. R. Russell Ltd., Windlesham, England. Very popular cultivar. ⊕

'**Macrophylla**' (Simon-Louis). Leaves ovate, to 14 cm long, somewhat bullate, to 7 cm wide on the basal third; inflorescences small. Found by Simon-Louis. Before 1866. Plate 122.

var. **ovalifolia** Franch. Leaves elliptic, glabrous and bluish beneath; flowers white (!), in 7–12 cm wide inflorescences. W. China. 1908. ⊕

'**Ruberrima**'. Habit more compact, to 1 m high, shoots later nearly glabrous; inflorescences finely pubescent, flowers dark pink. Before 1893. ⊕

S. lanceolata see: **S. alba**

S. lancifolia Hoffmanns. Dwarf shrub, 20–30 cm high, shoots often procumbent, gray pubescent (!); leaves elliptic, dentate at the apex, 1.5–2.5 cm long, gray tomentose beneath; flowers white, in small, 2.5–3.5 cm wide umbels, not exserted above the apical leaves, May, DL 3: 322 (= *S. hacquetii* Fenzl & Koch; *S. decumbens* var. *tomentosa* Poech). Tyrol, Krain, NE. Italy. 1885. z6 Fig. 253.

S. latifolia (Ait.) Borkh. Shrub, to 1.5 m high, young shoots glabrous; angular, red-brown; leaves broad elliptic to obovate or oblong, acute at both ends, 3–7 cm long, coarsely and often biserrate, bright green above, more blue-green and glabrous beneath, short petioled; flowers white to light pink, in glabrous (!!), broadly

conical, over 20 cm long panicles, often with horizontally spreading branchlets, stamens longer than the petals, disk usually pink, June–August; fruits glabrous, style remnants outspread. GSP 174; BC 3668; HyWF 89 (= *S. bethlehemensis* Hort.; *S. carpinifolia* Willd.). N. America. 1789. Hardiest species, but only slightly attractive. z2 Fig. 246.

S. laxiflora see: **S. canescens**

S. × lemoinei Zabel (*S. bumalda* × *S. bullata*). Low shrub, to about 50 cm; leaves ovate, somewhat rugose or bullate; flowers larger than those of the parents, pink, later becoming a dirty red (*S. bumalda* 'Ruberrima' Lemoine). Developed by Lemoine before 1892. Not to be confused with *S. japonica* 'Ruberrima'.

S. longigemmis Maxim. Shrub, 1–1.5 m high, branches spreading, slender, glabrous also when young, buds long acuminate, longer than the leaf petiole (!); leaves oval-lanceolate to more oblong, acute, 3–6 cm long, serrate to biserrate, teeth with a gland at the tip, bright green, glabrous; flowers white, 6 mm wide, in rather loose, 5–7 cm wide, pubescent corymbs, stamens longer than the petals, July; fruits nearly glabrous, style remnants outspread. BC 3666; GF 7: 345. NW. China. 1887. z5 Fig. 252.

S. lucida Dougl. ex Greene. Upright, to 1 m high shrub, glabrous, sparsely branched, shoots ascending from a creeping rootstock, cylindrical, brown or more yellowish; leaves ovate to obovate, usually acute at the apex, occasionally round, 2–6 cm long, base round to broad cuneate, coarsely serrate or also biserrate, entire on the basal half or third, glossy above (!); flowers in glabrous, rather dense, 3–10 cm wide, flat cymes, white, June–July. NW. USA. z6 ⊕

Fig. 253. *Spiraea lancifolia* (from Dippel)

S. × margaritae Zab. (*S. japonica* × *S. superba*). Shrub, to 1.5 m high, shoots finely pubescent, dark brown, rounded, finely striped; leaves oval-elliptic, 5–8 cm long, 3–4 cm wide, acute, coarsely serrate to biserrate, dull dark green above, lighter beneath and somewhat pubescent; flowers finely pubescent, 7–8 mm wide, bright pink, fading lighter, in 15 cm wide, loose, flat inflorescences, petals half as long as the stamens, July and August to September; fruits small, parallel, style remnants usually erect. DB 10: 14. Developed by Zabel before 1890 and named for his daughter. z5 Fig. 254. ⊕

S. media Schmidt. Upright shrub, similar to *S. chamaedryfolia*, but more tightly upright and with terete (!) branches, 1–1.5 m high, shoots straw-yellow to brown, pubescent when young; leaves ovate-oblong, 3–5 cm long, incised serrate on the apical half, occasionally entire, dark green above, lighter and more or less pubescent beneath; flowers white, 8 mm wide, many in umbellate, terminal racemes on small, foliate lateral shoots, occasionally grouped into small panicles, petals circular, shorter than the stamens, April; fruits pubescent. DRHS 2002; BS 3: 357; HM 1010 (= *S. confusa* Rgl. & Koern.). E. Europe to NE. Asia. 1789. z5 Fig. 251. ⊕

ssp. **media.** Inflorescences glabrous, petals white, entire (= ssp. *oblongifolia* [Waldst. & Kit.] Dost.). Throughout the range of the species.

ssp. *oblongifolia* see: ssp. **media**

ssp. **polonica** (Blocki) Pawl. Inflorescences soft pubescent, petals somewhat yellowish, margin fringed (fimbriate) (= *S. polonica* Blocki). Poland, Czechoslovakia.

S. menziesii Hook. Stoloniferous shrub, about 1 m high, young shoots brown, striated, finely pubescent when young; leaves oblong to obovate, obtuse at both ends, 3–7 cm long, coarsely serrate on the apical half (!), underside lighter green with pubescent venation or totally glabrous, petiole 3–5 mm long; flowers pink, small, in dense, narrow, 10–20 cm long, pubescent panicles, stamens over twice as long as the petals, June to August; fruits glabrous, style remnants spreading, sepals reflexed. Western N. America, Alaska to Oregon. 1838. z6 Fig. 246.

var. *macrothyrsa* see: **S. × billardii 'Macrothyrsa'**

S. micrantha Hook. f. Small to medium-sized shrub; leaves ovate-lanceolate, 8–15 cm long, long acuminate at the apex, base rounded, scabrous or biserrate, pubescent beneath; flowers only 4–5 mm wide, pale pink, densely brown tomentose, in loose, foliate, to 15 cm wide corymbs, June; follicles pubescent. E. Himalayas. 1924. z6 ⊕

S. millefolium see: **Chamaebatiaria millefolium**

S. miyabei Koidz. Similar to *S. chamaedryfolia ulmifolia*, but with compound corymbs. Shrub, to 1 m high, erect, shoots finely pubescent and somewhat angular; leaves ovate to elliptic, acute, 3–6 cm long, base round to cuneate-rounded, biserrate, green and glabrous on both

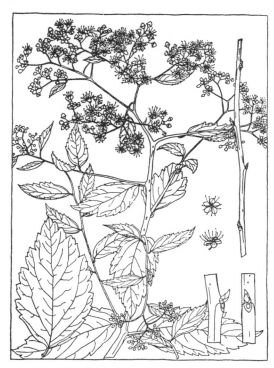

Fig. 254. *Spiraea × margaritae* (from Nose)

sides, petiole 2–5 mm long; flowers white, 8 mm wide, in pubescent, 3–6 cm wide corymbs, stamens 2–3 times longer than the circular petals, June; fruits tomentose, style remnants outspread. NK 4: 5 (= *S. silvestris* Nakai). Japan. 1915. z6

S. mollifolia Rehd. Very similar to *S. gemmata*, but silky pubescent. Shrub, 1.5–2 m high, branches drooping, very angular, reddish, very silky pubescent when young, winter buds long and acute; leaves short petioled, elliptic-obovate to oblong, 1–2 cm long, occasionally with a few teeth at the apex, both sides densely silky pubescent (!!); flowers 8 mm wide, white, in pubescent, about 2.5 cm wide umbels, on short, foliate stalks, June–July; fruits erect, pubescent, style remnants erect to outspread. W. China. 1909. z6 Fig. 255.

S. mongolica Maxim. (non Koehne!). Very closely related to *S. crenata*, but the leaves always entire, 3 veined; follicles longer than the erect calyx lobes; otherwise like Fig. 255. S. Mongolia, N. China, Kansu Prov. Existence in cultivation uncertain. See also: **S. gemmata.** z5

S. monogyna see: **Physocarpus monogynus**

S. × multiflora Zab. (*S. crenata* × *S. hypericifolia*). Shrub, about 1.5 m high, shoots thin, brown, finely pubescent; leaves obovate, base long cuneate, basal half nearly entire, gray-green, lighter beneath, 2–3 cm long, 1–1.5 cm wide, base 3(5) veined, underside finely pubescent when young; flowers white, very numerous, in sessile

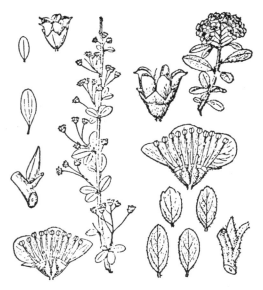

Fig. 255. **Spiraea.** Left *S. mongolica;* right *S. mollifolia* (from ICS)

umbels, the latter partly stalked (!) and foliate at the base, May. Before 1884. z6 ✣

S. nicoudiertii see: **S.** ✕ **pikoviensis**

S. nipponica Maxim. Shrub, 1.5–2.5 m high, shoots stiffly erect and bowed outward at the tips, red-brown, angular glabrous; leaves obovate to elliptic, 1.5–3 cm long, rounded at the apex, crenate, base broadly cuneate, dark green above, bluish green beneath; flowers 8 mm wide, many in hemispherical corymbs, stalk foliate, petals circular, longer than the stamens, May–June; ovaries ciliate on the apical ventral suture, style remnants usually spreading at a right angle to the elongated dorsal suture. MJ 1416; BC 3662; GC 130: 9 (= *S. bracteata* Zab. non Raf.). Japan. 1908. Despite the stiff habit, one of the best species of the genus. z5 Plate 122; Fig. 251. ✣

'Halward's Silver'. More compact habit, but erect, about 80 cm high in 5 years, very densely branched; corymbs with 8–12 flowers, the individual flowers to 9 mm wide, flowering abundantly. Developed from seed in 1960 at the Royal Botanic Garden, Hamilton, Ontario, Canada; given to the trade in 1971. ✣

var. **rotundifolia** (Nichols.) Mak. Leaves larger, broad obovate to more circular; flowers somewhat larger. BM 7429; GF 7: 305; MJ 3560. Japan. 1882. Plate 124. ✣

'Snowmound'. An American cultivar of particularly low habit and abundant flowers, but only slightly different (if at all) from var. *rotundifolia.* ✣

var. **tosaensis** (Yatabe) Mak. Leaves oblanceolate to oblong-obovate, 1–3 cm long, entire or somewhat crenate at the apex; flowers smaller, in dense umbels (= *S. tosaensis* Yatabe). Japan. 1935.

S. nobleana see: **S.** ✕ **sanssouciana** and **S.** ✕ **watsoniana**

S. obovata see: **S. hypericifolia** ssp. **obovata**

S. obtusa see: **S. blumei**

S. opulifolia see: **Physocarpus opulifolius**

S. pallasii see: **Sorbaria grandiflora**

S. pectinata see: **Luetkea pectinata**

S. ✕ **pikoviensis** Bess. (*S. crenata* ✕ *S. media*). Closely related to *S. crenata,* but the shoots nearly glabrous, cylindrical, yellow-brown; leaves oblong, 2.5–5 cm long, with a few small teeth at the apex or entire, 3 veined or pinnately veined, underside only slightly pubescent; flowers many in nearly glabrous corymbs, on 1.5–3 cm long stalks, white, petals circular, shorter than the stamens, mid May; style remnants usually straight, erect, situated just under the apex (= *S. nicoudiertii* Hort.). Found in the wild in 1816 by Besser near Pikow in Podolien, western Ukraine, USSR. z6

S. polonica see: **S. media** ssp. **polonica**

S. pruinosa see: **S.** ✕ **brachybotrys**

S. prunifolia S. & Z. Bridalwreath Spirea. Upright shrub, to 2 m high, shoots thin, long rodlike, nodding, finely pubescent at first; leaves oblong-elliptic, 2.5–4 cm long, finely dentate, bright green above, soft gray pubescent beneath, orange to red-brown in fall; flowers pure white, 3–6 in sessile umbels, double, about 1 cm wide, May. MJ 1420; DB 1953: 109; FS 153 (= *S. prunifolia* var. *plena* Schneid.). Japan, China, in cultivation, but also found in the wild in Hupeh Prov. 1843. z5 Fig. 256. ✣

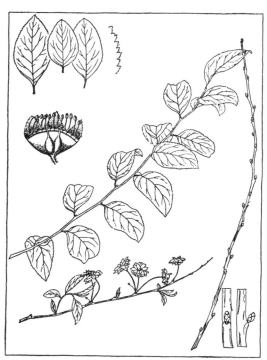

Fig. 256. *Spiraea prunifolia* (from Nose)

Fig. 257. **Spiraea.** Left *S. fritschiana;* center *S. rosthornii;* right *S. chamaedryfolia* (from ICS)

f. simpliciflora Nakai. The single flowered wild form. SH 1: 288 g–h. Korea, China, Taiwan. 1864. Insignificant for the garden.

S. pubescens Turcz. Shrub, 1–2 m high, branches slender, drooping, cylindrical, tomentose when young; leaves oval-rhombic-elliptic, 3–4 cm long, incised serrate to slightly 3 lobed, pubescent above, gray tomentose beneath; flowers white, 6–8 mm wide, in nearly hemispherical, glabrous corymbs, petals about as long as the stamens, May; fruits only ciliate on the ventral suture, otherwise glabrous, style remnants outspread. z6 GF 1: 331; NK 4: 10. N. China. 1883.

S. pumila see: **S. × bumalda**

S. × pumilionum Zab. (*S. decumbens* × *S. lancifolia*). Dwarf shrub, very similar to *S. lancifolia,* but also resembling *S. decumbens* in the leaf form, sparse pubescence and the totally glabrous flower rachises; leaves often entire; flowers white. Developed by Zabel before 1897. z6

S. × pyramidata Greene (*S. lucida* × *S. menziesii*). Upright, usually glabrous shrub, to 1 m, shoots cylindrical, red-brown; leaves elliptic-oblong, 3–8 cm long, obtuse to acute, only on the apical half coarsely (sometimes doubly) serrate, glabrous beneath, petiole 2–5 mm; flowers in rather dense, conical, pubescent or also glabrous panicles, white to lightly pink, July. NW. USA. Occasionally occurring among the parents in the wild. 1911. z6

S. reevesiana see: **S. cantoniensis**

S. × revirescens Zab. (*S. amoena* × *S. japonica*). Shrub, to 1 m high, shoots finely to angularly striated, brown, soft pubescent at first; leaves light green, oval-oblong, 5–9 cm long, incised to biserrate, bluish beneath, venation densely yellowish pubescent (!); inflorescences like *S.*

japonica, but more pubescent, flowers pink, 5–7 mm wide, petals somewhat shorter than the stamens, disk more distinctly lobed, late June to July and September–October. Before 1893. z5

S. rosthornii Pritz. Similar to *S. longigemmis,* to 2 m high, branches spreading, pubescent at first (!), buds elongated, acute; leaves oval-oblong, acuminate, 3–8 cm long, incised biserrate to slightly lobed, often soft pubescent on both sides or only on the venation beneath; flowers white, 6 mm wide, in loose, 5–8 cm wide corymbs on elongated stalks, inflorescences pubescent, June; fruits pubescent, style remnants outspread. W. China. 1909. z6 Fig. 257.

S. rotundifolia see: **S. trilobata**

S. salicifolia L. Narrowly upright shrub, stoloniferous and rank growing, shoots somewhat angular, yellowish brown, finely pubescent when young; leaves elliptic to oblong-lanceolate, acute at both ends, 4–7 cm long, scabrous and densely (occasionally doubly) serrate, glabrous on both sides, lighter green beneath; flowers pink, in slender, finely tomentose panicles with an ascending rachis, petals half as long as the stamens, June–July; fruits nearly parallel, ciliate on the ventral suture, style remnants reflexed. MJ 1418; BB 1883; NM 1012. SE. Europe to NE. Asia and Japan. 1856. Naturalizes rapidly and has unattractive foliage. z5 Fig. 246.

S. × sanssouciana K. Koch. (*S. douglasii* × *S. japonica*). Shrub, to 1.5 m high, shoots angular, finely pubescent when young; leaves oblong-lanceolate, biserrate, 6–9 cm long, entire on the basal half (or third), base acute (!), light green and tomentose beneath; flowers pink, in terminal, multi-tipped cymes compounded from several panicles, petals half as long as the stamens, June–August;

fruits glabrous, somewhat longer than the reflexed calyx. BM 5169 (= *S. nobleana* Hook.). Developed in 1857 at the Royal Nursery in Sanssouci, Japan; 2 years later also occurring in the garden of Noble in Bagshot, Surrey, England. z6 Plate 123.

S. sargentiana Rehd. Shrub, to 2 m high; shoots slender, broad and bowed outward, only pubescent when young, cylindrical; leaves narrowly elliptic to narrow to obovate, 1–2.5 cm long, finely serrate at the apex, finely pubescent above, shaggy beneath; flowers cream-white, 6 mm wide, in dense, shaggy, 3–4 cm wide, numerous corymbs, petals as long as the stamens, June; fruits nearly glabrous, style remnants outspread. W. China. 1909. z6

S. × schinabeckii Zab. (*S. chamaedryfolia* × *S. trilobata*). Most similar to *S. chamedryfolia*, medium-sized; shoots flexuose, brownish yellow, striped toward the apex, base pentagonal, scattered pubescent; leaves oblong to ovate, 4.5–5 cm long, doubly to incised serrate, dark green above, bluish beneath, glabrous; flowers white, large, in corymbs, petals rounded, longer than the stamens, June; style remnants terminal, somewhat outward curving. Before 1884. (Schinabeck was the Nursery Manager in Weihenstephan, W. Germany).

S. × semperflorens Zab. (*S. japonica* × *S. salicifolia*). Shrub, to 1.5 m high; shoots cylindrical, finely striated, glabrous; leaves oblong-lanceolate, 6–10 cm long, scabrous and biserrate nearly to the base, acuminate, bluish and rather glabrous beneath; flowers pink, rather large, in well branched, broadly conical, finely pubescent panicles, stamens twice as long as the petals, July–September; fruits glabrous (= *S. spicata* Dipp.). Around 1870. z4

S. silvestris see: **S. miyabei**

S. sinobrahuica see: **S. yunnanensis**

S. sorbifolia see: **Sorbaria sorbifolia**

S. spicata see: **S. × semperflorens**

S. splendens see: **S. densiflora** ssp. **splendens**

S. × superba (Froeb.) Zab. (*S. albiflora* × *S. corymbosa*). Low, nearly glabrous shrub, shoots erect, dark brown, striated; leaves narrowly elliptic to oblong, short acuminate, 4–7 cm long, about 2 cm wide, serrate to biserrate, dull dark green above, light green beneath; flowers light pink, 7–8 mm wide, in solitary, terminal umbellate panicles, stamens twice as long as the circular petals, disk conspicuous, lobed, late June; fruits nearly glabrous, parallel style remnants bowed-erect (= *S. callosa* var. *superba* Froeb.). Before 1873. Utilized only for its low growth habit and the late flowering time. z5 ✦

S. thunbergii Sieb. Shrub, seldom higher than 1 m high in cultivation, allegedly higher in its habitat, young shoots glabrous, new growth appears early, bright green, branches rodlike, cylindrical, the youngest more or less floccose, later totally glabrous; leaves narrowly lanceolate, 2.5–3 cm long, acute, scabrous and finely serrate, particularly toward the apex, usually yellow in

fall; flowers pure white, about 8 mm wide, in few flowered sessile umbels, late April–May. MJ 1411; GF 8: 84. China, Japan. 1863. z5 Fig. 251. ✦

S. tobolskiana see: **Sorbaria sorbifolia**

S. tomentosa L. Upright shrub, to 1.2 m high, shoots angular, brown tomentose (!); leaves acutely oblong-ovate, to 7 cm long, coarsely serrate, rugose with a rich green, gray-yellow tomentum beneath (!!); flowers purple-pink, in 20 cm long, narrowly conical, brown tomentose (!) panicles, late July–September. RWF 168; HyWF 84; GSP 170. Eastern N. America. 1736. Likes a moist site; without which the plant is always sickly in cultivation. z5 Fig. 246.

f. **alba** Rehd. Flowers white.

S. tosaensis see: **S. nipponica** var. **tosaensis**

S. trichocarpa Nakai. Very closely related to *S. nipponica*, but somewhat smaller, 1–2 m high, shoots thinner; leaves oblong to more lanceolate (!), 3–5 cm long, entire (!) or with a few teeth at the apex; flowers in pubescent, 3–5 wide corymbs, the lower branchlets of the inflorescence with 2–7 flowers, white, June; fruits pubescent. NF 1: 12; GC 134: 6; BS 3, Pl. 30. Korea. 1920. Very attractive species. z6 ✦

'**Snow White**' (*S. trichocarpa* × *S. trilobata*). Similar in appearance to *S. × vanhouttei*; leaves larger, lighter green, also the individual flowers somewhat larger. Hybridized by F. L. Skinner, Dropmore, Manitoba, Canada. Very winter hardy. ✦

S. trilobata L. Shrub, to 1 m high, shoots thin, glabrous, outspread, flexuose; leaves nearly circular, 1.5–3 cm long, incised crenate, usually 3 lobed, base round to somewhat cordate, blue-green above, particularly intense beneath; flowers pure white in many-flowered umbels, petals longer than the stamens, May–June; fruits somewhat outspread, style remnants ascending. BC 3663; GF 1: 452 (= *S. aquilegiifolia* Hort.; *S. rotundifolia* Hort.; *S. grossulariifolia vera* Hort.). N. China to Siberia and Turkestan. 1801. z5 Fig. 251. ✦

S. ulmifolia see: **S. chamaedryfolia** var. **ulmifolia**

S. vaccinifolia see: **S. canescens** and **S. crenata**

S. × vanhouttei (Briot) Zab. (*S. cantoniensis* × *S. trilobata*). Shrub, to 2 m high; long, rodlike branches gracefully nodding, glabrous; leaves ovate-rhombic, slightly 3–5 lobed, 3–4 cm long, crenate, dark green above, bluish beneath, glabrous; flowers pure white, 8 mm wide, in flat corymbs, in rich abundance along the shoot, petals circular, twice as long as the often partly sterile stamen filaments, late May–June; fruits somewhat outspread, style remnants semi-erect. GF 2: 317; Gs 1934: 136; DB 11: 7. Developed around 1862 by Billard in Fontenay-aux-Roses, France. One of the best forms of the entire genus today! z5 Plate 121. ✦

S. veitchii Hemsl. Very closely related to *S. wilsonii*, but taller, 3–4 m high, branches long drooping, reddish, pubescent, striated; leaves elliptic to oblong, occasionally obovate, 2–4 cm long, obtuse, base broadly cuneate, entire, glabrous above, bluish and finely pubescent beneath; flowers pure white, 4–5 mm wide, in 3–6 cm wide, finely pubescent corymbs, petals shorter than the stamens, June to July; fruits glabrous, parallel. BM 8383. Central and W. China. 1900. z6 Plate 124. ⊕

S. virginiana Britt. Shrub, about 1 m high or more, well branched, glabrous; leaves oblong-lanceolate, acute, rounded to cuneate at the base, entire or with a few teeth on the apical half; 2–5 cm long, lighter to bluish green beneath; flowers in dense, glabrous, to 5 cm wide corymbs, white, June. BB 2: 246. Eastern USA. z5

S. × watsoniana Zab. (*S. douglasii* × *S. splendens*). Similar to *S. sanssouciana*, but leaves elliptic-oblong, obtusish, usually rounded at the base (!), only serrate on the apical half, gray tomentose beneath; flowers pink, in dense, conical, finely tomentose panicles; fruits small (= *S. nobleana* Zab. non Hook.). Developed in cultivation before 1890, but also found in the wild in Oregon, USA. z6

S. wilsonii Duthie. Shrub, 2–2.5 m high, branches drooping, reddish, soft pubescent when young; leaves very short petioled, elliptic-obovate, 2–5.5 cm long, with only a few coarse teeth at the apex, otherwise entire, base cuneate, pubescent on both sides, but more densely and longer haired beneath (!); flowers white, in dense, glabrous, hemispherical, 3–5 cm wide corymbs, terminal on short, foliate, lateral shoots, petals as long as the stamens, calyx glabrous, June; fruits pubescent. BM 8399. Central and W. China. 1900. z6 Plate 124. ⊕

S. yunnanensis Franch. Elegant shrub, about 2 m high, young shoots thickly tomentose (!!), buds white woolly; leaves oval-rounded to obovate, 1–2 cm long, doubly dentate to finely lobed or occasionally entire on the apical half, tapering and entire toward the base, soft pubescent and dull green above, whitish or more gray tomentose beneath (!); flowers 10–20, in 1–2 cm wide, densely tomentose pubescent corymbs at the tips of short, foliate shoots, calyx and flower stalk tomentose, stamens 20, June (= *S. sinobrahuica* W. W. Sm.). W. China; Yunnan Prov. 1923. z7 ∅ ⊕

The spireas are generally very easy to cultivate; many species will become rank growing if not occasionally cut back. All like a very sunny site and fertile soil; only *S. tomentosa* requires a moist site.

Lit. Maximowicz: Adnotationes de Spiraeaceis; in Act. Hort. Petrop. 6, 105–261, 1879 (not seen by the author) ● Zabel, H.: Die strauchigen Spiräen der deutschen Gärten; Berlin 1893 (128 pp.) ● Ascherson & Graebner: Syn. Mitteleurop Fl. 6, 9–27, 1900 (Section *Spiraea*) ● Cambessedes, J.: Monographie du genre *Spiraea*; in Ann. Sci. Nat. **1**, 225 to 243; 352–392, 1824 (Plates 15–17, 25–28; not observed) ● Krüssmann, G.: Die wichtigsten *Spiraea*-Arten und -Formen unserer Gärten; Deutsche Baumschule, 10, 222–233; 278–282, 1966 ● Wyman, D.: The best ornamental Spiraeas; in Arnoldia **21**, 51–52, 1961.

STACHYURUS S. & Z. — STACHYUARACEAE

Deciduous shrubs; leaves alternate, thin, membranous, simple, serrate; flowers in terminal and axillary racemes or spikes, the individual flowers small, nearly sessile, usually hermaphroditic, but also unisexual flowers occurring in cultivation, sepals and petals 4, stamens 8, distinct, ovaries 4 locular; fruit a globose berry. — 10 species in E. Asia and the Himalayas.

Stachyurus chinensis Franch. Shrub, to 2.5 m high and wide, shoots green to brown, occasionally reddish; leaves ovate to oval-oblong, 3–15 cm long, abruptly short acuminate, crenate, base rounded to slightly cordate; flowers in 5–10 cm long, pendulous racemes, light yellow, petals more outspread than those of the following species and opening 2 weeks later, style as

Fig. 258. **Stachyurus**. Left. *S. himalaicus;* right *S. chinensis* (from ICS)

long or somewhat longer than the petals; fruits 6 mm thick. GC 79: 229. China. 1908. z9 Fig. 258. ✛

'Magpie'. Leaves gray-green above with an irregular, cream-white limb and light green, pink tinged spots. Developed in 1945 by Hillier.

S. himalaicus Hook. f. & Thomson ex Benth. Strong growing, with long, yellow-green shoots, to 3 m high; leaves semi-evergreen, oblong to oblong-lanceolate, 13–23 cm long, very long acuminate, margins finely serrate, petiole and midrib reddish; flowers in 4–5 cm long racemes, corolla cupulate, wine-purple to pink-red, early April (some of the old leaves still on the plant). W. China; Yunnan, Szechwan, W. Hupeh Provs., in the mountains; Taiwan. z8 Fig. 258. ✛

S. japonicus see: **S. praecox**

S. lancifolius see: **S. praecox** var. **matsuzakii**

S. matsuzakii see: **S. praecox** var. **matsuzakii**

S. ovalifolius see: **S. praecox** var. **matsuzakii**

S. praecox S. & Z. Shrub, 1–2 m high, to 4 m in its habitat, shoots slender, spreading, red-brown (!), glabrous, glossy; leaves elliptic-ovate to oval-lanceolate, long acuminate, rounded at the base, serrate, teeth somewhat outspread, glabrous and glossy beneath; racemes 5–8 cm long, flowers campanulate, yellow, 8 mm long, style shorter than the petals (!), March–April; fruits green-yellow with a red cheek. BS 3: 367; BM 6631; JRHS 84: 167 (= *S. japonicus* Steud.). Japan. 1864. z7 Plate 129. ✛

'Gracilis'. Female clone, otherwise only slightly differing from the species. ✛

var. **matsuzakii** (Nakai) Makino. Coastal form with thicker, light green and bluish shoots; leaves long petioled, oval-oblong to lanceolate, 13–25 cm long, gradually caudate acuminate, light green above, bluish green beneath; flowers yellow, early April; fruits larger, 10–15 mm long (= *S. lancifolius* Koidz.; *S. ovalifolius* Nakai; *S. matsuzakii* Nakai). Japan; coast of Honshu and other islands. z9 ✛

Illustrations of other species:

S. obovatus FIO 99	*S. szechuanicus* FIO 103
S. retusus FIO 102	*S. yunnanensis* FIO
S. salicifolius FIO 97	

Cultivated somewhat like *Rhododendron*, in humus soil, with peat and sand.

STAPHYLEA L. — Bladder Nut — STAPHYLEACEAE

Deciduous shrubs or small trees; branches with smooth, striped bark; leaves opposite, pinnate, with 3–5–7 leaflets, these serrate; flowers in terminal panicles, white or reddish; sepals and petals 5 each, erect, drawn together in campanulate form; stamens 5, about as long as the petals; fruit an inflated, 2–3 lobed, membranous capsule with 2–3 pea-sized, smooth, glossy, stone-hard seeds. — 12 species in the Northern temperate zone.

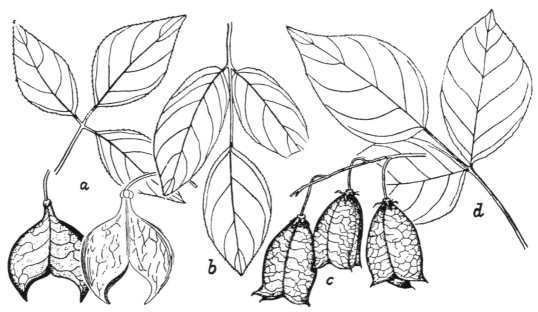

Fig. 259. **Staphylea**. a. *S. bumalda*; b. *S. holocarpa*; c. *S. colchica*; d. *S. trifolia*

Fig. 260. **Staphylea.** a. *S. × elegans;* b. *S. colchica;* c. *S. bolanderi;* d. *S. pinnata*
(from Gfl, GF and Lauche)

Key to the most Important Species

★ Leaflets 3;

> Middle leaflets 1.5–4 cm long stalked; panicles stalked;

× Flowers appear before the leaves; fruits not lobed:

S. holocarpa

×× Flowers appearing after the leaves;

) Leaflets elliptic-ovate, pubescent beneath:
S. trifolia

)) Leaflets broad elliptic-rounded, glabrous beneath:

S. bolanderi

>> Middle leaflets short stalked; panicles sessile:
S. bumalda

★★ Leaflets 5–7 (occasionally only 3);

> Leaflets 5, only 3 on flowering shoots; flowers in panicles; sepals outspread:
S. colchica

>> Leaflets 5–7; flowers in pendulous racemes; sepals erect:

S. pinnata

Staphylea bolanderi Gray. Erect, glabrous shrub, 1.5–2 m high, branches olive-brown, pruinose at first; leaflets 3, broadly elliptic to rounded, acute, 5–7 cm long, scabrous serrate, nearly gray-green above, light green beneath; flowers white, about 9–15 in nodding panicles, stamen filaments and pistils exserted, sepals and petals erect, April–May; capsule 5–6 cm long, inflated, 3 lobed with long awned tips. MS 315; GF 2: 545. USA; California. 1879. z7 Fig. 260. ⊕

S. bumalda DC. Bushy, to 2 m high shrub, branches broadly spreading, brown-red, greenish speckled; leaflets 3, elliptic-ovate, 4–6 cm long, crenate, light green, middle leaflets short stalked; flowers 8 mm long, in loose, erect, 5–7 cm long panicles, sepals yellowish white, somewhat shorter than the white petals, June; fruit usually bilabiate, 1.5–2.5 cm long, seeds yellowish. CIS 85; NF 4: 263; LF 207. Japan. 1812. z5 Fig. 259.

S. colchica Stev. Upright shrub, to 4 m high; leaflets 5, but only 3 (!) on flowering shoots, ovate-oblong, 5–8 cm long, scabrous serrate, bright green above, glossy light green beneath; flowers in 5–10 cm long and equally wide, erect, stalked panicles, sepals narrowly oblong, outspread, yellowish white, petals erect, narrowly spathulate, pure white, stamens glabrous, late May; fruit capsules obovoid, 2–3 lobed, 5–8 cm long, seeds 8 mm long. BM 7383; NF 6: 39; HL 392. Caucasus. 1850. z6 Fig. 259, 260. ⊕ ⚭

'Coulombieri'. Larger in all respects, luxuriant grower; leaves on long and short shoots, 3–5 parted, leaflets long acuminate, to 12 cm long; stamen filaments totally glabrous, anthers short acuminate; capsules to 6 cm long and 3 cm thick, apexes of the locules curved outward. BS 3: 370. Developed in 1872 in the Coulombier Nursery, Vitry, France. ⊕ ⚭

'Grandiflora'. Shrub, to 4 m high; flowering very abundantly, flowers to 2 cm long, panicles to 18 cm long. ⊕

var. kochiana Medwed. Leaves on the long shoots always 5 parted, the flower shoots sometimes 3 parted; filaments nearly totally pubescent (!!); capsules 5–6 cm long, to 3 cm thick, apexes usually bowed outward, some also inward curving. HL 393 (= var. lasiandra Dipp.).

var. lasiandra see: var. kochiana

'Laxiflora'. Leaves 3–5 parted, but predominantly 3 parted (!); flowers in slender, pendulous panicles, stamen filaments pubescent at the base. MD 1921: 127. Discovered in Wageningen, Holland around 1910.

'Pyramidalis'. Habit narrowly and densely erect. Origin unknown. Plate 129.

S. × elegans Zab. (S. colchica × S. pinnata). Similar in habit to S. pinnata, but the leaves usually 5 parted, oblong, acuminate, to 11 cm long, teeth outspread, dark green above, lighter beneath; panicles long, narrow, loose, pendulous, petals white, sepals pale brown-red on the dorsal side and the apex, later white, late April to May; capsules only rarely developed, irregular, 4–5 cm long to 3 cm wide with 2–3 straight lobes at the apex. GC 128: 62; HL 393. Developed around 1871 by Zabel. z6 Fig. 260. ⊕

'Hessei' (Hesse). Panicles more or less nodding, sepals white or reddish on the base, petals bright pink, lighter toward the apex, stamen filaments glabrous, flowering very abundantly; fruits 3–6 cm long, 3–4 cm wide, very uneven, lobes inward curving at the apex. Developed by Hesse, Weener, W. Germany before 1895. ⊕

S. emodi Wall. Closely related to S. trifolia. Shrub, 1.5–3 m high, occasionally a small tree in its habitat, shoots glabrous; leaflets 3, quite variable in size, elliptic, 5–14 cm long, middle leaflet occasionally larger, acute, finely serrate, scattered pubescent beneath when young; flowers 12 mm long, white, in pendulous, 5–10 cm long, long stalked panicles, sepals and petals erect, May; fruits 5–8 cm long. SH 2: 120b. Himalayas. 1890. z9

S. holocarpa Hemsl. Tall shrub, but also a tree to 5–7 m high; leaflets 3, oblong to more elliptic or lanceolate, 3–10 cm long, finely serrate, deep green and glabrous above, midrib pubescent beneath; flowers pink in bud, quickly becoming pure white, 12 mm long, in 3–10 cm long, pendulous panicles, appearing before the leaves (!!), May; fruits pear-shaped, 3–5 cm long, normally not lobed. BM 9074; LF 208; FIO 10. Central China. 1908. Quite hardy. z6 Fig. 259. ⊕ ⚭

f. rosea Rehd. & Wils. Leaflets white tomentose beneath when

young, later only long pubescent along the midrib; flowers somewhat larger, pink. GC 134: 36. Central China. 1908. ⊕

S. pinnata L. Upright shrub, 2–5 m high; leaflets 5–7, oval-oblong, acuminate, 6–10 cm long, scabrous serrate, bright green above, somewhat bluish green beneath, glabrous; flowers 1 cm long, petals oblong, white, sepals whitish, greenish at the base, reddish at the apex, ovate, erect, panicles to 12 cm long, pendulous, May to June; fruit nearly globose, 3 cm thick, 2–3 lobed, seeds yellow-brown, 1 cm long. HW 3: 52; HF 2182; MH Pl. 179. Central and S. Europe, Asia Minor. 1569. z6 Fig. 260. ⊕

S. trifolia L. Upright shrub, to 5 m high; leaflets 3, elliptic to ovate, acute, 5–8 cm long, scabrous serrate, dark green above, soft pubescent beneath, middle leaflets long stalked; flowers campanulate, to 8 mm long, white, in 3–5 cm long, nodding racemes, sepals somewhat shorter than the petals, greenish white, May; fruits 3–4 cm long, usually 3 lobed, seeds yellowish, 5 mm long. BB 2371; GSP 307. Eastern N. America, in moist thickets and along river banks. 1640. Not a highly valued garden plant. z5 Fig. 259.

'Pauciflora'. Stoloniferous; leaflets wider, only slightly pubescent, eventually glabrous; flowers 3–8 in short racemes; fruits 3 cm long. 1888.

All species and cultivars like a fertile, moist soil and a sunny site; with the exception of S. emodi, all species are winter hardy; S. holocarpa and its f. rosea are particularly attractive but utilized much too little.

Lit. Zabel, H.: Beiträge zur Kenntnis der gattung Staphylea L.; in Gartenflora 1888, 499 ● Zabel, H.: Weitere Beiträge zur Kenntnis der Gattung Staphylea L.; in Mitt. DDG 1897, 318–319 ● Zabel, H.: Zwei neue Staphylea-Formen; in Mitt. DDG 1898, 383.

STAUNTONIA DC — LARDIZABALACEAE

Evergreen, twining shrubs; leaves alternate, 3–7 parted; flowers in few-flowered small racemes; 6 petals, the outer ones fleshy and wider than the 3 inner ones; male flowers with 6 connate stamens, female flowers with 3 ovaries; nectaries absent; fruit a walnut-sized, sweet, watery berry. — 15 species in E. Asia, from Burma to Taiwan and Japan.

Stauntonia hexaphylla Decne. Twining to 10 m high; leaves long petioled, leaflets oval-elliptic, one side usually oblique, leathery tough, 6–10 cm long, abruptly acuminate; flowers whitish, turning violet, about 2 cm long, April; fruits violet-purple, edible, ovate, 3–5 cm long, juicy. NK 21: 2. Japan, Korea. 1874. z9 Plate 129. # ⊕

var. obovata Wu. Leaves obovate to oblong-lanceolate, 6–10 cm long, with a drawn out, caudate tip, base tapered to obtuse. Japan, Taiwan, in the mountains. Fig. 261.

Generally only suitable for overwintering in a temperate greenhouse or for very mild climates. Otherwise cultivated like Akebia.

Fig. 261. *Stauntonia hexaphylla* var. *obovata* (from LWT)

Fig. 262. *Stellera alberti* (from Gfl and Koehne)

STELLERA Gmel. — THYMELAEACEAE

Small shrubs or perennials; leaves alternate, simple; flowers tubular with 4–6 outspread limb tips; stamens 8–12, in 2 rows inside the tube, filaments very short; ovaries very short stalked; fruit a nutlet. — 8 species in temperate Asia.

Stellera alberti Regel. Shrub, 0.3–0.5 m high, very well branched, branches smooth, glabrous, young shoots green, finely appressed pubescent; leaves alternate to nearly opposite, sessile, spathulate to obovate, 1–4 cm long, bright green above, lighter beneath and finely pubescent; flowers in nearly sessile, capitate umbels, tube yellow, about 1 cm long, June; fruits ellipsoid. Buchara (Uzbek, USSR) in the mountains. Before 1893. Hardy. Fig. 262.

S. chamaejasme L. Subshrub or perennial, with long, fleshy roots, 30 cm high; leaves lanceolate, 1.5–2 cm long; inflorescences terminal, globose, many flowered, 4 cm wide, flowers white, red in bud, fragrant, June. BM 9028; JRHS 90: 54. Himalayas, central Asia; on gravelly soil. z5

Culture and hardiness like the alpine *Daphne* species.

STENOCARPUS R. Br. — PROTEACEAE

Evergreen shrubs, also a tree in its habitat; leaves alternate, entire or deep pinnately cleft; flowers hermaphroditic, in umbels, perianth tubular, opened on the underside, limb globose, red, yellow or white; fruit a narrow, leathery follicle. — 25 species in E. Australia and New Caledonia.

Stenocarpus sinuatus (A. Cunn.) Endl. A 30 m high tree in its habitat, but flowering abundantly as a shrub; leaves either deeply pinnately lobed and then 25–30 cm long, with 1–4 pairs of oblong lobes, or oblong-lanceolate and completely unlobed and 15–25 cm long; flowers 12–20 in about 7 cm long and 5 cm wide umbels, these either solitary or several in a compound umbel, perianth bright red, 25 mm long, 3 segments pendulous, 1 erect, limb yellow, style scarlet-red, inclined together in a "crown"-like fashion over the umbel, August to November. BM 4263. Australia; Queensland, New South Wales. 1830. z10 # ∅ ✛

STENOLOBIUM

Stenolobium alatum see: **Tecoma alata**

S. stans see: **Tecoma stans**

STEPHANANDRA S. & Z. — ROSACEAE

Delicately textured, deciduous shrubs; leaves alternate, distichous, usually lobed; flowers small, white, thin petioled, in small, terminal corymbs or panicles; calyx tube cupulate, sepals 5, petals 5; stamens 10–20; carpel only 1 (!), styles situated laterally; fruits only dehiscent at the base, with 1–2 seeds. — 4 species in E. Asia.

Stephanandra flexuosa see: **S. incisa**

S. incisa (Thunb.) Zab. Shrub, scarcely over 1.5 m high in cultivation (occasionally to 2.5 m in its habitat), branches flexuose, nodding outward, bright brown-red;

leaves ovate, 4–6 cm long, lobes incised and coarsely serrate, long acuminate, bright green above, lighter and pubescent beneath, deep brown-red in fall; flowers greenish white, 4–5 mm wide, in loose, to 6 cm long, numerous panicles, June. DB 9: 15; MJ 1422 (= *S. flexuosa* S. & Z.). Japan, Korea. 1872. z5 ⊕

'Crispa' (Jensen). Shrub, only 0.5 m high, much wider, shoots bowed downward; leaves triangular ovate, 3 lobed, lobes coarsely biserrate. Found around 1930 in the nursery of A. M. Jensen, Holmstrup, Denmark, but first given to the trade in 1949.

S. tanakae (Franch. & Sav.) Franch. & Sav. Shrub, to 2 m high and wide, shoots thin, glabrous; leaves broadly ovate to triangular, scabrous and biserrate, 5–10 cm long, caudate acuminate, also both small basal lobes, fall foliage orange to red; flowers white, in loose, 10 cm long panicles, stamens 15–20, June–July. BM 7593; MJ 1423; DB 9: 20. Japan. 1893. z6 ⊕

STEPHANOTIS Thouars. — ASCLEPIADACEAE

Evergreen, often high climbing shrubs; leaves opposite, leathery tough; flowers axillary in umbellate cymes; corolla rotate or infundibular, tube long, cylindrical, widest at the base, throat also widened, limb with 5 lobes, with a corona composed of 5 distinct, erect scales; fruit a fleshy follicle. — 5 species in Madagascar, of which the following is utilized as a potted plant or a landscape plant in frost free climates.

Stephanotis floribunda Brongn. Shrub, to 5 m high twining; leaves elliptic to more ovate, about 8 cm long, thick, glossy green, with a short mucro; flowers in large clusters, white, waxy, very fragrant, tube about 4 cm long, limb to 5 cm wide, segments oval-oblong, sepals obtuse ovate, about 1 cm long, lobes of the corona shorter than the anthers, June–September. BM 4058; PBl 2: 404. Madagascar. 1839. z10 # ⊕

STERCULIA

Sterculia platanifolia see: **Firmiana platanifolia**

STEWARTIA L. — Mountain Camellia — THEACEAE

Tall, deciduous shrubs, bark exfoliating *Platanus*-like; leaves alternate, simple; flowers solitary, large, terminal or axillary, shell-form; sepals ovate to oblong-ovate, also persisting at fruiting; petals white, connate at the base; filaments ring-like connate at the base; fruit a 5 lobed capsule, dehiscing from the apex, without a middle column; seeds with or without narrow limbs. — About 10 species in E. Asia and Eastern N. America.

According to many authors the spelling of *Stewartia* should be changed to *"Stuartia"*. Such advocates include T. A. Sprague in the Kew Bull. 1928, 362; J. R. Sealy in Bot. Mag. (1948), pl. 20, and indeed, Article 57 of the Internat. Rules of Bot. Nomenclature. Nevertheless, the former spelling will be retained here since it has yet to be proven whether or not this was the spelling intended by Linnaeus.

Key

+ Styles all distinct; petals occasionally 6; leaf base round:
  S. ovata

++ Styles connate, with 5 stigmas; petals usually 5;

> Shoots glabrous;

  × Corolla cupulate; leaves elliptic-lanceolate to obovate; shoots straight:
    S. pseudocamellia

  ×× Corolla shell form; leaves broadly elliptic; shoots zigzag form:
    S. pseudocamellia var. koreana

>> Shoots pubescent, at least when young;

  × Filaments purple, anthers bluish; leaves ovate to obovate, ciliate:
    S. malacodendron

  ×× Filaments white, anthers violet or yellow;

    § Filaments connate at the base;

      * Leaves elliptic to obovate, 5–10 cm long:
        S. sinensis

      ** Leaves oval-lanceolate, 4–6 cm long:
        S. monadelpha

    §§ Filaments totally distinct; petal exterior red at the base:
      S. serrata

Stewartia grandiflora see: **S. pseudocamellia**

S. koreana see: **S. pseudocamellia** var. **koreana**

S. malacodendron L. Small tree or shrub, 3.5 m high or more, young shoots soft pubescent; leaves oval-elliptic to obovate, 6–10 cm long, finely serrate and ciliate, light green above, pubescent beneath; flowers 8–10 cm wide, petals obovate, snow-white, widespreading, filaments purple, anthers bluish, style shorter than the stamens, June–July; fruits 1.5 cm thick. BM 8145; BS 3: 375; JRHS 100: 31; BB 2439 (= *S. nobilis* Salisb.; *S. virginica* Cav.). SE. USA; coastal region. 1741. Rare! Likes moist sites in semi-shade. z9 Fig. 263.

Plate 145

Trochodendron aralioides
in Poulsen Park, Kvistgard, Denmark

Ulmus carpinifolia 'Umbraculifera'
in the Morton Arboretum, USA

Ulmus glabra 'Crispa'
in the Royal Botanic Garden, Edinburgh, Scotland

Ulmus glabra 'Insularis'
in the Wageningen Arboretum, Holland

Plate 146

Ulmus glabra in Hohenheim Exotic Garden
Stuttgart, W. Germany
Photo: Dietrich

Ulmus glabra 'Exoniensis' (very old specimen)
in Nysoe, Denmark

Ulmus glabra 'Camperdownii'
in the Royal Botanic Garden, Edinburgh, Scotland

Ulmus parvifolia
in the Morton Arboretum, Illinois, USA

Plate 147

Ulmus procera 'Argenteovariegata' in the Prince
Schönaich Carolath Park, Hamburg, W. Germany

Ulmus procera 'Viminalis Aurea'
in the Copenhagen Botanic Garden, Denmark

Vaccinium glaucoalbum
in the Royal Botanic Gardens, Kew, England

Vella spinosa in its native habitat
in the Sierra Nevada, Spain

Plate 148

Tilia petiolaris in Dortmund, W. Germany

Tilia henryana in Les Barres Arboretum, France

Umbellularia californica in its native habitat in Oregon, USA
Photo: U.S. Forest Service

Plate 149

Vaccinium vitis-idaea
Photo: C. R. Jelitto, Berlin-Dahlem

Vaccinium macrocarpon
in the Dortmund Botanic Garden, W. Germany

Vaccinium arctostaphylos
in the Royal Botanic Garden, Edinburgh, Scotland

Plate 150

Verbascum dumulosum
in the Royal Botanic Gardens, Kew, England

Verbena tridens
in the Royal Botanic Garden, Edinburgh, Scotland

Viburnum atrocyaneum
in the Royal Botanic Gardens, Kew, England

Viburnum buddleifolium
in the Wageningen Arboretum, Holland

Plate 151

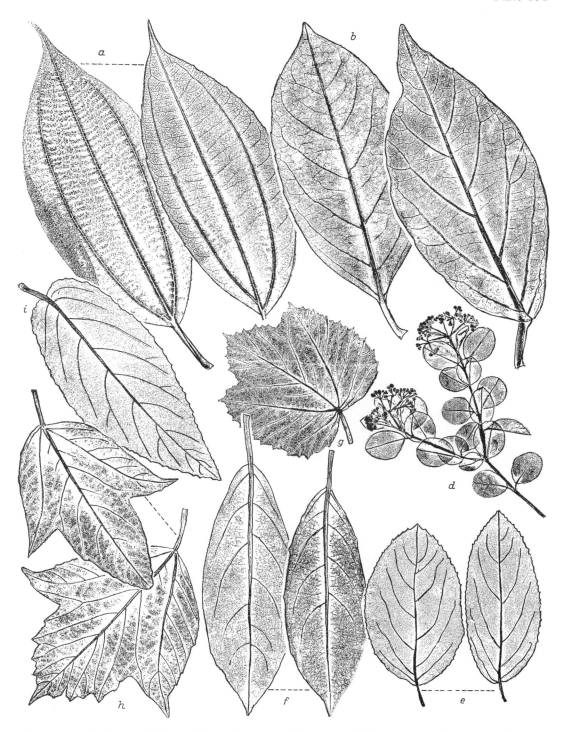

Viburnum. a. *V. cinnamomifolium*; b. *V. odoratissimum*; c. *V. japonicum*; d. *V. harryanum*; e. *V. macrocephalum*; f. *V. cylindricum*; g. *V. edule*; h. *V. sargentii* 'Flavum'; i. *V. buddleifolium* (material from cultivated plants)

Plate 152

Viburnum × burkwoodii
in the Späth Arboretum, Berlin, W. Germany

Viburnum carlesii
in the Späth Arboretum, Berlin, W. Germany

Viburnum burkwoodii 'Chenault'
in Knighthayes Court Park, England

Viburnum cinnamomifolium
in the Dublin Botanic Garden, Ireland

Plate 153

Viburnum cylindricum
in the Hillier Arboretum, England

Viburnum farreri
in the Berlin Botanic Garden, W. Germany

Viburnum davidii in the Royal Botanic Garden, Edinburgh, Scotland

Plate 154

Viburnum furcatum
in the Göteborg Botanic Garden, Sweden

Viburnum juddii
in the Wageningen Arboretum, Holland

Viburnum henryi in the Copenhagen Botanic Garden, Denmark

Plate 155

Viburnum lobophyllum
in the Copenhagen Botanic Garden, Denmark

Viburnum macrocephalum
in the Dortmund Botanic Garden, W. Germany

Viburnum plicatum in the park at Locarno, Switzerland

Plate 156

Viburnum propinquum
in the Bern Botanic Garden, Switzerland

Viburnum prunifolium
in the Späth Arboretum, Berlin, W. Germany

Viburnum × rhytidophylloides
in the Mlynany Arboretum, Czechoslovakia

Viburnum rigidum
in the Hamburg Botanic Garden, W. Germany

Plate 157

Viburnum. Left. *V.* 'Pragense'; center *V. utile;* right *V. rhytidophyllum*
Photo: J. Vik, Prague

Viburnum 'Pragense'
in the Hillier Arboretum, England

Viburnum rhytidophyllum
in the Dortmund Botanic Garden, W. Germany

Plate 158

Viburnum sargentii in its habitat
Photo: Dr. Watari, Tokyo

Viburnum sargentii 'Flavum'
in the Späth Arboretum, Berlin, W. Germany

Viburnum suspensum
in the Eden Panorama Park, Pallanza, N. Italy

Viburnum trilobum
in the Dortmund Botanic Garden, W. Germany

Plate 159

Viscum album and *Hedera helix* on an apple tree in central France

Viscum album
Photo: C. R. Jelitto, Berlin

Plate 160

Vitis aestivalis
in Les Barres Arboretum, France

Vitis amurensis
in the Leningrad Botanic Garden, USSR

Vinca difformis
in the S'Avall Garden, Majorca, Spain

Villaresia mucronata
in the Dublin Botanic Garden, Ireland

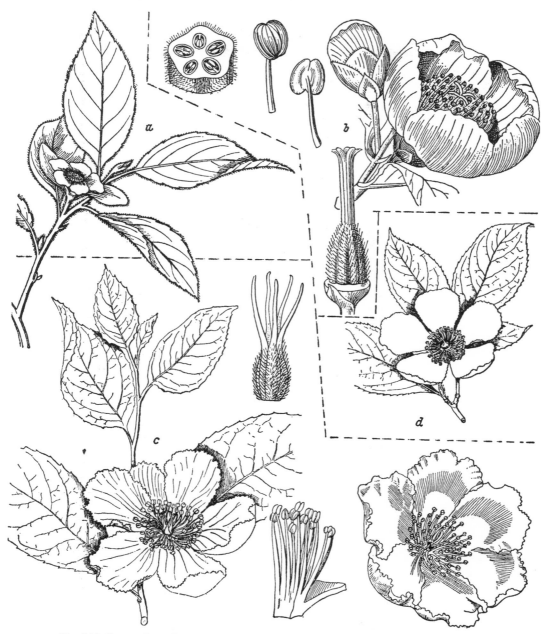

Fig. 263. **Stewartia.** a. *S. monadelpha;* b. *S. pseudocamellia;* c. *S. ovata;* d. *S. malacodendron*
(from B. M., Siebold & Zuccarini, Sprague & Gray)

S. monadelpha S. & Z. Generally a shrub in cultivation, a
tree in its habitat, to 10 m high, young shoots finely
pubescent; leaves ovate-lanceolate, 4–6 cm long,
sparsely finely serrate, appressed pubescent beneath,
fall foliage carmine; flowers very small, 3–4 cm wide,
white, petals outspread, filaments white, connate at the
base, anthers violet, July–August; fruits ovate, beaked, 1
cm long. MJ 982; KIF 1: 90; YTS 2: 87. Japan. 1903. z7–8
Fig. 263. ⌀

S. montana see: **S. ovata**

S. nobilis see: **S. malacodendron**

S. ovata (Cav.) Weatherby. Shrub, 4–5 m high, shoots
glabrous; leaves oval-elliptic, 6–12 cm long, rounded at
the base (!), sparsely finely serrate, gray-green beneath
and somewhat pubescent; flowers cream-white, cupulate, 6–7 cm wide, petals 5, occasionally 6, obovate, concave, filaments white (!), anthers orange, styles all dis-

tinct (!!), July–August; fruits sharply pentagonal, to 2 cm long, acute, pubescent. BB 2440; AB 17: 11; BM 3918; NH 1955: 220 (= *S. pentagyna* L'Hér.; *S. montana* Bartr.). SE. USA; Kentucky to Alabama. Around 1800. z6 Fig. 263. ⌀ ✧

var. **grandiflora** (Bean) Weatherby. Fall foliage orange to scarlet-red; flowers 8–10 cm wide, usually only a few opening, petals occasionally 6–8, filaments purple (!), anthers orange. NF 8: 23; AB 17: 4 (14–17). Georgia. 1914. The best of the entire genus. ⌀ ✧

S. pentagyna see: **S. ovata**

S. pseudocamellia Maxim. Shrub, 3–4 m high, a tree in its habitat, to 10 m high or more, bark red, exfoliating in large pieces, branches erect, young shoots thin, glabrous, straight (!); leaves elliptic-lanceolate to obovate, 3–8 cm long, cuneate at the base, sparsely crenate, thickish, bright green above, glabrous or with scattered pubescence beneath, dark red in fall; flowers broad cup-shaped, 5–6 cm wide, petals nearly circular, filaments white, anthers orange, July–August; fruits ovate, pentagonal, 2 cm long. BM 7045; NH 1955: 218; KIF 2: 64; YTS 2: 86; MJ 983; AB 17: 9 (= *S. grandiflora* Carr.). Japan. 1874. Very winter hardy. z5–6 Fig. 263. ✧ ⌀

var. **koreana** (Nakai) Sealy. Shoots zigzag form; leaves broad elliptic, short and scabrous acuminate, 4.5–6.5 cm long, base broad cuneate to rounded, sparsely pubescent beneath, more densely so toward the base; flowers broadly shell form, 6–7 cm wide, petals circular to broad obovate, limb finely undulate; fruits and seeds like those of the species. BMns 20; BS 3: Pl. 31; NH 1955: 221 (= *S. koreana* Nakai). Korea. (Included with *S. pseudocamellia* by Spongberg!) ✧ ⌀

'**Minterne Narrowleaf Form**' (Digby). Selection with conspicuously narrower leaves, these scarlet-red in fall. ⌀

S. serrata Maxim. Tall shrub to small tree, 7 m high or more, young shoots reddish, pubescent at first, later glabrous; leaves elliptic to obovate, 4–7 cm long, serrate, teeth inward curving, base cuneate, midrib and vein axils pubescent beneath; flowers solitary, axillary, 5–6 cm wide, cream-white, exterior somewhat reddish, distinctly red at the base, filaments totally distinct, white, anthers yellow, ovaries glabrous, June–July; fruits ovate, 2 cm long. BM 8771; MJ 3434; KIF 3: 50. Japan. 1908. z7 ✧ ⌀

S. sinensis Rehd. & Wils. Shrub or tree, 7 m high or more, the brown bark exfoliating in large plates, showing gray beneath, young shoots usually pubescent at first; leaves elliptic to oval-oblong, 5–10 cm long, acuminate, sparsely serrate or more crenate, base cuneate to nearly round, occasionally somewhat pubescent at first, petiole 5–8 mm long; flowers 5 cm wide, cup form, fragrant, white, petals broadly obovate, filaments connate on the basal third and pubescent, anthers yellow, ovaries pubescent, July; fruits nearly globose, pentagonal, 2 cm high. BM 8778. Central China. 1901. z6 Plate 130. ✧⌀

S. virginica see: **S. malacodendron**

All species, except the very rare *S. malacodendron*, are relatively

winter hardy, but unfortunately underutilized. An excellent summer blooming plant. Cultural preference somewhat like that of *Rhododendron*; i.e., a fertile, humus soil and sufficient moisture.

Lit. Spongberg, S. A.: A review of Deciduous-leaved species of *Stewartia* (Theaceae); Jour. Arnold Arbor. 55, 182–214, 1974.

STRANVAESIA Lindl. — ROSACEAE

Evergreen trees or shrubs; leaves petiolate, alternate, entire or serrate, with awl-shaped stipules; flowers white, in terminal corymbs; calyx top-shaped, 5 toothed, petals 5; stamens about 20, styles 5, connate to the middle; fruit a small pome; calyx teeth persisting on the fruit, inclined together; core easily separated from the fleshy pulp when the fruits are ripe. — 10 species in China and the Himalayas.

Stranvaesia davidiana Decne. Evergreen shrub, 8–9 high in its habitat, usually not over 2–3 m in cultivation, young shoots silky pubescent at first, quickly becoming glabrous; leaves oblong-lanceolate, acuminate, base cuneate, entire, about 12 cm long, 2–3 cm wide, glabrous on both sides, petiole 1–2 cm long, often reddish; flowers small, white, in about 5–8 cm wide, flat corymbs, June; fruits red, pea-sized, fall. BM 9008 (= *S. henryi* Diels). W. China. 1917. z7 Plate 130. # ⌀ ✧

'**Lutea**' (Donard). Seedling of var. *undulata* with orange-yellow fruits. Developed in the Slieve Donard Nursery, Belfast, N. Ireland around 1920. # 🜛

var. **salicifolia** (Hutchins.) Rehd. Leaves narrowly lanceolate, more distinctly veined, stipules abscising very early; inflorescences densely pubescent. BM 8862 (= *S. salicifolia* Hutchins.). W. China. 1907. z8–9 # 🜛

var. **undulata** (Decne.) Rehd. & Wils. Lower growth habit; leaves smaller, usually more oblong to somewhat obovate, 3–8 cm long, margins undulate; inflorescences smaller, usually totally glabrous; fruits smaller, orange, BM 8418 (= *S. undulata* Decne.). Central and W. China. 1901. # 🜛

S. glauca see: **S. nussia**

S. glaucescens see: **S. nussia**

S. henryi see: **S. davidiana**

S. nussia Decne. Evergreen shrub, to 5 m high or more; leaves tough, leathery, lanceolate to obovate, finely dentate, acute, 6–10 cm long, 3–5 cm wide, glossy dark green above, densely white woolly beneath at first; flowers white, 12 mm wide, in 10–15 cm wide, flat, somewhat nodding cymes, inflorescence white woolly at first, June; fruits globose, orange, pubescent. BR 1956 (= *S. glaucescens* Lindl.; *S. glauca* Baill.). Himalayas, Nepal to E. Bengal. 1828. z9 # ⌀ ✧ 🜛

S. salicifolia see: **S. davidiana** var. **salicifolia**

S. undulata see: **S. davidiana** var. **undulata**

All species do well in a normal garden soil, but prefer additional peat and sufficient moisture. *S. nussia* needs more heat and therefore prefers a warmer climate.

STRELITZIA Ait. — Bird of Paradise — STRELITZIACEAE

Banana-like, woody, multistemmed, low shrub with palm-like stems or only herbaceous without an actual stem; leaves of the species mentioned here are banana-like, distichous, leathery, large, long stalked; flowers of the mentioned species only slightly exserted past the leaf sheaths, bracts 1 or 2, navicular, the 3 blades of the outer perianth ring narrowly lanceolate, long acuminate, petals 3, of these 1 small and 2 grouped into a sagittate organ in whose fold lie the 5 stamens and the pistil; fruit a 3 locular capsule with many seeds. — 5 species in S. Africa.

Strelitzia alba (L. f.) Skeels. Tree Strelitzia. Stem woody, to 5 m high; leaves to 1.2 m long, 50 cm wide, petiole about 1 m long or longer, channeled above and somewhat winged, blade bright green, cordate at the base; flowers on a short stalk in the leaf axils, sheath purple, all other flower parts pure white, petals rounded at the base. BM 4167 and 4168; FS 1846: 173 (= *S. augusta* Thunb.). S. Africa; Cape Province and Natal. 1791. z10 Plate 130. # Ø ✛

S. augusta see: **S. alba**

S. nicolai Regel & Koern. Similar to *S. alba,* but taller and more tree-like, 6–8 m high; leaves similar to those of *S. alba,* but the blade base rounded; flower spathe and flowers conspicuously larger, with 4 superimposed bracts in the axillary inflorescences, bracts reddish brown, outer sepals white, inner blue, base hastate, May. FS 1858: 1356; BM 7038. S. Africa; Cape Province. 1849. z9 Plate 130. # Ø ✛

Lit. Moore, H. E., & P. A. Hyypio: Some comments on *Strelitzia;* Baileya **17,** 65–74, 1970 (with ills.!!).

STREPTOSOLEN Miers — SOLANACEAE

Monotypic genus with the characteristics of the species.

Streptosolen jamesonii (Benth.) Miers. Evergreen, roughly pubescent, climbing shrub; leaves alternate, 3–5 cm long, elliptic to ovate, acute at both ends, entire, somewhat bullate, petiole 1 cm; flowers in terminal umbellate panicles, calyx tubular, 1 cm long, with 5 acute teeth, corolla funnelform, with a long, narrow tube and 4 or 5 lobed, wide limb, bilabiate, the lobes semicircular, bright orange, flowering very abundantly, stamens 4, in 2 pairs, June; fruit a bivalved capsule with many, very small seeds. BM 4605; FS 436 (as *Browallia jamesonii*). Columbia. 1847. Outside of the tropics a good shrub for the conservatory. z10 Plate 125. # ✛

STYRAX L. — Storax, Snowbell — STYRACACEAE

Evergreen or deciduous trees or often only shrubs in cultivation, with stellate pubescent shoots; leaves alternate, short petioled, entire or serrate, usually stellate pubescent; flowers white, in terminal racemes or clusters on short lateral shoots, or solitary; corolla 5–8 parted or lobed, calyx campanulate, shallowly 5 lobed, to entire; ovaries nearly superior, stamens 10–14, anthers linear; fruit a globose drupe. — About 130 species in the warmer Americas, Asia and SW. Europe.

Key to the more Important Species
(from Perkins, simplified)

★ Corolla tube longer than the lobes; leaves nearly circular, coarsely serrate:
  S. shiraianus

★★ Corolla tube shorter than the lobes;
  ✕ Flowers few in clusters or racemes;
    > Flower stalk as long as the calyx, pubescent;
      + Leaves 3–9 cm long:
        S. americanus
      ++ Leaves 1–2.5 cm long:
        S. wilsonii
    >> Flower stalk 1.5–2.5 cm long:
        S. japonicus
  ✕✕ Flowers in many-flowered racemes;
    > Leaves tomentose or densely pubescent beneath, 6–20 cm long;
      + Petiole base not widened; inflorescences 6–10 cm long:
        S. grandifolius
      ++ Petiole base sheath-like, surrounding the leaf bud; inflorescences 9–20 cm long:
        S. obassia
    >> Leaves glabrous or sparsely pubescent on the underside, 5–14 cm long;
      + Petiole 5–15 mm long; corolla lobes imbricate in the bud stage:
        S. hemsleyanus
      ++ Petiole 1–3 mm long; corolla lobes valvate in the bud stage:
        S. dasyanthus

Styrax americanus Lam. Shrub, to 3 m high, branches red-brown, glabrous; leaves elliptic to ovate, 3–9 cm long, acute, entire to finely serrate, bright green, sparsely stellate pubescent; flowers grouped 1–4 together, nodding, on a 6–12 mm long, pubescent stalk, calyx with tiny, triangular teeth, corolla about 1.5 cm long, lobes outspread to reflexed, April–June; fruits obovoid, 8 mm long. BB 2834; BR 952; BM 921; KTF 170. SE. USA, in swamps and moist forests. 1765. Particularly tender as a young plant. z6–7 Fig. 265. ✛

f. **pulverulentus** (Michx.) Perk. Leaves sparsely stellate pubescent above, much more densely so beneath; calyx and flower stalk tomentose. BB 2835 (= *S. pubescens* Michx.). Virginia to Texas. 1794. z8

S. dasyanthus Perk. Shrub, a tree in its habitat, to 8 m, young shoots pubescent at first; leaves elliptic-oblong to obovate, 6–10 cm long, base cuneate, finely dentate, glabrous above, also eventually beneath; flowers in slender, 5–10 cm long racemes, stalks 6–8 mm long, corolla 1–1.5 cm long, corolla lobes lanceolate, valvate in the bud stage, style longer than the corolla, July. China; Hupeh Prov. 1900. z9 ⊕

S. grandifolius Ait. Shrub, usually only 1.5–3 m high, young shoots soft gray-yellow pubescent; leaves elliptic to obovate, 6–18 cm long, finely dentate to entire, thin, cuneate at the base, finely gray stellate pubescent beneath, petiole 5–10 mm long; flowers in 8–15 cm long, stellate tomentose racemes, fragrant, corolla 2–2.5 cm wide, lobes outspread, May; fruits obovoid, pubescent. GC 138: 230; BB 2836; KTF 171. SE. USA. 1765. z8–9 Fig. 265. ∅ ⊕

S. hemsleyanus Diels. Shrub, to 5 m high, also tree-like, to 10 m high, shoots stellate pubescent at first, quickly becoming glabrous; leaves obliquely obovate, acuminate, 7–13 cm long, 5–7 cm wide, sparsely finely serrate, base cuneate to round, glabrous above, underside slightly stellate pubescent; flowers in pubescent, 8–15 cm long racemes, corolla 1.5–2 cm long, limb lobes imbricate in the bud stage (!), stalk 3–4 mm long, June; fruits obovoid, 1.5 cm long. GC 129: 78; BM 8339; FIO 47; BS 3: 381. Central and W. China. 1900. z8–9 ⊕

S. huanus Rehd. Tree, 6–15 m high; leaves obliquely obovate, 6–10 cm long; flowers 8–16 together in terminal, 12 cm long racemes. NF 12: 149. China; SE. Szechwan Prov. Not yet cultivated, but very floriferous and notable. z7 ⊕

S. japonicus S. & Z. Tall shrub or small tree, to 10 m high, branches outspread, thin, gray stellate tomentose at first, like the leaves, later glabrous; leaves rounded-elliptic, 2–4(7) cm long, sparsely dentate; flowers 3–6 in clusters or racemes, pendulous, corolla 2 cm wide, stalks 2–3 cm long, glabrous, June–July; fruits ovate, 1 cm long. BM 5950 (as *S. serrulatus*); LF 259; MJ 668; KIF 1: 95; FIO 48. China, Japan. 1862. z6 Fig. 265. ⊕

S. obassia S. & Z. Shrub or tree, to 10 m high, branches ascending, floccose at first, quickly becoming glabrous; leaves usually nearly circular to broadly obovate or elliptic, 7–15 cm long, abruptly acuminate, sparsely dentate on the apical half, dark green above, densely pubescent beneath, petiole 6–20 mm long; flowers in 10–20 cm long, nodding racemes, partly hidden by the foliage, fragrant, corolla deeply 5 lobed, 2 cm long, calyx soft pubescent, May–June; fruits ovate, 2 cm long. BM 7039; KIF 1: 96; MJ 669; NK 13: 13. Japan. 1879. Generally quite hardy. "Obassia" is the Japanese name for the plant. z6 Fig. 265. ∅ ⊕

S. officinalis L. True Storax Tree. Shrub or small tree, 3–7 m high in its habitat, branches yellowish gray-green, stellate pubescent; leaves ovate, 3–5 cm long, obtuse,

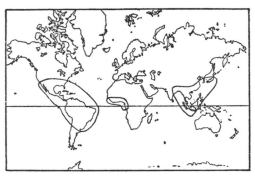

Fig. 264. Range of the Family Styracaceae

rounded at the base, stellate pubescent when young, entire; flowers in terminal, pendulous clusters of 3–6 together, corolla to 3 cm wide, 5(7) lobed, fragrant, densely white pubescent, May. BM 9653. SE. Europe, Asia Minor. 1957. Storax resin is obtained by tapping the stems and is used as an incense. A gorgeous flowering tree in the Orient. z9 Fig. 265, 266. ⊕

S. pubescens see: **S. americanus** f. **pulverulentus**

S. shiraianus Mak. Small tree, shoots soft stellate pubescent; leaves obovate to nearly circular, base cuneate, 3–10 cm long, very coarsely dentate toward the apex, soft pubescent beneath; flowers in 5–6 cm long, terminal racemes, short stalked, on short lateral shoots, corolla 2 cm long, nearly funnelform, lobes ovate, soft pubescent, half as long as the tube, June. MJ 670. Japan. 1915. z7 Fig. 265. ∅ ⊕

Fig. 266. *Styrax officinalis* (from Dippel)

Fig. 265. **Styrax.** a. *S. americanus*; b. *S. obassia*; c. *S. japonicus*; d. *S. grandifolius*; e. *S. officinalis*;
f. *S. shiraianus* (from Herb. Amer., Nose, Perkins, Siebold & Zuccarini, Watson)

S. shweliensis W. W. Sm. Shrub or small tree, 5–8 m high, shoots reddish brown, pubescent; flowers ovate-elliptic, 5–10 cm long, 2–5 cm wide, acute, base cuneate, margins shallowly dentate, dull green above, gray-green beneath, soft stellate pubescent on both sides (!), stalk 4 mm long; flowers 1–2 on short shoots, pendulous, corolla to 2.5 cm wide, calyx campanulate, very tomentose, nearly entire, June–July. China. 1913. z9 ⊕

S. veitchiorum Hemsl. & Wils. Small tree, 5–9 m high, young shoots, leaf petiole and calyx densely gray stellate pubescent; leaves elliptic-lanceolate, 7–12 cm long, long acuminate, base cuneate, sparsely and shallowly dentate, thin, stellate pubescent on both sides, but denser on the venation beneath; flowers in terminal and axillary racemes at the shoot tips, 10–20 cm long, corolla 2.5 cm wide, calyx short 5 toothed, June. Central China. 1900. z6 ✧

S. wilsonii Rehd. Densely branched shrub to 3 m high, branches stellate tomentose at first; leaves rhombic-ovate, 1.2–5 cm long, entire or with 3–5 teeth at the apex, slightly pubescent above, bluish and densely stellate pubescent beneath; flowers 3–5 or solitary on short lateral shoots, corolla 1.5–1.8 cm wide, short stalked, calyx stellate pubescent, May–June; fruits ovate, 8 mm long. BM 8444; GC 131: 93; 134: 175. W. China. 1908. A plant well worth a trial for its abundant flowers on young plants, but hardy only in z8–9. ✧

With the exceptions of *S. japonicus* and *S. obassia*, all species require a very well protected site; all species are beautiful specimens when in full bloom. A good garden soil is recommended.

Lit. Perkins, J.: Styracaceae; in Engler, Pflanzenreich, IV, 241, 17–88, 1907.

SUAEDA Forsk. — CHENOPODIACEAE

Upright or prostrate, salt-loving shrubs or perennials; leaves alternate, fleshy, sessile, nearly terete; flowers hermaphroditic or unisexual, inconspicuous; perianth 5 parted, stamens 5, ovaries ovate to cylindrical, with 2–5 short, sessile stigmas; fruit a small nutlet enclosed within the perianth. — About 110 species, cosmopolitan on the seacoasts and the salt plains.

Suaeda fruticosa Forsk. Evergreen shrub, 0.5 m high or more, upright, branches white barked, smooth greenish at first; leaves densely clustered at the apical end of the shoots, thickish, semi-terete, about 1 cm long, blue-green; flowers grouped 1–3 in globose clusters, June–July, inconspicuous. Seacoast of S. and W. Europe. z8 #

Only of botanical interest.

SUTHERLANDIA R. Br. — LEGUMINOSAE

Monotypic genus (according to other authors composed of several species) with the characteristics of the following species.

Sutherlandia frutescens (L.) R. Br. Deciduous, upright, gray pubescent shrub, to about 1 m high or also procumbent, also occasionally to 2 m high; leaves odd pinnate, 6–8 cm long, with 13–21 leaflets, these oblong-lanceolate, small, thinly pubescent; flowers 6–10 together in short, axillary racemes, attractive, standard, wing and keel scarlet-red, to 2.5 cm long, calyx campanulate, with 5 triangular lobes, June; fruits ovate, very inflated, similar to those of *Colutea*. BM 181. S. Africa, hills and dry mountain slopes of Cape Province. 1683. z10 Plate 125. ✧

Easily cultivated in a sufficiently warm climate and very floriferous.

SUTTONIA

Suttonia chathamica see: **Rapanea chathamica**

S. nummularia see: **Rapanea nummularia**

× SYCOPARROTIA Endress & Anliker (PARROTIA × SYCOPSIS) — HAMAMELIDACEAE

Inter-generic hybrid; only one species known to date.

× **Sycoparrotia semidecandra** Endress & Anliker. Semi-evergreen shrub, 4 m high (perhaps also becoming taller); leaves intermediate between the parents (*Parrotia persica* and *Sycopsis sinensis*), elongated obovate, about 10–12 cm long, 4–5 cm wide, widest at or above the middle, slightly acuminate, with about 5 small teeth on the apical half of either side, base somewhat truncate to lightly cordate, leathery; flowers intermediate between the parents, petals dark brown, tomentose, anthers vermilion carmine-red, April. Developed from seed around 1950 in the nursery of P. Schönholzer, Basel, Switzerland. z6 # ∅ ✧

Lit. Endress, P., & J. Anliker: × *Sycoparrotia semidecandra*; in Schweiz. Beitr. Dendrol. **16–18,** 11–23, 1968 (with ills.)

SYCOPSIS Oliv. — HAMAMELIDACEAE

Evergreen shrubs or trees; leaves oblong, entire or finely dentate, with stipules; flowers rather inconspicuous, monoecious, without petals, with small calyx lobes, grouped into heads or short racemes; staminate flowers in heads, surrounded by pubescent bracts; stamens 8, styles 2; fruit a pubescent, dehiscent capsule. — 7 species in China, Himalayas and the Philippines.

Sycopsis sinensis Oliv. Evergreen shrub, 4–6 m high; leaves leathery tough, elliptic-lanceolate, acuminate, 5–10 cm long, sparsely shallow dentate, glossy green above, lighter beneath, glabrous; flowers small, yellowish, anthers red, surrounded by dark brown, tomentose bracts, February–March; fruit a bivalved, ovate, beaked capsule. LF 160; BS 3: 386; BMns 655; HI 1931. Central and W. China. 1901. z8–9 # ∅

The flowers resemble *Parrotia*, but the plant is evergreen and much more tender. Cultivated like a *Hamamelis*.

Lit., see: *Distylium*, Vol. I, p. 443.

SYMPHORICARPOS Duham. — Snowberry, Coralberry — CAPRIFOLIACEAE

Low, deciduous shrubs; leaves opposite, short petioled, entire or lobed on long shoots; flowers small, inconspicuous, in short terminal or axillary spikes or racemes; calyx cupulate, with 4–5 teeth; corolla campanulate or infundibular, throat glabrous or pubescent, limb rather regularly 4–5 lobed; stamens as many as the corolla lobes; ovaries 4 locular; fruit a berry with 2 seeds. — 18 species in N. America, southward to Mexico, and one in W. China. The species are difficult to distinguish!

Key to the Important Species

Fruits blue-black:
S. sinensis

Fruits red with white spots, small leaved:
S. × chenaultii

Fruits red:
S. orbiculatus

Fruits white or pink;

● Pistil and anthers exserted:
S. occidentalis

●● Pistil and anthers not exserted;

= Upright habit:
S. albus

== Habit procumbent:
S. hesperius

Symphoricarpos acutus see: **S. hesperius**

S. albus (L.) Blake. Common Snowberry. Shrub, to about 1 m high, branches thin, erect, finely pubescent; leaves ovate, 2–5 cm long, often lobed on long shoots, dark green above, lighter and soft pubescent beneath; flowers in terminal and axillary spikes or clusters, corolla campanulate, 6 mm long, reddish white, pistil and anthers not exserted, tube pubescent on the interior, June–September; fruits oval-rounded, snow-white, 8–12 mm thick, in dense clusters, persisting from fall into winter. BB 3452; GSP 461 (= *S. racemosus* Pursh; *S. pauciflorus* Brit.). Northern N. America. z3 Fig. 269.

var. **laevigatus** (Fern.) Blake. To 2 m high, branches glabrous; leaves ovate, nearly glabrous, usually somewhat larger, lobed on long shoots; flowers in short racemes, corolla lobes as long as the tube, pink to white; fruits very numerous, white, globose. BB 3451; BM 2211; Add 94 (= *S. rivularis* Sukad.). Alaska to California. 1906. Often cultivated as "*S. racemosus*"! Ⓕ Czechoslovakia, USA; in screen plantings. Fig. 267. ⊗

f. **ovatus** (Späth) Rehd. More vigorous than var. *laevigatus,* over 2 m high; leaves broad ovate, bluish dark green, cuneate to rounded at the base; flowers light pink, 7–8 mm long; fruits somewhat larger (= *S. ovatus* Späth). 1888. Distributed to the trade by Späth in 1908. ⊗

'**Turesson**' (Doorenbos). Branches distinctly nodding; flowers in elongated racemes, corolla 4–5 mm long, pink, interior pubescent; fruits ellipsoid, 1–2 cm long (!). DB 1953: 74. Selection with particularly long, narrow fruits, brought into the trade by S. G. A. Doorenbos in 1953. Plate 131. ⊗

S. × chenaultii Rehd. Chenault Coralberry (*S. microphyllus* × *S. orbiculatus*). Fine textured shrub, 1.5–2 m high or more, erect, abundantly and open branched, whole plant densely and finely pubescent, young shoots reddish; leaves ovate, 1–2 cm long, dark green above, blue-green beneath, densely soft pubescent; flowers in short, terminal spikes, corolla campanulate-funnelform, pink, interior somewhat pubescent, June–July; fruits globose, red with white spots, often only white with red spots on the dorsal side. Gs 16: 36. Developed around 1910 by R. Chenault of Orléans, France. The best species of the genus. z5 ⊗

'**Elegance**' (Sport of *S. × chenaultii*). More upright and dense, shoot tips brown-red, new growth reddish; leaves oblong, 25–27 mm long, deep green above, blue-green beneath; flowers

Fig. 267. **Symphoricarpos.** Leaves, left *S. occidentalis* var. *heyeri* (3), right *S. albus* var. *laevigatus* (4) (from Schneider)

Fig. 268. **Symphoricarpos.** a. *S. microphyllus*; b. *S. occidentalis*; c. *S. rotundifolius*;
d. *S. hesperius*; e. *S. oreophilus* (from Dippel, B. M.)

inconspicuous, pink; fruits red, but only rarely developed.
Brought into the trade by P. de Bruin, Boxtel, Holland. ∅

'Hancock'. Branches procumbent and rooting, vigorous but
only 30–50 cm high. Developed around 1950 at the Woodland
Nurseries, Cookville, Ontario, Canada. Patented in the U.S.
Good ground cover. Plate 131.

S. × doorenbosii Krüssmn. (*S. albus* var. *laevigatus* × *S. ×
chenaultii*). Shrub, to 2 m high, vigorous growing, shoots
short pubescent; leaves elliptic to broadly ovate, obtuse
with a short tip, base obtuse to acute, 2–4 cm long, 1–2.5
cm wide, dark green and glabrous above, lighter and
more or less pubescent beneath, petiole 1–2 mm long,
pubescent; flowers in short racemes, calyx 5 parted,
corolla campanulate, 5–7 mm long, turning somewhat
pink; fruits in dense clusters, globose, 10–13 mm thick,
white with a pink cheek. z5

'Mother of Pearl' (Doorenbos). The type of the above hybrid. A
color plate may be seen in DB 10: 324. Developed in Den Haag,
Holland by S. G. A. Doorenbos in 1950. ⚲

S. giraldii see: **S. orbiculatus**

S. hesperius Jones. Shrub, prostrate or procumbent, but
the shoots erect, young shoots pubescent; leaves ovate,
1–3 cm long, glabrous and dark green above, underside
gray-green with pubescent venation, openly sinuate
lobed on the long shoots; flowers 2–6 axillary, corolla
campanulate, 4–5 mm long, pink, style and stamens as
long as the corolla tube, June–July; fruits white, globose,
6–8 mm thick. DL 1: 185 (= *S. acutus* Dipp.). Western N.
America. 1896. z6 Fig. 268.

S. heyeri see: **S. occidentalis** var. **heyeri**

S. microphyllus H. B. K. Upright shrub, 1–2 m high,
shoots soft pubescent, hairs curved (!); leaves acutely
ovate, 1–2.5 cm long, blue-green and pubescent

beneath; flowers solitary or paired, pink, axillary or in
short, terminal spikes, August; fruits translucent (!), pink
or white, 8 mm thick. BM 4975; DL 1: 188 (= *S. montanus*
H. B. K.). Mexico. 1829. z9 Fig. 268, 269.

S. mollis Nutt. Procumbent shrub, 30–90 cm high,
shoots velvety pubescent with curved hairs; leaves
nearly circular to elliptic, 1–3 cm long, pubescent above,
velvety pubescent and gray-white beneath; flowers in
small, axillary clusters, corolla pink, lobes as long as the
tube, stamens shorter than the tube, April–May. MS 635
(= *S. nanus* Greene). USA; California. z7

S. montanus see: **S. microphyllus**

S. nanus see: **S. mollis**

S. occidentalis Hook. Upright, 1–1.5 m high shrub,
somewhat stiff, shoots pubescent; leaves ovate, 2–7 cm
long, obtuse, entire or undulate, tough, gray blue-green
above, underside somewhat lighter and more or less
pubescent; flowers many in 1–3 cm long, dense, axillary
and terminal spikes, corolla pale pink, campanulate,
deeply lobed, interior densely pubescent, pistil and
anthers somewhat exserted, June to July; fruits globose,
1 cm thick, greenish white, quickly becoming brown. BB
3453; RMi 380; BC 3752; VT 951. Western N. America.
1880. Dry sites. Ⓕ USA, for erosion control. z3 Fig. 268,
269.

var. **heyeri** Dieck. Only slightly differing from the species;
leaves thinner, not so distinctly veined, somewhat more
obtuse; pistil and stamens somewhat shorter. DL 1: 187 (= *S.
heyeri* Dipp.). Colorado. 1888. Fig. 267.

S. orbiculatus Mnch. Coralberry. Shrub, 1–2 m high,
narrowly upright, shoots pubescent; leaves oval-
rounded, 2–4 cm long, dull dark green above, more gray-
green and pubescent beneath, often reddish in fall;

flowers in small, dense, axillary clusters or short spikes, corolla campanulate, 4 mm long, yellowish white, turning pink, interior sparsely pubescent, July–August; fruits nearly globose, purple-red, 4–6 mm thick, persistent. BB 3454; GSP 461; VT 948; Add 111 (= *S. vulgaris* Michx.; *S. giraldii* Hesse). N. America. 1727. Ⓕ USA, for erosion control. z2 Fig. 269. ♂

'Leucocarpus' (D. M. Andrews). Flowers greenish yellow; fruits white or whitish. Distributed to the trade in 1927 by D. M. Andrews of Rockmont Nurseries, USA.

'Variegatus'. Leaves golden-yellow margined and veined, occasionally reverting back to the species. 1902. ⌀

S. oreophilus Gray. Shrub, to 1.5 m high, erect, shoots thin and spreading, young shoots finely pubescent to glabrous; leaves elliptic, 1.4 cm long, acute, usually pubescent on both sides, but denser and more gray

beneath; flowers either in axillary pairs or in small, terminal spikes, corolla tubular-funnelform, 1 cm long, pink, tube 4–5 times longer than the lobes, interior nearly totally glabrous, June–July; fruits white, ellipsoid, 8 mm long. VT 946. SW. USA. 1894. z6 Fig. 269. ♂

S. ovatus see: **S. albus f. ovatus**

S. pauciflorus see: **S. albus**

S. racemosus see: **S. albus**

S. rivularis see: **S. albus var. laevigatus**

S. rotundifolius Gray. Shrub, 0.6–1 m high, erect, young shoots finely pubescent at first; leaves nearly circular to elliptic-ovate, 1–2.5 cm long, obtuse, occasionally sinuately dentate, pubescent on both sides, more gray beneath; flowers in terminal and axillary spikes of 2–5

Fig. 269. **Symphoricarpos.** a. *S. orbiculatus;* b. *S. occidentalis;* c. *S. albus;* d. *S. microphyllus;* e. *S. oreophilus* (from Schneider, Koehne, Kunth, Schmidt)

together, corolla pink-white, tubular-campanulate, 6–8 mm long, tube pubescent on the interior, May–June; fruits ellipsoid, white, 1 cm long. VT 950; MS 637. SW. USA. 1896. z7 Fig. 268. ⚥

S. sinensis Rehd. Glabrous shrub, to 1.5 m high, branches thin, red-brown; leaves rhombic to oval-elliptic, 1.5–2.5 cm long, bluish beneath, glabrous; flowers small, white, campanulate, solitary, axillary, July; fruits ovate, blue-black (!) and pruinose, 7 mm long. Central China. 1907. Hardy. Existence in cultivation to date unknown. Should be interesting for hybridization. z6 ⚥

S. vulgaris see: **S. orbiculatus**

Cultivars

'Erect' (Doorenbos 1940) (= *S. albus* var. *laevigatus* × *S. orbiculatus*?). Shrub, narrowly upright, the lateral shoots also erect, dense, young shoots short and erect pubescent; leaves broadly ovate to elliptic, obtuse, base rounded, 2–3 cm long, deep green above, more gray to yellow-green beneath, venation pubescent; flowers in dense racemes, calyx 5 parted, corolla campanulate, pink, interior pubescent; fruits very densely clustered, magenta-red, 1 cm thick. ⚥

'Magic Berry' (Doorenbos, around 1940). To 1 m high, bushy, shoots dense and erect pubescent; leaves broader ovate to elliptic, obtuse, 2–3 cm long, base round, dark green above, the whitish midrib short pubescent, light green and loosely pubescent beneath; flowers in short, pubescent racemes, corolla campanulate; fruits lilac-red, somewhat ellipsoid, showing color already in July, in dense clusters. ⚥

'White Hedge' (Doorenbos, 1940). Upright shrub, to 1.5 m high, branches ascending, glabrous; leaves elliptic to slightly obovate, obtuse, 2–3.5 cm long, base acute to cuneate, light green beneath, petiole 2–3 mm long; flowers in glabrous, elongated racemes, corolla campanulate, 4 mm long, somewhat reddish; fruits white, 10–13 mm thick, in erect racemes. Plate 131. ⚥

Not particular as to soil type, even thriving in dry and gravelly soil; the new cultivars are quite valuable for hedging and fruit color.

Lit. Jones, G. N.: A monograph of the genus *Symphoricarpos*; in Jour. Arnold Arb. **21**, 201–252, 1940.

SYMPLOCOS Jacq. — Sweetleaf — SYMPLOCACEAE

Deciduous or evergreen trees or shrubs, usually glabrous, occasionally pubescent; leaves alternate, simple, entire or dentate; flowers mostly in axillary spikes or racemes; calyx tube short at flowering time, enlarging when in fruit; stamens numerous, ovaries with 2–5 locules; fruits berrylike or drupaceous, usually with only one seed. — About 350 species, most in the tropics and subtropics. Only the following species generally cultivated.

Symplocos crataegoides see: **S. paniculata**

S. paniculata (Thunb.) Miq. Sapphire-berry. A deciduous shrub in zone 7, scarcely over 3 m high, branches outspread, pubescent at first; leaves ovate-elliptic to obovate-oblong, finely and scabrous serrate, 3–7 cm long, bright green above, glabrous and rugose, underside usually slightly pubescent; flowers in terminal, pubescent, 4–8 cm wide panicles on short shoots, white, scented about like *Crataegus*, May–June; fruits pea-sized, sapphire blue, in large inflorescences. BMns 149; GF 5: 89 (= *S. crataegoides* Buch.-Ham.). Japan, China to the Himalayas. 1824. z5 Plate 131. ⚘ ⚥

References to other illustrations:

S. glauca	LWT 300; KIF 2: 74
S. myrtacea	KIF 3: 69
S. prunifolia	KIF 3: 70
S. theophrastifolia	KIF 3: 75
S. tinctoria	KTL 172

For warm, sunny, somewhat protected sites; valued for its gorgeous blue fruits. Where possible plant several together to insure cross pollination and abundant fruit set.

Lit. Brand: Symplocaceae; in Engler, Pflanzenreich **6**, 13, 1901.

SYRINGA L. — Lilac — OLEACEAE

Deciduous, rarely evergreen shrubs, occasionally a small tree; leaves opposite, usually simple, occasionally lobed, or pinnate; flowers in terminal or laterally arranged panicles on the previous year's shoots, occasionally on the current year's shoots; calyx small, campanulate, with 4 teeth, persistent; corolla with a cylindrical tube and 4 erect lobes; stamens 2, inserted beneath the mouth of the corolla tube; fruit an oblong, leathery, terete or compressed capsule; seeds obliquely winged at the base. — About 30 species in E. Asia and SE. Europe.

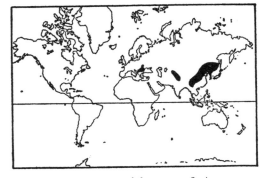

Fig. 270. **Range of the genus** *Syringa*

Outline of the Genus

Subgenus I. **Syringa**
Corolla tube much longer than the calyx; stamens nearly sessile;

Series 1. **Villosae** Schneid.
Panicles arising from the terminal bud, foliate at the base:
> *S. emodi, henryi, josikaea, komarowii, nanceiana, prestoniae, reflexa, swegiflexa, sweginzowii, tomentella, villosa, wolfii, yunnanensis*

Series 2. **Pubescentes** (Schneid.) Lingelsh.
Leaves more or less pubescent, often particularly dense beneath, occasionally totally glabrous or nearly so, upper surface without stomata; panicles more or less pubescent, arising from lateral buds, terminal buds usually absent; flowers usually very fragrant, rather small, limb about 6 mm wide; anthers yellow to bluish or violet; fruits warty to nearly smooth:
> *S. julianae, meyeri, microphylla, patula, pinetorum, potaninii, pubescens, skinneri, wardii*

Series 3. **Vulgares** Rehd.
Leaves glabrous or finely pubescent and ciliate on long shoots, with stomata on both sides; panicles finely pubescent to glabrous, arising from the lateral buds, terminal buds usually absent; flowers usually very fragrant, rather large, limb to 12 mm wide; anthers yellow; fruits smooth:
> *S. afghanica, chinensis, hyacinthiflora, laciniata, oblata, persica, rhodopea, vulgaris*

Series 4. **Pinnatifoliae** Rehd.
Leaves pinnate:
> *S. diversifolia, pinnatifolia*

Subgenus II. **Ligustrina** (Rupr.) K. Koch
Corolla tube short, scarcely longer than the calyx, shorter than the limb lobes; anthers yellow, exserted, filaments longer than the anthers; flowers white to cream-white, not fragrant, or unpleasantly scented; panicles arising from lateral buds, leafless at the base; fruits smooth:
> *S. pekinensis, reticulata*

Syringa affinis see: **S. oblata 'Alba'**

S. afghanica Schneid. Small shrub, branches short, thin, dark; leaves delicate, linear-lanceolate, to oval-lanceolate, pinnatisect, 1–3 cm long, 2–13 mm wide, to 5 cm long and 2 cm wide on long shoots, rather leathery tough, glabrous; flowers in slender, terminal and axillary, to 4 cm long panicles, corolla tube slender, to 10 mm long, blue-lilac, May. Afghanistan to Tibet. z5 Fig. 272.

S. amurensis see: **S. reticulata** var. **mandschurica**

S. × chinensis Willd. (*S. persica* × *S. vulgaris*). "Chinese Lilac" (the name is misleading since the plant originated in cultivation in France and does not occur in China). Bushy, thin-branched shrub, 3 m high and wide, occasionally higher, branches drooping; leaves ovate-lanceolate, acute, 4–8 cm long; flowers in large, limp panicles along the branch, lilac, fragrant, corolla tube 7–8 mm long, corolla lobes ovate, obtuse or acuminate, May. NF 7: 45; MLi 138 (= *S. rothomagensis* Hort.). Originated around 1777 in the Rouen Botanic Garden, France. z3 ⊕

'Alba'. Flowers white. MLi 137–139. 1817.

'Metensis' (Simon Louis 1871). Flowers bluish white. Rarely found in cultivation.

rubra see: **'Saugeana'**

'Saugeana'. Flowers red-lilac, darker than the species, occasionally also with lighter shoots appearing on the plant. MLi 134–136 (= *S. chinensis rubra* Lodd.). Around 1836. ⊕

S. + correlata Braun ([*S. chinensis* + *S. vulgaris*] × *S. chinensis* 'Alba'). Graft chimera, outer cell layer from *S. vulgaris* (white-flowering form), inner from *S. chinensis*; flowers in erect panicles, like *S. chinensis*, but totally light lilac, nearly white, but occasionally with shoots of normal lilac *S. chinensis* flowers occurring on the same shrub. z6

S. dielsiana see: **S. microphylla**

S. × diversifolia Rehd. (*S. oblata* var. *giraldii* × *S. pinnatifolia*). Medium-sized shrub, branch tips with or without a terminal bud; leaves partly oval-oblong, simple, with a rounded base, partly pinnatisect with 2–5 long acuminate lobes. Developed at the Arnold Arboretum, USA in 1929. z6

Including:

'William H. Judd'. The type of this cross. Flowers paired in panicles at the shoot tips, to 11 cm long, white, fragrant, early May. Fig. 272.

S. emodi Wall. Himalayan Lilac. Tightly upright shrub, 4–5 m high, branches steeply erect, rather thick, lighter warty punctate; leaves oblong-elliptic, tapered to both ends, 8–15 cm long, dark green above, blue-green beneath, glabrous; flowers pale lilac, unpleasantly scented, corolla lobes reflexed, anthers exserted, May to June. MLi 1 to 5; BR 31: 6; BS 3: 392; Bai 20: 80. Afghanistan, Himalayas. 1840. z7 Fig. 273.

'Variegata' (Ottolander 1877). Leaves very large, with wide light yellow margins in spring, later with more yellow-green margins.

S. formosissima see: **S. wolfii**

S. × henryi Schneid. (*S. josikaea* × *S. villosa*). Shrub, similar to *S. villosa* in habit, otherwise intermediate; inflorescences larger and more limp, flowers light violet-red, corolla tube gradually widening toward the apex, late May–June. MLi 40–44; Bai 20: 80. z2

'Lutèce' (Lemoine). The type of this cross. Flowers pale purple to nearly white. MFl 15. The often included cultivar 'Floréal' belongs to *S. nanceiana*!

S. × hyacinthiflora (Lemoine) Rehd. (*S. oblata* × *S. vulgaris*). Intermediate between the parents; leaves broad ovate, coloring purple in fall (!). z3
The so-called "Early Flowering Hybrids" or "Praecox Hybrids" must be included here; all cultivars of V. Lemoine, Nancy, France (from *S. oblata* var. *giraldii* × *S. vulgaris*), with flowers appearing 1–2 weeks earlier than *S. vulgaris*, panicles more open, all forms very similar to one another.
> Also included here are the cultivars 'Catinat', 'Lamartine', 'Mirabeau', 'Montesquieu', 'Necker' and 'Vauban' (description may be found in the cultivar list following species' description). 'Esther Staley' (W. B. Clarke) should also be included here.

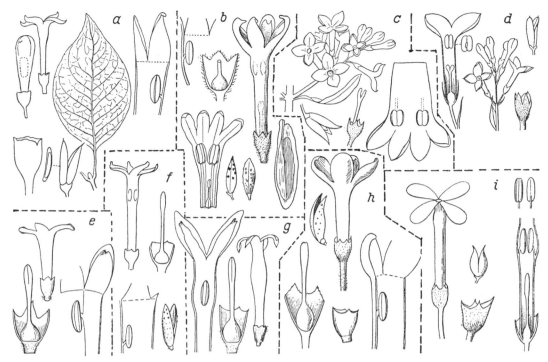

Fig. 271. **Syringa.** a. *S. sweginzowii;* b. *S. patula;* c. *S. vulgaris;* d. *S. × persica;* e. *S. julianae;* f. *S. pubescens;* g. *S. potaninii;* h. *S. oblata* var. *giraldii;* i. *S. oblata* (from Koehne, Schneider, H. Smith)

S. × josiflexa (Preston 1920) (*S. josikaea × S. reflexa*). Very similar to *S. reflexa,* but with other colors and better winter hardiness. The type ('Guinevere') originated from the above-mentioned cross, while the other cultivars are simply seedlings of the type.

(Descriptions of the cultivars may be found on p. 384.)

S. josikaea Jacq. f. Hungarian Lilac. Shrub, stiffly upright, 3–4 m high, branches stiff, glabrous, with a few lenticels; leaves broad elliptic, 6–12 cm long, finely ciliate, dark green above, blue-green to whitish beneath (!), venation with scattered pubescence; flowers in narrow, 10–15(20) cm long, finely pubescent, normally erect panicles, dark violet, corolla tube 10–15 mm long, corolla lobes usually more or less erect, not outspread even on faded flowers (!), anthers not exserted. MLi 11–15; BM 3278. Hungary, Galicia. 1830. z4 Fig. 273.

'Eximia' (Froebel 1898). Panicles and flowers larger, light red at first, later more pink. MG 16: 561; MD 1907: 262.

'H. Zabel' (Froebel 1899). Habit more compact; flowers more reddish, fading to whitish.

'Rubra' (Hartwig 1885). Flowers reddish violet.

S. julianae Schneid. Shrub, scarcely over 2 m high, sprawling habit, branches thin, very tomentose (!!); leaves elliptic-ovate, finely acuminate, 3–6 cm long, base rounded, dark green, appressed pubescent above, underside very pubescent; flowers in 5–10 cm long, very fragrant (!) panicles, violet-purple, tube 6–8 mm long,

calyx violet, May–June, MLi 61–66; BM 8423 (= *S. verrucosa* Schneid.). W. China. 1900. z6 Fig. 271.

S. koehneana see: **S. patula**

S. komarowii Schneid. Shrub, 3–4 m high, shoots light brown, warty, soft pubescent at first; leaves oval-oblong to oblong-lanceolate, 7–15 cm long, tapered to both ends, acuminate, glabrous above, soft pubescent beneath; flowers purple-pink, lighter exterior, in dense, ovate, nodding panicles, corolla lobes erect, not reflexed (!), anthers usually somewhat exserted, June. MLi 29–33 (= *S. sargentiana* Schneid.). W. China. 1911. z6 Fig. 273.

S. laciniata Mill. Shrub, very similar to *S. persica,* but the first leaves on the new growth pinnately cleft or 3–9 lobed, later leaves unlobed (!!), summer leaves simple; flowers light purple, in loose, lateral, 7 cm long panicles, fragrant, corolla tube 7 mm long. BS 2: 570; MLi 140–147 (= *S. persica* var. *laciniata* West.). NW. China, Kansu. 1768. z5 Plate 133; Fig. 272.

About 20 hybrids of *S. laciniata × S. vulgaris* ('Lavender Lady') were developed and named by J. Sobeck in Descano Gardens, La Canada, California, USA in 1955. They are listed, but not described, in Arnoldia 1966: 13–14.

S. meyeri Schneid. Small, dense growing shrub, 1–1.5 m high, branches slightly quadrangular, somewhat pubescent at first; leaves elliptic-ovate, 2–4 cm long, green on both sides, pubescent on the venation beneath, with 2 parallel vein pairs running from the base nearly to the apex; flowers violet, in about 8 cm long, dense, pubescent panicles, corolla very slender tubular, 15 mm long, May–June. MLi 86–91. N. China; Chile; 1923. Cultivar, not known in the wild. Very valuable in cultivation for its ability to flower on very young plants (rooted cuttings!). z5

'Palibin'. Lower, densely bushy shrub; flowers in small, but very numerous panicles at the shoot tips, buds purple-red, opening whitish pink, very attractive, June. Introduced by the Wayside Gardens Nursery, Mentor, Ohio, USA as *S. palibiniana*, later also introduced by Skinner of Dropmore, Manitoba, Canada as *S. microphylla* 'Minor'.

S. microphylla Diels. Small, bushy, broadly upright shrub, 1–1.5 m high, branches thin, soft pubescent; leaves rounded-ovate to elliptic-ovate, 1–4 cm long, rounded at the base, gray-green beneath, somewhat pubescent and ciliate; flowers in 4–7 cm long, finely pubescent panicles, corolla narrowly tubular, to 1 cm long, lilac, very fragrant, lobes lanceolate, calyx "helmet"-shaped, June; fruits frequently curved, warty. MLi 74–79 (= *S. dielsiana* Schneid.; *S. schneideri* Lingelsh.). N. China. 1910. z4 Fig. 273.

'Minor' see: **S. meyeri** 'Palibin'

'Superba' (Cassegrain). Primarily differing in the very long flowering period, May–October, and the pink-red, later lighter flowers. Grandes Rosaries du Val de Loire, Orléans, France. 1934.

S. × nanceiana McKelvey (*S. henryi* × *S. sweginzowii*). Shrub, to 3 m high; leaves like those of *S. henryi*, but somewhat smaller; inflorescence and flower form like *S. sweginzowii*. Developed before 1925 by Lemoine in Nancy, France.

'Floréal'. The type of the cross. Plate 132.

'Rutilant'. (Description, see cultivar list p. 385.)

S. oblata Lindl. Shrub, 2.5–4 m high, occasionally also a small tree, branches glabrous; leaves rounded cordate to kidney-shaped (!), 4–10 cm wide, sharply acuminate, tough, bronze-green, later glossy green on both sides, somewhat lighter beneath, wine-red in fall; flowers pale purple-lilac, in 6–12 cm long, loose, wide panicles, fragrant, corolla 10–12 mm long, late April–May. BM 7806; MLi 92 to 94; GF 1: 221. N. China. 1859. Similar to *S. vulgaris*, but flowering much earlier, leaves differing in form. z4 Fig. 271.

'Alba'. Shoots more gray; leaves thinner, green on the new growth; flowers somewhat smaller, white (= *S. affinis* L. Henry). Before 1902.

var. **dilatata** (Nakai) Rehd. Leaves ovate, acuminate, to 12 cm long, base rounded, totally glabrous; inflorescences looser, with leaves interspersed throughout, corolla 10–12 mm long, purple-violet. MLi 100–106; NK 10: 18. Korea. Differing from the species in the foliage and open habit. ⌖

var. **giraldii** (Lemoine) Rehd. Taller than the species; leaves much more acuminate, base more often broadly cuneate than cordate, soft pubescent, young leaves ciliate; inflorescences glabrous, slender, 10–15 cm long, calyx and flower stalks purple-violet, corolla purple-lilac. MLi 95–99; RH 1909: 335. N. China. 1895. Fig. 271.

var. **hupehensis** Pamp. Leaves broad cordate-ovate, 5.5–7 cm long, 3.5–6 cm wide, underside more or less persistently pubescent; limb finely ciliate; fruit capsule rather short, beaked, 11 mm long. China; Hupeh Prov.

S. palibiniana Nakai, see: **S. patula**

S. palibiniana Hort. non Nakai, see: **S. meyeri** 'Palibin'

S. patula (Palib.) Nakai. Shrub, to 3 m high, young shoots purple, often glandular, angular, finely pubescent; leaves ovate to lanceolate, 6–8 cm long, base broadly cuneate, dull green above, finely loosely pubescent, gray beneath, densely finely tomentose; flowers in 10–15 cm long, finely pubescent panicles, corolla 8–10 mm long, narrowly tubular, lilac, white interior, fragrant, lobes acute and narrow, recurved, anthers violet, May–June. MLi 67–73; NK 10: 20 (= *S. velutina* Komar.; *S. palibiniana* Nakai; *S. koehneana* Schneid.; *Ligustrum patulum* Palib.). Korea, N. China. 1910. z4 Plate 136; Fig. 271.

S. pekinensis Rupr. Shrub, 2.5–5 m high, glabrous, broadly sprawling, bark mirror smooth (!), young shoots brownish, thin, warty; leaves ovate to more lanceolate, 5–10 cm long, long acuminate, base usually cuneate, rich green above, more gray-green beneath, totally glabrous; flowers yellowish white, in 10–15 cm long, dense panicles, scented like *Ligustrum*, glabrous, anthers distinctly exserted, June. MLi 166–171; GF 3: 165. N. China. 1881. z5

S. × persica L. (earlier considered a separate species, but regarded today as a hybrid of *S. afghanica* × *S. laciniata*, possibly the fixed juvenile form of *S. laciniata*). Shrub, to 2 m high, bushy, young branches somewhat angular, smooth; leaves lanceolate, 3–6 cm long, acuminate, occasionally somewhat pinnate or 3 lobed; inflorescences 5–8 cm long, glabrous, corolla purple-lilac, 1 cm long, fragrant, May. BM 486; MLi 143, 146, 148; DB 1954: 122. Distributed throughout western Asia, but not in the wild, rather somewhat naturalized. 1640. z5 Plate 133; Fig. 271. ⌖

'Alba'. Flowers white to whitish. 1770.

var. *laciniata* see: **S. laciniata**

S. pinetorum W. W. Sm. (similar to *S. julianae*). Shrub, to 2 m high; branches densely pubescent; leaves oval-lanceolate, 2–4 cm long, thinly pubescent to glabrous above, venation pubescent beneath; flowers purple-violet, in 10–18 cm long panicles, calyx glabrous, teeth ciliate, anthers yellow, May–June. SW. China. 1923. z7

S. pinnatifolia Hemsl. Small shrub, to 3 m high in its habitat, delicately branched, bark exfoliating; leaves pinnate, 8 cm long, leaflets 9–11, sessile, ovate to lanceolate, 1–3 cm long, finely ciliate; flowers white to pale pink, in 3–7 cm long, axillary panicles, corolla narrowly tubular, 10 mm long, early May. MLi 149–154. W. China. 1906. Attractive plant, but of no particular garden value. z5 Plate 136; Fig. 272.

S. potaninii Schneid. Closely related to *S. julianae*, but to 3 m high; leaves ovate to more elliptic, 3–6 cm long,

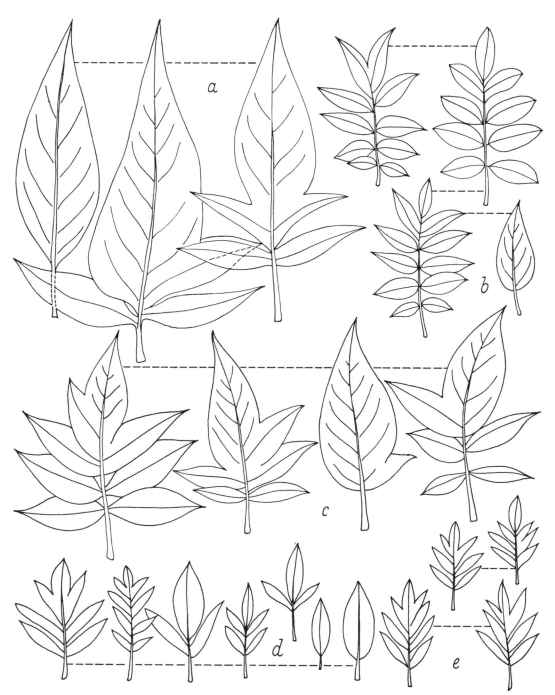

Fig. 272. **Syringa** with pinnate leaves. a. *S. diversifolia* 'William H. Judd'; b. *S. pinnatifolia*
c. *S. diversifolia* 'Nouveau'; d. *S. laciniata*; e. *S. afghanica* (Original)

rather thinly pubescent above, long haired beneath, usually short acuminate, petiole 2–5 mm long; flowers white to purple-pink, in erect, loose, conical, 7–15 cm long panicles, fragrant, calyx often pubescent, anthers yellow, June. BM 9060; MLi 144. W. China. 1905. z6 Fig. 271.

S. × prestoniae McKelvey (*S. reflexa* × *S. villosa*). Tall shrubs, similar to *S. villosa* in foliage and habit, but the inflorescences nodding like those of *S. reflexa*. Hybridized by Isabella Preston in Ottawa, Ontario, Canada since 1920. Very significant plant for northern N. America for its hardiness since *S. vulgaris* cultivars are often not sufficiently hardy. z2 ⊕

For the cultivars, see p. 384.

S. pubescens Turcz. Shrub, to 2 m high or more, broadly erect habit, branches thin, angular, glabrous, flushed with violet at first; leaves rounded-ovate, 3–7 cm long, short acuminate, ciliate, dark green and glabrous above, underside gray pubescent, particularly on the venation; flowers lilac-pink, conspicuously fading, in 7–12 cm long, dense panicles, tube thin, 1.5 cm long, very sweetly scented, April–May. BM 7064 (as *S. villosa*); MLi 80–85; DRHS 2070. N. China. 1881. Valued for its early flowering period. z6 Fig. 271. ⊕

S. reflexa Schneid. Shrub, about 3 m high, erect; leaves oblong-ovate, 8–15 cm long, acuminate, tough, dark green above, glabrous, gray-green beneath, soft pubescent on the venation; flowers in narrow, 10–16 cm long, nodding panicles, wine-red to dark pink on the exterior, interior nearly white, limb whitish; fruits 1.2 cm long, recurved, June. BM 8869; MLi 21–28; Bai 20: 81. Central China. 1910. Very attractive, abundantly flowering, hardy. z5 Plate 132; Fig. 273. ⊕

S. reticulata (Blume) Hara. Japanese Tree Lilac. Large shrub to small tree, stem short, crown oval, branches glossy, reddish, older branches with exfoliating bark; leaves broad ovate, 5–14 cm long, long acuminate, bright green, blue-green and soft pubescent beneath (at least when young); flowers yellowish white, in up to 30 cm long, strongly scented inflorescences, late June–July. DL 1: 18; KIF 1: 99; BM 7534; GF 2: 293 (= *S. amurensis* var. *japonica* [Maxim.] Franch. & Sav.). N. Japan. 1876. z4 ⊕

var. **mandschurica** (Maxim.) Hara. Amur Lilac. Usually a broad shrub, 3–4 m high and wide, branches gray; leaves ovate to broadly elliptic, abruptly long acuminate, 5–12 cm long, base round to cuneate, glabrous, dark green above, underside lighter to more bluish green; flowers white to cream-white, in 10–18 cm long, terminal panicles, not fragrant, erect to outspread, corolla lobes spreading outward, later reflexed, anthers somewhat exserted, June. MLi 155–159; GF 2: 271 (= *S. amurensis* Rupr.). Manchuria, N. China. 1876.

S. rhodopea Velenovsky. Medium-sized shrub, intermediate in appearance between *S. vulgaris* and *S. oblata*; leaves broadly ovate, base slightly cordate; panicles to 20 cm long, outspread, calyx short campanulate, as long as wide, very short toothed, corolla tube 8 mm long, lilac, limb very often with 5 (!) lobes; fruit acuminate. Bulgaria; Rhodope Mts. 1922. z6

S. rothomagensis see: **S. × chinensis**

S. sargentiana see: **S. komarowii**

S. schneideri see: **S. microphylla**

S. × skinneri F. Skinner. Hybrids between *S. patula* and *S. pubescens*, intermediate between the parents in general appearance; flowers mauve-lilac, usually opening to white, in large, to 20 cm wide panicles, fragrant. 1966. z4

S. × swegiflexa Hesse (*S. reflexa* × *S. sweginzowii*). Similar to *S. reflexa*, but with larger and denser inflorescences, buds deep red, flowers dark pink, later lighter. Developed by Hesse of Weener, W. Germany in 1935. z6 Plate 132.

S. sweginzowii Koehne & Lingelsh. Shrub, to 3 m high, branches purple-brown, glabrous; leaves ovate to oblong, 5–10 cm long, abruptly acuminate, dark green above, lighter green beneath; panicles erect, loose, glabrous to finely pubescent, to 20 cm long, corolla 11 mm wide, exterior flesh-pink, whitish on the interior, throat carmine-red, tube 8 mm long, anthers stopping at the corolla limb, style 2 mm longer than the calyx margin, June. MD 1932: 53; Gw 28: 41; MLi 55–60; Bai 20: 81. NW. China. 1914. z6 Plate 132; Fig. 271.

'Superba' (Lemoine). Leaves long acuminate, oblong-elliptic, 10–14 cm long, much lighter beneath, venation more pubescent, petioles reddish; inflorescences like those of the species, flowers whitish, pink on the interior, anthers terminating about 2 mm from the corolla limb, styles only slightly longer than the calyx. MD 1932: 53. Selected by Lemoine. 1915. ⊕

S. tigerstedtii H. Sm. Shrub, to 3 m high, divaricate, similar to *S. yunnanensis*, but lower, branches thin; leaves ovate, acuminate, 3–8 cm long, base round, widest beneath the middle, glabrous above, greenish white beneath, venation pubescent; flowers in terminal, foliate, to 20 cm long panicles, corolla whitish lilac, 8 mm long, fragrant, June. W. China. 1934. Can or possibly should be included in *S. yunnanensis*. z6 Fig. 273. ⊕

S. tomentella Bur. & Franch. Shrub, to 3 m high, young shoots thin, brownish, thinly pubescent; leaves oblong and ciliate; flowers in 15 cm long and 12 cm wide, terminal, foliate panicles, corolla pale lilac-pink on the exterior, interior white, to 10 mm long, lobes lanceolate, fragrant, anthers reaching to the throat, June. MLi 48–54; BM 8739 (= *S. wilsonii* Schneid.). W. China. 1904. z6 Fig. 273. ⊕

S. velutina see: **S. patula**

S. velutina 'Excellens' see: **S. × prestoniae** cultivars, 'Excellens'

S. verrucosa see: **S. julianae**

S. villosa Vahl. Shrub, 3–4 m high, branches rather thick, glabrous; leaves broad ovate, 5–15 cm long, rich green above, blue-green and loosely pubescent beneath, at least on the midrib; flowers pink-lilac, in 10–25 cm long, dense, finely pubescent panicles, corolla tube 12 mm long, lobes erect, late May–June. MLi 34–49; BM 8292 (as

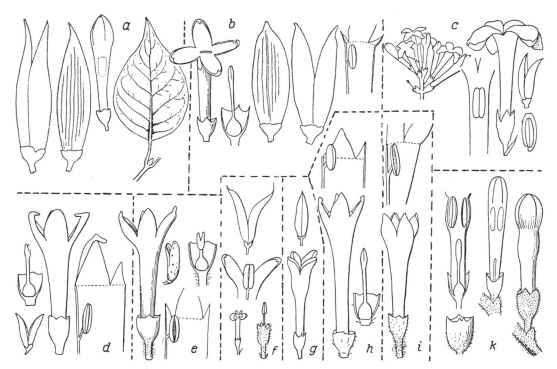

Fig. 273. **Syringa**. a. *S. tigerstedtii;* b. *S. yunnanensis;* c. *S. villosa;* d. *S. wolfii;* e. *S. reflexa;* f. *S. emodi;* g. *S. josikaea;* h. *S. komarowii;* i. *S. tomentella;* k. *S. microphylla* (from Koehne, Schneider, H. Smith)

S. bretschneideri); Bai 20: 80. N. China. 1885. See also: **S. wolfii.** z2 Fig. 273. ✣

S. vulgaris L. Lilac. Shrub or small tree, seldom higher than 7 m; leaves ovate to broad ovate, acuminate, 5–12 cm long, glabrous; flowers in 10–20 cm long panicles, lilac on the type. MLi 119–133; BM 183. SE. Europe. Cultivated since antiquity. Available today in about 800 cultivars including white, lilac, bluish, reddish and violet colors, single and double. Ⓕ Norway, W. Germany, Denmark, in windbreaks. z4 Fig. 271. ✣

For cultivar descriptions, please refer to the cultivar list at the end of this section.

S. wardii W. W. Smith. Shrub, 2–4 m high, shoots thin, pale gray pubescent when young; leaves broad ovate to nearly circular, 1–2 cm long and wide, apex and base rounded, deep green above, glabrous, lighter beneath, reticulately veined, petiole 2–3 mm; flowers in about 10 cm long and 7 cm wide, loose, erect, densely white pubescent panicles, corolla tube 6–10 mm long, tubular, limb tips round to acute, apex distinctly hooked, limb 6–10 mm wide, anthers yellow. China; Yunnan Prov. Closely related to *S. microphylla.* z6

S. wolfii Schneid. Shrub, to 5 m high, branches smooth, with only a few lenticels; leaves elliptic-oblong, 10–15 cm long, dark green above, gray-green beneath, long acuminate, underside with finely pubescent venation; flowers in 20–30 cm long, foliate and finely pubescent panicles, corolla 15–18 mm long, lilac, fragrant, lobes

erect, anthers light yellow, enclosed within the tube, not exserted. MLi 16–20; NK 10: 24 (= *S. villosa* Komar. non Vahl; *S. formosissima* Nakai). Korea, Manchuria. 1909. z4 Fig. 273.

S. yunnanensis Franch. Shrub, to 3 m high, thinly branched, shoots reddish, warty, glabrous; leaves oblong-lanceolate, acute at both ends, 3–8 cm long, slightly ciliate, bluish green beneath; flowers light pink, in erect, loosely pubescent, 8–15 cm long panicles, corolla lobes directed upward, fragrant, calyx reddish, glabrous, June. MLi 6–10. China; Yunnan Prov. 1907. z6 Fig. 273. ✣

'Rosea'. Flowers an attractive pure pink, fading somewhat lighter, in long, slender panicles. Developed by Hillier.

List of the Cultivars
of *Syringa vulgaris* including the Early Flowering Hybrids

Hybridizing of lilacs has only been done primarily over the last 100 years. As pointed out by Meyer, only 25 cultivars were known in 1850. Around 1875, V. Lemoine began hybridizing lilacs in Nancy, France. He brought no fewer than 214 new hybrids into the trade. Of these, many are not only still widely cultivated today, but have never been surpassed by more recent hybrids. Other hybridizers include Späth (Berlin, W. Germany), Pfitzer (Stuttgart, W. Germany), Stepman (Belgium) and Dunbar (USA). After 1920 many more American hybrids were developed by Klager, Havemeyer and Clarke. The first double flowering form ('Azurea Plena') was developed in 1843 by Libert-Darimont in Belgium.

Of the approximately 900 cultivars grown today, a much larger number are no longer in cultivation because of their small or less attractive flower panicles. The largest lilac collections and largest selection of lilacs is found in the USA. The only significant collections in Europe are in Aalsmeer, Holland (neglected in recent times and hardly worth seeing!) and Dortmund, W. Germany.

Many years of experience and systematic testing of lilac hybrids has been done in the USA. This has resulted in well evaluated and appraised cultivars, as is evidenced in the following list (the more asterisks, the better the plant).

All hybrids of uncited parentage belong to *S. vulgaris;* the "early flowering hybrids" are noted by "*giraldii* Hybrid" (for *S. vulgaris* × *S. oblata* var. *giraldii*). For cultivars not listed here, see the late flowering cultivar list on p. 384.

'Adelaide Dunbar' (Dunbar, named in 1916) [Seedling of 'Alaine Mocqueris']. Panicles long, narrow, loose, individual flowers semidouble, occasionally double, lobes irregularly twisted, deep purple. ***

'Alice Harding' (Lemoine 1938) [Earlier known as 'Souvenir d'Alice Harding"]. White. A novelty but not well known. **

'Alphonse Lavallée' (Lemoine 1885). Panicles conical, medium-sized, flowers star-shaped, medium-sized, lobes acute, a good lilac-blue, buds purple. Very popular plant. ***

'Ambassadeur' (Lemoine 1930). Flowers light azure-blue, center nearly white. Pretty, but the panicles are easily broken by rain and wind. ***

'Ami Schott' (Lemoine 1933). Flowers deep cobalt-blue with a lighter back side. ***

'Andenken an Ludwig Späth' (Späth 1883). Panicles to 30 cm long, narrow, symmetrical, flowering abundantly, individual flowers large, lobes somewhat hood-like and inclined together in a cupulate fashion, dark purple-red. Never surpassed for color. ***

'Buffon' (Lemoine 1921) [*giraldii* Hybrid]. Panicles loose, flowers pink, lobes reflexed. ***

'Capitaine Baltet' (Lemoine 1919). Panicles stout, broad at the base, lateral branchlets spreading, loosely covered with flowers, individual flowers very large, lobes wide, often curved, acute and convex, but not turned up at the margins, eventually forming a flat flower, tube slender, anthers easily visible, dull light purple-lilac. The whole flower attractive and evenly colored. ***

'Capitaine Perrault' (Lemoine 1925). Panicles large, flowers densely double, large, mauve-pink, very late, buds the same color. **

'Catinat' (Lemoine 1923) [*giraldii* Hybrid]. Panicles large, loose, individual flowers medium-sized, lobes narrow, acute, reflexed, anthers exserted, pink. *** Plate 134.

'Cavour' (Lemoine 1910). Panicles long, erect, full, conical, individual flowers medium-sized, lobes somewhat convex, violet-blue. DB 12: 94. ***

'Charles Joly' (Lemoine 1896). Panicles short and compact, flowers very abundantly, individual flowers large, asymmetrical, well developed double, lobes wide or narrow, round or acute, purple-red, the inner lobes often curve inward showing the lighter back side, giving the flower a bicolored appearance. Very popular!

'Charles X'. (Audibert, before 1831). Panicles medium-sized, symmetrical, lobes wide, convex, round to somewhat acute,

lilac-red. A strong grower but the panicles are not as good today (according to reports from Holland) as they were on plants 40–50 years ago; flower color and panicle size become less effective with age, doubtlessly a degeneration phenomenon. Less utilized in Europe today but still rating *** in the USA.

'Cheyenne' [*S. oblata*]. Shrub, to 2.5 m high and wide; flowers soft blue, very fragrant. Developed from seed collected in China in 1930 and given to the trade by the USDA in 1971.

'Christophe Colomb' (Lemoine 1905). Panicles usually in double pairs at the branch tips, long, conical, dense and well formed, individual flowers large, symmetrical, lobes round, salverform spreading, soft lilac. DB 12: 98. A gorgeous form. ***

'Clarkes Giant' (Clarke 1948). Panicles very large, conical, flowers single, soft blue, to 3 cm (!) wide, buds pink-lilac; the leaves are also larger than those of the other forms.

'Congo' (Lemoine 1896). Habit not particularly good; panicles compact, loose, individual flowers large, lobes wide, convex, symmetrical, anthers easily visible, purple-red, fading to a dull purple, lighter limbed on the backside. Not always true to name in the trade! ***

'Decaisne' (Lemoine 1910). Compact habit; panicles medium-sized to large, light blue, buds more lilac-blue, easily sets buds and extraordinarily floriferous. DB 12: 58. One of the bluest forms. ***

'De Miribel' (Lemoine 1903). Panicles large, densely conical, lobes broadly rounded, buds blackish violet, violet-blue when fully open. ***

'Diderot' (Lemoine 1915). Panicles very long and narrow, segmented, individual flowers very large, lobes conspicuously pouch form, anthers visible, dull purple, dorsal side somewhat darker, therefore giving a bicolor impression, mid to late season.

'Diplomate' (Lemoine 1930). Flowers blue, lasting very well, particularly through rain and wind. ***

'Duc de Massa' (Lemoine 1905). Panicles large, wide, lateral branchlets spreading, dense, individual flowers very large, 2 corollas (one inside the other), lobes wide, acute, eventually widespreading, bluish lilac, exterior also somewhat white, buds purple. ***

'Edith Cavell' (Lemoine 1916). Inflorescences large and long, individual flowers semidouble, very large, lobes somewhat inward curving, cream-white, milk-white when fully open. DB 12: 62. Highly valued. Plate 135.

'Edmond Boissier' (Lemoine 1906). Panicles large, long, broadly conical, individual flowers very large, asymmetrical, lobes narrow or wide, acute or round, light purple at first, then darkening, becoming more violet-purple. ***

'Emil Gentil' (Lemoine 1915). Panicles short, dense and wide, individual flowers very large, tube short, lobes wide and acute, occasionally round, spreading at right angles, light cobalt-blue. A rare color among the forms. **

'Esther Staley' (Clarke 1948) [*giraldii* Hybrid]. JRHS 1959: 161. In America generally considered to be the best single flowered, clear pink form.

'Etna' (Lemoine 1927). Weak grower; panicles not particularly well developed, flowers deep purple-red. Perhaps the darkest red form, but not yet perfected.

'Firmament' (Lemoine 1932). Similar to 'Ambassadeur'. Light azure-blue. ***

'General Pershing' (Lemoine 1924). Panicles very long, with long lateral branchlets at the base, dense, individual flowers partly double (2 corollas inside one another), partly single and with only a few lobes at the tube opening, asymmetrical, lobes wide or narrow, rolled distinctly inward, occasionally convex, purple-pink, dorsal side whitish lilac, bicolor effect from the easily visible backside. Garden merit quite variable.

'Gilbert' (Lemoine 1911). Panicles long, loose, branches widespreading, individual flowers usually particularly large, lobes wide, acuminate, distinctly hook form at the apex, horizontally spreading, bluish, anthers hardly visible.

'Henri Martin' (Lemoine 1912). Panicles long, dense, heavy, widely branched, individual flowers semi- to fully double, lobes spreading at right angles or inward curving, rounded, pure lilac, buds purple. ***

'Hippolyte Maringer' (Lemoine 1909). Panicles long, narrow, with ascending lateral branchlets, loose, individual flowers large, lobes round, somewhat crispate, lilac-pink, exterior whitish, buds carmine.

'Hugo de Vries' (K. Keessen 1927). Vigorous habit, erect; panicles large and very long, loose, individual flowers large, dark purple, even somewhat darker than 'Andenken an Ludwig Späth', but not surpassing the latter. Particularly good for forcing.

'Hugo Koster' (Koster 1914). Panicles medium-sized, loose, conical, individual flowers small, lilac, flowering rather abundantly. Particularly good for forcing.

'Hyazinthenflieder' (Späth 1906). Panicles long, narrow, somewhat irregular, individual flowers large, lobes narrow, recurved, purple-lilac with a light blue center, buds light red. Not to be confused with *Syringa hyacinthiflora*!

'Jacques Callot' (Lemoine 1876). Panicles large and loose, individual flowers very large, lobes convex, distinctly lilac colored. ***

'Jan van Tol' (van Tol 1916). Panicles long, but too heavy for the rather slight stalk, individual flowers pure white, 2.5–3 cm in diameter, fragrance very strong, pure white. Popular for forcing, not particularly for the garden. *** Plate 135.

'J. de Messemaeker' (Stepman 1908). Panicles long, narrow, symmetrical, loose, individual flowers large, lobes wide, convex, overlapping, spreading salverform, deep wine-red, somewhat darker on the backside.

'Jean Macé' (Lemoine 1915). Panicles large, long, broadly pyramidal, dense, individual flowers large, asymmetrical, lobes wide or narrow, acute, either spreading at right angles or recurved, mauve-pink, fading to bluish, buds purple-red. **

'Jeanne d'Arc' (Lemoine 1902). Buds cream-white, opening white, usually with 2 corollas superimposed and wider lobes, globose at first, later more flat spreading, late. ***

'Jules Ferry' (Lemoine 1907). Panicles wide branched at the base, irregularly double, loose, individual flowers double or semidouble, large, asymmetrical, lobes round, occasionally convex, inward curving, silvery pink, buds carmine-pink. **

'Katherine Havemeyer' (Lemoine 1922). Strong grower; panicles medium-sized to large, often interrupted with foliage at the base of lateral branchlets, broadly conical, individual flowers semi- to densely double, lobes rounded or acute, cobalt-lilac, with a trace of pink, purple-pink on the dorsal side,

buds lilac-pink. Generally very meritorious. ***

'Lamartine' (Lemoine 1911) [*giraldii* Hybrid]. Shrub, strong growing, erect; panicles about 20 cm long, flowers large, lobes rounded, light lilac-pink, buds light purple, late April. Very meritorious.

'Laplace' (Lemoine 1913) Panicles very large, lateral branchlets widespreading, loose, individual flowers very large, purple-red, lobes wide, margin conspicuously raised and tabular, anthers not visible, somewhat lighter limbed on the backside.

'Lavender Lady' (W. E. Lammerts, Livermore, California, 1954) [*S. vulgaris* × *S. laciniata*]. Open habit; flowers purple, single, fragrant. Patented in the USA.

'Léon Gambetta' (Lemoine 1907). Panicles narrow, long, symmetrical, individual flowers large, densely double, lobes wide or narrow, mostly acute, lilac-pink, buds red, very early. DB 12: 61. Also good for forcing. *** Plate 135.

'Louvois' (Lemoine 1921 [*giraldii* Hybrid]. Panicles attractively erect, with wide branching at the base, individual flowers medium-sized, normally single, but also occasionally with a few lobes at the opening of the corolla tube, lobes narrow, asymmetrical, purple-violet with a bluish trace. ***

'Lucie Baltet' (Baltet, before 1888). Panicles large, erect, loose, individual flowers medium-sized, lobes round, convex, nearly flesh colored or dark pink, more brownish red in bud, anthers distinctly visible. Very distinct and popular color. ***

'Lutèce' (Henry 1900) [*S. Henry*]. Flowers pale violet, eventually nearly white. Popular late flowering form.

'Macrostachya' (Lefièvre, before 1874). Panicles long, narrow, conical, erect, loose, individual flowers medium-sized, symmetrical, lobes convex, anthers visible, soft pink, fading to nearly white. DB 12: 99. One of the oldest forms and still very popular. ***

'Maiden's Blush' (F. L. Skinner 1966) [*S. microphylla* 'Superba' × (*S. oblata dilata* × *S. vulgaris*) hybrid]. Shrub, to 1.5 m high, habit very compact; leaves like those of *S. oblata*, but smaller; flowers medium-sized, pure pink, usually in several erect panicles at the shoot tips, in large clusters.

'Marceau' (Lemoine 1913). Somewhat tall thin habit; panicles somewhat conical, loose, individual flowers large, lobes wide, acute, convex, anthers easily visible, deep purple. ***

'Marc Micheli' (Lemoine 1898). Panicles long, narrow, dense, often with leaves at the base of the panicle branchlets, individual flowers large, very densely arranged, globose, with 2 distinct corollas at first, later less conspicuous, lobes often curved inward, interior soft lilac-pink, nearly white on the exterior, bicolored in effect. ***

'Maréchal Foch' (Lemoine 1924). Good habit, good bud set; panicles very large, lateral branchlets widespreading, individual flowers very large, symmetrical, lobes wide, round or somewhat acute, occasionally convex and inward curving, carmine-pink, becoming more mauve-lilac. Generally quite meritorious. ***

'Maréchal Lannes' (Lemoine 1910). Panicles dense and wide, erect and a good double, individual flowers double to occasionally single, pale violet, buds more violet-red. ***

'Marie Legraye' (Legraye 1879). Panicles medium-sized, pure white. DB 12: 97. Distinctive in the nursery for its crooked branches. Recently more and more surpassed by 'Mme. Florent Stepman', but still significant as an early, dependable form for forcing. ***

'Masséna' (Lemoine 1923). Low growing, resembling 'Marceau' (but lower), poorly branched; panicles wide at the base, loose, individual flowers very large, symmetrical, lobes wide, round, convex, margin nearly tabular, upturned at the margin, deep purple. DB 12: 65. Attractive as an old plant.

'Maurice Barrès' (Lemoine 1917). Panicles large, loose, well branched, individual flowers particularly large, lobes narrow, inward curving, convex, light azure-lilac, flowering very abundantly. DB 12: 3. ***

'Maximowicz' (Lemoine 1906). Panicles very long, broadly conical, loose, flowers semidouble, occasionally also single, lobes wide, acuminate, curved, purple-violet, somewhat lighter on the dorsal side. DB 12:95.

'Michel Buchner' (Lemoine 1885). Panicles long, narrow, with spreading lateral branchlets, individual flowers very consistent, about 1.5 cm wide, with 3 superimposed corollas, lobes imbricately overlapping, lilac, interior with a white "eye". Still propagated primarily for its ease of cultivation in the nursery.

'Mirabeau' (Lemoine 1911) [giraldii Hybrid]. Panicles large, double, individual flowers large, lobes widest in the middle, reflexed, lilac-pink, very early. *** Plate 134.

'Miss Ellen Willmott' (Lemoine 1903). Snow-white, flowers very large and and fully developed, late. Generally very meritorious.

'Mme. Abel Chatenay' (Lemoine 1892). Panicles asymmetrical, with leaves at the base, flowers white, semidouble, lobes acuminate or rounded.

'Mme. Antoine Buchner' (Lemoine 1909). Panicles long and narrow, but stout, individual flowers densely double, usually with 3 superimposed corollas, therefore more lobed at the tube opening, lobes narrow, often curving inward, a soft mauve-pink, late, buds large, oblong dark purple-brown. DB 12: 100. Quite meritorious form. Plate 134.

'Mme. Casimir Perier' (Lemoine 1894). Buds cream-white, opening to just short of a pure white, double. Despite the good habit and abundant flowers, surpassed today by 'Edith Cavell'. ***

'Mme. Lemoine' (Lemoine 1890). Shoots stout and long; flowers pure white, lobes round and curved, late. DB 12: 59. Always one of the best double white forms; excellent for forcing. Generally highly meritorious. ***

'Monge' (Lemoine 1913). Panicles long, symmetrical, pyramidal, loose, individual flowers very large, lobes narrow, inward curving, dark purple-red, flowering very abundantly. ***

'Montaigne' (Lemoine 1907). Panicles long and narrow, loose, individual flowers distinctly with 2 corollas, lobes acute, often inward curving, soft pink, turning to lilac-white, buds purple-pink. ***

'Monique Lemoine' (Lemoine 1939). Flowers pure white, double, in very large panicles. Plate 125.

'Mont Blanc' (Lemoine 1915). Panicles very large, symmetrical, lobes round, late. DB 12: 60. *** Plate 134.

'Montesquieu' (Lemoine 1926) [giraldii Hybrid]. Panicles large, well branched, individual flowers large, lobes nearly circular, forming an even surface, purple-lilac. DB 12: 106. ***

'Monument' (Lemoine 1934). Quite meritorious cultivar. ***

'Mrs. Edward Harding' (Lemoine 1923). Panicles large, broad at the base, flowers large, double, asymmetrical, lobes long, narrow, distinctly inward curving, light purple-red, turning an attractive purple-pink. Perhaps the best of the double reds. Generally highly valued.

'Mrs. W. E. Marshall' (Havemeyer 1924). Panicles narrowly pyramidal, individual flowers medium-sized, lobes narrow, limb raised, acute, somewhat inward curving, opens deep purple, then slowly becoming lighter, flowers abundantly. ***

'Murillo' (Lemoine 1901). Panicles medium-sized, obtuse, individual flowers medium-sized, with 3 superimposed corollas, buds oblong, light red, opening purple-lilac with a white "eye".

'Necker' (Lemoine 1921) [giraldii Hybrid]. Young leaves very slightly bronze; panicles large, wide at the base, but loose, individual flowers large, symmetrical, lobes convex, pale pink, very early. Flower color very similar to that of 'Lucie Baltet'. ***

'Oliver de Serres' (Lemoine 1909). Panicles very large and well formed, individual flowers very large, asymmetrical, outer lobes broad and rounded, inner ones narrow, acute or round and often inward curving, lavender-blue when fully open, buds purple-blue, abundantly flowering only on older plants. Generally highly rated.

'Pasteur' (Lemoine 1903). Panicles long and narrow, always with 2 heads, individual flowers very large, symmetrical, lobes wide, convex, limb raised, dark purple. BD 12:67.

'Paul Deschanel' (Lemoine 1924). Panicles elegant, attractive, abundantly flowering, flowers light purple to purple-pink, a good double, buds carmine.

'Paul Hariot' (Lemoine 1902) Panicles long and narrow, a good double, individual flowers large, asymmetrical, lobes acute or rounded, wide, globose, interior deep violet-red, silvery on the dorsal side, hence bicolor in effect.

'Paul Thirion' (Lemoine 1915). Panicles large, nearly hemispherical, with a broad base, densely double, individual flowers large, asymmetrical, with 2 superimposed corollas, lobes broad, rounded or acute, occasionally inward curving, corolla tube short, dark purple-red, buds darker. ***

'Pocahontas' (Skinner 1935). Flowers single, purple. ***

'Président Fallières' (Lemoine 1911). Panicles large, open, lateral branchlets outspread, individual flowers large, a good double, lobes wide, round or abruptly acuminate, inward curving, pure lilac-pink to whitish in the middle, late. Still valued in the USA but nearly surpassed by 'Rosace'.

'Président Grévy' (Lemoine 1886). Somewhat irregular in habit, poorly branched in the nursery; panicles large, pyramidal, loose, individual flowers large, semi- or fully double, asymmetrical, lobes round or obtusely acuminate, convex, nearly cobalt-blue, but lilac in the center, buds globose, thick, red-violet. ***

'President Lincoln' (Dunbar 1916). Panicles long, narrowly pyramidal, medium-sized to large, individual flowers medium-sized, symmetrical, lobes acute, convex, anthers easily visible, very early, pure light blue. Very unusual color. ***

'Président Loubet' (Lemoine 1901). Panicles very wide and compact, flowers abundantly, individual flowers large, semi- or fully double, asymmetrical, lobes wide or narrow, round or acute, occasionally convex, bright purple-lilac, buds carmine.

'Président Poincaré' (Lemoine 1913). Panicles often in 3 pairs, large, dense, conical, individual flowers good doubles, large, lobes round, frequently also acute, limb somewhat undulate, purple-lilac, buds purple. *****

'Président Viger' (Lemoine 1900). Panicles long and narrow, usually forked, distinctly erect, somewhat angular, individual flowers double or semidouble, light lilac-blue, buds thick, dark violet-red.

'Primrose' (Maarse 1949). [Sport of 'Marie Legraye']. Conspicuously light primrose-yellow, simple, buds more greenish yellow. First significant yellow form. ***** Plate 125.

'Princesse Clémentine' (Mathieu, before 1908). Large, loose panicles, flowers double, white, opening yellowish.

'Prodige' (Lemoine 1928). Purple-red, individual flowers to 3.5 cm across.

'Purple Heart' (Clarke 1949) [giraldii-Hybrid]. Large flowered, deep purple, single, early.

'Réaumur' (Lemoine 1904). Strong growing, bushy; panicles wide, large, long, individual flowers very large, lobes wide, round, convex when fully open, "petunia" violet. Generally highly rated.

'René Jarry-Desloges' (Lemoine 1905). Panicles large, loose, lateral branchlets spreading, individual flowers large, double or semidouble, lobes acute, somewhat convex at first, later spreading flat, azure-lilac with a trace of lilac and pink, buds purple.

'Rochester' (Grant 1971) [Seedling of 'Edith Cavell']. Slow growing, low; flowers glossy white, corolla often with 5 limb lobes, often observed with more (up to 17) lobes.

'Rosace' (Lemoine 1932). Flowers large, double, an attractive lilac-pink. Considered an improvement on 'Président Fallières'.

'Ruhm von Horstenstein' (Wilke 1921). A strong grower with good bud set; panicles somewhat short and compact, flowers deep lilac-red, buds red. MFl 33. *****

'Sensation' (D. E. Maarse 1938) [Sport of 'Hugo do Vries']. Purple-red, with broad silvery margined flowers. DB 12: 104. Plate 134.

'Thunberg' (Lemoine 1913). Panicles narrow, long, erect, very large, lateral branchlets spreading, individual flowers good doubles, often with 3 superimposed corollas, lobes acute, curving inward, dark lilac. *****

'Tombouctou' (Lemoine 1913). Panicles long, heavy, therefore often nodding, individual flowers very large, lobes wide, overlapping, spreading salverform, limb hood-shaped, violet-red, whitish on the dorsal side, limb visible. Unique.

'Toussaint-l'Ouverture' (Lemoine 1898). Panicles particularly long and narrow, segmented, leaves, rachises, calyces and young leaves on the lateral branches always bronze-red, individual flowers medium-sized, symmetrical, lobes long and narrow, anthers visible, dark purple-violet, interior somewhat lighter than the exterior.

'Vauban' (Lemoine 1913) [giraldii Hybrid]. Habit narrowly upright; panicles presented well, individual flowers semi- or fully double, lobes wide and round, soft pink. DB 12: 105.

'Vestale' (Lemoine 1910). Shrub, flowering well from base to peak, panicles pyramidal with a wide base, individual flowers somewhat similar to those of 'Mont Blanc', lobes somewhat acute and asymmetrical, tube long and thin, flowering well and early, pure white. *****

'Victor Lemoine' (Lemoine 1906). Panicles narrowly conical, long, side branchlets spreading, individual flowers large, good double, globose at first, later more spreading, lobes acute, soft lilac, buds flesh-pink. *****

'Violetta' (Lemoine 1916). Panicles long, narrow, conical, loose, flowers double to semidouble, asymmetrical, particularly large, lobes wide or narrow, round or acute, dark violet. The darkest of the double violet forms. *****

'Volcan' (Lemoine 1899). A poor grower in the nursery; panicles long, loose, very attractive form, individual flowers very large, lobes widest above the middle, conspicuously hook-form, deep purple-red.

'Waldeck-Rousseau' (Lemoine 1904). Panicles long, wide branched, loose, individual flowers medium-sized, double, round, lobes round, imbricately arranged, soft lilac-pink, white in the center. *****

Late Flowering Cultivars
(S. × prestoniae)

Covered here are North American hybrids, not as attractive as the vulgaris forms but flowering 2 weeks later, in different colors and flowering abundantly. The hybridizers are Isabella Preston, Central Experimental Farm, Ottawa, Canada (begun in 1920, but named much later) and Dr. F. L. Skinner of Dropmore, Manitoba (mostly darker to red tones).

In Poland, W. Bugala hybridized a few lilacs and named 9 prestoniae cultivars. Since these are hardly cultivated outside of Poland, the descriptions will be eliminated but their names are as follows; 'Telimena', 'Jaga', 'Basia', 'Jagienka', 'Nike', 'Goplana', 'Esterka', 'Danusia' and 'Diana'. These were developed from seed of 'Octavia' × 'Ursula'.

Parentage of cultivars belonging to S. × prestoniae is not indicated; all the others have the parents listed in brackets.

⊕ = the best forms.

'Audrey'. Purple-lilac, later nearly white on the interior, exterior pink, in dense, to 22 cm long and 12 cm wide panicles. Preston 1927.

'Bellicent' [S. josiflexa; seedling of 'Guinevere']. Reddish purple, whitish pink when fully open, panicles 15 cm long, 12 cm wide, loose. Preston.

'Coral'. The best pink form, but later fading very light, panicles to 20 cm long. Preston 1937. ⊕

'Dawn'. Reddish purple in bud and when opening, then becoming much lighter, panicles to 22 cm long, 12 cm wide, loose. Preston 1937. ⊕

'Desdemona'. Buds purple, eventually with a white interior and purple exterior, in 15 cm long and equally wide, loose panicles. Not a particulary attractive color. Preston 1927.

'Donald Wyman'. Dark pink-red, retaining its color well, panicles about 15 cm long, 12 cm wide, dense. Very attractive form. Skinner 1932. ⊕

'Elinor'. Interior light violet, exterior pale lilac, distinctive, panicles to 20 cm long. CG 130: 4. Preston 1928.

'Enid' [S. josiflexa]. Cyclamen-purple in bud and when opening, panicles to 25 cm long, 17 cm wide, loose to dense. Preston. ⊕

'Ethel M. Webster' [probably a S. henryi Hybrid]. Shrub, medium-sized, but compact; flowers in loose, wide panicles, flesh pink, May–June. Preston.

'**Excellens**' [*S. patula*]. Phlox-purple in bud but opening pure white, in 15 cm long and 10 cm wide, loose panicles (= *S. velutina* 'Excellens'). Lemoine 1931. ⊕

'**Floréal**' [*S. nanceiana*]. Delicate and open habit; buds pentunia-purple, opening whitish, panicles 20 cm long, 15 cm wide, dense, fragrant, very late (!). Lemoine 1925. ⊕

'**Francisca**'. Cyclamen-purple, later becoming lighter. Panicles 20 cm long, 15 cm wide. Preston 1928.

'**Guinevere**' [*S. josiflexa*]. Lilac in bud and when opening, in 22 cm long and 20 cm wide panicles, but unattractive when faded. Preston 1925. ⊕

'**Hecla**'. Dark pink, panicles narrow, long, somewhat nodding. AB 1951: 19. Skinner 1932. ⊕

'**Hedin**' [*S. villosa* × *S. sweginzowii*]. Purple-lilac, nearly white when fully open, panicles 19 cm long, 10 cm wide, loose. Skinner 1935.

'**Hiawatha**'. Shrub, only about 1.5 cm high; flowers lilac-pink, darker in bud, panicles 15 cm long, dense, flowers earlier than the other forms. Skinner 1932. ⊕

'**Isabella**' [The type of the *prestoniae* Hybrids]. Lilac-red, interior lighter, panicles to 27 cm long, 20 cm wide, dense. MLi 45; Bai 20: 82; AB 1951: 19. One of the best forms of this group. ⊕

'**Jessica**'. Interior light purple, exterior more purple-lilac, panicles to 18 cm long and 12 cm wide. One of the darkest forms. Preston 1928.

'**Juliet**'. Lilac-pink. Preston 1928.

'**José**' (Morel, before 1970) [(*S. patula* × *S. microphylla*) × *S. meyeri*]. Medium-sized shrub; leaves small, acutely ovate; flowers in loose, very long panicles at the branch tips, pink, buds darker. (Minier 1974).

'**Katherina**'. Purple-lilac in bud, opening whitish, panicles to 19 cm long, 10 cm wide, loose. Preston 1930.

'**Kim**' [*S. josikaea*]. Medium-sized, elegant shrub; leaves oblong-lanceolate, large, deep green; flowers in large, branched panicles, pale lilac, May to June. Preston.

'**Lutèce**' [*S. henryi*]. Phlox-purple in bud, opening light violet, panicles to 20 cm long, 10 cm wide, loose. Lemoine 1910. ⊕

'**Lynette**' [*S. josiflexa*]. Buds and flowers reddish purple, not fading lighter, panicles to 15 cm long, 10 cm wide, dense. Preston 1924. ⊕

'**Minuet**' ['Redwine' × 'Donald Wyman']. Very dense habit, upright, to 2 m high, rather small leaved; buds light purple, soft whitish pink when in full bloom, floriferous, late June. Introduced in 1972 by the Morden Research Station, Manitoba, Canada.

'**Miranda**'. Flowers violet-lilac on the exterior, opening somewhat lighter, panicles to 25 cm long, 12 cm wide. Preston 1928.

'**Nerissa**'. Exterior magenta-pink, lighter on the interior, panicles to 25 cm long, 20 cm wide, dense. Preston 1928. ⊕

'**Nocturne**'. Bluish lilac, retaining its color well in full bloom, panicles to 20 cm long, 10 cm wide, dense. Preston 1936.

'**Octavia**'. Buds purple, opening much lighter, panicles to 10 cm wide, 15 cm high, dense. Preston 1928.

'**Olivia**'. Buds and flowers cyclamen-purple, later much lighter, panicles to 22 cm long, 20 cm wide, loose. Preston 1928.

'**Paulina**'. Buds purple-lilac, opening eventually whitish, panicles to 12 cm long, 15 cm wide, loose. Preston 1927.

'**Prairial**' [*S. henryi* × *S. tomentella*]. Buds purple-lilac, opening whitish, panicles to 20 cm long, 15 cm wide, dense. Lemoine 1933. ⊕

'**Redwine**'. Carmine-pink, buds darker, panicles long. The strongest red form. Preston 1936.

'**Regan**'. Pink. Preston 1928.

'**Romeo**'. Buds and flowers reddish purple, not fading lighter, panicles 22 cm long, 20 cm wide, loose. Preston 1926. ⊕

'**Royalty**'. Buds deep violet, opening blue-lilac, later becoming somewhat lighter, but still the darkest of all, panicles to 17 cm long, 10 cm wide, very dense. For a long time erroneously known as *S. josiflexa*. Preston 1935. ⊕

'**Rutilant**' [*S. nanceiana*]. Flowers and buds cyclamen-purple, panicles to 25 cm long, 22 cm wide. Lemoine 1931.

'**Silvia**'. Purple-lilac in bud, opening whitish, panicles to 25 cm long, 15 cm wide, loose. Preston.

'**Titania**'. Purple-lilac in bud, opening whitish, panicles to 25 cm long, 15 cm wide, loose. Preston 1928.

'**Ursula**'. Buds purple, then pink-lilac, opening whitish, panicles to 25 cm long, 15 cm wide, dense. Preston 1928. ⊕

'**Valerie**'. Soft violet, later nearly white, in dense, 20 cm long panicles. Preston 1930.

'**Virgilia**'. Flowers pale lilac, panicles medium-sized, delicate, loose. Preston 1928.

'**W. T. Macoun**'. Flowers lilac-pink, opening whitish, panicles to 20 cm long, 12 cm wide, dense. Preston 1927.

All lilacs like a deep, fertile garden soil, preferably heavier rather than lighter, in full sun. On grafted plants, prompt removal of root suckers is important to avoid suppression of the desirable traits.

Registration of new cultivars. The international registration authority for lilacs since 1974 has been the Royal Botanical Gardens, Box 399, Hamilton, Ontario, Canada L8N 3H8. All new cultivars should be registered here before their introduction.

Lit. Bugala, W.: The Ottawa Lilac and its varieties (in Polish); in Arboretum Kornickie **1**, 131 to 141, 1935 ● Davies-Preston: The Lilac in Canada; in Rep. R. H. S. Conf. Ornamental Flowering Trees and Shrubs, 135–140, 1940 ● Harding, A.: Lilas de mon Jardin; Paris 1947 ● Hillier, H. G.: *Syringa* etc.; in Rep. R. H. S. Conf. Report (l. c.), 101–111 ● Knight, F. P.: Lilacs; in Jour. R. H. S. 1959, 486 to 499 ● McKelvey, S. D.: The Lilac; a Monograph; London 1928 (563 pp., 172 plates) ● Meyer, F.: Flieder; Stuttgart 1952 (98 pp.) ● Lilacs for America; Report 1941 and 1953 (48 pp.) ● Lingelsheim: *Syringa*; in Engler, Pflanzenreich **72**, 74–95, 1920 ● Starcs, K.: Übersicht über die Arten der Gattung *Syringa* L.; in Mitt. DDG 1928, 31–49 ● Wein, K.: Die Geschichte der *Syringa persica*; in Mitt. DDG 1928, 245–257 ● Rogers, O. M.: Tentative International Register of Cultivar names in the genus *Syringa*; Res. Rep. No. 49 N. Hampsh. Agr. Exp. Sta., Durham, New Hampshire, USA, 1976 (81 pp.) ● Pringle, J. S.: Interspecific Hybridization Experiments in *Syringa* Series Villosae; in Baileya **20**, 40 to 91, 1977 (with many ills., but the mentioned hybrids have not yet been given cultivar names) ● Bugala, W.: Nowe odmiany lilaka ottawskiega (*Syringa* × *prestoniae* McKelvey) otrzymane w Arboretum Kórnickim (In Polish with an English summary); in Arboretum Kórnieckie Rocznik **15**, 61–96, 1970 ● Wyman, D.: The Preston Lilacs; in American Nurseryman from Dec. 1, 1970, 10–12 (with ills.).

SYZYGIUM Gaertn. — MYRTACEAE

Evergreen trees; leaves opposite, pinnately veined; flowers in terminal or axillary cymes or panicles; sepals 4–5, petals 4–5 either all distinct or fused into a cap or abscising all together, stamens numerous, anthers laterally opening; ovaries inferior; fruit usually a single seeded berry. — 400–500 species, most in the tropics of the Old World.

Syzygium paniculatum Gaertn. A tree in its habitat, to 12 m; leaves oblong-lanceolate, to 7.5 cm long, deep green, glossy, reddish when young; flowers cream-white, 12–25 mm wide, few in terminal and axillary panicles; fruit a purple-red, ovate, 2 cm thick berry. BMns 529 (= *Eugenia australis* J. C. Wendl.; *Eugenia myrtifolia* Sims; *Jambosa australis* [J. C. Wendl.] DC.). Australia. Variable in habit, size of the flowers and form of the leaves; widely utilized as a hedge in California and Florida. z10

TACSONIA See: **PASSIFLORA**

Tacsonia exoniensis see: **Passiflora × exoniensis**

T. manicata see: **Passiflora manicata**

T. mollissima see: **Passiflora mollissima**

T. van-volxemii see: **Passiflora antioquiensis**

TAMARIX L. — Tamarisk — TAMARICACEAE

Deciduous or evergreen shrubs or trees with cylindrical, rodlike branches, the youngest lateral shoots abscising with the leaves; leaves scale-like, sheath-like or stem-clasping, alternate, sessile, imbricately overlapping, green or bluish; flowers small, pink, mostly in terminal racemose panicles; sepals and petals 4–5 each, stamens 4–12, occasionally fused ring-like at the base; fruit a small, usually 3–4 valved capsule, occasionally with 2 or 5 valves; seeds with a feathery tuft of hairs. — 54 species from W. Europe, the Mediterranean region to E. Asia; only a few being hardy.

Key to the More Important Species

● Flowers 4 parted; racemes axillary on the previous year's shoots;

  x Petals spreading; styles usually 3:
    T. parviflora

  xx Petals erect, abscising, styles 4:
    T. tetrandra

●● Flowers 5 parted;

  * Racemes laterally arranged on the previous year's shoots:
    T. juniperina

  ** Racemes grouped into large, terminal panicles;

    > Leaves glabrous;

      x Petals persistent;

        ★ Bracts oval-lanceolate:
          T. pentandra

      ★★ Bracts subulate;

        + Inflorescences nodding, tree:
          T. chinensis

        ++ Inflorescences erect, shrub:
          T. ramosissima

      xx Petals abscising:
        T. gallica

    > Leaves finely pubescent:
      T. hispida

Tamarix africana Poir. Very closely related to the much hardier *T. juniperina*. Flowers in dense, wide, 5–8 cm long racemes, 8–9 mm thick, nearly sessile, style much longer than the ovary. PEu 78. Mediterranean region. True existence in cultivation unknown. z8 Fig. 274.

T. anglica Webb. Closely related to *T. gallica*. Upright shrub, 1–5 m high, shoots thin, young shoots red-brown; leaves tiny, oval-lanceolate, glabrous, bright green; flowers white, somewhat reddish, in 3–5 cm long, slender racemes, petals 5, abscising, stamens 5, filaments widened at the base, August to October. CF 287. SW. England and W. France along the coast; also cultivated as a small street tree. 1877. z7

T. aphylla (L.) Karst. From NE. Africa and Asia Minor, not winter hardy! LAu 369 (= *T. articulata* Vahl; *T. orientalis* Forsk.). Ⓟ Israel, N. Africa.

T. articulata see: **T. aphylla**

T. chinensis Lour. Shrub or tree, to 5 m, branches very thin, often nodding; leaves blue-green, lanceolate, keeled, very small; flowers pink, in 3–5 cm long racemes, these grouped into large, weeping panicles on the current year's wood, disk 10 lobed, style clavate in form, July–September: DL 3: 5; HKS 97. China. 1907. See also: **T. juniperina**. z9 Fig. 274. ⊘ ⊕

T. gallica L. Shrub, occasionally a small, 10 m high tree in its habitat, branches thin, erect to spreading, purple; leaves ovate-lanceolate, blue-green, with a membranous margin; flowers pink, in dense, cylindrical, 3–5 cm long racemes, buds nearly globose, carmine-pink, stamens

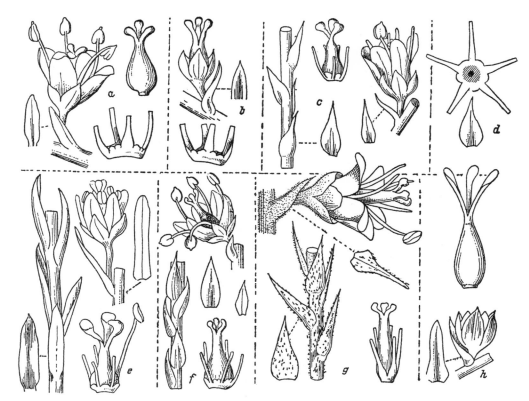

Fig. 274. **Tamarix**. Branch segments, flowers and flower parts. a. *T. parviflora*; b. *T. tetrandra*; c. *T. chinensis*; d. *T. gallica*; e. *T. juniperina*; f. *T. pentandra*; g. *T. hispida*; h. *T. africana* (most from Schneider, altered; much enlarged)

inserted into the rounded disk, June–August. RMi 313; HM 2022. The Mediterranean coast. 1596. z7 Plate 137; Fig. 274.

T. germanica see: **Myricaria germanica**

T. hispida Willd. Shrub, about 1 m high, erect, compact, conspicuously blue-green, easily distinguished by the finely pubescent branches and leaves; leaves ovate-lanceolate, sharply acuminate, tiny, rounded at the base; flowers attractively pink-red, in erect, 5–7 cm long, racemes, these grouped into long, terminal panicles, petals 5, abscising, much larger than the sepals, August–September. SH 2: 228 a-d; SDK 4:125 (= *T. kaschgarica* Lemoine). Caspian Sea to Manchuria. 1893. Ⓕ New Zealand, in dunes. z8 Fig. 274 ⊘ ✧

f. *aestivalis* see: **T. pentandra**

T. juniperina Bge. Tree-like habit or a tall dense shrub, branches somewhat nodding, annual shoots very thin, very closely spaced (giving a feathery effect !!); leaves green, oblong-lanceolate, membranous at the apex; flowers light pink, in 3 cm long, slender racemes on the previous year's shoots, petals persistent, disk 5 lobed, May (= *T. chinensis* sensu S. & Z. non Lour.; *T. plumosa* Hort.). China. 1875. z6 Plate 136; Fig. 274. ⊘

T. kaschgarica see: **T. hispida**

T. odessana see: **T. ramosissima**

T. orientalis see: **T. aphylla**

T. pallasii see: **T. pentandra**

T. parviflora DC. Shrub or also a small tree, shoots thin, deep red-brown, mostly drooping, nearly black in winter; leaves scaly, ovate, acuminate, half stem-clasping; flowers pink, 4 parted, on the previous year's wood, in slender, 3–4 cm long, racemes, petals erect, persistent, styles 3, May. FS 898; RH 1855: 401 (= *T. tetrandra* var. *purpurea* Hort.). SE. Europe. 1853. Often confused with the very similar *T. tetrandra*, whose petals abscise after flowering. z5 Plate 137; Fig. 274 ✧

T. pentandra Pall. Shrub or small tree, 3–5 m high, branches purple at first; leaves oval-lanceolate, blue-green to pale green; flowers pink-red, in small spikes, these grouped into large, terminal panicles, petals elliptic, inclined together, August–September. BM 8138 (= *T. pallasii* Desv.; *T. hispida* f. *aestivalis* Hort.). SE. Europe to central Asia. 1883. The best and most attractive species. Ⓕ Romania, for sand stabilizing. z5 Fig. 274. ✧

'Rubra' (Barbier). Sport with darker flowers, but not very consistent and occasionally reverting back to the parent form (= *T. hispida aestivalis rubra* Barbier; *T.* 'Summer Glow' Hort.).

Originated around 1935 by Barbier, Orléans, France. ✛

T. plumosa see: **T. juniperina**

T. ramosissima Ledeb. Upright shrub, shoots slender, yellowish brown in winter; leaves lanceolate, decurrent, gray-green; flowers small, light pink, in 3 cm long racemes, petals obovate, spreading, disk 5 lobed, with round lobes, styles often 4, nearly linear, July–September. SDK 128 (= *T. odessana* Stev.). SE. Russia, Caspian Region. 1885. Ⓕ China. z2 Plate 137.

T. tetrandra Pall. Shrub or also a small tree, usually about 3 m high, branches rodlike, nodding, red-brown, thin, feathery; leaves scale-form, ovate-lanceolate, bright green; flowers 4 parted, light pink, in small, laterally arranged spikes along the previous year's shoots, petals abscising on faded flowers (important characteristic from the simultaneously flowering *T. parviflora!*), stamens 4, late April–May. BS 3: 407; SDK 4: 121. SE. Europe, Orient. 1821. Often erroneously labeled in cultivation. z6 Plate 136; Fig. 274. ✛

var. *purpurea* see: **T. parviflora**

Since many *Tamarix* species occur in the Soviet Union, many good illustrations may be found in Sokolov, Derevja i kustarniki, Vol. 4:

> *T. androssowii* 121; *arceuthoides* 128; *bungei* 127; *elongata* 124; *florida* 127; *gracilis* 125; *hohenackeri* 128; *kotschyi* 121; *laxa* 122; *leptostachys* 125; *meyeri* 122; *passerinoides* 124; *szovitziana* 122.— Also *T. senegalensis* in TFA 101 and *T. gallica* var. *canariensis* in KGC 35.

For full sun and a good garden soil, although they are occasionally seen thriving on the steppes and salt flats. Easily cultivated and effective in bloom. The species can only be distinguised under a magnifying lens.

Lit. Ahrendt, G.: Beiträge zur Kenntnis der Gattung *Tamarix*; Diss. Univ. Berlin, Leipzig 1926 (56 pp., 2 plates) ● Gorschkova, S. G. (translated by L. H. Shinners): Salt Cedars in the Soviet Union; in The Southwestern Naturalist **2**, 48–73, 1957 ● Zohary, M.: The genus *Tamarix* in Israel; in Tropical Woods **104**, 24–60, 1956 ● McClintock, E.: Studies in Calif. ornamental plants. 3. The Tamarisks; in Jour. Cal. Hort. Soc. **12**, 76–83, 1951 ● Baum, B. R.: Introduced and naturalized Tamarisks in the United States; Baileya **15**, 19–25, 1967 ● Baum, B. R.: A monograph of the genus *Tamarix*; Jerusalem 1968 (220 pp.).

TAPISCIA Oliv. — STAPHYLEACEAE

Monotypic genus with the characteristics of the following species. Plants either all male with 10–15 cm long panicles, or hermaphroditic and then with up to 10 cm long panicles.

The inclusion in the family Staphyleaceae is unfortunate and the genus should have its own family "Tapisciaceae".

Tapiscia sinensis Oliv. Deciduous shrub or small tree, to 8 m high, shoots glabrous; leaves alternate, odd pinnate, to 40 cm long, leaflets 5–7(9), ovate, acute, to 13 cm long, 5 cm wide, serrate, base cordate, gray with somewhat tufted pubescence beneath, petiole about 1 cm; flowers very small, in axillary panicles, yellow, fragrant, 5 parted, calyx campanulate-tubular; fruits ovate, about 1 cm long, black, glossy. HI 1928. Central China; Szechwan, Hupeh Provs. 1908. Cultivated in England, but rare. z9 Fig. 275. ✛ ⌀

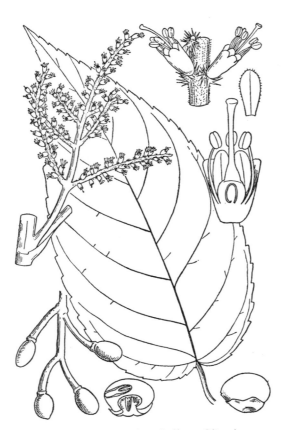

Fig. 275. *Tapiscia sinensis* (from Oliver)

TECOMA Juss. — BIGNONIACEAE

Upright shrubs (not climbing!!); leaves opposite, pinnate, leaflets thin, dentate; flowers in terminal racemes or panicles; calyx tubular campanulate, corolla infundibular; stamens enclosed, anthers diverging, with a leaflike widened connective; disk cupulate, with a crenate limb; fruit a linear capsule, with 2 leathery valves and numerous narrowly elliptic, winged seeds.— 16 species in the warmer Americas, from Mexico to Peru and Argentina.

Tecoma alata DC. Upright shrub; leaves pinnate, with 11–17 leaflets, these oblong, to 5 cm long, serrate; flowers in 20 cm long and equally wide panicles, corolla tube to 5 cm long, tubular infundibular, gradually tapering to the base, yellow with a trace of orange (!), limb tips reflexed. BC 3783; LWTP 502; MCL 87 (= *T. smithii* W. Wats.; *Stenolobium alatum* [DC.] T. Sprague). Australia. Possibly a hybrid of *T. stans* van. *velutina* × *Tecomaria capensis*. z10 # ✣

T. jasminoides see: **Pandorea jasminoides**

T. mollis see: **T. stans** var. **velutina**

T. radicans see: **Campsis radicans**

T. ricasoliana see: **Podranea ricasoliana**

T. smithii see: **T. alata**

T. stans (L.) HBK. Shrub or occasionally a small, 6 m high tree; leaflets 5–13, lanceolate to oblong-ovate, to 10 cm long, serrate; flowers in terminal racemes or panicles, corolla infundibular-campanulate, abruptly constricted at the base, golden-yellow, 5 cm long, summer. BM 3191 (= *Bignonia stans* L.; *Stenolobium stans* [L.] Seem.). West Indies, and from Mexico to Peru; Florida. 1730. z10 Plate 137; Fig. 276. # ✣

var. **velutina** DC. Leaves soft pubescent beneath (= *T. mollis* HBK.).

Lit. Melchior, H.: Beiträge zur Systematik und Phylogenie der Gattung *Tecoma*; in Ber. dt. Bot. Ges. **59**, 12–31, 1941.

Fig. 276. *Tecoma stans*

TECOMANTHE Baill. — BIGNONIACEAE

Evergreen, twining shrubs, leaves opposite, pinnate; flowers in short clusters on older wood (!) over the leaf scars; calyx campanulate to urceolate, more or less lobed, corolla tube more or less infundibular with large, irregular limb lobes; stamens 5, including 1 rudimentary; ovaries bilocular; fruit a leathery, bivalvate capsule with navicular halves, seeds winged. — 17 species from the Moluccan Islands to Australia and New Zealand.

Tecomanthe speciosa W. R. B. Oliver. Glabrous, open shrub, twining to 9 m high in its habitat, shoots thick, green, smooth, glossy; leaves pinnate, leaflets leathery, dark green, glossy above, terminal leaflets broadly elliptic to more obovate, 9–15 cm long, 5–8 cm wide, obtuse, the 4 lateral leaflets regularly formed, but 5–12 cm long, 3–7 cm wide, petiole thick, 7 cm long; flowers to 30 together in short corymbs, cream-white with a trace of green, calyx 1 cm long, green, velvety, corolla tube 3 cm long, bilabiate, tomentose on the exterior, May–July; fruit capsule to 18 cm long. BMns 618; GC 1954: 76 to 77, with ills. First discovered in New Zealand in 1945. z9 # ✣

TECOMARIA Spach — BIGNONIACEAE

Evergreen, usually upright shrubs, branches occasionally somewhat climbing; leaves opposite, odd pinnate, leaflets serrate; flowers in terminal panicles or racemes; calyx campanulate, regularly 5 toothed; corolla infundibular, somewhat curved; stamen filaments usually exserted, with spreading, pendulous anthers; fruit a linear, compressed capsule. — 2 species in Central and S. America and S. Africa.

Tecomaria capensis (Thunb.) Spach. Evergreen, leaves somewhat resembling *Campsis radicans*, but only about 8–10 cm long; flowers usually grouped 4–8 together, about 5 cm long, vermilion red, tube very narrow, limb nearly 3 cm wide, September–November. MCL 127; HV 25; DRHS 2085. S. Africa. 1823. z9 # ✣

Including some cultivars normally only grown in S. African gardens:

'Apricot'. Habit more dense and compact, only 1–1.5 m high; flowers bright orange. ✣

'Coccinea'. Bright red. ✣

'Lutea'. Habit lower than that of the species, only 1–1.5 m high; flowers an intense yellow. ✣

'Salmonea'. Strong growing; flowers salmon color. ✣

TELINE

Teline linifolius see: **Cytisus linifolius**

T. maderensis see: **Cytisus maderensis**

T. monspessulana see: **Cytisus monspessulanus**

T. stenopetala see: **Cytisus stenopetalus**

TELOPEA R. Br. — PROTEACEAE

Tall, evergreen shrubs; leaves alternate, entire or finely dentate; flowers very attractive, red, hermaphroditic, perianth quickly splitting open on the underside; style reaching through the opening; fruit a 5–10 cm long, curved pod. — 4 species in Australia, one in Tasmania.

Telopea speciosissima R. Br. Glabrous, evergreen shrub, 1.5–2 m high; leaves obovate, 12–20 cm long, 3–6 cm wide, obtuse and coarsely dentate (!) nearly to the base, very seldom entire; flowers in a dense, globose, 7–10 cm wide capitulum, coral-red, surrounded by many narrow, acute, carmine-red bracts, these 3–7 cm long, corolla tube of the individual flowers 2.5 cm long. BM 1128 (as *Embothrium speciosissimum*); JRHS 1964: 14. Australia; New South Wales. 1789. More difficult to cultivate than the following species; needs heat and plenty of water in the growing season, dryness in the dormant period. z9 Plate 126. # ✛

T. truncata R. Br. Evergreen shrub, 2–5 m high, shoots pubescent; leaves oblanceolate, tapered or rounded at the apex, occasionally with 2–3 teeth or 2 lobed, stiff and leathery, 5–12 cm long, dull green above, bluish beneath; flowers carmine, in 5–7 cm wide, many-flowered capitula, the individual flowers like *Embothrium* in appearance, June. CFTA 141; BM 9660. Tasmania. 1930. z9 # ✛

Wonderful flowering plants, unfortunately only suitable for warm climates; thriving in the cooler mountain regions of the habitat.

Lit. Willis, J. L.: The genus *Telopea;* in Australian Plants **1**, 7–10, 1959 (with 4 ills.; pp. 1–16 of this work are devoted to *Telopea* and its culture).

TEMPLETONIA R. Br. — Leguminosae

Evergreen shrubs; leaves alternate or with only 1 leaflet; flowers solitary or few axillary, attractive; stamens connate, alternating in 2 lengths; fruit a flat, leathery, dehiscent pod. — About 10 species in Australia.

Templetonia retusa (Vent.) R. BR. Coral Shrub. Glabrous shrub, 2 m high; leaves stiff-leathery, oblanceolate to obovate, to 3 cm long, obtuse, blue-green, occasionally incised at the apex, subsessile; flowers red, occasionally yellow, over 2.5 cm long, standard erect, 2.5 cm long, wings often folded inward, keel narrow, March–June; pod linear-oblong, 5 cm long. BM 2334. S. and W. Australia. 1817. z10 # ✛

TERNSTROEMIA Mutis — THEACEAE

Evergreen trees and shrubs; leaves alternate, leathery, entire or with undulate, obtuse teeth; flowers usually hermaphroditic, axillary, solitary or in clusters; sepals 5, overlapping, persistent; petals 5, overlapping, connate at the base, stamens many, attached at the base of the petals; fruits fleshy, not dehiscent, usually with a few, large seeds. — About 100 species in the tropics of Asia and America, some in Africa, 1 in Japan.

Ternstroemia gymnanthera (Wight & Arn.). T. Sprague. Small, glabrous tree, branches reddish brown; leaves elliptic to oblanceolate or obovate, to 7 cm long and 4 cm wide, obtuse to rounded, entire, petiole 7–10 mm long, reddish; flowers axillary, yellowish white, 2 cm wide, stalk 12–20 cm long, drooping, July; fruits globose, red, 1 cm thick, dehiscing later on this species. KIF 2: 65. India to Malaysia and Japan. z10 # ∅ ✛ ⚭

TETRACENTRON Oliv. — TETRACENTRACEAE

Monotypic genus. Deciduous tree; leaves alternate, petiolate, ovate; flowers in slender, pendulous spikes, inconspicuous, small, sessile, hermaphroditic; sepals 4, overlapping, ovate, stamens 4, exserted, carpels 4; fruit a deeply lobed capsule; seeds linear-oblong.

Tetracentron sinense Oliv. Deciduous tree, 10–20 m high or more, lower in cultivation, young shoots dark brown, with light lenticels, glabrous; leaves usually distichous, ovate, acute, dense and obtusely crenate, 7–12 cm long, base cordate, palmately veined with 5–7 veins; flowers yellowish, in terminal, pendulous, 10–15 cm long spikes, June. LF 138; CIS 23; FIO 58; HAL 157–158 (!). China; Hupeh Prov.; N. Burma. 1901. z7 Fig. 277. ∅

Cultivated somewhat like *Cercidiphyllum.*

Lit. See: *Trochodendron*

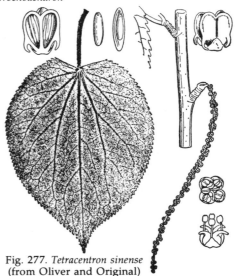

Fig. 277. *Tetracentron sinense*
(from Oliver and Original)

TETRAPANAX K. Koch— Rice-Paper Plant—ARALIACEAE

Only one species with the characteristics as described below:

Tetrapanax papyrifer (Hook.) K. Koch. Small shrub, 1–2 m high, stems regularly thick, thornless, with stolons; leaves alternate, thin to somewhat leathery, with a long, thick petiole, blade 30–50 cm wide, palmately lobed, with 7–12 lobes, these rather deeply incised, otherwise entire to coarsely serrate, the middle lobes 3 parted, deep green above, rust-red to white stellate tomentose beneath; flowers small, 4 parted, white, tomentose on the exterior, in umbels, these grouped into large, terminal panicles, 50 cm long, densely stellate tomentose, flowering in summer; fruit a small drupe. LWT 281; BM 4897 (= *Fatsia papyrifera* Hook.). S. China, Taiwan. z8 Plate 138.

TEUCRIUM L.— Germander—LABIATAE

Herbaceous, subshrub or also shrubs; leaves opposite, entire, dentate or incised or multi-incised, deciduous or evergreen, the bracts often very similar to the normal leaves, often also much smaller; flowers in whorls of 2, occasionally more, axillary or in spikes, racemes or capitula; calyx tubular or campanulate, 10 veined, 5 toothed, corolla tube usually totally enclosed, occasionally exserted, limb appearing 1 lipped, the lower lip is very large while the upper lip is tiny or incised and then appearing to be absent; stamens 4, in 2 pairs; nutlets obovoid, reticulately veined and rugose.— About 300 cosmopolitan species, but most from the Mediterranean region.

Teucrium chamaedrys L. True Germander. Deciduous subshrub, 15–25 cm high, with root sprouts, many branched, dense, more or less pubescent; leaves short petioled, ovate to oblong, 1–3 cm long, incised crenate, base cuneate, green or more gray-green on both sides, bracts smaller and dentate; flowers in whorls of 2–6, in

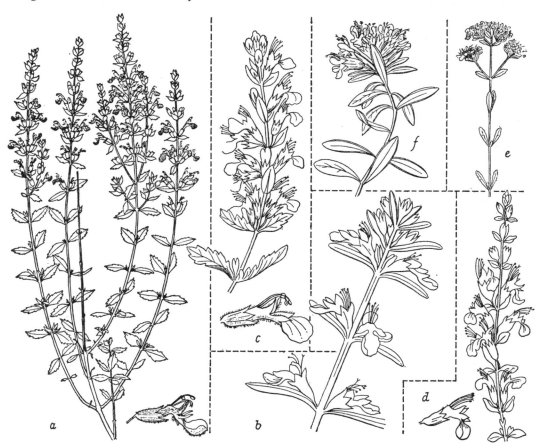

Fig. 278. **Teucrium.** a. *T. massiliense* (= *T. lucidrys*); b. *T. creticum*; c. *T. chamaedrys*; d. *T. marum*; e. *T. polium*; f. *T. montanum* (from Reichenbach, Briquet, Hayne, Boom, Sibthorp & Sm.)

apical racemes, purple-pink or light pink, with red and white spots, 2 cm long, July to September. Central and S. Europe, on dry gravelly slopes, particularly on limestone. Not indentical to the evergreen *T. "chamaedrys"* of garden culture; this is *T. massiliense!* z6 Fig. 278.

T. creticum L. Shrub, 25–30 cm high, spreading; leaves linear-oblong, similar to *Rosmarinus*, entire, somewhat involuted, eventually dark green above, white tomentose beneath, densely clustered at the base; flowers in 2's or more in erect, elongated racemes, calyx white tomentose, corolla reddish purple (= *T. hyssopifolium* Schreb). Eastern Mediterranean region. z8 Fig. 278.

T. flavum L. Closely related to *T. chamaedrys,* but more shrubby, to 50 cm high; leaves nearly triangular-ovate, about 2.5 cm long, thick, yellow-green. Dalmatia, Istria, S. France and the Mediterranean region. z8

T. hyssopifolium see: **T. creticum**

T. × *lucidrys* see: **T. massiliense**

T. lucidum L. Also similar to *T. chamaedrys,* but the shoots are totally glabrous; leaves oval-rhombic, crenate on the apex, glabrous; flowers purple, 1.5–2 cm long, calyx glabrous. N. Italy, S. France, in the maritime Alps. z8

T. massiliense L. Evergreen shrublet, 20–40 cm high, not stoloniferous, stems erect or ascending, pubescent, spreading branches; leaves ovate, crenate, petiolate, the apical ones lanceolate, entire, shorter than the calyx; flowers in long, terminal false spikes, pink, corolla about 1 cm long, white pubescent, calyx glandular-floccose, with rather large teeth, June–July (= ? *T. chamaedrys* Hort., non L.; *T.* × *lucidrys* Boom). West. Mediterranean region. It is still not completely clear whether *Teucrium chamaedrys* of common garden culture in actually identical to *T. massiliense* or, as suggested by Boom, if it is a hybrid between *T. chamaedrys* × *T. lucidum* or *T. divaricatum,* in Amsterdam around 1899. z5 Fig. 278. # ⊕ ∅

T. montanum L. Procumbent-ascending subshrub, not creeping, shoots abundantly branched, 5–10 cm long, gray-tomentose; leaves linear-oblong, entire (!), 1–2 cm long, 2–4 mm wide, margins usually involuted, dull green above, gray-tomentose beneath, petiole 1–3 mm; flowers in dense, terminal heads, white, later yellow, summer, calyx tubular-campanulate, teeth lanceolate. S. Europe, Asia Minor. z6 Fig. 278.

T. polium L. Procumbent, evergreen dwarf shrub, pubescent or tomentose or prickly tomentose, to 20 cm high, many branched, the shoots about 10–15 cm long; leaves cuneate or obovate or linear, 12–25 mm long, margins more or less involuted and crenate, both sides with short and gray-yellow, yellow or reddish colored tomentum, occasionally only gray-green; flowers in terminal heads of several whorls, small, white or purple. Mediterranean region, Asia Minor. 1562. z7 Fig. 278. # ∅

All species tolerate a wide range of soils, but like heat and the pubescent species need a dry site in winter. *T. massiliense* (often *T. chamaedrys* in cultivation!) is a popular, widely used plant for low, tightly sheared hedges or enclosures.

THEVETIA L. — APOCYNACEAE

Evergreen trees or shrubs with a milky sap; leaves alternate, entire, single veined or slender pinnately veined; flowers in large, terminal cymes, hermaphroditic, calyx 5 parted, with acute, spreading lobes, corolla tube infundibular, tube cylindrical, calyx abruptly widened campanulate form, throat with 5 pubescent scales, stamens 5, alternating with the scales at the tip of the corolla tube; fruit a drupe, wider than high. — 9 species in the tropical Americas and West Indies.

Thevetia neriifolia see: **T. peruviana**

T. peruviana (Pers.) K. Schum. "Yellow Oleander". Evergreen shrub or small tree, to 8 m; leaves linear to more lanceolate, to 15 cm long, 6 mm wide, gradually long acuminate, deep green and glossy above, lateral veins indistinct; flowers yellow to orange, fragrant, about 7 cm long, to 5 cm wide, in nearly sessile, terminal, few-flowered cymes, shorter than the leaves, June; fruits angular, hardy, about 2.5 cm wide, red, eventually black. BM 2309; LWTP 834 (= *T. neriifolia* A. Juss. ex Steud.). Tropical America, but widely planted throughout the tropics today. 1735. z10 # ⊕

Also occasionally including a white flowering form, '**Alba**'.

Likes a sandy, but fertile soil and also tolerates a light frost. All parts of the plant are poisonous!

THIBAUDIA

Thibaudia acuminata see: **Cavendishia acuminata**

THUNBERGIA Retz. — THUNBERGIACEAE

Upright or twining shrubs or herbs; leaves opposite, ovate to lanceolate or elliptic to cordate, cuneate at the base, obtuse to hastate; flowers solitary in the leaf axils, the calyx and usually also the corolla surrounded by the enveloping prophylls, calyx tiny, ring-form, with 10–15 small teeth or lobes; corolla attractive, corolla tube widened on one side, curved, limb spreading, with 5 round, wide lobes, twisted in bud, stamens 4; fruit a leathery, thick, globose capsule with an abrupt beak, dehiscence loculicidal. — About 200 species in tropical S. Africa, Madagascar and warmer Asia.

Thunbergia grandiflora Roxb. Evergreen, high twining shrub, shoots rather glabrous; leaves ovate to lanceolate, thick, 12–20 cm long, the uppermost usually lanceolate, caudate toothed to slightly lobed or entire, palmately 5–

7 veined, either glabrous or soft pubescent on either side, flowers light or dark blue (also a white form), 7 cm long and wide, most in pendulous clusters, occasionally solitary, summer to fall, prophylls nearly as large as the corolla tube. BM 2366; NV 27; BC 3339. N. India. 1820 z10 Plate 126. # ∅

Good plant for frost free climates.

TIBOUCHINA Aubl. — MELASTOMATACEAE

Evergreen shrubs, upright but occassionally also climbing or herbaceous; leaves often large, 3–7 veined, ovate or oblong, leathery, petiolate, flowers mostly in terminal, 3-forked panicles, violet or purple, usually 5 parted, calyx tube ovate or campanulate or cylindrical; petals 5, obovate, often uneven sided; stamens 10, with glabrous, pubescent or glandular filaments and awl-shaped anthers, filaments geniculate. — About 200 species in tropical S. America, mostly in Brazil.

Tibouchina urvilleana (DC.) Cogn.　Pubescent, evergreen, 4–6 m high climbing shrub, shoots 4 sided, reddish pubescent; leaves ovate-elliptic, acute, 5–12 cm long, 2.5–3 cm wide, finely serrate, 5 veined, somewhat erect pubescent above; flowers about 7 cm wide, attractive, solitary or in groups of 3, in branched, terminal panicles, with 2 prophylls to each flower, stamens purple, flowering over a long period, (particularly under glass), otherwise also flowering in the fall; fruit a 5 valved, 12 mm wide capsule with a persistent calyx tube. FS 2430; MCL 88. Brazil. This species is always confused with *T. semidecandra* (DC.) Cogn. (not generally cultivated), which has 4–6 prophylls on each flower. z10 Plate 126. # ⊕

'**Grandiflora**'. Flowers to 15 cm wide. # ⊕

Cultivated in the landscape only in frost free climates; likes a fertile, clay soil and lots of water in the summer.

Lit. Wurdack, J. J.; The cultivated Glorybushes, *Tibouchina* (Melastomataceae); Baileya **15**, 1–6, 1967.

TILIA L. — Linden — TILIACEAE

Deciduous trees, branches commonly stellate pubescent; leaves alternate, distichous, long petioled, usually cordate and serrate; flowers yellowish or whitish, most in small, pendulous cymes; stalk of the inflorescence usually adnate for half its length to a membranous, pale green bract; sepals and petals 5 each, often with 5 petaloid staminodes situated opposite the petals; stamens many, filaments forked at the apex, either all or some fertile; ovaries with 5 locules, style slender, with a 5 lobed stigma; fruit a small, globose to pear-shaped nutlet. — About 50 species in the northern temperate zone.

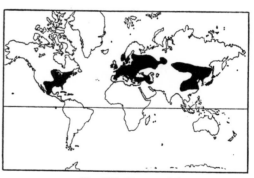

Fig. 279. Range of the genus *Tilia*

Key to the most important Species and Hybrids

● Leaves green or bluish beneath, glabrous or pubescent with simple (!) hairs;

　✕ Leaf undersides and young shoots pubescent; flowers without staminodes:
　　　T. platyphylla

　✕✕ Leaf undersides glabrous except for the hair fascicles in the vein axils;

　　v Hair fascicles at the blade base (!) and in the other vein axils;

　　　+ Finely serrate on the margins; flowers without staminodes;

　　　　§ Leaves green beneath; tertiary veins raised;

　　　　　★ Leaves dull green above, margin teeth short:
　　　　　　　T. europaea

　　　　　★★ Leaves glossy green above; margin teeth long acuminate:
　　　　　　　T. euchlora

　　　　§§ Leaves blue-green beneath; tertiary veins not raised;

　　　　　★ Cymes 5–11 flowered; flowers without staminodes:
　　　　　　　T. cordata

　　　　　★★ Cymes 8–40 flowered; flowers with staminodes:
　　　　　　　T. japonica

++ Margins coarsely serrate, leaves often 3 lobed, flowers with staminodes:
  T. mongolica

vv Hair fascicles present in the vein axils, but absent at the blade base; leaves 10–12 cm long; flowers with staminodes:
  T. americana

● ● Leaves stellate pubescent beneath (!) or stellate tomentose; flowers with staminodes;

  ✕ Young shoots glabrous;

    v Hair fascicles in the vein axils on the gray or gray-green leaf undersides:
      T. neglecta

    vv Hair fascicles absent from the vein axils on the white or whitish underside;

      + Underside densely white tomentose;

        § Leaves ovate to oval-oblong, 10–17 cm long, margins scabrous serrate:
          T. heterophylla

        §§ Leaves ovate, 5–10 cm long, margins sinuately serrate:
          T. oliveri

      ++ Leaves thinly gray tomentose or stellate pubescent beneath, usually with long hairs on the venation:
        T. moltkei

  ✕✕ Young shoots pubescent;

    v Leaf undersides without hair fascicles in the vein axils;

      + Leaves rounded ovate, with a persistent white tomentum;

        § Tomentum on the young shoots, buds and petioles gray to whitish; leaves finely serrate, teeth short and acute:

          ★ Habit upright; leaf petiole shorter than half of the blade length; fruit slightly pentagonal:
            T. tomentosa

          ★★ Habit pendulous; leaf petiole longer than half of the blade length; fruit with 5 furrows:
            T. petiolaris

        §§ Tomentum on the young shoots, buds and petioles yellowish or brownish; leaves coarsely serrate, teeth long acuminate:
          T. mandshurica

      ++ Leaves ovate-triangular, irregularly and coarsely serrate, teeth short acuminate, often eventually becoming glabrous beneath:
        T. miqueliana

    vv Leaf undersides with hair fascicles in the vein axils; leaves rounded-ovate, gray tomentose beneath, venation and midrib brownish:
      T. maximowicziana

Parentage of the Cultivars

'Blechiana'	→ T. moltkei
'Chancellor'	→ T. cordata
'Dropmore'	→ T. flavescens
'Fairview'	→ T. cordata
'Greenspire'	→ T. cordata
'Handsworth'	→ T. cordata
'June Bride'	→ T. cordata
'Longevirens'	→ T. europaea
'Mrs. Stenson'	→ T. varsaviensis
'Orebro'	→ T. playtphylla
'Pallida'	→ T. europaea
'Rancho'	→ T. cordata
'Redmond'	→ T. americana
'Rhodopetala'	→ T. tomentosa
'Wratislaviensis'	→ T. europaea

Tilia alba see: **T. petiolaris** and **T. tomentosa**

T. americana L. American Linden. A tall tree in its habitat, occasionally to 40 m, crown broad ovate to nearly globose (in an open site!), young shoots glabrous, green; leaves broad ovate, 10–20 cm long, abruptly acuminate, base cordate to truncate, coarsely serrate, teeth long acuminate, dark green above, lighter beneath with light brown axillary pubescence in the lateral vein axils, but not at the base (!), petiole 3–5 cm long; flowers 1.5 cm wide, 6–15 in pendulous cymes, stamens shorter than the petals, late July; fruits ellipsoid to nearly globose, not ribbed, thick shelled. BB 2411; GTP 303; SM 659; SS 24 (= *T. glabra* Vent.; *T. nigra* Borkh.). Central and Eastern N. America. 1752. z2 ⌀

'Ampelophylla'. Leaves very large, lobed, coarsely and irregularly serrate, teeth acuminate (= *T. incisodentata* Hort.; *T. longifolia dentata* Hort. p. p.).

'Convexifolia'. Slow growing form; leaves spathulate-convex, to 12 cm long, smaller than those of the species.

'Dentata'. Very strong growing habit, stem straight; leaves large, coarse and irregular, often biserrate, rich green (= f. *megalodonta* V. Engl.). MG 39: 274. Plate 139. ⌀

'Fastigiata'. Narrowly conical form, branches ascending (= *T. glabra* f. *fastigiata* Slavin). 1931.

'Macrophylla'. Leaves very large, to 25 cm long and nearly as wide. 1864. ⌀

f. *megalodonta* see: **'Dentata'**

var. *pendula* see: **T. petiolaris**

'Redmond' (Plumfield). Selection with a much denser, conical habit. Discovered around 1920. Distributed by the Plumfield Nurseries, Fremont, Nebraska, USA about 1926.

T. amurensis Rupr. Closely related to *T. cordata*, but with thin, scaly bark; leaves broad ovate, coarsely serrate with acuminate teeth; inflorescences 3–20 flowered, occasionally with incompletely developed staminodes; fruits nearly globose. NK 12: 7; PDR 9: 161; SDK 4: 111; CIS 177 (= *T. cordata* var. *mandshurica* Maxim.). Manchuria, Korea. 1909. z5

T. argentea see: **T. tomentosa**

T. baroniana see: **T. chinensis**

T. beaumontia × *pendula* see: **T.** × **europaea 'Pallida'**

T. begonifolia see: **T. dasystyla**

T. carlsruhensis see: **T.** × **flaccida**

T. caucasica see: **T. dasystyla**

T. chinensis Maxim. Closely related to *T. maximowicziana*, but to only 15 m high, young shoots glabrous; leaves ovate to broad ovate, 6–10 cm long, coarsely and scabrous serrate, totally glabrous above, thinly gray tomentose beneath, with rust-red hair fascicles in the vein axils; fruits 5 ribbed. CIS 186; SDK 4: 102 (= *T. baroniana* Diels). China; Kansu, Szechwan, Hupeh Provs. 1925. See also: **T. tuan** var. **chinensis.** z5

T. chingiana. Hu & Cheng. Similar to *T. tuan*, but the leaves more scabrous serrate, underside only sparsely stellate pubescent to nearly glabrous, vein axils not pubescent, inflorescences few flowered, flowers with oblong-lanceolate to more elliptic petals. Tree, 8–15 m high, often multistemmed at the base; leaves broad ovate, short acuminate, base obliquely truncate to cordate, scabrous serrate, 5–10 cm long, 5–9 cm wide, with about 4 vein pairs, deep green above, underside slightly stellate pubescent to glabrous, petiole 3–5 cm long; flowers 4–10 together, stamens 40–50; fruits ovate, 9–11 mm long, acute, finely warty, appressed pubescent. China; Kiangsi, Lushan, Kuling. z6

T. cordata Mill. Littleleaf Linden. Tree, to 30 m high, crown spreading outward, stem often with sucker sprouts, shoots glabrous or somewhat pubescent only at first; leaves rounded cordate, short acuminate, finely and scabrous serrate, rich green above, blue-green beneath with red-brown axillary pubescence (!!); flowers yellowish white, very fragrant, 5–9 in pendulous to erect cymes, first half of July; fruits globouse, with or without slight ribs, 6 mm thick, thin shelled. GPN 569 to 570; HM 1954 (= *T. parvifolia* Ehrh.; *T. ulmifolia* Scop.). Europe. Cultivated for ages. Ⓕ W. Germany. z3–7 Fig. 280. ⌀

Including a large number of selections, most from the USA:

'Chancellor'. Dense crown, conical, with a straight, central leader and with lateral shoots 360° around the stem; leaves like those of the species, somewhat glossy. Introduced around 1968 by the Cole Nursery, Ohio, USA. Patented. Very tolerant of dryness and therefore particularly well suited to street tree use.

f. *columnaris* see: **'Pyramidalis'**

'Fairview.' Selected as a seedling. Very strong growing; leaves larger than those of the species, much tougher and darker green. Introduced in 1973 by A. McGill & Son, Fairview, Oregon, USA. US. Patented. ⌀

'Greenspire'. Selection. Conspicuously pyramidal (even on young trees in the nursery), very symmetrical, fast growing; leaves remaining green for the whole summer. Selected by Princeton Nurseries, USA. Patented. ⌀

'Handsworth'. Attractive form with light yellow bark on the new growth. Developed before 1950 in the Handsworth Nursery near Sheffield, England.

'June Bride'. Narrowly conical, shoots arising 360° around the main stem, very dense crowned; leaves like those of the species but glossier; flowers much more numerous, the last week of June. Introduced by the Manbeck Nurseries, New Knoxville, Ohio, USA. Patented. ⌀ ✣

var. *mandshurica* see: **T. amurensis**

'Pyramidalis'. Habit narrowly conical. Gfl 45:38 (= f. *columnaris* Schwer.). ⌀

'Rancho'. Selection with a conical crown, supposed to reach only 9 m high with a 5 m width, well branched early, developing a dense crown. Introduced by Edward S. Scanlon, Olmstead Falls, Ohio, USA. Patented. Plate 138. ⌀

T. dasystyla Stev. Tall tree, to 30 m high, crown broadly conical, stem straight, new growth glabrous, red; leaves tough, ovate, abruptly acuminate, 8–14 cm long, obliquely cordate, scabrous serrate with awn-shaped teeth, very glossy dark green above, lighter beneath with whitish hair fascicles in the vein axils; flowers in cymes of 3–7, styles pubescent or glabrous; fruits oval-globose, 1 cm long, slightly 5 ribbed. SH 2: 254 e–f; 255e; PDR 9: 163 (= *T. rubra* Stev.; *T. caucasica* Rupr.; *T. begonifolia* Stev.). SE. Europe to the Caucasus and Iran. 1880. z6

T. diversifolia see: **T.** × **flaccida 'Diversifolia'**

T. × **euchlora** K. Koch. Crimean Linden (*T. cordata*? × *T. dasystyla*). Tree, to 20 m high, crown ovate, branches nodding, basal branches very pendulous, young shoots glabrous; leaves rounded ovate, base obliquely cordate, short acuminate, finely and scabrous serrate, 5–10 cm long, glossy above (!), dark green, with light green and brownish tufted pubescence beneath; flowers 3–7 in pendulous cymes, July; fruits densely shaggy-tomentose, short ellipsoid, somewhat 5 ribbed. HM 1965; MD 1920: 67 (= *T. europaea* var. *dasystyla* Loud. p. p.). Around 1860. Valuable street tree. z3 Plate 139; Fig. 280. ⌀

T. × **europaea** L. Common European Linden (Lime). (*T. cordata* × *T. platyphylla*). Tree, to 40 m high, crown conical, young shoots glabrous; leaves obliquely

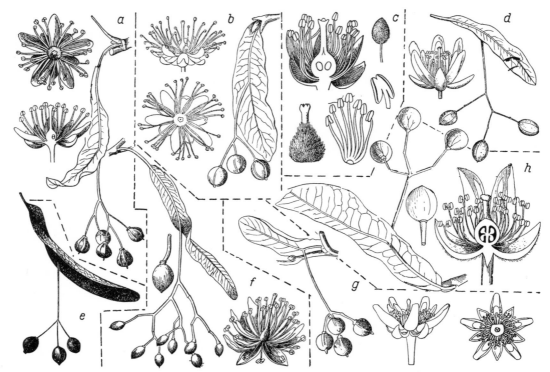

Fig. 280. **Tilia.** Flowers and fruits and their parts. a. *T. cordata;* b. *T. platyphylla;* c. *T.* × *euchlora;* d. *T. mongolica;* e. *T.* × *europaea;* f. *T. japonica;* g. *T. tomentosa;* h. *T. miqueliana* (from Hempel & Wilhelm, Koehne, Shirasawa, Kerner, Rehder)

cordate, short acuminate, scabrous serrate, dark green and glabrous above, lighter beneath with a few axillary tufts, petiole 3–5 cm long; flowers grouped 5–10 in pendulous, 7–8 cm long cymes, late June–early July; fruits nearly globose, indistinctly ribbed, tomentose, hard shelled. HM 1964; GF 2: 256 (= *T. vulgaris* Hayne; *T. hollandica* K. Koch; *T. intermedia* DC.). Cultivated for ages and surpassing the parents in beauty. Needs a large open site. z3 Fig. 280. ⊘

var. *dasystyla* see: **T.** × **euchlora**

'Longevirens' (Timm). Selection with particularly persistent foliage, somewhat yellowish on the new growth. Selected around 1930 by Timm & Co., Elmshorn, W. Germany. ⊘

'Pallida'. Branches and bud particularly reddish in the fall; leaves larger, bright green, yellowish to bluish-green beneath. MG 39: 274 (= *T. pallida* Simonkai). Cultivated for ages and also known as the "Kaiser Linden". ⊘

'Pendula'. Branches slightly pendulous (= *T. beaumontia pendula* Hort.).

'Wratislaviensis'. New growth and young leaves yellow, mature leaves greening. Found in 1898 in the Breslau Municipal Nursery.

T. × **flaccida** Host. (*T. americana* × *T. platyphylla*). Similar to *T. platyphylla,* but the leaves usually with acute to somewhat acuminate teeth, venation beneath only slightly pubescent, vein axils on the secondary veins with hair fascicles; flowers to 3 in cymes, stamens as long as the petals. SH 2: 254 a–b, 256 e–f (= *T. carlsruhensis* Simonkai; *T. praecox* A. Br. non Host). z3 Plate 138.

'Diversifolia'. Tree, to 6 m high, narrowly upright, shoots glabrous or eventually so; leaves large, 5–20 cm long, quite variable in form, very similar to those of *T. platyphylla* 'Laciniata', but much larger, most leaves with narrow middle lobes, dark green, glabrous, underside somewhat pubescent, petiole 3–6 cm long; flowers not observed (= *T. diversifolia* Wrobl.). Plate 139.

T. × **flavescens** A. Br. (*T. americana* × *T. cordata*). Tree with a strong, straight stem and a rounded crown; leaves 6–8 cm long, coarsely serrate, teeth acuminate, glabrous and green beneath, remaining green long into the fall; inflorescences many flowered, staminodes partly present, stamens shorter than the petals. SH 2: 252 p–q (= *T. spaethii* Schneid.). z3

Including the following selection:

'Dropmore'. Selected by F. L. Skinner in Dropmore, Manitoba, Canada. Supposedly resistant to red spider mites and leaf diseases. ⊘

T. floridana (V. Engl.) Small. Medium-sized tree, similar to *T. americana,* to 18 m high, shoots glabrous, reddish brown or yellowish; leaves broad ovate, coarsely serrate, developing leaves tomentose or pubescent beneath, but quickly becoming glabrous, eventually dark yellow-green, lighter or bluish green beneath, with or without very small hair fascicles in the vein axils; flowers few in

Plate 161

Vitis coignetiae
in the Dortmund Botanic Garden, W. Germany

Wigandia caracasana
in a garden in Marbella, Spain

Vitis pentagona var. *bellula*
in Les Barres Arboretum, France

Vitis davidii
in Les Barres Arboretum, France

Plate 162

Weigela decora
Photo: Dr. Watari, Tokyo

Weigela coraeensis
Photo: Dr. Watari, Tokyo

Weigela 'Gustave Malet'
in the Boskoop Experiment Station, Holland

Weigela 'Bristol Ruby'
in the Boskoop Experiment Station, Holland

Plate 163

Weigela florida 'Purpurea' in the Dortmund Botanic Garden, W. Germany

Wisteria sinensis 'Alba' in the Villa Favorita, Castagnola, Lake Maggiore, Italy

Plate 164

Xanthoceras sorbifolia
in the Berlin Botanic Garden, W. Germany

Wisteria floribunda 'Shironoda'
in the Jindai Botanic Garden, Tokyo, Japan

Xanthorrhoea arborea, in its Australian habitat
Photo: Australian News & Information Bureau

Plate 165

Yucca aloifolia
in the S'Avall Garden, Majorca, Spain

Yucca desmetiana
in the S'Avall Garden, Majorca, Spain

Yucca baccata
in the Darmstadt Botanic Garden, W. Germany
Photo: A. Purpus (1913)

Xanthorrhiza simplicissima
in the Dortmund Botanic Garden, W. Germany

Plate 166

Yucca flaccida
in the Aarhus Botanic Garden, Denmark

Yucca glauca
in the Lausanne Botanic Garden, Switzerland

Yucca filamentosa 'Variegata
in Les Barres Arboretum, France

Yucca elephantipes
in the S'Avall Garden, Majorca, Spain

Plate 167

Yucca gloriosa
in the Batumi Botanic Garden, USSR

Yucca smalliana
in the Dortmund Botanic Garden, W. Germany

Yucca treculeana var. *canaliculata*
in the Suchumi Botanic Garden, USSR

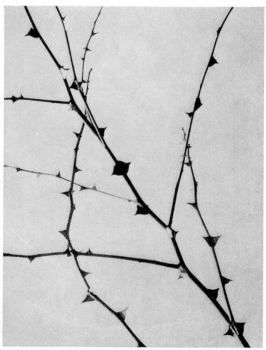

Zanthoxylum simulans
in the Dortmund Botanic Garden, W. Germany

Plate 168

Zelkova carpinifolia
in Bicton Park, England

Zelkova schneideriana
Photo: Bärtels

Zelkova serrata in its habitat
Photo: Dr. Watari, Tokyo

Zenobia pulverulenta var. *nitida*
Photo: C. R. Jelitto, Berlin

pubescent, compact cymes, bracts nearly sessile; fruits rusty-tomentose. SM 738. SE. USA. 1915. z6

T. glabra see: **T. americana**

T. grandifolia see: **T. platyphylla**

T. henryana Szysz. Tree, 9–15 m high, young shoots stellate pubescent at first, later glabrous; leaves broadly ovate or ovate, 5–12 cm long, short acuminate, finely dentate with bristly, 1 cm long teeth, base obliquely cordate to truncate, midrib and venation somewhat pubescent above, underside brownish stellate pubescent with axillary tufts, petiole 2–4 cm long, pubescent; flowers whitish, 10–20 or more in 10–15 cm long, pendulous cymes, bracts stellate pubescent; July to August, fruits short ellipsoid, 5 ribbed. PDR 9: 167; SDK 4: 101; CIS 185. Central China. 1901. z6 Plate 139, 148. ∅ ✤

T. heterophylla Vent. Large tree, to 30 m high, crown conical, shoots red, glabrous; leaves ovate, 8–13 cm long, gradually acuminate, base obliquely truncate, occasionally nearly cordate, finely awn-like serrate, glabrous and glossy above, thickly white tomentose beneath, also often brownish tomentose on the upper leaves (!) and with small, red-brown hair fascicles, petioles 3–4 cm long, glabrous; flowers 10–20 in 6–8 cm long cymes, bracts tomentose beneath at first, July; fruits ellipsoid, 8 mm long, acuminate, brown tomentose. BN 2413; SM 671; SS 27. Eastern USA. 1755. z5 Plate 139.

var. **michauxii** (Nutt.) Sarg. Young shoots red-brown, glabrous; leaves oval-oblong, 8–15 cm long, acute to abruptly acuminate, base cordate, occasionally obliquely truncate, coarsely serrate, short gray or white tomentose beneath, petiole pubescent at first; fruits nearly globose, 6–8 mm thick. SM 672; BB 2846; PDR 9: 165 (= *T. michauxii* Nutt.). N. America. 1800.

T. hollandica see: **T. × europaea**

T. incisodentata see: **T. americana 'Ampelophylla'**

T. insularis Nakai. Closely related to *T. japonica,* but the leaves larger, nearly kidney-shaped, 6–8 cm long, coarsely serrate, with whitish axillary pubescence beneath, thickish; inflorescence 4.5–7 cm wide, the individual flowers 12–14 mm wide, bracts 5 cm long; fruits obovoid. NK 12: 10; PDR 9: 159. z5 Korea.

T. intermedia see: **T. × europaea**

T. intonsa Rehd. & Wils. Tall tree, to 20 m high in its habitat, with a thick stem, young shoots densely yellowish brown pubescent; leaves rounded cordate, abruptly acuminate, evenly serrate, 4–10 cm long, densely stellate pubescent beneath, with 7–9 vein pairs, pubescent in the vein axils beneath; flowers solitary or in 3's, yellowish white, bracts narrowly oblong, pubescent; fruits ovate, 1 cm long, distinctly 5 ribbed, densely tomentose (= *T. tonsura* Hort. Veitch). China; W. Szechwan Prov. 1903. Very attractive species, particularly conspicuous for the persistent pubescence on the branches. z6

T. japonica (Miq.) Simonkai. Closely related to *T. cordata,* to 20 m high, young shoots somewhat pubescent at first; leaves nearly circular, abruptly acuminate, 5–8 cm long, cordate at the base, scabrous serrate, bluish beneath and with pubescent venation when young, with axillary tufts, petiole 2.5–5 cm long; flowers 4–40 (!) in pendulous cymes, bracts stalked, July; fruits short ellipsoid, thin shelled, slightly ribbed. MJ 1015; CIS 179; KIF 1: 88. Japan. 1875. z6 Plate 140; Fig. 280.

T. × juranyana Simonk. (*T. tomentosa* × *T. cordata*). Leaves very glossy above, scattered stellate pubescent beneath, margins densely serrate, teeth with a small mucro; fruits ovoid, somewhat ribbed. Found in Hungary in 1886 but its existence in cultivation is unknown. z4

T. kinashii see: **T. miqueliana**

T. kiusiana Makino & Shiras. Medium-sized tree, young shoots soft pubescent; leaves oblique, broadly ovate to oval-elliptic, occasionally more oblong, 5–8 cm long, 3–5 cm wide, abruptly long acuminate, base on one side wide and obtusely cuneate, the other side truncated to flat cordate or round, serrate, soft pubescent on both sides, with yellow-brown hairs on the vein axils beneath, petiole 8–12 mm long (!); inflorescences eventually glabrous, flowers with 4 mm long sepals and 5–6 mm long petals, July; fruits nearly globose, 4–5 mm, dense brownish pubescent, without ribs or furrows. KIF 2: 59. Japan. z6

T. longifolia dentata see: **T. americana 'Ampelophylla'**

T. mandshurica Rupr. & Maxim. Tree, to 20 m high, winter buds and young shoots densely brown tomentose; leaves ovate, 8–15 cm long, short acuminate, coarsely serrate with long acuminate teeth, occasionally somewhat lobed, base usually cordate, bright green and scattered pubescent above, underside densely gray-white tomentose, petiole 3–7 cm long, tomentose; flowers 7–10 in pendulous brownish tomentose cymes, July; fruits globose, tomentose, slightly 5 ribbed or distinctly ribbed toward the base. NK 12: 12; SDK 4: 103; CIS 182; KIF 4: 30. NE. Asia. Around 1860. ⓕ NE. China. z5

T. maximowicziana Shiras. Tall tree, 20–30 m high, young shoots tomentose; leaves ovate to broadly ovate, 8–10 cm long, abruptly short acuminate, coarsely serrate, teeth wide, with short tips, base obliquely cordate, deep green above and somewhat pubescent at first, gray tomentose with brownish hair fascicles beneath, but eventually partly glabrous, petiole 3–7 cm long; flowers 10–18 in pendulous, tomentose cymes, bracts 7–10 cm long, styles exserted, June; fruits nearly globose, 1 cm thick, 5 ribbed. BC 3815; MJ 1017; GF 6: 113 (as *T. miqueliana*); SDK 4: 102; KIF 2: 60 (= *T. miyabei* Jack). Japan. 1818. z6 Plate 141.

T. michauxii see: **T. heterophylla** var. **michauxii**

T. miqueliana Maxium. Tree, to 15 m high, young shoots tomentose at first; leaves triangular ovate or only ovate, long acuminate, 6–8 cm long, to 12 cm long on long shoots, longer than wide, coarsely serrate with wide teeth, with short mucronate tips, base obliquely cordate, dark green and nearly glabrous above, gray tomentose beneath, without axillary pubescence (!); flowers 10–20 in tomentose, pendulous cymes, stamens 60–75, styles shorter than the petals, June; fruits nearly globose, 5 ribbed at the base. PDR 9: 166; MJ 1016; SDK 4: 102; CIS 183 (= *T. kinashii* Lév. & Van.). Introduced from Japan; not known in the wild. Before 1900. First linden to leaf out in spring and therefore occasionally damaged by frost. z6 Plate 140; Fig. 280.

T. miyabei see: **T. maximowicziana**

T. × **moltkei** Späth (*T. americana* × *T. petiolaris*). A vigorous tree, crown open, branches more or less nodding, young shoots glabrous or slightly pubescent at first; leaves circular-ovate, 10–18 cm long, very similar to those of *T. americana*, but somewhat gray tomentose beneath, venation often pubescent, without axillary pubescence, petioles 5–6 cm long; cymes 5–8 flowered, dense, stalk finely tomentose, July; fruits nearly globose or flattened, indistinctly furrowed. EH 407 (11); SH 2: 256g (= *T. spectabilis* Dipps. non Host). Originated by Späth of Berlin, W. Germany. Before 1880. z5

'Blechiana' (Dieck). Corolla more ovate, denser; leaves large, broad ovate, 15–20 cm long, scabrous awn-toothed, dark green above, greenish white pubescent beneath; flowers in long-stalked small cymes, July; fruits globose, 1 cm thick, with 5 flat furrows, short pubescent. Introduced in 1885 by Dr. Dieck of Zöschen, E. Germany. Perhaps *T. americana* × *T. tomentosa*?

T. mongolica Maxim. Small tree, occasionally to 10 m high, branches nodding, brownish red; leaves on new growth reddish, later glossy green, bluish beneath, oval-rounded, coarsely and irregularly serrate, often 3–5 lobed (like a small *Vitis* leaf!), to 7 cm long; flowers in many-flowered cymes, July; fruits globose, 6–8 mm thick, finely pubescent. LF 226; CIS 180. Mongolia, N. China. 1880. Very interesting species. z3 Plate 140; Fig. 280. ⌀

T. monticola Sarg. Closely related to *T. heterophylla*. A tree to 20 m high, young shoots thick (!), usually red in the first year, winter buds pruinose; leaves ovate to oval-oblong, 10–18 cm long, gradually acuminate, finely serrate with straight or somewhat inward curving teeth, base obliquely truncate or cordate, dark green and glossy above, densely white tomentose (!) beneath, never brownish tomentose, petiole 3–7 cm long (!); flowers about 1 cm wide, 7–10 in glabrous cymes, July; fruits ellipsoid, 6–8 mm long, brown tomentose. SM 747. USA; mountains of Virginia, Tennessee to North Carolina. 1888. z6

T. neglecta Spach. A tall tree, 20–30 m high, annual shoots glabrous, red; leaves broad ovate to ovate, 10–20 cm long, acuminate, coarsely serrate with acuminate, forward-directed teeth, base obliquely cordate to truncate, dark green, glabrous and glossy above, underside gray or greenish and loosely stellate pubescent, venation often brownish with scattered, simple hairs, petiole glabrous, 3–6 cm long; flowers in loose, 5–15 flowered cymes, bracts decurrent to the base, July; fruits globose-ellipsoid, 8 mm thick, occasionally

somewhat angular. GTP 305; SM 673 (as *T. michauxii*); PDR 9: 163 (= *T. stellata* Hartig). N. America. 1830. z4

T. nigra see: **T. americana**

T. nobilis Rehd. & Wils. Small tree, 8–12 m high, young shoots thin, glabrous; leaves ovate, abruptly acuminate, 15–20 cm long, 11–15 cm wide, base obliquely cordate or truncate, sharp bristly serrate, base 5 veined, tough and somewhat leathery, dark green and glossy above, light green with reticulate venation beneath, with raised venation and silky brown hairs in the vein axils, petiole thick, 4–6 cm long, glabrous; flowers 2–5 together, bracts about 12 cm long, 2.5 cm wide; fruits ellipsoid, 1.5 cm long, 1 cm thick (!), pubescent, 5 ribbed. CIS 189; FIO 198. China; W. Szechwan Prov. This species has the largest leaves of all the Chinese lindens; existence in cultivation outside of China is unknown. z6 ⌀ ⊕ ⌂

T. oliveri Szysz. Small tree, 10–15 m high, young shoots glabrous (!), red-brown; leaves broad ovate to ovate, 7–10 cm long, with a short apex, sinuately toothed with short, gland-tipped teeth, base obliquely cordate to truncate, deep green and glabrous above, white tomentose beneath, without axillary tufts of pubescence (!), petiole 3–5 cm long; flowers small, 3–20 in pendulous cymes, flower stalks short, thickened, bracts sessile, June; fruits globose, acuminate, 8 mm long, warty, thick shelled. SDK 4: 102; SH 2: 259c; PDR 9: 165; CIS 184 (= *T. pendula* V. Engl.). Central China. 1900. z6 Plate 140.

T. × **orbicularis** (Carr.) Jouin (*T. euchlora* × *T. petiolaris*). Tree, crown conical, branches nodding, but not as much as those of *T. petiolaris*, with it otherwise very much resembles; leaf petioles also shorter, leaves ovate, short acuminate, scabrous serrate, 5–7 cm long, base cordate, very glossy and glabrous above, underside gray tomentose (not white!). SH 2: 252 l–m. Found around 1870 in the nursery of Simon-Lous in Metz, France. z6 Plate 140.

T. pallida see: **T.** × **europaea 'Pallida'**

T. parvifolia see: **T. cordata**

T. pendula see: **T. oliveri**

T. petiolaris DC. Tree, to 25 m high, branches nodding (!), round crowned, young shoots tomentose at first; leaves acute oval-rounded, 7–11 cm long, regularly and scabrous serrate, base obliquely cordate, dark green above, white tomentose beneath, pendulous on 5–6 cm long petioles (!), fall color golden-yellow; flowers whitish, 3–10 in tomentose cymes, July; fruits warty, flat globose, with 5 furrows. BM 6737; HM 1952 (= *T. americana pendula* Hort.; *T. alba* K. Koch non Michx.). Cultivated before 1840, but the origin unknown, presumably from SE. Europe to Asia Minor or only a cultivar of *T. tomentosa*. Plate 140, 141, 148.

T. platyphylla Scop. Summer Linden. Tree, to 40 m high, crown conical, stem rough, young shoots red-brown, pubescent; leaves rounded-cordate to ovate, short acuminate, scabrous and regularly serrate, to 12 cm long, bright green, lighter and soft pubescent beneath with straight, erect, white hairs (!); flowers yellowish white, mostly in 3's in pendulous cymes, in late June; fruits tomentose, with 5 ribs. GPN 571–572; HM 1960; MD 1917: 6 (= *T. grandifolia* Ehrh.). Central and S. Europe. Cultivated for ages. Ⓕ Czechoslovakia and Bulgaria. Fig. 280. ⌀

The following cultivars are known:

Differing in growth habit
Dwarf globose: 'Compacta'
Narrowly conical: 'Fastigiata', 'Örebro'

Differing in the branches
Bark red in winter: 'Rubra'
Bark yellow in winter: 'Aurea'
Branches twisted: 'Tortuosa'

Differing in the leaf form
Leaf base very oblique: 'Obliqua'
Blade 3 lobed: 'Vitifolia'
Blade very much incised: 'Laciniata'

f. *asplenifolia* see: **'Laciniata'**

'Aurea'. Bark of the annual shoots a pretty light green, particularly in winter. PDR 9: 156. 1838. ⌀

'Compacta'. Habit broadly globose, very slow growing (2 m high in 30 years); leaves broad ovate, deeply biserrate, base obliquely cordate, 4–6 cm wide. NDJ 20: 12a. Around 1930. Known only from the Wageningen Arboretum, Holland.

f. *corallina* see: **'Rubra'**

'Fastigiata'. Narrowly conical habit, branches slanting upright (= f. *pyramidalis* Hort.). 1864. ⌀

f. *filicifolia* see: **'Laciniata'**

'Laciniata'. Leaves deeply incised and often crispate. MD 1920: 67; PDR 9: 156 (= f. *asplenifolia* Hort.; f. *filicifolia* Hort.). 1835. Plate 140. ⌀

'Obliqua'. Leaves very oblique at the base. Boom, Ned. Dendr. (4th): 90d. 1853.

'Örebro' (Lundstrom). Narrowly conical, like 'Fastigiata', but the branches very tightly upright. NDJ 14: 73. Found in 1935 in the K. A. Lundstrom Nursery in Östansjö, near Örebro, Sweden.

'Rubra'. Branches with orange-red to coral-red bark in winter (= f. *corallina* Hartwig & Ruempl.; *T. rubra* DC.). Discovered in France in 1755. ⌀

f. *pyramidalis* see: **'Fastigiata'**

'Tortuosa'. Young shoots uniquely twisted and twining corkscrew-like. Discovered in England before 1888.

'Vitifolia'. Normal, tree-like habit; leaves slightly 3 lobed and scabrous serrate. Boom, Ned. Dendr. (4): 90c. 1875.

T. praecox see: **T. × flaccida**

T. rubra see: **T. dasystyla** and **T. platyphylla 'Rubra'**

T. spaethii see: **T. × flavescens**

T. spectabilis see: **T. × moltkei**

T. stellata see: **T. neglecta**

T. tomentosa Moench. Hungarian Silver Linden. Tree, to

30 m high, crown dense and widely conical, branches stiffly erect (!!), young shoots gray-tomentose; leaves rounded cordate, short acuminate, to 10 cm long, scabrous serrate, occasionally slightly lobed, base cordate to truncate, dark green above, light gray tomentose beneath, petiole 2–3.5 cm long (!!), fall color golden-yellow; flowers 7–10 in pendulous cymes, July; fruits acutely ovate, about 1 cm long, finely warty and slightly 5 ribbed. HM 1951; HW 3: 43 (= *T. alba* Ait. non K. Koch; *T. argentea* Desf.). SE. Europe, Asia Minor. 1767. Particularly pollution tolerant tree; very good street tree. Ⓕ Romania, Bulgaria. z4 Plate 139; Fig. 280. ⌀

var. *inaequalis* f. *rhodopetala* see: **'Rhodopetala'**

'Rhodopetala'. Flower buds red, petals violet-pink in full bloom, becoming yellowish toward the base, inflorescences more abundantly flowering than the species, also the fruits somewhat larger. DB 1965: 161–162 (= *T. tomentosa* var. *inaequalis* f. *rhodopetala* Borb.). Known before 1900 from several locations in Hungary, but first propagated in 1930. The best trees are at Vérmezö in Budapest. ⊕

T. tonsura see: **T. intonsa**

T. tuan Szysz. Tree, 10–15 m high, young shoots glabrous or quickly becoming so; leaves broad ovate, 6–13 cm long, acuminate, base very oblique, occasionally somewhat cordate, sparsely and finely toothed, usually entire on the basal half (!), glabrous above, densely gray tomentose beneath, with small axillary tufted pubescence, petiole pubescent, 3–6 cm long; flowers 15–20 in 7–10 cm long, pendulous cymes, yellowish white, bracts stellate pubescent, July; fruits globose, 8 mm thick, warty, thick shelled. LF 227; PDR 9: 165; SDK 4: 101; CIS 191; FIO 197. Central China. 1901. "Tuan" is the Chinese word for "linden". z6 Plate 140.

var. **chinensis** (Syzsz.) Rehd. & Wils. Young shoots tomentose, winter buds densely pubescent; leaves more ovate to oblong-ovate. SH 2: 257 l–m (= *T. chinesis* sensu Schneid.). 1907.

T. ulmifolia see: **T. cordata**

T. × varsaviensis Kobendza (*T. platyphylla* × *T. tomentosa*). Tree, similar to *T. tomentosa*, but the crown is more compact, conical, young shoots reddish, tomentose at first, tips of the uppermost shoots pendulous; leaves like those of *T. tomentosa*, glossy above, gray-green beneath, occasionally with a particularly large tooth on one or both blade halves; fruits occasionally wider than long, only slightly fertile. PDR 7: 160–169. Originating spontaneously around 1924 in the Warsaw Botanic Garden, Poland. z4

Including the clone:

'Mrs. Stenson. Tree, to 12 m, crown broadly conical, shoots dark red, tomentose when young, eventually glabrous; leaves rounded, abruptly acuminate, 6.5–10 cm long, tomentose on both sides in spring, later green and persisting so until late in the fall; flowers cream-yellow, very fragrant. Introduced from Poland into the USA by J. Vilhelm Stenson, 1965; distributed by the Woodland Nurseries, Cooksville, Ontario, Canada. ⌀

T. vulgaris see: **T. × europaea**

Illustrations of further species:

T. begoniifolia	CIS 214
T. omeiensis	FIO 198
T. paucicostata	CIS 181

All species will thrive in any good soil, but are sometimes damaged by red spider mites. Very valuable pollen source for honey bees, particularly *T. cordata* and *T. platyphylla*.

Lit. Szymanowski, T.: The fruits of the Lime-trees cultivated in Poland; in Ann. Sect. dendr. Soc. Bot. Pol. **9**, 151–169, 1956 (in Polish) ● Wagner, J.: Die Linden des historischen Ungarn; in Mitt. DDG 1932, 316–345; 1933, 5–60 ● Burret, M.: Beiträge zur Kenntnis der Tiliaceen; in Notizbl. Bot. Gart. Berlin **9**, 592–880, 1926 ● Engler, Vict.: Monographie der Gattung *Tilia;* Berlin 1909 (159 pp.) ● Schumann, V.: *Tiliaceae;* in Engler & Prantl, Nat. Pfl. Fam. III (6), 8–30, 1893.

TIPUANA Benth. — Yellow Jacaranda — LEGUMINOSAE

Montypic genus with the following characteristics:

Tipuana speciosa see: **T. tipu**

T. tipu (Benth.) O. Ktze. Attractive, deciduous, thornless tree; leaves odd pinnate, without stipules, leaflets 11–21, oblong, emarginate, 3.5 cm long, somewhat parallel veined; flowers in open-branched, terminal panicles, attractive, calyx top-shaped, teeth short and wide, standard ovate to nearly circular, yellow with reddish center, wings obliquely obovate, keel oblong, obtuse; fruits samara-like, indehiscent, with 1–3 seeds, 6 cm long, veined. MCL 34 (= *T. speciosa* Benth.). S. America; utilized as a street tree in the tropics. z10 ⊕

TRACHELOSPERMUM Lem. — Star Jasmine — APOCYNACEAE

Evergreen twining shrubs, shoots and leaves containing a milky sap; leaves opposite, leathery, distinctly pinnately veined; flowers white to yellowish, in terminal axillary clusters, corolla salverform, with a long, narrow tube and an outspread, 5 lobed limb, the lobes somewhat twisted together on the left side, overlapped on the right side; stamens very short, anthers united and appressed to the stigma. — About 30 species in E. Asia, only one in the Southern USA.

Trachelospermum asiaticum (S. & Z.) Nakai. Evergreen shrub, climbing 3–5 m high, shoots densely foliate, with a persistent pubescence; leaves elliptic, 2–5 cm long, obtuse, glabrous, glossy green; flowers yellowish white, fragrant, in terminal cymes, corolla 2 cm wide, calyx tips small and erect (!!), July–August. (= *T. divaricatum* Kanitz; *T. crocostemon* Stapf.) Korea, Japan. Much hardier than the following species. z9 # ⊕

T. crocostemon see: **T. asiaticum**

T. divaricatum see: **T. asiaticum**

T. jasminoides (Lindl.) Lem. Evergreen shrub, twining to 5 m high, young shoots pubescent; leaves elliptic-oblong, 2–6 cm long, obtuse, tapered to both ends, deep green and glossy above, underside somewhat pubescent at first; flowers pure white, very fragrant, corolla 2.5 cm wide, in terminal and axillary racemes, sepals outspread (!!), sinuate, July. FS 615; FIO 89; HV 28; BM 4737; MJ 622. China. 1844. z9 Fig. 282. # ⊕

'Variegatum'. Very attractive plant with white leaf margins, white speckled leaves, often turning somewhat carmine in winter. ⊕

'Wilsonii'. Leaves variable, from ovate to nearly linear-lanceolate, attractively veined, often carmine-red in winter. Introduced by E. H. Wilson from China. ⊕

Only suitable for very mild climates; particularly good wall climber or greenhouse plant.

Lit. Hatusima, S.: A revision of Japanese *Trachelospermum;* in Jour. Jap. Bot. **16**, 20–30, 1940.

TRACHYCARPUS Wendl. — PALMAE

Tall, relatively thornless palms with single trunks, upper portion of trunk covered with a fibrous netting and leaf sheaths; leaves terminal, petiolate, circular or hemispherical, with many short, radiating lobes, rachis absent; ligule very short, leaf sheaths with a fibrous layer inside; petiole flat above, with only small thorns on the margin; flowers monoecious, small, yellow, in large stiff panicles, petals and sepals 3 each; fruits 1–3 drupes together. — 8 species from W. Himalayas to China and Japan.

Trachycarpus fortunei Wendl. 4–12 m high, (depending upon site and climate), stem cylindrical, upper portion densely covered with coarse fibers; leaves nearly circular, to 60 cm long and 90 cm wide, composed of many narrow segments, light green, petioles 40–90 cm long, firm, finely dentate on the margins, with a tough fibrous net at the base; flowers small, yellow, many in thick-stalked, drooping, 30–60 cm long panicles, May–June; fruits blue-black, globose, 12 mm thick. BM 5221; MJ 2337, 3733 (= *Chamaerops excelsa* Mart.). Upper Burma, China, Japan. 1844. z9 Plate 142. # ∅ ⊕

TREMA Lour — ULMACEAE

Evergreen trees, similar to *Celtis;* leaves alternate, short petioled, 3 veined or pinnately veined, with stipules; flowers monoecious or dioecious, in small, nearly sessile clusters, petals absent, usually 5, occasionally only 4, parted; sepals on the staminate flowers valvate at the base, imbricate at the apex; stamens 4–5; ovaries unilocular, style with 2 linear arms; fruit a small, ovate to nearly globose drupe. — 30 species in the tropics and subtropics.

Trema orientalis Bl. Small tree, young shoots soft pubescent; leaves stiff, oval-oblong to more lanceolate,

Fig. 281. *Trema orientalis*

7–15 cm long, long acuminate, finely crenate, base cordate and 3–7 veined, rough above, appressed silvery pubescent beneath; fruits ovate, 4 mm long, black. S. Asia. z10 Fig. 281. # ∅

No particular requirements except for a frost free climate.

TRICUSPIDARIA

Tricuspidaria dependens see: **Crinodendron patagua**

T. lanceolata see: **Crinodendron hookerianum**

TRIPETALEIA S. & Z. — ERICACEAE

Deciduous shrub; leaves alternate, entire, short petioled; flower corolla with 3(sometimes 4–5) petals and as many sepals; petals somewhat spirally twisted; fruit a 3 locular, loculicidal capsule. — One species in Japan.

Easily distinguished by the 3-part corolla from the closely related genera *Elliotia* (with 4 petals) and *Cladothamnus* (with 5 petals). Distinguised from *Botryostege* by the 5 connate sepals, cupulate calyx and distinctly stalked fruit capsules.

Tripetaleia bracteata Maxim. see: **Botryostege bracteata**

T. paniculata S. & Z. 2 m high in its habitat, shoots red-brown, angular to slightly winged; leaves rhombic-ovate, 2.5–6 cm long, acute, base cuneate, glabrous; flowers in 5–10 cm long panicles at the end of the current year's densely foliate shoots, petals about 8 mm long, white with a trace of pink, twisted, calyx cupulate, indistinct and shallowly 3(5) lobed, July–September. MJ

772. Japan. 1877. z6 ✿

Winter hardy, but not particularly ornamental; cultivated somewhat like azalea.

TRIPTERYGIUM Hook. f. — CELASTRACEAE

Deciduous climbing shrubs; leaves alternate, simple, large; flowers small, in large, terminal panicles, polygamous; calyx 5 lobed, petals 5, stamens 5; fruit single seeded, with 3 wide, membranous wings. — 4–5 species in E. Asia, of these only one is winter hardy.

Tripterygium regelii Sprague & Takeda. Shrub, to 2 m high, branches long ascending-nodding, brownish green, densely punctate; leaves ovate, 10–17 cm long, long acuminate, regularly crenate, light green above, paler with a pubescent midrib beneath; flowers yellowish-white, 8 mm wide, in up to 25 cm long panicles, June–July; fruits greenish white (!), 15 mm long. Gfl 612; NF 1: 5; MJ 1079 (= *T. wilfordii* Regel non Hook. f.). Japan, Korea. 1509. Quite hardy. z5 Plate 141; Fig. 281. ✿ ⚥

T. wilfordii Hook. f. Climbing 7–10 m high; leaves 5–12 cm long, often blue-green beneath; panicles to 25 cm long; fruits purple-red (!!), to 2 cm long. BM 9488; DRHS 2149; LWT 182; GC 132: 60 (fruit). S. China, Taiwan, Burma. 1913. Not winter hardy! See also: **T. regelii**. z9 ✿ ⚥

Cultivated like *Celastrus*.

TROCHODENDRON S. & Z. — TROCHODENDRACEAE

Monotypic genus. Evergreen, aromatic shrub or tree; leaves alternate, clustered together, long petioled, margins crenate; flowers without sepals and petals, stamens numerous, spreading from the margin of a broad, green disk, filaments long, carpels 5–11; fruit composed of 6–10 follicles inserted in a fleshy calyx cap.

Trochodendron aralioides S. & Z. Evergreen tree, to 20 m high in its habitat, branches glabrous, bark aromatic; leaves ovate to obovate or oval-oblong, leathery, 8–15 cm long, obtusely acuminate, crenate, dark green and glossy above, lighter beneath, petiole 3–7 cm long; flowers green, 2 cm wide, anthers yellow-brown, in erect, terminal, 6–8 cm long panicles, June; fruits brown, 1.5–2 cm wide. BS 3: 439; BM 7375; MJ 1731; LWT 56. Japan, Korea; mountain forests. 1894. z8 Plate 145; Fig. 282. # ∅ ✿

Very attractive in a protected site; cultivated somewhat like *Magnolia* or *Rhododendron*.

Lit. Smith, A. C.: A taxonomic revision of *Trochodendron* and *Tetracentron*; in Jour. Arnold Arb. **26**, 123–142, 1945.

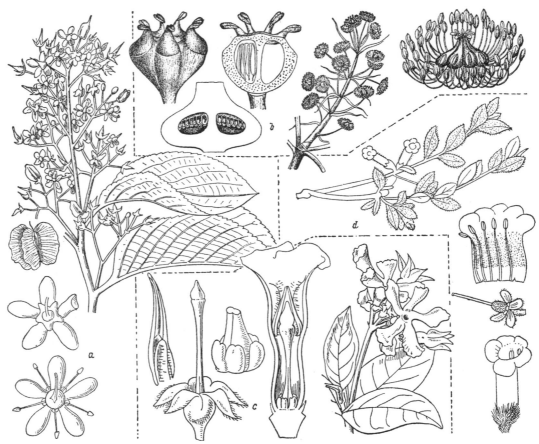

Fig. 282. a. *Tripterygium regelii*; b. *Trochodendron aralioides*; c. *Trachelospermum jasminoides*; d. *Tsusiophyllum tanakae* (from Maximowicz, Prantl, Siebold & Zuccarini, Regel, B. M.)

TSUSIOPHYLLUM Maxim. — ERICACEAE

Monotypic genus. Dwarf shrub, appressed pubescent; leaves alternate, entire; flowers in clusters of 2–6, corolla tubular, with a narrow, erect limb, calyx lobes 5, densely strigose, stamens 5; fruit a 3 locular, hard, loculicidal capsule.

Differing from *Rhododendron* in the longitudinally splitting anthers (not opening at the apex) and the 3 locular (not 5 or 10) capsule.

Tsusiophyllum tanakae Maxim. Semi-evergreen, broad growing dwarf shrub, 30–40 cm high, young shoots densely appressed pubescent, particularly on the leaf upper surface; leaves ovate to lanceolate or oblanceolate, 1–2 cm long; flowers in small, terminal clusters of 2–6, white, tubular, the small limb lobes rugose, tube silky pubescent on the interior, 15 mm long, June. MJ 746. Japan. z7 Fig. 282. #

Cultivated like *Rhododendron*.

TWEEDIA

Tweedia versicolor see: **Oxypetalum caeruleum**

ULEX — Furze, Gorse — LEGUMINOSAE

Thorny shrub with striped branches terminating in a thorny tip; leaves reduced to a thorny leaf petiole or a small scale, without stipules; flowers yellow, in the apical thorn axils, with a membranous, 2-part calyx; ovaries sessile, pods ovate, oblong or short linear, compressed, bivalvate; seeds appendaged at the hilum (strophiolate). — 20 species in W. Europe, N. Africa.

Key

+ Major thorns 2.5–5 cm long; calyx densely shaggy, 12–14 mm long:

         U. europaeus

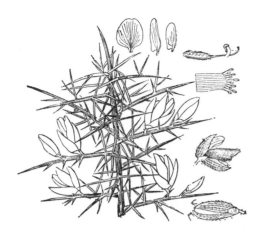

Fig. 283. *Ulex europaeus* (from Lauche)

++ Major thorns usually shorter than 2.5 cm; calyx softly pubescent, 7–12 mm long;

    * Thorns soft; wings bowed, about as long as the keel petal;

        U. nanus

    ** Thorns stiff; wings straight, longer than the keel:
        U. gallii

Ulex europaeus L. To 1 m high, occasionally twice as high, branches densely thorny and stiff, shoots furrowed, pubescent at first, green; leaves modified into 6–12 cm long, sharp thorns; flowers golden-yellow, solitary, but numerous, primarily at the branch tips, May–June, but also flowering somewhat throughout the year; pod 1 cm long. HF 2292. Originally only found in Portugal, but disseminated throughout Spain, France, Belgium, Holland and the British Isles, primarily along the coast and in pastures. Ⓕ Europe; for dune stabilizing. z6 Fig. 283. ⊕

'Plenus'. Lower growing; flowers double, seedless. First found in 1828 in the nursery of John Miller in Bristol, England. Flowers well only on poor soil. ⊕

var. **strictus** (Mackay) Webb. Irish Gorse. Tightly upright habit, narrower, often nearly columnar, flowering less abundantly (= *U. hibernicus* G. Don). Ireland.

U. gallii Planch. Dense, thorny shrub, 40–50 cm high in the wild, larger in cultivation, shoots pubescent, thorns only 1–2.5 cm long (!); flowers golden-yellow, 1.5 cm long, wings slightly bowed and longer than the keel (!), August–October (!); pods 1–1.2 cm long. CF 470; FS 441 (= *U. jussieui* Webb.). Portugal, England, primarily along the west coast. z9 Plate 142. ⊕

U. hibernicus see: **U. europaeus** var. **strictus**

U. jussieui see: **U. gallii**

U. minor Roth. Dense, compact shrub, 0.3–0.5 m high, shoots soft pubescent and densely thorny, thorns 6–12 mm long, soft; flowers golden-yellow, 12 mm long, calyx soft pubescent, wings about as long as the keel, bowed, July–October (!!); pods 12 mm long, pubescent. BS 3: 496; CF 471; PEu 53 (= *U. nanus* Forster). W. Europe, England. z7 ⊕

U. nanus see: **U. minor**

U. parviflorus Pourret. Shrub, 60–150 cm high, quite variable in habit, long shoots densely shaggy or crispate pubescent or also eventually glabrous, short shoots and thorns crispate pubescent to glabrous, thorns straight or bowed, 4–30 mm long, phyllodes 2–5 mm long, triangular; flowers yellow, standard and keel as long as the calyx, wings shorter. PSw 19. SW. Europe, Portugal to S. France. z7

Difficult to transplant, hence best seeded or moved with a ball of soil; likes a sandy acid soil.

Lit. Rothmaler, W.: Revision der Genisteen. I. Monographien der Gattungen um *Ulex*; in Bot. Jahrb. 72, 69–116, 1941 ● Vicioso, C.: Revision del genero "*Ulex*" en España; Madrid 1962 (57 pp., 13 plates).

ULMUS L. — Elm — ULMACEAE

Tall, deciduous trees, occasionally semi-evergreen shrubs; leaves distichous, alternate, short petioled, simple, never 3 veined (!), usually biserrate, usually very oblique at the base; flowers hermaphroditic, unattractive, most appear before the leaves, some species flower in fall; corolla campanulate, with 4 or 5 lobes and an equal number of stamens; fruit a flat nutlet, surrounded by a membranous, more or less broad, encircling winged margin, ripening very soon after flowering. — About 45 species in the north temperate zone.

NOTE ON NOMENCLATURE: While the nomenclature of the American and Asiatic species have undergone large revision, this is not the case with the European species. The European species have been treated in various ways by individual authors for over 200 years. The line is not sharply drawn even today and it appears that a total revision will not occur within the near future. In this work, the nomenclature of the European *Ulmus* (so far as is applicable) is taken from the new edition of Clapham-Tutin-Warburg (Flora of the British Isles).

R. H. Richens (1976, 1977) lumped all the European field elms under the name **U. minor** Mill. sensu latissimo (= *U. carpinifolia* Suckow). He established the following combinations:

U. minor var. **vulgaris** (Ait.) Richens
    (= *U. procera* Salisb.)

U. minor var. **cornubiensis** (West.) Richens
    (= *U. carpinifolia* var. *cornubiensis* [West.] Rehd.; *U. stricta* Lindl.)

U. minor var. **sarniensis** (Loud.) Richens
    (= *U. carpinifolia* var. *sarniensis* [Loud.] Rehd.; *U. stricta* var. *sarniensis* [Loud.] Moss)

U. minor var. **lockii** (Druce) Richens
    (= *U. glabra* var. *lockii* Druce; *U. plotii* Druce)

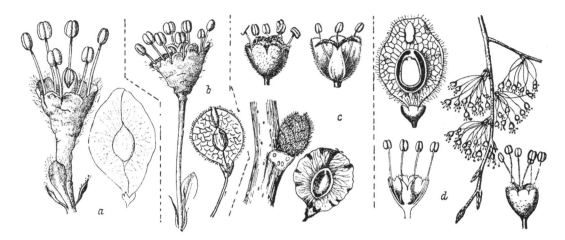

Fig. 284. **Ulmus.** Flowers and fruits. a. *U. glabra;* b. *U. laevis;* c. *U. rubra;* d. *U. americana*
(from Hempel & Wilhelm, Sargent)

Outline of the Genus

Section 1. **Blepharocarpus** Dumort.
Flowers appear before the leaves, in pendulous clusters, stalks of uneven length; calyx with 5–8 uneven, short lobes; fruits glabrous, but ciliate margined:
     U. americana, laevis

Section 2. **Chaetoptelea** (Liebm.) Schneid.
Flowers appear before the leaves, on long stalks, in racemes; fruits pubescent and ciliate along the margin, seeds near the apex:
     U. alata, thomasii

Section 3. **Madocarpus** Dumort.
Flowers in erect clusters before the leaves, nearly sessile to short stalked; calyx with 4–7 evenly short lobes; fruit only occasionally ciliate on the margin:
     U. bergmanniana, canescens, carpinifolia, davidiana, elegantissima, elliptica, glabra, hollandica, japonica, laciniata, macrocarpa, plotii, procera, pumila, rubra, villosa, wallichiana, wilsoniana

Section 4. **Microptelea** (Spach) Benth. & Hook.
Flowering in the fall, in erect clusters, on short, stout stalks; leaves semi-evergreen or falling very late; fruit wings pubescent or glabrous:
     U. crassifolia, parvifolia

Section 5. **Trichoptelea** Schneid.
Flowers in pendulous racemes in the fall; fruit wings pubescent and ciliate:
     U. serotina

Outline of the Parentage of the Cultivars

Some commonly used synonyms are also included in these lists.

'Argenteovariegata'	→ *U. procera*
'Atropurpurea'	→ *U. glabra*
'Augustine'	→ *americana*
australis	→ *U. procera*
'Bea Schwartz'	→ *U. hollandica*
'Belgica'	→ *U. hollandica*
'Berardii'	→ *U. pumila*
'Camperdownii'	→ *U. glabra*
'Christine Buisman'	→ *U. hollandica*

'Commelin'	→ *U. hollandica*
concavifolia	→ *U. carpinifolia* 'Webbiana'
'Coolshade'	→ *U. pumila*
'Cornubiensis'	→ *U. carpinifolia*
'Cornuta'	→ *U. glabra*
'Crispa'	→ *U. glabra*
'Dampieri'	→ *U. hollandica*
'Dauvessei'	→ *U. hollandica*
'Den Haag'	→ *U. pumila*
'Dicksonii'	→ *U. carpinifolia*
'Dumont'	→ *U. hollandica*
'Exoniensis'	→ *U. glabra*
'Gracilis'	→ *U. carpinifolia* 'Umbraculifera Gracilis'
Groenveld'	→ *U. hollandica*
'Hamburg Hybrid'	→ *U. pumila*
'Hansen'	→ *U. parvifolia*
Hillieri'	→ *U. hollandica*
'Hoersholm'	→ *U. carpinifolia* 'Hoersholmiensis'
Horizontalis'	→ *U. glabra*
'Huntingdon'	→ *U. hollandica* 'Vegeta'
'Improved Coolshade'	→ *U. pumila*
'Insularis'	→ *U. glabra*
italica	→ *U. carpinifolia* var. *italica*
'Jacqueline Hillier'	→ *U. elegantissima*
'Klemmer'	→ *U. hollandica*
'Koopmannii'	→ *U. carpinifolia*
'Louis van Houtte'	→ *U. procera*
'Major'	→ *U. hollandica*
'Lake City'	→ *U. americana*
'Littleford'	→ *U. americana*
'Marginata'	→ *U. procera* 'Viminalis Marginata'
'Moline'	→ *U. americana*
'Monstrosa'	→ *U. glabra*
montana horizontalis	→ *U. glabra* 'Pendula'
montana pendula	→ *U. glabra* 'Camperdownii'
'Monumentalis'	→ *U. carpinifolia* 'Sarniensis'
'Myrtifolia'	→ *U. carpinifolia*
'Pendula'	→ *U. glabra* 'Pendula'

'Pendula'	→ *U. hollandica* 'Smithii'
'Pitteurs'	→ *U. hollandica*
plumosa pyramidalis	→ *U. glabra* 'Exoniensis'
'Princeton'	→ *U. americana*
'Propendens'	→ *U. carpinifolia*
'Purpurascens'	→ *U. procera*
'Purpurea'	→ *U. procera*
'Purpurea'	→ *U. glabra*
'Rueppellii'	→ *U. carpinifolia*
'Sarniensis'	→ *U. carpinifolia*
'Serpentina'	→ *U. glabra*
'Smithii'	→ *U. hollandica*
'Superba'	→ *U. hollandica*
'Umbraculifera'	→ *U. carpinifolia*
unbraculifera gracilis	→ *U. carpinifolia* 'Umbraculifera Gracilis'
'Vegeta'	→ *U. hollandica*
'Viminalis'	→ *U. procera*
'Viminalis Aurea'	→ *U. procera*
'Viminalis Marginata'	→ *U. procera*
'Webbiana'	→ *U. carpinifolia*
wentworthii	→ *U. carpinifolia* 'Pendula'
'Wheatleyi'	→ *U. carpinifolia* 'Sarniensis'
'Wredei'	→ *U. hollandica*
'Wredei Aurea'	→ *U. hollandica* 'Wredei'

Other important Synonyms

U. angustifolia	→ **U. carpinifolia**
U. campestris	→ **U. carpinifolia**
U. coritana	→ **U. carpinifolia**
U. effusa	→ **U. laevis**
U. foliacea	→ **U. carpinifolia**
U. fulva	→ **U. rubra**
U. montana	→ **U. glabra**
U. montana 'Fastigiata'	→ **U. Glabra** 'Exoniensis'
U. minor Mill.	→ See notes at p. 403
U. nitens	→ **U. carpinifolia**
U. nitens 'Stricta'	→ **U. carpinifolia** 'Cornubiensis'
U. nitens 'Wheatleyi'	→ **U. carpinifolia** 'Sarniensis'
U. pinnato-ramosa	→ **U. pumila arborea**
U. praestans	→ **U. glabra** 'Superba'
U. sarniensis	→ **U. carpinifolia** 'Sarniensis'
U. scabra	→ **U. glabra**
U. stricta	→ **U. carpinifolia**
U. stricta goodyeri	→ **U. carpinifolia** 'Cornubiensis'
U. vegeta	→ **U. hollandica** 'Vegeta'

Ulmus alata Michx. Small tree, to 15 m high, crown oblong-globose, branches rather short, spreading, young shoots glabrous, usually with 2 wide, opposite corky wings (!); leaves oval-oblong to more oblong-lanceolate, 3–6 cm long, somewhat leathery, biserrate, glabrous above, venation pubescent beneath, petiole 1–3 mm long; fruits oval-elliptic, 8 mm long, narrowly winged, with 2 inward curving beaks at the apex. SS 313; BB 1252; HH 186; KTL 65. SE. USA. 1820. Rare in cultivation. z5 Fig. 288.

U. alba see: **U. americana**

U. americana L. American Elm. Tall, stately tree, 20–40 m high, crown nearly vase-shaped, branches diverging from each other and drooping in a wide arch, young shoots pubescent at first, winter buds ovate, acute or obtuse; leaves oval-oblong, widest in the middle, 7–15 cm long, acuminate, base very oblique, biserrate, glabrous and rough above, usually somewhat pubescent beneath, with about 18 vein pairs, petiole 5–8 mm long; flowers usually 3–4 together, pendulous on 1–2 cm long stalks, stamens 7–8, exserted, stigmas white; fruits elliptic, 1 cm long, incised to the nutlet, ciliate. SS 311; BB 1250; HH 182; GTP 193; KTL 66 (= *U. alba* Raf.). Eastern N. America. 1752. One of the most attractive of all park trees! Fast growing, but unfortunately easily damaged by wind and seriously threatened by the Dutch Elm Disease! Ⓕ USA, Canada. z2 Plate 143; Fig. 284. ∅

'Augustine'. Columnar form, very fast growing, branches obliquely spreading. Developed around 1920 in Normal, Illinois. Widely distributed throughout the USA.

Some other American selections include 'Lake City', 'Littleford', 'Moline' & 'Princeton'.

U. angustifolia see: **U. carpinifolia** 'Cornubiensis'

U. androssowii see: **U. pumila** f. **androssowii**

U. antarctica see: **U. procera** 'Viminalis'

U. asplenifolia see: **U. glabra** 'Crispa'

U. belgica see: **U. × hollandica** 'Belgica'

U. bergmanniana Schneid. Tree, 9–18 m high, branches stout, divaricately spreading, bark dark gray with shallow furrows, rather finely scaly, showing a brown inner bark beneath, young shoots thin, gray-brown, glabrous, punctate; leaves oblong-ovate, 8–14 cm long, 4–7 cm wide, long acuminate, base oblique, coarsely biserrate, glossy green above and long silky pubescent when young, later glabrous and light green, tough, nearly leathery, venation raised beneath, petiole 1 cm long; flowers 5–9 together, reddish green, clustered; fruits obovoid, deeply incised at the apex, nutlet in the middle of the surrounding wing, long stalked, wings ovate, pubescent and ciliate, greenish. China; Kansu, W. Hupeh, Szechwan Provs., 800 m. z6 Fig. 287. ∅

U. campestris see: **U. carpinifolia, U. glabra** and **U. procera**

U. campestris dampieri see: **U. × hollandica** 'Dampieri'

U. canescens Melville. Tree, very similar to *U. carpinifolia* in appearance, but the young shoots with a dense, soft, white pubescence in the first year; leaves oval-elliptic, crenate, densely gray pubescent, with 12–16(18) vein pairs. Central and Eastern Mediterranean region; Greece, Yugoslavia, Italy and Sicily. z7

U. carpinifolia Gleditsch. Smooth-leaved Elm. Tree, to 20(30) m high, quite variable in habit and leaf form, branches usually glabrous, erect to outspread, thin, often long and more or less pendulous; leaves usually 4–10 cm long, oblanceolate to nearly circular, usually smooth and glossy above, glabrous beneath with axillary pubescence, biserrate, base uneven, with 9–12 vein pairs, petiole 6–12 mm long, usually pubescent; flowers

Fig. 285. *Ulmus carpinifolia*, branch with flowers
and fruits (from Kerner and Hempel & Wilhelm)

in dense clusters, stamens 4–5, stigmas usually white,
February–March; fruits elliptic to obovate, cuneate at the
base, seeds located near the closed apex. HTr 86; CF 49;
HW 37 (= *U. campestris* L. p. p.; *U. foliacea* Gilib.; *U. nitens*
Moench; *U. coritana* Melville; *U. diversifolia* Melville).
Europe to the Mediterranean region. Cultivated for ages.
Ⓕ USSR, Czechoslovakia, Yugoslavia. z5 Fig. 285.

Many cultivars:

Varying in crown form;
  Conical;
    'Hoersholmiensis', 'Sarniensis'

  Narrowly conical:
    'Cornubiensis', 'Dicksonii' (yellow), 'Webbiana'

  Ovate:
    'Koopmannii'

  Globose form:
    'Rueppellii', 'Umbraculifera', 'Umbraculifera Gracilis'

  Weeping:
    'Pendula', 'Propendens'

  Branches very corky:
    f. *suberosa*

  Leaves variegated:
    'Dicksonii' (yellow), 'Variegata' (white variegated)

  Leaves with 14–18 vein pairs, leathery:
    var. *italica*

'Berardii' see: *U. pumila* 'Berardii'

'Cornubiensis'. Tree, narrowly conical, 18–20 m high, young
shoots more or less pubescent or only so at the nodes; leaves
somewhat leathery, elliptic to broadly obovate, 5–7 cm long,
dark green and smooth above, petiole about 8 mm long;
flowers usually 4 parted, stigma pink; fruits obovate, narrower

than those of the species. HTr 84; EH 397 (= *U. campestris stricta*
Ait.; *U. stricta* Lindl.; *U. campestris fastigiata* Spach; *U. angustifolia*
var. *cornubiensis* [West.] Melville). S. England; Cornwall, S.
Devon. In cultivation a long time.

'Dicksonii'. Tightly upright habit; similar to 'Cornubiensis', but
with golden-yellow leaves, holding its color well until fall.
Originated in Dickson's Nursery around 1900. ∅

'Hoersholm'. Tall tree, stem short, quickly separating into
several, tighly upright branches, narrowly ovate crown,
branches slightly nodding at the tips; leaves oblong, 8–14 cm
long, coarsely biserrate, acuminate, 3–4.5 cm wide; fruits
obovate, seeds in the middle of the wing. Lu 1950: 61–69.
Originated around 1885 in the L. Nielsen Nursery in
Hoersholm, Denmark. Widely disseminated in Denmark
today. Plate 144.

var. italica (Henry) Rehd. Large tree, similar to the species, but
the leaves more leathery, tough, with 14–18 vein pairs, totally
glabrous beneath except for some axillary tufts, petiole about 6
mm long. EH 411 (= *U. nitens* var. *italica* Henry). Italy, Spain,
Portugal. Plate 144.

'Koopmannii'. Very similar to 'Umbraculifera', but with an
ovate crown (!), just as dense, young shoots lighter, often
corky; leaves 2.5–3.5 cm long, more gray-green beneath,
petiole 3–5 mm long (= *U. koopmannii* Späth.). Introduced in
1883 by Lauche from Turkestan.

'Pendula'. Shoots thin, pendulous; leaves glabrous (= *U.
campestris wentworthii* Hort.). Before 1890.

'Propendens'. A form of var. *suberosa*, but the branches are
widespreading and nodding, corky; leaves only 2–3 cm long.
MG 1901: 163 (= *U. suberosa pendula* Lav.).

'Rueppellii' (Späth). Very similar to 'Umbraculifera', with a
dense, globose crown, slow growing, but with corky branches,
young shoots soft pubescent; leaves rather small, rough above.
Introduced by Späth from Tashkent, USSR.

'Sarniensis'. Jersey Elm. Only slightly different from
'Cornubiensis', shoots more tightly upright; leaves wider,
flatter, 4–6 cm long, dark green and glossy above, without
distinct axillary pubescence beneath, somewhat glandular, as is
the petiole. GC 41: 67; MD 1910: 273; HTr 85 (= *U. campestris
sarniensis* [Lodd.] Loud.; *U. campestris wheatleyi* Sim.-Louis; *U.
× sarniensis* [Loud.] Melville). England. 1836. Possibly a
hybrid, *U. angustifolia* × *U. glabra* × *U. carpinifolia* × *U. plotii*.
Plate 143.

var. suberosa (Moench) Rehd. Habit usually only shrubby,
branches erect, very corky winged; leaves smaller, somewhat
rough above (= *U. suberosa* Moench; *U. campestris suberosa*
[Ehrh.] Wahl.). Central Europe.

'Umbraculifera'. Small tree, crown globose, very dense,
branches thin, only somewhat pubescent when young; leaves
elliptic to more ovate, 3–7 cm long, somewhat rough above,
petiole 4–8 mm long. MD 1910: 73 (= *U. densa* Litvin.).
Turkestan. 1879. Plate 144, 145.

'Umbraculifera Gracilis' (Späth). Very similar to
'Umbraculifera' and a form of this with a more rounded habit,
thinner branches and smaller leaves (= *U. campestris
umbraculifera gracilis* Späth). 1897.

'Variegata'. Leaves white variegated, usually finely and
densely white punctate (= *U. campestris marmorata* Hort.). ∅

'Webbiana'. Habit narrowly conical; leaves longitudinally
folded (navicular) (= *U. campestris concavifolia* Hort.).

U. chinensis see: **U. parvifolia**

U. coritana see: **U. carpinifolia**

U. crassifolia Nutt. Resembles *U. parvifolia*. A tree to 25 m high in its habitat, young shoots soft pubescent, often with 2 corky wings; leaves ovate to oval-oblong, 3–5 cm long, acute to obtuse, coarsely and nearly single serrate, leathery tough, very rough above, soft pubescent beneath, petiole 2–3 mm long; flowers in axillary clusters in the fall (!); fruits 8 mm long, elliptic, deeply incised, pubescent. SS 315; VT 210. S. USA, on alkaline soil. 1876. z7 Fig. 286, 288.

U. dampieri aurea see: **U. × hollandica 'Wredei'**

U. davidiana Planch. Tree, 12–15 mm high, bark gray, fissured, branches thin, glabrous, often with large corky ridges, youngest shoots densely yellow pubescent; leaves ovate, 5–10 cm long, 4–7 cm wide, short acuminate, biserrate, base cuneate, tough, both sides soft pubescent at first, eventually rough on both sides, petiole 1 cm long, densely silky pubescent; fruits oblong-ovate, somewhat incised at the apex, tapered to the base, silky pubescent, nearly sessile. China; Hupeh, Shantung, Kiangsi, Anhwei Provs. z6 Fig. 287. ∅

U. densa see: **U. carpinifolia 'Umbraculifera'**

U. diversifolia see: **U. carpinifolia**

U. effusa see: **U. laevis**

U. elegantissima Horwood (*U. glabra* × *U. plotii*). Only the following clone in cultivation:

'Jacqueline Hillier'. Stoloniferous, slow growing shrub, about 2 m high in 10 years, very densely branched; leaves distichous in arrangement, elliptic-lanceolate, 2.5–3.5 cm long, biserrate, roughly pubescent, very densely arranged. Discovered in 1966 in a private garden in Selly Park, Birmingham, England; brought into the trade by Hillier. Excellent for hedging. Plate 126. ∅

U. elliptica K. Koch. Tree, closely related to *U. rubra*, young shoots pubescent; leaves elliptic-oblong, 8–14 cm long, smooth above, slightly pubescent beneath; fruits obovate, pubescent in the center. Transcaucasus, Armenia. True existence in cultivation is uncertain; often confused with *U. rubra*. z6

U. exoniensis see: **U. glabra 'Exoniensis'**

U. foliacea see: **U. carpinifolia**

U. fulva see: **U. rubra**

U. glabra Huds. Scotch, Wych Elm. Tall, broad crowned tree, usually without root sprouts, 30–40 m high, trunk more or less straight, bark remaining smooth for a long time (hence the name *glabra*), but eventually rough and furrowed, branches widespreading, young shoots red-brown and thickly pubescent at first, without corky ridges, totally glabrous only in the 3rd year; leaves broad ovate or elliptic to obovate, 5–16 cm long, gradually or abruptly acuminate, coarsely biserrate, base uneven, the long side (as a rounded auricle) covers the 3 mm long petiole, dark green and rough above, lighter and pubescent beneath; flowers in dense clusters, stamens 5–6, somewhat exserted, stigmas red, February–March; fruits obovate to broadly elliptic, 2–2.5 cm long, somewhat incised, seed in the center. SH 1: 136 u–v; 137 h–l; EH 400–401; HTr 78 (= *U. scabra* Mill.; *U. montana* Stokes; *U. campestris* L. p. p.). N. and central Europe, Asia Minor. Cultivated since antiquity. z5 Plate 146; Fig. 284.

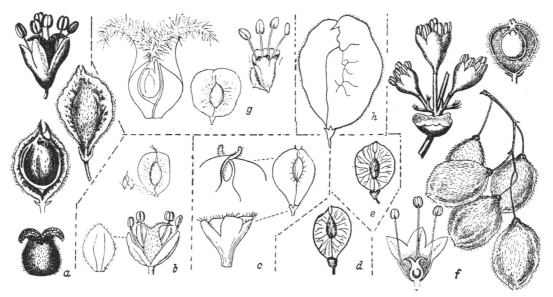

Fig. 286. **Ulmus.** Flowers and fruits. a. *U. crassifolia*; b. *U. parvifolia*; c. *U. wilsoniana*; d. *U. × hollandica*; e. *U. × hollandica* 'Vegeta'; f. *U. thomasii*; g. *U. pumila*; h. *U. macrocarpa* (from Franchet, Sargent, Hempel & Wilhelm, Schneider and Original)

Including many cultivars.

Differing in growth habit;

Conical:
'Exoniensis'

Ovate:
'Insularis'

Pendulous:
'Camperdownii' (branches nearly vertical)
'Pendula' (umbrella form)
'Serpentina' (branches spirally twisted)

Dwarf:
'Nana' (globose)

Branches differing;

Branch tips fasciated:
'Monstrosa'

Inner bark red:
'Rubra'

Leaves differing;
Green:
'Cornuta' (apex 3 lobed)
'Crispa' (margins deeply incised)
f. *nitida* (totally glabrous)

Variegated:
'Atropurpurea' (persistent dark red)
'Lutescens' (yellow)
'Purpurea' (new growth red)

'Atropurpurea' (Späth 1904). Leaves dark brown-red at first, gradually greening in the summer (= *U. montana atropurpurea* Späth). ∅

'Camperdownii'. Slow growing, branches quickly curving downward, crown nearly hemispherical, branch tips often lying on the ground; leaves densely covering the entire shoot. BC 3881 (= *U. montana pendula* Kirchn. non Loud.; *U. scabra pendula* Dipp.). Found around 1850 at Camperdown House near Dundee, Scotland. Plate 146.

'Cornuta'. Leaves broad obovate, to 10 cm long and wide, particularly on long shoots, 3(5) lobed-acuminate at the apex, the lobes narrowly triangular, unlobed at the apex on short shoots (as opposed to the similar *U. laciniata* on which all the leaves are lobed, also the shoots are glabrous). HW 3: 231 (= *U. tridens* Hort.; *U. montana* var. *triserrata* Lav.; *U. glabra* f. *tricuspis* Rehd.; *U. glabra* var. *grandidentata* Moss). Before 1845. ∅

'Crispa'. Slow growing with a divaricate habit; leaves narrowly oblong (!), margins deeply incised, the teeth hook-form. SH 1: 136y (= *U. montana* var. *crispa* Loud.; *U. scabra* f.*crispa* Dipp.; *U. asplenifolia* Hort.; *U. urticifolia* Hort.). Before 1800. Plate 145.

'Exoniensis'. Exeter Elm. Rather slow growing, narrowly conical, stiffly erect, to 7 m, eventually broadly globose; leaves deeply and irregularly dentate particularly on the apical half, teeth somewhat crispate, deep green (= *U. montana fastigiata* Hort.; *U. exoniensis* K. Kock; *U. glabra* var. *fastigiata* [Loud.] Rehd.; *U. plumosa pyramidalis* Hort.). Found around 1826 in the Ford Nursery in Exeter, England. Somewhat resistant to Dutch Elm Disease. Plate 143, 146. ∅

var. *fastigiata* see: 'Exoniensis'

var. *grandidentata* see: 'Cornuta'

'Insularis'. Crown oval-oblong-rounded, branches rather erect, densely arranged, large leaved. Distributed from Sweden. 1949. Plate 145.

'Lutescens'. Leaves yellowish green on new growth, later more bronze-yellow (= *U. scabra* f. *lutenscens* Dipp.). ∅

'Monstrosa'. Compact habit, shoots often fasciated at the apex; leaves 5–8 cm long, often funnelform connate at the base (= *U. scabra* f. *nana monstrosa* Schneid.).

'Nana'. Dwarf, globose bush, scarcely 2 m high; leaves usually obovate, 5–9 cm long, frequently with 1–2 lobe-like teeth at the apex, deep green.

f. *nitida* (Fries) Rehd. Young shoots glabrous; leaves smooth above; otherwise like the species (= *U. montana nitida* Fries). Norway.

'Pendula'. Weeping Elm. Flat crowned, broadly umbrella-shaped, branches horizontally spreading, nodding at the tips, usually foliate only at the branch tips. GC 50: 221 (= *U. montana horizontalis* Kirchn; *U. montana* var. *pendula* Loud.). Before 1816.

'Purpurea'. Leaves elliptic to more obovate, large, new growth reddish blue-green, later dark green (= *U. scabra purpurea* Hort.).

'Rubra' (Simon-Louis). Inner bark of the branches red (= *U. montana libero-rubro* Planch.). 1869.

'Serpentina'. Weeping form, foliage like 'Camperdownii', but the branches twisted corkscrew-like. Rather rare.

f. *tricuspis* see: 'Cornuta'

U. heyderi see: **U. rubra**

U. × *hillieri* see: **U.** × **hollandica 'Hillieri'**

U. × **hollandica** Mill. (*U. carpinifolia* × *U. glabra*). Collective name for a number of alleged hybrids between the mentioned species. Leaves usually medium-sized to large, 6–12 cm long, broadly oval-elliptic, smooth above. z5 Fig. 286.

Including:

Broad crowned forms:
'Bea Schwarz', 'Belgica', 'Christine Buisman', 'Commelin', 'Dauvessei', 'Groeneveld', 'Major', 'Pitteurs', 'Vegeta'

Narrow crowned forms:
'Dumont', 'Klemmer', 'Superba'

Very narrow conical forms:
'Dampieri' (green), 'Wredei' (yellow)

Globose dwarf form:
'Hillieri'

Weeping form:
'Smithii'

Bea Schwarz' (Went). Habit broadly upright, shoots nodding, young shoots persistently rough pubescent; leaves rather small, somewhat reddish at the shoot tips, ovate, 4–10 cm long, short acuminate, with 9–11 vein pairs, deep green above, somewhat lighter beneath, petiole 0.5–10 mm; fruits about 2 cm long, light green, seeds in the center of the wing. Selected around 1935 in the Baarn Experiment Station by Dr. Went. Very resistant to Dutch Elm Disease.

'Belgica'. Dutch Elm (despite the name!). Large tree, straight trunked, wide crowned, bark rough, young shoots more or less pubescent; leaves elliptic-obovate or narrowly obovate, 8–12

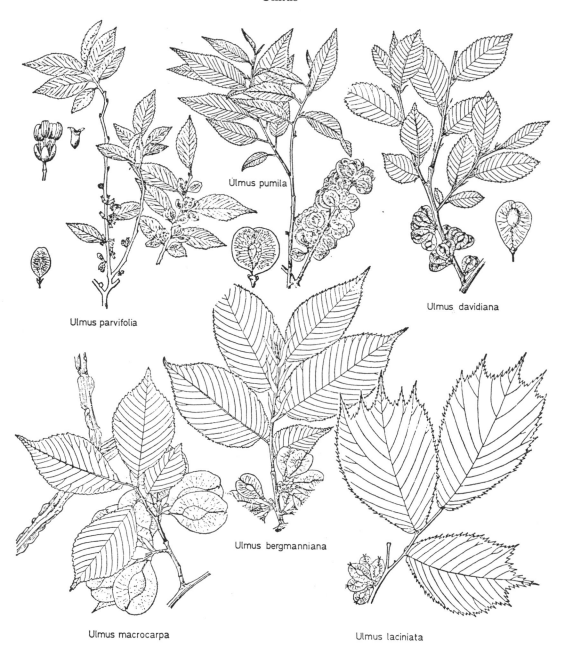

Ulmus pumila

Ulmus parvifolia

Ulmus davidiana

Ulmus macrocarpa

Ulmus bergmanniana

Ulmus laciniata

Fig. 287. *Ulmus* species of Asia (from ICS)

cm long, acuminate, with 14–18 vein pairs, base very uneven, somewhat rough above, underside soft pubescent, occasionally only on the venation, petiole 4–6 mm long; fruits elliptic, 2–2.5 cm long, seeds situated on the apical half. EH 412 (= *U. belgica* Burgsd.; *U. montana* var. *hollandica* Huberty). Belgium. 1694. Very susceptible to Dutch Elm Disease!

'Christine Buisman' (Went.) Tree, broadly erect, shoots limply nodding; leaves ovate, 5–8 cm long, base very oblique, with axillary pubescence beneath. Developed in the Boskoop Experiment Station around 1945. Very resistant to Dutch Elm Disease.

'Commelin' (Baarn Experiment Station). Straight stemmed when young (older specimens not yet observed!), open crowned, but more regular than 'Vegeta', shoots are like those of 'Vegeta', but brown and not glossy; leaves short ovate, to 10 cm long, with 8–12 vein pairs, more or less short pubescent beneath. Developed around 1950 in the Baarn Experiment Station, Holland. Very vigorous cultivar.

'Dampieri'. Very narrow conical form, eventually becoming wider; leaves crispate, clustered on the short shoots, broadly ovate, deeply biserrate, the teeth crenate serrate, 5–6 cm long, deep green, somewhat rough (= *U. campestris dampieri* Wesm.;

U. nitens f. *dampieri* Henry). Originated in Belgium around 1863. Rather resistant to Dutch Elm Disease.

'Dauvessei'. Crown broadly conical, young shoots more or less pubescent; leaves to 12 cm long, base more oblique, soft pubescent beneath, petiole 5 mm long; seeds near the apex (= *U. montana* var. *dauvessei* Nichols.). Before 1877.

'Dumont'. Very similar to 'Belgica', but with a much narrower crown, branches ascending (= *U. montana* var. *dumontii* Aigret). 1898.

'Groeneveld' (Bosbouw Experiment Station, Holland). Resembles 'Commelin', but with a tighter upright habit and remaining lower, 12–15 m high, crown dense, well and regularly branched. Very resistant to wind damage and Dutch Elm Disease. Not for wet soil! ∅

'Hillieri'. Dwarf form, scarcely 1.2 m high, widely branched, graceful, compact; leaves small, carmine and yellow in fall (= *U.* × *hillieri* Hillier). Developed in 1918 by Hillier.

'Klemmer'. Tall tree, crown narrowly conical, stem with a smooth bark, young shoots short pubescent; leaves ovate, 5–10 cm long, short acuminate, with 12 vein pairs, margins somewhat crispate, glabrous and rough above, finely pubescent beneath, petiole 5–10 mm long; seeds nearing the incision (= *U. klemmeri* Späth; *U. montana* var. *klemmer* Gillekens). Belgium. 1891.

'Major'. The type of the cross. A tall tree, to 40 m, stem short, crown wide, branches often nodding, with root sprouts, bark deeply fissured, young shoots glabrous or only slightly pubescent; leaves elliptic-ovate to broadly elliptic, 8–12 cm long, acuminate, deeply biserrate, teeth directed forward, with 12–14 vein pairs, base very uneven, dark green and rather smooth above, pubescent and somewhat glandular beneath, with axillary pubescent and somewhat glandular beneath, with axillary pubescence, petiole 6–10 cm long; flowers usually 4 parted; fruits elliptic-ovate, 2–2.5 cm long, seeds touching the incision. EH 42; HL 66; HTr 79–80; NF 2: 226 (= *U. scabra* var. *major* Dipp.; *U. major* Sm.; *U. montana major* Syme). Origin unknown.

'Pitteurs'. Strong growing tree, crown broadly ovate, one season's growth in the nursery 2–3 m long (!), very large leaved (= *U. scabra* var. *patteursii* Rehd.). Discovered before 1848 on the Pitteurs Estate in St. Troud, Belgium.

'Smithii'. Small tree, branches ascending at first, shoots pendulous, young shoots pubescent; leaves tough, elliptic, 8 cm long, long acuminate, smooth and glabrous above, underside sparsely pubescent, petiole 8 mm long; stamen filaments 3–5; fruits obovate, 2 cm long, incision open, seeds above the middle. EH 412 (= *U. montana* var. *pendula* Hort.; *U. smithii* Henry). Before 1830 in England.

'Superba'. Narrowly conical crown, stem with smooth bark, young shoots glabrous, somewhat glossy, gray-brown; leaves ovate to elliptic-obovate, 8–12 cm long, with 15–18 vein pairs, base very oblique, glabrous and smooth above, underside sparsely pubescent, persisting long into the fall, petiole 5–10 mm long; flowers usually 5 parted; fruits elliptic, 1.5–2 cm long, seeds nearly in the middle. HL 66 (= *U. montana* var. *superba* Morr.; *U. praestans* Schoch). Belgium. Plate 143.

'Vegeta'. Hintingdon Elm. Tall tree, trunk short, usually forked (!), bark rough, open crowned, branches erect, later more outspread and nodding, young shoots glabrous or only sightly pubescent, olive-green and somewhat glossy; leaves light green, elliptic, 8–12 cm long, acuminate, biserrate, teeth directed forward, with 14–18 vein pairs, base very uneven, smooth and glabrous above, underside glabrous with axillary pubescence, petiole 6–8 mm long; fruits elliptic-obovate, incision closed, seeds on the apical half. EH 395, 412; HTr 81; NF 2: 227 (= *U. vegeta* Lindl.; *U. montana vegeta* Kirchn.). Found around 1750 in the Wood Nursery in Huntingdon, England. Fig. 186.

'Wredei' (Jühlke). Golden Elm. Like 'Dampieri', but with golden-yellow leaves. MG 13: 160 (= *U. dampieri aurea* Hort.). Developed from seed around 1877 by Inspector Wrede in Geltow, near Potsdam, E. Germany. Resistant to Dutch Elm Disease. Plate 143, 144. ∅

U. japonica (Rehd.) Sarg. To 30 m high, broad crowned tree, young shoots yellow-brown, very densely pubescent and warty, occasionally also with corky ridges (!); leaves elliptic to obovate, 8–12 cm long, biserrate, with 12–16 vein pairs, rough above and somewhat pubescent, lighter beneath and soft pubescent primarily on the venation, petiole 4–5 mm long, pubescent; flowers with 4 stamens; fruits obovate-elliptic, gradually tapering to the base, 2 cm long, incised to the nutlet. GF 6: 323 (as *U. campestris*); MJ 1958. Japan, NE. Asia. 1895. Ⓕ NW. China; Mongolia; in reforestation. z5

U. klemmeri see: **U.** × **hollandica 'Klemmer'**

U. koopmannii see: **U. carpinifolia 'Koopmannii'**

U. laciniata (Trautv.) Mayr. Small tree, scarcely over 10 m high, young shoots totally glabrous or nearly so (!), later yellow-brown (!); leaves obovate to more oblong, 8–18 cm long, usually 3 lobed as the apex (occasionally also 5 lobed), base very oblique, biserrate, dark green and rough above, soft pubescent beneath, petiole 2–5 mm long; fruit elliptic, 2 cm long, glabrous, nutlets sessile in the middle. NK 19: 2–3; KIF 1: 59; ICS 930; LF 106; MJ 1960. Manchuria, N. China, Japan. 1900. Ⓕ NW. China; Mongolia. z5 Fig. 287.

var. **nikkoensis** Rehd. Primarily differing in the smaller leaves, usually obovate, 6–11 cm long, reddish on the new growth, venation of the underside short pubescent. Central Japan. 1905.

U. laevigata see: **U. wallichiana**

U. laevis Pall. Tree, 10–30 m high, branches nodding, young shoots more or less pubescent (!), winter buds slender, acute (!); leaves elliptic to obovate, widest above the middle (!), acuminate, scabrous and biserrate, base very oblique, usually glossy green and smooth above, underside soft pubescent, with 12–19 vein pairs, petiole 4–6 mm long; flowers with 6–8 stamens, stigmas white; fruits rounded to ovate, 1–1.2 cm long, ciliate (!), seed in the middle, the incision not touching the seed. HW 2: 39; GPN 248 (= *U. effusa* Willd.; *U. racemosa* Borkh.). Central and SE. Europe, Caucasus. z5 Fig. 284.

U. macrocarpa Hance. Small tree or also a shrub, young shoots pubescent at first, usually with 2 corky ridges; leaves elliptic to broad obovate, 3–7(10) cm long, usually short and slender acuminate, with 10–14 vein pairs, rough above, somewhat pubescent beneath with axillary tufts; fruits nearly circular or obovate, to 2.5 cm long (!), soft pubescent and ciliate, nutlet in the center. NK 19: 5; ICS 928; DB 1926: 70; SH 2: 556h. China. 1908. Hardy.

z5 Fig. 286, 287.

U. major see: **U. × hollandica 'Major'**

U. mandshurica see: **U. pumila**

U. minor see: **U. plotii**

U. montana see: **U. glabra**

U. nitens see: **U. carpinifolia**

U. nitens f. *dampieri* see: **U. × hollandica 'Dampieri'**

U. parvifolia Jacq. Chinese Elm, Lacebark Elm. Small tree with a broad globose crown (!), 10–15 m high, fast growing bark of older stems smooth, exfoliating in large, rounded pieces (!), the brown inner bark highly visible beneath, young twigs pubescent; leaves elliptic or ovate to obovate, 2–5 cm long, acute or obtusish, usually serrate, base irregularly rounded, eventually rather leathery and tough, glossy and smooth above, underside soft pubescent at first, petiole 2–4 mm long; flowers in axillary clusters in August–September (!!); fruits elliptic ovate, 1 cm long, incised at the apex, nutlet in the center. DB 1914: 26; KIF 2: 18; ICS 934; NK 19: 11 (= *U. chinensis* Pers.). China, Korea, Japan. 1794. Very valuable tree, much better than *U. pumila,* holding its green color long into the fall and resistant to Dutch Elm Disease. Ⓕ USSR and USA. z5–9 Plate 146; Fig. 286, 287.

Including 2 shrubby forms from Japan, only 1 m high, with very small leaves; leaves only 1 cm long, white variegated: **'Frosty'** and **'Chessins'**.

'Hansen'. Fast growing, shoots broadly ascending, with a ring-shaped bulge under each branch base (provides more stability in wind); leaves ovate, long acuminate, 8 cm long, biserrate, base rounded. GC from 2/18/1972: 38. Collected by N. E. Hansen in E. Siberia and further developed in South Dakota, USA. ∅

'Pendens'. Shoots drooping to the ground; leaves nearly semi-evergreen in mild climates (= f. *sempervirens* Hort.). Found in S. California before 1930.

f. *sempervirens* see: **'Pendens'**

U. pinnato-ramosa see: **U. pumila** var. **arborea**

U. plotii Druce. Medium-sized, rather narrow crowned tree, 12–25 m high, branches short and thick, horizontal to ascending, young shoots long, thin, pendulous, scattered pubescent, glabrous in the 2nd year, central leader nodding, particularly on young trees; leaves small, obovate to elliptic, 3–7 cm long, 2–3.5 cm wide, asymmetrical and often cordate at the base, acute to acuminate, dull and finely rugose above, densely short pubescent beneath at first, but later smooth except for the axillary pubescence, with 8–10, often forked vein pairs, margins entire to biserrate, petiole 5 mm, pubescent; flowers 20–25 together in short stalked clusters; fruits narrowly obovate, wing emarginate at the apex with a triangular incision, seed on the apical half. EH Pl. 411 (as *U. minor*); GC 50: 168 (1911) (= *U. minor* sensu Henry. non Miller 1786). Central England, primarily along the River Trent and its tributaries. z7 ∅

Fig. 288. **Ulmus.** a. *U. serotina;* b. *U. crassifolia;* c. *U. alata* (from Sargent)

U. plumosa pyramidalis see: **U. glabra 'Exoniensis'**

U. praestans see: **U. × hollandica 'Superba'**

U. procera Salisb. English Elm. Upright tree to 30 m high, with few, but thick, stiff branches on the basal portion, crown irregular and dense, tight, trunk fissured, root sprouts numerous, also with many suckers on the trunk, young shoots rather thick, persistently pubescent (!!), often corky; leaves nearly circular to ovate, always more or less rough above, 4.5–9cm long, evenly pubescent beneath and with axillary pubescence, base uneven, round to nearly cuneate, scabrous serrate, teeth directed forward, with 10–12 vein pairs; flowers short stalked, stamens 3–5, February–March; fruits nearly circular, 10–17 mm long, with a small incision at the apex, seed near the incision, glabrous. CF 48b; EH 405; HTr 82, 83 (= *U. campestris* L. p. p.; *U. campestris* Mill.). England to central and S. Europe. In cultivation a long time. z6 Plate 143.

Including the following forms and selections:

Differing in growth habit

Conical:

var. *australis*

Leaves green, differing in form

Very small leaved:
'Myrtifolia'

Narrowly obovate:
'Viminalis'

Leaves variegated

White:
'Argenteo-Variegata' (white speckled)
'Viminalis Marginata' (white margined)

Yellow:
'Louis van Houtte' (yellow toned)
'Viminalis Aurea' (narrow leaved)

Red;
'Purpurascens' (reddish toned)
'Purpurea' (red-brown)

'Argenteo-Variegata'. Leaves white speckled and veined (= *U. campestris argenteo-variegata* West). 1770. Plate 147.

var. **australis** (Henry) Rehd. Conical habit; leaves tougher and thicker, more abruptly acuminate, venation more protruberant beneath. EH 412. S. Europe. Long in cultivation.

'Louis van Houtte' (Van Houtte). Tree-like, open crowned, wide; leaves broad ovate, golden-yellow, petiole golden-yellow. Developed in Ghent, Belgium around 1880. Plate 143. ∅

'Myrtifolia'. Leaves ovate to oval-rhombic or more oblong, 2–3(5) cm long, scabrous and usually serrate, loosely pubescent on both sides; fruits obovate, 12–15 mm long (= *U. campestris* var. *myrtifolia* Hort.). 1880.

'Purpurascens'. Leaves like those of 'Myrtifolia', but reddish (= *U. campestris myrtifolia purpurea* De Smet). Before 1877.

'Purpurea'. Leaves 5–6 cm long, dark red on new growth, later greening (= *U. campestris purpurea* Wesm.). Before 1860. ∅

'Viminalis'. Small tree, 7–10 m high, occasionally taller, branches graceful and nodding, thin; leaves oblanceolate to narrow ovate, cuneately tapered at the base, 2.5–6 cm long, 3–20 mm wide, very deeply incised serrate, very rough above, venation pubescent beneath (= *U. viminalis* Lodd.; *U. antarctica* Hort.; *U. campestris viminalis* Loud.). Discovered in England around 1817.

'Viminalis Aurea'. Leaves 4–7 cm long, to 3 cm wide, finely scabrous to incised serrate, attractive and always yellow. IH 513 (= *U. campestris* var. *aurea* Morr.; *U. rosseelsii* K. Koch; *U. viminalis aurea* Bean). Developed in Loewen, Belgium before 1866 by E. Rosseels. Plate 147. ∅

'Viminalis Marginata'. Like 'Viminalis', but the leaves white on the margins (= *U. viminalis* var. *variegata* Bean).

U. pubescens see: **U. rubra**

U. pumila L. Siberian Elm. Small tree, 3–6(10) m high, rough barked, branches brittle (messy in wind!!), fast growing, young shoots thin, gray-brown, pubescent to nearly glabrous when young; leaves elliptic to more lanceolate, acute to acuminate, 2–7 cm long, normally serrate or the apical teeth with a few small secondary teeth, base usually nearly even, deep green and smooth above, underside somewhat pubescent only when young, tough, petiole 2–4 mm long; flowers very sort stalked, with 4–5 violet anthers, flowering in February–March (!); fruits circular, to obovate, 1–1.5 cm long, deeply incised, seed situated above the middle. LF 107; EH 411; VT 212 (= *U. mandshurica* Nakai). E. Siberia, N. China, Turkestan. 1860. Much used in the USA and confused with *U. parvifolia* which is a far superior tree. Resistant to Dutch Elm Disease. Ⓕ USSR, Romania, Bulgaria, USA, Canada, N. China, in screen plantings. z3 Fig. 286, 287.

f. **androssowii** (Litvin.) Rehd. Only slightly differing from the species, crown dense and wide, branches spreading, older branches corky (= *U. androssowii* Litvin.). 1934.

var. **arborea** Litvin. Tall tree, habit conical at first, young shoots distichous in arrangement; leaves elliptic-ovate to more lanceolate, longer acuminate, 4–7 cm long, serrate, but the teeth usually with 1–2 small secondary teeth, glossy above, petiole 4–8 mm long (= *U. turkestanica* Regel; *U. pinnato-ramosa* Dieck). Turkestan. 1894. Good resistance to Dutch Elm disease. Plate 143.

'Berardii' (Simon-Louis). Bushy, small tree, branches thin, erect, new growth appears very late; leaves very similar to those of *Zelkova*, elliptic to narrowly oblong, 2–5 cm long, each side with 2–6 coarse teeth, base cuneate and with equal halves (!), both sides somewhat rough pubescent. DL 3: 7 (= *U. carpinifolia* 'Berardii'). Found in Metz in 1863.

'Coolshade' (Wild). Slower growing, branches more resistant to wind damage. A selection of Wild Bros. Nursery, Sarcoxie, Missouri, USA. 1946.

'Den Haag'. Selection with a loose, open crown, to 20 m high. Very frequently planted in The Hague for its resistance to Dutch Elm disease, dryness and winds.

'Pendula'. Branches thin, pendulous. BD 1926: 70.

Further selections in the USA include hybrids with *U. rubra*; e.g. 'Improved Coolshade; 'Hamburg Hybrid', etc.

U. racemosa see: **U. laevis** and **U. thomasii**

U. rosseelsii see **U. procera 'Viminalis Aurea'**

U. rubra Muehl. Slippery Elm. Broad crowned tree, 15–20 m high, young shoots thin, rough pubescent, gray-brown, winter buds thick, dark brown pubescent, more orange on the tips (!); leaves broad ovate to obovate, 10–18 cm long, long acuminate, biserrate, with 10–14 vein pairs, base very uneven, very rough above, densely pubescent beneath, petiole 4–8 mm long; flowers in short stalked, dense clusters, stamens 5–9, stigmas reddish; fruits broad elliptic to rounded, 1–2 cm long, slightly incised, rust-red pubescent on the centrally situated seed (!). BB 1253; KTF 68; HH 188; VT 208 (= *U. fulva* Michx.; *U. heyderi* Späth.; *U. pubescens* Walt.). Central and southern USA. 1830. Inner bark produces a "slippery", mucilaginous substance when the young shoots are chewed. z3 Plate 143; Fig. 284.

U. × *sarniensis* see: **U. carpinifolia 'Sarniensis'**

U. scabra see: **U. glabra**
  —var. *major* see: **U.** × **hollandica 'Major'**
  —var. *pitteursii* see: **U.** × **hollandica 'Pitteurs'**

U. serotina Sarg. Broad crowned tree, 10–20 m high, branches often nodding, densely white pubescent only when young, 2–3 year old shoots with irregular corky ridges; leaves elliptic to obovate, 5–9 cm long, with 14–19 vein pairs, acuminate, biserrate, base very oblique, dark green and rough above, underside yellow-green with short white hairs until fall, petiole 6 mm long; flowers in pendulous, glabrous, stalked, 3 cm long racemes (!!) in September; fruits elliptic, about 1 cm long, deeply incised, densely ciliate, ripening in November. SS 718; VT 211. S. USA. 1903. Rare in cultivation. z6 Fig. 288.

U. smithii see: **U.** × **hollandica 'Smithii'**

U. stricta see: **U. carpinifolia 'Cornubiensis'**

U. suberosa see: **U. carpinifolia** var. **suberosa**

U. suberosa pendula see: **U. carpinifolia 'Propendens'**

U. thomasii Sarg. Rock Elm. Slow growing tree, to 20 m high, inner bark lemon-yellow (!), branches pubescent until the 2nd year, then developing corky ridges; leaves elliptic to oblong-obovate, 5–10 cm long, short acuminate, with 17–21 vein pairs, biserrate, without axillary pubescence (!), petiole 2–6 mm long; flowers few in 3–5 cm long, pendulous racemes, stamens 5–8, widely drooping, April; fruits elliptic, 2 cm long, only slightly incised, seed situated above the middle, margin thickened and ciliate, surface scattered pubescent. SS 312; BB 1251; RM 125; HH 184 (= *U. racemosa* Thomas non Borkh.). NE and central USA. 1875. Finest wood of all the elms. z2 Fig. 286.

U. tridens see: **U. glabra 'Cornuta'**

U. turkestanica see: **U. pumila** var. **arborea**

U. urticifolia see: **U. glabra 'Crispa'**

U. vegeta see: **U.** × **hollandica 'Vegeta'**

U. villosa Brandis. Large tree, bark rather smooth, dark gray-brown, inner bark ocher-brown, young shoots yellowish red, finely rough, later smooth and brown; leaves obovate or more oblong, only slightly asymmetrical, with a small protruding apex, upper surface more or less rough, lighter beneath, soft pubescent, the large leaves 8–12 cm long and 5–6 cm wide, the smaller 4–7 cm long and 3–4 cm wide; with 11–14 vein pairs, sharply biserrate, with white axillary pubescence beneath, petiole 3–7 mm long; flowers 10–15 in dense, sessile clusters. BMns 742. Himalayas; India, Kashmir, Afghanistan, 2500–3000 m. 1935. Very attractive elm with delicate, partly pendulous young shoots. (Kew). z5 ⌀

U. viminalis see: **U. procera 'Viminalis'**

U. wallichiana Planch. Medium-sized to tall tree, bark gray, rough, rhombic scaly, young shoots reddish, pubescent; leaves elliptic to obovate, long acuminate, 10–20 cm long, rough above, soft pubescent beneath, with 15–20 vein pairs, terminating at the teeth, petiole 3–4 mm long; flowers in dense, globose clusters in the axils of the fallen leaves; fruit wings thin, membranous, elliptic, 18 mm long, seed in the center (= *U. laevigata* Royle). NW. Himalayas; India, Kashmir. Ⓕ India. z6 ⌀

U. wilsoniana Schneid. Similar to *U. japonica*. Tree, to 20 m high, young shoots soft pubescent, later often corky; leaves elliptic to more obovate or ovate, 4–10 cm long, acute, rough above, finely pubescent to nearly glabrous beneath, with obovate fruits, glabrous, incision reaching to the nutlet. SH 565e, 566 c–d. China. 1910. Hardy. z6 Plate 143; Fig. 286.

The elms thrive in any good garden soil, but not excessive moisture. The species with small, tough leaves will tolerate dry sites. Their popularity as street trees stems not only from their rapid growth but their ability to heal quickly when wounded. Since the outbreak of Dutch Elm disease (*Ceratocystus ulmi*), many elms have had to be excluded from the recommended plant list (particularly in the USA). *Ulmus americana* is particularly susceptible. A reliable cure has yet to be developed, but work is being done on resistant hybrids. Three resistant (not immune) clones have been developed at the Baarn Experiment Station in Holland; 'Bea Schwartz', 'Christine Buisman', and 'Commelin'. The Asiatic species *U. parviflora* and *U. pumila* are also very resistant.

Lit. Clapham-Tutin-Warburg: Flora of the British Isles, 562–566, 1962 (2nd ed.) ● Hadfield, M.: British Trees, 226–247, 1957 ● Jackson, A. B.: The British Elms; in New Flora and Silva, **2**, 219–229, 1930 (with 8 plates) ● Rehder, A.: Neue oder kritische Gehölze; in Mitt. DDG 1915, 215–218 ● Wyman, D.: Elms grown in America; in Arnoldia **11**, 79–90, 1951 ● Wyman, D.: A second look at the popular Elms; in American Nurseryman, January 1, 1961, 12–13, 78–82 ● Green, P. S.: Registration of Cultivar names in *Ulmus*; Arnoldia 1964, 41–80 ● Melville, R.: The names of the Cornish and Jersey Elms; in Kew Bulletin **14**, 216–217, 1960 ● Touw, A.: Een voorlopig overzicht van de Nederlandse iepen; Jaarb. Ned. Dendr. Ver. **22**, 57–72, 1963 ● Melville, R.: Ambiguous Elm Names. II. *Ulmus minor* Mill.; in Jour. Botany 1939, 266–270 ● Richens, R. H.: Variation, cytogenetics and breeding of the European Field Elm (*Ulmus minor* Miller s. lat. = *U. carpinifolia* Suckow); Annales Forestale 7/4, Acad. Scie. Art. Slav. Meridional., Zagreb 1976 ● Richens, R. H.: Designations in *Ulmus minor* Mill.; Taxon **26**, 583–584, 1977.

UMBELLULARIA (Nees) Nutt. — California Laurel — LAURACEAE

Monotypic genus, classified between *Laurus* and *Sassafras*. Evergreen tree; leaves alternate, entire; flowers hermaphroditic, unattractive, in short stalked, many-flowered umbels; corolla with a very short tube and 6 equal lobes, 9 fertile stamens, of these the 3 inner ones with 2 basally situated glands; fruit a cherry-sized berry.

Umbellularia californica (Hook. & Arn.) Nutt. Evergreen shrub or tree, strongly aromatic, to 15 m high or more in mild climates; leaves narrowly elliptic to oblong, tapered to both ends, 5–12 cm long, tough and leathery, entire, totally glabrous; flowers yellow-green, in stalked, 2 cm wide umbels, April; fruits obovoid-globose, eventually purple-green. SS 306; BM 5320. SW. USA. 1830. Dislikes alkalinity. Smelling the crushed leaves can result in a headache. z9 Plate 148; Fig. 289. # ∅

Cultivated somewhat like *Laurus*.

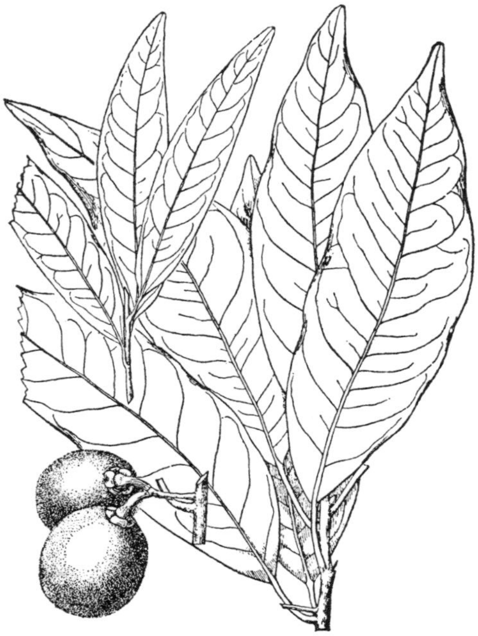

Fig. 289. *Umbellularia californica* with fruits (from Sudworth)

UNGNADIA Endl. — SAPINDACEAE

Monotypic genus. Deciduous shrub to small tree, leaves alternate, odd pinnate, without stipules; flowers polygamous or dioecious; calyx 5 toothed, petals 4, evenly formed, with a comb-like disk at the base; stamens 7–10; fruit a 3 valved capsule similar to that of *Aesculus*.

Ungnadia speciosa Endl. Shrub, 3–6 cm high, young shoots and leaves soft pubescent; leaflets 5–9, oblong to oval-lanceolate, 8–12 cm long, acuminate, finely crenate, nearly sessile, terminal leaflets long stalked, tomentose on new growth, later glabrous and glossy; flowers many in small clusters, calyx campanulate, 4–5 parted, pubescent, petals pink, corolla 2.5 cm wide. SS 73; FS 1059. Texas. z9 Fig. 290. ✿

Very attractive, from a distance appearing nearly like *Cercis siliquastrum* when in flower, but only for very mild climates.

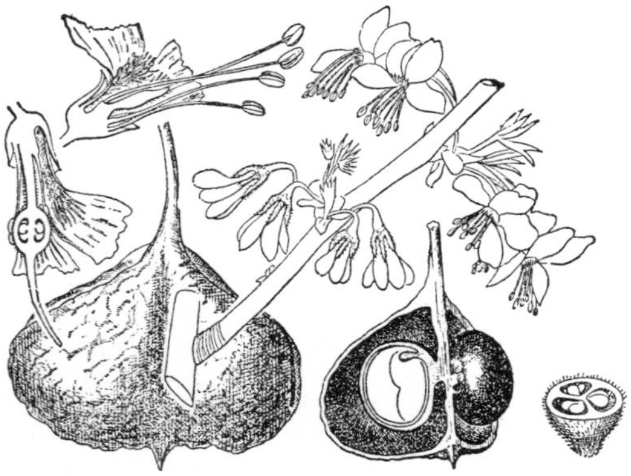

Fig. 290. *Ungnadia speciosa*. Flowering branch, sectioned flowers and fruits (from Sargent, Lauche)

URTICA

Urtica arborea see: **Gesnouinia arborea**

UVARIA

Uvaria japonica see: **Kadsura japonica**

VACCINIUM L. — Blueberry, Cranberry — ERICACEAE

Evergreen or deciduous shrubs; leaves alternate, short petioled, entire or serrate; flowers terminal or axillary, solitary or in racemes; corolla tubular, campanulate, urceolate or incised with 4–5 lobes, white, pink or red; calyx 4 or 5 parted; stamens 8–10, anthers tubular, opening with a pore on the apical end, often with an awn-like appendage; fruit a many seeded berry with a persistent calyx. — About 300–400 species in the Northern Hemisphere, from the Arctic Circle to the higher mountains of the tropics; some species of considerable economic importance.

Fig. 291. **Vaccinium**. a. *V. arboreum*; b. *V. stamineum* var. *neglectum*; c. *V. melanocarpum*;
d. *V. stamineum* (from BM, BB and Andr.)

Outline of the Mentioned Species

Subg. I Batodendron (Nutt.) Klotzsch
Corolla campanulate, 5 lobed; stamens enclosed, style
exserted; flowers in racemes, calyx and stalk separated;
ovaries incompletely 10 locular; fruit black:
V. arboreum

Subg. II Polycodium (Raf.) Sleumer
Corolla campanulate, 5 lobed; stamens exserted; calyx
continuous with the stalk (not separated!), flowers in foliate
racemes; ovaries incompletely 10 locular; fruits greenish or
yellowish to nearly black:
V. melanocarpum, neglectum, stamineum

Subg. III Herpothamnus (Small) Uphof
Creeping evergreen shrub; corolla urceolate, 5 lobed;
stamens without appendages, sepals very wide; flowers in
compact racemes in the axils of scale-like bracts; fruits black:
V. crassifolium

Subg. IV. Cyanococcus (Gray) Klotzsch
Corolla urceolate to cylindrical or oval-campanulate, with 5
short lobes; anthers without appendages, filaments
pubescent; flowers in racemes or clusters from special buds;
ovaries usually incompletely 10 locular:
*V. angustifolium, atlanticum, corymbosum, hirsutum,
myrtilloides, oldhamii, pallidum, praestans, smallii,
vaccillans, virgatum*

Subg. V. Vaccinium Klotzsch
Ovaries 4–5 locular;

Sect. 1. Myrtillus Koch
Leaves deciduous; corolla urceolate; anthers with
appendages, filaments glabrous; flowers grouped 1–4
axillary:
*V. caespitosum, deliciosum, membranaceum, myrtillus,
ovalifolium, parvifolium, uliginosum*

Sect. 2 Hemimyrtillus Sleumer
Leaves deciduous; corolla campanulate, anthers with or
without small appendages; flowers in long racemes:
V. arctostaphylos

Sect. 3. Vitis-idaea (Moench) Koch
Leaves evergreen, corolla campanulate, filaments
pubescent; flowers in short racemes:
*V. delavayi, intermedium, mortinia, moupinense,
myrsinites, nummularia, ovatum, vitis-idaea*

Subg. VI. Epigynium (Klotzsch) Drude
Leaves evergreen, corolla campanulate or conical, filaments
pubescent, anthers with appendages, disk distinctly 5
lobed; ovaries 5 or 10 locular; fruits leathery, with a few
seeds:
V. bracteatum, fragile, merrillianum (Fig. 292), *sprengelii,
urceolatum*

Subg. VII. Oxycoccoides (Benth. & Hook.) Sleumer
Corolla deeply 5 incised, lobes linear-oblong and revolute;
ovaries 4 locular; fruits solitary, axillary, nodding; leaves
deciduous:
V. erythrocarpum, japonicum

Subg. VIII. Oxycoccus Drude
Creeping, evergreen shrubs; corolla incised to the base in 4
linear-oblong, revolute lobes; ovaries 4 locular; flowers on
thin stalks, axillary or in racemes:
V. macrocarpon, oxycoccus

Vaccinium angustifolium Ait. Low Bush Blueberry.
Low, deciduous shrubs, shoots glabrous or somewhat
pubescent; leaves lanceolate, 7–20 mm long, acute at
both ends, finely bristly serrate, glossy green and
glabrous on both sides; flowers in short, dense clusters,
corolla tubular-campanulate, somewhat constricted at
the limb, 6–7 mm long, greenish white, calyx lobes acute,

April–May; fruits globose, blue-black, pruinose, 6–12 mm thick, sweet. GSP 427 (= *V. pensylvanicum* var. *angustifolium* Gray). Northeast N. America. 1772. z2 Fig. 298. ⊗ ✕

var. **laevifolium** House. Shrub, 50–60 cm high; leaves narrow elliptic to oblong-lanceolate, 1.5–3.5 cm long; flowers in short, compact, axillary panicles, corolla usually white and more tubular, 6 mm long; fruits light blue, 1–1.2 cm thick, good tasting. BM 3434; BB 2791 (= *V. pensylvanicum* Lam. non Mill.). Eastern USA, in dry, stony and sandy places. Fig. 298. ⊗ ✕

V. arboreum Marsh. Farkleberry. Tall, divaricate, deciduous shrub (tree-like and evergreen in its habitat), branches usually only finely pubescent when young; leaves evergreen or (in cooler regions) deciduous, oval-elliptic to obovate, 2–5 cm long, acute to obtuse, entire or indistinctly finely dentate, tough, glossy above, somewhat pubescent beneath; flowers solitary and axillary along the entire branch or in terminal, foliate racemes, corolla white, campanulate, 6 mm long, with 5 reflexed lobes, stamens much shorter than the pistil, ovaries 10 locular, July–August; berries globose, black, 6 mm thick, bitter, not edible. MD 48: 25; HyWF 133; BM 1607; KTF 164. S. to SE. USA. 1765. z7 Fig. 291. (#)

V. arctostaphylos L. Deciduous, upright shrub, 1–3 m high, young shoots red, later yellow-brown, glabrous; leaves oval-oblong to elliptic, acute at both ends, 3–10 cm long, margins undulate and finely serrate, venation somewhat pubescent, a gorgeous carmine-red in fall; flowers in loose, pubescent, axillary racemes, corolla greenish white with a reddish trace, campanulate, 6–7 mm long, May to June; fruits globose, purple, 8–10 mm thick. BM 974; BS 3: 461. N. Asia Minor, W. Caucasus. 1880. Hardy. z6 Plate 149; Fig. 292. ∅ ⊕ ⊗ ✕

V. ashei Reade. Shrub, 1–5 m high, usually deciduous, but also semi-evergreen to evergreen in its habitat; leaves broadly elliptic to broadly obovate, 4–8 cm long, 2–3.5 cm wide, serrate or entire, darker or lighter green to bluish above, usually densely glandular and soft pubescent or glabrous beneath; flowers usually broadly urceolate, lighter or darker pink to red or only white, about 1 cm long; fruits black, dull tasting, but also good selections available in cultivation, 1–1.5 cm thick. SE. USA. z8 ⊗

V. × atlanticum Bicknell (*V. angustifolium* × *V. corymbosum*). Similar to *V. corymbosum*, but only 1 m high; leaves elliptic-oblong to more lanceolate, 3–5 cm long, finely serrate and ciliate, usually pubescent only on the midrib beneath, occasionally glabrous; corolla more urceolate; fruits blue, pruinose. Eastern USA. 1905. z3

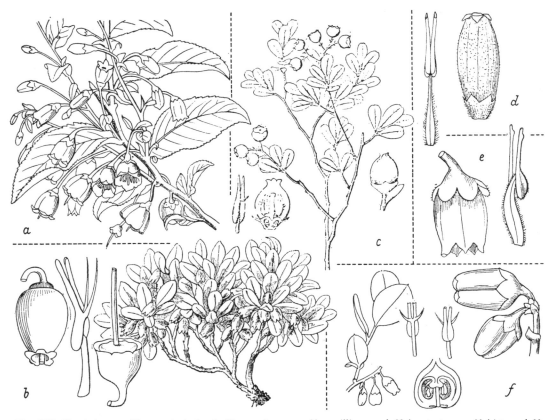

Fig. 292. **Vaccinium.** a. *V. arctostaphylos*; b. *V. caespitosum*; c. *V. merillianum*; d. *V. bracteatum*; e. *V. hirtum*; f. *V. uliginosum* (from ICS, Schneider and BM)

Fig. 293. **Vaccinium.** a. *V. membranaceum;* b. *V. parvifolium;* c. *V. myrtillus;*
d. *V. ovalifolium* (from Hooker, Schroeter and BM)

V. atrococcum Haller. Deciduous shrub, abundantly branched. 1.5–3 m high; leaves elliptic to oblong, apex entire, 3.5–7 cm long, 1.2–3 cm wide, glabrous above, densely pubescent beneath; flowers in short, axillary and terminal, compact, foliate racemes, corolla cylindrical-urceolate, pink or green with a trace of red, with 5 small, triangular, erect or spreading lobes, May; fruits black, globose, 6–8 mm thick, sweet. BB 702. Eastern N. America, from Canada to Alabama. 1898. z4 Fig. 299. ⚭✄

V. bracteatum Thunb. Evergreen shrub, about 1 m high, young shoots usually glabrous; leaves thin, leathery, elliptic to more oblong, acute, 2.5–6 cm long, sparsely dentate; flowers in axillary, 3–5 cm long racemes with persistent, acutely lanceolate, leaflike bracts, corolla white, tubular-urceolate, 6 mm long, fragrant, with 5 short, triangular limb lobes, calyx lobes triangular, pubescent, July–August; fruits globose, red, 6 mm thick, finely pubescent. NK 8: 22; MJ 270; KIF 2: 70; LWT 290. China, Japan. 1830. z9 Fig. 292. # ⊘ ✧ ⚭

V. caespitosum Michx. Deciduous, 10–25 cm high, rapidly spreading, densely branched shrub, shoots glabrous; leaves elliptic to obovate, 1.5–3.5 cm long, glabrous, entire or finely serrate; flowers solitary in the axils of the basal leaves and nodding, corolla pink to nearly white, oval-urceolate, 5 mm long, usually with 5 small, usually erect limb lobes, calyx margin more undulate than toothed, May to July; fruits globose, blue-black, pruinose, sweet, 6 mm thick. BM 3429; DL 1: 127; BB 2784; RMi 346. Northern and Western N. America. 1823. Hardy. z2 Fig. 292. ⚭

V. canadense see: **V. myrtilloides**

V. ciliatum see: **V. oldhamii**

V. corymbosum L. American Blueberry. Deciduous, upright shrub. 1–2 m high, branches glabrous or somewhat pubescent, warty, yellow-green; leaves ovate to lanceolate, 3–8 cm long, entire, glabrous above, venation somewhat pubescent beneath, an attractive orange to scarlet in fall; flowers in dense clusters, corolla tubular-urceolate to narrowly ovate, 6–10 mm long, white or slightly reddish, calyx bluish, May; fruits globose, 8–15 mm thick, blue-black, very pruinose, sweet and good tasting. DL 1: 219; HyWF 137; BB 2788. Eastern USA, on wet soils, in swamps and bogs. 1765. Very significant economically. z2 ⊘ ⚭✄

Including the garden blueberries, generally considered to be more fruitful: 'Earliblue', 'Blueray', 'Bluecrop', 'Herber', 'Berkeley' and 'Coville'. For further information, see Liebster, G.: Die Kulturheidelbeere; Berlin 1961 (229 pp., bibliography with 543 titles) or consult the fruit literature.

V. crassifolium Andr. Evergreen, procumbent shrub, shoots to 60 cm long, wiry; leaves thick and leathery, oval-elliptic to rounded, obtuse, 8–15 mm long, finely serrate, dark green above, lighter beneath; flowers in somewhat nodding, axillary and terminal racemes with scale-shaped bracts, corolla campanulate-urceolate, 4 mm long, pink or white with pink stripes, May–June; fruits globose, black, 3–4 mm thick. BM 1952; MK 1936: 17. SE. USA. 1794. z9 # ✧

V. cylindraceum Sm. Semi-evergreen or deciduous shrub, medium-sized to large; leaves narrowly elliptic to more oblong, bright green, finely dentate and reticulately veined; flowers in short dense racemes along the previous year's shoots in the summer or fall,

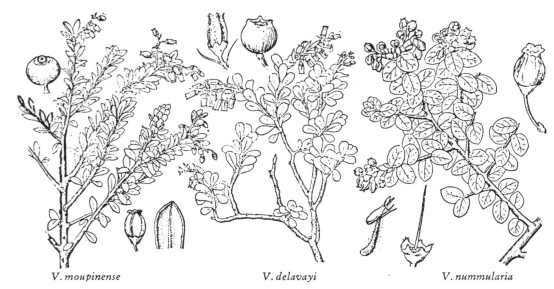

V. moupinense   *V. delavayi*   *V. nummularia*

Fig. 294. **Vaccinium** species (from ICS)

corolla cylindrical, 12 mm long, red in bud, later more yellow-green with a trace of red; fruits oblong, blue-black, pruinose. Azores. z10 ⊘ ☉ ☙

V. delavayi Franch. Compact, evergreen shrub, 0.3–0.5 m high, young shoots bristly; leaves clustered, obovate-cuneate to broad obovate, usually incised on the apex, 6–12 mm long, entire, glabrous; flowers in short, 1.5–2.5 cm long, axillary or (more commonly) terminal racemes, corolla cream-white, pink toned, globose-urceolate, 4 mm long, with 5 ovate or triangular lobes, June; fruits globose, carmine, 5 mm thick. China; Yunnan Prov. 1915. z7 Fig. 294. # ☉ ☙

V. deliciosum Piper. Small, deciduous shrub, very similar to *V. caespitosum*, 0.3 m high, but the leaves tougher, obovate to elliptic, thickish, bluish beneath, sparsely finely serrate; flowers more globose-urceolate, pink, solitary, nodding, May–June; fruits globose, black, sweet. MD 1936: 17. Western N. America. 1920. z6 ☙

V. erythrocarpum Michx. Deciduous shrub, 0.7–1.5 m high, branches pubescent, spreading; leaves oval-oblong to lanceolate, 3–7 cm long, acute, finely bristly serrate, green on both sides and pubescent on the venation; flowers solitary, axillary, nodding, corolla 1 cm long, light red, deeply parted into 4 narrow, reflexed lobes, calyx lobes acutely triangular, June; fruits nearly globose, red, later purple-red, sour. BM 7413; BB 2801; JRHS 1935: 154. SE. USA. 1806. z6 ☉ ☙ Fig. 297.

V. floribundum see: **V. mortinia**

V. fragile Franch. Evergreen shrub, 0.3–0.5 m high, young shoots cylindrical, densely bristly; leaves oval-elliptic, acute at both ends, 1.5–3 cm long, finely serrate, glandular pubescent on both sides; flowers in axillary, 2.5–5 cm long racemes at the branch tips, corolla urceolate, white to dark pink, 6 mm long, with 5 small, reflexed lobes and red bracts, calyx lobes ciliate, May–

June; fruits globose, black, 6 mm thick (= *V. setosum* Wright). W. China. 1909. z9 # ☉

V. gaultheriifolium Hook. f. Small to medium-sized, evergreen shrub, loosely branched, similar to *V. glaucoalbum*, but more delicate in habit and with large, long acuminate leaves, shoots pruinose; leaves elliptic, 7.5–13 cm long, long acuminate, glossy green above and reticulately veined, lighter and blue-white pruinose beneath, entire or finely dentate; flowers white, in corymbs, August–September. Himalayas. z10 # ⊘ ☉

V. glaucoalbum Hook. f. Evergreen shrub, 0.5–1 m high, young shoots smooth; leaves ovate-oblong to obovate, bristly serrate, leathery, acute, smooth and green above, more blue-green beneath with bristly venation, 3–6 cm long; flowers in axillary, 5–7 cm long racemes, corolla tubular-ovate, white with pink, 5–6 mm long, May–June; fruits globose, black, very pruinose, 6 mm thick. BM 9536; GC 129: 90; 133: 109; NF 4: 158. Himalayas; Sikkim. z9 Plate 147. # ☙

V. hirsutum Buckl. Upright deciduous shrub, about 0.6 m high, young shoots very pubescent; leaves ovate to elliptic-oblong, 2–6 cm long, entire, dull green above, lighter beneath, pubescent on both sides; flowers in short, crowded, axillary racemes, corolla tubular-ureolate, 10–12 mm long, white with pink, calyx lobes acute, pubescent, May to June; fruits globose, blackish red, glandular bristled, 6 mm thick, edible. GF 2: 365; MD 1936: 13. SE. USA. 1887. z6 Fig. 298. ☙

V. hirtum Thunb. Closely related to *V. smallii*, but lower, only 0.5 m high, young shoots and leaves soft pubescent; leaves elliptic-lanceolate, 1.5–3.5 cm long; calyx tubular, angled. MJ 716; NT 1: 247. Japan. z6 Fig. 292.

V. × intermedium Ruthe (*V. myrtillus* × *V. vitis-idaea*). Evergreen or semi-evergreen shrub, variable, 20–25 cm high, shoots slightly angular, finely pubescent when young; leaves obovate to elliptic, acute at both ends, 1.5–2.5 cm long, apex somewhat leathery, finely dentate, bright green above, lighter beneath, with only a few dark spots; flowers solitary or a few in terminal and axillary racemes, corolla globose-campanulate, pink, with 5 triangular, outspread limb tips, calyx lobes broadly ovate, acute, June; fruits globose, dark violet, 6 mm thick. DL 1: 121. Europe, occurring among the parents and variously resembling one or the other. 1870. z6 #

V. japonicum Miq. Deciduous shrub, 0.5–0.7 m high, young shoots glabrous, angular; leaves oval-oblong, 2–6 cm long, very short petioled, acute, base round to somewhat cordate, finely bristly serrate, bright green and somewhat rugose above, bluish beneath, totally glabrous; flowers solitary, axillary, on very thin, 12–15 mm long stalks, corolla pink, deeply incised into 4 narrow, revolute lobes, 8 mm long; June–July; fruits somewhat pear-shaped to globose, red, 6 mm thick, pendulous. MJ 725; LWT 289. Japan, Korea. 1892. z6 ♂

V. lanceolatum see: **V. ovatum**

V. macrocarpon Ait. American Cranberry. Evergreen shrub, procumbent, stems to 1 m long, creeping, developing large, flat mats; leaves elliptic-oblong, 1–2 cm long, flat or with slightly involuted margins, dark green above, whitish beneath; flowers light purple, few axillary, long stalked, corolla deeply 4 lobed, reflexed, stalk with 2 bracts, calyx cupulate, with 4 short lobes, June–August; fruits 1–2 cm thick, red, sour and unpalatable. BB 2800; GSP 436; BM 2586; HM 2689. Eastern N. America, N. Asia. 1760. Extensively cultivated in the USA on moist, peaty soil. Also available in a large number of selections. z2 Plate 149; Fig. 297. # ♂✗

V. maderense see: **V. padifolium**

V. melanocarpum (Mohr) Mohr. Deciduous shrub,

about 1 m high, young shoots very white pubescent; leaves ovate, elliptic to oblanceolate, acute, 3–10 cm long, usually finely white tomentose beneath; flowers in axillary racemes, with large bracts, corolla open campanulate, white to greenish, 6 mm long, with 5 wide lobes, calyx white tomentose, with 5 broadly ovate lobes, stamens exserted, May–June; fruits globose, violet-red, glossy, edible. SE. USA, in mountain forests. 1909. z6 Fig. 291. ♂

V. membranaceum Dougl. Deciduous, upright shrub, 0.5–1 m high, shoots angular, pubescent when young; leaves elliptic to oval-oblong, usually acute at both ends or with a rounded base, finely serrate, 2.5–6 cm long, very thin, petiole very short; flowers usually solitary, axillary, stalks reddish, short, glabrous, corolla globose-urceolate, greenish to white-pink, 6 mm long, calyx entire, June–July; fruit globose, dark purple, not pruinose, edible, but rather sour. BM 3447; BB 2785; MD 1936: 13 (= *V. myrtilloides* sensu Hook. non Michx.). Western N. America. 1828. Of only slight garden merit. z6 Fig. 293. ♂

V. mortinia Benth. Evergreen, procumbent shrub, 0.3–1 m high, shoots long outspread, rooting, young shoots dark brown tomentose; leaves very densely crowded, acutely ovate, base rounded, 8–15 mm long, very regularly formed, finely glandular serrate, tough and leathery, dark green above, lighter beneath with scattered glandular pubescence; flowers in dense, axillary racemes at the branch tips, usually hidden beneath the flowers, corolla tubular-urceolate, pink-white, 5–8 mm long, stamens pubescent, anthers without appendages, June; fruits 5 mm thick, red, pruinose, edible. BM 6872; GC 129: 91 (= *V. floribundum* H. B. K.). Andes of Ecuador. 1840. z9 # ✛ ∅ ♂

V. moupinense Franch. Dense, evergreen shrub, 0.3–0.6 m high, young shoots pubescent, furrowed, very similar to *V. delavayi*, but the leaves not incised on the apex;

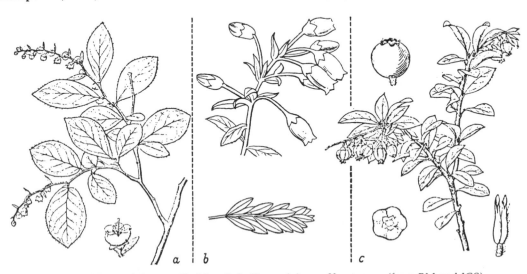

Fig. 295. **Vaccinium**. a. *V. oldhamii*; b. *V. myrsinites*; c. V. retusum (from BM and ICS)

leaves crowded, elliptic-oblong to obovate, leathery-tough, entire, 6–12 mm long, acute to rounded, base tapered, margins somewhat involuted, glabrous; flowers in glabrous (!), axillary, red-brown, 2–2.5 cm long racemes, corolla urceolate, pentagonal, red to brown, 5 mm long, calyx dark red, glabrous, with short, triangular lobes, May–June; fruits globose, black-red, 6 mm thick. China; W. Szechwan Prov. 1909. z9 Fig. 294 # ⌀ ⊕

V. myrsinites Lam. Evergreen shrub, more or less procumbent, to 0.5 m high, shoots thin, usually pubescent when young; leaves elliptic-oblong to obovate, tapered toward the base, acute, 1–2 cm long, irregularly and finely glandular serrate, glabrous and deep green above, lighter beneath with scattered pubescence; flowers in terminal and axillary clusters or short racemes, corolla ovate to urceolate, 6 mm long, white to pink, with 5 small, obtuse, spreading limb tips, April–May; fruits blue-black, globose, 6 mm thick. BM 1550. SE. USA; in sandy pine forest soil. 1813. z7 Fig. 295. #

V. myrtilloides Michx. Deciduous shrub, well branched, 0.3–0.5 m high, young shoots angular, pubescent; leaves lanceolate to narrowly oblong, 2–4 cm long, acute, entire, finely pubescent on both sides (!), particularly on the venation beneath; flowers in axillary, compact, nodding racemes, corolla greenish white to reddish, tubular-campanulate, 4–6 mm long, with 5 erect lobes, calyx lobes green with red tips, acutely ovate, July–August; fruits globose, blue-black, pruinose, 6–8 mm thick. DL 1: 128; BM 3446; BB 2790 (= *V. canadense* Richard). Canada; N. America. 1834. See also: **V. membranaceum.** z2 Fig. 296, 299.

V. myrtillus L. Bilberry, Whortleberry. Strictly upright, deciduous shrub, 30–50 cm high, shoots green, glabrous, sharply angular; leaves oval-elliptic, short stalked, 1–3 cm long, finely serrate, venation glandular pubescent

Fig. 296. *Vaccinium myrtilloides* (from Dippel)

beneath; flowers solitary, axillary, corolla globose-urceolate, 6 mm wide, greenish, often turning red, calyx green, scarcely lobed, May; fruits black-blue, globose, 6–10 mm thick, pruinose, good tasting, with a colored juice. GPN 664–665; HM 2682–2685. Europe to N. Asia, in open forests on acid soil. Of economic use but not significantly used in gardens. z3 Fig. 293. ⊛✳

'Leucocarpum'. Ripe fruits a dirty white.

V. neglectum see: **V. stamineum** var **neglectum**

V. nummularia Hook. f. & Thoms. Evergreen shrub, divaricately branched, 30–40 cm high, branches nodding, densely covered with brown bristly hairs when young; leaves nearly circular to elliptic, 1.2–2.5 cm long, leathery, rugose above, smooth beneath, bristly, finely serrate; flowers in axillary racemes at the shoot tips, corolla urceolate, pink, with 5 small, erect lobes, calyx lobes small, obtusely triangular, ciliate, April–May; fruits black, broadly ovate, 6 mm long, edible. JRHS 60: 155; BMns 470; Snp 98. Sikkim, Bhutan, in the mountains. 1850. Very meritorious garden plant. z7 Plate 127; Fig. 294. # ⊕ ⊛

V. oldhamii Miq. Bushy, deciduous shrub, 1–2 m high, to 3 m high or more in its habitat, young shoots glandular pubescent; leaves oval-elliptic to obovate, 3–8 cm long, finely serrate and ciliate, venation bristly pubescent on both sides, fall color carmine-red; flowers in 3–6 cm long, axillary, pubescent racemes, with bracts, corolla campanulate, green-yellow, somewhat reddish, 4 mm long, with 5 short limb tips, calyx lobes broadly ovate, June–July; fruits globose, 6 mm thick, black, edible. MJ 718 (= *V. ciliatum* G. Don non Thunb.). Japan, Korea. 1892. z6 Fig. 295. ⊛

V. ovalifolium Sm. Deciduous shrub, open branched, 1–3 m high, young shoots angular, glabrous; leaves elliptic to ovate, obtuse, entire, 2.5–6 cm long, pale green above, bluish beneath; flowers solitary, axillary on short stalks, corolla oval-urceolate, pink, 9 mm long, calyx cupulate, with very short lobes, June; fruits nearly globose, dark blue, pruinose, about 1 cm thick, mildly sour. BB 2786; MJ 719. Canada, N. USA. 1880. z3 Fig. 293. ⊕ ⊛

V. ovatum Pursh. Deciduous, bushy, upright shrub, 1–4 m high, broad growing when young, young shoots densely pubescent, red; leaves oval-oblong, acute, base cuneate to nearly cordate, 12–30 mm long, glossy green and scattered pubescent above, lighter beneath, midrib bristly, leathery tough, serrate; flowers solitary or in short, axillary racemes, corolla campanulate, white, somewhat reddish, 6 mm long, with 5 outspread lobes, calyx with 5 wide, shallow lobes, April–May; fruits globose, black, 6 mm thick, sour. DL 1: 220; BB 2700; BM 4732 (= *V. lanceolatum* Dun.). Western N. America. 1826. z7 Fig. 298. #

V. oxycoccos L. European Cranberry. Dwarf evergreen shrub, prostrate, shoots filamentous; leaves ovate-oblong, 5–10 mm long, margins involuted, deep green above, bluish beneath; flowers 1–4 in clusters, more rarely in small, erect racemes, corolla light purple,

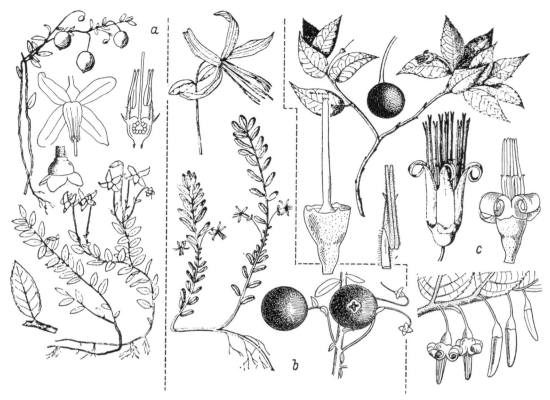

Fig. 297. **Vaccinium**. a. *V. oxycoccus;* b. *V. macrocarpon;* c. *V. erythrocarpum*
(from MB, BB and NBB)

deeply incised, the 4 corolla lobes reflexed, calyx
cupulate with 4(5) lobes, May–July; fruits globose, pea-
sized, dark red, sourish, persisting on the plant the entire
winter without rotting (benzoic acid!). BB 2799; GSP
436; HM 2689; HF 2039 (= *Oxycoccos quadripetala* Gilib.).
N. Europe, N. America, N. Asia, in peat bogs. 1789. z2
Fig. 297. # ⚭ ✕

V. padifolium Sm. Evergreen or semi-evergreen shrub,
densely branched, upright, scarcely over 2 m high in
cultivation, a small tree in its habitat; leaves ovate to
elliptic-oblong, 2.5–5 cm long, acute or round, base
cordate to cuneate, somewhat pubescent only at the
base, particularly beneath; flowers in 2.5–5 cm long,
axillary racemes, with bracts, corolla yellowish, red
striped, campanulate, 1 cm long, with 5 somewhat
reflexed lobes, calyx lobes broad and shallow, June;
fruits globose, black, 12 mm thick, sweet. BM 7305 (= *V.
maderense* Link). Madeira, found in the mountains in
1777. z9 # ⊘ ⊕ ⚭

V. pallidum Ait. Dryland Blueberry. Deciduous shrub,
to 1 m high, young shoots pubescent, yellow-green;
leaves elliptic-ovate; 3–5 cm long, acute, dull green
above, bluish beneath, finely serrate and ciliate; flowers
in dense clusters at the shoot tips, corolla short tubular,
5–8 mm long, white, often reddish, calyx usually
reddish, May; fruits blue, pruinose, 6–8 mm thick, sweet.

BB 2794; GSP 430; MD 1936: 11. E. USA, on dry sites. z4
Fig. 299. ⚭

V. parvifolium Sm. Deciduous, upright shrub, 1.5–2 m
high, often much higher in its habitat, shoots thin,
glabrous, angular; leaves thin, ovate-elliptic to oblong,
1.5–3.5 cm long, obtuse, base round, entire, glabrous;
flowers usually solitary, nodding on short stalks, corolla
flat globose, greenish, with a red trace, 6 mm wide, with 5
tiny, reflexed lobes, May–June; fruits ellipsoid, coral-
red, somewhat translucent, 12 mm long, edible. Western
N. America. 1881. z6 Fig. 293. ⚭

V. pensylvanicum see: **V. angustifolium** var. **laevifolium**

V. praestans Lamb. Deciduous dwarf shrub, similar to *V.
caespitosum*, about 15 cm high, shoots creeping and
ascending, glabrous or finely pubescent; leaves broad
elliptic to obovate, obtuse to acute, 2.5–5 cm long,
tapered toward the base, indistinctly serrate, glabrous
above, venation somewhat pubescent beneath; flowers
grouped 1–3 in axillary clusters on pubescent stalks,
with 2 lanceolate bracts, corolla campanulate, 6 mm
long, white with pink, with 5 erect, rather large lobes,
June; fruits bright red, globose, 12 mm thick, sweet and
fragrant. MJ 721. NE. Asia. 1914. z4 ⊕ ⚭

V. retusum Hook. f. Evergreen shrub, to 30 cm high,

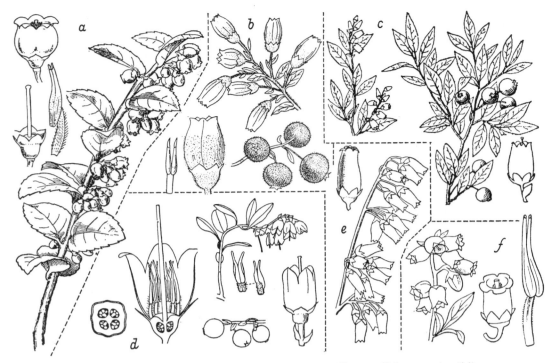

Fig. 298. **Vaccinium.** a. *V. ovatum;* b. *V. hirsutum;* c. *V. angustifolium* var. *laevifolium;* d. *V. vitis-idaea;* e. *V. virgatum;* f. *V. angustifolium* (from BM, BB, NBB and Schneider)

young shoots pubescent; leaves oblong, obovate or elliptic, 1.2–2.5 cm long, obtuse or more or less incised at the apex, entire, margins somewhat recurved, tapered to the base; flowers partly solitary, partly in 3–5 cm long clustered racemes, corolla ovate-urceolate, white with red stripes, 5 mm long, with 5 short lobes, May; fruits globose, 5 mm thick, black. BM 9291; SNp 96. Himalayas. 1882. z9 Fig. 295. # ✛

V. setosum see: **V. fragile**

V. smallii Gray. Deciduous shrub, closely related to *V. angustifolium,* to 1.5 m high, shoots glabrous; leaves elliptic to more lanceolate, 3–6 cm long, acute, base broadly cuneate to round, midrib pubescent beneath; flowers 1–3 together, nodding, corolla campanulate, 5–6 mm long, white to reddish, stamens as long as the corolla, May–June; fruits blue-black, 5–7 mm thick. NT 1: 247. Japan. 1915. Hardy. z6

V. sprengelii (G. Don) Sleumer. Upright, evergreen shrub, to 3 m high, branches thin, young shoots glabrous or soft pubescent; leaves lanceolate-oblong, acute at both ends, 3–7 cm long, finely serrate; flowers in 3–10 cm long, axillary racemes, corolla tubular-urceolate, 6 mm long, white to pink, interior pubescent, May; fruits black-red, globose, 5 mm thick. NE. India, central and W. China. 1908. z7 # ⊘ ✛

V. stamineum L. Deciduous shrub, 0.8–1.5 m high, densely branched, young shoots pubescent; leaves elliptic to oval-oblong, 3–6 cm long, usually bluish beneath, somewhat pubescent on both sides, entire; flowers in axillary, pubescent, 6 cm long racemes, corolla campanulate, 6–8 mm wide, yellowish green to whitish or reddish, stamen filaments widely exserted, April to June; fruits 8–10 mm thick, green or yellow, globose to pear-shaped, unpalatable. NF 11: 297; BB 2796; GSP 424; GC 132: 81. Eastern N. America, in dry, open forests. 1772. Hardy. z5 Fig. 291.

var. **neglectum** Small. Deciduous shrub, to about 1.5 m high, young shoots glabrous; leaves oval-lanceolate to obovate, acute, base rounded, entire, 2.5–8 cm long, glabrous, often bluish beneath at first; flowers in axillary racemes with bracts, corolla campanulate, about 6 mm long, pink to white, with 5 rather large limb tips, stamens widely exserted, sepals glabrous, May; fruits globose to obovoid, green to yellow, 6 mm thick, good tasting. MD 1936: 13 (= *V. neglectum* [Small] Fern.). SE. USA. z9 Fig. 291. ⚥

V. torreyanum see: **V. vaccillans**

V. uliginosum L. Bog Whortleberry. Stiffly erect, deciduous shrub, to 0.5 m high, densely branched, shoots cylindrical, usually glabrous; leaves elliptic to obovate, nearly sessile, 1–3 cm long, entire, bluish green on both sides, somewhat pubescent beneath; flowers solitary or paired, corolla urceolate, white-pink, 4 mm long, with 4 short, spreading lobes, 4 calyx tips, stamens glabrous, May–June; fruits blue-black, pruinose, 6 mm thick, sweet, juice not colored. GPN 662; BB 2763; HF 2027. N. America, N. Europe. 1789. z2 Fig. 292. ⚥

V. urceolatum Hemsl. Evergreen shrub, to 1.8 m high in

its habitat, young shoots densely tomentose at first; leaves oval-oblong, acuminate, leathery, 5–10 cm long, entire, rounded at the base, venation very indented above, dark green; flowers in axillary, 2.5–3 cm long racemes, corolla urceolate, pink, 6 mm long, with 5 (or only 4) lobes, stamens somewhat exserted, calyx with triangular lobes, June; fruits globose, black, 6 mm thick. China; Szechwan Prov. 1923. z9 # ⊕

V. vaccillans Torr. Deciduous shrub, similar to *V. pallidum*, but only to 30 cm high, shoots spreading, green or yellow-green; leaves elliptic spathulate to broad elliptic, 1.5–3 cm long, obtuse, entire or finely serrate; flowers few in racemes, corolla tubular, 5–7 mm long, green-yellow, somewhat reddish, calyx usually somewhat reddish; fruits globose, blue, somewhat pruinose, 4–5 mm thick. MD 1936: 11; BB 2793 (= *V. torreyanum* Camp). E. USA. 1884. z6 Fig. 299.

V. virgatum Ait. Upright, deciduous shrub, 0.4–1 m high, to 4 m high in its habitat, young shoots usually pubescent; leaves oblanceolate to narrowly elliptic, 3–6 cm long, acute, scabrous serrate, glandular above, glabrous beneath or somewhat pubescent on the venation; flowers in short, axillary or terminal racemes, corolla tubular urceolate, 5 mm long, with 5 short, reflexed lobes, May–June; fruits black, globose, 5 mm

thick. MD 1936: 11; BB 2787; RFW 284. E. and SE. USA. 1770. Similar to *V. corymbosum* and often confused with it, but with more urceolate (!) flowers. Highly valued. z6 Plate 149; Fig. 298. # ⚭ ✂

V. vitis-idaea L. Cowberry. Evergreen creeping shrub, 10–30 cm high; leaves leathery, obovate to obtusely ovate, often emarginate at the apex, glossy green above, lighter beneath with black punctate spots (!); flowers in small, nearly terminal racemes, corolla campanulate, white to pink, usually with 4 rather large lobes, calyx 4 lobed, May–June; fruits pea-sized, bright red, bitter. BB 2795; HM 2677; HF 2038. N. Europe to Siberia and Japan, arctic North America. 1789. Not actually in garden cultivation, but very economically important. z5 Plate 149; Fig. 298. # ⚭ ✂

'Erntedank'. Selected wild plant, particularly fruitful. Introduced by Albert Zillner.

'Koralle'. To 30 cm high; leaves 15–25 mm long, obovate, dull dark green; fruits 5–12 together, 7–9 mm thick, very abundant. Selected before 1969 by H. van der Smit, Reeuwijk, Holland. Plate 126.

'Leucocarpum'. Fruits dirty white.

var. **minus** Lodd. Mountain form, only 10–20 cm high, developing a dense mat; leaves only 8–15 mm long; corolla pink to red. Arctic N. America. z2

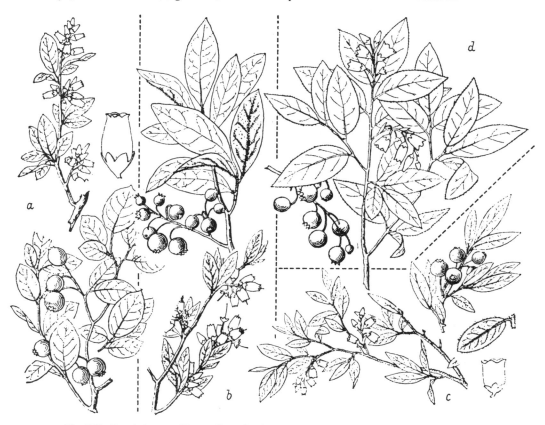

Fig. 299. **Vaccinium**. a. *V. vaccillans;* b. *V. atrococcum;* c. *V. myrtilloides;* d. *V. pallidum* (from BB)

The low species are very well suited to underplanting with *Rhodoendron* and Azaleas. All species thrive in a moist, sandy-humus, acid soil; many species also succeed in swampy sites. The evergreen Chinese and Indian species are generally suitable only for very mild climates.

Lit. Camp, W. H.: The North American Blueberries with notes on other groups of Vacciniaceae; in Brittonia 1945, 203–275 ● Uphof, T.: Die belangreichsten *Vaccinium*-Arten von Nordamerica; in Mitt. DDG 1936, 7–26 ● Sleumer, H.: Vaccinoiden-Studien; Bot. Jahrb. **71**, 375–510, 1941 ● See also the notes at *Vaccinium corymbosum.*

VANIERA

Vaniera tricuspidata see: **Cudrania tricuspidata**

VELLA L. — CRUCIFERAE

Evergreen or deciduous, low shrubs, similar to *Iberis,* but the flowers yellow; shoots thorny or thornless; leaves alternate, entire, usually rough haired; flowers in racemes; the longer filaments connate at the base; fruit pod (silique) ovate, somewhat compressed, with convex valves; seeds globose. — 3 species in the Mediterranean region.

Vella pseudocytisus L. Evergreen, densely branched shrub, usually only 30–40 cm high, also higher in very mild areas, shoots erect, covered with short, thorny bristles in the first 2–3 years, but later totally smooth and thornless (!); leaves usually several, axillary, obovate, 12–18 mm long, rounded above, tapered to a short petiole at the base, both sides and the margins with stiff bristly hairs; flowers in erect, elongated racemes, 10–20 cm long, petals yellow, somewhat spathulate, calyx green, May–June. BR 293. Mountains of central Spain. 1759. z9 Plate 127. # ✛

Fig. 300. *Vella spinosa* (from Kerner)

V. spinosa Boiss. Upright, deciduous shrub, to 30 cm high, dense and compact, shoots divaricate, erect, the upper shoots thorned, glabrous; leaves dull gray-green, linear, 15–20 mm long, fleshy, glabrous; flowers few in terminal corymbs, the individual flowers with 4 petals,

yellow with brown veins, 15 mm wide, June (= *Pseudocytisus spinosus* [Boiss.] Rehd.). Spain. z9 Plate 147; Fig. 300. ✛

Suitable for the rock garden in a sunny, dry site; similar to *Iberis,* but much more tender.

VERBASCUM L. — Mullein — SCROPHULARIACEA

Biennial or perennial or subshrubby plants, often with a thick taproot; leaves alternate, often very soft, entire or crenate or sinuately curved, often in large, basal rosettes; flowers yellow, red-brown, purple or red, occasionally white, in long spikes or racemes; calyx deeply 5 lobed, corolla with a very short tube and 5 lobed limb, stamens 5, attached at the base of the corolla; fruit a globose, many seeded capsule. — 360 species in the northern temperate zones.

Verbascum dumulosum P. Davis & Hub.-Mor. Subshrub, to 30 cm high, branched, the basal shoots prostrate on the ground, densely tomentose, white or gray; leaves elliptic to more oblong, rather thick, tomentose on both sides, entire or finely crenate; flowers in 5–10 cm long racemes, corolla disk form, 2.5 cm wide, lemon-yellow with a red throat, filaments purple pubescent. BMns 258. SW. Turkey; growing in the ruins at Antalya. 1847. z8 Plate 150. ∅ ✛ ○

V. pestalozzae Boiss. Very similar to the above species, but only to 20 cm high; leaves thick white or brownish tomentose, only 10 cm long; flowers about 2 cm wide, filaments yellow pubescent. Asia Minor. z7–8 ∅ ✛ ○

Both species occasionally found in rock gardens and alpine conservatories. Requires full sun and a dry site; winter protection advisable.

Lit. Murbeck, S.: Monographie der Gattung *Verbascum;* in Lunds Univ. Arssksr. **29**, No. 2, 1933.

VERBENA L. — Vervain — VERBENACEAE

Perennials or shrubs; leaves usually opposite, dentate or lobed, occasionally entire; flowers in racemes, panicles or umbels; calyx tubular, 5 toothed, 5 ribbed; corolla somewhat bilabiate, with a straight or bowed tube and 5 spreading lobes; stamens 4, enclosed; fruit surrounded by a dry calyx, divided into 4 parts when ripe. — About 100 species, mostly in tropical America, only a few in the Old World.

Verbena caroo see: **V. tridens**

V. juncea see: **Diostea juncea**

V. tridens Lag. "Matre Negra". Evergreen, divaricate shrub, to 2 m high; leaves densely crowded, very small, 3 lobed, 2–4 mm long, black-green, the lobes rather stiff, acute; flowers sessile, white to lilac-pink, grouped 6–12 in short, terminal spikes, fragrant, July. GC 90: 378 (= *V.*

caroo Spegazz.). Patagonia. 1928. z9 Plate 150.

Modest shrub for full sun, needs a protected site and a good garden soil. A very notable shrub for its unusual appearance.

VERONICA

Veronica bidwilii see: **Parahebe × bidwillii**

V. catarractae see: **Parahebe catarractae**

V. decussata see: **Hebe elliptica**

V. glaucocaerulea see: **Hebe pimeleoides**

V. lyallii see: **Parahebe lyallii**

V. traversii see: **Hebe brachysiphon**

VESTIA Willd. — SOLANACEAE

Monotypic genus with the following characteristics of the species.

Vestia lycoides Willd. Upright, evergreen shrub, unpleasant smelling, 1 m high, shoots soft pubescent; leaves alternate, oblong-elliptic to obovate, 2.5–5 cm long, glabrous, entire, tapered to the base; flowers axillary, nodding, tubular, 2.5–3 cm long, greenish yellow, calyx green, with 5 teeth, April–July; fruits small, yellow. Chile. 1815. z9 Plate 127. # ⊕

VIBURNUM L. — CAPRIFOLIACEAE

Deciduous or evergreen shrubs, occasionally small trees; leaves opposite, occasionally in whorls of 3, entire, serrate, dentate or lobed; flowers usually white, occasionally also pink, in corymbs, with or without sterile ray florets, or in axillary and terminal panicles; calyx very small, 5 toothed; corolla rotate, 5 lobed, stamens 5; stigma 3 lobed, sessile; fruit a dry or juicy drupe. — About 200 species in the temperate or subtropical zones, particularly in Asia and N. America.

Outline of the species mentioned in this work

Section 1. **Thyrsoma** (Raf.) Rehd.
 Leaf petiole without stipules; inflorescences in panicles, with opposite branching; drupes ovoid to ellipsoid, blue-black to purple; stone slightly compressed, deeply furrowed on the ventral side:
  V. bodnantense, erubescens, foetens, fragrans, grandiflorum, henryi, hillieri, odoratissimum, sieboldii, suspensum

Section 2. **Lantana** Spach
 Shrubs with stellate tomentum and naked winter buds; leaves deciduous, occasionally evergreen, usually finely dentate; stone distinctly flattened, with (occasionally indistinct) 3 furrows on the ventral and 2 furrows on the dorsal side:
  V. bitchiuense, buddleifolium, burejaeticum, burkwoodii, carlcephalum, carlesii, cotinifolium, juddii, lantana, macrocephalum, mongolicum, pragense, rhytidocarpum, rhytidophylloides, rhytidophyllum, schensianum, urceolatum, utile, veitchii

Section 3. **Pseudotinus** Clarke
 Deciduous shrubs, with stellate tomentum, leaves finely dentate; winter buds naked; inflorescences terminal, usually with enlarged marginal flowers; fruits purple-black, stone compressed, with a deeper furrow on the ventral side:
  V. cordifolium, furcatum, lantanoides, sympodiale

Section 4. **Pseudopulus** Dipp.
 Deciduous shrubs with dentate leaves and stellate tomentum; winter buds with 2 scales; inflorescences with enlarged marginal flowers, on short lateral shoots; fruits blue-black; stone compressed with a wide furrow on the ventral side:
  V. plicatum

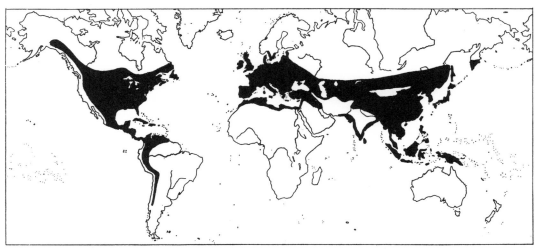

Fig. 301. Range of the genus *Viburnum* (from Egolf)

Section 5: **Lentago** (Raf.) DC.

Deciduous shrubs; leaves entire or finely serrate, venation bowed and diverting before reaching the margin; winter buds with 1 pair of scales; inflorescences without enlarged marginal flowers; fruits blue-black or black; stone convex on the dorsal side, with 3 shallow furrows on the ventral side:

V. cassinoides, jackii, lentago, nudum, obovatum, prunifolium, rufidulum

Section 6. **Tinus** (Borkh.) Maxim.

Evergreen, normally glabrous shrubs; leaves entire to indistinctly dentate, often 3 veined at the base, secondary veins curved and diverting before reaching the margins; petiole without stipules; winter buds with 1 pair of scales; corolla rotate; drupe nearly globose to ellipsoid, blue to blue-black; stone without furrows:

V. atrocyaneum, cinnamomifolium, davidii, harryanum, propinquum, rigidum, tinus

Section 7. **Megalotinus** (Maxim.) Rehd.

Leaves evergreen, entire or finely dentate, pinnately veined, diverting before reaching the margins; petiole without stipules; corolla rotate or tubular-campanulate; drupe blue-black or purple; stone compressed, with dorsal and ventral furrows; winter buds with 1 pair of scales:

V. cylindricum, ternatum

Section 8. **Odontotinus** Rehd.

Leaves deciduous, occasionally evergreen, dentate, venation straight and terminating in the marginal teeth, occasionally diverting before reaching the margins, occasionally 3 veined and lobed; petiole with or without stipules; corolla rotate; stone with 3 or 1 ventral and 2 (often indistinct) dorsal furrows; shrubs with clustered pubescence or glabrous; winter buds with 2 pairs of outer scales:

V. acerifolium, betulifolium, bracteatum, corylifolium, dasyanthum, dentatum, dilatatum, ellipticum, erosum, foetidum, hupehense, ichangense, japonicum, lobophyllum, molle, mullaha, orientale, phlebotrichum, rafinesquianum, sempervirens, setigerum, wilsonii, wrightii

Section 9. **Opulus** DC.

Leaves deciduous, 3–5 veined on the base, lobed, occasionally unlobed, with stipules; fruits red; stone flat, not or slightly furrowed; winter buds with 2 connate outer scales; glabrous shrubs or pubescent with simple hairs:

V. edule, kansuense, opulus, sargentii, trilobum

Outline of the Parentage of the Cultivars

'Alleghany'	→ V. rhytidophylloides
'Anne Russell'	→ list p. 443
'Aurora'	→ V. carlesii
'Candidissimum'	→ V. farreri
'Carlotta'	→ V. burkwoodii
'Cascade'	→ V. plicatum
'Catskill'	→ V. dilatatum
'Cayuga'	→ list p. 443
'Charis'	→ V. carlesii
'Charles Lamont'	→ V. bodnantense
'Chenault'	→ V. burkwoodii
'Dawn'	→ V. bodnantense
'Deben'	→ V. bodnantense
'Diana'	→ V. carlesii
'Erie'	→ V. dilatatum
'Eva Price'	→ V. tinus
'Froebelii'	→ V. tinus
'Fulbrook'	→ list p. 443
'Holland'	→ V. rhytidophylloides
'Iroquois'	→ V. dilatatum
'Lanarth'	→ V. plicatum
'Lucidum'	→ V. tinus
'Mariesii'	→ V. plicatum
'Mohawk'	→ list p. 443
'Mohican'	→ V. lantana
'Notcutt'	→ V. opulus
'Oneida'	→ list p. 443
'Onondoga'	→ V. sargentii
'Park Farm'	→ V. burkwoodii
'Pink Beauty'	→ V. plicatum; V. lentago
'Praecox'	→ V. alnifolium
'Pragense'	→ list p. 443
'Rosace'	→ V. plicatum
'Rowallane'	→ V. plicatum
'Seneca'	→ V. sieboldii
'Snow White'	→ V. grandiflorum
'St. Keverne'	→ V. plicatum
'Susquehanna'	→ V. sargentii
'Tatteri'	→ V. opulus
'Trewithen'	→ V. betulifolium
'Versicolor'	→ V. lantana
'Winton'	→ V. billieri

Viburnum acerifolium L. Upright, deciduous shrub, 1.5–2 m high, young shoots pubescent; leaves circular to ovate in outline, 3 lobed, 6–10 cm long, lobes acuminate, coarsely dentate, slightly pubescent above, densely so beneath with black punctate markings, a good carmine in fall; flowers yellowish white, all hermaphroditic, in 3–8 cm wide, long stalked cymes, May to June; fruits reddish black, ellipsoid, 6–8 mm long, BB 3437; NBB 3: 292; GSP 488. N. America. 1736. Likes dry sites. z3 Fig. 315. ∅

V. affine see: **V. rafinesquianum var. affine**

V. alnifolium Marsh. Deciduous shrub, branches forked (!), often also procumbent and rooting, young shoots tomentose-lepidote; leaves broad ovate, in widely spaced pairs, 10–20 (!) cm long, irregularly dentate, short acuminate, base cordate, stellate pubescent on both sides, eventually glabrous above, a good red in fall, petiole 3–6 cm long; flowers in 8–12 cm wide, stellate tomentose cymes, the sterile marginal flowers to 2.5 cm wide, stamens as long as the corolla lobes, May to June; fruits 8 mm long, red at first, then black. BM 9373; GSP 472; GF 2: 535 (= V. lantanoides Michx.). N. America; in moist mountain forests. 1820. z3 Fig. 307. ∅ ✧

'Praecox' (Hesse). Flowers 3 weeks earlier. MD 1912: 370. Selected by Hesse in Weener, W. Germany before 1912. ∅

V. americanum see: **V. trilobum**

V. atrocyaneum C. B. Clarke. Dense, evergreen shrub, 1(3) m high; leaves ovate, acute, to 5 cm long or smaller, somewhat resembling *Buxus*, glabrous, smooth, glandular dentate; young leaves coppery, all leaves bronze-green in winter; flowers in terminal cymes, but only few flowered, late May; fruits elliptic, blue-black. NH 1963: 38. Himalayas. z9 Plate 150. # ∅ ✧

V. awafuki see: **V. odoratissimum**

V. betulifolium Batal. To 4 m high, deciduous, glabrous

shrub, shoots eventually red-brown; leaves ovate to more rhombic or elliptic-oblong, 3–8 cm long; acuminate, coarsely dentate nearly to the broadly cuneate base, rich green above, lighter beneath, slightly pubescent and often also glandular in the axils of the 4–5 vein pairs, petiole 1–1.5 cm long; flowers white, in short stalked, rather loose, usually 7 rayed, 6–10 cm wide cymes, stamens longer than the corolla, June; fruits nearly globose, 6 mm long, bright red, in heavy, nodding clusters. DRHS 2226; BM 8672; ST 2: 147. Central and W. China. 1901. Hardy. Abundant fruiting only on older plants and then one of the best species. z5 Fig. 319. &

'Trewithen'. Taller growing; particularly abundant fruiting, fruits persist until January. An English selection. &

V. bitchiuense Mak. Deciduous, open upright shrub, to 3 m high, young shoots densely pubescent; leaves ovate, 3–7 cm long, usually obtuse, somewhat dentate, base nearly cordate, pubescent on both sides, underside particularly dense, with 5–7 vein pairs; flowers in loose, 7 cm wide inflorescences, pink at first, then white, corolla nearly 1 cm wide, tube very narrow, 8 mm long, filaments twice as long as the anthers (!), May; fruits black. BS 3: Pl. 37. Japan; Bitchiu Province. 1909. z6 ☉

V. × bodnantense Aberconway (*V. farreri* × *V. grandiflorum*). Deciduous, upright, well branched shrub, about 3 m high, rapid growing; leaves lanceolate to ovate or obovate, acute, 3–10 cm long, serrate, quickly becoming glabrous, with 6–9 deep vein pairs; flowers in 5–7 cm wide, dense clusters, corolla 1 cm long, limb about 1 cm wide, deep pink in bud, later more white, fragrant, October–March. Developed in Bodnant, North Wales. Around 1933. z7 ☉

'Charles Lamont' (*V. grandiflorum* × *V. farreri*). Inflorescences somewhat larger than those of the mother plant, dark pink.

'Dawn' (Aberconway). The type of the cross. BMns 113. ☉

'Deben' (Notcutt 1959). Habit stiff and divaricate, 2.5–3 m; flowers whitish, turning red, slightly fragrant, January–April. ☉

V. bracteatum Rehd. Deciduous shrub, closely related to *V. rafinesquianum*, to 3 m high; leaves circular to ovate, 5–12 cm long, coarsely and sinuately dentate, base cordate, venation pubescent beneath, petiole 1.5–2 cm long; inflorescences 4–8 cm wide, with distinct bracts (!); fruits 1 cm long, blue-black. ST 68. Georgia. 1904. z5 Fig. 307.

V. buddleifolium Wright. Upright, semi-evergreen shrub, to about 2 m high, shoots densely pubescent; leaves oblong-lanceolate, 7–15 cm long, shallowly dentate, acuminate, base rounded to slightly cordate, light dull green above, underside densely light gray stellate tomentose, very soft to the touch (!); flowers in about 8 cm wide cymes, corolla white, about 8 mm wide, May–June; fruits red at first, later black. Central China. 1900. z6 Plate 150, 151. (#) ∅

V. buergeri see: **V. japonicum**

V. burejaeticum Rgl. & Herd. Deciduous shrub, to 5 m

Fig. 302. *Viburnum burejaeticum* (from Dippel)

high, young shoots stellate pubescent, glabrous and white in the 2nd year (!), leaves oval-elliptic to obovate, 4–10 cm long, acute to obtuse, finely and sinuately dentate, base rounded to somewhat cordate, loosely stellate pubescent beneath, particularly on the venation, eventually nearly totally glabrous (!), petiole 3–8 mm long, lepidote; inflorescences 5 rayed, 4–5 cm wide, pubescent, white, May; fruits ellipsoid, 1 cm long, black. Gfl 384; DL 1: 116. Manchuria, N. China. 1900. Often erroneously labeled in cultivation. z5 Fig. 302.

V. × burkwoodii Burkw. & Skipwith (*V. carlesii* × *V. utile*). Evergreen shrub, open and divaricate, 1–2 m high, similar to *V. utile*, branches densely brown stellate tomentose, gradually becoming glabrous and olive-green; leaves often only semi-evergreen, ovate to elliptic, 4–7 cm long, indistinctly sparsely dentate, glossy dark green and rough above, gray-green tomentose beneath; inflorescences about 6 cm wide, very fragrant, pink at first, then white, corolla 1 cm wide, tube as long as the limb lobes, stamens inserted into the base, as long as the tube, March–April, normally producing a few secondary flowers in the fall (!). DB 4: 67. Developed in 1924 by Burkwood & Skipwith in Kingston-on-Thames, England. z5 Plate 152. # ☉

'Carlotta' (W. B. Clarke, San Jose, Calif.). Seedling of *V. burkwoodii*, once described as an improved *V. carlesii*. No longer cultivated.

'Chenault' (Chenault). Denser habit; leaves less glossy above, more gray pubescent beneath, more dentate, fall color often bronze-brown; flowers pale pink, later white, about 2 weeks earlier than the species (= *V. chenaultii* Hort.). Developed in France around 1930. Plate 152. # ☉

'Park Farm' (Johnson). Broader habit; leaves more ovate to lanceolate, 7–10 cm long, entire to somewhat serrate, pubescent beneath; flowers in 10–12 cm wide cymes, pure white (!) flowering only in spring (!), very fragrant. Developed in England around 1925. # ☉

V. burkwoodii × **carlesii.** Included here are 3 clones in the trade. See the list at p. 443 for: 'Anne Russell', 'Fulbrook', 'Mohawk'.

V. × **carlcephalum** Burkw. (*V. carlesii* × *V. macrocephalum* f. *keteleerii*). Deciduous shrub, similar to *V. carlesii* in appearance, about 1.5–2 m high; leaves to 12 cm long, lighter beneath, reddish in fall; flowers in large, 13 cm wide, globose inflorescences, pure white, only slightly reddish in bud, not always very floriferous, less fragrant than *V. carlesii*, tube shorter than that of *V. carlesii*, only about 2.5 mm long, anthers exserted, April. JRHS 1947: 132. Around 1932. z5 ⊕

V. carlesii Hemsl. Deciduous shrub, to about 1.5 m high, open stellate tomentose on all parts, habit broadly globose; leaves broad ovate, 3–10 cm long, acute, base usually rounded, irregularly dentate, dull green above, lighter and densely pubescent beneath, with 5–7 vein pairs; flowers in dense, 5–7 cm wide, hemispherical cymes, corolla 1–1.4 cm wide, tube 6–10 mm long, white, exterior pink-red, very fragrant, stamens enclosed, filaments shorter than the anthers, April–May; fruits blue-black, 1 cm long, ellipsoid. BM 8114; DB 1950: 153. Korea. A very attractive shrub. z5 Plate 152. ⊕

'**Aurora**'. Buds intensely red, opening to pink, then white, very fragrant. ⊕

'**Charis**'. Very similar to 'Aurora', but strong growing; buds red, opening pink at first, then white. ⊕

'**Compactum**' (Hoogendoorn). Slower growing, more compact; leaves darker green; flowering abundantly on older plants, flowers like the species. Discovered around 1950 by C. Hoogendoorn in Newport, R.I., USA. ⊕

'**Diana**'. Strong growing, but remaining compact; buds red, opening pink, then white, very fragrant. ⊕

> 'Aurora', 'Charis' and 'Diana' are selections by L. Slinger of the Slieve Donard Nursery in Newcastle, N. Ireland grown from Korean seed. All 3 forms are very similar, but much more vigorous than the old form. Around 1950.

V. cassinoides L. Deciduous shrub, usually not over 2 m high, shoots brownish lepidote at first, tightly erect, buds yellow-brown; leaves acutely oval-oblong, 3–10 cm long, light green, lighter and nearly glabrous beneath, margins indistinctly dentate (!), fall color an attractive red to orange; flowers white, in dense, to 12 cm wide, flat-arched cymes, stalks usually shorter than the inflorescence width (!), corolla 5 mm wide, July–August; fruits blue-black. GF 9: 305; NF 10: 40; BB 3442. N. America. 1761. z4 Fig. 309. ⌀ ⋇

'**Nanum**'. Compact habit, branches and shoots twisted; leaves crispate and twisted.

V. ceanothoides see: **V. foetidum** f. **ceanothoides**

V. cinnamomifolium Rehd. Evergreen shrub, tall, similar to *V. davidii*, but to 6 m high; leaves less tough, elliptic-oblong, distinctly 3 veined, abruptly long acuminate, nearly entire, dull dark green above, lighter with axillary pubescence beneath; flowers in loose, 7 rayed, long stalked cymes, 12–15 cm wide, cream-white, June; fruits 4 mm long, ovate, blue, glossy. ST 119.

China; Mt. Omei. 1904. z7 Plate 151, 152. # ⌀ ⊕

V. cordifolium Wall. A small tree in its habitat, resembling *V. sympodiale*, but with ovate leaves, rounded to cordate at the base; inflorescences without sterile outer flowers, pure white, stamens only half as long as the corolla. ST 2: 138; SNp 78. W. China; E. Himalayas. 1932. z9 Fig. 307.

V. coriaceum see: **V. cylindricum**

V. corylifolium Hook. f. & Thoms. Very similar to *V. dilatatum*, but with a long, rust-brown pubescence (!). Upright, deciduous shrub, to 3 m high, shoots densely red-brown pubescent; leaves nearly circular to obovate, 3–8 cm long, abruptly short acuminate, base cordate, dentate, with 6–9 vein pairs, pubescent on both sides, denser and longer beneath; flowers white, fragrant, very small, in 3–7 cm long cymes, June; fruits ovate, 8 mm long, scarlet-red. E. Himalayas, W. China. 1907. Hardy. z6

V. cotinifolium D. Don. Broad growing, deciduous shrub, to 4 m high, branches stellate pubescent at first; leaves rounded-ovate, 5–12 cm long, abruptly acuminate, finely crenate to nearly entire, base rounded to cordate, finely rugose above, gray stellate pubescent beneath; inflorescences usually 5 rayed (!); convex, 5–7 cm wide, corolla tubular-campanulate, 6 mm long, June; fruits ovate, to 1 cm long, red at first, then black. BR 1650; GF 5: 245; SNp 81. Himalayas. 1830. z6 Fig. 303.

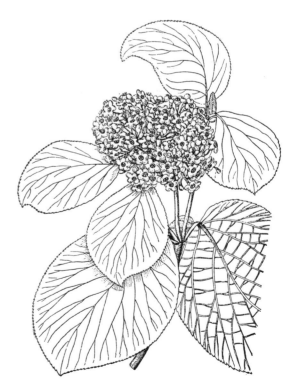

Fig. 303. *Viburnum cotinifolium* (from BM)

'Dwarf Form'. Low habit, compact; flowers light pink. ⊕

V. cylindricum D. Don. Evergreen shrub, also a tree in its habitat, to 12 m, shoots warty; leaves elliptic-oblong, 8–15 cm long, sparse and indistinctly dentate on the apical half, dull green above with a thin waxy coating (it is possible to write in this coating with a fingernail!), with 3–4 vein pairs; flowers white, usually in 7 rayed, 8–12 cm wide cymes, on 2–6 cm long stalks, corolla tubular-campanulate, with erect lobes (!), anthers lilac, July–September; fruits ovate, 5 mm long, black. ST 143 (= *V. coriaceum* Bl.). W. China, Himalayas. 1881. z6 Plate 151, 153; Fig. 312. # ⊘

V. dasyanthum Rehd. Deciduous shrub, to 2.5 m high, young shoots glabrous, red-brown; leaves oval-elliptic to oblong, 6–12 cm long, acuminate, sparsely shallowly dentate, with 6–7 vein paris, base usually rounded, petiole 1.5–2 cm long, with small stipules (!); flowers white, in loose, 7 rayed, 8–10 cm wide cymes, corolla densely long haired on the exterior, stamen filaments longer than the corolla, June; fruits ovate, 8 mm long, bright red. ST 149. Central China. 1907. z6 Fig. 312.

V. davuricum see: **V. mongolicum**

V. davidii Franch. Very densely branched, evergreen shrub, to 1 m high in its habitat (often only half as tall in cultivation), shoots warty; leaves tough, elliptic to more obovate, 5–14 cm long, short acuminate, entire to indistinctly dentate, distinctly 3 veined, deep green above, lighter with axillary pubescence beneath; flowers pink-white, in dense, 8 cm wide cymes, usually 7 rayed, June; fruits oval rounded, to 6 mm long, a good dark blue. BM 8980. W. China. 1904. Best planted in groups to insure good fruiting. A particularly good fruiting type exists in the trade called "femina". z7–8 Plate 153. # ⊘ ⊕ ⊗

V. dentatum L. "Arrow wood". Deciduous shrub, 1–5 m high, bark tight on the branches, gray-brown to reddish; leaves oval-lanceolate to circular, 4–10 cm long, with a sharp apex or short acuminate or rounded, dentate, the teeth triangular with a prominent apex, glabrous or nearly so above, underside somewhat stellate pubescent or glabrous, petiole very thin, 8–25 mm long, glabrous or stellate pubescent, usually without stipules; cymes 5–7 rayed, rachis 3–6 cm long, calyx glabrous or glandular or bristly, style pubescent, May–July; fruits blue-black, nearly globose to ovate, 5–10 mm long, seed with a narrow, deep furrow on one side. GSP 484; NBB 295. N. America; Maine to Illinois, southward to Florida and Texas. A polymorphic species from dry or wet soils or sand dunes, quite variable in the form of the leaves, with or without stipules, also varying in the degree of pubescence. Some decisively different types have been raised to the rank of species. This volume recognizes the work of Gleason in New Britton and Brown, Ill. Flora of the NE. USA and Canada, Vol. **3**, 1958. z2 Fig. 304.

Outline

× Leaf petiole glabrous; leaf undersides glabrous or only pubescent in the vein axils:
var. *lucidum*

×× Leaf petiole more or less stellate pubescent; leaves stellate pubescent on the underside, at least on the venation;
  v Stipules and stalked glands absent:
var. *dentatum,* var. *scabrellum,* var. *venosum*

  vv Stipules present on many leaf petioles; stalked glands often present:
var. *deamii,* var, *indianense*

var. **deamii** (Rehd.) Fern. Leaves circular, with many sharp teeth, somewhat similar to var. *lucidum,* but more or less

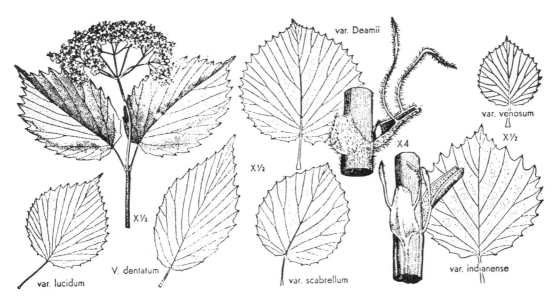

Fig. 304. *Viburnum dentatum* and its varieties (from NBB)

pubescent beneath, petiole pubescent on the underside (!), often intermixed with stalked glands. NBB 295. S. Ohio to Missouri. Fig. 304.

var. **dentatum**. Leaves relatively thin, usually ovate, thinly pubescent to glabrous beneath; calyx glabrous to glandular. NBB 295 (= *V. scabrellum* Gray; *V. semitomentosum* Small). Primarily along the coastal regions, New Jersey to Florida and Texas; extending northward but gradually changing to a form with larger, more green leaves and nearly or totally glabrous undersides (= *V. venosum* var. *canbyi* Gray; *V. pubescens* var. *canbyi* Blake).

var. **indianense** (Rehd.) Gleas. Resembling var. *deamii*, leaves nearly or totally glabrous beneath, leaf petiole only stellate pubescent in the furrow, with stalked glands above. NBB 295. S. Indiana to Illinois. Fig. 304.

var. **lucidum** Ait. Leaves thin, oval-lanceolate to rounded, scabrous and short acuminate, with 10–20 sharp teeth on either side; calyx glabrous. NBB 295; GSP 486 (= *V. dentatum* Gray; *V. recognitum* Fern.). Maine and New York to Ohio, in the mountains to Georgia, in moist forests and swamps. Fig. 304, 309. Ø

var. **scabrellum** Torr. & Gray. Resembling var. *dentatum* in foliage; but the calyx and corolla densely bristly or rough haired on the exterior. NBB 295. Coastal regions of Florida to Louisiana, also in Ohio. Fig. 304.

var. **venosum** (Brit.) Gleas. Leaves relatively tough, usually circular in outline, often wider than long, densely stellate pubescent with raised venation beneath; calyx glabrous or glandular. NBB 295(= *V. venosum* Gray p. p.). Sandy soil in the coastal regions of Massachusetts and the pine forests of New Jersey. Fig. 304.

V. dilatatum Thunb. Upright, deciduous shrub, to 3 m high, young shoots pubescent; leaves nearly circular to obovate or broadly ovate, 6–12 cm long, with 5–8 vein pairs, abruptly short acuminate, coarsely dentate, base round to somewhat cordate, pubescent on both sides, petiole 6–16 mm long; flowers very abundantly with 8–12 cm wide, pubescent cymes, stamens longer than the pubescent corolla, May to June; fruits broadly ovate, 8 mm long, scarlet-red. KIF 4: 46; NF 10: 38; BM 6215; MJ 310; BC 3924. Japan. z5 Fig. 319. ⚭

'Catskill'. Broad, compact habit, to about 1.8 m high, 2.7 m ·wide, branches light gray-brown and pubescent when young, later glabrous; leaves oval to obovate, 11–14 cm long, 7–10 cm wide, with 6–10 vein pairs, finely dentate, base round to slightly cordate, somewhat pubescent on both sides, dull dark green, orange-yellow to red in fall, petiole 1–3 cm; flowers usually in a 5 armed cyme, 8–10 cm wide, mid May; fruits dark red, persisting into the winter. Developed in 1954 by D. R. Egolf in the U.S. National Arboretum from Japanese seed. Ø ⊕ ⚭

'Erie'. Shrub, to 1.8 m high, to 3 m wide, broadly divaricate; leaves rather variable in size and form, dull green, a good yellow, orange and red in fall; abundantly fruiting, fruits pale pink at first, then coral-pink, later becoming somewhat lighter. Developed in the U.S. National Arboretum from Japanese seed by D. R. Egolf and introduced to the trade in 1975. Ø ⚭

'Iroquois'. A cross of 2 *dilatatum* clones. Bushy shrub, 2.5 m high to 3.5 m wide, branches erect and widespreading; leaves rounded to broad ovate or obovate, 11–16 cm long, 7–9 cm wide, abruptly short acuminate, coarsely dentate, with 8–14 vein pairs, base slightly cordate, glossy green in summer,

orange-red to red-brown in fall, petiole 1.5–3.5 cm; inflorescences very numerous, 8–12 cm wide, cream-white, mid May; fruits coral-red, 50–150 together, August, persisting long after leaf drop. Selected in 1958 by D. R. Egolf in the U.S. National Arboretum. Ø·⊕ ⚭

'Xanthocarpum'. Fruits yellow. 1919. ⚭

V. edule (Michx.) Raf. Deciduous shrub, loosely spreading 1–1.5 m high, young shoots glabrous; leaves nearly circular to broad elliptic, with 3 short lobes at the apex, 5–8 cm long, unevenly serrate, base rounded to truncate and 3 veined, glabrous or somewhat pubescent on the underside, petiole 1–2.5 cm long; cymes only 1.5–2.5 cm wide, May; fruits oval-globose, red, 8 mm long. BB 3436; GSP 492; RWF 356 (= *V. pauciflorum* Raf.). N. America, NE. Asia; in moist, cool, semishaded sites. 1880. z5 Plate 151; Fig. 315.

V. ellipticum Hook. Deciduous, 1.5–2.5 m high shrub, shoots somewhat pubescent at first, green-yellow; leaves thickish, eventually nearly leathery, elliptic-oblong, 3–7 cm long, obtuse, coarsely serrate above the middle, base 3 veined and somewhat cordate, pubescent beneath, at least on the venation; flowers in long stalked, pubescent, 4–5 cm wide cymes at the shoot tips, corolla nearly 1 cm wide; fruits ellipsoid, 12 mm long, black. DL 1: 113. Western N. America. 1908. Hardy. z6 Fig. 306.

V. erosum Thunb. Deciduous shrub, thinly branched, about 2 m high, young shoots soft pubescent; leaves oval-elliptic to more oblong or obovate, 4–8 cm long, acuminate, sharply dentate, base round to broadly cuneate, usually glabrous above, underside usually pubescent only on the 7–10 vein pairs, petiole 2–6 mm long, with stipules; flowers in rather loose, 5 rayed, slightly pubescent, usually 6–8 cm wide cymes, stamens somewhat longer than the corolla, ovaries glabrous, May–June; fruits nearly globose, 6 mm long, red. GF 9: 85; MJ 311. Japan. 1844. z6

V. erubescens Wall. Deciduous shrub to small tree; leaves elliptic, acuminate, base cuneate to round, 5–10 cm long, serrate, incised nearly to the base, with 5–7 glabrous or pubescent vein pairs beneath; flowers in sessile, 5 cm long, loose, pendulous panicles, corolla about 1 cm long, limb spreading, lobes rounded, white with a pink trace, fragrant, early June (!); fruits red at first, then black. SNp 80. Himalayas, W. China. Around 1925. Not particularly attractive. z6 Fig. 305. ⊕

var. **gracilipes** Rehd. Leaves usually elliptic, rounded at the base, glabrous; inflorescences 7–12 cm long (!), loose, pendulous. Central China. 1910. ⊕

V. farreri Stearn. Deciduous, tightly upright shrub, densely branched, to 3 m high, branches red-brown; leaves acutely elliptic, 4–7 cm long, tough, scabrous serrate; flowers in 3–5 cm long, dense panicles, corolla tubular, limb about 1 cm wide, pink to white, very fragrant, appearing before the leaves (!), March–April; fruits ripening already in late June, red at first, then black. BM 8887; DB 1955: 19a; ST 106 (= *V. fragans* Bge.). N. China. 1909. Selection is important since there are many poorly flowering types in cultivation. z6 Plate 153. ⊕

Fig. 305. **Viburnum.** Left *V. erubescens;* center *V. foetidum* var. *rectangulatum;* right *V. setigerum* (from ICS)

'Album' see: 'Candidissimum'

'**Candidissimum'.** Like the species, but the flowers are pure white, corolla somewhat larger, leaves lighter green; fruits light yellow (= 'Album'). Found in the wild in N. China. ⊕

'**Nanum'** (Cl. Elliot). Only about 50 cm high; leaves smaller; not as abundantly flowering as the species. 1937.

V. foetens Dcne. Deciduous shrub, closely related to *V. grandiflorum,* but lower, to 1.5 m high, wider and more open; leaves large, smooth, with a pungent scent (particularly when crushed, or dead); flowers white, in loose, 5 cm long panicles, very fragrant, January–March; fruits red at first, then black. Himalayas; Kashmir; Korea. z6 ⊕◑

V. foetidum Wall. Semi-evergreen, densely foliate shrub, 1.5–3 m high, young shoots stellate pubescent; leaves elliptic-oblong, 4–10 cm long, acute, base cuneate and 3 veined (!) and with 1–2 other vein pairs, dentate on the apical half to nearly entire, glabrous above, venation pubescent beneath, unpleasant smelling when crushed, 5–10 mm long; flowers on short, spreading lateral shoots in small, pubescent, 5–8 cm wide cymes, white, June; fruits scarlet-red, 7 mm long. Wall. Pl. As. Rar. 1: Pl. 61, Himalayas; Burma. z9 (#)

f. **ceanothoides** (Wright) Hand.-Mazz. Upright habit, to 2 m high; leaves obovate to elliptic-oblong, acute to rounded, base cuneate, petiole 2–6 mm long; flower stalks 5–15 mm long. GC 96: 313 (= *V. ceanothoides* Wright). W. China. 1901. z9

f. **rectangulatum** (Graebn.) Rehd. To 3 m high, branches widespreading and often nodding; leaves lanceolate to oblong obovate, acuminate, sparsely dentate or finely denticulate, 3–7 cm long; cymes usually nearly sessile on normally short, horizontal lateral shoots. BM 9509 (= *V. rectangulatum* Graebn.). W. China. z8–9 Fig. 305.

V. fragrans see: **V. farreri**

V. furcatum Bl. Very similar to *V. lantanoides,* more upright habit, young shoots soft pubescent; leaves circular to ovate, 7–15 cm long, with a short tip, base cordate, with 9–10 vein pairs; inflorescences quite flat, to 10 cm wide, sterile flowers only on the margin, these to 2.5 cm wide, white, stamens about half as long as the corolla, May; fruits ovate, red, then black. ST 119; KIF 4: 47. Japan; in moist and shady woodlands. 1892. Useless in full sun! z6 Plate 154.

V. grandiflorum Wall. Deciduous shrub, occasionally a small tree in its habitat, broad and somewhat stocky habit, branches thick, shoots soft pubescent at first; leaves elliptic-oblong, tapered to both ends, 7–10 cm long, with 6–10 vein pairs, these very pubescent beneath; flowers in dense, 5–7 cm wide cymes, corolla to 12 mm wide and long, white, turning pink, January–March; fruits red to black. Snp 79; NF 6: 202; BM 9063 (= *V. nervosum* sensu Hook. f. & Thoms.). Himalayas. 1914. z6 Fig. 308. ⊕

'**Snow White'.** Corolla tube white, occasionally turning pink-red, calyx green (!), in 5–7 cm wide cymes, very fragrant. JRHS 95: 172. Developed in England in 1950 by Lowndes from seed collected in Nepal. ⊕

V. harryanum Rehd. Evergreen shrub, 1–3 m high, open, *Ligustrum*-like in appearance (!), young shoots totally finely stellate tomentose, thin; leaves circular to ovate or obovate, 8–25 mm long or wide, tough, dull and dark green above, lighter beneath, glabrous; inflorescences usually 7 rayed, only about 3 cm wide, pure white; fruits 4 mm long, black. W. China. 1904. z9 Plate 151. # ∅

V. henryi Hemsl. Evergreen (or semi-evergreen) shrub, to 3 m high, tightly upright, shoots glabrous; leaves elliptic-oblong to more obovate, to 12 cm long, acute, flat toothed, glossy dark green above, glabrous beneath except for a few scattered stellate hairs; flowers in broadly conical, 10 cm long panicles, corolla white, about 6 mm wide, May to June; fruits ovate, red at first, then black, 6 mm long. BM 8393; BS 3: 502. Central China. z7 Plate 154; Fig. 316. #

V. hessei see: **V. wrightii** var. **hessei**

Fig. 306. *Viburnum ellipticum* (from Dippel)

V. × hillieri Stearn (*V. erubescens* × *V. henryi*). Loose, open, evergreen shrub, about 2 m high and wide; somewhat similar to *V. henryi*, but with wider leaves, 5–15 cm long, narrow elliptic, short acuminate, sparsely shallow serrate with 4–5 vein pairs, these indented above; flowers in conical, ascending, 6 cm long and wide panicles, corollas regularly funnelform, white, tube 4–5 mm long, flowering very abundantly, June; fruits red to black. BMns 680. Developed in cultivation at Hillier Nurseries, England in 1950. z6 # ⊕ ⊘

'Winton' (Hillier). The type of the cross. JRHS 81: 153. Originated as a chance hybrid around 1950 at Hillier Nursery, Winchester, England. # ⊕

V. hupehense Rehd. Similar to *V. dasyanthum*, but with stellate pubescent young shoots, later glabrous, purple-brown; leaves broadly ovate, 5–7 cm long, long acuminate, coarsely dentate, base truncate to somewhat cordate, pubescent on both sides, particularly dense beneath on the 7–8 vein pairs, petiole 8–15 mm long; flowers white, in mostly 5 rayed, long pubescent, 4–5 cm wide cymes, corolla soft pubescent on the exterior, May–June; fruits ovate, red, 8–10 mm long, fruiting very abundantly. BMns 41; GC 132: 56. Central China. 1907. z6 ⌘

V. ichangense (Hemsl.) Rehd. Deciduous shrub, 1.5–3 m high, very closely related to *V. erosum*, branches thin, pubescent at first, later glabrous and gray-brown; leaves ovate to more lanceolate, 3–6 cm long, acuminate, margins with widely spaced teeth, somewhat rough above, persistent pubescence beneath; flowers yellowish white, in 4–5 rayed, pubescent, 2.5–4 cm wide cymes at the branch tips, ovaries densely woolly (!) stamens shorter than the corolla, June; fruits red, 6 mm long, pubescent. ST 150. Central and W. China. 1901. z6 Fig. 319.

V. involucratum see: **V. mullaha**

V. × jackii Rehd. (*V. lentago* × *V. prunifolium*). Intermediate between the parents, but more similar to *V. lentageo*, more densely branched, winter buds shorter, leaves more broad ovate, more obtuse, more finely serrate, more green beneath, not light green, leaf petiole

not as broad winged. Originated before 1900. z5

V. japonicum (Thunb.) Spreng. Evergreen shrub, about 1.5–2 m high, shoots thick and glabrous; leaves leathery, broad ovate to rhombic, 8–14 cm long, acute, base broad cuneate to rounded, sparsely and shallowly dentate on the apical half, with 5–6 vein pairs terminating in the dentate margin (! see *V. odoratissimum*), very glossy above, dark green; flowers white, very fragrant, in dense, convex cymes, 7–10 cm wide, June; fruits globose to somewhat ovate, 8 mm long, bright red. MJ 321; NF 4: 265; KIF 3: 78 (= *V. buergeri* Miq.; *V. macrophyllum* Bl.). Japan. 1859. z7 Plate 151. # ⊘ ⌘

V. × juddii Rehd. (*V. bitchiuense* × *V. carlesii*). Resembles *V. carlesii* in appearance, but with more oblong leaves, larger but loose inflorescences. Broad, deciduous shrub, 1–2 m high, branches densely stellate pubescent; leaves ovate-oblong to elliptic, acute, shallowly dentate, 4–6 cm long, pubescent beneath; flowers in 5–9 cm wide cymes, pink at first, then white, very fragrant, corolla 1 cm long, 6 mm wide, filaments 1.5 times longer than the anthers, these situated in about the middle of the tube or deeper, April–May. GC 132: 18; JRHS 77: 52. Developed in the Arnold Arboretum around 1920. z5 Plate 154. ⊕

V. kansuense Batal. Deciduous shrub, to 3 m high, young shoots glabrous; leaves broad ovate, deeply 3–5 lobed (!), only 2.5 cm long, somewhat cordate at the base, the lobes acute, coarsely dentate, somewhat pubescent above, vein axils with tufted pubescence beneath, petioles thin, 1–2.5 cm long; cymes 3 cm wide, 5–7 rayed, pink-white, stamens longer than the corolla; fruits ellipsoid, 1 cm long, red. W. China. 1908. z5–6

V. laevigatum see: **V. obovatum**

V. lantana L. Wayfaring Tree. Deciduous, upright shrub, to 5 m high, strong growing, branches stellate tomentose; leaves ovate to oval-oblong, 6–12 cm long, acute to obtuse, densely and finely dentate, rugose and dark green above, underside dense gray stellate tomentose; flowers in up to 10 cm wide, stellate pubescent cymes, May–June; fruits oval-oblong, 8 mm long, red, later becoming black, glossy. HM Pl. 251; HF 2911. Europe, Asia Minor; on sunny forest edges, in thickets on gravelly, limestone soil. Ⓕ W. Germany, Austria (Tyrol; in green screens). z3 Fig. 316. ⊕ ⌘

'Aureum'. New growth and young leaves attractively golden-yellow, later green with a trace of yellow. Distributed to the trade by Späth of Berlin in 1921. ⊘

var. **discolor** Huter. Leaves smaller and tougher, white tomentose beneath. SH 2: 419 n–o. Balkan Mts.

'Mohican'. Particularly compact and dense habit, to 1.5 m high, 2.5 m wide, foliage deep green; fruits remaining orange-red for a long time, from early July, eventually black. Selected from Polish seed in 1952 by D. R. Egolf in the U.S. National Arboretum. ⌘

var. **rugosum** Lge. Leaves larger, more rugose; with larger inflorescences.

'Variegatum'. Leaves yellow variegated. England. 1770. ⊘

'Versicolor'. New growth light yellow, later golden-yellow,

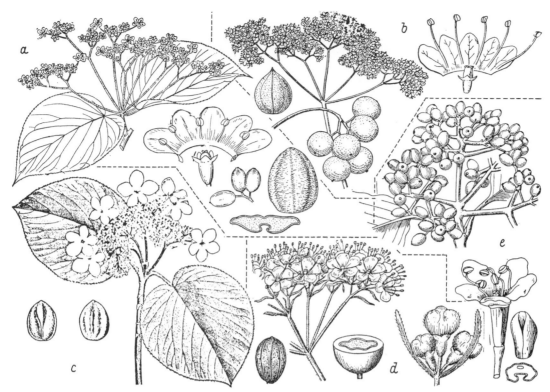

Fig. 307. **Viburnum**. a. *V. cordifolium;* b. *V. wrightii;* c. *V. alnifolium;* d. *V. bracteatum;*
e. *V. sieboldii* (from NBB, Sargent and Shirasawa)

bright variegated in fall. Different from 'Aureum'. Ø

V. lantanoides see: **V. alnifolium**

V. lentago L. Tall, deciduous shrub, occasionally a tree in
its habitat, to 10 m, branches thin, somewhat lepidote,
winter buds gray, terminal buds long acuminate; leaves
ovate to elliptic-obovate, 5–10 cm long, finely
denticulate, petiole undulately winged (!), light green,

Fig. 308. *Viburnum grandiflorum*
(from Gard. Chron.)

lighter beneath, and often somewhat lepidote on the
venation, fall color bright red-brown; flowers in sessile,
6–12 cm wide cymes, May to June; fruits blue-black,
pruinose, to 1.5 cm long. SS 223–224; DB 1955: 77; BB
3444. N. America. 1761. Needs a moist, somewhat
shaded site; does poorly in a dry site. z2 Fig. 310. Ø ☉

'**Pink Beauty**'. Fruits pink, eventually more violet. Very
attractive. ☿

V. lobophyllum Graebn. Deciduous shrub, very similar
to *V. betulifolium,* but the leaves usually broad ovate to
obovate and the cymes longer stalked. Glabrous shrub,
to 5 m high, shoots eventually deep red-brown; leaves
broad ovate to broad obovate, 5–11 cm long, acuminate,
base broad cuneate, rather glabrous except for the 5–6
somewhat pubescent vein pairs beneath, petiole 1–3 cm
long; flowers in 7 rayed, 5–10 cm wide, usually finely
pubescent and glandular, 1–2.5 cm long stalked (!)
cymes, stamens longer than the corolla, anthers yellow,
June to July; fruits nearly globose, 8 mm long, red. BMns
164; NF 10: 40; ST 148. Central and W. China. 1901. Very
meritorious for its fruit; however fruits only on older
plants. z6 Plate 155. ☿

V. macrocephalum Fort. Open branched, deciduous
shrub, about 1.5 m high, branches divaricate, somewhat
stellate tomentose at first; leaves thin, ovately oblong, 5–
10 cm long, finely dentate, obtuse, deep green and
nearly glabrous above, stellate pubescent beneath;

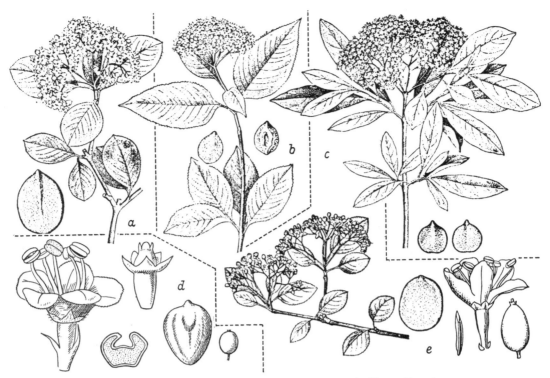

Fig. 309. **Viburnum.** a. *V. rufidulum;* b. *V. cassinoides;* c. *V. nudum;*
d. *V. dentatum* var. *lucidum;* e. *V. prunifolium* (from Koehne and NBB)

flowers in globose, 8–15 cm wide, dense inflorescences, all sterile, snow-white, May, much larger and more attractive than on the other *Viburnum* species! FS 263; NF 2: 274 (= f. *sterile* Dipp.) Garden form from China. 1844. z6 Plate 151, 155. ✧

f. **keteleerii** Carr. The wild form of this plant with flat inflorescences of small, fertile flowers, surrounded by large, white marginal flowers. China. Around 1860. Fig. 316

V. macrophyllum see: **V. japonicum**

Fig. 310. *Viburnum lentago* (from Guimpel)

V. molle Michx. Deciduous, 2–4 m high shrub, older stems with a thin, exfoliating bark (!!); leaves nearly circular to broad ovate, 6–12 cm long, short acuminate, coarsely dentate, deeply cordate at the base, dark green above, lighter and pubescent beneath, petiole 1.5–3 cm, with stipules; flowers in long stalked, 5–8 cm wide cymes, June; fruits blue-black, 1 cm long. BB 3441; DB 1955: 81. N. America; in gravelly forests and hills. 1923. Seldom cultivated and often incorrectly labeled. z6 Fig. 315.

V. mongolicum (Pall.) Rehd. Deciduous shrub, to 2 m high, branches spreading and stellate pubescent when young, gray-yellow and glabrous in the 2nd year; leaves broad ovate, 3–6 cm long, rounded at the base, shallowly dentate, densely stellate pubescent beneath; inflorescences only few flowered, 2–4 cm wide, stalked, flowers usually on the primary axis, corolla tubular campanulate, 6–7 mm long, with short, spreading lobes, ovaries glabrous, May; fruits ellipsoid, black. DL 1: 126 (= *V. davuricum* Pall.). E. Siberia. 1785. z5 Fig. 321.

V. mullaha Hamilt. Tall shrub, branches long, bark dark gray, young shoots, leaf petiole and inflorescence rachis gray-yellow stellate pubescent; leaves ovate to oval-lanceolate, long acuminate (!), 9–15 cm long, margins sparsely dentate, glabrous above, loosely stellate pubescent beneath, petiole 1–2.5 cm long; flowers small, but in large, sessile or to 5 cm long stalked cymes, calyx pubescent, corolla rotate, white, April–July; fruits yellow-red (= *V. stellulatum* Wall. ex DC.; *V. involucratum*

Wall.). Himalayas; Kashmir to Sikkim, in the mountains at 1500–3500 m. z9 ⌀ ⌘

V. nervosum see: **V. grandiflorum**

V. nudum L. Upright, deciduous shrub, 4–5 m high, young shoots somewhat lepidote; leaves elliptic, laurel-like, 8–15 cm long, thin bright glossy green, usually entire (!), bright scarlet to dark brown-red in fall; flowers white, in up to 12 cm wide, long stalked cymes, June–July; fruits globose, blue-black, 8 mm long. BM 2281; BB 3443; NBB 3: 293. Eastern N. America in lowlands near the coast. 1752. z5 Fig. 309, 311. ⌀

V. obovatum Walt. Deciduous shrub, broad, bushy, 1–2 m high, branches thin, gray; leaves somewhat leathery, very short petioled, obovate, 1.5–4 cm long, acute, entire or with a few small teeth on the basal half, glossy dark green above, lighter beneath; flowers in small, convex cymes, white, hardly showing above the leaves, June–July; fruits ovate, black, not pruinose. DL 1: 124 (= *V. laevigatum* Ait.). z9 Fig. 313.

V. odoratissimum Ker. Often confused with *V. japonicum*, which has however, more globose inflorescences and leaf venation which ends in the dentate margins. Evergreen shrub, to 5 m high, shoots stiff, warty, glabrous; leaves stiff leathery, elliptic, 10–20 cm long, acute at both ends, indistinctly sinuate dentate, dark green and very glossy above, underside with axillary pubescence on the venation; flowers in broadly conical, 7–15 cm long panicles, corolla pure white, 6 mm wide, fragrant, May; fruits red at first, then black. BR 456; KIF 2: 80; HKT 101; NH 1963: 45 (= *V. awafuki* Hort.). India to Japan. 1818. z8 Plate 151; Fig. 314. # ⌀ ⌘

V. opulus L. European Cranberrybush. Upright, deciduous shrub, 2–4 m high, bark thin and light gray, young shoots glabrous; leaves rounded, 3–5 lobed, to 12 cm long, irregularly dentate, light green, gray-green and pubescent beneath, a gorgeous wine-red in fall; flowers cream-white, in 8–10 cm wide, flat cymes, surrounded by a ring of sterile outer flowers, May–June; fruits ovate, bright red, 1 cm long. HM Pl. 251. Europe, N. Africa; in

Fig. 311. *Viburnum nudum* (from Schmidt)

forests, on moist sites. Cultivated since antiquity. ⑤ Austria (Tyrol; in green screens). z3 Fig. 315. ⌘ ⌘

Including the following cultivars:

Flowers double
  Leaves green: 'Roseum' (= "Sterile")
  Leaves white variegated: 'Tatteri'

Dwarf habit
  Flowers and fruits: 'Compactum'
  Not flowering: 'Nanum'

Leaves variegated
  Leaves yellow variegated: 'Aureum'
  Leaves white variegated: 'Tatteri', 'Variegatum'

Fruits differing:
  Fruits yellow: 'Xanthocarpum'
  Fruits yellow and red: 'Notcutt'

var. *americanum* see: **V. trilobum**

'Aureum'. New growth an attractive bronze, then dark yellow, finally light yellow, eventually greening. Yellow leaves easily burnt in full sun. ⌘

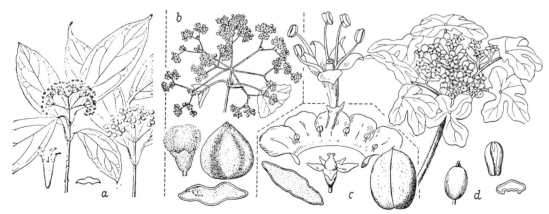

Fig. 312. **Viburnum.** a. *V. cylindricum;* b. *V. dasyanthum;* c. *V. phlebotrichum;* d. *V. plicatum* var. *tomentosum* (from ICS, Sargent and Shirasawa)

Fig. 313. *Viburnum obovatum*
(from Loddiges, altered)

'Compactum'. To 1 m high, very slow growing, dense, low; small leaves, but flowering and fruiting well. ⊕ ⊗

'Nanum'. Scarcely over 50 cm high, nearly like a witches'-broom in appearance; leaves very small, rarely blooming (= f. *pygmaeum* Hort.). Originated in France around 1841.

'Notcutt' (Notcutt). Strong growing, similar to the species; leaves deeply lobed; fruits very large, bright red. Probably a hybrid of *V. opulus* × *V. trilobum*. ⊗

f. *pygmaeum* see: **'Nanum'**

'Roseum'. The double "Snowball" with glabose cymes, these greenish at first, occasionally fading to slight pink (= var. *sterile* DC.). Known in Holland since 1594. ⊕

var. *sargentii* see: **V. sargentii**

var. *sterile* see: **'Roseum'**

'Tatteri' (Tatter). Foliage attractively white variegated; flowers double. Before 1896. Still cultivated? ⊘ ⊕

'Variegatum'. Leaves white variegated. 1770. ⊘

'Xanthocarpum'. Leaves much lighter, tougher; fruits bright green to light brown-yellow. JRHS 91: 251. Austria. 1842. ⊗

V. orientale Pall. Deciduous shrub, similar to *V. acerifolium*, but somewhat more vigorous in habit, 1.5–2.5 m high; leaves rounded 3 lobed, 7–12 cm long, base more or less deeply cordate, underside with pubescent tufts in the vein axils, but completely lacking the black punctate markings (!!); flowers white, in long stalked, 5 cm wide cymes, June; fruits deep red, eventually nearly black. Asia Minor, Caucasus. 1827. z6

V. oxycoccus see: **V. trilobum**

V. pauciflorum see: **V. edule**

V. phlebotrichum S. & Z. Deciduous shrub, similar to *V. setigerum,*to 2 m high; leaves narrowly ovate-oblong, 3–6

cm long, tapered to the base, regularly triangular dentate, with 6–9 vein pairs, glabrous above, venation silky pubescent beneath, petiole 2–5 mm long; inflorescences 2–4 cm wide, few flowered, nodding, thin stalked, stamens very short, filaments shorter than the anthers, May–June; fruits ovate, red. ST 2: 120; MJ 316; KIF 4: 48. Japan. 1890. z6 Fig. 312.

V. plicatum Thunb. Deciduous shrub, broad rounded habit, branches often nearly horizontally spreading, stellate tomentose when young; leaves broad ovate to elliptic-obovate, 4–10 cm long, short acuminate, crenate, base round to broad cuneate, dark green above, stellate pubescent beneath, fall color dark red to violet-brown, with 8–12 nearly straight vein pairs; flowers in globose, 6–8 cm thick, pure white cymes along the branch, May to June. MJ 315; DB 1951: 79; FS 278. (= *V. tomentosum* var. *sterile* Dipp.). China, Japan; known only in cultivation. 1844. z5–6 Plate 155. ⊕

Including the following cultivars and selections:

'Cascade' (Schoemaker 1970). Taller than 'Mariesii', but lower than 'St. Keverne', branches widespreading; inflorescences umbrella-shaped, very large, 8–10 cm wide, with large sterile outer flowers, white, May–June; red fruits in fall, fruits very abundantly. ⊕ ⊗

'Grandiflorum'. Like the species, but slower growing; leaves wider, venation reddish beneath; inflorescences globose, all flowers sterile, larger than those of the species and flowering 2 weeks earlier (= *V. plicatum* 'Grandiflorum' Hillier 1900; *V. tomentosum sterile grandiflorum* Hesse 1902). ⊕

Fig. 314. *Viburnum odoratissimum*
(from Bot. Reg. and Shirasawa)

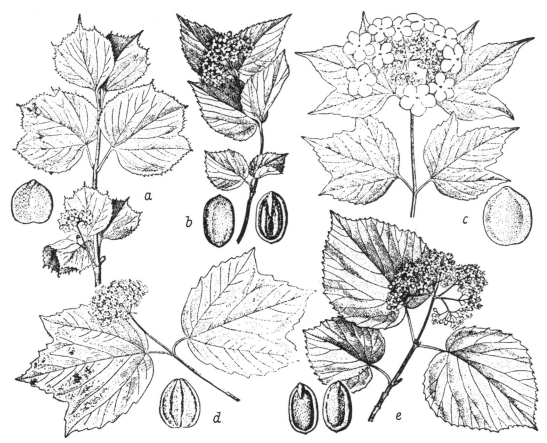

Fig. 315. **Viburnum.** a. *V. edule;* b. *V. rafinesquianum;* c. *V. opulus;* d. *V. acerifolium;*
e. *V. molle* (from NBB)

'**Lanarth**' (Williams). Very similar to 'Mariesii', but more vigorous, branches more ascending, to 4 m high and wide; leaves somewhat larger, more acute. Before 1930. ⊕

'**Mariesii**' (Veitch). Very low growing, branches and twigs spreading nearly horizontally; leaves always somewhat yellowish toned in summer (important characteristic!!); inflorescences umbrella-shaped, outer flowers somewhat larger, flowering abundantly, but hardly ever fruiting (!). Somewhat difficult to cultivate and therefore not always true to name! ⊕

'**Pink Beauty**'. Selection of f. *tomentosum*. Rather slow growing, small leaved; inflorescences small, umbrella-shaped, the sterile outer flowers white at first, later light pink toned. Not exceedingly attractive.

var. plicatum. The type (= *V. tomentosum* var. *plicatum* [Thunb.] Maxim.).

'**Rosace**'. Mutation of var. *plicatum*. New growth bronze-brown, leaves later particularly deep green; inflorescences globose, partly white, partly light pink (on the same shrub), all sterile. Developed around 1953 by C. E. Kern of Wyoming Nurseries, Cincinnati, Ohio, USA. (Actually 'Pink Sensation'?) ⊕

'**Roseum**'. Inflorescences umbrella-shaped, sterile outer flowers white at first, later coloring dark pink, allegedly only a good pink on acid soil. Originated in the Brooklyn Botanic

Garden, USA. Not sufficiently tested.

'**Rowallane**'. Selection of f. *tomentosum*, slower growing than the otherwise similar 'Lanarth', branches slightly nodding; leaves smaller; inflorescences umbrella-shaped, the marginal flowers somewhat pink, regularly fruiting (as opposed to 'Mariesii'). JRHS 67: 100; 81: 135. Selected before 1942 in Rowallane Park, N. Ireland. ⊕ ⚭

'**St. Keverne**' (Williams). Selection of f. *tomentosum*, coarser in habit and foliage, 3–4 m high and wide, branches and twigs widely divaricate; inflorescences umbrella-shaped; rarely producing fruit. Meritorious and better than the normal f. *tomentosum*. ⊕

f. **tomentosum** (Thunb.) Miq. The wild form, 2–3 m high, branches horizontally spreading and overlapping, usually wider than high; leaves deep wine-red in fall; inflorescences only with sterile marginal flowers, arranged in 2 rows on the horizontal branches, long stalked, May–June; fruits blue-black. KIF 4: 49; GF 4: 594; MJ 314 (= *V. tomentosum* Thunb.). Japan, China. 1865. Considerably improved upon by the cultivars. Fig. 312. ⊕

V. × 'Pragense', see p. 443.

V. propinquum Hemsl. Evergreen shrub, about 1 m high, branches glossy red-brown; leaves attractively bronze-brown on the new growth, oblong-elliptic,

Fig. 316. **Viburnum.** a. *V. macrocephalum* f. *keteleerii;* b. *V. henryi;* c. *V. rhytidophyllum;*
d. *V. lantana* (from Sargent and Loddiges)

Fig. 317. **Viburnum.** Left *V. sempervirens;* right *V. ternatum* (from ICS and Sargent)

acute, 6–9 cm long, base broadly cuneate, sparsely denticulate, distinctly 3 veined (!), thin and leathery, dark green above, lighter beneath; flowers greenish white, in 7 cm wide cymes, June; fruits ovate, 5–6 mm long, glossy blue-black. ST 115. Central and W. China. 1901. z7 Plate 156. #

V. prunifolium L. Upright, tall shrub, occasionally a 5 m high small tree, lateral branches horizontally spreading and open, winter buds short acuminate, green, somewhat reddish pubescent; leaves broad elliptic to ovate, 3–8 cm long, acute, base rounded, finely serrate, dark green above, light green beneath, glabrous, dark brown-red in fall, petiole not winged or very narrowly winged; flowers pure white, in sessile, 5–10 cm wide cymes, corolla 5–6 mm wide, April–May; fruits nearly globose, about 1 cm long, blue-black, pruinose. SS 225; BB 3445; GTP 340; DL 1: 195. N. America. 1727. z3 Plate 156; Fig. 319.

V. pubescens see. **V. rafinesquianum**

V. pubescens var. *canbyi* see: **V. dentatum** var. **dantatum**

V. rafinesquianum Schult. Deciduous shrub, to 2 m high, young shoots glabrous, later gray-brown; leaves ovate to nearly elliptic, 3–5 cm long, acute, base round to nearly cordate, coarsely dentate, underside densely soft pubescent, with 4–6 vein pairs, petiole 2–6 mm (!); flowers usually in 5–7 rayed, dense, glabrous, 3–6 cm wide cymes, May–June; fruits ellipsoid, 8 mm long, blue-black. GF 3: 125; GSP 482; DL 1: 114 (= *V. pubescens* sensu Gray non Pursh). Northern N. America. 1830. Flowering very abundantly! z2 Fig. 315. ✧

var. **affine** (Schneid). House. Leaves 3–8 cm long, glabrous beneath or the venation somewhat pubescent, petiole 2–10 mm long. SH 2: 415 l–m (= *V. affine* Bush). Eastern N. America.

V. recognitum see: **V. dentatum** var. **lucidum**

V. rectangulatum see: **V. foetidum** f. **rectangulatum**

V. × rhytidocarpum Lemoine (*V. buddleifolium* × *V. rhytidophyllum*). Shrub, semi-evergreen or deciduous, young shoots brown lepidote; leaves intermediate between the parents, somewhat stiffer than those of *V. buddleifolium*, bright green above, somewhat rugose and sparsely pubescent, glossy, underside densely white pubescent, entire or with a few crenate teeth; inflorescences similar to those of *V. buddleifolium*; fruits eventually black and rugose. Developed in 1936 by Lemoine in Nancy, France. z6 (#)

V. × rhytidophylloides Suring. (*V. lantana* × *V. rhytidophyllum*). Leaves usually abscising in winter (!), similar to *V. rhytidophyllum*, but somewhat wider, more ovate-elliptic, to 20 cm long, not rugose above, margins finely dentate; stamens about as long as the corolla. NDJ 1927: 10. z6 Plate 156. #

'Alleghany' (= *V. rhytidophyllum* × *V. lantana*). Rather globose habit, dense, to 3 m; leaves leathery tough, nearly evergreen, smaller than those of *V. rhytidophyllum*, but thicker than those of *V. lantana*, finely rugose, very dark green; flowers yellowish white, flowering abundantly, May; fruits red at first, eventually black, very abundantly fruiting. Selected in 1958 by D. R. Egolf

in the U.S. National Arboretum, Washington, D.C. Leaves very disease resistant. ∅ ✧ ☸

'Holland'. The type of the cross. Developed in Holland around 1925.

V. rhytidophyllum Hemsl. Evergreen shrub, tightly upright, to 4 m high, branches thick, densely light brown stellate tomentose at first; leaves ovate-oblong to more lanceolate, 8–18(25) cm long, glossy green and very rugose above, with raised reticulate venation and a dense gray or yellowish stellate tomentum beneath; flowers in 7–11 rayed, 10–20 cm wide, flat cymes, axis very brown stellate tomentose, corolla cream-white, 6 mm wide, flower buds developed already in the previous fall, May to June; fruits 8 mm long, short ellipsoid, red at first, then black, glossy. BM 8382; NF 5; 55. Central and W. China. 1900. Thrives in semishade and moist, humus soil. z6 Plate 175; Fig. 316. # ∅ ✧ ☸

'Roseum'. Vigorous grower; flower buds intense pink-red, but the flowers white. GC 104: 171. England. 1938. ✧

'Variegatum' (Chenault). Leaves irregularly light and dark yellow speckled, easily burning in full sun. Discovered before 1935 by Chenault in Orléans, France.

V. rigidum Vent. Evergreen shrub, similar to *V. tinus*, but the branches bristly pubescent. A loose, globose shrub, 1.5–2.5 m high and wide, young shoots bristly; leaves broad ovate to oblong, acute, 5–15 cm long, entire, both sides pubescent when young, later nearly glabrous above and somewhat rugose; flowers pure white, in 7–10 cm wide cymes, February–April; fruits ellipsoid,

Fig. 318. *Viburnum rigidum* (from BM)

blue-black. DL 1: 125; BM 2082; KGC 49; TFA 145 (= *V. rugosum* Pers.). Canary Islands. 1778. z9 Plate 156; Fig. 318. #

V. rufidulum Raf. A tall, deciduous shrub, also a small tree in its habitat, somewhat resembling *V. prunifolium* in appearance, but the winter buds rust-brown pubescent (!); leaves elliptic, 5–10 cm long, finely serrate, glossy deep green, light green and somewhat rust pubescent beneath, petiole usually narrowly winged; flowers pure white, in 8–12 cm wide cymes, May–June; fruits dark blue, pruinose, ellipsoid, to 1.5 cm long. SS 225; NBB 3: 293; BB 3446. N. America; in dry, gravelly spots along river banks. 1883. z6 Fig. 309. ⌀

V. rugosum see: **V. rigidum**

V. sandankwa see: **V. suspensum**

V. sargentii Koehne. Deciduous shrub, similar to *V. trilobum*, 2–3 m high, bark somewhat corky and thick; leaves 3 lobed, the apical ones usually with a distinctly elongated middle lobe and short, outspread lateral lobes, to 12 cm long, new growth dark brown, later a rich yellow-green, lighter and pubescent beneath, petiole 2–3.5 cm long, with large disk-shaped glands; flowers in 8–10 cm wide, 2–6 cm long stalked cymes, anthers purple (!), the sterile marginal flowers to 3 cm wide, May–June; fruits nearly globose, 1 cm long, light red. ST 42 (= *V. opulus* var. *sargentii* Takeda). NE. Asia. 1892. z3 Plate 158. ⚬

'**Flavum**'. Leaves very light green; anthers yellow; fruits yellow. DB 1950: 273: 1904. Plate 151, 158. ⚬

'**Onondaga**'. Selected from a cross between 2 *V. sargetii* clones. Shrub to 2 m high, globose habit, branches dark gray, corky, young shoots densely and finely pubescent, with large lenticels; leaves usually 3 lobed, 3 veined, 10–14 cm long, 9–14 cm wide, lobes acuminate, coarsely and irregularly dentate, base round to truncate, young leaves chestnut-brown, also more or less brown when mature (!), petiole 1.5–4 cm, with large, disk-shaped glands; flowers in 5–12 cm wide, flat cymes, buds red, opening cream-white with a pale pink trace, with 10–17 sterile, 1.3–2 cm wide marginal flowers, later May–early June; fruits red, but not very abundant, persisting for 3 months. Selected in 1959 by D. R. Egolf in the U.S. National Arboretum. ⌀ ⌀ ⚬

'**Susquehanna**'. Stems more stoutly branched, and with a more corky bark; leaves deep green, very tough; flowers cream-white, with a crown of sterile outer flowers, late May; fruits remain yellow-green for a long time, later becoming deep red and persisting so until winter. Selected from Japanese seed by D. R. Egolf of the U.S. National Arboretum, 1959. ⌀ ⚬

V. scabrellum see: **V. dentatum** var. **dentatum**

V. schensianum Maxim. Deciduous, thinly branched shrub, similar to *V. lantana*, but small leaved, young shoots stellate pubescent; leaves oval-elliptic, 2–5 cm long, obtuse, finely dentate, base round to broad cuneate, stellate pubescent beneath, with 5–6 vein pairs, these curving before reaching the dentate margin or sometimes reaching the margin, petiole 5–10 mm long; inflorescences 5 rayed, 5–8 cm wide, stellate pubescent, partly sessile, partly with a 5–25 mm long stalk, corolla rotate-campanulate, white, 6 mm long, May–June; fruits short ellipsoid, 8 mm long, red, later black. ST 140. NW. China. 1910. z6 Fig. 321.

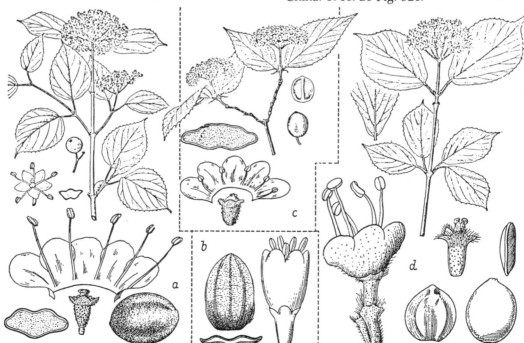

Fig. 319. **Viburnum**. a. *V. betulifolium*; b. *V. urceolatum*; c. *V. ichangense*; d. *V. dilatatum*
(from ICS, Sargent, Koehne)

V. semitomentosum see: **V. dentatum** var. **dentatum**

V. sempervirens K. Koch. Tall, evergreen shrub, young shoots 4 sided, pale yellow, cylindrical and red-brown in the 2nd year; leaves leathery, elliptic-lanceolate, 4–9 cm long, 2–3.5 cm wide, glossy green above, lighter beneath with fine black punctate markings, petiole 5–10 mm; flowers in 4–5 cm wide cymes; fruits red (= *V. venulosum* Benth.). Hong Kong, China; Yunnan Prov. z9 Fig. 317. # ⌀ ⬧

V. setigerum Hance. Upright, deciduous shrub, to 4 m high, young shoots glabrous, later gray; leaves oval-oblong, 5–12 cm long, long acuminate, widest beneath the middle (!), base round, sparsely dentate, with 6–9 vein pairs, dark green above, lighter and glabrous beneath except for the silky pubescent venation, petiole 1–2 cm long; inflorescences 3–5 cm wide, 5 rayed, stalk 1–2.5 cm long, stamens as long or shorter than the corolla (!), calyx purple, glabrous, May–June; fruits 6 mm long, ovate, bright red. ST 121 (= *V. theiferum* Rehd.). Central and W. China. 1901. Hardy and attractive. z6 Fig. 305. ⊕

'Aurantiacum'. Fruits orange-yellow. 1931. ⬧

V. sieboldii Miq. Deciduous shrub, 3–5 m high and wide, or also a small tree, narrowly erect, stiffly branched, young shoots pubescent; leaves elliptic to obovate, to 12 cm long, coarsely crenate, rich green and glossy above, scabrous veined beneath, with 7–10 vein pairs, these somewhat stellate pubescent, often rounded at the apex, cuneate at the base, crushed leaves scented (like green peppers !); flowers in 7–10 cm long panicles, often covering the entire plant (!), corolla cream-white, campanulate, 8 mm wide, late May; fruits oval-oblong, red at first, then black, fruit stalks a good red. GF 2: 559; MJ 313; DB 1955: 82; KIF 3: 79. Japan. 1880. Quite meritorous, abundantly flowering species. z5 Fig. 307. ⊕ ⬧

'Seneca' (*V. sieboldii* × *V. sieboldii*). Tall shrub or tree, to 10 m high, branches stiff, broadly spreading, shoots gray, stellate pubescent when young; leaves elliptic to lanceolate-obovate, 11–20 cm long, 3–8 cm wide, acute to rounded at the apex, margins crenate except for the basal third, base broadly cuneate, with 8–12 raised vein pairs on the underside, crushed leaves strongly scented; panicles 8–12 cm long and equally wide, with 200–700 waxy, white flowers, May–early June; fruits orange-red, later becoming blood-red and persisting so for 3 months, finally blue-black and then dropping. Selected in the U.S. National Arboretum and introduced in 1967. ⌀ ⊕ ⬧

V. stellulatum see: **V. mullaha**

V. suspensum Lindl. Evergreen shrub, 1.5–3 m high, shoots slender and warty; leaves oval elliptic, acute, 5–12 cm long, entire or dentate, acute, glossy green and glabrous, with 4–5 vein pairs; flowers in 5–10 cm long and equally wide panicles, corolla pink-white, fragrant, March–May; fruits globose, red to black. BM 6172; NH 1963: 48 (= *V. sandankwa* Hassk.). S. Japan. 1850. z8 Plate 158; Fig. 320. ⌀

V. sympodiale Graebn. Very similar to *V. furcatum*, but with smaller leaves, more ovate and with small stipules

Fig. 320. *Viburnum suspensum* (from Bot. Mag.)

on the petioles (!), leaves narrowly ovate to more elliptic, more finely serrate, base round to nearly cordate; inflorescences 6–9 cm wide. ST 2: 138. China. z6

V. ternatum Rehd. Closely related to *V. cylindricum*, but with thin leaves. Shrub, 1–4 m high; leaves usually in groups of 3 together, oppositely arranged only on weak shoots, elliptic to obovate-oblong, 8–22 cm long, 4–10 cm wide, yellow-green above, glabrous, lighter beneath, appressed pubescent on the venation, with 5–7 vein pairs, petiole 2–5 cm; inflorescences loose, 12–17 cm wide, flowers small, disk form, yellowish white; fruits red. W. China. z9 Fig. 317. ⊕ ⬧

V. theiferum see: **V. setigerum**

V. tinus L. Very dense, evergreen shrub, 1.5–2.5 m high or more, shoots glabrous or somewhat pubescent; leaves narrow ovate to oblong, acute at both ends, 3–10 cm long, entire, dark green and glossy above, lighter beneath with thin axillary pubescence; flowers white to pink-white, somewhat fragrant, in convex, 5–7 cm wide, terminal cymes, flowering from November to April in its habitat; fruits ovate, deep blue, later black, rather dry. BM 38. S. Europe, Mediterranean region. Cultivated since antiquity, primarily in the milder regions of Europe. z7 # ⌀ ⊕ ⬧

'Eva Price'. Flowers with a strong carmine-pink blush (HCC 21/1). Selected by Sir Henry Price, Wakehurst Place, Ardingly, Sussex, England. First named in 1960, but observed since 1905 and quite meritorious. ⊕

Fig. 321. **Viburnum.** Left *V. utile;* center *V. schensianum;* right *V. mongolicum* (from ICS)

'Froebelii'. Particularly compact habit; leaves light green; flowers pure white (= var. *froebelii* Nichols.). ⊕

'Lucidum'. More vigorous habit, more open, shoots glabrous; leaves larger and very glossy; inflorescences larger (= var. *lucidum* Ait.). More tender than the species. ⊕

'Purpureum'. Leaves with a dull reddish green blush. ∅

'Srictum'. Habit tightly and narrowly conical upright.

'Variegatum'. Leaves partly yellow variegated, occasionally half of the blade is yellow.

V. tomentosum var. *sterile* see: **V. plicatum**

V. trilobum Marsh. American Cranberry Bush, Highbush Cranberry. Deciduous shrub, to 3 m high, very similar to *V. opulus,* young shoots glabrous; leaves broad ovate, 5–12 cm long, 3 lobed, the lobes acuminate, middle lobes elongated and coarsely dentate or occasionally entire, light green above, lighter and somewhat pubescent beneath, turning carmine-red early in the fall and persisting for a long time, petiole 1–3 cm long, usually with small stalked glands (!); flowers white, in 7–10 cm wide cymes, stamens about twice as long as the corolla, anthers yellow, May–June; fruits nearly globose, 9 mm long, scarlet-red. GSP 490; DL 1: 105 (= *V. americanum* sensu Dipp.; *V. oxycoccus* Pursh.; *V. opulus* var. *americanum* Ait.). N. America, in swamps and moist, cool forests. 1812. Also utilized in the USA for its fruit. z2 Plate 158. ∅ ⚭ ✕

For a complete list of the cultivars see: Egolf 1962: 223.

V. urceolatum S. & Z. Sprawling, deciduous shrub, to 1 m high, shoots procumbent and rooting, usually totally glabrous when young, later yellow-brown; leaves ovate to lanceolate, 6–12 cm long, acuminate, crenate, base usually round, venation somewhat lepidote beneath, otherwise glabrous on both sides; flowers usually in totally glabrous, 5 rayed, 3–6 cm wide cymes, long stalked, corolla tubular-campanulate, 3–4 mm long, pink-white, with short erect lobes, May; fruits ovate, 6 mm long, black, stone furrowed on both sides. ST 141;

MJ 318. Japan. 1916. z6 Fig. 319.

V. utile Hemsl. Loose, evergreen, thinly branched shrub, to 2 m high, shoots stellate pubescent at first; leaves ovate-elliptic, 3–7 cm long, obtuse, entire, dark green and very glossy above, white stellate tomentose beneath, with 5–6 vein pairs; flowers in 5 rayed, 5–8 cm wide cymes, white, densely stellate pubescent, May; fruits blue-black. BM 8174; ST 143. Central China. 1901. On limestone in its habitat! z7 Plate 157; Fig. 321. # ∅

V. veitchii Wright. Deciduous shrub, tightly upright, 1–2 m high, young shoots and petioles stellate tomentose, as are the leaf undersides and flower stalks; leaves ovate, acuminate, 7–12 cm long, sparsely dentate, base cordate to round, loosely stellate tomentose and rugose above, densely stellate tomentose beneath; flowers in short stalked, flat, 5–12 cm wide cymes, usually 7 rayed, corolla white, about 6 mm wide, My–June; fruits 8 mm long, short ellipsoid, red, then black. China. 1901. z6

V. venosum see: **V. dentatum** var. **venosum**

V. venulosum see: **V. sempervirens**

V. × vetteri Zab. (*V. lentago × V. nudum*). Similar to *V. lentago* in habitat, but the cymes on short, 1.5 cm long stalks; fruits blue-black. Developed before 1879 in Germany, but cultivated today only in the Cambridge Botanic Garden, England.

V. wilsonii Rehd. Deciduous shrub, closely related to *V. dilatatum,* but differing in leaf form, 1.5–3 m high, shoots very pubescent; leaves ovate to round-elliptic, widest beneath the middle (!), long acuminate, 4–8 cm long, with 6–7 vein pairs, serrate nearly from the base up, usually pubescent beneath, new growth bronze-brown, petiole 1–1.5 cm long; flowers in 6 rayed, yellowish pubescent, 5 cm wide cymes, stalk velvety, 2 cm long, stamens about as long as the pubescent corolla, June; fruits ovate, 8 mm long, bright red, with scattered hairs. China. 1908. z7

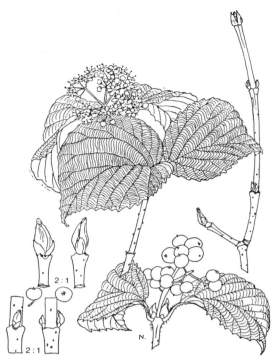

Fig. 322. *Viburnum wrightii* var. *hessei* (from Nose)

V. wrightii Miq. Upright, deciduous shrub, 2–3 m high, young shoots rather glabrous; leaves broad obovate to nearly circular, widest above the middle (!) on flowering shoots, more ovate to broad ovate on long shoots, 8–14 cm long, abruptly acuminate, coarsely dentate, rich green above, lighter beneath with small axillary pubescence on the 6–10 vein pairs, fall color dark brown-red, petiole 6–20 mm long; flowers white, in 5 rayed, 5–10 cm wide cymes, stalks 6–20 mm long, stamens longer (!) than the corolla, May–June; fruits nearly globose, 8 mm thick, bright red, glossy. MJ 312; ST 19; KIF 4: 50; NH 1962: 216. Japan 1892. One of the best fruiting species; only seedling plants have the typical upright growth habit, generally not evident on vegetatively propagated plants. z5 Fig. 307. Ø ✤ ⊗

var. **hessei** (Koehne) Rehd. Remains low; leaves more ovate, to 11 cm long, flatter and more sparsely dentate, fall foliage a brilliant red; inflorescences only to 6 cm wide, flat arched, stamens about as long as the corolla; fruits glossy scarlet-red. Gfl 58: 91; DB 1955: 80 (= *V. hessei* Koehne). Japan. Before 1909. Fig. 322. Ø ⊗

Other Viburnum hybrids not mentioned in the text:

'Anne Russell' (*V. burkwoodii* × *V. carlesii*). About 1.5 m high; leaves similar to those of *V. burkwoodii*, in globose corymbs, March–April; flowers white, very fragrant, buds pink. JRHS 83: 15. Hybridized by L. R. Russell, Windlesham, Surrey, England. 1951. Very abundant flowering. ✤

'Cayuga' (*V. carlesii* × *V. carlcephalum*). Deciduous shrub, to 1.5 m high, branches outspread; leaves ovate-ellipic, 5–12 cm long, 5–7 cm wide, dull green above, more resistant to foliage diseases than the parents, fall color a dull orange; flowers in hemispherical cymes, smaller than those of *V. carlcephalum*, but more abundant, waxy, outer flowers intensely pink-red, fragrant, late April; fruits dark blood-red at first, then black. Developed by D. R. Egolf in the U.S. National Arboretum. ✤ ⊗

'Fulbrook' (*V. burkwoodii* × *V. carlesii*). Similar to 'Anne Russell', but the inflorescences are somewhat larger, looser, slightly conical, flowering 2–3 weeks later, no difference in color and fragrance; leaves obovate, light green, to 5 cm long. Developed around 1950 by Miss Florence Paget; distributed to the trade by Mrs. Douglas Gordon, Fulbrook House, Elstead, Surrey, England. ✤

'Mohawk' (*V.* × *burkwoodii* × *V. carlesii*). Deciduous shrub, to 2 m high, branches outspread, stellate pubescent at first, later glabrous; leaves thin leathery, ovate to elliptic, 6–12 cm long, 3–8 cm wide, acute, base cuneate to cordate, margins serrate, small and glossy above, densely stellate pubescent beneath, with 5–7 vein pairs, fall foliage a bright orange-red; flowers appearing with the young leaves, 15–40 together in cymes, 6–8 cm wide, buds bright red, opening white, very fragrant, late April; fruits red, later black. Developed in 1959 by D. R. Egolf in the U.S. National Arboretum. ✤ ⊗

'Oneida' (*V. dilatatum* × *V. lobophyllum*). Upright deciduous shrub, to 3 m wide; leaves deep green, light yellow and orange in fall; flowers cream-white, very numerous, May, occasionally with a few scattered flowers in the summer; fruits deep red, August. Developed in 1961 by D. R. Egolf in the U.S. National Arboretum. ✤ ⊗

'Pragense' (Vik) (*V. rhytidophyllum* × *V. utile*). Evergreen shrub, about 2.5 m high, shoots rather thin, spreading to somewhat nodding; leaves elliptic-ovate, thin, 5–10 cm long, glossy green and rugose above, densely stellate tomentose beneath; inflorescences somewhat smaller than those of *V. rhytidophyllum*; fertile. Developed in the Prague Municipal Nursery around 1955 and quite winter hardy. Plate 157. # Ø

Most species of this wide ranging genus are rather easily cultivated; the evergreen species generally require a milder climate with the possible exception of *R. rhytidophyllum*. A large number of species prefer particularly moist soils and a cool site.

Every new cultivar of *Viburnum* should be registered with the U.S. National Arboretum, Washington, D.C., 20002, USA before its introduction into the trade.

Lit. Egolf, D.: A cytological study of the genus *Viburnum*; in Jour. Arnold Arb. **43**, 132–172, 1962 ● McAtee, W. L.: A review of the nearctic *Viburnum*; Chapel Hill, N.C. 1956 (125 pp.) ● Morton, C. V.: The Mexican and Central American species of *Viburnum*; in Contr. U.S. Natl. Herbar. **26**, 339–366, 1933 ● Wyman, D.: Viburnums; in Arnoldia 1959, 47–56 ● Egolf, D. R.: The cultivated Viburnums; U.S. Nat. Arbor. 1962 (14 p. index) ● Egolf. D. R.: Ornamental deciduous flowering Viburnums; Am. Hort. Mag. **41**, 139–155, 1962 ● Egolf, D. R.: Ornamental fruiting and autumnal foliage Viburnums; Am. Hort. Mag. **41**, 209–224, 1962 ● Egolf, D. R.: Evergreen Viburnums; Am. Hort. Mag. **42**, 39–51, 1963 ● Egolf, D. R.: Eight new *Viburnum* cultivars; Baileya **14**, 107–122, 1966 ● Egolf, D. R.: National Arboretum releases ten new Viburnums; American Nurseryman, February 1, 1967, 16; 46–56.

VILLARESIA Ruiz & Pavon — ICACINACEAE

Evergreen climber or a small tree; leaves alternate, oblong, entire or thorny dentate, thick-leathery; calyx 5 parted, petals 5, white ribbed inside, stamens 5; flowers in small panicles; fruits ovate, a fleshy drupe. — About 7 species in Central and tropical S. America.

Villaresia mucronata Ruiz & Pav. Upright, evergreen tree, to 18 m high in its habitat (often only a tall shrub in cultivation), young shoots furrowed and pubescent; leaves tough and leathery, resembling *Ilex*, ovate to oblong, 4–8 cm long, 2–5 cm wide, entire on flowering shoots, otherwise (on younger plants) much larger and thorny dentate, base round, glossy green, glabrous, petiole 3–6 mm; flowers yellowish white, in 5 cm long panicles in the apical leaf axils, fragrant, the individual flowers very small, June; fruits ovate, about 15 mm long, 10 mm thick, developed on very young plants. PFC 112; BM 8376. Chile. z9 Plate 160. #

VINCA L. — Periwinkle, Creeping Myrtle — APOCYNACEAE

Evergreen, creeping subshrubs; leaves decussate in arrangement, simple, entire; flowers solitary, axillary, attractive; calyx 5 parted, lobes acute; corolla salverform, limb 5 parted to 5 lobed, tube narrow, interior pubescent; stamens 5, the tube with enclosed short filaments, anthers with a tuft of pubescence; styles with a capitate, glandular pubescent stigma; 2 ovaries with a common style; fruit a double follicle. — 12 species in Europe to Asia Minor.

Vinca difformis Pourr. Dwarf, evergreen subshrub, shoots procumbent, flowering shoots erect; leaves ovate, 3–6 cm long, glabrous, stalk 6 mm long; flowers solitary, on 3 cm long stalks in the apical leaf axils, pale blue, 3 cm wide, sepals linear, fall. BM 8506 (= *V. media* Hoffmanns. & Link). Mediterranean region. z9 Plate 160. #

V. major L. Shoots more woody, to 30 cm high; leaves ovate, 3–7 cm long, glossy dark green and ciliate, base often nearly cordate; flowers bright blue, 3–4 cm wide, calyx lobes ciliate (!), about 1 cm long, May–September. HM 3030. S. Europe, Asia Minor. 1789. z8–9 Fig. 323. # ✿

f. *elegantissima* see: **'Variegata'**

'Maculata' Leaves with a large yellow-green blotch in the middle, particularly on young leaves. # ∅

var. **pubescens** Boiss. Shoots and leaves somewhat bristly pubescent beneath; leaves narrower; flowers blue, corolla tips narrow, acute. 1822. #

'Reticulata'. Leaves yellow veined. Rare.

'Variegata'. Leaves yellowish white speckled and bordered (= f. *elegantissima* Nichols.). 1838. ∅

V. media see: **V. difformis**

V. minor L. Flowering shoots to only 15 cm high; leaves oval-elliptic, 2–4 cm long, tapered to the base, totally glabrous (!); flowers lilac-blue, 2–3 cm wide, calyx lobes glabrous, May–September. BB 2814; HM 3031. Europe to Asia Minor. Cultivated for ages. Fig. 323. #

'Alba'. Leaves smaller; flowers pure white, single. 1770.

'Alba Plena'. Flowers white and double. 1770.

'Argenteovariegata'. Leaves white speckled and bordered. 1770. ∅

'Atropurpurea'. Leaves small, deep green; flowers variable in color, wine-red to purple. 1826. ✿

f. *aureo-variegata* see: **'Variegata'**

'Azurea'. Flowers sky blue (= f. *azurea* Mill.). 1889. ✿

'Azurea Plena'. Shoots thin, wiry; leaves small, light green; flowers dark blue, double.

'Bowles' (E. A. Bowles). More bushy upright habit; flowers deep azure-blue, 3 cm wide, corolla lobes rounded (!), flowering very abundantly. Perry 1926. ✿

'Gertrude Jekyll'. Shoots densely covering the ground; leaves deep green with a light bluish shimmer; flowers white, nearly translucent, flowering very abundantly (= 'Miss Jekyll', 'Miss Jekyll's White'). ✿

'La Grave'. Very similar to 'Bowles', also azure-blue, 3

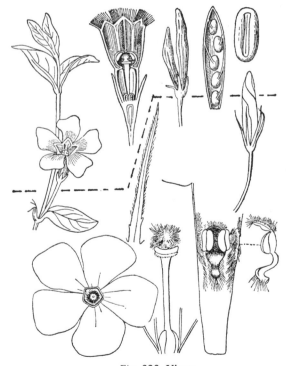

Fig. 323. **Vinca.**
V. minor above; *V. major* beneath (from Thomé)

cm wide, but the corolla tips narrow and apexes at an truncated angle. ⊕

'Miss Jekyll', 'Miss Jekyll's White' see: **'Gertrude Jekyll'**

'Multiplex'. Flowers purple, the first appearing often single, not actually double, but with a few extra small petals in the throat, next to the anthers (= f. *purpurea plena* West.). 1770.

f. *purpurea plena* see: **'Multiplex'**

'Rosea'. Leaves smaller; flowers violet-pink (= f. *rubra* Hort.).

'Rosea Plena'. Flowers violet-pink, double. ⊕

f. *rubra* see: **'Rosea'**

'Variegata' Leaves yellow variegated (= f. *aureo-variegata* West.). ∅

Easily cultivated in any moist, fertile soil, does best in a wooded site; propagated by division.

Lit. Lawrence, G. H. M.: *Vinca* and *Catharanthus*; in Baileya **7**, 113–119, 1959.

VIRGILA

Virgila lutea see: **Cladrastis lutea**

VISCUM L. — Mistletoe — LORANTHACEAE

Evergreen, parasitic shrub; leaves opposite, often thick and leathery, occasionally reduced to scales; flowers dioecious or monoecious, usually in sessile clusters in the leaf axils or terminal, inconspicuous; fruit a single seeded berry, with remnants of the perianth. — About 70 species in the warm and temperate zones of the earth, garden merit insignificant.

Viscum album L. Parasitic on trees of all species, a shrub to 1 m high, shoots green, cylindrical, segmented; leaves nearly sessile, oval-oblong, 3–5 cm long, leathery and tough; flowers yellowish, dioecious, sessile, March–April; fruit a white, translucent, pea-sized berry with one glutinous seed. HM Pl. 88. Europe. Within this species, 3 races are distinguished, one associated with *Pinus* and other conifers, another is found on *Abies*, the third and most common race is found on all deciduous trees. This latter race is further composed of subraces; see Tubeuf. z6 Plate 159. # ⚭

Lit. Heinricher: Die Aufzucht und Kultur der parasitischen Samenpflanzen; Jena 1910 ● Tubeuf, K. von: Monographie der Mistel; Berlin 1923 (832 pp., 35 plates).

VITEX L. — VERBENACEAE

Deciduous or evergreen, aromatic trees or shrubs; leaves opposite, 3–7 parted palmate, occasionally reduced to one leaflet; flowers small, white, blue or yellowish, often in panicle-like cymes; calyx campanulate, often 5 toothed, corolla tubular-infundibular, with an obliquely 5 lobed or nearly bilabiate limb; 4 stamens, 2 shorter and 2 longer, style incised at the apex; fruit a small, 4 chambered drupe with a persistent calyx. — About 250 species, in all the tropical and subtropical regions, only a few in the temperate zones.

Vitex angus-castus L. Chaste Tree. Deciduous shrub, to 3 m high, shoots gray tomentose, aromatic (quite pungent), 4 sided; leaflets 5–7 (!), lanceolate, 5–10 cm long, 0.6–1.5 cm wide, mostly entire or with a few large teeth, gray tomentose beneath; flowers fragrant, light violet, usually in sessile, dense spikes (!!), these grouped into 10–15 cm long panicles, corolla to 8 mm long, interior and exterior pubescent, September–October; fruits globose, 3–4 mm thick, very sharp tasting. HM 3169; BMns 400. S. Europe, Asia Minor. Probably cultivated long before the 16th century. z7 ⊕

'Alba'. Flowers white, 1770.

f. **latifolia** (Mill.) Rehd. Leaflets usually oblong-lanceolate, to 2.5 cm wide (= *V. macrophylla* Hort.). 1756. Total plant stronger growing, more winter hardy. ∅ ⊕

'Rosea'. Flowers pink. 1939.

V. incisa see: **V. negundo 'Heterophylla'**

V. lucens Kirk. Puriri. A tall tree in its habitat, to 18 m; leaves 3–5 parted, leaflets obovate to elliptic, to 12 cm long entire, glabrous, glossy; flowers dull red and pink-red, 4–15 in branched, axillary panicles, flowering very abundantly, corolla 2.5 cm long, bilabiate; fruit a red drupe, 1.8 cm thick. BMns 487. New Zealand; a much valued lumber species. z9

V. macrophylla see: **V. angus-castus f. latifolia**

V. negundo L. Shrub, to 5 m high, occasionally a small tree; leaves usually 5 parted (!), occasionally only trifoliate, oval-elliptic to lanceolate, 3–10 cm long, entire to serrate, gray tomentose beneath; flowers lilac, in loose clusters, these grouped into spikes and finally forming 12–20 cm long, terminal spikes, September; fruits only 2 mm thick. China, India. Around 1697. z6 ⊕

'Heterophylla'. Open and somewhat tall habit; leaflets usually only 3–5 parted, 2–8 cm long, incised serrate to pinnatisect, segments very narrow; flowers in loose panicles. BM 364 (as *V. negundo*); DRHS 2250 (= *V. incisa* Lam.). N. China, Mongolia, Korea. ∅

V. ovata see: **V. rotundifolia**

V. rotundifolia L. Shrub, only 1 m high, prostrate to ascending; leaves simple, obovate to ovate, 2–6 cm long, round, base broadly cuneate, deep green above, finely white tomentose beneath; flowers blue, 1–1.5 cm long, upper lip longer than the lower lip, in 4–12 cm long and 4 cm wide panicles. MJ 558; NK 14: 11 (= *V. ovata* Thunb.;

Fig. 324. *Vitex rotundifolia* (Original)

V. trifolia var. *simplicifolia* Cham.). E. Asia to Korea. 1930. Apparently totally winter hardy. z6 Fig. 324.

V. trifolia L. Shrub or a shrubby tree, to 6 m high; leaves grouped 1–3, oblong-elliptic to oblanceolate or obovate, to 7 cm long, entire, white tomentose beneath; flowers many in 15–18 cm long panicles, corolla blue to purple, bilabiate, July, somewhat resembling lilac flowers. BM 2187. SE. Asia to Japan, Philippines, Australia. 1739. z9

var. *simplicifolia* see: **V. rotundifolia**

For sunny sites and warm, light soil; a good late summer bloomer, but only suitable for mild climates.

Lit. P'ei, C.: The Verbenaceae of China; in Mem. Sci. Soc. China **1** (3), 1–193, 1932 (33 plates).

VITIS L. — Grape — VITACEAE

Deciduous climbing shrubs, with tendrils, bark longitudinally shredding, pitch brown; leaves simple, usually lobed, dentate, occasionally penniform; flowers 5 parted, panicles opposite the leaves; fruit a 2–4 seeded berry with pear-shaped seeds. — About 60–70, very similar species in the northern temperate zone.

Subgenus I. **Vitis**
   Bark of older shoots exfoliating in strips and shreds; lenticels absent; with a distinct or faint partition (diaphragm; Fig. 325); tendrils forked; seeds pear-shaped:
      V. acerifolia, aestivalis, amurensis, berlandieri, baileyana, candicans, cinerea, coignetiae, davidii, flexuosa, labrusca, monticola, palmata, pentagona, piasezkii, riparia, romanetii, rupestris, thunbergii, vinifera, vulpina, wilsoniae

Subgenus II. **Muscadinia** (Planch.) Rehd.
   Bark always tight, not exfoliating in strips, with lenticels; without a partition (diaphragm) at the nodes; tendrils simple, not forked:
      V. rotundifolia

Vitis acerifolia Raf. Procumbent, only occasionally climbing shrub, bark exfoliating only on older wood, tendrils only at the tips of fruiting shoots, young parts floccose pubescent; leaves leathery, triangular-ovate to nearly circular, to 12 cm long, indistinctly lobed, very coarsely serrate, underside remaining somewhat pubescent until fully ripe, eventually glossy above; fruits

in about 7 cm long racemes, berries about 12 mm thick, black, pruinose, sweet, quickly abscising (= *V. longii* Prince). USA; from Oklahoma to Texas and New Mexico. z6 Fig. 328.

V. aestivalis Michx. Summer Grape. High climber, internodes usually rather short, partition walls (diaphragm) thick, young shoots floccose; leaves broad ovate, 10–30 cm wide, basal lobes often overlapping, coarsely dentate, dull green and eventually glabrous beneath, underside rusty tomentose, eventually usually only on the venation; panicles 10–25 cm long, slender, June; fruits black, 8 mm thick, dry and bitter to juicy and sweet. BB 2399; GH 3: 110, 111; GSP 287. E. USA. 1784. z5 Plate 160; Fig. 327. ∅

V. amurensis Rupr. Amur Grape. Strong growing, young shoots slightly angular, reddish, floccose-tomentose at first (!); leaves broad ovate, 12–25 cm (!) long, cordate, with a broad sinus (!), usually 3–5 lobed, with rounded sinuses, acutely dentate, green and glabrous beneath or with pubescent venations, fall color carmine-red to purple; flowers in elongated, long stalked panicles, June; fruits black, 8 mm thick, edible, sourish, with 2–3 seeds. Gfl 339; NK 12: 6; DL 2: 256. Manchuria, Amur River region, Korea, Japan. Around 1854. z5 Plate 160. ∅

V. antarctica see: **Cissus antarctica**

V. armata see: **V. davidii**

V. baileyana Munson. High climber, shoots with short internodes and frequently with many short lateral shoots; leaves ovate to broad elliptic, 5–10 cm long, base cordate, usually finely dentate, normally distinctly 3 lobed at the apex, lobes short, bright green above, but not glossy, gray and pubescent beneath, eventually only on the venation; panicles compact, 8–12 cm long, June; fruits to 10 mm wide, black, lacking or only slightly pruinose, seeds broadly pear-shaped. BB 2405; GF 3: 475; GH 3: 102e, 124, 125 (= *V. virginiana* Munson non Poir.). E. USA. 1890. z6

V. berlandieri Planch. Very closely related to *V. baileyana*, but the leaves glossy above, gray pubescent beneath at first, eventually only on the venation; panicles 10–20 cm long; fruits purple, somewhat pruinose, pleasant tasting. GH 3: 126. Texas to Mexico. Hardy. z7 ⚭

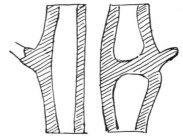

Fig. 325. *Vitis.* Longitudinal section through the nodes, left without, right with a partition wall (diaphragm) (Original)

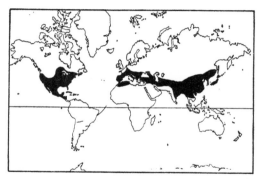

Fig. 326. Range of the genus *Vitis*

V. candicans Engelm. Similar to *V. thunbergii,* but the young shoots are cylindrical and white tomentose like the leaves, high climbing, partition wall very thick; leaves oval-kidney-shaped, 6–12 cm wide, indistinctly lobed or angular, deeply 3–5 lobed only on long shoots, both sides white tomentose at first, later only beneath, petiole white woolly, 3–6 cm long; panicles 5–12 cm long, June; fruits purple, thick shelled, unpleasant tasting. GH 3: 108 (= *V. mustangensis* Buckl.). USA. 1860. z5 Fig. 327.

V. chaffanjonii see: **Ampelopsis chaffanjonii**

V. cinerea Engelm. High climber, young shoots gray tomentose (!), partition wall thick; leaves broadly ovate, 8–20 cm wide, with a wide basal sinus, usually distinctly 3 lobed or triangular, dentate with short, wide teeth, upper leaf surface with a spider web-like indumentum at first, later dull green, underside with a persistent gray web-like indumentum; panicles irregular, 15–30 cm long, June; fruits 10–14 mm thick, black, scarcely pruinose. GH 3: 122; BB 2400. USA. 1883. z5 Fig. 327. Ø

V. citrulloides see: **Ampelopsis brevipedunculata 'Citrulloides'**

V. coignetiae Pull. Strong grower, young shoots rust-brown tomentose; leaves rounded-ovate, 10–25 cm wide, deeply cordate with a narrow sinus, irregularly and shallowly dentate, indistinctly lobed, dull green and rugose above, gray or brown tomentose beneath, a gorgeous scarlet to carmine-red in fall; fruits to 8 mm thick, black, purple pruinose, inedible. MJ 1025 (= *V. kaempferi* Rehd.). N. Japan, Korea. 1875. A very attractive species. z5 Plate 161. Ø

V. cordifolia see: **V. vulpina**

V. davidii (Roman.) Foex. Strong growing, branches glabrous, but covered with straight or hooked prickles; leaves broadly ovate, 10–20 cm long, acuminate, cordate, finely sinuate and indistinctly angular, bright carmine-red in fall; panicles usually longer than the leaves, June–July; fruits black, about 15 mm thick. DRHS 2251 (= *V. armata* Diels & Gilg.). China. 1885. z7 Plate 161. Ø

V. delavayana see: **Ampelopsis delavayana**

V. dissecta see: **Ampelopsis aconitifolia**

V. elegantissima see: **Ampelopsis brevipedunculata 'Elegans'**

V. flexuosa Thunb. Slow growing, very graceful, young shoots red-brown tomentose (!); leaves triangular-ovate, 5–8 cm wide, long acuminate, basal sinus broad and open, irregular sinuate or also 3 lobed, glossy above, venation and vein axils pubescent to floccose-tomentose beneath, tough; panicles slender, 5–14 cm long, June; fruits 8 mm thick, black, with 2–3 seeds. MJ 1027; NK 12: 4. Japan, Korea, China. 1880. Hardy. z6 Fig. 328.

V. flexuosa wilsonii see: **Ampelopsis bodinieri**

V. hederacea see: **Parthenocissus quinquefolia**

V. heterophylla variegata see: **Ampelopsis brevipedunculata 'Elegans'**

V. indivisa see: **Ampelopsis cordata**

V. kaempferi see: **V. coignetiae**

V. labrusca L. Fox Grape. Strong growing and high climbing, shoots with a tendril at each node and very floccose; leaves rounded to broadly ovate, 7–16 cm wide, with an open basal sinus, unlobed or slightly 3 lobed, usually shallowly and irregularly dentate, white beneath at first, later brownish tomentose, tough veined; panicles only slightly branched, 5–10 cm long, June; fruits purple-black, 1.5–2 cm thick, thick shelled and with a sweet musky taste. BB 2348; GSP 285; GH 3: 98, 99, 102b, 107. E. USA. 1656. z5

The origin of most of the American fruit varieties.

V. laciniosa see: **V. vinifera 'Apiifolia'**

V. leeoides see: **Ampelopsis chaffanjonii**

V. longii see: **V. acerifolia**

V. megalophylla see: **Ampelopsis megalophylla**

V. monosperma see: **V. palmata**

V. monticola Buckl. A graceful, 10 m high climber, young shoots angular, usually floccose, occasionally glabrous, partition wall thin; leaves rounded-kidney-shaped, 5–10 cm wide, base rounded to nearly truncate, coarsely dentate, often somewhat 3 lobed, dark green and glossy above, more or less pubescent beneath, sometimes spider web-like when young; panicles short and wide, June; fruits black or light, sweet, seeds broadly pear-shaped, 5–7 mm long. GH 3: 129, 130 (= *V. texana* Munson). Texas. 1887. z6 Fig. 328.

V. mustangensis see: **V. candicans**

V. odoratissima see: **V. riparia**

V. orientalis see: **Ampelopsis orientalis**

V. pagnuccii see: **V. piasezkii** var. **pagnuccii**

V. palmata Vahl. Cat Grape. Strong growing, but thin branched, young shoots glabrous, bright red at first, angular, with a thick partition wall at the nodes; leaves ovate, 8–12 cm wide, deeply 3–5 lobed, with rounded

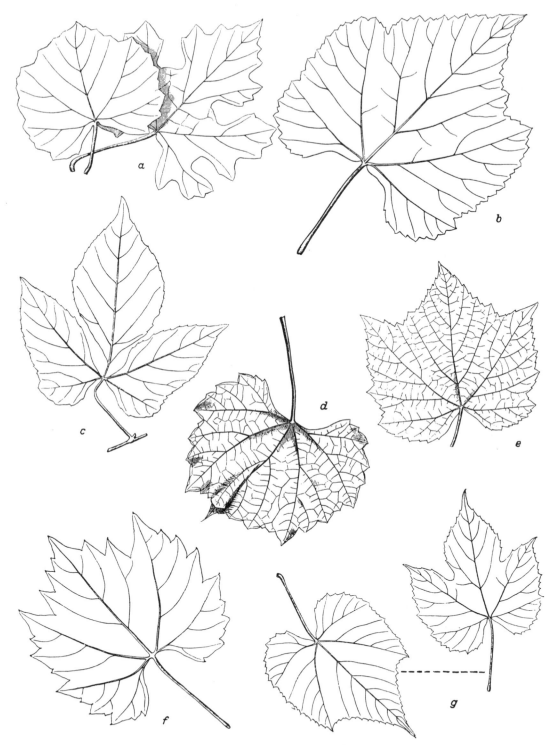

Fig. 327. **Vitis.** a. *V. candicans;* b. *V. aestivalis;* c. *V. piasezkii* **var.** *pagnuccii;* d. *V. rupestris;* e. *V. vulpina;* f. *V. riparia;* g. *V. cinerea* (from Dippel)

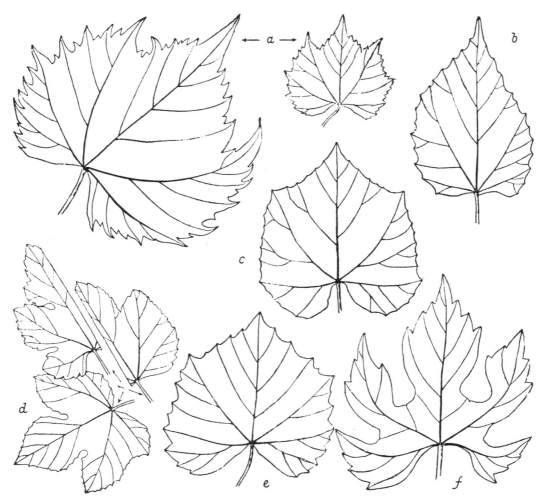

Fig. 328. **Vitis.** a. *V. acerifolia;* b. *V. flexuosa;* c. *V. wilsoniae;* d. *V. thunbergii;*
e. *V. monticola;* f. *V. palmata* (from Sokolov)

sinuses, lobes long acuminate and coarsely dentate, glossy above, petiole red; panicles long stalked, July–August; fruits black, 8–10 mm thick, not pruinose, eventually sweet, seeds nearly globose (!), often solitary. BB 2403; GH 3: 127 (= *V. rubra* Michx.; *V. monosperma* Michx.). N. America. 1633. Hardy. z5 Fig. 328.

V. pentagona Diels & Gilg. Strong growing, young shoots, tendrils and leaf undersides densely white tomentose; leaves ovate, 8–12 cm long, cordate to truncate at the base, finely sinuate and somewhat pentagonal, venation slightly pubescent above, gray-white beneath to reddish tomentose, petiole 4–9 cm long; panicles to 16 cm long, June; fruits blue-black, 6–7 mm thick, seeds pear-shaped, 4 mm long. SH 2: 2071 (= *V. quinquangularis* Rehd.). Central and W. China. 1890. Hardy. z6

var. **bellula** Rehd. Leaves only 3–5 cm long, tomentose beneath. 1907. Plate 161. ∅

V. persica see: **Ampelopsis vitifolia**

V. piasezkii Maxim. An elegant shrub, branches and leaf petioles rust-brown pubescent and glandular bristled; leaves quite variable on the same shoot, partly ovate or deeply lobed, 4–8 cm long, with a cordate base, also sometimes 3–5 parted (!), middle leaflets stalked, the others sessile and very oblique, white tomentose beneath, eventually persisting at least on the venation; panicles loose, to 15 cm wide, May–June; fruits 1 cm thick, black, pruinose. BM 9565; DRHS 2251; SDK 4: 97. W. China. 1903. z6 ∅

var. **pagnuccii** (Planch.) Rehd. Like the species, but the young shoots glabrous; leaves glabrous beneath or nearly glabrous. DL 2: 264 (= *V. pagnuccii* Roman.; *Ampelopsis davidii* Carr.). Central China. 1885. Fig. 327. # ∅

V. quinquangularis see: **V. pentagona**

V. repens see: **Ampelopsis bodinieri**

V. riparia Michx. River Grape. Strong growing and high clibing, young shoots glabrous, partition wall in the nodes very thin; leaves broadly ovate, 8–18 cm long, with a wide, open basal sinus, usually 3 lobed with short, acuminate lobes, irregularly and coarsely dentate, glossy above, bright green and glabrous beneath; flowers fragrant, in 8–15 cm long panicles, staminate flowers with long, erect stamens, pistillate flowers with much shorter, reflexed stamens, June; fruits purple-black, pruinose. DL 2: 260; BB 2402; GSP 290; BM 2429 (= *V. odoratissima* Donn.; *V. vulpina* sensu Leconte). Central and eastern N. America. 1806. See also: **V. vulpina.** z3 Fig. 327.

V. romanetii Roman. ex Foex. Strong grower, branches, leaf petiole and the very long, branched tendrils violet-red, floccose and covered with long, red glandular bristles; leaves rounded, 10–25 cm wide, deeply cordate, indistinctly 3 lobed, shallowly dentate, dark green above, slightly pubescent, gray tomentose beneath, tough and leathery; berries 1 cm thick, black, edible. RH 1890: 444 (= *V. rutilans* Carr.). China. 1881. z6 ∅

V. rotundifolia Michx. Muscadine Grape. Very strong growing, occasionally to 30 cm high in its habitat, bark densely covered with lenticels (!), occasionally also with aerial roots, never with a partition wall at the nodes; leaves nearly circular to broadly ovate, 5–12 cm wide, acute, with a shallow basal sinus, with large, triangular teeth, glabrous and glossy above, light green and glabrous beneath; panicles small and dense, June; fruits 1.5–2.5 cm thick, purple, not pruinose, shell very tough, with a musky taste. DL 2: 265; BB 2: 509. E. USA. 1806. z5

V. rubra see: **V. palmata**

V. rubrifolia see: **Parthenocissus himalayana** var. **rubrifolia**

V. rupestris Scheele. Sand Grape. Only 2 m high, usually a bushy shrub and hardly climbing, shoots glabrous or sparsely pubescent, more or less violet, tendrils sparse or stunted; leaves rounded, to 10 cm wide, irregularly coarsely serrate, usually nearly glabrous, somewhat bluish on both sides, tough and stout; panicles slender, 4–10 cm long, June; fruits purple-black, 7–14 mm thick, pleasant tasting, black, thin shelled. GH 3: 129; GSP 296; BB 2406. E. USA. Around 1860. Important in grape hybridizing for its disease resistant qualities. z5 Fig. 327.

V. rutilans see: **V. romanetii**

V. semicordata see: **Parthenocissus semicordata**

V. sieboldii see: **V. thunbergii**

V. texana see: **V. monticola**

V. tinctoria see: **V. vinifera 'Purpurea'**

V. thunbergii S. & Z. An elegant shrub, medium vigor, young shoots angular, rust-brown tomentose; leaves cordate, deeply 3–5 lobed, 6–10(14) cm wide, lobes broad ovate, with rounded sinuses, shallowly and irregularly dentate, dull dark green above, rusty tomentose beneath, carmine-red in fall; panicles 5–8 cm

long, July–August; fruits black, purple pruinose, 10 mm thick. BM. 8558; MJ 1026; DRHS 2252 (= *V. sieboldii* Hort.). Japan, China. 1879. z6 Fig. 328. ∅

V. veitchii see: **Parthenocissus tricuspidata 'Veitchii'**

V. vinifera L. Wine Grape. Shrub, climbing 10–20 m by means of tendrils, young shoots glabrous or also floccose-tomentose (depending on cultivar); leaves rounded-cordate, 7–15 cm wide, 3–5 lobed, sinuses rounded, basal sinus narrow (!), lobes coarsely dentate and often overlapping, glabrous or floccose beneath, petiole 4–10 cm long; fruits blue and pruinose or green or red. HM 1916. Habitat presumably the Caucasus region. Cultivated throughout history. z5 Fig. 329.

'Apiifolia'. Leaves deeply 3–5 slitted, incised lobed, segments further deeply incised (= *V. laciniosa* L.). 1648. ∅

'Purpurea'. Leaves attractively red at first, later a dull purple (= *V. tinctoria* K. Koch). England. 1838. Plate 127. ∅

var. **sativa** DC. All the wine cultivars are included here.

var. **silvestris** (Gmel.) Willd. The wild form.

Fig. 329. *Vitis vinifera.*
Flowering shoots and individual flowers

V. virginiana see: **V. baileyana**

V. vulpina L. Winter Grape. Strong growing, thick stemmed, stems of very old plants reaching 50–60 cm in diameter, partition walls in the nodes very thick, often incomplete; leaves broad ovate, 10–12 cm wide, cordate, with an open, but narrow and acute basal sinus, unlobed or shallowly 3 lobed, glossy above, light green beneath, irregularly and coarsely serrate, teeth acute; flower panicles 10–25 cm long, July; fruits black, somewhat bluish pruinose, with a thick rind, edible only after a good frost. BB 2404; GSP 292; GH 3: 102d, 124, 125, 132 (= *V. cordifolia* Lam.). SE. USA. 1806. Often confused with *V. riparia*. z5 Fig. 327.

V. wilsoniae Veitch. High climber, young shoots

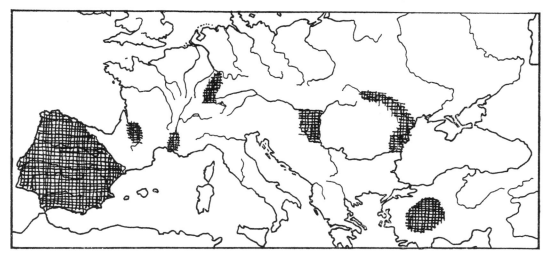

Fig. 330. Distribution of the wild grape (*Vitis vinifera* var. *silvestris*) in Europe
(from Zukovskij, in J. M. Renfrew, Palaeoethnobotany)

floccose; young leaves reddish, leaves broad ovate, 7–15 cm wide, base more or less cordate, both lobes forming a right angle sinus, sinuately dentate with tiny teeth, floccose at first, later glabrous above, venation beneath reticulate and with a cobweb-like indumentum; panicles narrow and long, 10–20 cm long with the stalk, June; fruits black, pruinose, 10 mm thick. SDK 4: 93. Central China. 1907. z6 Fig. 328.

All the species mentioned here thrive in a sunny, warm site on a heavy soil. All species generally quite hardy and suitable for planting on a pergola.

Lit. Bailey, L. H.: The Species of Grapes peculiar to North America; in Gent. Herb. **3**, 151–244, 1934 (34 ills.) ● Moog, H.: Einführung in die Rebensortenkunde; Stuttgart 1957 (93 pp.; for the cultivars of *V. vinifera* and hybrid grapes).

WASHINGTONIA Wendl. — Washington Palm — PALMAE

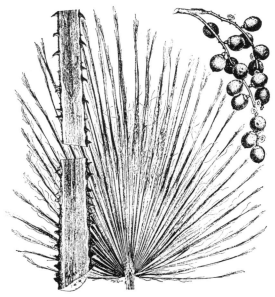

Tall palm trees; upper stem densely clothed in the pendulous remnants of the old leaves; leaves terminal, large, outspread, circular, pleated, incised nearly to the middle of the blade, segments with filaments along the margin; petiole long, tough, convex, margin very thorny; flowers white, hermaphroditic. — 2 species in the southwestern USA.

Washingtonia filifera (Linden) Wendl. 6–12 m high in its habitat or other mild climates, stem cylindrical; leaves circular, fan-shaped, deeply incised and pleated, segments with many filaments, petiole with hooked marginal thorns. SPa 77–78 (= *Pritchardia filifera* Linden). S. California. z9 Fig. 331. # ⌀

W. robusta Wendl. Stem more slender than the previous species, to 22 m high in its habitat; petiole brown and prickly for its entire length on young plants (*W. filifera* petioles green and prickly only at the basal end), leaves glossy green (the other species more gray-green), ligule not over 6–8 cm long, underside covered with a glossy, brown tomentum (= *W. filifera* var. *robusta* Parish). California; NW. Mexico. Around 1880. z10 # ⌀

Fig. 331. *Washingtonia filifera* (from Sudworth)

WEIGELA Thunb. — CAPRIFOLIACEAE

Tall, upright, deciduous shrubs, without stolons, branches with a solid pith; leaves opposite, short petioled, serrate, without stipules; flowers rather large, solitary or several in axillary cymes on short lateral shoots of the previous year's wood, white, pink to red or yellowish; corolla large, funnelform-campanulate, with a broad limb, not bilabiate, calyx 5 lobed, pistil often with a capitate stigma, stamens 5, shorter than the corolla; fruit a bivalved, woody, beaked capsule; seeds small, angular, often winged. — 12 species in E. Asia.

Key (from Rehder)

(This key cannot be used for the cultivars since they are tertiary and quarternary hybrids with intermediate qualities)

A. Anthers either clinging or inclined together, calyx not bilabiate, central column exserted from the fruit;

   B. Calyx incised to the base in linear, usually pubescent lobes, seeds narrowly winged:

Section 1. **Utsugia** (A. DC.) Bailey

   ● Leaves and branches pubescent;

      1. Flowers stalked, pink, carmine or white, pistil not or only slightly exserted past the corolla;

         a) Leaves primarily pubescent on the venation beneath; corolla funnelform-campanulate, gradually widening:
            W. japonica

         b) Leaves gray tomentose or densely white pubescent beneath, corolla tubular at the base, campanulate at the apex:
            W. hortensis

      2. Flowers sessile, dark red (except a few deviants) pistil widely exserted, ovaries pubescent:
            W. floribunda

   ● ● Flowers sessile, leaves and branches glabrous:
            W. coraeensis

   BB. Calyx incised only to the middle, lobes lanceolate, seeds not winged:

Section 2. **Calysphyrum** (Bge.) Bailey

      1. Leaves glabrous above, venation or only the midrib pubescent beneath:
            W. florida

      2. Leaves pubescent above, soft pubescent beneath:
            W. praecox

AA. Anthers pubescent, grouped ring-form over the pistil or inclined together and partly distinct, stigma mitre-shaped, calyx bilabiate, central column not exserted out of the fruit capsule;

      1. Valves of the fruit capsule separated at the apex by the persistent central column, seeds with narrow side wings;

Section 3. **Weigelastrum** (Nakai) Rehd.
            W. maximowiczii

      2. Valves of the fruit capsule connected at the apex, seeds winged at the ends:

Section 4. **Calyptrostigma** (Koehne) Rehd.
            W. middendorffiana

Weigela amabilis see: **W. coraeensis**

W. arborea grandiflora see: **W. coraeensis 'Alba'**

W. aborescens see: **W. floribunda 'Grandiflora'**

W. coraeensis Thunb. A shrub to 5 m high in its habitat, usually 2–3 m in cultivation, branches glabrous, stiff; leaves broad ovate to obovate, 8–12 cm long, abruptly short acuminate, base broadly cuneate, finely crenate, glossy and glabrous above, but pubescent on the venation, venation sparsely pubescent or totally glabrous beneath, petiole 5–10 mm long; flowers several in stalked cymes, more numerous on the short lateral shoots, corolla campanulate-funnelform, abruptly narrowed beneath the middle, 2.5–3 cm long, whitish to light pink at first, later coloring carmine-red, sepals linear-lanceolate, glabrous to ciliate, May–June; ovaries glabrous. DL 1: 179; GH 2: 26d; FS 855; BM 4893; KIF 4: 51 (= *W. amabilis* van Houtte; *W. grandiflora* K. Koch). Japan. 1850. z6 Plate 162. ⊕

'Alba'. Flowers yellowish white, later turning pink. RH 1861: 331 (= *W. arborea grandiflora* Hort.).

W. decora (Nakai) Nakai. Very similar to *W. japonica*, but the basal leaves shaggy pubescent on the venation; flowers short stalked, ovaries nearly glabrous, corolla greenish at first, then becoming whitish, eventually pink, styles slightly exserted. GH 2: 26c (as *W. versicolor*) (= *W. floribunda* var. *versicolor* Rehd. p.p.). Japan. 1933. z6 Plate 162. ⊕

W. floribunda (S. & Z.) K. Koch. Shrub, to 3 m high, shoots thin, pubescent when young (!) or at least with 2 rows of hairs; leaves elliptic-oblong to more obovate, 7–10 cm long, acuminate, serrate, base broadly cuneate, sparsely pubescent above, underside mainly shaggy pubescent on the venation; flowers sessile, several on short lateral shoots, corolla tubular at the base, gradually widening toward the apex, to 3 cm long, exterior pubescent, dark carmine, brownish carmine in bud, stamens as long as the corolla, style exserted, occasionally 1 cm longer than the limb tips, May–June; ovaries and capsule pubescent. DL 1: 181; BS 1: 624; YTS 2: 138. Japan; mountains. 1860. z6 Fig. 332. ⊕

'Grandiflora'. Flowers larger, brownish carmine (= *W. arborescens* Hort.).

var. *versicolor* see: **W. decora**

W. florida (Bge.). A. DC. Shrub, to 3 m high or more, young shoots with 2 pubescent strips or rows; leaves short petioled to nearly sessile, oval-elliptic to oval-oblong, 5–10 cm long, acuminate, serrate except for the rounded base, glabrous above, underside more or less pubescent to tomentose; flowers usually 3–4, without a common stalk, axillary, calyx lobes half as long as the tube, corolla campanulate above, abruptly narrowed beneath the middle, 3 cm long, dark pink or only pink, interior lighter to white, exterior more or less pubescent, limb lobes large and spreading, ovaries pubescent, but the capsule glabrous, May–June. BM 4396; FS 211; RH 1849: 381 (= *W. rosea* Lindl.). N. China, Korea. 1845. The most widely distributed species in cultivation; easily recognizable for the large limb lobes. z3–8 Fig. 332. ⊕

'**Alba**'. Flowers white at first, turning to light pink. RH 1861: 331.

'**Purpurea**'. Low, leaves deep brown-red; flowers dark pink, very attractive. Found in Holland, cultivated since 1930. Plate 163. ∅·⊕

'**Variegata**'. Leaves yellowish white limbed; flowers deep pink. BS 1: 490; FS 1189. ∅·⊕

'**Venusta**'. Leaves smaller than those of the species, oblong-elliptic, 3–5 cm long, longer on long shoots, nearly totally glabrous; flowers in dense clusters along the branch, corolla campanulate at the apex, gradually narrowing to a long, narrow, clyindrical tube, corolla lobes small, obtuse, equal in size, purple-pink, limb lighter, calyx 8 mm long, bilabiate to the middle; capsule short, glabrous. BM 9050; NK 11: 39 (= var. *venusta* [Rehd.] Nakai). Korea. ⊕

W. grandiflora see: **W. coraeensis**

W. hortensis (S. & Z.) C. A. Mey. Shrub, to 3 m high, young shoots pubescent; leaves ovate to obovate-oblong, 5–10 cm long, finely serrate, both sides pubescent at first, later glabrous above, gray pubescent to tomentose beneath, petiole 2–5 mm long; flowers in 3's on elongated, pubescent stalks, corolla tubular-campanulate, carmine, ovaries pubescent, May–June; capsule glabrous. GH 2: 26a; DL 1: 178; NT 1: 701; KIF 3: 80. Japan. Very much disputed species, possibly identical to *W. japonica*. It is uncertain whether or not a plant with the characteristics described by Siebold & Zuccarini exists in cultivation! z7

W. japonica Thunb. Shrub, 2–3 m high, young shoots glabrous or with pubescent lines; leaves short petioled, elliptic to ovate, more or less long acuminate, 5–10 cm long, serrate, either fully or soft gray haired only on the venation beneath; flowers usually in 3's on very short, common stalks, calyx lobes very narrow, separated to the base, pubescent, corolla funnelform-campanulate, 2–3 cm long, exterior pubescent, greenish to whitish at first, later light carmine-red, lobes of the corolla tips rather regular, obtuse, styles somewhat exserted, May–June; capsule glabrous, seeds winged. GH 2: 23–24; DL 1: 180; GF 9: 405. Japan, in the mountains. 1892. Probably only rarely true to name in cultivation. z6

'**Alba**'. Flowers white. Fig. 332.

W. maximowiczii (S. Moore) Rehd. Shrub, scarcely over 1.5 m high, young shoots with 2 pubescent lines; leaves nearly sessile, ovate-elliptic to more oblong, 4–8 cm long, acuminate, base broadly cuneate, scattered pubescent above, venation pubescent beneath; flowers usually in pairs, sessile, corolla funnelform-campanulate, 3.5 cm long, the narrow part of the calyx lobes exserted, greenish yellow, styles and stamens shorter

than the corolla, anthers inclined together, ovaries rather glabrous, May–June; capsule dehiscing at the apex, seeds with narrow lateral wings. NT 1: 692. Japan. 1915. Very similar to *W. middendorfiana*. For cool, moist sites. z6 Plate 127. ⊕

W. middendorffiana (Trautv. & C. A. Mey.) K. Koch. Shrub, about 1–1.5 m high, branches gray-yellow, with 2 pubescent stripes when young; leaves nearly sessile, ovate-lanceolate, 5–8 cm long, finely serrate, bright green above, finely rugose, venation short pubescent on both sides; flowers grouped 1–3 in terminal and axillary clusters, calyx bilabiate, corolla sulfur-yellow, the lower limb lobes orange speckled, funnelform, 3–3.5 cm long, stamens pubescent, anthers connate, May–June; capsule glabrous. BM 7876; DL 1: 182; GF 6: 183; FS 1137. N. China; Manchuria. 1850. For cool, moist areas. z5 Fig. 332. ⊕

W. praecox (Lemoine) Bailey. Shrub, to 2 m high, tightly upright, densely branched, branches glabrous or pubescent; leaves very short petioled, ovate-elliptic, 5–8 cm long, pubescent above, soft pubescent beneath; flowers grouped 3–5 in short, axillary clusters on short lateral shoots, nodding, but also terminal, corolla narrowly funnelform, exterior pubescent, 2.5–3 cm long, abruptly narrowed beneath the middle, corolla lobes rather small, nearly equal in length, purple-pink to carmine, throat yellow, calyx and ovaries pubescent, early May (!); capsule glabrous. Gfl 1441; RH 1905: 314; NK 11: 36. Korea, Manchuria. 1894. Flowers before all the other species. z5 Fig. 332. ⊕

W. rosea see: **W. florida**

W. × wagneri Bailey ([*W. coraeensis* × *W. florida*] × *W. middendorffiana*). Similar to *W. middendorffiana*, but with oval-oblong leaves and glabrous on the venation beneath; calyx lobes lanceolate, partly distinct, partly connate, corolla pink with yellow. Gfl 1899: Pl. 1461. True existence in cultivation unknown; often erroneously labeled! z6

List of the Cultivars

There are about 170 known hybrids. The first ones were named around 1860 by L. van Houtte in Ghent, Belgium ('Isoline', 'Stelzneri'). Soon afterward Billard of Fontenay-aux-Roses, France, began to introduce about 20 hybrids of which 'Gustav Malet' is still cultivated. In 1867, Lemoine of Nancy, France, began his hybridizing. His first cultivars were given Latin names ('Arborea Purpurata', 'Carminea', 'Kermesina', 'Lavallei', 'Incarnata', etc.), while those after 1875 were given French names. 'Edouard André' was the first to be introduced and another 60 hybrids followed until 1930. Around 1900, Rathke of Pruszcz near Gdansk, Poland, produced 'Eva Rathke', still a very popular cultivar today. Currently, the hybridizing of weigelas is carried on in the Boskoop Experiment Station, Holland.

Around 150 *Weigela* hybrids have been grown by the L. Späth Nursery in Berlin, W. Germany, at various times. Since the weigelas are very long-lived and transplant well even as old plants, it is presumed that many old hybrids are still in cultivation.

'**Abel Carrière**' (Lemoine 1876). Large flowered, early, bright

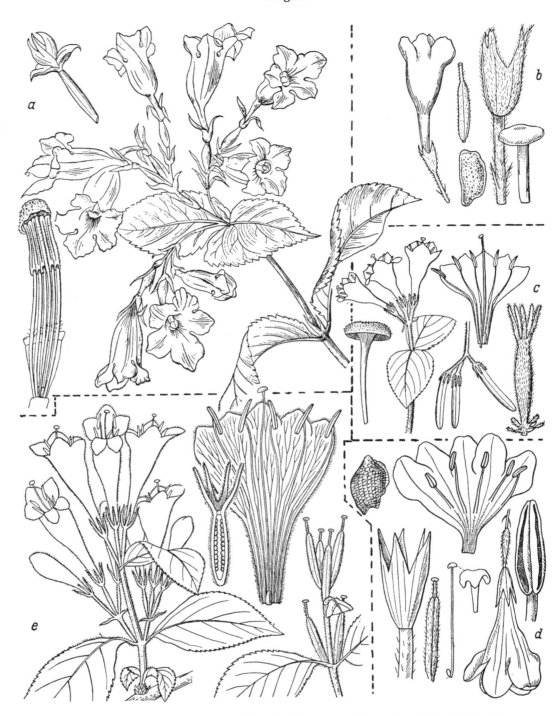

Fig. 332. **Weigela.** a. *W. middendorffiana;* b. *W. praecox;* c. *W. japonica* 'Alba'; d. *W. florida;*
e. *W. floribunda* (from Koehne, Regel, Siebold & Zuccarini)

pink to carmine-red, throat yellow speckled, buds purple-carmine. Gs 1934: 121. ✧

'André Thouin' (Lemoine 1882). *W. coraeensis* × *W. florida*. Flowers medium-sized, tube narrow, with a brownish red exterior, interior pale purple.

'Arléquin' (Hybridizer unknown, 1879). Milk-white intermixed with lilac or pink flowers in individual inflorescences. Long persisting.

'Augusta' (Dieck 1887). Carmine-pink, limb turning white, buds bright carmine-red.

'Aug. Wilhelm' (Lemoine 1881). Flowers wide open, broadly campanulate, orange-red.

'Avalanche' (Lemoine 1909). *W. praecox* form. Strong growing; flowers in small panicles, pure white, exterior somewhat soft pink, flowering very abundantly. ✧

'Avante-garde' (Lemoine 1906). *W. praecox* form. Flowers in large, horizontal clusters, large flowered, interior pink marbled and yellow speckled, later bright pink, floriferous. ✧

'Ballet' (Boskoop Experiment Station 1958). Developed from 'Boskoop Glory' × 'Newport Red'. Growth medium high, strong; corolla 3 cm wide, dark pink, tube long and narrow, floriferous. ✧

'Béranger' (Lemoine 1881). Medium-sized; flowers dark brown-red, interior purple limbed, throat yellow speckled.

'Biformis' (Baudriller 1880). Bearing 2 types of flowers at the same time; large dark pink and small or medium-sized light pink, often with stripes.

'Boskoop Glory' (R. Ramp, Boskoop, 1954). Salmon-pink, large flowered. ✧

'Bouquet Rose' (Lemoine 1899) *W. praecox* form. Large flowered, carmine-pink, limb whitish pink, throat yellowish striped, buds carmine-red. ✧

'Bristol Ruby' (A. Cummings, Bristol, Conn., USA, 1941). *W. rosea* × 'Eva Rathke'. Similar to 'Eva Rathke', flowers carmine-red, but not so intense, stronger habit. Patented. Plate 162. ✧

'Caméléon' (Billard 1868). Leaves caudate acuminate; pure white at first, then gradually turning dark pink, very floriferous.

'Candida' (Thibault & Keteleer 1879). Foliage light green; flowers only medium-sized, pure white even on older blooms. RH 1879: 130.

'Carminea' (van Houtte 1870). Buds black-red, opening wine-red.

'Congo' (Lemoine 1886). Crimson-purple, the limb tips often remaining closed (!), the large, white stigma usually exserted, large flowered, floriferous.

'Conquerant' (Lemoine 1904). *W. praecox* form. Good foliage; very large flowered, an attractive corolla form, red to wine-red, exterior and throat carmine. ✧

'Conquête' (Lemoine 1896). Buds carmine-pink, opening dark pink. Has the largest flowers of all cultivars, to 47 mm wide(!). ✧

'Dame Blanche' (Lemoine 1902). Foliage light green; buds yellowish white with a somewhat lilac trace, opening white, exterior lightly reddish, large flowered. ✧

'Daubenton' (Lemoine 1886). Interior dark yellow without any red, exterior carmine-red, large flowered, floriferous.

'De Jussieu' (Lemoine 1882). Flowers yellow in the throat, the corolla tips light pink, carmine exterior.

'Desboisii' (van Houtte 1861). Flowers dark crimson-red, wide open, limb lobes yellow speckled at the base, small flowered, very eary, buds blood-red. Gs 1934: 121. (Debois was the head gardener for van Houtte in Ghent, Belgium).

'Descartes' (Lemoine 1891). Bright brown-red, large flowered.

'Diderot' (Lemoine 1886). Bright red, very large flowered.

'Dr. Baillon' (van Houtte 1878). Dark brown-red, limb with a purple interior, medium-sized.

'Dropmore Pink' (F. L. Skinner, Canada, 1951). Pink. Selected from Manchurian seed for its winter hardiness.

'Ed. André' (van Houtte 1878). *W. arborea* × 'Lavallei'. Flowers black-brown on the exterior, interior purple-brown, stamens white.

'Elisabeth' (Späth 1892). Lilac-pink, limb turning white.

'Emile Gallé' (Lemoine 1881). Bright dark brown-red, medium-sized, slender tube.

'Espérance' (Lemoine 1906) *W. praecox* form. Flowers white with a salmon-pink blush, buds more salmon-pink, very large flowered, early, floriferous. ✧

'Eva Rathke' (Rathke in Pruszcz, near Gdansk, Poland, 1892). Growth medium high; flowers bright carmine-red to brown-red, floriferous. Unfortunately a rather weak grower. ✧

'Eva Supreme' (Boskoop Experiment Station 1958). 'Newport Red' × 'Eva Rathke'. Strong growing; flowers pure red, more or less glossy, interior somewhat lighter, corolla 3.5 cm wide at the limb, tube long and wide. ✧

'Excelsa' (Carrière 1873). Very strong growing, to 3 m high, but only sparsely branched; flowers pink with a violet trace.

'Féerie' (Lemoine 1926). Flowers light pink, flowering abundantly even on small plants. Gs 1930: 228. ✧

'Fiesta' (Boskoop Experiment Station 1958). 'Eva Rathke' × 'Newport Red'. Rather vigorous habit, loose; flowers monochrome, red, corolla 3 cm wide, tube narrow. ✧

'Flavo-fusca' (Dieck 1885). Flowers greenish. Of little interest.

'Fleur de Mai' (Lemoine 1899). *W. praecox* form. Flowers pink and purple on the exterior, interior white with pink marbling, buds purple, greatly fading, medium-sized, very early and abundant. ✧

'Floréal' (Lemoine 1901). *W. praecox* form. Carmine-pink, limb whitish pink on the interior, throat carmine-red, large flowered, floriferous, buds purple-red. ✧

'Fraîcheur' (Lemoine 1904). *W. praecox* form. Corolla irregular, exterior pink with a white limb, interior cream-yellow, rather large flowered.

'Gavarni' (Lemoine 1884). Flowers carmine-red, attractively formed, medium-sized.

'Giganteiflora' (Hesse-Weener 1908). Dull carmine, particularly large flowered, somewhat translucent.

'Gloire des Bosquets' (Lemoine 1881). Bright brown-red, interior purple with a yellow throat, large flowered, floriferous.

'Glorieux' (Lemoine 1904). *W. praecox* form. Slow growing;

flowers carmine, medium-sized, limb somewhat lighter, buds dark red.

'Gracieux' (Lemoine 1904). *W. praecox* form. Upright habit; flowers soft pink, corolla limb whitish, throat sulfur-yellow, buds salmon color, large flowered, very abundant. ⊕

'Groenewegenii' (van Houtte 1859). Strong growing; foliage glossy; flowers similar to those of 'Biformis', but with a dark red exterior and a pink interior.

'Gustave Malet' (Billard 1868). Flowers large, pink-red, long tubular, limb wide, buds bright pink, extraordinarily floriferous. Plate 162. ⊕

'Héroine' (Lemoine 1896). Upright habit; flowers rather large, soft flesh-pink, interior white.

'Idéal' (Lemoine 1926). Bright carmine exterior, interior carmine-pink, medium-sized, early.

'Isoline' (van Houtte 1875). Flowers white, partly also pink, with a large yellow spot. FS 1445. Not as good as 'Dame Blanche'.

'Jean Macé' (Lemoine 1882). Flowers deep purple, buds black-red, large flowered. Has the darkest flowers of all, but not very floriferous.

'Juvénal' (Lemoine 1893). Flowers dark brown-red, medium-sized, buds blackish red.

'J. Wittwer' (van Houtte 1878). Small flowered, carmine-purple.

'Kosteriana Variegata' (presumably van Houtte; cultivated since at least 1871). Leaves attractively yellow-white variegated.

'Lacépède' (Lemoine 1886). Fuchsia-pink, large flowered, wide open, buds carmine.

'Lavallei' (Lemoine 1871). Flowers bright crimson-red, small flowered.

'Le Printemps' (Lemoine 1901). *W. praecox* form. Buds light carmine, flowers pink with a whitish pink limb, very abundant.

'Looymansii Aurea' (van Houtte 1876). Leaves attractive and always golden-yellow, finely red limbed; flowers carmine-pink, abundant, very attractive. ⊘

'Lowii' (Lemoine 1870). Flowers small, brownish purple.

'Majestueux' (Lemoine 1930). Upright habit, tall; flowers amaranth-red, corolla limb somewhat lighter, anthers conspicuously red, very abundant, early.

'Memoire de Mme van Houtte' (Lemoine 1884). Pink, limb yellowish white on the interior, medium-sized.

'Mme Couturier' (Billard 1868). Flowers yellowish white at first, then bright pink.

'Mme Lemoine' (Späth 1887). Flowers intensely pink, white speckled, later becoming darker.

'Mme Teillier' (Billard 1868). Strongly upright habit; leaves very pubescent beneath; large flowered, soft whitish pink at first, later dark carmine-red.

'Monsieur André Leroy' (Billard 1868). Strong growing; foliage deep green; flowers with a pink exterior, interior flesh colored with a yellow blotch, very abundant.

'Monsieur Lemoine' (Billard 1868). Flowers light flesh-pink, later pink, eventually dark wine-red, with all 3 colors on one shoot.

'Mont-Blanc' (Lemoine 1898). Flowers very large, pure white, turning somewhat pink, buds greenish. The best white form. ⊕

'Montesquieu'. (Lemoine 1886). Flowers soft pink with a broad, white marbled limb, medium-sized, buds dark red.

'Nana Variegata' (Baudriller 1880). Low growing, rather globose; leaves attractively yellow bordered; flowers medium-sized, pink. ⊘

'Newport Red' (V. A. Vanicek, Newport, Rhode Island, USA, distributed in Europe in 1946 by B. Ruys, Dedemsvaart, Holland). Similar to 'Eva Rathke', but more vigorous, flowers not as bright, rather more purple-red (= 'Vanicek'). Easily recognizable in the winter by the green stems. ⊕

'Othello'. (Lemoine 1882). Flowers light carmine-red, darker veined, with a yellow center, tube narrow, buds dark red.

'P. Duchartre' (van Houtte 1878). New growth yellowish bronze (!); flowers medium-sized, deep brown-red, limb undulate, purple, very abundant.

'Pavillon Blanc' (Lemoine 1901). Soft flesh-pink with a wide, white, crispate limb, flowering in large clusters.

'Perle' (Lemoine 1902). Strong growing; flowers milk-white, light pink veined, throat pure yellow, large flowered, grouped 10–20 together in hemispherical clusters.

'Rosabella' (Boskoop Experiment Station 1958). 'Eva Rathke' × 'Newport Red'. More open habit, somewhat stiff; flowers pink, limb pink-white, large, wide open, tube short, flowering abundantly. ⊕

'Saturn' (Waterer Sons & Crisp 1892). Large flowered, bright deep red, darker than 'Eva Rathke', opening wide.

'Séduction' (Lemoine 1908). *W. praecox* form. Bright carmine-red, limb somewhat lighter, buds dark red, very abundant. ⊕

'Stelzneri' (van Houtte 1861). Flowers dark red, opening more purple-red, in clusters of 15–20 together. One of the most floriferous forms. ⊕

'Striata' (van Houtte 1861). Corolla light pink, white striped and blood-red speckled. FS 1446.

'Styriaca' (Klenert, Graz, Austria, 1908). Shrub, stays low; foliage light green; flowers carmine-pink, later more carmine-red, only medium-sized, but flowers abundantly. ⊕

'Van Houttei' (van Houtte 1861). Flowers carmine flushed with pink, limb white, throat lilac-purple. FS 1447.

'Vanicek'. Commonly used name for 'Newport Red' in the USA.

'Voltaire' (Lemoine 1882). Flowers dark brown-red, limb interior light purple, opening wide, tube flared outward at the base with a yellow exterior.

All the weigelas are easily cultivated and long-lived; 50 year old specimens have been transplanted and thrived with renewed vigor. They prefer full sun and a good, fertile soil.

Lit. Bailey, L. H.: The case of *Diervilla* and *Weigela*; in Gent. Herb. **2**, 39–54, 1929 ● Schneider, C.: Die Gattungen *Diervilla* und *Weigela*; in Mitt. DDG 1930, 13–24 ● Grootendorst, H. J.: Het *Weigela*-Sortiment; in De Boomkwekerij **5**, 20, 1949; 12, 79, 1957 ● Wyman, D.: *Weigela* list reflects changing styles; in Americ. Nurseryman, July 1, 1959, 12, 13, 30–33 ● Howard,

R. A.: A check-list of Cultivar names in *Weigela*; Arnoldia **25**, 49–69, 1965 ● Nakai, T.: *Weigela* and its akins in Japan proper and Korea; Jour. Jap. Bot. **12**, 1–17, 71–88 (ill.); Tokyo 1936 (excerpts in Jour. Roy. Hort. Soc. 1939, 156).

WEINMANNIA L. — CUNONIACEAE

Evergreen trees or shrubs; leaves opposite, simple or odd pinnate, leaf rachis commonly winged, stipules quickly abscising; flowers small, in terminal and axillary, upright racemes, with 4 or 5 sepals and petals, 8 or 10 stamens, ovaries superior, with 2 styles; fruit a 2 locular capsule. — About 100 species in the Southern Hemisphere, with the exception of Africa.

Weinmannia racemosa L. f. Towai or Kamahi. A small, graceful tree, but to 20 m high or more in its habitat; leaves of older trees simple, oblong-lanceolate to elliptic, to 10 cm long, coarsely serrate, 3–5 parted or 3 lobed or partly simple on young plants, coarsely serrate; flowers white to light pink, in narrow, about 10 cm long racemes, May–June; fruits small, red-brown capsules. KF 73; MNZ 71. New Zealand. z9 # ∅

W. trichosperma Cav. Small to medium-sized tree or a large shrub; leaves pinnate, 8–10 cm long, rachis rhombic (triangular winged on either side) between the 11–13 leaflets, leaflets broadly elliptic, with 3 coarse teeth on either side, acute, 1–2.5 cm long, sessile, oblique at the base, deep green and glossy above, glabrous, underside somewhat pubescent; flowers in loose racemes, May. PFC 79. Chile. z9 Fig. 333. # ∅

Cultivated in the landscape only in mild climates.

Fig. 333. *Weinmannia trichosperma* (from Dimitri)

WESTRINGIA Sm. — Victorian Rosemary — LABIATAE

Small, evergreen shrubs, shoots usually rectangular in cross section, leaves opposite or in whorls of 3–4, stiff, narrow, small, entire; flowers usually axillary or in terminal heads, calyx campanulate, 10 veined, with 5 teeth; corolla attractive, longer than the calyx, with a short tube and a pubescent interior, upper lip erect, stamens 4, of these, the bottom 2 are sterile; fruit composed of 4 reticulately veined, rough nutlets. — About 26 species in non-tropical Australia.

Westringia rosmariniformis Sm. Evergreen shrub, to 1.5 m high; leaves in whorls of 4, narrowly lanceolate to elliptic, to 2.5 cm long, margins involuted, underside densely white pubescent; flowers all axillary, nearly sessile, white with a lilac trace, brown speckled, floriferous, May–July. SE. Australia. 1791. z9 # ✧

For a very sunny, warm site and a well drained soil.

WIGANDIA Kunth — Wigandia — HYDROPHYLLACEAE

Tall herbs or subshrubs, leaves alternate, very large, rugose, double dentate, rough pubescent; flowers in large, terminal, forked-branched cymes (often helicoid), situated to one side of the rachis, corolla broad campanulate, with a large, wide, 5 lobed limb, the lobes imbricate before the flowers open; calyx lobes linear; stamens 5, rough pubescent, styles 2, filamentous; fruit a bivalved capsule with many seeds. — 6 species in Mexico, Peru and the West Indies.

Wigandia caracasana H. B. K. To 3 m high in cultivation, shoots shaggy-tomentose; leaves to 1 m long and 0.5 m wide, cordate-elliptic, double crenate, short tomentose above, densely gray-white pubescent beneath, long petioled; flowers revolute at the apex, curling up to one side, corolla small, violet-blue, August–September. FS 755; BM 4575. S. Mexico to Venezuela and Columbia. 1836. z10 Plate 161. ∅ ✧

Sometimes found in the parks and gardens of frost free climates; otherwise grown from seed as a summer annual for its foliage.

WIKSTROEMIA Endl. — THYMELAEACEAE

Deciduous or evergreen shrubs, occasionally trees; leaves simple, opposite or alternate; flowers terminal in spikes, racemes, heads or umbels, occasionally in panicles, hermaphroditic; calyx lobes 4, outspread, corolla tube with 4 spreading limb tips, throat without scales, stamens 8, in 2 rings; fruit a berrylike or dry drupe. — About 70 species in S. China, Indonesia, Australia and on the Pacific Isles.

Wikstroemia canescens Meissn. Small shrub, 30–90 cm

high; leaves opposite and alternate, oblong-lanceolate, 2.5–7.5 cm long, thin, venation indented above; corolla tube 8 mm long, yellow, flowers in loose, terminal heads; fruits silky pubescent. SNp 135. Himalayas; China; Ceylon. z10 ⊕

W. ganpi (S. & Z.) Maxim. Shrub, young shoots, inflorescences and stalks appressed white pubescent; leaves thin, oblong to oval-oblong, 2–4 cm long, 8–20 mm wide, obtuse or somewhat acute, loose scattered pubescent beneath, petiole 1–2 mm; flowers in dense racemes, very short, terminal and axillary, corolla tube 7–8 mm long, pink, white pubescent, August; fruit oval-spindle-form, 4 mm long, loose white pubescent. Japan; Honshu. z9 ⊕

W. shikokiana Franch. & Sav. Shrub, silky pubescent; leaves more or less alternate, thin, 3–5 cm long, 1.5–2 cm wide, densely silky pubescent on both sides, especially on the underside, petiole 2–3 mm; flowers few in heads at the shoot tips, calyx yellow, white silky pubescent, tube 8 mm long, May–June; fruit oval-spindle-form, 6 mm long, sparsely white pubescent. Japan; Honshu. z9 ⊕

Cultivated somewhat like *Daphne* in a moist, humus soil in a shady site and a mild climate.

WILLEMETIA

Willemetia africana see: **Noltea africana**

WINTERA

Wintera colorata see: **Pseudowintera colorata**

WISTERIA Nutt. — Wisteria — LEGUMINOSAE

Deciduous, high climbing shrubs; leaves alternate, odd pinnate, stipules insignificant, leaflets entire; flowers large, in pendulous, terminal and axillary racemes, blue, white or lilac; standard large and reflexed, normally with 2 appendages at the base, wings sickle-shaped, keel curved, obtuse; anther apexes distinct or half connate with each other, ovaries stalked, style glabrous; calyx campanulate, bilabiate; pod oblong, knotty, dehiscent, bivalvate. — 10 species in N. America and E. Asia.

Key to the Species covered in this book

● Plant twining to the left (clockwise);

  Pods glabrous; flowers in terminal racemes on the new shoots in June;

    + Racemes 4–10(15) cm long, without or nearly without glands:
        W. frutescens

  ++ Racemes (15)20–30(35) cm long, glandular;
        W. macrostachys

  Pods velvety pubescent, usually with several seeds; flowers in axillary racemes in May (with secondary flowers in July and August); leaflets 11–13 (never 15 or more); racemes 15 (or occasionally 30–40) cm long; flowers larger, 2.2–2.5 cm, standard petal over 2 cm wide, occasionally to 2.8 cm:
        W. sinensis

●● Plants right twining (counterclockwise); pods velvety; flowers in axillary racemes, May, with a few secondary flowers in July–August;

  + Racemes short to very long, from 10–75 cm long; leaves with 13–15(19) leaflets; flowers smaller, (1.2)1.7–1.9(2) cm long, standard usually less than 2 cm wide; pod usually with several seeds:
        W. floribunda

  ++ Racemes to 25 cm long; leaves with (7)11 to 13(15) leaflets; flowers about 2 cm wide; pod usually single seeded; a cultivated hybrid:
        W. × formosa

Wisteria brachybotrys see: **W. floribunda**

W. floribunda (Willd.) DC. Twining to 8 m high; leaflets 13–19, ovate-elliptic to more oblong, 4–8 cm long, acuminate, appressed pubescent at first, eventually nearly totally glabrous; flowers violet, 1.5–2 cm long, in 20–50 cm long racemes, gradually flowering from the base toward the apex, stalk 1.5–2.5 cm long, pubescent, May–June; pod 10–15 cm long, velvety pubescent. FS 880; LT 482; YTS 1: 130 (= *W. brachybotrys* S. & Z.). Japan. 1830. z5 Fig. 334.

Including the following forms:

Flowers white
  'Alba', 'Kuchi Beni', 'Longissima Alba', 'Shiro Noda'

Flowers pink
  'Rosea'

Flowers light reddish violet to violet
  'Ben Fugi', 'Kyushaku', 'Longissima', 'Macrobotrys', 'Murasaki Noda', 'Naga Noda', 'Royal Purple', 'Russelliana', 'Violaceo-plena', 'Ushi Jima'

Flowers blue-violet
  'Geisha', 'Sekine's Blue'

'Alba'. Racemes 25–27 cm long, dense, flowers white, medium fragrance; leaflets 13. RH 1891: 109: BS 2: 682.

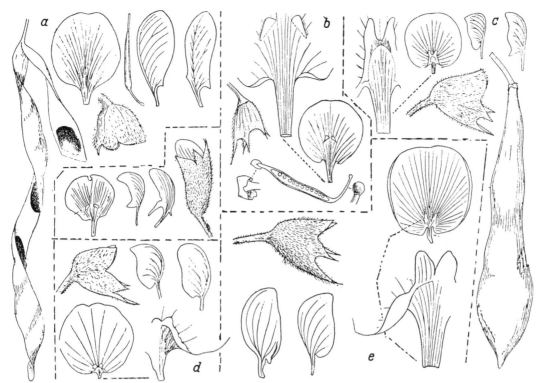

Fig. 334. **Wisteria.** Flowers and fruits and their parts. a. *W. japonica;* b. *W. macrostachys;* c. *W. floribunda* 'Macrobotrys'; between a. and d. *W. frutescens;* d. *W. sinensis;* e. *W. floribunda* (from Schneider)

'Beni Fugi'. Racemes 30–35 cm long, violet, only slightly fragrant; leaflets 19.

'Geisha'. Racemes 30 cm long, standard whitish, wings and keel petals blue-violet, fragrance medium; leaflets 13.

'Issai'. Flowers bluish, in 60–80 cm long racemes, also on young shoots. Possibly a hybrid of *W. floribunda* × *W. sinensis.* While the shoots are clockwise twining (like *W. sinensis*), the inflorescences are more similar to *W. floribunda.* ✧

'Kuchi Beni'. Racemes to 30 cm long, flowers not totally pure white, with a very light pink trace (appearing faded), medium fragrant; leaflets 15.

'Kyushaku'. Racemes to 65 cm long, flowers blue-violet (like 'Macrobotrys'), slightly fragrant.

'Longissima'. An unclear form; probably identical to 'Macrobotrys' or 'Kyushaku'.

'Longissima Alba'. Racemes 35 cm long, white, good fragrance; leaflets 13. Presumably a sport on the violet 'Longissima'.

'Macrobotrys'. Racemes 45–90 cm long and longer, standard petals cobalt-violet, wings and keel somewhat darker, excellent fragrance. FS 1002 (= *W. multijuga* van Houtte). This cultivar has the longest racemes. Plate 128; Fig. 334. ✧

'Murasaki Noda'. Racemes to 25 cm long, flowers violet like 'Macrobotrys', but the standard is somewhat larger and lighter, slightly fragrant; leaflets 15. ✧

'Naga Noda'. Racemes to 55 cm long, standard violet, wings and keel somewhat lighter, excellent fragrance. ✧

'Rosea'. Racemes to 35 cm long, flowers light pink, apex of the keel and the wings purple, fragrance excellent. ✧

'Royal Purple'. (W. B. Clarke). Racemes 30–35 cm long, standard violet, wings and keel lighter, slightly fragrant; leaflets 15. 1937.

'Russelliana'. Racemes 20 cm long, standard nearly white, wings and keel violet, slightly fragrant; leaflets 15.

'Sekine's Blue'. Racemes 17 cm long, standard whitish, wings and keel violet-blue, slightly fragrant.

'Shiro Noda'. Racemes 20 cm long, flowers white, medium fragrant; leaflets 15. Plate 164.

'Ushi Jima'. Racemes about 30 cm long, standard white with violet, wings and keel violet, slightly fragrant; leaflets 15.

'Violacea-plena'. Racemes 25–30 cm long, flowers double, reddish violet, slightly fragrant; leaflets 13. Flowers easily damaged in foul weather.

W. × formosa Rehd. (*W. floribunda* × *W. sinensis*). High climbing, twining from right to left, shoots silky pubescent; leaflets 9–15, usually 13; racemes about 25 cm long, flowers 2 cm long, standard pale violet, wings and keel somewhat darker, fragrance excellent, all flowers appearing nearly at the same time (!). Developed in Massachusetts, USA in 1905. z6

W. frutescens (L.) Poir. Twining 10–12 m high; leaves 20–30 cm long, leaflets 9–15, oval-lanceolate, 3–6 cm

long, finely appressed pubescent when young, later dark
green and glabrous above; flowers purple-lilac, small,
somewhat fragrant, in 4–10 cm long, finely pubescent,
often somewhat erect racemes, July–September, ovaries
and pods glabrous. BM 2103; RWF 203. Eastern USA.
1724. z5 Fig. 334.

'**Magnifica**'. Flowers soft lilac, with a large, sulfur-yellow blotch
on the standard petal. FS 1151. A seedling selection of M.
Delaville, Clermont, Oise, France. 1856.

'**Nivea**'. Flowers pure white, on short, very pubescent stalks,
appearing in late May. 1854. z9

W. japonica S. & Z. Thin branched, high twining, young
shoots glabrous; leaves 15–20 cm long, glabrous and
glossy; flowers yellowish white, in many-flowered, 30
cm long racemes, calyx glabrous and ciliate, July–
August; pod glabrous, to 10 cm long, with 6–7 seeds. DL
3: 698. Japan 1878. z8–9 Fig. 334.

W. macrostachys (Torr. & Gray) Nutt. Twining to 8 m
high, young shoots somewhat shaggy pubescent at first,
quickly becoming glabrous; leaflets normally 9, ovate-
elliptic to lanceolate, 3–7 cm long, acuminate, pubescent
at first, eventually only so beneath; flowers lilac-red, in
20–30 cm long racemes, stalks glandular, June–July;
pods glabrous, 7–10 cm long, somewhat twisted. FS
1151. Central USA. 1853. z6 Fig. 334.

W. multijuga see: **W. floribunda 'Macrobotrys'**

W. sinensis (Sims) Sweet. Twining to 10 m high; leaves
25–30 cm long, leaflets 7–13, ovate-oblong to more
lanceolate, abruptly acuminate, 4–8 cm long, appressed
silky pubescent at first, eventually totally glabrous;
flowers blue-violet, 2.5 cm long, slightly fragrant, in
dense, 15–30 cm long racemes, stalk shaggy pubescent,
April–May; pods 10–15 cm long, densely velvety, with
1–3 seeds. BM 2083; BR 680; MCL 125 (= *Glycine sinensis* Sims). China. 1816. z5 Fig. 334. ☉

'**Alba**'. Like the species, but with white flowers. Plate 163. ☉

'**Black Dragon**'. Flowers deep purple, double.

'**Jako**'. Racemes nearly 30 cm long, very dense, fragrance
excellent; leaflets 11. Much more attractive than 'Alba', but
often mistakenly labeled as such in cultivation. ☉

'**Sierra Madre**'. Racemes to 20 cm long, with a whitish standard,
wing and keel lavender-violet, very fragrant; leaflets 13. Found
in Sierra Madre, California. Perhaps a hybrid.

W. venusta Rehd. & Wils. Twining to 9 m high, very
similar to *W. sinensis*, but the shoots pubescent when
young; leaves 20–35 cm long, leaflets 9–13, elliptic to
ovate, short acuminate, rounded at the base, 3–10 cm
long, pubescent on both sides, particularly beneath;
flowers white, in 10–15 cm long and 10 cm wide
racemes, very fragrant, standard auricled at the base,
keel truncated at the apex, May–June; pod 15–20 cm
long, densely velvety, compressed. BM 8811; SDK 4: 17.
Japan; known only in cultivation. 1912. Very floriferous
and attractive. z5 Plate 128.

'**Violacea**'. Racemes 15 cm long, standard whitish, wings and
keel violet, flowering abundantly, quite fragrant; leaflets 13.
☉

All species and cultivars like a sandy soil. Seedling plants are
often poor bloomers. Performs best when provided with
support in full sun. Through continuous pruning, one can
supress the twining tendancy and encourage flowering. The
seeds are poisonous!

Lit. Sprengel, K.: Neue Mitteilungen über *Wisteria chinensis*; in
Mitt. DDG 1911, 237–240 ● Wyman, D.: Showy *Wisteria* still a
problem vine; in American Nurseryman, June 1, 1961, 10–11,
68–76 ● Bowden, W. M.: A survey of Wisterias in Southern
Ontario Gardens; Roy. Bot. Gard. Hamilton (Ontario, Canada)
Techn. Bull. **8**, 1–15, 1976.

XANTHOCERAS Bge. — SAPINDACEAE

Trees with alternate, pinnate leaves; flowers appear
before the leaves; sepals and petals 5 each, disk with 5
hornlike projections; ovaries 3 locular; fruit a 3 valved,
thick walled, large capsule. — 2 species in N. China.

Xanthoceras sorbifolium Bge. Deciduous tree, usually
only a shrub in cultivation, erect, later more wide to
globose; leaves to 30 cm long, leaflets 9–17, lanceolate,
4–5 cm long, scabrous serrate, persistent, abscising very
late; flowers polygamous, somewhat campanulate, 2 cm
wide, petals white, greenish yellow at the base at first,
later carmine, in dense, erect racemes to 25 cm long,
May–June; fruit a 4–6 cm long, 3 valved, thick walled
capsule, seeds chestnut-like, thick, globose, brown. BM
6923; FS 1819. N. China. 1866. z5 Plate 164. ☉

For any good garden soil; quite hardy and very attractive,
although seldom cultivated.

XANTHORRHIZA Marsh. — Yellow Root —
RANUNCULACEAE

Monotypic genus. Deciduous shrub, inner bark and
roots yellow; leaves alternate, pinnate, clustered at the
shoot tips; flowers insignificant, in terminal panicles,
polygamous, sepals 5, 5 nectaries, 5 or 10 stamens and
carpels, each carpel later becoming a single seeded
follicle.

Xanthorrhiza apiifolia see: **X. simplicissima**

X. simplicissima Marsh. Very stoloniferous, to only 60
cm high, a thinly branched shrub, stems hardly
branched; leaves pinnate, leaflets usually 5, ovate to
oblong, occasionally only trifoliate, incised dentate;
flowers red-brown, without petals, in terminal panicles,
5–10 cm long, appearing before the leaves, April–May.
BB 1553; GSP 130 (= *X. apiifolia* L'Hér.). Eastern N.
America. 1766. z3 Plate 165; Fig. 335.

Best suited for a woodland situation where it quickly spreads.
Hardy.

Fig. 335. *Xanthorrhiza simplicissima* (from Lauche)

XANTHORRHOEA Sm. — Grass Tree — XANTHORRHOEACEAE

Characteristic sample of Australian vegetation. Usually a well developed stem with terminal crest of evergreen, long persisting, narrow-linear, long leaves, similar to *Dasylirion*, but finer; flower small, white, in a very long, cylindrical, terminal spike; the individual flowers not very conspicuous, perianth with 6 lobes, 6 stamens; fruit a capsule. — 15 species in Australia.

Xanthorrhoea arborea R. Br. Grass Tree, Botany Bay Gum. Stem about 1–1.5 m high, 15–20 cm thick; leaves flat or triangular in cross section, about 1 m long or more, 3–4 mm wide; flowers 1.2 cm wide, inflorescences 1–1.2 m long, 2.5–3 cm wide, the peduncle 1.5–1.8 m long, April. Queensland. z9 Plate 164. # ⊘

X. preissii Endl. Black Boy. Stem to 4 m high, often shorter; leaves 60–120 cm long, 2–4 mm wide, stiff, very brittle when young; flowers 12 mm wide, inflorescences 30–90 cm long, 2.5 cm thick, the peduncle 30–90 cm long, April. BM 6933. W. Australia. z9 # ⊘

Found in some of the larger botanic gardens of the warmer regions. Requires heat and dryness.

XYLOSMA G. Forst. — FLACOURTIACEAE

Evergreen, dioecious or polygamous trees or shrubs, with axillary thorns; leaves alternate, simple, leathery and tough; flowers small, in axillary panicles, sepals usually 4–5(7), slightly connate at the base, petals absent, stamens numerous; disk glandular or ring-shaped and surrounding the stamens; fruit a small, 2–8 seeded berry. — About 100 species in the warmer regions.

Xylosma congestum see: **X. japonicum**

X. japonicum (Walp.) A. Gray. Evergreen shrub, with thorn-like short shoots on young plants, shoots red-brown, short pubescent when young; leaves ovate to more oblong, 4–8 cm long, 3–4 cm wide, acuminate, base acute, rounded on young plants, margins dentate, glabrous; flowers not very conspicuous, yellowish white, 2.5 mm wide, in short, axillary, short stalked racemes, Sepember; fruits 2–3 together, ovate, 4 mm wide, brown with black stripes. LWT 241 (= *X. racemosum* [S. & Z.] Miq.; *X. congestum* Merr.). Japan, Taiwan, China. 1907. z7 # ⊘

X. racemosum see: **X. japonicum**

Garden merit only slight; winter hardy in milder climates.

YUCCA L. — Adam's Needle, Spanish Dagger — LILIACEAE

Evergreen plants with a simple or branched, thick stem or lacking a stem; leaves swordlike, in terminal, densely packed clusters, usually long and narrow, often with a thorny tip, margins often tough and more or less shredded; flowers in terminal, many-flowered panicles; corolla globose to broadly globose, pendulous, short stalked, petals 6, fleshy, nearly distinct; stamens 6, ovaries oblong, style thick with 6 stigmas; fruit 6 locular, capsule-like to fleshy; seeds large, with a thin shell. — About 40 species in southern N. America and Central America.

Positive identification is not simple, and many transitional forms exist in cultivation.

Outline of the more Prominent Species

- Leaves not dentate, margins with more or less fine filaments;

    x Stem absent; style oblong, white;
    + Leaves tough as reeds:
        Y. filamentosa

    ++ Leaves weaker:
        Y. flaccida

    xx Stem short; style thick, green:
        Y. glauca

- • Leaves entire or very slightly and temporarily denticulate or sparsely and indistinctly filamentous;

    x Leaves to 5 cm wide in the center, stiff, inflorescence 1–2 m high; flowers pendulous:
        Y. gloriosa

    xx Leaves to 5.5 cm wide, limp; inflorescence narrow, loose:
        Y. recurvifolia

● ● ● Plants usually multistemmed, tall, stems very swollen at the base:
Y. elephantipes

Yucca aloifolia L. Tree-like, stem thin, erect, 3–6 m high, only rarely branched, crest of leaves 60–90 cm wide; leaves stiff, dagger-like, 30–45 cm long, 2.5–3.5 cm wide, widest in the middle, deep green with a bluish trace, with a hard, sharp thorned tip, margins finely and scabrous serrate; flower panicles dense, 30–60 cm long, flowers about 5 cm long, cream-white, turning purple at the base, May–June. BM 1700. SE. USA to E. Mexico, Jamaica, etc. One of the most commonly cultivated species. z10 Plate 165. # Ø ⊕

Including a number of cultivars of which the following 2 are frequently seen:

'Quadricolor'. Leaves green, with white, yellow and red longitudinal stripes. # Ø

'Tricolor'. Leaves green, with white and yellow longitudinal stripes. # Ø

Y. angustifolia see: **Y. glauca**

Y. baccata Torr. Stem short or absent or prostrate; leaves 60–90 cm long, swordlike, very thick and stiff, to 5 cm wide in the middle, channeled above, blue-green on both sides, with a thorned tip, margins red-brown, with rough filaments; total inflorescence about 1 m high, flowers to 8 cm long, white, the lobes narrowly lanceolate, 12–20 mm wide, August; fruits edible. USA; from Arizona to Nevada and New Mexico, and northward to Utah and Colorado. z6 Plate 165. # Ø ⊕

Y. brevifolia Engelm. Joshua Tree. An open-branched tree, stem and branches forked, with a rough, thick bark; leaves in short, dense heads at the branch tips, outspread, about 25 cm long, 15 mm wide, slightly convex to triangular in cross section, very stiff, prickly, margins finely denticulate; inflorescences sessile, dense, flowers greenish white, 3–5 cm wide. MCL 196. USA; California, Arizona, Utah, in dry regions. z7 # Ø ⊕

Y. californica see: **Y. whipplei**

Y. desmetiana Bak. Very slow growing, stem single, to 3 m high or more, slender, with a 30–40 cm long, leafy apex; leaves rather loosely arranged, linear, flat, purple when young, later blue-green, without a thorny tip, margins without teeth, dead leaves hanging on the stem for years, about 30 cm long, 12–20 mm wide in the center, only 6–9 mm wide at the base; hardly flowering. Mexico. 1868. z10 Plate 165. # Ø ⊕

Y. elephantipes Regel. Globose crowned tree, usually multistemmed, 6–12 m high in its habitat, stem swollen at the base (!); leaves glossy green, 60–120 cm long, 5–10 cm wide, indistinctly toothed, apex soft; flowers cream-white, 6–7.5 cm long, in very dense, 60–80 cm long, erect panicles in the summer. TY 51, 82; BM 7977 (= *Y. guatemalensis* Baker). Central America. 1873. Occasionally found in cultivation and very attractive. z9 Plate 166. # Ø ⊕

Y. filamentosa L. Without a stem, with only short, lateral shoots at the base; leaves stiffly erect to spreading, 30–70 cm long, 3–10 cm wide, oblong-lanceolate to oblanceolate, acuminate, somewhat blue-green, margins with numerous, 5–7 cm long, curling filaments; flowers yellowish white, pendulous, 5–7 cm long, in a conical, erect, glabrous panicle, 90–180 cm high, July–August. BM 900; TY 8, 12. S. USA. 1675. Hardy. Often confused in cultivation with *Y. smalliana*. z5 # Ø ⊕

var. *antwerpiensis* see: **Y. flaccida 'Major'**

'Variegata'. Leaves yellow and white striped. Plate 166. Ø

Y. flaccida Haworth. Stem absent, with short lateral shoots at the base; leaves green or blue-green, 30–60 cm long, 2.5–3 cm wide, acuminate, the apical part of the leaves hanging downward, margins with 5 cm long, curly filaments as on *Y. filamentosa*; flowers yellowish white, 5–6 cm long, in erect, pubescent panicles, July–August. TY 12, 16. SE. USA. 1816. Hardy. z5 Plate 166. # Ø ⊕

'Major'. Leaves more blue-green, wider; panicles soft pubescent, petals narrower. BM 6316 (= *Y. filamentosa* var. *antwerpiensis* Hort.). Ø

Y. glauca Nutt. Stem absent or prostrate; leaves narrowly linear, 30–70 cm long, 12–28 mm wide, blue-green, drawn out to a very long tip, all leaves in a horizontal (!), 1.2 m wide rosette, leaf margins white, with only a few filaments; flowers pendulous, greenish white, 5–7 cm long, in erect, 90–150 cm long panicles, July–August. TY 23–24; NF 10: 60; HyWF 15 (= *Y. angustifolia* Pursh). Central USA. 1811. z5 Plate 166. # Ø ⊕

Y. gloriosa L. Stem short and thick, occasionally branched; leaves 40–60 cm long, 5–7 cm wide, stiff, flat, straight, thorn tipped, blue-green; flowers cream-white, exterior often purple or red toned, pendulous, in dense, narrow, conical panicles 90–180 cm long (in some cases to 4.5 m high!), July–September. BM 1260; GC 132: 57; TY 43–44, 46. SE. USA. 1550. z7 Plate 167. # Ø ⊕

Y. guatemalensis see: **Y. elephantipes**

Y. × karlsruhensis Graebener (= *Y. filamentosa* × *Y. glauca*). Leaves to 1.5 cm wide, blue-gray, flexible, with marginal filaments; flowers white, exterior with a reddish trace. Gw 8: 7; NF 1: 36. Developed before 1906 by Graebener, chief city gardener in Karlsruhe, W. Germany. Very meritorious. z5 # Ø ⊕

Y. longifolia see: **Nolina longifolia**

Y. recurvifolia Salisb. Plants with a 1.8 m high stem, single or branched; leaves 60–90 cm long, 3–6 cm wide, drawn out to a thorny tip, blue-green at first, all leaves (except the youngest) distinctly reflexed; flowers cream-white, 5–7 cm wide, in erect, 90–150 cm long, branched panicles. BS 3: Pl. 40; NF 8: 42, TY 46–47. SE. USA. 1794. Hardy. z6 # Ø ⊕

'Marginata'. Leaves yellow margined. Ø

'Variegata'. Leaves with yellow midstripes. Ø

Y. smalliana Fern. Stem absent; leaves tough, 30–90 cm long, 20–30 mm wide; linear-lanceolate, acuminate, with many white filaments along the margins; flowers pendulous, nearly white, 4–5 cm long, in erect, finely pubescent panicles. SE. USA. Very similar to *Y. filamentosa* and often confused with such in the garden. z6 Plate 167. # Ø ⊕

Y. treculeana Carr. Stem single or branched, 4–5 m high, then with a 30–60 cm thick stem and branched; leaves densely arranged, 60–100 cm long, thick, stiff, blue-green, 5–7 cm wide, rough, margins often with wiry filaments and red-brown, indistinctly finely serrate at the base; flowers white, occasionally turning somewhat purple, 3–6 cm long, densely packed into narrow, conical, 50–100 cm long panicles, June. Texas, Mexico. 1858. z9 # Ø ⊕

var. **canaliculata** Hook. Leaves wider yet, deeply channeled above; flowers smaller, yellowish white. BM 5201 (as *Y. canaliculata*). Plate 167. # Ø ⊕

Y. whipplei Torr. Stem absent, stoloniferous, dies after flowering; leafy crest composed of 150–200 densely packed, 30–80 cm long leaves, these 15 mm wide, nearly triangular, stiff, taut, linear, green with a gray-blue trace, apex sharp and prickly, margins finely and scabrous denticulate; inflorescence a 1–3 m high, dense, oblong-lanceolate panicle, secondary axes 15 cm long or longer, flowers pendulous, 3–4 cm long, white, exterior greenish. MCL 197 (= *Hesperoyucca whipplei* Baker; *Y. californica* Lem.). USA; California. 1854. z10 # Ø ⊕

All the above-mentioned species like a medium-heavy soil and full sun.

Lit. McKelvey, S. D.: Yuccas of the Southwestern United States; Jamaica Plain, USA, (I) 1938; (II) 1947 ● Sprenger, K.: *Yucca* auf Korfu; in Mitt. DDG 1931, 281–287 ● Sprenger, K.: Mitteilungen über meine *Yucca*-Hybriden und -Formen; in Mitt. DDG 1920, 96–138 ● Sprenger, K.: Beobachtungen an einigen *Yucca*-Arten; in Mitt. DDG 1920, 138–149 ● Trelease, W.: The Yuccaceae; in Mo. Bot. Gard. Ann. Rep. **13**, 27–133, 1902 (99 plates) ● Webber, J. M.: Yuccas of the Southwest; Agr. Mon. 17, Washington 1953.

YUNNANEA Hu — THEACEAE

Monotypic genus. Evergreen tree, similar to *Camellia*, differing in the evergreen, persistent sepals and bracts; flowers solitary, large; sepals similar to the bracts but larger; petals 5, basal portion fused into a tube; stamens numerous, adnate to the tube; fruit a thick, woody drupe with very small, single seeded locules.

Yunnanea xylocarpa Hu. Evergreen tree, about 6 m high; leaves elliptic to broad lanceolate, 6–10 cm long, tough and leathery, long acuminate, ridged, finely serrate, glabrous; flowers red, about 5 cm wide; fruits globose, dark brown, about 3.5 cm thick, seeds 6 mm long. RYB 11: 46. China; Yunnan Prov., discovered in the mountains at 2400 m in 1983, but not totally familiar. Existence in cultivation unknown. z6 # ⊕ ⊗

ZANTHOXYLUM L. — Prickly Ash, Hercule's Club — RUTACEAE

Trees or shrubs with more or less prickly stems; leaves deciduous or semi-evergreen, alternate, odd pinnate or trifoliate, translucent punctate and aromatic; flowers unisexual, small, inconspicuous, with a single perianth, yellow-green; fruits compound, composed of (2)–3–5 fruitlets together; these bivalvate, dehiscent, dry. — About 20–30 species in the tropical and subtropical regions of both hemispheres, only a few in the temperate zone of E. Asia and N. America.

Outline of the Species covered in this work

● Flowers appearing before the leaves in axillary clusters; leaflets 5–11, pubescent beneath:
  Z. americanum

● ● Flowers appearing after the leaves, in corymbs at the ends of lateral shoots, occasionally on terminal shoots; leaflets glabrous or nearly so;

  x Rachis broadly winged; leaflets 3–5, 3–12 cm long:
    Z. alatum

  xx Rachis not winged or only slightly winged;

    v Leaflets nearly sessile; prickles straight; fruits beaked;

      + Prickles stout, base distinctly flattened; leaflets 7–11, 1.5–5 cm long:
        Z. simulans

      ++ Prickles slender; leaflets 11–21, not over 3 cm long;

        § Prickles paired; flowers with a single perianth:
          Z. piperitum

        §§ Prickles solitary; flowers with sepals and petals:
          Z. schinifolium

    vv Leaflets short stalked, 7–13 together, 3–7 cm long; prickles usually hook-form:
      Z. stenophyllum

Zanthoxylum alatum var. **planispinum** (S. & Z.) Rehd. & Wils. Deciduous shrub, 2–4 m high, shoots glabrous, thorns paired, broad and flat, 6–12 mm long; leaves 12–25 cm long, rachis broad winged (!), leaflets 3 or 5, ovate to lanceolate, 3–12 cm long, dentate; flowers yellowish, in 3–5 cm long corymbs, spring; fruits red, warty, globose. BM 8754; FIO 78. Japan, China, Korea. 1865. The type, **Z. alatum** has 3–15 leaflets and is indigenous to the Himalayas. z6 Ø ⊗

Z. americanum Mill. Toothache Tree. Shrub or small tree, to 8 m high, young shoots pubescent, prickly, prickles paired beneath the leaf buds; leaflets 5–11, ovate-elliptic, 3–6 cm long, acuminate, dark green above, lighter and pubescent beneath; flowers yellow-green, inconspicuous, in small, axillary clusters, appearing before or with the new foliage in spring; fruits small, blackish. BB 2269; GSP 249; KTF 120 (= *Z. clava herculis* L.; *Z. fraxineum* Willd.). Eastern N. America. 1740. The fruits and bark were once chewed to relieve toothaches;

Fig. 336. *Zanthoxylum americanum* (from Lauche)

the sharp, numbing taste would supposedly displace the pain of a toothache. z3–7 Fig. 336.

Z. bungei see: **Z. simulans**

Z. clava herculis see: **Z. americanum**

Z. fraxineum see: **Z. americanum**

Z. piperitum DC. Compact shrub to small tree, young shoots pubescent, prickles paired, flat, 12 mm long; leaves 7–15 cm long, rachis pubescent, prickly, leaflets 11–23, ovate, 1.5–3 cm long, glabrous, dentate, terminal leaflets incised at the apex; flowers small, green, in 2–5 cm long cymes, terminal on short side shoots; fruits reddish. HM 1691; KIF 3: 31. N. China, Japan, Korea. 1877. z6 ⚭

Z. schinifolium S. & Z. Deciduous shrub or small tree, shoots glabrous, prickles solitary, 12 mm long; leaves 7–17 cm long, leaflets 11–21, lanceolate, 2–3 cm long, obtusely dentate, incised at the apex, glabrous, rachis prickly; flowers 12 mm wide, green or brown; seeds blue-black. LF 187. China, Japan, Korea. 1872. z6 ∅

Z. simulans Hance. A broad shrub, only about 3 m high, shoots somewhat pubescent or glabrous, prickles very wide (to 15 mm), very compressed at the base; leaflets 7–11, broad ovate, 2–5 cm long, obtusely dentate, glabrous, glossy, rachis and midribs prickly; flowers in loose cymes appearing after the leaves, May–June; fruits reddish, darker punctate. LF 188; HM 1690 (= *Z. bungei* Hance). China. 1869. z6 Plate 167. ∅ ⚭

Z. stenophyllum Hemsl. Somewhat climbing, to 2.5 m high, shoots and leaves glabrous, prickles short-hooked, stiff; leaflets 7–13, oval-oblong to lanceolate, 3–10 cm long, abruptly slender acuminate, very finely dentate,

rachis prickly; fruits reddish, glossy, globose and beaked. FIO 80. W. China. 1908. z9

All hardy except the last species; with no particular cultural requirements but of little ornamental merit.

ZAUSCHNERIA Presl. — California Fuchsia — ONAGRACEAE

Low subshrubs; leaves opposite at the branch base, alternate toward the tip, entire; flowers resembling those of *Fuchsia*, in racemes, scarlet-red; calyx tubular, base globose-inflated, with 4 limb tips, petals 4, stamens 8, exserted; fruit an elongated capsule. — 4 species in western N. America.

Zauschneria californica Presl. To 30 cm high, shoots somewhat woody at the base; leaves clustered, linear-lanceolate, 1–2 cm long, sessile, entire to totally finely serrate, pubescent; flowers scarlet-red, in large, loose racemes at the shoot tips, July–September. BMns 19; FS 414. California. 1847. z8 Plate 128; Fig. 337. ☉

Z. cana Greene. Similar to the above species, but differing in the leaves. 30–60 cm high in its habitat or other favorable climate, total plant gray tomentose; leaves narrowly linear to nearly filamentous, not over 2 mm wide, entire, in clusters together; flowers scarlet-red, 2–3 cm long, August–October. MCL 178. California. z9 ∅ ☉

A very attractive subshrub for very sunny, warm sites in light soil; should be protected well in winter.

Lit. Hilend, M.: A revision of the genus *Zauschneria*; in Amer. Journ. Botany **16**, 58–88, 1929 ● Clausen-Keck-Hiesey: Experimental studies on the nature of Species; 1. 213–259, 1940; in Carnegie Inst. Publ. no. 520.

Fig. 337. *Zauschneria californica* (from Raimann)

ZELKOVA Spach — ULMACEAE

Deciduous, (elm-like) trees or shrubs; leaves alternate, short petioled, base not oblique, simple, parallel veined, serrate; flowers inconspicuous, monoecious, axillary, in small clusters on the current year's shoots; fruits drupaceous, oblique. — 6–7 species in W. and E. Asia.

Key

- Shrub or small tree;

  ✕ Leaves 12–30 mm long, bristly pubescent at first, later glabrous:
  Z. abelicea

  ✕✕ Leaves 3–7 cm long, soft pubescent beneath;
  Z. verschaffeltii

- • Larger trees;

  ✕ Shoots nearly glabrous; leaves with 8–14 vein pairs:
  Z. serrata

  ✕✕ Shoots pubescent; leaves with 8–14 vein pairs;

    v Shoots very pubescent; leaves 3–8 cm long, with 6–8 vein pairs:
    Z. carpinifolia

    vv Shoots gray woolly at first; leaves 3–6 cm long, with 8–12 vein pairs:
    Z. sinica

Zelkova abelicea (Lam.) Boiss. Small, fine textured shrub, 2.5–3.5 m high, strongly branched, branchlets very thin, short bristly pubescent at first; leaves ovate-oblong, 12–25 mm long, with 7–9 large, triangular teeth, both sides bristly pubescent at first (like the branchlets), later totally glabrous or nearly so, nearly sessile (= *Z. cretica* Spach). Crete, in the mountains. 1924. z7 Fig. 339. ∅

Z. acuminata see: **Z. serrata**

Z. carpinifolia (Pall.) K. Koch. Tree, to 25 m high, often multistemmed, crown ovate to ellipsoid (!!), bark *Fagus*-like, gray, scaly-exfoliating, young shoots thin, pubescent; leaves elliptic-oblong, 2–5(9) cm long, acute,

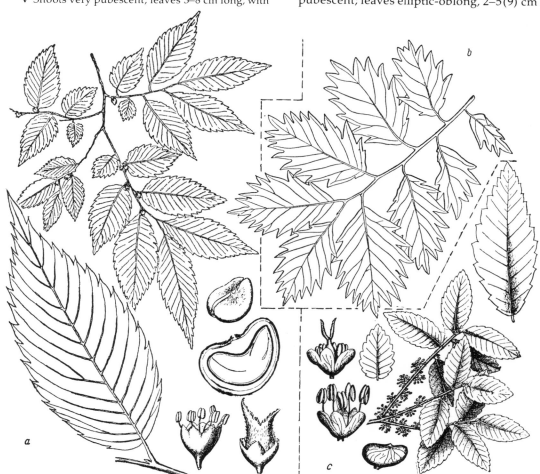

Fig. 338. **Zelkova.** a. *Z. serrata;* b. *Z. verschaffeltii;* c. *Z. carpinifolia*
(from Engler, Dippel, Shirasawa, Graebner)

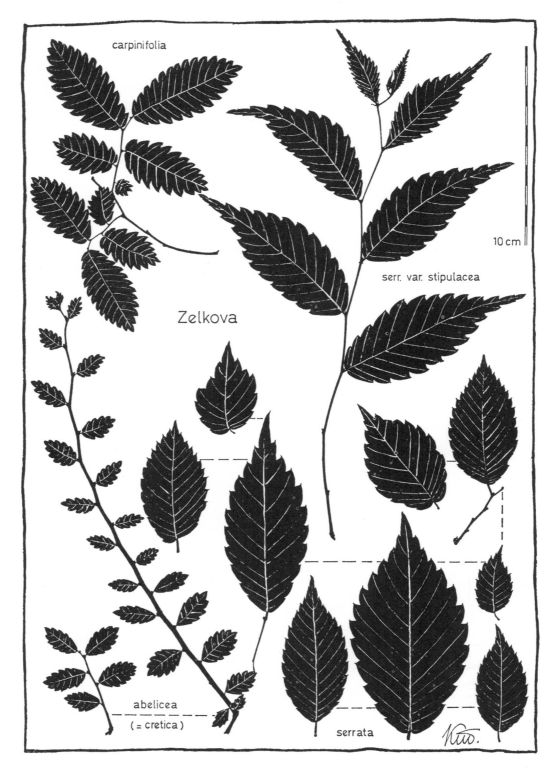

Fig. 339. **Zelkova** (from material out of the Dortmund Botanic Garden, W. Germany)

base round to somewhat cordate, coarsely crenate, with 6–8 vein pairs, deep green and somewhat rough above, venation pubescent beneath, petiole 1–2 mm long; fruits 5 mm thick. EH 249; BS 3: Pl. 41 (= *Z. crenata* Spach; *Z. ulmoides* Schneid.). Caucasus. 1760. Ⓕ USSR (Aserbeidshan). z7 Plate 168; Fig. 338, 339. ∅

Z. crenata see: **Z. carpinifolia**

Z. cretica see: **Z. abelicea**

Z. davidii see: **Hemiptelea davidii**

Z. keaki see: **Z. serrata**

Z. schneideriana Hand.-Mazz. Tree, 8–15 m high, bark gray and scaly, shoots dark gray, thin, glabrous; leaves oval-oblong to oblong-elliptic, 4–9 cm long, 1.5–5 cm wide, long acuminate, base round to rhombic, crenate, with 7–14 indented vein pairs above, gray silky beneath, thick, slightly leathery, petiole 5–10 mm, densely gray haired; fruits irregularly ovate, 3 mm long and wide, solitary, axillary (= *Z. serrata* var. *stipulacea* Makino). Ⓕ E. and central China. z6 Plate 168.

Z. serrata (Thunb.) Mak. Tree, to 30 m high, stem short and often parted into many, erect, main branches, crown broad and globose (!!), stem gray, branches brown-red, glabrous, thin, nodding; leaves oval-oblong, 3–6 cm long, to 12 cm long on long shoots, long acuminate, base round to cordate, scabrous serrate with acute teeth, with 8–14 vein pairs, rough above, rather smooth beneath, petiole 2–5 mm long; fruit 4 mm thick. EH 250; NK 19: 12; CIS 20 (= *Z. keaki* Maxim.; *Z. acuminata* Planch.). Japan. 1861. Occasionally suffers from "Dutch Elm Disease". Ⓕ Japan. z5–6 Plate 168; Fig. 338, 339. ∅

'Pulverulenta'. Leaves much smaller, yellow variegated. Introduced from Japan by Lefeber, Boskoop, Holland.

var. *stipulacea* see: **Z. schneideriana**

Z. sinica Schneid. Tree, 15–18 m high, young shoots gray woolly at first, later smooth and brown; leaves ovate to more lanceolate, 2.5–6 cm long, base obliquely rounded or broadly cuneate, margins ciliate, crenate, with 7–12 vein pairs, dull green and rough above, soft pubescent beneath, petiole short pubescent; fruits obovoid, 5–6 mm thick. China. 1920. z5–6

Z. ulmoides see: **Z. carpinifolia**

Z. verschaffeltii (Dipp.) Nichols. Shrub or small tree, branches thin, spreading, young shoots very thin, slightly pubescent at first; leaves elliptic-ovate, 3–6 cm long, with 6–9 vein pairs and an equal number of triangular, coarse, deeply incised teeth, rough above, underside soft pubescent; fruits nearly like those of *Z. carpinifolia*. SH 1: 141; DH 2: 14. Origin unknown, perhaps the Caucasus (or only a juvenile form of *Z. carpinifolia*), 1886. z6 Fig. 338. ∅

Cultivated like the elms. A very nice park tree.

Lit. Czerpanov, S.: Revisio specierum generis *Zelkova* Spach et *Hemiptelea* Planchon; in Botan. Material. **18**, 58–72 (in Russian).

ZENOBIA D. Don — ERICACEAE

Monotypic genus. Shrub, only semi-evergreen, deciduous in colder regions; leaves leathery; flowers at the shoot tips, grouped into long racemes; calyx 5 parted, corolla campanulate, with 4 awn-like, erect appendages; fruit a flat-globose capsule.

Zenobia pulverulenta (Willd.) Pollard. Upright shrub, 0.5–1 m high, branches somewhat bowed outward, more or less bluish pruinose; leaves ovate-oblong to elliptic, 2–7 cm long, finely crenate to entire, obtuse, base usually rounded, finely bluish pruinose on both sides (!); flowers campanulate, pure white, in clusters, these grouped into long racemes, May to June; fruits globose, 5 valved, seeds numerous, angular. BM 667; BR 1010 (= *Andromeda pulverulenta* Bartr.; *Andromeda dealbata* Lindl.). SE. USA, in moist forests. 1801. z6 ☼

f. **nitida** (Michx.) Fern. Leaves usually semi-evergreen, glossy green on both sides (without the pruinose layer!), ovate to oblong-elliptic, obtuse, entire, also slightly crenate on the flowering shoots. BB 2769; BM 970; RWF 267 (= *Z. speciosa* D. Don). Occurring together with the species. 1801. Plate 168. ☼

Z. speciosa see: **Z. pulverulenta** f. **nitida**

Soil preference and hardiness about like the winter hardy hybrid azaleas. The "Lily of the Valley"-like flowers are very attractive.

Lit. Wood, C. E.: The genera of Ericaceae in the S.E. United States; 9. *Zenobia*; in Journ. Arnold Arb. **42**, 45–47, 1961 (with a further bibliography and ills.)

ZIZIPHUS Mill. (= *Zizyphus* Adans.) — Jujube — RHAMNACEAE

Deciduous to evergreen trees or shrubs, stipules thorny; leaves distichous-alternate, short petioled, 3–5 veined from the base up, entire to serrate; flowers usually hermaphroditic, 5 parted, yellow, in axillary cymes; ovaries usually 2 locular; style usually 2 parted; fruit a nearly globose to more oblong drupe. — About 40 species, most in Indomalaysia and S. Asia, the tropics of Africa, Mexico and S. America; one species in the Mediterranean region.

Zizyphus jujuba Mill. Jujube. Deciduous shrub or tree, to 9 m, shoots flexuose, glabrous, thorny, with an occasional 3 cm long straight thorn, the others short and hook-like, shoots often clustered and then appearing like bipinnate leaves; leaves elliptic to oval-lanceolate, 2.5–6 cm long, obtuse to round, base oblique and 3 veined, crenate, tough, glabrous, petiole 1–5 mm long; flowers yellow, 2–3 axillary, April–May; fruits ovate-oblong, 1.5–2.5 cm long, dark red, eventually black, edible. HM 1884; SNp 7 (= *Z. vulgaris* Lam.; *Z. sativa* Gaertn.). Southeastern Europe and E. Asia. 1640. Often cultivated for its fruits in warmer climates. z6 ⚘ ✗

Z. sativa see: **Z. jujuba**

Z. vulgaris see: **Z. jujuba**

APPENDIX

Addenda to Volume I:

page 89
Acer palmatum 'Dissectum Chitoseyama'. Upright habit; leaves deeply incised, bronze-green (de Jong, Boskoop, Holland 1977).

p. 90
Acer palmatum 'Oregon Sunset'. Leaves larger than those of 'Atropurpureum', attractive fall color (Spaargaren, Boskoop, Holland 1977).

p. 95
Acer platanoides 'Royal Red'. Improvement on 'Crimson King'. Stronger growing; leaves dark red the entire summer, glossy. Originated by J. Holmason, Pacific Coast Nursery, Portland, Oregon, USA. 1964.

p. 132
Alnus × 'Cordinca' (*A. cordata × A. incana.*) Leaves cordate. Rarely cultivated (Boot & Co., Boskoop, Holland, since 1971).

p. 273
Caragana arborescens 'Tidy'. Originated as a bud mutation on a seedling, very similar to 'Lorbergii', but with a stiffer, more upright habit. First named *C. microphylla* 'Tidy', later disseminated by the Morden Research Station, Manitoba, Canada.

p. 376
Corylopsis willmottiae 'Spring Purple'. Leaves on the young shoots an attractive violet-red from bud break to early summer, then gradually turning green. JRHS 1977: 390. Selected as a seedling by Hillier in Winchester, England, 1969.

p. 376 (Lit. section addition)
Morley, B.: *Corylopsis*, spring flowering shrubs in JRHS **109**, 105–107, 1977 ● Morley, B., & Chao, Jew-Ming: The genus *Corylopsis*; in Jour. Arnold Arboretum 1977.

p. 398
Crataegus laevigata 'Crimson Cloud' is practically identical to 'Punicea', but allegedly more vigorous in the USA than the latter.

p. 414
Daboecia × scotica D. McClintock. Hybrids between *D. azorica* and *D. cantabrica*, originated in Scotland and more winter hardy than the parents. Shoots 50 cm high, exceptionally to 1 m; leaves to 9 mm long; flowers to 11 mm long, with a few glandular hairs, flowers from May to June and August to winter.

'William Buchanan'. The type of the hybrid. See the description in Vol. I: p. 415. JRHS 1978:114.

'Silverwells'. Low growing; flowers white. JRHS 1978: 114.

Cross references for Volume I:

A. linearifolia see: **Rhododendron macrosepalum 'Linearifolium'**
A. macrosepala see: **Rhododendron macrosepalum**
A. mollis see: **Rhododendron japonicum**
A. nudiflora var. *alba* see: **Rhododendron alabamense**
A. nudiflora var. *coccinea* see: **Rhododendron flammeum**
A. oblongifolia see: **Rhododendron oblongifolium**
A. pontica see: **Rhododendron luteum**
A. pontica var: *sinensis* see: **Rhododendron molle**
A. rosaeflora see: **Rhododendron indicum 'Balsaminiflorum'**
A. sinensis see: **Rhododendron molle**
A. yodogawa see: **Rhododendron yedoense**

Bambusa aurea see: **Phyllostachys aurea**
B. disticha see: **Sasa disticha**
B. flexuosa see: **Phyllostachys flexuosa**
B. nigra see: **Phyllostachys nigra**
B. palmata see: **Sasa palmata**
B. viridi-glaucescens see: **Phyllostachys viridi-glaucescens**

Bignonia alba see: **Pithecoctenium cynanchoides**
B. echinata see: **Pithecoctenium muricatum**
B. stans see: **Tecoma stans**

Bryanthus breweri see: **Phyllodoce breweri**
B. empetriformis see: **Phyllodoce empetriformis**
B. erectus see: **× Phyllothamnus erectus**
B. glanduliflora see: **Phyllodoce glanduliflora**

CERASUS See: **PRUNUS**

Cerasus brachypetala see: **Prunus prostrata** var. **brachypetala**
C. decumana see: **Prunus avium 'Decumana'**
C. juliana pendula see: **Prunus avium 'Pendula'**
C. nicotianifolia see: **Prunus avium 'Decumana'**

Chamaerops excelsa see: **Trachycarpus fortunei**

Citrus trifoliata see: **Poncirus trifoliata**

Cocculus heterophyllus see: **Sinomenium acutum**

Crataegus glabra see: **Photinia glabra**
C. pyracantha see: **Pyracantha coccinea**

CYCLOCARYA See: **PTEROCARYA**

Cyclocarya paliurus see: **Pterocarya paliurus**

Cydonia sinensis see: **Pseudocydonia sinensis**
C. veitchii see: **Pyronia veitchii**

Cytisus ramentaceus see: **Petteria ramentacea**
C. weldenii see: **Petteria ramentacea**

DASIPHORA See: **POTENTILLA**

Dasiphora fruticosa see: **Potentilla fruticosa**

DOLICHOS See: **PUERARIA**

Dolichos japonicus see: **Pueraria lobata**

Drimys colorata see: **Pseudowintera colorata**

Errata Volume I

p. 124, in Lit. correct spelling is Landbouwhogeschool.

p. 124, in Lit. correct spelling is Hensen.

p. 159, at heading for *Anopterus,* insert Escalloniaceae for Saxifragaceae.

p. 172, at top left of page, correct spelling is *setchuenensis.*

p. 173 **Aronia arbutofilia** should read **Aronia arbutifolia.**

p. 175 insert Gramineae for Bambusaceae, at heading for *Arundinaria.*

p. 187 Bambusaceae should read Bambusoïdeae.

p. 208, **'Auricoma'** belongs under **B. × ottawensis.**

p. 215, correct spelling is 'Vermilion', bottom-left.

p. 233, in Lit. should read Fontaine, F. J.

p. 245 strike Plate 85 from **B. nivea.**

p. 261, text of **'Spicata'** should read "flowers purple-pink."

Same page, add **'Spicata Alba'.** Flowers white.

p. 267, **Camellia sinensis** var. **assamica** should have a reference to Plate 138 in Vol. III.

p. 273, **B. boisii** should read **C. boisii.**

Same page, at **B. boisii,** should read *crasse-aculeata.*

p. 369, for possible addition to *Cornus* 'Eddie's White Wonder': presumed to be a hybrid between *C. nuttallii* and *C. florida,* is actually (according to Herman Grootendorst, Boskoop, Holland) a form of *C. nuttallii,* despite the 4 bracts; such forms are found occasionally in the habitat of *C. nuttallii.*

p. 375, at **griffithii,** should read *himalayana.*

p. 386, **'Robusta'** should read **'Robustus'.**

p. 408, at **C. linifolius,** should read *Teline linifolia.*

p. 410, left column, middle at "The latter 2 cultivars . . .", should read "The cultivars **'Hollandia'** and **'Zeelandia'.**

Same page, at **C. scoparius** should read *Spartium scoparium.*

p. 413, **C. supranubius'** should read **supranubium.**

p. 415, at **Danae racemosa,** *Ruscus racemosa* should read *racemosus.*

p. 443, under **Docynia delavaya,** *Pirus* should be spelled *Pyrus.*

Taxonomic Outline of the Families and Genera Covered in this Work

from A. ENGLER, Syllabus der Pflanzenfamilien, 12th ed., revised by H. MELCHIOR and E. WERDERMANN, Berlin 1958 (with some alterations according to J. C. WILLIS, A Dictionary of the Flowering Plants and Ferns, 8th ed., Cambridge 1973)

Other than for some particularly extensive Families, their respective Genera are alphabetized.

Division **PTERIDOPHYTA,** Ferns
  Cyatheaceae
    Cyathea, Dicksonia

Division **GYMNOSPERMAE,** Naked seeds

  Cycadaceae
    Cycas

  Zamiaceae
    Encephalartos

Division **ANGIOSPERMAE,** Covered seeds

1. CLASS: DICOTYLEDONAE

1. Subclass: ARCHICHLAMYDEAE

  1. Order: **Casuarinales**

    Casuarinaceae
      Casuarina

  2. Order: **Juglandales**

    Myricaceae
      Comptonia, Myrica

    Juglandaceae
      Carya, Juglans, Platycarya, Pterocarya

  4. Order: **Leitneriales**

    Leitneriaceae
      Leitneria

  5. Order: **Salicales**

    Salicaceae
      Chosenia, Populus, Salix

  6. Order: **Fagales**

    Betulaceae
      Alnus, Betula

    Corylaceae
      Carpinus, Corylus, Ostrya, Ostryopsis

    Fagaceae
      Carpinus, Castanea, Castanopsis, Chrysolepis, Fagus, Lithocarpus, Nothofagus

  7. Order: **Urticales**

    Ulmaceae
      Aphananthe, Celtis, Hemiptelea, Planera, Pteroceltis, Trema, Ulmus, Zelkova

    Eucommiaceae
      Eucommia

    Moraceae
      Broussonetia, Cudrania, Ficus, × Macludrania, Maclura, Morus

  Urticaceae
    Boehmeria, Gesnouinia

8. Order: **Proteales**

  Proteaceae
    Banksia, Dryandra, Embothrium, Gevuina, Grevillea, Hakea, Leucadendron, Leucospermum, Lomatia, Protea, Stenocarpus, Telopea

9. Order: **Santalales**

  1. Suborder: Santalineae

    Oleaceae
      Abeliophyllum, Chionanthus, Fontanesia, Forestiera, Forsythia, Fraxinus, Jasminum, Ligustrum, Notelaea, Olea, Osmanthus, Osmarea, Parasyringa, Phillyrea, Syringa

    Santalaceae
      Osyris, Buckleya, Pyrularia

  2. Suborder: Loranthineae

    Loranthaceae
      Loranthus, Viscum

12. Order: **Polygonales**

  Polygonaceae
    Atraphaxis, Brunnichia, Calligonum, Eriogonum, Homalocladium, Muehlenbeckia, Polygonum

13. Order: **Centrospermeae**

  1. Suborder: Phytolaccineae

    Phytolaccaceae
      Ercilla, Phytolacca

    Nyctaginaceae
      Bougainvillea

  3. Suborder: Caryophyllineae

    Caryophyllaceae
      Drypis

  4. Suborder: Chenopodiineae

    Chenopodiaceae
      Atriplex, Camphorosma, Eurotia, Haloxylon, Suaeda

15. Order: **Magnoliales**

  Magnoliaceae
    Aromadendron, Liriodendron, Magnolia, Manglietia, Michelia

  Winteraceae
    Drimys, Pseudowintera

Annonaceae
Annona, Asimina

Schisandraceae
Kadsura, Schisandra

Illiciaceae
Illicium

Monimiaceae
Peumus

Atherospermataceae
Atherosperma, Laurelia

Calycanthaceae
Calycanthus, Chimonanthus

Lauraceae
Actinodaphne, Apollonias, Cinnamomum, Laurus, Lindera, Litsea, Machilus, Neolitsea, Ocotea, Persea, Phoebe, Sassafras, Umbellularia

Tetracentraceae
Tetracentron

Trochodendraceae
Trochodendron

Eupteleaceae
Euptelea

Cercidiphyllaceae
Cercidiphyllum

16. Order: **Ranunculales**

1. Suborder: Ranunculineae

Ranunculaceae
Clematis, Xanthorriza

Berberidaceae
Berberis, × *Mahoberberis, Mahonia*

Nandinaceae
Nandina

Sargentodoxaceae
Sargentodoxa

Lardizabalaceae
Akebia, Decaisnea, Holboellia, Lardizabala, Sinofranchetia, Stauntonia

Menispermaceae
Calycocarpum, Cocculus, Sinomenium, Menispermum

17. Order: **Piperales**

Chloranthaceae
Chloranthus

18. Order: **Aristolochiales**

Aristolochiaceae
Aristolochia

19. Order: **Guttiferales**

1. Suborder: Dilleniineae

Dilleniaceae
Hibbertia

Paeoniaceae
Paeonia

Eucryphiaceae
Eucryphia

Actinidiaceae
Actinidia, Clematoclethra

2. Suborder: Ochnineae

Ochnaceae
Ochna

3. Suborder: Theineae

Theaceae
Camellia, Cleyera, Eurya, Franklinia, Gordonia, Schima, Stewartia, Ternstroemia, Yunnanea

Rhodoleiaceae (distinction unclear!)
Rhodoleia

Hypericaceae (= Guttiferae)
Ascyrum, Hypericum

21. Order: **Papaverales**

1. Suborder: Papaverineae

Papaveraceae
Dendromecon

2. Suborder: Capparineae

Capparidaceae
Capparis

Cruciferae
Aethionema, Alyssum, Aurinia, Iberis, Ptilotrichum, Vella

23. Order: **Rosales**

1. Suborder: Hamamelidineae

Plantanaceae
Platanus

Hamamelidaceae
Corylopsis, Disanthus, Distylium, Fortunearia, Fothergilla, Hamamelis, Liquidambar, Loropetalum, Parrotia, Parrotiopsis, × *Sycoparrotia, Sycopsis, Sinowilsonia*

2. Suborder: Saxifragineae

Crassulaceae
Sedum

Saxifragaceae
Ribes

Baueraceae
Bauera

Philadelphaceae
Carpenteria, Deutzia, Fendlera, Fendlerella,

Jamesia, Philadelphus

Hydrangaceae
Decumaria, Hydrangea, Pileostegia, Platycrater, Schizophragma

Iteaceae
Itea

Escalloniaceae
Anopterus, Escallonia

Cunoniaceae
Caldcluvia, Cunonia, Weinmannia

Pittosporaceae
Billardiera, Bursaria, Hymenosporum, Pittosporum, Sollya

3. Suborder: Rosinae

Rosaceae

I. Spiraeoideae
Chamaebatiaria, Exochorda, Luetkea, Neillia, Neviusia, Pentactina, Petrophytum, Physocarpus, Sibiraea, Sorbaria, Spiraea, Stephanandra

II. Pomoideae
Amelanchier, × Amelasorbus, Aronia, Chaenomeles, Cotoneaster, + Crataegomespilus, Crataegus, × Crataemespilus, Cydonia, Dichotomanthes, Docynia, Eriobotrya, Lindleya, Malus, Mespilus, Peraphyllum, Osteomeles, Photinia, Pyracantha, × Pyracomeles, × Pyrocydonia, × Pyronia, Pyrus, Pseudocydonia, Rhaphiolepis, × Sorbaronia, × Sorbocotoneaster, × Sorbopyrus, Sorbus, Stranvaesia

III. Rosoideae
Adenostoma, Cercocarpus, Chamaebatia, Coleogyne, Cowania, Dryas, Fallugia, Kerria, Lyonothamnus, Margyricarpus, Polylepis, Potentilla, Poterium, Purshia, Rhodotypos, Rosa, Rubus

IV. Prunoideae
Maddenia, Osmaronia, Prinsepia, Prunus

4. Suborder: Leguminosineae

Leguminosae

I. Mimosoideae
Acacia, Albizia, Calliandra, Prosopis

II. Caesalpinioideae
Bauhinia, Caesalpinia, Cassia, Ceratonia, Cercidium, Cercis, Delonix, Gleditsia, Gymnocladus, Parkinsonia

III. Papilionoideae (= Fabiodeae)
Adenocarpus, Alhagi, Amicia, Ammodendron, Amorpha, Anagyris, Argyrolobium, Astragalus, Calicotome, Calophaca, Campylotropis, Caragana, Carmichaelia, Cladrastis, Clianthus, Colutea,

Corallospartium, Coronilla, Cytisus, Desmodium, Dorycnium, Erinacea, Erythrina, Genista, Halimodendron, Hedysarum, Indigofera, Kennedia, + Laburnocytisus, Laburnum, Lespedeza, Lupinus, Maackia, Medicago, Notospartium, Ononis, Petteria, Piptanthus, Podalyria, Psoralea, Pueraria, Robinia, Sesbania, Sophora, Spartium, Sutherlandia, Templetonia, Tipuana, Ulex, Wisteria

26. Order: **Geraniales**

2. Suborder: Geraniineae

Zygophyllaceae
Nitraria

Linaceae
Linum

3. Suborder: Euphorbiineae

Euphorbiaceae
Acalypha, Aleurites, Andrachne, Codiaeum, Euphorbia, Glochidion, Mallotus, Ricinus, Sapium, Securinega

Daphniphyllaceae
Daphniphyllum

27. Order: **Rutales**

1. Suborder: Rutineae

Rutaceae
Acradenia, Adenandra, Barosma, Calodendrum, × Citrofortunella, × Citroncirus, Citrus, Choisya, Coleonema, Correa, Euodia, Fortunella, Orixa, Phellodendron, Poncirus, Ptelea, Ruta, Skimmia, Zanthoxylum

Cneoraceae
Cneorum

Simaroubaceae
Ailanthus, Picrasma

Meliaceae
Cedrela, Chuniodendron, Melia

3. Suborder: Polygalineae

Polygalaceae
Polygala

28. Order: **Sapindales**

1. Suborder: Coriariineae

Coriariaceae
Coriaria

2. Suborder: Anacardiineae

Anacardiaceae
Cotinus, Pistacia, Rhus, Schinus

3. Suborder: Sapindineae

Aceraceae

Acer, Dipteronia

Sapindaceae
  Alectryon, Dodonaea, Koelreuteria, Sapindus,
  Ungnadia, Xanthoceras

Hippocastanaceae
  Aesculus

Sabiaceae
  Meliosma

Melianthaceae
  Melianthus

30. Order: **Celastrales**

  1. Suborder: Celastrineae

  Cyrillaceae
    Cliftonia, Cyrilla

  Aquifoliaceae
    Ilex, Nemopanthus

  Corynocarpaceae
    Corynocarpus

  Celastraceae
    Celastrus, Euonymus, Maytenus, Pachistima,
    Tripterygium

  Staphyleaceae
    Euscaphis, Staphylea, Tapiscia

  Bischofiaceae
    Bischofia

  2. Suborder: Buxineae

  Buxaceae
    Buxus, Nothobuxus, Pachysandra, Sarcococca

  3. Suborder: Icacinineae

  Icacinaceae
    Villaresia

31. Order: **Rhamnales**

  Rhamnaceae
    Berchemia, Berchemiella, Ceanothus, Colletia,
    Discaria, Hovenia, Noltea, Oreoherzogia,
    Paliurus, Phylica, Pomaderris, Rhamnella,
    Rhamnus, Ziziphus

  Vitaceae
    Ampelopsis, Cissus, Parthenocissus, Vitis

32. Order: **Malvales**

  1. Suborder: Elaeocarpineae

  Elaeocarpaceae
    Aristotelia, Crinodendron, Elaeocarpus,
    Sloanea

  3. Suborder: Malvineae

  Tiliaceae
    Grewia, Sparmannia, Tilia

  Malvaceae
    Abutilon, Hibiscus, Hoheria, Lagunaria, Lava-

tera, Malvaviscus, Plagianthus, Sphaeralcea

Bombaceae
  Chorisia

Sterculiaceae
  Brachychiton, Dombeya, Firmiana, Fremento-
  dendron, Reevesia

34. Order: **Thymelaeales**

  Thymelaeaceae
    Dais, Daphne, Dirca, Edgeworthia, Ovidia,
    Stellera, Wikstroemia

  Elaeagnaceae
    Elaeagnus, Hippophae, Shepherdia

35. Order: **Violales**

  1. Suborder: Flacourtiineae

  Flacourtiaceae
    Azara, Berberidopsis, Carrierea, Idesia, Polio-
    thyrsis, Xylosma

  Violaceae
    Hymenanthera, Melicytus

  Stachyuraceae
    Stachyurus

  Passifloraceae
    Passiflora

  2. Suborder: Cistineae

  Cistaceae
    Cistus, Fumana, × *Halimocistus, Halimium,*
    Helianthemum, Hudsonia

  3. Suborder: Tamaricineae

  Tamaricaceae
    Myricaria, Reaumuria, Tamarix

  Frankeniaceae
    Frankenia

  4. Suborder: Caricineae

  Caricaceae
    Carica

36. Order: **Myrtiflorae**

  1. Suborder: Myrtineae

  Lythraceae
    Decodon, Heimia, Lagerstroemia

  Myrtaceae
    Acca, Callistemon, Calothamnus, Chamaelau-
    cium, Eucalyptus, Eugenia, Leptospermum,
    Melaleuca, Metrosideros, Myrtus, Psidium,
    Syzygium

  Punicaceae
    Punica

  Melastomataceae
    Tibouchina

  Onagraceae

Fuchsia, Zauschneria

37. Order: Umbelliflorae

Alangiaceae
Alangium

Nyssaceae
Camptotheca, Nyssa

Davidiaceae
Davidia

Cornaceae
Aucuba, Cornus, Corokia, Griselinia, Helwingia

Garryaceae
Garrya

Araliaceae
Acanthopanax, Aralia, Dendropanax, × Fatshedera, Fatsia, Hedera, Kalopanax, Neopanax, Nothopanax, Oplopanax, Pseudopanax, Schefflera, Tetrapanax

Trochodendraceae
Trochodendron

Umbelliferae
Aciphylla, Bupleurum

2. Subclass: SYMPETALAE

1. Order: Diapensiales

Diapensiaceae
Diapensia, Pyxidanthera

2. Order: Ericales

Clethraceae
Clethra

Pyrolaceae
Chimaphila

Ericaceae

I. Rhododendroideae
Andromeda, Botryostege, Bryanthus, Cladothamnus, Daboecia, Elliottia, Enkianthus, Kalmia, Kalmiopsis, × Ledodendron, Ledum, Leiophyllum, Loiseleuria, Menziesia, × Phylliopsis, Phyllodoce, × Phyllothamnus, Rhododendron, Rhodothamnus, Tripetaleia, Tsusiophyllum

II. Ericoideae
Bruckenthalia, Calluna, Cassiope, Erica, Pentapera

III. Vaccinioideae
Agapetes, Arbutus, Arcterica, Arctostaphylos, Cavendishia, Chamaedaphne, Chiogenes, × Gaulnettya, Gaultheria, Gaylussacia, Leucothoe, Lyonia, Oxydendrum, Pernettya, Pieris, Vaccinium, Zenobia

IV. Epigaeoideae
Epigaea, Orphanidesia

Empetraceae
Corema, Empetrum

Epacridaceae
Cyathodes, Dracophyllum, Epacris, Leucopogon, Richea

3. Order: Primulales

Myrsinaceae
Ardisia, Myrsine, Rapanea

4. Order: Plumbaginales

Plumbaginaceae
Acantholimon, Ceratostigma, Plumbago

Limoniaceae
Limoniastrum

5. Order: Ebenales

1. Suborder: Sapotineae

Sapotaceae
Argania, Bumelia

2. Suborder: Ebenineae

Ebenaceae
Disopyros

Styracaceae
Alniphyllum, Halesia, Huodendron, Pterostyrax, Rehderodendron, Sinojackia, Styrax

Symplocaceae
Symplocos

6. Order: Oleales

Oleaceae
Abeliophyllum, Chionanthus, Fontanesia, Forestiera, Forsythia, Fraxinus, Jasminum, Ligustrum, Notelaea, Olea

7. Order: Gentianales

Loganiaceae
Gelsemium

Desfontainiaceae
Desfontainia

Asclepiadaceae
Allamanda, Beaumontia, Carissa, Elytropus, Mandevilla, Nerium, Plumeria, Thevetia, Trachelospermum, Vinca

Asclepidiaceae
Araujia, Gomphocarpus, Marsdenia, Metaplexis, Oxypetalum, Stephanotis

Periplocaceae
Periploca

Rubiaceae
Bouvardia, Cephalanthus, Coprosma, Emmenopterys, Gardenia, Leptodermis, Luculia, Mitchella, Paederia, Pinckneya, Plocama, Serissa

8. Order: **Tubiflorae**

1. Suborder: Convolvulineae

Polemoniaceae
Cantua

Convolvulaceae
Convolvulus, Ipomoea

2. Suborder: Boraginineae

Boraginaceae
Lithodora, Lithospermum, Moltkia

Ehretiaceae
Ehretia

Hydrophyllaceae
Wigandia

3. Suborder: Verbenineae

Verbenaceae
Aloysia, Callicarpa, Caryopteris, Citharexylum, Clerodendron, Diostea, Duranta, Lantana, Petrea, Rhaphithamnus, Verbena, Vitex

Labiatae
Ballota, Colquhounia, Elsholtzia, Lavandula, Leonitis, Perovskia, Phlomis, Prostanthera, Rosmarinus, Sphacele, Teucrium, Westringia

4. Suborder: Solanineae

Solanaceae
Brunfelsia, Cestrum, Datura, Fabiana, Iochroma, Lycium, Nicotiana, Nierembergia, Solandra, Solanum, Streptosolen, Vestia

Buddleiaceae
Buddleia

Scrophulariaceae
Antirrhinum, Bowkeria, Calceolaria, Freylinia, Hebe, Isoplexis, Jovellana, Mimulus, Parahebe, Paulownia, Penstemon, Phygelius, Russelia, Verbascum

Globulariaceae
Globularia

Bignoniaceae
Anemopaegma, Bignonia, Campsis, Campsidium, Catalpa, Chilopsis, Clytostoma, Distictis, Doxantha, Eccremocarpus, Jacaranda, Pandorea, Phaedranthus, Pitecoctenium, Pleonotoma, Podranea, Pyrostegia, Spathodea, Tecoma, Tecomanthe, Tecomaria

Thunbergiaceae
Thunbergia

Acanthaceae
Adhatoda

Gesneriaceae
Asteranthera, Mitraria, Sarmienta

5. Suborder: Myoporineae

Myoporaceae
Myoporum

9. Order: **Plantaginales**

Plantaginaceae
Plantago

10. Order: **Dipsacales**

Caprifoliaceae
Abelia, Diervilla, Dipelta, Kolkwitzia, Leycesteria, Linnaea, Lonicera, Sambucus, Symphoricarpus, Viburnum, Weigela

11. Order: **Campanulales**

Compositae

1. Heliantheae
Iva

2. Astereae
Baccharis, Chrysothamnus, Grindelia, Haplopappus, Microglossa, Olearia, Pachystegia

3. Anthemideae
Artemisia, Chiliotrichum, Chrysanthemum, Hertia, Santolina

4. Inuleae
Asteriscus, Cassinia, Helichrysum, Pertya, Ozothamnus

5. Senecioneae
Brachyglottis, Euryops, Felicia, Senecio

6. Calenduleae
Osteospermum

7. Eupatorieae
Eupatorium

8. Mutisieae
Mutisia, Oldenburgia

2. CLASS: MONOCOTYLEDONEAE

3. Order: **Liliiflorae**

1. Suborder: Liliineae

Liliaceae
Aloe, Asparagus, Asteiia, Smilax, Yucca

Xanthorrhoeaceae
Xanthorrhoea

Agavaceae
Agave, Beschorneria, Cordyline, Dasylirion, Dracaena, Nolina, Phormium

Ruscaceae
Danae, Ruscus

Philesiaceae
Lapageria, Luzuriaga, × Philageria, Philesia

5. Order: **Bromeliales**
Bromeliaceae
Puya

6. Order: **Commelinales**

  3 Suborder: Restionales

    Restionaceae
      Restio

7. Order: **Graminales**

    Gramineae
      Arundinaria, Arundo, Chusquea, Phyllo-
      stachys, Pseudosasa, Semiarundinaria,
      Shibataea, Sinarundinaria

8. Order: **Principes**

    Palmae (= Palmaceae)

Butia, Chamaerops, Erythea, Jubaea, Phoenix,
Roystonea, Sabal, Trachycarpus,
Washingtonia

11. Order: **Pandanales**

    Pandanaceae
      Pandanus

13. Order: **Scitamineae**

    Musaceae
      Musa

    Strelitziaceae
      Strelitzia

Alphabetical List of the Families with their Genera

Acanthaceae
Adhatoda

Aceraceae
Acer
Dipteronia

Actinidiaceae
Actinidia
Clematoclethra

Agavaceae
Agave
Beschorneria
Cordyline
Dasylirion
Dracaena
Nolina
Phormium

Alangiaceae
Alangium

Anacardiaceae
Cotinus
Pistacia
Rhus
Schinus

Annonaceae
Annona
Asimina

Apocynaceae
Allamanda
Beaumontia
Carissa
Elytropus
Mandevilla
Nerium
Plumeria
Thevetia
Trachelospermum
Vinca

Aquifoliaceae
Ilex
Nemopanthus

Araliaceae
Acanthopanax
Aralia
Dendropanax
× Fatshedera
Fatsia
Hedera
Kalopanax
Neopanax
Nothopanax
Oplopanax
Pseudopanax
Schefflera
Tetrapanax
Trochodendron

Aristolochiaceae
Aristolochia

Asclepiadaceae
Araujia
Gomphocarpus
Marsdenia
Metaplexis
Oxypetalum
Stephanotis

Atherospermataceae
Atherosperma
Laurelia

Bambusaceae
→ **Gramineae**

Baueraceae
Bauera

Berberidaceae
Berberis
× Mahoberberis
Mahonia

Betulaceae
Alnus
Betula

Bignoniaceae
Anemopaegma
Bignonia
Campsis
Campsidium
Catalpa
Chilopsis
Clytostoma
Distictis
Doxantha
Eccremocarpus
Jacaranda
Pandorea
Phaedranthus
Pitecoctenium
Pleonotoma
Podranea
Pyrostegia
Spathodea
Tecoma
Tecomanthe
Tecomaria

Bischofiaceae
Bischofia

Bombaceae
Chorisia

Boraginaceae
Lithodora
Lithospermum
Moltkia

Bromeliaceae
Puya

Buddleiaceae
Buddleia

Buxaceae
Buxus
Nothobuxus
Pachysandra
Sarcococca

Calycanthaceae
Calycanthus
Chimonanthus

Capparidaceae
Capparis

Caprifoliaceae
Abelia
Diervilla
Dipelta
Kolkwitzia
Leycesteria
Linnaea
Lonicera
Sambucus
Symphoricarpos
Viburnum
Weigela

Caricaceae
Carica

Caryophyllaceae
Drypis

Casuarinaceae
Casuarina

Celastraceae
Celastrus
Euonymus
Maytenus
Pachistima
Tripterygium

Cercidiphyllaceae
Cercidiphyllum

Chenopodiaceae
Atriplex
Camphorosma
Eurotia
Haloxylon
Suaeda

Chloranthaceae
Chloranthus

Cistaceae
Cistus
Fumana
× Halimiocistus
Halimium
Helianthemum
Hudsonia

Clethraceae
Clethra

Cneoraceae
Cneorum

Compositae
Artemisia
Asteriscus
Baccharis
Brachyglottis
Cassinia
Chiliotrichum
Chrysanthemum
Chrysothamnus
Eupatorium
Euryops
Grindelia
Felicia
Haplopappus
Helichrysum
Hertia
Iva
Microglossa
Mutisia
Oldenburgia
Olearia
Osteospermum
Ozothamnus
Pachystegia
Pertya
Santolina
Senecio

Convolvulaceae
Convolvulus
Ipomoea

Coriariaceae
Coriaria

Cornaceae
Aucuba
Cornus
Corokia
Griselinia
Helwingia

Corylaceae
Carpinus
Corylus
Ostrya
Ostryopsis

Corynocarpaceae
Corynocarpus

Crassulaceae
Sedum

Cruciferae
Aethionema
Alyssum
Aurinia
Iberis
Ptilotrichum
Vella

Cunoniaceae
Caldcluvia
Cunonia
Weinmannia

Cyatheaceae
Cyathea
Dicksonia

Cycadaceae
Cycas

Cyrillaceae
Cliftonia
Cyrilla

Daphniphyliaceae
Daphniphyllum

Davidiaceae
Davidia

Desfontainiaceae
Desfontainia

Diapensiaceae
Diapensia
Pyxidanthera

Dilleniaceae
Hibbertia

Ebenaceae
Diospyros

Ehretiaceae
Ehretia

Elaeagnaceae
Elaeagnus
Hippophae
Shepherdia

Elaeocarpaceae
Aristotelia
Crinodendron
Elaeocarpus
Sloanea

Empetraceae
Corema
Empetrum

Epacridaceae
Cyathodes
Dracophyllum
Epacris
Leucopogon
Richea

Ericaceae
Agapetes
Andromeda
Arbutus
Arcterica
Arctostaphylos
Arctous
Bejaria
Botryostege
Bruckenthalia
Bryanthus
Calluna
Cassiope
Cavendishia
Chamaedaphne
Chiogenes
Cladothamnus
Daboecia
Elliottia
Enkianthus
Epigaea
Erica
× Gaulnettya
Gaultheria
Gaylussacia
Kalmia
Kalmia
× Rhododendron
Kalmiopsis
× Ledodendron
Ledum
Leiophyllum
Leucothoe
Loiseleuria
Lyonia
Orphanidesia
Oxydendrum
Menziesia
Pentapera
Pernettya
× Phylliopsis
Phyllodoce
× Phyllothamnus
Pieris
Rhododendron
Rhodothamnus
Tripetaleia
Tsusiophyllum
Vaccinium
Zenobia

Escalloniaceae
Anopterus
Escallonia

Eucommiaceae
Eucommia

Eucryphiaceae
Eucryphia

Euphorbiaceae
Acalypha
Aleurites
Andrachne
Codiaeum
Euphorbia
Glochidion
Mallotus
Ricinus
Sapium
Securinega

Eupteleaceae
Euptelea

Fagaceae
Castanea
Castanopsis
Chrysolepis
Fagus
Lithocarpus
Nothofagus
Quercus

Flacourtiaceae
Azara
Berberidopsis
Carrierea
Idesia
Poliothyrsis
Xylosma

Frankeniaceae
Frankenia

Garryaceae
Garrya

Gesneriaceae
Asteranthera
Mitraria
Sarmienta

Globulariaceae
Globularia

Gramineae
Arundinaria
Arundo
Chusquea
Phyllostachys
Pseudosasa
Sasa
Semiarundinaria
Shibataea
Sinarundinaria

Greyaceae
Greya
Guttiferae
→ **Hypericaceae**

Hamamelidaceae
Corylopsis
Distylium
Disanthus
Fortunearia
Fothergilla
Hamamelis
Liquidambar
Loropetalum
Parrotia
Parrotiopsis
Sinowilsonia
× Sycoparrotia
Sycopsis

Hippocastanaceae
Aesculus

Hydrangeaceae
Decumaria
Hydrangea
Pileostegia
Platycrater
Schizophragma

Hydrophyllaceae
Wigandia

Hypericaceae
Ascyrum
Hypericum

Icacinaceae
Villaresia

Illiciaceae
Illicium

Iteaceae
Itea

Juglandaceae
Carya
Juglans
Platycarya
Pterocarya

Labiatae
Ballota
Colquhounia
Elsholtzia
Lavandula
Leonitis
Perovskia
Phlomis
Prostanthera
Rosmarinus
Sphacele
Teucrium
Westringia

Lardizabalazeae
Akebia
Decaisnea
Holboellia
Lardizabala
Stauntonia
Sinofranchetia

Lauraceae
Actinodaphne
Apollonias
Cinnamomum
Laurus
Lindera
Litsea
Machilus
Neolitsea
Ocotea
Persea
Phoebe
Sassafras
Umbellularia

Leguminosae
Acacia
Adenocarpus
Albizia
Alhagi
Amicia
Ammodendron
Amorpha
Anagyris
Anthyllis
Argyrolobium
Astragalus
Bauhinia
Caesalpinia
Calicotome
Calliandra
Calophaca
Campylotropis
Caragana
Carmichaelia
Cassia
Ceratonia
Cercidium
Cercis
Cladrastis
Clianthus
Colutea
Corallospartium
Coronilla
Cytisus
Delonix
Desmodium
Dorycnium
Erinacea
Erythrina
Genista
Gleditsia
Gymnocladus
Halimodendron

Hedysarum
Indigofera
Kennedia
+ Laburnocytisus
Laburnum
Lespedeza
Lupinus
Maackia
Medicago
Notospartium
Ononis
Parkinsonia
Petteria
Piptanthus
Podalyria
Prosopis
Psoralea
Pueraria
Robinia
Sesbania
Sophora
Sutherlandia
Templetonia
Tipuana
Ulex
Wisteria

Leitneriaceae
Leitneria

Liliaceae
Aloe
Asparagus
Astelia
Smilax
Yucca

Limoniaceae
Limoniastrum

Linaceae
Linum

Loganiaceae
Gelsemium

Loranthaceae
Loranthus
Viscum

Lythraceae
Decodon
Heimia
Lagerstroemia

Magnoliaceae
Aromadendron
Liriodendron
Magnolia
Manglietia
Michaelia

Malvaceae
Abutilon
Hibiscus

Hoheria
Lagunaria
Lavatera
Malvaviscus
Plagianthus
Sphaeralcea

Melastomataceae
Tibouchina

Meliaceae
Cedrela
Chuniodendron
Melia

Melianthaceae
Melianthus

Menispermaceae
Calycocarpum
Cocculus
Menispermum
Sinomenium

Monimiaceae
Peumus

Moraceae
Broussonetia
Cudrania
Ficus
Maclura
× Macludrania
Morus

Musaceae
Musa

Myoporaceae
Myoporum

Myricaceae
Comptonia
Myrica

Myrsinaceae
Ardisia
Myrsine
Rapanea

Myrtaceae
Acca
Callistemon
Calothamnus
Chamaelaucium
Eucalyptus
Eugenia
Leptospermum
Melaleuca
Metrosideros
Myrtus
Psidium
Syzygium

Nandinaceae
Nandina

Nyctaginaceae
Bougainvillea

Nyssaceae
Camptotheca
Nyssa

Ochnaceae
Ochna

Oleaceae
Abeliophyllum
Chionanthus
Fontanesia
Forestiera
Forsythia
Fraxinus
Jasminum
Ligustrum
Notelaea
Olea
Osmanthus
× Osmarea
Parasyringa
Phillyrea
Syringa

Onagraceae
Fuchsia
Zauschneria

Paeoniaceae
Paeonia

Palmea (Palmaceae)
Butia
Chamaerops
Erythea
Jubaea
Phoenix
Roystonea
Sabal
Trachycarpus
Washingtonia

Pandanaceae
Pandanus

Papaveraceae
Dendromecon

Passifloraceae
Passiflora

Periplocaceae
Periploca

Philadelphaceae
Carpenteria
Deutzia
Fendlera
Fendlerella
Jamesia
Philadelphus

Philesiaceae
Lapageria
Luzuriaga
× Philageria
Philesia

Phytolaccaceae
Ercilla
Phytolacca

Pittosporaceae
Billardiera
Bursaria
Hymenosporum
Pittosporum
Sollya

Plantaginaceae
Plantago

Platanaceae
Platanus

Plumbaginaceae
Acantholimon
Ceratostigma
Plumbago

Polemoniaceae
Cantua

Polygalaceae
Polygala

Polygonaceae
Atraphaxis
Brunnichia
Calligonum
Homalocladium
Muehlenbeckia
Polygonum
Rumex

Proteaceae
Banksia
Dryandra
Embothrium
Gevuina
Grevillea
Hakea
Leucadendron
Leucospermum
Lomatia
Protea
Stenocarpus
Telopea

Punicaceae
Punica

Pyrolaceae
Chimaphila

Ranunculaceae
Clematis
Xanthorrhiza

Restionaceae
Restio

Rhamnaceae
Berchemia
Berchemiella
Ceanothus
Colletia
Discaria
Hovenia
Noltea
Oreoherzogia
Paliurus
Phylica
Pomaderris
Rhamnella
Rhamnus
Ziziphus

Rhodoleiaceae
Rhodoleia

Rosaceae
Adenostoma
Amelanchier
× Amelasorbus
Aronia
Cercocarpus
Chamaebatia
Chamaebatiaria
Chaenomeles
Coleogyne
Cotoneaster
Cowania
+ Crataegomespilus
Crataegus
× Crataemespilus
Cydonia
Dichotomanthes
Docynia
Dryas
Eriobotrya
Exochorda
Fallugia
Holodiscus
Kerria
Lindleya
Luetkea
Lyonothamnus
Maddenia
Malus
Margyrocarpus
Mespilus
Neillia
Neviusia
Osmaronia
Osteomeles
Pentactina
Peraphyllum
Petrophytum
Photinia
Physocarpus

Polylepis
Potentilla
Poterium
Prinsepia
Prunus
Pseudocydonia
Purshia
Pyracantha
× Pyracomeles
× Pyrocydonia
× Pyronia
Pyrus
Rhaphiolepis
Rhodotypos
Rosa
Rubus
Sibiraea
Sorbaria
× Sorbaronia
× Sorbocotoneaster
× Sorbopyrus
Sorbus
Spiraea
Stephanandra
Stranvaesia

Rubiaceae
Bouvardia
Cephalanthus
Coprosma
Emmenopterys
Gardenia
Leptodermis
Luculia
Mitchella
Paederia
Pinckneya
Plocama
Serissa

Ruscaceae
Danae
Ruscus

Rutaceae
Acradenia
Adenandra
Barosma
Boenninghausenia
Calodendrum
× Citrofortunella
× Citroncirus
Citrus
Choisya
Coleonema
Correa
Euodia
Fortunella
Orixa
Phellodendron
Poncirus
Ptelea

Ruta
Skimmia
Zanthoxylum

Sabiaceae
Meliosma

Salicaceae
Chosenia
Populus
Salix

Santalaceae
Buckleya
Osyris
Pyrularia

Sapindaceae
Alectryon
Dodonaea
Koelreuteria
Sapindus
Ungnadia
Xanthoceras

Sapotaceae
Argania
Bumelia

Sargentodoxaceae
Sargentodoxa

Saxifragaceae
Ribes

Schisandraceae
Kadsura
Schisandra

Scrophulariaceae
Antirrhinum
Bowkeria
Calceolaria
Freylinia
Hebe
Isoplexis
Jovellana
Mimulus
Parahebe
Paulownia
Penstemon
Phygelius
Russelia
Verbascum

Simaroubaceae
Ailanthus
Picrasma

Solanaceae
Brunfelsia
Cestrum
Datura
Fabiana
Iochroma
Lycium

Nicotiana
Nierembergia
Solandra
Solanum
Streptosolen
Vestia

Stachyuraceae
Stachyurus

Staphylaceae
Euscaphis
Staphylea
Tapiscia

Sterculiaceae
Brachychiton
Dombeya
Firmiana
Fremontodendron
Reevesia

Strelitziaceae
Strelitzia

Styracaceae
Alniphyllum
Halesia
Huodendron
Pterostyrax
Rehderodendron
Sinojackia
Styrax

Symplocaceae
Symplocos

Tamaricaceae
Myricaria
Reaumuria
Tamarix

Tetracentraceae
Tetracentron

Theaceae
Camellia
Cleyera
Eurya
Franklinia
Gordonia
Schima
Stewartia
Ternstroemia
Yunnanea

Thunbergiaceae
Thunbergia

Thymelaeaceae
Dais
Daphne
Dirca
Edgeworthia
Ovidia
Stellera
Wikstroemia

Tiliaceae
Grewia
Sparmannia
Tilia

Trochodendraceae
Trochodendron

Ulmaceae
Aphananthe
Celtis
Hemiptelea
Planera
Pteroceltis
Trema
Ulmus
Zelkova

Umbelliferae
Aciphylla
Bupleurum

Urticaceae
Boehmeria
Gesnouinia

Verbenaceae
Aloysia
Callicarpa
Caryopteris
Citharexylum
Clerodendron
Diostea
Duranta
Lantana
Petrea
Rhaphithamnus
Verbena
Vitex

Violaceae
Hymenanthera
Melicytus

Vitaceae
Ampelopsis
Cissus
Parthenocissus
Vitis

Winteraceae
Drymis
Pseudowintera

Xanthorrhoeaceae
Xanthorrhoea

Zamiaceae
Encephalartos

Zygophyllaceae
Nitraria

Index to the Botanical Authors and Horticulturists
(Arranged by their abbreviated names)

(Included are primarily authors of dendrologic works and the more prominent hybridizers.)

A. Br., see Braun, Alexander Karl Heinrich.

Abrams—LeRoy Abrams, 1874–1956, American botanist; wrote the 4 volume *Illustrated Flora of the Pacific States.*

Adam—Jean-Louis Adam, 1777–1830, nurseryman in Vitry, near Paris; known for originating the grafted chimera *Laburnocytisus adami* in 1825.

Adans.—Michel Adanson, 1727–1806, French botanist and zoologist; after whom the genus *Adansonia* was named.

A. DC., see De Candolle, Alphonse.

Ahrendt—Leslie Walter Allan Ahrendt, born in 1903, English clergyman and botanist; wrote a revision of the genera *Berberis* and *Mahonia* in 1961.

Airy Shaw—see Shaw, Herbert Kenneth Airy.

Ait.—William Aiton, 1731–1793, director of the Royal Botanic Gardens, Kew, England; wrote *Hortus Kewensis;* one of the more famous botanists of his time.

Ait. f.—William Townsend Aiton (the son), 1766–1849, English gardener; succeeded his father at Kew Gardens; wrote the 2nd edition of *Hortus Kewensis.*

Aitch.—James Edward Tierney Aitchinson, 1836–1898, English plant collector in Asia; later director of Kew Gardens.

Allan—Henry Howard Allan, 1882–1957, New Zealand botanist; wrote *Flora of New Zealand.*

Alphand—Jean Charles Adolphe Alphand, 1817–1891, French garden architect during the Kaiser Realm [1871–1918].

Alschinger—Andreas Alschinger, 1781–1864, Austrian schoolteacher in Vienna, later in Zara, Dalmatia (Yugoslavia); wrote a *Flora Jadrensis.*

Ambrózy—Count Stephan Ambrózy-Migazzi, 1869–1933, Hungarian dendrologist and proprietor of the Mlynany Arboretum in Slowakei, Czechoslovakia [earlier Malonya, Hungary].

Anders., T.—Thomas Anderson, 1832–1870, born in Scotland; director of the Botanic Gardens in Calcutta, India.

Anderss.—Nils Johan Andersson, 1821–1880, professor of botany in the National Museum in Stockholm, Sweden; specialist in *Salix* and the flora of Lapland.

Andr.—Henry C. Andrews, 1752–1828, English botanist and flower painter, illustrator of famous plates of African Erica, geranium and roses; published the *Botanist's Repository*, London.

André—Edouard André, 1840–1911, French gardener; first publisher of the *Revue Horticole* in Paris.

Ant.—Franz Antoine, 1815–1866, director of the Imperial Gardens in Vienna-Shönbrunn, Austria.

Arends—Georg Arends, 1863–1951, German gardener in Wuppertal-Ronsdorf; developed many new herbaceous plants and *Rhododendron.*

Armstr.—John B. Armstrong, 1850–1926, New Zealand botanist born in England; wrote about New Zealand plants.

Arn.—George Arnold Walker Arnott, 1799–1868, Scottish botanist; director of the botanic gardens in Glasgow.

Aschers.—Paul Friedrich August Ascherson, 1834–1913, German botanist; curator of the Botanical Museum in Berlin; collaborated with Engler and Prantl on *Die natürlichen Pflanzenfamilien.*

Aschers. & Graebn., see under both names.

Ashe—William Willard Ashe, 1872–1932, North American botanist; specialist in *Crataegus.*

Aubl.—Jean Baptiste Christophe Aublet, 1720–1778, French botanist and pharmacist; wrote about the plants of French Guiana.

Audib.—Audibert Frères, between 1810–1830, proprietor of a well-known nursery in Tonelle, near Tarascon, France.

Baas-Beck.—Louise Henriette Baas-Becking, Dutch botanist; concentrated on *Ulmus.*

Bab.—Charles Cardale Babington, 1808–1895, English professor of botany, wrote a *Manual of British Botany.*

Bachelier was a poplar hybridizer in Chateauroux, France; the *Populus* 'Bachelieri' was named for him.

Backhouse—James Backhouse, 1794–1869, founder of a nursery in York, England, well-known for its winter hardy selections of *Erica.*

Bailey—Liberty Hyde Bailey, 1858–1954, professor of botany in the USA; author of many botanical and gardening works including the *Standard Cyclopedia of Horticulture* and *Manual of Cultivated Plants.*

Baill.—Henri Ernest Baillon, 1827–1895, French doctor and botanist, Paris; wrote a 13 volume *Histoire des Plantes* and an *Iconographie de la Flore Française.*

Baker—John Gilbert Baker, 1834–1920, curator of the Kew Herbarium; wrote primarily about tropical plant genera.

Baker, R. T.—R. T. Baker, Australian botanist, 1854–1949; published in 1910 with H. G. Smith, *A research of the Pines of Australia.*

Bal. — Benedicte Balansa, 1825–1891, French botanist.

Balf. — John Hutton Balfour, 1808–1884, Scottish doctor and botanist; director of the Royal Botanic Gardens, Edinburgh; wrote about the plants of the Bible, among others.

Balf. f. — 1853–1922, son of the preceding, professor of botany in Glasgow, then Oxford and Edinburgh; specialist in *Rhododendron* and *Primula*.

Banks — Sir Joseph Banks, 1743–1820, president of the Royal Society in London, from 1772–1820 the director of Kew Gardens; instrumental in the production of *Illustrations of the Botany of Captain Cook's voyage round the world*, etc.

Banks & Soland. — see under both names.

Barbier — Barbier & Fils, 1845–1931, nursery in Orléans, France.

Barratt — Joseph Barratt, 1796–1882, American botanist; specialist in *Salix*.

Bartl. — Friedrich Gottlieb Bartling, 1798–1875, professor of botany and director of the Göttingen Botanic Gardens, W. Germany.

Bartr. — John Bartram, 1739–1823, North American botanist in Pennsylvania; founded the first botanic garden in North America at Kingsessing, Pa., near Philadelphia.

Batal. — Alexander Batalin, 1847–1896, Russian botanist at the St. Petersburg Botanic Garden [Leningrad today].

Batsch — August Johann Georg Karl Batsch, 1761–1802, professor of natural history in Jena, E. Germany and the director of the botanic gardens; author of a number of botany texts.

Batt. — Jules Aimé Battandier, 1848–1922, French doctor and botanist in Algeria; wrote a *Flore d'Alger* including an atlas together with Trabut.

Baudrill. — Baudrillart, French authority on forestry subjects, wrote around 1825.

Baumann — The brother of Charles A. (born ?) and Constantin Auguste Napoléon Baumann, 1804–1884; of a French-German nursery in Bollweiler, Alsace; published *Les Camellias de Bollweiler*, etc.

Baumg. — Johann Christoph Gottlob Baumgarten, 1765–1843, German botanist, born in Lusatia, E. Germany; wrote *Verzeichnis der Pflanzen Transsilvaniens*, etc.

Bausch — Jan Bausch, born in 1917, Dutch botanist; wrote a revision of the Eucryphiaceae.

Beauv. — Ambroise Marie Francois Joseph Palisot de Beauvois, 1752–1820, French botanist and explorer; specialist in the mosses and grasses as well as African flora.

Bean — William Jackson Bean, 1863–1947, Curator of Kew Gardens, London; author of several dendrology works of which the most popular is the 3 volume *Trees and Shrubs hardy in the British Isles*, in its 8th edition since 1973 and now in 4 volumes.

Beadle — Chauncey Delos Beadle, 1866–1950, North American botanist and director of the Biltmore Herbarium in North Carolina.

Bebb — Michael Schuck Bebb, 1833–1895, American botanist and plant collector.

Becc. — Odoardo Beccari, 1843–1920, Italian botanist; specialist in palms.

Bechst. — Johann Matthäus Bechstein, 1757–1822, director of the Dreissigacker Forestry Academy, near Meiningen, E. Germany; wrote a forestry botany.

Beck — Günther Beck from Managetta and Lerchenau, 1856–1931, Austrian-Czechoslovakian botanist; director of the Botanic Garden at the German University in Prague; author of a flora of Bosnia and Herzegowina, etc.

Behnsch — Reinhold Behnsch, nursery in Duerrgoy, near Breslau [now Wroclaw, Poland] (firm no longer in existence).

Beij. — Willem B. Beijerinck, 1891–1960, Dutch botanist; specialist in *Calluna*.

Beissn. — Ludwig Beissner, 1843–1927, Inspector at the Botanic Garden in Bonn, W. Germany; co-founder of the Deutschen Dendrologischen Gesellschaft [German Dendrological Soc.]; wrote *Handbuch der Nadelholzkunde*.

Benth. — George Bentham, 1800–1884, one of the more prominent English botanists; president of the Linnean Society; wrote *Genera Plantarum* together with Hooker.

Benth. et Hook. — see under both names.

Bercht. — Count Friedrich von Berchtold, 1781–1876, Austrian botanist; traveled in South America, wrote an *Economic-technical Flora of Bohemia*.

Berg — Otto Karl Berg, 1815–1866, German pharmacist and botanist, in Berlin; wrote, among other works, an *Anatomischen Atlas zur pharmazeutischen Waarenkunde*.

Berl. — Jean Louis Berlandier, 1805–1851, Swiss botanist from Geneva; explored Texas, and Mexico where he died, wrote on the Saxifragaceae and Grossularieae, etc.

Bernh. — Johann Jakob Bernhardi, 1774–1850, professor of botany in Erfurt; wrote a botany text, etc.

Bert. — Carlo Guiseppe Bertero, 1789–1831, Italian doctor, botanist and plant collector from Torino; discovered many plants in South America; drowned on a trip between Chile and Tahiti.

Bertin — Pierre Bertin, 1800–1891, proprietor of a nursery in France.

Bertol. — Antonio Bertolini, 1775–1869, professor of botany in Bologna, Italy; wrote a 10 volume flora of Italy.

Bess. — Willibald Swibert Joseph Gottlieb von Besser, Austrian professor in Lvov, and Krakow [Poland] and Wilna [USSR], later a Russian advisor and professor of botany in Kiev, Ukraine; specialist in *Artemisia*.

Bge. — see Bunge.

Bieb. — Friedrich August Marschall von Bieberstein, 1786–1826, born in Stuttgart, German-Russian botanist, later a Russian advisor; traveled in the Caucasus and Taurus, wrote a flora of that region.

Bigel. — Jacob Bigelow, 1787–1879, professor of botany and pharmacology in Boston, Mass., USA; wrote an *American Medical Botany*.

Bignon — Abbé Jean Paul Bignon, 1662–1743, French clergyman and scholar in St. Quentin.

Billard — L. C. B. Billard, French nursery from 1860–1870 in Fontenay-aux-Roses, near Paris; specializing in *Spiraea*.

Bitt. — Friedrich August Georg Bitter, 1873–1927, German botanist; wrote a *Monograph of the genus* Acaena.

Bl. — Carl Ludwig Blume, 1796–1862, born in Braunschweig [formerly central Germany], founded the National Herbarium in Leiden, Netherlands; wrote a *Flora Javae*, also wrote on *Magnolia* and contributed to *Flora von Niederlandisch Indien* [Dutch Indies].

Blackburn — Benjamin Coleman Blackburn, born in 1908, American botanist; wrote on the magnolias.

Blake — Sidney Fay Blake, 1892–1959, American botanist in Maryland; specialist for the American Compositae and Polygalaceae; wrote the very significant work, *Geographical Guide to Floras of the World*.

Blakely — William Faris Blakely, 1875–1941, Australian botanist; *Eucalyptus* authority.

Blanch. — William Henry Blanchard, 1850–1922, teacher in Vermont, USA; specialist in *Rubus* of the USA and Canada.

Blytt — Matthias Numsen Blytt, 1789–1862, curator of the Botanical Museum in Christiania [Oslo], Norway; wrote a *Norsk Flora*.

Boehmer — Louis Boehmer, owner of a German export nursery in Japan from 1882–1908.

Boenn. — Clemens Maria Friedrich von Boenninghausen, 1785–1864, Privy Councillor, doctor and director of the Münster Botanic Gardens, Germany.

Bois — Désiré Jean George Marie Bois, 1856–1946, dendrologist and editor of the *Revue Horticole* in Paris; wrote *Fruticetum Vilmorinianum*, etc.

Boiss. — Edmond Pierre Boissier, 1810–1885, Swiss naturalist, born in Geneva; wrote *Flora Orientalis, Icones Euphorbiarum*, a *Monographe der Plumbaginaceae*, etc.

Bolle — Carl August Bolle, 1821–1909, dendrologist and independent scholar on Scharfenberg Island near Berlin-Tegel, Germany.

Bong. — August Heinrich Gustav von Bongard, 1786–1839, born in Germany, a botanist, later a Russian Privy Councillor in St. Petersburg [now Leningrad]; compiled a flora of Russia.

Bonpl. — Aimé Jacques Alexandre Bonpland (known as Larousse, a pseudonym for Aimé Goujad), 1773–1858, French traveling companion of A. von Humboldt; later director of the Imperial Gardens of Malmaison; professor in Buenos Aires in 1818; died in Santa Ana Corrientes, Argentina.

Boom — Boudewijn Karel Boom, born in 1903, a Dutch botanist; wrote a 3 volume *Flora der Cultuurgewassen van Nederland*.

Booth — John Booth, 1836–1908, German gardener from Hamburg; his father, John Richmond Booth (1799–1847), immigrated from England and started a very famous nursery in Hamburg, W. Germany.

Borb. — Vincze tól Borbás, 1844–1905, Hungarian botanist; director of the Cluj Botanic Gardens, Rumania after 1902.

Borkh. — Moritz Balthasar Borkhausen, 1760–1806, officer at the Forestry College and public official in Darmstadt, W. Germany; wrote various works on forest botany.

Bornmuell. — Joseph Friedrich Nikolas Bornmueller, 1862–1948, professor of botany at Weimar, E. Germany; outstanding authority on the flora of the Mediterranean and the Orient, acquired from his extensive collecting trips into these regions.

Bosc. — Louis Augustin Guillaume Bosc, 1759–1828, French botanist; supervisor at the gardens and nursery of Versailles, and the Paris Botanic Garden; traveled in North America, wrote on *Quercus,* etc.

Bouleng. — Georges-Albert Boulenger, 1858–1937, Belgian botanist and zoologist; employed at the British Museum in London from 1882–1920, then at the Brussels Botanic Garden; wrote primarily on wild roses.

Boynt. — Frank Ellis Boynton, born in 1859, botanist at the Biltmore Herbarium in the USA; specialist in the flora of the southern Appalachians.

Br. A. — Alexander Karl Heinrich Braun, 1805–1877, born in Regensburg, German professor of botany; director of the Berlin Botanic Gardens after 1851.

Br. J. E. — John Ednie Brown, Australian botanist; wrote between the years 1869–1896.

Br. N. E. — Nicholas Edward Brown, 1849–1934, English botanist at Kew Gardens; author of many taxonomic works, particularly on succulents.

Br. R. — Robert Brown, 1773–1858, born in Scotland; 1801–1805 in Australia, later curator of the British Museum in London; one of the most famous of English botanists, wrote a flora of Australia.

Brand — August Brand, 1863–1931, German botanist; specialist in the Boraginaceae, etc.

Brandeg., K. — Mary Katherine Brandegee, 1844–1920, North American botanist; plant collector and spouse of the following.

Brandeg., T. S. — Townshend Stith Brandegee, 1843–1925, North American botanist; collected primarily in California.

Brandis — (Sir) Dietrich Brandis, 1824–1907, German dendrologist from Bonn; worked for many years in India and wrote *The Forest Flora of North West and Central India.*

Bretschn. — Emil Vasiljevitsch Bretschneider, 1833–1901, embassy doctor in Peking and botanist; specialist in Chinese flora, wrote *Botanicon Sinicum* and *History of European botanical discoveries in China.*

Briot — Charles Briot, 1804–1888, French national nursery in Trianon near Paris.

Briq. — John Isaac Briquet, 1870–1931, Swiss botanist; director of the botanic gardens in Geneva, wrote on *Cytisus* and a *Prodromus de la Flore Corse.*

Britt. — Nathaniel Lord Britton, 1859–1934, North American geologist and botanist at Columbia University; director of the New York Botanical Garden; wrote (with A. Brown) *An illustrated Flora of the Northern States and Canada,* etc.

Brongn. — Adolphe Theodore Brongniard, 1801–1876, French professor of botany; wrote on the Rhamnaceae, otherwise on paleobotany.

Brot. — Felix da Silva Avelar Brotero, 1744–1828, professor of botany in Coimbra, Portugal; later director of the Royal Garden in Ajuda, Lisbon; wrote a *Phytographie Lusitaniae* and *Flora Lusitanica.*

Broussonet — 1761–1801, French doctor in Montpellier; later a professor of botany.

Buch.-Ham. — Francis Buchanan, later Lord Hamilton, 1762–1829, Scottish doctor and botanist; traveled in Nepal, director of the Botanic Gardens of Calcutta; wrote primarily on Indian plants.

Buchholz — John Theodore Buchholz, 1888–1951, American botanist; conifer specialist, from the University of Illinois.

Buckl. — Samuel Botsford Buckley, 1809–1884, North American botanist.

Buddle — Adam Buddle, 1660–1715, English botanist in London.

Buhse — Friedrich Alexander Buhse, 1821–1898, Latvian botanist from Riga; traveled with Boissier (see also).

Bunge — Alexander Andrejewitsch von Bunge, 1803–1890, Russian professor of botany from Kiev; later, director of the Dorpat Botanic Garden; traveled in central Asia and the Altai region, wrote a *Flora Altaica,* etc.

Bur. — Edouard Bureau, 1830–1918, professor of botany in Paris; wrote *Monographie des Bignoniacées,* etc.

Burgsd. — Friedrich August Ludwig von Burgsdorf, 1747–1802, professor of botany in Berlin and head forester; made an attempt at writing a complete history of the prominent woody species.

Burkw. — Arthur Burkwood, 1888–1951, co-owner of the English nursery, Burkwood & Skipwith, Kingston-on-Thames; introduced many new plants.

Burm. — Johannes Burman, 1707–1779, professor of botany in Amsterdam; wrote *Thesaurus Zeylanicus,* etc.

Burret — Carl Ewald Max Burret, 1883–1964, German botanist in Berlin; wrote on palms and Tiliaceae, traveled in Brazil.

Burvénich — Frédéric Burvénich, 1857–1917, Belgian gardener; wrote extensively in the *Revue Horticole Belge* between 1880–1902.

Bush — Benjamin Franklin Bush, 1858–1937, North American botanist.

Cabrera — Angel Lulio Cabrera, born 1908, Spanish botanist from Madrid; worked in Argentina.

Callier — Alfons Callier, 1866–1927, pharmacist and botanist in Carolath, Silesia; specialist in *Alnus.*

Cambage — Richard Hind Cambage, 1859–1928, Australian botanist.

C. A. Mey., see Carl Anton Meyer.

Cambess. — Jacques Cambessèdes, 1799–1863, French botanist; wrote a monograph of *Spiraea,* 1824.

Camus, A. — Aimée Antoinette Camus, 1879–1965, French botanist from Paris; wrote on the Gramineae, *Castanea, Cupressus,* orchids, *Salix* and a 6 volume monograph of the genus *Quercus.*

Camus, E. G. — Edmond Gustave Camus, 1852–1915, father of the previous Camus, French botanist and pharmacist; wrote on the bamboos, *Salix,* orchids, sometimes co-authoring with his daughter.

Cardot — Jules Cardot, 1860–1934, French botanist; wrote on the flora of Madagascar and on some of the Rosaceae.

Carr. — Elie Abel Carrière, 1816–1896, head gardener at the nursery of the Museum d'Histoire Naturelle (Jardin des Plantes) in Paris; wrote *Traité général des Conifères.*

Carruth. — William Carruthers, 1830–1922, English botanist and paleontologist.

Cass. — Alexandre Henri Gabriel Comte de Cassini, 1781–1831, French botanist in Paris.

Catesb. — Mark Catesby, 1682–1749, English botanist and traveler in the USA; wrote *Natural History of Carolina, Florida and the Bahama Islands.*

Cav. — Antonio José Cavanilles, 1745–1804, Spanish professor of botany in Madrid; wrote *Icones et descriptiones plantarum.*

Cavalerie — Pierre Julien Cavalerie, 1869–1927, French priest and botanist; lived in Yunnan Province, China from 1894 to his death.

Celak. — Ladislav Josef Celakovsky, 1834–1902, professor of botany in Prague, Czechoslovakia; wrote *Prodromus der Flora von Bohemia,* etc.

Cels — Jacques Philippe Martin Cels, 1743–1806, founded a nursery which was carried on by his descendants until 1888 in Montrouge near Paris; an arboretum was contained within the nursery.

Chaix — Dominique Chaix, 1731–1800, French abbott and botanist in Mont-Auroux; wrote on the plants of Dauphiné.

Cham. — Adelbert von Chamisso (actually Louis Charles Adelhaide Chamisso de Boncourt), 1781–1838, born in France, but lived in Germany from 1790 onwards, German writer, botanist and explorer; curator of the Botanical Museum of Berlin-Dahlem, wrote about his travels around the world.

Cham. et Schlecht., see under both names.

Chapm. — Alvan Wentworth Chapman, 1809–1899, American doctor and botanist in Florida; wrote on the flora of the southern United States.

Cheesem. — Thomas Frederick Cheeseman, 1846–1923, botanist from New Zealand; wrote *Manual of the New Zealand Flora.*

Chenault — Léon Chenault, 1853–1930, proprietor of a well-known nursery in Orléans, France; introduced many plants from East Asia (firm now out of existence).

Chéng — Wan-chün Chéng, born in 1903, Chinese botanist; wrote between 1930–1950 on the Chinese woody flora, particularly flora in the mountains of Szechwan and Sikang.

Chitt. — Frederic James Chittenden, 1873–1950, secretary of the Royal Horticultural Society in London, prominent plantsman; published the 4 volume *Dictionary of Gardening.*

Chmelar — Jindrich Chmelar, born in 1926, Czechoslovakian botanist in Brno; specialist in *Salix.*

Chois. — Jacques Denis Choisy, 1799–1859, Swiss clergyman and professor of philosophy in Geneva; wrote various monographs (Convolvulaceae, Selaginellaceae, *Hypericum,* and others).

Christ — Hermann Christ, 1833–1933, Swiss lawyer and botanist in Basel; authority on ferns and alpines; wrote *Monographie der schweizer Wild-Rosen.*

Chun — Woon-young Chun, born in 1894, Chinese botanist; wrote since 1922 on the Betulaceae, Juglandaceae, flora of Kwangtung, etc.

Clarke, C. B. — Charles Baron Clarke, 1832–1908, English botanist; wrote on the Commeliaceae, Cyperaceae, etc.

Clarke — W. B. Clarke, nursery in San Jose, California; known for his many hybrids of *Chaenomeles,* etc.

Clementi — Guiseppe Clementi, 1812–1873, Italian botanist from Turin.

Cock. — Leonard C. Cockayne, 1855–1934, English botanist; lived in New Zealand after 1881 and wrote *The vegetation of New Zealand, The trees of New Zealand,* and other works.

Cockerell — Theodore Dru Alison Cockerell, 1866–1948, born in England, botanized in the USA.

Col. — William Colenso, 1811–1899, English clergyman and botanist; lived in New Zealand after 1834.

Colla — Luigi Aloysius Colla, 1766–1848, Italian botanist from Turin.

Comber — Harold Frederick Comber, born in 1897, English gardener and plant collector; traveled primarily in South America and Tasmania.

Coss. — Ernest Saint-Charles Cosson, 1819–1889, French doctor and botanist, explorer; wrote on the plants of North America.

Coste — Hippolyte Jacques Coste, 1858–1924, French minister and botanist.

Cottet — Michel Cottet, 1825–1896, clergyman in Gruyères, Canton Frieburg, Switzerland.

Coutinho — Miguel Pereiro Coutinho, born 1915, Portuguese botanist from Lisbon.

Cov. — Frederik Vernon Coville, 1867–1937, American botanist.

Cowan — John MacQueen Cowan, Scottish botanist; specialist in *Rhododendron.*

Craib — William Grant Craib, 1882–1933, English botanist; wrote on *Primula, Indigofera, Enkianthus* as well as the flora of Siam.

Crantz — Baron Heinrich Johann Nepomuk von Crantz, 1722–1799, born in Luxembourg, Austrian doctor and professor of botany in Vienna; adversary of Linnaeus.

Crép. — François Crépin, 1830–1903, Belgian botanist from Rochefort; later, director of the Brussels Botanic Garden; best authority of his time on wild roses, wrote *Primitiae Monographiae Rosarum.*

Cripps — Ph. Cripps, 1810–1888, English gardener.

Crisp — Sir Frank Crisp, 1843–1919, English gardener in Henley-on-Thames.

Cubitt — G. E. S. Cubitt, English plant collector in N. Burma.

Cunn. — Allan Cunningham, 1791–1839, born in England, botanized in New Zealand and Australia, died in Sydney.

Cunn, R. — Richard Cunningham, 1793–1835, brother of the previous, also botanized in Australia; director of the Sydney Botanical Gardens, was murdered on a plant expedition in Australia.

Curt. — Willam Curtis, 1746–1799, English pharmacist and botanist; first publisher of the modern *Botanical Magazine,* also wrote *Flora Londinensis,* etc.

Dalechamp — Jacob, 1513–1588, French doctor and botanist in Lyon.

Dallim. — William Dallimore, 1871–1959, English gardener and forester, eventually curator of the Kew Museum; wrote *Handbook of Coniferae.*

Dammer — Carl Lebrecht Udo Dammer, 1860–1920, German botanist; specialist in the palms and Polygonaceae at the Botanic Garden and Museum in Berlin.

Dandy — James Edgar Dandy, 1907–1976, English botanist; authority on the Magnoliaceae at the British Museum in London.

Dansereau — Pierre Dansereau, born in 1911, Canadian botanist from Quebec.

Davidson — Anstruther Davidson, 1860–1932, American botanist.

DC. — Augustin Pyramus De Candolle, 1778–1841, famous Swiss botanist, taxonomist from Geneva; wrote a 13 volume *Prodromus systematis naturalis regni vegetabilis,* etc.

DC. A. — Alphonse De Candolle, 1806–1893, son of the former, Swiss botanist; wrote *Monographie des Campanulacé*es, etc.

D. Don, see Don, D.

Debeaux — Jean Odon Debeaux, 1826–1910, French pharmacist and botanist; specialist in the flora of China.

Denhardt — Friedrich Denhardt, 1787–1870, German botanist in Nepal.

den Boer — Arie F. den Boer, 1898–1962, American gardener, born in Gouda, Holland; the best *Malus* authority of his time.

Decne. — Joseph Decaisne, 1807–1882, born in Brussels, Belgium, worked himself from a simple gardener to a professor of botany; active at the Jardin des Plantes in Paris, wrote *Le Jardin fruitier du Museum,* 7 volumes.

Delavay — Abbé Jean M. Delavay, 1838–1895, French missionary and plant collector in China.

Delile — Alire Raffenau Delile, 1778–1850, French

botanist; went to Egypt with Napoleon's campaign; later a professor at Montpellier; wrote a flora of Egypt.

Desbois — Fr. Desbois, 1827–1902, Belgian gardener.

Déséglise — Pierre-Alfred Déséglise, 1823–1883, French independent scholar; later lived in Geneva, Switzerland where he died; worked on the genus *Rosa* and others.

Desf. — René Louiche Desfontaines, 1750–1833, professor at the Jardin des Plantes in Paris, France; wrote *Flora Atlantica.*

Desp. — Narcisse Henry François Desportes, 1776–1856, French botanist, curator at the museum in Paris; wrote *Rosetum Gallicum.*

Desrouss. (Desr.) — Louis Auguste Joseph Desrousseaux, 1753–1838, French botanist; worked in Paris, colleague of Lamarck.

Desv. — Augustin Nicaise Desvaux, 1784–1856, professor of botany in Angers, France; wrote *Traité général de Botanique.*

Dieck — Georg Dieck, 1847–1925, German gardener and botanical explorer; founded a national arboretum in 1870 at Zöschen near Merseberg; collected plants primarily in the Caucasus and Siberia.

Diels — Friedrich Ludwig Emil Diels, 1874–1945, professor of botany and director of the Botanic Garden and Museum in Berlin-Dahlem, Germany; wrote *Flora von Zentral-China, Pflanzenwelt von West-Australien* and many significant monographic works.

Dierville — French surgeon and friend of Tournefort; traveled in Canada from 1699–1700.

Dietr. — Friedrich Gottlob Dietrich, 1765–1850, garden director in Eisenach, E. Germany; wrote a 10 volume *Lexikon der Gärtnerei und Botanik,* etc.

Dietr. D. — David Nathanael Friedrich Dietrich, 1799–1888, nephew of the previous, a prolific writer, botanist and gardener; curator of the Jena Botanic Garden; wrote a large number of floras and manuals.

Dipp. — Leopold Dippel, 1827–1914, born in the Palatinate region of SW. Germany, professor of botany and director of the Darmstadt Botanic Gardens; wrote a 3 volume *Handbuch der Laubholzkunde.*

Dirken — B. W. Dirken, Dutch gardener in Oudenbosch in the 19th century.

Dode — Louis-Albert Dode, 1875–1943, French attorney and botanist; specialist in *Populus, Juglans, Platanus, Sorbus,* etc.; longtime secretary of the Société Française de Dendrologie.

Doerfl. — Ignaz Doerfler, 1866–1950, curator of the Botanical Institute of Vienna, Austria; traveled in the Balkans and Crete, wrote *Botaniker-Adressbuch* [Botanists Directory], *Botaniker Porträts,* etc.

Don, D. — David Don, 1799–1841, librarian and professor of botany at the King's College in London,

England; wrote a flora of Nepal.

Don, G.—George Don, 1798–1856, brother of the previous, also a botanist, gardener and plant collector in London; wrote a monograph of the genus *Allium,* etc.

Donn—James Donn, 1758–1813, curator of the Cambridge Botanic Garden, England; published *Hortus Cantabrigiensis.*

Doorenb.—Simon Godfried Albert Doorenbos, born in 1892, garden director in The Hague, Holland; dendrologist, specialist in *Fraxinus, Ulmus, Malus, Symphoricarpos* and roses.

Dougl.—David Douglas, 1799–1834, famous Scottish plant collector; traveled in North America; died in an accident in Hawaii.

Druce—George Claridge Druce, 1850–1932, botanist and pharmacist in Oxford; published several plant lists and floras.

Drummond—J. Drummond, 1800–1863, Scottish botanist and traveler.

Dryander—Jonas Carlsson Dryander, 1748–1810, Swedish botanist from Göteborg, died in London.

Duchartre—Pierre Etienne Simon Duchartre, 1811–1894, French botanist in Paris; wrote a monograph of the Aristolochiaceae, *Élémens de Botanique,* etc.

Duham.—Henri Louis DuHamel de Monceau, 1700–1781, French naturalist and marine inspector; wrote *Traité des Arbres et Arbustes,* 7 volumes with many plates, the second edition is known as *Nouveau Duhamel.*

Dum.-Cours.—George Louis Marie DuMont de Courset, 1746–1824, French garden writer; wrote *Le Botaniste Cultivateur.*

Dumort.—Barthélemy Charles Dumortier, 1797–1878, president of the Belgian congress; wrote a Belgian flora, a monograph of the Belgian *Salix,* etc.

Dunn—Stephen Troyte Dunn, 1868–1939, English botanist at Kew; wrote 2 English floras.

Durand—Elias Magloire Durand, 1794–1873, American botanist from Philadelphia, Pennsylvania.

Durazz.—Antonio Ippolito Durazzini, 1750–1818, Italian botanist and doctor in Florence (listed as Ippolito Durazzo in the "Bio. Dict." of the Hunt Inst., 1972).

DuRoi or **Duroi**—Johann Philipp DuRoi, 1741–1785, German doctor in Braunschweig; occasional steward for the Count of Veltheim on Harbke near Helmstedt where he wrote *Harbkesche wilde Baumzucht.*

Duthie—John Firminger Duthie, 1845–1922, English botanist; wrote about the grasses of northwestern India, the orchids of the northwestern Himalayas; was also the director of the Botanical Gardens in Saharanpur, India.

Eastw.—Alice Eastwood, 1859–1953, American botanist in California; wrote *Handbook of the Trees of California.*

Eat.—Amos Eaton, 1776–1842, American botanist, professor in Albany, N.Y.; wrote *Manual of Botany for North America.*

Edgew.—Michale Pakenham Edgeworth, 1812–1881, from Ireland, an English civil servant and botanist in India; explored the flora of Bengal.

Edwards—Sydenham Teast Edwards, 1769–1819, botanical artist; primarily did work for the *Botanical Magazine* and *Botanical Register,* produced 2702 plates for the last 33 volumes.

Ehrenb.—Christian Gottfried Ehrenberg, 1795–1876, doctor and professor of botany in Berlin; traveled to Egypt and Arabia; wrote a microgeology and various botanical works.

Ehrh.—Friedrich Ehrhart, 1742–1775, Swiss by birth, but a pharmacist in Hannover, Stockholm and Uppsala; a student of Linnaeus and eventually the overseer at the Herrenhäuser Garden in Hannover.

Ell.—Stephen Elliot, 1771–1830, botanist in Charleston, S.C., USA; wrote a flora of South Carolina and Georgia.

Ellw.—Georg Ellwanger, 1816–1906, born in Württemberg, W. Germany, co-owner of the Mt. Hope Nursery (Ellwanger & Barry) in Rochester, N.Y., USA.

Elwes—Henry John Elwes, 1846–1922, English botanist, forester and plant collector; produced, along with Augustine Henry, the 7 volume plate work, *The Trees of Great Britain and Ireland.*

Elwes & Henry, see under both names.

Endl.—Stephan Ladislaus Endlicher, 1804–1849, born in Bratislava, Czechoslovakia, professor of botany and director of the Botanic Garden in Vienna, Austria; wrote *Synopsis Coniferarum,* etc.

Engelm.—Georg Engelmann, 1809–1884, born in Frankfurt, W. Germany, doctor, botanist and plant collector in St. Louis, USA; wrote on the Cactaceae, etc.

Engl.—Heinrich Gustav Adolf Engler, 1844–1930, professor of botany in Kiel, Breslau and Berlin; director of the Botanic Garden and Museum in Berlin; founded the system of botanical classification bearing his name; wrote the voluminous work *Die natürlichen Pflanzenfamilien* and *Das Pflanzenreich* and many other very basic works, sometimes with other authors such as Diels, Graebner, Prantl, Irmscher, Krause, Warburg.

Engl. V.—Viktor Engler, 1885–1917, botanist at the Botanic Garden of Breslau; area of specialty, *Tilia.*

Esch.—Johann Friedrich von Eschscholtz, 1793–1831, born in Tartu, Estonia, Russian physician and naturalist; accompanied Kotzebue on his world voyage.

Espinosa—Marcial Ramon Espinosa-Bustos, 1874–1959, Chilean botanist and plant collector from Santiago.

Everett — Thomas Henry Everett, born in England in 1903; worked at the New York Botanic Garden, USA.

Exell — Arthur Wallis Exell, born in 1901, English botanist and plant collector; employed by the British Museum in London.

Faber — Ernest Faber, 1839–1899, English clergyman; collected plants in China from 1887–1891.

Fang — Wen-Pei Fang, born in China in 1889, wrote between 1930–1960 and published a comprehensive monograph of the Chinese Aceraceae.

Farr. — Reginald John Farrer, 1880–1920, English garden writer, wrote the *English Rock Garden;* plant collector in Tibet and Burma, where he died.

Faurie — Urbain Jean Faurie, 1847–1915, French missionary and plant collector in China; died in Taiwan.

Fedde — Friedrich Karl Georg Fedde, 1873–1942, teacher in Berlin, botanist; founded and published the *Repertorium specierum novarum* and the 2nd edition of several volumes of Engler's *Pflanzenreich* and *Natürliche Pflanzenfamilien.*

Fedtsch. — Boris Alexewitsch Fedtschenko, 1872–1947, Russian botanist; wrote, together with his wife Olga, primarily on the plants of Turkestan, Altai, Tien Shan, *Revisio generis Hedysari,* etc.

Fenzl — Eduard Fenzl, 1808–1879, imperial Privy Councillor and professor; curator of the Botanical Museum in Vienna, Austria; wrote *Illustrierte Botanik,* also wrote on the plants of Syria and the Taurus Mts.

Fern. — Merritt Lyndon Fernald, 1873–1950, director of the Gray Herbarium in Cambridge, Mass., USA; published *Rhodora* and *Gray's Manual of Botany.*

Fiesser — H. G. Fiesser, 1848–1940, head gardener in Schwetzingen, W. Germany.

Fife — James Duff, Earl of Fife, 1729–1809, English plant collector.

Finet — Achille Finet, 1862–1913, French botanist.

Fisch. — Friedrich Emmanuel Ludwig von Fischer, 1782–1854, born in Halberstadt, Prussian Saxony, director of the Botanic Garden in St. Petersburg (now Leningrad), USSR; authored many works.

Fisch. & Mey. see under both names.

Fitsch. — Jost Fitschen, 1861–1947, school headmaster, botanist and authority on conifers from Hamburg; compiled a revised edition of Beissner's *Handbuch der Nadelholzkunde* and wrote a woody plant flora.

Fletcher — Fletcher & Sons, Ottershaw Nurseries in Chertsey, England.

Florin — Carl Rudolf Florin, 1894–1965, Swedish botanist and director of the Bergianska Trädgarden in Stockholm; specialist in the conifers and wrote *The distribution of Conifer and Taxad genera in time and space.*

Fluegge — Johann Flügge, 1775–1816, doctor and botanist in Hamburg; wrote a monograph of grasses.

Focke — Wilhelm Olbers Focke, 1834–1922, doctor and botanist in Bremen, Germany; specialist in *Rubus* and wrote a *Synopsis Ruborum Germaniae,* etc.

Forb. (Forbes) — James Forbes, 1773–1861, head gardener for the Duke of Bedford; wrote *Hortus Woburnensis, Salicetum Woburnense* and *Pinetum Woburnense.*

Forrest — George Forrest, 1873–1932, Scottish botanist; collected plants in China, died in Yunnan Province; introduced many new species.

Forssk. — Pehr Forsskal, 1732–1763, Swedish botanist, born in Helsinki, Finland; travelled in Egypt and Arabia, where he died; wrote *Flora Aegyptiaco-Arabica.*

Forsyth — William Forsyth, 1737–1804, famous English gardener; director of the Royal Garden in Kensington.

Fort. — Robert Fortune, 1812–1880, born in Scotland, botanist and gardener; later director of the Chelsea Gardens, London; undertook many great collecting trips to China and was one of the most successful plant collectors; introduced the tea plant into India.

Forst., G. — Johann Georg Adam Forster, 1754–1794, son of Johann Reinhold Forster, German botanist from Nassenhuben, near Gdansk [now Poland]; accompanied his father on his world travels and wrote together on the plants of Australia.

Forst., J. R. — Johann Reinhold Forster, 1729–1798, German botanist from Dirschau [now Tczew, Poland]; participated in Captain James Cook's circumnavigation of the globe; spent 1773 in New Zealand; later a professor in Halle, E. Germany, where he died.

Forst., J. R. & G. — see under both names.

Foug. — Auguste Denis Fougeroux, 1732–1798, French botanist.

Franch. (Fr.) — Adrien Rene Franchet, 1834–1900, French botanist at the Muséum d'Histoire Naturelle in Paris, prominent taxonomist; wrote *Plantae Davidianae, Plantae Delavayanae,* and others.

Franch. & Sav. — see under both names.

Franco — João Manual Antonia Pais do Amaral, born in 1921, Portuguese botanist in the Agricultural College in Lisbon; international authority on nomenclature.

Fr. R. E. — Robert Elias Fries, 1876–1966, Swedish botanist; wrote on the Annonaceae and the history of botany.

Freyn — Josef Franz Freyn, 1845–1903, Austrian botanist; lived in Prague, Czechoslovakia.

Froeb. — Karl Otto Froebel, 1844–1906, Swiss gardener in Zurich; hybridized new plants (firm nonexistent today).

Gadeceau—Emile Jules Arthur Gadeceau, 1845–1928, French botanist from Nantes.

Gaertn.—Joseph Gaertner, 1732–1791, doctor and botanist in Calw, near Stuttgart, W. Germany; wrote a 3 volume work on the fruits and seeds of plants; died in Tübingen.

Gaertn. f.—Carl Friedrich von Gaertner, 1772–1850, son of the above, doctor and botanist in Calw, near Stuttgart; completed his father's work and wrote on hybridization in plants.

Gagnep.—François Gagnepain, 1866–1952, French botanist at the Muséum National d'Histoire Naturelle in Paris; wrote primarily on Asiatic plants.

Gamble—James Sykes Gamble, 1847–1925, English botanist in India; wrote a flora of Madras and about the bamboos of India.

Gams—Helmut Gams, born 1893, Austrian botanist and plant collector from Brünn; professor of botany in Innsbruck; wrote primarily on alpine plants and cryptogams.

Gand.—Michel Gandoger, 1850–1926, French clergyman and botanist, died in Lyon; wrote *Conspectus dichotomus Rosarum,* one of the most extensive botanical "splitters."

Gatt.—Augustin Gattinger, 1825–1903, born in Munich, W. Germany; North American botanist and doctor in Tennessee.

Gaud.—Jean François Aimé Philippe Gaudin, 1766–1833, Swiss clergyman and botanist in Nyon, Waadt Canton; wrote *Flora Helvetica,* and others.

Gaylussac—1778–1850, French professor of chemistry at the Museum of Natural History in Paris.

Gebler—Fr. August Gebler, 1782–1850, born in Zeulenroda, Vogtland, E. Germany.

Geert—August van Geert, 1818–1880, Belgian azalea breeder in Ghent; wrote 2 important works on azaleas.

Gibbs—Vicary Gibbs, 1853–1932, well-known English plantsman and plant collector in Aldenham.

Gilg—Ernst Gilg, 1867–1933, born in Baden, German botanist, curator and professor at the Botanical Museum in Berlin; wrote several textbooks, revised many families for Engler's *Natürliche Pflanzenfamilien.*

Gilib.—Jean Emmanuel Gilibert, 1741–1814, French botanist in Lyon; once a professor in Wilna; wrote a flora of Lithuania and *Histoire des plantes d'Europe.*

Gilmour—John Scott Lennox Gilmour, born in 1916, English botanist from London; director of the Cambridge Botanic Garden.

Gouan—Antoine Gouan, 1733–1821, French botanist from Montpellier.

Gleditsch—Johann Gottlieb Gleditsch, 1714–1786, born in Leipzig, E. Germany, doctor, professor of

medicine and botanist; director of the Berlin Botanic Garden.

Gmel., C. C.—Carl Christian Gmelin, 1762–1837, German doctor and botanist from Badenweiler; director of the Karlsruhe Botanic Garden.

Gmel., J. F.—Johann Friedrich Gmelin, 1748–1804, German doctor and botanist from Tübingen, died in Göttingen; wrote various botanical papers, including a complete botanical dictionary.

Gmel., S. G.—Samuel Gottlieb Gmelin, 1743–1774, German doctor and botanist from Tübingen; later with a university in St. Petersburg [Leningrad, USSR]; travelled with Pallas in southern Russia and around the Caspian Sea, died as a prisoner of the Chaitak tribe in the Caucasus.

Godr.—Dominique Alexandre Godron, 1807–1880, professor in Nancy, France; wrote a flora of Lorraine.

Goepp.—Heinrich Robert Goeppert, 1800–1884, professor of medicine; wrote primarily on fossil plants.

Goldring—W. Goldring, 1854–1919, English gardener.

Gord.—George Gordon, 1806–1879, born in Ireland, botanist; superintendent of the Royal Horticultural Society in Chiswick, later at Kew; colleague of Loudon; wrote a conifer book.

Grab.—Heinrich Emmanuel Grabowski, 1792–1842, pharmacist from Oppeln in Silesia; wrote a flora of upper Silesia.

Graebn.—Karl Otto Robert Peter Paul Graebner, 1871–1933, began as a gardener and was later curator and professor at the Berlin-Dahlem Botanic Garden; wrote, together with Ascherson, *Synopsis der mitteleuropäischen Flora,* etc.

Gray, A.—Asa Gray, 1810–1888, professor of botany at Harvard University in Cambridge, Mass., USA; wrote *Manual of Botany of the Northern United States.*

Green, P. S.—Peter Shaw Green, born in 1926, English botanist at Kew.

Greene—Edward Lee Greene, 1842–1915, North American botanist; wrote *Illustrations of Western American Oaks,* etc.

Gremli—August Gremli, 1833–1899, Swiss botanist; earlier a pharmacist, then curator of the herbarium in Nant-sur-Vevey; wrote a Swiss excursion flora and various other monographs.

Gren.—Jean Charles Marie Grenier, 1808–1875, professor of botany in Besançon; wrote together with Godron *Flore de France.*

Gren. & Godr.—see under both names.

Griff.—William Griffith, 1810–1845, English doctor with the English East India Company in Singapore; produced a plate work on Asiatic plants and also wrote about palms of the region; died in Malacca.

Grig. — G. T. G. Grignan, French gardener; wrote between 1903–1914.

Grisebach — August Heinrich Rudolph, 1814–1879, from Hannover, professor of botany in Göttingen; wrote *Flora of the British West Indian Islands*, etc.

Groenewegen — Nurseryman in Amsterdam, Holland.

Grootend. — Herman Johannes Grootendorst, born in 1911, Dutch gardener and dendrologist in Boskoop; wrote a book on *Rhododendron* and others.

Grosser — Wilhelm C. H. Grosser, 1869–(?)1942, German botanist; director of the federal seed control authority in Breslau; wrote *Monograph der Cistaceae*.

Grossh. — Alexander Alfonsovitch Grossheim, 1888–1948, Russian botanist; wrote a flora of the Caucasus, etc.

Guinea — Emilio Lopez Guinea, born in 1907, Spanish botanist from Bilbao; worked in Madrid.

Gumbleton — W. E. G. Gumbleton, 1830–1911, English botanist.

Guimpel — Friedrich Guimpel, 1774–1839, German botanical illustrator in Berlin; illustrated several works for Hayne (see also).

Hacq. — Balthasar (Balsazar) Hacquet, 1739–1815, born in Brittany, a royal advisor and professor in Lemberg [now Lvov, Poland]; wrote on alpine plants; died in Vienna, Austria.

Hagerup — Olaf Hagerup, 1889–1961, curator of the Botanic Garden and Museum in Copenhagen, Denmark.

Hance — Henry Fletcher Hance, 1827–1866, British Consulate in China; wrote a large number of papers on East Asiatic plants.

Hand.-Mazz. — Baron Heinrich von Handel-Mazzetti, 1882–1940, Austrian botanist and explorer in East Asia; curator of the Museum of Natural History in Vienna; wrote *Symbolae Sinicae* among others; discovered many new *Rhododendron* species.

Hara — Hiroshi Hara, born 1911, Japanese botanist at the University of Tokyo; wrote a flora of Karuizawa, etc.

Harding — Alice Harding (Mrs. Edward Harding), North American plant collector; wrote books on *Paeonia* and *Syringa* between 1917 and 1933.

Hardw. — Thomas Hardwicke, 1757–1835, English general, zoologist and botanist; wrote about South African plants, etc.

Hariot — Paul Auguste Hariot, 1854–1917, French botanist from Paris; wrote on *Ligustrum*, etc.

Harms — Hermann August Theodor Harms, 1870–1942, German botanist at the Botanical Museum in Berlin; revised, among others, the Araliaceae, Hamameli-

daceae, Leguminosae, Bromeliaceae; for many years was the editor of Engler's *Pflanzenreich.*

Hartig — Theodor Hartig, 1805–1880, forester in Braunschweig, E. Germany.

Hartm. — Carl Johan Hartmann, 1790–1849, Swedish botanist; wrote a handbook of the Swedish flora.

Hartw. — Karl Theodor Hartweg, 1812–1871, from Karlsruhe, head gardener in Schwetzingen, Germany; collected plants in Mexico for the Royal Horticultural Society in London; wrote *Hortus Carlsruhensis.*

Hartwig — August Karl Julius Hartwig, 1823–1913, German gardener; wrote primarily on fruit tree hybridizing.

Hartwig & Ruempl. — see under both names.

Hartwiss — Nikolaus von Hartwiss, 1791–1860, director of the Botanic Garden in Nikita, Jalta, Crimea.

Hassk. — Justus Carl Hasskarl, 1811–1894, born in Kassel, W. Germany; director of the Botanic Garden in Bogor, on Java; died in Cleves, Germany.

Hauskn. — Heinrich Karl Hausknecht, 1838–1903, Privy Councillor in Weimar, E. Germany; wrote a monograph of the genus *Epilobium.*

Havemeyer — Theodore A. Havemeyer, 1868–1936, New York, owner of a large *Syringa* collection; hybridized between 1920 and 1930.

Haw.-Booth — Michael Haworth-Booth, English gardener in Haslemere, Surrey; wrote on *Hydrangea*, etc.

Hayashi — Yasaka Hayashi, born 1911, Japanese dendrologist.

Hayata — Bunzo Hayata, 1874–1934, Japanese botanist; wrote on the flora of Formosa [Taiwan].

Hayne — Friedrich Gottlob Hayne, 1763–1832, professor of botany in Berlin; wrote a dendrologic flora of Berlin.

H. B. K. — see Humboldt, Bonpland and Kunth.

Hedl. — Johan Theodor Hedlund, 1861–1953, professor of botany in Alnarp, Sweden; wrote a monograph of the genus *Sorbus.*

Hegi — Gustav Hegi, 1876–1932, Swiss botanist, professor in Munich, W. Germany; wrote the 7 volume *Illustrierte Flora von Mitteleuropa.*

Heldr. — Theodor von Heldreich, 1822–1902, German botanist; director of the Athens Botanic Garden, Greece.

Hemsl. — W. Botting Hemsley, 1843–1924, curator of Kew Gardens, London; wrote, along with Forbes, the *Index Florae Sinensis.*

Henders, M. D. — Mayda Doris Henderson, born in 1928, South African botanist.

Hendr. — Willem Johan Hendriks, 1889–1967, municipal landscape architect in Amsterdam, Holland; wrote a Dutch dendrology.

Henkel—Johann Baptist Henkel, 1815–1871, Professor of Pharmacology and botany at the University of Tübingen; wrote, with Hochstetter (see also), on the conifers.

Henry—Augustine Henry, 1857–1930, Irish botanist, first in Cambridge, England, later in Dublin, Ireland; authority on the Chinese flora; wrote, together with Elwes (see also), a 7 volume dendrology.

Henry, L.—Louis Henry, 1853–1913, French gardener; wrote between 1890 and 1911.

Herincq—François Hérincq, 1820–1891, French gardener; wrote an 8 volume work, *Le Règne végétal,* and others.

Herrm.—Johann Herrmann, 1738–1800, Alsatian botanist from Strasbourg; wrote on the roses and medicinal plants.

Hers—Joseph Hers, Belgian botanist; lived in China for many years as General Secretary of the Railway Administration at Pien-Lo and Lung-Hai; wrote between 1922 and 1938 on Chinese woody plants.

Hesse—Hermann Albrecht Hesse, 1852–1937, Commerce Advisor and nursery owner in Weener-Ems, W. Germany; a well-known plant authority.

Hibb.—James Shirley Hibberd, 1825–1890, English gardener.

Hickel—Paul-Jean Hickel, 1861–1935, French forest botanist; wrote *Dendrologie Forestière.*

Hill—Elsworth Jerome Hill, 1833–1917, American botanist; wrote on the flora of the Midwest.

Hillier—Hillier & Sons, Nursery in Winchester, England; Edwin Lawrence H., 1865–1944; Harold George H., born in 1905, one of the best dendrologists of our time.

Hochst.—Christian Fredrich Hochstetter, 1787–1860, municipal pastor and professor of botany in Esslingen, W. Germany.

Hochstetter—Wilhelm Hochstetter, 1825–1881, University garden director in Tübingen, W. Germany; wrote, together with Henkel (see also), *Synopsis der Nadelhölzer.*

Hodgins—A nurseryman in Dunganstown near Wicklow, England.

Hoefk.—Hinrich Hoefker, 1866–1945, born in East Friesland, school teacher and botanist in Dortmund, W. Germany; a past president of the German Dendrological Society.

Hoey Smith—see van Hoey Smith.

Hoffm.—Georg Franz Hoffmann, 1760–1826, professor of botany in Göttingen, W. Germany, later in Moscow; wrote on lichens, *Salix* and others.

Hoffmgg.—Count Johann Centurius von Hoffmannsegg, 1766–1826, German botanist in Dresden; published a catalogue of the plants in his garden and (together with Link) a Portuguese flora.

Hohenack.—Rudolph Friedrich Hohenacker, 1798–1874, born in Zurich, Austria, clergyman and plant collector; explored the Caucasus region.

Holdt—Friedrich von Holdt, nurseryman in Alcot, near Denver, Colorado, USA.

Hook.—William Jackson Hooker, 1785–1865, English botanist; first Regius Professor of Botany at the University of Glasgow, Scotland; director of Kew Gardens from 1841–1865; wrote a British flora and many other works.

Hook. f.—Joseph Dalton Hooker, 1817–1911, son of the above, director of Kew Gardens from 1865–1885; wrote a number of significant works on East Asiatic plants collected by himself, particularly *Rhododendron.*

Hook. & Thoms.—see Hook. f., and Thoms.

Host—Nicolaus Host, 1761–1834, Imperial personal physician in Vienna, Austria; published a volume of plates on East Asiatic plants.

Houtzag.—Gijsbertus Houtzagers, 1888–1957, professor of forestry at the agriculture college in Wageningen, Holland; wrote on poplars and forest trees.

Houzeau—Jean Houzeau de Lehaie, 1820–1888, Belgian gardener; wrote about bamboos.

Houtte—Louis van Houtte, 1810–1876, famous Belgian nurseryman, botanist and traveler from Ghent; publisher of *Flore des Serres.*

Hovey—Charles Mason Hovey, 1810–1887, gardener and author in Cambridge, Mass., USA.

Hu—Hsen-Hsu Hu, born in 1894, Chinese botanist in Peking; specialist in the woody flora of China.

Hu, S-Y.—Shiu-Ying Hu, born in 1910 in Suchow, Chinese botanist; worked at the Arnold Arboretum of Harvard University in Cambridge, Mass., USA.

Huds.—William Hudson, 1730–1793, pharmacist and botanist in London; wrote *Flora Anglica.*

Hueg.—Carl Alexander Anselm (Baron) von Hügel, 1794–1870, Austrian diplomat and botanist.

Hughes—Dorothy Hughes, later Mrs. Wilson Popenoe, 1899–1932, English botanist, later in Washington D.C., USA; collected plants in Guatemala.

Hultén—Oskar Eric Gunnar Hultén, born 1894, Swedish botanist at the Museum of the University of Lund; wrote, among others, *Flora of Alaska and the Yukon.*

Hulthem—Ch. Jos. Emanuel van Hulthem, 1764–1821, Belgian city councilor and famous bibliophile in Ghent; instrumental in the founding of the city's botanic garden.

Humboldt—Friedrich Heinrich Alexander von Humboldt, 1769–1859, most famous naturalist of his time; wrote numerous works on the plants collected by himself and Bonpland in South America (also together with Kunth).

Hume — Hardrada Harold Hume, 1875–1965, Canadian botanist, later living in Florida; wrote primarily on *Ilex* and *Camellia*.

Hutchins. — John Hutchinson, 1884–1972, leading English botanist, from Kew Gardens; wrote *The Families of Flowering Plants,* established a new system of plant evolution.

Hylander — Nils Hylander, 1904–1970, Swedish botanist and curator at Uppsala.

Ingram — Collingwood Ingram, born in 1884, English officer, ornithologist and botanist; wrote *Ornamental Cherries.*

Inokuma — Taizo Inokuma, born in 1904, Japanese forest botanist; after 1931 wrote about Japanese forest plants.

Jack — John George Jack, 1861–1949, professor of dendrology at the Bussey Institute in Jamaica Plain, Mass., USA.

Jackm. — George Jackman, nurseryman in Woking, Surrey, England; known for many *Clematis* hybrids originated between 1864 and 1882.

Jacks., A. B. — Albert Bruce Jackson, 1876–1947, English conifer authority; general secretary of the Linnean Society in London.

Jacob-Mackoy — More correctly Lambert Jacob, 1790–1873, Belgian gardener; founded a nursery together with another gardener, Makoy, in Liège and dealt primarily in azalea breeding.

Jacq. — Nicolaus Joseph Jacquin (Baron von J. after 1806), 1727–1817, born in Leiden, Holland, botanist and professor of chemistry in Vienna, Austria; director of the Botanic Garden in Schönbrunn; collected plants in South America; published a famous work of plates, *Icones Plantarum Rariorum.*

Jacquemont — Victor Jaquemont, 1788–1831, French botanist from Paris; traveled through North America and the East Indies.

Jaeg. — Hermann Jaeger, 1815–1890, Saxon nursery inspector and plant authority in Eisenach, E. Germany.

James — Edwin P. James, 1797–1861, American botanist; reported on the plants of the Rocky Mountains.

Jancz. — Eduard Janczewski Ritter von Glinka, 1846–1918, Russian botanist, born in Lithuania; an advisor and professor in Krakow, Poland; wrote *Monographie des Grosseillers [Ribes].*

Jaennicke — Friedrich Jaennicke, 1831–1907, German botanist; wrote studies on the genus *Platanus.*

Janka — Victor Janka von Bulcs, 1837–1890, Hungarian botanist, born in Vienna, Austria; revised the *Flora des Donaugebeites.*

Janko — Johan Jankó, Hungarian botanist; wrote around 1890.

Jaub. — Count Hippolyte François de Jaubert, 1798–1874, French minister of public works and botanist; published, together with Spach (see also), a large plate work on oriental flora.

Jaub. & Spach — see under both names.

Jeffrey — Scottish gardener from the Royal Botanic Garden, Edinburgh; collected seed in Oregon, USA from 1850–1853, then was overcome with "gold fever" and vanished.

Jens. H. — Holger Jensen, a Swedish gardener in Ramlösa; died around 1955.

Jepson — Willis Linn Jepson, 1867–1946, American botanist in California; wrote *The Silva of California,* etc.

Johnst. — Ivan Murray Johnston, 1898–1960, American botanist at the Gray Herbarium of Harvard University in Cambridge, Mass., USA.

Jones — George Neville Jones, 1904–1970, professor of botany at the University of Illinois; wrote a monograph of the American *Amelanchier* species.

Jouin — Victor Jouin, 1839–1909, director of the nurseries of Simon Louis Frères in Plantières near Metz, France.

Jühlke — Ferdinand Jühlke, 1815–1893, garden director in Potsdam, E. Germany.

Judd — William H. Judd, 1888–1946, born in England, worked at the Arnold Arboretum in Jamaica Plain, Mass., USA.

Jundzill — Bonifaciusz Stanislaw Jundzill, 1761–1830, Polish professor of botany from Lithuania; authored a Polish botany.

Jurrissen — Johannes Josephus Jurrissen, 1839–1928, Dutch nurseryman.

Juss. — Antoine Laurent de Jussieu, 1748–1836, French botanist from Lyon; professor at the Jardin des Plantes in Paris; most significant plant taxonomist of his time, developed a system of classification which bears his name.

Juss., A. — Adrien Henri Laurent de Jussieu, 1797–1853, son of the above, French botanist, also in the Jardin des Plantes in Paris; wrote various monographs on the Euphorbiaceae, Meliaceae, Rutaceae and others.

Juss., B. — Bernard de Jussieu, 1699–1776, French botanist from Lyon, uncle of Antoine; overseer for the Trianon Botanical Gardens, Paris.

Juss., J. — Joseph de Jussieu, 1704–1779, French botanist from Lyon; collected in the American tropics for 36 years; died in Paris.

Kache — Paul Kache, 1882–1945, garden director in Potsdam, E. Germany; temporary publisher of *Gartenflora.*

Kalm — Pehr Kalm, 1716–1779, Swedish professor of economics in Abo, Finnish botanist in Nerpio, Finland; student of Linneaus; traveled in North America from 1748–1752.

Kalmbacher — George Anthony Kalmbacher, born in 1897, American botanist; wrote on magnolias, etc.

Karst. — Gustav Karl Wilhelm Hermann Karsten, 1817–1908, from Stralsund, E. Germany, later professor of botany in Vienna, Austria; wrote about Central and South American flora.

Keller — Robert Keller, 1854–1939, Swiss botanist from Winterthur; revised particularly the roses and *Hypericum*.

Ker (or **Ker-Gawl.**) — John Bellenden Ker (penned under the name John Gawler before 1804, later as John Ker Bellenden or John Bellenden Ker), 1764–1842, was a captain in the English Army until 1793, forced out as a result of his sympathy for the French revolution; later became the publisher of the *Botanical Register,* for which he wrote most of the plant descriptions.

Kern. — Anton Joseph Kerner von Marilaun, 1831–1898, Austrian professor of botany in Innsbruck and Vienna; wrote *Pflanzenleben* and others.

Kesselr. — Friedrich Wilhelm Kesselring, born 1876 in St. Petersburg (Leningrad), died in 1966 in Darmstadt, director of the Darmstadt Botanic Garden from 1926 to 1947; his father founded a notable nursery with E. von Regel in Leningrad.

King — Sir George King, 1840–1909, Scottish botanist in India; wrote a monograph of the genus *Ficus;* died in San Remo, Italy.

Kingdon-Ward — Frank Kingdon-Ward, 1885–1958, from Manchester, England, botanist and plant collector in China, Burma and Tibet, the most notable of the more recent plant collectors; wrote a number of books on his travels.

Kirchn. — Georg Kirchner, 1837–1885, gardener at the arboretum of Prince Pückler in Muskau, Silesia; wrote the botanical portion of *Arboretum Muscaviense.*

Kirk — Thomas Kirk, 1828–1898, forest botanist and plant collector, born in England, lived and worked in New Zealand; wrote *Forest Flora of New Zealand.*

Kit. — Paul Kitaibel, 1757–1817, Hungarian professor of botany in Budapest; wrote, with Waldstein (see also), about Hungarian plants.

Kobendza — Boleslaw Kobendza, 1886–1955, Polish professor of botany at the University of Warsaw.

Kobuski — Clarence Emmeren Kobuski, 1909–1963, American botanist at the Arnold Arboretum in Jamaica Plain, Mass.; specialist in Theaceae, *Jasminum,* etc.

Koch — Wilhelm Daniel Josef Koch, 1771–1849, from Zweibrücken, W. Germany, later professor in Erlangen; wrote a synopsis of the German and Swiss flora.

Koch, F. — Friedrich Koch, contemporary from Northeim (Harz Mts.), Germany; concentrated on *Ribes* breeding.

Koch, K. — Karl Heinrich Emil Koch, 1809–1879, from Weimar, E. Germany, professor of botany in Berlin; wrote a 3 volume dendrology.

Koehne — Bernhard Adalbert Emil Koehne, 1848–1918, from Silesia, later a professor in Berlin; prominent dendrologist, wrote many taxonomic works and a German dendrology.

Koelreuter — Joseph Gottlieb Kölreuter, 1733–1806, professor of botany in Karlsruhe.

Koerb. — Gustav Wilhelm Koerber, born in 1817, German botanist in Breslau [now Wroclaw, Poland].

Koern. — Friedrich August Körnicke, 1828–1908, German botanist from Pratau near Wittenberg; wrote on the Ericaceae, Marantaceae, etc.

Koidz. — Gen'ichi Koidzumi, 1883–1953, Japanese botanist in Yonezawa; wrote monographs on the Aceraceae, Rosaceae, etc.

Komar. — Vladimir Leontyevitch Komarov, 1869–1945, Russian botanist in Leningrad; wrote *Flora Manschuriae* and 13 volumes of *Flora U.R.S.S.*

Koopm. — Karl Koopmann, 1851–1924(?), nursery inspector in Geisenheim, later in the game preserve near Potsdam, E. Germany; wrote between 1879–1900.

Kordes — Wilhelm Kordes, 1891–1976, prominent German rose breeder, also hybridized *Rhododendron* and *Malus; Rosa kordesii* was named for him.

Korsh. — Sergei Ivanovitch Korshinsky, 1861–1900, Russian botanist; published a Russian flora.

Koster — M. Koster & Sons, nursery family in Boskoop, Holland; well-known azalea breeders.

Kotschy — Karl Georg Theodor Kotschy, 1813–1856, Austrian botanist, curator of the Botanical Museum in Vienna; collected more than 300,000 specimens in his travels to the Orient; wrote about the plants of Arabia and the oaks of Europe and the Orient.

Krasser — Fridolin Krasser, 1863–1922, Austrian botanist in Vienna; wrote about *Fagus* and *Nothofagus.*

Krassn. — Andrej Nikolajewitch Krassnow, 1862–1915, Russian botanist.

Krishtofovitch — Afrikan Nikolajevitch Krishtofovitch, 1885–1953, Russian botanist, geologist and taxonomist.

Krüssm. — Gerd Krüssmann, 1910–1980, born in Dinslaken, W. Germany, dendrologist; director of the Botanic Garden and German National Rosarium in Dortmund from 1950–1975; editor of the periodical *Deutsche Baumschule;* wrote *Handbuch der Nadelgehölze, Laubgehölze, Rosen-Rosen-Rosen,* etc.

Ktze. — Carl Ernst Otto Kuntze, 1843–1907, from Freiburg, German botanist; wrote the 4 volume *Revisio*

Generum Plantarum, strongest advocate of the priority principle in nomenclature.

Kunth — Carl Sigismund Kunth, 1788–1850, professor of botany in Berlin; wrote a textbook of botany, the 5 volume *Enumeratio Plantarum,* and edited some of the works of Humboldt and Bonpland.

Kunze — Gustav Kunze, 1793–1851, professor of botany and director of the botanic garden in Leipzig, Germany; wrote primarily on ferns and grasses.

Kurz — Wilhelm Sulpiz Kurz, 1824–1878, German botanist and dendrologist in India; curator of the herbarium in Calcutta.

Kusnez. — Nikolai Ivanovitch Kusnezov, 1864–1932, professor of botany in Dorpat, later Leningrad; wrote on *Gentiana,* etc.

L. — Carl Ritter von Linné, (Latin, Linnaeus), 1707–1778, famous Swedish botanist, the "Father of Botany;" founded the Linnaean System, introduced the method of binomial nomenclature generally accepted today; wrote *Systema Naturae, Species Plantarum,* and others.

L. f. — Carl von Linné, 1741–1783, son of the above, successor to his father's office; wrote primarily on ferns and mosses as well as a supplement to his father's system.

Labill. — Jacques Julien Houttou de Labillardière, 1755–1834, French botanist; wrote on the plants of Syria, Australia and medicinal plants.

Lag. — Mariano Lagasca y Segura, 1776–1839, Spanish professor of botany in Madrid; wrote primarily on Spanish plants.

Lam. — Jean Baptiste Antoine Pierre Monnet (Chevalier) de Lamarck, 1744–1829, French botanist; wrote a 13 volume flora of France; famed for his philosophy of the variability of species.

Lamb. — Aylmer Bourke Lambert, 1761–1843, from London, vice president of the Linnean Society; published a splendid work on *Pinus.*

Lambert — Peter Lambert, 1860–1939, German rose breeder in Trier.

Lauche — Friedrich Wilhelm G. Lauche, 1827–1883, German gardener, director of the Wildpark Educational Institute; wrote *Deutsche Pomologie, Deutsche Dendrologie,* etc.

Lav. — Pierre Alphonse Martin Lavallée, 1836–1884, French gardener, dendrologist, was general secretary of the French Horticulture Society; wrote *Arboretum Segrezianum, Les Clématites à grandes fleurs,* etc.

Lawson — Peter Lawson, 1730–1820; Charles Lawson, 1774–1873; owners of a once famous nursery in Edinburgh, Scotland; Peter L. wrote *Pinetum Britannicum.*

Lecomte — Paul Henry Lecomte, 1856–1934, French botanist; wrote on the Sabiaceae, Simaroubaceae, flora of Indochina, etc.

Ledeb. — Carl Friedrich von Ledebur, 1785–1851, German botanist from Greifswald; professor of botany in Dorpat, then an official for Russia in Siberia and elsewhere; wrote *Flora Russica, Flora Altaica,* etc.; died in Munich, W. Germany.

Lehm. — Johann Georg Christian Lehmann, 1792–1860, German botanist, professor and director of the Hamburg Botanic Garden; wrote a monograph on *Potentilla, Primula,* etc.

Lem. — Charles Antoine Lemaire, 1801–1871, born in Paris, professor in Ghent, Belgium; edited the *Flore des Serres, L'Illustration Horticole,* etc.

Lemm. — John Gill Lemmon, 1832–1908, American botanist; wrote primarily on the conifers of the Pacific West.

Lemoine — Pierre Louis Victor Lemoine, 1823–1911, prominent French gardener and breeder of many woody ornamentals; his son Emile Lemoine, 1862–1943, continued his work; nursery does not exist today.

Leroy — André Leroy, 1801–1875, and Louis Leroy, 1808–1887, French nurserymen in Angers.

Leschenault — Louis Théodore Leschenault de la Tour, 1774–1826, French naturalist-explorer; traveled in southern Asia and South America.

Less. — Christian Friedrich Lessing, 1810–1862, from Silesia, German doctor and botanist; wrote on the Compositae.

Lév. — Auguste Abel Hector Léveillé, 1863–1918, French botanist and missionary; wrote extensively, from 1894 until his death, on East Asiatic flora.

Leyb. — Friedrich Ernst Leybold, 1804–1864, Austrian botanist; wrote on alpine plants.

Lge. (Lange) — Johan Martin Christian Lange, 1818–1898, Danish botanist, director of the Copenhagen Botanic Garden; wrote a handbook of the Danish flora, also on Spanish plants and *Crataegus.*

L'Hér. (L'Hérit.) — Charles Louis L'Héritier de Brutelle, 1746–1800, French government official, lawyer and botanist, murdered in Paris; wrote a work on *Geranium, Sertum Anglicum,* and others.

Liebl. — Franz Kaspar Lieblein, 1744–1810, professor of botany in Fulda, W. Germany; wrote *Flora Fuldensis.*

Lindl. — John Lindley, 1799–1865, famous professor of botany in London; wrote a British flora, monographs on *Digitalis, Rosa,* orchids, medicinal plants; editor of the *Botanical Register,* first publisher of *The Gardeners Chronicle* (still being published).

Lingelsh. — Alexander von Lingelsheim, 1874–1937, German botanist in Breslau; specialist in the Oleaceae (Fraxineae and Syringeae).

Link — Johann Heinrich Friedrich Link, 1767–1851, professor of botany and director of the Berlin Botanic

Garden; published many plates of the garden's rare plants.

Lipsky — Vladimir Ippolitovitch Lipsky, 1863–1937, Russian botanist; wrote a flora of central Asia, Tien Shan, etc.

Little, Jr. — Elbert Luther Little, Junior, born in 1907, American dendrologist with the U.S. Forest Service; wrote many dendrological works on North American woody plants.

Litvin. — Dimitri Ivanovitch Litvinov, 1854–1929, Russian botanist; continued the work of Korshinsky (see also), wrote on the flora of Turkestan, a bibliography of the flora of Siberia, etc.

Liu — Tang-Shui Liu, born 1910, Chinese dendrologist; wrote a 2 volume woody flora of Taiwan and a monograph of the genus *Abies*.

Lobb — William Lobb, 1809–1863, English plant collector for James Veitch & Sons, was in North and South America for many years; his brother Thomas Lobb, 1817–1894, collected in SE. Asia for the same firm.

Lodd. — Conrad Loddiges, 1732–1826, allegedly born in Holland, founded a nursery in Hackney, near London, England (the birthplace of Conrad Loddiges according to R. Maatsch [in Schlechter, *Die Orchideen*, 3rd edition, Volume II: 9] has been contested; in any case, he is not from Holland and also not from Hannover, W. Germany or the surrounding area); George Loddiges, 1784–1846, son of the above, continued the nursery; in London published the *Botanical Cabinet* with 2000 plates.

Löbner — Max Löbner, 1870–1947, first director of the Horticultural Institute in Friesdorf near Bonn, W. Germany; worked in hybridizing *Syringa* and *Philadelphus*.

Loes. — Ludwig Eduard Theodor Loesener, 1865–1941, curator and professor at the Botanical Museum in Berlin; wrote *Monographia Aquifoliacearum,* etc.

Loisel. — Jean Louis Auguste Loiseleur-Deslongchamps, 1774–1849, French botanist and doctor; wrote a flora of France, a history of roses, etc.

Lombarts — Pierre Lombarts, 1873–1949, Dutch nurseryman in Zundert, North Brabant; Jacques Lombarts, son of the above, 1904–1971, dendrologist and first president of the International Dendrology Society. Firm now out of business.

Lonicer (Lonitzer) — Adam, 1518–1586, German doctor in Frankfurt; known for his herbal.

Looymans — P. J. Looymans, Dutch gardener in Oudenbosch.

Lorberg — H. Lorberg, German nurseryman in Biesenthal, later in Berlin-Lichtenrade.

Loud. — John Claudius Loudon, 1783–1843, Scottish gardener and writer; wrote an 8 volume dendrology, the *Arboretum and Fruticetum Britannicum.*

Lour. — Joao de Loureiro, 1710–1796, Portuguese Jesuit and botanist from Lisbon; in East Asia for 30 years, wrote a flora Cochinchinensis.

Lucombe — Trade gardener in Exeter, England.

Maack — Richard Maack, 1825–1886, Russian botanist in Petersburg [Leningrad]; traveled in the Amur and Issuri regions.

Macartney — George Macartney, 1737–1806, English statesman; led an expedition into China in 1792 and collected many plants.

Mackay — James Townsend Mackay, 1775–1862, Irish botanist, founder and first curator of the Dublin Botanic Garden; wrote a flora of Ireland.

MacBride — James Francis MacBride, born 1892, North American botanist.

McKelvey — Suzan Delano McKelvey, 1883–1964, American botanist at Harvard University; wrote a monograph on *Syringa.*

MacNab — William MacNab, 1780–1848, from Scotland, curator of the Royal Botanic Garden Edinburgh; wrote on the South African *Erica.*

Märklin — Georg Friedrich Märklin, died in 1823, pharmacist in Wiesloch, W. Germany; co-author of a review of Heidelberg's wild plants, published in 1827.

Magnol — Pierre Magnol, 1638–1715, professor of botany and director of the Botanic Garden in Montpellier, France.

Maiden — Joseph Henry Maiden, 1859–1925, born in England, botanist and plant collector in Australia.

M'Mahon — Bernard M'Mahon, 1775–1816, Irish gardener; traveled to the USA and founded a popular nursery and seed firm specializing primarily in seed of American plants; wrote the first significant American garden book, the *American Gardeners Calendar.*

Mak. — Tomitaro Makino, 1862–1956, lecturer at Tokyo University; wrote a very large number of works on Japanese flora.

Mak. & Shib. — see under both names.

Manetti — Guiseppe Manetti, 1831–1858, administrator of the imperial garden in Monza, Lombardy, Italy.

Manetti, X. — Saverio (Xavier) Manetti, 1723–1784, Italian doctor and botanist; director of the Florence Botanic Garden.

Maries — Charles Maries, English plant collector, 1877–1879 for J. Veitch & Sons, London, in China and Japan; died in 1902 in Gwalior, India.

Markgr. — Friedrich Markgraf, born in 1897, German botanist in Berlin, then Munich, eventually in Zurich, Switzerland; revised the Gnetaceae and others.

Marsh. — Humphrey Marshall, 1722–1801, American botanist and dendrologist.

Mars. — Giovanni Marsili (Marsilius), 1727–1795, professor of botany in Padua, Italy.

Martelli — Niccola Martelli, professor of botany in Rome, Italy; died in 1829.

Mast. — Maxwell Tilden Masters, 1833–1907, English botanist in London; publisher of *Gardeners Chronicle,* wrote *Pinetum Britannicum* and many monographs.

Matsuda — Sadahisa Matsuda, 1857–1921, Japanese botanist; wrote between 1917 and 1927 on the Ulmaceae, *Chimonanthus* and questions of nomenclature.

Matsum. — Jinzo Matsumura, 1856–1928, Japanese botanist; wrote *Index Plantarum Japonicarum,* also a standard work on Chinese plant names, etc.

Mattf. — Johannes Mattfeld, 1895–1951, curator and professor at the Botanical Museum in Berlin-Dahlem; traveled the Balkans and Asia Minor; wrote on *Quercus,* Caryophyllaceae, etc.

Mattuschka — Count Heinrich Gottfried von Mattuschka, 1734–1779, German botanist, landowner in Plitschen, Silesia; wrote a Silesian flora.

Maxim. — Carl Johann Ivanovitch Maximowicz, 1827–1891, Russian botanist, curator of the Petersburg [Leningrad] Botanic Garden; wrote on the *Hydrangea, Rhamnus, Rhododendron;* also an explorer.

Mayr — Heinrich Mayr, 1865–1911, professor of forestry at the University of Munich, W. Germany; traveled in North America, Japan, China, India, etc.; wrote a book on exotic forest and park trees for Europe.

M. & B. — Maxwell & Beale, nursery in Broadstone, Dorset, England, specializing in *Erica* and *Calluna.*

McClintock — Elizabeth May McClintock, born in 1912, American botanist in San Francisco; specialist in *Hydrangea, Teucrium,* and questions of nomenclature.

McClure — Floyd Alonzo McClure, 1897–1970, American botanist; specialist in bamboo.

Med. (Medic.) — Friedrich Casimir Medicus [Medikus], 1736–1808, doctor, government official and director of the garden in Mannhein and Schwetzingen, W. Germany; wrote *Philosophische Botanik,* etc.

Medwed — Yakov Sergejevich Medwedew (Medvedev), 1847–1923, Russian botanist.

Meeh. — Thomas Meehan, 1826–1901, gardener in Philadelphia, USA.

Meissn. (Meisn.) — Carl Friedrich Meissner, Swiss botanist from Bern, professor of botany in Basel; wrote monographs of the Polygonaceae, Proteaceae, Thymelaeaceae, etc.

Menzies — Archibald Menzies, 1754–1842, born in Scotland, botanical explorer; discovered *Pseudotsuga menziesii* on Nootka Sound, Canada; died in London.

Mérat — François Victor Mérat, 1780–1851, French botanist and doctor; wrote several floras of Paris and the surrounding area.

Merr. — Elmer Drew Merrill, 1876–1956, American botanist, prominent plantsman; director of the New York Botanical Gardens in Bronx Park, New York, USA, later with the Arnold Arboretum; wrote, among others, a *Bibliography of Eastern Asiatic Botany.*

Metcalfe — Charles Russell Metcalfe, born in 1904, English botanist; Jodrell Laboratory in Kew, worked on the comparative anatomy of angiosperms.

Mey., C. A. — Carl Anton von Meyer, 1759–1855, Russian botanist, director of the botanic garden in St. Petersburg [Leningrad]; traveled in the Caucasus, Altai and Dzungaria regions; wrote monographic works on *Cornus, Ephedra,* etc.

Meyer — Ernst Heinrich Friedrich Meyer, 1791–1858, professor of botany in Königsberg [East Prussia, now Russia], wrote a history of botany.

Mez — Karl Christian Mez, 1866–1944, German botanist from Freiburg, W. Germany, later Königsberg [now Kaliningrad, USSR]; wrote primarily on the South American flora as well as the Lauraceae and Myrsinaceae.

Michx. — André Michaux, 1746–1802, French botanist in Paris; wrote on the North American *Quercus;* lived for a long time in Madagascar, where he died.

Michx. f. — François André, Michaux, 1770–1855, son of the above, French botanist in Paris, continued the work of his father; wrote on North American forest trees and *The North American Sylva.*

Middendorff — Alexander Theodor von Middendorff, 1815–1894, Russian doctor and botanist; traveled in northern India and Siberia.

Mielichhofer — M. Mielichhofer, Austrian municipal advisor, served in his knowledge of the flora of Salzburg.

Miers — John Miers, 1789–1879, English botanist in London; published a plate work on South American plants and also a monograph of the Menispermaceae.

Mill. — Philip Miller, 1691–1771, English gardener and botanist; director of the Pharmacology Society's garden in Chelsea, near London; wrote a garden dictionary, which has appeared in many editions and translations.

Millais — John G. Millais, English botanist; wrote an excellent book on *Rhododendron,* also on magnolias, between 1917–1927.

Milne-Redh. — Edgar Milne-Redhead, born in 1906, English botanist at Kew; wrote primarily on the flora of tropical East Africa.

Miq. — Friedrich Anton Wilhelm Miquel, 1811–1871, German botanist, born in Hannover, later professor of botany in Utrecht, Holland, director of the Rijksherbarium in Leiden; wrote monographs on *Cycas,*

Piper, Casuarina and several floras.

Mirbel — Charles François Brisseau de Mirbel, 1776–1854, French botanist, director of the Jardin des Plantes in Paris; wrote primarily on plant anatomy and physiology.

Misak — Josef Misak, 1893–1963, supervisor at the Malony Arboretum, Slovakia (now Mlyňany, Czechoslovakia); wrote on evergreens.

Mitford — Algernon Bertram Freeman-Mitford, Lord Redesdale, 1837–1916, English botanist; wrote on the bamboos.

Miyabe — Kingo Miyabe, 1860–1951, Japanese botanist at the Sapporo University Botanic Garden; wrote on the flora of the Kuril Islands and Hokkaido.

Miyoshi — Manabu Miyoshi, 1861–1932, Japanese professor of botany at the University of Tokyo; published an atlas of Japanese vegetation and a prominent work on Japanese cherries.

Moçino — José Mariano Moçiño Suares Losada, 1757–1820, Spanish botanist; traveled in Mexico.

Moerloose — Nursery in Ledeberg, near Ghent, Belgium; went out of business in 1850.

Moench (Mnch.) — Conrad Moench, 1744–1805, professor of botany in Marburg, W. Germany; wrote on the plants of Hessen, etc.

Molina — Juan Ignacio Molina, 1738–1853, missionary and botanist in Chile.

Moore — Thomas Moore, 1821–1887, English gardener, curator of the Chelsea Physic Garden; wrote primarily on the ferns and orchids.

Moore, L. B. — Lucy Beatrice Moore, born in 1910, New Zealand botanist.

Moquin-Tandon — Christian Horace Benedict Alfred Moquin-Tandon, 1804–1863, French gardener and botanist from Montpellier, died in Paris; wrote on the *Eurotia,* etc.

Moricand — Stefano Moricand, 1779–1854, Swiss naturalist-explorer and botanist from Geneva.

Morr. — Charles Jacques Edouard Morren, 1833–1886, professor of botany in Liège, Belgium; published the periodical, *La Belgique Horticole.*

Moser — Jean Jacques Moser, 1846–1934, French gardener.

Mott. — Seraphin Mottet, 1861–1930, head gardener at Vilmorin-Andrieux in Paris; wrote a dendrology and many smaller articles in the *Revue Horticole.*

Mouillef. — Pierre Mouillefert, 1846–1903, professor of forestry in Grignon, France.

Muell. Arg. — Johannes Müller (Müller-Argoviensis, Jean), 1828–1896, Swiss botanist from Aargau Canton; wrote monographs on *Reseda,* Buxaceae, Rubiaceae etc.; director of the Geneva Botanic Garden, where he died.

Muell., F. v. — (Sir) Ferdinand Jacob Heinrich (Baron) von Mueller, 1825–1896, born in Rostock, E. Germany, botanist and government official in Melbourne, Australia; wrote on the flora of Australia, published *Eucalyptographia.*

Muenchh. — Otto (Baron) von Münchhausen, 1716–1774, regional governor in Kalenberg, W. Germany, creator of the Schwöbber Landscape Park near Hameln; published an index to the plants in this park.

Muhlenb. (also **Muehlenb.**) — Gotthilf Henry Ernest Muhlenberg, 1753–1815, American Evangelical-Lutheran minister and botanist in Lancaster, Pennsylvania; in 1813 published a guide to the known North American plants.

Mullig. — Brian O. Mulligan, born in 1907 in northern Ireland, director of the Botanical Gardens at the University of Washington in Seattle, Washington, USA; specialist in *Acer* and *Sorbus.*

Munro — William Munro, 1818–1880, English botanist; wrote a monograph on bamboo.

Munz — Philip Alexander Munz, 1892–1974, North American botanist; director of the Santa Ana Botanic Garden, California, USA; wrote *A California Flora,* etc.

Munoz — Carlos Muñoz, 1913–1976, Chilean botanist, later in New York.

Murray — Johan Andreas Murray, 1740–1791, born in Stockholm, Sweden, professor of medicine and botany in Göttingen.

Murray, E. — Albert Edward Murray, born in 1935, American botanist; wrote a monograph on the genus *Acer.*

Mut. — José Celestino Mutis, 1732–1809, Spanish doctor and botanist in Santa Fe, Columbia; collected plants in Central America.

Nakai — Takenoshin Nakai, 1882–1952, Japanese professor and director of the Tokyo Botanical Gardens; author of several large works on the flora of Korea and Japan.

Nash — George Valentine Nash, 1864–1919, American botanist in New York.

Nees — Christian Gottfried Daniel Nees von Esenbeck, 1776–1858, president of the Leopoldian Academy and professor of botany in Wroclaw, Poland; wrote a manual of botany and a number of works on the cryptogams.

Neilr. — August Neilreich, 1803–1871, Austrian high court judge and botanist; wrote a flora of Vienna and lower Austria.

Nemoto — Kwanji Nemoto, 1860–1936, Japanese botanist.

Nichols. — George Nicholson, 1847–1908, curator of Kew Gardens, London; published a 4 volume garden dictionary.

Niedenzu — Franz Josef Niedenzu, 1857–1937, professor of botany at the Theologic-Philosophical Academy in Braunsberg, east Prussia; revised 3 editions of Garcke, *Flora von Deutschland,* etc.

Niedzwetzky — J. Neidzwetzky, born 1845, Austrian geologist and traveler; collected plants in Turkestan around 1880, hence *Malus niedzwetzkyana.*

Noble — Charles Noble, English nurseryman in Bagshot, Surrey, around 1850.

Norrlin — Johann Peter Norrlin, 1842–1917, doctor in Oslo, later a forester in Tromsö, northern Norway.

Nutt. — Thomas Nuttall, 1786–1859, English botanist; from 1808–1841 lived and traveled in North America, was also a professor of botany in America; wrote *The North American Sylva;* died in England.

Oeder — Georg Christian Edler von Oeder, 1728–1791, born in Ansbach, Germany, botanist, lived in Copenhagen for 20 years; published *Flora Danica,* was eventually a magistrate in Oldenburg, W. Germany where he died.

Oerst. — Anders Sandoe Oersted, 1816–1872, professor of botany in Copenhagen, Denmark, botanist and zoologist; wrote on Central American plants, Gesneriaceae and oaks.

Ohwi — Jisaburo Ohwi, 1905–1977, Japanese botanist; wrote *Flora of Japan,* translated into English.

Oliv. — Daniel Oliver, 1830–1916, English botanist, curator of Kew Gardens; wrote *Flora of tropical Africa.*

Oliv., W. R. B. — Walter Reginal Brook Oliver, 1883–1957, Australian botanist, born in Tasmania, later lived and worked in New Zealand.

Olivier — Guillaume Antoine Olivier, 1756–1814, French botanist, zoologist and doctor; traveled in Egypt and Persia collecting plants; died in Lyon.

Orph. — Theodoros Georgios Orphanides, 1817–1886, professor of botany and gardener in Athens, Greece.

Osborn — Arthur Osborn, born in 1878, English gardener.

Ostenf. — Carl Emil Hanse Ostenfeld, 1873–1931, Danish botanist, director of the Copenhagen Botanic Garden; wrote a flora of Iceland and *Flora Arctica.*

Otto — Christoph Friedrich Otto, 1782–1852, supervisor at the Berlin Botanic Garden for nearly 40 years, collaborated with several botanists.

Ottolander — Cornelius Johannus Ottolander, 1822–1887, Dutch gardener in Boskoop.

Ouden — Pieter den Ouden, 1874–1963, Dutch gardener in Boskoop, conifer authority; wrote a book on conifers.

Palibin — Ivan Vladimirovitch Palibin, 1872–1940, Russian botanist; wrote a flora of Mongolia, otherwise an authority on the Korean flora.

Pall. — Peter Simon Pallas, 1741–1811, German doctor and botanist, from Berlin; later a Russian government advisor in St. Petersburg [Leningrad]; wrote *Flora Russica,* etc.

Palmer — Ernest Jesse Palmer, 1785–1862, North American botanist specializing in dendrology, particularly *Crataegus* and *Quercus.*

Pamp. — Renato Pampanini, 1845–1949, Italian botanist; revised *Artemisia,* wrote a flora of San Marino.

Pardé — Léon Gabriel Charles Pardé, 1865–1944, French dendrologist; wrote an inventory of all the plants in the National Arboretum at Les Barres, including an atlas.

Parl. — Filippo Parlatore, 1816–1877, professor of botany in Florence, Italy; wrote a flora of Italy.

Parrot — F. W. Parrot, 1792–1841, German professor of surgery, born in Karlsruhe; first to climb Mt. Ararat in Turkey (1829), later worked in Tartu, Estonia.

Parsons — Samuel Bowne Parsons, 1819–1906, American nurseryman in Flushing, Long Island, USA.

Paul — William Paul, 1814–1905, well-known nurseryman in Waltham Cross near London, rose authority; wrote a popular book on roses, which appeared in many editions; also wrote on *Hedera.*

Pav. (Pavon) — José Antonia Pavon, 1754–1844, Spanish botanist, colleague of Ruiz (see also); traveled in South America.

Pax — Ferdinand Albin Pax, 1858–1942, born in Königinhof, Bohemia, German botanist; professor and director of the Breslau Botanic Garden; wrote monographic works on the Aceraceae, Primulaceae, Euphorbiaceae, etc.

Paxt. — (Sir) Joseph Paxton, 1803–1865, English botanist, gardener and architect; built the Crystal Palace in London; published a 16 volume *Magazine of Botany.*

Pelkw. — A. J. ter Pelkwijk, Dutch botanist from Utrecht.

Pennell — Francis Whittier Pennell, 1886–1952, American botanist from Pennsylvania; specialist in the Scrophulariaceae of North America and western Himalayas.

Perk. — Janet Russell Perkins, 1853–1933, North American botanist; revised the Styracaceae in Engler's *Pflanzenreich.*

Pernet — Jean Pernet, 1832–1896, French rose breeder in Lyon.

Perrier (Perr.) — J. O. Eugéne Perrier, 1853–1916, French botanist; authority on alpine plants in Chambéry, Savoy, France.

Pers. — Christiaan Hendrik Persoon, 1762–1836, South African botanist from Cape Town; later a doctor and botanist in Göttingen, W. Germany and Paris, France; wrote *Synopsis Plantarum.*

Petter — Franz Petter, Austrian professor of botany in Split (Spalato), Dalmatia, Yugoslavia; died in 1958.

Petrović — Sava Petrović, 1839–1889, Serbian botanist.

Petzold — Eduard Petzold, 1815–1891, park superintendent in Muskau, Silesia [E. Germany]; wrote, together with G. Kirchner (see also), the *Arboretum Muscaviense*.

Pfitzer — Ernst Hugo Heinrich Pfitzer, 1839–1906, professor of botany and director of the Heidelberg Botanic Garden; orchid specialist.

Phil. — Rudolf Amandus Philippi, 1808–1904, German botanist from Berlin-Charlottenburg; later a plant collector in Chile and museum director in Santiago.

Pilg. — Robert Knud Friedrich Pilger, 1876–1953, born in Helgoland, W. Germany, botanist and director of the Berlin Botanic Garden and Museum; specialist in the Coniferae, Gramineae, Plantaginaceae and several tropical Families.

Piper — Charles Vancouver Piper, 1867–1926, Canadian botanist and plant collector; later lived in Washington D.C.; wrote a flora of the state of Washington.

Pissard — M. Pissard, head gardener for the Shah of Persia around 1880; sent a *Prunus* form to France in 1881 which is named for him (see *Prunus cerasifera* 'Pissardii').

Pitteurs — Belgian farmer and senator in St. Truiden.

Planch. — Jules Emile Planchon, 1823–1888, French professor of botany in Montpellier; co-author of *Flore des Serres;* revised the Ulmaceae for De Candolle.

Planer — Johann Jakob Planer, 1743–1789, German doctor in Erfurt.

Plot — Robert Plot, 1640–1696, English naturalist and book dealer.

Poech — Joseph Poech, 1816–1846, Austrian botanist; wrote on the plants of Cyprus; died in Prague.

Poepp. — Eduard Friedrich Poeppig, 1798–1868, German botanist and zoologist; traveled in Chile and Peru from whence he collected about 4000 plant species, described these with Endlicher (see also).

Poir. — Jean Louis Marie Poiret, 1755–1834, French clergyman and botanist; traveled North Africa in 1785/86.

Pojark. — Antonia Ivanovna Pojarkova, born in 1879, Russian botanist.

Pourret — Pierre André Pourret de Figeac, 1754–1818, French clergyman and botanist; later lived in Spain and wrote a flora of the Pyrenees as well as a monograph of the genus *Cistus*.

Prain — (Sir) David Prain, 1857–1944, Scottish botanist; later worked at Kew Gardens; occasional publisher of the *Botanical Magazine*.

Prantl — Karl Anton Eugen Prantl, 1849–1893, German botanist and director of the Breslau Botanic Garden; co-editor of the compilation by Engler & Prantl, *Die natürlichen Pflanzenfamilien*.

Preiss — Ludwig Preiss, 1811–1883, botanist in Australia.

Presl — Karel Boriwog Presl, 1794–1852, Czechoslovakian professor of natural history and technology in Prague; wrote *Symbolae Botanicae,* etc.

Preston — Isabella Preston, 1881–1965, British born botanist who worked at the Central Experimental Farm in Ottawa, Canada; hybridized *Syringa* around 1920.

Purdom — William Purdom, 1880–1921, English botanist; collected in Kansu, China together with Farrer.

Pursh — Frederick Pursh (actually Friedrich Traugott Pursch), 1774–1842, born in Grossenhain, Saxony; lived in North America and wrote an American flora; died in Montreal, Canada.

Puvill. — Puvilland, French nursery, around 1800.

Pynaert — Edouard Christophe Pynaert van Geert, 1835–1900, Belgian gardener.

Purp., C. A. — Carl Anton Purpus, 1853–1914, German botanist and plant collector in Mexico. — His brother Joseph Anton Purpus, 1860–1932, was employed in the St. Petersburg [Leningrad] Botanic Garden, then from 1888–1932 was superintendent at the Darmstadt Botanic Garden.

Radde — Gustav Ferdinand Richard von Radde, 1831–1903, born in Gdansk [in Poland today], botanist; collected plants in Siberia; after 1867 director of the Tiflis Botanical Gardens.

Raddi — Guiseppe Raddi, 1770–1829, Italian botanist; traveled in Brazil.

Raf. — Constantin Samuel Rafinesque-Schmaltz, 1783–1842, born in Galata near Istanbul, Turkey, later a professor of botany at Transylvania University in Kentucky, USA; wrote several floras of North American plants.

Raffill — Charles Percival Raffill, 1876–1951, English gardener and botanist in Kew Gardens.

Raoul — Edourd Fiacre Louis Raoul, 1815–1852, French ship's doctor and botanist; wrote about Australian plants.

R. Br. — see Brown, Robert (Br. R.).

R. E. Fr. — see Fries, Robert E. (Fr. R. E.).

Redouté — Pierre Joseph Redouté, 1759–1840, born in St. Hubert, Belgium, famed botanical artist in Paris; produced valuable plates of lilies, roses, etc.

Regel (Rgl.) — Eduard August von Regel, 1815–1892, born in Gotha, W. Germany, first gardener-director of the Zurich Botanic Garden in Switzerland, then a

Russian advisor and director of the St. Petersburg [Leningrad] Botanic Garden; wrote many dendrological works and monographs (all in Russian); founder of *Gartenflora.*

Rehd. — Alfred Rehder, 1863–1949, born in Waldenburg, Saxony, a gardener in Berlin, Muskau and Göttingen, then a dendrologist in the USA; professor and curator of the herbarium at the Arnold Arboretum; wrote a manual and 2 extensive dendrological bibliographies; one of the more prominent dendrologists of his time.

Reichenb. — Heinrich Gottlieb Ludwig Reichenbach, 1793–1879, government advisor and professor of botany in Dresden, E. Germany; wrote a monograph on *Aconitum, Flora Exotica, Icones Florae Germanicae et Helveticae* with 2800 plates, as well as many other works.

Reichenb. f. — Heinrich Gustav Reichenbach, 1824–1889, son of the above, professor of botany in Hamburg, orchid authority; wrote *Xenia Orchidacea,* co-authored *Icones Florae . . .* with his father.

Retz. — Anders Johan Retzius, 1742–1821, Swedish professor of botany in Lund; wrote a Swedish botany, etc.

Reuter — Georges François Reuter, 1815–1872, Swiss botanist in Geneva; wrote *Catalogue Plant. Vasc. Genève,* 1862.

Rinz — German nursery firm in Frankfurt am Main, firm expired around 1860; introduced many new plants between 1830 and 1860.

Ririe — B. Ririe, English clergyman and missionary to the Chinese interior; friend and helper of E. H. Wilson (see also).

Riv. — Auguste Rivière, 1821–1877, French gardener; wrote on ferns and bamboo.

Rivers — Thomas Rivers, 1798–1877, English gardener and nurseryman.

Robson — Norman Keith Bonner Robson, born in 1928, Scottish botanist from Aberdeen; worked at the Kew Herbarium; specialist in *Hypericum.*

Rock — Joseph Francis Charles Rock, 1884–1962, born in Vienna, Austria, later with the U.S. Dept. of Agriculture as a botanist, geographer, ethnographer, explorer and expedition leader; traveled in China and Tibet and collected a large number of new plants; finally lived in Hawaii.

Rodway — Leonard Rodway, 1853–1936, English botanist; later lived in Tasmania where he died.

Roem. — Johann Jakob Roemer, 1763–1819, Swiss doctor and professor of botany in Zurich; published a magazine and established a botanical archive.

Roezl — Benedikt Roezl, 1824–1885, born in Prague, Czechoslovakia, an Austrian botanist and plant collector in South America, Mexico and California.

Rogers — W. H. Rogers, gardener in Basset near Southhampton, England.

Rolfe — Robert Allen Rolfe, 1855–1921, English botanist in Kew Gardens; revised the orchids.

Roth — Albrecht Wilhelm Roth, 1757–1834, German botanist; wrote a 3 volume manual of botany.

Rothr. — Joseph Trimble Rothrock, 1839–1922, American dendrologist and forester in Pennsylvania.

Rouy — Georges C. Ch. Rouy, 1851–1925, French botanist from Paris; wrote *Flore de France,* etc.

Rovelli — Renato Rovelli, 1806–1880, Italian gardener in Pallanza on Lake Maggiore, Italy, with 2 brothers, Carlo and Achille.

Rowley — Gordon D. Rowley, born in 1921, English botanist at the University of Reading; wrote frequently on the development of roses.

Roxb. — William Roxburgh, 1751–1815, born in Scotland, botanist and doctor; director of the Botanical Gardens in Calcutta; wrote several floras of India.

Royle — John Forbes Royle, 1799–1858, English doctor and botanist born in India; at various times director of the Botanical Gardens in Saharanpur, India; later, professor at the Queen's College in London; published a work of plates on the plants of the Himalayas and Kashmir.

Rümpl. — Theodor Rümpler, 1817–1891, German gardener and garden writer; published *Vilmorins Blumengärtnerei* as well as *Illustriertes Gartenbau-Lexikon;* general secretary of the Gartenbauvereins Erfurt.

Ruiz — Hipolito Ruiz Lopez, 1754–1815, Spanish botanist from Madrid; wrote several floras on Peru and Chile, where he also collected plants with Pavon (see also).

Ruiz & Pavon — see under both names.

Rupr. — Franz Joseph Ruprecht, 1814–1870, born in Freiburg, W. Germany, doctor and botanist; curator of the Herbarium at the Academy of Science in St. Petersburg [Leningrad]; wrote a flora of the Caucasus, the northern Ural region, as well as a monograph on bamboo.

Ruys — Jan Daniel Ruys, 1897–1954, Dutch gardener and botanist in Dedemsvaart.

Rydb. — Pehr Axel Rydberg, 1860–1931, born in Sweden, an engineer, later a botanist in the USA and a prominent plant collector for the New York Botanical Gardens, wrote a flora of the Rocky Mountains and a monograph on North American *Potentilla.*

S. & Z. — see Siebold, and Zuccarini.

Sakata — Sakata & Company, Japanese nursery.

Salisb. — Richard Anthony (Markham) Salisbury, 1761–1829, English botanist from Leeds, later in London; wrote an excellent 4 volume work, *The Paradisus*

Londinensis, and others.

Sarg. — Charles Sprague Sargent, 1841–1927, founder and first director of the Arnold Arboretum in the USA; wrote *The Silva of North America;* editor of the periodical *Garden and Forest;* specialist in *Crataegus.*

Sav. — Ludovic Savatier, 1830–1891, French botanist; wrote, along with Franchet (see also), on Japanese plants.

Savi — Gaetano Savi, 1769–1844, professor of botany in Pisa; wrote a flora of Italy.

Sax — Karl Sax, 1892–1973, American botanist from Spokane, Washington, dendrologist and breeder of many new plants; director of the Arnold Arboretum.

Schau. — Johann Konrad Schauer, 1813–1848, professor of botany in Greifswald, Germany; collaborated on Martius' *Flora Brasiliensis.*

Scheidecker — J. P. Scheidecker, trade gardener in Munich, W. Germany around 1890.

Schelle — Ernst Schelle, 1864–1945, born in New York, later a garden superintendent in Tübingen, W. Germany; co-founder of the German Dendrological Society; wrote on conifers.

Schenk — Joseph August von Schenk, 1815–1891, from Hallein, Tyrol, professor of botany in Würzburg, otherwise primarily involved in paleontology.

Schinz. — Hans Schinz, 1858–1941, Swiss botanist from Zurich, director of the botanic garden; wrote, together with Keller (see also), a flora of Switzerland.

Schlechtd. (Schlechtend.) — Diederich Franz Leonhard von Schlechtendal, 1794–1866, born in Xanten in Niederrhein, W. Germany, professor of botany in Halle-Saale; published a 32 volume flora of Germany as well as a monograph of the Elaeagnaceae; was editor of the periodical *Linnaea* for 40 years.

Schleich. — Johann Christoph Schleicher, 1768–1843, born in Hofgeismar, Hesse, W. Germany, later worked as a botanist in Bex, Switzerland; wrote an index to the indigenous plants of Switzerland.

Schmalh. — Johannes Theodor Schmalhausen, 1849–1894, Russian botanist from St. Petersburg [Leningrad], later in Kiev; worked with Regel (see also).

Schmidt, F. — Friedrich Schmidt, 1832–1908, Russian botanist and officer from Livonia, later in St. Petersburg [Leningrad]; wrote about his travels in the Amur region.

Schneid. — Camillo Karl Schneider, 1876–1951, from Gröppendorf, Saxony, later in Vienna and Berlin, prominent dendrologist and garden designer; traveled in East Asia; wrote *Handbuch der Laubholzekunde,* and others.

Schott — Heinrich Wilhelm Schott, 1794–1865, born in Brno, Czechoslovakia, later director of the Imperial Garden at Schönbrunn near Vienna; wrote on ferns, *Ranunculus, Primula* and the Araceae.

Schrad. — Heinrich Adolph Schrader, 1767–1836, professor of botany in Göttingen; wrote *Hortus Gottingensis,* etc.

Schrefeld — Gustav Schrefeld, 1831–1891, park superintendent in Muskau, Silesia.

Schreib. — Beryl O. Schreiber, born in 1911, American botanist.

Schrenk — Alexander Gustav von Schrenk, 1816–1876, Russian botanist at the St. Petersburg Botanic Garden [now Leningrad]; traveled in Turkestan and Russia.

Schumacher — Heinrich Christian Friedrich Schumacher, 1757–1830, from Glückstadt/Holstein, W. Germany, later a government advisor in Copenhagen and professor; wrote a flora of Copenhagen and a medicinal flora.

Schwedler — Carl Heinrich Schwedler, 1807–1880, garden supervisor for Prince Hohenlohe of Slawentitz, upper Silesia.

Schwein. — Ludwig David von Schweinitz (Lewis David de S.), 1780–1834, superior of the Moravian Brothers in Bethlehem, Pennsylvania; traveled in the northwestern USA, collected plants and wrote many papers.

Schwenckf. — Kasper Schwenckfeld, 1563–1609, city physicist in Hirschberg, Silesia; wrote a flora of the Hirschberg region.

Schwerin (Schwer.) — Count Fritz von Schwerin, 1856–1934, manor owner in Wendisch-Wilmersdorf near Berlin, president of the German Dendrology Society for many years; revised *Sambucus* and *Acer.*

Scop. — Giovanni Antonio (Johann Anton) Scopoli, 1723–1788, born in Cavalese, Tyrol, doctor and professor of mineralogy, later a professor of botany in Pavia, Italy; wrote on the flora of Italy and Austria.

Sealy — Joseph Robert Sealy, born in 1907, English botanist at Kew Gardens; wrote a revision of the genus *Camellia,* and others.

Seem. — Berthold Carl Seemann, 1825–1871, born in Hannover, W. Germany, in London he published the periodical *Bonplandia;* wrote on the palms, *Hedera,* a flora of Hong Kong, etc.

Seemen — Karl Otto von Seemen, 1838–1910, German cavalry officer from East Prussia, honorary professor; specialist in *Salix.*

Sénécl. — Adrien Sénéclause, French gardener and dendrologist; wrote from 1840–1867.

Ser. — Nicolas Charles Seringe, 1776–1858, French professor of botany in Lyon; wrote on the Rosaceae, *Salix* and a 3 volume *Flore des Jardins.*

Servettaz — Camille Servettaz, 1870–1947, French botanist; wrote *Monographie des Elaeagnaceae.*

Shaw (Airy-Shaw) — Herbert Kenneth Airy Shaw, born in 1902, English botanist, at Kew Gardens.

Shibata — Keita Shibata, 1876–1949, Japanese botanist in Tokyo.

Shiras. — Homi Shirasawa, 1868–1947, Japanese botanist at the Meguro Forestry Academy in Tokyo.

Sibth. — John Sibthorpe, 1758–1796, born in Oxford, England, professor of botany and a doctor; traveled twice to Greece and Asia Minor where he collected plants, which were the basis for *Flora Graeca,* later published by J. E. Smith.

Sieb. — Philipp Franz von Siebold, 1796–1866, born in Würzburg, German doctor, botanist and ethnologist; spent 7 years in Japan during his service as a doctor with the Dutch East India Company; upon his return to Europe he founded a nursery in Leiden, Holland; also wrote *Flora Japonica.*

Silv. Tar. — Count Ernst Silva Tarouca, 1860–1936, Austrian Agriculture Minister, a chairman of the Austrian Dendrological Society, owner of a famous garden in Pruhonice near Prague, Czechoslovakia (still exists today and is owned by the Czech government); wrote 3 books on woody ornamentals and perennials together with Camillo Schneider.

Sim.-Louis — Léon Simon Louis, 1843–1913, proprietor of a well-known nursery in Plantières near Metz, France.

Simmonds — Arthur Simmonds, 1892–1968, English gardener; secretary of the Royal Horticultural Society in London.

Simonkai — Lajos tol Simonkai, 1851–1910, Hungarian botanist; one of the best authorities on the plants of his country.

Simpson — Joseph Herman Simpson, 1841–1918, American botanist and plant collector, born in Illinois, died in Florida.

Simpson, G. — G. Simpson, 1880–1952, New Zealand botanist.

Sims — John Sims, 1749–1833, English botanist; long-time publisher of the *Botanical Magazine* in London.

Skinner — Frank Leith Skinner, 1882–1967, gardener and lilac breeder in Dropmore, Manitoba, Canada.

Sleum. — Hermann Otto Sleumer, born in 1906 in Saarbrücken, W. Germany, botanist; first in Berlin, then in San Miguel de Tucuman, Argentina, finally in the Rijksherbarium in Leiden, Holland.

Sm. (Sm. J. E.) — Sir James Edward Smith, 1759–1828, English botanist and doctor, founder of the Linnean Society; wrote a number of significant floras, including *Flora Graeca.*

Sm. H. — Karl August Harald (Harry) Smith, born in 1889, Swedish botanist at the Institute for Taxonomic Botany in Uppsala; traveled East Asia, specializing in *Gentiana,* Asiatic *Saxifraga,* etc.

Sm. W. W. — Sir William Wright Smith, 1875–1957, Scottish professor of Botany, director of the Royal Botanic Garden Edinburgh, Scotland; traveled in Sikkim and Nepal; prominent authority on *Rhododendron* and *Primula.*

Small — John Kunkel Small, 1869–1938, American botanist at the New York Botanic Garden; wrote several floras of the southeastern states.

Smirn. — Michael Smirnow, 1849–1889, Russian botanist from Odessa; explored the flora of the Caucasus.

Smith — Peter Smith, nurseryman in Bergedorf (now Hamburg) W. Germany, a nursery well-known in its time for great variety; liquidated by its last owner, Rüppel around 1900.

Soland — Daniel Carl Solander, 1736–1782, born in Sweden, lived in England after 1760, botanist and librarian; curator of the botanical department of the British Museum in London; participated in Capt. James Cook's first world voyage.

Soul.-Bod. — Etienne Soulange-Bodin, 1774–1846, a French diplomat at first, later founded a nursery in Froment, near Paris.

Soulié — Jean André Soulié, 1858–1905, French missionary with the outer mission in Tibet; collected plants between 1890 and 1895.

Spach — Edouard Spach, 1801–1879, from Strasbourg, Alsace [France], botanist; later, adjunct to the Museum of Natural History in Paris; wrote a Natural History of Plants in 14 volumes.

Späth — Ludwig Späth, founded the well-known Berlin nursery in 1720; it became the largest nursery in the world under Franz Ludwig Späth from 1839 to 1913; the last owner, Hellmuth Späth (1885–1945) wrote the Späth Book. The nursery exists today under state ownership.

Sprague — Thomas Archibald Sprague, 1887–1958, Scottish botanist from Edinburgh, later at Kew Gardens; traveled in India, Venezuela and Columbia; edited the *Index Kewensis* for many years.

Spreng. — Curt Polycarp Joachim Sprengel, 1766–1833, professor of botany and doctor in Halle-Saale, E. Germany; wrote a history of botany and papers on the Umbelliferae, etc.

Standish — John Standish, 1814–1875, English gardener; founded a nursery together with Charles Noble.

Standl. — Paul Carpenter Standley, 1884–1963, North American botanist at the Chicago Natural History Museum; primarily dealt with the plants of Mexico and Central America; wrote *Trees and Shrubs of Mexico;* died in Guatemala.

Stapf — Otto Stapf, 1857–1933, born in Ischl, Austria, but worked in London at Kew Gardens from 1891–1922; publisher of the *Botanical Magazine;* wrote on the flora of Cape Province [S. Africa] as well as on tropical Families; died in Innsbruck.

Staunton—Sir George C. Staunton, 1737–1801, from Ireland; wrote a 2 volume work on his botanical trips through China.

Stearn—William Thomas Stearn, born 1911, English botanist at the British Museum in London; wrote many taxonomic and historical papers and the book *Botanical Latin*.

Stern—Sir Frederick Claude Stern, 1884–1967, English gardener, botanist and officer from London; wrote a study on the genus *Paeonia* and further works on *Galanthus*, *Leucojum*, etc.

Steud.—Ernst Gottlieb von Steudel, 1783–1856, chief physician in Esslingen, W. Germany and botanist; wrote *Nomenclatur Botanicus* and others.

Stev.—Christian von Steven, 1781–1863, Finnish botanist from Frederiksham; later a Russian advisor and inspector for the silk industry in Moscow, then director of the Nikita Botanical Gardens in Crimea; traveled the Taurus Mts.; died in Simferopol, USSR.

Steyerm.—Julian Alfred Steyermark, born in 1909, American botanist; wrote primarily on the flora of Missouri, Guatemala, Honduras and Ecuador.

Stokes—Jonathan Stokes, 1755–1831, English botanist and doctor from Chesterfield; wrote on medicinal plants.

Sudw.—George Bishop Sudworth, 1864–1927, dendrologist in the U.S. Forest Service in Washington; wrote *Forest trees of the Pacific Slope*, etc.

Summerh.—Victor Samuel Summerhayes, born in 1897, English botanist at the herbarium in Kew Gardens.

Sw.—Olof Peter Swartz, 1760–1818, Swedish professor of botany in Stockholm; wrote on West Indian plants, ferns, orchids, etc.

Sweet—Robert Sweet, 1783–1835, English gardener and botanist in London; wrote *Cistineae*, *The British Flower Garden*, *Geraniaceae*, etc.

Swingle—Walter Tennyson Swingle, 1871–1952, botanist in the U.S. Dept. of Agriculture; specialist in *Citrus*.

Syme—John Thomas Irvine Syme (Boswell), 1822–1888, Scottish botanist from Edinburgh.

Szysz.—Ignaz von Szyszlowicz, 1857–1910, Polish botanist; revised *Tilia*, Theaceae, etc.

Täckholm—Gunnar Täckholm, 1891–1933, Swedish botanist; notable for his cytological research on roses.

Tagg—Harry Frank Tagg, 1874–1933, English botanist at the Royal Botanic Garden Edinburgh; specialist in *Rhododendron*.

Takeda—Hisayoshi Takeda, born in 1883, Japanese botanist in Tokyo; wrote on *Mahonia*, etc.

Talbot—Milo (Lord) Talbot of Malahide, 1912–1972, English diplomat in Laos, later working solely as a botanist; collected plants primarily in Tasmania and South America; established the largest collection of Australian, New Zealand and South American plants at Malahide Castle near Dublin, Ireland.

Tanaka—Yoshio Tanaka, 1838–1915, Japanese botanist; wrote on the economic plants of Japan.

Tantau—Mathias Tantau (the father), 1882–1953, German rose breeder in Uetersen, Holstein; Mathias Tantau (the son), born in 1912, successor.

Taub.—Paul Hermann Wilhelm Taubert, 1862–1897, German botanist; specialist in the Leguminosae.

Tausch—Ignaz Friedrich Tausch, 1793–1848, Austrian professor of botany in Prague, Czechoslovakia; wrote *Hortus Canalius*.

Taylor, G.—Sir George Taylor, born in 1904, Scottish botanist from Edinburgh, was director of Kew Gardens.

Ten.—Michele Tenore, 1780–1861, professor of botany in Naples, Italy; wrote an extensive *Flora Napolitana* and many other works.

Teusch.—Heinrich (Henry) Teuscher, born in 1891 in Berlin, later moved to the USA, then became curator of the Montreal Botanic Garden, Canada.

Thell.—Albert Thellung, 1881–1928, Swiss botanist from Zurich, employed at the Zurich Botanic Garden; wrote, together with Schinz (see also), and Keller (see also), the *Flora der Schweiz*.

Thomas—Friedrich August Wilhelm Thomas, 1840–1918, German botanist and high school teacher in Ohrdruff.

Thoms.—Thomas Thomsen, 1817–1878, English botanist, plant collector in India; superintendent of the Calcutta Botanic Garden for several years; collaborated with J. D. Hooker (see also).

Thory—Claude Antoine Thory, 1759–1827, French gardener; wrote a rose monograph.

Thuill.—Jean Louis Thuillier, 1757–1822, French botanist in Paris; wrote a flora of Paris.

Thunb.—Carl Pehr Thunberg, 1743–1822, doctor and professor of botany in Uppsala, Sweden; traveled in Europe, Africa, Asia and particularly in Japan; wrote *Flora Japonica*, *Flora Capensis*, etc.

Tiegh.—Philippe Edouard Léon van Tieghem, 1839–1914, French botanist in Paris; wrote on the *Buxus*, *Stachyurus* and anatomical works.

Tobler—Friedrich Tobler, 1879–1957, Swiss botanist, born in Berlin, Germany; later a professor in Münster, then director of the Dresden Botanic Garden; wrote a monograph of the genus *Hedera* and on colonial economic food plants.

Tolm.—Alexander Innokentvich Tolmatchev, born in

1903, Russian botanist; wrote a woody flora of Sachalin.

Torr. — John Torrey, 1796–1873, North American botanist and chemist from New York; wrote on the plants of the northern and central states as well as *Flora of North America* with Asa Gray (see also).

Torr. & Gr. — see Torrey, and Gray.

Tourn. — Joseph Pitton de Tournefort, 1656–1708, from Aix, French botanist; wrote *Histoire des Plantes,* also wrote on medicinal plants; traveled in Asia Minor.

Transon — Transon Frères, French nursery in Orléans, around 1900.

Tratt. — Leopold Trattinnick, 1764–1849, Austrian botanist; curator of the herbarium in Vienna; published many valuable plates and wrote a monograph of roses.

Trautv. — Ernst Rudolph von Trautvetter, 1809–1889, Russian botanist; born in Mitau, founder of the Kiev Botanic Garden, Ukraine; later, director of the St. Petersburg [Leningrad] Botanic Garden; traveled in Siberia.

Trel. — William Trelease, 1857–1945, North American botanist at the University of Illinois; specialist in American oaks.

Tschonoski (actually Chonosuke) — Sukawa Thschonoski, 1841–1925, Japanese botanist and collaborator with Maximowicz (see also).

Tulasne — Charles Tulasne, 1816–1884, French botanist.

Turcz. — Nicolaj Stepanovich Turcaninov, 1796–1864, Russian justice and finance official, later botanist at the University of Charkow; wrote a flora of Siberia.

Turner — William Turner, 1508–1568, doctor and garden owner in Kew, England; wrote *A New Herball;* also called the "father of English botany."

Turra — Antonio Turra, 1730–1796, Italian botanist; wrote a flora of Italy.

Turrill — William Bertram Turrill, 1890–1961, curator of the Kew herbarium and publisher of the *Botanical Magazine.*

Ungnad — Baron Freiherr von Ungnad, Austrian envoy to Constantinople [now Istanbul, Turkey] in the first half of the 16th century; brought the first seeds of *Aesculus hippocastanum* to Vienna.

Usteri — Alfred Usteri, born in 1869, Swiss gardener in Zurich; wrote on *Berberis.*

Uyeki — Homiki Uyeki, born in 1882, Japanese botanist and dendrologist; worked on the woody flora of Korea.

Vahl — Martin Hendriksen Vahl, 1749–1804, Danish botanist from Aarhus, later professor of botany in Copenhagen; wrote *Symbolae Botanicae.*

Van Eseltine — Glen Parker van Eseltine, 1888–1938, botanist in New York; specialist in *Malus.*

Van Hoey Smith — James Richard Pennington van Hoey Smith, born in 1921 in Rotterdam, Holland, director of the Trompenburg Arboretum; worked mostly on *Quercus* and *Fagus.*

Van Steenis — Cornelius Gijsbert Gerrit Jan van Steenis, born in 1901, Dutch botanist; director of the Rijksherbarium in Leiden, established the "Flora Malesiana [Malaysia]."

Van Volxem — Jean van Volxem, Belgian gardener, around 1870.

Vatke — Georg Carl Wilhelm Vatke, 1849–1889, from Berlin, botanist in the Berlin Botanic Garden.

Veillard — Veillard (first name and dates not determined), French botanist, collaborated with Nouveau Duhamel, 1800–1819.

Veitch — John Gould Veitch, 1839–1870, English gardener from Exeter; traveled in Japan, Australia, China etc.; carried on the nursery established by his forefathers in Combe Wood, Surrey. — James Veitch (Sr.), 1792–1863; Sir Harry James Veitch, 1840–1924; James Veitch (Jr.), 1815 to 1869; James Herbert Veitch, 1868–1907.

Vent. — Etienne Pierre Ventenat, 1757–1806, professor of botany in Paris, librarian in the Panthéon; wrote a monograph on *Tilia* and *Jardin de la Malmaison.*

Verlot — Pierre Bernard Lazare Verlot, 1836–1897, French botanist from Longvic near Lyon; wrote on alpine plants.

Verschaffelt — Ambroise Verschaffelt, 1825–1886, Belgian gardener from Ledeberg near Ghent; wrote a 13 volume plate work on *Camellia.*

Vervaene — Domien Vervaene, about 1810–1870, ancestor of a famous Belgian nursery family noted for their breeding of azaleas, *Camellia* and *Rhododendron;* his son Jozef lived from 1845–1914.

Vill. — Dominique Villars, 1745–1814, French doctor and botanist in Grenoble; wrote on the plants of Dauphiné.

Vilm. — Pierre Philippe André Lévèque de Vilmorin, 1776–1862, and Maurice Lévèque de Vilmorin, 1849–1919, members of a famous nursery family in Paris, founded the National Arboretum in Les Barres, and the Arboretum in Verrières-le-Buisson near Paris; introduced many plants from China.

Viviani — Domenico Viviani, 1772–1840, Italian professor of botany in Genoa; wrote about the plants of Italy, Egypt and Libya.

Vos — Cornelis de Vos, 1806–1895, Dutch gardener.

Voss — Andreas Voss, 1857–1924, born in Lyke near Bremen, E. Germany, gardener and writer in Berlin; revised the 3rd edition of *Vilmorins Blumengärtnerei.*

Vuyk — Tenuis Vuyk, 1851; Pieter Vuyk, 1878 to 1942; Aart Vuyk; Dutch nurserymen in Boskoop, breeder of azaleas.

Wada — Kiyoshi Wada, born in 1911; Hakoneya Nurseries, Numazu-Shi, Japan, well-known Japanese nursery, brought many new plants into the trade.

Wahl. (Wahlenb.) — Georg (Göran) Wahlenberg, 1780–1851, Swedish doctor and professor of botany in Uppsala; wrote floras of Sweden, Lapland, Carpathian Mts.

Wahlb. — Pehr Frederik Wahlberg, 1800–1877, Swedish professor of botany from Göteborg, later in Stockholm.

Waitz — Karl Friedrich Waitz, 1774–1848, from Altenburg, Thüringia, E. Germany, a high government official; wrote a monograph of the genus *Erica*.

Waldst. — Count Franz Adam von Waldstein-Wartenberg, 1759–1823, Austrian officer and botanist, born in Vienna; wrote, together with Kitaibel (see also), on the rare plants of Hungary.

Waldst. & Kit. — see Waldstein, and Kitaibel.

Wall. — Nathanael (or Nathaniel) Wallich, actually Nathan Wolff, 1786–1854, born in Copenhagen, Denmark, later a doctor in the Danish colony Frederiksnagore (Serampore) near Calcutta, India and curator of the Calcutta Botanic Garden; wrote about the rare plants of Asia; died in London.

Wallr. — Carl Friedrich Wallroth, 1792–1857, German botanist and doctor in Nordhausen; wrote on roses, cryptogams, etc.

Walp. — Wilhelm Gerhard Walpers, 1816–1853, Thüringian doctor and botanist from E. Germany; wrote a number of works on taxonomic botany.

Walt. — Thomas Walter, 1740–1789, born in England, went to North America; wrote a flora of Carolina.

Wanger. — Walter Leonhard Wangerin, 1884–1938, German botanist from Halle-Saale; wrote monographs on the Cornaceae, Nyssaceae, Alangiaceae, etc.

Wangh. — Friedrich Adam Julius von Wangenheim, 1749–1800, born in Coburg-Gotha, later head forester in Gumbinnen, E. Prussia; wrote on the North American woody flora.

Warburg — Otto Warburg, 1859–1938, German botanist from Hamburg; collaborated on Engler's *Pflanzenreich* and Engler & Prantl's *Die Natürlichen Pflanzenfamilien.*

Ward — see Kingdon-Ward.

Warsz. — Józeph Warszewicz, 1812–1866, born in Vilnius, Poland, Polish-Lithuanian plant collector in Asia and South America; later superintendent of the Krakow Botanic Garden.

Waterer — John Waterer Sons, nursery in Bagshot, Surrey, England; Anthony Waterer, 1823–1896.

Wats., S. — Sereno Watson, 1826–1892, from Connecticut, North American botanist at Harvard University, curator of the Gray Herbarium; wrote a manual of botany.

Weatherby — Charles Alfred Weatherby, 1875–1949, North American botanist at the Gray Herbarium; plant collector.

Weigel — Christian Ehrenfried von Weigel, 1748–1831, botanist and chemist with the Greifswald University, Germany.

Wender. — Georg Wilhelm Franz Wenderoth, 1774–1861, professor of botany at Marburg University, W. Germany; wrote a flora of Hessen.

Wendl. — Johann Christoph Wendland, 1755–1828, born in Landau, W. Germany, later garden superintendent in Hannover-Herrenhausen; wrote a popular plate work on South African *Erica.*

Wenz. — Theodor Wenzig, 1824–1892, German botanist; wrote a monograph on *Spiraea* and papers on *Fraxinus.*

Werderm. — Erich Werdermann, 1892–1959, from Berlin, German botanist; director of the Berlin Botanic Garden, specialist in cacti, revised the Dilleniaceae, Actinidiaceae, etc.

Wesm. — Alfred Wesmael, 1832–1905, Belgian dendrologist and gardener, wrote on *Populus, Fraxinus, Acer,* etc.

West. — Richard Weston, 1733–1806, English dendrologist; wrote on the woody plants cultivated in British nurseries (*The English Flora*).

Wettst. — Richard Ritter von Wettstein von Westersheim, 1863–1931, Austrian botanist; wrote *Handbuch der systematischen Botanik,* etc.; director of the Vienna Botanic Garden; died in Tirol.

Wieg. — Karl McKay Wiegand, 1872–1942, American botanist at Cornell University.

Wier — D. B. Wier, gardener in Lacon, Illinois, USA; found a maple and named for him in 1873, *Acer saccharinum* 'Wieri'.

Wierzb. — P. Wierzbicki, 1794–1847, doctor and botanist in Orawicza in the Banat region of eastern Europe.

Wies. — Albert Everett Wieslander, born in 1890, American botanist and forester in California.

Wight — Robert Wight, 1796–1872, born in Scotland, ship's doctor at first, later director of the Madras Botanic Garden [India]; wrote on Indian plants.

Wight, W. F. — William Franklin Wight, 1874–1954, North American botanist.

Wikström — Johann Emmanuel Wikström, 1789–1856, professor of botany in Stockholm, Sweden; wrote on *Daphne, Rosa, Equisetum,* etc.

Willd. — Karl Ludwig Willdenow, 1765–1812, professor of botany and director of the Berlin Botanic Garden; wrote *Berlinische Baumzucht* and the plate work *Hortus Berolinensis*.

Willkomm — Moritz Willkomm, 1821–1895, from Saxony, later in Prague, Czechoslovakia, then a Russian advisor and professor of botany; director of the Tartu Botanic Garden, Estonia [USSR]; wrote a flora of Spain with J. Lange, and a forest flora.

Willm. — Ellen Ann Willmott, 1860–1934, English rose authority; wrote "The genus *Rosa*," an excellent work.

Wilmott — Alfred James Wilmott, 1888–1951, English botanist, curator of the British Museum in London.

Wils. — Ernest Henry Wilson, 1876–1930, born in England, later a botanical explorer for the Arnold Arboretum of Boston, Mass., USA; traveled several times to Japan and China; wrote many smaller botanic works and several gardening books.

Wimm. — Christian Friedrich Heinrich Wimmer, 1803–1868, school superintendent in Breslau, Silesia [now Wroclaw, Poland]; wrote a flora of Silesia and papers on *Salix*.

Winkl. — Hubert Winkler, 1875–1941, botanist in Breslau, Silesia [now Wroclaw, Poland]; wrote on the Betulaceae.

Wistar — Caspar Wistar, 1761–1818, professor of anatomy and naturalist at the University of Philadelphia, USA.

Wittm. — Max Carl Ludwig Wittmack, 1839–1919, German botanist; specialist on South American flora; publisher of *Gartenflora* for many years.

Wolf, E. — Egbert Wolf, 1860–1931, born in Berlin, gardener, later professor at the Forestry Institute in St. Petersburg [Leningrad, USSR]; authority on the genus *Salix*.

Wood — Alphonso Wood, 1810–1881, North American botanist; wrote *A Class-book of Botany* which sold 100,000 copies in just one edition.

Woot. — Elmer Otis Wooton, 1865–1945, North American botanist from Arlington, Virginia; wrote *Flora of New Mexico*.

Wright — Charles Henry Wright, 1864–1941, English botanist at the Kew Herbarium; plant collector.

Wulf. — Franz Xaver Freiherr von Wulfen, 1728–1805, born in Belgrade, Yugoslavia, an Austrian professor of botany in Klagenfurt.

Wyman — Donald Wyman, born in 1903 in California, a noted botanist at the Arnold Arboretum; wrote *Trees for American Gardens, Shrubs and Vines for American Gardens,* etc.

Yaltirik — Faik Yaltirik, Turkish botanist in Istanbul; worked on the genus *Acer*.

Yatabe — Ryokicki Yatabe, 1851–1899, Japanese botanist; published an iconography of the Japanese flora.

Young — Maurice Young, 1834–1890, nursery in Epson, Surrey, England.

Zab. — Hermann Zabel, 1832–1912, gardener from Germany, garden administrator in Hannover-Münden, prominent dendrologist; wrote on *Spiraea*.

Zahlbr. — Johann Zahlbruckner, 1782–1850, Austrian botanist in Vienna; plant geographer.

Zauschner — Johannes Baptist Joseph Zauschner, 1737–1791, professor of natural history in Prague, Czechoslovakia; particularly chemistry and mineralogy.

Zenari — Silvia Zenari, 1896–1956, Italian botanist, director of the Botanical Institute and Botanic Garden in Padua; wrote a flora of northern Italy.

Zengerl. — Zengerling, Austrian author, wrote around 1889.

Zeyher — Johann Michael Zeyher, 1770–1843, garden director in Schwetzingen, W. Germany.

Zuccagni — Attilio Zuccagni, 1754–1807, Italian botanist and natural historian from Florence.

Zucc. — Joseph Gerhard Zuccarini, 1797–1848, professor of botany in Munich, W. Germany; wrote papers on dormancy in the woody flora of Germany, a flora Japonica, an *Oxalis* monograph and many other works.

LITERATURE

The biographical notes have been found in many periodicals and articles as well as in the following works:

Bailey, L. H.: The Standard Cyclopedia of Horticulture; New York 1950 (3 vols., pp. 1563–1603, on American gardeners).

Bailey: Hortus Third; New York 1976.

Biographical Dictionary of Botanists represented in the Hunt Institute Portrait Collection; Pittsburgh 1972.

Glaser, L.: Taschenwörterbuch für Botaniker; Leipzig 1885.

Hegi: Flora von Mitteleuropa (footnotes in all volumes).

Koch, K.: Dendrologie; Erlangen 1869–1873 (3 vols., footnotes).

Leunis, J.: Synopsis der Pflanzenkunde 1, IX to LXXIX; Hannover 1877.

Nissen, C.: Die botanische Buchillustration; Stuttgart 1951.

Ohwi, J.: Flora of Japan; Washington, D.C., 1965.

Pritzel, G. A.: Thesaurus literaturae botanicae; Leipzig 1871.

Scheerinck, H.: De *Azalea indica,* 447–473; Antwerpen 1938 (primarily on Belgian gardeners).

Zander: Handwörterbuch der Pflanzennamen, 10th edition, revised by F. Encke and G. Buchheim; Stuttgart 1972.

Registration Authorities for Cultivar Names

Article 53 of the International Code of Nomenclature for Cultivated Plants (1969) states that the cultivar name must be approved by a legitimate registration authority before its introduction.

To this end, please note below a list of international and national registration authorities for woody ornamentals. The appropriate authorities are often given in the text at the end of a particular genus section, however, a summary seems appropriate at this point.

Berberis

The Institute for Horticultural Plant Breeding, Postbus 16, in Wageningen, Holland.

Bougainvillea

Division of Horticulture, Indian Agriculture Research Institute, New Delhi 12, India.

A cultivar list with about 300 names is being prepared.

Buxus

American Boxwood Society, Box 85, Boyce, Virginia 22620, USA.

Camellia

International *Camellia* Society, Mr. J. T. Gallagher, Secretary, Oldfield, Moorlands Road, Verwood, Dorset, England.

Cultivar list in preparation.

Carissa

Arnold Arboretum, Jamaica Plain, Massachusetts 02130, USA

Chaenomeles

Arnold Arboretum, Jamaica Plain, Massachusetts 02130, USA.

Cultivar list is in Arnoldia 1963: 17–75 and 116.

Conifers, dwarf etc.

Royal Horticultural Society, Vincent Square, London SWIP 2PE, England.

Coprosma

Royal New Zealand Institute of Horticulture, Attn. Nomenclature Committee, P.O. Box 450, Wellington, New Zealand.

Cornus

Arnold Arboretum, Jamaica Plain, Massachusetts, 02130, USA.

Cultivar list appeared in Arnoldia 1963: 88–89; 1967: 61; 1969: 2; 1970 and 1972.

Cotoneaster

The Institute for Horticultural Plant Breeding, Postbus 16, Wageningen, Holland.

Escallonia

California Academy of Sciences, Dr. Elizabeth McClintock, Golden Gate Park, San Francisco, California 94118, USA.

Fagus

Arnold Arboretum, Jamaica Plain, Massachusetts 02130, USA.

Cultivar list appeared in Arnoldia 1964: 1–8: 1967: 62.

Forsythia

Arnold Arboretum, Jamaica Plain, Massachusetts 02130, USA.

Cultivar list appeared in Arnoldia 1967: 39–42; 1967: 62.

Fruits & Nuts (non-ornamental)

(National Registrar) Dept. of Viticulture & Enology, University of California, Davis, California 95616, USA.

Fuchsia

American *Fuchsia* Society, Hall of Flowers, Golden Gate Park, San Francisco, California 94122, USA.

The Society has published a number of lists.

Gleditsia

Arnold Arboretum, Jamaica Plain, Massachusetts 02130, USA.

Cultivar list may be found in Arnoldia 1961: 31–34.

Heather

Heather Society, Yew Trees, Horley Row, Surrey, England.

A preliminary list of the genera *Andromeda, Bruckenthalia, Calluna, Daboecia* and *Erica* is in preparation.

Hebe

Royal New Zealand Institute of Horticulture, Attn. Nomenclature Committee, P.O. Box 450, Wellington, New Zealand.

Hydrangea

California Academy of Sciences, Dr. Elizabeth McClintock, Golden Gate Park, San Francisco, California 94118, USA.

Hypericum

The Institute for the Development of Ornamental Plants in Wageningen, Holland has ceased registration work.

Ilex

Holly Society of America, Attn. Gene Eisenbeiss, Registrar, U.S. National Arboretum, Washington, D.C. 20002, USA.

Bulletin No. 13 from the Society contains a list of the registered cultivars.

Lagerstroemia

Dr. Donald R. Egolf, U.S. National Arboretum, Washington, D.C. 20002, USA.

Lantana

Arnold Arboretum, Jamaica Plain, Massachusetts 02130, USA.

Leptospermum

Nomenclature Committee, Botanic Gardens, Rolleston Ave., Christchurch 1, New Zealand.

Magnolia

American *Magnolia* Society, Dr. John M. Fogg, Registrar, Box 128, Merion, Pennsylvania 19066, USA.

A check list of cultivated magnolias was published in 1975.

Malus (ornamental types)

Arnold Arboretum, Jamaica Plain, Massachusetts 02130, USA.

"Crab Apples of America" was published by D. Wyman in 1955; also, lists appear in Arnoldia 1963, 1966, 1967 and 1970.

Paeonia

American Peony Society, Mr. G. M. Kessenich, Editor, 150 Interlachen Road, Hopkins, Minnesota 55343, USA.

A "National Listing" appeared in 1976.

Penstemon

American Penstemon Society, Miss Aileen McWilliam, Registrar, 711 Magnolia Avenue, Mena, Arkansas 71935, USA.

An official list of named varieties and hybrids registered by the American *Penstemon* Society was published in 1973.

Philadelphus

Arnold Arboretum, Jamaica Plain, Massachusetts 02130, USA.

Pieris

Arnold Arboretum, Jamaica Plain, Massachusetts 02130, USA.

Registration lists of cultivar names may be found in Arnoldia 1961, 1963, 1966 and 1967.

Populus (forestry types)

International Poplar Commission, Via delle Terme di Caracalla, 01000 Rome, Italy.

A list is being planned for publication.

Potentilla

The Institute for Horticultural Plant Breeding, Postbus 16 in Wageningen, Holland is no longer involved in registration.

Pyracantha

U.S. National Arboretum, Attn. Dr. Donald E. Egolf, Washington, D.C. 20002, USA.

A cultivar list is being prepared.

Rhododendron (including Azaleas)

Royal Horticultural Society, Vincent Square, London SW1P 2PE, England.

The International *Rhododendron* Register was published in 1958 with supplementary lists published nearly annually in the *Rhododendron* Year Books.

Rosa

American Rose Society, Mr. Harold S. Epstein, Registrar, P.O. Box 30,000, Shreveport, Louisiana 71130, USA.

The international list, Modern Roses VIII, is currently in print.

Syringa

Royal Botanical Gardens, Attn. Mr. Freek Vrugtman, Registrar, Box 399, Hamilton, Ontario, Canada L8N 3H8.

In 1976, Mr. O. M. Rogers published the Tentative International Register of Cultivar Names in the Genus *Syringa.*

Ulmus

Arnold Arboretum, Jamaica Plain, Massachusetts 02130, USA.

Registration lists of cultivar names may be found in Arnoldia 1964 and 1967.

Viburnum

U.S. National Arboretum, Attn. Dr. Donald R. Egolf, Washington, D.C. 20002, USA.

Weigela

Arnold Arboretum, Jamaica Plain, Massachusetts 02130, USA.

Check lists of the cultivar names appeared in Arnoldia in 1965, 1967 and 1969.

For all the other genera with no established registration authority, the Arnold Arboretum would be the source to contact.

Lit. cited for this section:

Vrugtman, F.: Bibliography of Cultivar Name Registration; in Chronica Horticulturae **12**, 47–50, 1972. — Addendum 1: **13**, 54, 1973. — Addendum 2: **17**, 29–30, 1977.

American Nurseryman: Naming and Registering new Cultivars, 16 pp.; Washington, D.C. (1974).